1940

1950

1960

1970

WAR

WAR

THE SOARING
SIXTIES?

ECONOMICS
an
Introduction
to
Analysis and Policy

ECONOMICS

GEORGE LELAND BACH

*Frank E. Buck Professor
of Economics and Public Policy,
Stanford University*

Seventh Edition

an Introduction to Analysis and Policy

Prentice-Hall, Inc., Englewood Cliffs, New Jersey

SEVENTH EDITION

ECONOMICS
An Introduction to Analysis and Policy

George Leland Bach

SBN 13-227272-5
Library of Congress Catalog No. 76-140764

Current printing (last digit):
10 9 8 7 6 5 4 3 2 1

PRENTICE-HALL INTERNATIONAL, INC., *London*
PRENTICE-HALL OF AUSTRALIA, PTY. LTD., *Sydney*
PRENTICE-HALL OF CANADA, LTD., *Toronto*
PRENTICE-HALL OF INDIA PRIVATE LIMITED, *New Delhi*
PRENTICE-HALL OF JAPAN, INC., *Tokyo*

Preface

This edition is, like its predecessors, frankly and enthusiastically a book on political economy. It is a book on economic theory, but equally a book on how students can use economic theory in thinking about complex problems for themselves. It is a book designed for either a full-year or a one-semester course, for instructors who wish to put either micro- or macroeconomics first.

The focus throughout is on what the *student* does. The evidence is overwhelming that students retain little of what they learn in college economics courses unless they become interested enough to continue to use it as they read the newspaper and vote, after they leave the classroom. If we do not manage to kindle a real interest in economics, we have lost the battle at the outset. If we don't give students concepts and methods which they can use *for themselves* after graduation, little will last.

Thus, the emphasis here is on key central concepts, principles, and models—and on how to apply these analytical tools to current, real-world, "relevant" problems. This is a big book, not because its goal is to cram students full of information, but to provide teachers a rich menu of lively applications from which they can choose to fit the interests of their students. Theory, and how students can apply it for themselves, is the theme throughout.

This edition not only looks new. It is new, with the following innovations.

It stresses "National Goals and Priorities" as the key to Part I, and as the framework for the whole book, in keeping with today's student interests and the temper of the times.

It has ten new chapters or appendixes applying economic theory to big, "relevant" national and world problems:

Pollution and the Environment
The Population Explosion
Economic Growth and the "Quality of Life"
Black Economic Development and Black Capitalism
Poverty and Insecurity
Economics of the Draft
The Military–Industrial Complex
Marx, Radical Economics, and Profits
The Urban Crisis
Economics of Minimum-Wage Laws

With these, the book can provide readings for a whole course without the need for additional outside assignments, but it is also suited for use with outside materials.

It stresses economics as a modern empirical science.

It has a thorough, up-to-the-minute treatment of money and modern monetary analysis—and of the "monetarist"-fiscal policy controversy, including quantitative evidence on the debate.

Public goods, externalities, and the public sector are greatly expanded and tied into the discussion of shifting national goals and priorities—all in relation to market processes and alternative means of resource allocation.

It builds on new developments in learning theory and research:
Student motivation—big and little current problems to involve students.
Clear focus on objectives—what the student should learn and keep.
Learning retention—through repeated, explicit use of concepts and principles.

It offers a rich menu of up-to-the-minute supplementary teaching aids:
A big, new *Teacher's Manual and Question Bank*, providing about 2,000 easy-to-grade objective and discussion questions, plus suggested examinations and teaching hints (prepared jointly with Professor William Moffat).
A new *Workbook* and new readings volume (*Economic Analysis and Public Policy*), both based on experience-tested earlier editions (prepared jointly with Professors Myron L. Joseph and Norton Seeber).
New editions of "programmed-learning" texts covering micro and macro theory (*Microeconomics* and *Macroeconomics*) (prepared jointly with Professors Richard Attiyeh and Keith Lumsden).
Color and black-and-white transparencies of major charts for use with large classes (prepared by Professor Phillip Saunders).

Suggested divisions of the text for two different one-semester courses are included immediately after the Table of Contents.

Over successive editions, my indebtedness to colleagues and friends in the profession has become so vast that it is patently impossible to list all those who deserve credit. For this seventh edition, however, I must thank especially Professor William Moffat, who has provided innumerable perceptive suggestions and kept me from many errors; and my present and former colleagues, Professors Richard Attiyeh (University of California, La Jolla), William Dunkelberg (Stanford), Myron Joseph (Carnegie-Mellon University), Keith Lumsden (Stanford), Phillip Saunders (Indiana University), and Norton Seeber (Oakland University). Professor Michael Lovell of Wesleyan University continues to share authorship of the mathematical appendixes. Professor Stewart Lee of Geneva College has been helpful on several editions. The usual warning that only I am responsible for the final outcome needs to be added, however, for I have accepted only some of the suggestions advanced. Lastly, I want to add my appreciation to James Bacci, Eloise Starkweather, and Marvin Warshaw of Prentice-Hall for their help in making the book more readable and attractive throughout; to Lynette Sweet for her many hours of expert secretarial assistance throughout; and to Lorian Marlantes for his valuable assistance in preparing the index.

CONTENTS

---

part three Markets, the Price System, and the Allocation of Resources

---

---

part four The Distribution of Income

---

part five   Public Goods and the Public Sector

part six   The International Economy

part seven   Perspectives on Economic Change

Suggested Outlines
for
Alternative Courses

course A   Emphasizing Microeconomics
(one semester—about 440 pages)

course C   Suggested Division of Text for Year-Long Course

First Semester *(About 360 pages)*

PART I

The Foundations of Economic Analysis

PART III

Markets, the Price System, and the Allocation of Resources

PART IV

The Distribution of Income

*PART V

Public Goods and the Public Sector

Second Semester *(About 350 pages)*

PART II

National Income, Employment, and Economic Growth

PART VI

The International Economy

PART VII

Perspectives on Economic Change

*Some instructors may prefer to shift this to the beginning of the second semester.

course D Alternative Division for Year-Long Course

First Semester *(About 340 pages)*

PARTS I, II, AND V.

Second Semester *(About 370 pages)*

PARTS III, IV, VI, AND VII.

part one

The Foundations of Economic Analysis

Economics in the Modern World

Economics is the study of how the goods and services we want get produced, and how they are distributed among us. This part we call economic analysis. Economics is also the study of how we can make the system of production and distribution work better. This part we call economic policy. Economic analysis is the necessary foundation for sound economic policy. This is a book about both economic analysis and policy. It is a book about the big economic problems of our time.

Without concrete examples, such a definition conveys little meaning. Consider the following examples, chosen to give you some impression of the range of problems with which economics deals. Then we shall turn in later chapters to how economists analyze such problems, large and small, through the use of theory and its application.

International Living Standards

Over the face of the earth, over 3 billion human beings live in widely varying economic circumstances. Look at Table 1–1 for a summary picture.

The figures in the table are obtained by adding together the money value of all the goods and services produced in each country in 1970 (clothes, food, buildings, machinery, automobiles, defense products), and dividing each total by the number of people in that country. The figures shown are rough, but, with the possible

table 1-1
World Output per Capita, 1970*

Country	Dollars	Country	Dollars
United States	$4,800	Italy	$1,400
Canada	3,450	Mexico	550
Sweden	3,300	Brazil	370
West Germany	2,750	Egypt	180
France	2,550	India	115
United		Communist	
Kingdom	2,300	China	115**
USSR	1,700	Nigeria	110
Japan	1,500	Ethiopia	65

*Converted to U.S. dollars in 1970 prices. For source, more complete data, and an explanation of what is included and excluded, see Table 19-1.

**Extremely rough estimate.

exception of the so-called underdeveloped or less-developed countries, they are usable approximations. For the major Western countries, we know they are reasonably accurate.

Compare the U.S. per capita output of $4,800 with the figures for Communist China, India, and Ethiopia, all under $125. The United States has been called an affluent society; no word other than poverty can describe the living standards of the hundreds of millions in the less-developed nations. We are the "haves," they are the "have-nots." Although most of the industrialized Western world falls in the $1,000-and-up per capita output group, nearly two-thirds of the world's population—nearly 2 billion human beings—live in countries with per capita incomes of $150 per year or less.

The figures in Table 1-1 to some extent compare incomparables. The Indian or Chinese peasant lives in a rough hut in a tiny village, with no clothes except what he wears, and with a monotonous diet of fish or rice. He lives out his years never going more than twenty-five miles from his birthplace. He has so little in common with the American or West European that the figures may have little real meaning. The same is true for the African tribesman. But the figures do say unmistakably that we are extremely rich by comparison with the billions who live in the

less-developed countries, and that they are bitterly poor.

Why is this so? And why has the United States, a relatively new nation, raced ahead of the other major industrial nations of the Western world, most of whom were there long before us? Casual observation suggests that all the high-income countries in Table 1-1 are predominantly "capitalist" or "free enterprise." Not until we reach the USSR about halfway down the list, do we come to a "Communist" country, while the very poor nations shown are either Communist or have placed much less reliance on private-enterprise institutions than we. Is this the answer? Or is there another reason?

Why nations, and individuals in those nations, receive the incomes they do is one of the big questions to be answered by the use of economic analysis throughout this book.

Incomes in the United States

The United States is the richest nation in the world. In 1970, for example, we produced some $980 billion worth of goods and services. About $225 billion of this total went for national defense, education, highways, and other government services. Another $140 billion consisted of "producers' goods"—factories, machinery, new buildings, and other equipment for producing more and better consumer goods in the future. The biggest chunk, two-thirds of the total, was made up of consumer goods and services—autos, beefsteak, clothing, medical services, and the like.

Against this background, consider Figure 1-1, which shows the incomes received by American families in 1970. The median family income was $9,400 for a statistically average family; half of all families received more than this and half less. At the top, nearly 20 percent of all families received incomes over $15,000, and the 10 million families in this group received over $300 billion, about 40 percent of the national income of all families. Over 40 percent of all families had incomes above $10,000.

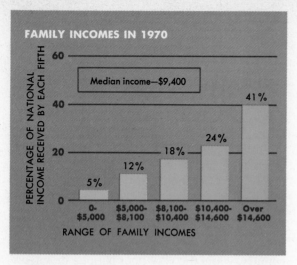

fig. 1-1

The United States has a wide range of family incomes. Each bar shows one-fifth of all families. Three-fifths of all families had incomes between $5,000 and $14,600, but the 20 percent with higher incomes received 40 percent of the national total. Half got more than $9,400, half less. (Source: U.S. Census Bureau; preliminary data for March, 1970.)

But at the bottom, even with America's affluence, nearly 10 percent of all families and single individuals received incomes under $3,000, and those families received less than 2 percent of the nation's total income. Why is poverty still

fig. 1-2

The past century has seen a dramatic change in the way Americans earn their livings. Today over 60 percent of all jobs are in service industries; less than 40 percent work at producing physical goods. Note the decline in agriculture. (Sources: National Resources Committee and U.S. Department of Commerce.)

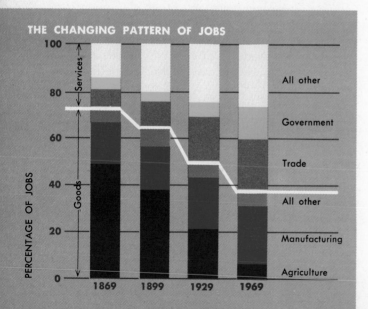

a massive social problem in our prosperous economy? Many social observers have written that the world of poverty is a world of desolation, of hopelessness, of bitterness and resentment, of slums, of discrimination. It is a world of Negroes and Puerto Ricans living in the great slums; of old men and women living alone in rented rooms; of poor southern farmers living in ramshackle huts without plumbing; of fatherless families whose mothers struggle to support their children; of failures and rejects for a dozen other reasons.

Economists ask: Why these income differentials? Why are the poor, poor, and the rich, rich? They also ask: If we don't like it, what can we do about it? These are two central themes in Part Four.

Changing Job Patterns in the United States

Figure 1-2 shows the jobs Americans work at today, and the great changes in our job patterns that have occurred over the past century. A hundred years ago, nearly 75 percent of all jobs involved the production of goods (coal, steel, food, clothing, and so on), only one-quarter the production of services (doctors, lawyers, amusements, transportation, and so on). Today, the picture is reversed. Only 40 percent of all jobs are devoted to producing physical goods, 60 percent to producing services. And the trend toward more services continues.

What will job patterns be in 1975 or 1980 when you enter the labor market? Economic analysis says they will depend largely on consumer demands for different goods and services, on technological changes, and on public wants expressed through government taxing and spending, plus a variety of other factors. Parts Three, Four, and Five all contribute to answering this question.

Government and the Economy

Most people in the United States—about five-sixths of the total—work for themselves or for private employers. But looked at another way, one worker out of six is on a government payroll (if we include the armed services)—over 14 million people.

In 1970, governments (federal, state, and local) bought nearly one-fourth of all the goods and services produced in the economy. Government spending included not only salaries of government jobholders, but primarily payments for missiles, highways, schools, and other things bought for the benefit of the citizens. In addition, governments made about $100 billion of "transfer payments"—payments like old-age pensions, unemployment benefits, and interest on the national debt, for which the recipient renders no direct service. To get the money for these expenditures, governments took a huge chunk of our incomes in taxes—about $330 billion in 1970. Figure 1–3 shows the picture for that year.

In addition, governments make and enforce a maze of regulations as to what we may and may not do in our economic activities. They regulate banks and financial institutions. Federal law sets the minimum wage employers must pay, and prescribes that business must deal with workers and unions when the workers so choose. Governments set elaborate standards of performance for businesses and specify that businesses cannot discriminate against employees on the basis of race, creed, or color. Government says businesses cannot agree to fix prices and cannot merge together to form bigger businesses if this would substantially reduce competition.

How big should government be? How much should it intervene in the economic processes of our basically private market economy? These are questions that will recur over and over through the chapters to come. Parts Three and Five focus on these issues.

Big Business in the Economy

Ours has been called a business economy. Most of us earn our livings by working for businesses. We buy most of our products from businesses. Many of us own parts of businesses, directly or through ownership of stock.

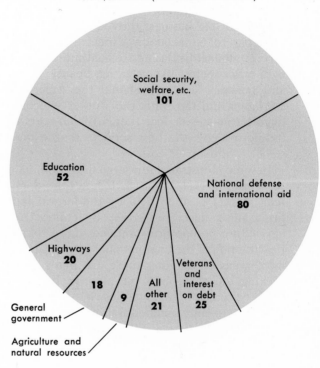

GOVERNMENT SPENDING, 1970

Total: $326 billion (slices in billions of dollars)

Social security, welfare, etc. **101**

Education **52**

National defense and international aid **80**

Highways **20**

Veterans and interest on debt **25**

All other **21**

18

9

General government

Agriculture and natural resources

fig. 1–3

Of $326 billion of federal, state, and local government spending in 1970, nearly one-third went for social security and welfare payments, another nearly one-third for national defense and such related items as international aid and veterans' benefits. (Sources: U.S. Budget and U.S. Department of Commerce, preliminary estimates.)

In total, there are some 10 million business firms in the United States. About 9 million of these are relatively small businesses run by individual owners, 3 million of them in agriculture and most of the others as small-scale retail outlets, cleaning establishments, service stations, professions, and the like. About 1 million are business "corporations." These business corporations, generally owned jointly by many people, do the bulk of the nation's business, employ over 60 percent of its workers, and account for about two-thirds of all privately produced output. The biggest modern corporations are true Goliaths. In 1970, for example, the assets of the American Telephone & Telegraph Company (the world's largest business) exceeded $30 billion, and General Motors' sales of over $20 billion were larger than the entire output of most of the world's nations.

Why has big business thrived so mightily in some parts of our economy (especially manufacturing), while little businesses continue to dominate other sectors like retailing, beauty shops, and personal services? Should the American consumer and the American worker welcome huge businesses or fear them? Which sorts of businesses give the best services to the consumer at the lowest cost?

In some industries a few large firms dominate the entire market. Figure 1–4 shows the dominant market position held by the largest four firms in six major industries. By contrast, in agriculture no one firm produces more than a tiny fraction of the total national output, and in most areas of retailing there are many firms seeking the consumer's business. In between these extremes are many industries that have a moderate to large number of firms, but far from the huge number of small firms that characterize agriculture.

What are the results of market concentrations like those pictured in Figure 1–4? Is such concentration a danger to the consumer? What kinds of firms and market arrangements are most efficient in producing the goods and services we as consumers want? Part Three provides the analysis needed to answer these questions, and some suggestions on policy to make such markets work better.

Unemployment and Inflation

Over the past two centuries, the American economy has been the greatest economic success story in the history of mankind. The evidence is vividly presented in Table 1–1. But American history also tells a story of intermittent booms and depressions.

Figures 1–5 and 1–6 picture two sides of this problem. In a private-enterprise economy we have never completely eliminated unemployment, and intermittently the percentage of our labor force out of work has risen to 5, 10, and even, in the Great Depression of the 1930s, to nearly 25 percent. Depression and massive unemployment bring immeasurable hardship and waste. Idle men and idle machines mean hunger and desolation, famine and want in the midst of potential plenty, the erosion of human dignity.

On the other hand, there have been intermittent "booms," with sharply rising prices—inflation. When prices rise, the amount of goods and services you can buy with a dollar falls correspondingly, though incomes rise, so most people have more dollars to spend. Figure 1–6 shows the intermittent erosion over the past century in the purchasing power of a dollar, as prices have, on the average, risen much more than they have fallen. A close look at the chart suggests that the big inflations (that is, the big drops in the purchasing power of a dollar) have come during and soon after major wars—in the early 1920s and again in the 1940s, 1950s, and 1960s; but remember that these have also been periods of booming prosperity, which has also often been associated with inflation. Clearly, inflation is a more complex issue than merely the question of how much less one dollar will buy when prices rise.

fig. 1–4

The largest four firms dominate the market in many leading American industries. (Source: Federal Trade Commission. Data are for 1966.)

MARKET POSITION OF LEADING FIRMS

Aluminum
Electric lamps
Linoleum
Breakfast cereals
Cigarettes
Autos and parts

0   25   50   75   100
PERCENTAGE OF INDUSTRY OUTPUT

fig. 1–5

Unemployment soars in depressions, and even in recessions. What is a reasonable minimum level of unemployment for us to shoot at? (Source: U.S. Department of Labor.)

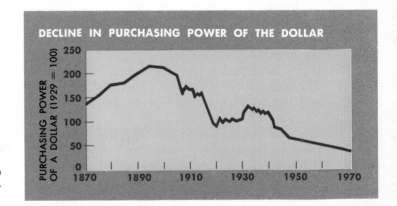

fig. 1–6

Inflation has repeatedly eroded the value of the dollar, with the biggest price increases coming during and after wars. (Source: U.S. Department of Labor.)

Why does our economy intermittently generate periods of unemployment and depression, and then periods of prosperity and inflation? Must a private-enterprise economy accept such economic instability or have we now learned how to eliminate unemployment and inflation through the use of government monetary and tax-expenditure policies? Dare we risk increasing the national debt to increase government spending aimed to fight unemployment? These questions have loomed large in economics since the 1930s. The interacting questions of economic analysis and economic policy they pose form the core of Part Two.

Economic Growth—National Priorities and the Future

The American standard of living today is the world's highest. We have achieved this posi-

tion of eminence in only two short centuries. Will our economy continue to grow at the rate of the past two centuries? Will other nations catch us and overtake us, or will we widen the gap? What will be the future of the economic race between the United States and the USSR, between capitalism and communism?

Table 1–2 shows, for a number of leading nations, the annual percentage increase in output per capita over the past century, and over the last decade. Will the recent higher growth rates persist with their rapid improvement in living standards? What accounts for some of the fascinating differences among the nations shown —for example, the remarkable surge of Japan?

Table 1-2 does not include the less-developed countries, which hold over two-thirds of the world's people. India and Communist China alone contain about one out of every three human beings alive. Yet there is little evidence that the average standard of liv-

table 1-2

Growth in per Capita Production*

Country	1865—1965	1960—1970
Japan	3.0	10.0
Sweden	2.2	3.3
United States	2.1	3.8
USSR	2.0	3.7
France	1.6	3.7
Germany	1.6	4.6
United Kingdom	1.2	2.2
Italy	1.2	4.4

*First column based on data for approximately 100 years. For sources, see Chapter 16.

ing of the Indian or Chinese peasant is much higher now than it was a thousand years ago. The gap between the less-developed nations and the Western world is widening dramatically, not closing!

Is there an answer in the experience of the Western industrialized world for the poverty-stricken masses of the less-developed nations? What can those nations do to help themselves, or what can we do to help them to get started on the path towards self-sustaining economic growth? What are the key factors in rapid economic growth? Perhaps no questions in economics are more important than these, for it is only through growth in output per capita that the living standards of the people of the world can rise over the long run. Part Two focuses on these issues.

Recently many Americans, especially college students, have challenged the validity of per capita incomes as measures of economic well-being. They demand more stress on the "quality of life," less on the "quantity of goods and services." They assert that our industrialized economy is producing alienation, dirty air and water, and unneeded consumer goods, while the gross-national-product (total-output) figures soar.

How effectively our economy meets our national priorities is a very important question. Reduction in air, water, and noise pollution has recently become a pressing national goal. So

have elimination of poverty, and of urban slums and blight. But other Americans prefer freedom to spend their incomes individually to paying the taxes needed to finance the new national priorities of clean air, slum removal, and the like. Economic analysis throughout the text stresses the central problem of allocating our limited resources to producing efficiently the most wanted goods and services. There is never enough to go around—for everyone to have all he wants of everything. Will the optimal allocation of resources be best achieved by relying on the business profit motive in responding to consumer spending, on government intervention through regulations, taxing, and spending, or on other approaches? There are no easy answers, but Parts Two, Three, and Five provide the analysis you will need to think the problem through for yourself.

A Sampler of Smaller Problems

All the preceding examples have been big problems, at the national or international level. But economics is equally concerned with "little" problems, close to home in everyday life. You work summers as a resort waitress; why is your hourly wage what it is? You are studying to be an accountant; will electronic computers replace people in many middle-management jobs, and what will they do to accountants' salaries?

Most big cities require licenses to operate taxicabs. For example, in New York City there is a fixed supply of some 12,000 such licenses, which can be bought and sold by taxi operators. Is the public better served by such a system of limited licenses than by one of open entry for anyone who will obey city-specified rules on rates and service? Many cities regulate the rates parking-lot operators can charge, to prohibit their "gouging" the public on special occasions such as big ball-game days; others have rent ceilings for apartments in low-income areas. What are the real effects of such regulations? Whom do they help and whom do they hurt? Your city has to raise more tax revenues to finance its spending on education and general services; what are the relative advantages and disadvantages of a city sales tax, a wage tax, and higher property taxes? Economic issues are everywhere in everyday life. Part Three provides the analysis for such problems.

Economics in a Democracy

These are the problems of economics. They, and many others like them—big and little, national and local, public and personal—are the problems of this book. Some are difficult and complex, some are simple. All are problems of the real world around us every day. To understand them, it is necessary both to understand some basic economic concepts and principles and to understand how to use those concepts and principles in analyzing different problems. In order to reach intelligent conclusions on government policy and private policy, economic analysis is the essential foundation. For without such analysis, debates may be lively, but they are likely to generate more heat than light—to be primarily an airing of hunches and emotions, rather than rational analysis of issues involved.

Throughout your life, economics will play a major role in determining what you do and how happy you are doing it. If there are depressions or inflations, you will not be able to escape them. Your income will depend largely on how effectively you participate in the economic process. Thus, from a purely selfish point of view, it will pay you to understand how your economic system works.

But the main reason citizens in a democracy need to understand the economic system is that they are voters as well as active participants in the economy. Not long ago governments didn't interfere much in economic life, but that time has passed. Today, almost everybody agrees that the government should provide national defense, social security, education, and a score of other services not forthcoming through the private-enterprise economy; that it should regulate the supply of money; that it should protect consumers against the excesses of monopoly; that it should prevent depressions and inflations. Fill out the list for yourself. Many people believe the government should do many more things—provide medical protection for the poor, support the prices of farm products, legislate minimum wages, even guarantee full employment.

This is a book on "political economy." It is concerned with using economic analysis to find answers to the problems above and to many more. The goal is to understand how our economy works now and how to make it work better. The political economist doesn't sit on the sidelines. He is interested in what to do about the big and little problems we face.

But if you expect to find the answers in this book to what you or the government should and should not do, you're in for a disappointment. The job of a course in economic analysis is to give you the tools and the background for making up your own mind on the important economic issues of the day, and to teach you how to use the tools—not to tell you what to think. Better understanding of how the system works will go a long way toward making you a more intelligent citizen. But you should recognize from the outset that even with a thorough understanding of economics, not everybody will come out with the same answers on the problems of public policy. This is because we have different ideas on where the nation ought to be headed. Some people, for example, think that avoiding inflation is the most important thing. Others believe that assuring everyone a reasonable minimum income should have first priority. Any respectable economist will advise the government to do different things, depending on which of these objectives is placed first. Such conflicts among the goals of different individuals and groups are an important part of the modern American democracy in action.

Objectives of the Book

If you're going to spend several months or a year studying a book, you deserve to know what the author thinks he is trying to accomplish. A good deal of the flavor of this book has been given in the preceding pages. It's a mixture of analysis and policy. But specifically, the book is aimed at these objectives.

1. To provide an overview of the way our individualistic, largely private-enterprise but mixed economic system works.

2. To focus attention on the big problems faced by our economic system, and to arouse an interest in economic problems that will last after you leave college. If your use of the concepts in this book ends with the final exam, the book will have failed. Its real goal is to help you read the newspaper, argue understandingly with your neighbor, and vote intelligently on economic issues over the years ahead.

3. To provide a few fundamental analytical concepts and principles that will stick with you and help you in thinking about economic problems for yourself. You need an economic tool kit.

4. To help develop an orderly, systematic way of thinking through economic problems— of applying the concepts and theories in your economic tool kit. There's nothing unique about straight thinking in economics. But heated emotions, prejudices, and gossip are especially likely to get in the way of objectivity in discussing labor relations, the national debt, and other such subjects. In economics, as elsewhere, you have to know what the problem is before you can solve it. You need to marshal your analytical tools and use them carefully and systematically, instead of rushing blindly ahead on the first tack that comes to your mind. You need to check your conclusions against other evidence and against other conclusions on the same question. And, if you want to understand more in the future than you do now, you need to stop frequently and ask yourself: What have I learned by thinking through each problem?

The habit of orderly, careful thinking is something you can't learn in any one course alone. But a major purpose of this book is to repeat the process over and over in economics, in the hope that it will stick both here and in other fields. Chapter 2 has a good deal more to say on this important subject.

5. To provide enough descriptive material on the present economic system to give you a foundation for understanding what the problems are. Without understanding a problem in its whole setting, there's little chance of solving it effectively. And knowing the facts is a first step. But the book makes no pretense of supplying an encyclopedic description of the modern economy. It takes the position that your main job is to learn how to think straight for yourself, not to cram your head full of facts. A mind cluttered with transient details seldom sees the major issues. And few things will be deader ten years from now than many of today's facts. In any case, the evidence is clear that we don't remember most of the facts we memorize anyway. So learn the main outlines of the economic system and the facts you need to understand each problem that you study. But don't make a fetish of facts.

Throughout the book, whenever policy issues are posed, you will find a recurring theme: Decide for yourself what you think should be done! This is not because economists have no ideas on what should be done, or because economic analysis does not suggest strongly what ought to be done. We do have ideas, lots of them, on public policy issues, and on many of these issues economic analysis points a clear path. But the main goal of the book is to give you the tools you will need, and experience in using those tools to reach your own conclusions.

Some Suggestions on How To Use the Book

The most important suggestions on how to use this book are contained in the preceding sections. But there are some tricks in using a book like this that may help you do a better job than just plowing through the assignment each day.

1. Know where you're going before you start reading. Before you start a chapter, go back and look at its place in the table of contents. Then skim through the chapter itself. Every chapter is organized so that the major headings mark off the main parts. These headings are designed to give a summary picture of what is covered, and to provide an outline of the chapter to help you

keep the main points in focus. With this framework in mind, then study the chapter thoroughly.

2. As you read, keep asking yourself, "What is the main point of this paragraph and of this section?" Try to put the ideas in your own words. Some sections are largely descriptive. Some are full of tightly reasoned analysis, usually supplemented by an example of how the analysis might apply. It's important to remember that the analysis is the main point; don't let the example become the center of your attention except as an example. To help you, main ideas are set in different-colored type so they will stand out. In addition, the old-fashioned devices of underscoring main points in the text and making notations in the margins can help in studying and reviewing throughout the book.

3. Much of economics is cumulative. So if you don't understand a paragraph or a section the first time you read it, don't kid yourself. Be sure you understand as you go along. Otherwise, as the course goes on, things are likely to get progressively foggier, not clearer.

4. When you've finished reading, review to see what you've really learned. A tough but very useful test is to shut the book, put aside any notes you have taken, and then write down in a few sentences the fundamental points of the chapter. If you can do this, you've read the right way—concentrating on the fundamentals and using the rest of the chapter as a setting for understanding them. If it takes you more than a page, you may have read the chapter well, but you had better recheck to be sure you have the central points clearly in mind.

Review

FOR ANALYSIS AND DISCUSSION

Throughout the text, these end-of-chapter questions are designed as a basis of class and out-of-class analysis and discussion. They are "think" questions. Drill and self-test questions, to test whether you understand the mechanics of the theory presented and its use are available in M. Joseph and N. Seeber, *Workbook in Economics*, 4th ed. (Englewood Cliffs, N.J.: Prentice-Hall, Inc., 1971), designed specifically for use with this text.

1. What factors seem to you most important in explaining why our standard of living is so high compared with India's? With England's? Can you explain the order of the countries in Table 1–1?
2. Why has employment in agriculture declined so steadily over the past century relative to that in other major sectors of the economy like manufacturing and services?
3. What do you think are the main reasons why many Americans are so poor, as indicated by Figure 1–1, while others receive such high incomes?
4. Is the government spending shown in Figure 1–3 too large? How can you decide whether it is too large compared to the private sector of the economy?
5. If another major depression like that of the 1930s occurs, how seriously do you think it will affect you and your family? What if a rapid inflation occurs, in which prices double over the next few years? From your own point of view, which is the more serious problem for the economy to avoid? Why?
6. Suppose you are visiting abroad and are alarmed to find a large amount of anti-American sentiment, on the ground that America is

extremely wealthy and could well afford to give more aid to less-wealthy peoples, rather than selfishly clinging to most of the goods we produce. How would you go about explaining to the local residents why the present distribution of real income among the nations is a fair and proper one?

7. What are the "national priorities" that you would give top emphasis in deciding what our economic system ought to achieve?

two

Economics as an Empirical Science

Straight thinking is hard work. Few of us have acquired the careful, orderly mental habits and disciplines demanded by straight thinking.

For many people, straight thinking in economics is especially difficult. Not that economics is inherently more difficult or more complex than many other fields. But economics is so mixed up with our everyday lives that, without realizing it, we've accumulated a mass of opinions, ideas, hearsay, and half-truths that subtly dominate our minds when economic questions arise.

When we want to build a bridge, it never occurs to us to start without calling in expert engineers to design it. If we want expert advice on physics, we ask the physicists. Few people consider themselves experts on bridge building just because they drive across a bridge every day going to work, or on physics just because they live in the physical world. Yet many people, especially if they've "met a payroll," somehow feel that they're experts on economics simply because they successfully earn a living in the economic world.

It's not surprising that most people have views on the big economic issues outlined in Chapter 1. They're in the newspapers every day, in every election campaign. And the tendency for every man to be his own economist is strengthened by the fact that economics is close to the pocketbook. It is especially hard to be objective about things that affect us intimately. But merely living in the economic world or meeting a payroll doesn't make us experts on

13

how the economy operates, any more than having teeth makes us experts on dental health and how to fill cavities. Economics is concerned with the way the whole economy operates, not with the way in which to run a better grocery or bank. And these are quite different things.

The purpose of this chapter is to provide a broad-brush picture of the way economics can help you to do your own intelligent thinking about economic issues. It's about the way economists analyze these problems, and how you can analyze them for yourself.

The Tax Cut of 1964—An Example

Consider an example—a highly simplified analysis (since this is merely an introductory overview) of the way economics helped us to understand a major economic issue and to predict the consequences of an important tax change. After this introduction, we will look more systematically at modern economics as an empirical science, and at the problem of doing your own straight thinking in economics.

In the early 1960s, the economy was performing reasonably well. Most people had jobs with good pay, profits were substantial. Yet over 5 percent of the labor force was unemployed. If this figure could have been reduced to 3 or 4 percent, the nation could have had perhaps $30 to $40 billion worth of additional goods and services. Productive capacity in men and machines was wasted because total demand for goods and services was not large enough to make it profitable for businessmen to hire workers and produce this extra output.

To remedy this situation, presidents Kennedy and Johnson, following the advice of many economists, recommended a major cut in income taxes on individuals and businesses, without a corresponding reduction in federal spending. They reasoned that if consumers had more money left to spend after paying their tax bills (that is, if their "disposable incomes" were larger because of lower tax bills), total spending on goods and services would increase and businesses would hire more workers and increase output to meet this demand.

They proposed a tax cut of about $10 billion. They argued that, in fact, aggregate spending and hence incomes received by workers and others in the society would actually rise by more than $10 billion—possibly by $20 or $25 billion as a result of this tax cut. This would occur because the new consumer expenditures would be received by others who would in turn spend more, hire more workers, and buy more goods. This spending would in turn increase the incomes of others, who would in their turn have more to spend. This respending effect, called the "multiplier" effect by economists, would thus help substantially to raise incomes and reduce unemployment.

Consider the essential steps in the reasoning. In essence, these economists had a "model," or "theory," of how the economy functions, and of how the effects of the tax cut would work their way through this economy. Their first assumption was that if consumers received an increase in disposable incomes (because their tax bills were reduced), **other things equal** they would spend a large portion (probably over 90 percent) of this increased disposable income on consumer goods and services, rather than use it to pay off debts or just hold on to it. Second, the economists had a model of typical business firms that indicated that in response to increased consumer spending these firms would hire more workers and furnish more goods, in the process paying out more incomes to those whom they hired and to suppliers from whom they bought raw materials.

Third, in the economists' model, the government would borrow funds to maintain government spending unchanged after the tax cut, and this borrowing would not produce an offsetting reduction in private spending by drawing away spendable funds from private consumers or businesses. If the borrowing should correspondingly reduce private spending, obviously the desired increase in total spending on goods and services would not result. Fourth, to provide the specific estimate that total national income would rise by about $25 billion as a result of the $10 billion tax cut, their model had to include estimates showing how much consumer spending would rise per dollar of additional disposable income (perhaps ninety-five cents), how many new workers would be hired per dollar of additional consumer spending, and the like.

Many people were skeptical of the argument for the tax cut. For example, they argued that consumers would in fact not increase their spending on goods and services by anything like ninety-five cents for each dollar of new disposable income, but would in effect hoard the additional income they received or use it to pay off debts. Skeptics raised other objections as well, but let us focus attention for now on this particular counterargument.

Most economists firmly rejected the counterargument. Why? Because economists have made elaborate empirical (factual) investigations of the relationship between consumers' disposable income and their spending. These studies have consistently shown that other things equal for high-employment periods of moderately stable growth, such as we had during the 1960s, consumers spend a remarkably stable proportion of additional disposable incomes—generally around 94–96 percent, given some months to adjust to larger incomes. Sophisticated economists know that this figure is only a first approximation, and that it reflects a complex interplay of forces behind the scenes. But as a rough approximation it was a safe assumption that, barring other special forces at work, consumers would spend the largest portion of their new disposable income on goods and services within, say, six months to a year.

Who was right? After the tax cut was passed by Congress in early 1964, the effects on the economy were very close to the predictions of the economists who advocated the cut. Although it is difficult to measure precisely the results of any action in a complex economy, consumers did behave almost exactly as the model predicted, and the national income did rise by almost exactly the $25 billion predicted. The tax cut was widely acclaimed a great success.

What is the point of this example? It is both (1) to show you, in a very simplified way, how economists use models of major economic relationships to predict what will happen under different circumstances, and (2) to emphasize that such models must rest on careful empirical research about the behavior patterns assumed if they are to be reliable. Without such a model of consumer and business behavior and of the interactions between them, the impact of the tax cut would have been pure guesswork.

The results in 1964 were impressive. But a warning! We have only seen that employment and national income in 1964 following the tax cut turned out about the way many economists predicted they would. This result lends credibility to the economic analysis used and to the claim that the good results were caused by the tax cut. But this is not necessarily so. The cause may have been something else. In fact, some economists argue that the happy results came about primarily because another part of the government, the Federal Reserve System, rapidly increased the supply of money available to consumers and businesses through the banking system, and that more money led to increased spending and employment. These other economists have a different model (which we shall spell out later), and the results were also consistent with their model. Thus, it is not clear from this evidence which of the two big causes (the tax cut or increased money in the economy) deserved the most credit.

In our complex world it is never possible to be absolutely sure about the consequences of major public actions when several things are going on at once. But the stakes are large, and we must make decisions on economic policy issues, like those aimed at eliminating undesirable unemployment. The better our models are, the more fully validated they are by empirical evidence on the major interactions among the variables, the more confident we can be of our ability to predict the consequences of alternative economic policies.

Economics as an Empirical Science

Against the backdrop of this oversimplified example, turn now to a more systematic look at how modern economics operates as an empirical science, and how it can help you toward straight thinking on economic issues.

Use of Simplified Models: Theory

The most apparent fact about economic reality is its complexity. There are millions of businesses, 200 million consumers, hundreds of thousands of different products, multiple stages in the production of nearly every product. Faced with this overwhelming complexity, we obviously have to find some way of simplifying things down to manageable proportions. The first job is to simplify.

In order to do so, the economist, like other scientists, begins by developing an analytical framework, or model, of the reality he wants to analyze. This model focuses on the main elements and main relationships in the complex real economic world he is studying. For example, in the tax case above the main elements of the model were consumer behavior, business behavior in response to increased demand, and the responding cycle in response to the original increase in disposable incomes.

Such simplified models are often called "theories." They make no pretense of being accurate descriptions of any part of the economy. If they were completely accurate, they would defeat their own purpose by getting back to all the detail. Instead, they are intended as highly simplified abstractions of the main elements of the reality to which they apply.

The notion of a model or theory can be illustrated by a noneconomic example. Suppose you want to understand how a bicycle works—a theory of its operation. You could study every detail of a single bicycle, or a large number of them, examining the tires, the handlebars, the sprocket, the paint, and so on. But if you could instead get a simple diagram, or a stripped-down working model of a bicycle, you'd get to the essentials quicker. This diagram wouldn't be concerned with all the details of paint, style, quality of steel, and so on. Instead, it would show the fundamental parts of the bicycle—wheels, frame, sprockets, driving chain, brake—and the basic relationships among these parts. The diagram would show how foot pressure applied to the pedals turns the sprocket wheel; how the chain connects this large sprocket to a smaller one at the center of the back wheel of the bicycle; and how, because of

the difference in the size of the sprocket wheels, pressure on the foot pedal exerts a multiplied pressure in turning the back wheel. The diagram should also indicate the important numerical relationships, for example, between the sizes of the large and small sprockets of the pedal and the back wheel.[1] People have used such a model of a bicycle many times, and its predictions have been thoroughly validated by empirical evidence. The theory, or model, is thus a good one in that it helps us to understand the way a bicycle works and to predict the consequences of changing the main variables—for example, the sizes of the two sprocket wheels. The theory "works."

So it is in economics. A model is a simplified diagram indicating the main elements in any situation, and the main interactions among these elements. The more firmly validated these relationships are by empirical observation of many cases, the safer we feel in using them in our model. Some models are very sketchy, merely identifying the main elements and loosely stating their interrelationships. Others specify precisely the relationships connecting the main variables, as when specific physical principles are used in explaining the operation of a bicycle. Unless we are reasonably precise as to the main economic forces at work and their interactions, with empirically validated quantitative statements of these relationships, we cannot safely predict how the economy will react to particular events or policy measures like the tax cut.

An economic model may be stated as a diagram, and many graphs are used in the pages ahead. It may be stated in words, as in the bicycle case above. Or it may be stated in mathematical terms, but except for a little simple algebra and geometry used in the diagrams, we shall use little mathematics.[2] Most economic

---

[1] In terms of basic physics, it might help to have explanatory notes on the diagram indicating that the principles of mechanical advantage are used, with the pedal being a second-class lever and the relative sizes of the gear wheels being crucial in determining the speed and power resulting from any given foot pressure on the pedals.

[2] However, there is a set of special mathematical appendixes at the end of the book for students familiar with calculus. References are indicated in the chapters to which these appendixes apply.

models can be stated in any of these three ways.

Last, it is important to emphasize that the economist doesn't apologize for the fact that his theories don't describe the real world precisely and in detail. On the contrary, like any other scientist, he says that any theory is a skeleton, or a framework, to help simplify and understand the intricate complexity he is attempting to understand and predict.

"Other Things Equal" and "Equilibrium"

The real world is far too complex for us to analyze everything at once. Thus, in common with many other scientists, economists use the concept of holding "other things equal," or "constant."

In the chemistry laboratory, we hold "other things equal" through controlled experiments. We put two elements (say hydrogen and oxygen) together in a test tube **under controlled conditions**, and get water if the proportions are two to one. In the bicycle example above, we hold friction, gravity, air pressure, and various other factors constant (or assume them away altogether) in analyzing the way the bicycle works. So it is in economics. To understand, say, what happens when consumers receive larger disposable incomes because of a tax cut, we may want to assume that many other things are "constant"—for example, the stock of money in the economy, political conditions, and the like—in order to simplify the job of analyzing the result of the tax cut. If at the same time that taxes are cut, war should break out, obviously consumers might use their additional disposable income in another way than under peacetime conditions. In the real world, "other factors" may not stay constant; but by assuming temporarily that they will do so, we can isolate the impact of the tax change in which we are interested.

This idea is closely related to the concept of "equilibrium," which is also widely used by scientists. In chemistry, for instance, after we've combined hydrogen and oxygen to form water, this equilibrium state is maintained until something disturbs it. In the same way, economists generally think of the economic system as tending to move toward equilibrium when some disturbing change occurs; and in analyzing the

movement of any sector of the economy toward equilibrium after it is disturbed, they commonly hold many "other things equal" in order to isolate the effects of the change being studied.

Consider a simple example related to the tax cut above. We may say a household (a consumer) is in equilibrium when it spends just that proportion of its income on all different products that bring it the greatest total satisfaction and saves the rest. Say the household is receiving $100 per week and spending $95 on a variety of goods and services while saving $5 per week. Now its disposable income rises to $110 weekly because of the tax cut. It is now obviously out of equilibrium because, unless it increases its spending on consumer goods and services, it will be saving $15 per week, a large increase in the percentage saved. This saving increase may well occur temporarily, because it takes time to adjust to changes in our economic affairs. But the household will presumably want to adjust toward a new equilibrium pattern of spending with its larger income. At the new higher level of income, it may decide to save a larger proportion of its disposable income, or it may decide that 5 percent is still about right. Either way, once it has adjusted its spending to the desired allocation of its income among all possible uses, it is again "in equilibrium." **We mean by equilibrium a situation in which everybody is satisfied to keep on doing what he is doing. In economic equilibrium, there's nothing at work to change the economic behavior under consideration.**

To repeat, "equilibrium" and "other things equal" are purely analytical concepts. No one believes that in the real world "other things" do always stay equal when we are trying to analyze the behavior of the economy, or that economic units are always in equilibrium. Use of these concepts simply helps us to trace through what **would** happen **if** all "other things" in the economic system remained unchanged until the new factor under consideration (such as the tax cut) had fully worked itself out. But don't think that this makes economic analysis just an intellectual game. Such analysis can give us powerful conclusions as to the **direction** the economy, or parts of it, will move in response to different individual actions or government policies, even if it can't tell us just what the end result will be some time hence in a world of many simultaneous crosscurrents.

Empirical Foundations for Economic Analysis

The social scientist, unfortunately, seldom can run controlled experiments. We can't get everything else in the economy to stand still while we lower income taxes 10 percent to see just what would happen. Nor can we get at the results by putting a few people off in a closed room and lowering their income tax 10 percent. So the social scientist is never as sure and precise as the physical and natural scientist can be.

But it's easy to overstate the differences, too. Economics is increasingly an empirical science, which is building up a vast body of quantitative knowledge about the behavior of economic units and the interactions among them.

How, for example, can we be **sure** about what proportion of their new disposable income consumers will spend in the event of a tax cut? The answer is, there is no way to be **sure**. But through intensive empirical analysis of consumer behavior in the past, we can greatly increase our confidence in the prediction we may make. And modern statistical techniques make it increasingly possible for us to use past information as a basis for predicting the future.

Suppose we speculate ("hypothesize") that the amount people spend on goods and services in any year will depend on the disposable income they have in that year. We hypothesize that consumer spending is a "function of" disposable income. That is, we hypothesize that consumer spending depends on, or is predictably related to, the disposable income they receive. Economists might write this functional relationship:

$$C = f(DI)$$

where C stands for consumption, f for "a function of" (perhaps with a value of .95 in this case), and DI for disposable income. To say that C is a "function of" DI means it "depends on" DI.

Suppose now that we get records showing the disposable incomes and consumption spending of a large number of families over the past ten years. Looking at these records, we find that many families have spent about 95 percent of their disposable incomes on consumption in most years, but there are lots of exceptions. For example, young families seem consistently to spend more than 95 percent, families in their fifties spend less, and retired families spend more. (These differences make sense if you think about it; young families are just starting up, buying new durable goods and raising babies, so they are able to save little; older families, once their homes are established and the children raised, find it easier to save out of their incomes; while retired families have reduced incomes and spend down past savings.) We also find that in years when incomes have risen rapidly, the percentage spent on consumption falls below 95. (Again, this seems reasonable, because it takes time for people to adjust their spending to new higher incomes.) And so we might examine many other special forces at work. But overall, for the average of all families in periods of reasonably stable, prosperous times, consumption hovers around 94 to 96 percent of disposable income.

In addition, we might observe a sample of families this year to see how they behave. Looking at them one at a time, we find wide diversity. But again, on the average, they seem to come out at about the 95 percent level for this year.

What could we infer from this statistical analysis? We should have to be careful, because we have seen exceptions to our general presumption. Certainly we could not safely predict the behavior of any particular family without knowing a lot about that family. But on the imaginary evidence cited just above, we would be increasingly comfortable in saying that, **other things equal**, in reasonably stable, prosperous periods consumers as a group will spend about 95 percent of any new disposable income on goods and services, given a reasonable amount of time to adjust to the new income.

This is an oversimplified example, but it suggests the way in which we must go about building up reliable quantitative information on economic behavior. Actually, as we shall see in

Part Two, consumer behavior is a good deal more complex then this, and we need a more elaborate theory to explain and predict it satisfactorily. So it is with most other parts of economic life. Economics, like any other empirical science, must continually develop new theories, test them out against the world, and reformulate them in the light of empirical evidence.

Prediction with Economic Theories

Thus far we have been talking mainly about a simple economic relationship—how much families will spend on consumption out of an additional dollar of disposable income. If we return now to the more complex issue of the total economic results of a tax cut like the one in 1964, the problem is more intricate. Here we need a theory with several subparts and a complex set of interactions among them.

How can we test how good a total theory is? There are two ways. One is to examine the assumptions on which the theory rests and the internal logic that it builds on those assumptions. The other is to make a pragmatic test of how well it actually predicts in the real world the variables in which we are interested (here employment and income). Both are valuable.

In the first approach, we ask two questions: (1) Do the assumptions of the theory correspond to the reality to which it is being applied? (2) Is the internal reasoning of the theory logically correct? If both these conditions are met, the theory should be useful for explanation and prediction. But there are problems. Most important, the world is so complex that it's hard to be sure that our assumptions are correct and that they are the only relevant ones for our problem. Remember that in the tax-cut example above, some economists suggested that leaving the money stock out of the analytical model left out the really important causal factor.

As a practical matter, therefore, many economists now rely more on the second test—how well does the theory actually predict? Economists thus try a model out to see what it predicts, and then check the prediction against the real world they are trying to explain. If the prediction is poor, they distrust the model, no mat-

ter how beautiful its logic. If a model based on dubious assumptions gives good predictions, they are inclined to use it, but only tentatively. For then they are uncertain about whether it predicts well because it is sound, or merely by chance. Alas, we can never be absolutely sure a model is "correct," even if it has predicted correctly in a number of past situations. It is always possible that the result may be the consequence of some other set of factors that we haven't thought about and don't have in our model. But the more frequently a model predicts correctly, the more confident of it we have a right to be.

Lastly, we can never be sure of our predictions for another reason—we can never know that the future will be like the past. Even though consumer spending of disposable income has been extremely consistent in the past, it may change tomorrow. It may change because consumers simply decide to behave differently. Or, more likely, it may change because of a change in other circumstances that affect consumer behavior. For example, international tensions may grow, and in such an uncertain world consumers might decide to save more than in the past.

All these warnings are important. There are many uncertainties about our understanding of the economic world. But much of economic theory has met both the tests discussed above. And there is no uncertainty about the path to better understanding. It is the path of economics as an empirical science, which involves an interacting pattern of basic empirical research, the development of better analytical models, and continuing checks on the predictive power of the new models. Happily, modern economics is making rapid progress as an empirical science, and much of this progress underlies the chapters to come.

One last introductory comment concerning theory and practice. You often hear someone say, "That's good theory, but it doesn't work in practice." What the speaker must mean, if he is talking sense, is either that it is not good theory because it doesn't help explain the real world, or that it is good theory but it is being inexpertly used. A theory (the use of an abstract model) is good only when it does work in practice—that is, when it is useful in helping to understand the problem to which it is being applied.

Economic Analysis and Public Policy

This book focuses on both analysis and its use in helping you think through the public-policy issues America faces. There is no one best way of thinking straight about policy problems—for instance, what should be done to check an inflation or avoid unemployment. But most experts agree that an orderly, systematic job of thinking through a "decision" problem of this sort (be it in economics or any other field) must include the following broad interacting steps:

1. First, define the problem. In economic policy issues, defining the problem usually has two parts: (a) understanding the situation in which the problem exists, and (b) clarifying the objectives you want to achieve. In simple words, you need to clarify where you are and where you want to go. In 1964, for instance, what was the basic economic situation, and what specific goals did we want to accomplish with the proposed tax cut? Unless you're straight on these two questions, you're likely to behave like a headless horseman, rushing this way and that, trying one tack after another, but getting more exercise than results. Unless we know where we are and where we want to go, our chances of getting there are poor.

2. Second, map out the main alternative ways of achieving the desired goals—the alternative paths from where we are to where we want to be. In the 1964 unemployment case, for example, there might have been three major approaches: increase the public's spending power through cutting taxes, increase the money supply, or raise government spending. No one can see in advance what all the fruitful alternatives may be, but a plan that covers systematically the major alternatives suggested by preliminary analysis will usually save time and help keep the main issues uppermost.

3. Third, analyze carefully the alternate policies outlined in step 2. "To analyze" means to trace through carefully the effects of the different policies. Here the analytical models you've learned will come in handy. Economic theory should help you make a tentative choice on the best steps to take. Perhaps in the analysis of your main three alternatives you'll hit on a fourth one you hadn't thought of at first. Although it's important to systematize your thinking, it's equally important to remain flexible and alert for new solutions.

4. When you finally have a tentative solution to the problem (for example, pass a law that sets a minimum wage for all workers), don't stop! The fourth step is: Check your solution—both against flaws in your own analysis resulting from fallacies or blind spots, and against past experience. The world has had recessions and unemployment before, and governments have tried to eliminate them before. If your preferred alternative has failed before, why? It's no fun to have to throw out a solution after you've gone through a lot of analysis to get it. But if your checking suggests that something is wrong, take another look.

Review

CONCEPTS
TO
REMEMBER

Be especially sure you understand the following concepts introduced in this chapter:

model	function
theory	hypothesis
"equilibrium"	statistical generalization
"other things equal"	

1. What is a "theory"? A "model"?
2. Why should we assume "other things equal" in economics when we know they aren't that way in the real world?
3. We suspect that ten-year-olds' demand for ice-cream cones depends on the temperature, their allowances, and the price of ice-cream cones. Can you write an equation showing the demand for cones (D_c) as a function of these three explanatory variables? How might we go about determining the relative importance of the explanatory variables for ten-year-olds in a particular community?
4. According to the "laws" of probability, if you toss an unbiased penny 100 times, it will come down heads and tails about 50 times each. How does this compare with an economic "law"—for example, that with people's wants for a commodity unchanged, an increase in the amount produced will, in competitive markets, lead to a lower price?
5. "Theory is all right for college professors, but not for me. I'm a practical man. Give me the facts and they'll speak for themselves." Do you agree or disagree with this sentiment? Why? How do facts speak for themselves?
6. (*Based on the appendix*) Analyze the validity of the following statements. In each case, explain carefully why you accept or reject the statement.
   a. What goes up must come down. (True about prices?)
   b. Sales taxes burden the poor, so they are inequitable taxes.
   c. In the past, booms have always been followed by depressions, so we can look forward to a real depression in the next few years.
   d. Millions are hungry in Asia, but government-owned wheat rots in storage bins. The administration's farm policy couldn't be more nonsensical.
   e. American industry is owned by the man in the street. A recent study by the New York Stock Exchange shows that 25 million Americans own stock in corporations.

APPENDIX   *SOME COMMON FALLACIES*

The preceding sections have outlined the positive job of straight thinking in economics. But the buzzing, booming, confusing world of economics seems to produce controversy everywhere. This appendix is intended to point up some of the common fallacies lying in wait for the unwary. Many of these fallacies, incidentally, show up everywhere you go, not merely in economics.

Wishing It Were So.   One of the commonest of human frailties is to believe the things we want to believe. The boss believes his employee-education program is opening the worker's eyes to the necessity of large profits for continued prosperity—and he may be a surprised man the next time the wage contract comes up for renewal if he's just been wishing it were so.

This is one of the most insidious fallacies. We tend to talk to people who agree with us, to read the newspaper that reports things the way we like, and to run away from information and conclusions that are painful to us. Confronted with two interpretations of an event, one favorable and the other unfavorable, most of us will choose the favorable one. The union members believe the company could pay lots higher wages if only it would. Top management believes that all right-thinking people see that management is right and labor wrong in most wage disputes. Just wishing it were so?

Post Hoc, Propter Hoc.   Suppose there's a bad depression. The government pays out large sums on public-works projects. Six months later we're on the way up. Was the government spending the cause of the recovery?

Many people would say "yes." The government spent, and recovery came. What could be clearer? But maybe the recovery was on its way anyhow, and the government spending did no good at all. The observed evidence tells us that government spending **may** have caused the recovery. But the mere fact that one event precedes another doesn't necessarily mean the first caused the second. They both may have been caused by some third factor. To assume that causation can be determined so simply is the fallacy of **post hoc, propter hoc**—"after this, therefore because of it." Keep your ears open and notice how often people rely on this sort of reasoning, especially in discussing economic problems.

The Fallacy of Composition. Next, perhaps the most dangerous fallacy of all in economics—the fallacy of composition. Suppose one rancher increases his cattle production. He can reasonably expect that the increase will bring him more money when marketing time comes round. But suppose that all ranchers decide to raise more beef cattle this year. Will they get more money for the cattle in total? Quite possibly not. More cattle coming to market will, other things equal, push down the price of cattle. If prices fall a long way because of the increased production, the total revenue to all cattle farmers may be less for the larger output of cattle. Clearly what is true for one rancher alone is not necessarily true for all ranchers taken together.

Consider another example. Saving is obviously a sensible procedure for most families. But suppose that in a depression everyone decides to increase his savings. What this will mean, other things equal, is that everyone cuts down on his consumption expenditures. Unless someone else spends more, merchants' sales will fall off. People may lose their jobs. Incomes fall, and with lower incomes people may actually find they are able to save **less** than before. How can a decision that is so obviously sound as an individual matter have such unintended, perverse results in the aggregate?

There are examples elsewhere too. Suppose you're in a crowded hall and can't see the stage very well. So you stand on your chair, and can see beautifully. But now suppose everyone else stands on his chair too. As a result, no one is better off. You can't conclude that what worked for you will work for the whole crowd.

To assume that what is true of one part will necessarily be true of the whole is the fallacy of composition. It may not seem reasonable that when we aggregate everybody together, everything may go topsy-turvy from the way it looked when we considered one person alone. But it does in economics, in a surprising number of cases. It's easy but fallacious to assume that what you know about the individual family or business is necessarily true for the whole economy.

Reasoning by Analogy. One of the most effective ways to explain something is to use an analogy. For example, in trying to explain the effect of continued repression on human behavior you may say, "Not letting someone express his feelings is like building up steam in a boiler." This conveys a vivid impression; if those feelings aren't let out, the person is going to burst like an overheated boiler.

Is the analogy a fallacy, or a very useful means of communication? It may be either, depending on how closely a human being with repressions actually corresponds to a steam boiler. It would be difficult to communicate without using analogies, but don't let the analogies lead you farther than can be justified by careful analysis. Analogies are everywhere. For example, are big businessmen in economic life robber barons?

The Dog and The Bone. Consider the following syllogism, as this particular form of reasoning is called:

Major premise: All dogs like bones.
Minor premise: Roger likes bones.
Therefore: Roger is a dog.

How about it? Is Roger a dog? You should see in a minute that the conclusion doesn't follow from the premises at all. Roger may be a man, or a woodchuck, or anything else that likes bones. Maybe he's a dog, but this reasoning doesn't give you any basis for believing it.

Now try this syllogism:

Major premise: All dogs like bones.
Minor premise: Roger is a dog.
Therefore: Roger likes bones.

Here the logic is airtight. If the first and second statements (the premises) are true, it necessarily follows that the conclusion is true: Roger likes bones. Why? Because the major premise states that **all** dogs like bones; and the minor premise states that Roger is a dog and hence included in the group covered by the major premise. If Roger is included in the group described by the major premise, anything that is true of all the major-premise group must be true of Roger.

The fallacy in the first syllogism is called the fallacy of the "undistributed middle." The minor premise doesn't get Roger included under the major premise. Hence, we don't know whether statements about the major-premise group are also true of Roger.

This may seem to have very little to do with economics, but in fact syllogistic reasoning crops up constantly in our daily conversations. Consider this example: "Necessities shouldn't be taxed, so potatoes should be exempted from sales taxes." If you look at it, this is nothing but a syllogism with a missing minor premise:

Major premise: Necessities shouldn't be taxed.
Minor premise:
Therefore: Potatoes should be exempted from taxation.

Set up this way, it is obvious that the minor premise has to be, "Potatoes are a necessity," to make the reasoning sound. If in fact potatoes aren't a necessity, the conclusion won't necessarily follow. It may be desirable to avoid taxing potatoes, but the conclusion cannot be demonstrated from the major premise alone.

This example is a very simple one. Most syllogisms are not quite so easy to detect and clear up; often the conclusion is stated first, with the premises following "Because" or some other similar word. For example, "Potatoes shouldn't be taxed because we shouldn't tax necessities." Keeping your eye out for fallacious logic is an effective way to ferret out crooked thinking.

Facts That Aren't Facts. The second syllogism above looks airtight, but can we really be sure that Roger likes bones? The answer is, yes—if . . . only if the statements in the major and minor premises are in fact true. Do all dogs really like bones, and is Roger really a dog?[3]

When is a fact a fact? In the economic world, there are very few facts like the major premise above: "All things are this way," or "this is *always* thus and so." Such statements are called universal propositions. It is important to recognize that a universal proposition can never be completely validated by evidence. We can never examine all the cases to find out whether it was always true in the past, but even more important we can never be sure that it will always be true in the future even if it has always been true in the past.

An accurate statement is much more likely to be: "Most dogs like bones," or "The best evidence is that about 80 percent of all dogs like bones," or "Nearly all collies chew on bones when they are hungry." This fallacy of accepting a general assertion as a fact when it isn't necessarily always so is closely related to the discussion above on statistical verification or rejection of theories. For most economic statements, we need to specify carefully the conditions under which they are said to be true, and to look hard at the empirical evidence on how true they have been in the similar situations in the past. We need to be especially careful about extending the "facts" of the past into the future, unless we are confident that the circumstances that produced the facts in the past will be reproduced in the future.

These warnings immediately play havoc with airtight syllogistic logic, but unfortunately that's the way the world is. Don't throw your knowledge about syllogisms out the window, however. You can still use

it just as before, except that your statements generally need to be *probabilistic* rather than absolute. If 80 percent of all dogs like bones (assumed to be an established proposition) and if Roger is a dog, we have a priori a four-out-of-five chance that Roger will like bones. This a pretty high likelihood, but you still have to be cautious about the fifth chance.

It is impossible here to go into statistics and the rules of statistical inference that tell just what it's safe to conclude from combinations of probabilistic statements. But you should get used to the fact that facts are seldom absolute—that they are usually "almost always" true, or maybe only 60 percent true. Often they're true under some circumstances and false under others. This kind of world makes flatly "right" or "wrong" conclusions less common than many people like to think.

Generalizing from Small Samples. Another warning related to the same problem of using empirical evidence. "Redheaded people are hot-tempered. I know! I have two red-haired friends and they're both hot-tempered." Or, to go back to the dog-and-bone case: "I know that dogs like bones, because I have a dog and he likes bones!" Such statements are a favorite way of backing up your position that you "know for a fact."

To generalize about all redheaded people or about all dogs on a sample of one or two is extremely dangerous, unless you have some convincing reason to suppose that this tiny sample is representative of the whole universe of red-haired people or dogs. There is probably no commoner fallacy than that of generalizing unthinkingly from small samples. We are continually learning from what we see and do; this is the commonest way of extending our knowledge. Thus, we inevitably build up tentative generalizations about the world from our everyday experience. But your own limited experience may or may not be typical. The safest generalizations have been established by careful, systematic observation of a large number of cases. The same question again: When is a fact a fact?

Black, or White, or Gray? There is another related fallacy. If one is not wary, he can go astray by (explicitly or implicitly) assuming that there is no middle ground between two extremes. On a foggy day, someone asks, "Is it raining?" You reply, "No." "Then," he may retort, "you mean it is sunny." But of course it may just be foggy. Often there is a perfectly logical middle ground between what appear at first glance to be two mutually exclusive alternatives; the alternatives stated may not exhaust the possible situations. The wise observer of the economic scene is the one who sees the grays in their proper shadings —not the one who sees everything as black or white, true or false.

---

[3]Note that these are the same two warnings stressed a few pages back in evaluating theoretical models. Be sure the basic assumptions are sound, and that the reasoning is logically correct.

National Goals and Priorities

We live, it is said, in an affluent society. The United States is, indeed, rich by comparison with other nations. Table 1–1 in Chapter 1 shows per capita output of goods and services in this country as compared with a dozen other nations. We lead the Canadians and Swedes, the next most affluent nations, by over $1,000 per person in total output, and we have roughly double the output per capita of most of the Western European nations. Our lead over the so-called developing countries is enormous.

For example, in recent years most Americans have been deeply concerned about the poverty of Negro Americans, which is partly the result of discrimination against them in the marketplace. But in the late 1960s, the per capita income of the average American Negro, while only about 60 percent that of the average white, was substantially larger than that of the average Englishman. It was five times larger than that of the average Spaniard, and more than fifteen times that of the average Nigerian. Even the destitute black sharecroppers of the Mississippi Delta had per capita incomes that exceeded the per capita incomes of most countries outside Western Europe.

But many Americans are not satisfied. Our living standards are not high enough for a big part of the population. We have too few good schools, too little leisure. These critics feel that our national priorities need reexamination—that we are not allocating our rich productive resources properly. Some allege that the "quality" of American life is inferior to that of many other nations, certainly inferior to what it might be. They point to pollution, to the slums in our cities, to poverty, discrimination, and social immobility for minority groups. During recent years they have pointed especially to our heavy expenditures on national defense and the unpopular war in Vietnam, when we have other pressing goals at home, such as better education and housing for our own poor. But even apart from national defense, there is today a clamor that the nation reexamine its goals and its national priorities. The fact that we are so well-off economically makes our failure to devote adequate resources to important national goals doubly unacceptable.

National Goals

In 1960, a commission of a dozen distinguished Americans, appointed by President Eisenhower, produced a widely acclaimed statement, *Goals for Americans*.[1] After two years of study and large amounts of staff work by experts in every phase of American life, the commission listed fifteen major goals that should receive national priority. These goals were the following:

1. Freedom and opportunity for every individual.
2. Equality of status and opportunity.
3. Achievement of a truly democratic political process.
4. Better education for all, especially for those who do not have adequate access to higher education.
5. More resources for the arts and sciences; strengthening of knowledge and innovation on every front.
6. A democratic economic system, involving freedom of individual choice and diffusion of economic power.
7. Economic growth at the maximum rate consistent with primary dependence upon free enterprise and the avoidance of marked inflation.

8. Promotion of technological change as a powerful force for advancing our economy.
9. A more efficient, market-determined agricultural sector, providing a fair return to the farmers and adequate food at reasonable prices for the public.
10. Improvement of living conditions—primarily in the slums where low-income minority groups are concentrated, but also in suburban and rural areas.
11. Raising health and welfare standards for most of the population.
12. Abroad, furthering freer world trade and providing greater aid to the less-developed nations.
13. Participation in the defense of the free world and devoting adequate resources to our national defense.
14. Disarmament—a major foreign policy goal—to lessen the likelihood of destructive wars and to reduce the volume of resources drawn away from civilian uses.
15. Effective support for the United Nations to encourage international peace and cooperation.

Three aspects of this list of national goals deserve special note. First, many of them cut across economic, political, and social lines; obviously, they are difficult to cost out economically. Second, some of the goals deal with processes (for example, freedom of choice for the individual and maintenance of a democratic political system), while others deal directly with ends (for example, higher levels of health and welfare for most Americans). Third, this list of goals obviously calls for a major increase in our resource commitment to several of the goals listed—for example, better education for all, higher standards of health and welfare, more aid to the less-developed nations, and reconstruction of the urban ghettos.

A decade later, another group of distinguished Americans prepared for the U.S. Department of Health, Education, and Welfare, a thoughtful document, *Toward a Social Report*.[2]

[1]President's Commission on National Goals, *Goals for Americans* (Englewood Cliffs, N.J.: Prentice-Hall, Inc., 1960).

[2]Department of Health, Education, and Welfare, *Toward a Social Report* (Washington, D.C.: U.S. Government Printing Office, 1969).

While the nation has a mass of economic statistics to permit careful measurement of our economic progress, adequate data on the extent to which we approach many of our other social goals are scanty. This commission chose seven major goals, or sets of goals, for emphasis:

1. Health and illness—are we becoming healthier?
2. Social mobility—how much equality of opportunity do we have?
3. Physical environment—are conditions improving?
4. Income and poverty—are we as a nation, and particular groups within the nation, better off economically?
5. Public order and safety—are we achieving a more equitable and orderly society?
6. Learning, science, and art—are they enriching society as they should?
7. Participation and alienation—does our system lead to participation or toward alienation for significant groups?

Still a different list of goals has been suggested by many economists, focusing more directly on economic aspects of life:

1. Progress: a rising average standard of living.
2. Production in accordance with individual (consumer) demands.
3. Equitable distribution of income.
4. Economic security.
5. Individual freedom and opportunity, in economic and in other aspects of our lives.

Obviously, there are many sets of national goals that might reasonably be specified. In the last analysis, each individual must choose his own. And, as we shall see in a moment, nearly every list poses difficult problems of priorities, since, affluent though we may be, we clearly cannot have all of everything that we would like for the nation. Moreover, there are direct conflicts between some of the goals, so we can have more of one only by having less of another.

There is a further problem with such lists of national goals—they are broad and full of ambiguities. What does "individual freedom" mean? You and your roommate may have quite different ideas. What is an "equitable" distribution of income? The answer of an activist member of a minority group is likely to be very different from that of a comfortably situated white lawyer or businessman. What does "economic security" mean? Does it mean a guaranteed job, a guaranteed above-poverty standard of living, the right to a job, protection against loss of jobs because of ill health?

Make your very own set of national goals, and try to define them operationally. As we shall see in a moment, such an operational definition is in many cases very difficult. But without such goals against which to measure the performance of our economy, it will be impossible for you to make rational evaluations of how well it works and of measures proposed to make it work better. Much more of this in chapters to come.

National Priorities

If nature somehow provided everything each of us wants, there would be no need to economize—no need to choose among alternative uses of our resources. But in fact, this is not by any means the case. Affluent though we are by historical and comparative standards, our resources are far short of assuring that each of us can have all he wants without working for it. In this fundamental sense, ours is very much an economy of scarcity.

For example, a major national goal on just about everyone's list is better housing for all. We might set as a national goal a modern $30,000 house or apartment for each family in the United States, a pleasant but certainly not luxurious home. But to achieve merely this one national goal would require the equivalent of about $1.2 trillion worth of new housing—the equivalent of about forty years of our total housing production at peak construction rates. To achieve this goal in only one year or in a few years is obviously impossible, even if we gave it a top-ranking priority. We have neither the materials and labor, nor manufacturing capacity for the components that it would take to meet such a goal, however high priority we might give it. Nor, indeed, is it clear how we could find the land on which to build all these houses in areas that would be pleasant and also reasonably convenient to the jobs of all the people concerned. It would mean reconstructing and dispersing virtually every one of the great urban centers that now mass people together in congested areas.

Consider another type of goal. One thing the typical American wants is lots of electricity. He has a passion for gadgets that freeze, defrost, mix, blend, toast, roast, iron, sew, wash, dry, open garage doors, trim hedges, entertain with sound and picture, heat his house in winter, and cool it in summer. Residential use of electricity has been growing at some 12-15 percent per year, to which must be added the large increases for industrial and commercial use. The proportion of American homes with some air conditioning rose from about 10 percent a decade ago to over 45 percent today. The whole northeastern section of the country was shut down for hours in the great electric blackout of 1965.

But, unfortunately, electric generating plants are unsightly and often pollute both the air and water around them. Electric transmission lines cut great scars across the countryside. Nuclear and fossil plants occupy scenic sights along the rivers and shores because their condensers require huge amounts of cooling water. The growth in private demand for electricity alone will, by 1980, mean that an amount equal to one-sixth of all fresh flowing water in the United States will pass through, and be heated by, the condensers of generating plants. Which goal should dominate—enough electricity to fulfill our wants, or landscapes and rivers free of the pollution and unsightliness of generating plants?

Following the report of the Presidential Commission on National Goals in 1960, the National Planning Association set about costing out the list of goals the commission had suggested, to see whether they were within the range of economic feasibility. Obviously many of the goals are impossible to quantify—for example, freedom for all individuals and an effectively operating democratic political system. But most of

the goals did involve an economic cost, and, albeit very roughly, the NPA attempted to set prices on them. This involved, of course, quantifying what is meant by adequate housing, by an improved educational system, and the like. In this study, the NPA set two standards—one a base minimum and the other a higher "aspiration level." Including a steady growth in consumer standards of living at about the historical rate, the NPA estimated the 1970 minimum requirements would cost about $1.2 trillion (in 1970 prices), and "aspiration standards" about $1.6 trillion. Actual g.n.p. in 1970 was about $1 trillion. There was thus a shortfall of somewhere between a quarter and a half trillion dollars worth of output in 1970.[3]

Such figures should not be taken too seriously; they provide only the roughest orders of magnitude, and clearly others' interpretations of the Eisenhower goals might differ widely from those used by the NPA in making its estimates. But the central lesson comes through. There is not enough productive power even in our incredibly productive system to enable us to meet all the national goals we set as long as ten years ago. Since today's national aspirations are far higher than those envisaged by the Eisenhower commission a decade ago, the production gap is now even larger than is indicated by the cost estimates above. Ours is still an economy of scarcity, albeit also one of affluence compared to most other nations. With our escalating aspirations for such goals as urban reconstruction, better education, an end to poverty, and clean air and water, on top of the long-standing goal of steadily rising real income for everybody, the decade of the seventies may well turn out to be the decade of the great crunch on economic resources, as well as the decade of affluence.

Thus, we need both to clarify what our national goals are and to establish priorities among them. The priorities problem is made still more difficult by the fact that there is not only a shortage of total production to meet all our goals, but that the very essence of some of the goals is contradictory to the achievement of others. For example, suppose that to eliminate poverty

[3]Leonard Lecht, *Goals, Priorities, and Dollars: The Next Decade* (New York: The Free Press, 1966).

each four-person urban family was guaranteed a $3,800 annual income, with corresponding amounts to families in other environments. It is probable that this would lead at least some individuals to stop working, especially those who were earning only that amount or less by working. This would mean less total national output to raise our overall standard of living, surely another major national goal. Which goal should dominate in such a case—economic security, or economic progress through increased production?

Setting National Goals and Priorities

How do we set our national goals and priorities? How should we set them?

One answer denies that it is meaningful to formally list "national goals" in a nation of 200 million individuals where individual freedom is the overriding goal. If individual freedom is dominant, the only meaningful national goals are those that arise out of the combined free actions of individuals acting in accord with their own wishes. Thus, they argue that the marketplace provides the best means of setting and ranking national goals. What we are willing to pay is the best measure of what we want; therefore, the goods and services produced by a system responding effectively to millions of individual wants expressed in the marketplace provide the most meaningful approach to an optimal achievement of national goals and priorities. If people want something else more than what is now produced, they will shift their spending accordingly.

Another approach to determining national priorities is through the democratic political process. Through the political system, we vote for representatives who will support those goals we consider most important. If your senator votes to spend too much on national defense and not enough on urban reconstruction, you can vote for his opponent in the next election. If you believe your government should allocate more resources to highways and fewer to schools, you tell your representative in Washington or the state capitol. If you feel that big corporations are getting too powerful, you push your representative to strengthen the laws that regulate business. You, plus 80 million other voters, hold the ultimate power in determining what the government should do or not do, and what regulations the government places on the activities of citizens and institutions in our society.

These examples make it clear that defining national goals and priorities is far from simple. Arguments that we should alter our national priorities—for example, devote fewer resources to the military budget and more to urban reconstruction and the abolition of poverty—touch a responsive chord in many American hearts. Polluting the streams and the air through industrial processes, many argue, doesn't make sense in a nation that can, and should, be concerned about maintaining its natural resources and the environment in which people live. But, if so, what decision must we make in the electricity generating–pollution problem above? Who shall decide how much the cost of electricity should be increased to provide clean streams and unmarred scenery?

Once in a while, the president will establish a major national objective and mass support behind it—for example, President Kennedy stated that we would send a man to the moon before 1970. But mainly the political process operates through adjustments at the margin— more for educational benefits next year, less for dams and highways; an increase in the income tax on high-income groups, a decrease on low-income groups.

The American political process is ad hoc, pragmatic. Those who are most concerned over issues take steps to get their viewpoints across to Congress and the administration, and to state and local governments. Those who don't care so much are apt to be silent. The net result is very uneven; sometimes it seems as if the lobbyists can get anything through, however contrary it may be to the "public interest". But in the long perspective the American democratic political system works well. It is a far-from-perfect instrument for fine-tuning national policy, but it works, albeit slowly sometimes, on the big issues. Most Americans feel there is no obviously superior political process that might replace it, though many reformers are happy to suggest improvements here and there.

How does this compare with other main channels for determining national goals and priorities—balloting with dollars in the marketplace, instead of with votes at the ballot box. With over 200 million consumers, no one person has appreciable individual market power over what gets produced and what not. But if large numbers of individuals are willing to lay their dollars on the counter for automobiles, automobiles will be produced in response to consumer demand. If consumers decide, for whatever reason, they don't like cigarettes, the profits in the cigarette industry will fall, and fewer resources will be devoted to cigarette production and sales. How much is produced of any good or service depends directly on how many dollars are spent on that good or service, so those with many dollars have many votes, those with few dollars correspondingly little influence. There is no formal statement of national goals, no formal ranking of alternatives.

The market process is imperfect, as is the political process. We shall have a great deal more to say about that in the chapters to come. Advertising sways consumers' choices, perhaps away from what they really want. Big businesses and big labor unions sometimes grab off for themselves more of the increase in consumer spending than is justified by the workings of competitive markets. Most important, the market doesn't work adequately when big "externalities" exist—for example, where production of some good (say autos) involves social costs (smog) not included in the economic costs to the producers and hence not included in the price of autos to consumers. By and large resources flow into the uses that consumers value most highly as signaled by their market demands, but the exceptions are important as well.

How are the political and market processes linked? In many ways. First, the political process basically sets the rules of the game within which the market process must operate. It decrees through the antitrust laws that monopolies, which might keep consumers from getting what they want at the lowest cost, are illegal. It

decrees that businessmen must bargain collectively with their workers, if the workers vote for a union. It imposes safety regulations on auto manufacturers. Through these regulations it implements national priorities. Equally important, the government through its power to tax and spend channels resources away from private (marketplace) uses into "public sector" uses. Nearly one-fourth of our total national production of goods and services each year reflects resources transferred by taxes out of the private sector into public-sector uses. Governments take away private buying power through taxes and spend the money for education, or national defense, or cancer research. Actually the government produces very little itself. For the most part it spends tax collections to induce private firms and individuals to produce what the voters want—rockets, research, school teaching.

These political and economic processes do not represent neat, orderly ways of establishing and implementing national goals and priorities. The American economy and political system are pragmatic, adaptive mechanisms. With 200 million people, they disperse power widely among many groups and individuals—though, in the eyes of some, not widely enough. The "military-industrial complex" seems to many to have too much political and economic power. Madison Avenue is said to mold consumer preferences. Some lobbyists are more effective than others, some representatives more responsive than others. Inefficient businesses may exist for extended periods before the pressures of competition drive them to greater efficiency or bankruptcy.

How does this way of setting goals and priorities square with the proposal in Chapter 2 that orderly problem solving should begin with a clear statement of objectives or goals? The answer is, we ought to proceed that way, but often we don't. The president and Congress, if they consider alternative policies carefully and rationally, will make just such an analysis—attempting to clarify what are the most important national goals and what are te most efficient ways of achieving those goals. The president's budget each year is an example of such a choice through comparison of alternatives. At the same time, the president's budget generally works on the margins—it starts from where we are and accordingly adjusts tax and expenditure programs upward or downward moderately. Similarly, in an election the voters presumably judge candidates primarily on the basis of their main commitments to different programs, but voters cannot register their views on the many issues on which their senators and representatives will have to vote separately.

Much of the rest of this book is devoted to analyzing how goals and priorities are set and implemented in the market economy, and through governmental action in the public sector. How well the combined economic-political system reflects people's wishes on national goals and priorities is a central question to keep in mind throughout the book. Even more important is the question how we can induce either the market or the political process to reflect our individual and national goals and priorities more effectively.

Review

FOR ANALYSIS AND DISCUSSION

1. What is your list of national economic goals?
2. Can you establish priorities among those goals? If so, what are they?
3. Is.it inconsistent to say that we are the wealthiest nation in the world, but that scarcity—since resources are limited relative to our wants—is still the fundamental economic problem we face?
4. How should we as a nation set our national goals and establish operational priorities among them?

four

Private Enterprise, Profits, and the Price System: An Overview[1]

How is it that we in America are, by and large, well fed, well clothed, and well housed, while most of the world is dismally poor? What explains the incomes we receive—$125,000 for Willie Mays, $20,000 for a master plumber, $2,000 for an itinerant fruit picker? What has brought about rapid changes in job patterns over the years in the United States? Why has big business boomed in some sectors of the economy, while in others it has made little headway against small concerns? Why do we have air and water pollution?

There are no simple answers to these questions. Indeed, most of the book is aimed at answering them and others like them. As an introduction to the more detailed analysis that follows, this chapter sketches out briefly the foundations upon which our economic welfare rests and provides a simple overview of the way our modern American economy operates.

[1]Instructors who wish to include a brief introductory unit on the market mechanism, supply and demand, and resource allocation through the price system, before proceeding to Part Two of the text, can do so by assigning this chapter, followed by Chapters 20 (optional), 21, 22, 23 (optional), and 24. The material is written to be used in either order. (The appendices should be omitted if Chapters 21–24 are assigned here.)

The Foundations of Economic Progress

Our ability to produce the goods and services we want depends on the resources at our disposal and our knowledge of how to use them. The United States is rich in natural resources; it is rich in produced resources, such as factories, houses, and machinery; and it is rich in human resources, the most important of all. The American worker on the production line is the best educated, the best fed, and the most productive in the world. American engineering and mass-production know-how have produced Detroit's fabulous auto plants, Pittsburgh's steel mills, Oak Ridge's atomic energy installation. Vast research expenditures generate a steady stream of new products and new methods. And the American businessman, watched over by the government and consumers, manages somehow to keep the whole combination going in a way that excites the mixed envy, dismay, and sometimes disdain of his less-aggressive counterparts in the rest of the world. These resources and this technology are the real foundations of the American standard of living—of our sweeping growth over the centuries. (Some would add, they are also the foundations for some of our major problems, such as the deteriorating environment.)

In addition, we have developed a high degree of economic specialization and a complex exchange system. How many people do you depend on to get your everyday economic wants satisfied? You may say, not many. But think a minute. Who built the house you live in, and who provided all the materials to build it? How about the car that you drove to school, or the shoes if you came afoot? Where did your breakfast come from? Suppose you take in a movie tonight or watch TV. How many people have had a hand in making this possible?

To produce all the things we want takes many people, each specializing on what he can do best. Charlie Chaplin immortalized the forlorn worker on the assembly line, day after day screwing his single bolt onto the cars as they went by. But specialization goes far deeper than this. The engineer who designs the plant is a specialist. So is the banker who lends part of the money for the construction. So are the accountant who keeps the records and the secretary who does the typing. Only by dividing up tasks and developing highly specialized

human skills and equipment can the economy obtain the benefits of "mass production."

But specialization and division of labor would be fruitless without a system for exchanging the goods and services produced by the specialists. The lawyer, the banker, the truck driver, the engineer—all would starve if the intricate system of exchange we take for granted didn't enable them to buy the food they need with the incomes they earn. Even the farmer who might eat his own carrots and potatoes would be in desperate straits if he were really cast on his own—without electricity, new clothing, gas and repairs for his car, mail delivery, and the thousand things he gets from other specialists. Every minute of our daily lives we depend on the specialization and exchange all of us take for granted. None of us would dare specialize if we couldn't count on being able to exchange our services and products for the wide range of things we want.

(1) Productive resources, (2) technology, (3) specialization, and (4) exchange. These are the four foundation stones of the productive power of the American economy—and of every other highly developed modern economy, Communist or capitalist. These four basic factors make the difference between poverty and plenty. Many of the commonest economic fallacies are rooted in the neglect of these simple truths.

Limited Resources Mean We Must "Economize"

Limited resources—which force us to choose among alternative uses of them—are the basic economic problem in every economy. There is not enough of everything for everyone to have all he wants, so that we can simultaneously achieve all our national goals. If nature somehow provided bountifully all the things we want, there would be no need to work, no need to arrange for economic production, no need to choose among alternatives. We could have all we want of everything free, without working. But very few things are so plentiful. Human wants are vast, perhaps infinite. Resources to fulfill these wants are limited. They are "scarce."

For most of the world, economic scarcity is painfully evident; millions live on the edge of starvation. Even we in the United States are far from rich enough to escape the ever present need to "economize." We must choose between alternatives when we would like to have both. At the individual level, few of us have all the money we want. If you have a vacation trip to Florida this year, you can't afford a new suit. If you buy a new car, you can't afford a new hi-fi too. Time is a scarce resource too. It would be nice this afternoon to play golf, to go to the movies, to study, and to pick up some spare cash by working. But you can't do them all at the same time.

Scarcity, and the problem of choice it raises, is as ever present at the group and national level as in our individual lives. If we use land for a shopping center, we can't use it for a school. If we use steel for autos, we can't use it for refrigerators. If we use engineers to design missiles and intercontinental rockets, they can't work on air pollution control devices.

For the nation, the heavy hand of war points up vividly this fundamental dilemma of scarcity. Modern war is fantastically expensive, in money and, more fundamentally, in men and materials. In 1970 we spent over $75 billion— about 10 percent of our national income—directly on war and preparation for war. If the government had merely left this money in the hands of the taxpayers, on the average every American family would have had nearly $1,500 more to spend on clothes, housing, and the like. "Poverty," as it is usually defined, could have been eliminated. Behind the diversion of money to military spending is the diversion of productive resources—men, machines, and materials. In a fully employed economy, we must choose between guns and butter, between bungalows and bombers. If we use a big chunk of our productive resources for national defense, our standard of living in civilian goods is going to be correspondingly lower. There is enough electronic equipment in one space missile to provide a telephone system for a small city.

The Need to Economize

Because resources are scarce relative to what we want to do with them, we must "economize" them. That is, we must choose among alternative ways of using our resources so as to satisfy the largest possible share of human wants with them. We need to economize time, money, and productive resources, anything that is scarce, if we are to achieve our national goals. So far in history, no economy has been rich enough to escape this problem of economizing —of choosing between alternative uses of resources that are too limited to satisfy all human wants. Probably no society ever will be. This is the central problem of economics—though it takes a strange twist in depressions, as we shall see presently.

It is easy to see that we must choose among the products we would like to have produced with our limited resources. But it may be less obvious that how fast the economy grows—that is, how fast we increase our total output—also depends on where we allocate our limited resources. To grow, an economy must use part of its productive resources to build up future productive capacity. If we use steel to make autos and refrigerators for today, we cannot use it to build factories that will increase production in future years. If our engineers build TV sets, they cannot spend their time on basic research to raise our future standard of living. Thus, one of the choices every economy must make is between present and future. To grow fast means foregoing consumption today. Shall we live less well today so we and our children can live better tomorrow?

Unemployment and Depression: An Exception?

Few deny the basic fact of economic scarcity in the world today. Yet in America the newspaper headlines sometimes tell of millions unemployed, of auto factories idle because the public doesn't buy enough cars, of massive waste of men and machines because there isn't enough demand to buy the goods and services that could be produced with everyone at work. How can this be reconciled with the proposition that limited resources and scarcity are the basic economic problem?

Widespread unemployment of men and factories reflects a breakdown in our economic machinery. Resources are still limited relative to the vast unsatisfied human wants they might help to fulfill. People still desire better houses, more food, more of almost everything—if only they had the incomes to buy them. The unemployed want jobs. Businessmen want to increase production and give them jobs—if only they could sell the products. A million men involuntarily unemployed for a year mean between $5 billion and $10 billion worth of potential output lost forever.

The problem of depression and unemployment, which generally reflects insufficient total demand to induce profit-seeking businesses to keep our resources fully employed, has been a central one for America. In depression, we mistakenly and involuntarily allocate part of our scarce productive resources into unemployment and waste.

Choosing among Alternatives

When resources are limited relative to wants, we face the need to economize.

Economists are fond of illustrating this problem with a simple example—an economy that must choose between guns and butter, between bombers and bungalows. These symbolize any two competing groups of commodities for which we might use our resources.

The Production-Possibilities Curve

Assume that our economy has a fixed stock of productive resources (land, labor, machines, and the like) and of technological knowledge about how to use these resources in producing the things we want. With these resources and this technological know-how, we can produce guns or butter—military or civilian goods—or some combination of the two. To simplify, assume that only these two commodities (our groups) can be produced.

Table 4–1 shows the hypothetical range of possibilities open to us. If we use all our resources to produce bungalows (houses), we can have 1 million bungalows a year. Or if we use all

our resources to produce bombers, we can have 50,000 bombers. In between various combinations are possible—for example, .8 million bungalows and 15,000 bombers, or .6 million bungalows and 25,000 bombers, and so on.

The point of this table is to show the many production possibilities open to us, even when we assume a very simple economy producing only two products. Of course, bombers and bungalows are merely arbitrary examples. We might have used highways (a public good) and refrigerators (a private good), or any other pair of products to illustrate the same point. The important thing to see is that there is a tradeoff between the two commodities. With limited resources we can get more of one thing only by giving up some of the other. We face the problem of economizing.

It is convenient for many purposes to put the production-possibilities table in the form of a curve, or graph. This is done in Figure 4–1.

Economists use graphs a great deal, so it is important to understand how to read them. In Figure 4–1, we show millions of bungalows along the horizontal axis and thousands of bombers along the vertical axis. Each heavy dot plots one of the production-possibility combinations from Table 4–1. For example, the top dot shows that we may produce 50,000 bombers and no bungalows (alternative 6 in Table 4–1). The next dot shows we may produce 45,000 bombers and .2 million bungalows, and so on for the other dots. The figure is merely a graphical representation of the table.

table 4-1
Production Possibilities for Bungalows and Bombers

Alternatives	Bungalows (Millions)	Bombers (Thousands)
1	1.0	0
2	.8	15
3	.6	25
4	.4	40
5	.2	45
6	0	50

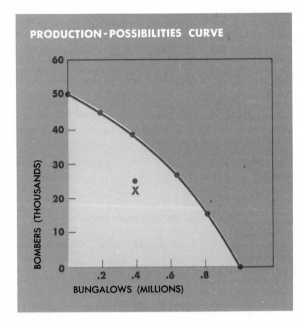

fig. 4–1

The curve shows how many bombers, how many bungalows, or what combination of the two we could produce with our limited stock of resources.

It is generally convenient to join the dots together with a line, or curve, to show approximately what the situation would have been if we had plotted all the dozens of possible intermediate combinations, instead of merely the six shown in the table. As the table indicates, the more bombers we make, the less new housing we can have, and vice versa. The production-possibilities curve shows the alternatives open to us, given our limited stock of resources.

Some Applications

The production-possibilities curve can help illuminate a variety of economic problems. Suppose that, possibly because of a depression, the economy only produces 25,000 bombers and .4 million bungalows, as shown by the dot labeled x to the left of the production-possibilities curve. This dot shows that the economy is not fully utilizing its productive capacity, as in fact happens during depressions. To operate at point x is clearly to waste productive resources. We could have had an additional .2 million bungalows and the same number of bombers, or an

additional 15,000 bombers and the same number of bungalows, if we had employed all our resources.

Economists sometimes say that when an economy operates at point x it is operating inside the production-possibilities frontier. That is, the production-possibilities curve shows the largest amounts of production that we can have with our limited resources. We are inside the frontier when for some reason we don't fully utilize our productive capacity.

Now suppose that the population increases, so that we have more workers than before, or that scientists improve technology, so that we can obtain more output from the same amount of resources. Thus in the second year, there will be a new production-possibilities curve to the right of the first-year curve. This can be illustrated as in Figure 4–2. The curve labeled "first year" is the same as in Figure 4–1. The curve labeled "second year" is farther out, to the right. It shows that the production possibilities are larger than before; the production frontier has moved out. This new curve for the second

fig. 4–2

If a nation's resources expand or its technology improves, its production-possibilities curve moves out, to the right. This expansion of productive capacity is the essence of economic growth.

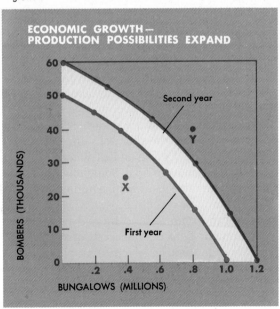

year shows economic growth. The economy can now produce a larger total output—more houses and the same number of bombers, or vice versa, or a combination involving more of both.

Suppose the economy tries to produce 40,000 bombers and .8 million houses (shown by point *y*). Clearly this is impossible. Production will fall short of one target or the other, or both. The economy cannot produce more than its production-possibilities curve permits.

An economy producing only two goods may seem extremely oversimplified. Yet many times throughout the chapters ahead, a production-possibilities curve will prove a useful simplification—to illustrate the possibilities of moving the production frontier out, the results of operating inside the production frontier, or the ever present need to choose among alternative uses of resources in a fully employed economy. Unless we can move the production-possibilities curve out, we can have more of one product only at the cost of accepting less of another.

Cooperation and Competition in a Private-Enterprise Economy

How in fact do we decide among alternative uses of resources, and how does the economy's total production frontier move out?

Man lives by cooperating with his fellow men. In all economics there is no more basic truth. And in the modern American economy this cooperation is indescribably broad and complex. To satisfy our simplest wants, we rely upon the efforts of innumerable people in all parts of the world, and on the labors of generations past. Yet this vast cooperative system, as a system, has not been consciously designed by man. No human director tells the 80 million workers in the United States where to work, what to do, or how to do it. Somehow the system seems to organize itself, with a minimum of central planning or directing.

Man can organize, and indeed he has organized much. Tens of thousands of workers are employed in some large industrial plants. Often many of these huge plants are joined together in a single organization. The American Telephone and Telegraph Company, for example, spreads over the entire United States, with over half a million employees and assets of over $45 billion. But in spite of the immense power of such huge aggregations, each business concern plays a tiny part in the total picture of organizing economic resources to satisfy human wants. And in spite of the great expansion of government controls, the private-enterprise economy still does the bulk of the job in its long-established unplanned way—in contrast to the central plans that control our biggest rival, the Soviet economy.

The Incredible American Economy

It's easy to find things the matter with a basically private-enterprise, "unplanned" economy, like ours. But thoughtful observers have long been impressed by its remarkable efficiency in producing the infinite variety of goods and services consumers want.

Consider New York City, teeming with 8 million people crowded into a few square miles. As Bastiat, a famous economist, remarked about the Paris of 100 years ago, here are millions of human beings who would all starve in a short time without a constant flow of provisions into the metropolis. Hardly one could support himself for more than a few days without help from the far corners of the nation. "Imagination is baffled," Bastiat wrote, "when it tries to appreciate the vast multiplicity of commodities which must enter tomorrow in order to preserve the inhabitants from falling prey to the convulsions of famine, rebellion, and pillage. Yet all sleep, and their slumbers are not disturbed for a single minute by the prospect of such a frightful catastrophe."

Every day, New York City gets hundreds of tons of meat, huge amounts of fresh vegetables, coal, oil, furniture. Every year, it gets millions of shirts, automobiles, rugs, hairnets, movie films, and more other goods and services than you can think of. Yet no individual, business, or government agency plans it that way. The same is true, on a smaller scale, of every city and village throughout the country.

Who sees to it that all these millions of products are where they're needed when they're needed? What organizes this indescribably complex economy?

Suppose for a moment that you have just been made complete economic dictator, and that for some unfortunate reason you have no idea of the quantity of everything now being produced. You have to tell every one of 80 million workers just what to do, decide how much of each commodity and service shall be produced, and determine who shall get how much of what is made—all this so that the amount of everything produced will be equal to the amount wanted, and so that no productive resources will be wasted through involuntary unemployment!

How, for example, would you decide whether Joe Smith ought to spend his time grinding fine edges on a machine tool later to be used in manufacturing tractors later to be used in producing corn later to be fed to hogs later to be eaten as pork; or whether he ought to spend his time making TV cabinets, or flying an airplane, or operating a corner grocery store? What would you do about the minor problem of how many sheep to raise, when each sheep yields both wool and mutton, the demands for which are almost completely independent? Wool is used for clothing, blankets, rugs; mutton is used for dinner. How are you going to make them come out even, even if you have somehow decided on the total number of sheep to be raised? How would you decide who is to have the tractors and corn and cabinets and mutton and wool once they are produced? Or, to take an apparently simple problem, how would you decide how many raincoats to make next year? This is the merest suggestion of the problems faced—and it matters not whether the economic system is capitalist, Communist, Fascist, or what not. Somehow these decisions have to be made. We must discover what our production possibilities are, make full use of them, and do so in a way that will go as far as possible toward satisfying the mixture of wants of some 200 million people, remembering that the wants may include clean air as well as more automobiles.

The Organizers: Self-Interest and Competition

In a basically private-enterprise economy like ours, we rely chiefly on private initiative, in search of wages and profits, to get the job done.

If we as a group want something badly enough, we are willing to pay for it. If we want shoes, there will be a profit to be made in producing shoes. Businessmen, recognizing this potential profit, begin producing more shoes. People go to work where businesses will pay the best wages, in general where consumer demands are strongest. As output increases, a point is reached when just as many shoes are being produced as consumers are willing to pay for at a price that is just high enough to cover the full production costs. If businessmen compete actively, prices will be held down to a level that just covers the costs of production. Consumers get the shoes they want at the lowest possible price through the search of businessmen for profits.

The same general pattern of production in search of profits goes on for thousands of other products simultaneously. Consumer spending guides profit seekers to where the potential profits are largest. Where profit prospects look brightest, they offer jobs and bid raw materials and capital in to increase production. Millions of workers work where they will, generally where wages are best but taking into account working conditions and the like. Consumer demands through the market process determine where on the production-possibilities curve we operate.

This is the mechanism by which the "private-enterprise, free-price system" does this indescribably complex job. It decides what's to be produced, how to get it produced, and how to distribute it among 200 million consumers. As Adam Smith pointed out in his famous *Wealth of Nations* back in 1776, the desire for personal profit within the framework of a competitive economic system works almost like an "invisible hand" to guide the system toward the greatest possible welfare of all.

Perhaps Adam Smith was overenthusiastic in relying so heavily on individual self-interest and competition as a beneficent invisible hand. But the first big lesson to learn about a private-enterprise economy is that it gets its vast job done for the most part automatically and impersonally, through the profit-and-price system. Nobody decides any more than his own affairs. Yet everyone deciding in his own self-interest seems to do the trick. In a private-enterprise economy, absence of planning and control does not mean chaos. Rather, it means order in an economy so complex that no mind could comprehend it and bring order without the price system or something like it to do the job.

But this is a lesson that must not be overlearned. We can understand and admire the way the private-enterprise, free-price system ticks on year after year, impersonally solving its millions of intertwined problems, and still not shut our eyes to its failings. And failings there are—drastic ones, some people think. The public has looked increasingly to government intervention to assure competition among businessmen; to set minimum standards for wages and working conditions; to regulate industries (like broadcasting and telephone service) where the public interest is paramount and free competition is not feasible; and to provide a wide range of services (like education, highways, national defense, and police protection) that can't reasonably be obtained on a private-profit basis for the bulk of the public. In fact, government is now so involved in the economy that many people call ours a "mixed" rather than a "private-enterprise" economy. For the moment, however, leave the government out, while we get a slightly more complete overview of how a private-enterprise economy solves the basic economic problems. It all comes back to the central economic problem—how to use our limited resources to satisfy the public's vast human wants as fully as possible.

How a Private-Enterprise System Solves the Basic Economic Problems

Consider now how a private-enterprise system allocates resources to solve four basic economic problems.

How the Market System Decides What To Produce

Under a private-enterprise, free-price system, consumers control what is produced. Consumers register their preferences through the amount of money they spend on various goods and services. The more you want something, the more money you will spend on it and the higher price you will be willing to pay for it. This is how the price system decides which are the most important goods and services to produce. The price of each good is a signal of how much of it consumers want produced.

But one point is vital. In order to count, consumers' demands have to be backed up with dollars. No matter how badly you want a Buick and a fine house, your desires become effective in the market only to the extent they are backed up by the ability to pay. The price mechanism is hard-boiled, impersonal. It produces Cadillacs for millionaires when poor youngsters have no toys. Prices reflect not how much consumers "need" goods and services, but how much they are willing and able to pay for them.

How the Market System Gets the Goods Produced

Businessmen are out to make profits, and they find profits where selling prices are higher than costs. Thus, businessmen move to those industries where consumers bid prices up, and where their own ingenuity and other factors, such as plentiful labor and materials, can bring costs down. Workers and owners of other productive resources generally move toward higher-pay, away from lower-pay jobs, though their decisions are also influenced by their preferences on location, working conditions, and the like. This combination of consumers' demands, workers' job preferences, and businessmen's desire for profits gets the goods produced that consumers want most, at the lowest possible cost.

Thus, the businessman is essentially a link between consumers and productive resources. His social function is to organize productive activity in the most efficient (lowest-cost) way possible, and to channel productive resources toward industries where consumer demand is strongest. Profits are the mainspring of the system—the carrot in front of the profit seeker. In seeking profits, the businessman performs a vital social function. And prices play a key role in allocating resources to where consumers want them most.

How the Market System Distributes Products

Who gets the goods that are produced? The price system allocates them to those who have the desire and the income to buy them. There are two steps in this process.

The first is the distribution of money incomes. We earn our incomes primarily by working for businessmen, helping to produce the goods and services consumers want. The prices we get for our services depend on how much we are worth to the businesses we work for. Competition forces the businessman to pay each of us about what we contribute to the sale value of what he is producing. The incomes we receive in this way largely determine what we can afford to buy.

The second step is the distribution of goods and services among those with money income to pay for them. The price of each commodity is bid up until the buyers least able and willing to pay for it are eliminated. This does not necessarily mean that low-income buyers are eliminated completely. Often it means that they can afford only a few units at the price established, while higher-income groups can afford more. Poor people buy steaks, but not many. In other cases, such as mink coats and country estates, the poor are eliminated from the market. Here again prices play a vital role; they ration final products among consumers.

How the Market System Decides Between Present and Future: Economic Growth

As was indicated above, we can use our productive resources either for current consumption or for capital accumulation. By building new factories and other productive facilities, we can shift the economy's production-possibilities curve out. In the same way, we can send our children to school rather than putting them directly to work, thereby increasing the nation's future productive potential at the cost of lower present output. Here again, the private-enterprise system depends largely on the free decisions of consumers and profit seekers to allocate resources between present and future.

Looking at the growth process in money terms, we must save some of our incomes and invest in building new factories and the like, rather than spending everything on consumption. In our individualistic economy, each person and each businessman decides how much of his income he wants to save. If these savings are a large proportion of our total income, investment in factories and people can be large relative to current consumption and the economy will grow rapidly. If we save only a small portion of our total income and investment is correspondingly small, the growth in productive capacity will be slow.

But here the private-enterprise system may have trouble. Sometimes when people save, businessmen don't see enough potential gain in making new investments in capital goods to match, or use up, the savings. Then the savings "lie idle" instead of being spent. This means unemployment and recession. The economy wastefully operates inside the production-possibilities frontier. Other times, businessmen grow unduly enthusiastic over future prospects and invest far beyond the rates at which people plan to save. This speeds up capital accumulation and economic growth. But it also may bring overinvestment and inflation. Excess productive capacity develops; factories can't sell their output; investment is cut back; workers are laid off. Thus, miscalculations and overbuilding can mean uneven growth, with inflationary booms and ensuing depressions.

Solving All the Problems Simultaneously

These four major decisions are not made separately. Rather, they are all interdependent. The economic system is a huge, interconnected set of markets, each with many buyers and sellers. All four big decisions are simultaneously the outcome of millions of free, individual choices by people largely concerned with their own private welfare. Since most buyers buy in many different markets, what they buy of one good affects what they will buy of another. Most sellers must compete with many other sellers for the labor they hire, the raw materials they use, the dollars they borrow to build their plants. The process of production both provides goods to meet consumer demands and generates incomes for workers who are in turn consumers. And each consumer constantly chooses between saving or buying something now with his income.

The private-enterprise, free-price system, then, makes all four of its major decisions simultaneously, each composed of millions of concurrent self-interest subdecisions by consumers, workers, businessmen, bankers, and other participants in the economic process. How all these complex decisions are simultaneously and continuously made and how they interact in our economic system is the core of the study of economics.[2] (Remember that we're temporarily omitting a big group of desired goods and services—those produced by governments—where demand is reflected through different channels.)

[2]In mathematical terms, it may be helpful to think of all these interdependent markets and decisions as a large system of simultaneous equations. In fact, one of the first clear perceptions of the entire process was by Leon Walras, one of the first mathematical economists, who saw it just that way about a century ago.

fig. 4–3

THE CIRCULAR FLOW OF ECONOMIC ACTIVITY

Finished goods and services

Consumption expenditures ($'s)

THE PUBLIC
(Income receivers and consumers)

BUSINESSES
(Hirers and income payers)

Wages, interest, etc. ($'s)

Productive services

The Circular Flow of Spending and Production

It is important to see that income in a private-enterprise economy flows around a circle. Businesses pay wages, interest, and other income to the public. The public, as consumers, spends this income back to businesses in payment for finished goods and services. This demand, in turn, leads businessmen to hire workers to produce more goods and services for consumers.

Figure 4–3 shows this circular flow of income. The inner line shows consumers spending to businesses (top half) and businesses spending back to the public through paying wages and interest (bottom half). The outer line shows the corresponding reverse flow of productive services and final products. On the bottom half, labor and other productive services are being hired by business from the public. On the top half, finished goods are moving from businesses to consumers.

Which comes first, business hiring and spending or consumer spending? This is a chicken-and-egg question. The main point is that neither can go on for long without the other. Consumers without jobs and incomes make for very poor business. And a business with products that no one buys is a good bet for bankruptcy. Economic activity in a private-enterprise system is a continuous flow of productive services and finished products, facilitated by a matching counterflow of money spending, and guided by the price system into thousands of different product channels within the main streams shown in the diagram.

You can readily see that this picture is oversimplified. The government has been left out. And there's no place for savings and production of capital goods that aren't sold to consumers. But the simple picture points up the central role of the circular-flow process. Unless there is a continuous flow of money spending by businesses to the public and by the public to businesses, we're in trouble. If something dams up the flow of spending, depression and unemployment result, and the economy wastefully operates inside its production frontier.

The National-Output Pie and Who Gets It

One last way of looking at the economy, its output, and who gets it. We can think of the nation's output each year as a huge pie (totaling about $1 trillion worth of goods and services in 1970). The pie was made up of thousands upon thousands of different goods and services—by and large the things consumers wanted most as signaled by their expenditures. And the pie was sliced into many pieces—the real incomes received by millions of wage and salary earners, rent and interest receivers, profit takers, and others, all of whom used their incomes to buy the parts of the pie they wanted.

Many of the big issues faced in any economy —capitalist, Communist, or other—can be illuminated by remembering these three questions. What does the proposed action (say, a new income tax) do to the size of the total national pie, to its composition of particular goods and services, and to the way it is sliced up in income shares? Clearly, there's only so much real pie to go around at any given time, so a bigger income slice for A means less for B. But if the pie grows, both can have more. To have a smaller pie because of unemployment and depression is pure waste. Similarly, we may argue over what should be in the pie—more milk and less beer, more education and fewer houses, more bombers and fewer health services, more autos and less clean air? The national pie—its size, composition, and division— provides a useful central focus for analysis throughout much of economics.

Individual Freedom and the Role of Government

The French and American revolutions that gave us political democracy provided the ideological framework for economic individualism. Political democracy and modern private-enterprise economics arose in the same historical setting, part of the same broad sweep of history.

Individual freedom and self-interest were at the core of this revolution of the eighteenth and nineteenth centuries. In politics, every man should be free to vote as he pleased—to look out for his own interests at the ballot box. In economic life, every man should be free to seek his own self-interest—to work where he wished, and to spend his money on whatever he wanted most. Self-interest and individual initiative were the driving forces for the common good. The ballot box in politics and the market in economics were the ultimate, impartial arbiters of differences of opinion.

This philosophy assigned to government only a small role. The less government interfered with individual freedom, the better. This was the laissez-faire philosophy of the nineteenth century. To be sure, individualism never went so far as to exclude government intervention altogether. True freedom necessarily involves some restrictions on freedom. A society that gave you freedom to murder your neighbor whenever you felt like it would be anarchy.

So it was in the economic sphere. Clearly the government needed to establish and enforce a few "rules of the game" for the free-enterprise system. One basic rule was the guarantee that no one should be deprived of life, liberty, or property without due process of law. Another was the long-standing rule against fraud and against default on contracts. But the rules should be simple, and government should have no business in economic life outside these rules.

As time passed, the public's outlook changed. More and more questions were raised about the ability of an automatic, uncontrolled price system to make vital economic decisions acceptably. Mass production and the modern corporation swept away the possibility of an economy of tiny, highly competitive firms. Powerful unions replaced the individual worker in bargaining with big business. Throughout the economy, concentration of economic power and reliance on group activity spread steadily. Many new products brought objectionable side effects, e.g., smoke from factory chimneys.

Moreover, with a wealthier, more complex society, people wanted more things that couldn't be readily provided through private profit-incentive in the marketplace—schools, highways, national defense, parks, and the like.

Besides setting the rules of the private-enterprise game, governments were called on to do more and more things directly. Today federal, state, and local governments buy one-fifth of all the goods and services produced in the economy.

At the same time, common concern grew for the individual who couldn't take care of himself. Willingness to abide by the impersonal income allocations of the market steadily diminished. Desire to "do something" about booms and depressions became widespread. A subtle shift in the meaning attached to the words "individual freedom" marked the changing tenor of the times. The rules of the game have grown into an intricate mass of law and administrative controls. The government has become a major participant in the economic game, as well as the umpire.

The Mixed Economy

Today, ours is a mixed economy—still basically private-enterprise but with large areas of government control and direct participation. It's up to you to decide whether you like what's been going on—whether you want to move back toward the traditional private-enterprise system, or on toward a more administered, planned economy, or in some other direction.

This is no ivory-tower, academic issue, dreamed up for college classrooms. It is a basic issue of public economic policy today. Should we try to shore up the individualistic free-price system and its individualistic implications? Or should we accept new power groupings and set up government procedures to work with them toward a more administered economy? Clearly the government must step in to provide national defense and highways, but how about slum clearance, public housing, and air pollution? Nearly everyone agrees the government should provide free schooling for all children, but how about assuring minimum health standards and old-age security? Everyone agrees that we need to level off booms and depressions. Can the government take on this job and still perform in a manner consistent with the basic philosophy of

private-enterprise nonintervention? Individual freedom is no longer a simple concept.

At the end of this book, we shall step back and compare our private-enterprise system with the Communist approach, which is a powerful economic, social, and political force in the world today. Some people feel that the American economy is already far down the primrose path to socialism, that the government has a hand in everything. But compared with most of the rest of the world, private enterprise is still rampant in America. As a college student and as a citizen, you need to do a lot of careful, unemotional thinking about where the American economy really is, and which way you want it to go. Some economists put the problem this way—how far shall we rely on a free-market economy, how much on one run by government "commands"?

Capitalism Today

"Capitalism" is a term often used but seldom defined. Words so used often generate more heat than light, and "capitalism" has over the years become a fighting word for many who advocate and oppose it. Recourse to dictionaries and learned treatises of economists and historians unfortunately does not resolve the dilemma of just what we should mean when we say capitalism, for these authorities are far from agreement.

So, instead of talking about capitalism, this book uses such less-colorful but more descriptive terms as the "private-enterprise, free-price system" and "market system" in referring to the big private sector of the modern American economy. But, though we shall generally eschew the emotionally colored term, a brief note on "capitalism" may be useful. Many writers agree that a "capitalist" economy is marked by at least these major characteristics:

1. Private ownership of property prevails.
2. Property has been accumulated by individuals and businesses, and this accumulated "capital" provides incomes to its owners.
3. Individuals and businesses are free to seek

their own economic gain; the profit motive plays a central role in economic life.

4. Some writers add to this list a highly developed banking and credit system.

This list gives the basic flavor of such a system. But once we look at the points in detail, the trouble begins. How free must individuals be to own and use property if a system is to be termed "capitalism"? Is an income tax that takes away part of your income each year, depending on how much you earn, consistent with capitalism? Does a federal law that limits the monopoly power you can attain violate the essential freedoms of capitalism? Is government operation of the postal system enough to make the system "noncapitalist"? Many people may accept substantially the above definition of capitalism, yet disagree widely among themselves about how

"capitalist" the American economy actually is.

We shall be concerned with all these questions and others like them. But there is little to be gained by debating just which measures are and which are not consistent with "capitalism" when there is so little agreement on what the term means. Instead, we will concentrate on trying to decide whether proposed policy measures are good or bad on their merits, taking into full account the different social goals held by different groups in America today. In talking about a "basically private-enterprise, free-price system" throughout most of the book, we will be talking about the system many writers call "modern capitalism." If you like the term, use it. But don't let your emotional attachment or antagonism toward it get in the way of thinking objectively about the issues.

Review

CONCEPTS TO REMEMBER

This chapter has introduced some important concepts that will be reused many times throughout the book. Recheck especially the following to be sure you have them firmly in mind:

productive resources
technology
specialization
exchange
scarcity
economizing
production-possibilites curve

production-possibilities frontier
private-enterprise, free-price economy
market system
economic growth
circular flow
laissez-faire
"capitalism"

FOR ANALYSIS AND DISCUSSION

1. "Man lives by cooperating with his fellow men. In all economics there is no more fundamental truth than this." "The core of the competitive, free-market system is the driving urge of most men to get ahead in the world, to rise above their fellow men."

   Are these two statements about the American economic system consistent or contradictory? If they are consistent, how do you reconcile their apparent contradiction?
2. The price system allocates resources where consumers spend their dollars. Thus the rich man has far more influence than the poor man. Is this compatible with the democratic presumption that every man is equal?

3. The federal government and most state governments levy heavy taxes on liquor. This increases the price of liquor and tends to discourage drinking. Should the government influence how you spend your money this way?

4. Look back at Figure 1–2. Can you explain better now why the big changes in employment shown there have occurred?

5. Does the present level of government spending tend to raise or lower our standard of living? Use a production-possibilities curve in explaining your answer.

6. Suppose American college students were to develop a craze for pork-chop sandwiches, instead of hamburgers. Trace through as carefully as you can the impact of this craze on the allocation of the economy's productive resources. Would such a shift be good or bad?

7. Leading movie stars receive annual salaries up in the hundreds of thousands of dollars. Some baseball players receive $50,000 to $100,000 for the eight-month season. Yet an intelligent, skilled, hardworking nurse or farmer will ordinarily earn not more than $6,000 or so per year.

   a. Are such differences predictable results of the free-market system, or do they reflect breakdowns in the functioning of the system?

   b. Do you approve of such inequalities in the distribution of income? Why or why not?

National Income, Employment, and Economic Growth

five

National Income, Production, and Prices[1]

The economic history of the United States is a great success story. In less than 200 years, our country has grown from a few struggling colonies into the world's richest nation. In the present century alone, our total national output (adjusted to eliminate the effect of price inflation) has risen sixfold.

But it has been a bumpy ride up. There was a major financial crisis in 1907; a big inflation after World War I; a terrible depression from 1929 to 1939; and another big inflation during and after World War II. We can be proud of our success, but we must face the fact too that our rapid economic growth has been marred by inflationary booms and by depressions.

Economists once took it for granted that our, largely private, enterprise system would automatically restore itself to full-employment prosperity whenever it got far off the track. But no more! Today we have grave doubts that the system is self-stabilizing, and since the 1930s the biggest economic issue has been how to device government policies that will eliminate both depressions and inflations.

Part Two analyzes what determines the overall levels of production, income, and employment in our economy. In nontechnical terms, the big problems are: what makes us grow rapidly or slowly, why do we have booms and depressions, and how can we make the

[1]Some instructors may prefer to use Parts Three and Four on microeconomics and the distribution of income before Part Two on macroeconomics. These parts are written to be equally usable in either order.

economy perform better? The purpose of this first chapter is to provide some of the major analytical concepts we need to understand these problems—basically, the concepts of the national income accounts.

Measures of National Production and Income

Modern economics is an empirical science. To understand and regulate the behavior of an enormously complex economy, we need measures of its performance—just as a business needs accounts to measure its performance. We need a measure of its total output of goods and services, and a measure of the total income received by all its people. We also need more detailed measures—of how much people have left to spend after paying their taxes, of corporate profits, of family and business savings, and so on.

The "national income accounts" provide these measures. We'll start with the "gross national product," the measure of the economy's total production of goods and services, and work down to some of the more detailed measures. The primary goal is to lay a foundation for explaining why people and businesses receive the incomes they do, and why they spend their incomes as they do. For the combined spending of individuals, businesses, and governments largely explains, in our market-oriented economy, why sometimes there's inflation and sometimes unemployment.

To begin, a basic question: What do economists mean by "production"?

Economic Production Defined

To the economist, production is the creation of any good or service that people are willing to pay for. Raising wheat is production, and so is making the wheat into flour and the flour into bread. It is also production for the local grocer to have the bread on his shelf when you want it, or to deliver it to your door. The agricultural, manufacturing, and marketing services all satisfy human wants, and people are willing to pay for them.

In fact, over half the people employed in the United States today render services rather than manufacture or raise anything. Over half of what you pay goes for middlemen's services—the retailer, the wholesaler, the banker, the trucker, and many others. Lots of people object to this situation. "There are too many middlemen!" they say. Maybe there are. But if you stop to think about it you'll run head-on into this question: Are there too many manufacturers, or too many farmers? The real economic test for all producers of goods or services is whether they satisfy a consumer demand—not how many pounds of physical stuff they produce.

Production as the economist defines it is not a moral or ethical concept. Making and selling cigarettes is production, just like raising and selling food. The test of the private-enterprise economy is the test of the market. If an act helps satisfy a want that someone is willing to pay for, that act is production.

Gross National Product

Gross national product is the nation's total production of goods and services (usually for a year), valued in terms of the market prices of the goods and services produced. This concept goes directly back to the definition of production above: Production is whatever people will pay for, and what they pay is an economic valuation of the worth of the product or service. Gross national product (abbreviated "g.n.p.") includes all the economic production in the country in any given time period.

Gross national product is stated in money terms, since this is the only meaningful way of adding together the output of such diverse goods and services as carrots, machine tools, maid service, air travel, and Fords. Strictly, then, g.n.p. is the money value of total national production for any time period.

Gross national product is also the nation's total expenditures on goods and services produced during the year. Each unit produced is matched by an expenditure on the unit. Most goods and services produced are bought outright. But how about the ones produced but not sold? Economists regard these as having been bought by the producers who hold them, as inventories. Then it is clear that the production and expenditure totals are identical.

G.n.p. is also the total income received by all sellers of goods and services. What someone spends on current output, someone else receives as income. This is g.n.p. seen from the receipts side.

Thus, it doesn't matter whether we look at gross national product as (1) the value of all goods and services produced, (2) the sum of all expenditures on those goods and services, or (3) the (gross) incomes received for producing the goods and services. They are all the same thing, and we get the same total each way.

There are two ways to calculate g.n.p., each designed to avoid the danger of double counting in a complex economy. One way is to sum up all expenditures on final products sold to consumers or to businesses for final use as producers' goods—all spending on potatoes, factories, missiles, legal services, and so on. Note the word "final." Miners dig iron ore out of the ground and sell it to U.S. Steel. The latter makes the ore into steel and sells the steel to Westinghouse. Westinghouse makes refrigerators and sells them to you and me. We don't count the value of the iron ore, plus the value of the steel, plus the value of the refrigerator. That would involve counting the iron ore three times. Instead, everything that is used in another product during the years show up and is counted only in the final product (in this case, refrigerators), since the value of the final product will reflect the value of all the raw materials, labor, and other productive services included in it.

Producers' goods, like machinery, which are bought by businesses, pose an obvious problem here, since they are not directly incorporated into the final consumers' goods the way raw materials are. We count machinery and other producers' goods once, when they reach their final buyer—for example, when Ford buys a new machine tool. Remember that goods in process at the end of the time period are counted as inventories (purchased by the owner) in the latest stage they have reached. This process of summing up all final purchases is called the "final-products approach" to estimated g.n.p.

Gross national product can also be estimated in another (equivalent) way: by the "value-added" method. Here the estimators establish the value added to each product by each producer, then sum up all these values. For example, in converting the iron ore to steel above, U.S. Steel adds something to the value of the product it passes along. This added value is the difference between what it pays for the ore, coal, and other products that it uses and the price at which it sells the steel to Westinghouse; roughly, it is the wages, interest, and rents paid by U.S. Steel plus the profit it earns. Similarly, we can compute the value added by Westinghouse. And so on for each productive unit in the economy. By summing up all the values added, we come out with the gross national product, again avoiding double counting.

Table 5–1 shows who buys the goods and services in the g.n.p., a useful breakdown in a market-directed economy where production is mainly in response to market demand. Purchasers are divided into three big groups: consumers, businesses (buying "investment," or "producers'," goods), and governments. To provide historical perspective, Figure 5–1 then presents the same data from 1929 to 1970. Take a look at the three major segments.

1. The biggest part of total production has consistently been made up by goods and services for consumers—electric fans, stoves, dresses, movies, medical services, hats, and all the other things that consumers buy.

2. The next group is private investment in "producers'" or "capital" goods. These are

table 5-1

U.S. Gross National Product, 1969*

Components	In Billions
Consumer purchases	$576
Business investment expenditures (including foreign)	141
Government purchases	215
Total	$932

*Data from U.S. Department of Commerce.

MAJOR COMPONENTS OF GROSS NATIONAL PRODUCT SINCE 1929

Government purchases

Private investment

Consumption purchases

BILLIONS OF DOLLARS

fig. 5-1

Consumers buy most of the g.n.p. The other third is divided between private investment and government purchases. (Source: U.S. Department of Commerce.)

buildings, machinery, equipment, and other capital goods used in the production of further goods or services. Such producers' goods are purchased primarily by businesses. But houses are also included in the investment-goods category, on the grounds that they are so durable that in effect they represent investment goods rendering consumer services, even though they are often owned directly by consumers.[2] Business investment also includes—as inventories—any increase in unsold goods in process or final form.

Three important warnings about the private-investment category.

First, "investment" means the purchase of investment goods (buildings, machinery, and so on) **produced during the year.** For example, if someone buys a ten-year-old factory, this is not investment; the factory was included in the gross national product ten years ago, when it was built.

Second, investment does **not** include mere financial transfers, such as the purchase of stocks and bonds. For example, if you buy a share of General Motors stock from me, this is not investment for purposes of the national income accounts, since it does not pay for any new production.

Third, note that investment includes **gross** purchases of investment goods. It includes production that merely replaces depreciating buildings, machinery, and equipment, as well as production that represents a net increase in society's stock of capital goods. We come to the **net** increase in the nation's capital goods in the section on "net national product" below.

3. Government purchases of goods and services include both consumption and investment goods. Federal, state, and local governments buy food, police services, and other current consumption items, as well as investment goods such as roads, buildings, and parks. But notice that government purchases of goods and services do not include all government expenditures. Governments also spend large sums on "transfer payments" (such as unemployment insurance and social security payments) that are not payments for currently produced goods and services and are hence not included in gross national product.

4. We have included "foreign investment," or "net exports," in private investment here, although it is often shown as a separate item. In 1969, for example, the United States exported $2 billion more than it imported, and to be complete we must include this **net** production in g.n.p. We will pull it out for special attention in Part Six on "The International Economy."

To summarize, g.n.p. is made up of: (1) consumer goods and services bought by individuals

[2]Although it is reasonable to treat new private housing as investment, note that houses differ only in degree from such durable consumer goods as autos, refrigerators, and vacuum cleaners, which are treated as consumption goods.

49

and households, (2) investment goods bought mainly by businesses, and (3) both consumer and investment goods and services bought by federal, state, and local governments. In all three categories, remember that only goods and services produced during the current year count; transfer of existing assets are excluded. G.n.p. may be thought of as the total national pie for each year, with the big slices going to consumers, businesses, and governments.

Net National Product

Gross national product is the most widely used measure of the total production of goods and services in the economy. But, as was noted above, it includes some producers' goods that just replace already existing producers' goods that are "depreciating," or wearing out. If a truck lasts ten years, we might say that one-tenth of it is used up every year, and the oil company that owns it would consider this tenth as an annual cost that year.[3] So it is with all other producers' goods; they wear out. Thus, before a firm or the economy as a whole adds anything net to its stock of producers' goods, part of the new trucks and buildings each year must go to replacing the ones wearing out.

Net national product (n.n.p.) is the net production of goods and services.

tional product, less those goods that merely replace depreciating buildings and machines. In 1969, for example, gross national product was $932 billion. Depreciation (sometimes called "capital consumption allowances") was estimated at $80 billion. Thus, net national product was $854 billion, about 9 percent less than gross national product. In other words, about 9 percent of our total output went to replace depreciating producers' goods and houses. Net national product measures the total production of goods and services available for current consumption and for adding to our stock of producers' equipment, including housing.

[3]Accountants have more complicated depreciation plans, which recognize the fact that buildings and machines do not necessarily wear out at constant rates.

National Income

National income is the total of all income earned by the "factors of production"—land, labor, capital, and management. The national income is basically the net national product viewed from the income side. National income is always less than the net national product, however. The factors of production (laborers, managers, machinery, and so forth) do not actually receive as income the full value of their output, because businesses that hire them must pay indirect taxes (sales taxes, excises, and property taxes) to the government, which cut down on the income left to pay to the factors of production. If we subtract indirect business taxes from n.n.p., we have left the national income that goes to all factors of production. In 1969, the indirect tax deduction was $87 billion. Deducting this from net national product of $854 billion, we get a national income of $771 billion.[4]

Table 5–2 shows the share of the national income earned by each major factor of production. Note the large share of salaries and wages —70 percent in 1969. This percentage hasn't varied far from two-thirds of the total national income over several decades, though there seems to have been a gradual upward trend.

table 5-2

U.S. National Income, 1969*

Source of Income	In Billions
Total	$771
Wages and salaries	564
Net income of unincorporated business**	66
Corporation profits***	88
Interest	31
Rental income	22

*Data from U.S. Department of Commerce.
**Mainly farmers and professional men in business for themselves.
***Of which $43 billion was paid out in income taxes and $26 billion was plowed back as reinvested earnings. Dividends paid out to stockholders were $25 billion.

[4]This omits some minor items with which we needn't be concerned.

The other main sources of income fluctuate more widely over business cycles.

Personal Income and Disposable Personal Income

"Personal income" is the total income received by all individuals in the country—what individuals actually have to spend, save, or pay taxes with. Personal income is less than the national income, mainly because national income includes total corporation profits whereas individuals receive only part of these profits in dividends. As the last footnote to Table 5–2 indicates, nearly half of corporation profits go to Uncle Sam as corporation income taxes, and part of what's left is plowed back into businesses rather than paid out to stockholders. We must subtract these amounts from national income to get income actually paid out to individuals; in 1969 their dividends were only $25 billion out of total profits of $88 billion. On the other hand, individuals receive large net "transfer payments" (social security, interest on the national debt, and so forth), which are personal income to them although they are not part of the national income (since they don't reflect any current production). We must add these transfer payments in to get total personal income. (Details are shown in Table 5–4.)

In 1969, total personal income was $747 billion. Table 5–3 shows what people did with this income: First, they paid their income taxes. What they had left we call "disposable personal income." Most of this they spent on consumption and the rest they saved. The concept of "disposable personal income" (what people have left after they pay their taxes) will be important later on in analyzing consumer spending and saving behavior.

The Integrated National Income Accounts[5]

If you have the concepts of gross national product and personal income well in hand, you're prepared to cope with a good many

[5]Within the last few years, a new set of social accounts has been released by the Federal Reserve System. These are called the "flow of funds accounts." They include all finan-

cial transactions in the economy, including payments in the stock market, for other financial transfers, for existing assets, and for a variety of other purposes not included in the national income accounts. These new money-flows accounts can be integrated with the national income accounts, and now provide a complete picture of money payments throughout the economy.

---

table 5-3

U.S. Personal Income, 1969*

		In Billions
Total personal income		$747
Less: Personal income taxes	$117	
Equals: Disposable personal income		630
Of which:		
Consumer outlays		592
Personal saving		38

*Data from U.S. Department of Commerce. Consumer outlays include $15 billion of consumer interest payments, which are excluded from the "consumer purchases" shown in Table 5-1. The Department of Commerce defines "consumer expenditures" to include only consumer payments for goods and services.

---

table 5-4

The National Income Accounts for 1969*

		In Billions
Gross national product		$932
Deduct: Capital consumption allowances (mainly business depreciation allowances)	$ 78	
Net national product		854
Deduct: Indirect business taxes	87	
National income		771
Deduct: Corporation profits taxes	43	
Corporate savings (undistributed profits)	26	
Social security taxes	54	
Add: Transfer and interest payments	91	
Personal income		747
Deduct: Personal taxes	117	
Disposable personal income		630
Of which: Consumer outlays**		592
Personal saving		38

*A few minor items are omitted, which explain the apparent discrepancies in the table.

**Includes $15 billion of interest paid by consumers not considered an expenditure on goods and services.

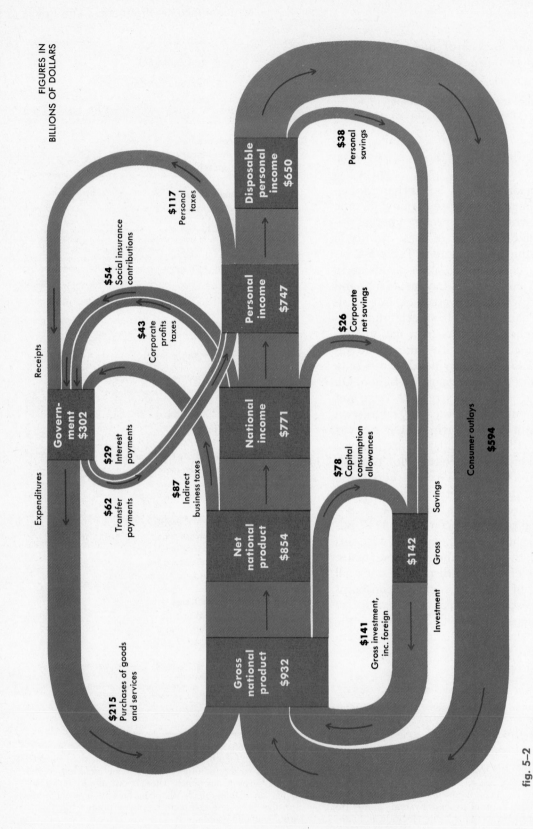

fig. 5-2

National income and expenditure make essentially a circular flow, with many side loops. This is a
more complete version of the simple circular money flow introduced in Fig. 4–1. Some minor items
are omitted; "consumer outlays" include $16 billion consumer interest payments generally excluded
from "consumer expenditures" and g.n.p., so totals will not add exactly to g.n.p. Figures shown are
for 1969.

problems. For example, most newspaper stories and business magazines focus on these measures. But for clear thinking in some of the following analysis, you need to have a more detailed grasp of the relationships between the various parts of the total income and product accounts. Table 5–4 summarizes the complete set of interconnections for 1969 just explained, beginning with the gross-national-product total. Figure 5–2 shows the same set of interconnections as a flow diagram, tracing the entire income-and-payments flow. This figure ties the circular flow of gross national product back to the simple, fundamental circular-flow diagram in Figure 4–2. (A few minor items are omitted, which explains the apparent discrepancies.)

In Figure 5–2, begin with gross national product of $932, as in Table 5–4. Then $78 billion of capital consumption (depreciation) allowances drains off as a form of private saving, leaving $854 billion of net national product. From n.n.p., another $87 billion drains off to the government through indirect business taxes, leaving national income of $771 billion. From this, corporate income taxes, social security taxes, and corporate saving (undistributed profits) are drained off; while interest on the government debt and other transfer payments are added back into the income stream, to make up $747 billion of personal income. The resulting personal income total is reduced to personal disposable income by the payment of personal income taxes, and then part of disposable income goes into personal savings while the bulk flows on into consumption expenditures. These consumption expenditures in turn become part of gross national product.

Now add back in the private-investment and government-spending flows—the private savings that flow on into investment expenditures and the government tax receipts that flow on into government spending. Together these three types of spending make up gross national product, the three big components of aggregate demand for currently produced goods and services—consumption, investment, and government spending. Remember them, for they provide the analytical core of Chapters 7–9.[6]

Changing Price Levels and Price Indexes

When prices change, g.n.p. expressed in terms of dollars is no longer an adequate measure of the real goods and services produced. A 100 percent increase in real national output would mean a great rise in the national standard of living. But doubling g.n.p. merely through doubling prices is no real economic gain at all. In order to separate "real" from merely "dollar" changes in individual and national incomes, we have to make an adjustment for price-level changes.

Figure 5–3 indicates the big fluctuations in prices in the United States over the last two centuries. The problem of price-level changes is no minor one.

fig. 5–3

Prices have fluctuated sharply throughout our history. The big peaks have come during or after major wars. So far, there has been no price slump since World War II. (Source: U.S. Department of Labor.)

What Is a Price Index?

In 1929, a family income of $1,300 would have bought a group of goods and services called a "subsistence standard of living." In

---

[6]It is important to note that the private investment in the bottom loop need not exactly equal the private saving flow, nor need government spending in the top loop equal tax collections. Either sector may run a surplus or a deficit, as will be explained in Chapter 7.

1933, you could have bought the same collection of goods and services for about $900. By 1970, you would have needed about $2,800.

If all prices changed in the same proportion in the same direction at the same time, measuring price-level changes would be simple. But the world of real prices is not simple and orderly. Even in the big price rises shown in Figure 5–3, some prices declined and others rose at very different rates. Yet, even though not all prices rose, we say that the "price level" rose because the average of all prices rose. The price of the same market basket of goods was higher than before.

Table 5–5 shows how to calculate a simple "price index" for a "market basket" of four commodities, to show whether their price level went up or down between 1960 and 1970. A price index is a measure of price-level changes.

With 1960 as the "base year," the price of each item in that year is 100 percent of itself. This is what people mean when they say, "Take 1960 as 100." Then we compute what percentage each 1970 price is of the 1960 price. For example, eggs at 6 cents each are 120 percent of the 1960 price. This 120 percent is the 1970 "price relative" for eggs, since it shows the 1970 price relative to that in 1960. To find the change in the price level (the average of all four prices), we simply take the average of the four 1970 price relatives, which gives us 108 percent for the 1970 price level. (The percentage sign is usually omitted for convenience.) Of course, most price indexes include more commodities, but they are made in a generally similar way.[7]

This simple method of calculating price-level changes may give misleading results, however. It tacitly assumes that eggs, hamburger, turnips, and apples are equally important. A 10 percent change in the price of hamburger influences the index exactly as much as a 10 percent change in the price of turnips. Actually, hamburger is more important than turnips in most budgets, and it seems logical that the price of hamburger should affect the index more.

Thus, in most price indexes, each price is "weighted" according to its importance. For example, the U.S. Bureau of Labor Statistics weights the prices in its widely used consumers' price ("cost-of-living") index as follows. The statisticians take a "market basket" of the goods and services bought during the 1960s by typical urban wage earners' families. Choosing some 400 of the most important prices, they weight each roughly in accordance with the proportion of the family's total expenditure for that commodity. If the family bought lots of potatoes, potatoes make up a sizable part of the weekly market basket; rent is a big item in the basket. In effect, the market-basket approach weights

[7]The final index numbers merely indicate the relation of average prices in the two years. We could just as well have taken 1970 as 100, in which case the 1960 index would have been 93. Although the actual index numbers would have been different, either set shows equally well the relative price levels in the two years: $93/100 = 100/108$. Thus the year chosen as 100 has little significance.

table 5-5

Price Index for 1970 with 1960 as Base Year

Product	1960	1970	
Eggs, each	5¢ = 100%	6¢ = 120%	of the 1960 price
Hamburger, per lb	40¢ = 100%	50¢ = 125%	"
Turnips, per lb	9¢ = 100%	6¢ = 67%	"
Apples, per lb	10¢ = 100%	12¢ = 120%	"
	4) 400%	4) 432%	
	100% = price level in 1960	108% = price level in 1970	

the price of each commodity according to the amount spent on that commodity weekly.

Having decided on the contents of the hypothetical market basket, the B.L.S. gets its price index by comparing the cost of the basket from one week to the next. If the index uses 1957–59 as a base period (100), a weekly index reading of 120 means that the cost of the market basket is up 20 percent from the 1957–59 price level for those goods and services.

Price Indexes for Different Price Levels

Since a price level is merely an average of some group of prices, we can speak of many different price levels. One may reflect the prices paid by a group of consumers (their cost of living); another, the prices paid by wholesalers; another, the level of wages in manufacturing.

Figure 5–4 shows the movements of four important price indexes from 1929 through 1969. What price level is most significant depends on what you are talking about. If you want to measure changes in the cost of living for a particular group, the logical choice is an index of the prices of the goods and services the group buys. Given the wide diversity of price movements, it is hard to devise a single price index that will be a significant measure for the whole economy. The closest approach is an index developed by

the Department of Commerce to eliminate the effects of price-level movements from the gross national product. This adjustment is spoken of as "deflating" the g.n.p. In it, first special indexes are computed for the different major sectors of g.n.p., and then these are combined to obtain a "g.n.p. deflator." The result is a price index for all goods and services in the gross national product.

Figure 5–5 compares g.n.p. since 1870 in the actual (current) prices that prevailed each year with g.n.p. in constant (1964) prices.[8] We often speak of the constant-price g.n.p. as "real" g.n.p., since with the elimination of price-level changes the g.n.p. index measures real changes in output of goods and services. In periods of rapidly changing prices, like World War II, the money g.n.p. figures give a seriously misleading picture of how rapidly real g.n.p. is rising.

How Good Are the Price Indexes?

How accurately do the well-known price indexes mirror the price changes they are intended to summarize? The most widely used

[8]Remember from above that we could have chosen some year other than 1964 as the "base" year for calculating constant-price g.n.p. over the years. Another base year would give different absolute levels for the constant-price g.n.p. but would not change the relative movements in the two curves.

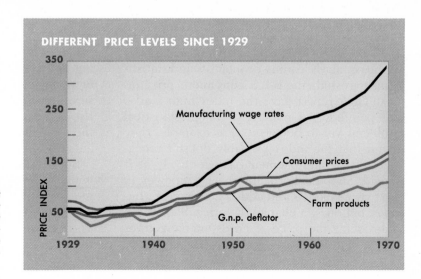

fig. 5–4

Different prices move diversely in the American economy. The g.n.p. deflator series comes closest to showing the price changes for all currently-produced goods and services. Note the wage-rate index. (Sources: U.S. Departments of Labor and Commerce.)

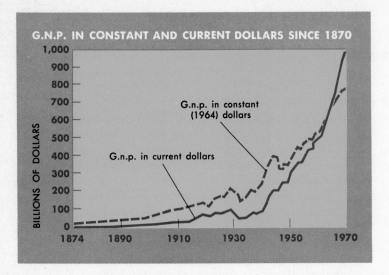

G.N.P. IN CONSTANT AND CURRENT DOLLARS SINCE 1870

G.n.p. in constant (1964) dollars

G.n.p. in current dollars

BILLIONS OF DOLLARS

1,000
900
800
700
600
500
400
300
200
100
0

1874 1890 1910 1930 1950 1970

fig. 5–5

G.n.p. has grown rapidly, but in spurts, over the past century. The solid line shows g.n.p. in current dollars, while the dashed line shows g.n.p. in dollars of constant (1964) purchasing power. The dashed line thus shows the growth in real output over the century. (Sources: National Bureau of Economic Research and U.S. Department of Commerce.)

indexes are prepared by the government—the consumers' price index, the wholesale price index, and the g.n.p. deflator. These are the product of years of hard work and millions of dollars, and they're as good as the experts can make them. Many privately made indexes fall short of these standards of excellence, even though they may serve useful purposes. Others are extremely accurate, though they measure only a few prices—for example, the well-known Dow Jones index of a small group of leading stock prices.

How good the price indexes are is no mere academic question. Millions of workers' wages are adjusted periodically under their union contracts for changes in the "cost of living," which are usually measured by the B.L.S. consumers' price index. Other indexes are used daily in business and government decision making. In 1959 President Eisenhower appointed a group of the country's leading economists and statisticians to restudy the B.L.S. consumers' price index. Their report gave the index high marks, but pointed to a number of tough statistical problems yet to be solved. For example, they found that the index probably doesn't recognize quality improvements as effectively as it should. Suppose Ford ups the horsepower in next year's models and adds a new type carburetor, but doesn't change the price. Should the index show the price of Fords unchanged, or lower (because you get more car for your money)? If lower, how much? Many economists

believe the B.L.S. consumers' price index shows prices rising perhaps 1 percent a year too fast because of the difficulty of reflecting promptly such changes due to new products and quality improvements, but this is a highly debatable issue. Moreover, the price indexes are largely based on prices formally quoted by sellers and fail to reflect many cases where actual prices are shaded below formal quotations to get business, especially in recessions.

Price Levels and the Value of Money

The value of money varies inversely with the general price level. Suppose that all prices (retail, wholesale, wages, rents, securities, and so forth) exactly doubled. There would be no question about the purchasing power, or value, of a dollar. It would be cut exactly in half. And if all prices were to fall by 50 percent, the purchasing power of a dollar would double. The value of money, like the value of other things, is measured by what we can get in exchange for it. A rise in the average level of all prices is a fall in the value of money. The two are simply different ways of saying the same thing.

But to measure changes in the value of money in the real world is much harder than this example suggests. Money represents generalized purchasing power over all goods and services. To measure changes in the value of money itself, therefore, we ideally need an index that summarizes the movement in all prices, and no such index exists. Remember that prices of all existing assets, as well as g.n.p. items, would have to be covered. But we can construct indexes accurate enough to show that the value of money has fluctuated sharply. The rough data on wholesale prices back to 1750 shown in Figure 5–3 demonstrate vividly that the dollar has not been a stable standard of value. On the contrary! It is as if our yardstick had intermittently contracted to eighteen inches and then stretched to six feet.

Growth in the American Economy

America's economic success story can be told in two simple statements:

1. Total real g.n.p. has grown rapidly and vigorously, far more so than in any other country over the past two centuries.

2. Real g.n.p. has grown far more rapidly than the number of people at work—that is, output per person has also risen rapidly.

But a black mark has to be chalked up too:

3. Growth has been spasmodic and uneven, interrupted by depressions and recessions with wasteful unemployment of men and productive capacity.

Growth in Total Output

Figure 5–5 shows the growth in gross national product over the past century. The graph tells the story. Gross national product in actual prices rose from $7 billion to nearly $1 trillion. If you take out the price inflation, the growth is less, but it's still phenomenal—from about $25 billion to about $850 billion in constant (1964) dollars. This is a more than thirtyfold increase. Real g.n.p. grew between 3 and 3½ percent per annum. This rate doesn't sound like much in a single year, but it compounds fast as the decades go by, in a geometric progression. Take $1 to start and do the arithmetic to see what it amounts to in 100 years. An annual growth rate of 3½ percent will more than double g.n.p. every two decades.

Growth Rates—A Digression

Figure 5–6, which takes an even longer look at American economic history, emphasizes the importance of thinking about annual growth rates—i.e., about the percentage increase per year. The left-hand portion shows real national income—in constant prices—from 1800 to 1970. This chart makes it look as if the growth rate had speeded up enormously in the last half century. The line goes almost straight up, with an increase of over $500 billion in the last fifty years.

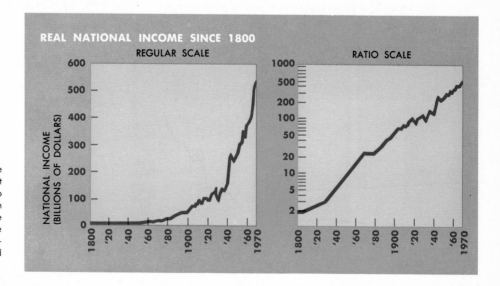

fig. 5–6

Both halves of the chart show the same data—national income in constant 1956 dollars since 1800. But the ratio scale shows that the annual growth rate has been quite stable over the past century, not rising sharply as the regular scale suggests. (Sources: National Industrial Conference Board and U.S. Department of Commerce.)

But take a look at the right-hand portion. This shows exactly the same data (national income since 1800, in constant prices) on a "ratio," or "logarithmic," scale. In contrast to regular charts, which give equal vertical distance to equal absolute increases, this ratio scale on the vertical axis gives equal distance to equal percentage increases. Thus, on the ratio scale an increase from five to ten takes about a third of an inch vertically, and an increase from 100 to 200, or from 500 to 1,000, takes exactly the same distance.

A ratio scale permits easy comparison of annual growth rates over the long period. A constant percentage increase—say 3 percent per year—will show as an equal vertical increase each year—a steadily rising straight line. If the growth rate is 4 percent, the line will be steeper. If it is only 2 percent, the line will be flatter.

Thus when we look at the right-hand section of Figure 5–6, we see the past in different perspective. What looks on the regular-interval scale like a big increase in the recent growth rate turns out on the ratio scale to be just about the same annual growth rate as over most of our history.

Growth in Output per Worker and per Capita

This growth in national output reflects in part the steady increase in the number of people working. But over the past century, only somewhat over 1 percent of the roughly 3+ percent annual growth in real output has come from more workers. The other 2+ percent a year represents increased output per worker, which in turn reflects more capital, improving technology, and better management, as well as improved worker skills and education.

Look at the chart just inside the front cover of this book. The top line shows real gross national product soaring upward. But right under it is output per man-hour, climbing steadily too. A worker today turns out over three times as much per hour as he did in 1900, and six times as much as a century ago. Who deserves the credit for this extraordinary advance? By the end of the book you should be able to answer.

Figure 5–7 shows the growth in real income (or output) per capita since 1800. As in the other charts, data before the present century are rough, and are plotted only once each decade to give a picture of major trends. Note the big increase in recent decades—but remember that this is a regular-interval, not a ratio, scale. On a ratio scale, the speedup has been moderate, between ½ and 1 percent per annum.

Booms and Depressions

Figures 5–5, 5–6, and 5–7 also illustrate how spasmodic our economic growth has been. Connect the peaks of the real g.n.p. curve in Figure 5–5 since 1929, and you'll have roughly the growth in full-employment capacity of the economy. The area between your line and ac-

fig. 5–7

Per capita real income has grown rapidly but erratically over the past century, apparently less rapidly during the early 1800's. Note the big World War II spurt, but remember that this is not a ratio scale. (Data from Fig. 4–6 divided by population.)

tual g.n.p. roughly measures the potential output lost because the economy operated below potential. It may not look like much, but it has been estimated that we lost at least $200 billion worth of output (in today's prices) in the 1930s alone through unemployment. This was equal to three full years of actual output during the ten depression years. Recent estimates show a waste of $30–50 billion a year over the 1958–64 period because the economy fell short of full-capacity output, even in those reasonably prosperous years. (The booms and depressions don't show before the 1920s, since the earlier data are plotted only once each decade.)

G.n.p. and Economic Well-Being

Growth in g.n.p. is a widely used measure of economic well-being. It's the figure you see most frequently in the newspapers, and we will use it too because it is an important and useful measure. But it has important shortcomings, and recent years have heard angry denunciations of American "idolization" of growth in g.n.p. A "zero-growth economy" has rallied student support as an alternative to the widely supported belief that more g.n.p. (output) is better than less. Eight warnings on the use of g.n.p. are in order. The first five rouse little disagreement; controversy grows with the last three.

1. For many purposes, gross national product is more useful on a per capita or per family basis. Ultimately, g.n.p. has economic usefulness to the individuals in a nation. A big nation like China is poor with a large g.n.p.; a small one like Switzerland is well off with a small g.n.p. Total g.n.p. figures alone can be seriously misleading.

2. As we have seen, price levels have fluctuated. To get a meaningful measure of actual growth in output, we must use data valued in constant prices—i.e., real g.n.p.

3. Durable consumers' goods (for example, autos and refrigerators) are included in gross national product when they are produced. Yet many of them are used over several years. The statistics imply that all consumers' durables are used up and represent income only in the year

in which they are produced. Thus, the real income (services) actually received by using durables is greater in depression years than is shown by the g.n.p., since few new durables are produced but many old ones are in use. Conversely, it is lower than reported by g.n.p. in booms when consumers' durables are produced faster than they are used.

4. G.n.p. data cover for the most part only goods and services that pass through money transactions. They take no account of such important items as nonpaid housewives' services. If Mrs. A. and Mrs. B both do their own housework, neither's services show up in gross national product. If they simply exchanged housework and paid each other $5,000 a year, neither would be better off; yet g.n.p. would be $10,000 higher. For the economy as a whole this factor alone has been estimated at $200–250 billion annually.[9] In only a few cases, such as the estimated value of services from owner-occupied homes, has it provided practicable to include real production that is not sold for money.

5. G.n.p. places no value on leisure. Over the past century, the average workweek has been cut in half—from seventy-five hours to thirty-nine—and vacations have lengthened greatly. No accurate monetary value can be placed on this gain, but to disregard it would be a gross error indeed. It is at least as important as the housewives' services noted above.

6. G.n.p. says nothing about what goods and services get produced. Most economists presume that goods produced through the private economy reflect roughly the desires of the buying public, weighted by the size of their pocketbooks. But there are some questions about this, and still more when the decision is made through the government. Is a dollar spent on national defense or highways, financed through taxes, more or less important to our economic well-being than a dollar spent privately on food or clothing? For example, real g.n.p. in 1944 was about twice the 1929 peak level. About half

[9]For estimates of the entire range of excluded nonmarket income see I. A. Sirageldin, *Non-Market Components of National Income* (Institute for Social Research, University of Michigan, 1969).

the total 1944 output was munitions, services of troops, and other war activities. Was the country twice as well off economically? Should schools and highways be included dollar for dollar with beefsteak and Buicks? The g.n.p. accounts say yes.

A comparable problem arises as modern life becomes more complex. Now we build elaborate subways, elevated, and street transport systems in our cities. They provide incomes to thousands and serve millions daily, contributing billions to the annual g.n.p. Do these billions reflect increased well-being for our city dwellers, or do they reflect instead a huge amount of resources devoted to the painful necessity of getting around in crowded cities? Many argue that our larger g.n.p. gives a misleading picture of how much better off we actually are than, for example, a rural nation with no complex transportation system.

7. G.n.p. gives no negative weight to those side effects of g.n.p. that do harm rather than good. Air and water pollution is a vivid case. Big factories that spew out smoke and dirty water as well as wanted products get overcounted. Their products increase g.n.p. dollar for dollar, but there is no negative charge for all the damage done by the pollutants. Such side effects (called "externalities" by economists) are common in our modern, crowded, high-technology society. But don't jump to the conclusion that this necessarily means that modern technology and more g.n.p. are bad. Economists point out that it is perfectly possible to have the larger quantity of goods we want and to preserve clean air and clean water if we as a society are willing to pay the cost of avoiding the unwanted pollution.

8. G.n.p. measures only economic production, which is only one part of what makes us happy or unhappy, contented or alienated. Whether people are happier now than they were a century ago with vastly lower per capita g.n.p. is impossible to say. Critics of modern life point to high suicide rates, alienation on the campuses, and what they see as the dull monotony and broad discontent of middle-class American life. But defenders counter that comfortable homes, modern plumbing, healthy children, an automobile, modern mass education, and a good office or factory job look very good compared to the lives of their grandfathers—and that the alienated critics had better be careful not to throw out the baby with the bath water. Are we happier—better off—with our high g.n.p. per capita than if we were poorer? This controversy will seldom be far from the surface through the chapters to come.

National Priorities and the "Quality of Life"

The economic quality of life depends on both per capita g.n.p. and the composition of that g.n.p. U.S. per capita g.n.p. of about $4,800 means that our total output (income) is very large compared to other nations. But total g.n.p. may include any percent of military output, education, health services, automobiles, and the like. Most, but not all, of the talk about redirecting our national priorities and improving our quality of life logically deals with the composition of g.n.p., with how we allocate our resources among different priorities through the market mechanism and through the political process. But the broad issue of work versus leisure bears directly on how hard we want to work to obtain more goods and services—and of leisure for what, if we choose more leisure instead of more output. Not least, those who challenge growth in g.n.p. argue that modern science and technology should be slowed down, and/or better controlled. To study all these questions, the concept of g.n.p. (its size and its composition) provides a useful analytical tool.

The national income accounts, however useful, clearly measure only part of the activities of modern society. In 1966, John Gardner, then Secretary of Health, Education, and Welfare, established a distinguished Task Force to study what new measures could be developed to provide better information on the state of the nation's physical environement, its social mobility, its health, its public order and safety, its feeling of participation or alienation, and the like. The Task Force found rough going; we have no adequate national data, comparable to the g.n.p.

accounts, on such issues. But its *Toward a Social Report*[10] plots some paths toward collection of such information for the future, to complement

[10]U.S. Department of Health, Education, and Welfare, *Toward a Social Report* (U.S. Government Printing Office, 1969).

the economic measures established over the last half century. Ten or twenty years hence we will surely have vastly better data on these other aspects of life. In the meantime it is important not to overstress g.n.p. as a social measure just because g.n.p. is what we have the best data on.

Review

CONCEPTS TO REMEMBER

This chapter introduces some of the most important concepts in economics. The following checklist is to help you make sure that you have them firmly in mind:

production	disposable personal income
gross national product	personal savings
"real" gross national product	gross private investment
"value added"	producers', or capital, goods
"final-products approach"	personal consumption
net national product	ratio, or logarithmic, scale
capital consumption allowance	per capita income and output
depreciation allowance	price level
national income	price index
personal income	value of money

FOR ANALYSIS AND DISCUSSION

1. Which of the following is production, as defined by the economist?
   a. Delivering milk.
   b. Making steel.
   c. Selling cigarettes to minors.
   d. Flying an airplane.
   e. Going to school.

2. In the national income accounts, production is measured by what people pay for it. Is it therefore true that a dollar spent on liquor, on missiles for defense, and on bread are all equally important?

3. Using Figure 5–2, explain each diversion from the main circular flow of income, and trace through the way in which it returns to the main stream. Did government add to or deduct from the flow of spending in 1969?

4. A recent congressional investigation found that over half the consumer price of many food products went to middlemen at different levels—retailers, wholesalers, and so on. In some cases, as little as 20 percent of the final price represented payments to the farmer who originally produced the food. Farm and consumer groups testifying before the committee urged action to rectify this situation.
   a. Do you agree that Congress should take some action? Why or why not?
   b. If Congress should act, what should it do?

5. Is gross national product, net national product, or disposable personal income after taxes the best measure of the overall performance of the economy? Why?

6. The steady growth in service workers is a sign of weakness in our economy, because they produce no *real* goods output comparable to farm output of food and raw materials. (True or false? Why?)
7. From the data below on disposable personal income and the consumer price index, compute disposable personal income for the years shown in constant (1947–49) dollars. Did "real" disposable income fluctuate more or less than money disposable income?

	Current Disposable Personal Income	Consumer Price Index (1947-49 = 100)	Disposable Personal Income in 1947-49 Dollars
1929	$ 83 billion	73	_____
1933	46 "	55	_____
1939	70 "	60	_____
1959	337 "	126	_____
1969	630 "	156	_____

8. Suppose that prices for certain products in 1960 and 1970 were as follows:

	1960	1970
Round steak (per pound)	$ .70	$ 1.00
Butter (per pound)	.90	.75
Men's suits (each)	40.00	60.00
Ford sedans (each)	1,600.00	2,800.00
Student notebooks (each)	1.00	1.00

a. Construct a price index showing the change in the price level of these commodities from 1960 to 1970. If you feel you need further data, explain why, make a reasonable assumption on the data, and then construct the index.
b. Does this index give a reasonably good picture of the change in the cost of living between 1960 and 1970? Why or why not?
c. Would the index reflect reasonably the change in your own (individual) cost of living? If not, what changes would need to be made to have the index reflect accurately changes in your own cost of living?

APPENDIX   *DATA FOR NATIONAL INCOME ACCOUNTS*

This appendix presents some background information on the g.n.p. accounts, and the actual data over most of the past century.

Table 5–6 presents some of the major national income accounts since 1869, the first year for which reasonably reliable g.n.p. estimates are available. Data for the related series not shown in the table may be found in *Historical Statistics of the United States* (Washington, D.C.: U.S. Government Printing Office, 1960); in the annual *Economic Report of the President;* and in the monthly *Economic Indicators* (Joint Economic Committee of Congress) for recent years. *Economic Indicators* provides the best simple, up-to-date summary of most important national economic series.

How accurate are the data that make up the national income accounts? Nobody knows exactly. The Department of Commerce and private research workers have spent years improving techniques for estimating the magnitudes involved. Most of the components are estimated directly from sample information. For example, the business inventory estimates rest on current samples of businesses maintained by the Department of Commerce and the Securities and Exchange Commission. Wages and salaries are estimated from samples of different sectors of the economy. Tax payments are taken directly from current government tax receipts. Personal savings are estimated by the Department of Commerce and the Securities and Exchange Commission. All these estimates are cross-checked as thoroughly as possible, both by employing two methods of estimating and by using different sources. After a year or so, more complete data for checking is available from individual and business federal income-tax returns. At longer intervals, detailed census data provide checkpoints.

But the series are only estimates, and sometimes

table 5-6

U.S. National Product, Income, and Employment

Year or Yearly Average	Gross National Product * (In Billions of 1964 Dollars)	Gross National Product †	National Income †	Disposable Personal Income †	Consumer Expenditures †	Total Employment ** (In Millions)
		(In Billions of Current Dollars)				
1869-78		7	7			19
1879-88		11	10			23
1889-98		15	13			27
1899-1908	90	22	20			32
1909-18	121	40	36			39
1919-28	162	85	70			44
1929	218	104	87	83	79	48
1931	184	76	59	63	61	42
1933	153	56	40	45	46	39
1935	183	72	57	58	56	42
1937	219	90	74	71	67	46
1939	227	90	73	70	67	46
1941	287	125	104	92	82	51
1943	374	193	168	132	102	55
1945	393	214	182	150	123	53
1947	337	234	198	170	166	58
1949	352	258	218	190	181	59
1951	412	329	279	228	210	61
1953	449	365	306	253	233	62
1955	473	398	330	274	257	63
1957	493	442	367	309	285	65
1959	518	483	400	337	314	66
1960	531	504	415	352	329	67
1961	542	520	427	365	339	66
1962	579	560	458	385	355	67
1963	595	590	481	404	374	68
1964	631	631	517	437	401	69
1965	677	681	559	469	436	71
1966	731	740	610	505	465	73
1967	763	794	654	547	492	74
1968	803	866	714	590	537	76
1969	829	932	772	630	576	78

* Data before 1929 based on John Kendrick, in *Studies in Income and Wealth*, Vol. 16 (National Bureau of Economic Research); thereafter from U.S. Departments of Commerce and Labor.
† Data before 1919 from National Bureau of Economic Research and National Industrial Conference Board; thereafter from U.S. Department of Commerce.
** Total civilian employment. Data prior to 1914 from National Industrial Conference Board; thereafter from Bureau of Labor Statistics.

estimates are based on skimpy samples. Perhaps large chunks of income are omitted entirely (though this seems unlikely). The absolute level of the aggregates is hard to check, because only during national censuses do we get complete coverage of the population, and census information only partially meets the needs of the national income calculators. Income-tax returns fill in a mass of data, but they miss part of the population—and there is always a question about how much income goes unreported. Probably the year-to-year changes in the national income data are more accurate than the absolute levels, since any classes of income missed probably stay missed. Certainly, the farther back the figures go beyond the last half century, the less reliable they become. But whatever their failings, these national income accounts are the best we have, and they are probably superior to those available anywhere else in the world.

Aggregate Supply and Aggregate Demand

A Simple Model
Aggregate Supply and Demand
Aggregate Demand,
Unemployment, and Inflation
Growth in Productive Capacity

Why do we have booms, depressions, inflations, and unemployment? What determines how fast an economy grows? For over a century economists have examined these problems. Today, we have a reasonably good understanding, though enough unanswered questions remain that they get more attention in current economic research than does any other area.

The next five chapters present the basic theory of income, employment, and prices—the general analytical model that has proved most useful in understanding what determines the overall level of income, employment, and prices in the American economy. No section of the book is as important to read and understand thoroughly. Chapters 10–15 then turn to the question of stabilization policy—how to avoid unemployment and inflation in our economy, using the basic analysis to evaluate alternative government stabilization policies. Last, Chapters 16–19 focus on long-run economic growth; what determines the rate at which different economies grow over the long run, both here and in the less-developed world; what we can do to speed or slow our rate of economic growth; and what we can do to speed economic growth in the developing nations, where growth holds the key to a rising standard of living for the world's impoverished billions.

A Simple Model

To understand the complex real economic world, it is useful to begin with a very simple model. You will recall from Chapter 2 that the essence of a model is that it focuses on a few critical variables and the relationships among them, abstracting from many details in order to highlight these essentials.

We want to understand the determinants of real g.n.p., of aggregate employment, and of the price level. Let us begin by focusing on two major variables—aggregate demand and aggregate supply. Aggregate demand simply consists of the combined expenditures of consumers, businesses, and governments that make up g.n.p., though at first we shall simplify even further by leaving the government out of the picture. Thus, aggregate demand is simply the sum of consumption and investment expenditure on currently produced goods and services.

Aggregate supply consists of the total amounts of goods and services that will be produced (supplied) in response to different levels of aggregate demand. In our private-enterprise economy (leaving government aside for the moment), goods and services are produced only when they can be sold at a profitable price. If there is no market demand, businesses will soon stop producing. Thus, we think of supply as a schedule of different amounts that will be produced in response to different levels of aggregate demand.

Obviously, as we look back on any time period, aggregate demand and the amount produced (supplied) will be the same. What is produced (measured in dollars) is identical with what is spent on it. This is simply g.n.p. looked at from the production and expenditure sides. But whether the two sides are equal at a high or low level of g.n.p.—whether at full employment and prosperity or at unemployment and depression—will depend in this simple model entirely on the level of aggregate demand. The amount produced (aggregate supply) responds directly to aggregate demand only.

Now let us spell out the model in a little more detail.

Aggregate Supply and Demand

What determines the economy's aggregate supply schedule? The "real" productive ca-

pacity of any economic system sets the upper limit to its real g.n.p. at any time. This productive capacity—the economy's production-possibilities curve for total output from Chapter 4 —depends on its underlying real productive resources, its technology, and its economic organization.[1] But an economy may not achieve this full production potential. History shows that nations often fall short of obtaining the maximum production possible from their economies, for example in the Great Depression of the 1930s. This failure reflects a shortage of aggregate demand. There is not enough total spending by consumers and businesses to buy all the goods that could be produced at full employment.

Conversely, aggregate spending may exceed the productive capacity of the economy at existing prices. If that occurs, prices are bid up and there is inflation.

The Short-Run Supply Schedule and Supply Curve

At any given time, the production-possibilities curve for an economy is given. The economy may produce less than the maximum indicated by its production-possibilities frontier, but it cannot produce more. Given this fact, let us make up an aggregate-supply schedule for the economy, assuming that the full-employment production limit is $400 billion. Column 1 in Table 6–1 simply shows different assumed levels of aggregate demand; column 2 shows the amount that will be produced in response to each level of demand. As long as the economy is below its capacity limit, rising demand calls forth more output, dollar for dollar. But after full capacity is reached, more demand cannot increase output further. The result will be inflation, but this doesn't show in Table 6–1, because the aggregate-supply schedule there is in real (constant price) terms. Above $400 billion of aggregate demand, total real output is unchanged at $400 billion, although money g.n.p. rises with inflation.

[1] Over time, some economies have been able to increase their productive capacity rapidly, while others seem to get nowhere. But for the moment we take the nation's production-possibilities curve as given. This is reasonable, since we want to begin by analyzing the behavior of the economy at a given point in time.

table 6-1

Aggregate Demand and Aggregate Supply

Aggregate Demand	Aggregate Supply (in Real Terms)
$100 billion	$100 billion
200 "	200 "
300 "	300 "
400 "	400 "
500 "	400 "
600 "	400 "

It is useful to represent this aggregate-supply schedule graphically as an aggregate "supply curve" for the economy. This curve will show how much will be produced (supplied) in response to different levels of aggregate demand.[2]

In Figure 6–1, we show on the horizontal axis the amount supplied—that is, real g.n.p. (in initial prices). On the vertical axis we show aggregate demand—total spending by all those who buy goods and services in the economy in this period. (We investigate in detail the forces determining aggregate demand in Chapters 7 and 8.) Equal distances show equal amounts on both axes.

At one extreme, if there is no demand, nothing will be produced in our profit-motivated economy. At the other extreme, OQ_3 shows the maximum real output possible for the economy in this period. Output OQ_3 corresponds to $400 billion in Table 6–1. More generally, it corresponds to a point on the nation's production-possibilities frontier, since OQ_3 is the maximum output feasible for the economy this year. No matter how much people spend and try to buy, more than this cannot be produced. Below OQ_3, as people spend more or less, businesses will increase or decrease output in response to this demand.

[2]We shall see the terms "supply schedule" and "supply curve" are used somewhat differently here from Parts Three and Four, where they apply to individual business firms and markets. Here, the supply schedule shows the aggregate amounts that will be produced in response to different levels of *aggregate demand*. Later, supply schedules for individual firms will show the amounts produced in response to different *prices* for the product concerned.

For example, if aggregate demand is zero, output will be zero. If aggregate demand is OD_1, businessmen will produce real g.n.p. OQ_1. At OQ_1, the economy would be operating far inside its production-possibilities frontier. If aggregate demand rises to OD_2, output will rise to OQ_2. Thus, if we can imagine the output levels called forth by all possible levels of aggregate demand from zero to OD_3, we would have the line OA, rising at a forty-five-degree angle from the zero point in Figure 6–1. It rises at a forty-five-degree angle because for each level of OD, real output on the horizontal axis is an identical amount. We call this line OA the economy's aggregate-supply curve; it shows how much the economy would produce at each different level of aggregate demand.

But once the economy has reached its full-employment g.n.p. (here OQ_3), it cannot increase output further, no matter how high aggregate demand rises. Thus, the aggregate-

fig. 6–1

Curve OA suggests that as aggregate demand rises, output will be increased proportionately without any price increase (inflation) up to full-employment output OQ_3. If demand increases further, however, the result will be purely rising prices since output cannot be expanded further in the short run.

THE ECONOMY'S AGGREGATE SUPPLY CURVE

supply curve OA becomes perpendicular at that point; Figure 6–1 extends it up to become OAB. Further increases in demand, say aggregate demand of OD_4, will simply bid up prices rather than calling forth more output. Intuitively, it is easy to see that if aggregate demand rises into this range, inflation will be the result. Figure 6–1 suggests that the total money g.n.p. will now be OD_4, of which OD_3 is real output corresponding to OQ_3, while the rest is simply higher prices. Actually, we shall see later that demand OD_4 might generate a cumulative rise in prices rather than an equilibrium g.n.p. of OD_4, but we postpone this problem temporarily.

It is important to recognize that by the same reasoning as above, we are assuming that if aggregate demand falls, the results are just the reverse of those that occur when demand rises. Given the aggregate supply curve OAB, when aggregate demand falls from OD_4 to OD_3 the result is purely lower prices. But when demand falls from OD_3 to OD_2 or to OD_1, the result is purely reduced real g.n.p., not falling prices. That is, we assume temporarily that below full-employment output, rising or falling aggregate demand will alter only real g.n.p., while after full employment has been reached changes in demand will affect only the price level. We shall see later that this is not strictly true, but it is a useful temporary assumption.

Thus, at any given time, in this simplest model the level of aggregate demand determines the aggregate output of this economy. Given supply curve OAB, if demand is less than OD_3, real g.n.p. is less than potential full-employment g.n.p., and productive resources are wasted. If aggregate demand is more than OD_3, there will be full employment but there will be inflation in addition. Only if aggregate demand is just OD_3, the economy will operate precisely at full employment without inflation.

Aggregate demand and aggregate supply are key concepts to remember through all of economics. Much of the next eight chapters center around the determinants of these big, key variables. Changes in their relationship to each other provide the framework for analyzing booms and depressions, inflation and unemployment, economic growth and stagnation.

Remember them and the simple little model we have just developed. For it underlies all the more complex, detailed analysis that follows.

Aggregate Demand, Unemployment, and Inflation

Our model is of course a highly oversimplified representation of the real world. Let us now make it a little more complex, to show how to analyze more fully when rising demand will call forth additional output, when inflation, and when a mixture of both.

In the real world, it is not true that rising aggregate demand will always call forth solely dollar-for-dollar increases in real g.n.p. up to full employment, and pure inflation thereafter. Actually, we would expect some prices to begin to rise before full employment is reached, because increases in demand might cause production bottlenecks and shortages in some sectors of the economy before full employment occurred in others. Demand would normally rise faster for some products than for others.

To show this situation, Figure 6–2 reproduces the aggregate-supply curve from Figure 6–1, as solid line OAB. But it adds a dashed segment which rounds off the corner where solid OAB has a sharp kink at A. If this dashed segment is correct, it shows that prices will begin to rise before we reach full employment. Put otherwise, it shows that we can reach full-employment output OQ_3 only with aggregate demand OD_4 and the considerable inflation that implies.

Try using Figure 6–2 to predict the consequences of different levels of demand. If demand rises from OD_1 to OD_2, the result is still purely rising output and employment as before; note that real g.n.p. of OQ_1 implies massive unemployment with the economy operating at less than half its capacity. But suppose demand moves on up to OD_3. Now, with the new dashed supply curve, some of the growth in aggregate demand will still induce more output but some will go into higher prices. To push the economy all the way to its full-employment output of OQ_3, we must now have aggregate demand of

fig. 6–2

As the dashed section of *OB* shows, when an economy approaches full employment prices ordinarily begin to rise before full-capacity output is reached. Here full-employment output *OQ*₃ can be achieved only with aggregate demand *OD*₄, which would imply substantial inflation.

OD₄, and with it a lot of inflation. Demand *OD₃* won't do the job any more.

This situation can pose a difficult dilemma for economic-policy makers. As we approach *OQ₃,* is it desirable to expand aggregate demand further in order to reduce unemployment to a bare minimum, even though this brings on some inflation? Or is it better to keep aggregate demand at a lower level, accepting some unemployment but also avoiding inflation? This is a problem that will be very much in the picture when we come to stabilization policy problems in Chapters 10–15.

A second modification of our Figure 6–1 model is in order if we want to use it in analyzing the impact of rising demand on unemployment and prices. In the real world, full-employment g.n.p. is never the precise amount implied by the vertical section of the aggregate-supply curve in Figures 6–1 and 6–2. As wages

and prices rise, housewives, students, and older people enter the labor force. Workers put in longer hours. Industrial engineers find ways of increasing output per man-hour. Production managers push plants beyond their quoted capacities for months, even years. With enough pressure, there are many ways of getting a little more output. As demand rises, the full-employment ceiling on output is a mushy one, rather than a precise production-possibilities frontier. To reflect this accurately, the vertical segment of *OAB* should bend over a little to the right. Eventually it must become vertical for any given time period, but the full-employment ceiling is less definite than it appears at first glance.

The Output Gap and the Inflation Gap

If aggregate demand falls short of the economy's full-employment capacity level, unemployment of men and factories will result. For example, if aggregate demand is only *OD₂* on Figure 6–2, output will be only *OQ₂* and there will be an "output gap" of *Q₂–Q₃* by which output falls short of full capacity. Sometimes this is called the "employment gap." It is the case of recession or depression if the gap is large.

If, on the other hand, aggregate demand exceeds full-employment capacity output at existing prices, there will be an "inflation gap." If demand is *D₄,* for example, clearly prices will rise. Thus the inflation gap would be *D₃–D₄,* showing the rise in prices as a result of excess aggregate demand. Actually, as Figure 6–2 suggests, the concept of the inflation gap is a slippery one. Since prices would begin to rise once demand exceeded *D₂,* we might call *D₂–D₄* the inflation gap even though output *Q₂* is far short of full employment. Or we might say there is no real inflation gap at *D₄,* since only at that demand level is full-employment output achieved. But the most common usage is to call *D₃–D₄* the inflation gap.

Growth in Productive Capacity

The aggregate-supply curves in Figures 6–1 and 6–2 are for a given time period—say a

AGGREGATE SUPPLY CURVE SHOWING GROWTH IN CAPACITY

fig. 6–3

With more productive resources and improved technology, an economy's productive capacity increases. With increased capacity, more aggregate demand is required to call forth full-employment output. In years two and three, here full-employment capacity has risen to OQ_4 and OQ_5 respectively.

year before—the production-possibilities frontier moves out. It is important to note that if productive capacity grows this way, what is full-employment aggregate demand for one year will be inadequate to call forth full-employment output the next year.

We can show this readily in Figure 6-3. It reproduces supply curve OAB from Figure 6-1, and adds on extended segments ACC and ADD to show how potential real g.n.p. moves out year after year with new investment, more labor, and advancing technology. By the same token Figure 6–3 shows that larger aggregate demand will be needed each year to call forth full-capacity g.n.p.

Thus, the aggregate-supply curve for year 2 is OCC. Potential real g.n.p. has moved out to OQ_4, and demand OD_4 is required to assure full employment. In year 3 the aggregate-supply curve becomes ODD. Potential real g.n.p. has now moved out to OQ_5, and the necessary aggregate demand up to OD_5. In terms of Chapter 4, the economy's production frontier moves out.

Chapters 7 to 15 are primarily concerned with the short-run behavior of the economy. They generally take the productive capacity of the economy as substantially fixed, although you can see that this short-run fixed-supply curve model is not quite accurate. Then, in Chapters 16 through 19 we will turn specifically to the question of long-term economic growth, and the expansion of capacity will be the center of attention. It is important both to utilize our existing capacity fully in the short run and to expand this productive capacity over the long run.

year. They are what economists often call short-run supply curves. Over longer periods, of course, the productive capacity of an economy can grow—for example, through investment in new factories, increases in the labor force, and technological progress. In that event, full-employment output each year is larger than the

---

Review

This chapter introduces two basic concepts that will be used over and over. Be sure you understand:

aggregate supply	inflationary gap
aggregate demand	output gap

1. Explain the relationship between an economy's production-possibilities curve and its aggregate-supply curve.
2. Does the aggregate-supply curve in Figure 6–1 or that in Figure 6–2 make it easier for the economy to achieve full employment without inflation? Explain.
3. In a private-enterprise, profit-motivated economy, why is it reasonable to say that aggregate production will depend on the level of aggregate demand?
4. After an economy reaches full employment, raising aggregate expenditure must always cause inflation. (True or false? Does the time period involved influence your answer?)
5. What are the main ways by which a nation can move its production-possibilities curve out (to the right)?

The Modern Theory of Aggregate Income, Employment, and Prices

In the short run, whether we have depression, prosperity, or inflation depends largely on the level of aggregate demand. What determines the level of aggregate demand is thus an extremely important question. In Chapter 6 we simply assumed different levels of total spending. We need to examine in detail what determines aggregate demand under different circumstances.[1]

Two general approaches have been stressed. One emphasizes the supply of money as a, or the, dominant force determining the level of total spending. This is sometimes called the "monetarist," or neoclassical, approach. It is examined in Chapter 9. The other, sometimes called the "income–expenditures," or neo-Keynesian, approach, emphasizes that spending depends on incomes received.[2] It is the main topic in Chapters 7–8. Then, we shall

[1]Section I of the Mathematical Appendix, at the end of this text, presents the central argument of this chapter in mathematical terms. Students who know calculus and find mathematical formulations helpful may find the appendix a useful aid, but it is recommended for use only *after* the following text sections have been read.

[2]This general approach was first popularized by a noted economist, John Maynard Keynes, during the depression of the 1930s. Keynes achieved wide fame because he was one of the earlier outspoken advocates of fighting depressions with deficit spending. Whatever you think about that issue —it's a central issue in Chapter 14—you should understand that the present chapter deals only with neutral analytic tools that can help you understand the determinants of aggregate demand; but they don't tell you what we should do about the problem of depressions and inflations.

merge parts of both approaches into a "modern synthesis," which many economists now agree seems to provide the best explanation of changes in aggregate demand.

This chapter, then, focuses on the income–expenditures model. It stresses that one big part of aggregate demand—what people spend on consumption—depends primarily on the incomes they receive. What businesses spend is determined mainly by their profit outlook, which in turn depends heavily on consumer buying. What governments spend is determined by other forces. This analysis focuses attention on the three big components of gross national product from Chapter 5—on private consumption spending, private investment spending, and government spending, on their determinants, and on their interrelationships. (We shall continue temporarily to ignore international considerations, postponing them to Part Six.)

Simple Static G.n.p. Model

To simplify, first assume temporarily that there is no government spending or taxation. Thus, aggregate demand is the sum of consumption *(C)* plus private investment spending *(I)*. Since aggregate demand is also equal to gross national product, we can also say that g.n.p. equals $C + I$. (Economists typically use Y to represent national income or g.n.p., and so will we. Thus $Y = C + I$.)

Second, assume (what many economists consider a crude first approximation to reality) that consumption spending depends entirely on the incomes that people receive, and not on any other factor. Moreover, the portion of their income households don't spend on consumption, they save. Since saving is defined as simply that income received that is not spent on consumption, savings also depend on the amount of income people receive. Obviously, saving equals income minus consumption $(S = Y - C)$.

Third, assume temporarily that business investment spending is autonomously determined. That is, businessmen decide how much to invest on the basis of considerations other than consumer spending and saving. What this means as a practical matter is that we simply take business investment spending as fixed for any time period at this stage of the analysis.

Thus, given these assumptions, in this simple income–expenditures model aggregate demand in each year will be the sum of two parts: business investment spending (a given amount determined autonomously) and consumption spending (which is dependent on the incomes that households receive). But income, which determines consumption, is in turn partially made up of consumption spending. Thus it should be clear that g.n.p., consumption, and investment are all interacting in what we may call a simultaneously determined system. Given these assumptions, we can readily show how consumption and investment spending interact to produce an equilibrium level of aggregate demand (and hence g.n.p.) each year. The reasoning can be presented verbally, graphically, or algebraically. It's done all three ways below, because different people find different approaches most helpful. Note therefore that the following sections repeat the same analysis in these different forms.

Algebraic Presentation

We have defined aggregate demand as being equal to g.n.p., which is equal to consumption plus investment spending. Let Y stand for aggregate demand and g.n.p. Then:

$$Y = C + I$$

Now assume that consumption spending is always just .75 of income (that is, people spend three-fourths of their incomes on consumption and save one-fourth), so that:

$$C = .75 \cdot Y$$

Saving (S) is the portion of their income that households don't spend on consumption. Thus, $S = .25Y$.

Remember that investment (I) is autonomous; it is independently determined. That is, business investment spending depends on expected profits, on new inventions, or some other forces, but not on consumption spending or saving. Suppose, now, that business investment spending is 100 this year, so:

$$I = 100$$

Now, substitute the values for C and I in our original equation, $Y = C + I$. We get:

$$Y = .75 \cdot Y + 100$$

Using the rules of elementary algebra, move the $.75Y$ to the left side of the equation. This changes the sign from plus to minus, and we have:

$$Y - .75Y = 100, \text{ or}$$
$$.25Y = 100, \text{ or}$$
$$Y = \frac{100}{.25}, \text{ and}$$
$$Y = 400$$

Equilibrium aggregate demand, or g.n.p., will be 400 if investment is 100 and people spend three-fourths of all the income they receive on consumption.

This is the "equilibrium" level of g.n.p., given our assumptions. That is, it is the level to which aggregate demand and output will move, and the level at which they will stay once they get there, unless something new comes along to change them. It is this equilibrium level of g.n.p. (aggregate demand) we are trying to explain in this chapter.

Verbal Presentation

Put the reasoning in words. Given our assumptions about consumption and investment decisions, g.n.p. couldn't stay lower than 400. To see why not, suppose g.n.p. were 300. Then people would be spending 225 on consumption (.75 of 300) and saving 75 (.25 of 300). But business investment spending of 100 added to consumption spending of 225 would give a g.n.p. of 325. This 325 $C + I$, or g.n.p., is obviously more than 300. Given our basic assumptions about C and I, g.n.p. cannot be as low as 300; it rises to 325, toward 400.

Now try g.n.p. at 325; it is also too low to be

consistent with our assumptions, by the same reasoning, and it would also rise. So is any other level below 400. At any g.n.p. below 400, the savings being withdrawn from current income would be less than the 100 of investment spending being spent into g.n.p., and thus larger investment spending would push g.n.p. up toward 400. This statement puts the reasoning in terms of the lower loop of Figure 5–2 and lets you see the economic reasoning rather than just stating the logical requirements for an equilibrium g.n.p.

Conversely, try any level of g.n.p. higher than 400—say, 500. Then consumption plus investment spending on our basic assumptions about C and I would be less than 500. Consumption would be 375 (.75 of 500) and investment 100, totaling only 475. At a 500 level of g.n.p., people would want to save 125, more than is being invested. Hence g.n.p. would fall toward 400. Only at 400 will the sum of investment (100) plus consumption (three-fourths of g.n.p.) just equal the current g.n.p. of 400, so g.n.p. will remain unchanged. To put it another way, equilibrium is reached only when the amount being withdrawn from the income stream through saving each period just offsets the amount being inserted through investment.

We can look at this adjustment mechanism another (equivalent) way. Assume again that g.n.p. is 500. This means that businesses are producing 500. But on the demand side buyers would purchase only 475, i.e., 375 of consumption goods (three-fourths of 500) plus 100 of investment goods. Unsold inventories would pile up, and businesses would reduce production (g.n.p.). And so it would be for any other g.n.p. above 400. Conversely, if we assume a g.n.p. less than 400, then demand $(C + I)$ would be larger than production. For example, if g.n.p. (production) were 300, demand would be 325— 100 of investment plus the 225 people would consume if their incomes were 300. Inventories would be used up and businesses would increase production (g.n.p.) to meet the larger demand. G.n.p. would thus rise toward 400.

Work out as many examples as you like and you'll always get one and only one equilibrium value of aggregate demand and g.n.p. Equilibrium requires that the public decide to save just the amount businesses have decided to invest. Of course, the particular numbers in our example are arbitrary. If business investment is higher, say 150, the equilibrium g.n.p. is higher. If consumers spend 80 instead of 75 percent of their income on consumption, equilibrium g.n.p. will be higher. Try it and see. But the reasoning—the underlying economic adjustment process—is unchanged.

Graphic Presentation

The same reasoning can be presented in graphical terms. Note that this presentation adds nothing to the reasoning above. It's just another way of presenting the same analysis. But in doing so, let us change the numbers and let us make the model more realistic by introducing a more realistic "consumption function," which is what economists call the relation between people's income and their consumption spending. The only difference from the example above is a slightly different assumption, that people consume a lower percentage of their incomes at high than at low incomes, instead of always just three-fourths. This shift will, of course, change the equilibrium level of g.n.p. Again, consumption and saving depend entirely on g.n.p. and investment is fixed at 100.

The Consumption and Saving Schedules

Figure 7–1 shows these new consumption and saving functions. On the left-hand chart,

line *CC* plots consumption spending against g.n.p. at different levels of g.n.p. In addition, the chart has a 45° line, every point on which is equidistant from the two axes. Thus, at any point on it, total consumption would just equal total g.n.p. If line *CC* coincided with the 45° line, there would be no saving. Whenever the consumption curve *(CC)* is below the 45° line, part of g.n.p. is being saved. For example, at a g.n.p. of 200, the economy would spend 160 on consumption and save 40. However, if g.n.p. were as low as 50, people would spend more than their full incomes on consumption; they would "dissave" by borrowing or drawing on past savings.[3]

The right-hand part of Figure 7–1 shows the corresponding saving schedule *(SS)*. This is drawn simply by taking the amount saved at each level of g.n.p. from the left-hand portion. Saving will be negative at low income levels

[3]For readers who know mathematics, the equation of this consumption function is: $C = a + b(Y)$, where a and b are constants with $a = 40$ and $b = .6$. Therefore, $C = 40 + .6Y$. That is, consumption is always 40 plus .6 of the amount of income received. The basic $Y = C + I$ equation can be solved just as before by making the new substitution for C. Thus:

$$Y = (40 + .6Y) + 100, \text{ or}$$
$$Y - .6Y = 40 + 100$$
$$.4Y = 140, \text{ so}$$
$$Y = 350$$

The Mathematical Appendix at the end of the book and the appendix to this chapter on "Econometric Models" show more fully how simple mathematical systems can be used to determine equilibrium g.n.p. levels under more complicated conditions.

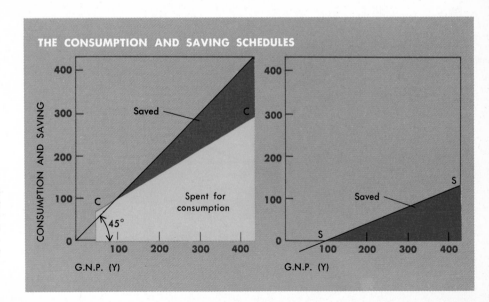

THE CONSUMPTION AND SAVING SCHEDULES

fig. 7–1

The left-hand portion of this figure shows that people will spend a smaller proportion of their income on consumption as income rises, and save a larger proportion. The right-hand portion shows the same saving behavior by itself.

when *CC* exceeds total g.n.p., and will be positive at higher income levels. The *SS* curve will, of course, cross the zero line at the same income level as the *CC* curve cuts the 45° line, where all g.n.p. is spent on consumption—at 100 on Figure 7–1.

By adding investment to Figure 7–1, we can see graphically how equilibrium is determined. This can be done in two ways. First, plot the saving curve *(SS)* in Figure 7–2, from the right-hand portion of Figure 7–1. Now add investment *(II)*. It is a horizontal line at 100, since we have assumed that investment is (temporarily) fixed at that level. *II* intersects *SS* at a g.n.p. of 350, and this is the equilibrium level. Given our new assumptions on consumption and investment behavior, aggregate demand and g.n.p. will move to 350 if it is at any other level. Note that equilibrium g.n.p. here is different from the preceding example, because we have assumed a different consumption function. People no longer spend just 75 percent of their incomes on consumption.

Why is 350 the equilibrium level? The reasoning is the same as before: because at this level of g.n.p. the amount businessmen invest is exactly offset by the amount people want to save. Thus, the circular flow of income will be complete and stable. Consumers will receive 350 each year, and (reading from the left-hand por-

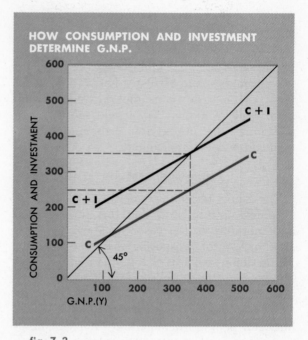

fig. 7–3

Equilibrium g.n.p. is established where the sum of consumption- and investment-spending (on the vertical axis) just equals g.n.p. (on the horizontal axis). This gives the same equilibrium level as Fig. 7–2.

tion of Figure 7–2) they will save 100 and spend 250 on consumption. Each year, businesses will invest 100, just equal to the amount people save; and so on for each succeeding time period. Equilibrium will be achieved only at the income level where consumers want to save just enough to match business investment spending.

Now a second way of showing the same results graphically. Figure 7–3 shows the consumption and investment functions on the same graph. It adds to consumption spending (the *CC* curve of Figure 7–1) 100 of investment spending at each income level each year. Thus, *C + I* is the amount that households and businesses will spend on consumption plus investment at each level of g.n.p. Now, since consumption and investment spending are on the vertical axis, and total g.n.p. is on the horizontal axis, the 45° line shows all the points where aggregate demand *(C + I)* will just equal total production (g.n.p.).

In Figure 7–3 aggregate demand *(C + I)* just equals g.n.p. (cuts the 45° line) at 350. At 350

fig. 7–2

Equilibrium g.n.p. is established where the public wishes to save just enough to match the amount being invested.

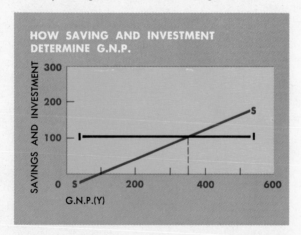

and only at 350 does the sum of consumption and investment spending just equal g.n.p. (production).

Test the result. As before, assume any g.n.p. lower than 350 (say 300), and you will see that it can't last. At a g.n.p. of 300, consumption plus investment spending, shown by $C + I$, would be above the 45° line. Thus, business sales would exceed production, inventories would be drawn down, and businesses would increase production. G.n.p. would rise toward 350. The opposite is true if we assume g.n.p. is anything higher than 350, say 400. At a g.n.p. of 400, $C + I$ would be less than 400; people would not buy all the goods being produced; unsold inventories would pile up; and production would fall toward 350.

A crucial reminder: All the above analysis assumes that consumption and saving are functions solely of income received. If consumption spending changes for any other reason, the equilibrium level of income will be changed. In the model, such a change would be shown as a shift in the consumption function (on the chart, a shift of the CC line to the right or left).

Equilibrium Not Necessarily Full Employment

It is important to recognize that an equilibrium g.n.p. does not necessarily imply that there is full employment. Look back at the aggregate-supply curve in Figure 6–1. If our equilibrium g.n.p. level is less than OD_3 and OQ_3, there will be unemployment and the economy will be operating inside its production-possibilities frontier; there will be an output gap. If equilibrium g.n.p. is above OD_3, the result will be inflation; there will be an inflation gap. "Equilibrium" g.n.p. as we have defined it is thus a neutral analytical concept. It does not imply anything, either good or bad, about the level of employment or how well the economic system is performing.

Changing Investment— the Multiplier

Suppose now that businessmen decide to increase their spending on investment, perhaps because of a new invention. This decision will raise the II curve in Figure 7–2 and the $C + I$ curve in Figure 7–3. The result, common sense tells you, will be a higher equilibrium level of g.n.p. after the increase in investment. Conversely, a decrease in investment spending will lead to a lower equilibrium level.

These results are obvious enough, but one additional fact may not be: **Each dollar of increase in autonomous investment will increase aggregate demand and g.n.p. by a larger, or multiplied, amount.** This is because each new dollar of investment, as it is spent, becomes income to a consumer who saves part but respends the rest on consumption. This respending constitutes income to someone else, who in turn saves part but respends the rest. And so on. The number of times the final increase in income (g.n.p.) exceeds the new investment is called the "multiplier." For example, if one additional dollar of investment spending generates four additional dollars of g.n.p., the multiplier is four.

Marginal Propensity To Consume

To explore this process more fully, we now need to be more precise about the consumption function, and to distinguish between the "average propensity to consume" and the "marginal propensity to consume." Suppose that total income (g.n.p.) is 100 and people are spending 75 on consumption and saving 25 each period. Then the average propensity to consume is .75; people are spending .75 of their incomes on consumption. However, it does not necessarily follow that if they receive additional income they would maintain this same consumption–income ratio. Suppose their incomes now rise to 110 but they only consume .5 of this additional 10 of income. Then the marginal propensity to consume is .5. The marginal propensity to consume is the proportion of additional, or marginal, income that is spent on consumption. It is the marginal propensity on which we need to focus our attention when we are analyzing changes in the level of g.n.p., since it is the marginal propensity to consume that tells us what percentage of additional income people spend on consumption.

The Multiplier

Begin with an equilibrium g.n.p. level of 350 and assume that the marginal propensity to consume is .75. Suppose now that businessmen increase their investment spending by 10. When the 10 is spent on new investment (say, building a new plant), it becomes income to the recipients, who then spend 7.5 on consumption and save 2.5. The 7.5 of consumption spending becomes income to someone else who in turn responds 75 percent (5.6) on consumption and saves 25 percent (1.9). The 5.6 becomes income to someone else, and so the process goes. Remember that savings are withdrawn from the income stream and are not respent in this model; nor do they stimulate more business-investment spending. We get a table like the following.[4]

	New Income	New Consumption	New Saving
Initiating New Investment	10.0	7.5	2.5
On Round 2	7.5	5.6	1.9
On Round 3	5.6	4.2	1.4
On Round 4	4.2	3.2	1.0
	.	.	.
	.	.	.
	.	.	.
	40	30	10

The table shows only the first four rounds, but it gives the general picture. The 10 of new investment generates a chain of responding on consumption—called the "multiplier" effect—that leads to new income of much more than 10. Each round makes a smaller net addition to income than its predecesor, because part of the new income is drained off into saving by each recipient, and by assumption these savings are not respent nor do they stimulate additional business investment. If you carry the arithmetic to its conclusion, you will find that the total new g.n.p. generated is 40 (including the 10 of new investment). Of this total, 30 is spent on con-

[4]Assume for this example that the businesses get the funds for the extra 10 of investment by borrowing newly created funds from the banks, rather than by saving out of their own current incomes.

sumption and 10 is saved, in accordance with our marginal propensity to consume of .75. The new equilibrium g.n.p. is 40 higher, total consumption 30 higher, and total savings and investment each 10 higher than before. The expansion process has continued until the amount people want to save of their higher income just matches the 10 of new investment. Adding these increments to the original equilibrium values, we get a new equilibrium total g.n.p. level of 390. The multiplier is four, since income has risen by 40 in response to 10 of new business investment.

This result is shown graphically in Figure 7–4. The CC and $C+I$ curves before the increase in investment are shown as solid lines, reproduced directly from Figure 7–3. Now we add 10 more of investment at each level of income. In other words $(C+I)'$ (the solid black line) now represents consumption plus 110, instead of plus 100, at each level of realized g.n.p. The CC line is unchanged because it was originally drawn to show what households would spend on con-

fig. 7–4

An additional 10 of investment raises the $C+I$ curve to $C' + I'$ and brings a new equilibrium level of g.n.p. of 390, up 40 from the previous equilibrium. The investment multiplier is 4.

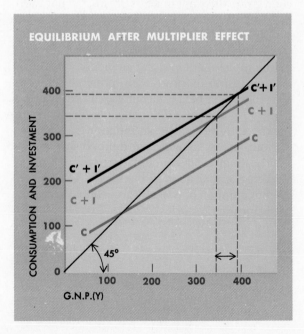

sumption at each level of g.n.p. But the new equilibrium level of g.n.p. is 390, up 40. This is where the new $(C + I)'$ curve cuts the 45° line, even though investment has increased only 10.

If this looks like graphical trickery, consider the economic common sense of this multiplier effect of new investment on consumption and g.n.p. Under what conditions is the effect powerful, and when is it weak? Just how does it work? There are four important points:

1. The multiplier effect hinges on the fact that people respend on consumption part of each increment of income they receive. If at any point they save all their new income, the respending spiral stops short.

2. The larger the proportion of its additional income that the public respends each round, the larger will be the multiplier effect. Conversely, the larger the proportion saved each round, the smaller will be the multiplier effect.

3. The size of the multiplier is given precisely by the formula:

$$M = \frac{1}{1 - \text{Marginal propensity to consume}}$$

Thus, if the marginal propensity to consume is .75, the multiplier will be

$$M = \frac{1}{1 - .75} = \frac{1}{.25} = 4.$$

Hence, an increase of $1 in investment would mean an increase of $4 in g.n.p. If the economy's marginal propensity to consume out of g.n.p. were .90, the multiplier would be 10. (Work out the .90 case in the equation, and check yourself by working out a table like the one in the preceding section. You will find that the formula merely summarizes the arithmetic.) An easy way to look at it is this: The multiplier is the reciprocal of the marginal propensity to save, still using our simple assumptions. Thus, if consumers save one-fourth of their new income, the multiplier is 4. If one-tenth, the multiplier is 10. And so on.

4. Last, review again the economic reasoning behind this formula. For example, with a marginal propensity to consume of .75, why is the new equilibrium level of g.n.p. higher by just four times the level of additional investment spending? Because at any assumed g.n.p. level below equilibrium, people would want to save less than the new level of investment, and the respending rounds would continue to raise g.n.p. Equilibrium is achieved only when the public's income is such that it wants to save just enough to offset the amount being invested. Only if these two just match will the circular flow of income be continuous and stable.

This is the basic multiplier process. But a warning is needed. In the real world, with government taxes and spending and with business as well as consumer saving, the picture becomes more complex. To calculate real-world multipliers, wait for the section, "The Multiplier in the Real World," a few pages later on.

The Paradox of Thrift

This reasoning suggests a curious paradox. If consumers decide to save a larger percentage of their incomes, other things equal this increased propensity to save will lead to a lower multiplier, lower consumption, a lower g.n.p., a decrease in induced investment, and a lower level of aggregate saving in the new equilibrium. Here is an example of the fallacy of composition. More saving out of any given level of income may be a very good thing for the individual household, but a simultaneous attempt by many households to save more out of their incomes may throw the economy into a recession which makes us all worse off, and where we actually save less because of our lower incomes. This is the paradox of thrift.

But note that an increase in the economy's propensity to save need not throw us into recession. If the increased thriftiness comes in a period of inflation, it can have the happy result of pulling aggregate demand down toward maximum potential real g.n.p. and reducing inflationary pressure. And even in noninflationary periods, the drop in consumption relative to income may be offset by increased private investment or government spending—which leads us on to the next section. But the paradox of thrift may pose a real problem when the economy is on the verge of unemployment or in a recession.

Induced Investment and Dynamic Processes

Thus far we have assumed that investment decisions are autonomous—that is, determined independently of the level of consumption. But actually, the level of sales and the resulting business profits are surely an important determinant of business-investment plans. If we say that business investment is dependent on consumer spending in the preceding period, we get what economists call "dynamic" analysis. In that case, the new equilibrium level in Figure 7–4 would not be a lasting equilibrium, since the higher consumer spending would in turn induce more business investment. The new induced investment in turn would lead to a further multiplier effect on consumption and g.n.p. Intuitively, you might expect such a process to spiral upward indefinitely—and under some conditions it would. But under others, we can explain why the spiral would die out, or even reverse itself and start downward.

This study of dynamic processes is the essence of the study of booms and depressions (business cycles). But it is better to postpone such dynamic analysis until we have equilibrium analysis firmly in hand. We shall return to dynamic processes in detail in Chapter 10.

Government Taxes and Expenditures (Fiscal Policy)

Now let us put government taxes and spending into our model, to bring it into closer correspondence with the real world. Government taxes take away part of the spendable income of households and businesses, and governments spend on current output. Thus, we need to add government on both the spending and saving sides of the picture.

Up to this point we have said that the equilibrium condition is:

$$G.n.p. = C + I = C + S$$

If consumer plans to save differ from business plans to invest in the private economy, the level of g.n.p. will move up or down until people want to save just enough to offset business investment. Now add government to this equation.

We can treat government tax collections as being similar to private savings; they constitute a leakage out of the respending stream. Similarly, we can treat government spending on goods and services as being similar to private investment spending; government spending constitutes effective demand for goods and services. At least to a first approximation, government spending may be considered as autonomous spending; that is, it can be viewed as determined by forces other than the current level of g.n.p.

We now have a slightly more complex model in which both private investment and government spending are autonomous expenditures whereas consumption spending is an induced expenditure; and on the other side both private savings and government tax receipts are withdrawals from the income stream. Thus the new equilibrium condition is:

$$I + GE = S + GR$$

where GE is government expenditure and GR is government tax receipts. That is, if the sum of private investment plus government expenditures (autonomous spending) exceeds the "leakages" from the spending stream through private savings and tax receipts, g.n.p. will rise. Conversely, g.n.p. will fall if investment plus government spending is less than the leakages through saving and tax receipts.

This reasoning can also be readily presented in graphic form. Look back at Figure 7–3. To get the new $(C + I + GE)$ aggregate-demand curve, merely reduce the $(C + I)$ curve there by the amount taxes reduce private spending, and add government spending to the new $(C + I)$ curve so obtained. This new $(C + I + GE)$ curve may fall directly on the previous $(C + I)$ curve, or above or below it, depending on whether government spending is more or less than the amount by which taxes reduce private spending.[5] Where the new total $(C + I + GE)$ curve cuts the 45° line will be the equilibrium level of g.n.p., for exactly the same reasons as those that explained the previous equilibrium level for an entirely private economy. The equilibrium condition is: **Gross national product must be such that private savings plus government tax collections just match autonomous expenditure (private investment plus government spending).**

Obviously, this statement suggests that higher government spending without offsetting tax increases may be used to raise aggregate demand and real g.n.p., because of the help given by the multiplier effect. Look ahead to Figure 14–1. There we have added 10 of government spending from new money, which therefore does not reduce private spending through tax collections. With a marginal propensity to consume of .75, the multiplier is 4, and total income is increased by 40, to a new equilibrium level of 390. Increasing government spending by 10 has raised g.n.p. by 40, just as 10 of increased private investment would do. To repeat, the equilibrium condition with the government in the picture is $C + I + GE = C + S + GR$. If government spending continues at its new level, g.n.p. will stay at 390. If government spending drops back to its original level, equilibrium g.n.p. will fall back to 350.

Surpluses and Deficits—Public and Private

There is no reason, of course, why government taxes and spending must exactly balance in each time period. Neither, once we introduce government into our model, is there any reason why private saving and private investment must exactly balance in each time period. Thus, the private part of the economy may be investing more than it saves at equilibrium g.n.p., while the government is collecting more taxes than it spends. In that case the private economy would be running a "deficit" and

the government a "surplus." Conversely, the private economy might be running a surplus by saving more than it invests while the government is running a deficit by spending more than it collects in taxes.

It should be clear, then, that it is the combined $(I + GE)$ which is the base for our multiplier effect, once we put the government in. This fact provides the base for modern "fiscal policy." If government spending rises without an offsetting reduction in private investment spending, the resultant multiplier effect will raise g.n.p. by more than the amount of the government spending. More on this in Chapter 14.

The Multiplier in the Real World

Once we introduce government spending as a base for multiplier effects, we must also introduce government taxes as a leakage from the income stream comparable to private saving. And there is another leakage from the spending stream we have also thus far neglected—the fact that business firms, as well as households, may save. If we want to estimate the multiplier effect of any increment of private or government spending in the real world, therefore, we must, in effect, calculate the marginal propensity to consume out of total g.n.p. That is, we must allow for all the leakages, not just consumer saving.

For example, if consumption spending is $400 billion, disposable personal income is $450 billion, and g.n.p. is $600 billion, then the average propensity to consume out of disposable income is approximately .9, but only .67 out of g.n.p. The relevant multiplier for estimating the impact of new investment on g.n.p. if we assume the marginal propensity is the same as the average, would be 3. To use a multiplier of 10 (based on households' .9 propensity to consume out of disposable personal income) would be wrong, because it would neglect all the leakages from the circular spending flow except household saving. Specifically, it would neglect business savings and all government tax collections, and hence would give a much too high multiplier.

---

[5]Actually, the problem is a little more complicated. Since in the real world, consumption is a function, as we shall see, of disposable personal income rather than of g.n.p., a change in taxes may affect the ratio of consumption to g.n.p. But this complication may be temporarily postponed.

CONCEPTS
TO
REMEMBER

This is a major chapter. Its analytical concepts and models are used through all the rest of the book. Be sure you understand the basic reasoning in the chapter, and the following new concepts:

income—expenditure approach	equilibrium g.n.p.
consumption function	underemployment equilibrium
average propensity to consume	the multiplier
marginal propensity to consume	autonomous investment
saving function	induced investment
average and marginal	paradox of thrift
propensities to save	

FOR ANALYSIS
AND DISCUSSION

1. Assume that gross national product is $900 billion. Investment is $200 billion. Consumption expenditures are $700 billion. Assume no government participation in the income stream:
   a. If investment rises to $225 billion, with the marginal propensity to consume = .8, what will be the new equilibrium level of gross national product?
   b. Explain why this will be an equilibrium level.
2. Would you expect that decisions to save for the year ahead in the economy would ordinarily be about the same as decisions to invest? Why or why not?
3. Changes in investment cause changes in saving for the economy as a whole, rather than vice versa. (True or false? Why?)
4. What is the "paradox of thrift"? Explain why its strange result occurs.
5. Suppose that in a hypothetical economy g.n.p. is running at an annual rate of $600 billion. Other major items in the national income accounts are as follows:

Consumption	$400 billion
Investment	70 "
Savings	100 "
Government expenditures	130 "
Taxes.	100 "

The marginal propensity to consume is three-fourths. (For purposes of this problem, take the three-fourths marginal propensity to consume against income before taxes.)

   Suppose that the government now balances its budget through a reduction in government expenditures while maintaining taxes at the level of $100 billion. What will be the effect on the levels of income, consumption, and savings? Explain.
6. Assume the following conditions in an economy that includes a government sector.

Government spending	$44 billion
Government tax receipts (obtained from a tax that is independent of the level of g.n.p.)	44 "
Consumption expenditure = $30 billion plus 8/9 of the g.n.p. remaining after payment of taxes	
Investment expenditure	24 "
G.n.p. = C + I + G	

    a. Calculate the equilibrium levels of g.n.p., consumption, and savings.

    b. Investment increases to an annual rate of $29 billion and remains constant at that level. Calculate the new equilibrium levels of g.n.p., consumption, and savings.

    c. Under the conditions first described, government spending increases to an annual rate of $80 billion and annual tax receipts are raised to $80 billion. Both figures then remain constant. Calculate new equilibrium levels of g.n.p., consumption, and savings.

7. Explain why if the private sector runs a "deficit" (i.e., invests more than it saves) the public sector must run an exactly offsetting "surplus" (i.e., collect more in taxes than it spends).

APPENDIX   *ECONOMETRIC MODELS*

Modern economics, like other sciences, has come increasingly to use precisely stated analytical models, which are often most conveniently put in mathematical form. Modern economics also has become increasingly empirical—that is, concerned with measuring its variables in the real world, as distinguished from merely theorizing about them. Thus, "econometrics" has become an increasingly important branch of economics.

Econometrics deals with the science of economic measurement, as is obvious from its components, "econo" and "metrics." Broadly, econometrics involves setting up precise models of economic phenomena in mathematical form; then measuring in the real world the variables and relationships included in the model; and then solving the model to see how closely it conforms to or can predict actual economic behavior.

Simple Income-Determination Models.[6] The simple model back on page 73 provides an example. We specify a model:

$$Y = C + I, \text{ and}$$
$$C = f(Y), \text{ where } f \text{ stands for "function."}$$

So this equation says that C is a function of (or depends on) Y. The model is obviously too simple to represent the real world precisely, but assume for the moment that it does. Next we have to measure in the real world the crucial variables and relationships specified by the model. Suppose we find that I is always 100 and is independent of Y and C; and estimate that C is always just .75 of Y. Then we can insert these values in $Y = C + I$, as on page 74, and get our final equation: $400 = 300 + 100$.

[6]These are technically called "single-equation" models, since, although they begin with more than one equation, they reduce to one equation for statistical fitting to the real-world situation they represent.

But note that our model, if it is a true model of the real world, can tell us other things. If I rises to 125, we can predict that, other things remaining unchanged, g.n.p. will rise to 500; this follows directly by inserting the new value for I in the model—since C is always .75 of Y, I must always be .25 of Y. So an econometric model is in effect a forecasting device, which ways that *if* we know the values of some of the crucial variables and relationships, then we can predict others—in this model, g.n.p. and consumption.

More Complex Simultaneous-Equation Models.[7] More complex econometric models involve precisely the same basic steps: specification of the model, measurement of the relationships and variables, and solution of the model (system of equations). Some years ago, *Business Week*, while poking a little fun at econometricians, summed up the method of econometrics effectively in the sketch on page 84.

Note that the basic model is stated in the system of multiple equations in #3. Equations 1, 2, and 3 are "behavioral" equations; that is, they describe the behavior of units in the economy. Equations 4 and 5 are "identities"; that is, they merely state what we have defined as being identical. For example, we define g.n.p. as the sum of consumption plus investment plus government spending. Obviously, equations 1 through 3 are the critical ones. The solution of the model (that is, the value of g.n.p.) depends on solving the set of five equations simultaneously, just as in the real world all the factors are interacting simultaneously to determine g.n.p.

This a more complex model than was used in Chapter 7, though it is still too simple to represent the real world effectively. The government is added, and investment is made a function of profits in the preced-

[7]These are called "simultaneous equation" models, since several equations must be fitted statistically on a simultaneous basis.

The Junior Econometrician's Work Kit.

Predict the U.S. Economy for 1956.
Build Your Own Forecasting Model.

DIRECTIONS:

1. Make up a theory. You might theorize, for instance, that (1) next year's consumption will depend on next year's national income; (2) next year's investment will depend on this year's profits; (3) tax receipts will depend on future Gross National Product. (4) GNP is the sum of consumption, investment, and government expenditures. (5) National income equals GNP minus taxes.

2. Use symbols for words. Call consumption, C; national income, Y; investment, I; preceding year's profits, P_{-1}; tax receipts, T; Gross National Product, G; government expenditures, E.

3. Translate your theories into mathematical equations:

(1) $C = aY + b$ (4) $G = C + I + E$
(2) $I = cP_{-1} + d$ (5) $Y = G - T$
(3) $T = eG$

This is your forecasting model. The small letters, a, b, c, d, e, are the constants that make things come out even. For instance, if horses (H) have four legs (L), then $L = aH$; or $L = 4H$. This can be important in the blacksmith business.

4. Calculate the constants. Look up past years' statistics on consumption, income, and so on. From these find values for a, b, c, d, and e that make your equation come out fairly correct.

5. Now you're ready to forecast. Start by forecasting investment from this year's profits. Look up the current rate of corporate profits — it's around $42-billion. The model won't tell what federal, state, and local governments will spend next year — that's politics. But we can estimate it from present budget information — it looks like around $75-billion.

6. Put all available figures into your model. (We've put in the constants for you.)

(1) $C = .7Y + 40$ (4) $G = C + I + 75$
(2) $I = .9 \times 42 + 20$ (5) $Y = G - T$
(3) $T = .2G$

7. Solve the equations. You want values of C, I, T, G, Y. Hints: Do them in this order — (2), (1), (4), (3), (5). In solving (1), remember that I and E are both part of G, $Y = G - T$, and $T = .2G$.

8. Results. (See if yours are the same.) For 1956, consumption will be $260.0-billion; investment, $57.8-billion; GNP, $392.8-billion; tax receipts, $78.6-billion; national income, $314.2-billion. These results are guaranteed — provided that the theories on which they're based are valid.

Reprinted with permission from *Business Week*, September 24, 1955 ing time period. (*P__* means profits in the preceding time period; most econometricians label all their variables with time subscripts, since time is so important in most economic relationships.) This model will predict this year's national income and consumption if we know last year's profits (to predict *I* in equation #2) and government expenditures. These two—last year's profits, and government spending—turn out to be the crucial "independent variables" that control the predicted level of national income, given the relationships specified in the model. In fact, if we want to predict more than one year ahead we need a more complex model, since profits this year will obviously depend partly on the levels of *C, I,* and *G* this year (as well as on other variables). Thus, a more complete model would need a behavioral equation to integrate the determinants of profits into the system. Then, only government spending would remain a truly independent variable; and even that might turn out to depend on some of the other variables, such as tax receipts of the government. If so, the model would then require another behavioral equation to specify government spending.

All this may begin to sound complex, and it is. There are now several econometric models of the economy involving 20 to 150 equations. Moreover, a nationwide group of economists has recently completed, in preliminary form, a massive econometric model of the economy that involves over 400 equations. How well it "works" remains to be seen; it was developed by building up a large number of submodels of particular sectors of the economy and then putting them together in the overall model.[8]

Problems of Statistical Estimation. Building an econometric model requires an underlying theory. But equally it requires careful statistical estimation of the variables and relationships in the equations. A good econometrician is thus as much a statistician as an economist. Statistical estimation of complex economic relationships is a difficult job indeed, as was suggested in Chapter 2 and is pointed out in more detail in Chapter 8. Interactions among important variables in our economy—for example, among personal consumption, disposable income, the money stock, holdings of liquid assets, and the like—are complex and sometimes shifting.

Modern statisticians are gradually developing methods to handle such complex interrelationships and forecasting problems. They are too intricate to consider here. But remember that progress in understanding what determines what in the economy depends heavily on this kind of behind-the-scenes interacting theoretical and empirical work.

---

[8]A substantial econometric model of the economy is described in nontechnical language in "A Quarterly Econometric Model of the United States," *Survey of Current Business*, May, 1966.

eight

The Determinants of Consumption and Private Investment

Consumption Expenditures
Private-Investment Expenditures
Money in the
Income–Expenditures Model

Chapters 6 and 7 provided a simple model showing how real g.n.p. is determined by the interaction of aggregate supply and aggregate demand. In the short run, since the aggregate-supply curve is essentially fixed, the level of aggregate demand largely determines the level of real output and employment. In that model, consumption spending is entirely a function of the level of g.n.p. (income), while both private investment and government spending are considered autonomous—that is, unaffected by the level of g.n.p. Thus, the simple multiplier effects in Chapter 7 depend on the partially unreal assumptions that private investment and government spending are autonomously determined, and that consumption spending is passively dependent on income received.

Obviously that model is oversimplified. You may reasonably suspect that consumption spending is affected by factors other than income. Moreover, Chapter 7 did not look into the actual determinants of private-investment spending, which you may safely suspect are complex. And we have left money out of the picture. It is the purpose of this chapter to examine in more detail the determinants of consumption and private-investment spending.

Consumption Expenditures

The Relation of Consumption to Income

It seems intuitively reasonable to suppose that consumption expenditures depend heavily on the incomes that people receive. Careful studies have been made of what happens to aggregate consumption expenditures when aggregate disposable personal income rises and falls. As far back as our data go, they show aggregate consumption rising and falling with aggregate disposable personal income; and, of course, they show that, on the average, this same relationship holds for individual families. However, if we look at individual families one by one and at different time periods, we find widely varying behavior masked by the average figures.

Consider first the aggregate relationships. Figure 8–1 plots the relationship between total disposable personal income and total consumption expenditures in the economy in each year from 1922 through 1969. For example, in 1960, d.p.i. (read off the bottom scale) was about $352

billion and personal consumption expenditures (read off the vertical scale) were $329 billion. For 1933, the lowest year, d.p.i. was only $45 billion while personal consumption expenditures were $46 billion, actually more than disposable personal income. People used accumulated savings and went into debt to keep themselves fed, clothed, and housed when incomes plummeted in the depression.

The line running from southwest to northeast on the chart is drawn to "fit" the dots plotted. The fact that most years fall about on the straight line shows that the relationship between disposable income and consumption spending has been a rather stable one. But the fact that some years are substantially off the line shows equally that the stable relationship has not always held. During World War II, for ex-

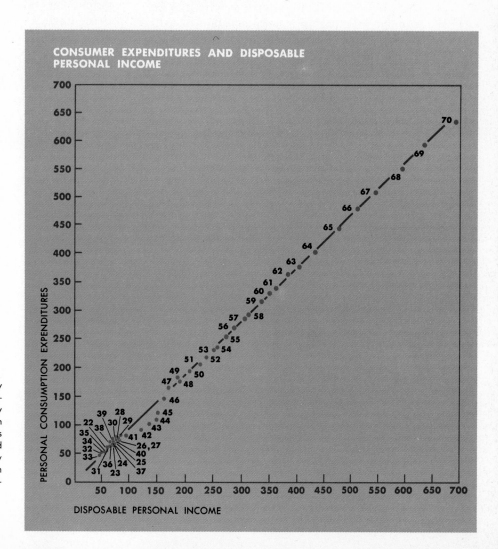

fig. 8–1

In the depression people spent nearly all their disposable income on consumption. During World War II they saved a large proportion. Since then their spending-saving behavior has been quite stable. Note that the trend line leans over a little, showing how much consumption spending is less than disposable income. (Source: U.S. Department of Commerce.)

ample, consumption spending fell far below what would normally have been expected for the high incomes received during those years.

Put in common-sense language, this evidence says that the percentage of d.p.i. spent on consumption rose as incomes fell in the depression; people tried hard not to cut back their living standards as much as their incomes fell. Conversely, when incomes are much higher in a boom, the percentage spent on consumption is much lower (around 94–96 percent in the generally prosperous years since 1950). And under special circumstances like World War II, when many goods were unavailable and the government urged everyone to save more to avoid inflation, the consumption percentage may fall much further—down to about 75 percent in 1943 and 1944. The fact that the "fitted" line leans over toward the right shows that the percentage relationship is not a constant one, like $C = .9$ (d.p.i.). Such an equation would give us a line that shows zero consumption at zero d.p.i. But we see that households in fact raised their consumption to over 100 percent of d.p.i. in 1932, when income was well above zero. Try fitting a shorter straight line to the years through 1945 only, and you will see that it leans over much more to the right, reflecting experience in a more sharply cyclical period.[1]

Such analysis of historical relationships is an

[1] For readers who know a little mathematics, the equation that approximately fits the solid line is $C = a + b(Y)$, where a and b are constants that show the relationship between consumption (C) and disposable income (Y). This is the consumption function used on page 75 above.

example of the research that provides sound empirical foundations for the models used in economic analysis, as in Chapter 7. However, we shall see in the following sections that the consumption–income relationships are in fact more complex than those shown in Figure 8–1, and to get useful predicting relationships we need to take more factors into account.

The Saving Function

By definition, consumers save that portion of their disposable income that they do not spend on consumption. The relationship between consumer saving and disposable personal income is shown in Figure 8–2, which gives the percentage of d.p.i. saved each year. The underlying data are the same as those for Figure 8–1. The percentage saved is of course one minus the percentage consumed for each year.

Figure 8–2 indicates vividly the high percentage of d.p.i. saved in the war years, and the negative savings in the years 1932 and 1933 at the bottom of the Great Depression. But more significantly it stresses the nearly constant percentage saved (about 4–7 percent) during the entire period of reasonably stable, prosperous times since 1950.

What Determines Consumption Expenditures?

The preceding data reinforce our intuitive presumption that consumption spending depends mainly on disposable personal income. But they also warn us that other forces may shift

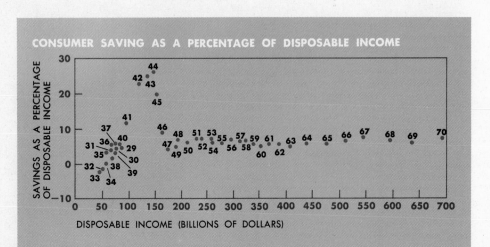

fig. 8–2

Personal saving has been a quite stable percentage of disposable personal income in peacetime prosperity, but has fluctuated sharply in depressions and wars. (Source: U.S. Department of Commerce.)

the propensity to consume, slightly or dramatically. We need now to take a more detailed look at the forces that have influenced consumption spending over the past half century.

Income—Present, Past, and Future. Empirical studies show a close relationship between present income and current consumer spending. But sophisticated statistical work over the past decade has suggested that adding past income and income expectations gives a better explanation of consumer spending than does present income alone.

The influence of past income is persistent. Once families have become used to any real consumption level, they are reluctant to slide back down to a lower level, even if their income drops. Rather than reduce their standard of living as income falls, they will (at least temporarily) reduce their saving levels to well below the amount they would have saved at that income on the way up.

Similarly, when incomes rise sharply, consumption spending rises more slowly. That is, with rising incomes the marginal propensity to consume is lower in the short run than in the long run. For example, following the big federal income tax cut in 1964 that directly increased disposable personal incomes, the percentage of d.p.i. saved rose temporarily, and then gradually shifted back to its earlier level, as previous studies of consumption indicated it would do. Consumption spending takes time to adjust.

Recently, some research workers have advanced a more sophisticated hypothesis. They suggest that consumption spending is a substantially constant and similar proportion of disposable income for average families at all income levels—if we exclude major disruptions like war and mass depression, if we include consumer durables (especially houses, autos, and household furnishings) with saving (investment), and if we consider their "permanent" or "life-span" incomes rather than the particular income of any given year, which may be distorted by special factors. It is the last clause which is the crucial one.

One version of this approach (the life-cycle hypothesis) says that families, consciously or subconsciously, estimate their long-range income over the years ahead (over their entire life cycle), and adjust their current consumption spending and saving to their rough expectations for the entire period. As a college professor, I have a pretty good idea how my salary will rise over the years ahead to retirement, barring major calamities and other such special factors. I base my estimate especially on my income during the recent past. The same is true for many other families. Thus, during their early married years most couples spend most of their income and even go into debt to start families and set up households. A little later, as income rises and these special expenses have passed, they begin to save more, for retirement, to send their children to college, and so on. After their houses are well furnished and their children are educated, they commonly save at a much higher rate. Late in life, after they retire, the saving ratio drops again and often becomes negative. Looking over this life-span, the average ratio of consumption to income is, if the investigations of this group stand up under further scrutiny, surprisingly similar for typical families at different income levels. By the same token, this suggests that consumption is a quite stable function of income for the population as a whole.

The "permanent income" hypothesis is similar. It says that families base their consumption on what they expect their "permanent" income to be. Temporary deviations in income up or down from this permanent expectation will usually not affect consumption much. Rather, if income falls temporarily, the family will cut back its savings, use up its liquid assets, or go into debt to maintain consumption. If income bulges temporarily, the bulge is likely to go mainly into saving (including purchase of consumer durables). Just how families actually decide what their "permanent," or life-span, income is, is not clear; past incomes presumably provide the best indicator.

What is the evidence on the life-span and permanent-income models? Good statistical evidence is hard to get, and interpretation of the data in relation to these models is a tricky problem. Most economists believe that the evidence to date generally supports the models, but with enough contradictory data to require a suspended judgment so far as practical use of the model is concerned.

Money and Wealth

Other things equal, a family with large wealth (ownership of economic assets such as money, stocks, bonds, houses, and consumer durables) will spend more on consumption than will a low-wealth family with the same income. For example, suppose a family receives an annual income of $10,000 and has accumulated wealth of $25,000. Imagine now that a wealthy relative dies and leaves the family another $25,000. We would expect its level of consumption to rise even if the father's salary stayed at $10,000. Note, incidentally, that this effect is closely related to the "permanent" income hypothesis above. With more wealth, the family's permanent, or life-time average, income has increased, since the family's income now includes the interest, dividends, or other yield on the additional $25,000 of wealth.

Money is one form of wealth, and more money, other things equal, will surely lead households to spend more on consumption (and possibly on other things as well). But money is a special form of wealth—the only one that can be freely used to buy other goods and services. Some economists (the "monetarists") argue that this special quality of money makes it an especially powerful determinant of consumer spending. They contend that the stock of money in the economy is the main determinant of consumption, and indeed of total aggregate demand.

This alternative approach to explaining aggregate demand is examined in detail in Chapter 9, and it is combined with Chapters 7–8 in a modern synthesis there. In the meantime, remember that money may be a very important variable, which is being temporarily set aside here.[2]

[2]The period immediately following World War II is often cited to show the importance of money and other liquid assets. During World War II, government borrowing placed nearly $250 billion of new liquid assets (money and government securities) in the hands of the public. After the war,

Consumer Credit. One way of getting around the limitation of income is to borrow money or buy on credit. A net increase in consumer credit correspondingly increases consumer spending power, beyond that provided by current income. Until the last couple of decades, consumers did little credit buying except in purchasing homes. But since World War II a huge volume of houses and consumer durables (especially automobiles) has been bought on credit. By 1970, families were over $125 billion in debt on consumer goods, compared to $6 billion in 1929 and in 1946. This growth thus represented a net addition of $120 billion to total consumer spending power over the period. Mortgage debt on houses passed $275 billion in 1970, up over $225 billion since 1946. In total, such new credit to households thus increased family buying power by nearly $350 billion over the 1946–70 period.

But there is a counterforce at work here too. The deeper consumers are in debt, the less they can count on increasing this supplement to current income in future periods, and the greater is the potential inroad on current consumption spending from required payments on the debt. If you are in debt, interest and debt repayments must be met before current income can be devoted to consumption expenditures. By 1970, the proportion of current disposable income committed in this way exceeded 15 percent, which correspondingly restricted consumers' power to spend disposable income on goods and services.

Availability of Goods. During World War II, you just couldn't buy lots of "hard goods" like refrigerators and automobiles, because their production was cut back or eliminated by the war. Reflecting this and other factors, the

this huge accumulation began to burn a hole in the public's pocket. Between 1945 and 1947, consumption spending rose from 80 to 98 percent of d.p.i. Then, as incomes and prices caught up to a more normal relationship to liquid assets, the consumption–income relationship eased back down to previous high-employment peacetime levels.

The facts are clear. But just how much weight should be given to money and other liquid assets is debatable. Skeptics point out that other factors (especially the pent-up demand for consumer durables unavailable during the war) may also help explain the postwar spending burst.

economy's consumption ratio dropped to below 75 percent of d.p.i. in 1943 and 1944. By 1946, consumers had accumulated an enormous backlog of demand for such consumer durables, which undoubtedly helps explain the big postwar buying surge. Such shortages of goods are rare, but they may exert a powerful force on the consumption function when they occur.

Consumer Stocks of Durable Goods. The converse effect occurs when consumers have built up unusually large stocks of durable goods. Consumer spending on nondurables (food, clothing, and so on) and on services (housing, utilities, and so on) is relatively stable, but spending on durables (automobiles, refrigerators, TV sets, and so on) fluctuates sharply with fluctuations in income. Since such durables last, their purchase can be postponed far more readily than the purchase of nondurable goods or services. Thus, after consumers have engaged in a big buying spree on durables (for example, 8 million autos in 1955), they are likely to slack off their buying until the new durables are at least a few years old, even though consumer income holds up. Note that this example applies to only one sector of consumer spending, not necessarily to total consumption expenditures. Remember, too, that the permanent-income hypothesis includes most durable-goods purchases as saving-investment, not as consumption.

Price Expectations. If you expect prices to rise, the time to buy is now, before things go up. If you expect deflation, you had better hold off postponable purchases until prices go down. Changing expectations of future prices can thus bring violent shifts in the consumption–income relationship. Immediately after the outbreak of the Korean War in 1950, for example, current consumer saving dropped almost to zero as consumers rushed to stock up before prices skyrocketed and goods vanished from the market. Such drastic shifts in price expectations are rare, but when they do occur, they can dominate the more stable consumption–income relationships that generally prevail. Unfortunately, there is no one simple expectations–spending relationship. Some consumers reduce buying of nonessentials when they expect inflation, to conserve their funds for the most urgent needs.

Long-run Stability and Short-run Instability. Where do all these considerations leave us on the determinants of consumer spending? Some modern statistical efforts to answer this question are presented in the following section. But at the risk of oversimplification, we can say that over the long pull the ratio of consumption to disposable personal income has been quite stable. At high-employment levels, it has seldom varied from the 93–96 percent range, moving outside that range for long only in response to strong, identifiable special forces, such as war. In spite of short-run fluctuations in business cycles, consumers as a whole appear to adjust their consumption habits to rising incomes over the long run so as to maintain about the same average ratio of consumption to disposable income as in past prosperity periods. Will this tendency persist over the years ahead? Nobody knows. But the historical relationship has prevailed long enough to make it a reasonably good bet.

The Consumption Function—Modern Statistical Evidence

While the above generalizations give us some guides to consumption behavior, they are too rough to be satisfactory for national forecasting purposes—for example, when we want to predict the probable effects of a tax cut or tax increase. Thus, modern econometricians have devoted a great deal of attention to analyzing precisely the empirical relationship between the various causes listed above and consumption spending the past.

A number of modern studies agree that we can generally get a good approximation of the likely change in consumption for the quarter or year ahead if we can predict changes in disposable income and changes in wealth (or perhaps money) held by consumers. As is suggested above, this prediction seems to improve if we substitute for current disposable income a somewhat more sophisticated measure of "permanent" or "life-cycle" income. Rough approximations of these concepts have been made by assuming that people will take an average of their income over the past several years as a predictor of their permanent or life-cycle income, once adjustments are made for their age, family status, and the like.

Another approach is to break down consumer spending into a number of major components—spending on services, on nondurable goods, on automobiles, on other durable goods, and the like. One well-known econometric model, for example, relates changes in spending on nondurable goods to disposable income, the level of spending on nondurables in the preceding period, and holdings of liquid assets in the preceding period, plus a "catch-all" factor for other variables. Note that the inclusion of spending on nondurables in the preceding period reflects the importance of previous consumption levels; this reflects the fact that consumers' current consumption spending is considerably influenced by what they spent last quarter or in other recent quarters. They are reluctant to cut back their spending drastically, even if their income level falls.

Econometricians write this relationship in the following way. Actual numbers are inserted for the relationship from one well-known study:

$$\Delta ND = .224\ \Delta Y + .205\ \Delta ND_{-1} + .143 \Delta L_{-1} - .149$$

In this equation, Δ means change from the last quarter to this one; ND means spending on nondurables; Y means disposable personal income; L means liquid asset holdings; $_{-1}$ means in the quarter preceding this one; and no subscript means in the present quarter, or the one being predicted. Thus ΔND in any quarter is .224 of the change in income, plus .205 of the change in spending on nondurables over the past quarter, plus .143 of the change in liquid assets over the past quarter, minus .149. Similar, but separate, equations have been worked out in this model for consumer spending on automobiles, other durables, services, and housing.[3]

We cannot yet confidently forecast just what consumer spending will be, even when we abstract from such special forces as war. But careful econometric work is rapidly building up our knowledge and increasing our ability to predict the consequences of changes in tax rates or other actions that influence consumer spending.

Private-Investment Expenditures

So far we have assumed that investment spending is autonomous. Thus we have been able to consider private-investment spending (together with government spending) as an independent driving force, to which (through the multiplier effect) total g.n.p. and consumer spending adjust. Now we must look at the determinants of private-investment expenditure in more detail. We shall see that while private-investment expenditure is partly autonomous, it is also related closely to the level of consumer spending. That is, rising consumption may induce more investment, as well as the other way around. Thus, a more thorough look at the system will require us to complete the circle: Investment spending → more consumption → more private investment → more consumption . . . and so on.

Investment spending is largely business spending—on plant, equipment, machinery, and inventories. Only one component of private investment is made directly by households—new single-family housing—and this seldom accounts for over a quarter of the total. Private-investment spending reflects primarily the decisions made by businessmen—presidents, finance committees, boards of directors, and others, all the way down to the corner grocer.[4]

Private-investment spending has been the most dynamic and unstable major component of the gross national product. Most economists think it plays a central role in explaining both

---

[3]See D. B. Suits, "Forecasting with an Econometric Model," *American Economic Review*, March, 1962, p. 113. For students who know mathematics, all of this article may be interesting. It includes comparable forecasting equations for all major sectors of the economy and for many of the

subsectors in those major groupings. See especially the last section of the article, which lists all the forecasting equations.

[4]If most spending on consumer durables is included in investment, the proportion determined directly by households is higher, but still only about one-half.

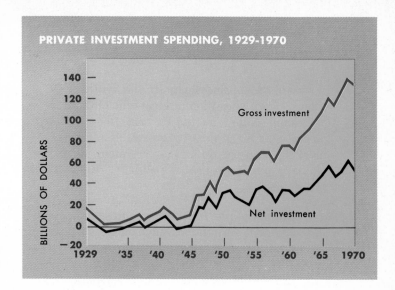

PRIVATE INVESTMENT SPENDING, 1929-1970

fig. 8–3

Private investment spending fluctuates sharply. It is now higher than ever before, but gross investment is roughly the same percentage as g.n.p. as in other prosperous periods.

economic growth and fluctuations. Figure 8–3 shows the fluctuation in private-investment spending since 1929. The top line is gross, or total, investment. The lower line is net investment, which subtracts the allowance to replace capital goods worn out (depreciated) during that year. Only the lower line represents the net addition to our capital stock each year.

What Determines Private-Investment Spending?

What determines private business investment spending? As with consumer expenditure, the answer is gradually being clarified through both theoretical and empirical work. Begin again with a simplified model. Later we shall look at some of the modern empirical evidence.

Fundamentally, expected profits determine how much a business will spend on investment in any given year. When a businessman thinks he can invest in a new machine and get back over the life of the machine what it costs, plus running expenses, plus interest on the money invested, plus some extra return (profit), he will probably make the investment. He will invest when the expected rate of return on his invested capital exceeds the going rate of interest (cost of capital) he must pay for funds to make the investment.

The Marginal Efficiency of Investment

Economists call the expected rate of return on investment the "marginal efficiency of investment" (m.e.i.). Suppose, for example, a busi-

nessman is thinking of buying a new milling machine for his plant. He knows the machine will cost $10,000 and his engineers estimate that it will increase the annual output of the plant by about $2,000, with unchanged costs for labor and materials. To maintain the machine, however, will cost about $500 a year. (To make the example easy, assume the machine lasts indefinitely.) Thus, the expected annual net return on the $10,000 investment in the machine will be $1,500. The marginal efficiency of investment would thus be 15 percent (that is, $15 return annually on every $100 invested). If he could borrow money at, say, 5 percent to buy the machine, it looks like a good investment.[5]

What factors determine the marginal efficiency of investment in typical cases? Some of the major ones are:

Expected Product Demand. The dominant consideration is the expected demand for the firm's product. Note that it is expected net return on investment that matters. Thus, whenever a businessman expects the demand for his product to rise, this anticipation increases the expected rate of return he can get by investing in new plant and equipment that will increase his output or improve the quality of his product. The fact that expectations govern the marginal efficiency of investment makes it subject to wide fluctuations, depending on how things

[5]For a more complex and precise analysis of how to compute the net rate of return on investments and how businessmen sometimes look at the investment problem, see Chapter 33.

93

look to the businessman. If the world looks black, down goes the marginal efficiency of investment. Note here the tie back to consumer spending. One of the big forces influencing the expected return on new investment is consumer spending—the demand for business' products.

Technology and Innovation. Research and development push the marginal efficiency of investment up. If a new machine promises to lower costs or improve product quality, this promise will be reflected in a larger expected net return on the investment. Some investment is justified just to replace old machinery with duplicate equipment, but technological advance is the foundation of most present-day investment in plant and equipment.

Taxes. With modern corporation income tax rates, businessmen are primarily concerned with the expected rate of return on investment after taxes. In 1970, nearly all corporations except the smallest paid income taxes of about 50 percent on their profits. (If we take this factor into account, the milling-machine investment above loses a lot of its glamour.) An increase in corporation tax rates, other things equal, will lower the marginal efficiency of investment; a decrease will raise it.

General Outlook. A businessman can never estimate precisely all the factors involved over the life of a major investment. Will demand for the final product really be what he expects? Will tax rates stay the same? Will the government step in and regulate his business? Will a new machine come along that will make this one obsolete? With all this uncertainty, the general outlook of the businessman often plays a big role in his final decision on whether or not to invest.

Interest Rates—"The Cost of Money"

The other side of the picture is the interest rate—the cost of the money needed to make the investment under consideration. If the businessman has to borrow the funds needed, we can get a direct figure for the cost of money— maybe it's 5 percent. But even if he has the money already, possibly in retained earnings from previous profits, he must still figure "implicit" interest on the funds used, since when he ties them up here he will be foregoing interest he could earn by investing them elsewhere. Then the proper interest rate to charge is harder to estimate, but he must settle on some figure for his calculation. We'll look at the details presently.

The Investment Schedule and Investment Decisions

At any time, many alternative investment opportunities are open to any business, some promising high rates of return, some low. We can graph these investment opportunities as in Figure 8–4. Suppose we list all the possible investment opportunities that the firm foresees for next year. A few projects will promise a high rate of return; more will promise at least a medium rate; many will be available that promise at least a very low rate. Plot these in curve *II*. A few investments (about $140,000) promise 5 percent or more; about $300,000 promise 4 percent or more; and so on. Note that the

fig. 8–4

The curve, *II*, shows the amount of investment it will pay to undertake at each level of the interest rate.

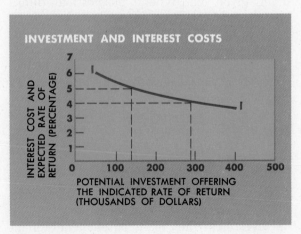

INVESTMENT AND INTEREST COSTS

$300,000 includes all that promise 4 percent or higher; it includes the $140,000 that promise 5 percent.

Now we easily see how much a rational, profit-seeking businessman will invest. Suppose the interest rate he must pay or charge himself is 4 percent. Then any investment opportunity on his investment schedule that will yield above 4 percent is profitable. Figure 8–4 shows that this business should invest about $300,000 if the interest cost is 4 percent, taking on all the projects promising to yield 4 percent or higher. If the interest cost is 5 percent, it will only pay to invest about $140,000 this year—only in those projects above where the 5 percent line intersects *II*. Each point on *II* shows how much will be invested at that interest rate. It shows investment as a function of the interest rate $[I = f(i)]$.

A Modification. This analysis is straightforward enough, and the logic is impeccable. In the business world, however, most businessmen seem to insist on introducing a big "safety factor," or they may call it something else. Company after company requires an expected return of 15 or 20 percent on new investment before taking action, even though it can go to banks or the open market and borrow at 6 or 7 percent. What is the answer to this paradox?

Taxes are part of the story. They take about half of most business profits. Another answer is the safety factor suggested above. Businessmen say they never know whether things will turn out as well as expected. Another answer is the reluctance of many businessmen to go into debt, even when it is directly profitable to do so. A fourth possibility is that businessmen calculate the effective cost of money to themselves as much higher than current market interest rates, especially if they must issue new stock to get funds. But these questions get further into business finance than we can go at this point. All we can do is note the real-world fact that most businesses want an expected rate of return well above the market rate of interest before they will invest. This fact does not change the gen-eral principle indicated above, but it does reduce the number of investment opportunities that many businessmen will consider attractive at any given time.

To summarize: Business investment spending in any given time period is determined by the marginal efficiency of investment in relation to the interest rate (cost of capital). Many business firms consciously go through the type of analysis outlined above for each major investment considered. Others make their calculations much more roughly. Some operate by hunch and intuition. For present purposes, assume that our model gives a rough approximation for the economy as a whole.

Business Investment in Inventories. The above analysis of business investment applies basically to business investment in plant and equipment—buildings, machinery, and the like. Business investment in inventories (raw materials, goods in process, and finished goods still on hand) raises other special problems, which become especially important when we consider booms and depressions—short-run economic fluctuations. For the moment, only a warning that inventory investment is a special problem, one we will examine in more detail in Chapter 10 on business fluctuations. This warning does not change the general principle stated in the preceding sections.

Business Saving: A Digression

Thus far we have assumed that all savings are made by households. What people don't spend on consumption they save. But of course businesses also save. And business savings constitute a leakage from the income stream, just as do household savings. Business savings reduce the size of the multiplier effect of any autonomous spending in the economy.

Business savings come from two sources: profits not paid out to owners ("undistributed profits") and depreciation reserves (to replace wearing-out capital equipment). Since World War II, such business savings have made up well over half of the economy's total gross saving. In

1969, for example, business gross saving totaled $106 billion, compared to $38 billion of personal saving. But business net saving was only about $26 billion through its retention of undistributed profits; the other $80 billion consisted of depreciation allowances.

Although business savings constitute a leakage from the income stream, most of them are reinvested directly by the business firms themselves, as indicated above. Businesses generally prefer to use their own savings before going out to borrow from others. Eastman Kodak and du Pont are examples of companies that have grown mainly through reinvestment of retained earnings. But in the g.n.p. accounts and for multiplier analysis in our model, business saving must be added to personal saving as a leakage that reduces the economy's marginal propensity to consume out of g.n.p. This parallels the way we include gross business investment in g.n.p., even when it is financed by internally generated savings.[6]

Money in the Income–Expenditures Model

Money has entered the analysis of the last two chapters only peripherally. In conclusion, it is important to clarify the role of money in the income–expenditures (neo-Keynesian) model.

In this model, changes in the stock of money influence the interest rate (which neo-Keynesians think of as the price of money). Thus an increased supply of money lowers its price (the interest rate), and a decreased supply raises its price, other things equal. A higher or lower interest rate in turn decreases or increases investment, which, you will recall, depends on the interest rate compared to the marginal efficiency of investment. The level of investment in turn determines the level of aggregate spending (g.n.p.) through the multiplier.

The way money fits into the income–expenditures model can be easily seen from the following causal chain. If the government adds more money to the system, it affects g.n.p. as follows:

$$+\,M \rightarrow -\,i \rightarrow +\,I \rightarrow +\ \text{g.n.p.}$$

where M stands for money, i stands for interest rate, I stands for investment, and g.n.p. is aggregate spending. Note that in this approach more money does not directly stimulate consumption spending; its only effect is to lower the interest rate, thereby stimulating investment.

Moreover, Keynes argued, often changes in M won't affect interest rates very much, especially in depressions (for reasons to be explored in the next chapter). Besides, he found that fluctuations in interest rates are generally smaller than variations in the marginal efficiency of investment, which depends on expectations of profits and other factors in the future —and these may swing widely. Thus, moderate changes in the stock of money, bringing about only moderate changes in interest rates, generally have a rather unimportant influence on total investment spending. According to Keynes investment spending is thus relatively insensitive to changes in interest rates, and hence indirectly to changes in the money stock. But this degree of sensitivity is a factual issue, on which the evidence is mixed. Some of the relevant information is presented later in the next chapter.

If we accept this analysis of the place of money in the determination of aggregate spending, then government-induced changes in the stock of money may influence aggregate spending somewhat, but only indirectly, and in general the role of the money in the model is a minor one.

Chapter 9 looks in more detail at the role of money in explaining aggregate output and prices. And Chapter 10 goes on to the complex dynamic problem of economic fluctuations (inflations, booms, and depressions), including the important role money plays in such fluctuations.

---

[6]Net foreign investment, one of the categories in the g.n.p. accounts, is neglected throughout this chapter, even though it may have a multiplier effect on g.n.p. similar to that of domestic private investment. Net foreign investment has been relatively small since World War II, and it is more convenient to leave it for consideration in Part Six on "The International Economy."

Review

CONCEPTS TO REMEMBER

Be sure you understand the following new analytical concepts introduced in this chapter.

"permanent income"   implicit interest
"life-cycle income"   "cost of capital"
marginal efficiency of investment investment schedule
interest rate   business saving

FOR ANALYSIS AND DISCUSSION

1. What are the main factors which determine your personal consumption expenditure? What forces would you expect to shift your consumption function over the next ten years?

2. How would you expect the marginal propensity to consume to compare for families at the same income level (say $8,000 per year) at the following ages for the head of the family: 25, 40, 60, 75? Explain your answer.

3. During part of 1969, consumption outlays totaled only about 93 percent of disposable personal income. How would you have gone about determining whether this unusually high savings ratio was likely to be permanent or temporary?

4. Investment spending has often fluctuated sharply during booms and depressions. Using the model of business investment decision making in the chapter, can you explain why this is likely?

5. Explain how you would decide whether to invest in a new set of store furnishings if you were the owner of an ice cream parlor.

6. Would you expect higher interest rates to stimulate or retard business investment? Explain why, using a graph like Figure 8–4.

Money, Aggregate Demand, and the Price Level: the Modern Synthesis

Chapters 7 and 8 explained aggregate demand with little mention of money. There, spending depended largely on incomes received. But we receive our incomes in the form of money, and somehow it seems that money must be more than peripheral. It is! This chapter focuses on money and the important role it plays in determining aggregate demand, real output, and the price level.[1]

The chapter has three main sections. The first points out the major facts about money and its relationship to g.n.p. and prices during this century. The second summarizes the "monetarist" analysis of the central role money plays in explaining aggregate demand and prices. The third puts both the income–expenditures and monetarist models together in a "modern synthesis," which recognizes that both have important elements of truth in explaining aggregate spending, real g.n.p., and prices in the modern economy.

The Facts

What is money? What controls its supply? What are the facts about money in relation to aggregate demand, real output, and the price level?

[1]Teachers who want their students to understand monetary mechanics (the operations of the banking system) before considering money in relation to aggregate demand should assign Chapter 12 here, before Chapter 9.

What Is Money and Who Controls It?

In today's economy, money is composed of bank demand deposits (which we spend by writing checks) and currency (coins and paper money). Together, as of 1970 they totaled about $200 billion. Contrary to the common impression, bank deposits make up the bulk of our money (nearly 80 percent); currency plays only a minor role.

It is important to distinguish between money and income. A man with an income of, say, $10,000 annually, may possess only a few hundred dollars of money at any given time. (He might have even more than his $10,000 income in money, though that would be untypical.) Money is a form of wealth, an asset; income is a flow or stream of payments made by exchanging money. Each dollar of money may thus be spent many or a few times a year, creating "income" when it is spent on transactions that enter the national income accounts.

For example, in 1970 the average amount of money outstanding (currency and checking deposits) was about $200 billion, while g.n.p. was $980 billion. Thus, on the average people and businesses held money equal to only about one-fifth of their total incomes at any given time. Put another way, on the average each dollar of money was spent on a g.n.p. transaction about five times during the year.

The Constitution gives Congress the power to create money and regulate the value thereof. Congress has delegated this power, under certain restrictions, to the U.S. Treasury and to the Federal Reserve System, a partially "independent" agency within the federal government. The Treasury mints coins, a routine function. The Federal Reserve issues paper currency, and, more important, regulates the supply of bank deposits by controlling the "reserves" that commercial banks must hold behind their deposits.

Broadly speaking, therefore, the government (including the Federal Reserve) controls the supply of money. This is not entirely accurate, as we shall see, but as a first approximation assume that the stock of money is set by the government. Chapter 12 explains money and the banking system in detail, including the way the Federal Reserve and Congress do regulate the money stock. That chapter can equally well be studied here by those who want to understand more thoroughly what money is and where it comes from before analyzing the effects of monetary changes on the economy. However, this chapter considers the impacts of money on aggregate demand, real output, and prices, without considering in detail how the supply of money is determined.

Some Historical Facts

Figure 9–1 summarizes some important relationships among money, aggregate demand, real output, and prices since 1900. The bottom line shows the growth in the stock of money, averaging 5½ percent per annum since 1900. The next two lines show that "real" gross national product (that is, g.n.p. in constant prices) rose at about 3¾ percent per annum over the same period, while money g.n.p. rose at about 5½ percent annually. The top line shows that the price level rose by an average of about 2¼ to 2½ percent annually, the difference between money gross national product and real gross national product.

It is clear that the increase in the money stock on the average paralleled closely the growth in money g.n.p.; and that about two-thirds of the growth in money g.n.p. was growth in real output, while about one-third was inflation.

Deviations from these average (trend) growth lines are as interesting as the trends themselves. The big inflation of World War I is clearly visible. The money stock shot up from 1915 to 1920 as new money was created to finance the war, and prices soared roughly apace. About 1927, the money stock began to fall below the economy's 3+ percent real long-term growth rate, and the long depression of the 1930s began two years later. The great collapse (in both output and prices) came between 1929 and 1933, when the money supply was contracting severely.

World War II was different from World War I. Again, much of the war was financed by newly created money. But widespread price

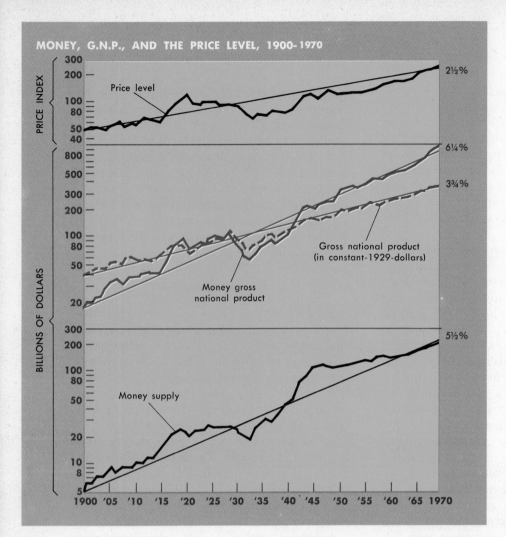

MONEY, G.N.P., AND THE PRICE LEVEL, 1900-1970

PRICE INDEX

Price level — 2½%

BILLIONS OF DOLLARS

6¼%

3¾%

Gross national product
(in constant-1929-dollars)

Money gross
national product

5½%

Money supply

1900 '05 '10 '15 '20 '25 '30 '35 '40 '45 '50 '55 '60 '65 1970

fig. 9-1

The money stock has risen about 5 1/2 per cent annually, and money g.n.p. a little faster. G.n.p. in constant dollars has grown only about 3 3/4 percent annually, however, and a price rise of about 2 1/2 percent per annum accounts for the difference. Has the excess of money supply over the growth in real g.n.p. caused the inflation? (Sources: Federal Reserve Board, U.S. Department of Commerce, and National Bureau of Economic Research.)

and wage controls held inflation to a creep during the war, and it was not until their removal after 1946 that prices rose rapidly. Thus, the inflationary pressure generated by new money was more spread out than during World War I. Strikingly, the growth in the money supply leveled off around the mid-1950s; it rose only about 1 percent a year over the next several years. This period included the "weak" recoveries of 1956–1957, 1959–1960, and 1961–1964, and the recessions of 1958 and 1960–1961. The money supply began to rise rapidly again in 1965, and so did money g.n.p. and prices.

Some economists infer from these facts that the money supply exercises a powerful effect on the level of both real output and prices. When the money supply rises much faster than the growth in the economy's real output potential,

inflation results. Growth in the money supply parallel to growth in potential real g.n.p. (about 3+ percent per annum over the past half century) would go far to ensure stable economic growth. Slower growth in money means recession. But others say that this is too simple an analysis of a highly complex problem, and that it overstates the role of money.

Money, Aggregate Demand, and Prices

The classical economists—the long tradition from Adam Smith through David Ricardo and Alfred Marshall, up to the decade of the 1920s—gave money a central role in explaining aggregate spending. They had two main points. First, the amount of money will determine aggregate money spending; and second, variations in aggregate money spending will generally affect the price level but not real g.n.p. except for temporary aberrations.

First, if people have more or less money, they will spend more or less. People don't hold money for its own sake, but for what it will buy. In general, the rate at which they spend the money they receive will be stable, or change only gradually. Thus, changes in the amount of money will generally lead to proportional changes in total spending.

Second, these variations in total spending will mainly just bid the price level up or down, without changing the level of real output and employment. The classical economists argued that a free-market economic system would ordinarily tend to be self-equilibrating at approximately full employment. They reasoned that whenever resources are unemployed or unsold, their market price will move down until it falls low enough, so that everything offered is hired or sold—just as will the price of wheat or coal. There may be temporary deviations from full employment and, indeed, these deviations may involve booms and depressions. But they will be aberrations, explained largely by special external factors such as wars or famines; by cumulative, herdlike sweeps of expectations that lead to gluts of overproduction or to depressions; and especially by the erratic behavior of the monetary system. Over the long pull, the economic system will always tend toward full employment. More or less money will change spending proportionately, and more or less spending will lead to a correspondingly higher or lower price level, not to a change in real output.

In terms of our earlier diagrams, this classical position can be put as follows. The economy will always tend to operate on its production-possibilities frontier—i.e., at full employment. Thus, in Figure 6–1 the economy's short-run aggregate-supply curve is, as a practical matter, not *OAB*, but instead a vertical line rising from the horizontal axis at *OQ₃*. This is because the economy will tend to operate at full employment whatever the level of aggregate demand is. If aggregate demand falls, prices will

fall but output and employment (real g.n.p.) will be unchanged; if aggregate demand rises, prices will rise but real g.n.p. will remain unchanged. Money-induced fluctuations in aggregate spending would lead primarily to fluctuations in the general price level. This was called the "quantity theory of money," because in it the quantity of money roughly determined the price level. It contradicts the neo-Keynesian analysis of Chapters 6–7, which says that rising aggregate demand in an underemployed economy will raise output and employment and will cause inflation only after substantially full employment is reached.

"Say's law," named for early economist J. B. Say, summed up in a related but different way the argument why a "shortage" of aggregate demand could never cause more than transitional unemployment. Any production creates its own demand, he argued, since payments to the factors of production (including profits) equal the value of the product. If some income recipients save instead of consume, this saving must of course be offset by investment to avoid trouble; but in such a case the interest rate (which is the price that equilibrates saving and investment) will fall because of the increased flow of savings. This drop in the interest rate will stimulate investment while discouraging saving. The savings-investment market will thus be cleared by the interest rate, just as price variations act to clear the market for goods and labor, unless restricted by monopolies or laws that produce inflexible prices.[2]

Money, Velocity, and Aggregate Demand

How are changes in money linked with changes in aggregate demand (money g.n.p.)? The classical economists asked, (1) how much money do people have, and (2) how fast do they

----

[2]These remarks do less than justice to the classical economists, but the purpose here is merely to give some background on their view of money's role, not to paint a complete picture of what different economists thought. In particular, they realized that severe booms or depressions could occur while these long-run forces were gradually moving the economy back toward full-employment equilibrium, and that "sticky" prices (because of monopoly or other market imperfections) could keep the equilibrating price adjustments from occurring.

spend it? A simple "equation of exchange" (proposed by Professor Irving Fisher a half century ago) points up the relationships involved in this approach. The equation is:

$$MV = PT = \text{g.n.p.}$$

M stands for the amount of money in the hands of the public; V for the average "velocity of circulation," or the number of times each dollar is spent per time period; P for the price level, or average price per unit sold; and T for the number of units sold during each time period. If we think of T as the real goods and services produced in any year, it becomes the real g.n.p. of the economy; and P can be thought of as the "g.n.p. deflator" from Chapter 5. Then V is called "income velocity" because it shows the average number of times a dollar is spent each year on income-creating transactions in the g.n.p. accounts.[3]

For example, in a very simple hypothetical economy, suppose M is $1,000. Suppose further that during some year 2,000 units of physical goods are sold, and that their average price is $2. The T (real g.n.p.) in our equation would then be 2,000, and the P would be $2; PT equals $4,000, the total amount paid for the goods sold. This leaves the V, the average number of times per year each dollar is spent. Here the V is obviously 4, since total expenditures on the goods sold were $4,000 (P times T), so each of the 1,000 dollars must have been spent four times during the year on the average to account for the $4,000 of expenditures. The whole equation is then:

[3]Obviously we could include in T all transactions during the period, adding in purchases of stocks and bonds, of existing houses, of secondhand automobiles, and so on. Then MV and PT would not be equal to money g.n.p., but to a larger total that would include sales of existing assets as well. This would greatly increase the dollar figures on each side of the equation, since there is a huge volume of transactions each year that do not represent expenditures on current output. In 1970, g.n.p. was about $980 billion, whereas total expenditures on all transactions were estimated roughly at $8 or $9 trillion—perhaps ten times g.n.p. If we use this broader approach, V reflects spending on all transactions, and is called "transactions velocity." We would have to use this approach, for example, if we were interested in a general price level that includes prices of existing assets as well as of currently produced goods and services.

$$MV = PT, \text{ or}$$
$$\$1,000 \times 4 = \$2 \times 2,000$$

The two sides of the equation are defined so that they will always be equal. MV is simply the total amount spent on goods and services during the time period—the total number of dollars multiplied by the average number of times each dollar is spent in the period. PT is the total amount received for goods and services during the period—the number of units sold multiplied by the average price per unit. The two are identical; what someone spends, someone else receives. If we now add another $1,000 of money in our example, and keep V and T unchanged, clearly P will have to be $4 to make the equation balance at $8,000. Prices would be twice as high on the average because expenditures doubled but only the same physical volume of goods was sold.

The equation of exchange is obviously a truism. It just says that every dollar spent by someone is received by someone else. Why, then, is it a useful analytical tool? The answer is, because it sets out four important variables for analyzing booms and depressions, inflations and deflations. And it sets forth these variables in a way that points up some of their broad relationships—for example, it is the amount of money people have, multiplied by the average number of times each dollar is spent, that gives the total annual amount of spending. The equation certainly doesn't provide any answers, but it is a framework for looking at the complex real world. It skips over the whole detailed analysis of consumer and business spending decisions in Chapters 7–8. But it suggests that behind the scenes, the quantity of money may be a basic factor controlling the level of spending.

How Important Are M and V?

Assume that the receipts (PT) side is by and large passive, as the classical economists did. Then the equation says that an increase in the amount of money will lead to a higher volume of expenditures, unless it is offset by a decrease in the velocity at which the money is spent.

World War II provides a historical example. The money stock increased from about $36 billion to $110 billion, largely because we financed the war in considerable part by creating new money. The equation of exchange suggests that with such a big increase in the money supply, g.n.p. should have risen in the same proportion unless income velocity increased or decreased during the war.

What did happen? Money g.n.p. rose rapidly. But V declined substantially over the war period, and total spending rose much less than in proportion to the money supply. On the average, people held more dollars in proportion to their incomes. This was partly because many goods were unavailable, partly because there was a lot of patriotic pressure against spending, and partly because interest rates were so low that holding securities was a relatively unattractive alternative to holding money. As a result, money g.n.p. *(MV)* rose only from $91 billion to $211 billion, as indicated in the lines for 1939 and 1946 in the table below:

1929: M ($ 26 billion) $\times$ V (4.0) = g.n.p. ($104 billion)
1939: M ($ 36 billion) $\times$ V (2.5) = g.n.p. ($ 91 billion)
1946: M ($110 billion) $\times$ V (1.9) = g.n.p. ($211 billion)
1970: M ($204 billion) $\times$ V (4.8) = g.n.p. ($980 billion)

The 1929 and 1970 lines of the table provide some historical perspective. Back at the peak of the boom in the 1920s, V was high. People were spending their money fast, holding their idle money balances to a minimum. Then came the big drop of the depression and war years, as billions were piled up in temporarily idle balances. After World War II, people began to spend down their accumulated balances, and V rose persistently. Higher interest rates provided an inducement to put idle money into securities and other assets, and as money became "tighter" both businesses and individuals were again forced to "economize" their cash balances, cutting them back to the minimum consistent with their needs.

If V were stable, changes in M would be a good predictor of g.n.p. Indeed, by controlling M we could control g.n.p. Professor Fisher argued that by and large his V (which was a little different from ours) was relatively stable over long periods, so that changes in M could be expected to have roughly proportionate effects on PT.[4]

Has the evidence borne Fisher out? Yes and no. The table above makes V look highly unstable. But over the long pull, except for the long dip from 1930 to the 1960s, V has been reasonably stable with a gradual upward trend that may reflect increasing efficiency in our payments mechanism (e.g., use of credit cards and computers). Figure 9–2 provides the data since 1900. If we eliminate the Great Depression and the World War II period, V has generally stayed in the 3–4 + range. But that's a fairly

[4]In fact, Fisher went further and argued that changes in M would generally lead to corresponding changes in P, since T as well as V would be roughly stable—a simple version of the "quantity theory of money." But he recognized that V might fluctuate substantially in the short run.

fig. 9–2

Income velocity has shown a gradual updrift over the long run. It rises and falls sharply in booms and depressions, and sometimes falls dramatically for special reasons—note the World War II period. (Calculated by dividing money stock into money g.n.p. for each year.)

wide range, and prediction is insecure. Both M and V have dropped sharply in depressions and have increased in booms. However, the long-term trend looks more stable.

Why Do People Hold Money? V and the Demand for Money

We understand reasonably well what controls the supply of money (M). But the classical economists were never very satisfactory in explaining changes in V. Why do people hold money instead of exchanging it for something directly useful? You can't eat money, drink it, or use it directly for anything. Money yields no concrete return unless it is invested. Thus people presumably will spend the money they get unless there is some special reason for holding on to it. In explaining V, therefore, the crucial question is: How much money do people feel they need to hold?

People hold money because of the buying power it gives them over goods and services, now and in the future. If John Doe decides he doesn't need to hold as much money as he has on hand, he will spend it. But if he feels that he needs a larger money balance, he will hold down his expenditures relative to his income to build up his money balance. Thus, changes in the desired level of money balances will have a direct impact on current spending. If we combine the stock of money with this analysis of the demand for money to hold buying power over real goods and services, we have an explanation how money affects the level of spending.[5]

Modern economists have tried to simplify and clarify the public's demand for money balances through empirical research. Presumably, people are primarily interested in the real buy-

ing power of their money, and research has focused on the demand for real (price-level-adjusted) money balances. Recent studies suggest that the demand for such "real money" is basically a function of two variables: the level of real income and the interest rate on close money substitutes like bonds. Thus, they write the demand for real-money balances as follows:

$$M^d = f(Y,i),$$

where M^d is the demand for money balances, Y is income, and i is the interest rate. First, higher income (Y) means that people and businesses will want to hold more money.[6] Total wealth (W) of households and businesses can be substituted for Y, with about equally good results. Either way, the better off people are economically, the larger will be their demand for money balances, other things equal. Second, a higher interest rate on money substitutes induces people to hold less money, i.e., to shift from money to interest-yielding assets; conversely, a lower interest rate will increase the public's demand for money to hold.

This demand-for-money equation (using either Y or W) appears to fit past experience well, and hence, presumably, can provide a reasonable forecast of how much of any additional M people will choose to hold or to spend at any time. Put in other words, it will predict V if we know Y, i, and M. But the research results are not conclusive, and more econometric work is needed before we can be sure of the results.

Equilibrium and the Demand for "Real-Money" Balances.

Suppose that we all decide to build up our real-money balances by decreasing our expenditures relative to our incomes; as a group we want to hold more purchasing power in the form of money balances. We want to increase our "real balances"—i.e., our buying power over goods and services.

[5]Recent variations have singled out a variety of motives for holding money: the "transactions" motive (having enough money for day-to-day individual and business purposes); the "precautionary" motive (having money on hand to be prepared for unforeseen contingencies); and the "speculative" motive (holding money because you think the prices of things you want to buy are coming down). When these motives grow stronger, total expenditures by individuals and businesses drop, given any fixed amount of money for the public to hold, because people will hold on to more of their money rather than spend it. Conversely, when the motives for holding money weaken, other things equal, you can look for more spending.

[6]If we take Y to stand for "permanent," or average life-long, income, the accuracy of the equation improves substantially, since people's demand for money apparently does not vary with all short-run fluctuations in incomes received.

Will the result be higher money balances all around? If your inclination is to say yes, stop and think again. With any given supply of money, there can be no change in the total amount of nominal money balances held, because there isn't any more money for the public to hold and every existing dollar must be held by someone. Thus, the result of a general attempt to build up money balances is a decrease in total expenditures as V decreases, not an increase in total balances, as long as the total amount of money is unchanged. (Remember the fallacy of composition.)

Will this concerted attempt to accumulate buying power over goods and services be completely thwarted? The answer is no. By pulling down total expenditures, the public's desire to build up its real balances will ultimately decrease prices (and probably production and employment as well). As prices fall, the existing amount of money will command more real goods and services. Thus, even though the total stock of money remains unchanged, the public will succeed in increasing its "real balances." People don't plan it that way, but they increase the real value of their money balances by bringing on deflation, and possibly depression with it. When prices have fallen enough to give existing money balances the desired amount of real purchasing power in relation to incomes and other assets, the public's demand for money balances will again be in equilibrium. People (households, businesses, and others) will again be satisfied to hold just the amount of money that exists.[7]

This can be put in equilibrium terms, comparable to others we have seen. Suppose there is some fixed amount of nominal money (M). If people have more money than they want to hold, M^s will exceed M^d. That is, there will be an excess supply of money, which people will spend on goods, bonds, or whatnot. They will continue to try to spend down their money bal-

ances. Spending and prices will thus rise until $M^s = M^d$, that is, until the amounts of money demanded and supplied are equal. Only then is there monetary equilibrium.

Conversely, if M^d exceeds M^s, people will try to build up their real balances. Spending and prices will decrease until at the lower prices M^d just equals M^s. This is the reasoning of the modern "monetarists."

In conclusion, it is important to recognize the two separable parts of the modern monetarist analysis. The first part is the proposition that changes in M will change the level of aggregate money demand in a predictable way. The second is that such changes in aggregate money spending will generally lead, in the long run, to changes in prices rather than to changes in real g.n.p., although the short-run effect may be on both real output and prices in periods of unemployment. Monetarists are in far more complete agreement on the first than on the second part of the analysis.

The Modern Synthesis

Both the income–expenditures model of Chapters 7 and 8 and the preceding monetarist model of this chapter provide plausible explanations of how aggregate demand is determined. Both have something to contribute; we now have to merge them.

The income–expenditures model says that equilibrium can be attained only when households are spending in relation to their incomes at the rate they prefer, and only when businessmen are investing at the rate they judge will maximize their profits. This is an analysis in terms of income flows—through consumption and investment expenditures—not in terms of equilibria between supplies and demands of assets held. Money (an asset) is ignored or introduced only indirectly through its effect on the interest rate.

The monetarist (portfolio-balancing) model says that the system will be in equilibrium only when households and businesses are content to hold just the existing stock of money and other assets. This equilibrium will occur when each

---

[7]It is important to note that if prices are flexible downward as spending falls, the attempt to increase real balances will succeed without any decrease in real output and employment. But if prices and costs are inflexible downward, the result is likely to be a big decline in output and employment before prices fall far enough to satisfy the increased demand for real balances.

economic unit has allocated its total wealth (assets) among money, other liquid assets (bonds, savings accounts, and so on), and real assets (houses, durable goods, and so on) so that the marginal return from the last dollar invested in each kind of asset is the same. If this were not so, it would pay to shift out of the low-yield assets into higher-yield assets. For example, if a family had more money than it wanted to hold, it would use this "excess" money to acquire other assets, such as an auto, clothes, or bonds. It would spend down its money balance until the marginal satisfaction obtained from the last dollar held in money just balances that received from the last dollar invested in bonds, housing, and any other asset the family wants. Then its asset portfolio would be in equilibrium. If MU is the marginal utility, or satisfaction, obtained from the last dollar invested, then equilibrium is obtained when:

$$MU \text{ (money)} = MU \text{ (bonds)} =$$
$$MU \text{ (clothing)} = MU \text{ (autos)}\ldots \text{ and so on.}$$

for all assets held.

Thus, for equilibrium to be obtained in the economy, both the "flows" of the income–expenditures model and the "stocks" of the portfolio-balancing model must be in equilibrium. Unless all economic units are in equilibrium on both accounts—that is, unless they are content to keep on doing what they are doing —they will change their behavior and bring about a movement in spending, output, and prices toward the desired equilibrium state.

Portfolio Balancing and Aggregate Money Demand

Consider in more detail how the portfolio-balancing analysis explains aggregate money demand. Every asset held yields some return, or satisfaction. Money provides generalized, risk-less, immediately available buying power, but no interest return. Securities provide interest or dividends and possibly the expectation of capital gains, although they also involve some risk. Capital goods (like machinery) provide a direct contribution to business profits. Consumers' durable goods provide current services to their users. Each individual will maximize his satisfaction (or yield)—that is, his portfolio of all his assets will be "balanced"—when he obtains equal satisfaction from the last dollar allotted to each kind of asset. When he achieves this position, he is in equilibrium, since he cannot increase his total satisfaction by changing the mix of assets he holds. Then, MU (money) = MU (autos) = MU (bonds)... and so on.

Note that this portfolio balancing may lead households or businesses to spend either more or less. Suppose that an individual can obtain more satisfaction by spending a dollar on consumer durables than by holding that dollar as money. Then, if he is rational, he will spend the dollar. He can increase his total satisfaction (yield) by doing so. The same proposition is true about business-asset portfolios—they are "balanced" only when the marginal return per dollar obtained on all types of assets held is equal. If, therefore, individuals or businesses find that the marginal returns on different assets are different, they will always move toward equilibrium by shifting out of assets with lower marginal yields into higher-yielding ones. And this will lead them to spend more or less on different assets.

It is important to note also that this increased spending may or may not directly increase money g.n.p. If you reduce your money balance by buying General Motors stock, U.S. bonds, or an existing house, this is merely an exchange of existing assets. Your expenditure does not directly increase g.n.p. But if you buy a new coat, or have your car repaired, your money expenditure does directly increase g.n.p. Similarly, a business may shift out of money into new plant and equipment, thus directly increasing the investment component of g.n.p. Or it might simply invest the excess money in bonds. It is this portfolio balancing that provides the linkage between money stocks on the one hand and the flows of consumption and investment spending in the g.n.p. accounts on the other.

M Increases Wealth and Aggregate Demand: An Example

Suppose the government simply prints up some new money and gives it to the public, say in the form of unemployment relief. This increases the total assets (wealth) of the public and simultaneously increases disposable personal income. Let us trace through the effects of this increase in M.

The public now has more money than previously. If it was previously satisfied with its money holdings (i.e., its asset portfolios were balanced), it now has too much money compared to other assets, such as consumers' goods or securities. The marginal satisfaction from holding money has fallen relative to that on other assets, since the public has more money but no more of other things. It therefore will spend some of the new money for other assets. This will bid up prices of other things and thus gradually decrease the satisfaction obtainable by spending an additional dollar on them. The public will continue to spend its new money balances until rising prices restore an equilibrium in the rates of return provided by a marginal dollar held in money and in all other assets. Thus, on the asset side, more M leads to more spending, as people act to rebalance their portfolios.[8]

On the income-flows side, the increase in disposable income will lead to more consumption, and through the multiplier to a higher g.n.p. Equilibrium is reestablished when g.n.p. reaches a new level where consumers are at their desired consumption–income ratios and businesses are at their desired investment levels relative to their receipts and profit expectations given their larger income.

Thus, households and businesses throughout the economy adjust both their asset portfolios and their current spending patterns until they

are content with new equilibria attained on both fronts. Both adjustments go on simultaneously.

M Increases Without Increasing Wealth

Now, a harder example. Suppose the government increases M by buying up bonds owned by the public. This increases the public's money balances and reduces the interest rate through bidding up the price of bonds, but it does not increase the public's total wealth. Does this lead to more spending, via either the portfolio-balancing or income-flows route?

The neo-Keynesians would say no, or at least only indirectly. It would have no effect on disposable income and hence no effect on consumption. It might indirectly increase g.n.p. by stimulating investment through the lower interest rate, though this effect is problematical. The monetarists disagree. They concur that the stimulus to money g.n.p. would be less than in the preceding increased-wealth case. But they argue that the new money will spill over at least in part to other assets, like consumer goods, investment goods, and equities. This difference of opinion is an important one for governmental monetary-policy makers who must determine how much money we should have and how to introduce it.

Money and Income Flows as a Basis for Government Policy

Nearly everyone agrees that both money and the income-flow factors of Chapter 7 and 8 are important determinants of aggregate demand, and that we must take both into account. But which is more powerful, and which relationship is more stable, so we can rely upon it in predicting the future behavior of the system? Suppose, for example, there is unemployment and we want to raise aggregate demand by $10 billion. One approach: We might print up $2.5 billion of new money and give it out in the form of relief payments, on the reasoning that income velocity in 1970 was about 4.7, so the new money would raise g.n.p. by little over $10 billion. Another approach: We might not change M at all but instead reduce personal income

---

[8]To see why a rise in the price of a security or other asset is the same thing as a decline in the yield on it, consider the following. Suppose the security is a $100 government bond paying 3 percent (that is, $3 a year), and is due in ten years. If the price is bid up to $110, the annual real yield falls to about 2 percent. This is because, offset against the annual interest payment of $3, the bond buyer must consider the $10 he will lose when he gets back in ten years only $100 instead of the $110 he paid. Spreading this "capital loss" evenly over the ten years takes away $1 return per year, lowering the effective annual yield to $2, which is an effective interest rate of 2 percent. (Actually, it is a little less than 2 percent, since you get $2 per year on an investment of $110.) This same type of effect holds for other assets that provide a given yield.

taxes by $4–5 billion without correspondingly reducing government expenditures. This increase in d.p.i. would increase consumer spending by nearly as much, and neo-Keynesians suggest that the multiplier on autonomous spending is about 2–2½, given stable interest rates. Thus, the result should be an increase of about $10 billion in g.n.p. Which approach is better? Is the figure for income velocity (4.8 in this example) more reliable than the figure for the multiplier (2–2½ in this example) in predicting the new g.n.p.?

The answer from econometric studies is mixed. Neither income velocity nor the multiplier is as predictably stable as their advocates would like. As a practical matter, if we want an increase of $10 billion in aggregate demand, to use either increased M or decreased taxes alone risks partial success. For example, the tax reduction may increase g.n.p., but if M stays constant, the growing transactions demand for money will raise interest rates, which will partially check the upswing by reducing businesses' incentive to invest. To increase M alone (say, by buying up outstanding bonds with new money) does not increase anyone's disposable income or profits, and the income–expenditures advocates question whether the policy will accomplish more than slightly reduce the interest yield on bonds. Depending on the particular circumstances, either the tax or the monetary approach may be the more appropriate one if we must choose. But most experts agree that it is safer to use them both simultaneously if this is feasible.

In the meantime, more research is needed to clarify the quantitative importance of the income and money factors in household and business behavior. The simple income–expenditures model of Chapters 7 and 8 (before money was introduced) implicitly implied that either the stock of M or V (i.e., the demand for money) would passively adjust to permit the equilibrium level of g.n.p. predicted by the income–expenditures model. If, for example, we cut taxes by $1 billion but did not change the money stock, the multiplier described by the Chapter 6 model would provide an increase of $4 billion in g.n.p. But if there is no more M, this rise in g.n.p. would imply that V automatically rises to permit the $4 billion increase in g.n.p. Conversely, the monetary approach implicitly assumes a passive adjustment in m.p.c. to permit g.n.p. to follow changes in M. Suppose, for example, we increase the money stock by $1 billion but make no change in taxes, government expenditures, or the other income-flow variables. The monetary approach tells us that, if V is stable at, say, 4, g.n.p. will rise by $4 billion. But this increase implies a facilitating upward adjustment in the public's marginal propensity to consume or in businesses' marginal propensity to invest. To decide whether tax or monetary policy is a more powerful device to regulate aggregate demand, we need to know more about the relative stabilities of the demand for money and the economy's propensity to spend out of disposable income. The evidence is simply not yet clear.[9]

[9]Modern econometricians are working hard to determine the relative influence on g.n.p. of changes in M and in autonomous expenditure (often roughly defined as private investment plus most government spending). For example, to oversimplify, they say: Suppose we statistically relate changes in g.n.p. to changes in M, and then separately relate changes in g.n.p. to changes in A (autonomous expenditure). The results look like this, for the ten-year period ending with 1967. (In the equations, t stands for time period, so t is this quarter, $t-1$ is one quarter back, and so on; and Δ stands for "change in.")

$$(1) \quad \Delta\text{GNP}_t = 5.61\text{b.} + 3.94\ (\Delta M)_{t\text{-}3} \qquad r^2 = .553$$
$$(2) \quad \Delta\text{GNP}_t = 4.94\text{b.} + 1.08\ (\Delta A)_{t\text{-}1} \qquad r^2 = .400$$

Equation (1) says that the quarterly change in g.n.p. equaled $5.61 billion plus $3.94 for each $1 increase in M three quarters previously. Put otherwise, a $1 increase in M was associated with a $3.94 increase in g.n.p. three quarters later. Equation (2) says that a $1 increase in A was associated with a $1.08 increase in g.n.p. one quarter later. The r^2 in each case is called the "coefficient of determination." It shows how much of the total actual change in g.n.p. each quarter is explained by the M or A, respectively. Thus, ΔM in this simple test explained a little more of Δg.n.p. than did ΔA.

But actually, of course, both M and A exert influence on g.n.p. simultaneously. If we put both variables in the same equation, we get:

$$(3) \quad \Delta\text{GNP} = 4.00\text{b.} + 2.52\ (\Delta M)_{t\text{-}3} + .670\ (\Delta A)_{t\text{-}1}$$
$$r^2 = .658$$

This equation shows that ΔM and ΔA together explain appreciably more (65.8 percent) of Δg.n.p. than does either alone. Quarterly changes in g.n.p. (annual rates) over the ten years were $4 billion plus $2.52 for each $1 increase in M and 67 cents for each $1 increase in A, with the time lags shown.

The modern synthesis reminds us that the economic system simultaneously responds to two aspects of the public's behavior. (1) The public receives incomes, and it spends, saves, and invests out of these incomes (an analysis in terms of income "flows"). (2) The public has a portfolio of assets (money, securities, capital goods, and consumer goods), and it balances the assets in its portfolio to achieve the most desirable "mix" at all times (an analysis in terms of asset "stocks"). Whenever the public is not satisfied with its position on either assets or income–expenditure relationships, it will readjust accordingly, buying or selling assets and spending or saving more or less. It is important to recognize that these two aspects of economic behavior proceed simultaneously and interact continuously. The system will move toward a new equilibrium whenever the public is out of equilibrium on either set of accounts.

Prices or Real Output

The preceding paragraphs have avoided the question as to when increased money demand will lead to more real output and when merely to higher prices. Clearly, if there is full employment already, the short-run effect must be mainly on prices. If there is massive unemployment, most economists argue that much of the short-run effect will be on real output and employment, contrary to the extreme monetarists.

But the longer-run effects are less clear in both cases. Let us postpone this issue until the chapters on monetary and fiscal policy, when it

becomes a central problem—especially in Chapter 15.

Money, Interest Rates, and Expectations: Dynamics

One further complication must be added. Everyone agrees that the first direct effect of introducing more money into the economy will, other things equal, be to reduce the interest rate —directly if the government introduces the money by buying up bonds, or indirectly through portfolio balancing if the money is inserted some other way. But one of the main lessons of economics is: don't stop with the first effect; second and third effects may also be important! And so they may be here.

More M will almost certainly raise money g.n.p. This, in turn, will increase the demand for money, and this second effect will tend to raise the interest rate, partially offsetting the original downward pressure of more M. This is called the "income effect." But there may be a still further, third effect—the "inflation effect." If the rising income comes at a time of full employment, it will stimulate further inflation. If this leads the public to expect more inflation, it will lead lenders to demand higher interest rates to offset the expected inflation. It will also increase the demand of borrowers for loans because they can repay in dollars of reduced buying power; borrowers will be willing to pay a higher interest rate if they anticipate inflation. The third effect of more M may, therefore, be higher interest rates, not lower ones, as both lenders and borrowers include an inflation allowance in their bargains. The final combined effect will depend on the relative size of the three effects.

In fact, rapid increases in M have generally been associated with rising, not falling, interest rates. The 1965–1969 period is an example. M, commodity prices, and interest rates all rose rapidly, apparently reflecting strong expectations that more M created by the government would lead to more inflation and hence to substantial inflation allowances by both lenders and borrowers in interest-rate bargains. This direct relationship between changes in M and interest rates is often called the "Gibson para-

---

This example suggests how econometricians go about using historical evidence to judge how much different factors influence g.n.p. But the example is greatly oversimplified, and it is important to remember that the figures shown do not provide a satisfactory answer on the relative importance of M and A for real-world use. Different time periods and different definitions of M and A give significantly different results. And a dispute rages among the experts as to whether more meaningful answers are obtained from relatively simple models like this one or complex models including many more variables.

For references to more complex models, see the appendix to Chapter 6. For an analysis of the results of simple ("reduced form") models, see Leonell Anderson, "Money and Economic Forecasting" and Edward Gramlich, "The Role of Money in Economic Activity," *Business Economics*, September, 1969.

dox"; M and interest rates move together rather than in opposite directions.

The Gibson paradox can make life difficult for government officials. Suppose they wish to restrain an inflationary economy. The standard advice would be to reduce M, thereby raising interest rates and discouraging investment. But given Gibson paradox conditions, reduced M would probably reduce, not raise, interest rates, insofar as it reduced the public's expectations of further inflation. Suppose, on the other hand, the government wanted to lower interest rates. Would you advise it to increase or decrease M, given the uncertain dynamics of inflation expectations? This problem will be a certral one when we come to monetary policy making in Chapters 13–15.[10]

Money in Perspective

So how important is money? Clearly money matters—and matters a lot. Money has played a vital role in all the big inflations. Runaway increases in the money stock have invariably been associated with soaring prices, usually in a dog-chasing-his-own-tail upward spiral where more money leads to higher prices, which leads the government to print more money to pay its bills, which leads to still higher prices, and so on. The expected yield on M becomes negative, because people expect inflation to erode its value. People reduce their holdings of M to barest minima needed for transactions and precautionary purposes.

Just how important changes in M are in explaining smaller fluctuations is less clear. Although changes in M and in g.n.p. are closely correlated, as we shall see in Chapter 13, it is not always clear which causes which. But one historical fact stands out: real g.n.p. has grown stably in this country only when the money supply was growing at least roughly at the same rate as the productive capacity of the economy. Nearly everyone agrees that a growing money supply is a necessary condition for a growing real g.n.p. Some believe that it is a sufficient condition to induce stable growth in our economy. The implications of the two conclusions for long-run monetary policy are, happily, similar. But until we have clearer evidence, most economists are not prepared to rely solely on stable growth in M to provide stable growth in aggregate demand and real output.

[10]The picture is actually not as black as it seems, as we shall see later on. If the government reduces M and actually lowers the market rate of interest, it may nonetheless succeed in raising the *real* rate (that is, the rate after the inflation allowance is removed) and hence in restraining real investment and inflation.

Review

CONCEPTS TO REMEMBER

The following new concepts in this chapter are worth careful review:

equation of exchange	transactions motive
velocity of circulation	speculative motive
income velocity	precautionary motive
transactions velocity	quantity theory of money
nominal money	portfolio balancing
"real" money	Say's law
demand for money	Gibson paradox

FOR ANALYSIS AND DISCUSSION

1. By and large, would you expect prices to rise in proportion to any major increase in the supply of money? Explain.

2. Suppose the government holds the stock of money roughly constant over the next decade. Would you expect constant, rising, or falling price and income levels? Explain.
3. Is your own spending rate primarily a function of your recent income, of your cash balance, or of other factors? Which of the approaches described in this chapter is most helpful in explaining your own spending behavior?
4. Suppose the 1975 full-employment potential g.n.p. is $1.5 trillion. How big a money supply do you estimate will be needed to finance this g.n.p.?
5. Suppose the public's demand for money balances increases because of fear and uncertainty at the beginning of a recession. If the government wants to keep prices and employment stable, what should it do about the stock of money?
6. "In depression an increase in the money supply leads to more jobs; in prosperity to inflation." Is this quotation correct? Does the equation of exchange help in analyzing it?
7. Explain why an equilibrium level of g.n.p. requires equilibrium in **both** the "flow" decisions that consumers and businesses make about their spending **and** the "stock" decisions as to the form in which consumers and businesses hold their assets.
8. In a period of inflation, would an increase in the money stock lower or raise interest rates? Would your answer be different in a noninflationary period? Explain.

APPENDIX   *SIMULTANEOUS EQUILIBRIUM IN GOODS AND MONEY MARKETS*

The latter sections of Chapter 9 emphasize that both money and income flows are important in understanding the level of g.n.p. Equilibrium requires (a) that households and firms be satisfied to hold just the amount of money that is in existence, and also (b) that they be spending and saving the amounts that they prefer in relation to their incomes. That is, there must be equilibrium in the money market (the demand for and supply of money) and in the goods market (the demand for and supply of real g.n.p.).

If we assume that interest rates play a crucial role in equilibrating M_s with M_d and that there are no

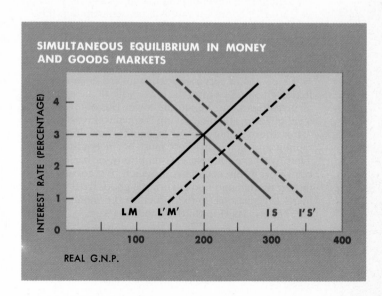

SIMULTANEOUS EQUILIBRIUM IN MONEY AND GOODS MARKETS

fig. 9–3

Intersection of *IS* and *LM* curves shows the level of g.n.p. and the interest rate which simultaneously equate supply and demand in the markets for both money and goods.

price-level changes (i.e., that all variables are in real terms), this dual equilibrium condition can be illustrated by a simple diagram. Suppose there is some given stock of money (M_s = constant) and the public has a fixed demand function for real money balances $[M_d = f_1\,(i,Y)]$. In Figure 9–3, then, curve LM shows the combination of interest rates and levels of g.n.p. that are consistent with this given stock of money and the given demand of the public to hold real balances. For example, if the interest rate is 2 percent, the LM curve shows that this will be consistent with a real g.n.p. of $150 billion. If the interest rate is 4 percent, the consistent real g.n.p. is $250 billion. At each point on the LM curve the amount of M demanded by the public just equals the amount in existence, i.e., $M_d = M_s$.

Why does LM slope upward—that is, why are higher levels of g.n.p. consistent with higher interest rates? The reason is that higher interest rates will lead the public to economize on money; at high interest rates, it will want to hold a smaller stock of money for speculative and precautionary purposes than it would at lower interest rates. This will release more of the total money stock for transactions purposes, raising the level of g.n.p. consistent with the given money stock. To translate this into traditional monetary terms, the income velocity of circulation of any given money stock will be higher, the higher the interest rate is that can be obtained on substitutes for money.

Now consider the IS curve. This shows all the different levels of investment-saving equilibria that will be consistent with different interest rates and different levels of g.n.p. Here again, there are two underlying assumptions: The consumption function $[C = f_2\,(Y)]$ and the investment function $[I = f_3(i)]$ are both fixed. Then at an interest rate of 4 percent, the equilibrium level of g.n.p., where I equals S, will be 150. If the interest rate is 2 percent, the equilibrium level of g.n.p., where I equals S, will be 250.

The IS curve thus shows the possible equilibrium levels in the goods market (real g.n.p.) for different levels of the interest rate; at each point on IS, $I = S = Y - C$. The IS curve slopes downward because the higher the interest rate, the lower will be the amount of investment and hence the lower the equilibrium level of g.n.p. at which saving is equal to investment.

For the economy to be in equilibrium, both the money and goods markets must be in equilibrium. Thus, we have four basic assumptions, or basic relationships, in the economy, of which two govern the money market and two govern the goods (real g.n.p.) market. Equations (1) to (3) picture the money market, equations (4) to (6) the goods market.

(1) M_s = constant

(2) $M_d = f_1(Y,i)$

(3) $M_s = M_d$ (equilibrium condition)

(4) $C = f_2(Y)$

(5) $I = f_3(i)$

(6) $I = S = Y - C$ (equilibrium condition)

If the basic functions are as pictured by the IS and LM curves in Figure 9–3, then equilibrium g.n.p. must be $200 billion and the equilibrium interest rate must be 3 percent. Only at these levels of g.n.p. and the interest rate will **both** the money market and the goods market simultaneously be in equilibrium.

To see why this must be so, suppose the interest rate were 4 percent. Then the goods market (g.n.p.) would be in equilibrium only at an output of 150. But with a 4 percent interest rate the money market would be in equilibrium only with g.n.p. at 250. Clearly 4 percent is not a sustainable level for the interest rate. At that rate, the public would attempt to reduce its money balances and the rate would fall toward 3 percent. As the interest rate falls, investment rises and g.n.p. increases from 150 toward 200. That is, both the interest rate and real output will move toward the equilibrium position indicated by the intersection of the curves.

Or suppose the level of g.n.p. is 250. This is also clearly an unsustainable level. In the goods market this would imply an interest rate of about 2 percent for equilibrium. But if the interest rate were 2 percent, the LM curve says there would be insufficient money spending to sustain the 250 g.n.p. The public's demand for money would force the interest rate up, and the higher interest rate would produce a lower level of real g.n.p. To repeat, only at an interest rate of 3 percent and a gross national product of about 200 would there be simultaneous equilibrium in both the goods and the money markets.

This IS-LM diagram can help in predicting the effects of policy changes *under the simplified assumptions given*—for example, an increase in the money stock or in the public's marginal propensity to consume. Suppose, for example, that the government increases the money stock, the demand for money balances remaining unchanged. This will move the entire LM curve to the right, to L^1M^1. The new L^1M^1 curve shows a higher level of g.n.p. consistent with each interest rate, since there is more money. With the LM curve shifted to the right, the new equilibrium g.n.p. for the economy (where L^1M^1 and IS intersect) will be higher than before, and the new interest rate lower than before.

Or suppose the public's marginal propensity to consume rises. This will shift the IS curve to the right (to I^1S^1), because now a higher equilibrium level of g.n.p. will be associated with each level of investment and hence with each interest rate. The new equilibrium for the economy will be at the new intersection between I^1S^1 and LM, with both g.n.p. and the interest rate higher than before. If both LM and

IS shift as indicated above, check for yourself to see the effect on the interest rate and g.n.p.

It is important to note that the quantitative effects of such changes will depend on the slopes of the *IS* and *LM* curves. Try drawing a flatter *IM* and steeper *IS* curve, and trace out the effects of the same changes in *M* and in m.p.c. analyzed in the preceding two paragraphs. How different are the resulting equilibrium-g.n.p. and interest-rate levels?

Lastly, and most important, remember that these conclusions hold only insofar as the underlying assumptions are valid. They are highly simplified assumptions, so that many economists question the applicability of such *IS* = *LM* analysis.

ten

Economic Fluctuations and Forecasting[1]

The long pull of American economic growth is impressive. But that growth has come spasmodically, in spurts separated by recessions and sometimes major depressions. Prosperity, with heavy investment spending, means a surge in economic growth. Unemployment and recession mean lagging economic growth.

In perspective, the booms and depressions of American history are thus fluctuations around a long-term growth trend. And this is the right way to look at them. For seldom has the trough of a recession been lower than the peak of the boom before last. Growth dominates fluctuations in our history. But this doesn't mean that repeated booms and depressions have been unimportant. Far from it! Some economists believe we have conquered the business cycle, and wise use of monetary and fiscal policy can now produce stable economic growth. But even if this belief happily turns out to be true, we need to understand the forces producing economic fluctuations so we can counteract them effectively. And the theory of the preceding chapters gives us the basis for this understanding.

Growth and Fluctuations in America

The long sweep of growth in America, interrupted by repeated recessions, is shown by

[1]Some instructors may prefer to assign Chapter 16 on growth theory at this point. It is written to be usable in either order.

Figure 17–1 and by the top line of the graph inside the front cover. Figure 10–1 points up both these characteristics another way. The fluctuations of real g.n.p. around its growth rate of about 3–4 percent per year are bounded on the top and bottom by two trend lines, roughly connecting the peaks of the booms and the troughs of the depressions. Growth is the basic process, with the economy pushing up toward the bounds of productive capacity in boom periods and slumping down toward an (ill-defined) floor in depressions and milder recessions. The vertical shaded areas are recession or depression periods. Note that the light (up-swing) periods are substantially longer than the shaded (recession) areas. This emphasizes that growth is the basic process that dominates our economic history, and that growth occurs in the recovery-prosperity periods.[2]

Business-cycle experts have dissected the upward sweep of g.n.p. into its component parts. The fluctuations are commonly called "business cycles," but this is clearly a misnomer if the

term connotes a truly regular "cycle" of fluctuations.

One way of studying economic fluctuations is to separate the fluctuations from the long-term upward trend, or growth. Figure 10–2 does this for industrial production, a major, volatile sector of the modern American economy. This sector is also one that fluctuates widely in booms and depressions. To construct Figure 10–2, we first draw a "trend" line through the actual monthly data for industrial production (per capita) over the period, a rapidly, irregularly rising series. A trend line is a line drawn roughly through the middle of the fluctuating series—so the readings on the industrial-production curve above the trend line about equal those below it.[3] If, then, we lay the trend line out flat, it becomes the zero line in Figure 10–2. Thus, periods when industrial production was above the trend line are shown above zero, and conversely for those below.

All the data are shown as percentage deviations from trend. Thus, the moderate prosperity of the years 1961 to 1964 runs about 10–15 percent above "normal," as does that of the

[2]The top of the World War II boom (1942–1945) is shown above the dashed line because the economy was then clearly operating beyond its normal capacity level. Housewives, old people, and children were temporarily pulled into the labor force, and workers were called on for vast amounts of overtime to meet wartime production goals.

[3]Any elementary statistics book provides information on the statistical techniques used in "fitting" trend lines to data. There are several techniques, which may be considered substantially equivalent for our purposes.

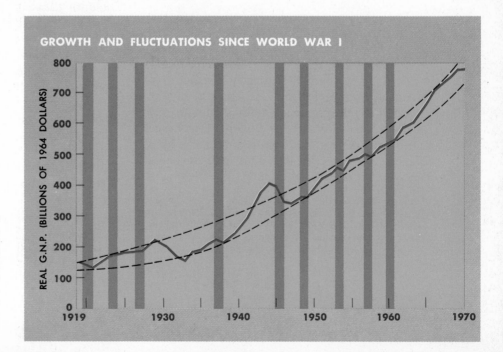

fig. 10–1

The shaded areas show the recessions and depressions since 1919. Recessions since World War II have been mild, hardly more than a flattening out of the growth in real g.n.p., though quarterly data would show sharper fluctuations. (Sources: U.S. Department of Commerce and National Bureau of Economic Research.)

U.S. INDUSTRIAL OUTPUT—DEVIATIONS FROM TREND

fig. 10–2

The curve shows percentage deviations from the long-term upward trend of U.S. industrial production. Areas above the zero line are above trend, and conversely for readings below. (Source: Cleveland Trust Company.)

years 1905 to 1907. In absolute terms, of course, industrial production for the period from 1961 to 1964, and its expansion from the preceding low, were many times what they were for the period from 1905 to 1907. The vast area below normal in the 1930s and those above normal since the 1940s on the chart are thus far smaller in comparison with earlier cycles than they would be plotted in terms of absolute, rather than percentage, deviations.

The huge depression of the 1930s and the great output expansion during World War II stand out. But most recessions and prosperities have involved smaller percentage deviations from the long-run growth trend.

The Anatomy of Economic Fluctuations

The big booms and depressions in America have all involved major swings in real g.n.p., employment, and money income. The great depressions, like that of the 1930s, have meant massive unemployment, vast grey idle factories, financial disaster for millions, endless days of increasingly desperate job hunting, hunger, and malnutrition. Most college students today cannot remember a great depression, for you have never seen one. Perhaps there will never be another, but we cannot be sure.[4] The big booms

[4]Some "feel" of the Great Depression is provided by "Black Depression" from Frederick L. Allen's *Only Yesterday* (New York: Harper & Row, Publishers, 1939) and the dreary, desperate saga "Job Hunters" from E. W. Bakke's *The Unemployed Worker* (New Haven: Yale University Press, 1940), both reprinted in M. L. Joseph, N. Seeber, and G. L. Bach's *Economic Analysis and Policy: Background Readings for Current Issues* (Englewood Cliffs, N.J.: Prentice-Hall, Inc., 1971).

have been the opposite—more jobs than workers, soaring wages and prices, big profits, speculation on the stock market, good times for everybody, but uncertainty about how long it all will last.

In the big booms and depressions, nearly everything goes up or down together. But underneath the surface, different parts of the economy expand and contract at different rates. In many fluctuations some sectors of the economy are actually contracting while others are expanding.

Figure 10–3 shows employment and three major components of real g.n.p. in the United States over the past forty years. Their roughly synchronous behavior is obvious. But production of durable goods fluctuates far more violently than nondurables, services, or employment. In fact, fluctuations in total production and employment occur largely in the capital-goods and durable consumer-goods industries—steel, electrical machinery, automobiles, refrigerators. Fluctuations are much milder in shoes, clothing, food, and other nondurable consumer goods. And the stability of spending on services is remarkable; the growth curve hardly wobbles since the 1930s, in spite of repeated recessions. This does not mean that services and nondurable consumer-goods industries are unaffected by cyclical fluctuations, but the heart of the problem lies in the capital and durable consumer-goods industries.

If this were a more advanced text on economic fluctuations, we would need to look at hundreds of series rather than only a few major ones. The National Bureau of Economic Re-

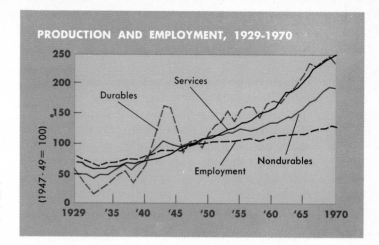

fig. 10-3

The major components of production and employment fluctuate roughly together, but with very different amplitudes. All curves except "Employment" show actual production, with 1947–49 = 100. Note the big fluctuations in output of durables. (Source: U.S. Department of Commerce.)

search, the leading private research organization on business cycles, has plotted hundreds of economic series and found that there is a wide spectrum of movements up and down. Some series normally lead the economy in both directions, some lag far behind, and others are spread out in between. Thus, orders for new machinery may turn down, the average workweek in factories may be just flattening off, national income may be rising strongly, and the unemployment rate may be falling gradually, all at the same time as a recovery moves upward. Since hundreds of different components of total economic activity are important and since their movements vary so widely, the Bureau generally defines a recession as a period in which over half of the important components are falling, and a recovery as a period in which over half of these components are rising. Most economists prefer to focus on a few big, critical measures, like real g.n.p., employment, industrial production, investment, and the like, but it is important never to forget the great complexity of movement in the real world.

Are There Business Cycles? Are there business cycles—regularly recurring booms and recessions? By now the answer should be clear. It is "no," if you stress the "regularly." Some upswings are long and strong, others short and weak. Some recessions are mild, others become massive depressions. But the answer is "yes," if you mean only that there are intermittent periods of prosperity and recession. Given these facts, many economists have dropped the words "business cycles" in favor of the term "fluctuations," which doesn't connote such regularity. A

few argue that there is no business cycle at all, only a series of responses to more-or-less random disturbances like wars, crop failures, and political changes—or surges and slowdowns in the growth rate.

Business-Cycle Theory

Ever since booms and depressions began, people have been trying to figure out why they occur. Professional economists have worked out a variety of theories. Businessmen, financiers, labor leaders, and the man in the street have their business-cycle theories too. The man who says, "The bigger the boom, the bigger the bust!" has an implicit theory about how booms and busts are related. The man who says, "What goes up must come down!" also has at least a partial theory about the relation of booms and depressions.

Different writers have emphasized everything from sunspots to Wall Street as the primary cause of booms and depressions. A theory that seems to explain all business cycles simply and neatly is heady stuff. But alas, no one has come up with one simple theory that does the job. However, there is widespread agreement on a central analytical framework for looking at the dynamically interacting variables.

This framework is provided by Chapters 6 to 9. It suggests that we should focus on changes in aggregate demand relative to the economy's growing productive capacity. Aggregate demand is made up of consumption and investment spending (if we temporarily ignore government spending), and these in turn are influenced by the supply of money and interest rates. Booms are **dynamic,** cumulative, interacting processes in which increased investment stimulates more consumption, which in turn raises business sales and profits and stimulates more investment. Similarly, depressions are cumulating downward processes in which the dynamic interaction between contracting consumption and contracting investment is the core of the contraction. In both, money and interest rates generally play important roles.

We shall, therefore, focus on these three major variables (consumption, investment, and money) and on their dynamic interactions—both because this approach provides a relatively simple framework and because it is the way most economists themselves go about explaining complex real-world economic fluctuations. This temporarily omits government.

1. The level of g.n.p. at any time is primarily determined by the level of investment and a multiplier whose size depends on consumption behavior and on the total leakages (saving and taxes) in the system.

2. Investment in any period is partly a function of income and consumption in the preceding period; thus there is a "feedback," or "accelerator," effect of consumption on investment as well as a causal link from investment to income and consumption.

3. Changes in the supply of and demand for money also importantly affect the equilibrium toward which the system moves at any time.

It is the dynamic interaction among these three, sometimes strongly affected by government policy and by random shocks such as wars, that is the essence of "business cycles."

Role of Government

The above model leaves the government out. But in fact government purchases and transfer payments equal nearly 30 percent of g.n.p., and taxes withdraw a comparable amount from the payments stream. Moreover, government control of the money supply exerts a major influence on the economy.

Government is omitted here because it is useful to separately analyze the way in which the private economy fluctuates as it grows. Government stabilization policy can counter these fluctuations only if we understand what they are and why they occur. We turn to stabilization policy in the next chapter.

But the government budget can be destabilizing too, a major cause of inflation or depression. For example, huge government expenditures on Vietnam and domestic problems in the period from 1965 to 1968 drastically increased aggregate demand without offsetting taxes. The result was an inflationary boom. In the years 1957 and 1958, increased taxes and sharply reduced government expenditures turned the economy down into recession. The wrong level of government spending can undercut stable economic growth, just as can the wrong level of private spending. Monetary policy, too, can be destabilizing. The government can be part of the economic stabilization problem, as well as part of its solution, as we shall see in Chapters 13–15.

The Cumulative Upswing

Let us begin with an economy recovering from a recession. Assume that something happens to start an upswing. We want to trace its progress. In examining the upswing, note how each expansive factor gradually develops self-limiting tendencies, which increasingly act to put a ceiling on the prosperity and to turn the economy down into recession.

Rising Consumption

Rising Consumption Through the Multiplier. To begin, assume that investment spending increases, perhaps because a new product or machine is invented. This new investment spending will generate a multiplied amount of income and consumer spending, through the multiplier. Just how much consumption rises for each dollar of new investment depends, of course, on the "leakages" through saving in each round of spending. Apparently a multiplier of two or so is not uncommon for the

American economy; remember, it's the relation of consumption spending to g.n.p., not to disposable personal income, that provides the relevant multiplier for explaining g.n.p. (see page 81).

The consumption–disposable-income ratio tends to be high in bad times. At the bottom of a depression, consumption may be nearly 100 percent of disposable income; if the marginal propensity to consume is similarly high, the multiplier will be relatively large. As incomes rise into prosperity, though, the marginal propensity to save typically rises, reducing the multiplier on each additional investment dollar. Whatever the m.p.c., rising incomes are the main foundation for rising consumption spending in the upswing. Consumption spending rises primarily because incomes rise; consumption plays a relatively passive role in the upswing.

Other Inducements to Rising Consumption. As the economy comes out of a depression, more spendable income is the only thing likely to give a major boost to consumption spending. But if the revival takes hold, there are three additional special factors that may increase the marginal propensity to consume, pushing toward a larger multiplier.

First, consumers may have a backlog demand for consumer durables—refrigerators, stoves, autos, and radios—piled up from the depression. You can use the same refrigerator a long time if you're good at minor repairs and don't mind foregoing the latest improvements, but you're not likely to be very happy about it. And try as you will to avoid it, the day will come when you have to buy another refrigerator or have the food spoil in hot weather. The postponement of purchases of durable goods is one reason why recessions last. Catching up on these postponed purchases is one of the big lifts in revival.

Second, as revival moves along and prices begin to rise, consumers may begin to expect still higher prices ahead. Expectations of rising prices can speed consumer buying, but this is a boost we can't count on with any confidence until the upswing is well under way.

Third, as times improve consumer credit may become more readily available to marginal borrowers. Such credit permits consumers to spend more in relation to current income than they otherwise might.

But remember: Rising consumption in the upswing depends largely on rising incomes, and thus indirectly on rising investment.

Rising Investment

The "Accelerator." Rising consumer spending means rising sales for businesses. This will deplete inventories and push firms toward capacity limits in factories and stores. Thus, rising sales sooner or later will stimulate more investment. This effect of more consumption spending in inducing more investment is called the "accelerator," or the "acceleration effect." It provides the link to complete the cumulative interaction in the upswing: more investment → more income → more consumption → more investment, and so on. In summary, the upswing is a cumulative multiplier-accelerator process.[5]

Unless the original burst of investment and its multiplied effect on consumption in turn induce more investment, there will be no cumulative upswing—only a hump on the floor of the depression. But if the rise in consumer spending does produce a substantial accelerator effect, then the revival is on. The further induced investment in turn produces its multiplier effect, which in its turn may induce further investment. How big and how repetitive the acceleration effect is, is a crucial question in determining whether the revival grows or withers. If both the multiplier and the accelerator are large, any revival that gets started will be an explosive one, with consumption and investment interacting vigorously. If either is zero, that's the end of the upswing.

How strong will the accelerator in fact be? The answer is, different at different times. Rising incomes and sales will induce new invest-

---

[5]Appendix B to this chapter presents a formal model of the cumulative multiplier-accelerator process that shows that under certain (not unrealistic) conditions, the combination of accelerator and multiplier effects can induce cyclical fluctuations in g.n.p. even when the original stimulus of investment does not fluctuate.

ment whenever they make the **desired** amount of plant and equipment larger than the **actual** amount on hand. Thus, if sales rise and the producer has no excess productive capacity, his desired stock of plant and equipment will clearly exceed his present stock, since without more capacity he can't meet the expanding demand. But if he begins with excess capacity, he has more plant and equipment than he currently needs, so even increased sales won't necessarily raise his desired stock above what he has.

Pragmatically, when the economy is just emerging from a serious recession, the outlook for a larger accelerator effect from rising sales is bad, for two reasons:

1. Idle capacity is widespread during depression, and moderate increases in demand can often be met by using existing idle equipment.

2. Businessmen, whatever the capacity situation is, may cautiously wait to see whether the increased demand is permanent. If they do, no acceleration effect will occur. Their desired stock of capital depends on the permanence they attach to the increased demand.

But if revival progresses and idle capacity vanishes, further increases in consumer spending are more and more likely to stimulate new investment. History and theory both suggest that the acceleration effect can be powerful.

In some cases, an increase in consumer demand may stimulate a much more than proportional increase in investment spending on plant and equipment, providing a large accelerator. Suppose, for example, that the shoe industry produces 100 million pairs of shoes per year; that it has 1,000 shoe machines, each producing 100,000 pairs per year; and that the average life of shoe machines is ten years. This means that 100 machines wear out and have to be replaced each year.

Now suppose that consumer demand rises by 10 percent next year, to 110 million pairs. To meet this demand, if they have no excess capacity or extra inventories, shoe manufacturers will have not only to replace the regular 100 machines wearing out but also to buy 100 new machines to produce the additional 10 million pairs demanded. In this case, a 10 percent increase in final product demand leads to a 100 percent increase in the demand for plant and equipment.

But the acceleration effect is not a stable booster for the upswing. Suppose consumer demand stays at 110 million in the third year. Now manufacturers will have the productive capacity needed to meet this demand if they replace only the regular 100 worn-out machines. (None of the extra new machines need replacement yet, of course.) Thus, the demand for new machines drops back to the original level of 100 per year, a drop of 50 percent, even though consumer demand stays unchanged at the new higher level.

Worse, assume that in the fourth year consumer demand for shoes drops below the original level, to 90 million pairs annually. Then manufacturers don't have to buy any new shoe machines at all. They don't even have to replace the ones that wear out that year. The demand for new machines drops to zero as a result of a relatively small drop in the demand for shoes.

This shoe illustration, though purely hypothetical, does indicate how modest shifts in consumer demand can, through the acceleration effect, give rise to sharp spurts of induced investment or to correspondingly steep slumps, even though neither is likely to be permanent.

The accelerator is likely to be especially large for long-lived investments. For example, if houses ordinarily last fifty years, each year about 1/50 of all houses may be replaced (say, 1 million houses annually). Assume that as the result of higher incomes in a recovery, 1 million young couples who had been living with relatives decide they want new homes. This increase of 1/50, or 2 percent, in the total stock of houses demanded will result in a 100 percent increase in the demand for new houses. Here again, note that the induced new investment in houses is a temporary lump that will vanish the next year unless there is a further increase in the number of young people setting up their own homes.[6]

[6]Examples like these two are tricky and are only illustrations of possible results. Small changes in the assumed conditions can give drastically different results.

The acceleration effect can account for a substantial part of changes in investment as consumption rises. But not for all of them. Some other determinants of the cyclical behavior of investment may be at least as important.

Shifting Cost–Price Relationships. Back in Chapter 8, we said that decisions to invest depend basically on the relationship between the marginal efficiency of investment and the interest rate (cost of money). Rising consumer demand will increase the marginal efficiency of investment and the desired stock of capital, other things equal. But common sense says that the marginal efficiency of capital also depends on the cost–price relationships involved in making the product concerned. If costs rise faster than selling prices, rising consumer demand won't stimulate much new investment, except possibly in cost-saving equipment.

When a revival is just beginning, businessmen can increase output and build new plants without incurring higher construction or unit operating costs—because there are still much unemployed plant capacity and manpower in the economy. Costs stay low as demand and prices rise in the upswing; unemployment tends to hold wage rates down, and higher plant-operating rates tend to reduce costs per unit of output in existing plants. Profit margins widen, increasing the marginal efficiency of capital and providing more funds to finance new investment.

But as the boom sweeps upward, excess capacity and unemployment vanish. Increasingly, **both** operating costs (e.g., wages and materials) **and** the cost of money (interest rates) rise as demands for funds increase. Thus, the return on investment is often squeezed by rising costs as the boom progresses. Businessmen complain about the "profit squeeze," and about the shortage of profits to finance new plant and equipment. Shifting cost–price relationships are an important factor in investment decisions over the cycle, and a profit squeeze per unit of output typically helps to check the upswing.

Rising labor costs in prosperity also stimulate businessmen to invest in labor-saving equipment. This fact helps account for large business investments even when there is substantial ex-

cess manufacturing capacity, for example in the years 1968 to 1970. Such investment does not contradict the comments about the acceleration principle above; it merely indicates that there are many different factors that influence investment decisions.

Innovation and the Development of New Industries. Historically, most big booms have centered around the development of a few important new industries. For example, during the 1800s railroad building, with the resultant demand for iron and steel products, was especially important. The boom of the 1920s centered around the auto and electrical industries. Actually, the inventions underlying these industries had been made years before. It was the utilization of these inventions on a large scale through developmental investment that produced the booms they dominated. And when the investment opportunities surrounding these new industries were temporarily exploited, the central thrust of the boom was gone.

Was the development of new industries at those particular times induced by the revivals then beginning, or were the revivals created by new industries? The effect ran both ways. Whether such innovations actually set off a revival or not, they play a major role in most major booms. Once a few entrepreneurs have successfully braved the uncertain paths of profit by introducing new products and new methods, others are eager to follow. With big new industries, booms are long and lusty. Without them, prosperities are weaker and growth slows down.

Inventory Investment and the Inventory Cycle. Investment in business inventories plays a special role in business fluctuations. Fluctuations in inventory investment constitute one of the most regular subcycles in economic activity. Many "business cycles" are predominantly inventory cycles. When inventories become scarce relative to rising sales, businessmen try to build inventories back up to desired levels. Businesses tend to overbuy in building them up, and thus overshoot what they consider desirable inventories. Trying to unload these excess inventories, they generally overshoot again,

FLUCTUATIONS IN INVENTORY INVESTMENT

fig. 10–4

The inventory cycle shows sharp, large fluctuations in inventory investment, which are a major factor in many of the smaller swings in aggregate economic activity.

plummeting themselves into a position where inventories are short—and they're all ready to start up again. This is too simple a picture, but it is reasonably accurate.

Figure 10–4 shows the persistence and vigor of these inventory fluctuations. Note that the chart shows changes in net inventory investment; this is in accordance with the national income accounts, which count as inventory investment the net increase or decrease in the total stock of inventories held by business. Thus, any figure above the zero line shows inventories building up; any figure below zero shows inventories being depleted. If you compare Figure 10–4 with the earlier data on total investment and g.n.p., you'll see that plummeting net inventory investment accounted for much of the recession drops of 1949, 1954, 1958, 1960, and 1970, and of the upswings in 1950, 1955, 1958, and 1961. If, as some argue, we are beginning to get major cyclical fluctuations under control, the inventory cycle may be our stickiest remaining cyclical problem.

In essence, the inventory cycle amounts to this: When businesses are accumulating inventories, production is running ahead of consumption. Obviously this can go on only for so long; the day of reckoning must come. Conversely, when business inventories are declining, consumption is running ahead of production. Obviously this too can go on for only so long. In 1970, business inventories in the whole economy (at

all levels—manufacturers, wholesalers, and retailers) totaled about $170 billion. Over the long pull this total can be expected to rise roughly with the growth in total sales—perhaps 4 percent a year assuming no inflation. But you can be sure that any inventory accumulation much faster than that won't last for long. And you can be equally sure that if inventory falls far short of that rate, there's going to be an upswing in inventory investment soon.

Money in the Upswing

The cumulative upswing in production, employment, and income may be financed by the existing money supply for a while, as businesses and consumers draw on "idle" balances and V rises. But before long, new money is needed to finance the growing volume of business. Businesses need more working capital to expand operations and longer-term funds to finance new investment in plant and equipment. With higher incomes, consumers want to hold larger money balances. On all sides, the demand for money rises.

Will the rising demand for money be met by more M, or will it result in higher interest rates and a growing drag on the upswing process? The commercial banks, and behind them the government (through the Federal Reserve), are the only source of new money for the system as a whole, as we shall see in Chapter 12. Every major upswing has been marked by a substantial increase in the volume of bank credit and money.

Early in the upswing, as demands for loans increase and as better times lessen the apparent risks in lending, bankers are glad to expand loans. But as revival progresses, loans rise and the public draws more currency from the banks. As banks' excess reserves are used up, interest rates rise and bankers begin to "ration" their remaining credit to preferred borrowers. Unless the Federal Reserve provides more money for the system, credit stringency will gradually impose a ceiling on the upswing as businesses cannot borrow the money they need to expand.

The ceiling is not a firm one. As money tightens and interest rates rise, businesses and families increasingly economize on the money balances they hold. When working capital is scarce, corporate treasurers squeeze their idle cash down to the lowest possible levels. Households put their unneeded money to work in securities or other ways when interest rates offered on such investments rise. Thus V rises and partially offsets the credit ceiling imposed by a shortage of money. But there are limits on how small cash balances can be and still meet the needs of expanding businesses. The rising V can slow the impact of the credit ceiling, but not eliminate it. Only the provision of more money by the Federal Reserve can do that (more details on the process in Chapter 12). More money is necessary for a lusty upswing.

Upper Turning Point: Why Doesn't Prosperity Continue Forever?

Prosperity is wonderful. Why can't it go on forever? Maybe it can, and there are good reasons for believing our chances now are a lot better than ever before. But history warns us to expect a downswing sooner or later. Some reasons have been suggested on the preceding pages.

The cumulative upswing is many-sided and interacting. Early in the rise, everything seems to work together toward prosperity. But as the boom continues, the economic system becomes increasingly "vulnerable" to shocks that may precipitate a downturn, especially if the upswing is a rapid one. Inflationary booms in particular typically produce distorted patterns of activity that are difficult to maintain indefinitely.

What actually turns economic activity downward? Sometimes there is a spectacular financial crisis, as in 1907 and 1929. But economic change is complex, and often some phases of economic activity turn down while others are still moving strongly upward. Sometimes it is hard to say whether the economy is still moving up or has turned down; it depends on where you look.

So the experts are wary of predicting just what particular factor is likely to spark the downturn. Rather, a series of developments gradually set the stage for a downswing, and in such a setting it becomes increasingly likely that something will give the push that sets the economy unmistakably downward, even though we may not recognize it until months later.

The main limiting "environmental" factors appear to be:

1. Piling up of business inventories.
2. Accumulation of large stocks of new durables in consumers' hands.
3. Consumer resistance to rising prices.
4. End of the upward "acceleration" effect, and resulting decline in investment spending.[7]
5. Rising costs and profit squeeze.
6. Accumulation of new productive capacity.
7. Utilization of available new technological developments, and growing scarcity of promising large-scale investment outlets.
8. Exhaustion of excess bank reserves.
9. Weakening of confidence and expectations.

Sometimes a boom keeps going until it faces all these hurdles simultaneously. Sometimes the downturn comes when only two or three seem to present serious problems. Basically, the boom

---

[7]In the multiplier-accelerator model in Appendix B to this chapter, the accelerator alone is sufficient to generate upper and lower turning points in g.n.p.

ends when the entire conjuncture gradually shifts over from favorable to unfavorable—when the driving forces of the upswing (especially spending on investment and consumer durables) give way to disappointed expectations in the face of increasingly saturated markets.

All this has left the government out of the picture. Yet increasingly, government action is a critical consideration in turning points. Government spending and tax policies and Federal Reserve monetary policy may be used to avoid the downturn and recession. Such government action is the focus of attention in the next five chapters. If we are to achieve stable high employment without inflation, it's clear we need positive government assistance to turn the trick.

The Downswing

A recession looks pretty much like a boom in reverse. The multiplier and accelerator work downward instead of upward. Decreasing investment pulls out the support for a multiplied amount of income. Falling incomes mean falling consumption expenditures, which in turn reduce the incentive to invest. The upward spiral that made hearts glad seems diabolically designed as it races downward into depression.

Once a downswing gets under way, the path toward depression may be direct and cumulative. Businessmen, somewhat disappointed in sales and profits as prosperity levels off, are uneasy. Under such conditions, it takes only a downturn in expectations to undermine investment and production plans. Attempts to unload inventories and to obtain cash lead to the very price declines that sellers are trying to "beat" and to still worse expectations for the future.

On the other hand, not all downturns turn into major depressions, just as not all recoveries soar into full-fledged booms. Since World War II, sustained consumer spending on nondurables and services has proved a massive block against a downward spiral. Business investment in plant and equipment has been more resistant to panic cutbacks than in earlier decades. Perhaps most important, government spending provides a big stable block of demand, and government tax and expenditure systems now automatically lead to quick tax-liability reductions when incomes fall and to increased unemployment-compensation transfer payments, which help to maintain personal incomes. And private unemployment-insurance plans supplement this support.

The behavior of the banking system is especially important in major downswings. Traditionally, recessions led to "runs" on the banks, as people lost confidence in their safety and withdrew their deposits. With deteriorating expectations, bankers called for repayments of loans, both to obtain funds to meet withdrawals and because they feared borrowers might become unable to repay. But at such times borrowers were in no position to pay. Bank pressure forced them to liquidate inventories and securities to obtain funds, just when the demand for both was sagging. This induced further declines in prices, employment, and incomes, speeding the downward spiral.

Since the monetary reforms of the 1930s, there is strong reason to hope that recession-period banking pressures that previously forced mass liquidation have been eliminated. Federal deposit insurance has substantially eliminated the likelihood of widespread runs on banks. And the Federal Reserve authorities now have both the power and the stated intention of providing to member banks the funds needed to avoid massive credit liquidation at such times. With the terrific downward monetary pressures of past depressions hopefully eliminated, our chances of avoiding major depressions have been greatly improved.

Upturn or Stagnation?

If a depression occurs, will business activity turn up again, or will the system bump along the bottom indefinitely?

Take the list of hurdles facing a boom as it reaches its peak, reverse them, and you have a picture of the potentially favorable forces that make an upturn increasingly likely as the downswing continues. The gradual buildup of potential demand for consumers' and producers' durables as old stocks wear out is one of the surest and most powerful forces. But many economists lack confidence that the economic system will turn itself up without a prolonged depression if it is again permitted to reach the depths of the 1930s. Positive government action to check the downswing and turn the system back up has become a dominant part of any consideration of lower turning points.

Some Special Factors

The Role of the Stock Market

In spite of its prominent position in the public eye, the stock market generally plays a minor role in business cycles. Rising security prices do help to speed the upswing, and a collapse of prices on the stock market may help set off or intensify a downswing. But usually these events bring more newspaper headlines than they justify on the basis of their importance in determining real output and employment.

The stock market has four main channels of impact. First, the biggest effect is probably psychological—a symbol of better or worse times for businessmen and the general public. How important all the talk is varies from time to time, with only big changes in the market probably having identifiable effects on investment and consumption spending. Second, rising stock prices mean paper profits for stockholders. With more wealth, at least on paper, stockholders probably are inclined to spend more out of their incomes or out of capital gains. Third, from the point of view of corporations, higher stock prices mean a lower cost of capital for expansion. If a firm needs long-term funds, it can sell new stock at a higher price; that is, it can obtain new funds at a lower cost for the money obtained. Fourth, if rising stock prices have been heavily financed by borrowed money, a downturn in the market may precipitate a major collapse in stock prices, as lenders call for cash, and may place serious financial pressure on banks and other lenders. A high market based on credit is thus far more vulnerable than a "cash" market, and is more likely to be a cyclically destabilizing force.

Stock prices have usually preceded cyclical movements in general business, though by no definite lead. As boom psychology spreads, speculative activity increases on the stock exchange. This was most spectacular in the boom of the years 1928 and 1929, when speculative activity reached heights completely out of touch with the actual profit possibilities or the general level of business activity. Such a speculative boom carried within itself the seeds of its own destruction.

Once the bubble was pricked in late 1929, security prices nosedived, pushed downward by calls of the New York bankers for repayment of loans that had financed most of the purchases. The result was a mass destruction of paper profits. The break in the market provided the psychological turning point of the boom— people found their airy dreams ruined, their financial security vanished, their confidence in permanent prosperity turned to utter uncertainty. Financial crisis has often characterized the upper turning point of the cycle. But with reforms in our financial system since the crash of 1929, financial crises seem likely to play a less-prominent role in the future. For example, severe stock-market breaks in 1962 and 1970 failed to trigger depressions.[8]

International Aspects of Business Fluctuations

One component of gross investment omitted above is net foreign investment. Current excess of exports over imports represents a net demand for U.S. output and is considered investment abroad in the national income accounts. The excess of exports over imports represents goods produced in this country that do not move into current U.S. consumption, just as inventories accumulated by domestic business are not currently consumed. Such a net export balance provides employment and incomes in the United States, just as does domestic investment; its multiplier effect is similar. The main difference is that with foreign investment the goods

[8]For a lively, popular account of the crash of 1929, see J. K. Galbraith, *The Great Crash* (Boston: Houghton, Mifflin, 1955).

produced go abroad rather than being used domestically.

How important is the foreign-trade multiplier? Not very, most of the time. The U.S. net export surplus has seldom exceeded $5 billion. Our foreign trade has seldom exceeded 5 percent of total g.n.p. But this is a far from trivial amount, and foreign trade is far more important for most other nations. In Brazil, for example, domestic income, jobs, and prices depend heavily on the international demand for coffee, lumber, and a few other main exports, and on the prices Brazil has to pay for her imports. We shall return to the whole problem of international interactions in detail in Part Six.

Growth and Fluctuations Again

Can we have rapid, stable growth without booms and depressions in our basically private-enterprise, profit-motivated economy? Look back at Figure 10–1. History warns against overoptimism, unless we've learned how to turn the trick through governmental monetary and fiscal policy. Some economists think we have.

In principle, there's no reason investment has to come in surges that overbuild. But as long as we rely on the private-profit motive to induce investments, the likelihood is high that investments will cumulate when times are good and slump when times are bad—even though the long-term trend is strongly upward. Increasingly therefore, we have turned to government monetary and fiscal policy for help in offsetting big swings in private aggregate demand $(C + I)$ so as to smooth out the inflationary booms and depressions that have plagued us in the past. If government stabilization policy can actually produce stable economic growth without depressions, unemployment, or inflation, the gain to mankind will be measured in hundreds of billions of dollars. Unfortunately, government spending and taxing sometimes turns out to be destabilizing instead. Chapters 11 to 15 look in detail at the prospects and at the problems we face.

Review

CONCEPTS TO REMEMBER	This chapter reuses most of the important concepts introduced in Chapters 5–9. In addition to those, be sure you have a firm understanding of the following:

business cycle	inventory cycle
boom	innovation
recession and depression	cycle turning points
deviations from trend	foreign-trade multiplier
accelerator	

FOR ANALYSIS AND DISCUSSION	1. Why can't a boom go on forever? Or can it? If your answer is "yes," what change promises to make the future different from the past?
	2. One group of business-cycle analysts argues that booms and depressions are caused by expansions and contractions in the quantity of money. Can you see any important weaknesses in this argument? If so, what are they?
	3. "The bigger the boom, the bigger the bust." Is this often-heard statement true or false? Support your answer by a careful analysis of reasons why or why not.

4. The following factors are generally agreed to play important roles in cyclical upswings. Analyze how the force of each changes as national income rises from depression levels to prosperity, and how each gradually helps set the stage for the upper turning point:
   a. The banking system.
   b. The public's propensity to consume.
   c. Consumer and business price expectations.
   d. Induced investment (the acceleration effect).
   e. Cost–price relationships as they affect investment.
   f. Inventory levels.
   g. Consumer and business "psychology."
5. How many factors can you list that might reasonably be expected to provide a strong impetus to an upswing from a long, deep depression? Evaluate the likely force of each.
6. *(Based on the appendix)* Forecast the g.n.p. over the year ahead, using the analytical framework provided by this chapter and by Chapters 6–9.

APPENDIX A *ECONOMIC FORECASTING*

All economic policy, public or private, involves making forecasts about the future. If the government is to help stabilize the economy, it must know whether next year promises unemployment or a boom. The businessman must forecast his sales for months ahead to plan purchases of materials, inventory levels, and sales quotas for his marketing department. He must forecast years ahead if he is to make his long-range plans soundly—when to expand plant and equipment, when the firm will need to obtain additional capital funds, what his needs will be for managers, engineers, and the like. And in most cases, the company's outlook is closely tied to the general level of business conditions.

Thus, both the government and the businessman have to make economic forecasts, like it or not. If they fail to make explicit forecasts, they are making implicit forecasts, perhaps without realizing it—that tomorrow will be about like today, that present trends will continue, that the outlook story in yesterday's *Wall Street Journal* was probably about right. Increasingly, both government and business officials have begun to face up consciously to the need for the best possible economic forecasts as a basis for their forward planning.

How Well Can We Forecast? How well can we forecast, using the models of the preceding chapters or other approaches as a foundation? First, no one can forecast **precisely** very far into the future, no matter how glibly he talks or how much he charges for his services. Second, real experts, using the latest tools and the mass of statistical data now available, can do a reasonably reliable job for perhaps six months to a year ahead for overall activity (say,

g.n.p.), but the reliability goes down rapidly as the distance into the future increases. Third, especially for longer-range forecasts, it is realistic to recognize that ranges (say, a real g.n.p. between $80 and $100 billion higher for two years hence) are more reliable forecasts than those that pick a specific figure. Unfortunately, there is no way of making reliable "point" forecasts far ahead in the complex real world; but happily, for many purposes "range" forecasts often provide much of the information we really need for making today's action decisions.

Short-range Forecasting. Suppose you are a congressman, voting on a proposal to cut taxes. Or suppose you are a businessman, manufacturing sewing machines and now facing production decisions on machines to be sold in the autumn–winter sales season that comes six months hence; you know that in the past your sales have fluctuated closely with disposable personal income. In each case, you'd face a similar forecasting problem. How could you go about it?

Maybe you'd want to spend your time reading the predictions of others—government economists, professional forecasting services, business magazines, academicians. But even if you rely on these, you need to have some criteria for judging among the conflicting predictions you're likely to find.

First, your economics should tell you that economic fluctuations are complex, everchanging phenomena, and that there is no foolproof way of predicting aggregate business activity, even six months ahead. Beware of the man who has the surefire answer!

Inertia Models. Economics also suggests that there is a large amount of inertia in such a huge, diverse economy as ours. Allow for gradual growth, and disposable personal income (or any other of the major aggregates) is unlikely to be enormously different next autumn from this spring, unless some big special development is in the offing. The economy is so large, with so many different factors influencing disposable personal income, that only in major expansions or contractions will most of them be moving strongly in the same direction over a short period. Employment in autos may be rising, but construction is easing off and the stock market is soft. Government spending moves up, but international developments have oils and chemicals in the doldrums. And so it goes. Moreover, "built-in countercyclical flexibility" in government taxes and expenditures, as we shall see presently, helps to offset short-term tendencies up or down in the economy.

So one simple type of short-run forecast, which has a higher batting average than many, is just to assume the next half year will be about the same as the past one, plus allowance for a 4 percent real-growth trend, unless there is a strong reason to modify this prediction. Another "inertia" approach is to extend the rate of change of the present six months out a half year; this assumes that the present direction will continue at about the same rate. Neither of these is very elegant, and obviously they give only rough approximations. But each recognizes the basic fact of inertia for short-run forecasting, and they don't miss because of mistaken judgments of forecasters based on hunches, waves of hearsay, and the like, which are common in the newspapers and magazines.

G.n.p. Models. If you want a more careful, thorough forecast, most leading economists (in industry, government, and the universities) now use the gross national product accounts as a framework, and try to estimate each major component separately. Then they fit the parts together to see whether they are consistent, and check for likely interactions that may have been missed in studying the individual parts. Chapter 5 provides the breakdown commonly used (though many forecasters look in considerably more detail); and Chapters 6–10 indicate most of the interrelationships among the major variables that forecasters typically work with.

For example, nearly everyone forecasts separately private investment, consumer expenditures, and government expenditures to get gross national product. Then they need separate estimates on government taxes and depreciation accounts to get to national income, and estimates of transfer payments and personal income taxes to get to disposable personal income.

How, for example, can we forecast that volatile item, business investment? For plant and equipment spending, we now have businessmen's own forecasts of their investment spending a year ahead, collected and published regularly by the U.S. Department of Commerce. These figures give a pretty good short-run bench mark. We can check them to see whether projected spending is way out of line with historical relationships to, say, consumer buying of final goods. The more extreme the estimates look, the more we may want to modify them. We know that investment seldom booms when there is substantial unused capacity. And we know that businessmen typically underestimate their reactions to upturns or downturns in aggregate demand.

For investment in inventories, we also have the published plans of businessmen from time to time. But these forecasts have proved less reliable. We need to look at the ratio of inventories to sales in relation to historical standards, and to whether purchasers are facing full-capacity production conditions that may force them to wait for deliveries. We need to look at how fast businesses have been accumulating or using up inventories over the past year or two. The "inventory cycle" (see Figure 10–4) is one of the more regular phenomena in business fluctuations. If real inventories have been accumulating at, say, a $10 billion annual rate for the past year or so, you can be pretty sure a drop-off in this rate isn't far away. Over the long pull, businesses won't continue to produce large inventories they don't sell. Nor will they be willing to deplete their inventories below what they consider sound business levels. On the average, we can expect that total inventories will grow at somewhere near the same rate as total real sales in the economy—say, 3–4 percent per annum in the absence of inflation.

To finish forecasting private investment, we'd need a separate analysis of home construction, of foreign investment, and so on in detail for all investment categories.

Similarly, we can estimate consumer spending from different sides, and thus cross-check. The University of Michigan's Survey Research Center examines consumer buying attitudes and intentions quarterly and publishes the results. These will give some clues. But consumer spending depends mainly on the disposable income consumers receive, so we need to rely heavily here on the forecasts of private and business investment plus transfer payments, adjusted by all the special factors that may affect the propensity to consume in the short run (consumer credit, the current stock of consumer durables, the rate of family formation, and so on—see Chapter 7).

Then we need to look at the government—at tax and expenditure rates, at monetary policy expectations, at special government activities in any field that might affect economic activity. The federal budget calls for careful attention, since federal spending and tax receipts exercise such a big effect on the economy. Happily, the government publishes detailed estimates semiannually.

Put this analysis of the individual categories together in the national income accounts, cross-check to see whether the individual estimates appear consistent with one another, and you should have a substantial improvement on the simpler inertia type of forecast we began with.

Econometric Models. The fastest growing modern forecasting method evolves out of the preceding one. It is the use of formal econometric models. It uses the same variables and relationships as those in the preceding paragraphs, but bases their relationships on statistical studies of past experience, and then obtains final estimates of the end variables (say, g.n.p.) by using a computer to solve the set of equations in the econometric model, which, in essence, assumes that the statistically validated relationships of the past will hold in the future.

This approach is for the experts, even more than the preceding one. But the essentials are presented nontechnically in the appendix to Chapter 7 on econometric models. If you are seriously interested in how modern economists forecast, see the references there, in Chapter 8, and especially on page 108 of Chapter 9 (which deals with alternative methods of assessing the monetarist and income–expenditures models for forecasting). Only hard empirical testing of the relationships among the key variables can give us a reliable basis for making forecasts in our complex economic system.

"Leading Indicators." A last approach emphasizes leads and lags. The National Bureau of Economic Research has studied the behavior of hundreds of economic series in business fluctuations since the middle 1800s, and has found that some economic series usually lead others. Typically leading series include construction contracts, new orders for producers' durables, new business incorporations, length of the workweek in manufacturing, common-stock prices, and business failures (inverted). No one alone is reliable, but if most or all of the so-called leading indicators are moving up or down together, this suggests that other parts of the economy will follow. Since most of the leading series exhibit irregular jags from month to month, it's often hard to separate out the false signals from the real ones they may be giving about turning points. For very short-range forecasts the leading indicators now provide valuable forecasting evidence, especially when interpreted by the experts. But don't be misled by the newspaper accounts; the leading indicators fall far short of providing a layman's guide to the future.[9]

It should be clear by now that short-run economic forecasting is a tough job. But substantial progress

has been made in the last quarter century, both through improved methods and vastly more data. How close do the experts come? The President's Council of Economic Advisers produces the most widely used regular forecasts, at the beginning of each year. They are sophisticated experts, with the full statistical resources of the government to draw on, and they use a combination of methods, cross-checking each against the other. By and large in recent years they have done well, only once missing by more than 2 percent for the year ahead. Their forecasts for 1964 and 1966 tell the story. In January, 1964 they forecast a 1964 g.n.p. of $624 billion, and the final figure was, almost too good to be true, $628 billion. But their forecast for 1966, using substantially the same methods, undershot the mark by $14 billion, when the war in Vietnam and booming private expenditures produced a g.n.p. of $740 billion, compared to their forecast of $726 billion. They were about 2 percent short of the actual g.n.p. Both public and private forecasters missed on late 1968, following the Johnson surtax at midyear. Results for 1970 were a mixture.

A miss of only $15 billion or so in a trillion dollar economy seems good to many observers, and it is. But $15 billion may mean the difference between satisfactory employment and economic slack. Moreover, $10–15 billion is a substantial percentage of an annual change of $60–70 billion, and the Council is dissatisfied unless it comes closer. Some private forecasters do about as well, sometimes better, often worse.[10]

Long-range Forecasting Long-range economic forecasts pose different problems. This is the problem of forecasting the growth rate of the economy, the topic of Chapters 16–19. Generally, a reasonably wide range of likely figures for five or ten years ahead will serve the government's or company's planning purposes about as well as a specific figure, since what is usually needed is an order-of-magnitude picture of the situation several years ahead. Many businessmen insist on having a specific figure for such long-range estimates, but this is pure wishful thinking. No economist, statistician, businessman, government official, or anyone else can be sure of his forecast for the g.n.p. or any other major economic variable five or ten years ahead within 5 percent (which would

---

[9] The leading, coincident, and lagging series are now published monthly by the U.S. Department of Commerce in *Business Conditions Digest*, together with a substantial amount of related information.

[10] The bookstores are full of books on forecasting, especially on forecasting the stock market. Measured scientifically by tests of what their success would have been had they been used in the past, many of them, alas, aren't much good. A recent basic text, with stress on modern quantitative and econometric approaches, is W. Butler and R. Kavesh, eds., *How Business Economists Forecast* (Englewood Cliffs, N.J.: Prentice-Hall, Inc., 1966); see especially Part I. The suggestions in the preceding column are likely to be more useful for beginners.

allow an error margin of some $75 billion on a $1.5 trillion g.n.p.).

A good economist can lay out the major factors determining the economy's long-term growth rate. He can point out the importance and likely effects of alternative government policies aimed at providing purchasing power sufficient to assure high employment. He can provide careful forecasts of the major variables involved, and of their interaction.

A concluding note if you're headed for business. These warnings need not be discouraging to the thoughtful manager. For long-range forecasts can be made that will provide reasonably reliable order-of-magnitude estimates for the total economy, estimates that are close enough to provide a rough basis for business long-range planning. In any case, individual industry forecasts (say, of sewing machine sales) are the critical requirements for the business firm. What the total-economy forecasts can do is only provide the general setting for the individual market studies required. The bare statement that g.n.p. in the years 1975 to 1977 will probably at least approach $1.5 trillion, in 1970 prices, and may be higher, is enough alone to pose the growth problem squarely to any firm that expects to hold or increase its share of the market.

Input–Output Models. Economists now have elaborate "input–output" models of the economy that show for past U.S. census years the interactions among the sales, and materials and labor utilization of hundreds of different industries. These interrelations are shown as matrices, listing the industries involved across the top and down the side of the matrix. One cell then shows, for example, how much steel the auto industry would buy from the steel industry to produce $1 million worth of autos. The relevant steel industry cell shows how much coal the steel industry would buy to produce that steel, and so on for thousands of other interlinkages in the economy.

While the statistical work involved in making such an input–output matrix is enormous, the principle is simple. If such matrices are accurate, they provide an unprecedented wealth of information on the ties among different industries. Moreover, if the relationships are reasonably stable over time, the effects of a billion dollars of new government spending on arms next year on all the affected industries in the country can readily be forecast from the matrix. The same is true for any other change in demand.

Note that the input–output matrix does nothing to help in forecasting the aggregates like g.n.p. But given a g.n.p. forecast, it helps to spell out the implications of that forecast for individual industries. Input–output economics provides a path toward relating aggregate forecasts to forecasts for individual industries.

How reliable are existing input–output matrices for individual industry forecasting? Experience thus far suggests that they can be helpful, but that they're far from foolproof yet. The two main problems are (1) the accuracy of the relationships based on the census data, and (2) the question of how fixed these interindustry relationships are over time. The census data are available only infrequently, so the base information is always several years out of date. With rapid technological change and shifting economic relationships it would be surprising if the interindustry relations did not shift substantially over a decade or so. But input–output, or interindustry, economics is one of the exciting new frontiers of economic forecasting.[11]

[11]For further information, see W. Leontief, "Structure of the American Economy," *The Scientific American*, April, 1965.

APPENDIX B   *A FORMAL MULTIPLIER-ACCELERATOR MODEL*

This appendix presents a simple formal model to illustrate the types of dynamic interaction that may occur between the multiplier and the accelerator. It will be most interesting to those who like precise, theoretical reasoning, and especially to those who know mathematics.

Suppose, in Table 10–1, that we begin with national income at 1,000. Now (say because there is a temporary war scare), businesses increase their investment rate by 100 in periods 1 and 2. The war scare then vanishes, and businessmen are prepared to drop their investment spending back to the original level. What will be the impact of this temporary surge of new investment?

Assume, for this example, that the marginal propensity to consume is .8 out of the income of the preceding period (perhaps a more reasonable assumption than that consumption is related to current income). Assume also that businessmen are led to make new investments in inventories, plant, and equipment when sales improve, and that such new induced, accelerator-type investment is just equal to the rise in consumption during the preceding time period.

On the basis of these illustrative assumptions, now trace through the dynamic results of this original surge of assumed autonomous business investment.

In Table 10–1, the 100 of new autonomous investment in period 1 becomes income to its recipients in that period, raising the period 1 total-income level to 1,100. This rise in income increases consumption in period 2 by 80, which is .8 of the new income in

table 10-1

Dynamic Income-Expenditure Model

	Total Income (1)	Change from Original Level in:		
		Investment (2)	Consumption (3)	Income (4)
Original level	1,000			
Period 1	1,100	+ 100		+ 100
Period 2	1,180	+ 100	+ 80	+ 180
Period 3	1,224	+ 80	+ 144	+ 224
Period 4	1,243	+ 64	+ 179	+ 243
Period 5	1,229	+ 35	+ 194	+ 229
Period 6	1,198	+ 15	+ 183	+ 198
Period 7	1,147	− 11	+ 158	+ 147

Assume: Original autonomous investment of 100 in periods 1 and 2 (in Col. 2).

Thereafter: To obtain change from original level: Consumption equals .8 of income during preceding period.

Investment equals the increase (+ or −) in consumption (i.e., business sales) in preceding period over the next preceding period. For example, investment in period 3 is −80, because consumption was 80 higher in period 2 than in period 1.

Thus: Col. 1 equals 1,000 (original income) plus Col. 4 (change in income).

Col. 2 equals 100 in periods 1 and 2 (new assumed investment), and changes in Col. 3 in preceding period for all succeeding periods (since induced investment equals the preceding change in consumption).

Col. 3 equals .8 of Col. 4 during preceding period (since consumption is always .8 of the national income of the preceding period).

Col. 4 equals Col. 2 plus Col. 3 (since national income equals investment plus consumption).

The same model in equations (as explained in appendix to Chapter 6, on "Econometric Models"):

$$C_t = .8 Y_{t-1}$$
$$I_t = C_{t-1} - C_{t-2}$$
$$Y_t = C_t + I_t$$

where C = consumption, I = investment, Y = income, and the subscript shows the time period. Thus $_t$ is any time period, $_{t-1}$ the preceding period, and so on.

period 1. The burst of autonomous business investment continues in period 2, by assumption. Adding together the new investment and new consumption in period 2, we get 180 of new income over the original level; this gives a total income of 1,180 for period 2. The higher income in period 2 in turn raises consumption in period 3; in addition, the preceding rise in consumption induces 80 of new business investment, raising total income to 1,224. And so the process goes.

This cumulative upward expansion arises out of the interacting multiplier and accelerator effects. Common sense tells us that if we increase the strength of either the multiplier or accelerator we will get a more rapid income expansion. If we weaken either, the rise in income will be slower. And these results can readily be checked by substituting a different propensity to consume or a different accelerator in the table.

This dynamic model provides a simple framework that may help you understand the cumulative upswing of the boom and the downswing of depression.

131

But, once it's started, why does national income ever stop going up or down? Notice that income rises ever more slowly from period 1 through period 4. Since induced investment depends on the **change** in consumption, induced investment gradually falls and the acceleration effect gradually weakens, in spite of the continued upward multiplier effect of whatever new investment there is. By period 5, new investment has dropped off substantially and the drop in investment is enough to more than offset the continued rise in consumption. Thus, total income falls slightly in period 5, and the expansion has passed its upper turning point. Moreover, once consumption begins to fall, investment becomes a negative figure (by our accelerator assumption). This sets off a negative multiplier effect, and the downswing is under way. The block of autonomous investment has set off an upswing, which has eventually checked itself and has become a downswing. And the accelerator has given us an upper turning point unaided by other factors. Moreover, if you trace the process further, you'll see that it also reverses the downswing a few periods later.

If you think easily in mathematical terms, putting the model in the simple system of equations shown under Table 10–1 may be helpful. These are "difference equations," and the solution of the system mathematically gives the pattern of changes in income worked out arithmetically in Table 10–1.

This dynamic model gives some idea of the possible results of interacting multiplier and acceleration effects. But don't be too impressed with it. Changing the values of the accelerator and multiplier can substantially change the pattern you get for national income over a series of time periods. If you increase both—the multiplier to a very high marginal propen-

sity to consume, and the accelerator to 3 or 4—you will find that national income "explodes" upward once anything starts it up. If you trace out the model given in Table 10–1 for about fifteen periods, you will find that income "damps" back down toward the original income level of 1,000. If you use lower values for the multiplier and accelerator, national income will return to the 1,000 level faster. Moreover, if you make induced investment a function of the **level** of national income in the preceding period, rather than of the **change** in national income, you will get a still different pattern of interaction.[12]

Thus, the purpose of this simple dynamic model is not to show how business fluctuations really work. Rather, it is to show how simple mathematics can be used to analyze economic problems; and to focus attention on the importance of the propensity to consume and on induced investment, on the factors that influence these key variables, and on some possible interactions among the critical factors.

---

[12]For *constant* values of the multiplier and accelerator, an autonomous rise in investment to a new higher level will induce (a) an explosive, continued rise in income when both the multiplier and accelerator are large, (b) no cumulative upward process when either the multiplier or accelerator is zero, and (c) cyclical fluctuations around the new income level if one is weak and the other strong. In some cases under (c), the fluctuations will be damped—that is, they will gradually die out. In others, they may be constant or expanding in amplitude. For a precise statement of these cases, given different constant values for the multiplier and accelerator, see P. A. Samuelson, "Interactions between the Multiplier Analysis and the Principle of Acceleration," in *Readings in Business Cycle Theory* (New York: McGraw-Hill Book Company, Blakiston Division, 1944).

Stabilization Policies: Goals and Costs

Economic Analysis as the Basis for Policy
The Goals of Stabilization Policy
The Costs of Unemployment
The Costs of Inflation
The Trade-off between High Employment and Stable Prices

Can we maintain high-level employment without inflation? Almost everyone agrees on this as a major goal. Depression and mass unemployment bring waste and human misery. Inflation erodes the value of savings and may lead to disruptive speculation. But there is less agreement on how to achieve this combined goal. And if we must give up one goal to achieve the other, which should give way?

On such complex problems, we don't know all the answers. But economics as an empirical science has made great headway in recent decades, both in building better analytical models of the economy and in checking out these models through extensive empirical investigations. Fortunately, by now there is substantial agreement (far more than the general public

often realizes) on some broad lines of monetary and fiscal policy to help achieve stable growth. We may not know exactly what leads people to venture over their depth in swimming, but we can agree that it's good policy to have a competent lifeguard on duty. In the same way, there remain disagreements about the causes of unemployment and inflation, but the disputants still agree on some major policies to minimize these problems.

This chapter looks in detail at some of the major goals of economic policy and at the issues involved in choosing among them. It presents empirical evidence on the advantages and costs of each of the major goals. Then the next four chapters consider specific governmental monetary and fiscal policies to help achieve the goals

—mainly to stabilize the economy at high employment without inflation.

Economic Analysis as the Basis for Policy

Economic policy is concerned with the problem of how we can make the economy serve us better. Economic analysis (that is, economic theory) is the necessary foundation for sound economic policy. Chapters 6 to 10 have been devoted largely to economic analysis—to developing theoretical models that help to explain the levels of aggregate demand, real output, employment, and prices in our basically private-enterprise economy. Now comes the chance to use the theory that you have learned. For this is the theory that should provide a foundation for deciding what governmental policies are most likely to help us achieve our economic goals.

Chapter 2 stressed that there are four big steps in thinking through most policy problems.

1. First, define the problem. This usually involves two parts: (a) understanding the existing situation, and (b) clarifying the objectives you want to achieve through policy action. You need a clear picture of where you are and where you want to go.

2. Second, map out the main alternative ways of achieving the stated objectives—the main alternative paths from where you are to where you want to be.

3. Third, analyze carefully the alternative policies outlined broadly in step 2, and make a judgment as to which promises to help most in achieving the goals specified in the first step.

4. Fourth, check your solution, both for flaws in your own analysis and against past experience. History has a way of throwing light on flaws in even the most careful analysis of contemporary problems.

The Goals of Stabilization Policy

There is widespread agreement on two overriding goals for domestic macroeconomic policy.

1. High-level employment of men and machines, avoiding the wastes of large-scale involuntary unemployment.
2. A reasonably stable price level.

Virtually everyone agrees, moreover, that policies to achieve these goals must be consistent with a high level of freedom for individuals and businesses in our economic life. Our basic presumption in favor of extensive economic freedom establishes a framework within which acceptable governmental policies must fit, except for periods of war or other national crisis.

Many, though by no means all, would add two other basic goals:

3. More rapid economic growth.
4. Maintenance of "equilibrium" in our international balance of payments.

More rapid growth (defined as higher g.n.p. per capita) seems to most economists a central goal for any economic system that is to raise the nation's standard of living. In recent years, however, some critics argued that we should stress the "quality of life," not just more output. Similarly, though many economists argue that every nation must keep its international balance of payments near equilibrium, just what constitutes equilibrium is in dispute, as are the appropriate steps for achieving this goal.

Analysis of these two controversial goals—faster growth and balance-of-payments equilibrium—is postponed to Chapters 16 to 19 and 41 to 44, respectively. Thus, this chapter and the immediately following ones are focused on the central problems of maintaining high employment and a stable price level in the domestic economy.

The Trade-off Problem—Conflicting Goals

High-level employment and a stable price level are both desirable. Hopefully, we can achieve both. But, alas, these goals may sometimes conflict—we can have one only at the cost of giving up the other.

Look back at Figure 6–2, at the dotted line that cuts across the corner at A. This shows that when aggregate demand rises, some inflation begins before we reach full employment. As unemployment is reduced, more demand is increasingly likely to lead to higher prices. Wages are bid up as labor becomes scarce. Unions demand higher pay and costs rise. Rising aggregate demand leads to full employment in some industries before unemployment and excess capacity are eliminated in others. Then further increases in aggregate demand bid up prices in the "bottleneck" industries before unemployment of men and machines is eliminated elsewhere.

What then? How shall we trade off the employment of 500,000 more men against a 1 percent increase in the consumer price index? This is no imaginary problem. Between 1953 and 1965 the economy persistently had more unemployment than in previous boom periods. But prices crept upward, fast enough to warn that more aggregate demand might produce substantial inflation. Expansionary monetary-fiscal policy to eliminate unemployment thus was continually restrained by the danger that too much aggregate demand could restart the substantial inflation that followed World War II.

Whether we can avoid this trade-off dilemma by sound economic policy is an unsettled issue, to which we shall return repeatedly. If in fact we face the dilemma, one path is to search for solutions that will eliminate it. But if we cannot find such a solution, an intelligent policy decision requires carefully weighing the relative advantages of achieving each of the goals. And it is interesting to see that as a practical matter, the choice is usually not all-or-none—not: what is more important, full employment or price stability? Instead, typically it is: Shall we seek a little more employment at the cost of a little more inflation? The real problems are marginal problems.

The Costs of Unemployment

The case for high-level employment of men and machines is clear. Involuntary unemployment means waste of productive capacity. It means less clothing, fewer refrigerators, highways, and factories than we could otherwise

have. It means human misery, resentment, shame, decay of skills, degrading deprivation for the unemployed and their families. It means a lower average standard of living for the nation today and in the future.

What Is Unemployment?

Unemployment is defined in the official U.S. statistics to include all those in the labor force who are not employed or self-employed. The labor force includes all those sixteen years old or over who have a job, are self-employed, or are looking for a job. Thus, in essence the unemployed are those who don't have a job and are looking for one.

How do we decide who is unemployed? Mostly, we ask. A scientific sample of the entire population in the relevant age group is asked: Do you have a job? If the answer is no, the respondent is asked: Are you looking for a job? If the answer is no, the respondent is not in the labor force and is not considered unemployed. If the answer is yes, he is in the labor force and is unemployed. The interview probes somewhat further, but this is the core of the matter. A person may be in the labor force, and unemployed, even though he is only looking for a part-time job; large movements of students into and out of the labor force often account for big swings in the unemployment totals during summer and other vacation periods.

How much has the waste of unemployment cost? Figure 11–1 gives a rough measure of this cost since 1953. The straight line is a rough measure of high-employment capacity output for the economy; it is drawn to show the growing capacity of the economy at 4 percent unemployment. The fluctuating line below shows actual g.n.p. during the same period (in constant purchasing-power dollars). Thus the colored area between the two lines is a rough measure of how far actual g.n.p. fell short of reasonably obtainable g.n.p. over the years shown. (Note that in 1953 and in the years 1967 to 1969 the actual-output line is above the capacity line; in those years unemployment went below 4 percent.)

These estimates suggest that the economy

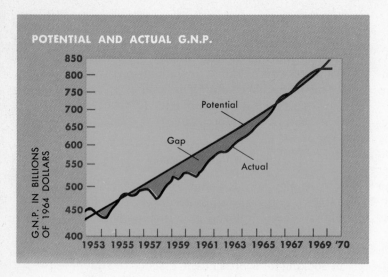

POTENTIAL AND ACTUAL G.N.P.

G.N.P. IN BILLIONS OF 1964 DOLLARS

Potential

Gap

Actual

1953 1955 1957 1959 1961 1963 1965 1967 1969 '70

fig. 11–1

Actual g.n.p. has not usually matched our productive potential, even when potential is defined (as here) as only 96 percent of full employment. (Source: Council of Economic Advisers.)

may have wasted as much as $50 billion per year through unemployment in the post–World War II recession years, such as 1958 and 1961. Over the 1955–1965 decade we wasted some $300–$500 billion in potential real output (at current prices)—or in terms of wasted man-power, the equivalent of some 20–30 million man-years of work.

Back in the Great Depression of the 1930s, the waste was a far greater proportion of our potential production. In 1933, for example, actual g.n.p. was less than two-thirds of potential, and many estimates indicate that as much as $200 billion of potential output was wasted through unemployment during the decade of the 1930s, compared to a total actual g.n.p. of less than $800 billion during the decade. Unemployment in 1932 and 1933 was between 20 and 30 percent of the total labor force, and many of the employed held only part-time jobs.

How Low Can Unemployment Be?

Figure 11–1 sets "high-level–employment" output as that attainable with 4 percent unemployment. But whether 3, 4, or 5 percent unemployment represents a reasonable goal is a hotly debated issue. Our aspiration levels vary with our achievements. During the early 1950s, when average unemployment fell to 3 percent or less, about 3 percent seemed a reasonable goal for stabilization policy to shoot at. With the discouraging results of the late 1950s and early

1960s, many people lowered their aspirations to 4 percent, or even to 5 percent, unemployment.

Clearly there is some unavoidable minimum of unemployment. In a large, free economy like ours, hundreds of thousands of people are always on the move. In 1969, for example, some 12 million people changed jobs. It takes time for people to move from one job to another. In seasonal industries such as agriculture and construction, there is certainly going to be some unemployment in the slack season. Such unemployment is often called "frictional" unemployment. Moreover, there are always some essentially "unemployable" people looking for jobs—individuals with very poor health, with very low mental capacities, with no training, and the like. Still others are potentially employable, but their skills and locations are badly out of line with job openings or their wage demands are unrealistically high for what they can offer; these are the "structurally" unemployed. There is some level of aggregate demand that will put all such individuals to work in short order, but it is very high indeed, and it would surely generate widespread inflation before it provided jobs for all.

How large is the unavoidable minimum unemployment? There is no precise answer, because clearly with enough pressure of aggregate demand (as in World War II) unemployment can be reduced to almost zero, and indeed millions of new workers can be drawn into the labor force by high wages. But such policies clearly involve massive inflationary pressures. Careful empirical studies suggest that perhaps 2–3 percent of the labor force may be taken as a reasonable approximation of frictional unemployment plus job seekers who are, for practical purposes, unemployable under normal conditions.[1]

Other nations set us a goal to shoot at. In all of Western Europe, since World War II unemployment rates have been much lower than we have achieved, in most cases varying between 1 and 2 percent of the labor force over the past decade. But these results have generally been achieved at the cost of somewhat higher inflation than in the United States.

One last general observation on the problem of unemployment rates. If actual unemployment is 6 percent and the frictional minimum is estimated at 3 percent, can we conclude that the economy is operating at 3 percent below capacity? No. More probably, output is 6–8 percent below the system's capacity. The reason is partly that with substantial unemployment many workers are on a part-time basis. As demand rises and unemployment falls, these people shift to a full-employment basis, so the number of man-hours of work rises more rapidly than the number of employed. More important, with widespread unemployment many persons drop out of the labor force because they become too discouraged to continue looking for jobs. When aggregate demand and employment opportunities rise, many, especially women and "marginal" workers, return to the labor force. Thus, in unemployment periods there is always a reservoir of potential labor force entrants and of "hidden unemployment," made up of workers who are not reported as unemployed in the statistics because they are not actually seeking work.

The Human Costs of Unemployment

Fewer than 15 percent of today's 200 million people were adults in 1930 at the onset of the Great Depression of the 1930s. Thus, most of today's Americans have no memory of that period and its devastating impact on human morale and well-being, as well as on the aggregate production of the economy.

Figure 11–2 presents the cold statistics. Unemployment reached a peak of approximately 25 percent of the labor force in 1933, and it averaged between 15 and 20 percent for the entire decade of the thirties. Moreover, it must be remembered that many of the people employed were on a part-time basis at drastically reduced rates of pay, and there were millions of "hidden unemployed" barely eking out an existence in agriculture. At the bottom of the depression surely not more than two-thirds of the total labor force had regular full-time jobs, and some estimates put the figure nearer one-half.

But statistics are bloodless things. Listen to the testimony given by an economist before a Senate subcommittee investigating unemployment in 1932: [2]

Mr. deSchweinitz: When I appeared before the subcommittee last December, I stated that there were 233,000 persons out of work in Philadelphia. . . . There are now 298,000 persons out of work. . . . In December I told you that 43,000 families were receiving relief, today 55,000 families are receiving relief.

In December, our per family grant was $4.39 per week per family. It is now $4.23 per family. Of this $4.23 per family, about $3.93 is an allowance for food. . . .

I want to tell you about an experience we had here in Philadelphia when our private funds were exhausted and before public funds became available. . . . There was a period of about eleven days when many families received nothing from us. We have received reports from workers as to how these families managed. The material I am about to give you is typical, although it is based on a small sample.

One woman said she borrowed 50¢ from a friend and bought stale bread for 3½¢ per loaf, and that is all they had for eleven days except for one or two meals.

One woman went along the docks and picked up

---

[1]See, e.g., *The Extent and Nature of Frictional Unemployment,* published by the Joint Economic Committee of Congress in 1959, and *Economic Report of the President,* January, 1970, pp. 147–56.

[2]*Federal Cooperation in Unemployment Relief,* Hearings before Senate Committee on Manufactures, 72nd Cong., 1st sess., 1932, pp. 20–26. This testimony and that which follows is reproduced more completely in D. A. Shannon, *The Great Depression* (Englewood Cliffs, N.J.:Prentice-Hall, Inc., 1960).

UNEMPLOYMENT AS A PERCENTAGE OF CIVILIAN LABOR FORCE

PERCENTAGE OF CIVILIAN LABOR FORCE UNEMPLOYED

fig. 11–2

Unemployment soars in depressions, and even in recessions. What is a reasonable minimum level of unemployment for us to shoot at? (Source: U.S. Department of Labor.)

vegetables that fell from the wagons. Sometimes the fish vendors gave her fish at the end of the day. On two different occasions this family was without food for a day and a half.

The gas company was careful not to turn off gas in the homes of a great many of these families, so in some instances food could be cooked.

Another family did not have food for two days. Then the husband went out and gathered dandelions and the family lived on them.

I should also like to say that when we talk to people to ask about unemployment, they say, "Well, people manage to get along somehow or other, don't they? You do not have very many people who really drop dead of starvation." That is true. Actually, death from starvation is not a frequent occurrence.... They live on inadequacies, and because they live on inadequacies the thing does not become dramatic, and we do not hear about it. Yet the cost in human suffering is just as great as if they starved to death overnight.

Now listen to the testimony of another witness, given before a House subcommittee at about the same time.[3]

Mr. Ameringer: The last thing I saw on the night I left Seattle was numbers of women searching for scraps of food in the refuse piles of the principal markets of that city. A number of Montana citizens told me of thousands of bushels of wheat left in the field uncut on account of its low price that hardly paid for the harvesting. In Oregon I saw thousands of bushels of apples rotting in the orchards. Only absolutely flawless apples were still salable, at from 40–50¢ a box containing 200 apples. At the same time, there are millions of children who, on account of the poverty of their parents, will not eat one apple this winter.

While I was in Oregon, the *Portland Oregonian*

[3]*Unemployment in the United States*, Hearings before House Committee on Labor, 72nd Cong., 1st sess., 1932, pp. 98–99.

bemoaned the fact that thousands of ewes were killed by the sheep raisers because they did not bring enough in the market to pay the freight on them. And while Oregon sheep raisers fed mutton to the buzzards, I saw men picking meat scraps in the garbage cans in the cities of New York and Chicago. I talked to one man in a restaurant in Chicago. He told me of his experience in raising sheep. He said that he had killed 3,000 sheep this fall and thrown them down the canyon because it cost $1.10 to ship a sheep, and then he would get less than a dollar for it. He said he could not afford to feed the sheep, and he would not let them starve, so he just cut their throats and threw them down the canyon.

The roads of the West and Southwest teem with hungry hitchhikers. The campfires of homeless are seen along every railroad track.... Between Clarksville and Russellville, Arkansas, I picked up a family. The woman was hugging a dead chicken under a ragged coat. When I asked her where she had procured the fowl, first she told me she had found it dead in the road, and then added in grim humor, "They promised me a chicken in the pot, and now I got mine."

Most American families were not in such desperate straits. But fear was everywhere. In every American city, hordes of families were evicted from their apartments, often moving in with other families until ten or twelve people would be sharing three or four rooms, often shivering through the winter in heatless houses because they could afford little or no coal. Many fought to maintain respectability. Clerks put pieces of cardboard inside their shoes before setting out on endless job-hunting rounds; previously well-to-do families wiped out in the stock-market crash struggled back to get poorer jobs and to use part of their drastically reduced incomes to pay on their debts. But for many, long-continued failure wiped out self-respect and the will to try. Parks were sprinkled with desolate men in shabby clothes, merely sitting. Many more of them remained home.

John Steinbeck pictured the plight of thousands of migrant workers in his *The Grapes of Wrath*, a story of the bitter despair as families, pushed off their land by poverty and the great dust storms of the 1930s, wandered through the Southwest, looking for work anywhere, scraping by on almost nothing in their battered jalopies, homeless and often pursued by the police and "respectable" citizens in communities that did not want them.

These are the costs of massive unemployment and depression. Such conditions are hard to imagine today. Perhaps another great depression will never come; let us hope not.

Is such evidence on the human cost of unemployment relevant today? Today, unemployment is far more modest even at the depths of our postwar recessions. Nationwide unemployment insurance provides temporary financial support for regular workers laid off. Government relief payments help others. Many unions have obtained private unemployment-compensation plans to supplement government benefits. The impact of modern unemployment is far less devastating now than during the desperate days of the 1930s.

But at best, these unemployment-insurance plans provide only a fraction of regular wage incomes, and all have time limits, often as short as thirteen weeks. Moreover, to receive unemployment-insurance benefits, one must have held a regular job, and hundreds of thousands of unemployed persons fail to qualify on this test. In the depressed areas—for example in the soft-coal fields of the Appalachians—many workers have been out of jobs for years. Discouragement, and then despair, take over when no job is available month after month.

Who are the unemployed in prosperous times or in moderate recessions? Table 11–1 gives the answer for 1969, a highly prosperous year, when unemployment averaged only 3.5 percent.

Note that about 30 percent of the unemployed in 1969 were teen-agers, a ratio that

table 11-1 Unemployment, 1969*	Number Unemployed (Thousands)	Rate (Percent)
Total unemployment*	2831	3.5
Age:		
Teen-agers, 16-19	853	12.2
Adults, 20-44	1370	3.2
Adults, 45 and over	608	2.0
Race:		
White	2261	3.1
Negro and other races	570	6.4
Type of worker:		
Blue-collar	1154	3.9
White-collar	780	4.7
Sex:		
Male	1403	2.8
Female	1428	4.7
Marital status:		
Married	1271	2.8
Other	1560	6.5

*Data will not necessarily add to totals because of rounding. Source: U.S. Department of Labor.

rose sharply during the summer months, although many teen-agers were only seeking part-time jobs. They had far the highest unemployment rate of any age group; compare the 3.2 and 2.0 percent rates for adults. Minority groups (mainly Negroes) consistently showed unemployment rates about twice those for whites; unemployment averaged nearly 25 percent for minority-group teen-agers.

Why were the unemployed out of work? Table 11–2 provides one set of answers. Note that only about one-third had actually lost their last job; all the rest had either quit voluntarily or, more important, had just recently begun looking for a job. Rapid technological change, shifting consumer demands, and seasonal patterns in some industries all lead to continually shifting job patterns. Nearly 10 million people were unemployed at some time during the year, though the average was only 2.8 million.

Variations in unemployment are thus closely

table 11-2

Reasons for Unemployment, 1969*

Reason	Number Unemployed (Thousands)	Percentage Distribution
Total unemployment*	2,831	100
Lost last job	1,017	36
Voluntarily left last job	436	15
Reentered labor force	965	34
Entered labor force, first time	413	15

*Details may not add to totals because of rounding. Source: U.S. Department of Labor.

linked to variations in its duration. During prosperous 1969, the average unemployed worker was out of work for only about 4½ weeks. But in recessions this period rises sharply—for example to 9 weeks in 1958 and in 1960–1961. Figure 11–3 shows this close relationship.

These data say that unemployment is relatively short-lived for most workers; for most it reflects the need to adjust to a constantly shifting economic scene, so long as serious recessions are avoided. But it is of little solace to the unemployed worker that national unemployment totals only 4 percent of the labor force if he has no job and little hope of finding one.

Few years have as little unemployment as the peak-prosperity year 1969. Who lose their jobs first when recessions come? In most cases the uneducated, the unskilled, the young, the inexperienced—the least-productive and those with the least seniority. Employers naturally want to hold on to experienced, highly skilled workers who will be most valuable when demand revives, and union contracts further protect the workers with the most seniority. Thus, the hardest-hit in recession usually are teen-agers, blue-collar workers, and low-skill minority-group workers.

But there are exceptions. The slump of early 1970 reflected large cutbacks in military and aerospace spending. Thus unemployment rose rapidly among workers in those industries. High-skill technicians, engineers, and the like, joined the ranks of the unemployed (even men with ten and twenty years of experience and $20,000 salaries), and they lined up with the clerks and blue-collar workers for government unemployment benefits.

The Costs of Inflation

Nearly everyone agrees that big inflations and deflations are bad. But the case for stable prices is less obvious and clear-cut than that for high employment of human and other resources. Figure 11–4 presents the evidence on the price level.

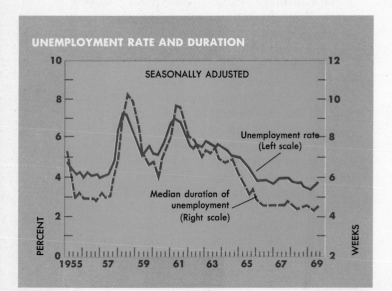

fig. 11–3

Mounting unemployment usually reflects longer out-of-work periods as much as newly unemployed workers. (Sources: U.S. Department of Labor and Council of Economic Advisers.)

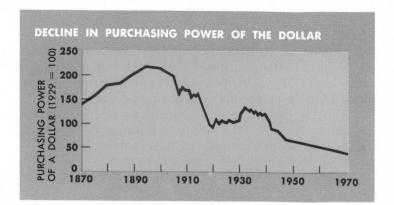

fig. 11–4

Inflation has repeatedly eroded the value of the dollar, with the biggest price increases coming during and after wars. (Source: U.S. Department of Labor.)

What Is Inflation?

Inflation is often discussed with more heat than light. One problem is definitions. When you use the word inflation to mean a rise in the price level and your neighbor uses it to mean more money printed by those irresponsible fellows in Washington, it's no wonder you don't succeed in talking much sense about it—especially if neither of you bothers to make clear how you are defining inflation. Socrates said, "If you want to argue with me, first define your terms." And he was right. There are several common definitions of inflation, so one must be clear about which he is using.

"Inflation," in this book, means a rise in the price level of all currently produced goods and services— that is, a rise in the average price of all goods and services in the gross national product. This definition is used because it is simple and direct, because we have a readily available index to measure it (the g.n.p. deflator), and because it is close to what the man in the street means when he talks about inflation.

But it is important to recognize what is *not* included in this definition. Higher prices in the stock market aren't included. Neither are higher wages. Neither is more money and credit. All these things are usually found when inflation, as we define it, occurs; but when we say inflation we shall mean the rise in g.n.p. prices per se.[4]

[4]Some people prefer more complex definitions—for example, one that says inflation is an overextension of credit. Such definitions often raise serious problems of measurement and clear analytical use; what is "overextension"? But the main point is to decide just what definition one is using, and then to stick to it.

Using this definition, who gains and who loses when price levels move up (or down)? Does inflation ruin everybody except a few sly profiteers? Is deflation a fine thing for creditors, who can then collect dollars that have stepped-up buying power? Broadly speaking, the economic impact of inflation can be analyzed by asking two questions: (1) Does inflation increase or decrease the total real g.n.p. of the economy? (2) How does it affect the distribution of the g.n.p. among various groups in the economy?

Hyperinflation

When inflation runs away and reaches astronomical proportions, it is often called "hyperinflation." Every American schoolboy learns about the great hyperinflation in Germany following World War I. The government had to make huge expenditures (including heavy reparation payments to the victorious Allies), and it chose to finance its expenditures by printing paper money rather than by drastically increasing taxes. This new money increased total spending and sped the upward price spiral, for the war-torn German economy could not rapidly increase its output of goods. As prices spiraled, so did government costs, requiring further recourse to the printing presses. People receiving money spent it as fast as they could, to convert it into goods before it fell further in value. Prices, government spending, and new money soared to fantastic levels.

Near the peak of the inflation in 1923, a box of matches sold for more than 6 billion marks, the total amount of German marks in circulation ten years before. Before the war all mortgages in Germany totaled 40 billion marks; at the peak of the inflation 40 billion marks were worth only a few cents. Things happened as in a feverish dream. Life insurance policies, when paid out, would not buy a handkerchief. No one wanted to lend, everyone wanted to borrow, because it would soon be so easy to pay off today's debts as the value of money fell. Interest rates rose to 900 percent, and even then lenders were often not protected. Wages, as well as prices, came to be adjusted every day, sometimes several times a day. Savings invested in fixed-income securities were completely wiped out, and much of the middle class became paupers while skillful speculators became fabulously wealthy. Prices rose so fast that productive activity was disrupted and real g.n.p. was reduced. The distribution of income and wealth was cruelly and arbitrarily altered.

Inflation can be a terrible thing. It *was* in the great German hyperinflation, and in the other great hyperinflations the world has known. Happily, there have not been many hyperinflations, and interestingly two common elements have linked all of them. They were associated with war or its aftermath, especially in defeated countries. And they were financed by great issues of new money to cover huge government expenditures. The big inflations in the United States (none of such virulence as the great hyperinflations) have also been associated with our wars and the creation of large amounts of new money.

Moderate (Creeping) Inflation

What are the effects of moderate, or "creeping," inflation of only a few percent a year—the kind of inflation most major industrialized nations have faced since World War II? It is this kind of inflation that some economists say we must accept if we are to achieve continuing high-level employment.

One introductory fact. You often hear the statement that we can't have "just a little" inflation, that inflation inevitably builds up and runs away, once started. This assertion is just wrong, on the evidence of history. Both here and in other nations, there have been many periods of

moderate or creeping inflation followed by stable or moderately declining prices; very few inflations have turned into hyperinflation. Most economists agree that inflation has some self-feeding elements, mainly the expectation that price increases will accelerate. But they need not do so.[5]

With this background, let us ask our two basic questions: (1) Do moderate inflations increase or decrease real g.n.p.? (2) How do they affect the distribution of income and wealth?

Effects on Total Output

Short-run Effects. May moderate inflation, at least temporarily, stimulate either a larger or smaller real g.n.p.? Consider first the possibility of stimulating an **increase** in output and employment.

First, we need to go back to some fundamentals. We can get more output only by (a) using the productive resources we have more effectively, or (b) increasing the quantity or quality of those productive resources. If there is already full employment of men and machines and we are using fully our technological and managerial know-how, there is nothing inflation can do in the short run to increase total output and employment.

But if we have unemployed resources, it is possible to increase real g.n.p. merely by putting them back to work. And increasing aggregate demand in an underemployed economy can put resources back to work. But we must separate the effects of increased aggregate demand from those of inflation, even though they may occur together. If we raised aggregate demand **without** bidding up prices, this would increase real g.n.p. (Look back at Figure 6–1.) Will inflation along with rising demand help? It may, **if** selling prices rise faster than the costs of businesses, since that will generally lead businessmen to increase investment and hire more

[5]Many of the less-developed countries have had repeated periods of rapid, though not hyper-, inflation. Brazil, for example, has had inflations varying between 50 and 100 percent annually over many decades. These have often been disruptive, but they have not escalated into hyperinflations, partly because of the special international positions of such countries. See Part Six.

workers. But wages and other costs may not lag in inflation, and the effects of inflation per se, as distinct from rising aggregate demand are problematical. Sometimes wages do lag behind rising prices in inflation, sometimes they don't. On this lag, history provides a mixed picture, as we shall see below.

May inflation **reduce** real output? In the big hyperinflations, it clearly did. Resources were diverted to speculation and spending money fast before it depreciated, instead of producing needed goods and services—though this effect apparently was not a serious drain on output until late in the inflations. But even in more modest inflations, speculative price increases are apt to set the stage for a collapse. The more rampant the speculation becomes, the more likely inflation is to lead to an economic bust. Such speculative spirals occur in commodity prices, the stock market, the real-estate market. But it is important to understand that there is nothing in higher prices per se that reduces real output. And in most cases, rising prices and increasing real output have come together, not the converse.

Conclusion: In the short run, inflation may help to stimulate more output in times of unemployment, but this effect is uncertain. In full-employment periods, it can do little good and may do harm by helping to precipitate a recession. Either way, remember it's the impact on the employment of real resources—on jobs and real output—that counts.

Long-run Effects—Growth. There is one big difference in the possible long-run effects of inflation. Then the quantity and quality of productive resources can be increased significantly —through growth in the labor force and technological progress (where inflation is unlikely to be an important factor), and through capital accumulation (where inflation may have a substantial effect). If inflation slows the rate of saving and capital accumulation, it reduces real output over the long run. If it increases the rate of saving and capital accumulation, it speeds economic growth.

What is the evidence? Mixed, and subject to lots of argument. But the evidence seems reasonably clear on three points: First, hyperinflation cuts down on saving and productive investment. Second, moderate, or creeping, inflation has little effect one way or the other on the level of saving and investment. Third, the critical relationship in determining the effect of moderate inflation on growth is that between selling prices and wages.

This third point is theoretical. With mixed historical evidence on whether inflations go together with fast or slow growth, we must look for a model that tells us under what conditions inflation will increase capital formation and when it will not. The theory says that if selling prices rise faster than wage costs, profits expand and more investment is induced. But if costs rise as fast as selling prices, inflation provides little inducement to more saving and investment.

Which relationship has predominated? Over the past several centuries, wages have frequently lagged behind rising prices, and inflation seems then to have stimulated economic growth. But in creeping inflation of the 1950s in the United States, wage costs rose faster than selling prices, reversing the traditional stimulus to growth. We need to look at the facts in each case individually.

Inflation and the Distribution of Income

In a full-employment economy, inflation cannot increase total output. But it can change who gets the output. Think of real g.n.p. as a big pie. Under full employment, inflation can't increase the size of the pie (except possibly over a long period through speeding growth), but it can affect the size of the pieces that different people get.

First, a very fundamental fact. Given the size of the real g.n.p. pie, inflation does not make people in the aggregate either better or worse off economically. If someone gets a smaller piece, someone else is bound to get a bigger one. Moving up from a $900 billion to a trillion dollar g.n.p. merely through higher prices does not make the economy either better or worse off in terms of real income, if the same level of employment prevails before and after.

The central principle about how inflation affects the distribution of income for a given real g.n.p. is this: Those whose incomes rise faster than the average get bigger pieces of the real g.n.p., and those whose incomes rise slower or not at all get smaller pieces. In a full-employment economy, inflation usually means that prices rise at about the same rate as money g.n.p. The man whose income just keeps pace with rising prices will keep about the same-sized piece of pie. The man whose income lags behind rising prices will get a smaller piece. Those whose incomes rise faster than prices will get a bigger share of the pie.[6]

Remember, however, that in an **underemployed** economy, real g.n.p. may expand with inflation. Then everybody's real income may rise. But the principle controlling the **distribution** of real income is the same: Those whose incomes rise fastest relative to the prices they pay increase their **percentage** shares of the national output; and those whose incomes rise slower relative to the prices they pay get smaller **percentage** shares. Since with unemployment the total pie may be growing, nobody has to lose just because someone else gains. And most people do find their real incomes improving when inflation comes in periods of rising total output, except for those people on fixed or badly lagging incomes.

The Importance of Anticipations. Whose income lags and whose leads depends heavily on how accurately different people anticipate the amount of inflation ahead. If everyone expected prices to rise 10 percent annually, everyone would presumably build this anticipation into his actions. Unions would demand 10 percent higher wages to avoid losing real purchasing power. So would lenders on interest rates they charged on loans. So would businessmen pricing their products, recognizing that

[6]To be strictly accurate, the principle must be modified to recognize that different people buy different things whose prices may rise faster or slower than the average. So how an *individual* is affected depends on the increase in *his income relative to the increase in the prices of the goods he buys,* not relative to some general price index. But the simple proposition in the text provides a good first approximation in a full-employment economy.

costs would rise that much. At the same time, businesses would be more willing to give big wage boosts, borrowers would pay higher interest rates, and the like. In principle, if there were no market barriers (such as long-term wage or interest-rate agreements), all prices would be adjusted upward by 10 percent in accordance with inflation anticipations, and relative income shares would remain unchanged. Everyone's money income and all prices would go up 10 percent; real incomes would be unchanged. By the same reasoning, inflation would have **no** effect on real output and employment, since all prices, costs, and asset values would increase proportionately.

In fact, of course, inflation anticipations are far from perfect. The uneducated, the poor, the unsophisticated are likely to be badly informed, compared to the educated and well-to-do. In addition, even with equally accurate anticipations different groups would be affected differently, because not all of them have the same ability to adjust. For example, long-term bondholders are stuck with a real loss on their fixed-interest bonds. So are workers covered by long-term wage contracts and many others with fixed commitments. However, over time these barriers to flexibility vanish.

These general principles are cold and abstract. What do they mean for four important income groups?

Fixed Incomes. At one end of the spectrum is the fixed-income receiver—for example, a widow living on a fixed pension or on interest on government bonds. If the price level goes up, her purchasing power goes down whether total output increases or not. She gets the same number of dollars and each dollar will buy less. Retired people appear to suffer most in mild inflations, though others on fixed incomes are in a similar position.

Salaries. In inflation, most salaries get adjusted upward, but often with a substantial lag. Temporarily, the stenographer or the schoolteacher is in the same position as the fixed-income widow, but not permanently. This is true of most salary earners. Their incomes lag, to varying degrees.

Wages. It is commonly said that wage earners lose buying power when prices go up, because wages lag behind rising prices. But today this statement is an uncertain one, for two reasons. First, even when wage rates lag behind rising prices, the real income of labor as a group often rises in inflation, because higher prices come with better business conditions that produce more jobs and higher total real wages even if money wage rates lag. Second, since the 1930s organized labor has grown much stronger, and wage rates have often not lagged behind rising prices.

Businessmen and Stockholders. Traditionally, businesses and their stockholders have gained from inflation (as long as the inflation is relatively mild), and suffered in deflation. Generally, profits have risen in inflation because businesses add a standard percentage markup on their rising costs in setting prices, and they sell more units in prosperous, rising-price periods. When wages and materials costs lag behind rising selling prices, business profits rise still faster. **But** if wages rise faster than prices in inflation, business profits may be squeezed (at least relatively and possibly absolutely), rather than enlarged. This was true in 1969–70.

Figure 11–5 shows the shifting shares of the national income over the past thirty years. The gradual rise in the wage and salary share during the postwar inflationary years is clear, and wage rates per hour or year have risen much faster than the return per unit of capital invested—the reverse of the standard statement that inflation cuts real wages. But remember two warnings in looking at the chart: First, it doesn't necessarily follow that inflation **caused** these income shifts, just because they occurred during an inflationary period. Second, remember that **all** the income shares rose substantially in real terms. Real g.n.p. more than doubled over the quarter century, so even the unincorporated business sector had a larger real income in 1970 than in 1939.

Figure 11–5 tells another story, too, and a very important one. Over the past quarter century of persistent inflation, most major income groups have managed to protect their positions surprisingly well. Wages, salaries, profits, and most other incomes have been moved up **roughly** apace. Most participants in the market, as workers or businessmen, have managed to put up their prices fast enough not to fall far behind, if at all. In perspective, the economy may have shifted substantially to an inflation-adjusting basis for creeping inflation. Even the traditional laggards have managed to shorten the lag. Retired people have brought pressure to increase federal old-age benefits, and they are converting their investments from fixed-income bonds into stocks. Universities are rais-

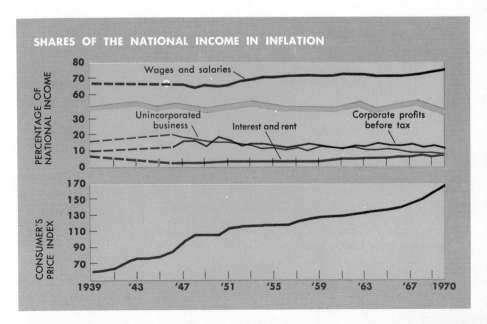

fig. 11–5

The shares of major groups in the national income have been reasonably stable over three decades of intermittent inflation, with a gradual rise in the share of wages and salaries. (Source: U.S. Department of Commerce.)

ing tuition and getting higher legislative appropriations to raise salaries. Governments are paying their workers more. It is easy to overstate this inflation anticipation and adjustment process as a protection against inflation, but equally misleading to overlook it.

Inflation and the Distribution of Wealth

The effect of inflation on the distribution of current income is complex. But its effect on the distribution of wealth is clear. Inflation transfers real purchasing power from creditors to debtors.[7]

The effect of inflation on money holdings is easiest to see. The saver who holds $1,000 in his safe-deposit box for a year while prices rise 5 percent has effectively lost 5 percent of his $1,000. Even if he has it invested in a safe security, like government bonds, he is robbed by the inflation. A hundred dollars invested in 3 percent government bonds in 1939 had a purchasing power of only $80 ten years later, even when about $40 of interest was added to the $100 originally invested. Or, the thrifty couple who save up enough to purchase a comfortable life-time annuity on retirement find that the generous figure of $2,000 a year planned in 1939 is not enough to keep them above destitution in 1970, with prices nearly three times as high.

Don't be tricked into thinking that the loss doesn't amount to much as long as inflation only creeps. Table 11–3 shows how long it takes for a dollar to lose half its purchasing power at different small rates of inflation. At only 5 percent inflation a year, half its purchasing power is gone in fourteen years.

If we add up all the assets with fixed dollar values (money, bonds, insurance policies, and so on) and calculate the loss in their purchasing power due to inflation between 1939 and 1970, the loss is nearly a trillion dollars. Of course this huge loss of purchasing power did not represent

table 11-3

Half-Life of a Dollar with Inflation

Annual Rate of Inflation	Years To Lose Half of Purchasing Power
1 percent	70
2 " "	35
3 " "	23
4 " "	18
5 " "	14

a loss of real wealth to society as a whole, since real income and wealth were not reduced correspondingly. However, it did reflect a massive shift of buying power over society's current output and accumulated assets from net monetary creditors to others whose buying power rose with the inflation.

If everyone could anticipate inflation accurately, most people could adjust their asset holdings to avoid this redistribution of wealth. For example, lenders would charge high enough interest rates to take into account the expected loss of purchasing power per dollar over the life of the loan. But in fact, many inflations are partially or completely unanticipated. And many people, especially the poor and uneducated, don't understand the process well enough to protect themselves even if they do think inflation is coming. The uneducated laborer can hardly take his life savings of $1,000 and go into the stock market instead of holding money or government bonds. If he is heavily in debt to buy a house, actually inflation may help him rather than harm him; but this is largely an incidental effect, not one he plans as an inflation hedge.

International Effects of Inflation

If costs and prices in any country rise faster than elsewhere, that country will have increasing trouble meeting competition in international markets. Conversely, as its own incomes rise, its people will import more from abroad.

[7]More accurately, we must calculate the *net* debtor or creditor position of each economic unit. For example, if Family A has $10,000 of money and bonds but owes $6,000, it is a "net monetary creditor" by $4,000.

Thus, it will end up with an international "balance-of-payments deficit"—it will owe more abroad than it has to collect from foreigners. For any nation heavily dependent on foreign trade (for example, most of Western Europe and many of the less-developed countries), this fact constitutes a major barrier against accepting more rapid inflation than that which prevails in other countries with which that nation trades. We postpone detailed consideration of the international aspects of inflation to Part Six, but it is important to recognize that inflation may involve major international costs to any country whose prices rise faster than those abroad.

How Bad Is Inflation?

How bad is inflation, putting all the above effects together? Try the following exercise to test how well you understand the central principles. Evaluate this statement by a well-known senator: "Inflation reduces the buying power of every dollar, and impoverishes the American people. It is a national disaster!"

There is no doubt about the first half of the first sentence. It is true by definition—by our definition, at least. We defined inflation as rising prices, and higher prices do reduce the purchasing power of any dollar. But the second half of the sentence needs a closer look, in spite of its apparent plausibility. Does it follow from the acceptable first portion that inflation impoverishes the American people? A reasonable first step is to look at history.

Consider the period from 1960 to 1970 as an example. Over the decade there was considerable inflation. The Bureau of Labor Statistics consumer price index rose from 100 to 130, using 1960 as the base year. In 1960, national income was $415 billion; in 1970, it was about $800 billion. If we adjust the 1970 national-income figure downward to eliminate the effect of inflation, we get a 1970 real income of $615 billion in 1960 prices. This was an increase of $200 billion (almost 50 percent) over the 1960 real income. Even allowing for possible error in the B.L.S. price index, it is hard to see how this inflation impoverished the American people as

a whole. Although one dollar would buy less in 1970 than in 1960, the increase in money incomes received far outdistanced the loss caused by rising prices. History shows clearly that inflation does not necessarily impoverish the American people.

To return to a first principle, the goods and services produced in an economy determine the national standard of living. Higher prices mean that the purchasing power of any given national money income is less than when prices are low. But what happens to real output produced and consumed is the fundamental test.

However, this historical evidence doesn't prove that inflation did no harm. Real output might have risen even more with a stable price level. Certainly history doesn't prove that inflation caused the increase in output, so we are not justified in giving inflation credit for the extra goods and services produced. Moreover, even though the public as a whole (and per capita) clearly had far more real income in 1970 than in 1960, many people were harmed by the inflation—people whose money incomes were relatively fixed and who were net monetary creditors. Inflation, as always, altered the distribution of the national output and wealth, so that even with a larger pie to divide some pieces were smaller in 1970 than in 1960.

Putting the whole picture together, was the senator right—is inflation a national disaster? It hardly looks that way for the 1960s, though some other examples could make inflation look a lot worse. In summary, in analyzing any inflation, first look at the impact on real output per capita as the best single guide to what happened to national economic well-being. Second, ask what happened to the distribution of real income, and decide whether the redistribution was good or bad. Third, ask what happened to the distribution of wealth—the differential impact on net monetary debtors and creditors, and the position of savers as against spenders. Last, look to the future, to see whether the inflationary developments have set the stage for an economic downturn or have slowed the rate of economic growth and whether international balance-of-payments problems threaten.

The Trade-off between High Employment and Stable Prices

High employment and a reasonably stable price level are both desirable social goals. Put the other way, the costs of both unemployment and inflation are real and substantial. But which goal should take precedence if we must choose —avoiding unemployment or avoiding inflation? Is reducing unemployment a little worth accepting a little more inflation?

Review

CONCEPTS TO REMEMBER

This chapter adds some important new analytical concepts to those developed in earlier chapters. Be sure that you understand especially the following:

unemployment	inflation
frictional unemployment	hyperinflation
structural unemployment	trade-offs between policy goals
bottlenecks	

FOR ANALYSIS AND DISCUSSION

1. If we face a choice between reducing unemployment further or avoiding inflation, which goal should have top priority? Why?
2. "The cost of unemployment is wasted resources, that of inflation merely a redistribution of income and wealth." Is this quotation correct? Is it a convincing argument for generally preferring high employment over stable prices in case of a conflict?
3. "So long as unemployment stays at moderate levels (say under 5 percent), it does not justify strong aggregate demand measures that risk inflation, since most of the unemployed are either loafers or temporarily unemployable because they lack the skills to fill the jobs that more aggregate demand would open up. Thus, the case for more demand to fight unemployment is a weak one." Analyze this argument.
4. "The American public as a whole is economically worse off today than in 1960 in spite of the apparent huge rise in national income, because inflation has eaten away more than the nominal increase in total income." True or false? Check the facts for yourself, using *Economic Indicators,* or the *Economic Report of the President.*
5. Suppose three classes of individuals constitute the total population of an economy: (1) Wealthy, high-income individuals who live entirely on income from their bond coupons; (2) low-income wage and salary earners; and (3) businessmen who employ the workers and live on the profits they make. Analyze the likely effects of an inflation on the three income groups in this economy. Who, if anybody, is hurt by the inflation? Who, if anybody, is helped by it? State clearly any assumptions you make in your analysis.
6. Who is really hurt by inflation, and who gains from it—when inflation is only a few percent a year? What is the effect on you?

twelve

Money, Financial Institutions, and the Federal Reserve

Without money, our complex exchange economy would grind to a halt. Without financial intermediaries like banks, insurance companies, and savings and loan associations to link savers and investors, the circular flow of income would stagnate. Thus, regulation of the supply of money and of the financial intermediaries provides a major channel for government control of aggregate demand. This chapter explains how our monetary and banking system works. Chapter 13 focuses on monetary policy—on how the monetary authorities can help us achieve stable economic growth without unemployment or inflation.

Money and Near-Monies

Think for a minute about what life would be like under a barter economy. Suppose you have a pig. But what you really want is a spool of thread, two new shirts, a movie, and a newspaper. You hear that B down the road has made some shirts. But unless B happens to want some pork chops, you're still out of luck. Your neighbor, C, wants a pig, but he has only lumber to trade. If you're lucky, you may be able to get lumber from C and swap that to B for shirts. But it's going to take some fancy haggling to work out a fair trade with such indivisible products, even if you all have a basic desire to swap. But with money as a medium of exchange and as a standard unit for quoting exchange prices, it's easy to avoid this kind of difficulty. Money is a universally accepted unit of purchasing power, freely spendable and easy to store if you want to postpone spending your income.

When you hear the word money, you think of

149

coins and paper bills. But for hundreds of years cattle served as money in the ancient world. In the late Roman Empire, small, square pieces of leather were used. Two hundred years ago, hides and wampum beads served as money in North America. Only recently has the world widely adopted the coins and paper notes that we now use; and today we are moving away from them to bank checks except for small transactions. Computer entries may be next. Money cannot be defined merely in terms of the substances that we use for it at any time.

A useful definition of money must be based on what money does, not on what it looks like. Actually, around 80 percent of all payments in the United States today are made by bank checks, only about 20 percent by currency (i.e., coins and paper money). We have become so accustomed to using bank checks as money that for practical purposes payment by check is the equivalent of payment by currency, even though the check is a "credit" instrument that is good only if the bank will pay the sum indicated.

Money, therefore, is defined here as the total of currency and bank checking deposits, since these two constitute the nation's generally acceptable media of payment. The top part of Table 12–1 shows the amount of these two major types of money in existence in 1970. It is very important to note that the bulk of our money is bank checking deposits, not currency, and that the great bulk of our payments are made by bank checks.

Only a thin line separates actual money from a variety of "near-monies," shown in the bottom half of the table, that are readily convertible into currency or checking deposits. Bank savings deposits, savings and loan shares, short-term U.S. government securities, U.S. savings bonds redeemable on the owner's demand, and the cash surrender value of insurance policies

table 12-1

Money and Near-Monies in the United States*

		In Billions
Money		$200
Currency	$ 47	
Checking deposits	159	
Important near-monies		723
Savings deposits	260	
Savings and loan shares	135	
Liquid U.S. government securities	170	
Insurance policies (cash value)	158	

* As of Jan. 1, 1970, Currency shown is that held by the public outside banks. Only government securities redeemable on demand or due within one year are included. Data from *Federal Reserve Bulletin* and *Life Insurance Fact Book.*

are probably the most important of these near-monies. But there are many more that are only a little less-easily convertible, including the great mass of longer-term government bonds.

Any of these near-monies serves one function of money reasonably well—that of a store of value. In one way, they are better than money, for the holder receives interest on most near-monies and none on money itself. Balanced against this, the near-money must be converted into actual money before it can be spent. This always involves some inconvenience or delay, and sometimes a risk that the near-money can be converted only at a loss—for example, when government securities must be sold before maturity. The factors that induce people and businesses to shift back and forth between money and near-monies often play an important role in determining how well the economic system works.

PART A: PRIVATE FINANCIAL INSTITUTIONS AND THE MONEY SUPPLY

Many kinds of private financial institutions have developed over the years to meet people's

changing needs. Some of these, such as savings and loan associations and insurance companies, receive long-term savings and channel them on into real investment in buildings, equipment, and the like. Others, such as the ordinary ("commercial") banks, serve as depositories for both currently used funds and longer-term savings.

Banks

There are now about 14,000 "commercial" banks in the United States, which accept both "savings" (or time) accounts and "checking" (or demand) accounts. The presumption is that savings accounts represent funds put in the bank for relatively long periods of time, while checking deposits are funds that you may want to use promptly. Thus banks generally feel freer to make long-term loans when their savings deposits go up than when their checking accounts increase. Technically, the banks can require depositors to give thirty or sixty days' notice before withdrawing savings deposits, but they almost never do. Actually, the dividing line between savings and checking deposits is not very sharp once the funds have been deposited in the bank. But there is one fundamental difference: Checking deposits are spendable money, since depositors can write checks on them. Depositors cannot write checks on savings deposits. A savings deposit can be spent only by withdrawing it in the form of hand-to-hand currency or by transferring it to a checking account.

Harking back to the circular-income-flow diagram in Figure 5–2, it's obvious that saved funds have to be matched by equal investment or government spending if money income is to continue to flow smoothly through the economy. Do the financial "intermediaries" succeed in connecting up savers with borrowers who will spend the savings back into the income stream? Sometimes they do, and sometimes they don't. Often the commercial banks actually increase or decrease the nation's money supply by their own actions, as we shall see below.

Other Financial Intermediaries

Financial middlemen have grown up to accommodate about every imaginable type of saver and borrower. Savings and loan associations are much like the savings departments of commercial banks; they draw mainly the savings of lower- and middle-income individuals, make mainly loans for home construction, and have grown enormously since World War II. Life-insurance companies are huge financial intermediaries. Total premiums paid on life-insurance policies and annuities in 1970 were over $20 billion, of which almost half represented savings—that is, accumulation of reserves by the insurance companies against future policyholder claims. Insurance companies use these funds in many ways—for government bonds, real-estate and business loans, and direct real-estate and business investments.[1] "Consumer finance," or "sales finance," companies get most of their funds secondhand from the banks and insurance companies, and then lend these funds directly to consumers at higher rates.

Federal, state, and local governments, though they're out of place in this section on private institutions, have become important financial middlemen between savers and investors. Whenever governments borrow from private savers to finance their expenditures, they're behaving much as private financial middlemen do, though the resulting forms of real investment are different—roads, schools, and space missiles, instead of factories and houses.

Direct Conversion of Savings

Often no financial intermediary is involved in the investment of savings. Every year, businesses reinvest billions of dollars of their own earnings in buildings, equipment, and other investment goods. Individuals buy new houses, which are considered a form of investment in the national income accounts. Individual savers also invest directly in new stocks and bonds, leading on toward real investment.

Financial Investment and Real Investment

In everyday conversation, the term "investment" is used in several different ways. Often it

[1] Total life insurance in force amounted to over $1.3 trillion.

means financial investment—that is, the process of taking funds and "investing" them in stocks, bonds, or the like. Sometimes it also means "investing" in real assets, like houses, as when you buy a new or used house. Each usage is justified by the dictionary, but it is important to remember that in the national income accounts of economics, harking back to Chapter 5, the term investment is defined specifically to mean real investment in currently produced capital goods—factories, machinery, housing, and the like. Thus, if you buy a government bond, this is often considered investment in the newspapers and everyday conversation, but it is not investment as the economist defines the term. In economics, if I use my savings to build a new house, that's real investment. But if I buy General Motors stock, that's only a financial transfer, which passes my savings on to the man who sells me the stock, or to General Motors if it's new stock issue. The question then is: What does that man, or General Motors, do with the funds? Only when the funds go on into real investment in newly produced capital goods or housing is there investment in the economic sense of the term.

The Supply of Currency (Government-Issued Money)

Most financial intermediaries take savers' funds and channel them on toward investment without increasing or decreasing the stock of money. But the commercial banks, unlike others, may actually increase or decrease the stock of money as they make and collect on loans and investments. In fact, the supply of money in our society depends largely on the lending activities of the commercial banks. Most of the rest of Part A of this chapter, therefore, is devoted to an analysis of the way commercial banks operate, and the way they may increase the nation's money stock through their lending activities.

But first, a brief section on the forces governing the supply of currency—government-issued coins and paper money. Currency makes up only about one-fifth of our money supply, and it

is used primarily to finance small transactions. As a practical matter, whenever you have a bank deposit account, you can readily get currency, merely by writing a check on your account. Indeed, this is the way currency is placed in the hands of the public. Although it is formally issued by the government (mainly the Federal Reserve Banks, to be explained presently), new currency is made available to the general public through providing it to the banks, which in turn pay it out to depositors on demand. In essence, the Federal Reserve always stands ready to print up enough currency to permit the public to get currency in exchange for any deposits it has.

Currency is comprised of Federal Reserve notes (paper money) and coins. Federal Reserve notes totaled $47 billion and coins $7 billion on January 1, 1970.[2] Note that paper money is nearly 90 percent of the total.

What Determines the Amount of Currency in Circulation?

What determines the amount of currency outstanding? The answer is, to repeat, the Federal Reserve always prints up enough money to give bank depositors all they want in exchange for their deposits. Thus, it is the stock of bank deposits that basically determines the size of the nation's money stock. Once the public has deposits, it can obtain more currency at will. If for some reason the public has more currency than it wants to hold, it simply puts the currency back in the bank and receives a deposit in exchange.

Thus, basically, it is the public's demand for currency that determines how many coins are minted and how much paper money is printed. Remember, though, that although many people think of currency as the main form of money, in fact it plays a minor role in our monetary system. People ordinarily keep about one-fifth of their total money holdings in the form of currency, and about four-fifths in demand deposits. Although this ratio varies from time to time, as a general rule the monetary authorities can pre-

[2]This total includes $7 billion of currency held in bank vaults, which was not included in Table 12–1.

dict that if households and businesses receive $100 of additional deposits, they will withdraw about $20 of it in the form of new currency.

The Supply of Bank Money: Checking Deposits

Commercial Banks and the "Creation" of Deposits

Currency is government money issued directly by the Treasury and the Federal Reserve. But the great bulk of our money is not issued by the government at all. Rather, it is provided by the commercial banks in their day-to-day business of making loans and "investments."[3] The distinguishing feature of modern commercial banking is its ability, through making loans and investments, to "monetize" the debts of others, and thereby in effect to create demand deposits (checking accounts) which serve as money.

Thus, the commercial banks (that is, the banks we all know and deal with) in good times generally lend out more than customers have previously deposited. In bad times, they may insist on repayment of the same loans, wiping out the deposits created when the loans were made. Far from being a passive link in the savings-investment process, commercial banks may drastically affect the flow of funds from savers into real investment.

[3]When banks make "investments," these are financial investments in government bonds or other securities. Banks make very few direct *real* investments.

To understand this rather startling statement that commercial banks "create" checking deposits, you need to know something about how a commercial bank works. The easiest way to get this picture is to look at a simplified balance sheet of a bank, and then to trace through a few transactions. This will give you an understanding of the nature of deposits and how they get created.

The Bank's Balance Sheet

Banks, like other business institutions, keep a running financial record of what they own and what they owe to other people. What they own and what is owed to them are their "assets." What they owe to other people are their "liabilities." The difference between the two is the "net worth" of the business to its owners, the stockholders. When these three main categories are put together in one statement, they are called a "balance sheet."

A typical bank balance sheet looks like the one below, except that we have omitted a lot of minor items to make the essential categories stand out.

What this balance sheet says is that on June 30, 1971, the bank owned cash of $400,000, bonds valued at $800,000, and a building and fixtures valued at $50,000. In addition, it had loaned out $400,000 to customers, who owed the money back to the bank. These are its assets.

Offsetting these assets, the bank had deposits of $1,500,000, partly demand and partly time

Report of Condition

VICTORY BANK AND TRUST COMPANY

June 30, 1970

Assets		Liabilities and Net Worth	
Cash	$ 400,000	Demand deposits	$ 900,000
Bonds	800,000	Savings deposits	600,000
Loans outstanding	400,000	Net worth	150,000
Building and fixtures	50,000		
	$1,650,000		$1,650,000

deposits. These deposits are liabilities, because they are sums the bank promises to pay to the depositors on demand or on due notice.

The difference between the assets and liabilities is $150,000, which is the estimated net worth of the bank. Part of this net worth was originally paid in by the stockholders as "capital" when they bought stock to start the bank. The rest is "surplus and undivided profits," which are mainly the profits made by the bank and not paid out to the owners. This breakdown of net worth is not shown on our simplified balance sheet.

Potential Creation of Credit by an Individual Bank

If we make some highly simplified assumptions, the basic operations of the Victory bank are laid bare. Assume for the moment that: (1) the bank is on an isolated island where there are no other banks and no communication with other countries; (2) all payments on the island are made by bank check, and no currency is used by the public (the "cash" item on the balance sheet may, for example, be gold); and (3) there are no laws to control the volume of loans the bank can make.

Suppose now that you, a substantial businessman on the island, go to the banker and ask to borrow $1,000. Your credit is good, and he agrees to make the loan. What happens to the bank's balance sheet?

On the assets side "Loans Outstanding" go up $1,000, and on the liabilities side "Demand Deposits" go up the same amount. Remember that all payments are made by check, so you will simply take your loan as an addition to your checking deposit at the bank. Instead of giving you currency, the banker gives you a checking account. The balance sheet still balances, as it always must. But now there is $1,000 more spendable money (checking deposits) in existence merely as a result of the bank's making a loan to you. There is no change at all in the amount of "cash" in existence. The bank has taken your promise to pay (which could not serve as money) and has given you its promise

to pay on the order of your check (which is widely acceptable money). It has "monetized" your debt.[4]

This result is shown readily by a simplified bank balance sheet (sometimes called a T-account), listing only the changes that take place in this transaction. It shows that loans have increased $1,000 on the assets side and that deposits have increased $1,000 on the liabilities side of the balance sheet.

Assets	Liabilities
Loans +$1,000	Deposits +$1,000

Chances are you've borrowed the money because you want to spend it. What happens when you do spend it? Say you buy some machinery from John Jones, and write him a check for $1,000. When Jones presents the check at the bank for payment, $1,000 is taken out of your account and put in his. Since all payments are made by check, he will not want any currency; he merely wants the $1,000 in his checking account so he can spend it when he likes. The new $1,000 of checking deposits has been spent once and is now available for Jones to spend again.

A few days later, Jones buys a new roof for his house, and pays for it with the $1,000. Then the $1,000 is transferred again, from Jones's account to the roofer's account. Now the $1,000 has financed $2,000 of transactions, and the money is as ready for spending again as if the bank had printed up a thousand one-dollar bills and lent them to you. Obviously the new deposit can be spent over and over as long as it is in existence.

In the meantime, what has been happening on the bank's balance sheet? Nothing. The

---

[4]Banks ordinarily deduct interest on loans in advance. Thus the bank would give you perhaps $970 and keep the other $30 for interest; you would repay the full $1,000. This process of deducting interest in advance is called "discount" rather than charging "interest." Suppose for simplicity, however, that the bank gives you the full $1,000.

$1,000 checking deposit has been moving from one account to another, but the overall totals on the balance sheet remain unchanged. The additional deposit was created by the loan to you. It remains outstanding until the loan is paid off, and may be spent (transferred) any number of times in the meantime.

Some day your loan will come due. If you're a sound businessman, you will have built up your own checking account in preparation for the day by holding on to receipts you get from your customers. On the due date, you go in to see the banker and write him a check for $1,000 on your own account. He returns your promissory note to you, and the loan is paid off. But look at what this does to the bank's balance sheet.

Loans are down by $1,000, since the loan to you is paid off. And deposits are down by $1,000, since you have written a $1,000 check against your account payable to the bank, and this check is not transferred to any other depositor. Repayment of the loan just reverses the original entries that were made when you borrowed the money. The loan was made by giving you a deposit account to write checks on. Repayment of the loan wipes out that checking account, and at the same time wipes out your debt to the bank. The whole transaction has been perfectly businesslike. It has thousands of counterparts every day in the United States. Yet, in effect, the bank has acted like a little mint, monetizing your debt and creating the checking deposit it lends you, and wiping the deposit out when you repay the loan.

Look at the T-account now. It still shows the + $1,000 in loans and deposits from the initial loan. But now we add a – $1,000 for both deposits and loans. The balance sheet is back to its original position, but the economy had an extra $1,000 of money while the loan was outstanding.

Assets		Liabilities	
Loans	+$1,000	Deposits	+$1,000
	− 1,000		− 1,000

How many other loans can the banker make simultaneously? Obviously, there is no reason why he has to stop with you. Since the public does all its business by check, and since there is no other bank on the island, he need not worry about currency withdrawals or loss of deposits to another bank. It is hard to see what will put a ceiling on the volume of loans the banker can extend. And he could just as well extend credit by buying bonds. Suppose that instead of lending $1,000 to you he buys a new $1,000 bond issued by the island government. The bank enters a $1,000 checking account for the government, which the government can spend when it pleases. The checking deposit is created in exactly the same way, and it stays in existence (however often it is spent) until the bank is repaid for the bond. Since the bank collects interest on every loan or investment made, this looks like a very good thing indeed for the banker and his stockholders.

But it all sounds a little like never-never land. You probably suspect there's a catch in it some place. If people could draw out currency, you say, the banker couldn't go around creating money like that just by writing down entries on his books. And you'd be right—partly right. We need to explore what happens when people can withdraw currency. But before you throw out this simplified example, remember that about 80 percent of all transactions in the United States today are made by bank check. The example is not far off on that score after all.

Limits to Credit Creation by an Individual Bank

Why don't banks keep on expanding their loans and earning more interest indefinitely, if all they have to do is create new checking accounts by making entries on their books? Now remove the simplifying assumptions of our island economy, one by one, to get a real-world situation like the one that exists in the United States today. But still assume there is no Federal Reserve to regulate the banks and to provide more currency; the amount is fixed.

Currency Withdrawals

Keep the other assumptions unchanged but assume now that the island's money-using habits are like those in the United States today. The people want to hold about a fifth of their total money supply in the form of currency. Suppose that the bank's "cash" account consists of currency—coins or paper currency originally printed by the government.

Now the banker has to be more careful. His balance sheet shows $400,000 of cash. If he is reasonably sure that the 4-to-1 ratio between deposits and currency wanted by the public will continue, he can calculate roughly how far he can safely go in extending new credit. Every time he adds $5 to his deposits the public will withdraw $1 of it in currency. Thus, he might be safe in expanding his deposits nearly $2,000,000, of which he would expect to lose about $400,000 in currency, if he didn't mind seeing his cash account go down to almost zero.

Actually, the banker wouldn't want to run anywhere near that close on his currency lest the bank be unable to meet unexpected depositors' demands and "go broke." Bankers are traditionally conservative people. Nevertheless, the basic relationship of currency to potential credit expansion is clear. Whenever there is a chance of a currency withdrawal, the bank must be sure it has enough currency to meet the requests of depositors. This public demand is typically small relative to the total volume of deposits, but the potential currency demand imposes a real restriction on the bank. After a banker has been in business a while, he develops a pretty good feel for how heavy currency drains will be at different times of the year and under different circumstances, and governs himself accordingly as a normal part of his business operations. But he also usually keeps a good margin of safety.

What if people lose confidence in the bank and all want their money in currency right now? The answer is painfully clear. The depositors who demand the first $400,000 can be paid off, but the rest are out of luck. In a fractional-reserve banking system—that is, one where the total cash reserves are only a fraction of the system's deposits—the banks cannot pay off all their depositors in currency, for the simple reason that they don't have that much currency. This fact was faced with painful regularity during past financial crises and depressions in the United States. The worst was in the years 1932–1933. A spreading panic of bank "runs" by people wanting to withdraw their deposits in currency forced the government to close all the banks in the country temporarily to protect them all from bankruptcy. At the end of the "bank holiday," public confidence had been restored enough to permit banks to reopen on a gradual basis.

This situation reemphasizes the basic fact: bank deposits largely represent credit extended through the making of loans and investments by banks, not through the deposit of currency in banks. This is obviously true in the Victory bank, since it has only $400,000 in cash but deposits of $1,500,000. It is equally true in the United States today, where the total "cash" reserves of all commercial banks are about $90 billion and total deposits (demand plus savings) are over $400 billion.

Legal Reserve Requirements

Suppose now that the islanders get to worrying about whether their bank is sound (or maybe they hear about the way things are done in the United States), and pass a law requiring the bank to hold cash reserves equal to at least 20 percent of its deposits. (Before reading further, ask yourself whether you would favor this law, and why you would or would not.)

This legal requirement puts a real crimp in the bank's expansion possibilities. With $400,000 of cash, the bank can have only $2,000,000 of deposits. It already has $1,500,000, so the limit of its new deposits (credit extension) is $500,000. The actual working limit is less, because the banker needs to worry about likely currency withdrawals as well as about the legal reserve requirement. Thus, a legal cash-reserve requirement against deposits puts an upper limit on the amount of credit the bank can extend, since new loans or investments mean new deposits.

How many deposits can be supported on any given cash reserve depends on the level of the reserve requirement. With a 20 percent reserve requirement, the bank legally can have five times as many deposits as it has reserves. If the reserve requirement is 50 percent of deposits, the bank can only have twice as many deposits as it has reserves. If the reserve requirement is 10 percent, deposits can be ten times reserves. In fact, the legal reserve requirement now averages about 15 percent for banks in the United States.

The real function of bank reserve requirements is, thus, to limit the total volume of bank credit that can be extended. Although bank reserve requirements do serve the purpose of protecting the security of customers' deposits to some extent, it should be clear by now that nothing short of 100 percent reserves would guarantee the continuous availability of cash for all depositors. With much smaller cash reserves, the thing that really keeps the banking system solvent is the confidence of the public in each other's checks. So long as nobody wants much more currency than usual, the banks get along fine. But if everyone tried to get currency for his deposits at the same time, the legal reserve requirement would be of only minor help in paying off the depositors. The basic purpose of reserve requirements is to limit the amount of credit the banks can extend, and hence to limit the amount of deposits they can create.

A few institutional details about legal reserve requirements in the United States are worth attention, although they don't change the basic principles stated above.

1. Only "cash" is counted in computing banks' legal reserves. Government securities and other assets may be nearly as liquid as cash, but they are not part of a bank's legal reserve.

2. When a bank has more cash reserves than the law requires it to have, the excess is termed "excess reserves." Whenever a bank has excess reserves, it feels some pressure to expand its loans and investments. Idle reserves earn no interest. Thus, the banker generally tries to keep excess reserves at the lowest level consistent with his liquidity needs and the availability of safe loans and investments.

3. There are different reserve requirements for different banks and for different types of deposits. Banks that are members of the Federal Reserve system (see Part B of this chapter) have their reserve requirements set by that federal authority. "Nonmember" banks have their requirements set by state laws or state authorities. In either case, reserve requirements are generally higher on demand deposits than on time deposits, and on large city banks than on small country banks.

Adverse Clearing Balances

Now drop the last special assumption—that there is only one bank—and put the Victory bank in the United States. Here there are lots of other banks in operation, and the Victory bank needs to take this fact into account. If the bank makes loans to its customers, there is a good chance that they will write checks to people who do business elsewhere. And when this happens, the Victory bank has to pay cash to the other bank. This is a most important change in the bank's position.

In a many-bank system, the most important limitation on the power of an individual bank to expand credit to the legal limit permitted by its reserves is the fear that it will lose reserves to other banks. If bank A has to pay cash to bank B when they settle up the checks written back and forth between their customers, we say that bank A has an "adverse clearing balance." And to bank A an adverse clearing balance is just like a currency drain—it takes away cash reserves.

Ordinarily, the checks written against any bank and the checks it has to collect against other banks roughly balance off. You send $500 to Philadelphia to pay a bill, and your neighbor gets a payment from Philadelphia. But if one bank expands its credit more rapidly than other banks do, it's likely to lose reserves on balance. Recognizing this fact, few bankers would make new loans and investments amounting to anything like $5,000 on $1,000 of excess reserves (assuming a 20 percent reserve requirement) unless they had some special reason to suppose that they would not lose reserves through adverse clearing balances. Indeed, bankers ordinarily hesitate to extend new credit much beyond their excess reserves.

To summarize what we have said so far about banks and the supply of money: (1) One function of financial institutions is to channel savings to borrowers. This activity has no direct effect on the volume of money. (2) Commercial banks are distinguished from other savings institutions in that, as a group, they do not simply lend out the money that people have deposited. They actually "create" money by giving borrowers current spending power in exchange for future promises to repay the bank. (3) The power of an individual commercial bank to expand credit on its reserves is limited by (a) legal reserve requirements, (b) the dangers of currency withdrawals by customers, and (c) adverse clearing balances.

Credit Creation and Contraction by the Banking System

Any one bank that expands loans when other banks are not expanding is checked by adverse clearing balances. But when we view the banking system as a whole, the limitation imposed by adverse clearing balances disappears. This is because the reserves one bank loses another gains. Since the banking system as a whole loses no reserves through adverse clearing balances, it can create deposits through lending up to the multiple permitted by the legal reserve-requirement ratio, just as could the island bank above. If, for example, the legal reserve requirement against deposits is 20 percent, the banking system can expand deposits up to five times its reserves.

Of course, the banking system faces limitations from the withdrawal of currency by depositors and from increases in reserve requirements, just as did the Victory bank above. For currency withdrawals reduce the volume of total reserves in the banking system. And higher legal reserve requirements reduce the multiple by which deposits can exceed reserves. But the apparent check of adverse clearing balances vanishes when we consider all banks together.[5]

[5]Since the Federal Reserve imposes higher legal reserve requirements against demand deposits than against savings

It is easy to see that adverse clearing balances don't limit the expansion power of the banking system. But since individual banks normally do not lend much beyond their excess reserves, the banking system normally only gradually expands deposits to the legal limit on new reserves.[6]

Sometimes, however, the banking system expands credit very rapidly. For example, during World War II the banking system created $100 billion of new deposits (money) by purchasing new government securities from the U.S. Treasury. During each "War Loan Drive" the commercial banks bought billions of dollars of new government bonds, and paid for them by giving the government demand deposits to spend. In a War Loan Drive, for example, the banks would buy $10 billion of new government bonds and a corresponding $10 billion of new deposits would be created in a single day. The banks would enter $10 billion of deposits for the U.S. government on their books, with a matching asset of $10 billion of new bonds they had acquired. The government then spent the money, and the new deposits became part of the money supply for spending and respending. Never before had this country seen such mass creation of deposits, and never before had the process of bank-credit creation been demonstrated with such simplicity.

The money-creation process works in reverse too. If one dollar of reserves is the basis for five dollars of outstanding bank deposits created by loans and investments, the loss of each dollar of reserves may force contraction of five dollars in deposits. Indeed, if banks are fully "loaned up" to their legal required-reserve limit, loss of reserves must cause a contraction of deposits, and hence of loans and investments.

Such a contraction is brought about when banks reduce their loans or investments; remember the $1,000 reduction in deposits

deposits, the power of the banking system to expand credit depends to some extent on whether the public chooses to hold its deposits in demand or saving accounts.

[6]For doubters, the appendix to this chapter explains in detail how the banking system can expand deposits fivefold on new reserves, assuming a 20 percent reserve requirement, even though no individual bank ever lends out more than its excess reserves.

when your Victory bank loan was paid off above. If the banks run short of reserves and cannot obtain more, they reduce their deposits by calling in loans as they come due or by selling bonds.

Sometimes, as with credit expansion, credit contraction snowballs in a massive way. In the Great Depression of the early 1930s, for example, nearly one-third of the nation's money supply (mainly demand deposits) was wiped out through the contraction of bank loans and investments. Banks lost reserves as the public withdrew currency in a scare wave, and this forced them to call for payment of loans and sell off their government bonds. Bank deposits plus currency fell from $46 billion to $30 billion between 1929 and 1933. Remember that each dollar of currency withdrawn removes the reserve base for several dollars of deposits and loans and investments.[7]

Money and the Creation of Near-Monies

Only commercial banks can "create" money by monetizing others' debts because by law only banks can hold demand (checking) deposits. But savings deposits, savings and loan shares, and other near-monies are close substitutes for money as a store of purchasing power. And other financial institutions can "create" near-monies, as banks "create" demand deposits. Moreoever, by shifting their savings between checking deposits and time deposits at

banks and savings and loan associations, the public can change the amount of checking deposits (money) in existence.

Suppose John Doe, seeing an ad promising 5 percent at a savings and loan association, saves part of his paycheck and buys a $100 savings and loan share, which is much the same thing as putting a $100 savings deposit in the savings and loan association. Or he may just withdraw $100 from his own checking account and transfer it to the S. and L. Either way, he transfers $100 from a commercial-bank demand deposit to the savings and loan association. Demand deposits are down, S. and L. time deposits are up correspondingly. But the S. and L. association will probably soon redeposit the $100 in its own checking account at a commercial bank so that it can spend or lend the money itself.

Look now at the results: First, commercial bank reserves and demand deposits are unchanged in total; the S. and L. has returned John Doe's deposit to the commercial bank. But second, John has a fine $100 money substitute in his savings and loan share; this will presumably decrease the amount of actual money (currency and checking deposits) he needs at any given time to have an adequate margin of liquidity. It thus frees a bigger share of demand deposits for "active" use in making payments for goods and services. Third, the savings and loan association has $100, most of which it will now feel free to lend out to new borrowers. John's decision to substitute a near-money for actual money in his own financial position has both increased the nation's total supply of money plus near-monies, and increased the total lending power of all financial institutions, since the commercial banks have lost no reserves and the savings and loan association has gained $100 in additional lending power (less whatever part of the total it feels it must hold as a ready cash reserve).

Thus, we must add to the money-creating powers of the commercial banks a similar power of other financial intermediaries to "create" near-monies, as individuals and businesses transfer money holdings into near-monies. In total, therefore, the power of the financial system to generate money plus near-monies far exceeds its power to create money alone.

---

[7]In view of the important part bank-credit expansion and contraction play in business cycles, some economists advocate requiring 100 percent reserves behind all bank deposits. They argue that this step would do much to lessen the severity of business fluctuations. They point out that businessmen and others who wish to borrow could continue to do so, through "savings and loan organizations." These organizations would receive savings from the public, but could lend only as much as savers deposited, rather than being able to create money as the banks do at present. The present banks might be split into two parts. One part would act as a storehouse for funds that savers simply wanted to keep idle for checking or other purposes (on which depositors would probably have to pay service charges). The other part would act as a savings and loan organization to receive savings (paying interest on them) and to lend these savings to borrowers at a higher rate of interest.

It is important to see that shifts of deposits between commercial banks and other financial intermediaries can thus influence the size of the money stock and the amount of total deposits supportable on any volume of bank reserves.

The money stock is, therefore, not entirely under the control of the government, although it is clear that by regulating the volume of reserves the government can generally control the volume of deposits that banks create.

PART B: | THE FEDERAL RESERVE SYSTEM AND THE MONEY SUPPLY

The Constitution gives to Congress the power to "coin money and regulate the value thereof." Congress has since delegated most of this power to the Federal Reserve system, which was established in 1914 after years of painful experience with repeated financial crises. The following pages first describe the Federal Reserve system and indicate briefly how it carries out its day-to-day activities. Then we analyze more fully how the Federal Reserve influences interest rates and the supply of money, the "Fed's" main channels for regulating the level of aggregate demand.

The Federal Reserve System

The Federal Reserve is the major agency established by Contress to provide currency for the nation; to furnish a wide variety of financial services to the government and to the economy; and, most important, to regulate the total amount of money and to maintain "monetary and credit conditions favorable to sound business activity in all fields—agricultural, industrial, commercial."[8]

Organization

The Federal Reserve system is made up of the following:

1. The Board of Governors.
2. The twelve Federal Reserve banks.
3. The Federal Open Market Committee.
4. The member banks.

[8]*The Federal Reserve System: Its Purposes and Functions* (Board of Governors of the Federal Reserve System), p. 23. This booklet provides an authoritative statement of the aims and operations of the Federal Reserve System.

1. The board of governors is composed of seven members, appointed by the president and confirmed by the Senate. Members are appointed for fourteen years. One term expires every two years, an effort to safeguard the board as far as possible from political pressure groups. In most matters, the board of governors is ultimately responsible for the major policies of the twelve Federal Reserve banks; and, since the Federal Reserve banks in turn supervise and regulate the member banks, ultimate responsibility for the entire system is largely centralized in the board of governors.

2. Each of the twelve Federal Reserve banks serves a certain district in the United States. The banks are located in Boston, New York, Philadelphia, Cleveland, Richmond, Atlanta, Chicago, St. Louis, Minneapolis, Kansas City, Dallas, and San Francisco. Each Federal Reserve bank was founded by the sale of stock to member banks, which are required to buy stock. Though technically they are thus privately owned, the Federal Reserve banks are operated in the public interest, not for profit.

3. The Federal Open Market Committee consists of the seven members of the board of governors, plus five of the presidents of the Federal Reserve banks. This twelve-member committee determines the system's policy on open-market operations—that is, the purchase and sale of government securities in the open market. These operations, explained below, are the primary means by which the Federal Reserve authorities attempt to control the volume of bank credit. Although the board of governors does not determine open-market policy independently, its seven members constitute a majority of the Open Market Committee.

4. The member banks include all national banks (chartered by the federal government) in the United States and those state banks that agree to conform to the requirements set up for member banks. In 1967, about 6,000 of the 14,000 commercial banks in the United States were member banks, but the nonmember banks were almost all small ones, holding only about 10 percent of the total deposits of the banking system.

Service Functions of the Federal Reserve

Before we turn to the major policy functions of the Fed, its important, though routine, service functions deserve a brief survey.

Holding Member-Bank Reserves. Each member bank must by law keep its legally required reserves on deposit at its Federal Reserve bank.[9] These reserve balances at the Reserve banks are essentially checking accounts that the member banks maintain with the Federal Reserve, just as an individual has a checking account with a commercial bank. A member bank must always keep the reserve required by law, but beyond this requirement it is free to draw on, or add to, its reserve account as it wishes. If it needs currency to pay out to its customers, it simply draws the needed amount from its reserve balance at the Federal Reserve bank. Member banks receive no interest on their reserve balances.[10]

Furnishing Currency for Circulation. All currency in the United States is issued either by the Treasury or by the Federal Reserve banks. Treasury currency—mainly coins—makes up about 10 percent of the total. It is issued by the Treasury but is placed in circulation largely through the Reserve banks and the commercial banks. The Reserve banks themselves issue Federal Reserve notes. These are liabilities of the issuing Federal Reserve bank, and also of the federal government. Each Federal Reserve note must be backed fully by collateral—gold, government bonds, or other designated acceptable security—but in essence the Fed has unlimited power to issue new Federal Reserve notes if the government agrees.

Furnishing currency for circulation is a continuing operation. New currency is constantly being put into circulation to replace old, worn currency. Currency in circulation grows gradually as the economy grows, and increases temporarily at certain periods of the year, such as Christmas and the Fourth of July, when people and businesses want more hand-to-hand money. Currency is put into circulation very simply. The banks get currency by drawing on their reserve accounts at the Reserve banks and pay out the currency to customers who make withdrawals from their deposit accounts. The Reserve banks always keep large supplies of paper money and coin on hand to meet the needs of member banks. If the public has more currency than it wants, it simply redeposits the currency in commercial banks, which in turn redeposit the excess in their reserve accounts at the Federal Reserve banks.

Clearing and Collecting Checks. Most payments in the United States are made by means of bank checks. And most bank checks drawn on out-of-town banks are "cleared" through the Federal Reserve system to avoid shipping currency. Suppose Jones in Chicago sells a $100 bill of goods to Smith in Detroit, and Smith pays by a check on his Detroit bank. Jones deposits the check at his bank in Chicago. The Chicago bank sends the check to the Chicago Federal Reserve bank, which increases the reserves of the Chicago bank by $100 and decreases the reserves of the Detroit bank by $100. The check is then sent to the Detroit bank, which decreases Smith's account by $100. Jones in Chicago has his $100; Smith in Detroit has $100 less. And since both banks keep their reserves with the Chicago Federal Reserve bank, the check is cleared simply by increasing the reserve account of the Chicago bank and decreasing the account of the Detroit bank. No

---

[9]Except for the "vault cash" (currency) which it keeps in its own vaults.

[10]The use of the word "reserve" in banking is quite different from that in ordinary business accounting, as we shall see in the appendix to Chapter 20.

currency has to be shipped around the country.

When Jones and Smith are in different Federal Reserve districts (say Chicago and New York), the process is identical except that the New York and Chicago Federal Reserve banks must settle their accounts. They offset the checks due to each other through an "Interdistrict Settlement Fund."

To give some idea of the magnitude of this clearing function, in 1969 the Federal Reserve system handled 7 billion checks, with a total value of $3 trillion. This total included many checks on nonmember banks, which are permitted to use the Federal Reserve check-clearing facilities.

Supervising Member Banks. Banks in this country are supervised by several authorities. The Federal Reserve supervises all member banks. Other federal and state authorities also supervise banks. The same bank may be subject to supervision by as many as three authorities. Generally these authorities cooperate, but not always.

Each Federal Reserve bank examines the member banks in its own district. The examiners make detailed reports to the Federal Reserve bank on the management, the loans and investments, and the general condition of each member bank. If any member bank refuses to conform to the standards of sound banking practice specified by the Federal Reserve, the board of governors may remove its officers and directors or take away its right to make use of Federal Reserve credit facilities. These sanctions seldom need to be used.

Fiscal Agent for the Federal Government. The Federal Reserve banks are bankers for the federal government. They carry most of the government's checking accounts, handle the issue and redemption of government securities, and act as fiscal agent for the government in numerous other ways. The government is continuously receiving tax funds, borrowing, paying out funds for salaries, planes, and so on. It issues and redeems huge volumes of securities. These activities comprise one major part of the Federal Reserve's operating responsibilities.

The Federal Reserve, Interest Rates, and the Supply of Money

In the United States, the Federal Reserve is the "central bank." Its major job is to maintain monetary conditions that will help achieve a stably growing, prosperous economy.

Federal Reserve control over the supply of money and interest rates is exercised largely by controlling the volume and use of member-bank reserves. Without excess reserves, commercial banks cannot extend more credit. Excess reserves make possible (but do not assure) expansion of bank earning assets and deposits. Thus, Federal Reserve powers are designed largely to provide or reduce excess reserves.

The Fundamental Nature of Central Banking

A Federal Reserve bank is a central bank—a banker's bank. Member-bank reserves are member-bank deposits at the Reserve banks. Thus, Federal Reserve control over the volume of member-bank reserves is, in fact, control over the volume of its own deposits. And the Fed can create or destroy the reserves that provide commercial banks' powers to lend and invest.

Before the establishment of the Federal Reserve as a central bank in 1914, the nation's commercial banks faced periodic crises. Mass currency withdrawals by depositors in times of panic exhausted reserves and forced widespread bank failures, because there was no way to convert good but nonliquid loans into currency on short notice. The Federal Reserve was established largely to remedy this situation. Member-bank reserves were to be held by the Reserve banks, and the Reserve authorities were given power to provide new reserves for member banks in times of need.

The ability to create new bank reserves and to provide liquidity to commercial-bank assets is the distinguishing feature of a true central bank. The Federal Reserve can create new reserves (member-bank deposits) by buying bonds or making loans to member banks, just as member banks create deposits by buying bonds or making loans to businesses and individuals. It does this the same way as commercial banks extend credit—by giving deposits in exchange for borrowers' promises to repay at a later date. If a member bank wants more reserves (i.e., deposits at the Fed), it can borrow at the Fed, giving its own promise to repay. Or it can sell some of its government bonds to the Fed, receiving reserves (deposits at the Fed) in payment. In either case, the Fed "creates" the new reserves, by giving the member bank a new deposit (reserve) in exchange for the assets it receives from the member bank.

Main Federal Reserve Powers

The Fed attempts to control the volume and direction of commercial-bank lending and investing, and hence the volume of bank deposits, through the following seven major channels. The first three (open-market operations, reserve requirements, and the rediscount rate) are aimed largely at controlling the total supply, or "quantity," of credit, through regulating the commercial banks' excess reserves. The others are aimed more at controlling the flow of credit to particular uses, such as speculation. These latter are thus called "selective," or "qualitative," credit controls. In regulating the supply of credit, the Fed also influences interest rates —the "cost" of credit.

Open-Market Operations

Purchase and sale of U.S. government securities in the open market is the major device used by the Fed to control the volume of member-bank reserves. By buying "Governments," the Fed increases member-bank reserves; by selling

Governments, it reduces member-bank reserves. To understand how this works, consider first the combined balance sheet of the Federal Reserve banks, shown at the bottom of this page.

This shows the two big assets of the Federal Reserve banks, gold and government securities. The offsetting major liabilities are member-bank deposits and Federal Reserve notes. It is essential to remember that the "cash reserves" shown on commercial-bank statements are mainly not actual currency but are instead deposits held at the Federal Reserve banks.

1. The Federal Reserve can create new reserves for the commercial banks by buying government bonds in the open market—thereby stimulating the commercial banks to make new loans and investments. If the Federal Reserve wants to encourage more bank loans, it goes into the open market and buys $1,000 worth of U.S. government bonds, say from a commercial bank.[11] To pay for these bonds, it simply gives the bank a $1,000 deposit credit (new reserve balance) at the Federal Reserve. The commercial bank has $1,000 of new reserves, and they are all excess reserves, since its deposits have not been changed by the transaction. The Federal Reserve has created a $1,000 member-bank deposit (reserve account) against the government bond. Since the commercial banks now have $1,000 of new excess reserves, they are in a position to expand their loans by four or

[11]Remember that the Fed, while part of the government, is quite separate from the U.S. Treasury. The Fed does not issue any bonds itself, but merely buys and sells government bonds that have been issued previously by the Treasury.

FEDERAL RESERVE BANKS			
April 30, 1970			
(In Billions of Dollars)			
Gold	$11	Member-bank deposits	$23
U.S. securities	56	Federal Reserve notes	47
	$67*		$70*

*Does not balance because minor items are omitted.

five times that amount, depending on legal reserve requirements.[12]

Consider the T-accounts for the commercial and the Federal Reserve bank. They show the $1,000 addition to excess reserves on the books of both the Fed and the commercial bank.

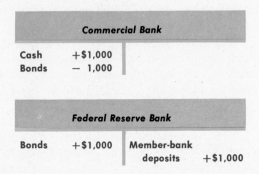

Commercial Bank		
Cash	+$1,000	
Bonds	− 1,000	

Federal Reserve Bank		
Bonds	+$1,000	Member-bank deposits +$1,000

Does all this seem a little like black magic—new commercial-bank reserves created out of nowhere by the Federal Reserve banks, reserves which in turn can provide the basis for a much larger amount of commercial-bank deposits, also created out of nowhere? In a sense, it is. But each dollar of new member-bank reserves at the Fed is matched by a newly acquired government bond, and each new deposit at the commercial bank will be matched by a borrower's promise to repay. There is no magic. But through this process the Fed is able to "create" new member-bank reserves, which are often called "high-powered money," since they can in turn serve as the reserves behind a larger volume of newly created deposits at commercial banks.

Is there a limitation on how many new reserves the Federal Reserve can create in this way? No direct limit. Until 1968 the Fed was required to have a 25 percent gold reserve against member-bank deposits and Federal Reserve notes respectively, but now there is no such requirement. Fundamentally, the reserve-creating powers of the Fed are now limited only by the good judgment of the Federal Reserve

authorities, and by the discretion of Congress, which can repeal or alter the Fed's powers anytime it wishes. Thus, control over the nation's money supply is ultimately subject to the control of the democratic process, just as are other government powers.[13]

How effective is the Federal Reserve in lowering interest rates and stimulating new commercial-bank loans when it provides new reserves? More reserves push a banker to extend new credit, for no banker likes to lose the interest he might earn on idle reserves. In those rare cases where excess reserves are already large because bankers don't see any "sound" borrowers looking for loans, still more excess reserves may not help much. But don't forget that banks can also buy government bonds. If their excess reserves are increased when no desirable loans are available, they may increase the volume of deposits by buying up government bonds. Bankers do vary the amount of excess reserves they wish to hold under different circumstances. But history suggests that with rare exceptions commercial bankers have increased their loans and investments about as far as their excess reserves permit. The big exception was the depression of the 1930s, when the commercial banks held billions of dollars of excess reserves for nearly a decade.

Note that the Fed's open-market purchases also directly push down interest rates on government securities. Fed purchases will tend to bid up the prices of bonds, which is equivalent to forcing down the interest yield on the bonds. (See the footnote on page 107 if you don't remember why.) Since lower interest rates also help to stimulate the economy, open-market purchases are a two-pronged weapon against recession.

2. When the Open Market Committee wants to decrease member-bank reserves, it sells government securities in the open market to whoever bids for them—individuals, businesses, or banks. This reduces commercial-bank reserves when the Federal Reserve is paid for the bonds. Consider how.

---

[12]There is substantially, but not quite, the same effect if the Fed buys the bond from a business or individual. Trace through the effect for yourself. Section (2) below will suggest the analysis if you need help.

[13]As a practical matter, international balance-of-payments problems may constrain the Fed's use of its powers, as we shall see in Part Six.

If a member bank buys the bond, it pays by giving $1,000 of its reserves to the Federal Reserve; on the member bank's balance sheet, "cash" goes down and "bonds" go up by $1,000. Thus, the bank loses a full $1,000 of excess reserves, since its deposits remain unchanged. If a business or individual buys the bond from the Reserve, the effect is almost the same. He pays by a check on his bank. His bank's reserves are reduced by $1,000 when the Federal Reserve presents the check for collection. The member bank's deposits also drop by the $1,000 transferred from the bond buyer's account to the Federal Reserve. Since the bank loses $1,000 in both deposits and reserves, its required reserves are $200 lower but its excess reserves drop by $800. Excess reserves contract a little less than in the bank-purchase case, but the general effect is similar.

If the bank buys the bonds, the T-account entries at the commercial bank are as shown above the dotted line. If an individual buys it, the entries are as shown below the dotted line.[14]

Cash	−$1,000		
Bonds	+ 1,000		
Cash	− 1,000	Deposits	− $1,000

Federal Reserve open-market sales can limit bank-credit expansion when they reduce excess reserves to low levels. The Federal Reserve might face a problem if banks had large excess reserves on hand, for the banks could then lose reserves and still have an adequate base for new loans and investments. But in recent decades excess reserves have been small, and the Fed has had plenty of government bonds to absorb all the excess reserves of the banking system if it wants to.

Rediscount Rate Changes

When a member bank runs short of reserves, it may borrow from its Federal Reserve bank, just as you and I borrow at a commercial bank. In such a case the member bank could "rediscount" notes. The member bank has made loans to customers against customers' promises to repay, called "notes," or "commercial paper." It can "rediscount" these notes with its Federal Reserve bank—that is, it can use the note as collateral to borrow additional reserves. The rate of interest, or discount, charged by the Federal Reserve to member banks is called the "rediscount rate." Or member banks may borrow using government securities as collateral. In rediscounting, the initiative is in the hands of the commercial banker to increase his reserves, while open-market operations are at the discretion of the Fed.

The Fed raises the rediscount rate to discourage member-bank borrowing and lowers the rate to encourage it. But few bankers like to borrow, and most borrow only when they badly need to in order to get additional reserves. Moreover, the Fed discourages member-bank borrowing except on a temporary basis. Thus, the rediscount rate is of relatively minor direct importance. But changes in the rediscount rate have an important psychological effect on the banking and business communities because they are viewed as evidence of the Fed's general position on monetary expansion or restraint.[15]

Changes in Member-Bank Reserve Requirements

In 1933, a drastic new power was given to the Board of Governors—the power to raise and lower legal reserve requirements for member banks. Reserve requirements against demand deposits can be varied between 10 and 22 percent for city banks and 7 and 14 percent for country banks, and against time deposits between 3 and 6 percent for all banks.

By raising reserve requirements, the Board wipes out member banks' excess reserves and

[14]If the buyer pays in currency, he reduces the amount of currency in circulation, also a reduction in the money stock. But payment in currency is very unusual.

[15]Sometimes you see the term "free reserves." These are excess reserves *less* commercial-bank borrowing from the Fed. Since each commercial bank must repay its borrowing promptly, many experts believe that free reserves are better than excess reserves as an indication of commercial banks' ability to extend new credit. When free reserves are negative, they are called "net borrowed reserves."

directly restricts credit expansion. Suppose a member bank has $1,000,000 deposits and $200,000 reserves, and the required legal reserve ratio is 16 percent. It has a comfortable $40,000 of excess reserves. If the Board raises the legal requirement to 20 percent, the reserve required jumps to $200,000 and the bank's excess reserve is wiped out. Conversely, lowering legal reserve requirements increases excess reserves.

Changing reserve requirements is a relatively heavy, blunt tool of credit control, compared with the gradual, flexible way open-market operations can be used. Thus, the Reserve authorities change reserve requirements only infrequently, depending instead primarily on open-market operations.

"Selective" Credit Controls

The preceding general controls over bank reserves are often called "indirect" or "quantitative" controls, since they only control the total volume of bank lending, the level of interest rates, and the stock of money. They leave the private banker free to allocate his funds as he wishes among different borrowers. In addition, the Fed has smaller "direct," or "selective," controls over particular bank loans and uses to which bank credit is put. These permit the Fed to influence directly the uses of bank credit. Many economists question the effectiveness of such controls, because money, once created, flows freely from one sector of the economy to the other, and it is very difficult to control any one sector by limiting lending directly to it. But such selective controls may have important temporary effects.

Maximum Interest Rates on the Deposits. The Fed has the power to set maximum interest rates on different classes of deposits, and other regulatory agencies have similar powers over other financial intermediaries, such as the savings and loan associations. By setting different ceilings on interest rates at different institutions, the bank supervisors can significantly influence their relative competitive positions, and thus indirectly influence where savers' funds go.

For example, in the 1960s, the S. and L.'s bid many deposits away from the commercial banks, and channeled these funds into mortgages to finance home building, especially in the West. Originally, there were no governmental ceilings on the rates that S. and L.'s could pay their depositors, but commercial banks had maximum rates on their savings deposits. In the mid-1960s, the Fed raised the maximum rates that commercial banks might pay, and thus permitted them to bid deposits back away from the S. and L.'s. This channeled funds away from the housing industry toward the broader uses made by commercial banks of their lending power. Rate ceilings were also used to affect the competitive power of big U.S. commercial banks vis-à-vis European capital markets.

Once detailed direct controls are instituted that influence the competitive position of different financial institutions, difficult questions of equity arise, and there is an unfortunate tendency for such direct controls to proliferate. Many economists argue that interest-rate ceilings do more harm than good. We shall return to the issue in the next chapter.

Control of Stock-market Credit: Margin Requirements. Often customers buy stocks and bonds "on margin." That is, they pay the broker a cash "margin" (down payment) and borrow the rest of the purchase price from the broker, leaving the newly purchased securities as collateral for the loan. The broker, in turn, typically borrows from commercial banks what the security buyer does not put up as margin (cash). The smaller the margin required, the more the buyer can borrow of the purchase price. If margin requirements are raised, therefore, the use of bank credit for purchasing securities is restricted. If margin requirements are lowered, it becomes easier to buy securities on credit.

The Fed has power to set minimum margin requirements for dealings on the major securities exchanges, ranging up to 100 percent cash payments. In the wild stock-market speculation of the late 1920s, most stock was bought on margins of 10 percent or less, so speculators found it easy to bid up prices on borrowed money. Now, with margin requirements much higher, most stock is bought with full cash payment, or with relatively little borrowing. Most economists believe that Federal Reserve margin requirements exercise a healthy restraint on speculative stock purchases under boom conditions.

"Direct Pressure" or "Moral Suasion." When the Fed wants to discourage bank lending, it may use "direct pressure," or "moral suasion," on the bankers. Bank examiners may be instructed to tighten up their requirements for "good" loans and investments. Reserve officials may frown when member banks come to the discount window for temporary loans. They may also make public statements warning against inflation and overexpansion of credit. In extreme cases, the Reserve banks may simply refuse to lend to offending member banks. There is not much evidence that such moral suasion is very effective. There is even less hope that it can do anything to persuade bankers to make more loans in hard times.

Consumer-Credit Controls. During World War II and in the Korean War, the Fed was temporarily given power to regulate consumer credit (on installment purchases and charge accounts) and real-estate credit. On both housing and consumer credit, the Fed imposed minimum down payments and maximum repayment periods. Raising down payments made it hard to buy without cash in hand; shortening the total payment period increased the monthly payment required.

The wartime goal was partly to restrain inflationary consumer demand, partly to divert demand away from the durables that competed directly with war production. But many people objected, especially the lower-income groups who couldn't afford to pay cash for everything. Why, they asked, should the few cars and refrigerators go exclusively to the rich? In wartime, shouldn't rationing or some other equitable system of distributing scarce goods be adopted, rather than merely shutting out the poor by imposing drastic controls on borrowing? Such consumer-credit controls lasted through the war and as long afterward as infla-

tionary pressure continued strong. But in 1952, Congress eliminated them, and repeatedly has refused to restore them in spite of requests from both the Board and the president for reinstatement at least on a "standby" basis.

Conclusion

In perspective, The Fed has enormous powers to check any credit expansion—indeed, to force mass contraction—if it chooses to use them. By dumping all its $56 billion of government securities on the market and by raising reserve requirements to their legal limits, the Fed could bring on a massive deflation sure to send the entire economic system into chaos. Of course, the Federal Reserve officials would never consider such a foolish action. But this points up the great power inherent in the Federal Reserve's restrictive measures. The main problem is to use the existing controls effectively, not to seek more powerful weapons.

The Fed's ability to stimulate bank lending is also great and it has substantially unlimited power to create new reserves through open-market operations. But success on the expansion side is less sure. Banks need not necessarily make new loans in recession merely because they receive new excess reserves. By flooding the banking system with excess reserves, the Fed can almost surely expand the nation's money stock, since the banks will buy government securities even if they won't lend to business concerns and consumers. But if direct loans to business and consumers are needed to stimulate investment and consumption, the problem may be a tough one. And, as Chapter 9 indicated, even if deposits are expanded, the public may choose to convert its new demand deposits into money substitutes like savings deposits or bonds, rather then spending new funds on goods and services.

But even with these limitations, the Fed's powers are great. The real issue is how to use these powers most effectively to achieve a stably growing, high-employment economy without inflation. This is the task of monetary policy, to which we now turn in Chapter 13.

CONCEPTS AND INSTITUTIONS TO REMEMBER

This chapter has introduced several important concepts and institutions. Be especially sure you understand the following:

money	credit contraction
currency	Board of Governors
demand (checking) deposits	Open Market Committee
savings and time deposits	Federal Reserve banks
near-monies	member banks
bank credit	"creation" of bank reserves
commercial bank	open-market operations
financial intermediary	rediscount rate
credit creation	selective credit controls
bank reserves	interest-rate ceilings
excess reserves	margin requirements
reserve requirements	consumer credit
adverse clearing balance	

FOR ANALYSIS AND DISCUSSION

1. Why is currency worth more than its value as paper and ink?
2. Get a copy of a recent balance sheet from one of your local banks. What main types of credit does this bank extend? Which of these types of credit would you expect to be most liquid (most readily convertible into cash) in case of a serious recession in overall business activity?
3. If banks hold "reserves" equal to only a small fraction of their deposits, are you safe in depositing your money in a bank? Explain why or why not.
4. If you were a banker, would you hold excess reserves? Why or why not?
5. In a small, isolated economy (i.e., no foreign trade) with money-using habits comparable to those of the United States, there are five identical banks. Each bank's balance sheet is as shown below. The law prescribes that banks must hold a 10 percent cash reserve against deposits. There is no central bank.

Cash	$ 4,000,000	Deposits	$30,000,000
Loans	14,000,000	Capital and Surplus	4,000,000
Government Securities	16,000,000		
	$34,000,000		$34,000,000

   a. A customer of bank A mines $1 million of gold (considered as cash for reserve purposes) and deposits it in his bank. Trace through any likely expansion of the money supply by bank A and by the entire banking system. What would be the maximum expansion possible? Specify clearly any assumptions that you make and state your reasoning carefully and precisely.
   b. Is the banking system in a more or less sound position as a result of the gold deposit and the consequences you have predicted above? Explain why or why not.
6. Explain how the transfer of your $100 deposit from a commercial bank to a savings and loan association can increase society's stock of liquid assets (money plus near-monies).
7. In what ways are the objectives of a central bank (like the Federal Reserve) different from those of a commercial bank?

8. Explain the main weapons the Fed has to check an inflationary boom.
9. The powers of the Federal Reserve to restrict credit expansion in booms are greater than those to stimulate credit expansion in a depressed period. (True or False? Why?)
10. Suppose the Federal Reserve takes the following actions. In each case, explain what will be the likely effect on the total money supply:
    a. It sells $2 billion of government securities to the banks.
    b. It lowers reserve requirements from 15 to 10 percent for all member banks.
    c. It buys $2 billion of government securities from individuals and business concerns.
    d. It buys direct from the United States Treasury $2 billion of newly issued government securities.
    e. It lowers rediscount rates by 1 percent.
11. Suppose the economy is in a serious depression. The commercial banks have substantial excess reserves. What steps would you advocate that the Federal Reserve take to help stimulate lending and recovery? Why?

APPENDIX   *THE INDIVIDUAL BANK AND THE BANKING SYSTEM*

If no individual bank lends more than its excess reserves, how can the banking system expand credit fivefold on its excess reserves (assuming a 20 percent reserve requirement)? An example can show how it works.

Assume, first, that the Victory bank has $1,000 excess reserves, and that all other banks are loaned up to their legal limits. As the Victory bank makes new loans and investments, its reserves are gradually drawn away to other banks, and its credit-expansion possibilities are limited. But the reserves the Victory bank loses, some other bank gains.

Suppose Victory makes a new loan of $1,000, just the amount of its excess reserves. The T-account then looks like this, including the original $1,000 of excess reserves but excluding the rest of the original balance sheet. Consider first only the entries above the dotted line.

matching $1,000 cash reserve from the Victory bank to B. On the Victory bank T-account, deduct $1,000 from cash and from deposits, as shown below the dotted line, to see the bank's new position. Victory is left with $1,000 of increased loans, on which it happily earns interest.

Bank B now has $1,000 of new reserves and $1,000 of new deposits. We can set up a T-account for bank B, showing (Stage 2) + $1,000 for both the new cash and deposits, above the first dotted line. Of the new reserves, only $200 is required to back the new $1,000 deposit, so $800 is excess. Obviously, B is now safe in extending at least $800 of new loans, since it has that much excess reserves.

So B makes a new $800 loan, creating $800 of additional deposits. This is shown on B's T-account, below the first dotted line.

Victory Bank — Stage 1			
Excess reserve	$1,000		
Loans	+ 1,000	Deposits	+ $1,000
. . . .	. . . .	. . . .	. . . .
Cash	− 1,000	Deposits	− 1,000

Bank B — Stage 2			
Cash	+ $1,000	Deposits	+ $1,000
. . . .	. . . .	. . . .	. . . .
Loans	+ 800	"	+ 800
. . . .	. . . .	. . . .	. . . .
Cash	− 800	"	− 800

Soon the borrower writes a check for the entire $1,000, and the check is deposited in bank B. This action transfers both the $1,000 deposit and the

Now the borrower spends the money to a customer of bank C. Bank B loses the $800 in deposits and in reserves to bank C. The loss is shown below the second dotted line on B's accounts. Note that on the liability side, B still has the $1,000 original deposit created by Victory bank; on the asset side, it still has a matching $200 of new reserves from Victory, plus $800 of its own new loans. It is earning interest on its new $800 loan.

But C now has $800 of new deposits and the $800 of new reserves from B (Stage 3). This is shown in a new T-account, set up for C; the items are shown above the dotted line.

Bank C — Stage 3			
Cash	+$800	Deposits	+$800
Loans	+ 640	"	+ 640

The total of new deposits has now risen to $1,800 ($1,000 in B and $800 in C), matched by $1,800 of new loans, even though no bank has lent a penny beyond its available excess reserves. Bank C, moreover, now has $640 of excess reserves ($800 new reserves, of which only $160 is required to back its $800 of new deposits). On these excess reserves it can safely make at least $640 of new loans, shown below the dotted line on its T-account. This will raise the total of new deposits to $2,440 against the original $1,000 of excess reserves. (The $2,440 total includes $1,000 in bank B and $1,440 in bank C at this stage.) And the expansion process can obviously continue. Trace it another stage for yourself, assuming

that C's borrower spends his deposit to someone who banks with D; or the effect is the same if the reserves go back to the Victory bank, or to any other. The expansion can continue until total deposits have risen to $5,000 against the $1,000 of excess reserves. Each individual bank rightly hesitates to lend out more than its excess reserves, but the reserves it loses go to some other bank.

This process of cumulative deposit expansion is diagramed in Figure 12–1. Assume that bank A receives $1,000 of new reserves, say because $1,000 of newly mined gold is deposited. This $1,000 deposit requires only $200 of new reserves, so bank A is entirely safe in expanding its loans and investments by $800, as shown in the dark-colored bar for bank A. (Note that the bank names don't match those in the preceding example.)

Now bank A's new borrower writes a check to a customer of bank B, and the $800 is transferred to bank B. Bank B now has $800 of new deposits and $800 of new reserves, which means that it has excess reserves of $640, since required reserves increase by only $160. It is perfectly safe in lending out an additional $640, and does so, as shown in the diagram. This $640 may now be transferred to a customer of some other bank (C), which then has new deposits and excess reserves on which to expand its loans. At each stage, the deposits created by previous transactions are piled on top, in the dotted sections, to show the cumulative increase.

As the diagram shows, this process can continue, piling up new deposits that arise from new loans, until a total of $5,000 of new deposits is reached (the tall light-colored bar at the right), including the origi-

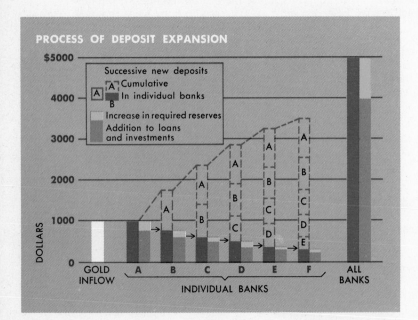

PROCESS OF DEPOSIT EXPANSION

Successive new deposits
- Cumulative
- In individual banks
- Increase in required reserves
- Addition to loans and investments

fig. 12–1

One thousand dollars of new reserves (gold) ultimately serves as the foundation for $5,000 of new deposits, as banks make new loans and investments —even though no bank ever lends out more than its own excess reserves.

nal $1,000 deposit produced by the gold deposit. This is just what we would expect: $1,000 of new reserves has been able to support $5,000 of new deposits, given a 20 percent legal reserve requirement against deposits and no currency drain. The tall dark bar at the right shows the $4,000 of new loans and the $1,000 of new required reserves, just using up the original $1,000 of new gold reserves, so the growth must now stop. Moreover, this expansion has taken place even though no individual bank has ever lent out more than the excess reserves it actually has on hand. So when your banker tells you that he would never lend out more money than he has in excess reserves, he may be quite correct. Yet the banking system as a whole creates deposits equal to many times its cash reserves.

The critical point is that the banking system is not limited by adverse clearing balances. The reserves one bank loses, another gains. For the banking system as a whole, the only overall drain on reserves comes from currency withdrawals, from international gold flows, or from Federal Reserve or Treasury policies.

thirteen

Monetary Policy

Can we maintain high-level employment and reasonably stable prices in a growing economy? The stakes are high, and the costs of failure are large.

To achieve these dual goals, aggregate demand must grow stably, just fast enough to take a growing high-employment output off the market at stable prices. The preceding analysis suggests little reason to suppose the private economy on its own will generate just this amount of aggregate demand. Thus, we must turn to government for help in achieving the needed level of total spending.

Monetary policy (control over the money supply and interest rates) and fiscal policy (government spending and taxing) are the two main tools the government has to help keep aggregate demand growing stably. Monetary policy is the subject of this chapter, fiscal policy the subject of the next.

The Theory of Monetary Policy

Under the "gold standard" that prevailed in the Western world during most of the century preceding World War II, the stock of money was largely controlled by an impersonal mechanism. The money supply increased and decreased when gold flowed in or out of a nation. But even in those days, many argued against leaving the supply of money solely to

172

this mechanism. Instead, they argued, a "central bank" should be responsible for controlling the money stock in order to minimize inflations and depressions. The Bank of England is generally considered the forerunner of other central banks, and the "Old Lady of Threadneedle Street" (as the bank is often called) has played a significant part in influencing British monetary conditions for three centuries. The United States was one of the last major nations to establish a central bank. Our Federal Reserve was set up in 1914.[1] But over the decades since, we have come to rely on Federal Reserve policy as one of our two big guns in the war against unemployment and inflation.

Monetary Policy, Interest Rates, and the Money Stock

Chapters 6 to 10 provided the analytical foundation for monetary policy. If we want to increase or decrease aggregate demand, the central bank should increase or decrease M. Remember the main channels of effect.

The neo-Keynesian model suggests that more M will act only by increasing investment spending through reducing the rate of interest. Then the chain of effects runs like this:

$$+M \rightarrow -r \rightarrow +I \rightarrow + \text{g.n.p.}$$

That is, an increase in M leads to a lower interest rate, which in turn leads to more investment, which in turn leads to a higher g.n.p. directly and through the multiplier.

The monetarists argue that money has a broader and more direct effect. More M may lead not only to more investment through lower interest rates but also directly to more consumption and investment spending. This occurs because an increase in M will lower the marginal return on money relative to other assets and will lead consumers and businesses to spend down their real money balances, acquiring other assets (including both consumer and investment goods) instead.

[1]Two earlier government-sponsored banks (the First and Second Banks of the United States) had only brief lives and did not act as full-fledged central banks.

What Is the Right Amount of Money?

If total real g.n.p. were a constant multiple of the stock of money (that is, if V were constant and real output varied proportionately with money g.n.p.), then the task of monetary policy would be relatively simple. Determine the desired level of g.n.p., and then move the stock of money up or down to obtain that desired level. But we know that the public's demand for money balances varies, and that the V in $MV = PT$ varies. Thus, to determine the right M to produce any desired level of aggregate money spending, we must take into account changes in the public's demand for money balances. Figure 9–2 pictured the fluctuations in income velocity since 1900. Moreover, we know that changes in spending sometimes raise or lower prices rather than real output.

In a growing economy, the amount of money needed will gradually rise. Prima facie, we might expect the need for more money to grow apace with the growth in real-output potential —say about 4 percent a year. But just how fast M needs to grow in a growing economy will depend on how fast the public's demand for money balances rises at full-employment levels.

The public's demand for money balances depends on its level of income (or wealth) and on interest rates on money substitutes. The higher the income (or wealth) of the public, the larger, other things equal, will be the money balances it wishes to hold. The higher the interest rate on money substitutes, the less the money it wishes to hold will be because higher interest rates will lead people to shift their assets out of money (which yields no interest) into securities or other assets. Thus, for any level of aggregate demand we want to achieve, the right amount of M is that amount that the public desires to hold at that desired level of g.n.p. and at existing interest rates. More M than this amount will lead to higher spending than we want; less M will lead to lower spending.

But even if the Fed could keep total spending growing at exactly the desired rate, this would not guarantee full employment without inflation. Sometimes, especially in the upsweep of a boom, more spending leads to rising prices before full employment is reached. Then, if the monetary authorities increase M further to raise spending in order to reduce unemployment, the undesired side effect is inflation. But to hold spending constant so as to avoid inflation is to accept undesired unemployment. Thus, even complete ability to control money g.n.p. would not be neough to guarantee full employment without inflation. But it would be a big step in that direction, and we shall focus attention here on the control of money g.n.p., leaving to Chapter 15 the difficult problem that arises when high employment and stable prices appear to be incompatible.

Summary: The right amount of money depends both on the desired level of real g.n.p. and on the public's demand to hold money balances at that level of g.n.p. and of interest rates. A rising g.n.p. without an increase in M will tend to raise interest rates and thus limit the growth in g.n.p. Thus, it is important that M grow gradually over the long pull—at roughly the growth rate of the economy's productive capacity, but possibly with variations to offset short-run disturbances.

Should the Fed Watch M or Interest Rates?

Monetary theory provides no decisive answer as to whether the Fed should focus on M or on interest rates in attempting to control aggregate spending. The monetarist analysis says M, since V will normally be relatively stable. The neo-Keynesians say interest rates, since interest rates influence the rate of investment, which in turn influences g.n.p.

If the public's demand for money varies, the Fed can fix the stock of money, or interest rates —but not both. It must choose. Suppose the public's demand for money decreases, but the Fed wants to keep g.n.p. constant. It can keep M constant, but if it does the interest rate will fall (since the supply of M is unchanged but the demand for money falls). Or it can keep the interest rate stable, but only by reducing the stock of money. Thus, which theory is right is no idle question for the monetary authorities. If they keep M stable but the neo-Keynesians are right, falling interest rates will stimulate investment and an inflationary boom will result. If

they stabilize interest rates but the monetarists are right, reduced M will produce falling spending and a recession.

Often no dilemma exists. For example, in depressions everyone agrees that both more M and lower interest rates are needed; conversely, to fight inflation tighter M and higher interest rates are both appropriate. But sometimes the dilemma does arise—be guided by interest rates or the money stock. The late 1960s were a case in point. As we shall see, until recently the Fed has watched primarily interest rates as indicators of the need for expansionary or restrictive action. But in the late 1960s both academic economists and the Fed began to place more stress on M. Today, the Fed clearly watches both—and, until the dispute is resolved, tries to analyze each case on its own merits when the two indicators conflict.

Policies To Restrain Aggregate Demand

If the Fed wants to restrain aggregate demand, it can sell bonds in the open market or raise required reserves to reduce excess reserves. Since commercial banks typically operate with small excess reserves, either action can have a direct and powerful restrictive effect on the extension of bank credit. The Fed can also raise the rediscount rate, which makes it more expensive for commercial banks to borrow additional reserves when they run tight. This is a less-powerful restraint, since banks are still able to borrow additional reserves if they are willing to pay the higher rate. But the rediscount rate is widely viewed as an indicator of the Fed's attitude on credit conditions, and thus has an important symbolic, psychological impact. The Fed has plenty of powers to restrain aggregate demand if it wants to use them.

The Impact of Monetary Restriction

When the economy is expanding, more money is needed. Businesses need more for "working capital" to finance larger inventories, to meet higher payrolls, to buy more materials. They need more to finance investment in machinery, equipment, and buildings. Consumers too need more money to finance the higher volume of transactions. These facts can be summed up in the demand-for-money function indicated above; the public needs more money to hold as the level of income and wealth rises. And the basic source of more money for the system is bank lending, which in turn rests on the availability of more reserves provided by the Fed. Note, therefore, that in an expanding economy, if the Fed merely does nothing to provide additional reserves, this policy of inaction implies a gradual tightening of the money markets and a rise in interest rates, since demand for M rises but its supply does not.

What do the banks do when their excess reserves are squeezed? They often raise their interest rates—the prices they charge on credit. Alternatively, banks often "ration" credit to their customers before they raise interest rates. Instead of using higher rates to eliminate the customers least willing to pay more for loans, they allocate their scarce credit to their oldest and best customers. They consider this sound long-run policy, just as many businesses don't try to squeeze the last penny out of good customers in periods of temporary shortages.

Either way, tight money tends to check the upswing.

Bankers hate to impose credit rationing on good customers. Instead, they often sell off part of their government securities and use the funds to meet customers' loan demands. But such switches from government securities to loans are limited by the volume of securities the banks already have and by falling government-bond prices if many banks try to sell simultaneously. Bankers may also get new reserves by borrowing at the Fed. But the Fed can close this loophole by raising the rediscount rate and frowning on rediscounting.

On their side, businesses and consumers try to avoid the pinch by economizing on money balances—that is, by reducing their money balances to the barest minimum needed to carry on their transactions and meet precautionary needs. The same amount of money thus does more work; V is speeded up, and the restraint of tighter money is partially avoided. The higher interest rates are forced by the credit squeeze, the greater the inducement is to put "idle" money to work.

Figure 13–1 shows this effect clearly. The dot for each year shows the average interest rate on

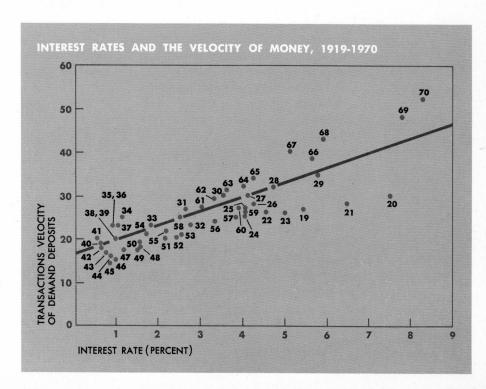

fig. 13–1

As interest rates rise, the turnover of demand deposits goes up. It pays people to economize on the use of money and to reduce their idle balances. (Source: Federal Reserve Board.)

"prime" short-term loans and the average turnover (or velocity) of demand deposits at some 400 city banks outside New York City (which is eliminated to avoid the huge volume of stockmarket transactions there). Velocity varies directly with interest rates. For example, note the low interest rates and velocity during the depression years. These velocity figures include many transactions not contained in the g.n.p. accounts and thus are only a very imperfect approximation to changes in income velocity. But in some respects they are more interesting, since they show what happens to the total use of demand deposits when interest rates rise or fall. If we plot income velocity against interest rates for the same years, the same general relationship is revealed.

But there are limits on how far working cash balances can be reduced. The public and the banks can avoid the pressure of Federal Reserve restraint temporarily, but only temporarily if the Fed keeps the pressure on. Ultimately the Fed can have as strong an impact as it wishes, by raising reserve requirements sharply and by selling a large enough volume of government securities.

Don't jump from this fact to the conclusion that the job of the Federal Reserve is easy. Its power to check economic expansion is enormous, but overly drastic action may throw the baby out with the bath water. The Fed's job is to check the inflation and level off the boom, not to plunge the economy into depression. Tightening up credit just enough to keep consumption and investment growing at exactly the right rate is a difficult and delicate task.

The Differential Effects of Tight Money

When money tightens, some borrowers are squeezed more than others. Banks naturally tend to allocate their scarce funds to established customers. Conversely, new small firms and individuals tend to be squeezed out, especially when their credit rating is not high. Tight money squeezes home construction especially, because high interest rates bulk large in total monthly mortgage payments and because many banks rank such loans below those to businesses that they see as long-run customers.

Bitter claims of inequity can be expected from potential borrowers who are shut out when interest rates rise and there aren't enough loans to go around. There is no way to restrict aggregate demand without turning away somebody, and the big, grade-A borrowers aren't likely to be the ones turned away.

A further complication arises when the monetary authorities use direct controls (interest-rate ceilings) to regulate the flow of savings to different financial institutions. S. and L.'s, for example, lend almost entirely to builders and home buyers. Thus, if they are permitted to pay high rates to the depositors while commercial banks are limited to lower rates, both S. and L.'s and the housing industry are favored relative to commercial banks and industries that borrow from the banks. But normally in tight money periods, interest rates obtainable elsewhere by savers rise above the rates S. and L.'s can pay, and funds are channeled away from the housing market. Housing is thus a prime victim of tight money in most cases.

Government use of direct controls to favor some sectors over others is questioned by some, defended by others. The former say the free market should govern the allocation of credit. The latter say the government should see to it that vital areas like housing should get the funds when money is scarce. Either way, tight money must shut out someone from credit if it is to do its job. There is no way it can avoid restraining some potential borrowers more than others.

The Problem of Timing and Lags

Consider now another Federal Reserve problem in deciding what to do at any given time. The problem breaks down into two big questions: First, what is the state of the economy now, and where is it going in the absence of further monetary policy action? Second, what shall we do to mold this pattern into one of stable economic growth without inflation? Look at Figure 13–2, which provides a very rough picture of a business cycle, and put yourself in the position of a member of the Federal Reserve Board.

First, you have to decide where you are now. At *A*, *B*, *C*, or *D*? You don't know for sure, and

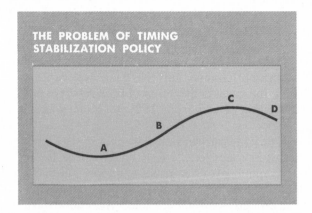

THE PROBLEM OF TIMING STABILIZATION POLICY

fig. 13–2

The Federal Reserve authorities seldom know where we are in the cycle, or just how long it will take their actions to exercise their full effects. What is the right monetary policy if you think we're probably at B, but there's a good chance it may be C instead?

neither does anybody else. Suppose you think we're probably well along in a strong business upswing—say at about *B*. Then the problem is, how near the top? And how long will the inflation and prosperity continue if you do nothing? Is the boom weakening, with a downturn just around the corner? Or does the upswing have months or years of healthy prosperity left in it, so that it would be a shame to damp it? If only you knew![2]

Second, given your best decision as to where we are and where we're headed, you have to decide what the Fed should do now. Suppose that you suspect we're at *B*, and that inflation poses a serious problem. Should you raise reserve requirements? Sell bonds in the open market to tighten reserves? Or is the safe thing just to wait till we're clearly at *D* if that comes, and then fight the recession, on the ground that it's better not to risk killing off prosperity?

Note that here you have two subproblems. One is how much effect will any Federal Reserve action have on business activity? If you sell $1 billion of government bonds, will this drastically check bank lending, or only slow it slightly? How about raising reserve requirements 10 percent? The second question is, even

[2]For a discussion of how government and other economists forecast economic conditions, see the appendix to Chapter 10.

if you know what the effect will be, how long will it take for the full impact of tighter money to be felt? If you sell bonds tomorrow, this may only gradually shut off lending and that in turn may reduce *C* and *I* still later. Thus, the full effects of your action will be spread over months, perhaps over a year or two. By that time the boom may have turned down. Then the lagged effect of tight money would be to speed the downturn into recession.

The lags and uncertainties between Federal Reserve actions and their final impact on total spending are substantial. How long will it take the banks to react to tighter reserves? Will they try to sell off government securities and thus evade the desired restriction on business borrowing? How fast will businesses react to tighter credit and higher interest rates? Will the Fed's action have a strong psychological effect that reduces business investment? Some economists estimate the total lag between Federal Reserve action on reserves and the ultimate major effect on g.n.p. as long as twelve to twenty-four months and suggest that the lag varies depending on prevailing conditions. Most agree that the major effect of Federal Reserve action is felt beginning immediately and spreading over some six to eighteen months. Researchers are hard at work on the problem, but the Fed doesn't know for sure. And it has to act, or let things go their way without control.

Federal Reserve officials have sometimes described their policy as "leaning against the wind." By this they mean that when the economy is moving up they tend gradually to impose a drag on the upswing; and when it is moving down they tend gradually to increase the monetary ease in the system to check the downswing. Question: Suppose the average lag of the effect of monetary policy is six months. Is a policy of leaning against the wind a sound one at all times?

Policies to Stimulate Aggregate Demand

Suppose aggregate demand is inadequate and the Fed wants to expand it. Its first act is to be sure the banks have plenty of reserves. It can lower reserve requirements and buy government securities in the open market, providing new bank reserves in paying for its purchases. In addition, it can offer to rediscount commercial paper the commercial banks may bring, thus guaranteeing liquidity to the banking system and eliminating the possibility of another debacle like that of the years 1929 to 1933 when mass liquidation of bank loans forced the downward spiral ever deeper.

If the Fed provides generous excess reserves, what will the bankers do? With growing excess reserves, they will want to lend, since idle reserves earn no interest. If times are reasonably good, history suggests that the banks will indeed increase their loans promptly. But in depression acceptable borrowers are scarce. Businesses need to borrow when they are expanding, not when they are contracting. With adequate reserves, banks will tend to lower their interest rates and make credit readily available to desirable borrowers. But that may or may not produce more loans.

Even in this case, however, bankers can put their reserves to work by buying government securities on the open market. These are always substantially safe, and they pay interest. And buying government securities increases the money stock, just as making new loans does. So flooding the banks with reserves will increase M, bidding up the price of bonds, and (what is the same thing) bidding down the interest rate (the effective yield on bonds).

History presents one big counterexample. After 1933, in the Great Depression, the inflow of gold plus Federal Reserve policy built up large excess reserves at the commercial banks. While bank credit in fact expanded rapidly as reserves built up, it did not expand nearly as rapidly as reserves grew. Thus, for the first time in history, the banking system held a huge volume of excess reserves over a period of years. Some economists suggest that this indicates a "liquidity trap" that we can expect to face again if we get into another serious depression. They argue that monetary policy is thus a very weak stimulant to expansion under such conditions. More excess reserves or more M will simply pile up in idle balances. But others point out that the large excess reserves of the 1930s were the exception to the general rule. Moreover, they stress that pumping reserves into the banking system did in fact increase M rapidly, and that in turn both money and real g.n.p. rose rapidly, once the great contraction of both reserves and M in the period from 1929 to 1933 was reversed.

Everyone agrees that easy money is a good thing in recessions, even though there is disagreement over its precise effects. The evidence suggests that lower interest rates are more likely to stimulate long- than short-term investment. On a long loan, like a thirty-year mortgage, a small reduction in the interest rate makes a big difference in the monthly payment. Thus, lower interest rates may be a substantial stimulus to long-term private and public projects like houses, public utilities, factories, highways, schools, and the like. Low short-term interest rates are less likely to stimulate investment. Cheaper money lowers the cost of borrowing for working-capital purposes—to meet payrolls, carry inventories, and so on. But here interest is a tiny part of the relevant costs. And the marginal efficiency of investment in inventories and the like depends heavily on volatile customer demand and profit expectations.

Since everyone agrees that easy money may help some to expand aggregate demand, why not just flood the banks with reserves to get whatever stimulus more M can produce? The answer is that here, as in fighting inflation, there may be danger of too much as well as too little. If the Fed pours excessive M into the economy, given the lags of policy it may be very hard to check the ensuing boom without very strong restrictive measures if "overheating" of the economy results. The timing problems faced in fighting recession are roughly comparable to those in fighting an inflationary boom. Just right is what's needed, not too much or too little!

The Dangers of Destabilizing Policy

Given the uncertainties outlined above, it is not surprising that the monetary authorities sometimes make mistakes. The monetarists, who generally support a reasonably stable growth in M, criticize the Fed for overreacting to short-run disturbances with big swings in M as it tries to keep interest rates and money-market conditions stable. In fact, they argue, such well-intentioned policies destabilize the economy. The neo-Keynesians, on the other hand, have recently criticized the Fed for letting interest rates swing too widely in misguided attempts to keep M growing reasonably stably.

The 1967 to 1970 period provides two lively case studies. By 1967, inflation had clearly become the economy's number one problem. The demand for credit soared with war spending and boom times. The Fed, seeing interest rates climbing toward historic highs, increased M rapidly to keep rates from soaring even faster. Nevertheless, borrowers complained of scarce and expensive credit. By 1968, long-term interest rates, which were only 2–3 percent during the 1930s, passed 7 percent on newly issued business bonds as the inflationary boom continued. Hoping to moderate this increase, the Fed increased bank reserves still further and M grew at over 7 percent per annum. Even so, both commodity prices and interest rates continued to climb—inflation reached a 5 percent annual rate and long-term interest rates on new grade-A bonds passed 8 percent.

Monetarists bitterly attacked the Fed. They argued that the rapid growth in M was feeding the inflation and was indeed the cause of the high interest rates because it led both lenders and borrowers to add a big inflation allowance to their interest-rate bargains. They claimed that in fact real interest rates were relatively low, since perhaps 5 percent of the quoted 8 percent rate was an inflation allowance. Thus, they said, actually money was very "easy." The only way to stop the inflation and lower interest rates was to reduce the rapid increase in M, just the opposite of the neo-Keynesian prescription for attaining lower interest rates.[3] In retrospect, the monetarists look substantially right in their criticism of the Fed in the 1967 to 1968 period.

[3]For the underlying monetarist analysis of the relation between M and interest rates in inflation, see page 109 (Chapter 9).

The rapid growth in M surely contributed substantially to the inflation, and probably helped to raise long-term interest rates through an inflation allowance, rather than to lower them.

But consider now the case of 1970. Very tight money (zero growth in M and very high interest rates) had checked the upswing in 1969, though inflation continued. The bloom was off the boom, unemployment was up to 5 percent, and industrial operating rates were below 80 percent. To keep the downturn from becoming a major recession, the Fed in early 1970 expanded M at a rate that temporarily exceeded 10 percent. Again the battle was on. Monetarists warned against stimulating a new inflationary boom, and urged reduction of the money growth rate to about the 4 percent long-term growth in the economy's productive capacity. Neo-Keynesians, pointing to growing unemployment and still peak interest rates (10 percent on new corporate bonds), pleaded for easier money and lower rates to avoid the danger of serious recession. They urged that the Fed not make a fetish of the growth rate of M but to pour in more reserves.

Who was right in mid-1970 is less than clear. History may have decided by the time you read this. To get interest rates down, would you have recommended that the Fed increase or decrease the growth rate in M? Whatever your answer, the monetary disputes of the years 1967 to 1970 suggest that well-intentioned monetary policy may be destabilizing—that government policy, however well meant, may be part of the problem as well as part of its solution.

Stable Growth in the Money Stock?

Some monetarists, led by Chicago's Milton Friedman, suggest a simple rule for monetary policy. Just increase the money stock about 4 percent a year through thick and thin. (The 4 percent is based on the assumption that this is about the rate of growth in the full-employment capacity of the economy. If the growth rate of the economy is more or less, the growth rate of the money stock could be adjusted accordingly.) These economists argue that, even with the best intentions in the world, the Fed cannot forecast business conditions effectively. Moreover, the lag in effect of monetary policy is uncertain, and the Fed generally pays too much attention to short-term interest-rate fluctuations. Thus, Federal Reserve discretionary action is likely to be wrong about as often as it is right, and in fact it has been destabilizing on many occasions in the past. A major example is the collapse of the years 1929 to 1933 when the Fed permitted the money stock to shrink by nearly one-third; another is that of the years 1967 and 1968.

Suppose we automatically increase M at about the full-employment growth rate of the economy, eschewing all attempts to forecast and to offset every real or imagined fluctuation. To be sure, this might not keep the economy exactly on a stable growth path. There might be small recessions and small booms, which might temporarily involve some unemployment and some inflation. But the policy would avoid big booms and big depressions. Whenever the economy began to fall into serious recession, continued increase in the money stock at the annual 4 percent rate would provide a massive support against collapse. Conversely, if inflation began, limitation of the growth in M to 4 percent annually would be a powerful restraint on the inflationary pressures. A constant-growth-in-M rule is not a counsel of perfection; it is advanced as a sensible precept of action that would give by and large good results and would avoid the danger of serious errors due to fallible monetary authorities.[4]

Few economists or laymen take the proposal to abolish the Federal Reserve and to substitute a completely inflexible rule of a stably growing money stock seriously. But many economists who have studied the evidence believe that the reasoning behind the rule has much to offer the Federal Reserve authorities. Whenever M is growing much faster or slower than the full-employment growth rate of the economy, that's

a warning flag, and there ought to be a good reason for the divergence.

The Lessons of Monetary Experience

What has history taught about the effectiveness of monetary policy in the United States, and about the problems of using it? Some historical vignettes may be helpful.

The 1920s—Boom and Bust

World War I was followed by a sharp inflationary boom and then by a short sharp inventory liquidation that drove prices spiraling down. By 1922, the economy had begun a long upward pull—almost a decade of good times and substantially full employment. In 1924 and again in 1927, prosperity was broken by slight hesitations. And increasingly as the boom continued, observers questioned whether times were not a little too good. Real-estate prices climbed as construction activity reached peaks never before dreamed of. After 1926, construction turned down. But the stock market soared as the public proclaimed permanent prosperity. The man in the street, the businessman, and the financier, became speculators "in the market." As stock prices spiraled upward, easy profits were available for the taking, especially since stocks could be bought on margin for only a tiny fraction of their sale price.

In the midst of this speculative fever, some questioned whether such a speculative boom could last. Industrial production leveled off in 1928 and construction activity slumped substantially. The general price level was stable. Federal Reserve authorities were divided among themselves on what was the best policy. Finally in 1929, they took mild deflationary action, in spite of widespread criticism, raising rediscount rates and speaking out against the excessive use of bank credit for speculative purposes. In late 1929 came the stock-market crash, triggering the worst deflation and depression of America's history.

Lesson: When times are good it's hard to know what's the right policy vis-à-vis specula-

---

[4]For a lively exposition of this proposal, see E. S. Shaw, "Money Supply and Stable Economic Growth," in M. L. Joseph, N. C. Seeber, and G. L. Bach, *Economic Analysis and Policy* (Englewood Cliffs, N.J.: Prentice-Hall, Inc., 1971).

tion and minor fluctuations—what would you have done? And when the boom gets roaring, steps to check it are generally unpopular. The life of a central banker is not easy!

The 1930s—Crash and Stagnation

As the economy spiraled downward, it was far from clear whether this was a major depression, a temporary stock-market setback, or merely a regular cyclical readjustment, after a long period of rapid economic growth. The Fed reduced discount rates to ease credit in the deflation. By early 1931, there was considerable evidence that the worst was over and that a new footing had been reached for recovery.

But European financial crises in mid-1931 set off worldwide hoarding of gold. Facing this gold loss, the Reserve authorities adopted a tight-money, high-interest policy to keep gold from flowing abroad. This made money hard to get at home in spite of widespread unemployment and the still uncertain recovery. Faced with a conflict of domestic and international goals, the Fed chose the latter. Within a few weeks, business turned down sharply again and the spiral of financial liquidation resumed. A quick return to easier money did not stem the tide. Unemployment soared. Runs on banks developed everywhere. On his inauguration day, Franklin Roosevelt's first major act was to declare a nationwide "bank holiday," closing all banks until the panic could be calmed and arrangements could be made to keep the financial system from complete collapse.

Following 1933, with Roosevelt's new appointees running the system, the Federal Reserve adopted easy money and low interest rates to fight the depression. Excess reserves were pushed up to $3 billion by late 1935, and then, as recovery seemed on the way, pulled back down to $1 billion in 1937. Soon after, the boomlet of 1936 to 1937 crashed precipitously back to mass unemployment in early 1938. Again there was widespread criticism of the preceding Federal Reserve increases in reserve requirements to restrain rising prices in spite of continued heavy unemployment.

From then on, the banks were flooded with reserves. Excess reserves exceeded $5 billion by the outbreak of war in 1939, in comparison to an average level of under $500 million through the 1920s. Total bank credit and the money stock rose in response to these added reserves. But by 1939, g.n.p. was still only back up to the level of 1929; 8 or 9 million people were unemployed; net private investment for the entire decade was a negative figure.

Lessons: (1) When mass deflation sets in, don't hesitate to flood the economy with liquidity. Hindsight makes it clear that the Reserve authorities made a fatal error in moving so slowly to eliminate the pressure of financial liquidation that swept the whole economy downward. (2) When times are bad, it's still hard to know what is the best policy vis-à-vis minor fluctuations. (3) In a major depression, flooding the economy with liquidity at least checks further financial liquidation and helps to stimulate total spending; but bankers may pile up excess reserves rather than correspondingly expanding loans and deposits. The life of a central banker is not easy!

World War II—War Finance, Gold, and the Congress

During the ten years before World War II, our gold reserves increased from $4 billion to $23 billion, as gold flowed in from abroad for investment and safekeeping during the troubled 1930s. The gold entering the United States was sold to the government through the Federal Reserve banks. Each dollar of gold increased the reserves of the commercial banks by $1, as the seller of the gold deposited the check paid to him by the government. It also increased the Fed's supply of gold by $1 as the member banks turned the gold over to it. By 1941 the commercial banks had huge excess reserves, and the Federal Reserve also had gold reserves far beyond the legal requirements against currency outstanding and member-bank reserves.

With soaring war expenditures, Congress raised taxes, but only enough to cover about 40 percent of the war's costs. The Treasury began to borrow to cover the difference. About half the government bonds were sold to the public, exchanging bonds for already existing money. The other half were sold to the commercial banks, which created new deposits to be spent by the government. This deposit expansion rapidly ate into the excess reserves of the commercial banks; withdrawal of currency into hand-to-hand circulation drained away reserves even faster (currency alone increased by over $20 billion during the war period).

By 1942, the commercial banks' excess reserves were nearly gone. The war blazed on and Treasury borrowing needs skyrocketed. What would you have done? You'd have found some way to permit the Treasury to sell more bonds to the banks in order to get money to finance the war, and that's just what the Federal Reserve authorities did. They could have lowered the reserve-requirement ratio to provide more excess reserves. But the currency drain was so rapid that it alone would have withdrawn all existing bank reserves in about two years. So the Reserve banks began to buy government securities in the open market, to create new bank reserves on which the commercial banks could then buy five times as many newly issued government bonds from the Treasury.

This was money-creation with a vengeance. Preceding a typical "war loan drive," for example, the Federal Reserve bought enough bonds in the open market to build up commercial banks' excess reserves. The banks could then buy all the bonds the Treasury could not sell to the nonbanking public. On a set day during the "drive," bank subscriptions for new bonds from the Treasury would be opened and the bonds allocated. Suppose the Treasury allocated $5 billion to the banks. Then the next day, the banks' balance sheets throughout the country would show $5 billion of new deposits for the Treasury, offset by $5 billion of new government bonds held by the banks. If you didn't quite believe that banks create deposits back in Chapter 12, World War II provided a vivid and irrefutable demonstration on a grand scale.

Between 1941 and 1945, the Federal Reserve created $23 billion of new member-bank reserves through open-market purchases. With these additional reserves, the commercial banks bought $70 billion of government securities and paid out $20 billion of new currency. As was to

be expected, each dollar of new reserves served to support about four dollars of new money.

But each new Federal Reserve note took 40 percent gold reserves, and new member-bank reserves took 35 percent gold reserves.[5] By 1944, therefore, the Federal Reserve itself began to run short of gold. It still had about the same amount of physical gold, but this gold was "used up" by legal requirements. Without more gold, its power to provide more currency and more bank reserves to help finance the war was threatened.

What would you have done? The Reserve and Treasury authorities went to Congress with a suggested solution. There was little dissent. Congress simply lowered the gold-reserve requirement to 25 percent against both Federal Reserve notes and deposits. The Fed again had excess gold reserves, though there was no more actual gold. The needs of war finance had triumphed over the tradition of gold and financial orthodoxy.

Lessons: (1) The Federal Reserve plus modern fractional-reserve banking provides an easy way to manufacture money in almost any amount desired. (2) In wartime, it's hard not to lose sight of the dangers of excess money issue and inflation in the press of winning the war. (3) Gold provided an ultimate limitation on the money-creating powers of the Fed under the law. But Congress makes the law and Congress can change it, even on gold.

Monetary Policy and the National Debt, 1946–1951

At the end of World War II, over $275 billion of government debt was outstanding, nearly $100 billion of it held by the banking system. Between $50 and $75 billion of this debt came due for refunding each year. The Federal Reserve faced a dilemma. (1) If it tightened bank reserves and raised interest rates to check the postwar inflation, the squeeze would induce banks to dump their low-yield government

---

[5]At that time, the Fed was required to hold gold reserves against both Federal Reserve notes and the deposits (reserves) of member banks.

securities on the market to get new reserves in order to make higher-yield business loans. This would force down the price of government bonds, with cries of anguish from the Treasury and the public. (2) On the other hand, if the Fed did nothing to check bank loans to private borrowers, it could ease the Treasury's job in refinancing the national debt by keeping bond prices up and interest rates down; but then it would be lying down on its job as the nation's monetary spearhead against inflation.

Until 1951, the Fed chose the latter path. It stood ready to buy all government bonds from the commercial banks at par, maintaining their price against decline. This action made it cheap and easy for the Treasury to refund the maturing debt. But it also meant that the banks' huge holdings of government securities were as good as excess reserves, since they could be converted into money at no risk at any time. Bank loans to private borrowers soared, as business boomed and prices climbed following the war.

The Treasury, anxious to maintain confidence in the goverment's credit, liked this policy. A huge volume of short-term securities was outstanding, and the holders might demand cash at maturity if government securities didn't remain attractive. Banks and nonbank holders might also lose confidence and try to sell their longer-term securities, drastically reducing prices. Treasury refunding would then have to be done at sharply increased interest rates, and the future market for government securities might be seriously weakened. Political repercussions from government-bond holders could be very unpleasant for the administration in power if bond prices slumped.

Many economists argued, however, that higher interest costs and sagging bond prices were a proper price to pay for the restoration of effective monetary restraint against inflation. The Fed increasingly took this view. If monetary policy was to check inflation, it argued, the Fed must tighten the overall credit supply, including a rise in interest rates to the federal government itself.

Thus, the Federal Reserve authorities tried gradually to tighten up the money market. Finally, in 1951, in an open break with the Treasury, the Fed withdrew its support for government-bond prices. Bond prices fell below par, but bank credit was tightened and interest rates rose. Federal Reserve control over the money supply was partially restored.

But even then, the Federal Reserve officials made it clear they would continue to work closely with the Treasury. Why? In spite of their "nonpolitical" status, Federal Reserve Board members are appointed by the president and are responsible to Congress. They recognize fully their primary role as part of the government. Their job is to work with other government agencies to produce a stably growing economy. Were they actively to combat the government's financial policy, or even fail to cooperate satisfactorily, the president might object strenuously and Congress could at any time alter the semi-independent status of the Federal Reserve. With a major portion of the nation's money supply outstanding against Treasury bonds, it is clear that Federal Reserve monetary policy and Treasury policy in handling the federal debt must be made cooperatively.

Lesson. There are many considerations that must be weighed in forming wise monetary policy. One of the most difficult problems is the weight to be given to Treasury financing needs when they conflict with other stabilization objectives. The life of a central banker is not easy!

The Dilemma of Inflation or Unemployment— The 1950s

Basically, the decade of the 1950s was a period of good times. But 1954 and 1958 brought short recessions reminiscent of 1924 and 1927. After 1954, unemployment hovered around 5 million, until the recession of 1958 shot the figure up to 7 million, the highest since the peak in the post–World War II conversion period. Recovery in the years 1959 to 1960 failed to restore high-level employment. Technological progress and greater managerial efficiency substantially reduced the number of workers needed to turn out any given output. In the meantime, the USSR grew at 7–10 percent annually compared to our 3–4 percent for the decade and consistently outpaced us in the space race. Yet, over the decade in America prices crept up nearly every year, and after 1958 we began to lose gold to foreign nations.

Was tight money—to avoid inflation and to keep up interest rates in order to check the gold outflow—holding down the rate of economic growth and causing unemployment? The Fed generally saw inflation and the gold drain as the major dangers, though it reiterated its goal of fighting both recession and inflation. From 1955 on, it permitted the money supply to grow only slowly, although it quickly eased credit in the recession of 1958. Increasingly, unions and Democratic politicians attacked the Fed as a barrier to a healthy, growing economy. They believed that tight money was shortsighted, for it put the "fetish" of a stable price level over the productivity and human happiness of full employment. Others, including the Reserve authorities, saw the problem differently. Only stable money could provide the foundation for continuing saving and prosperity, and we could not disregard the continuing gold outflow.

Lesson. Even prosperity has its problems. The hardest choices of all are between widely accepted goals that conflict. The central banker who places price stability above booming prosperity and rapid economic growth reaps many harsh words. The old refrain: The life. . . .

The Sagging and Soaring Sixties?

The next of these vignettes is the 1960s, first sagging, then soaring. During the early sixties the basic unemployment–inflation dilemma of the fifties persisted. And the problem was made more serious by our increasing concern over the loss of our gold stock to other nations. Beginning about 1963, however, the Fed, though moving cautiously, provided bank reserves so the money stock would rise at a faster rate, as both prices and interest rates remained relatively stable and the international position of the dollar improved gradually. Whether as effect or coincidentally, the growth rate in

g.n.p. stepped up; and by the mid-1960s the U.S. economy was again approaching full employment.

In 1965, soaring Vietnam war spending and private investment were superimposed on an already prosperous economy. Both prices and interest rates began to rise as unemployment fell. By year-end, inflation had emerged again as a major problem, and in 1966 the Fed hauled the growth rate in M down to zero to check the inflationary boom. Tight money worked, even against an economy fueled by rising Vietnam spending, and by late summer a "credit crunch" developed as credit became very scarce in mortgage and some bond markets. Talk of financial panic spread, inventories piled up, and consumer demand flattened.

In reaction, the Fed quickly stepped up the increase in bank reserves. M resumed its rise at 7–8 percent per annum, as government spending continued to rise rapidly. The result was resurgence of the inflationary boom by mid-1967, and the monetary policy dilemmas outlined in the "Dangers of Destabilizing Policy" section above were back again.

Again in the period from 1969 to 1970 tight money effectively slowed the boom, as the Fed held the growth in M to zero for much of 1969. But inflation persisted after excess aggregate demand had been eliminated, and unemployment rose rapidly to the 5 percent level. Monetary policy offered no clear—or at least no quick —answer to the unemployment–inflation dilemma, although it worked as planned on aggregate spending and real output. Inflation slowed, but only very gradually, as unemployment rose in the years 1969 and 1970.[6]

Lesson. Managing aggregate demand is very difficult when the economy is in the high-employment area. Tight money can check a boom; but if the dose is too strong, recession is the result. If inflationary expectations are deep-seated, monetary restraint is likely to slow real

---

[6]Every time the Fed tightens money to restrain economic expansion, the critics complain that the Fed is too "independent" and that it should be made directly subservient to the president. For both sides of this controversy, see the statements by Representative Wright Patman and G. L. Bach in *Economic Analysis and Policy*.

growth and employment much faster than it slows inflation.

Gold and Monetary Policy

The preceding pages say little about the fact that the United States lives in an increasingly interdependent economic world. During some periods, for example the quarter century following the mid-1930s, Federal Reserve policy needed to pay little attention to our economic relations with other nations. We had a lion's share of the world's gold reserves, and monetary policy could be focused almost entirely on domestic goals.

But over most of our history it has not been thus. And since the late 1950s our concern over gold and the international balance of payments has again played a major role in constraining our domestic monetary-policy actions. Although you can only understand the importance of gold and the balance of payments through a detailed look at the international economic relations (in Part Six), it is important in concluding this chapter on monetary policy to recognize briefly the role gold has often played.

What Was the "Gold Standard"?

The "gold standard" prevailed in the United States and most major European nations over a good share of the century preceding the 1930s. Although it varied from country to country, and from period to period, it had two major characteristics. First, changes in the total amount of money in each country were to be roughly proportional to changes in its gold holdings. Gold itself was not the only kind of money. But as new gold was received by a country, it would serve as the basis for additional money issued in the form of currency or deposits. On $1 worth of new gold, $2, $10, or some other number of dollars of new money might be issued. Similarly, an outflow of gold would reduce the nation's money supply.

Second, each unit of money was "worth" (freely convertible into) a certain number of grains of gold. Until 1934, for example, each U.S. dollar "contained" 23.22 grains of fine gold; that is, the price of gold was fixed so that 23.22 grains of gold could always be obtained at the Treasury for $1, and vice versa.

Thus, the gold standard in its pure form was essentially an automatic regulator of the supply of money. M would be largely dependent on the stock of gold in each nation. Actually, the gold standard was never as automatic in operation as in theory. But it did provide a strong constraining framework for almost all monetary-policy thinking and action over a long period of years.

The Gold Standard as a Safeguard against Inflation

The main argument for the gold standard in most people's minds is that it will safeguard the economy against overissue of money and inflation. Since the government must have gold to back each dollar, gold sets a limit to how much money can be created and provides value for the money issued.

But U.S. history shows clearly that as a practical matter the gold standard was no guarantee against sharp price-level changes. Figure 11–3 shows the big inflation that took place during and following World War I, the precipitous drop following that inflation, and the sharp drop from 1929 to 1933—all while we were on the gold standard. The quantity of money (M) fluctuated widely. This was partly because of swings in our gold stock. But also, as was noted above, as a practical matter the banking system could expand and contract the money supply over a wide range for any given amount of gold reserves, and in addition our monetary authorities often partially offset or augmented the effects of gold flows (not quite proper for the pure gold standard).

On the other hand, it is true that adherence to the gold standard would insure against any such runaway inflation as occurred in Germany after World War I, if sticking to the gold standard were politically and economically possible under such circumstances. Then the limited stock of gold would prevent a vast overissue of money. However, under such drastic circumstances it is hard to imagine that any country would remain on a gold standard. Remember from the discussion of hyperinflations in Chapter 11 the enormous political and economic pressures on the German government to pay its bills by creating new money. The drastic monetary disturbances of that period were as much a symptom as a cause of the difficulties of the German economy.

Most economists today deny that gold flows provide the best guide to how much money the economy needs. There is no reason to suppose that the optimal supply of money will correspond to how much gold is mined each year and how much goes into or out of speculators' hoards. Moreover, rigid adherence to a gold standard would tie the monetary authorities' hands against monetary action to combat unemployment and depression.

Abandonment of the Gold Standard

It was the desire to "do something" about the depression that largely explains the worldwide abandonment of the gold standard in the 1930s. Countries were increasingly loath to accept deflation as they lost gold. Getting men back to work became the major national goal. European countries faced huge gold drains into private hoards and to the United States. In 1931, England, long the financial center of the world, went off the gold standard. Remaining on gold meant intensified deflation as gold was withdrawn. Off gold, England could expand her money supply to check the depression and falling price level, regardless of gold flows.

Britain's abandonment of the gold standard was a terrific blow to the confidence of the financial world in those troubled times. The next major country to be hit by gold hoarding was the United States. Within a few months, our monetary authorities felt they must choose between staying on the gold standard (raising interest rates to keep capital from flowing out of the United States) or giving up the gold standard to be able to expand the money supply in the face of a falling gold stock.

They accepted the discipline of gold flows

and raised interest rates; and g.n.p. plummeted again. But finally, in 1934, as part of Roosevelt's emergency program to check the wave of bank failures, all gold was called out of monetary circulation into the Treasury. The United States officially went off the gold standard. Most of the countries of Europe had already taken this step. Today no major country retains the prewar gold standard.

The International Gold Reserve Standard

Today the United States and most other Western nations are on what might be called a limited "international gold reserve standard." Domestic monetary policy retains substantial freedom to counteract booms and depressions, regardless of international gold flows. The stock of money is not tied directly to gold reserves. But gold is used as a means of international payment among central banks and government treasuries and provides a basic international reserve for most nations to meet their commitments to other nations arising out of international trade and financial transactions. For many nations, American dollars have also come to be considered part of this international reserve, since dollars are widely acceptable in the payment of international obligations.

Since gold is one major means of international payment, gold tends to move from country to country when one owes more payments to another than vice versa. If a nation consistently spends more abroad (including capital investment and gifts) than it collects from abroad, it has a "deficit" in its international balance of payments, and tends to lose gold. The converse is true when it receives more payments than it makes. Thus, unless a nation has large gold reserves, there are limits to how long it can run a substantial deficit in its balance of payments, because of the danger that its gold reserves will be exhausted and that it will be unable to meet its international obligations. However, the major central banks (under a so-called "two-tier" gold system adopted in 1968) send gold only to each other, not to private individuals and businesses. Thus, there are two gold markets—one a set of exchanges among central banks, and the other a free market in which gold is bought and sold privately like other commodities.

The danger that we might lose gold to private speculators and other nations is thus a much weaker constraint on U.S policy makers than before 1968. But we still may see our gold drain away to other central banks if our international payments deficits are too large. And the Fed must always be aware of this danger. The details are provided in Part Six.

Review

CONCEPTS TO REMEMBER

Be sure you have a firm understanding of the following major new concepts and institutions. They supplement the list at the end of Chapter 12, most of which are essential also for this chapter.

"tight" and "easy" money
credit rationing
liquidity trap
M and interest rates as guides to monetary policy

differential effects of tight money
gold standard
international gold reserve standard
gold flows

FOR ANALYSIS AND DISCUSSION

1. Would you say that the Federal Reserve's chances of preventing a severe depression are better now than they were in 1929? Why or why not?
2. Suppose that prices are rising slightly, 5 percent of the labor force is unemployed, and a recovery in process seems to be running out of steam but you can't be sure. As a member of the Federal Reserve Board, what would you do?
3. Suppose you were a banker with a balance sheet roughly like that of the Victory bank in Chapter 12. Now the Federal Reserve raises reserve requirements to tighten credit just when the demand for loans from your long-standing business customers is rising. What would you do?
4. When inflation and unemployment coincide, sensible Federal Reserve action would be to raise reserve requirements while buying bonds in the open market. True or false? Explain.
5. If the Treasury must finance a federal budget deficit designed to stimulate the economy, what should the Federal Reserve do? Suppose it holds the stock of bank reserves constant; what would you expect to happen to interest rates and credit conditions?
6. If the Fed wishes to encourage stable growth in real g.n.p. and employment, what general rules should it follow in determining its policies? Can you see any serious objections to merely increasing the money stock about 4 percent per year?
7. When tight money is needed to check inflation, should the Fed provide special loopholes for housing borrowers, to avoid limiting home construction? If so, why? And how should they accomplish this goal?

fourteen

Fiscal Policy[1]

The Theory of Fiscal Policy
Expenditure versus Tax Changes
Discretion, Built-in Flexibility, and
    Politics
Does Fiscal Policy Work?
The Balanced-Budget Tradition
The Mix of Monetary and Fiscal
    Policy

Back in the pre-1930 days, government expenditures and taxes were only about 10 percent of the national income. But in World War II this figure soared to 50 percent, and during the 1950s it fell back only to around 30 percent. Federal, state, and local government spending of over $325 billion annually today exerts an enormous influence on the level and direction of the nation's economic activity. And there is little reason to expect a return to the 1920s.

Before the 1930s, almost no one questioned the wisdom of balancing the federal budget every year. Sometimes the government didn't manage to do it, but everyone was apologetic

[1]Some instructors may prefer to assign Chapter 38 on "The Public Sector" before Chapter 14, to provide further background for the discussion of fiscal policy.

about the failure. But as the depression deepened in the 1930s, the federal government just couldn't balance the budget, try as both Mr. Hoover and Mr. Roosevelt would. We had federal deficit financing because we couldn't help it. But an increasing number of people, led by economist John Maynard Keynes, began to argue that the government's excess spending was actually a good thing in depression. The argument went like this.

The government should "prime the pump" of private spending. Everyone can agree that it would be foolish to try to have government receipts just equal expenditures every week or every month. Why, then, should the budget be balanced every year, instead of every two, or five, or ten years? Wouldn't the sensible thing be to balance the budget roughly over the length of the business cycle? Government deficit spending in depression would help increase total spending and prime the private pump. Later, excess government taxes to pay off the debt in prosperity would help damp down the boom. The deficit would be a temporary expedient.

But as the long black years of the 1930s dragged on, faith in both monetary policy and government pump priming waned. Talk of a stagnant economy and a chronic deficiency in private investment spread. Emphasis shifted to a continuation of "compensatory" government spending, aimed at filling in the deficiency of private investment. According to the compensatory spenders, the private economy couldn't carry itself forward to prosperity even when primed by doses of government investment. Government deficit spending should be continued as long and as heavily as necessary to attain and maintain full employment.

The Theory of Fiscal Policy

Fiscal policy is the use of government spending, taxing, and borrowing to increase or decrease aggregate demand. Aggregate demand is the sum of private and government spending (g.n.p. $= C + I + GE$). The government can increase total expenditures by spending more than it currently takes away from private spending in taxes. Conversely, the government can reduce g.n.p. by taxing away more than it spends. Either way, the net change in autonomous spending triggers a multiplier effect.

Look back at the circular-flow diagram of Figure 5–2. The government may spend back more into the income stream than it currently withdraws from it, thus swelling the total. Or it may spend back less, thus reducing the flow of total spending. Obviously the net result depends on the expansionary effect of government spending offset against the depressive effect of tax collections.

An increase in government expenditures raises g.n.p. The increase per dollar of govern-

ment spending is determined by the multiplier. Each additional dollar of government spending on goods and services adds directly to g.n.p. and becomes income to an individual or a business. Part of this new income will be respent, in the familiar multiplier-respending process of Chapter 7. If the multiplier for the economy is two, for example, each dollar of additional government spending will generate an increase of $2 in g.n.p.

An increase in tax collections reduces g.n.p. The decrease per dollar of tax collections again depends on the multiplier. When individuals or businesses pay taxes out of their incomes, they reduce their spending on goods and services. This reduction has a negative multiplier effect, the reverse of the positive multiplier associated with government expenditures. The size of this negative multiplier will depend on much the same factors as those determining the positive multiplier on government spending, as was explained in Chapter 7.

The net multiplier effect of the government budget on the economy depends on the net result of these plus and minus factors. The larger the excess of government expenditures over tax receipts (i.e., the larger the deficit), the larger will be the effect of governmental fiscal policy on total g.n.p., other things equal. Conversely, the larger the excess of tax receipts over expenditures (i.e., the larger the government surplus), the lower g.n.p. will be, other things equal. These propositions will need to be qualified somewhat presently, but they provide a powerful first approximation. When we want the government to exert strong expansionary pressure on g.n.p., a larger government deficit is desirable.

Figure 14–1 presents the analysis graphically. Let the CC and $C + I$ lines be identical with the lines in Figure 7–4, back on page 78. Equilibrium income would then be 350, where $C + I$ cuts the 45° line. Now suppose the government enters the picture and begins to spend 10 each year without collecting any taxes (perhaps borrowing at the banks). We can thus draw a new government spending layer (GE) on top of the $C + I$ curve. This new $C + I + GE$ curve is 10 higher at every point. As indicated above, the

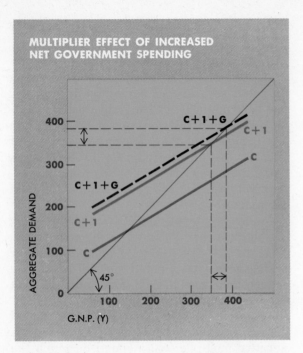

MULTIPLIER EFFECT OF INCREASED NET GOVERNMENT SPENDING

fig. 14–1

Net new government spending of 10 adds 10 of "investment" and, with a multiplier of 4, raises total income by 40—up to a new equilibrium of 390. This is identical with the multiplier effect of 10 of new private investment in fig. 7–4.

new government spending becomes income to the private economy and has a multiplier effect just like private investment. If the marginal propensity to consume is .75, the new equilibrium level of g.n.p. in Figure 14–1 will be 390, as the multiplier raises total income by four times the original government spending. Note that this new equilibrium income is identical to that in Figure 7–4, where the additional autonomous spending of 10 was private rather than government.

The Balanced-Budget Multiplier

It may appear intuitively that a balanced government budget (i.e., tax collections just equal to government spending) will always be neutral with respect to g.n.p. But this is not quite correct. An increase in government spending matched by an identical increase in tax collections provides some net expansionary multiplier effect, and a decrease in government expenditures exactly matched by tax reduction has a net deflationary multiplier effect. This is called the "balanced-budget multiplier." It works this way.

Assume that the government increases its spending by $10 million, and that the public's marginal propensity to consume is .5. Disregard any accelerator effects. The $10 million of new government spending immediately constitutes $10 million of new g.n.p., to which the multiplier adds another $10 million through respending. This gives a total increase in g.n.p. of $20 million in the new equilibrium level of g.n.p.

Now trace through the deflationary impact of the $10 million of new taxes to finance the expenditures. With a marginal propensity to consume of .5, private spending will fall by $5 million in the first round, $2.5 million in the second, $1.25 million in the third, and so on as in the preceding example. The total sequence of respending rounds ($5 million plus $2.5 million plus $1.25 million plus...) adds up to a total negative multiplied effect of $10 million for the tax increase.

Note that this negative tax multiplier is just $10 million less than the positive expenditure multiplier, just the amount of the budget increase. The respending effects after the first impact of the new government spending and of the new government taxes are the same, but the $10 million increase in government purchases of goods and services became a direct part of g.n.p. whereas the tax payment by the private economy to the government was simply a transfer of purchasing power that is not part of g.n.p. The "balanced-budget multiplier" is thus just 1 in this example; g.n.p. rises by precisely the amount of the increase in government spending financed by an identical increase in government tax receipts. The $20 million addition to g.n.p. exceeds the $10 million reduction by just the amount of the new government spending.[2]

Most economists agree that a balanced-budget multiplier effect of this sort occurs. But it need not be 1. This precise result depends on

[2]It follows from this reasoning that the tax multiplier will always be smaller than the expenditure multiplier per dollar of tax reduction or expenditure increase. Can you explain why?

190

two assumptions: that the government spending is on goods and services rather than on transfer payments, and that the propensity to consume out of disposable personal income is the same for taxpayers and recipients of government spending. In any event, the balanced-budget multiplier is, at most, only 1. Most economists believe that deficit-financed government spending is a far surer road to a higher g.n.p.

The Role of Money

In calculating private-investment or fiscal-policy multipliers, most neo-Keynesians say little or nothing about the assumed behavior of M. This does not necessarily mean, however, that money is unimportant. Implicitly, the usual assumption is that M or V adjusts somehow, so that interest rates remain constant while the multiplier effects are occurring. The adjustments in M or V may come automatically (perhaps because bank loans or the demand for money adjust automatically to changes in household or business expenditure), or because the central bank consciously adjusts M to keep interest rates stable.

To see why this assumption is crucial, assume that government increases expenditure without raising taxes, expecting thereby to expand g.n.p. through a multiplier effect. Rising incomes will increase the demand for money; therefore if M remains constant, the interest rate will rise, partially checking the desired multiplier effect. Thus, unless accommodating monetary expansion (in M or V) is assumed, the kind of fiscal-policy multiplier effects explained above are partially offset.

Given these facts, it is often difficult to tell whether rising g.n.p. reflects fiscal or monetary policies when government deficits and increases in M are engineered simultaneously. In any event, it is important to recognize that the apparent absence of money from multiplier analysis only means that the monetary role is being hidden behind the scenes—just as changes in g.n.p. induced by changes in M must implicitly assume accommodating changes in

household and business propensities to consume and invest, as was emphasized in the "Modern Synthesis" section of Chapter 9.

Price versus Real Output Effects

As with monetary policy, expansionary fiscal policy may raise the price level rather than real output, especially when the economy is near full employment. Unlike monetary theory (which stresses the distinction between money and real effects), early income–expenditure analysis simply stated all variables in real terms (g.n.p., consumption, investment, and the like) and assumed that inflation would occur only after full employment was reached. But no more! Both neo-Keynesians and monetarists faced the inflation-with-unemployment dilemma in the 1960s. Fiscal policy that succeeds in raising money g.n.p. may still find itself generating inflation rather than increased output and employment. Or, as in the 1969 to 1970 period, moves toward fiscal restraint may slow real economic activity without appreciably slowing inflation, just the reverse of the desired effect.

In this chapter, as in the last, we focus mainly on the powers of fiscal policy to keep aggregate money demand growing at some desired rate. The unemployment-with-inflation dilemma is postponed to Chapter 15.

Expenditure versus Tax Changes

If the government wants to change aggregate demand, will variations in expenditures or tax rates be more effective? Let us consider the problem in some detail when the goal is to reduce unemployment by raising g.n.p., and then consider more briefly the converse problem of checking inflation.

When the government wants to raise g.n.p., should it increase expenditures, cut tax rates, or both? The answer will depend partly on the relative flexibility of the two approaches, and partly on your socioeconomic preferences for "private enterprise" as against "public spending." Consider some of the issues.

Public-Investment Expenditures

"Regular" government expenditures in normal times include extensive investment in highways, education, parks, and so on. These public projects are presumably undertaken because they fill a greater social need than alternative private uses of the resources do. Citizens' dollars are diverted through taxation from private to government spending on goods and services. (Postpone for the moment such transfer payments as "welfare" and unemployment "insurance.")

Public spending in depression should be considered in the light of these "regular" needs. Such "net-social-gain" public projects should be the ones undertaken first in depression periods unless there are strong counterarguments. Next, projects that were marginal in periods of full employment may be worthwhile when expansionary public spending is needed. For example, a new highway that could not quite be justified on its own merits may become clearly desirable when it can double in brass as a recovery stimulant. But how effective is such spending against unemployment and underspending in the private sector?[3]

1. Outlays on public works directly stimulate the durable-goods and construction industries, where unemployment is often centered. Public expenditures "bunched" on public works can provide a big stimulus to demand in such industries (e.g., construction and steel).

2. Public works, unlike unemployment or relief payments, give us "something to show for our money." Modern schools, parks, and highways are valuable in their own right, beyond the help they provide in raising aggregate demand.

3. By providing jobs for otherwise unemployed workers, public-works projects help

[3]A more complete analysis of public expenditures will be found in Part Five.

maintain the morale, self-respect, and skill of workers. Even with a dole or unemployment compensation to avoid starvation, worker morale may suffer severely from unemployment; self-respect is lost; idleness becomes habitual; skills become rusty. Such social losses are a major cost of unemployment.

On the other hand, public-investment projects have serious limitations:

1. Most important, flexibility in timing is hard to attain. Public-works projects are generally slow to get started and hard to stop once the need for them is past, because of both their physical nature and their political setting. Every locality and political group demands its share. It takes a long time to draw plans and let contracts for major construction projects. Moreover, it is not practical to cut them off short of completion, once they are begun. A bridge halfway across a river or a partly-built schoolhouse must be completed to avoid flagrant waste even if depression has turned to inflation.

2. Public-works projects may perpetuate undesirable relative price–cost maladjustments in the industries where public-works spending is centered. Especially in the construction industry, wages and prices rise rapidly in boom times and stay up when demand slackens. Large government construction projects help keep these costs high.

3. Some types of public works may compete with private investment. This objection is advanced most strongly against government construction of low-cost housing and such combined power, reclamation, and flood-control projects as the Tennessee Valley Authority. Whatever the answer is on these public-works projects, a wide range of available outlets, such as education, highways, parks, and resource conservation, is clearly noncompetitive.

Some observers argue that in our rich society we starve the public sector of the economy. We desperately need better education, cleaner streets, slum clearance, and the like. Instead, we "waste" billions annually creating obsolescence through style changes on cars and refrigerators, on vast attempts to create demand for "unneeded" products. These observers argue that there is a presumption in favor of increased "public services" at all times, and that at a minimum we can obtain a balanced-budget multiplier effect by raising both expenditures and tax receipts. But others strongly oppose more government activities and favor leaving to individuals the choice of how they spend the dollars they earn. They say, cut taxes rather than increase government spending. Your preference will obviously depend heavily on your basic attitude about how far the government should go in allocating resources in our economy.

Transfer Payments and Unemployment "Insurance"

The government may also spend through transfer payments, especially direct relief or "unemployment insurance" payments to the unemployed. This is the cheapest and most direct way to get funds to the needy and to assure that they will be promptly spent. Few unemployed recipients will hold the funds they receive idle. And such payments, if authorized in advance, can begin automatically when unemployment occurs. There is no need for elaborate plans and negotiations over public-work projects. Indeed, we have built up a nationwide compulsory unemployment insurance plan, financed largely by payroll taxes collected while men are employed, that provides just such an automatic spending program. Transfer payments don't directly raise g.n.p. (give jobs), but their next-stage multiplier effects do. And their superior flexibility is a telling plus.

The problem of government transfer payments to fight recession is closely linked to that of lessening poverty, including poverty among the unemployed. Recently, widespread support has developed for a massive federal "minimum family-income plan," which would substantially guarantee a minimum income to all, whether or not they have jobs. (In one version, this is called a "negative income-tax plan.") If such a plan is adopted, federal payments will automatically be made to all whose incomes fall below the stated minimum for any reason, which will automatically provide government transfer payments to offset declining incomes, including those in recessions.[4]

Tax Cuts

Tax cuts are the alternative to increased spending when the government wants to expand aggregate demand. The multiplier effect of a tax cut, as was indicated above, is less than that of the same dollar increase in expenditures. This is because the expenditure counts directly as part of g.n.p., while the tax cut merely increases disposable income. Moreover, cuts in different taxes may have different respending effects. For example, a cut in personal income tax rates is guaranteed to increase disposable personal income accordingly, and the result is quite predictable. Household comsumption expenditures will rise roughy in accordance with the long prevailing propensity to consume, though there may be a lag as people take time to adjust their consumption spending to higher disposable incomes.[5] The effect of a cut in corporation income taxes is more difficult to predict; but there is widespread agreement that a cut in corporate income taxes is likely to stimulate investment spending.

Many economists favor tax cuts over increases in government spending, on grounds of greater flexibility. Taxes usually can be cut faster than expenditures can be increased, and they can be more readily reversed, at least in principle. A tax cut immediately increases disposable income and stimulates aggregate demand promptly. Moreover, tax cuts leave households and businesses free to spend their disposable income as they wish, in contrast to the government control over resource alloca-

---

[4]For details, see Chapter 37.

[5]If consumers believe the tax cut is a temporary one, and if the "permanent consumption" hypothesis explained in Chapter 8 is correct, they will increase their consumption spending less than for a permanent tax cut, since consumption under that hypothesis is a roughly stable proportion of *permanent* income.

tion when government spending on goods and services is increased.

Which is the better way to increase g.n.p., increased expenditures or tax cuts? To summarize, the first big issue is your basic preference for private spending against governmental provision of "public services." The second is the relative flexibility of the two plans. Suppose that some time soon you, a senator, were faced with the need to spur total spending because a recovery was topping off too soon, leaving 6 or 7 percent of the total labor force unemployed. The economy needs a $30 billion increase in aggregate demand. Would you vote to cut taxes or to increase government spending? Try justifying your recommendation to an opposition senator who says you are wrong.

Discretion, Built-in Flexibility, and Politics

Flexibility is crucial to the success of discretionary fiscal policy. For such fiscal policy to work well, the administration must recognize promptly what fiscal policy is needed. Then Congress must act promptly to change expenditures or tax rates, whichever it chooses. Although there have been some cases of successful, prompt action (for example, the excise-tax cut of 1965), these have been the exception rather than the rule. The two big income tax bills of the 1960s were both based on modern fiscal theory. But it took nearly three years, first to convince President Kennedy and then to get the widely applauded big tax cut of 1964 through Congress. The Johnson antiinflation surtax of 1968 was nearly as long in coming. Variations in government expenditures to combat economic fluctuations have also lagged notoriously behind the apparent need for them.

Thus, the record on using fiscal policy for stabilization has been a mixed one. Merely to guarantee against destabilizing fiscal effects (e.g., in the years 1961 to 1963 while the Kennedy tax cut was being debated) would mark a big step forward. Fiscal policy, notably a slow-moving, bickering Congress, is part of the stabilization

problem as well as of its solution. It is important to remember that the ultimate fiscal authority lies with Congress, not with the president. The president proposes, but Congress disposes.[6]

One way to reduce these lags would be for Congress to delegate limited power to the president to cut or raise tax rates temporarily (in some pattern previously specified by Congress) in case of rising unemployment or inflation. Recent presidents asked Congress for this power, to be exercised for a six-month period, subject to congressional veto at any time. But Congress has shown no interest whatsoever in giving away its exclusive power to vary tax rates. Nor has it shown much more willingness to give the president leeway to vary expenditure rates.

The most fundamental reform would be to persuade Congress to consider stabilization budget proposals promptly as such, and not to let them get bogged down in the usual tax and expenditure legislation procedures. The typical tax bill is subject to long hearings before House and Senate committees, with enormous pressures from lobbies and special-interest groups, each understandably out to protect its own interests. On the expenditure side, appropriations are largely controlled by some twenty-five powerful subcommittees, each dominant over its section of the budget, and often controlled by a congressman of long seniority who rules his domain almost as a private fiefdom. Little wonder that prompt overall budget swings to offset economic instability have proved difficult to obtain!

Perhaps Congress might be persuaded to consider separately as a stabilization proposal annual presidential recommendations for a flat percentage surtax (positive, negative, or zero) on personal and corporate income taxes, avoiding the issues of relative burdens and "inequities." Or conceivably Congress might be persuaded to adopt at the beginning of each year a total expenditure ceiling based on stabilization grounds, within which individual spend-

[6]For more detailed analysis with recommendations for change, see G. L. Bach, *Making Monetary and Fiscal Policy* (Washington, D.C.: The Brookings Institution, 1970), Chapters 7–8.

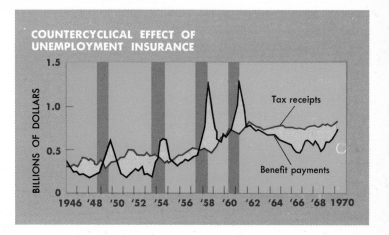

fig. 14–2

Unemployment insurance provides a strong, automatic coun-ter-cyclical force. While payroll tax collections are fairly sta-ble, benefit payments build up rapidly in recessions and fall rapidly as recovery develops. Data plotted quarterly. (Source: U.S. Department of Labor.)

ing decisions would have to fit. Today, such proposals are dreams. But dissatisfaction with present cumbersome congressional procedures that block effective stabilization policy is grow-ing, and change may come to facilitate more effective fiscal policy.

Another approach is "built-in flexibility" in taxes and government expenditures. Consider the tax side first. Suppose that the budget is balanced and that income and sales tax rates remain unchanged. If, now, a recession occurs and g.n.p. falls, tax collections will automati-cally fall. Thus, if government expenditures re-main constant, the declining tax collections will automatically generate a deficit to help halt the decline in g.n.p. Conversely, if g.n.p. rises and government expenditures stay constant, fixed tax rates will automatically generate a govern-ment surplus that will help to halt the rising aggregate expenditures. Since this built-in fed-eral flexibility apparently absorbs over a quarter of changes in g.n.p., it is a powerful automatic damper on fluctuations in the economy. Econo-mists dispute about the exact magnitude of the built-in stabilization effect, but all agree that, with the large size of the government budget in the modern economy, the damper is a powerful one.

On the expenditure side, as was indicated above, unemployment insurance provides a comparable automatic countercyclical varia-tion. As with the built-in flexibility of tax collec-tions, no one needs to forecast coming booms or depressions to obtain the stabilizing effect, nor does Congress or any official have to act to set

it in motion. The effect of unemployment insur-ance is much smaller in size than that of total tax collections, but Figure 14–2 illustrates its strong countercyclical nature.[7]

Built-in flexibility of taxes and expenditures provides a very useful countercyclical fiscal effect. Against minor recessions and booms it may be enough to keep the economy near an even keel. But few economists believe that we can count on built-in flexibility to protect us against big booms and depressions, if strong pressures toward either should develop. In such instances, discretionary policy is clearly required to supplement built-in flexibility. Im-proving our performance on discretionary changes is the number one problem in making stabilizing fiscal policy work better.

Does Fiscal Policy Work?

Some critics of modern fiscal policy argue that, however logical it all may sound, it just doesn't work, even aside from the long inside lag on congressional action. They cite the evi-dence of the 1930s, when there were large gov-ernment deficits but massive unemployment continued. They cite also the 1954–1964 decade, when the government ran persistent deficits but unemployment stayed above ac-

[7]Unemployment insurance has some special weaknesses. For example, if unemployment rises through new additions to the labor force there is no automatic countercyclical effect because the new entrants have built up no claims for unemployment-insurance payments.

195

ceptable levels. Advocates of modern fiscal policy counter these accusations, and further point with pride to the big tax cut of 1964, when the predicted stimulus to the economy worked out exactly according to plan. Who is right?

First, briefly note the evidence. During the 1930s, unemployment rose to a peak of about 13 million people by 1933, over 25 percent of the total labor force. Moreover, over the following years unemployment averaged over 18 percent of the total work force (nearly 10 million people) for the decade. The federal government ran a deficit in each year from 1931 to 1940, averaging about $3 billion annually—although the government clearly tried to avoid deficits until the last three or four years of the decade. The unemployment rate fell rapidly after 1939, as aggregate demand (and government deficits) rose with the onset of World War II.

During the 1954–1964 decade, the picture was much less dramatic, but in some respects similar. The federal budget showed a deficit in seven of the ten years, while the unemployment rate varied between 4.2 percent (in 1956) and 6.7 percent (in 1961). Unemployment never fell as low as the 3 percent level of the years 1952 and 1953 and of earlier prosperities.

Soon after 1960, President Kennedy's advisers began to urge a large tax cut to raise aggregate demand—in spite of the already substantial federal deficit. The economists predicted that the $10 billion tax cut would raise g.n.p. by $20–25 billion, through a combined multiplier-accelerator effect. And in fact almost exactly the predicted result occurred following the tax cut in 1964.

In 1968, a temporary (18-month) 10 percent surtax on all personal and corporate income taxes was passed by Congress to help check the inflation—after nearly three years of pleading by many economists. Result: consumers reduced their savings to pay the temporary tax, and the inflationary boom surged on—though probably less vigorously than without the tax increase.

How shall we assess this evidence? Defenders of fiscal policy contend that the 1930s were not a fair test of their proposals. First, what defi-cits did occur were the result of haphazard, unplanned actions. Indeed, government expenditures were cut and tax rates increased during the first three years of the decade when the depression was spiraling downward. Moreover, state and local governments were actually running surpluses big enough to offset the complete federal deficits until the mid-1930s. Even during the latter part of the decade, when President Roosevelt and the New Dealers finally became convinced that deficit financing was a sensible thing, deficits were still small, only 2 or 3 percent of g.n.p. With such a massive unemployment problem, they understandably didn't eliminate unemployment.

Again in the 1950s and early 1960s, government deficits were not part of a planned attack on unemployment. Rather, they came about haltingly, as the result of haphazard governmental fiscal measures on both tax and expenditure sides. And the temporary surtax of 1968 was both too late to halt a roaring boom and limited in effectiveness because it was announced as temporary.

The Full-Employment Budget

But the main argument of the supporters of fiscal policy is this—that in fact government fiscal policy in the 1930s, 1950s, and early 1960s was not expansionary in spite of the deficits. They argue that the deficits during these periods reflected mainly low incomes and employment in the economy, not positive government action to stimulate aggregate demand through a deficit. Thus to look at the actual government deficit during such a period is to look at the wrong measure of the impact of government fiscal policy.

Instead, they say that the proper measure of the effect of government fiscal policy is what surplus the federal budget would show at full employment—the "full-employment surplus (or deficit)." Although actual federal deficits occurred in most of those years, in all of them there was a large full-employment surplus. The federal budget on balance exerted a net drag on the economy before it could reach full employment, because with existing tax rates receipts

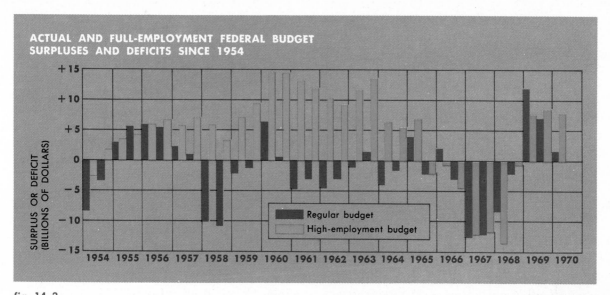

fig. 14–3

The "full-employment" and actual federal budget give very different pictures of the impact of the budget on the economy, especially during the last decade. Most economists believe the former gives a better indication of the net fiscal contribution or drag on the economy. Data are seasonally adjusted annual rates. (Source: Council of Economic Advisers.)

would exceed government spending before full employment was achieved. (Remember that total tax receipts rise with rising incomes, given any tax rates.)

In essence, this argument is that the persistent deficits of the 1930s, 1950s, and early 1960s reflected mainly the **involuntary** results of a depressed g.n.p. that pulled tax receipts below government spending levels. Tax rates were too **high** in spite of the deficit. Each time g.n.p. rose, rising tax receipts would have swung the budget to a surplus long before full employment was reached, given those tax rates.

In 1962, for example, the realized government deficit was $4 billion.[8] Yet, then existing tax rates would have produced a federal budget **surplus** of $10 billion, had the economy been at full employment. That is, existing tax rates put a heavy "fiscal drag" on the upswing long before it reached full-employment levels. And so it was for every year from 1954 up to the large tax cut of 1964.

Figure 14–3 shows this effect. The dark bars show the actual recorded federal deficits and

surpluses over the last decade—deficits for most years. The light bars show what the budget situation would have been had the economy been at full employment each year. In every year the federal budget would have shown a substantial surplus at full employment, and in some years (for example, from 1960 to 1963) there would have been a huge government surplus.

Some economists think of the federal budget as "neutral" when the full-employment surplus is zero. Whether or not one accepts this definition of neutrality, it is important to see that a balanced full-employment budget is not necessarily desirable. If in fact at full employment private investment would exceed private saving, then the ideal government full-employment surplus would be just large enough to offset the private-investment excess. Conversely, if at full employment private investment would exceed private saving, ideally the government full-employment budget should show a corresponding deficit.

With both the actual and the full-employment surplus (or deficit) it is important to see that it is only **changes** (plus or minus) in the level of the surplus that will induce **changes** in g.n.p. That is, only **changes** in the full-employment budget

[8]Data here and in Figure 14–3 for "actual" budgets are for the "national income and products account," rather than the "cash" budget.

will stimulate or depress g.n.p. A large government surplus will mean a lower g.n.p., other things equal, than would a smaller surplus or a deficit. But remember that if we want to raise aggregate demand, it is necessary to increase the government's deficit or decrease its surplus, and conversely to move the budget toward surplus if we want to lower g.n.p.

"Fiscal Drag," "Fiscal Dividend," and Economic Growth

Critics and advocates of modern fiscal policy alike agree on one major point. With our rapidly growing economy, given any level of government spending and any set of tax rates, the federal budget will rapidly move toward surpluses as g.n.p. increases. With a 4 percent annual increase in g.n.p., federal tax receipts rise by $8–10 billion annually. Thus, a budget in balance one year will show $8–10 billion surplus only a year later with stable federal spending. To avoid this "fiscal drag" resulting merely from the growth of the economy, we must cut federal tax rates by $8–10 billion annually, increase federal expenditures by this amount, or some combination of the two. Actually, with inflation added to real growth, the fiscal drag during the late 1960s was growing at about $15 billion per year.

Looked at another way, this fiscal drag can be seen as a huge "fiscal dividend" we can obtain by merely holding tax rates constant as the economy grows. Holding federal tax rates stable over the next decade would generate an annual surplus of perhaps $100 billion by 1980, assuming continued growth, unchanged government spending, continuing 4 percent unemployment, and no inflation. This potential surplus could finance a vast increase in federal spending on education, urban renewal, health, and the like. Alternatively, it would permit large tax cuts if we maintain an unchanged level of federal spending. But the fiscal-drag analysis warns us that we will build up massive deflationary pressure over the decade if we neither cut tax rates nor increase federal spending. The fiscal drag in that case would surely prevent rapid economic growth with full employment, and the fiscal dividend would never materialize.

The Balanced-Budget Tradition

This reasoning suggests that government deficits and surpluses are powerful tools in fighting unemployment and inflation. Yet until the 1930s scarcely anyone questioned the proposition that the government's budget should be balanced every year. And today many people still believe a balanced budget is the best thing. We need to take a more detailed look at the consequences of different budget policies.

Annual Budget Balance

A balanced-budget policy is, in one sense, a "neutral" government policy. The government feeds back into the income stream just what it withdraws—no more and no less. Thus, a balanced budget seems appropriate when we are satisfied with the existing level of g.n.p.— roughly, in periods of full employment without inflation.

But suppose recession appears. What does the annually balanced budget policy call for? With falling g.n.p. and unchanged tax rates, the government's tax receipts will fall. A deficit will be created automatically unless offsetting steps are taken. To avoid the deficit, the annual-budget balancers say: Raise tax rates to get more money or reduce spending to match reduced tax receipts. If you believe that the government ought to try to expand total spending in order to check the recession, the balanced-budget prescription is clearly wrong. To reduce tax rates and increase government spending would help raise the level of total spending, but the balanced-budget policy calls for exactly the opposite actions under recession conditions.

Similarly, inflation would generate budget surplus, calling for tax reductions and increased spending to avoid this surplus, under an annually balanced budget policy. Again, this seems clearly the wrong prescription for stabilization purposes. It would speed the inflation, rather than check it.

If an annually-balanced-budget fiscal policy is likely to give the wrong answer so often, why did it take so long to discover its weakness? There are probably three answers: (1) a faith that by and large the private economy will itself correct deviations from full employment without government intervention; (2) a belief that budget deficits always lead to inflation; and (3) an analogy that if private individuals should balance their own budgets, the government should do likewise. You should be able to form your own judgment on (1) by now. On (2), government deficits certainly tend to raise aggregate demand or keep it from falling, but whether this leads to inflation of course depends heavily on whether the economy is already near full employment. On (3), we shall have more to say in analyzing the effects of a large public debt in the next chapter. For the moment, keep an open mind.

A Cyclically Balanced Budget

The obvious difficulties of annual budget balancing led, during the 1930s, to the proposal that the budget should be balanced not annually, but over the length of the business cycle. There seemed no great virtue in one year as an arbitrary accounting period. A cyclically balanced budget would permit government fiscal policy to play a positive stabilizing role, running a deficit in depression and a counterbalancing surplus in the following boom—and at the same time maintain the basic character of a balanced budget.

How about this sensible sounding policy? History suggests one major problem. What if the government runs a big deficit fighting a long, severe depression, and then the following boom turns out to be a weak affair that never gets up to full employment? Should the government then try to collect a large surplus to offset the preceding deficit, even though to do so would depress the economy again? The advocate of a cyclically balanced budget policy would presumably say "yes," but common sense rebels at the idea of a big government surplus when the problem is to get out of a recession.

If inflationary booms just offset depressions, a cyclically balanced budget could work out precisely right. But if the two needs for fiscal policy turn out not to balance at all, the cyclically balanced budget philosophy exposes us to the same false prescriptions as annual budget balancing.

"Functional Finance"

"Functional finance" is the logical outcome of the new fiscal economics. The "functional finance" advocates say: Forget about balancing the budget as a separate goal. Use the government budget as needed to help provide full employment without inflation. If the private economy stagnates, more federal deficits than surpluses are appropriate; a rising government debt is a small price to pay for the avoidance of mass unemployment. If the private economy is too buoyant, we need continued government surpluses. The major goal is stable economic growth, and we shouldn't become so preoccupied with our tools that we lose sight of our basic objectives. This approach is called "functional finance" because it views the federal budget functionally, as a means toward the goal of stable economic growth.

This policy is the logical conclusion of looking at government fiscal policy as a means of compensating under- or overspending in the private sector of the economy. This theory says it's the right thing to cut tax rates even though we already face a big deficit if aggregate demand at present tax rates is too small to provide prosperity. To paraphrase Admiral Farragut, "Damn the deficits, full speed ahead!"

High-Employment Budget Balance Plus Built-in Flexibility

One last middle-of-the-road budget proposal is worth attention. It proposes that we should first determine federal spending (on nonstabilization grounds); then set tax rates to cover those expenditures at roughly full employment; and then, foregoing discretionary countercyclical fiscal policy, rely on built-in flexibility to keep the economy from swinging to either unemployment or inflation.

For example, suppose federal spending is set at $200 billion because that's the volume of public services we want the government to provide on the assumption we must pay for them through taxes. Then tax rates would be set to yield $200 billion when g.n.p. was at roughly full employment. With stable tax rates, tax yields would vary directly with any fluctuations in g.n.p.

Assume that we can begin with a full-employment situation. Then, if g.n.p. falls because of recession, tax collections would automatically fall below $200 billion. Government expenditures would be maintained, however, so that a deficit would automatically be created to check falling income and employment. If g.n.p. soars above the full-employment level, tax receipts would rise about $200 billion and an automatic budget surplus would result to damp the boom. Expenditures would be held at $200 billion in either case, except for unemployment benefits and other such automatically countercyclical expenditures. The plan would thus combine "built-in budgetary flexibility" with the basic virtue of making Congress face up to the need to balance expenditures with taxes—at full employment.

Proponents of this plan claim that they are facing political and economic realities that other approaches gloss over. The built-in flexibility plan would require no action on the part of Congress or the administration in forecasting business developments and in changing tax and expenditure policies to counter changing economic conditions. There would be no need to delegate congressional power over tax rates or spending to get quick action. Congress would need only to establish annually the basic level of government spending and set tax rates to cover those expenditures at high-level employment. The rest would be automatic; just don't try to change tax rates or expenditures to stabilize the economy, since, as a practical matter, you'll probably do as much harm as good.

But this plan has weaknesses too. First, there's no guarantee that the automatically created deficits and surpluses would be big enough to keep small swings from developing into big booms or depressions. Second, if the private economy is basically stagnant or over-buoyant, a federal full-employment budget balance won't compensate for this private under- or overspending. In those cases, the economy needs positive federal stimulus or response, not the federal neutrality of full-employment budget balance. Full-employment budget balance isn't necessarily a policy that will produce and maintain full employment.

The Mix of Monetary and Fiscal Policy

Fiscal and monetary policy must be effectively coordinated for optimum results. Unless they are, one may offset the other.

Suppose, for example, the government reduces tax rates to expand aggregate demand. Unless the money stock is simultaneously increased, interest rates will rise and the expansionary force of the tax cut will be partially offset. Why? Because government borrowing will tend to bid up interest rates, and as income rises the public's demand for money balances will also rise, further increasing interest rates. But if the Fed simultaneously provides more money for the system, interest rates can be held down and this offsetting effect can be avoided.

The 1964 experience shows the importance of such cooperation. The big tax cut led to rising incomes, to rising demands for money balances as transaction needs increased, and to upward pressures on interest rates from direct federal borrowing to finance the deficit. But simultaneously the Fed provided new bank reserves that permitted the money stock to grow about 5 percent during the year, which kept interest rates roughly stable and helped the inducement of more spending. Whether monetary or fiscal policy deserves more credit is not the main issue here; we needed both.

The late 1960s demonstrated the problems that arise if we rely too heavily on one policy instrument without help from the other. From 1965 through 1968, fiscal policy was highly expansionary, reflecting big increases in both Vietnam and domestic spending. The Fed had to undertake single-handed the job of slowing the inflationary boom. In 1966 rapidly tightening money shot up interest rates and produced a credit crunch, as the growth rate in M was dragged to a halt for almost six months. In particular, new credit for home construction nearly vanished as lenders channeled funds to more attractive borrowers. Similarly, rising interest rates made it very difficult for local governments to borrow; many were forbidden by law to pay more than stated rates, which were below soaring market rates. New and small businesses also found funds very hard to obtain.

Although the credit crunch of 1966 was alleviated by Federal Reserve provision of more bank reserves, the squeeze of tight money on particular sectors, notably housing, continued to the end of the decade. Almost exclusive reliance on tight money to check the inflationary boom threw the brunt of restriction on particular sectors of the economy. A more balanced stabilization program, including restrictive fiscal policy, would have permitted a broader, more equitable spreading of the burden.

The need to mesh international and domestic considerations raises different problems of determining the right policy mix. During the early 1960s, for example, our international position has called for high interest rates to keep funds invested here instead of abroad, while at home unemployment called for increased aggregate demand. Under these circumstances, many economists urged tighter money to raise interest rates in order to solve the international problem, combined with an expansionary fiscal policy to stimulate the domestic economy.

When we come to the problem of long-term economic growth, still another policy-mix problem will arise. Suppose, for example, we want to stimulate faster growth when we already have high-level employment and stable prices. We can do so by an easy-money policy, lowering interest rates to stimulate investment. But under these circumstances, this policy will produce excess aggregate demand and inflation. However, if we simultaneously raise taxes to generate a budget surplus, we can restrain demand and counteract the undesired inflationary pressure. Thus, an easy-money policy of low interest rates combined with a budget surplus could help stimulate growth while maintaining high-level employment without inflation. (But this low interest rate policy, alas, is just the opposite of what we may need for international purposes, if conditions are as described in the preceding paragraph.)

History shows that the world has an unpleasant way of throwing up new problems, every time we think we have the old ones well under control. Prudent economic policy will require flexibility in the way we use monetary and fiscal policy, and a changing mix of these policies to cope with new situations as they arise.

Review

FOR ANALYSIS AND DISCUSSION

1. You are asked to speak before a local businessmen's group on whether federal taxes should be increased, lowered, or left unchanged for the next year. Outline the talk you would give, indicating briefly how you would develop each of your major points.

2. If gross national product is $50 billion short of a full-employment level, the public's marginal propensity to consume is .8, and private investment is constant, about how much additional government investment, financed by bank borrowing, would be necessary to raise gross national product to a full-employment level? Explain why, indicating clearly any assumptions you make. Would your answer be different if the government spending is financed by borrowing from the general public? Explain.

3. Suppose the situation is as in the preceding question, but the level of private investment is not held constant. Would you then expect the amount of government investment required to be larger or smaller? Why?

4. "Since government officials can't forecast accurately what fiscal policy will be needed when, we are better off to rely entirely on built-in fiscal stabilizers." Do you agree? How could we increase the strength of our built-in stabilizers?

5. Does the "full-employment budget surplus" analysis convince you that federal fiscal policy can work effectively, in spite of the coexistence of large deficits and unemployment in the past?

6. State carefully all the advantages and disadvantages you can think of in balancing the federal budget (a) weekly; (b) annually; (c) over the cycle; (d) over a fifty-year period; (e) only when business conditions are at the desired level, regardless of how often this occurs. Which alternative is best on the basis of your analysis?

7. Assume that international tensions require a $50 billion increase in military expenditures over the next two years. Would you recommend that the federal government raise the $50 billion by borrowing, or by increasing tax rates? Why? Does the balanced-budget multiplier affect your answer?

8. Suppose you believe that a growth rate of 5 percent per annum is essential for the American economy. What federal fiscal measures would you advocate to achieve that growth rate?

9. As an economist for the President's Council of Economic Advisers, you are asked to prepare a set of recommendations for action in case a recession develops in the near future. Outline the recommendations, explaining your reasons for supporting these measures.

fifteen

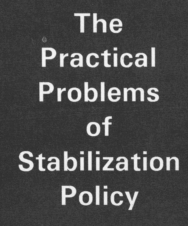

The Practical Problems of Stabilization Policy

Can We Have High Employment without Inflation?

The Problem of Forecasting and Flexibility

The Problem of Expanding Government Control

The Problem of the Public Debt

Are Depressions Obsolete?

In principle, monetary-fiscal policy to smooth out booms and depressions and to keep aggregate demand on a stable growth path is clear. But will it really work?

The first thing to note is that there isn't much evidence yet. We have had less than four decades of experience with conscious fiscal policy. Congressional and public opinion have only gradually accepted the idea of countercyclical budget policy, and advocates of an annually balanced budget are still powerful. Thus fiscal policy has been controversial, halting, and spotty—far from the orderly plan laid out by the functional-finance programmers. Even monetary policy has been used in a modern vein only recently.

The results thus far have been mixed. Chalk up the 1930s as poor, but hardly a reasonable test of combined monetary-fiscal policy; the 1940s and fifties as so-so; and the 1960s as mixed—sometimes promising. Four decades is a short period, and it would be surprising if our new stabilization tools had proved fully successful in their trial run, especially with such an unsystematic trial period. The World War II experience did demonstrate unmistakably the enormous expansionary power of large-scale deficit spending financed by bank credit. And since 1940 there has been no major recession— the longest generally prosperous period in our history. But we have had intermittent inflation and unemployment during the period.

This chapter looks at four important practical problems we face in trying to stabilize the

203

growth of the economy through monetary and fiscal policy.

Can We Have High Employment without Inflation?

Either unemployment or inflation alone can be attacked readily by monetary and fiscal policy. The former calls for easy money and an expansionary budget, the latter for the reverse action. But when unemployment and inflation occur together, there's trouble.

Is there a necessary connection between the rate of inflation and the amount of unemployment? For example, if we want only 3 percent unemployment, will we have to accept a 5 percent inflation rate? Worse, if we want only 3 percent unemployment, will we have to accept an ever-growing inflation—5 percent this year, 6 percent the next, and so on? If there is a "tradeoff" between inflation and unemployment, is it only a temporary phenomenon or one that we must face indefinitely?

The Short-Run Unemployment–Inflation Tradeoff

Until the 1950s, economists generally assumed that prices would not rise much until reasonably full employment prevailed. But no longer. Now just about everyone agrees that as we approach full employment and labor markets become tighter, higher wage costs and prices will appear in some sectors before the economy as a whole reaches "full" employment (even if full employment is defined to allow for 2 or 3 percent frictional unemployment). The lower the level of unemployment, the more inflation there will be. Moreover, the faster the growth in demand, the less time there will be for markets to adjust and the more inflation is likely to accompany rising expenditures. Thus, if we want to achieve full employment rapidly by expanding demand, a probable price is some degree of inflation.

Is There a Long-Run Tradeoff?

Whether there is a long-run (or permanent) tradeoff between unemployment and inflation is much less clear. The short-run trade-off problem can be minimized by increasing demand only gradually, or by accepting some inflation to get unemployment down but expecting prices to stabilize once the rapid expansion in spending is halted. But if the tradeoff is a long-run one, the policy problem is more serious. Then we can lower unemployment and keep it down by increasing aggregate demand only through continuing inflation.

A pioneering study by A. W. Phillips of the London School of Economics showed that in England over the past century, whenever unemployment fell below about 5 percent, wage rates tended to rise faster than was consistent with stable prices. Some American economists believe they see the same general relationship in our economy. This tradeoff between unemployment and inflation can be shown graphically in what is often called a "Phillips curve." Figure 15–1 plots the rate of inflation against unemployment; the curve suggests the tradeoff between the two during the 1960s. It is this kind of curve that supporters of

fig. 15–1

In general, prices rise fastest when unemployment is low. Curve is fitted to data for 1960s; note that it would fit less closely if 1950s were included. (Source: Council of Economic Advisers.)

the long-run trade-off theory cite to support their position. They argue that we can only keep prices stable by accepting substantial unemployment (as in the early 1960s). Conversely, lower unemployment can be bought only with faster inflation (as in the late 1960s).[1]

But most economists think the problem is more complex, and question any such simple 5 percent-unemployment-for-stable-prices trade-off. First, they point out that the curve would not fit so well if we included the 1950s, and even less if we included still longer periods. Equally important, there are serious unsettled analytical problems in the long-run trade-off theory.

(a) As the footnote to Figure 15–1 states, there is no simple relationship between wage rates and prices, even if an unemployment–wage-rate tradeoff were established.

(b) Theoretically, the inflation stimulus to employment presumably stems from the fact that in inflation selling prices rise faster than wage costs. This widening spread leads businesses to employ more workers. But the wage lag does not occur in all inflations. And if an inflation persists, both workers and businesses are likely to adjust their expectations accordingly. Workers include an inflation allowance in their wage demands; businessmen are increasingly willing to grant such inflation allowances to buy labor peace. Thus, as inflation is built into anticipations, the wage lag vanishes and with it businesses' incentive to hire more workers. Unemployment tends to rise back to its original level or at least does not decline any further as inflation continues. Therefore, if this reasoning is correct, any purchase of reduced unemployment by inflation is a purely transient, short-run phenomenon that can last only as long as inflation is not anticipated. A steady rate of inflation, once it has become anticipated, will not increase employment. Only an ever increasing rate of inflation that continually runs ahead of anticipations can further reduce unemploy-

ment. And it's hard to fool all the people all the time.

How much of a long-run tradeoff actually exists between inflation and unemployment is thus a complex, unsettled issue, on both empirical and theoretical grounds. Certainly we are unsafe in counting on more inflation to buy a continuing increase in employment. It is also apparent that under some circumstances more inflation may be a cost of achieving lower unemployment. More theoretical and empirical research is needed before the issue can be considered settled. In the meantime, easy talk about buying more employment by accepting more inflation must be viewed with reservations. Two distinguished experts on the problem have summarized the situation as follows: "Authors of Phillips curves would do well to label them conspicuously, *'Unstable. Apply with extreme care.'*"[2]

Wage–Price Guideposts and Incomes Policies

The problem of avoiding inflation in a high-employment economy is not unique to the United States. Nearly every major Western economy has faced it intermittently since World War II. Broadly, two approaches to handling the problem have been tried. One is the use of wage–price–profits "guideposts" developed by the government in cooperation with labor and business. In essence, these imply guidelines as to how the national income shall be shared, and they are often called "incomes policies." The other approach is through improvements in labor and product markets, information on jobs, training facilities, and the like, to shift the Phillips curve to the left by assuring that unemployed workers can move quickly into the jobs that open up when aggregate demand increases. Consider the wage–price guideposts' approach first.

In 1962 President Kennedy's Council of Eco-

[1]Actually, Phillips plotted the increase in wage rates against unemployment. But since wages are a big element in costs, many economists plot prices directly against unemployment, though logically this slides over a complex relationship between wage rates and prices.

[2]A. Rees and M. Hamilton, "The Wage-Price-Productivity Perplex," *Journal of Political Economy*, February, 1967, p. 70. For a good nontechnical summary of the controversy, see "The Relation Between Prices and Employment: Two Views," in *Federal Reserve Bank of St. Louis Monthly Review*, March, 1969, which also includes references to more detailed studies on both sides.

nomic Advisers suggested a set of wage–price "guideposts" for unions and businessmen.[3] The Council suggested that if unions and businesses would adhere to these guideposts, aggregate-demand policy by the government could bring full employment and prosperity without inflation. The Council didn't suggest government action to force unions and businesses to adhere to the guideposts, but it did urge them as useful guides to private behavior.

In essence, the guideposts suggested that annual wage increases in all industries should roughly equal the average increase in output per man-hour in the economy.[4] With such wage increases, prices of final products should be kept stable. Bigger wage increases would be inflationary, while smaller ones would give an undue share of the benefits of increasing productivity to profits. The guideposts were based on the general position that wage rates should behave about as they would in a highly competitive market where supply and demand would tend to produce wage increases equal to increases in "productivity."

Consider a simple example. Assume a stable population and an economy where all income goes to wages and profits. Total output is $300, of which wages are 2/3 and profits 1/3. Now suppose the total output increases by 3 percent

[3]See *Economic Report of the President*, January, 1962, chap. 4.

[4]Three details may help spell out the implications of the guideposts:

1. Wages in particular industries *should not* be directly related to productivity changes in that industry. Thus, if productivity in the automobile industry increases 5 percent per year, but only 3 percent for the economy as a whole, this does not justify a 5 percent wage increase in the auto industry. Rather, it calls for a decline in the price of automobiles.

2. Prices should remain approximately stable in industries that have an average rate of productivity increase. Where productivity increases faster than the national average (that is, where per-unit costs fall faster than the average), selling prices should decline. Prices should rise where productivity increases more slowly than the average.

3. Some exceptions are justified. Wages should rise less than the national average in industries where unemployment persists, to discourage additional workers from entering the industry and to encourage employers to use more labor in that industry. Wages should rise faster than the average where labor is especially scarce. (Again, these are the results to be expected from highly competitive markets.) Moreover, individual wages could rise more or less than the national average where deviation is needed to correct major inequities.

(that is, $9), and that wages are increased by 3 percent, as suggested by the productivity guidepost. Wages will now rise by $6 (that is, 3 percent of $200), leaving $3 for increased profits (that is, 3 percent of $100). Thus, the average-productivity increase guide would increase both wages and profits by the same percentage, maintaining whatever distribution of income prevailed before. It is important to see that increasing wage rates in proportion to productivity increase does not mean that all of the increase goes to labor, although this is a commonly held misconception.

The 1962 guideposts have been the source of violent disagreement. The critics make three main points.

First, if you don't think the present income distribution between wages and profits is fair, preserving it won't be very attractive. Many union members believe that profits are already exorbitant. Many businessmen believe profits are already too low. And at any time individual wage rates in particular firms or industries may be unfairly out of line, too high or too low.

Second, fixed-income people—the pensioners and old people—would like to see prices decline with advancing productivity, since unless prices fall they don't share in the fruits of progress.

Third, both unions and businessmen told the government to keep its nose out. They wanted no government control, and rebelled at the idea that they shouldn't take full advantage of their competitive positions, though some were reluctant to say so publicly. If productivity rises 5 percent annually in the auto industry, the auto workers are understandably reluctant to settle for only a 3 percent wage increase, just because productivity elsewhere has increased less than theirs. If you were head of the auto union, would you agree to take a 3 percent increase when by hard bargaining you could get 5? If you were president of General Motors, would you reduce prices just because the guideposts say that this is desirable when you believe you could make bigger profits by keeping prices up? Would you take a costly strike to hold wages down to help the nation fight inflation, when there's plenty of demand to support higher prices for autos and when wages are rising elsewhere?

Consider a more recent example. In the 1969–1970 period, the Federal Reserve resolutely set out to halt the growing inflation in a high-employment, booming economy. Tight money succeeded in slowing the growth in money g.n.p. from about 8 percent to 4 percent a year. But the slowdown brought the growth in real g.n.p. to a virtual halt while prices were temporarily rising at about 5 percent a year, the peak rate of the inflationary period. Everyone was in favor of stopping inflation. But the unions said (accurately) that inflation since 1965 had eaten away much of their nominal increases in wages. Thus they demanded wage increases equaling productivity advances plus allowances for expected future inflation and to make up for past real gains lost through past inflation. Businessmen argued (accurately) that such wage increases would sharply increase unit costs. Thus, they argued they would have no alternative to increasing prices. Whatever happened to current wage settlements, many union contracts had large built-in wage increases for two or three years ahead, far in excess of probable economywide productivity gains of 3 or 4 percent.

Again, wage–price guideposts, or an outright wage–price–profit freeze, were widely suggested to get everyone to go along in slowing inflation without generating a recession in the process. In 1970, no one seriously proposed cutting back wage increases immediately to the 3.2 percent level of the 1962 guideposts, or prices to absolute stability. Instead, most proposals involved getting workers to agree to a gradual slowdown in wage increases, and businesses to absorb part of these wage increases so as to slow down the rate of price increases. Advocates of a temporary wage–price–profit freeze proposed that it be used to break the spiral of inflationary psychology and to facilitate a move back to high employment without inflation.

But neither workers nor businessmen responded with any enthusiasm. Each pointed to the "excessive" income claims of the other. Guideposts that ask unions and businesses forego private gain for the national good, without any government-enforcement mechanism, obviously face serious problems. And most Americans have a deep distrust of giving the government power over individual wages and prices. Some guidepost advocates urge government "jawbone" intervention in pattern-setting wage bargains, and pitiless government publicity on inflationary wage and price behavior. But often such informal pressure hasn't been very effective, and the step from there to actual governmental dictation of key wage and price settlements is a short one.

Nearly everyone agrees that the broad guidepost results are sensible. But many economists reluctantly argue that only hard-boiled market pressures of weak aggregate demand can drive businessmen to bargain hard enough to slow wage increases to noninflationary rates and to set prices that seriously squeeze profits. They suspect we can drive out the inflationary psychology of workers, businessmen, and consumers based on the past inflationary decade only by accepting at least a moderate recession, with its painful unemployment, falling profits, and stable prices.

Many others are unwilling to pay this cost for breaking inflationary expectations. While they know the voluntary, or even compulsory, wage–price guideposts cannot be counted on to halt inflations fed by large excess demand, they argue that when excess demand has been eliminated (as in 1970) some form of guideposts can help modestly in easing wage rates and prices down to acceptable growth rates. Government publicity on inflationary wages and price policies can put pressure on both unions and businesses to moderate their behavior. Moreover, supporters see wage–price guidelines increasingly as vital educational ventures, largely aimed at building up public understanding and support for wage and price behavior consistent with both high employment and reasonably stable prices.

What has been the experience of foreign nations? Pretty much the same as ours, though on the average their unemployment rates were lower than ours since World War II, and they had somewhat more inflation. In some countries (for example, Holland) national incomes policies have apparently helped significantly for substantial periods, as long as three or four years, before support for them eroded. Some nations have given their guidelines the force of law; others have relied on joint responsibility for formation of the guidelines and public pressure for enforcement. In all cases, though, it is clear that such incomes policies work only when they seem reasonable to the major participants and when they have the force of public opinion behind them.

Manpower Policies, Structural Unemployment, and Inflation

Since neither aggregate demand nor incomes policies alone seem able to assure high employment without inflation, policy makers turn also to other measures that will shift the Phillips curve to the left—i.e., that will increase the level of employment consistent with any given level of spending and inflation. Better job-information exchanges, training and retraining facilities, moving allowances, and reduced monopolistic barriers to entry by unions are examples of such measures. All are aimed at improving the efficiency of labor markets; all whittle away the core of unemployed for any level of aggregate demand; all are complementary, not competitive with, aggregate demand policies for stable economic growth.

Unemployment that seems hard to eliminate through growth in aggregate demand is often called "structural unemployment." It reflects the failure of unemployed workers to move into jobs because of lack of information on job openings, inadequate skills, financial inability to move to other areas, low I.Q.'s, laziness, and the like—in contrast to unemployment caused by inadequate total demand. There are jobs available in the economy, but the structurally unemployed can't find or fill them. With an increased rate of "automation," many feel that structural problems have increased substantially—old skills rapidly become obsolete and major retraining is necessary if the unemployed are to find new jobs.

An example is the middle-aged West Virginia coal miner, thrown out of work a decade ago by mechanization of the mines, uneducated, unskilled except in coal mining, and abjectly poor, living on his little garden patch and perhaps a small government welfare check. Even though there are plenty of jobs for college graduates, for skilled machine-tool operators, for computer programmers, these have little relevance to him. And expanding aggregate demand further isn't going to make much difference to him. It will just bid up the wages of the skilled workers who fit the expanding job categories.

There is certainly some structural unemployment in our economy. But the evidence is strong that more aggregate demand effectively pulls most of the unemployed back into jobs, even when they appear to be structurally unemployed. If consumer demand is strong enough, businessmen somehow find the workers needed and train them on the job if there is no other way. The profit incentive is a powerful weapon against structural unemployment. While such unemployment is always a problem for some, there's little evidence that it's worse now than before.

The recent experience of Pittsburgh, a major steel center, is a good example. In early 1962 the unemployment rate in Pittsburgh was over 11 percent, compared to a national average of about 6 percent. Pittsburgh was a major "labor surplus" area. Employment in the steel mills had been declining persistently since World War II. The steel companies could produce one-third more steel than ten years previously, with fewer men. Pittsburgh was cited as a classic case of structural unemployment—unemployed steelworkers whose jobs were gone forever and who were ill-equipped to take on other jobs and unwilling or unable to move to other areas.

But after the strong economic expansion of 1964, Pittsburgh unemployment at year-end was only 3.7 percent, compared to over 5 percent for the nation. Rapidly growing aggregate demand boomed needs for steel in the economy. Mills called displaced workers back to their jobs. But more important, over the years 1960 to 1964 more than 100,000 people emigrated from the Pittsburgh industrial area as more jobs opened up elsewhere in the United States. Areas like Pittsburgh, specializing in production of durable goods, are especially susceptible to swings in aggregate demand. But the Pittsburgh experience emphasizes that what appears to be long-run structural unemployment may be eaten away rapidly by growing aggregate spending. The "hard core" of unemployed workers is of ice, not of iron. We can melt much of it away under the sun of strong aggregate demand.

But enough aggregate demand to do the job is likely to cause unacceptable inflation. Thus manpower policies to improve the efficiency of labor markets are fundamental steps toward high employment without inflation. This lesson has been forcefully brought home by the inflation–unemployment dilemmas we have faced since World War II. Moreover, most European nations have done far more than we, and their unemployment rates have averaged substantially lower than ours. More emphasis and dollars on manpower policies are clearly indicated if we hope to achieve our macroeconomic goals.

The Problem of Forecasting and Flexibility

Fine tuning the economy for stable economic growth depends on accurate timing of monetary and fiscal policies: knowing when to do what, and then doing it at the right time. This problem has come up repeatedly before.

Any honest economist will admit a lot of uncertainty about just what policy measure should be adopted when. First, economic forecasting is improving rapidly, but it's still a long way short of sure reliability.[5] It's sometimes hard to know for sure where we are, even more so to tell where we'll be six months hence. Second, even when we know what lies ahead we're not sure of the exact impact of different combinations of taxes, government spending, and monetary policy. Is a $10 billion surplus gentle restraint or a sledgehammer against inflation in a $1 trillion economy? Lastly, there's uncertainty about the lag before either monetary or fiscal policy has its full impact on real g.n.p. and employment.

[5]For a fuller discussion of forecasting methods, see the appendix to Chapter 10.

On monetary policy, the Fed can act promptly once the need is diagnosed. All the authorities need to do is buy or sell bonds in the open market, a matter of hours after the decision is made. So the "inside" lag between recognized need and action can be short. But the "outside" lag between Federal Reserve action and its final impact on output and employment is unfortunately longer, and worse, is uncertain in length. Most economists put the outside lag at from six to eighteen months on the average; some of the effect comes immediately but the rest spreads out over many months. If they're right, using monetary policy effectively against minor business fluctuations is tough. Before easy money stimulates more spending, the recession may be over; instead, its impact may come just in time to reinforce the next inflationary boom.

On fiscal policy, it's the "inside" lag that causes most of the trouble. Both the administration and Congress have to be convinced of the need to change taxes and spending to fight the boom or recession, and then they must act. It's a slow total process, especially if the need is to damp an overheating boom. Prosperity is nice. And the prospect of being blamed for a depression strikes horror to the heart of any elected official.

But don't put the blame too readily on "those politicians." Ask yourself what you'd do if you were president or a senator in 1970, when inflation was still unchecked by government policies, but unemployment had climbed to 5 percent. To make your answer easier, assume that you don't even plan to run for reelection, and that all you care about are the best interests of the people as a whole. What would you do?

The "outside" lag is shorter for fiscal than for monetary policy. With widespread tax withholding by employers, a change in personal income tax rates is reflected immediately in after-tax take-home pay (disposable personal income). Government spending, once it is begun, directly affects aggregate demand and employment.

Several proposals to improve the administrative-legislative flexibility of stabilization policy have already been noted. One would delegate more tax and spending powers to the president. A second suggests reform of congressional procedures in handling stabilization proposals. A third would adopt a simple, rigid rule, such as an annual 4 percent increase in the money stock, which would completely avoid administrative discretion. A fourth would increase the amount of built-in fiscal flexibility in the system. Alas, no one has a satisfactory answer, but we are gradually improving our ability to focus stabilization policy effectively on the economy.

The Problem of Expanding Government Control

If the economy persistently tends toward underemployment, compensatory fiscal policy might mean steadily rising government expenditures. Many Americans don't like this picture of larger government spending, because they feel that it would mean expanding government control over private economic affairs.

Views differ violently on whether increased government spending involves undesirable interference with the affairs of private individuals and businesses. One school points out that the government is directly responsible to the people, and we can always vote the rascals out if we don't like what they're doing to us. Another argues that increased government spending is the primrose path to socialism—step by step the government takes over direction of our economic lives. Still another says that the public sector is starved and that we need more government spending. Make up your own mind. Economics gives no clear-cut answer.

But don't forget that when expansionary government fiscal policy is needed, tax reductions can do the job too. So fear of growing government spending need not block active fiscal policy.

One thing is clear on the record to date. Most big expansions in government spending have come with war and preparations for war, not with attempts to stabilize the economy. Even the New Deal of the 1930s channeled only a small fraction of the national income through the government in this worst of all depressions, compared to the massive government spending

of World War II and the Vietnam conflict. Still, there is little doubt that it is much harder for the government to stop spending than to start. But social-welfare and income-maintenance programs soared in the 1960s and 1970s. And the antirecession projects of today can easily turn into the regular government expenditures of tomorrow—the farm price-support program of the 1930s is a prominent example.

The Problem of the Public Debt

Much of the controversy over fiscal policy arises because people fear the rising public debt that comes with deficit financing. Since the 1920s, the public debt has increased to nearly $400 billion. Should we view the public debt with alarm? The answer is, not with as much alarm as most people have, but with some. The first step toward an objective assessment of the problem is to look at the facts.

The Facts about the Public Debt

Figure 15–2 shows the public debt (the heavy black line), and the debt as a percentage of the g.n.p. (dashed red line), since 1920. It is clear that our present $380 billion federal debt came largely from World War II. It's also clear that as a percentage of g.n.p. the federal debt has steadily drifted downhill from a peak of about 130 percent at the end of World War II to below 40 percent now.

Another useful way of looking at the federal debt is in terms of the interest charges it involves. Figure 15–3 shows annual interest payments on the federal debt since 1920, and again those payments as a percentage of g.n.p. Interest rates have risen persistently since World War II, and the annual interest payments on the debt have grown to $18 billion. This growth has roughly matched the steadily growing g.n.p., so that interest payments have run about 1.5 to 2 percent of g.n.p. over most of the last decade.

It is also interesting to compare public and private debt. Figure 15–4 shows dramatically that private (corporate, household, and farm) debt accounts for most of the massive growth in total debt since 1929. Of the private-debt in-

G.N.P. AND THE FEDERAL DEBT, 1920-1970

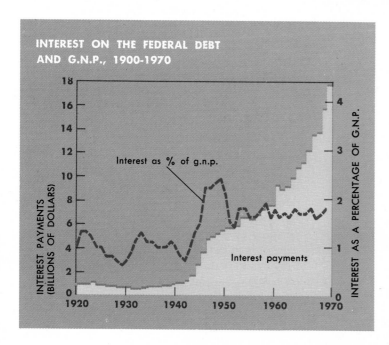

fig. 15–2

The federal debt has spurted upward in war periods, but has declined steadily relative to g.n.p. since World War II. (Sources: U.S. Treasury and Commerce Departments.)

INTEREST ON THE FEDERAL DEBT AND G.N.P., 1900-1970

fig. 15–3

Annual interest on the federal debt now exceeds $17 billion but it is less than 2 percent of g.n.p., and only a slightly higher percentage than during the 1920's. (Source: U.S. Treasury Department; data for fiscal years.)

PUBLIC DEBT AND PRIVATE DEBT, 1929-1969

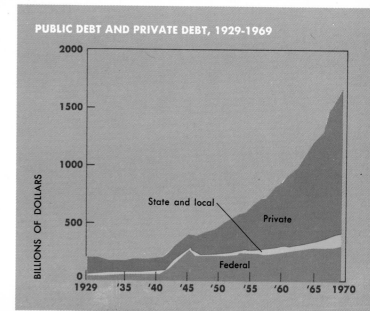

fig. 15–4

Net public and private debt combined are now nearly $2 trillion, but private debt accounts for three-fourths of the total and nearly all the huge increase since World War II. (Source: U.S. Department of Commerce.)

crease, about half is corporate debt and the other half is debt of individuals and unincorporated businesses. The biggest single item is real-estate mortgages, which now exceed the federal debt, having grown from about $30 billion in 1946 to nearly $400 billion in 1970. There's far more private than public debt to worry about.

Against these facts consider seven common objections to a large federal debt.

The Danger of Bankruptcy and Economic Collapse

May a big government debt bankrupt the government and lead to economic collapse? "Bankruptcy," as the word is generally used, means inability to pay one's debts when they are due. In this formal sense, the federal government need never go bankrupt, because it always has the power to tax, and the economic capacity of the entire economy to produce provides fundamental ability to pay taxes. Beyond this, the federal government has the power to create money to service or repay the debt. It never needs to default.

But can a big public debt bankrupt "the economy"? Extremely unlikely, is the answer. Payment of interest and principal involves essentially a redistribution of income and assets within the economy, so long as the debt is domestically held.[6] It is conceivable, of course, that the government debt might be so large as to lower drastically the credit standing of the government among investors. But U.S. government bonds are still the world's ultimate gilt-edged investment. Even with its huge debt, the government obtains funds in competitive markets at the lowest interest rates of any borrower. And whatever interest rate the government must pay to borrow, there is nothing involved that will "bankrupt the economy," whatever this vague term actually means.

In looking at the problems raised by a large government debt, most economists emphasize the need to look at the debt relative to current g.n.p. As the preceding section indicates, on

[6]If the debt is held by foreigners, then payments on interest and principal involve actual costs to the domestic economy rather than merely a redistribution.

this score the burden of the debt has steadily declined since World War II, while interest payments have remained a roughly constant percentage of g.n.p. If g.n.p. grows at only 4 percent annually over the years ahead, the increase will be over $40 billion annually. Thus the public debt could increase by nearly $20 billion a year, or over $200 billion in only ten years, and still merely maintain the present ratio of the debt to g.n.p.

Surely the dire predictions of economic collapse because of the public debt are overdone. But there are six more worries to consider.

"A Big Public Debt Must Cause Inflation"

Closely related to the economic-collapse argument is the assertion that a big public debt must necessarily cause inflation, sooner or later.

A government deficit, other things equal, surely has an expansionary effect on aggregate demand because government spending adds more to the income stream than taxes subtract. But the result may or may not be inflation, depending largely on how near the economy is to full employment and how many bottlenecks expanding aggregate demand encounters. In any case, it is important to recognize that any inflationary effect arises from the current expansion of total spending generated by the government's deficit spending, not from the existence of public debt per se.

But the "public debt causes inflation" claimants often argue that the larger debt will cause inflation sometime in the future, even if it doesn't now. This argument too is a dubious one. The expansionary pressure of the deficit occurs when the government spending occurs, as was indicated above. The mere existence of the resulting debt a decade later has little or no expansionary effect of total spending. Indeed, the transfer burden involved in interest charges may well be somewhat deflationary, since the transfer is generally from lower- to higher-income groups.

Is there no validity to the "inflation-in-the-future" fear? Two more arguments are advanced. The first is that when the public holds the new public debt among its assets, its propensity to spend out of current income will be increased. This may be true, but this could hardly generate major inflationary pressure without a huge increase in the public debt outstanding; current consumption is relatively insensitive to changes in holdings of liquid assets. The second is that the government, saddled with the public debt, will someday create new money to pay it off, and the newly created money will then create inflationary pressures. Obviously this second argument is difficult to rebut or support. How much weight you give it will depend heavily on your faith in governmental processes to produce responsible fiscal behavior. Certainly history shows that there need not be repudiation of a large debt through inflation, though some government debts have been eliminated this way.

"It Just Passes the Burden on to Future Generations"

Many people say that borrowing to pay our government bills just passes the cost on to future generations. But this concern is largely fallacious, as a little careful reasoning will show.

Suppose we are fighting a war. The real economic cost of war consists of the resources used up. If we use steel to produce jet engines and missiles, we can't use it for autos and refrigerators. A further real economic cost is the wartime disruption and destruction. However the war is financed—by taxation, by borrowing, or by just printing new money—these real costs are substantially the same. They are borne by the war generation. They cannot be passed on to future generations except insofar as wartime destruction may impoverish future generations because we pass on less real capital to them. The dollar cost of the war may be higher if deficit financing generates inflation, but the real cost in resources used up by the war is unaffected. If the new debt is accumulated through antidepression deficits that succeed in putting unemployed resources to work, there is little real burden of any sort on the generation involved.

But may not borrowing impose a special burden on future generations,[7] even if it cannot

remove the basic burden from the present generation? The answer is that payment of interest and principal by any future generation is just a transfer or redistribution of income within that generation. If the debt is paid off, the future generation is taxing itself to pay itself. If the debt is refunded, the result again is a redistributional one, and indirect transfer effects are minimized. Although the redistributional effects may be important, the crucial factors determining the economic well-being of the future generation are its accumulated real capital and its current real output. Having a money debt from earlier generations does not reduce either, and hence imposes no aggregate real burden on the future generation.[8]

There is one way that borrowing instead of taxing can pass a real burden on to future generations, even with an internal debt. This is on the assumption that people who buy bonds consider them as wealth, and base their lifetime consumption levels on the higher wealth they now hold. Thus, holding bonds from the war financing, after the war the present generation would consume more than if it had been taxed, and would accumulate correspondingly less capital to be passed on to following generations. In this way, borrowing rather than taxing might burden future generations and lessen the real consumption given up by the present generation because of the war. Some economists believe this is the way people behave; many others are doubtful. In any event, the main real costs of government spending and use of resources are as indicated above.

The Transfer Burden of Interest Payments

Large annual interest costs on a big public debt may impose a real burden, even though these are only transfer payments within the economy—from one of our pockets to the other, considering the nation as a whole. The taxpayer

---

[7]To simplify matters, a "future generation" is assumed to be one that does not overlap with the present generation. The basic reasoning is similar if the generations overlap, but

the results are more complicated because then we need to consider the relative positions of working and retired people in the two generations.

[8]If the war generation borrows outside the United States, and the future generation has to pay foreign bondholders, then it may be justifiable to speak of a burden of payment being placed on the future generation in the United States.

and the interest receiver may be different people. To the individual taxpayer, higher taxes to finance interest payments on the debt seem a very real cost.

Heavy taxation tends to distort people's behavior. If the government takes a big chunk of each additional dollar earned, your incentive to work may diminish. Taxes on particular items raise their cost relative to other items and shift demand away from the taxed goods. Nobody knows just how important such distortions are, but they look substantial. And they surely increase as the tax share of the national income goes up.

Lastly, given our present tax system, taxing to pay interest on the debt tends to shift income from active earners to rentiers, and (to a smaller extent) from the poor to the rich. Taxing the workers and the poor to pay bondholders sounds unjust to many people.

Psychological Deterrents to Private Investment

Many writers allege that concern over the government debt deters private investment. Direct facts on the issue are hard to come by, but most evidence suggests that the danger is easy to overstress. Business investment depends far more on consumer demand relative to productive capacity and on expected profits than on the size of the public debt.

The business community and the general public adjust surprisingly quickly to changes in the economic environment. One of the writer's first memories of economics is the bitter controversy that raged during the 1930s over whether a public debt as huge as $50 billion could conceivably be borne without utterly destroying organized economic activity. No one seriously dreamed the debt would ever go so high—the argument concerned a hypothetical ultimate upper limit. By 1936 or so, the $50 billion had been upped to $100 billion, as New Deal borrowing burgeoned. Fifty billion dollars no longer seemed to mean certain disaster. By 1941, the debt of $50 billion was forgotten in the mad scramble for materials, labor, sales, and profits as government and private spending soared with the war. Soon the question, no

longer an issue of burning interest, was: What about a $200 billion debt?—or $300 billion?

With the present national debt near $400 billion, per capita income at new highs each year, and the economy growing persistently, public concern over the debt is far less than it was a generation ago. Conservative financial circles still demand debt reduction. But there is little reason to believe that if a further increase in debt is required, we will not adjust "psychologically" to it as we have to previous increases. The businessman who foregoes otherwise profitable investments because of the debt item on the Treasury daily statement is hard to find.

Debt Management and Monetary Policy

A big federal debt may increase the difficulty of using monetary policy effectively. Billions of dollars of government bonds held by the commercial banks provide a facile base for inflationary credit expansion if the Federal Reserve supports government bond prices. Even if it does not, bank holdings of bonds represent a huge stock of semiliquid assets. The Governments held by the public also create a vast backlog of spending power for inflationary spending sprees, making control through monetary-fiscal policy more difficult.

If stagnation lies ahead, this liquidity may be helpful. But when inflation looms on the horizon and with continued Treasury refunding and new borrowing ahead, Federal Reserve officials can hardly help feeling hampered by the present big debt. When the Treasury needs to refund $100 billion of federal debt annually, in addition to any new borrowing, it hopes to have security prices high and interest rates low. But these are precisely the conditions that encourage inflation and increase the liquidity of the outstanding public debt. The Federal Reserve can only fight inflation by making the Treasury's job harder. Remember the monetary policy vignette following World War II.

Encouragement of Government Waste

As a matter of practical politics, too easy reliance on borrowing invites easy spending. Experience has shown that when Congress doesn't feel obliged to raise taxes to pay the bills, waste and inefficiency are likely results. This is a homely but important argument against too easy reliance on continued deficit financing.

How Big Can the Public Debt Be?

How big can the public debt be? There is no simple answer to this question. Government debt per se has certain disadvantages but they are not overwhelming. The most important principle is that changes in the level of public debt—either increases or decreases—ordinarily exercise a much more direct and forceful effect on the level of current g.n.p. than does any given level of existing debt.

Current fiscal policy (which may increase or decrease the public debt) is thus generally more crucial than the level of existing debt is. If our major aim is to maintain high-level output, the level of public debt in itself becomes a residual effect of stabilizing fiscal policy. Paying off the debt, viewed in this fundamental fashion, is a secondary reason for running a budget surplus. Whether a budget deficit or surplus is desirable depends predominantly on whether a deflationary or expansionary effect on current g.n.p. is needed. Once we have the public debt, its major effect has been felt. Similarly, the effect of paying off the debt will be largely through the impact of the current budget surplus.

Government Debt as an Offset to Saving

In a high-income economy, individuals and businesses save large amounts annually. These savings must be channeled back into the circular income flow if they are not to exert a deflationary effect. Savers may return the funds themselves by direct investments. But most do not, and instead put their savings into banks, buy bonds or stocks, or acquire other liquid assets. If financial intermediaries like insurance companies receive the savings, then they must channel the funds on into real investments.

To have a smoothly functioning economy, therefore, we must have liquid assets (bonds, stocks, and the like) available for savers and financial intermediaries to buy as part of the machinery for channeling savings on into real investment. Private businesses and individuals want to borrow a lot of savings. But if their demand for savings to make real investments falls short of the savings being made at high-income levels, g.n.p. will contract. New government debt (resulting from a government deficit) is one way of filling this shortage of liquid assets for savers to buy, with the government then making the real-investment expenditure.

Savers also want to hold money (deposits and currency) as one form of liquid asset. Again, growth in private borrowing at the banks may generate just the amount of money the public wants to hold at the desired high g.n.p. level. But if this is not the case, increases or decreases in the public debt provide a device for helping the Federal Reserve to provide just the amount of money the public wants to hold at the high-employment g.n.p. level. Remember that of our present money stock of about $200 billion, $100 billion represents money created against new government debt during World War II. As an interesting exercise, ask yourself what would happen if the government paid off this debt.[9]

Are Depressions Obsolete?

At the end of this long analysis of economic fluctuations and stabilization policy, a concluding question: Are depressions and inflationary booms obsolete? Are improved private practices plus the impressive arsenal of the government's monetary-fiscal tools sufficient to protect us against another debacle like the 1930s? Against smaller recessions? Against inflations?

It is clear from Chapters 13 to 15 that the problem of inflation with high employment is still unsolved. But on avoiding big depressions

---

[9] A difficult brainteaser: What growth in the supply of liquid assets will be required to facilitate a stably growing, high-employment economy? Answer: Just enough liquid assets each year to absorb savings made at high-employment g.n.p., less the amount that savers put directly into real investment themselves. In terms of financial-asset structure, the right mix of money and other financial assets is that mix that gives people just the amounts of money and other financial assets they want to hold at the growing high-employment levels of g.n.p.

the history of the last quarter century is encouraging. We weathered two wars, two reconversions to peace, and a wide variety of other economic shocks, without a major bust, albeit with a good deal of war-induced inflation. The post–World War II growth in real g.n.p. has been remarkably steady compared to its roller-coaster performance between World Wars I and II. And we surely know a lot more than we did about what makes business cycles tick and how to damp them down. The optimists list the following specific factors, in roughly ascending order of importance.

1. Businessmen now plan their investment on a longer-range basis. Thus, investment plans are less susceptible to short-term swings in expectations. Long-run growth is widely recognized as a dominant factor in business planning, and this factor will keep business investment plans from serious short-run collapse.

2. Consumers in America have become adjusted to a high and rising standard of living, and they will not be panicked into cutting back their spending even though business conditions weaken. If incomes slide, they draw on liquid assets and borrow to protect their living standards, looking to a resumption of better times in the near future. This fact has been demonstrated repeatedly during the postwar years when consumer expenditures have continued to increase through changing times.

3. Federal, state, and local government spending of nearly $350 billion annually provides a massive, stable component of g.n.p. Never before has there been such a huge, stable block of spending.

4. Federal tax and spending arrangements now have a large element of built-in countercyclical flexibility. Tax liabilities fall rapidly if incomes drop. Hence, disposable personal income drops far less than do wages, salaries, and other income before taxes. Similarly with business profits after tax. Moreover, spending on unemployment insurance and price-support payments to farmers increase automatically if employment and prices fall. All things considered, built-in federal fiscal flexibility will automatically absorb maybe a third of the shock of any drop in national income.

5. The banking and financial system has been greatly strengthened since the crash of 1929. We need never again have the enormous credit contraction that was the core of the 1929 to 1933 collapse and of every other great depression. Federal insurance of bank deposits has substantially removed the danger of runs on banks. Government supervision of banking practices is closer than before. But most important, the Federal Reserve now stands ready to convert bank assets into cash reserves in case of any major banking crisis, so a general financial collapse like that of the years 1929 to 1933 is no longer thinkable.

6. We have learned how to fight depression through government monetary and fiscal policy. We now understand business slumps far better than in 1929, and we have powerful tools to check any major slump in aggregate demand. The Federal Reserve has been greatly strengthened to prevent financial panic and to see that plenty of money is available. And there is now general recognition that government deficit spending can provide massive buying power if private spending slumps. This was the lesson of World War II, when mass government spending rapidly bailed us out of unemployment into peak production and employment.

How convincing are these arguments? We're surely in better shape than ever before to avoid major depressions. We seem to be protected against another liquidity collapse, and we have government deficit financing to greatly lessen the likelihood of another debacle like the 1930s. But while we have powerful cannons to wheel up against big depressions, our small artillery to fight minor fluctuations merits less confidence. The inventory cycle alone is big enough to give us some nasty bumps, and no one has much hope yet of eliminating inventory fluctuations. Best professional opinion places a good deal of weight on items 2, 3, and 4 above to moderate economic swings, but surely not to eliminate little recessions, or possibly even middle-sized ones. Effective stabilization policy still faces many problems.

Yet to end on a negative note would be mistaken. Combined monetary and fiscal policy, plus other improvements in our institutional arrangements, provide a powerful arsenal against instability that should eliminate massive depressions and help substantially to smooth out smaller fluctuations.[10]

[10]More thorough support for this analysis is presented in G. L. Bach, "The Search for Stability—What Have We Learned" in *Public Policy and Economic Understanding* (American Bankers' Association, 1970).

Review

FOR ANALYSIS AND DISCUSSION

1. As a practical matter, is the present level of unemployment as low as we can expect without substantial inflation? Explain.
2. In the last three decades labor unions have become much more powerful than before. Under these circumstances, according to some economists, government assurance that total spending will be kept up to high-employment levels would be in effect a guarantee of continued inflation. Why, if at all, would this be so? Is it a serious danger? How would you go about assuring high-level employment without inflation?
3. Do the wage–price guideposts provide an equitable solution to the persistent quarrel between management and labor over income shares? Do they provide an effective means of solving the dilemma of high employment without inflation? Do they represent a dangerous intrusion of government into the private economy?
4. How would you rate the following for quick action to fight a recession: monetary policy, tax reductions, and increased government spending?
5. If you were a congressman, would you vote to delegate the power to change tax rates to the president? To the Federal Reserve Board? To anyone? Explain. Would your answer be the same on delegating power to start previously approved public-works projects?
6. Can you devise a plan to make Congress behave more speedily and responsibly on tax and expenditure actions to stabilize the economy?
7. You are asked to give an hour's talk before your local Kiwanis Club on the subject, "What Should We Do About Our National Debt?" Outline your talk, indicating briefly under each point how you would develop it. Bear in mind the backgrounds and opinions of the group in planning your talk.
8. The National Association of Manufacturers has stated: "A government cannot continue indefinitely to run at a deficit without creating an inflationary trend which will in time undermine public confidence in its obligations." Do you agree or disagree with this statement? Why? To what extent does your answer depend on your expectation of persistent stagnation or inflationary pressures?
9. Is public debt more dangerous than private debt, or vice versa? Why?
10. Are depressions obsolete?

sixteen

The Theory of Economic Growth

For two-thirds of the world's population—over 2 billion people—the number one economic problem is getting enough to eat and a place to sleep. By our standards, they are desperately poor. For these people, economic growth—more goods and services per capita—offers the only real hope of rising above a bare subsistence level of food and shelter.

Few people in the United States today need fear starvation. Yet even here there are millions of poor, miles of squalid slums—and few in our population of over 200 million do not continually hope for more income to spend, for the better things in life. Thus, here too economic growth is a central issue, though a far less-pressing need than for the world's less-developed, poverty-stricken nations.

Today many young people, and their elders, argue that concern for the "quality of life" should replace our traditional stress on the quantity of g.n.p. Some advocate a zero-growth goal, others less-colorful policies to slow growth where this would significantly reduce pollution of the environment. Extremists allege that technology has taken over society, and man is now a mere slave to machines; their solution is often vague, in general somehow to slow technology and return to a simpler life. Others claim that mass starvation is around the corner because population is growing too fast, and even modern technology cannot increase food output fast enough to keep up with more mouths.

Carefully viewed, these antigrowth arguments turn out to rest on a variety of propositions, often contradictory. Some economists brush the criticisms aside, correctly pointing out that there is no **necessary** conflict between growth in national productive capacity and use of that capacity to assure a cleaner, more pleasant environment. But this is brushing away the criticisms too easily. We shall consider them in detail in Chapter 18 on "Growth Policy" and in later chapters.

The present chapter begins with some facts on economic growth, but it is concerned primarily with the theory of growth. Why do economies grow as fast or as slowly as they do? What are the major forces on which we, and the poverty-stricken nations, must rely for a long-term rise in per capita output? Chapter 17 then uses this theoretical framework to explain growth in today's American economy; and Chapter 18 turns to the policy issues we face—should we grow faster or slower, and how? Chapter 19 does the same for the less-developed economies, which contain the great bulk of the world's people.

Some Facts on Growth

Economic Growth Defined

Economic growth means growth in the amount of goods and services produced—in total, or per capita. For some purposes, growth in total output is most important—for example, in assessing a nation's economic potential for fighting a war, its ability to provide large amounts of foreign aid, and the like. But for most purposes we are more interested in output per capita (or per family)—that is, growth in the ratio: $\frac{\text{total output}}{\text{total population}}$. For output per capita provides a rough measure of the average standard of living of individuals in the economy. You will find "economic growth" used widely in both senses, but here economic growth will mean growth in output per capita unless growth in total output is specified.

The two definitions can color the facts quite differently. If total output grows but population grows even faster, the standard of living of the typical individual is sliding down, not rising. In this country, total output has risen on the average between 3 and 4 percent annually over the last century, while output per capita has risen only about 2 to 3 percent per annum as population grew about 1 percent per annum. In India, total output has grown too recently, at a rate not far under ours, but population has grown nearly as fast as output. Hence there has been little change in output per capita, and the Indian standard of living today is little higher than it was a century ago.

Economic Growth in Perspective

Look back at Table 1–1 and then ahead to Table 19–1 to get a first picture of the results of such widely varying economic growth rates over the world today. The United States stands at the top. We are far ahead of the nearest challengers—even though we are a much newer nation than many of the others shown. The success story of the American economy is written in these figures, in the spectacular results of our economic growth over a mere two or three centuries of the world's history.

Second, what about comparative growth rates for major industrialized countries over the last century? Table 16–1 tells the story. Growth rates have varied widely even among such industrialized nations. Although some rates are surprisingly close (for example, those of the United States and Sweden), don't forget the enormous difference that even a fraction of 1 percent annually can make when compounded over an entire century. Beginning from a level of 100, a growth rate of 1.5 percent per annum would give a total of 443 in 100 years; a growth rate of 2 percent 725; and a growth rate of 3 percent 1,922. Even a half percent difference in the annual growth rate can make a huge difference in comparative living standards in only a few generations.

Try matching up these rates with the present standings shown in Table 1–1. When, for example, did the United States gain its present big advantage over Japan, Sweden, and the USSR? Does our relatively late industrialization explain much of our excellent performance over

table 16-1

Long-Term Growth Rates in Output per Capita*

	Annual Percentage Increase
Japan	3.0
Sweden	2.2
United States	2.1
Russia	2.0
Canada	1.8
Denmark	1.7
France	1.6
Germany	1.6
United Kingdom	1.2
Italy	1.2

*Based on data for approximately 100 years. Exact beginning date varies slightly; for example, U.S. data begin in 1871 to avoid Civil War period. Data from D.C. Paige, "Economic Growth: The Last Hundred Years," *National Institute Economic Review*, July, 1961; Simon Kuznets, "The Pattern of U.S. Economic Growth," *The Nation's Economic Objectives* (E. Edwards, ed.; Chicago: University of Chicago Press, 1964); and United Nations. Inclusion of recent years would raise most of the figures shown appreciably, especially those for Japan.

table 16-2

Comparative Annual Growth Rates, 1950-1970*

	G.n.p. per Capita	G.n.p.
Japan	10.2	11.2
West Germany	5.1	6.4
Italy	4.5	5.3
USSR	3.9	5.5
Sweden	3.9	4.6
France	3.6	5.0
United States	3.0	4.4
Canada	2.9	4.6
United Kingdom	2.3	2.9

*Estimates based on United Nations and International Monetary Fund data; in real terms.

like these explain why economic historians and economic theorists have a fascinating time explaining the facts.

One last introductory look at the facts. What about recent comparative growth rates? Table 16–2 gives the answer. Since World War II we have grown nearly 50 percent faster than over the previous century. But a number of other nations have done still better, especially Japan and West Germany. And the order is very different from those of Tables 1–1 and 16–1.

A word of warning is needed here, however. Growth figures for any short period are tricky, and the years in Table 16–2 reflect partly special circumstances growing out of World War II. Indeed, in the last few years the European nations shown in the table have been slowing down, while the United States has speeded up. Certainly the long-term rates in Table 16–1 are of greater historical significance. But there's no getting around the fact that growth rates have varied widely since World War II.

The Difference between Growth and Cycle Upswings

It is important to distinguish between long-run growth rates and short-run swings reflecting business-cycle fluctuations. For example, output per capita usually rises rapidly as an economy moves from depression to high employment. But this is clearly a temporary factor, and should not be extrapolated out as a long-run growth rate. Thus, most economists look upon the long-run growth rate as something to be measured only over extended periods that cover at least the years from one cycle peak to another, and preferably several cycles. Alternatively, they look at the growth in the "full-employment capacity" of the economy—that is, its growing capacity to produce at "full employment" of men and machines.

The Theory of Economic Growth

Why have some nations grown so fast and others not at all? How do some nations push out their production-possibilities curves so much

the past century compared to most European nations, which had already partly industrialized by the 1860s? How about Japan, which began to industrialize very late? She now has the world's third largest g.n.p., behind only the United States and the USSR, and is growing far faster than either. When will she falter? Tables faster than others? What, in short, is the theory of economic growth? Only through answering this question can we really understand why some nations are rich and some are poor. Alas, there is no one simple theory that seems to explain everything. But there is growing consensus on some central factors in the growth process and it is on these that we shall concentrate.

Supply and Demand Factors in Economic Growth

As we shall see, the classical economists had a simple answer to questions about economic growth. The basic productive factors were land, labor, and capital. Growth in total output depended on the combined expansion of these productive factors, reflecting especially enterprise, hard work, and thrift. And the growth in output per capita depended largely on the growth in population relative to the growth in land and capital available for production. They stressed the supply factors—the ones that move out the nation's production-possibilities curve.

Nearly two centuries later the classical economists still look basically right. It is the "real" (supply) factors that matter most in economic growth—the accumulation of productive capital goods; growth in the size and efficiency of the labor force; the natural resources ("land") that a nation has; and its research, education, and technical advance, which permit it to produce more with any given amount of capital, labor, and natural resources.

Beyond land, labor, capital, and technology, many historians and economists point to other, more tenuous factors—the energy and "drive" of a nation's people, the social and economic mobility of its classes, the economic institutions it devises, its governmental and political structure and traditions. Although we set most of these forces aside for the moment, it is important not to forget them.

These "supply" factors matter most, but in a private-enterprise economy money demand matters too. Unless aggregate demand is adequate to take goods off the market, they will not long be produced. And unless prospective money demand promises reasonable returns, the new capital goods and research necessary for economic growth will not be forthcoming.

Summary: On the supply side, the problem of economic growth is to increase the productive capacity of the economy—basically through diverting resources from current consumption to investment in capital goods, research, education, and other activities that increase future productive capacity; through increasing the size and quality of the labor force; and through improving the economic and social-political organization of the society. On the demand side, the first problem is to be sure that there is always adequate total demand to induce high-level utilization of the productive capacity that exists; otherwise, potentially available output is wasted and the inducement to new investment is reduced. (This has been the focus of Chapters 12 to 15.) The second problem on the demand side is to channel spending from consumption into saving and investment so that society's stock of capital goods and human resources will be built up to increase future output. Thus, on the demand side, both the level of aggregate demand $(C + I + GE)$ and the proportion going into investment (private and governmental) influence the growth rate.

Almost all economists would agree with the preceding paragraphs. But just how these forces interact, and which are more important under what circumstances, are more difficult questions. A brief look at the historical development of the theory of economic growth is a good start toward answering them.

Adam Smith—Progress through Enterprise and Thrift

Men have long been concerned with progress, with a better life. This is not surprising, since man, for most of his history, has been hungry, often unprotected from the elements, bitterly poor by the standards we now know. How is it that in the last 200 years, only in a few now industrialized nations of the Western world, man has managed to rise rapidly from poverty to our present comfortable ways of living?

Adam Smith, in his famous *Wealth of Nations*

in 1776, first saw the central rationale of an individual self-interest, market-directed economy. Let each individual seek his own self-interest—the highest profit he can make, a job at the best wage he can command. But let there be competition in the market, so that no seller dares put his price above what others charge, and no buyer can drive down the price of labor he hires because workers will go elsewhere. Then, Smith wrote, self-interest, the most powerful motivating force of all, will be harnessed by the forces of competition to produce those goods men want to buy, at the lowest prices that cover their cost of production. Better than any planner or dictator could, self-interest, harnessed by competition, will produce the greatest good for all—as if directed by an invisible hand. This was the case for a self-interest, private-enterprise, market-directed economy—in dramatic contrast to the "command" economies of the lords, the kings, and the pharaohs who had ruled the world's economies through many centuries before.

But Smith was interested equally in the progress of society. Would these forces lead man to an ever better life? His answer was "yes"—because self-interest would produce not only hard work and enterprise, but also thrift and accumulation. As man saved part of what he produced, the savings of many individuals could mean new factories, new machines, better houses. Thus, thrift and accumulation, savings from the fruits of hard labor, were the foundations of economic growth, of progress toward a better life.

To be sure, more machinery and more capital would mean a larger demand for workmen, and this in turn would lead to higher wages, until profits—the special source of, and stimulus to, accumulation—were eaten away. But Smith saw no crisis in this process. He observed that higher wages and more food would lead to more people, and thus to more workers. This in turn would tend to push wages back down, lowering the costs of businessmen as it lowered the real wages of the worker. And so profits and accumulation would again become possible, with further progress.

While Smith was crystal clear on the role of the market in organizing a self-regulating economy, he was less explicit on just where this interacting process of accumulation and population growth would take society and on how fast it would raise real wages (output per worker). And little wonder. Economists still, 200 years later, debate the answer. But Smith's was an optimistic world, of self-interest and of order. It was a world of progress for those who worked hard and saved, and for societies made up of such men. And Smith's analysis still has fundamental lessons to teach us in the world of today.

Malthus, Ricardo, and Marx—Strife and Diminishing Returns

Two Englishmen, writing soon after Adam Smith, saw instead a gloomy world of conflict and strife—of workers, capitalists, and landlords climbing on each others' backs, each trying to increase his own share of the sustenance produced by society. T. R. Malthus and David Ricardo, two other great founders of modern economics, challenged the orderly world of Adam Smith with disturbing predictions that also have a modern look today, nearly two centuries later.

Malthus and the Specter of Famine. More people mean more productive power and more output. But more people also mean more mouths to feed, more backs to clothe. In 1798, Malthus, then a young British minister, wrote his now famous *Essay on the Principle of Population.* He gloomily predicted that population would rise far faster than the productive power associated with more people. Looking at rising birthrates, Malthus pointed out that the population could double every generation if each woman had only four surviving children, half of them girls who would produce more children in the next generation. Malthus felt that this might well give a geometrical population increase—2, 4, 8, 16, 32, 64, and so on—with a doubling each generation.

But the world's land could not possibly increase its food output at this rate over the long run, Malthus argued. Thus, unless population growth was checked by moral restraint, or by such disasters as war or disease, it must ultimately be checked by recurrent famines as the population outran the food supply. The British standard of living was hardly above the subsistence level for much of the population; unless steps were taken to control the growth of population, the outlook for growth in output per capita and for a better life was bleak.

Ricardo and the "Law of Diminishing Returns." David Ricardo, another famous British economist, provided a further intellectual justification for Malthus's fears. Ricardo first stated the "law of diminishing returns." Loosely, the law says that if the number of workers applied to any fixed supply of land is increased, the crops obtained from the land will increase, but sooner or later output will increase at a slower rate than the rate at which workers are added.

The implications of this "law" for the standard of living of a growing population seemed clear. Given the world's supply of tillable land, sooner or later food output per worker would fall when the point of diminishing returns was passed in the application of more and more workers to the limited supply of land. And as population grew thereafter, food output per capita (more accurately, per worker) would decline steadily, even though total food output might continue to grow.

But at the same time as diminishing returns pressed down on the food available for individual workers, it would enrich the landlords. For as more and more workers sought sustenance from the land, the price of each piece of land (in sale or in rent) would rise. Ricardo, the economic theorist par excellence, explained through the law of diminishing returns precisely how fast rents would rise and wage rates fall as more workers were applied to the increasingly scarce land.

Assume momentarily that all land and all workers are identical in productive power. Then basically the wage rate would be set by the (declining) contribution each additional worker added to total output. Rent per acre would be set in the same way by the (rising) contribution attributable to each increasingly scarce acre. In a market system, it would pay

profit-seeking businessmen and farmers to pay up to the amount added by each additional worker or acre; and competition for workers and land would drive wages and rents up to those levels. Here we need not be concerned about the details. You merely need to see that, under diminishing returns, with a growing labor force the nation's total output might grow, but marginal, or additional, output per worker (and therefore the worker's real wage) would fall. At the same time output per acre (which determines the rent paid to the landowner) would rise steadily.[1]

But what of capital accumulation, the path to progress in Smith's system? Ricardo saw the importance of thrift and accumulation in man's attempt to improve his lot. But here again, Ricardo wrote, the fact of diminishing returns rears its ugly head. As more and more capital is accumulated relative to scarce land, the return on capital (interest or profits) will be squeezed down more and more. In the end it is the landlords who wax ever richer, while both workers and capitalists find their individual returns (in the form of wages and of profits) squeezed to the barest minimum.

Were Malthus and Ricardo right? If history has proved them wrong in the nations of the Western world, where did they go astray? Have they been proved right in China and India, where starvation is an ever present threat for over a billion people? Will Malthus's specter reappear worldwide with the modern population explosion? As with Smith, Malthus and Ricardo have lessons for today. Their arguments will reappear in the modern analysis of growth.

Marx and the Collapse of Capitalism. Fifty years later came Karl Marx, the gloomy prophet of the downfall of the entire capitalist system that Adam Smith had praised so highly. Like his classical predecessors, Marx was interested in the grand dynamics—the progress of society or its road to collapse. But he saw no progress. Instead, he foresaw collapse, as capitalists

---

[1] If you don't want to accept this loose statement as intuitively right, look ahead to the appendix to Chapter 23 where the principle is stated precisely and explained more fully.

seized ever larger profits while forcing the workers into degradation and eventually to revolt, which would overthrow the capitalist system.

Marx built an elaborate theoretical structure on the fallacy that labor is the source of all value. He said that any return to another productive resource, such as capital or land, is merely a misappropriation of the "surplus value" produced by labor. But we need not be concerned with the details of this argument. To Marx, capital accumulation was again at the center of things. The desire for profit leads men to accumulate capital and to wring every ounce of effort out of the workingmen who must labor for their bread. Because capitalists are powerful and rich, whereas laborers are poor and divided, capitalists can in fact push down the real wages of their workers to the point where workers can barely subsist. The higher profits lead to more and more capital accumulation, as Smith and Ricardo had predicted before him.

But to Marx the end result of all this was quite different, though it had been hinted in the worryings of Parson Malthus. Capitalism will develop increasing crises, Marx wrote. Too much of society's income will go to the rich capitalists. Too little will be paid to the masses to permit them to buy the output of the new factories and machines. Thus capitalism will face increasingly severe crises and depressions, with resulting unemployment and chaos. Finally, the hungry workers, long ground under the heel of the wealthy capitalists, will rise in revolt and overthrow the capitalist system. So, wrote Marx, would come the downfall of capitalism, brought on by the very process of capital accumulation that the classical economists had praised as the foundation of economic growth.

Clearly, Marx has been wrong in the Western world. Real wages have not been ground down over the long run. Both they and profits have risen rapidly in total, and real wages per worker are vastly higher now than 100 years ago. Interestingly, the rate of return per dollar of capital invested (loosely, the profit rate or the interest rate) has apparently not increased, though of course the total return to capital has grown enormously with the vast accumulation of capi-

tal. And apparently modern monetary-fiscal policy has brought great depressions under control.

Let us stop now and examine more rigorously some of the issues that were exposed by Smith, Malthus, Ricardo, and Marx.

The Deepening of Capital and Diminishing Returns. It is relatively easy to explain the growth in total output of an economy as capital and labor grow. The production-possibilities curve moves out. Unless unbalanced ("excessive") capital accumulation brings on the crises suggested by Malthus and Marx, an increase in any or all of the factors of production will raise total output. Thus, more workers, more capital goods, or more natural resources will increase total production. (Note that increased natural resources are a real possibility in new nations; for example, until nearly 1900 the United States had continuous access to more land through the open frontier westward.) But how to increase output **per capita** is a much more difficult problem. For more workers, given the law of diminishing returns, will produce more total output, but output per worker will fall, assuming that the stock of capital and land remain constant.

Neglect for a moment the supply of land (natural resources) as of decreasing importance in the advanced economies. Then, if the number of workers increases, at least a parallel increase in the stock of capital would appear to be the only hope for avoiding declining real wages as a result of the law of diminishing returns. The stock of capital must rise faster than population grows, if output per worker is to rise.

This is what economists call the "deepening" of capital—more capital per unit of labor. It is this deepening of capital, the analysis of the preceding paragraphs suggests, that is the fundamental hope for progress, for economic growth.

Let us reconsider now, more analytically, the effects of capital deepening in a simple system. To take the simplest case, assume there is no land, but merely labor and capital as productive factors. Suppose capital grows faster than the labor supply. What then happens to per capita output? The answer is given by Ricardo's law of diminishing returns. Total output will grow, but not in proportion to the growth in the capital stock. Thus, the return per unit of capital (the interest rate or profit rate) will fall as capital deepens. Here labor is the relatively fixed factor (just as was land in Ricardo's case). Thus, the wage rate (the return to labor) will be bid up as labor becomes ever scarcer relative to capital; labor replaces the "greedy landlord" of Ricardo's system. But last, note that higher wage rates and lower interest rates in the system do not necessarily imply a higher percentage share of the total national output for labor. This is because there are more units of capital being used. The increased number of units may more than offset the lower return per unit of capital and thus keep the aggregate share of capital in the national output from falling absolutely, or even relatively to the share of labor.

It is important to be clear about the reasoning of the preceding paragraph. It is the foundation for much of the modern theory of growth, and for moving on now to a new factor—technological progress.

The New Look—Technical Advance and Innovation

Why have Malthus, Ricardo, and Marx proved wrong in nearly all of the Western world, although they may be discomfortingly right for 2 billion people in the less-developed nations? Is the answer a simple one—that Adam Smith was basically right in his optimistic prediction of growth in private-enterprise economies, but that the less-developed nations have not yet heeded his advice?

Most modern economists say that Smith deserves credit for a powerful analysis of some of the basic forces. But something else has been added to give the victory to Smith's optimism over Malthus's and Ricardo's gloom. This is technical advance and its handmaid, innovation, that bring to society the fruits of new ways of doing things, new products, new approaches. The revolution of science, technology, and education has saved us from diminishing returns!

The basic fact is that total output has grown much faster than the combined inputs of the factors of production. Only part of the growth in total U.S. output since 1900 can be explained by the growth in capital and labor inputs, disregarding land as substantially fixed in quantity. Similar patterns apparently prevail in other advanced industrial nations. And, modern economics says, the main reason is technical progress and innovation. New machines, better management methods, computers to do the work of adding machines, new fertilizers to double output of farm crops, new management techniques—these have more than offset the once-feared law of diminishing returns.

It is important to remember that technical change shows up in higher skills and better education for workers, scientists, and managers, as well as in new machines and methods. Modern computers drastically reduce business costs and make possible fantastic new scientific developments. Is the technical advance in the computers, or is it in the skills of the scientists who designed the computers and the programmers who apply them to new problems? Both, is the answer. Thus technical advance is introduced through education and training (investment in human beings) as well as through new capital goods and techniques (investment in research and development and in new capital).

Technical progress—embodied in new machines, new methods, and better skills for workers—has made Adam Smith right. It has gone far to prove that the pessimists were wrong, mainly because they overlooked the vast power of modern technical change. Joseph Schumpeter, a famous economist writing early in this century, first stressed innovation (in productive techniques and in new products) as the mainspring of economic growth. Modern research seems to be bearing Schumpeter out.

Growth in Developed Economies

A satisfactory modern theory of growth for the developed Western economies like the United States must explain at least the following facts.

1. The strong, upward movement in real wages in the face of a rapidly rising population

and labor force. (In the United States, population has tripled since 1900, whereas real wages have risen more than fivefold.)

2. A still more rapid increase in the capital stock, with a resultant deepening of capital, but (disregarding business-cycle fluctuations) with a roughly stable long-term interest rate, contrary to the falling expectation given by the law of diminishing returns.

3. A slightly falling ratio of capital to total output for the economy in the face of the rapid deepening of capital, where the law of diminishing returns would lead us to suppose that the capital–output ratio would rise.

4. A roughly constant division of the total national product between wages and salaries on the one hand and returns to property (profits, interest, and rent) on the other—with a gradual increase in the labor share in recent decades.

Supply Factors: Capital, Labor, and Technology

Modern growth theory stresses the fact that total output grows when capital and labor grow and technology improves, disregarding land as a relatively minor factor in highly developed countries.[2] In general, then, output per capita will grow only when capital grows faster than labor or when there is technical advance, or both. When capital is deepened, unless there is technical change the law of diminishing returns will reduce the rate of return on capital and increase the real wage of labor. But with technical advance, the rate of return on capital need not fall; it may be stable or even rise while the real wage rises even more rapidly. What happens to the relative shares of capital and labor in the total national income depends on the relative rates of growth of the two.

Saving and investment (diversion of real resources from consumption to increase investment) is thus central to the growth process. For investment is required both for capital deepen-

---

[2]Some economists like to summarize this relationship in a simple "production function" for the entire economy:

$$\text{Output} = a(A \cdot K \cdot L)$$

where K is the stock of capital; L is the stock of labor; and A is technical progress. Thus, output depends on the combined effect of all three. For a more complete discussion, see the appendix to this chapter.

ing and research and, in most instances, to incorporate technical advance. The larger the portion of its current output is that a society devotes to investment, the faster capital will deepen and the faster output per capita will rise. Moreover, the more of its resources it devotes to investment in research and development and to education, the faster technical progress will occur.

Demand Factors

Malthus and Marx warned of breakdowns in the growth process because aggregate demand might fall short of buying all the goods that could be produced as the stock of capital grows. Modern economists recognize that this was a valid warning. We now recognize that aggregate demand must grow roughly apace with the productive capacity of the economy if unemployment and inflation are to be avoided. It is clear, further, that when aggregate demand does fall short and depression occurs, the ratio of investment to g.n.p., and therefore the rate of economic growth, declines.

Equally important, decisions on money spending or saving within the total are vital to a stable growth process. This is because they largely control the division of the national output between consumption on the one hand and saving–investment on the other. For a brainteaser on the saving–investment rate needed to just maintain stable growth in g.n.p., see the appendix to this chapter.

Growth and Fluctuations

Schumpeter stressed the intimate relationship between growth and economic fluctuations. Partly, Schumpeter argued, this was a real phenomenon. As we saw in Chapter 10, the bunching of real investment is the essence of a boom and of rapid growth. But this very process usually involves overshooting the amount of real productive capacity needed to meet consumer demands. When the overshoot becomes obvious, private investment is cut back and a recession occurs until a better balance between capacity and growing consumption is restored. Partly, Schumpeter stressed, this is a monetary phenomenon. Excessive expansion of credit helps to speed investment booms, supplementing the intended savings of the public and thus intensifying the overinvestment beyond a sustainable growth rate. On both real and monetary scores, the theory of growth and the theory of fluctuations are inseparable, Schumpeter emphasized. Even if monetary-fiscal policy could assure the continuous smooth conversion of intended saving into real investment, we might still have real-investment booms (bursts of growth) that were extremely difficult to maintain without ensuing recession.

The Eclectic Consensus

Most modern economists thus look at the stock of capital, the stock of labor, and technical advance as a framework for analyzing growth in total output. The law of diminishing returns, partially or completely offset by technical advance and innovation, provides a powerful tool for understanding what happens to output per capita, and to the relative shares of capital and labor, in the growth process. The extent to which any growth is sustainable, rather than leading to "overinvestment" through excessive capital accumulation, depends partially on monetary-fiscal factors and partially on the bunching of real investment in the process. Throughout, there must be adequate demand to buy the growing full-employment output. This general theory, or framework, helps to explain the basic facts on growth listed at the beginning of this section. It is a modern eclectic consensus.

Other Factors

One last preliminary word is needed. Many economists believe that this framework is too narrow to explain the basic forces of economic growth, in either the United States or less-developed nations. They say that private initiative and our free-enterprise economic institutions have played a major role in explaining our rapid growth over the centuries. Our success breeds further success, since our markets are now so big that we can take full advantage of the economies of mass production, an important factor in making effective use of our resources. The "noneconomic" factors mentioned at the outset—the initiative of the people and their "drive," social and economic mobility in the system, the flexibility of economic and social institutions, religious traditions and ethical mores, and particularly the political stability and structure of a nation—may be as important as the purely "economic" factors stressed in the preceding pages. Certainly absence of these factors has seriously deterred growth in many of the less-developed nations (see Chapter 19). The simple theoretical framework sketched in this chapter provides a useful guide to thinking about economic growth. But it is only a framework for more thorough investigation of the complex process of economic growth in any particular case.

Review

CONCEPTS TO REMEMBER

Be sure you understand the following basic concepts introduced in this chapter. They are reused repeatedly in the rest of the book.

economic growth	demand (money) factors in growth
growth vs cycle upswings	technical advance
supply (real) factors in growth	capital deepening

FOR ANALYSIS AND DISCUSSION

1. Does Adam Smith or Malthus-Ricardo provide a better explanation of economic growth over the past century in the United States? In

India and the less-developed nations? If your answers are different, why?

2. Suppose you want to explain Japan's rapid economic growth. At what factors does the theory of Chapter 16 suggest you should look?

3. "Increased aggregate demand is a first-rate answer to the depression problem, but it can't help much to speed up long-term growth." Do you agree? Why or why not?

4. Suppose you want to speed up the rate of economic growth in the United States. What does the theory of Chapter 16 suggest as the most promising measures? Would your answer be different if you measured economic growth by total g.n.p. instead of g.n.p. per capita?

5. In what sense, if any, has modern technological advance repealed Ricardo's law of diminishing returns?

6. If the rate of population growth speeds up relative to the rate of capital accumulation, what effect, if any, would you predict on the shares of labor and capital in the national income?

APPENDIX   *SOME SPECIAL POINTS ON ECONOMIC GROWTH*

Growth theory raises a host of interesting problems. This appendix is intended for students who want to look a little further into the intricacies of the subject.

A Simple Growth Model. Shortly after World War II, Oxford's Sir Roy Harrod and M.I.T.'s Evsey Domar simultaneously developed a simple growth model that has since been widely used. It builds on the fact that investment (increase in the capital stock) is a prime cause of economic growth, and assumes for simplicity that the capital–output ratio is constant. Note that a constant capital–output ratio assumes away the existence of diminishing returns.

Let Y = output, K = capital stock, and designate changes in any variable by Δ. Suppose the constant capital–output ratio is β—for example, 3—so that 3 of additional capital means 1 of additional output. Suppose further that savings *(S)* are a constant proportion of income *(Y)*. Let that proportion be σ. Lastly, let us assume full employment; that is, we are concerned with the growth in full-employment potential output for the economy.

Since β is fixed, we know how much Y will increase for any increase in K:

$$\Delta K = \beta \Delta Y$$

But ΔK in any year is simply net investment in that year, and we know that saving equals investment in any year. Thus:

$$\Delta K = I = S = \sigma Y$$

Now combine the equations, substituting σY for ΔK.

Then:

$$\beta \Delta Y = \sigma Y, \text{ so}$$

$$\frac{\beta \Delta Y}{Y} = \sigma, \text{ or}$$

$$\frac{\Delta Y}{Y} = \frac{\sigma}{\beta}$$

Since $(\Delta Y//Y)$ is the growth rate, the full-employment growth rate for the economy is given by $\frac{\sigma}{\beta}$. Thus, if β is 3 and σ is 15 percent, the economy will grow at 5 percent per year ($\frac{.15}{3} = .05$).

This model stresses some important relationships. But remember the simplified assumptions before you conclude it will tell you just how much saving your favorite economy needs to grow at 5 percent annually. In the real world, we often don't know what the capital–output ratio for new capital will be, and the savings–income ratio also has a slippery way of sliding around. Moreover, we've abstracted from a lot of real-world factors, such as business savings, taxes, and the like.

How To Maintain Stable Growth. A difficult brainteaser: Is there some rate of saving and investment out of total output that is necessary for "balanced" or "sustainable" growth, avoiding too rapid or slow an increase of capital that might lead to an "oversupply" or "undersupply" of productive capacity? If there is a constant capital–output ratio given by technology, then we can show that there is indeed such a required rate. Suppose labor grows at 1 percent annually and technological advance at 2 percent, so the basic capacity of the system to produce grows at 3 percent. Suppose further that the fixed capital–output ratio is 3:1. That is, three dollars of additional capital will produce one dollar of additional output.

Then, using the highly simplified Harrod-Domar model above, we can show that the economy must save and invest just 9 percent of its output to grow stably. Why? Begin with a total output of 100. The extra nine units of capital (i.e., $\sigma = 9$ percent) will produce just the three additional units of output that match the 3 percent growth in potential output from more labor and technical change ($\beta = 3$). Less saving and investment would provide inadequate capital to produce the possible 3 percent annual growth in output, given the 3:1 capital–output ratio. Larger saving and investment would pile up more capital than could be used in producing the 3 percent growth in output. In this model, a knife-edge saving rate is required for stable economic growth. But remember that this is only one model, based on extremely limited assumptions, so the conclusion may not apply directly to the real world.

Is Technical Progress "Neutral"? Does technical progress tend to increase the share of Y going to labor or to capital, or is it "neutral" as between the two shares? Obviously, technical progress might be "labor saving" or "capital saving." That is, it might reduce or increase the relative amount of labor or capital needed to produce a given output. If the technical advance is labor saving, so that less labor is now needed for a given output, we might predict that the labor share of Y would fall.

In fact, we observe in the real world that the labor and capital shares of national income have been surprisingly constant (abstracting from cyclical fluctuations), with a small tendency for the labor share to rise. Can we infer that technical progress has been "neutral" in the above sense? Consider two possible explanations.

First, it is possible that in the absence of technical change the elasticity of substitution between K and L is 1. That is, if the wage rate falls relative to the cost of capital, businessmen will hire just enough more labor to offset the lower wage rate, and just enough less capital to offset the higher price per unit. Then the relative income shares of capital and labor will remain unchanged. We can write an aggregate "production function" to show this case as follows:

$$\text{Output} = A \ (L^{a} \cdot K^{1-a}),$$

where A is technical progress, L is the stock of labor, and K is the stock of capital. If this is the economy's production function, constant relative shares of total output for labor and capital are shown by the coefficients a and $1-a$; a is the fraction of total output earned by labor, and $1-a$ is the corresponding fraction for capital. This is sometimes called a Cobb-Douglas production function, after the economists who developed it to explain the apparent stability of relative income shares. If the elasticity of substitution between capital and labor is 1, the a and $1-a$ will be constant shares of total output going to labor and capital, and A is "neutral" with respect to the relative shares going to labor and capital.[3]

Alternatively, it may be that without technical change the elasticity of substitution is not 1. Then if investment produces a relatively faster growth in capital (as in the U.S. economy), the interest rate might fall enough and the wage rate might rise enough for the income share of capital to fall, that of labor to rise. Indeed, there seems little a priori reason to suppose the elasticity of substitution between K and L is just 1. But if so, how shall we explain the surprising relative stability of income shares? The answer, some modern economists argue, is that technical progress is not neutral, but instead it provides a built-in mechanism for keeping income shares roughly constant. If, for example, this second case occurs, businessmen will be induced by the profit motive to shift their technical change (innovations) toward the labor-saving type. They do so because labor is becoming relatively more expensive, capital relatively cheaper. Moreover, it is argued, this inducement will be roughly enough to offset any tendency for the relative shares of capital and labor to shift.

Is this induced-innovation theory of stable income shares right? Or is innovation generally "neutral," so that the observed rough stability in income shares comes from an elasticity of substitution between K and L of about 1? Answer: We don't know. This is the kind of research project on which modern economists work—both because it is intellectually challenging and because the conclusions may throw light on fundamental social issues.

[3]For a more complete account of the forces determining the incomes received by labor and capital see Part Four, and Mathematical Appendix IV which provides a rigorous analysis of the Cobb-Douglas production function.

seventeen

Economic Growth in the United States

We think of ourselves as the richest and most progressive nation in the world. We have a right to. Starting from nowhere only two centuries ago, the U.S. economy has produced results that are spectacular, by any standards. Our 1970 g.n.p. of nearly $1 trillion was one-third of the world's total, yet we have only 6 percent of the world's population. It was more than double that of our nearest competitor, the USSR; and on a per capita basis it led the world by a wide margin.

Since World War II, the American economy has grown at about 4.4 percent annually in total output, nearly 50 percent faster than over the preceding century. But many of the other advanced industrial nations have done even better.

How have we done so well over the long pull? What is the outlook for the future? This chapter tries to answer the first question. Chapter 18 looks to the future.

The U.S. Record

Figure 17–1 shows the record. Over the past century total U.S. real g.n.p. (in 1964 prices) has risen from about $18 billion to $850 billion, or fiftyfold. Over the same period per capita g.n.p. (also in 1964 prices) rose from about $450 to $4,200, or nearly tenfold. Total output has grown at a rate of about 3.5 percent, and per capita output at about 2.2 percent annually.

The historical record raises some intriguing problems. Table 16–1 showed our long-term

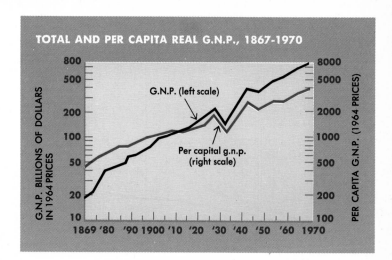

TOTAL AND PER CAPITA REAL G.N.P., 1867-1970

fig. 17–1

Both total and per capita real g.n.p. have risen persistently over the past century, faltering seriously only during the 1930s. Data are plotted only at five-year intervals to show the main growth trends. (Source: U.S. Department of Commerce.)

growth rate compared to those of other leading industrialized countries over the past century. We come off well, but some of the rates are surprisingly close. If these facts are correct, and they are the estimates of the best research workers in the world today, how shall we explain the wide lead of present U.S. output per capita over that of other nations such as Japan and the USSR? A plausible inference from the estimates would be that somehow the United States grew very fast during the first century of its existence, so that we had already established a substantial lead over the other nations by the middle of the nineteenth century. But many observers reject this explanation, arguing that the U.S. growth rate began to pick up with the Industrial Revolution here in the middle 1800s. Whatever the answer, don't forget one impressive fact. Only a fraction of a percentage point difference in annual growth rate can accumulate to enormous totals over a century or more.

To fill in the factual backdrop, let us take a closer look at the anatomy of U.S. economic growth since 1900. Figure 17–2 shows the trends since 1900 in the major variables in the growth process that were stressed in the theory of Chapter 16. Note that all curves are plotted on a ratio scale, so the slopes of the lines show comparative growth rates.

What can we see here? A rapid but jagged rate of growth in real g.n.p., reflecting a roughly similar rate of growth in the capital stock and a much slower growth in population. The theory of Chapter 16 would suggest rising real wages

relative to the return on capital, and this in indeed what we see in the lower part of the chart. Further, the theory would predict that without technical progress the rate of return on capital would fall absolutely. But, interestingly, the return on capital (the interest rate), though fluctuating widely in the Great Depression, is roughly flat in trend. Something, presumably technical advance, has buoyed up both real wages and the return to capital, as the theory suggests. And the capital–output ratio, not shown on the chart, was also roughly flat in trend, contrary to the increase we would expect with rapid capital deepening in the absence of technical advance. Our growth theory from Chapter 16, with technical advance included, is confirmed by the evidence.

Explaining U.S. Growth to Date

The Sources of Growth

What have been the main sources of economic growth in the United States? Table 17–1 gives one courageous expert's estimates of the quantitative importance of the big forces at work during this century. Although he doesn't pretend that these are more than crude approximations, they provide an interesting introduction to the rest of this chapter.

Note the significant differences between the pre- and post-1929 periods. The increasing quantity of labor and capital goods dominates

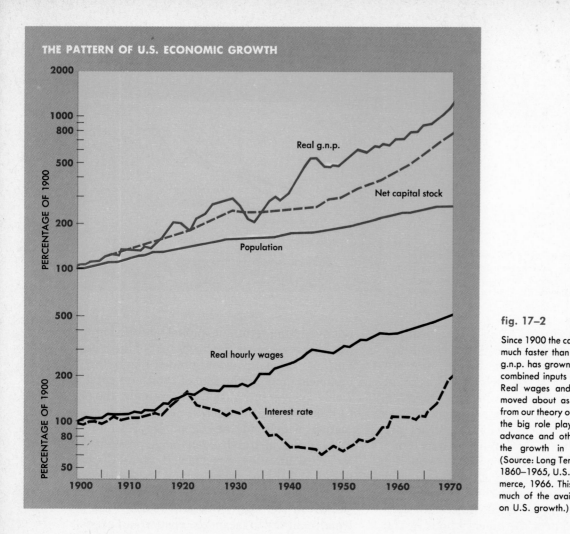

THE PATTERN OF U.S. ECONOMIC GROWTH

fig. 17–2

Since 1900 the capital stock has grown much faster than the labor force, and g.n.p. has grown faster than have the combined inputs of labor and capital. Real wages and interest rates have moved about as would be expected from our theory of growth, recognizing the big role played by technological advance and other elements beyond the growth in labor and capital. (Source: Long Term Economic Growth, 1860–1965, U.S. Department of Commerce, 1966. This volume summarizes much of the available statistical data on U.S. growth.)

table 17-1

Sources of U.S. Economic Growth, 1909-1957*

	Percentage of Total Growth	
Source	1909- 29	1929- 57
Total growth in national real income	100	100
Increase in labor force **	39	20
Improved education and training	13	27
Increased stock of capital goods	26	15
Improved technology	12	20
All other ***	10	11

* Edward Denison, *The Sources of Economic Growth in the United States* (Committee for Economic Development, 1962).

** Adjusted for decreasing number of working hours per year.

*** Mainly due to increased economies of large-scale production with growing total size of the market.

the pre-1929 picture. But since 1929, improvements in the quality of labor and capital (technical advance incorporated in both real capital and human beings) have accounted for over half of our total growth, according to these estimates. And if we eliminate growth in the labor force (population) because it doesn't significantly raise output per capita, these improvements in quality accounted for over two-thirds of the total increase.

These allocations are in dispute among research workers. Harvard's Zvi Griliches and Dale Jorgenson, using different methods, conclude that increased inputs account for nearly all the growth in output, leaving very little role for technical advance as a separate factor. Distinguishing between the contribution of more capital and improved technology is extremely difficult, because with advancing technology new machines almost always have higher productivity than their predecessors. How much of the increased output shall we attribute to more capital, how much to improved capital? The problem is almost as bad for labor. Today's workers are better fed, better educated, better trained than yesterday's. How much of today's increased output is due to more workers, how much to better workers?[1]

There is no undisputed way to draw the line. But nearly all research experts agree that Denison's factors are the right ones to look at, and that the truth since World War II lies in the area between him and Griliches-Jorgenson.

Now let us use the basic theoretical model of Chapter 16, which also lies behind Denison's table, as a framework for looking at the actual forces underlying U.S. economic growth over the past century.

Natural Resources

Natural resources—land, minerals, power resources, and the like—are the foundation that nature gave us for economic growth. They are substantially fixed in amount; for that reason Table 17–1 gives them no credit for our growth since 1909. We may use part or all of them, but we cannot increase their quantity. To be sure, by using fertilizers and irrigation we can improve the crop-bearing ability of land, but this is really capital investment. Through improved technology we may use natural resources that have previously been useless; solar power may run the factories of tomorrow. But it was the fixed supply of natural resources (especially productive land) that underlay Malthus's worries. Today we have broadened the category of land to include all natural resources, but they are still fixed in supply.

Strikingly, the law of diminishing returns has never seemed to drag seriously on U.S. economic growth, even though population has

grown rapidly. When the first settlers arrived in the New World they found a wealth of fertile land, plenty of vegetation and timber, and a temperate climate. Until nearly 1900 the steady westward movement of the frontier revealed ever more bountiful resources. Thus, in effect we could increase our natural resources—by moving west. But even today our natural resources are so vast, and the ratio of people to natural resources so low here compared to most of the rest of the world, that most experts doubt that the law of diminishing returns on natural resources will exert a major drag on our progress. But opponents now, as over the past century, proclaim major crises ahead, caused by exhaustion of our natural resources.

One reason many observers don't worry is our ingenuity in developing new ways to use the resources we have. Table 17–2 shows the revolutionary replacement of human beings and animals by inanimate energy sources. Figure 17–3 shows another way the economy has adjusted to the need for new and larger power sources. Is solar power the next big breakthrough? The old concept of a fixed stock of natural resources requires a new look in the light of our ever growing abilities to use existing resources more flexibly and efficiently. Accumulation of capital goods, technical progress, and education have swamped the law of diminishing returns over a period of three centuries.

[1] Denison has lumped together all "advances of knowledge" in a more recent study of growth in nine Western nations and has somewhat reduced the importance allocated to it in the United States since 1955. *Why Growth Rates Differ* (Washington, D.C.: The Brookings Institution, 1967), p. 299.

table 17-2

U.S. Energy Sources, 1850-1970*

	Percentage of Total		
	1850	1900	1970
Human power	13	5	0.8
Animal power	52	22	0.4
Inanimate power (water, petroleum, etc.)	35	73	98.8
Total	100	100	100.0

*Based on estimates of J. F. Dewhurst and Associates, *America's Needs and Resources* (Twentieth Century Fund, 1955).

fig. 17–3

Petroleum and natural gas have increased as major sources of energy for the modern economy. Will nuclear and solar power soon take over? (Source: National Industrial Conference Board.)

Capital Goods and Capital Accumulation

History suggests that the long-term economic growth rates of the major countries correspond roughly to the proportion of their total outputs they save and invest. When we recognize that most technical advance also requires investment (in research and development, in human beings, and as a vehicle for introducing technical changes), the need to save and invest for economic growth becomes doubly obvious.

Throughout the nineteenth century, the United States was a high-saving and high-investment economy. It paced the world in economic growth. During the present century,

though we have become ever richer, the proportion of our national product devoted to investment has dropped substantially—especially during the Great Depression of the 1930s and again after the Korean War.

Figure 17–4 tells the story. Gross and net capital formation were high percentages of g.n.p. during the last century, but both have clearly trended downward during the last half century, though with an upward surge again in recent years.[2]

Despite this downward trend, year after year American businesses have invested huge sums. Private homes and apartment houses have been built on an unprecedented scale. U.S. private investment in capital goods and housing (excluding investment in consumers' durables like automobiles) reached the staggering total of $135 billion in 1970. Government investment in highways, public buildings, and other civilian-type goods accounted for perhaps $25 billion more. This huge total was more than the entire g.n.p. of any other country in the world, except the USSR, Japan, and West Germany.

The result of this saving–investment process over the centuries is that America has an enormous stock of capital. Our capital goods are es-

[2]In principle, only net investment should contribute to the accumulation of capital and productive capacity. But in fact our measures of depreciation are rough and the replacement of depreciated capital goods often does increase our productive capacity because the new machines almost always embody technical advances. But even if we use gross investment, this rate too has fallen, and it is now well below those of the rapid-growth nations.

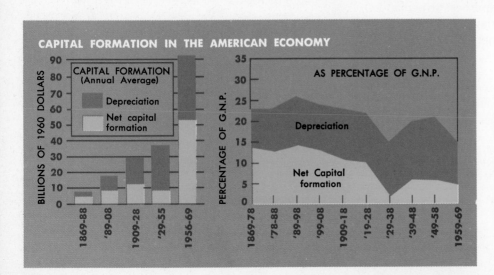

fig. 17–4

Gross capital formation has risen tenfold over the past century, but recently both gross and new capital formation have been much smaller percentages of g.n.p. than in earlier decades. (Sources: S. Kuznets, *Capital in the American Economy*, Princeton Univ. Press, 1961; and Council of Economic Advisers.)

timated at over $3 trillion (excluding stocks of goods held by consumers, such as furniture and clothing); this amounts to over $50,000 per family. A century ago, the figure was only $8 billion. In petroleum, capital investment exceeds $100,000 per worker. Capital has deepened steadily, except in the Great Depression of the 1930s. Remember that our capital stock has grown sixfold since 1900, while population has only tripled.

One more word on the process of saving and capital investment in the American economy. Private saving and investment decisions have produced most of this growth. But governments and the political process have played a big role too. When we levy taxes on ourselves and use the funds to build public capital goods like highways, we accumulate capital through diverting current output from use in current consumption, much as with private saving and investment.

Technical Change

Since 1900, national output has risen twice as fast as the input of labor and capital combined. Technical advance must account for a good share of the difference. Table 17–2 breaks down technical advance between improvement in the quality of capital and the quality of labor, but remember that these estimates are very

rough. Whatever the precise figures, American technology over the past century speaks for itself. Look at a modern oil refinery. Or walk through an automobile assembly plant. Visit a midwestern farm, complete with automatic farm machinery and fertilizers. This is modern technology, the trademark of America, and a source of never-ending amazement to visitors from abroad.

Increased investment in research and development is one major explanation for the rate of technological advance. Figure 17–5 shows the spectacular growth of spending on research and development in the United States since World War II. R & D spending by the government and private industry has grown by more than 10 percent annually. Since 1960, we have spent three-fourths as much on research and development as on total investment in fixed plant—perhaps a harbinger of a speeded growth rate in the future. Strikingly, about two-thirds of this total was paid for by the federal government; in basic research, over 90 percent was government-financed. Since 1940, the federal government has spent over $150 billion on R & D, though most of the work has been done in private industry, universities, and private research organizations. In 1970, the government financed $17 billion of the nation's $27 billion total, but the growth in federal financing of research slowed in the late 1960s—and when inflation is taken out of the figures, growth in real

fig. 17–5

Research is the newest major industry in the United States. It has developed largely since World War II, and is about two-thirds government financed. Most is applied and developmental, only a little basic, research. (Source: National Science Foundation.)

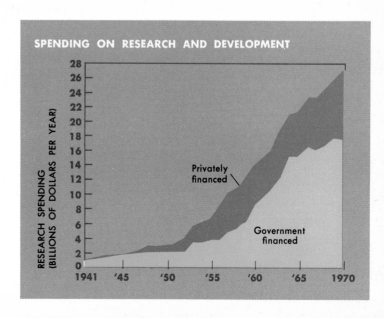

government spending on research was below 5 percent for the first time since World War II. Private industry has concentrated largely on developing the basic research of others into commercially profitable applications. Digital computers, many drugs, atomic energy, missiles, and modern aircraft are notable examples of major innovations originally stimulated and financed by government research funds.

The National Science Foundation suggests that research has a lagged effect on real output. Some observers argue that we are now seeing its accelerated impact, in computers and electronic devices, atomic and solar energy, satellites circling the earth, and modern chemistry and machinery on the farm where productivity has increased even faster than in industry. Perhaps Denison was wrong in giving so much credit to technological advance (20 percent of our total growth since 1929), more than to capital accumulation itself. Or perhaps he gave technical advance too little credit. But as best we can tell, technological advance has played a major role in U.S. economic growth.

Population and the Labor Force

Human beings are the most important productive resource of all. Denison allocated from 27 to 39 percent of total U.S. output growth to increased **quantity** of labor, and another 13 to 27 percent to improvements in its **quality**.

Figure 17–6 presents the facts on U.S. population growth rates since 1800. During the nineteenth century we were one of the world's high growth rate nations. Recently we have fallen far behind the less-developed nations, reflecting in part a gradual decline in birthrates here but primarily a dramatic extension of the life-span in the less-developed nations. During the first half of the 1800s our population grew at around 35 percent per decade, nearly 3 percent annually. During the depression decade of the 1930s, the rate was down to less than 8 percent for the entire ten years. Since then it has been back up a little, but there's little evidence of the world "population explosion" in the United States.

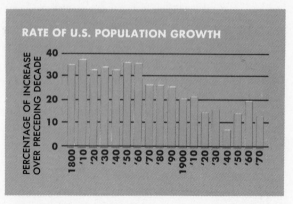

fig. 17–6

The postwar baby boom produced a big increase in our population growth rate. But the rate was higher still a century ago, and it has been slowing recently. Each bar shows percentage increase over preceding decade. (Source: U.S. Bureau of the Census.)

The Labor Force

Population growth means more mouths to feed and more backs to clothe, but not immediately an increase in the number of workers, since babies don't work. By definition the "labor force" includes all persons aged sixteen or older who hold or are looking for paid jobs, or who are self-employed. The concept thus provides a rough measure of the currently available work force. In the United States, this includes most men between sixteen and sixty-five except those who are in school, and over a third of all women.

Figure 17–7 shows what has happened to the labor force since 1900. It has grown steadily except for big bulges during the two major wars, averaging around 40 percent of total population. Now, as the postwar babies grow up, the average annual increase is over a million persons a year, far more than the economy has ever before had to absorb.

Beyond the 80 million people in paid civilian and military jobs of all sorts, there are now some 40 million housewives plus perhaps 20 million retired persons and young people in high school and college who are quite capable of performing productive work. The "labor force" is thus an obviously arbitrary, though useful, concept. What determines the proportion of the population in the labor force? Clearly, a lot of factors. A wealthy nation like ours can afford to keep its children in school until they are grown and thoroughly educated, in contrast with poor nations where everyone must turn to work at an early age. We have steadily increased the years of schooling before our youth enter the job market. Offsetting this drain, the proportion of women working has risen rapidly in recent decades. A century ago, few women worked at paid jobs. Once married, a girl retired sedately to her new home to keep the furniture dusted, get the meals ready on time, and raise a family. But today, over a third of all married women have paid jobs, and the 30 million women at work are over a third of the labor force. Earlier retirement age is a force pushing in the opposite direction.

Closely related is the question of the average number of the working hours per year for the labor force. A century ago, the average factory worker in the United States put in seventy-five to eighty hours a week—generally ten hours or more a day including Sundays. Today he works only around forty hours, and a standard thirty-five hour five-day workweek may not be far away. The New York electricians won a contract for a twenty-five-hour workweek in 1962.

fig. 17–7

The U.S. labor force has grown steadily, with bulges during major wars. Most have taken nonagricultural jobs. Note the big unemployment pocket during the 1930's. (Source: U.S. Department of Labor.)

U.S. LABOR FORCE, 1900-1970

Thus, over the decades America has faced a continual choice between work and leisure. We have chosen a steady increase in the amount of leisure, even though we may have thereby reduced somewhat the growth rate in real output. There is no obvious answer to the best balance between work and leisure for a society. Short hours and long vacations may produce fewer cars and houses, but leisure, though not sold in the marketplace, has a real value for the persons enjoying it. Remember that the g.n.p. figures place no value on the vast amount of added leisure achieved by the American people over the past century.

Investment in Human Capital

Investment in human capital—better education, training on the job, healthier workers, and the like—may have accounted for a quarter of our economic growth during the last quarter century, and it is growing in importance.[3] No other factor has been more important for American growth since 1929, if Table 17–1 is right.

The growth of education in America has been phenomenal. In colonial days, few people received any formal education beyond elementary reading and writing. By 1880, only one in 15 persons of high-school age was attending school. Today this figure is over 95 percent, with 12 million students in some 25,000 high schools, and with the proportion of illiterates in the population below 3 percent. Over 40 percent of all high-school graduates now go on to college, while only a generation ago a college education was a special privilege available only to the well-to-do.

Figure 17–8 shows the rapid growth in spending on education since 1900. During the first three decades of the century, the rate of growth in investment in human resources was more than twice that in nonhuman capital; the upward slope of the education line on the ratio chart is roughly twice that of the top line show-

[3]Chicago's T. W. Schultz argues that investment in education may be even more important than this. See his "Investment in Human Capital," *American Economic Review*, March, 1961.

ing investment in capital goods. (Query: How long is the time lag between more education and a resulting increase in output per capita?)

Figure 17–8 indicates some other interesting facts: (1) The growth in spending on education has been much more stable than on private investment in capital goods. (2) Since World War II, the rates of growth in investment in human and nonhuman resources have been roughly comparable, unlike the 1900 to 1930 period. (3) The overwhelming bulk of our expenditure on education goes into elementary and secondary schools. Even with our recent big increase in college education, it still accounts for only a minor portion of our total investment in human capital.

The scarcest resource has become not land or coal or even skilled workers, but brainpower. The achievements of modern science—atomic power, electronics, the "wonder drugs"—are worth the muscle power of millions of human backs, the output of untold acres of land. Will we run out of oil? If nuclear and solar energy take its place, the world may little care. Will human needs for food outrun the world's land supply? Not if the scientists' amazing accomplishments in producing new fertilizers, hybrid high-yield crops, and new types of cultivating machines continue. In the ultimate improvements of human welfare, one Einstein or Edison is worth thousands of ordinary mortals like most of us. Outstanding brainpower is beyond price.

But a major challenge in education still faces America today. Only three-fourths of the top fifth of high school graduating classes go on to college; only two-thirds of the second fifth. Although most boys and girls now finish high school, hundreds of thousands of youngsters are lost through pregraduation dropouts every year. To repeat the theme from above, brainpower is our scarcest resource. High-grade education and training that push our ablest people to their utmost are among the cheapest and surest investments in progress, both for the individuals and for the nation.

The American Entrepreneur[4]

One group in the labor force deserves a special section. One of the greatest "quality" superiorities in the United States has been the ingenuity and energy of its "entrepreneurs"— its business innovators, managers, and risk takers. The spirit of inquiry and innovation, and the organizing and operating energy of the American entrepreneur deserve much credit for our spectacular economic progress.

Later on, Parts Three and Four of this book look intensively at the function of the entrepreneur as a central organizer of economic activity in a private-enterprise economy. Pending this detailed look, this section represents only a passing bow to his special role in economic growth. The absence of a comparable spirit of entrepreneurship goes far to explain the slower

fig. 17–8

Investment in education has grown faster than private investment in capital goods since 1900, and at a much more stable rate. (Sources: U.S. Departments of Commerce, and Health, Education, and Welfare.)

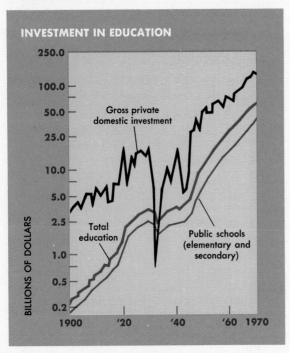

INVESTMENT IN EDUCATION

Gross private domestic investment

Total education

Public schools (elementary and secondary)

BILLIONS OF DOLLARS

[4]*Entrepreneur* is a widely used economic term. An entrepreneur is an enterpriser, loosely someone who is prepared to undertake the production of goods or services when there appears to be a potential profit in doing so. For a more complete analysis, see Part Three.

growth of many of the less-developed countries of Asia and Africa.

People and Productivity in American Growth

Average hourly or annual output per worker is often called worker "productivity." Thus, total output can be viewed as the number of workers times average output per worker. But don't let the common practice of using "productivity" to mean output per man mislead you into attributing all the increased output to workers. We could equally well do a productivity calculation showing output per unit of capital, by dividing total output by the number of units of capital employed. But like it or not, "labor productivity" is in the newspapers and labor–management arguments all the time. And you can understand the complex growth process better if you recognize the widely divergent patterns of change in productivity that make up the total.

Table 17-3 points up the wide fluctuations from decade to decade. Rough data going back to 1850 suggest similar fluctuations in the nineteenth century. Annual increases vary from as high as 12 percent (1919) to minus 8 percent (1917), though few years show a negative figure.

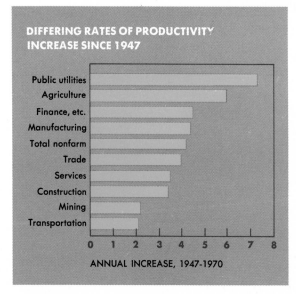

fig. 17–9

Since World War II, output per man-hour has increased at widely differing rates in different sectors of the economy. Excludes government sector. (Source: Council of Economic Advisers.)

Moreover, the economy-wide figure for any year covers up wide differences among different industries. For example, since 1929 average output per man-hour has increased about 3 percent a year. But Figure 17–9 shows the widely differing increases in different sectors of the economy. Separate data on individual firms within industries would show an even more dramatic spread.

Figure 17–9 also suggests that occupational shifts may significantly affect the national average growth rate. The persistent shift of manpower out of agriculture, for example, has recently meant a move for workers from lower- to higher-productivity industries (though productivity is growing faster in agriculture). The recent great increase in spending on services, where productivity is low and growing slowly, has held down the average growth rate. We may note, parenthetically, that rapid output growth in Western Europe following World War II reflected massive shifts of workers from low-productivity agriculture to high-productivity industry. Without this shift, their total

table 17-3

Average Annual Gain in U.S. Productivity, 1909-1970*

Period	Average Annual Gain (Percentage)
1909-1918	0.5
1919-1928	2.7
1929-1938	2.4
1939-1948	2.1
1949-1958	3.0
1959-1970	3.3

*Data from National Industrial Conference Board and Economic Report of the President; 1970 estimated by author. "Productivity" is output per man-hour in the private sector of the economy.

measured growth rates would have been little higher than ours.

Economic Organization and Social-Political Environment

How much of our economic growth is due to the individual-initiative, basically private-enterprise, free society that we prize so highly? There is no simple quantitative answer. Looking backward, it seems clear that America's economic, political, and religious atmosphere has been peculiarly favorable to individual initiative, hard work, and the pursuit of material rewards. Success in business has been a mark of distinction. The "Protestant ethic," which looks upon work as good in itself, has had an important role in establishing our mores. And the basic tradition of "each man for himself" has provided an inviting setting for individual attempts to move up the economic ladder. Experts trying to help the "less-developed" countries are increasingly impressed with the value of such traditions as a foundation for hard work and economic growth. If the recent opposition of many college protesters to work as a way of life should seriously affect adult behavior, the growth in the American standard of living would certainly slow and perhaps actually decline.

American economic institutions have shown unusual flexibility in adjusting to the needs of the growing economy. Banking and financial institutions developed rapidly in response to the need to accumulate savings for investment in business units, and to provide the money to finance the economy's growth. Development of the modern corporation facilitated the accumulation of capital for business ventures without undue risk for nonmanagerial investors. Risk taking was encouraged by financial intermediaries that spread the risk, thereby making investments more attractive to private savers.

Individual freedom to work where a man wished, to set up in business when he liked, to invest his savings as he preferred, provided a setting unique in the modern world. It was a setting ideally designed to stimulate initiative, risk taking, and personal effort. And it was coupled with unparalleled political freedom and social flexibility for the man who could win out in the open competition of the new economy.

Reflecting this climate, government has been generally friendly to vigorous, open competition. Preservation of peace and order, protection of property rights, general maintenance of laissez-faire conditions, and provision of necessary government services such as education, highways, and communications, all provided a foundation for vigorous economic activity. On the regulatory side, the government has largely limited itself to checking undue restrictions on competition. Only with the long depression of the 1930s did far-reaching governmental concern with economic security begin to encroach substantially on the strong tradition of individual initiative in the marketplace.

How much credit should Denison have given these factors back in Table 17–1? He couldn't measure them, so he didn't put them in. Yet many observers feel they deserve a lot of the credit for our superior performance.

Scale of Market

Mass production is obviously more efficient than small-scale output in many industries. Steel, aluminum, automobiles, glass, and dozens of other major products must be produced on a massive scale to permit use of the expensive capital equipment and sophisticated techniques that characterize modern mass production and underlie low prices. Long ago, Adam Smith spelled out the economies to be had from specialization and division of labor in making pins.

Thus, an economy must have large markets if it is to take advantage of economies of mass production. The very fact that the American economy grew so fast and became so large gave it an edge for still faster growth, compared to the smaller economies of the world. Again, no one can measure exactly how important these growing markets have been in permitting us to take advantage of what economists call "economies of scale." But historians and economists agree that they have played a large role.

growth of many of the less-developed countries of Asia and Africa.

People and Productivity in American Growth

Average hourly or annual output per worker is often called worker "productivity." Thus, total output can be viewed as the number of workers times average output per worker. But don't let the common practice of using "productivity" to mean output per man mislead you into attributing all the increased output to workers. We could equally well do a productivity calculation showing output per unit of capital, by dividing total output by the number of units of capital employed. But like it or not, "labor productivity" is in the newspapers and labor–management arguments all the time. And you can understand the complex growth process better if you recognize the widely divergent patterns of change in productivity that make up the total.

Table 17-3 points up the wide fluctuations from decade to decade. Rough data going back to 1850 suggest similar fluctuations in the nineteenth century. Annual increases vary from as high as 12 percent (1919) to minus 8 percent (1917), though few years show a negative figure.

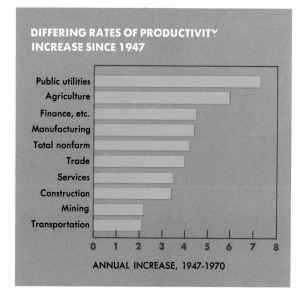

fig. 17–9

Since World War II, output per man-hour has increased at widely differing rates in different sectors of the economy. Excludes government sector. (Source: Council of Economic Advisers.)

Moreover, the economy-wide figure for any year covers up wide differences among different industries. For example, since 1929 average output per man-hour has increased about 3 percent a year. But Figure 17–9 shows the widely differing increases in different sectors of the economy. Separate data on individual firms within industries would show an even more dramatic spread.

Figure 17–9 also suggests that occupational shifts may significantly affect the national average growth rate. The persistent shift of manpower out of agriculture, for example, has recently meant a move for workers from lower- to higher-productivity industries (though productivity is growing faster in agriculture). The recent great increase in spending on services, where productivity is low and growing slowly, has held down the average growth rate. We may note, parenthetically, that rapid output growth in Western Europe following World War II reflected massive shifts of workers from low-productivity agriculture to high-productivity industry. Without this shift, their total

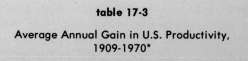

table 17-3

Average Annual Gain in U.S. Productivity, 1909-1970*

Period	Average Annual Gain (Percentage)
1909-1918	0.5
1919-1928	2.7
1929-1938	2.4
1939-1948	2.1
1949-1958	3.0
1959-1970	3.3

*Data from National Industrial Conference Board and *Economic Report of the President*; 1970 estimated by author. "Productivity" is output per man-hour in the private sector of the economy.

measured growth rates would have been little higher than ours.

Economic Organization and Social-Political Environment

How much of our economic growth is due to the individual-initiative, basically private-enterprise, free society that we prize so highly? There is no simple quantitative answer. Looking backward, it seems clear that America's economic, political, and religious atmosphere has been peculiarly favorable to individual initiative, hard work, and the pursuit of material rewards. Success in business has been a mark of distinction. The "Protestant ethic," which looks upon work as good in itself, has had an important role in establishing our mores. And the basic tradition of "each man for himself" has provided an inviting setting for individual attempts to move up the economic ladder. Experts trying to help the "less-developed" countries are increasingly impressed with the value of such traditions as a foundation for hard work and economic growth. If the recent opposition of many college protesters to work as a way of life should seriously affect adult behavior, the growth in the American standard of living would certainly slow and perhaps actually decline.

American economic institutions have shown unusual flexibility in adjusting to the needs of the growing economy. Banking and financial institutions developed rapidly in response to the need to accumulate savings for investment in business units, and to provide the money to finance the economy's growth. Development of the modern corporation facilitated the accumulation of capital for business ventures without undue risk for nonmanagerial investors. Risk taking was encouraged by financial intermediaries that spread the risk, thereby making investments more attractive to private savers.

Individual freedom to work where a man wished, to set up in business when he liked, to invest his savings as he preferred, provided a setting unique in the modern world. It was a setting ideally designed to stimulate initiative, risk taking, and personal effort. And it was coupled with unparalleled political freedom and social flexibility for the man who could win out in the open competition of the new economy.

Reflecting this climate, government has been generally friendly to vigorous, open competition. Preservation of peace and order, protection of property rights, general maintenance of laissez-faire conditions, and provision of necessary government services such as education, highways, and communications, all provided a foundation for vigorous economic activity. On the regulatory side, the government has largely limited itself to checking undue restrictions on competition. Only with the long depression of the 1930s did far-reaching governmental concern with economic security begin to encroach substantially on the strong tradition of individual initiative in the marketplace.

How much credit should Denison have given these factors back in Table 17–1? He couldn't measure them, so he didn't put them in. Yet many observers feel they deserve a lot of the credit for our superior performance.

Scale of Market

Mass production is obviously more efficient than small-scale output in many industries. Steel, aluminum, automobiles, glass, and dozens of other major products must be produced on a massive scale to permit use of the expensive capital equipment and sophisticated techniques that characterize modern mass production and underlie low prices. Long ago, Adam Smith spelled out the economies to be had from specialization and division of labor in making pins.

Thus, an economy must have large markets if it is to take advantage of economies of mass production. The very fact that the American economy grew so fast and became so large gave it an edge for still faster growth, compared to the smaller economies of the world. Again, no one can measure exactly how important these growing markets have been in permitting us to take advantage of what economists call "economies of scale." But historians and economists agree that they have played a large role.

Table 17–1 allocates 10 percent of our total growth this century to economies of scale. Other economists have come up with even larger estimates. Chalk up economies of scale as an obviously important factor, and one on which the United States has had a big advantage. But the figures are only the crudest of approximations.

Aggregate Demand

The preceding look at the sources of economic growth in the United States has stressed primarily the potential supply side, and properly so. For it is the "real" supply factors that basically determine how fast an economy grows. Enough aggregate demand to avoid the waste of unemployment is indeed critical. But once this condition is met, more aggregate demand will merely generate inflation.

Today we recognize that government monetary-fiscal policy can go a long way toward assuring roughly the right rate of growth in aggregate demand. Through most of our history, however, this was not true, and it is only since the 1930s that monetary-fiscal policy has been seriously mobilized to maintain a stably growing level of aggregate demand. To be sure, some attempts were made earlier to avoid monetary excesses in both expansion and contraction, but planned stabilizing monetary-fiscal policy is new.

Look back at Figure 9–1 to see what has happened to the growth in the money stock and aggregate money demand since 1900. Whether the growth in the money stock has been mainly cause or effect of the growth in real output, the end result has been somewhat faster growth in money and aggregate demand than in real output, with a resulting gradual inflationary trend. Except during the long depression of the 1930s, it is not clear that deficient aggregate demand has seriously held back our rate of economic growth.

Many observers point to our repeated booms and depressions, arguing that misbehavior of aggregate demand has indeed slowed growth. One test would be the average level of unemployment of men and machines over the long pull. Here we have little reliable information beyond a quarter century back. New figures by Wesleyan's Stanley Lebergott suggest that the decade of the 1930s was our big failure on unemployment; on the average we have had about 5 percent of our labor force unemployed over the past century. The factors summarized back in Figure 17–2 and Table 17–1, rather than monetary-fiscal policies, look like the critical forces in explaining U.S. economic growth over the past century.

Conclusion

In retrospect, does the theory of Chapter 16 do a good job of explaining U.S. economic growth? The answer appears to be, "yes." Growth in the United States has been a complex, shifting process, and no single, simple explanation can be satisfactory. But this basic analytical framework can go a long way in pointing up the main forces, and in keeping you from getting bogged down in details.

Review

FOR ANALYSIS AND DISCUSSION

1. Has the U.S. record on economic growth been satisfactory over the period since World War II? What criteria do you use in judging?
2. Make a list of the major factors likely to increase the labor force over the next twenty years, and those likely to decrease it. Which are likely to dominate?

3. How long should the workweek be? What seem to you the major considerations in answering this question?
4. Suppose today's college generation decides that it prefers the "simple life" to work for today's business firms. What would be the effect on the standard of living of (a) this college generation over the next decade? (b) the rest of the American public?
5. Is Denison right (Table 17–1) in giving no weight to natural resources in explaining the causes of U.S. economic growth since 1909? Explain.
6. Most Americans feel that private initiative and our market system deserve great credit for our high standard of living compared to other nations. Suppose you meet a foreigner who disagrees. What arguments can you advance to convince him?
7. Critics of the law of diminishing returns argue that the law must be unimportant or invalid in the United States since the U.S. population has grown enormously over the past century while the stock of natural resources has been fixed, yet output of food per capita has risen greatly. Are the critics right?
8. "More rapid growth of population in the United States would mean a decline in our standard of living." Do you agree? Explain.

Growth Policy in the United States

Now, a look to the future. How fast should the American economy grow? Four percent a year? Five percent? As fast as we can? Not at all? Most living things—trees, animals, people—grow more slowly as they mature. Is this true of economies too? If so, should we expect our past growth rate to slow down, or is the United States still a healthy growing youngster?

The optimal rate of growth has become a controversial issue. Most Americans want a higher standard of living—more income and the things that income can buy. They want better houses, automatic clothes washers and dryers, better education for their children, better highways—and to get rid of the slums and poverty that mar American life. We must produce more if we are to have more. But "Zero Growth" has become a rallying cry of the student activists and others who argue that modern technology and the economic growth it helps generate are dehumanizing society and destroying the environment. Our social values are perverted, the critics say. Not more g.n.p. but a higher quality of life should be our major goal.

Before examining the great growth controversy, it is important to distinguish between economic growth and population growth. Economic growth is growth in output, or output per capita—more output to consume or invest. Population growth means more people—more mouths to feed and backs to clothe, but not necessarily any more output. Thus, other things equal, economic growth means a higher standard of living, population growth a lower one.

As a practical matter, of course, economic and population growth often come together. But analytically they are separate phenomena, and to be clear we need to analyze them separately. The case for zero population growth is very different from that for zero economic growth. The main focus of this chapter is on policy toward economic growth, with the analysis of population growth mainly postponed until the next chapter.

The Great Growth Controversy

The Benefits of Growth

The growth rate of the American economy will largely determine your standard of living during your entire life. Consider Table 18–1, which shows U.S. real g.n.p. in 1980 and 2000, in case we grow at 3, 4, or 5 percent for the rest of this century.

Put simply, if we grow at 3 percent per annum, the average family's real income, as measured by real g.n.p. per family, will be about twice as high by the year 2000 as it is now—about $18,000–$20,000 compared to $9,400 in 1970. If we grow at 5 percent, this average family-income figure could soar to over $35,000 (all in 1970 prices). Five percent would be very high by historical standards, but it is the goal set by most West European nations in their recent planning. Even 4 percent, about our post–World War II rate, would yield an extra nearly trillion dollars annually by the year 2000, as compared to the 3 percent that marked our performance before World War II. This difference

is about as much as our total national income in 1970.

Figure 18–1 puts these same alternative growth rates in graphical form, to provide historical perspective. The stakes in the growth game are huge!

These figures are so large as to be almost beyond comprehension. The benefits of growth as a practical matter can be illustrated by looking backward, when the economy has grown at about 3.5 percent annually since 1900. Compare American living standards then and now.

The most obvious change is the dramatic reduction in hard physical labor, on the job, in housekeeping, and even on the farm. In 1900 the average factory workweek was fifty-five hours, now it is less than forty. In 1900, the typical householder fired a coal furnace several times a day; his wife cooked on a wood or coal kitchen stove, which she fired daily. To do the weekly wash, she carried a huge tub of water to boil on top of the stove. Today she spends far less time on backbreaking household work, far more on leisure. Today's family eats better (more meats, fruits, and dairy products), lives more comfortably, has hot running water and inside plumbing, is healthier, and lives longer. A child born today has a life expectancy of seventy years; at the beginning of the century it was less than fifty.

Today virtually every child goes to high school, nearly half to college. In 1900, an eighth-grade education was par for the course; only a tiny fraction got to college. Today's average American has an automobile, and goes more places, sees more things, in a year than his 1900 counterpart did in a lifetime. To cross the country then took a week, now it takes five hours. Then, slow surface mail, with a rare telegram, was the only effective means of communication outside the range of the human voice; now the telephone, radio, and television link all parts of the nation (even the world) almost instantaneously. Today's family has vastly more freedom as to the amusement, travel, and other leisure it enjoys, partly because of technical advances, partly because of the larger income it has left over after paying for necessities. With a four times higher real income, its economic security is far greater. The average family's life

table 18-1

U.S. Real G.n.p. For Alternative Growth Rates
(In billions, at 1970 prices)

	1970	1980	2000
With 3 percent annual growth	$980	$1,350	$2,400
With 4 percent annual growth	980	1,450	3,200
With 5 percent annual growth	980	1,620	4,300

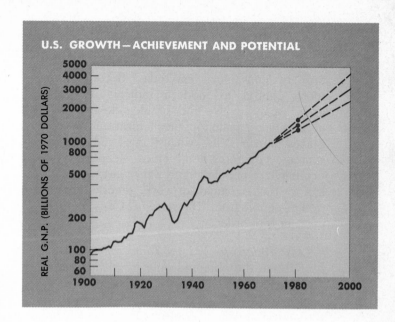

U.S. GROWTH—ACHIEVEMENT AND POTENTIAL

fig. 18–1

U.S. real g.n.p. has grown since 1900 at about 3 1/2 percent per annum. If we can raise the rate to 4 or 5 percent, the payoff in more output will be enormous over the years ahead.

insurance, for example, today totals nine times as much as in 1900, even after allowance is made for today's higher prices. All these facts are commonplace to us. But they are the envy of poorer nations, and they would have been utterly unbelievable to students in 1900.

Some, especially students from well-to-do families, argue that the United States is indeed now so affluent that we no longer need increase total output. Leaving to the next section the major costs these critics see in further growth, consider here merely the argument that we no longer need seek further benefits from growth —that we have plenty of economic goods and services.

It is striking that this cry for "Zero Growth" should come just when the nation appears to be establishing a new set of enormously expensive "national priorities." Chapter 3 listed some of these. To raze and rebuild the nation's city slums would cost, it has been estimated, at least a quarter to a half trillion dollars; other estimates are higher. Four million families now receive incomes below $3,000; to raise the 10 percent of the nation's families officially classified as poverty-stricken up above the poverty level would cost perhaps $25 billion annually. To extend Medicare and Medicaid to the entire population, as many argue would be desirable, would cost more than the entire antipoverty program just mentioned. To eliminate **existing** water pollution alone would cost, according to

widely varying estimates, somewhere between $50 billion and $200 billion. Add raised housing standards for those outside the slums, cleaned-up air, better education for all, improved mass transportation, and so on, and it becomes painfully clear that, instead of a surplus of economic productive capacity, we face a massive resource crunch if we hope to make significant headway on our new national priorities. Our aspirations have risen at least as fast as our achievements.

If we then add the vast needs for aid of the so-called less-developed nations (with over 2 billion people living barely above the existence level), the need for economic growth, here and in other nations, seems overwhelming. Even dramatic steps to redistribute today's U.S. incomes equally among all (leaving aside the probable large drop of total output with complete elimination of individual economic incentives to produce) could only redistribute what we have, not produce more to meet new national and international priorities. It is no accident that neither the lower-income groups nor economists are prominent among those proposing "Zero Growth" as our new national goal.

The Costs of Growth

Offset against these potential benefits of growth are two major types of costs. First, to grow faster requires saving and investing resources that could otherwise have raised current consumption. We can have more tomorrow only by consuming less today. Second, and more central to modern radical criticism, growth may involve undesirable side effects—air and water pollution, mechanization that replaces human skills, exhaustion of natural resources, overcrowded cities (caused by economic or population growth?), large organizations that dehumanize work, general alienation of people from "the system." Consider the costs in that order.

Less Today for More Tomorrow. Faster growth can be obtained only by either more and harder work or reduced consumption now to permit higher investment that will raise future output. Economists often say, "There is no such thing as a free lunch," to emphasize the fundamental economic problem. Given full employment of resources, we can have more of one thing only by having less of something else—we can grow faster only by accepting less leisure and lower consumption now than we could otherwise have had.

Of course, we can expand total output faster by having a larger population. But this does nothing to raise per capita output and the real standard of living. Indeed, a higher birthrate will decrease output per capita in the short run, because new babies eat but do not work. Even immigration doesn't help much, because it provides more workers only at the cost of more mouths to feed. Thus, only if we ourselves work more we can hope to speed growth per capita through the quantity-of-labor route.

It is to capital accumulation, to technical advance, and to investment in human beings that we must basically look for faster growth in output per capita. And these routes require more saving and investment—a cost now for a future benefit. The critical issue is how we weigh the present against the future—our work and our comforts against those of our children and our grandchildren.

Perhaps the payoff to investment in research and in education will prove to be quick and spectacular. Improved science and technology may produce more rapid growth with little further diversion of resources from current con-

sumption. But even with great research success, most technological advance requires capital investment to put it into effect. It seems unlikely that there is an easy road to faster growth that does not require saving and investment. Growth has a cost. The problem is to weigh the cost against the benefits.

Your inclination may be to say, "Of course we should save more today for a better tomorrow. We should sacrifice more for the benefit of our children and grandchildren." But don't be too quick. Even with the present growth rate, the average per capita income of your children a generation hence will be more than 50 percent higher than yours is today; that of your grandchildren two generations hence will be far more than double the present level. Given these facts, some observers don't find the case for paying the cost of faster growth every impressive. Why, they ask, should we squeeze down on consumption now to make the future even richer? Make up your own mind whether saving more today to assure a better tomorrow is worthwhile, individually and nationally.

Undesirable Side Effects of Growth

Destruction of the environment and deterioration in the quality of life are the charges now most often levied against economic growth. Meaningful analysis of such sweeping charges is impossible without more specific accusations. But it is clear that pollution of water and air is widespread in modern America. The Los Angeles smog is now an oppressive reality for many other cities as well. Many rivers are running waste disposals for sewage and industrial residues. The south shore of Lake Erie is dead, substantially devoid of normal marine life and unsafe for human swimming and recreation. Pollution of quiet is as common. Air hammers, jet aircraft, motorcycles, trucks, and electronically magnified rock bands blast one's eardrums at decibel levels specialists say will gradually deafen us. Major highways and streets are cluttered by unsightly neon signs, wires, and hot dog stands; parks are full of autos and empty beer cans.

Every newspaper and magazine is full of such

stories and pictures. The pollution story is so well known now that there is little need to continue the examples here. Indeed, an entire chapter (39) is devoted to pollution and its possible solutions later in the book, when we have the rest of the analytical tools needed to work the problem through. Here three points are important in a preliminary look at the costs of economic growth.

1) A lot of the unwanted pollution of the environment is associated with economic growth.

2) There is no necessary reason why this should be so. For example, Los Angeles smog is largely caused by auto-exhaust emissions. However, there is nothing in economic growth that requires use of just the present type of internal combustion engine and fuel; if we choose to do so, we can require auto manufacturers to meet "clean" emission standards for new autos and present owners to install and maintain smog filters in order to cut down emissions from existing cars. Both will cost money—almost certainly paid by all of us as car users. Thus, such laws would presumably reduce the amount of auto transportation attained from any given level of resource use, but dirty air is not a necessary condition of economic growth. We can, if we wish, buy more clean air (less pollution) and less transportation for our auto money. And so it is for ugly signboards, dirty rivers, noisy motorcycles, and most of the other examples of environmental pollution cited above. Clearly, the cleaner the air or water, the higher the cost will be. We neither need nor can afford a perfectly clean environment, whatever that would mean. The practical question is how much cleanliness we are willing to pay for, as an alternative to other uses of our resources.

3) As we shall see in Chapter 39, it is unlikely that we will obtain acceptably pollution-free growth without collective (governmental) action to require it. This is not because modern businessmen and consumers are evil people or we have been taken over by modern technology, but because of what economists call "externalities." Take the auto-exhaust problem. By putting an expensive smog-control device on my car and having it cleaned every six

months, I can drastically reduce my contribution to smog in California. But, alas, with over 10 million other cars in the state, the air I breathe will be, for all practical purposes, just as dirty as before. And so it is for any other driver acting alone. Unless I can count on it that others will do the same, there is little incentive for me to reduce my smog emission below the California legal maximum. If we want to eliminate auto-caused smog, the only practical way we can be sure 10 million auto owners will cooperate is by having a law that requires them to do so. So it is with most other cases of pollution. There are "external" effects of each consumer's or business' behavior that are not worthwhile for him to take into account unless others will do likewise. More details in Chapter 39.

Other alleged undesirable side effects of growth are harder to come to grips with—as to either cause or cure. Take the alleged dehumanization that modern technology is said to produce—machines eliminate meaningful human skilled jobs, and modern businesses are so big that the individual becomes only a routine cog in a huge organization. Obviously, the issues here go far beyond economics. But economics has something to say. First, although a lot of high-skilled jobs have been eliminated by machines, overall the mix between low-, intermediate-, and high-skill jobs in the economy has shown little change over the last quarter century. The modern computer is a good example. It has displaced mainly routine, low-skill, clerical jobs in banks, insurance companies, and the like. It has created mainly high-skill jobs, in making computers, in servicing them, and above all in programming (applying) them to solve problems in science and industry. The modern steel mill has eliminated mainly hard, low- and medium-skilled labor—though some skilled jobs as well. One of the biggest job shifts is from manufacturing to services—store clerks, travel agents, airline employees, beauty parlor operators. It's not obvious whether the shifts have been toward or away from more meaningful jobs. If the standard of comparison is the frontier pioneer of a century ago, there has indeed been a change in jobs. But even there it's not clear the present jobs aren't easier, and the drop in living standards in going back to the frontier is more than even most ardent zero-growth advocates are prepared to contemplate.

The charge that growth depends on bigness for efficiency, and that bigness means personal frustration and alienation from "the system," is largely beyond the bounds of economic analysis. Economic efficiency does demand big economic units in some businesses—e.g., steel production and public utilities. There is little doubt that some people find the large modern corporation an oppressive, dull master, and their jobs routine and meaningless. It is equally clear that others find it a comfortable if unexciting environment—a satisfactory place to earn a living with good pay and a good deal of leisure time to do what they like to do. Still others find big business an exciting challenge—a place where first-rate ability can bring big salaries and satisfying success. You'll have a good basis for making up your own mind only after you've faced the problem of earning a living for a few years after college. But don't forget two facts. First, less than a quarter of all Americans work for the huge corporations that are said to dominate the American economy (see Chapters 20 and 29–31 for details). Second, life consists of comparison of alternatives. What are the feasible alternatives to the kinds of jobs in today's economy if indeed we want to maintain, and even improve, our existing living standards—as it seems clear most Americans do.

Consider two other probable, unwanted, by-products of faster economic growth—over-crowding of our already crowded urban areas, and exhaustion of natural resources. On closer analysis, both turn out to be reflections of **population,** at least as much as **economic,** growth. Indeed, urban crowding seems primarily that. Modern business does see advantages in clustering head offices in major cities, where supplementary financial services are available and communication is easy. Moreover, these office clusters draw service workers, retail stores, amusement facilities, and the like. But modern business has increasingly moved to decentralize its production and distribution activities away from the cities to more pleasant and productive environments. If we continue to crowd more people into already jammed, noisy, dirty, crime-ridden cities, urban problems will get worse rather than better. But only a modest part of this blame should be chalked up against **economic** growth per se. It's more people who create the crowding problem. As with pollution, more crowded cities need not be a by-product of further economic growth.

Both population and economic growth use up natural resources. The American economy chews up an enormous volume of raw materials. If we want more material goods, we will probably use still more raw materials, primarily our own but also many from abroad. There is no obvious way to avoid this cost without growing slower or shifting the mix of final products from goods to services. However, the danger of exhaustion of natural resources is easy to overstate. The facts are in Chapter 17. Conservationists have predicted dire consequences from our "extravagant" use of our raw materials and energy reserves for at least a century. But in fact new reserves and, more important, substitute materials and energy sources have been discovered even faster than our uses have grown. Oil and natural gas are examples of the former; nuclear and solar energy of the latter. The massive substitution of artificial for natural rubber and of nylon and other man-made fibers for silk are other examples. Clearly natural resources are not limitless, but technical ingenuity has overcome all the major shortages and more to date. Most experts appear to take a middle position. We do indeed face problems ahead on some resources, but most doomsday predictions are badly overdone.

One last argument deserves attention here, though it is a major focus of analysis in Chapter 43, which deals with international economic policies. This is the common claim by growth critics that U.S. growth rests on exploitation of the "Third World" nations, that we are rapidly exhausting their natural resources, and that without this exploitation U.S. growth would grind to a halt. Such arguments carry heavy political overtones.

The economic facts are reasonably clear. (1) Total U.S. imports of all industrial raw materials from all so-called developing nations in 1969 (a boom year) were about $11 billion, roughly 1.2 percent of U.S. g.n.p. While loss of imports of some materials (notably tin) from the "Third World" would be highly disruptive in some U.S. industries, and while we import large quantities of others (notably petroleum) in addition to our own production and imports from other developed nations, roughly 1 percent of g.n.p. hardly looks like the foundation that keeps the whole U.S. economy from tumbling down. (2) Whatever the radical critics of the U.S. economy say, the views of the developing nations are clear. They desperately want the United States to buy their raw materials, for the proceeds are what they use to pay for the imports of food and capital goods they need for their own development. The bitterest cries against the United States come when U.S. purchases of such raw materials drop, because of U.S. recession or of U.S. import restrictions. Faster U.S. economic growth would almost surely use more raw materials from abroad, but both the magnitude of these uses and the costs to the "Third World" nations are often grossly overstated by critics of U.S. economic growth.[1]

Balancing the Benefits and Costs of Growth

Can we somehow obtain the important benefits of continuing economic growth but avoid the devastating side effects that endanger our environment? If we just go on as we have in the past, the answer is no. U.S. economic growth over the past half century has brought great benefits, but at major costs to our environment and our "quality of life." Using resources to reverse this deterioration (for example, by cleaning up our air, streams, and lakes) will mean less production of other things we might otherwise have—cleaner air and water but less transportation, paper, and chemicals from our existing stock of productive resources. Looking to the future, it will mean more of the growth in pro-

ductive capacity allocated to pollution control, less to more traditional goods and services.

Strikingly, more growth in productive capacity (through saving and investing) can mean both a cleaner environment and more output of goods and other services because of our expanded total productive ability. Without continued growth we can clean up the environment and avoid further deterioration only by taking less than we now have of other goods and services. Growth and a better environment are partly competitors for our resources; partly they are complementary. Undisciplined growth brings pollution. But the more growth we have in productive capacity, the more we can afford to clean up the environment without foregoing other goods and services.

Consider these very important propositions. The generalized productive capacity we call economic growth can produce leaded gasoline, or Beethoven quartets, or smog-control devices. That is, it can produce output that causes pollution while giving people a product they want; it can produce things that yield no pollution; or it can produce things that reduce pollution. Growth (more productive capacity) gives us the potential for having more of any combination of the three. Whether we use the growth wisely is a problem we must face as communities and as a nation. The addition of a cleaner environment to our list of national priorities increases rather than reduces the importance of our having a growing capacity to produce; there are never enough productive resources to provide everything we want. To reject growth because we are unwilling or unable to seize the potentialities for using it well would be a shortsighted conclusion indeed.[2]

Population Growth

The case for zero, or slower, **population** growth is very different from that for slower **economic** growth. Indeed, slower population growth means, other things equal, **faster** economic growth, if we mean by economic growth

---

[1]These two facts, of course, are only part of the complex problem of U.S. economic relations with the developing countries. The whole issue of alleged U.S. economic "exploitation" of the developing countries is examined in more detail in Chapter 43. Only the facts specifically relevant to U.S. growth policy are considered here.

[2]Parts Three and Five to come are entirely devoted to the complex issues of attaining an optimal use (allocation) of our limited stock of productive resources.

"growth in output per capita." Population is the denominator in the ratio: $\frac{\text{Output}}{\text{Population}}$. At best, more population can be only roughly neutral with reference to the average standard of living —more people produce more but also consume. As a practical matter, over any decade or two faster population growth is likely to reduce output per capita, since babies and children consume but don't produce.

This problem is painfully apparent in the less-developed countries, where the "population explosion" is at the core of their economic problem. Many of these nations have now succeeded in increasing their total output at a substantial rate (often as much as 4 to 5 percent per year), but population has grown almost as fast. All of Chapter 19, with its special appendix on "The Population Explosion," is devoted to the problems of the developing nations.

In principle, the relation of population to economic growth is similar in the developed countries. But there is no population explosion in those countries. In the United States, for example, there has been a persistent decline in the rate of population growth over the past century (see Figures 17–6 and 19–2), and the population growth rate is relatively slow in nearly all the highly developed countries. The U.S. population density of about 20 per square kilometer is tiny compared to most developed nations. Germany and the United Kingdom both have about 230 people per square kilometer, Belgium and Holland even more. Nonetheless, if you are concerned with overcrowding in the cities and place a high value on open spaces, the case for slower population growth here will seem strong. Slower population growth in the United States would probably raise average living standards here a little over the decades immediately ahead, compared to recent population growth rates.

How To Grow Faster: The Supply Side

Suppose we want to increase our total productive capacity faster. Leaving aside questions as to how to allocate this capacity among different public and private priorities, how can we grow faster?

Experts estimating long-run growth in the economy's full-employment productive capacity often use a two-stage process. First, they estimate what the labor force will be. This is not too difficult to forecast for a decade or two, because nearly all the labor force is already born and we know the age and sex distribution. When we adjust for a gradual reduction in the workweek, for longer education, and for more women in the labor force, a figure of 1 to 1.5 percent growth per annum emerges, depending on the period concerned.

Second, the experts estimate the growth in output per man-hour or man-year. This estimate of "productivity" is harder, since it lumps together the effects of capital accumulation, education, and improving technology—everything except the quantity of labor. Yet, over the century before World War II the growth in productivity was reasonably stable, around 2 percent per annum; since World War II it has averaged over 3 percent.

Lastly, they combine these two estimates and get an estimate of growth in aggregate output. With the postwar speedup in productivity and a higher labor-force growth, hopes have crept up, from 3 to 4 or even 5 percent. Remember, this is the growth in potential high-employment output. If there is substantial unemployment, actual g.n.p. will be correspondingly less.

This simple procedure gives a manageable framework for making rough estimates of total output potential for any future year. But it also should emphasize the need to look behind the two key figures, since they sum up the forces that will make the economy grow faster or slower. How can we speed economic growth for the future?

More Work

Population growth has been slowing down in America over the past century. But in any event, more people only raise total output, not output per capita. If we want to raise per capita g.n.p. through more work, we need to raise the labor-force participation rate (the proportion of the total population who work) or to increase the average number of working hours per year per worker.

Most of the experts expect a gradual increase in participation by women to be roughly offset by longer education for young people before they enter the labor force. The U.S. Department of Labor estimates that over the coming decade our labor force will grow at a high 1.7 percent annually, compared to only 1.3 percent over the preceding fifteen years. But this will be partly offset by a continuing drop in the average workweek. Labor Department experts estimate about an hour a week less by 1980. This estimate pulls down the effective growth in annual hours worked to about 1.5 percent, somewhat above the expected rate of population growth of perhaps 1.25 percent.

Ours is a free society. We believe that a housewife and her husband, not the government, should decide whether she stays home or looks for a job. How many hours a week you work is largely up to you and your employer. The government may plead and explain the facts of economic growth. But short of national emergencies like war, there is little it can do to change the long-term trends of labor-force participation and the gradually falling workweek. Indeed, government's main intervention has been through extending the period of free, or cheap, education, thereby reducing the labor-force participation rate. If we want to speed economic growth through national policy, we must probably look to other approaches.

Research and Technical Advance

Modern research has produced spectacular results. Basic research in chemistry is rapidly giving us, in essence, more usable resources—fertilizers for poor soil, means of refining low-grade metallic ores, and dozens of other such improvements. Science has opened up vast new power sources for economical use—oil, gas, nuclear energy. Food from seawater and power from the sun may be tomorrow's answer to the law of diminishing returns. Moreover, we have significantly speeded the translation of research into widespread use. One of the most important social changes of our time is the growing contrivance and management of change itself.

Figure 17–5 showed the explosion of spending on research and development since World War II. Half of all measured research in our history has occurred in the last ten years. Since research obviously has a lagged effect on actual production, perhaps we have already put a mighty force in motion—a force just beginning to show in modern "automation," computers, satellites, solar power, and the like. Output per worker has grown at over 3 percent annually, not its historical 2 percent, since World War II. But two decades is too short a period on which to generalize. How much modern R & D has speeded long-run economic growth remains to be seen.

Figure 17–5 indicated also that much of the research and development in America has been financed by the federal government. Almost all the funds for "basic" research have come from government sources. During the late 1960s the federal government was financing about two-thirds of all R & D spending (mainly through its defense and space budgets), although nearly three-fourths of the actual work was done in industry and much of the rest in universities. Industry itself financed only about a quarter of the total, and foundations and universities the rest.

Private industry can probably be counted on to finance most developmental and applied research leading directly to salable products. There is no obvious way to increase such private spending on research and development, short of providing a governmental subsidy. Firms already can charge off most research expenses as direct costs and hence as full tax deductions. But the case for direct government support of basic research is strong. The results of truly basic research are unpredictable; and they seldom have direct commercial profitability. Even more important, if a company does make a major basic breakthrough, it is seldom able to protect its discovery for long from use by its competitors and by others. Thus, it is hard to see why many firms will spend much money on such basic research. But history records that it is the basic research breakthroughs that have provided the foundation for the great scientific and practical benefits of our times.

Government support for the rapid dissemination of new knowledge and techniques also makes sense, on the same grounds. This is especially true for the outpouring of information from the government's own vast R & D spending on defense, space, and health projects. The agricultural experiment stations and extension services established at state universities throughout the nation a century ago have played a major role in speeding innovation in American agriculture. Similar aid in manufacturing, services, and other areas might produce similar results.

Saving and Capital Accumulation

How can public policy divert more of our current incomes and output to saving and investment—to the future as against the present? For the most part, this allocation is now determined by the individual decisions of millions of rich and middle-class families and by the managers of the nation's business firms. For it is they who make most of the nation's saving and investment decisions.

It is not easy to change the decisions of so many million savers and investors. If we want the economy to save and invest more, we can change the tax structure to lessen the burden on high incomes where most of the saving is done, and place more of the burden on the poor, where it will surely reduce consumption. But at the margin, the differences in the marginal propensities to consume out of income are surprisingly small. Similarly, reduced taxes on corporate profits would stimulate investment. Special provisions to permit corporations to charge off depreciation faster for tax purposes can raise profit rates and stimulate investment.

Still more directly, the government may collect more taxes and invest the money itself. Under our political process, presumably each man, rich or poor, has one vote, and society may vote this way to raise investment. Every year our governments already tax away billions of dollars to invest in public capital goods—schools, highways, airports, parks, and other such investments. In addition, some new military equipment might be viewed as a temporary accumulation of national capital. In 1969, some $20–$30 billion was channeled into public capital accumulation in this way through federal, state, and local governments. Here is a direct way social action can change the saving–current consumption mix.

But direct government intervention to increase investment relative to consumption faces a problem. Private citizens can offset the government action through switching their individual consumption–saving mixes by reallocating the income they have left after taxes so as to restore roughly their previous levels of consumption. Insofar as this happens, the government policy is thwarted, private saving is reduced, and the result is simply a substitution of public investment for private.

In a Communist economy like the USSR or China, the rate of capital accumulation is determined directly by the state. The Kremlin or Peking decrees that resources will be used to produce factories and dams rather than consumer goods. Current consumption by the masses has been held down by dictatorial planning that we would find intolerable. Yet the Russians and Chinese leaders argue that the people basically want heavy investment to raise living standards for the future. They say that state action makes it possible for the economy to grow faster than the vast unplanned chaos that they see in our capitalist system can. Few Americans favor direct government control over all investment. How far should we go in raising or lowering investment rate through governmental measures?

Investment in Human Beings

Human beings are capital to a society, just as buildings and machines are. Improvement in the quality of our human capital through education and training provides a social payout through increasing future output, just as does investment in research and development. Indeed, modern research suggests that the return on investment in human capital (through formal education, retraining, and the like) is considerably higher than the return on investment in capital goods. If this is true, both individuals and society would gain economically by spending more on education. In addition, we would get the large but immeasurable benefits of a better-educated population for a stable social-political system. The external economies again make a strong case for government action.

If education is such a good investment, why don't private individuals make the investment themselves voluntarily? Many do. Almost everyone now gets through grade school and into high school on public funds. Most finish high school. Over 40 percent of the population goes on to at least some college work, and a much higher proportion of upper-income families send their children to college. Anyone who has done the arithmetic knows that a good education for his son is likely to be a better investment than buying the best stocks and bonds.

Nevertheless, either most of the population hasn't done the arithmetic or doesn't believe it. Over half of our youngsters don't go to college, and most families and teen-agers are reluctant to borrow to make this investment in human resources, even though it is clearly profitable in the long run. Moreover, our society frowns on slavery; thus there is no sure way a capitalist with spare funds can get back a big return if he wants to invest in John Jones's education, instead of in a business venture.[3]

Improved Economic Efficiency

If we can increase the output obtained from any given capital and labor input through increased efficiency, obviously there is social gain. Two measures have been widely suggested to speed economic growth this way.

The first is to break up monopolies, because monopoly (as will be explained in Part Three) generally leads to an inefficient allocation of resources and thus to less output than could otherwise be obtained from any given amount of capital and labor. The second is to improve the labor markets so workers will move more promptly from declining to expanding industries and areas. This would help to lessen "frictional" and "structural" unemployment, which exist because of poor information or immobility. Better information on job openings, government subsidies to bring new industries to unemployed workers—all these have been used successfully in Europe, where unemployment since World War II has averaged lower than ours.

Clearly it is to everyone's advantage to get frictional and structural unemployment down. But the evidence of Chapter 15 suggests that strong aggregate demand may be the best tool of all. For then employers themselves take over the job of finding workers and training them if need be, under the spur of the profit motive.

The Economic Climate—Initiative and Enterprise

Everyone agrees that individual initiative, the spirit of enterprise, open markets with active competition, economic and social mobility, and a generally favorable economic social-political climate deserve much credit for America's growth record over the past two centuries. But how to make them contribute more to growth in the future is less clear.

Indeed, these conditions are challenged by many today. Today's student radicals reject the fundamental tenets of work to earn one's own living and competition with economic rewards to the winners. Others claim that the American economy has become confortable, affluent, and tradition-bound—less inclined to vigorous competition and less open to the newcomer and the new idea. They see a growing unwillingness to work—the desire for security replacing traditional American aggressive individualism.

---

[3]Some who resist public compulsion (which is involved in the expenditure of tax funds on more education) urge, instead, measures to improve borrowing arrangements for those who want an education and are willing to make an investment in it. They argue that we should provide everyone accurate information of the probable economic benefits of private investment in education. Then if people didn't choose to borrow to pay for their own education, there would remain no reason why society should provide the further education for them at public expense. But this argument overlooks the external economics point, and brushes over the great difficulty the poor would have in borrowing to finance their children's education.

Maybe the critics and worriers will turn out to be right; others, however, see in the American economic organization a still impressively vigorous, flexible, adaptive machine. But even in a wealthy, high-saving economy like ours, rapid growth is not automatic. Hard work and incentives are still important, as the spectacular growth of Japan and West Germany since World War II illustrates. Sir Henry Clay, a noted economist, two decades ago put the problem provocatively: "The so-called capitalist system, so far from failing, has been almost too successful in the interests of its own survival; it has encouraged the great mass of our population to believe that the increase of wealth is easy and inevitable, and depends no longer on incentives and appropriate organization but on scientific research, adequate education, and public direction."[4] His warning is appropriate today.

Demand Policy for Stable Growth

Increasing our productive capacity (moving out the production-possibilities frontier) is the main requisite for faster economic growth. But in a largely private-enterprise economy, the demand side matters too. For businessmen will not long produce goods they cannot sell at a profit. On the other side, excess aggregate demand will produce inflation and instability. What level of aggregate demand should monetary and fiscal policy encourage so as to assure stable economic growth, avoiding both depressions and inflations?

What Aggregate Demand Is Needed for Stable Economic Growth?

Assume that national productive capacity is growing 4 percent annually because of population growth, capital investment, and technological advance. We want continuous high-level employment with stable prices. What aggregate demand is needed, assuming that we begin from a stable, high-employment situation?

[4]Address at Wharton School of Finance and Commerce, University of Pennsylvania, January 10, 1947.

The answer is clear. Aggregate demand should rise at about 4 percent a year (the same rate as the expansion of productive capacity), and the division between consumption and investment spending should match the division between consumption and saving decisions (omitting government taxes and spending). More total spending will mean inflation. Less will mean underemployment and waste. A malallocation of spending between consumption and investment is likely to generate short-run fluctuations that may become serious booms or depressions.

Begin with the following simplified high-employment economy for 197X.

	In Billions
Total g.n.p.	$1,000
Consumption	620
Investment and saving	140
Government taxes and spending	240

We want to grow at 4 percent yearly. What must 197X + 1 look like? To simplify, let us assume arbitrarily that government taxes and spending increase just 4 percent. Then, clearly, private spending must also rise 4 percent if 4 percent more output is to be taken off the market at a stable price level. If the proportion between consumption and investment remains stable, 197X + 1 would look like this, with total spending up 4 percent.

	In Billions
Total g.n.p.	$1,040
Consumption	644
Investment and saving	146
Government taxes and spending	250

It does not necessarily follow, of course, that a 4 percent increase in investment any year will produce a 4 percent increase in capacity the next year; the capital–output ratio need not produce that result. Remember that capacity depends on other factors in addition to investment. Perhaps total 197X + 2 full-employment capacity will be up only 3 percent, perhaps 5 or 6. But whatever the percentage is, the full-employment-without-inflation level of aggregate demand rises by the same amount. And the same rule applies for following years.

In principle, there is no reason why we need to have a stable price level to achieve stable, full-employment growth. If, for example, total spending rises only 2 percent while capacity grows by 4 percent, full-employment output can still be achieved if the price level falls 2 percent. Conversely, if total spending rises 6 percent, full-employment output can be maintained with a 2 percent increase in average prices.

As a practical matter, however, as we saw in Chapters 10 and 15, substantial economy-wide price reductions without serious disruption seem unlikely in the modern American economy. With downward inflexibility of costs and prices, inadequate total spending means unemployment of men and machines. Thus, few economists now believe that aggregate demand can safely grow less than roughly in proportion to total capacity. Holding aggregate money demand constant with a 4 percent annual growth in capacity could mean something like 20 percent unemployment of men and capacity in only five years. This is, indeed, roughly what happened between 1929 and 1939, when the latter year saw 8 million unemployed with about the same money g.n.p. as in peak-prosperity 1929.

A look ahead to 1980 will illustrate some of the magnitudes involved in such growth. Assume stable prices at 1970 levels and roughly constant proportions between consumption, saving–investment, and government taxes–spending. Then a 4 percent growth rate gives a 1980 g.n.p. of about $1.5 trillion, divided roughly like this:

	In Billions
Total g.n.p.	$1,500
Consumption	930
Investment and saving	210
Government taxes and spending	360

Will Private Decisions Provide the Right Total Spending?

Can we count on consumers to buy nearly $1 trillion of food, clothing, washing machines, automobiles, and other goods and services, only a decade hence? Perhaps more important, since investment is a driving force of economic growth, can we count on private businesses and households to spend $210 billion in 1980 on new plant, equipment, and construction? Remember that this 1980 figure implies they spent nearly as much in 1979, only a little less in 1978, and so on back down to the then-peak level of around $140 billion in the late 1960s. And after $210 billion in 1980, will they invest the $218 billion in 1981 and $227 billion in 1982 that will be needed, on our assumptions, to maintain economic growth and offset the growing savings made at g.n.p. levels above $1.5 trillion? What industries will require investment of these astronomical sums year after year to produce the goods consumers want to buy? Lastly, will we want governments to take away $360 billion in taxes and spend it for us? If not, private spending will have to grow even faster to take up the slack.

A further problem needs to be noted. Where will the money come from for stable economic growth? Will the private economy automatically produce the right amount? Looking back to Chapter 9, we can see that M and V combined must increase enough to produce a 4 percent annual increase in money g.n.p.

Will private bank-borrowing and spending decisions automatically add up to just the required growth in money and in aggregate demand? Obviously, there is no necessary reason they will. The case for conscious stabilizing monetary-fiscal policy to keep aggregate demand on target is loud and clear.

Capital and Labor Shares in Stable Growth

Even if aggregate demand grows stably, may not the investment–consumption balance get out of kilter? And a closely related question: What balance between wages and profits (as rough surrogates for consumption and investment) is required for stable, sustained growth?

Clearly, the answer depends partly on how fast we want to grow. Fast growth requires a high-profit, high-investment economy. Wages shouldn't rise too fast. High profits are a fine thing for rapid growth. We'd better be sure the unions don't get too much at bargaining time.

But if profits and investment get too large relative to wages and consumption spending, excess capacity will develop and the boom will collapse. Indeed, when it comes to maintaining high-level employment, union leaders hammer away at one proposition: Wages are the biggest single source of buying power in our economy. The major cause of depression, they say, consist of wages that are too low. If wages don't rise fast enough, profits will swell and income will be saved, not spent. Every bargaining time, union leaders mount a public-relations campaign that a wage boost will really be a boon to everyone through the increased spending it will generate.

Are the unions right that higher wage rates are the way to fight underemployment and overinvestment? The answer hinges on some technical considerations. With higher wage rates, will employers spend more or less on total wages for labor? If more, the higher wage rates at least have a chance of increasing consumption spending. But if employers spend less on labor, clearly the higher wage rates will reduce consumer spending. Either way, higher wage rates, other things equal, mean higher costs and prices than would otherwise prevail for more workers. Over the long pull, moreover, it's clear that higher wages steadily push toward the substitution of machinery for labor.

In any case, don't be trapped by the obvious fallacy that business profits represent savings withdrawn from the income stream. Many business profits flow directly into investment spending, and there is no necessary reason to classify big profits as a deflationary force. What matters for economic health is total spending on consumption plus investment, not just consumption. Wages are purchasing power, but so are profits.

It should be clear that the investment–consumption balance issue is a thorny one. Econo-

mists have a variety of "growth models" that illustrate the relative paths of investment and consumption needed to assure stable, sustainable growth under different conditions—different propensities to consume, different capital–output ratios, different rates of technical progress, and the like. One such simple model was represented in the appendix to Chapter 16. But nearly all these models, and historical experience, tell us that growth must be reasonably balanced if it is to be stable. Consumption and investment must be kept growing at roughly the same rates. If either investment or consumption gets too far out of line with the other, we're in for trouble. And although profits and wages are by no means identical with investment and consumption spending, very roughly the same balanced-growth proposition holds for them.[5]

A Concluding Note

An interesting and provocative concluding note on national growth policy has been provided by Brookings' Herbert Stein:

We have had a good deal of talk about the desirability of economic growth, which has almost always been accepted as a good thing. There have been national policies which contributed to growth but also many which retarded it. There has been no national determination of a desirable rate of growth, no effort to formulate a comprehensive program to achieve any specified rate of growth, and few policy decisions that were dominated by growth considerations. Growth in America has been the outcome of the efforts of millions of families to improve their own conditions and the conditions of their children, rather than the outcome of a national policy. The picture of a government of tyrannical Philistines forcing economic growth upon a citizenry of Henry David Thoreaus is fantasy. The spontaneous and decentralized origins of the growth suggests how difficult it would be to influence its rate very much, in either direction, by national policy.[6]

[5]It is interesting to note that the 1962 "wage–price guideposts" (see page 205) provide for this rough stability in wage and profit shares of the national income.

[6]From "An Economist Looks at the 1970s," speech at Rider College, Trenton, New Jersey, May 15, 1970, pp. 5–6. At the time, Stein was a member of President Nixon's Council of Economic Advisers.

Review

FOR ANALYSIS AND DISCUSSION

1. How fast should the American economy grow over the decade ahead? What measures would you propose to achieve your desired growth rate?

2. How much of your personal income are you willing to use over the next decade to build up the economic capacity of the nation for future production? Does the government have a right to dictate to you a rate different from the one you prefer?

3. Can you see how we can have continued economic growth and also a cleaner, more attractive environment? Explain.

4. Are economic growth and a better "quality of life" competitive or complementary? Explain.

5. Why do many economists who favor slower *population* growth simultaneously support faster *economic* growth?

6. Since 1900 (see Figure 18–1), have money demand or real factors been more important in explaining our growth rate? If your answer is the real factors, how about the period of the 1930s?

7. Only about 3 percent of the g.n.p. is devoted to research and development. Would it be sound policy to double this amount? Who should decide? If the amount should be doubled, who should pay for it?

8. Can you suggest ways of increasing the nation's rate of capital formation that do not impinge on the freedom of individuals and businesses to spend or save their incomes as they please?

9. By 1980, the population of the United States may be 225 million. Assume that the same proportion (about 40 percent) of the population is in the labor force as in 1970, that the average propensity to consume out of g.n.p. remains at about two-thirds; that output per worker rises about 2 percent per annum; and that the price level remains constant:

   a. What level of gross national expenditure will be required in 1980 to assure full employment? Explain.

   b. What level of private investment will be required, assuming government expenditures on goods and services remain at their 1970 level of about $225 billion?

   c. Suppose that only 35 percent of the population is in the 1980 labor force. How would your answers to a. and b. change?

   d. Suppose now that the average workweek is reduced from forty to thirty hours. How would per capita real output compare with 1970, when population was just over 200 million?

10. Is Stein right in his last sentence, at the end of the text above?

nineteen

Growth in the Less-Developed Countries[1]

The Anatomy of
Underdevelopment

Policy for Economic Development

The Future of the
Less-Developed Nations

Appendix: The Population
Explosion

In the United States, economic growth is the road to raising further our already high standard of living. But for over 2 billion people who live in the economically less-developed (or "underdeveloped") countries, economic growth is a necessity if they are to escape from the bitter poverty that has been their lot through history. Per capita g.n.p. in the United States in 1970 was about $4,800. In the "less-developed" countries (sometimes called the "Third World") it averaged about $150.

Table 19–1 classifies the nations of the world

[1]Note to instructors: This chapter can equally well be combined with Chapter 46 as a closing unit on comparative economic systems.

into three groups, depending on their per capita annual g.n.p.'s. "Highly developed" countries are those with per capita g.n.p.'s above $1,000. The "intermediate" group are countries where the figure was between $500 and $1,000. The "less-developed" nations are those with per capita g.n.p.'s below $500.

The figures in Table 19–1 are very rough. They probably substantially underestimate income levels in the poorer nations on two counts. First, incomes there may be underestimated relatively because so much home-produced food and clothing does not go through the market. Second, prices of the staples that form the standard of living of the masses there are gener-

table 19-1
Countries Grouped by per Capita G.n.p. — in U.S. Dollars*

Highly Developed Countries (about 800 million people)
(Over $1,000 per capita)

In the Americas:		In Europe (cont'd):	
United States	$4,800	Netherlands	$2,500
Canada	3,450	Denmark	2,400
Puerto Rico	1,400	United Kingdom	2,350
Venezuela	1,100	Norway	2,300
		Belgium	1,700
In Oceania:		USSR	1,700
Australia	2,550	Finland	1,600
New Zealand	2,500	Austria	1,475
		Italy	1,425
In Europe:		Czechoslovakia	1,390
Sweden	3,300	East Germany	1,360
Switzerland	2,850	Hungary	1,060
West Germany	2,700	Ireland	1,040
France	2,600		

Intermediate Countries (about 500 million people)
($500 — $1,000 per capita)

In Africa:
Union of South Africa   680

In the Americas:		In Europe:	
Argentina	760	Poland	960
Uruguay	680	Greece	800
Chile	650	Bulgaria	750
Cuba	610	Spain	750
Mexico	550	Rumania	720
Panama	550	Portugal	500

Less-Developed Countries (over 2 billion people)
(Less than $500 per capita)

All of Africa except countries listed above	about 125	Middle East	about 250
		India	115
		Communist China	115**
All of the Americas except countries listed above	about 300	All of Asia except countries listed above	about 100
		Southeast Europe	450

*Figures are estimated 1970 gross domestic product for each nation, converted to 1970 U.S. dollars at official exchange rates and divided by population. Estimates are based on E. E. Hagen and O. Hawrylyshyn, "Analysis of World Income and Growth," *Economic Development and Cultural Change*, October, 1969, and United Nations data. Remember the text warning that data are very rough for the less-developed nations, and that figures for such nations are probably substantially understated by using official exchange rates — perhaps by as much as 100 percent. Several smaller nations are omitted.

**Figures for Communist China are extremely rough.

ally very cheap compared to items bought by higher-income families; thus, conversion of, say, Indian rupee incomes into U.S. dollars at the official exchange rate that is based on prices of a wide range of commodities will tend to give a misleading picture of actual comparative living standards. But even if the per capita incomes in the poor nations were doubled to adjust for these possible underestimates, the less-developed nations would still appear desperately poor. For most of the world, poverty is far and away the number one economic problem.[2]

Worse, this huge gap between rich and poor nations is widening rapidly, not closing. The following table for the United States and India since 1960 tells the story. Although it shows the extremes, it suggests the spectacular rate at which the Western industrial nations are pulling away from the less-developed world. A 2 percent annual increase on the U.S. base of $4,800 means a $96 increase in one year, about equal to the entire per capita g.n.p. in India. In India, the same 2 percent increase, if it could be achieved, would be about $2 per capita.

Why do these vast differences in standards of living exist? Why is the gap between the rich and the poor widening even further? Why have per capita incomes not grown at all over the past century for hundreds of millions of the poorest people? The theories of economic growth presented in Chapter 16 can help answer these questions, and most of the rest of this chapter is devoted to applying the same central theory of economic growth to the less-developed countries as was applied to the United States in Chapters 17 and 18. But, as we shall see, the situations are vastly different.

Development of these economically less-developed countries has become the most ex-

[2]Two good general references on the less-developed areas and their problems are J. Bhagwati, *Economics of the Underdeveloped Countries* (New York: McGraw-Hill Book Company, 1966), and Charles Kindleberger, *Economic Development* (New York: McGraw-Hill Book Company, 1965). They and many other experts believe that the very low per capita incomes reported in Table 19–1 for Asia and Africa are indeed underestimated substantially, for the reasons indicated. But expert views differ.

table 19-2

Per Capita Real G.n.p. in the United States and India*

	1960	1970
United States	$3,250	$4,800
India	109	115

*Data in 1970 U.S. dollars. Figures for India are probably understated relative to United States but the 1960-1970 change is roughly accurate.

plosive socioeconomic problem of our times. Poverty is a source of acute discontent for hundreds of millions of people aroused by their nationalistic leaders. In China and India alone there are nearly 1½ billion people—two huge nations awakening to their potential power and to the fact that poverty and misery may not be the inescapable lot of the masses in the Orient. A great change is moving Asia, Africa, and Latin America, a change compounded of growing nationalism and a desire for economic progress and power. A revolution of rising expectations —of economic progress, individual status, and national prestige and power—is sweeping the less-developed nations.

Are the Less-Developed Countries Really "Backward"?

Although economists sometimes refer to regions with low output per capita as "backward" and underdeveloped, some observers argue that this is mistakenly imposing our standards on other societies. They contend that others may prefer to devote themselves to aesthetic values and leisurely living rather than to accumulating material possessions. Perhaps they are happier than the Western industrialized nations. Part of our material wealth may be pointless in the eyes of other nations. Cars that crowd the highways; elaborate subways to get us around the teeming cities we have created. These raise the g.n.p., but do they really increase our happiness?

But having taken this warning to heart,

remember that poverty and hunger are very real and painful facts for hundreds of millions of people in other lands. The number of economies that have rejected additional material goods when given a practical choice is small indeed. Precisely the leaders of the newly awakening "less-developed" countries protest most violently against the poverty, disease, and misery that envelop the masses in their countries, and resent most bitterly the wide gap between their poverty and the affluence of the industrialized nations. Today the drive for increased material well-being dominates economic thinking in the less-developed nations.

The Anatomy of Underdevelopment

Poverty is the central economic fact of the less-developed areas. But there are many differences among them. Some are primitive; others, like India and China, boast civilizations that are far older than those of the West. Some have generous natural resources; others are bitterly poor in the endowments of nature. Some have a high ratio of population to land; others have vast open spaces. The poverty of a beggar on the streets of Calcutta is different from that of the Bushman of South Africa or the desert nomad of the Middle East. But in spite of these differences, there are some strong resemblances. And our theory from Chapter 16 can provide a useful framework for examining the problems of the less-developed nations.

Patterns of Economic Activity

First, a brief look at the economies of the less-developed nations as a backdrop for analysis of why they are poor, and of what can be done to raise their production.

Poverty and the Dominance of Low-Productivity Agriculture. In the less-developed countries, food is the main item of production and consumption. It has to be, for starvation hovers uncomfortably near. For the entire group of less-developed countries, about 70 percent of all production is food. In the United States, the comparable figure is below 20 per-

cent. Although diets in most nations are adequate to preserve life, they are often inadequate to fend off disease or, even allowing for the small bodily stature of many peoples, to provide enough energy for continued hard work.

A mud or a thatched hut and a little simple clothing make up most of the rest of the consumption pattern in many less-developed countries. Remember that only around $50 per year per capita is left to cover everything except food. Hospitals, plumbing, highways, and other such services that we take for granted have no place in such standards of living. The masses in these nations save little or nothing at all. In Calcutta, a teeming city, between a quarter- and a half-million people have no home or job whatsoever and simply wander the streets. Their food often comes from garbage in the gutter.

Outside a few modern industries in the cities, production is at the handicraft stage. Since human labor is very cheap and capital scarce, the most laborious details are often done by hand. Tractors and other mechanized farming equipment are little known, and would generally be unusable even if available, because of lack of fuel, maintenance facilities, and sufficient education to use them. Figure 19–1 shows vividly how little the poor nations rely on nonhuman energy (electricity, water, and minerals) compared to the developed nations. (In this and the following figures, income per capita is always shown on the vertical axis. Both income and energy use are plotted on ratio (logarithmic) scales to make relative comparisons easy.)

The nonagricultural population is crowded into a few large cities, where small-scale industry, services for the wealthy, and government employment provide most of the jobs available. Simple textiles, sometimes not much beyond the handicraft stage, are important in many less-developed economies; the cloth is used for clothing and home furnishings. In the more developed countries, modern large-scale industry (steel, chemicals, fertilizers, and the like) has begun to appear in the major cities. In a few cases, one basic industry dominates the economy—oil in the Middle East, rubber in Malaysia, copper in Chile.

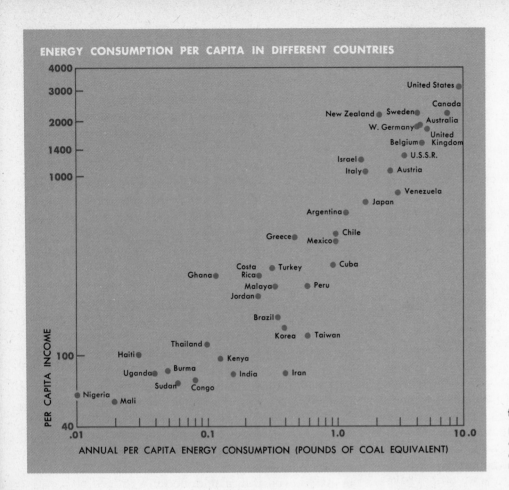

ENERGY CONSUMPTION PER CAPITA IN DIFFERENT COUNTRIES

fig. 19–1

Energy consumption per capita is closely correlated with the degree of economic development. (Source: United Nations. Data are for 1964.)

Dual Economies: Limited Development of Markets. Thus, many nations are in essence "dual economies." One part is a money, market-oriented economy centered in a few large cities, with modern industry mixed with crowded slums. The other part is a subsistence-level, rural, barter-type economy of hand labor and primitive superstitions, comprising 75 percent or so of the population, substantially isolated from the markets and industry of the cities. To go from one to the other is to go from one world to another, from the dark ages to the present.

Transportation is crude. The highways of the cities rapidly dwindle to dirt roads and to mere paths a hundred miles away. Religious and cultural barriers fragment the nation. One can scarcely call them "economies"—for economic life as we know it exists only around the cities and towns. Without roads and communication, there is little chance for a market economy to develop.

In some nations, one-product export econo-

mies have developed—coffee in Brazil, rubber in Indonesia, oil in Saudi Arabia. Much of the investment to develop these export enclaves is foreign, and resentment against foreign ownership and operation is common. Often it leads to nationalization, whether or not there is a native competence to operate the industry.

Unequal Distribution of Income. In most less-developed countries, income is very unequally distributed—far more unequally than in the highly developed, capitalist economies. There are often a few rich landholders, sometimes a few industrialists. The masses are dismally poor, mainly living just above subsistence level on farms or in villages. Strikingly, there is often no "middle class" of shopkeepers, professional men, and skilled workers, such as makes up a major portion of Western populations.

Weak Governments and Limited Government Services. A few less-developed nations have well-established democratic institutions, but they are the exception. Governments are typically unstable, revolutions are commonplace. There can be little long-range planning of basic government services such as schools, highways, and the like. Equally important, there is no basis for long-run planning by investors and businessmen. Often governments are dominated by the entrenched "haves," who block social and political change that might endanger them. Tribal chieftains, religious leaders, and other guardians of the traditional culture are likely to occupy positions of great influence.

Governments, which must provide leadership for many changes in development, are usually weakly staffed, reflecting the newness of the nations and the lack of education and traditions of honest civil service. Government jobs are often political perquisites, which mainly provide an accepted position for corruption. All too often, confusion, red tape, and bungling characterize government "programs." There is little chance for such governments to establish and administer effective tax systems to collect the funds needed to provide schools, highways, and sanitation.

So much for a general, if discouraging, overview. Now let us look more analytically at the problem, using the theory from Chapter 16. If the theory is right, low per capita output in the less-developed nations should reflect a high ratio of population to natural resources and to capital; a slow rate of capital accumulation and technical advance; an uneducated, low-productivity labor force; and a general environment unconducive to initiative, enterprise, and organized economic activity. And in fact, this is a reasonable description of most of the less-developed nations. Look now at these factors one at a time.

Natural Resources

Lack of natural resources does not explain the plight of the less-developed nations. Switzerland has one of the world's highest per capita incomes on virtually no natural resources; China has one of the lowest on vast natural resources. Africa is rich in natural resources. The Malthu-

sian hypothesis suggests that per capita incomes will be lowest where the ratio of population to natural resources is highest—where people outrun the ability of the land to feed them. But this is clearly too simple an explanation. The ratios of population to arable land for Switzerland, Belgium, and the Netherlands are about the same as those for Bolivia, Peru, and Egypt.

Plentiful natural resources can certainly help. The United States, Canada, and Australia all have rich resources and low ratios of population to land. Surely the vast western frontier helped to speed our early growth. Moreover, even the poor nations would be much worse off without generous resources—the copper and nitrates of Chile, the oil of the Middle East, the rubber of Sumatra. Perhaps climate, rather than natural resources in the usual sense, is critical. Most of the world's well-to-do nations lie in the temperate zone; none of them in the tropics. But within the temperate zone there are wide variations in economic development, as there are among tropical nations. Nor does primary reliance on agriculture, for whatever reason, necessarily characterize the poor nations. Denmark and New Zealand demonstrate that agricultural countries need not be poor. The poor nations are poor not because they are agricultural, but because productivity in their agriculture is so low.

Shortage of Capital and Primitive Technology

The stock of capital explains much more. No less-developed country has a large stock of capital goods per capita; every well-to-do nation does. Modern factories, machinery and equipment, highways, hospitals—all are scarce in the less-developed nations. Without them, high output per capita is very difficult.

The reason is easy to see. When nations are poor, they find it hard to save. Saving in India or Tanganyika means cutting back an already pitifully low standard of living. Saving in America is easy. The less-developed country can divert resources from producing consumption goods to investment only through greater want and privation. Yet without capital goods it can never hope to raise the standard of living of the masses very much.

Capital investment of over $20,000 per factory worker in America was cited above. In the poorest nations, the comparable figure is only a few dollars. Gross capital formation is only 5–10 percent of gross national product in such poor nations as Paraguay and Nigeria. In the well-to-do nations it runs 15–20 percent, and in the very rapidly growing nations, like Japan, up to 30–40 percent. It is easy for the rich to become richer. The poor, like the queen in *Through the Looking Glass,* must run as fast as they can merely to stay in the same place, as population grows constantly.

Closely related, most less-developed countries have little modern technology. Human beings and beasts do virtually all the work in agriculture. Handicraft methods dominate in small-scale industry in the towns and cities. To the illiterate native of Kenya or Yemen, Detroit's mass-production methods and Pittsburgh's steel mills have little relevance. For him the problem is to learn to use a plow. Where economic development is beginning, sometimes wild contrasts exist in the dual economies. In the cities of India and Venezuela, some of the world's most modern oil refineries and chemical plants loom against the sky. Fifty miles away there is the most primitive agriculture, unchanged for a thousand years.

Overpopulation and the Labor Force

In one fundamental sense, overpopulation is the crux of the less-developed economies' problem. The population is so large that, given the natural resources and capital available, there is barely enough output per person to maintain life. And when total output increases because of improved technology or capital accumulation, population increases nearly as fast, so there is little improvement in the average standard of living. This is not the picture in all the less-developed economies, but it is in most.

In recent years, total production has risen at substantial rates in many of the less-developed nations, apparently at 3–5 percent per annum in Latin America, Africa, and southeast Asia. This is near the growth rate of total output in the industrialized countries. Thus per capita incomes have risen little in most less-developed nations because population has grown nearly as fast as output.

What are the facts about population? In most less-developed economies, the annual birthrate is between thirty and fifty per thousand people; in the United States and Western Europe, the comparable rate has generally declined to around fifteen to twenty-five per thousand. But in the less-developed economies until recently death rates typically ran from twenty-five to thirty-five per thousand, compared to ten or below in the Western world. Malthus's specter of famine as population outruns the food supply has always been near, aided by inadequate diet and low resistance to disease. Since it is the difference between birth- and death rates that determines population growth, population growth rates in the two types of economies have until recently not been grossly different, running around ten to fifteen per thousand (1 to 1½ percent per year).

Since World War II, this picture has changed dramatically. Western methods of disease prevention have drastically reduced the death rate in many less-developed countries, especially the rate of infant mortality. DDT alone is estimated to have saved 50 million lives through checking the spread of infectious disease. In Ceylon, the death rate was cut almost in half in three years by the virtual elimination of malaria. During the 1940–1950 decade, the death rate declined by 46 percent in Puerto Rico, 43 percent in Formosa, 23 percent in Jamaica. But birthrates have dropped only slowly in most cases. The result is a population explosion in the less-developed nations. In Latin America and West Africa, population is doubling every twenty years, on the Asian mainland every twenty-five years. China's growth rate is nearly 2.5 percent. Her population of nearly 800 million is growing by 20 million every year, and at the present rate will reach 1 billion before 1980.

Figure 19–2 shows this contrast dramatically. Note the high birthrates in most less-developed

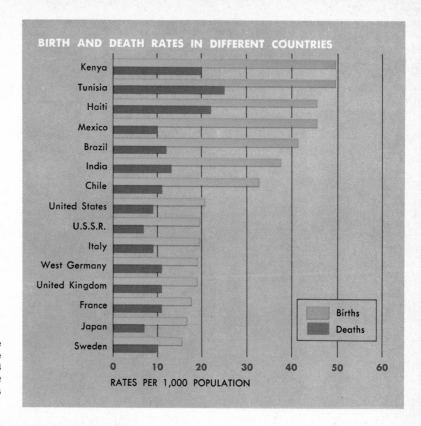

BIRTH AND DEATH RATES IN DIFFERENT COUNTRIES

Births
Deaths

RATES PER 1,000 POPULATION

fig. 19–2

The less-developed nations have the fastest-growing populations. For the whole world, the birthrate is about 34 per thousand and the death rate about 11. (Source: United Nations. Figures for 1964.)

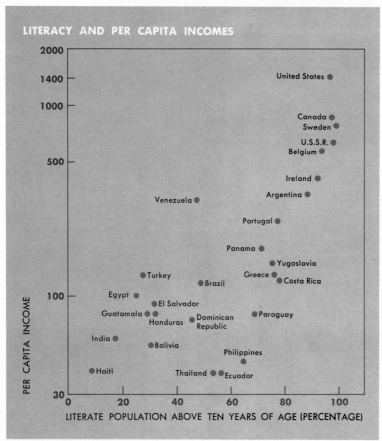

LITERACY AND PER CAPITA INCOMES

PER CAPITA INCOME

LITERATE POPULATION ABOVE TEN YEARS OF AGE (PERCENTAGE)

fig. 19–3

The degree of literacy is highly correlated with the extent of economic development, as both cause and effect. (Source: UNESCO. Figures for various dates in the 1950's and 1960's.)

countries, and their rapid rates of population growth implied by the big spread between birth- and death rates.

In many less-developed nations, most of the population is illiterate. New methods that involve even the simplest changes often meet barriers of superstition and inadequate understanding—for example, use of chemical fertilizers and crop rotation. In Africa, only about 25 percent of all children between five and eighteen go to school, about 40 percent in Asia. In the United States, the figure is over 95 percent.

Figure 19–3 shows the strong correlation between literacy and living standards. Plotting daily newspaper circulation per 1,000 inhabitants against per capita income gives an even more striking correlation (though here the causal chain may run strongly from income level to newspapers as well as the other way).

The absence of even qualified clerks and bookkeepers poses a major problem for any commercial or business activity. The habits of honesty and reliability that we take for granted are the foundation of economic activity as we know it in the Western world. In some of the poorest nations, witch doctors and primitive customs are still more common.

Environment and Initiative

Rapid economic growth, closely related to the Industrial Revolution, has occurred in the Western world where the social and economic groundwork was already well laid. Nowhere has there been rapid, continuing growth without reasonably stable government and financial and economic institutions. In all the countries of the "highly developed" group of Table 19–1 except the USSR, the profit motive and individual initiative have played a central role.

On these scores, the problems faced by the less-developed economies are enormous. Apathy and ignorance characterize the great mass of their populations. Except for government leaders and small educated groups, there is often little effective impetus for economic development; and all too often even the leaders appear more concerned with their own positions than with economic progress for the masses. In central Africa, the medicine man may have more influence than elected government leaders or outside experts. The head of a tribe may be held responsible for an adequate supply of rainfall as well as for selling the cocoa produced nearby. In some nations, manual labor is considered beneath the dignity of a man, certainly of an educated man, and is left entirely to women. In most of the poor nations, few of the peasants own much, if any, land. They see little reason to work harder to produce more when most of it must be given up to the absentee landlord. The tribesman in Africa has no idea of modern commercial or industrial activity, nor any interest in central government.

Thus, it is not surprising that the less-developed nations lack entrepreneurs—individuals with imagination and initiative to seize economic opportunities and develop them. In the traditional societies, such attitudes and activities are often frowned upon. It would seldom occur to most people in those nations to start a business, however small, or even to innovate in their day-to-day tasks of farming or handicraft work. Caste systems bar occupational changes, and class hierarchies prevent vertical mobility. Things have been done the same way since time immemorial.

Nor can such nations expect to surge upward without what economists call an "infrastructure" of "social overhead capital"—highways, schools, communications, hospitals, sanitation. These all require capital and planning—and their benefits to the whole economy far exceed the individual benefits that individual investors might see. Enforced saving through government tax collections is the only practical way to finance them. Thus stable, established governments, capable of collecting taxes and spending efficiently, are essential—but rare.

Absence of stable governments and well-established tax systems leads to persistent government deficits and inflation. There are vast needs. Roads, schools, fertilizer plants, irrigation projects—everything cries out to be done, and government action seems the only way. But tax systems are primitive and subsistence living standards make new taxes very difficult to impose and collect. The predictable result is government spending without corresponding tax revenues—and excess-demand inflation.

The resulting inflations are bad partly because of the inequities they wreak on the masses, who have little way to protect themselves from higher prices of essentials. Inflation thus becomes a kind of "forced saving" that substitutes for tax collections. But worse, inflation and financial instability repel foreign investors, whose capital is so desperately needed and make foreign purchases difficult.

The Vicious Circle of Poverty

The less-developed countries vary widely. But in most the problem seems to be a vicious circle of poverty: Incomes and living standards are so low that productivity is low and saving is impossible for the mass of the population. Producing food for subsistence is the main goal. Without more saving to accumulate more capital goods, build highways, and provide education, total output per capita cannot be increased. Total output does increase as population produces more workers, and some saving by the upper-income groups and through government investing provides some additional capital goods and public services. But population grows nearly as fast as does total output, thus holding down living standards and preventing the saving that might permit faster capital accumulations. Even if these barriers could be overcome, the domestic market is too small to permit the economies of mass production.

Throughout the less-developed economies, a significant part of the farm population is "surplus," in the sense that it could be removed from the farms of the countries concerned without any reduction in total farm output. But to move this surplus population to productive employment seems impossible. What will keep them from starving until they become established in industrial jobs? How can uneducated people be made into effective industrial workers? Where will the industrial jobs come from—who will provide the tools for new factory workers, capital for factory equipment, and the enterprise to establish new concerns? How could

the newly made industrial goods be sold either domestically or abroad without an established market and without adequate transportation and commercial facilities?

Lastly, government planning and taxation are required to enforce saving and channel investment into socially desirable channels; yet governments are weak, inefficient, unstable. Inefficient bureaucracies bungle rules and frustrate businessmen with morasses of red tape. Inflations and financial instability are commonplace. It seems that everywhere they turn, the less-developed nations face insoluble dilemmas. Their leaders may know the prescriptions of the theory of Chapter 16, but what shall they do?

Policy for Economic Development

How can the less-developed countries break out of the vicious circle of poverty and take off into self-sustaining growth? There is no simple answer. Indeed, there may be no answer at all for some of them. The main approaches suggested by the experts follow the lines of the theory suggested above.

Environment and Institutions for Economic Development

It is striking that everyone of the top ten countries in the "highly developed" group of Table 19–1 is either in Western Europe or has inherited much of Western European culture and traditions. Max Weber, a famous sociologist, in his *The Protestant Ethic and the Spirit of Capitalism* argued that the rapid economic development of Western Europe was linked intimately with what he called the "Protestant ethic"—the belief that work is good for its own sake and that the individual should be free to seek after his own welfare through work.

Weber emphasized the institutions of capitalistic society that have accompanied rapid economic development in the West: (1) private ownership and control of the means of production; (2) freedom of the market from such restrictions as guild monopolies, social-class barriers, and government price fixing; (3) the reign of calculable law, enabling people to know in advance what rules they operate under in economic life; (4) freedom of individuals to work for wages; (5) "commercialism" of economic life through a market system of wages and prices to mobilize and allocate productive resources; and (6) speculation and risk taking (which had been largely prevented in the preceding feudal and guild societies).

Were the Protestant ethic and the institutions of capitalism essential to the rapid economic growth of today's richest countries? The facts fit Weber's description reasonably well, but there are exceptions.

The rise of industrial Germany during the last half of the nineteenth century, for example, showed strong government encouragement of economic development within an essentially private-enterprise economy. The spectacular advance of Japan during the past century involved government leadership on at least a quasi-authoritarian basis. The most striking case far outside the Weber pattern is modern Russia, whose rapid economic development has been accomplished through a highly centralized economic control.

Everyone agrees today that sustained rapid economic growth is extremely unlikely without a stable government, law, and order. Without such stability, neither domestic nor foreign investors are willing to risk their funds. Without stable governments, the essential economic infrastructure of highways, communications, and other public utilities is unlikely to come. But revolution and instability have been common in the less-developed nations, especially in recent decades when the masses have increasingly challenged control by foreign nations and rich minorities. Struggles for power by competing military factions have been common. Illiterate, superstitious people find it hard to make democracy work effectively after they wrest power from rich dictators or foreign rulers. But difficult as it may be, establishment of stable government appears to be a *sine qua non* for the takeoff into economic growth.

Development of individual initiative and an entrepreneurial class, plus acceptance of a market economy, is also vital. There must be individuals who take leadership in establishing enterprises, who see potential gains in taking risks, who manage to mobilize capital, who have the drive to push ahead through difficulties and to organize the work of others. There must be organizers and administrators. Often immigrants from a different culture, who are materialistic, experimental, frugal, industrious, and ambitious for their families have provided entrepreneurial leadership. Acceptance of a profit motive apparently also helps, partly because profits provide a direct source of funds for further needed private investment.

Equally important, and perhaps most difficult, a spirit of greater initiative must be instilled in the masses. To be more productive, the individual must learn to want more and to work more efficiently to get it. Apathy and ignorance lead to acceptance of poverty and the status quo—to acceptance of the life of one's parents and their parents before them. No other problem seems more frustrating to the planners trying to pull economies up from poverty.

How private initiative, a market, and an entrepreneurial class develop in traditional tribal or village societies is far from clear. Sociologists, economists, and anthropologists have studied dozens of cases and find no single explanation. In some instances (e.g., Japan), an entrepreneurial class seems to develop from pressures of social and cultural change. Dissatisfied groups outside the ruling elite see trading and business as a way to rise to higher status. In other cases (e.g., Egypt), the spirit of entrepreneurship is imported through colonial rule, which later is thrown off. Increasing awareness of the outside world seems everywhere to be important. In many cases, the development of an entrepreneurial class has been a revolt against prevailing tribal or village mores, a social as well as an economic revolution.[3]

Capital Accumulation and Industrialization

As our theory would lead us to expect, substantial capital accumulation has marked every major case of rapid economic development. To

[3]E. E. Hagan has spelled out an entire theory of economic growth centering around these socioeconomic interactions, which also uses modern psychological analysis of personal behavior patterns in the emerging societies (*On the Theory of Social Change*; Homewood, Illinois: Dorsey Press, 1962).

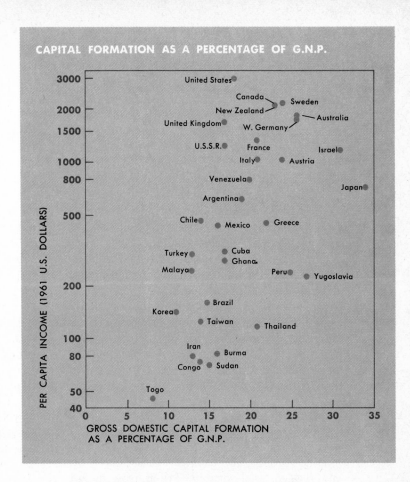

CAPITAL FORMATION AS A PERCENTAGE OF G.N.P.

fig. 19–4

High per capita incomes and high rates of capital formation generally go together, as interacting cause and effect. But there are exceptions; note Japan on the chart. (Source: United Nations. Data for 1964.)

rise from poverty, every nation faces the central problem of increasing saving and investment as a share of total output. Figure 19–4 shows the wide variation among countries in the ratio of gross investment to g.n.p. in the 1960s. Although a few of the nations with very high savings–investment ratios have relatively low per capita incomes (for example, Japan and Yugoslavia), they are now growing rapidly. The United States, with the highest per capita income, has a moderate savings–investment ratio but also a relatively slow rate of growth over recent years; we had a high savings ratio during the nineteenth century.

There is some evidence that it takes about $3 to $4 of new capital goods to increase current income by about $1 annually in these countries (a "capital–output ratio" of 3 or 4 to 1). With a 4 to 1 marginal capital–output ratio, an economy that saves 4 percent of its income to accumulate capital will, other things equal, increase its national income by about 1 percent annually. Then, if population grows at about 1 percent annually, per capita income is just held constant. To raise its living standard the economy must either save more or slow its population growth. Any saving rate below 4 percent of income will mean decreasing per capita incomes.

This relationship between the capital–output ratio and the rate of saving is illustrated by Table 19–3. If 4 percent of total income is saved,

table 19-3

Capital-Output and Savings Ratios

| Savings-Income Ratio | Annual Increase in Output (Percentage) with: | |
	Capital-Output Ratio = 3-1	Capital-Output Ratio = 4-1
.04	1.33	1.0
.05	1.67	1.25
.10	3.33	2.5
.15	5.0	3.75

there will be a 1.33 percent increase in total annual output in case the capital–output ratio is 3–1, but only a 1 percent increase with a 4–1 capital–output ratio. Similar differences exist for higher savings ratios. Obviously both higher saving ratios and lower capital–output ratios are good for economic growth. A few countries have apparently managed a capital–output ratio of 2, which has permitted them to expand output rapidly with modest saving ratios.

How can a nation be asked, or even forced, to save more when the great mass of its population is barely above subsistence level? Increasingly, the less-developed nations have turned to government tax and investment programs to obtain needed economic infrastructure—roads, schools, and sanitary facilities that aid development throughout the nation as a whole, even though no single investor could undertake them.

Foreign Investment and Imperialism

Some nations, for example India, have obtained substantial portions of their growth capital from abroad, through both private investment and government aid. The United Nations estimates that the provision of capital by the developed to the less-developed nations rose from $2 billion in 1950 to $13 billion in 1968. Of this total, $7 billion consisted of loans or grants from other nations or international agencies and $6 billion of private investment from the developed nations. Just under half came from the United States.

Poor nations desperately need capital from abroad. Economic analysis says there will be benefit to both borrower and foreign lender if the expected rate of return on the capital in the developing nation exceeds that which the lender can obtain elsewhere.[4] But nonetheless, many developing nations have invited foreign private investment only with stringent restrictions. With burgeoning national pride they want no part of foreign control, and they distrust foreign investors who may try to exploit them and withdraw their profits once made. The memories of many decades of colonialism

[4]The analysis is presented in Chapter 41.

are still strong. Thus, as badly as they need foreign capital, many of the poor nations have hedged foreign capital and companies around with restrictive controls reaching into day-to-day operations.

Are these fears of foreign imperialism irrational? There is little doubt that over the past century, foreign investors have often exploited native resources and workers, making large profits with little concern for the welfare of the less-developed nations. This economic domination was often paralleled by ruthless political and social repression of native populations. Although native living standards may well have been higher than they would have been with no foreign capital at all, bitter resentment was a predictable consequence.

Since the emergence of national independence for nearly all people since World War II, the pendulum has swung. Foreign companies (e.g., in petroleum) that formerly paid only 25 percent of their profits to local nations for the privilege of extracting natural resources have seen their shares fall to 50 percent, and then even lower. Restrictions on operations have been steadily tightened. Outright expropriation has become more common—sometimes to the serious loss of the developing nation, which has neither the technical skills nor managerial and marketing abilities to continue effective operation. Prospective foreign businesses have often been turned away because offers were considered inadequate, sometimes with the result that nothing happens—no foreign capital, no jobs for native people.

Socialist doctrine says that foreign "imperialist" investment will bleed the less-developed economy by withdrawing the profits it extorts from the native population. But, although this may sometimes occur, two counterarguments are important. First, at least in the last two decades when reliable figures have become available, only a moderate share of profits has actually been withdrawn, and these withdrawals have been vastly overbalanced by new foreign investments. Thus, there has been a continuous large net inflow of private foreign capital from developed to less-developed nations—note the $6 billion figure above for 1968.

Second, even if all profits were withdrawn by the foreign investor, the developing nation might well gain from the investment. Remember the desperate need for capital to raise output and provide jobs for the surplus native population. If native workers take jobs voluntarily in the foreign business, they presumably prefer that to their other alternatives. If local customers voluntarily buy the foreign product, they presumably prefer it to other alternatives, even though its price may have yielded a large profit to the foreign company. Hard-boiled realism would ask—whether I like the foreigner or not, am I better off with his capital invested here, or without it? Clearly, the developing nation would be still better off if part or all of the profits were reinvested there, as occurs in the great bulk of the cases. But what if the alternative is no foreign investment at all?[5]

Most of the developing nations have attempted to compromise this dilemma. They seek foreign capital, but on terms they dictate. Some compromises have been effective in attracting foreign capital on terms acceptable to the host countries; others have not. To the outsider, restrictions that lead foreign investors to turn away may seem shortsighted, for the less-developed nation ends up with its restrictions and no capital for development. But simple economic analysis is not always clear when emotions run strong. And fear of foreign exploitation is understandably strong indeed in many of the less-developed nations.

Technical Advance and Education

Technological advance and development of an educated, skilled labor force appear to have played a central role in the development of the Western economies. How can the poor nations achieve such technical advance?

Their problem may look easy—just borrow the technology of more advanced nations. Germany, as it developed industrially in the nineteenth century, was able to borrow productive processes developed in England. The USSR

[5]For a more complete analysis, see Charles Kindleberger, *American Business Abroad* (New Haven, Conn.: Yale University Press, 1969), chap. 5.

after World War II adopted industrial methods and techniques wholesale from the West—in some cases, whole factories were reproduced. Recently India and China have imported technology heavily from both East and West. But the problems of such importation were outlined above—the necessity for heavy capital investment; the need for skilled laborers, technicians, and managers; the need for mass markets to justify many modern methods.

Think, for example, how you would go about introducing modern technology into Somalia, an emerging African nation of about 2 million people, most of them illiterate nomads. Literacy: perhaps 10 percent. Total college graduates in the country: about 100. Per capita income: less than $75 a year. Politics: long-standing bitter rivalry among tribal groups. The problem is a far cry from the science, engineering, and management we think of in America as the solution to technological advance.

In fact, the biggest promise for technical change probably lies in agriculture rather than in industry. Primitive, low-productivity agriculture is the greatest millstone around the necks of the poor economies. Improving productivity in agriculture has led the way in nearly every case of growth. Here technology can be introduced in small stages, and with more modest capital costs—simple tools, fertilizers, improved irrigation.

Technological advance requires an educated labor force and willingness to accept change. Thus, mass education and development of a core of skilled technicians and teachers are goals of virtually every less-developed nation. Investment in education may not pay a fast return. But Figure 19–3 speaks for itself. The long-run payoff is big, in economic terms and in laying a foundation for a better life for all.

Steps toward mass education in the less-developed economies have been spectacular since World War II, in India and in many smaller nations. But schools are expensive and teachers are very scarce. Thus, educational efforts have been concentrated on the young. It will be generations before half the population in many of the less-developed nations is literate, much less educated to the point of being able to take on skilled jobs as we know them. In-donesia, with 110 million people, has two universities. The huge Republic of the Congo in Africa has one university. There are crying shortages of teachers in virtually every poor nation.

Population Policy

Growth theory suggests that output per capita will rise fastest when the ratio of capital to population increases. And history generally confirms this expectation. But it is precisely in the poorest countries that rates of population increases have been the highest. Look back at Figure 19–2.

Governments have moved increasingly to encourage birth control and family planning. In several nations, e.g. India, they have received high priority. But the problem of providing effective bases for family planning among hundreds of millions of illiterate, widely scattered people is great. Religious barriers appear to be less formidable than was previously believed. However, the social barriers are huge. In the less-developed economies tradition is strong. The family is often the economic and social unit, and parents must look to their children for support in old age. Once people in the poor nations recognize that with modern death rates they need not have seven or eight children to be reasonably sure three or four will survive, perhaps birth control will be more readily accepted in many of the less-developed areas. But progress is far from certain.

Until the less-developed nations slow their rates of population growth, they are unlikely to escape far from Malthus's dire predictions. Even high growth rates in aggregate output cannot outdistance high rates of population growth. For many nations, Malthus's gloomy predictions still look more right than wrong. But the population experts are at last beginning to advance cautious predictions of widespread success of new birth-control approaches within the next two or three decades. Appendix A, "The Population Explosion," explores this central problem in more detail.

Balanced vs Unbalanced Growth

In the less-developed nations and among the experts, the debate rages as to whether poor nations can grow faster by concentrating on the development of either industry or agriculture alone, or by striving to develop both sectors in balance.

Sooner or later, industrialization is necessary for full economic development. Every high-income nation in Table 19–1 has a major industrial and commercial sector. Transport and steel play prominent roles in industrialization. Adequate transport facilitates communication, permits specialization, and underlies mass production and mass markets. Steel is used in nearly every facet of modern industrial activity. Figure 19–5 shows the close correlation between miles of railroad per 10,000 people and per capita income levels. Figure 19–6 shows a similar correlation between per capita steel consumption and per capita incomes. Every growing nation longs for its own modern steel mill, as a symbol of national pride.

But mounting experience suggests that improving agricultural productivity is the first need if the less-developed nations are to break out of their vicious circle. With 70 or 80 percent of the population in agriculture, that's where the mass of the problem is. A more efficient agriculture could produce more food for domestic use and export. More workers would be freed for gradual transfer to other jobs. In most successful cases of development, a gradual, then rapid, improvement in farm productivity has preceded industrialization. The United States and Japan are examples.

Some simple arithmetic dramatizes the importance of improving farm productivity. Suppose a nation wants to increase total output 5 percent annually but finds it impossible to raise agricultural productivity. If the "modern," nonagricultural sector produces 20 percent of total output, its productivity would have to increase 25 percent a year in order to provide the desired overall 5 percent increase. Such a spectacular performance is hardly likely.

Thus, allocation of scarce capital to raising

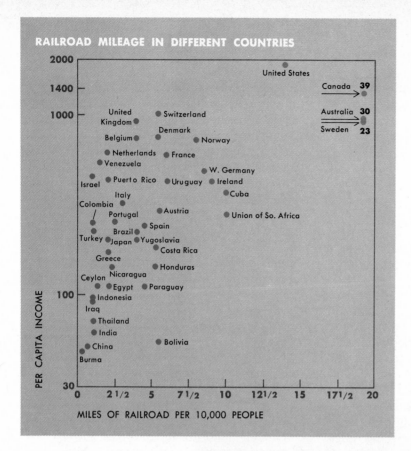

RAILROAD MILEAGE IN DIFFERENT COUNTRIES

PER CAPITA INCOME

MILES OF RAILROAD PER 10,000 PEOPLE

fig. 19–5

Railroad density is also correlated with the extent of economic development, again probably as both cause and effect. (Source: United Nations.)

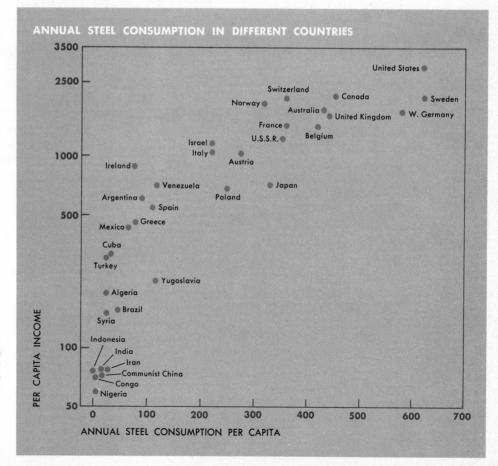

ANNUAL STEEL CONSUMPTION IN DIFFERENT COUNTRIES

PER CAPITA INCOME

ANNUAL STEEL CONSUMPTION PER CAPITA

fig. 19–6

The highly developed nations use much more steel per capita than the less-developed ones. (Source: United Nations. Data for 1964.)

agricultural output makes sense. Improving agricultural efficiency through fertilizer, simple tools, and improved methods requires little capital compared to mass industrialization. It requires less social disruption, less transfer of people, less infrastructure than does movement to a modern industrial sector.

Economic Planning or the Price System?

Many Americans, seeing the success of our essentially private-enterprise, market-directed economy, argue that the less-developed nations should rely on private initiative and let the marketplace decide what should be produced and who should produce it. But this view has found little sympathy in the less-developed countries. There is too much to be done and too little evidence that individual initiative and the marketplace will bring the desired changes fast enough—if at all. These nations do not trust the unseen hand of Adam Smith to guide the complex process of growth, to assess the long-range importance of alternative uses of resources. Admitting that private enterprise has been successful, it is too slow. They want roads, schools, fertilizers, and industrial plants now. Thus, government intervention on a wide scale is the active agent in less-developed nations. The main issue is whether it shall involve complete government control over economic life (as in Communist China) or merely government direction of broad lines of activity with wide scope left to private initiative (as in India).

Nearly everywhere it is agreed that government must provide infrastructure. Even where most of the economy stays private, basic investment priorities have become the province of the government. Nearly everywhere, foreign exchange is under government control, so that scarce foreign currencies are used for high-priority imports rather than for private luxuries.

But in recent years, the experts have increasingly turned back to the crucial importance of individual initiative, and the role of self-interest in providing that initiative. There is disenchantment with government planning to solve all the problems. Many government planners and native bureaucrats are incompetent; corruption is common. Some less-developed countries now try to regulate the behavior of individuals to a degree unknown in the Western world since mercantilism. All foreign trade and use of foreign exchange is regulated in detail. New businesses require government licenses. Rentals, wages, and basic commodity prices are controlled. Internal shipments of grains and other basic commodities require government permits. The amount of red tape horrifies both native entrepreneurs and foreign businessmen. With the best of intentions, such complex regulations plus widespread incompetence in their administration often succeed mainly in stifling business rather than in speeding development.[6]

Monetary-Fiscal Policy and Economic Growth

Chapters 6–15 stressed aggregate demand and expansionary monetary-fiscal policy as steps to eliminate underemployment and stimulate investment. Why don't the governments of the poor nations use deficit-financed spending to set up factories and lure the surplus farm population away from disguised unemployment into useful work, thereby increasing output and improving everybody's welfare?

The answer is that the main result would be inflation rather than increased output. As in the United States, speeding the long-term growth rate is basically a **real** "supply" problem, not one of inadequate demand.

Suppose the government of Peru or Afghanistan prints money to lure workers into industry. There are no idle factories where output can be increased by calling the unemployed back to work. First the government must build the factories and provide the tools for the new workers. Where will it get the steel, machinery, skilled labor, and management? Foreigners will not ship in the essential real capital and managerial services merely for freshly printed promises to pay. Who will train the workers and managers? How will the government provide new living quarters for the families drawn into the cities? How will it get food to the cities to feed them in a largely nonmarket economy, with no regular distribution channels? Suppose

[6]See P. T. Bauer, *United States AID and Indian Economic Development* (American Enterprise Foundation, 1969), for Indian examples.

all these obstacles are overcome. How long will it take before salable output begins to come out of factories manned by untrained workers, and where will the goods be sold when they are produced? Suppose the product is cloth; will there be a domestic market and distribution channels to tap the market, or will the government have to try to find markets abroad in the hectic international competition of the textile trade?

With all these obstacles to increasing real output, government spending without corresponding tax collections is likely to lead mainly to inflation as spending rises and output does not. Rapid inflation may endanger the stability of the government. Sound government finances are the first thing outside investors look for. And the higher domestic costs and prices make it harder to sell in world markets, a major blow when foreign exchange is badly needed to finance imports.

To repeat, the problems of the less-developed economies are basically "real" problems. They are sectoral problems, of transferring resources into more efficient uses as well as improving their efficiency in existing uses. There is little basis for supposing that these problems can be solved by using the modern monetary and fiscal policies that seem so promising against unemployment in the Western economies. But inflation from deficit-financed government spending is one of the commonest of the poor nations' ailments. It's not hard to understand why. The pressure on the government to "do something" is enormous. Taxes are already a painful burden on the poverty-stricken masses. Maybe this time deficit-financed government spending will manage to increase real output and growth—that is the ever present hope. But the common result is inflation and financial instability—an inequitable form of forced saving and a major barrier to the foreign investment that is so desperately needed.

Two Important Cases: India and China[7]

The less-developed areas are not just hard-to-remember small nations of Southeast Asia or Africa. More than one of every three living persons is Chinese or Indian. And these countries exemplify two drastically different approaches to the problem of economic development.

In many respects, India and China face similar problems. They are both vast land masses, heavily populated in many areas but with great reaches of mountains and wasteland. Both, in about 1950, had per capita incomes around $90–95 in present U.S. prices; China's was possibly lower. In both, around 80 percent of the total population is engaged in agriculture. And both, since World War II, have undertaken vigorous planned programs of economic development.

India. In her first four "five-year plans," covering 1951 to 1971, India has chosen an essentially democratic approach. This has left considerable freedom to private enterprise under government planning, while using government projects in such major areas as irrigation, transportation, and education. Nearly half of total investment has been private. Taxes were raised only a little, and in spite of India's claim to be a "socialist"state the great bulk of her economic activity remains in private hands. Government taxes and spending remain only about half as large a percentage of g.n.p. as in the United States and Western European nations. The plans pushed both industrialization and agricultural productivity—primarily the former at first, with more stress on agriculture recently. Industrial investment concentrated on both small-scale industry, such as textiles, and on larger projects, such as power development, fertilizers, coal, and heavy manufacturing. The plans called for increased capital accumulation in both agriculture and industry, plus added government services.

Results of the first three plans were mildly encouraging, but far from spectacular. Real national income rose 3 to 4 percent per annum and population about 2½ percent, giving perhaps a 1 percent annual increase in per capita income—perhaps $1 a year. This is pitifully

[7]John Lewis, *Quiet Crisis in India* (Washington, D.C.: The Brookings Institution, 1962) and *An Economic Profile*

of Mainland China (Joint Economic Committee of Congress, 1967), provide interesting overviews of the two economies in action.

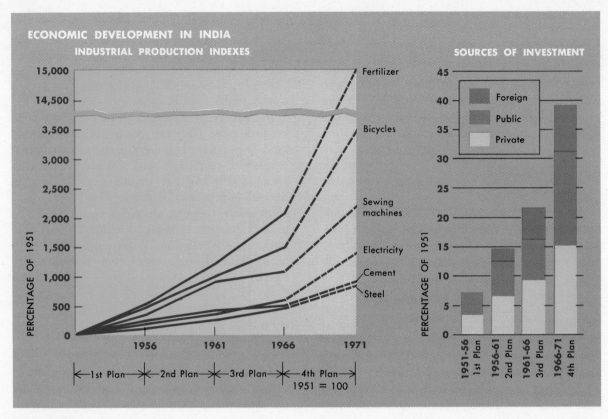

fig. 19–7

India hopes to double her investment under the 4th Five-Year Plan, and to increase sharply the output of such products as fertilizers, steel, and consumer goods. (Source: Indian Government.)

small, given the bitter poverty of India's masses. There was little increase in agricultural output, and it is not clear that the living standard of the Indian peasant is appreciably different from what it was a thousand years ago. The industrial improvement is more promising. Net investment rose from about 5 to over 10 percent of net national product, and saving is apparently rising.

But the achievements fell far short of the optimistic goals. Moreover, unemployment has risen from perhaps 10 to 20 million people in the cities, perhaps many more; no one has reliable statistics. Agriculture has been the great problem sector. And both the second and third plans would surely have foundered had not large-scale foreign aid been obtained to ease India's desperate foreign-exchange shortages as she tried to finance the imports required for food and capital investment. In the third plan, 25 percent of the investment was scheduled to

come from abroad, nearly half of it in the form of U.S. foreign aid. Figure 19–7 gives some impression of how far India had come by 1966. But remember that this picture omits the massive problem of lagging food production. And recently, heavy military expenditures, reflecting concern over Indian relations with both China and Pakistan, have cut the supply of civilian-type goods.

The fourth five-year plan calls for a 5.5 percent annual growth in output and a large step-up in both public and private investment. India hopes that foreign credits will finance about one-third of the investment. Strikingly, this plan shifts top priority to agriculture and agricultural-support activities like irrigation and fertilizers. It also calls for a massive population-control program; the first five-year plan budgeted 1.5 million rupees for birth control, and the fourth 950 million rupees.

Most observers think the goals are unrealistically high. But Table 19–4 shows some of them.

In the second and third plans, governmental regulation of investment, foreign trade, and other aspects of economic activity became more and more detailed. Complaints of bureaucratic red tape and corruption multiplied, from Indians, foreign businesses in India, and potential investors. The major failures of the third plan were attributed by many to this increasing bureaucracy and government inefficiency. The public sector and detailed government planning are thus strikingly less prominent in the fourth plan. Detailed industry "targets" have been replaced by planning estimates, except for a few key industries. Inducements to private investments are up. More stress is placed on encouraging initiative of individual farmers.

The hopeful view is that India is on the verge of her takeoff into self-sustaining growth. But her modest successes have been heavily dependent on foreign aid. Many Western observers, while admiring the humanistic, individualistic attitudes of India's leaders, believe she must have more firm, effective governmental leadership and more freedom for private initiative to make real progress in economic development. Bureaucracy, indecision, and red tape frustrate every foreign visitor who tries to help the Indi-

ans. Today India remains a restless giant, unsure of the success of her individualistic, humanistic program of mixed public-private enterprise.

China. China's first five-year plan, covering 1952 to 1957, called for drastic increases in industrialization, collectivization of agriculture, and ruthless suppression of consumption to obtain the resources required for capital accumulation. The plan centralized economic control in the Communist government. It called for rapid increases in agricultural output and mass transfer of agricultural population into industry. Voluntary private saving played only a small part; high government taxes on the masses and "profits" on government-monopolized necessities were used to seize a large portion of total income for government investment. Hard work and long hours were forced on the Chinese people.

This was followed by a second five-year plan for the period from 1957 to 1962, which continued the same policies and called for an even larger increase in total output by 1962, over 10 percent a year. This plan called for a "great leap forward" with the primary focus on heavy industry, although food targets were also up substantially. In 1958, government seizure of huge land masses and forced concentration of millions of agricultural families in huge "communes" virtually abolished individual family units and treated the peasants as hardly more than draft animals. Women were pressed into all areas of work on substantially the same basis as men, and children were placed in state nurseries. Communist dictation even of thought patterns made George Orwell's *1984* seem very real indeed.

Reliable information on China's recent economic progress is scarce. Western observers now agree that her economic advance during the years 1951 to 1958 was remarkable, though short of the claims of the Chinese leaders. From a centuries-long, stagnant, poverty level, with a primitive family-type economy, per capita output apparently rose 4 or 5 percent per annum during the decade, in spite of a huge growth in population. Industrial output appears to have risen at the spectacular rate of as much as 20

table 19-4

Indian Growth Targets—Third and Fourth Plans

	Third Plan	Fourth Plan
Food grains (millions of tons)	72	120
Irrigation (millions of acres)	18	26
Fertilizers (millions of tons)	.8	3.4
Steel (millions of tons)	6	12
Cement (millions of tons)	11	20
Cotton cloth (billions of meters)	4.4	5.5
Machine tools (value — millions of rupees)	23	105

percent per year. Net investment was pushed up to nearly 30 percent of net national product. Food output rose substantially.

China's annual growth in total g.n.p. was nearly twice that of India; China's growth in industrial production was four times that of India. China's dictatorial methods, her disregard of the individual, her total reliance on central planning seemed to be winning the race by an uncomfortably wide margin.

But Mao's great leap forward turned out to be China's great failure. After a first surge, industrial output collapsed. In the years 1959 to 1961 both industrial and agricultural output fell radically—food production apparently by nearly one-half, as bad weather compounded the Communists' troubles. The strains of the previous decade's massive conversion to industry and of the Communists' ruthless abolition of traditional family values apparently forced a massive retreat from the "communes" policy that had seized all private land and forced families into closely regulated agricultural communes. Some land was returned to individual family ownership, and some degree of family life was restored. More stress was placed on food production, and industrialization plans were revised downward radically.

Since 1959, the Communists have released no official data on the performance of the Chinese economy, although Western China-watchers have increasingly pieced together bits and pieces of information into consistent patterns of evidence. Apparently China gradually restored economic order in the early 1960s, although most estimates show total food and industrial output by 1967 and 1968 still below the levels of a decade earlier. What happened during the widespread political and social disorders of the 1968 to 1969 period is disputed. Apparently the disruptions again reduced economic output, but friendly observers argue that this disruption was slight and that the economy is again growing substantially. China still must import large quantities of grain to avoid starvation. Military production appears to be a substantial diversion from civilian output, which remains only slightly above subsistence levels for the rural masses.

What is the outcome of the race between China and India? The question is an important one, for in the eyes of much of the world it is a race between democratic and Communist ways, and between mixed and centrally planned approaches to economic development. During the 1950s, the results made bad reading for believers in Western democracy and private enterprise. China stumbled after 1959, and some Western observers thought they saw the beginning of a collapse of the Chinese economic revolution. The Communists' abolition of traditional Chinese family values and individual initiative has been ruthless, and their suppression of individual choice and pressure for ever more and harder work relentless. Many Americans (and Indians) believe that Chinese economic progress, even if it does outdistance India's, is not worth its high price in terms of human values. But although the Communist leaders have retreated and the Chinese economy has shown serious strains, apparently some economic growth has resumed.

India faces basic problems of human incentives, too. Can the Indian government implement its program of low consumption and capital accumulation among the people on a voluntary basis? Persuading a poverty-stricken population to hold down consumption in order to save is hard, perhaps impossible, in a democratic society; but to achieve sustained growth India must do it. India's success or failure will indicate whether social revolution and establishment of a balanced, prosperous economy are feasible without dictatorship and violence—whether democratic planning can effectively lay the foundations of the takeoff into economic growth of a huge free nation.

The Future of the Less-Developed Nations

A leading American economist has recently summarized the lessons of development policy over the past two decades:[8]

[8]Stephen Enke, in "Economists and Development," *Journal of Economic Literature*, December, 1969, p. 1135.

Both the practical and theoretical emphasis is now more on agriculture and less exclusively on industry, more on human and relatively less on physical capital investment, more on private enterprise and less on state industries, more on reducing birthrates and less on increasing national output, and more on cultural and technological change instead of making foreign loans and grants called "capital." The lack of real managers and technical specialists is seen as especially acute in the recently decolonized nations. The importance of efficient and honest government is becoming more appreciated.

So, what is the future of the less-developed nations? Can the "Third World" hope to "catch up" with the more developed nations?

Clearly many of the less-developed nations are economies in motion. And there is good reason to believe that two decades of investment are beginning to pay off in faster growth for much of the "Third World." Changing the rate of economic growth is slow business, and two decades is very little against the yardstick of history.

But for such nations to catch up with developed-nation per capita incomes in the foreseeable future is unbelievable. Even on the most optimistic assumptions of annual growth rates in the less-developed countries, the absolute gap between rich and poor nations is widening at a breakneck pace. A 2 percent annual increase on $4,800 (roughly the present U.S. per capita figure) is nearly $100, about the total present annual per capita income in India and China. Even if the Indian-Chinese growth rates were to be double ours (say 4 percent per capita as against 2 percent)—a most unlikely situation—by the end of the century U.S. per capita income would still be nearly $9,000, Indian-Chinese about $400. Clearly the less-developed nations can raise their living standards greatly. Some have done so in the past two decades—Israel, Thailand, and Taiwan are examples. But most have made pitifully little progress, some have slipped backward. And even if success surpasses their wildest dreams, the absolute gap between the "haves" and "have-nots" in our ever smaller world seems certain to widen spectacularly over the years ahead.

What would you advise Mme. Gandhi, Prime Minister of India, to do to raise the standard of living of the Indian people?

U.S. Policy

Mankind is passing through the most pervasive revolution it has ever known—the revolt of two-thirds of the world's people against the poverty, misery, and degradation of their present conditions of life, and against the domination of the industrialized, wealthy, Western powers. The speed and force of this revolution are hard to perceive, sitting in the comfort of an American home or classroom. But they may well do more than any other force to determine the kind of world in which we will live a half century hence.

What should American policy be? As the world's richest nation, and the proud leader of a democratic, humanitarian tradition in today's world, what should we do to speed or slow this revolution? What interests do we have in the less-developed nations, many of whose names we scarcely recognize?

First, we are engaged in a contest with communism for world leadership. If we want to maintain the prestige and attractiveness of the Western way, it is important that economic development in the free societies fare better than in China and the Communist satellites. Attempting to win political friendship through help in economic development is a precarious and uncertain business. The countries that take our aid one day sometimes seem to turn on us the next, almost before the money is spent; Egypt's startling seizure of the Suez Canal in 1956 following substantial Western aid is a striking case. And we have often failed to capture the imagination and support of the people themselves; Vietnam is a painful example. But other results, for example, Mexico and Taiwan, have been more promising.

Second, we have economic interests. But it would be foolish to overstress this element. Trade with all the less-developed nations amounts to only about 2 percent of U.S. g.n.p., although this trade provides useful imports and profitable export markets. Except for foodstuffs and raw materials, there is relatively little direct competition in world markets between the developing economies and American exports. International exchange with such areas thus looks favorable for us, though the facts are far from supporting the charge that U.S. economic interests vis-à-vis the developing nations provide a strong foundation for U.S. imperialism in those countries.

Third, many Americans feel that we have a humanitarian interest in the relief of starvation, the lessening of disease and misery, and the improvement of education and living standards of the billions of people in the less-developed areas. There but for the grace of God go I, they say. We are very rich and they are very poor, and they need our help. Others disagree, especially when the time comes to pay the taxes to finance help to the less-developed nations. Here obviously is a moral issue on which you must make up your own mind.

Channels of American Aid

If we want to help, for political, economic, or humanitarian reasons, it is well first to ask the question: Can we really make any difference? The task of helping 1 or 2 billion people to a better life is a huge one. And the preceding pages surely show that the task is not simply one of providing more dollars of foreign aid.

Yet we should remember some facts. The total income of all the billion people in the non-Communist less-developed nations in 1970 was less than $250 billion. The g.n.p. of the United States alone was $980 billion. In 1970 we spent over $70 billion on military purposes. Total arms spending in the world was perhaps $150 billion. Elimination of these war expenditures could have raised by over 50 percent the living standard of each of the billion people.

The United States has the economic ability to help significantly. What have we done? What should we do?

Total Aid and Private Investment. First, Table 19–5 provides a summary look at the entire flow of government and multinational aid, plus

table 19-5

Loans, Grants, and Private Investment in Less-Developed Countries, 1968*

Source	Amount
Government loans and grants:	
From United States	$3.6
From other Western countries	3.3
Subtotal:	$ 6.9
Private net long-term investment:	
From United States	$2.1
From other Western countries	3.8
Subtotal:	$ 5.9
Total	$12.8

* Data from Organization for Economic Cooperation and Development. Does not include aid from China, the USSR, and other Communist nations; or short-term credits and loans; but does include aid through international organizations.

private investment, to the less-developed countries in 1968.

The $12.8 billion total shown in Table 19–5 has grown gradually over the past decade; it was $8 billion in 1960. The United States provided about half ($5.7 billion) of the 1968 total, though this was only .8 percent of our 1968 national income. France, Germany, and the United Kingdom all totaled more than 1 percent of their national incomes, although their total volume of aid was much smaller than that of the United States.

Capacity of Less-Developed Nations To Absorb Aid. Obviously the less-developed nations have a vast need for assistance. But, as a practical matter, how much aid in the form of foreign capital could they currently absorb effectively? The experts have come up with widely varying answers. But most estimates range between $15 and $20 billion a year. These estimates reflect the fact that development in most of the poor nations is held back by many other factors as well as capital—by lack of education, skilled workers, and managers; by unstable governments; by absence of initiative, and the like. It is clear that on these grounds some less-developed nations are much more "ready" to absorb foreign aid than are others, and some experts advocate concentrating aid on these nations.

1. **Government loans and gifts.** The most direct way for us to help is by government loans or gifts. Since World War II, U.S. government aid to other nations has totaled over $100 billion, first to Europe through the Marshall Plan and since then mainly to the less-developed nations. About two-thirds of this has been non-military aid. During the 1960s, such direct government aid averaged between $3 and $4 billion annually, with the biggest shares to India and to Latin America. But recently Congress has cut the total regularly, to only about $1.7 billion for 1971, reflecting growing discouragement over the results of such aid. This steady reduction in U.S. aid runs counter to the recommendations of international organizations that all developed nations provide aid (including private investment) equal to at least 1 percent of g.n.p.

For the most part this aid is provided through low-interest loans or direct grants, most of which must be spent on U.S. goods and services. One other big part has been direct transfers of surplus food (mainly wheat) from U.S. stocks. Such food is technically "sold" to the recipient country—for example, India. The Indian government, however, pays in rupees, which we agree to spend only for special purposes in India. The food is thus in large part a gift, since we are unlikely ever to use up all the rupees we accumulate. Insofar as the food is U.S. surplus, however, there is little real cost to us in sending our massive food grants to the less-developed nations.

2. **Private U.S. capital investment.** The large growth potential of the less-developed economies might seem attractive to American capital seeking investment at good rates of return. But the problems of breaking the vicious circle of poverty are apparent. Moreover, many of the less-developed nations distrust foreign investment as threatening foreign intervention and control. Thus they place elaborate regulations,

special taxes, and restrictions on withdrawal of profits on foreign investments. Moreover, many governments are unstable, and the next regime may decide to seize foreign property. Returns to foreign investors are sometimes high, but risks are great.

Nevertheless, over the past decade private U.S. net investments in the less-developed nations have averaged around $2 billion annually, with nearly two-thirds of the total going into Latin America. Total accumulated U.S. private investments in the less-developed areas by 1969 were about $22 billion, nearly all of them made during the postwar period.

Private direct investments in less-developed nations can hardly be considered U.S. aid, since presumably they are made as voluntary profit-seeking business ventures. However, they do represent a major source of capital for the less-developed nations.

3. **Technical assistance.** After the postwar burst of enthusiasm for aid to the less-developed economies came the sobering recognition that many of the crucial problems were internal ones—ignorance and apathy among native populations, lack of real impetus for development, and unstable governments. Even billions of foreign aid might have little effect unless such factors were attacked vigorously and effectively by the less-developed nations themselves.

"Technical assistance" programs to help local governments and local peoples to help themselves have grown during recent years, partly because they seem to work well, partly because they are far cheaper than mass capital-investment grants. Assistance in establishing better schools, efficient local government administration, sanitation and public health projects, better farming techniques, and other such programs have generally proved successful.

U.S. and multinational technical-assistance programs stress training natives to teach other natives and to take over essential jobs themselves at the earliest possible moment. In most cases, U.S. technical assistance has been provided on a matching basis, with half the cost of the joint programs being borne by local governments. Technical assistance is a bright spot in our foreign-aid program.

4. Lowering of international trade barriers and purchase of local products. In order to grow, most less-developed countries must sell basic products abroad if they are to secure foreign exchange with which to finance needed imports. Many of their economies are centered around one or two basic products—oil, rubber, nitrates, coffee, tin. Trade barriers that shut these products out of American markets strike a serious blow at the economies concerned. They raise understandable resentment among natives who hear American propaganda that we are anxious to help the developing nations. We have led the way in reducing tariff barriers and in helping to provide stable international markets for such basic commodities, but many less-developed nations think we should do still more.

5. Military aid. Presumably military aid is given mainly for military purposes. But in a country that would otherwise spend part of its national product on military activities, U.S. military aid provides direct relief to the local government budget. It thus permits local government spending to be focused on economic development.

Perspective on U.S. Policy

How successful has American aid to less-developed countries been? If the test of success is maintenance of political and military alliances with America or neutrality vis-à-vis the Communist bloc, the verdict is favorable in some cases, but mixed. If the test is friendliness and gratitude for American generosity, the verdict is at best mixed. Few people like to think they are objects of charity, and we probably make a great mistake to expect thankfulness in return. If the test is economic improvement and lessening of human misery abroad, the verdict is—some progress.

To expect fast results from our foreign aid is unreasonable. Economic growth is at best a very slow process, even when the conditions are favorable. It is instructive to remember that the United States, with extremely favorable conditions for development, relied substantially on capital from abroad for nearly a century. It will probably be decades before substantial results become apparent from foreign aid to most of the less-developed nations. And even with this long lag, the results are far from certain. At most, foreign aid can only help. The real force for development must come from within the less-developed nations themselves.

What has our foreign aid to the less-developed nations really cost us? Although the total number of dollars is impressive in absolute size, it has been a small fraction of 1 percent of our annual g.n.p. Moreover, as indicated above, one big component of this aid is surplus food products. If we didn't send this food abroad, we would presumably just run up storage charges on it. Moreover, insofar as our foreign aid increases aggregate demand for American products when our economy is underemployed, such foreign aid may help increase our real g.n.p. Thus, it is by no means clear that the dollar totals reflect the real cost to the American public of providing aid to the developing nations.

Lastly, recognition of the powerful force of growing nationalism and the desire for status and respect in every less-developed country must be the cornerstone of successful aid, whatever our basic motives are. Increasingly, American experts have urged that all American foreign aid except technical assistance be channeled through international organizations, to remove any implication of political pressure or domination by the United States. Those who want to use foreign aid as a political weapon or who want direct recognition understandably oppose such proposals.

Economic analysis can tell you a lot about the problem of raising living standards for the world's impoverished billions. It can give some guidance on how our help can do the most lasting good. But the problem of U.S. aid is moral and political as much as economic. It is one of the biggest issues on which this nation must take a stand over the decades ahead.

Review

FOR ANALYSIS AND DISCUSSION

1. How well do the theories of Adam Smith and Malthus explain the plight of the less-developed nations? Has modern growth theory (from Chapter 16) added much to their analyses?

2. To develop rapidly, a nation must save and invest a substantial portion of its income. What steps would you advise the Indian government to take to increase India's saving rate when the majority of the population is on the brink of starvation?

3. Nearly everyone agrees that slower growth in population is essential to reducing poverty in the less-developed nations. Suppose you were prime minister of India or Colombia, how would you bring this about?

4. Development of an entrepreneurial class seems critical for nations trying to break out of the vicious circle of poverty. If you were a government official in Peru or the Congo, what would you do about this problem?

5. "Modern economics tells us to pump in purchasing power in order to eliminate unemployment when depression occurs in the Western world; but this approach has no relevance for the less-developed nations, where a shortage of real capital is the basic problem." Is this statement correct? Explain your answer.

6. The United States has spent over $70 billion annually for defense expenditures in recent years. Yet it has spent only about $2 to 3 billion annually on direct aid to the less-developed economies. Should we divert $10 billion annually from the military budget to an all-out effort to speed economic development and to win friends among the less-developed nations?

7. Will the gap between U.S. and underdeveloped nations' living standards narrow or widen over the next quarter century?

8. Suppose the U.S. government sends you out to a less-developed nation to assess its development prospects over the next decade. What would be the key information you would seek for your report?

APPENDIX   *THE POPULATION EXPLOSION*

Between the birth of Christ and 1650, the population of the world roughly doubled, from 250 million to 500 million people. Population doubled again, to 1 billion people, by 1850, in about 200 years. It doubled again in 80 years—to 2 billion people in 1930. And it will double again, from 2 to 4 billion people, by 1975, only 35 years. Such projection of future population growth is tricky business, but many estimates call for the next doubling, from 4 to 8 billion people, in perhaps 25 years, by the year 2000. Figure 19–8 shows the spectacular surge of population in the last century, compared to its slower growth over the preceding 2,000 years.

The world is presently adding about 70–75 million people each year, the equivalent of an entire U.S. population every three years. Most of this increase is in the less-developed nations, particularly China, India, Southeast Asia, and Latin America, areas where the standard of living hovers only a little above the survival level. The phenomenal increase in the present century reflects primarily not higher birthrates but rather a rapid decrease in death rates in the less-developed nations. As Figure 19–2 indicated, birthrates are much higher in the less-developed than in the highly developed nations, and with dropping death rates population in the less-developed nations has soared. Today it is common to estimate the present world-population growth rate at about 2.6 percent per annum. At this rate the 4 billion persons expected in 1975 would become 32 billion a century later.

Numbers of this size stagger the imagination. They would make the earth into a human anthill. But population will surely not reach anything like these levels, for one simple reason if no other. The world does not have natural resources, especially for producing food, to support a population of that size. Indeed, one biologist has argued that already "The battle to feed

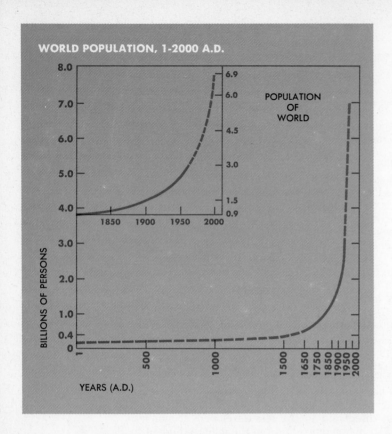

WORLD POPULATION, 1-2000 A.D.

POPULATION OF WORLD

BILLIONS OF PERSONS

YEARS (A.D.)

fig. 19-8

Estimated world population from 1 A.D. (Source: P. Hauser, ed., *The Population Dilemma,* 2nd ed., Prentice-Hall, Inc., 1969.)

all humanity is over. In the 1970s the world will undergo famines—hundreds of millions of people are going to starve to death in spite of any crash programs embarked upon now."[9] He writes that we have already lost the food race—famine is here already in the less-developed nations, which make up two-thirds of the world, and is just around the corner in the developed nations, such as the United States.

Not only does the world face mass starvation, the conservationists argue, it will soon run out of vital natural resources—minerals, fuels, water, clean air. Today's growing population, especially in the developed nations, produces an unbelievable quantity of waste that must somehow be disposed of. It fouls the air and pollutes the water. Its use of chemicals to increase crop yields will have a long-run effect of poisoning the environment. Partly because of rapid population growth, and partly because of the developed countries' rapidly rising aspirations for living standards, we are fast destroying the environment on which we must rely for life itself.

What can economic analysis tell us about the population explosion and its impact on people today and tomorrow? Are these dire warnings of catastrophe soundly based, or is catastrophe mainly in the minds of men who are honestly mistaken or given to extravagant statements in pursuit of their own values and goals?

[9]Paul Ehrlich, *The Population Bomb* (San Francisco: Sierra Club Books, 1968), p. 11. Few food experts accept this extreme statement.

The Presumptions of Economic Theory. Growth theory (in Chapter 16) and history tell us that total output is a function of the supply of labor, capital, and land (natural resources), and of the level of technology. A brief review may be useful. If we take the stock of natural resources as fixed, growth in total output depends on the other factors of production (labor and capital) and on the advances in technology. Given a fixed capital stock and technology, more people (labor force) will produce more total output (food), but total output will grow at a slower rate than labor, because of the law of diminishing returns. Thus the marginal output per person or per worker will fall. If we roughly equate output with food, it is clear that in this kind of situation rapidly growing population threatens poverty and ultimate famine for mankind.

Suppose, however, that parallel to the growth in the labor force the capital stock is also increased through saving. If capital and labor grow at about the same rate, total output will increase, but at a slower rate than the capital-labor growth rate because the law of diminishing returns comes into play as more capital and labor are combined with the same amount of land. Land will become increasingly expensive per unit as its scarcity rises; landlords will prosper, absolutely and relative to capitalists and workers. The sharing of income between capital and labor would depend on the relative rates of increase of the two.

Suppose now, however, that there is also technological advance. Now not only total output can increase with growing labor and capital, but output per unit of input of either labor or capital, or both, may continue to rise, even with a fixed stock of land. With technical advance and capital accumulation, mankind need never approach a famine condition (declining real output per capita), even with a rapid growth in population.

Casual observation of the world around us suggests that the developed nations, like the United States, fall into this last category. Although the amount of land (natural resources) is substantially fixed, population growth is much more than matched by growth in the capital stock, and rapid technological advance makes it possible for total output and the real shares of all three—land, labor, and capital—to rise. For the reasons noted in Chapter 16, the relative total income shares of labor and capital have remained relatively stable, although the returns per unit of land and of labor have risen rapidly compared to that per unit of capital, since capital has grown much faster than labor and natural resources.

The less-developed countries seem generally to fall in the earlier category—that of rapidly growing population unmatched by capital stock growth and with substantially fixed natural resources. For them, Malthus was right. In these economies, especially since most begin from a poverty level, rapid growth in population does indeed carry the threat of constant or even falling output per capita—of famine. Though technical advance (fertilizers, crop rotation, and the like) is in principle available, its utilization is difficult in the less-developed nations, because of inertia and because of the shortage of capital to facilitate introduction of modern technical methods. Total output grows little, if any, faster than population; if population growth speeds up, the immediate effect is likely to be a worsening of output per capita and, in food terms, famine.[10]

Population and the World Food Problem. Since Malthus's forecast, nearly two centuries ago, that population would be periodically checked by famine unless man found a voluntary way to halt population growth, the world has heard repeated dire predictions of impending famine. Professor Ehrlich's warning above is an example. What are the facts, and what is the outlook for the future?

In the United States and the other Western industrialized nations, food output has far outpaced the growth in population. While there is no doubt some

[10]Remember further that when the population growth rate rises, there are proportionately more children. Children eat, but they do not work. Thus, the short-run effect of faster population growth is to decrease per capita incomes relative to output per worker, since the total output must be spread over a large number of nonworking people. Conversely, a decline in the rate of population growth will, other things equal, help to raise output (food) per capita.

hunger among the poor, average consumption of calories is far above minimum levels, and the diet is rich in the proteins that are lacking in the diets of most less-developed nations. Indeed, American agricultural policy in the last half century has been focused on restricting agricultural output, in order to prevent "surpluses" that would depress market prices and incomes of farmers. With present resources and technology, the United States could readily feed twice its present population adequately. Clearly the starvation problem is not one of inadequate ability to produce food in the United States.

But in the less-developed countries, the picture is gloomy. Table 19–6 shows average calorie-consumption levels in a sample of the world's regions in the early 1960s. Experts do not agree on the precise calorie level needed for maintenance of health; this depends somewhat on the composition of the diet. But they do agree that diets below 2,000 calories per day are surely close to the minimum level for reasonable nutrition, while 2,400 calories a day or thereabouts may be needed to provide not only sustenance but also the basis for good health and energy.

Calories alone are an inadequate measure of nutrition. Protein and fat consumption provide other measures that supplement the calorie figures. Data on per capita protein and fat consumption do not substantially change the order of ranking of the countries and areas indicated, but they greatly widen the spread between them. For example, protein con-

table 19-6*

Country	Calorie Consumption per Day
Australia-New Zealand	3,260
United States	3,190
Canada	3,100
Northern Europe	3,060
USSR	3,040
Southern Europe	2,720
Brazil	2,710
Mexico	2,580
Central and Eastern Africa	2,410
Japan	2,360
Western Asia	2,350
Other South and Central America	2,250
India	2,060
Communist Asia	1,790
World	2,360

*Data from The World Food Budget, 1970 (U.S. Department of Agriculture), p. 25.

sumption in India and Communist Asia averaged about 50 grams per person per day, while that in the United States and Canada was nearly double this figure. Fat consumption in grams per day at the same time ranges from about 20 per day in Communist Asia to about 145 per day in the United States. Nutritionists generally agree that if cereals and other starchy foods make up more than 80 percent of the calories in the diet, malnutrition is likely. In well-fed countries like the United States, the United Kingdom, and France, hardly anyone derives 80 percent of his calories from cereals and sugar starches, while in less-developed nations as many as two-thirds of all households fell in this category.

Considering both calories and composition of diets, studies by the United Nations and by the U.S. Department of Agriculture have repeatedly shown that perhaps as many as 2 billion of the world's people live in the nations where average per capita food consumption is inadequate to avoid either malnutrition or undernourishment, although most actual starvation occurs only in years of extremely bad crops due to poor weather. Such diets are adequate to sustain life, but they do not provide an adequate basis for good health and energetic work.

The world food problem thus is not a single problem, but a very different one for different parts of the world. About 75 percent of the total world food deficit, as measured by the calorie indicators above, is centered in Asia, particularly in Communist China and India, which together include nearly 40 percent of the world's population. Average deficiencies in the other areas are much smaller; for example, the per capita deficit appears to be around 3 percent for South and Central America, perhaps 2½ percent for Africa, so that moderate increases in food per capita could substantially eliminate the deficits in the foreseeable future if population growth slows. But the case for slower population growth throughout the less-developed nations is strong if we want to improve diets and reduce poverty there.

Over the past half century, food consumption per capita has apparently increased gradually in the developed Western nations (with large shifts among food categories), and has shown little change in most of the less-developed nations. Total food production has risen substantially, but total world population has grown almost as fast. During the 1950s, it appeared that the world was slowly but surely solving its food problem. But in the early 1960s, population growth rates surged to frightening levels, and bad weather in Asia in the years 1965 to 1967 helped turn the picture, in many observers' eyes, to dark despair. Since 1967, however, there has been a resurgence of food output in the world; and with some startling technological developments in the production of wheat, rice, and other grains, the outlook has turned brighter once again. Agricultural output has increased at a spectacular rate in some countries, such as Israel, the

Sudan, Mexico, the Philippines, Yugoslavia, Taiwan, and Thailand. In all of these, total food production has increased recently at 4 to 5 percent a year or more. Studies by the United Nations and others make it clear that, thus far, the population explosion has not outrun the capacity of the world to produce food, in spite of the vivid phrases coined by many alarmists. On the other hand, there has been little progress in moving food levels much above minimum, and real plus potential hunger dominates the picture. What will happen over the years ahead is unclear.

While experts dispute over remedies, it is clear that the basic economics above constrains the possible alternatives. Unless nations can raise capital investment relative to labor, or assimilate rapidly improving technology, or slow their rates of population growth, there is little promise for substantial improvement in the lot of most of mankind. If they can do any one or all of these three, there is no reason why the "population explosion" need lead to famine or even to more severe undernourishment than now prevails. Nonetheless, nearly every expert on the developing economics pleads for steps to slow the population explosion there. The case against population growth in the developed economies gains little support from the starvation argument; it rests mainly on the issues considered in the following sections.[11]

Population and the Environment. The population explosion of the past half century has occurred largely in the less-developed nations—the "Third World"—and the world food problem is largely concentrated there. In the Western industrial, developed nations, the rate of population growth has been slowing over the past century, and especially in the last few decades. While the U.S. birthrate picked up sharply after World War II, it has again turned downward. Birthrates are generally much lower in the developed nations than in the rest of the world.

But for these nations, two other arguments are advanced against population growth. First, it will soon be checked—if not by famine, then by the exhaustion of our natural resources (minerals, oil, water, and the like). Second, the growing wastes of a more populous, technological society are increasingly polluting the atmosphere, water, and land, so that man will find the environment increasingly unpleasant, and ultimately too hostile to support him.

Pollution, overcrowding, and other such side effects of growing population and the modern technological age are indeed serious problems. For the highly developed nations they may be the greatest

[11]For authoritative analyses of the population and world food problems, see P. Hauser, ed., *The Population Dilemma* (Englewood Cliffs, N.J.: Prentice-Hall, Inc., Spectrum Books, 1963); and W. W. Cochrane, *The World Food Problem* (New York: Crowell Collier and Macmillan, Inc., 1969), which draw heavily on United Nations studies.

costs of population and economic growth. But since an entire chapter (39) is devoted to them in Part Five, they are temporarily set aside here.

Fear that Western industrialized society, especially the United States, will soon run out of natural resources to support its high standard of living is a separate argument, and one worth consideration here in connection with the population explosion.

First, what are the facts? U.S. per capita consumption of natural resources has grown steadily, with our rising standard of living. Over the past half century, growth in per capita consumption of all natural resources has been something less than 1 percent per year. Consumption of minerals has grown substantially faster, perhaps 1½ percent per year since World War II. Only for forest products has per capita consumption persistently fallen, reflecting growing scarcity of wood resources and a corresponding increase in their relative prices. Second, another indicator of resource scarcity is the share of energy provided by natural as against human resources; this has persistently risen in the United States over the last century (see Figure 17–3). Third, if resources were becoming relatively scarce, one would expect their prices to rise relative to the prices of other things. In general, again with the exception of forest products, the relative prices of natural resources (minerals, agricultural products, and the like) have fallen substantially. Fourth, if we were suffering from natural resource shortages, one would expect a rise in the proportion of raw materials and food imported from abroad. There has been a slight increase, especially for agricultural products where we were large exporters until the Great Depression. For minerals,

there has been relatively little change; imports total less than 10 percent of total consumption over the past century—less than 5 percent if we include agricultural products.[12] These facts do not support the doomsday predictions about natural resource exhaustion that are so frequently made today.

Many experts have ventured predictions as to the probable state of U.S. natural resources by the year 2000. Table 19–7 summarizes one widely used set of estimates made at "Resources for the Future," an independent research organization supported by foundation and government funds. The underlying assumption is that population will rise to 330 million by the year 2000.

Commenting on the estimated 2000 requirements, the authors report:

"Cropland will be adequate assuming that yields per acre increase in line with recent trends.... Meeting the increased demand for lumber will strain the economy's capacity to produce ... and perhaps we shall have to resort to additional imports and further substitutions.... Water problems are primarily regional; their solution will require more investment in developing supplies, reducing pollution, and more efficient use. Petroleum, now in oversupply ... may be short toward the end of the century.... Coal reserves remain plentiful. Very large nuclear resources await further reductions in cost.... Many areas of the world from which imports of nonfuel minerals

[12]J. L. Fisher and Neal Potter, "Resources in the United States and the World," in *The Population Dilemma*, provide references to the detailed underlying studies on which the information is based.

Table 19-7

U.S. Natural Resources and Requirements, 1960 and 2000*

	1960	2000
Crop and pasture land (million acres)	447	476
Timber (billion cubic feet)	11	32
Fresh water withdrawal depletions (billion gal./day)	84	149
Oil (billion bbls.)	3.2	10
Natural gas (trillion cu. ft.)	13	39
Coal (million tons)	436	718
Nuclear power (billion kilowatt hours)	. . .	2,400
Iron ore (million tons)	131	341
Aluminum, primary (million tons)	2	13
Copper, primary (million tons)	2	4.5

*From Fisher and Potter, "Resources in the United States and the World," p. 102. The underlying data are from H. Landsberg, L. Fischoman and J. Fisher, *Resources in America's Future* (Baltimore: The Johns Hopkins Press, 1963).

can be obtained have not been very well explored, some not at all, and the possibilities of using lower grade ones are reasonably bright...."

No such estimates, however objective, can provide more than rough orders of magnitude, and other estimates differ. But most such expert looks ahead paint a picture of neither despair nor large excess supplies.

Indeed, the density of population in relation to land and other natural resources is of dubious usefulness as a predictor of real per capita output and food consumption. Population density per square kilometer is highest in the central European nations—about 140 persons per square kilometer. In North America it is about 10 persons per square kilometer; in South Central Asia, mainly India, about 110 persons per square kilometer. Yet these nations range the entire world spectrum of affluence and poverty. Switzerland, Denmark, and the Netherlands, for example, have high per capita incomes with very limited natural resources, because they rely heavily on world trade, importing the raw materials and food they need and exporting finished goods. An extreme example is Hong Kong, which has an enormous population density but considerably higher per capita income than Mainland China and India. Within nations, trade again provides high per capita incomes for land-poor areas. The so-called Northeast Corridor in the United States, from Boston to Washington, has a very high density of population but a median family income well above the national average.

Thus, there is little evidence that population growth has yet run against the limits of natural resources in the United States or in the other developed Western economies, or even in the less-developed nations where lack of natural resources is seldom the critical barrier to development. These facts, of course, do not guarantee adequate world natural resources for the future. But they do suggest the fallacy in looking only at population in relation to natural resources within national boundaries, as long as international trade is a feasible alternative.

A related argument, especially by the new "activists," is that the United States already has more people than it can adequately maintain itself, and that we therefore are completely dependent on imports for our affluence. So we exploit the natural resources of the less-developed nations to support our affluence. U.S. economic growth will halt when those nations are no longer willing or able to supply our needs, the argument runs.

Again, the facts suggest that this is a fallacious argument. In 1969, total U.S. imports of all goods and services were about $40 billion. Of this total, all raw materials and agricultural products, from both developed and less-developed nations, totaled less than $12 billion, compared to a total gross national product of about $980 billion—a little over 1 percent. To say that the United States is completely dependent on imports for its wealth is thus an obvious misstatement. Clearly, without some imports of particular foods and raw materials (e.g., coffee and tin), we should have to change our pattern of living. But the total amount imported is tiny compared to the total output of the American economy.

In emotion-laden discussions of the population explosion, it is often hard to separate fact from fiction. Population has, indeed, grown by leaps and bounds in the less-developed nations, and it continues to grow substantially in the developed countries like the United States. Clearly the ratio of population to natural resources is rising, since natural resources are presumably fixed in quantity. Clearly, also, this development does, other things equal, restrain the growth in per capita output. However, steady discovery of resources hitherto unfound (for example the huge oil fields in northern Alaska), technical advances in using resources more efficiently, and development of synthetic substitutes, have more than offset the rising man–land ratio thus far in the developed nations. In most of the less-developed nations the picture is more bleak, and the case for slower population growth seems compelling to most economic observers. This is not to say that the same happy developments will continue for all future times even in the developed nations. But it does suggest the importance of careful analysis in examining extreme conclusions about population trends in both developed and less-developed nations.

One technological argument stands apart from the preceding data. Although it belongs mainly in Chapter 39, it deserves a brief concluding mention here. This is the biological argument that by using modern technology to increase output from our natural resources we are so altering the ecological balance that in fact we will radically change nature. For example, it is argued that we may so change the heat balance as to bring another ice age or turn the earth into a great desert. At a less-extreme but shorter-run level, the argument runs that modern pesticides and other chemical "advances" to increase food production are gradually poisoning both our natural resources and us.

Economists have no special expertise in analyzing these arguments. Many biologists say the danger is real; for example, the "death" of Lake Erie is attributed more to runoff of unabsorbed agricultural chemicals than to industrial wastes. Both economic theory and history suggest that adaptive political-economic processes may help to mitigate unwanted impacts of technological change and thus to reduce the probability of impending disaster from the indirect effects of population growth. (They have certainly done so in the past.) But environmental pollution may indeed be a highly undesirable side effect of population growth.

The main job of an elementary economics textbook is to stir an interest in economic problems, to present the central analytical tools of economics, and to provide some guided experience in using them to reach independent judgments on current economic developments and on public-policy measures. I hope that the preceding pages have conveyed some sense of the lively urgency of the problems with which economics deals, and some sense of the manner in which modern economics helps to solve them.

Economists spend much of their time using the tools presented here and helping to devise public policies that will make our economic system work better. But one of the further things that makes economics exciting is research—the fascination of probing for new knowledge and new insights into how the economic system works. Economics is far from a dead, stable body of theory and knowledge. It is the research of today that will make the better textbooks and the better world of tomorrow.

It is the purpose of these brief appendixes at the end of each part to convey a brief impression of the kinds of research currently under way in economics. Some of the research cited is readily understandable by a good student at the elementary level; other parts are more difficult. But the purpose is not to provide references that all beginning students should read. Rather it is to suggest some samples of economic research that may be intriguing to students who want to look beyond the text and who want to know more about what economics is and what economists do. Pick out two or three and look at them. If they don't hit the spot, try another. The goal is to interest you and make you want to read further.

The following paragraphs report briefly a small sample of research on some major problems covered by Part Two. There is no intention to imply that they represent the best, or the most important, research under way on the problems covered. They are merely samples of research that one economist thinks might be interesting to curious students getting acquainted with economics. A major criterion in selection has been variety. A half dozen other comparable lists could readily be provided—and, indeed, your instructor may be happy to provide one he feels is superior.[1]

Growth, Fluctuations, and Unemployment. Yale's James Tobin examines the case for faster growth as a major goal of national policy in "Economic Growth as an Objective of Government Policy" in the *American Economic Review* for May, 1964; look also at Herbert Stein's rejoinder. For perspective on growth

[1]A number of the following references, in this and other appendixes on current research, have been reprinted in M. Joseph, N. Seeber, and G. L. Bach, eds., *Economic Analysis and Policy*, 3rd edition (Prentice-Hall, Inc., 1971).

in the long sweep of the history of the world, try Simon Kuznets's fascinating "Notes on the Pattern of U.S. Economic Growth," in *The Nation's Economic Objectives* (University of Chicago Press, 1964). A quite different view of growth is given by A. D. Chandler's *Ford, G.M., and the Automobile Industry* (Harcourt, Brace & World, Inc. 1965), a case study of one major industry; and by Chapter 6 of W. Baumol's provocative little book, *Business Behavior, Value and Growth* (The Macmillan Company, 1967). Lastly, the role of technology in growth is thoroughly assessed by R. R. Nelson, M. J. Peck, and E. Kalachek in *Technology, Economic Growth, and Public Policy* (The Brookings Institution, 1967).

Monetary and Fiscal Policy. The great debate between the monetarist and income-employment approaches to macroeconomic analysis and policy has spawned a huge literature. For a starter, try "Two Views of the Role of Money," by Yale's James Tobin and Carnegie-Mellon's Allan Meltzer, in *Controlling Monetary Aggregates* (Federal Reserve Bank of Boston, 1969). A good statement of the current fiscal policy approach is offered by W. W. Heller and others, *Fiscal Policy for a Balanced Economy* (Organization for Economic and Cultural Development, Paris, 1968). Herbert Stein provides a fascinating historical study in *The Fiscal Revolution in America* (University of Chicago Press, 1969); sample two or three chapters. Milton Friedman's *A Program for Monetary Stability* (Fordham University Press, 1969) is an authoritative statement of the monetarist viewpoint. Stanford's E. S. Shaw adds a lively statement of the case for a stable-money-growth rule in "The Money Supply and Stable Economic Growth," in *United States Monetary Policy* (American Assembly; Columbia University Press, 1958). G. L. Bach's *Making Monetary and Fiscal Policy* (The Brookings Institution, 1971) is a study of political and economic interactions in the policy-making process.

Inflation and Unemployment. A number of readable references on the "Phillips Curve" controversy (whether we must accept inflation to have full employment) are cited in the footnotes to Chapter 15. The controversy is summed up in "The Relation between Prices and Employment: Two Views," in the Federal Reserve Bank of St. Louis *Review*, March, 1969. A broader approach, which combines economic, social, and political factors, is illustrated by G. L. Bach's *Inflation: A Study in Economics, Ethics, and Politics* (Brown University Press, 1958).

The Less-Developed Economies. There is a flood of research on the less-developed economies, why they are less-developed, and how they might grow faster. For a starter, try Albert Hirschman's *Journeys Through Progress* (Doubleday & Company, Inc.

1963), on Latin America; or John Lewis's *Quiet Crisis in India* (The Brookings Institution, 1962). Stephen Enke sums up recent experience in "Economists and Development; Rediscovering Old Truths," *Journal of Economic Literature*, December, 1969. On Communist China, see N. R. Chen and W. Galenson, *The Chinese Economy Under Communism* (Aldine Publishing Company, 1969); and at a more detailed, and more controversial, level, the compendium of the Joint Economic Committee of Congress, *An Economic Profile of Mainland China* (two volumes, 1967), which presents the views of a number of experts on recent developments in mainland China; see especially Volume 1. Lastly, on the controversial food–population problem, balanced analyses are presented by W. Cochrane's, *The World Food Problem* (Crowell, 1969), and P. Hauser (ed.), *The Population Dilemma* (Prentice-Hall, Inc., Spectrum Books, 1963).

Forecasting. If you're interested in some of the newer developments in economic forecasting and know a little mathematics, two recent studies will give you a good introduction; "Forecasting with an Econometric Model," by Daniel Suits *(American Economic Review*, March, 1962), and "A Short-term Forecasting Model," by Pennsylvania's I. Friend and P. Taubman *(Review of Economics and Statistics*, August, 1964). W. W. Leontief's "The Structure of the U.S. Economy," *The Scientific American*, April, 1965, describes "input–output analysis." A survey of all the modern forecasting techniques is provided by Part One of W. Butler and R. Kavesh, *How Business Economists Forecast* (Prentice-Hall, Inc., 1966).

Markets, the Price System, and the Allocation of Resources

prologue to part three

In Part Two we were concerned mainly with macroeconomics—with economic growth, fluctuations, unemployment, the price level, and the big public policy questions they raise. We paid little attention to the individual goods and services that make up g.n.p.—to how many cars and carpets are produced, to the incomes different individuals receive, to the behavior of individual businesses, and the like. Now, in Parts Three and Four we turn to microeconomics—to look at the individual units that make up our economy, at their functioning, at the prices they pay and charge, and at incomes that different individuals receive.

Imagine you are flying over America, looking down at the economy in operation. You would see millions of individual consumers spending their incomes on what they want most. You would see these purchases providing signals to businessmen on where the largest profits could be made, and businessmen responding to those signals by producing what consumers want to buy. You would see competition among sellers forcing prices down toward the lowest possible cost of producing those goods and services. You would observe that each worker generally earns the most by working where he can contribute the most to producing what consumers demand, because that is where businesses can afford to pay him the most. You would see a constantly shifting mix of goods and services being produced, as consumers change their minds as to what they want, and as businessmen try to meet these shifting consumers' demands.

For the most part, no one guides this vast, interlinked process. Workers' self-interest in trying to earn a good living, businessmen's self-interest in trying to earn large profits, consumers' self-interest in spending their incomes on what they want most—these millions of free choices are meshed together through many interlinked markets, where prices and quantities produced move up and down in response to changing demand and supplies. Viewed from above, Adam Smith wrote, it is as if a beneficent invisible hand were guiding the system so as to allocate our scarce productive resources to yield the most of what we want at the lowest possible costs.

Today's economy is far from Adam Smith's competitive ideal. And today a lot of people feel that Adam Smith was too optimistic, that any market-type economy falls short on many scores. They feel that collective (government) action is needed to make it work better, both through government regulation of the economy and through direct government provision of goods and services (such as education, highways, and national defense). We can appreciate the virtues of a private-enterprise market-type economy, and still recognize the strength of these reservations. Indeed, Part Five is devoted entirely to "The Public Sector," where the government takes over from private markets.

The following chapters take up the main actors in the American market system, beginning with the business firm, then the consumer, and then the interaction of consumer demands and business responses in different markets. Seeing the individual parts and how the individual actors behave is important. But as you go along, don't lose sight of the big picture of how the whole system fits together. For that's where we will come out at the end. And it's against that backdrop that you need to see today's issues, and to make up your mind on the policy problems America will face in the rapidly changing economy of the 1970s.

Business Enterprise in the Modern Economy

In a private-enterprise economy, the business-man is at the center of the economic process. He decides what will be produced in response to market demand, and how much of it. He decides how many employees to hire and how much he is willing to pay them. It is he who responds to consumer demands, and pays out most of the incomes. Within the framework of rules established by society, his decisions and policies determine most directly how effectively the private-enterprise economy functions.

In America today, government controls over business operations are numerous—so numerous that some businessmen protest that their traditional freedom is gone. Government produces some goods and services itself, in addition to its controls; and its demands in the market (for missiles, highways, schools, and many thousands of other products) give it important powers over the businesses from which it buys. Labor unions press increasingly for a share in the traditional prerogatives of management. But the businessman, harassed though he may be, remains the organizing agent at the center of our economy.

The purpose of this chapter is to provide a factual background on modern business enterprise, what it is and how it operates.

Entrepreneurs, Plants, Firms, and Industries

Business enterprises are called "firms." John Brown and his family run a farm; the farm is a firm. United States Steel is a firm, with steel mills in many cities, with iron and coal mines, with ore ships on the Great Lakes. The important characteristic of the firm is that it is owned and controlled essentially as a unit, however diverse its parts.

The function of making fundamental policy decisions in a firm is generally called "entrepreneurship." The entrepreneur decides when to establish a firm, what goods to produce, how the concern will be financed, what price policies to follow, when to expand or contract, and so on. A firm is thus a business unit under one coordinated "entrepreneurship."

In the independent corner grocery store, the proprietor is the entrepreneur. He decides whether to borrow funds to remodel his store, what prices to set on his merchandise. In bigger businesses, it is harder to pick out the entrepreneur. For example, who is the entrepreneur of American Telephone and Telegraph? The 3 million stockholders? The board of directors? The finance committee of the board? The president? Here it is impossible to pick out any person or group of persons as the entrepreneur; the functions of the entrepreneur are performed in a coordinated way by the various individuals and groups concerned.

A "plant" is a building or a group of buildings, along with other more or less fixed physical equipment, that are used together in producing something—such as a shoe-manufacturing plant or an auto-assembly plant. The Ford Motor Company is a firm with plants in Dearborn, St. Louis, Kansas City, and so forth. John Brown's farm, on the other hand, is a firm with only one plant.

An "industry" is harder to define. Usually we use the word to mean all the producers of any "commodity." Farmer Brown is part of the wheat industry if he produces wheat, part of the corn industry if he produces corn; he may be in both simultaneously. General Motors is part of many industries. The trouble comes when we try to be precise. Shall we consider a "motor-vehicles industry," or an "auto industry," or a "low-priced auto industry"? For many purposes, how finely we divide up commodities is not a major problem. You will seldom get in trouble if you let common sense be your guide and if you stick to the same definition of "commodity" and the associated "industry" in analyzing any problem.

The Shifting Legal Organization of Firms

The legal forms of business firms have changed with the times. When small-scale business was the rule, the individual proprietorship was dominant. This is a simple arrangement in which an individual puts up the money, starts his own business, runs it himself, and has the profits and losses to himself. There are still more individual proprietorships in the United States than any other form of business organization— some 9 million in all. Of these, 3 million are in agriculture, and most of the rest are small-scale retail concerns and service enterprises, such as cleaning establishments, filling stations, doctors, lawyers, and so on. Ninety-nine percent of all farms are still single-proprietorships, but the 1 percent that are corporations do about 20 percent of all the business. In wholesale and retail trade, the 82 percent of all firms that are single-proprietorships do only about 25 percent of the business; remember Sears and the big grocery chains.

As the need for larger capital funds increased, partnerships became popular. In these, two or more people assume joint proprietorship —usually joint provision of funds, joint management, and joint financial responsibility. This arrangement has substantial advantages over the single-proprietorship, but it still falls short of providing enough capital for really large-scale business operations. And it shares one serious drawback with the single-proprietorship: The partners are personally liable for all the debts of the business. Thus, in most cases, each partner is personally liable to an unlimited amount for the deeds of the other partners—a somewhat precarious position at best, and definitely not suited to drawing in funds from absentee investors. Partnerships are not very important in the United States today, though there are some 900,000 in existence. About half of them are in retailing; the rest are widely scattered.

The Modern Corporation

The modern corporation, which was conceived to meet the needs of large-scale business organization and to avoid the drawbacks of the other arrangements, has become the dominant form of American business enterprise. Although there are only about 1.5 million business corporations, they do the bulk of the nation's business, employ over 50 percent of the workers, account for about two-thirds of the nation's privately produced income, and pay out over 50 percent of the total national income. They do virtually all the business in public utilities, manufacturing, transportation, and finance; around half in trade and construction; but less than a quarter in services and agriculture.

The biggest modern corporations are truly Goliaths. In 1969, for example, the assets of the American Telephone and Telegraph Company (the world's largest business) were $44 billion. Those of Standard Oil of New Jersey and of General Motors were $17 and $15 billion, respectively. G.M.'s 1969 sales of $24 billion were larger than the entire gross national product of most of the world's nations. In all, in 1969 there were 115 nonfinancial corporations with sales over a billion dollars.

Many financial corporations (banks and insurance companies) are as large, though most of their assets consist mainly of investments in corporate and government securities and of direct loans to businesses and individuals. In 1969, the total assets of the Prudential Life Insurance Company, the largest insurance company, approached $28 billion. Those of the Bank of America, the biggest bank, were $25 billion.

Modern finance and industry are heavily con-centrated in the hands of large firms, as we shall see in Chapter 29. Nevertheless, there are still many more small firms than large ones, and big business has been only gradually increasing its share of the total market in manufacturing over recent decades. And if we include government and other nonprofit service industries (e.g., health and education), the share of the total national income produced by private corporations has declined gradually since hitting a peak of 55 percent in the mid-1950s.

What Are Corporations?

A corporation is an organization that exists as a "legal person" apart from the individuals who own and control it. A corporation may carry on business in its own name, enter into contracts, sue and be sued, own property, borrow and lend money. In general, it may as a business unit do all the things that any individual person may legally do in business.

For a long time, corporation charters specified the purpose of the corporation rather closely. Today, however, the corporation charters granted by most states are broad grants of power with only vague statements of corporate purposes that exercise little restraint over what corporations do or where they operate.

The main advantages of the corporate form of organization center around its financial arrangements. Briefly, they are the following:

1. Stockholders who invest money in corporations have no liability for the debts of the corporation; at worst, they can lose their original investment. Thus, corporations can obtain funds by selling "stock" and "bonds" to many investors who merely want to earn a return on their investments without further financial involvement. These advantages are spelled out below.

2. In a corporation, management is delegated to a board of directors elected by the stockholders. The directors in turn supervise the salaried officials who actually run the business. Thus, the individual stockholder need not concern himself with the details of managing the concern unless he wishes to—quite another

story from the continuous attention required in a single-proprietorship or partnership. Freedom to delegate power and responsibility to expert "managers" is essential to the operation of today's mammoth business enterprises.

3. Corporate securities are readily transferable. No matter how many individual stockholders die or lose interest in the corporation, the business can go on unaffected.

Financing Corporate Enterprise— Stocks and Bonds

Corporations obtain funds by selling "stocks" and "bonds" to savers. Individual investors who buy these securities may be part owners of the corporation, or they may simply lend money to the business. Stocks represent ownership in the corporation. Bonds represent money lent to the corporation by bondholders. There are many variations within each class, and at the margin they run together. The most important differences are: (1) the priority of security-owner's claim on the income of the enterprise; and (2) the owner's right to vote on personnel and corporate policy, and hence his power to control the corporation.

Common stockholders are the owners of a corporation. They own the company's stock. They have the right to elect the board of directors and hence to control the policies of the corporation. They are entitled to any income remaining after prior claims of creditors have been met. If the corporation is dissolved, they get all that remains (if anything) after everyone else has been paid. The common stockholders are the "residual claimants" to the corporation's income and property. They gain the most when income is high, and they are the first to lose when things go badly.

Profits paid out to stockholders are called "dividends." Although the profits of the business "belong" to the stockholders, often the corporation does not pay them all out, but instead reinvests part in the business. This is called "plowing back" earnings. Whether the net income is paid out or reinvested, however, it accrues to the benefit of stockholders, since reinvested earnings increase the value of the business.

Bondholders are creditors of the corporation. When corporations want to borrow large sums for long periods, they commonly issue bonds that are sold to people or institutions with funds to invest. Bonds are promises by the corporation to repay the funds to bondholders, at some specified future date with a set rate of interest.

If you own a bond, you are merely a creditor. You ordinarily have no voting power to elect directors and control the corporation's policies. You take less risk than the stockholders, since the interest on your bonds must be paid before they get any dividends. On the other hand, you will receive only your set rate of interest no matter how big profits are. Bondholders also have a prior claim on the assets of the corporation in case of liquidation. Some bonds provide that if a corporation fails to pay interest when due, voting power is automatically given to bondholders so that they can protect their interests by having a voice in directing the policies of the business.

Preferred stockholders have a position intermediate between common stockholders and bondholders. Preferred stock sometimes carries a vote; more often it does not. Typically, it has a set rate of dividends, say $6 per share, that must be paid before any dividends can be paid on the common stock. It also has priority over common stock in case of liquidation. But preferred stock stands behind bonds in priority of claim on income and assets.

Who Controls the Corporations?

Suppose you own 100 shares of General Electric stock. How much control do you have over how General Electric is run?

The answer is, for practical purposes, none. Not because anyone is cheating or hoodwinking you—least of all the G.E. management, which makes a continuous effort to keep stockholders informed and to get them interested in company affairs. It is because of a combination of factors. In the first place, you own only a tiny fraction of 1 percent of the company's stock.

Moreover, you don't and can't know much about the operations and internal policies of G.E., an $8 billion corporation producing thousands of products, most of them involving complex scientific processes and know-how. Besides, G.E. pays good dividends on your 100 shares, and that's what you bought them for. You haven't the slightest intention of spending a lot of money and time on an obviously fruitless trip all the way to Schenectady, New York, to try to tell the management how to run G.E., or to throw them out for a new management.

To be sure, even if you don't go to the annual stockholders' meeting, you are entitled to send a "proxy," a person of your choice whom you designate to vote for you. Before each annual meeting, you will receive from the management a proxy form, suggesting that you designate someone to vote for you in case you don't plan to be present. You may throw the proxy in the waste basket. If you do send it back, the chances are you'll designate the person suggested—partly because you don't know whom else to designate—thereby giving the present management the votes to reelect themselves.

Surprisingly enough, you will be acting like the typical stockholder when you do this, even though you assume there are many other interested "big" stockholders who are keeping a sharp eye on the operating management from a stockholder viewpoint. A.T. & T. now has 3 million stockholders, no one of whom owns as much as 1 percent of its stock. U.S. Steel has over 300,000 stockholders, Westinghouse over 175,000. On the other hand, a few well-to-do people and large investment institutions (like pension and trust funds) own large blocks of stock in many well-known companies.

This wide dispersion of stock ownership, coupled with the lethargy of most stockholders, goes far to explain the substantial control over most large corporations exercised by small groups of active stockholders, and often by the operating management "insiders" who may themselves own very little stock. This divorce of active control from ownership is a major development of modern business enterprise. It is probably inevitable in the large corporation. It

certainly does not provide a "democratic" government of corporation affairs in most cases, however good the intentions of the management on this score.

Of course, stockholder lethargy does not always exist. In some smaller companies, stockholders take an active interest in the conduct of the business. Even in large corporations, conflicts and sharp struggles for proxies sometimes occur, with control of the corporation at stake. But for the most part, minorities retain effective control without holding more than a small fraction of the voting stock. They are on the scene; most of the stockholders are far away and little interested.

Less than 10 percent of the voting stock is enough to assure working control of most major corporations. Indeed, most existing managements operate with less. A 1966 study on this point covered the largest 200 nonfinancial corporations in the United States. In 85 percent of the corporations, control was exercised by the management without material stock ownership. None of the corporations was directly controlled by a private family through ownership of over 50 percent of the stock; and in only 12 percent was direction exercised by a particular family or other special group of stockholders with a substantial share of the stock—say 20 to 50 percent. Cases where the "management" (directors and officers together) hold more than 5 percent of the company's common stock are the exception rather than the rule. By contrast, in 1929 only 44 percent of the top 200 companies were management-controlled, while 50 percent were controlled by families or other special groups through substantial blocks of stock holdings. Clearly, there has been a change in the way our major corporations are controlled.[1]

What proportion of the public owns corporation stock? By 1970 there were about 30 million individual stockholders in "publicly owned"

[1]The data are from R. J. Larner, "Ownership and Control in the 200 Largest Nonfinancial Corporations," *American Economic Review*, September, 1966. See also R. A. Gordon, *Business Leadership in the Large Corporation* (Washington, D.C.: The Brookings Institution, 1964), Chap. 2.

corporations, plus probably 1 to 2 million more in "privately owned" companies whose stock was held entirely by family or private control groups. The comparable total for 1955 was only 6 or 7 million.

Thus, perhaps 25 percent of all adults now own stock in business corporations. This is a large number, and many big companies have more stockholders than employees. But it is still a small fraction of the population. This fact, together with minority and "insider" control even in the most widely owned corporations, makes it clear that America's corporations are still largely controlled by a few people. Most of the 30 million stockholders are small owners. A large portion of all individually owned stock, as we shall see in the next section, is held by only a few thousand wealthy individuals and families. More important, huge blocks are increasingly held by financial institutions like trust, insurance, pension, and mutual funds, most of which so far have exercised little direct control over the management of the corporations whose stock they own.

Business Consolidations and Combinations

Many of today's big corporations are the result of consolidations and mergers of separate companies. Over the past century, business combination has been a persistent, though irregular, trend. Today, the once-popular business "trusts" of the 1800s have almost vanished from the scene. But "holding companies" remain a prevalent form for organizing financial control over large aggregations of capital. And mergers and consolidations of existing firms have reached record-breaking levels.

The Trusts

In a "trust," property is held by a trustee who has power to administer it and to dispense the income from it, as directed by the owners of the property. This scheme has often been used by people who want to have funds held safely for the benefit of their children, and for other simi-

lar purposes. The business trust was ordinarily a corporation formed to hold stocks in a number of other corporations. Owners of stock in the controlled corporations turned their securities over to the trustee corporation and received "trust certificates" on which dividends were paid. Technically, they remained owners of the stock, but their power to vote was transferred to the trustee organization which could then eliminate competition among the individual companies.

In the decade of the 1880s, the trusts grew rapidly. The most famous was the Standard Oil Company, under John D. Rockefeller. Some of the others were the whiskey, cordage, national lead, and sugar trusts.

The Holding Companies

The Sherman Antitrust Act of 1890 outlawed many trusts, and the holding company became the dominant tool for concentrating control.

A holding company is similar to a trust, with one primary difference. The trust simply holds the shares of the controlled companies as trustee; it does not own them outright. The holding company buys up stock in the companies it wants to control. As the name indicates, the holding company typically owns and holds securities of other corporations; it frequently owns no land, machinery, or other such operating property itself.

Figure 20–1 illustrates how a holding company might be used to concentrate control over a vast amount of capital with a minimum of investment. Suppose there are twelve railroads, A through L. Each is capitalized at $100 million, of which half is bonds, one-fourth is nonvoting preferred stock, and one-fourth is common stock. Suppose we want to get control of these railroads, but we don't have enough money to buy control of each. The maximum total investment required to get control of railroad A is just over $12.5 million, which is the value of half the voting stock. We would need the same amount for each of the other railroads, if we assume that half the common is actually needed to maintain control. Actually, a smaller amount would probably do.

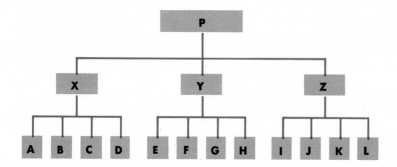

fig. 20–1

Holding companies provide a device for holding control over a large amount of corporate assets with a relatively small investment.

In this situation, we can form holding company X to buy up control of railroads A, B, C, and D. The total capital required is $50 million, since $12.5 million is needed to get control of each of the four roads. To raise this fund, suppose we sell $25 million of bonds, $12.5 million of preferred, and $12.5 million of common, in a new holding company X. Since only half the common stock is required to control company X, we need buy only $6.25 million of the common ourselves to hold control. We obtain the rest of the funds from the public. Then suppose we do the same with holding companies Y and Z to buy up control of railroads E, F, G, and H, and I, J, K, and L, respectively. We now have control of all twelve railroads, with a capital of $1.2 billion, through investing only $19 million, the amount necessary to control holding companies X, Y, and Z.

But we can go further. To control the three holding companies, about $19 million is necessary. Suppose we form another holding company, P, capitalized at $20 million, to raise these funds (as shown in the table). In forming company P, we issue $10 million of bonds, $5 million of preferred, and $5 million of common. Since only half the common is needed to control, we need put up only $2.5 million to retain control of P, with the remainder of the securities sold to the public. With this $2.5 million investment, we now have control over the entire $1.2 billion set of operating railroads. Since many stockholders fail to vote their holdings, we might be able to do the job with even less cash.

This hypothetical example may seem fantastic. As a matter of fact, it has historical parallels.

For example, in the 1930s a court found that Howard Hopson, a shrewd promoter, had managed to maintain control of the billion-dollar Associated Gas and Electric holding-company system with approximately $100,000 of voting stock. Holding companies in the public utilities and railroad fields attained almost unbelievable complexity. A diagram of the companies included in the famous billion-dollar Insull utility holding-company empire in the late 1920s would take up three or four of these pages in this size print. This was one of the most blatant cases of "insider" control and self-seeking. Small and large investors lost every cent of their investments in the Insull holding-com-

Total investment of $1.2 billion controlled by an investment of $2.5 million in the second-degree holding company, P:

Each operating company (A—L) has:	
Total capitalization of	$100,000,000
Bonds	50,000,000
Preferred stock	25,000,000
Common stock (voting)	25,000,000

Each "first-degree" holding company (X,Y,Z) has:	
Total capitalization of	$ 50,000,000
Bonds	25,000,000
Preferred stock	12,500,000
Common stock (voting)	12,500,000

The "second-degree" holding company (P) has:	
Total capitalization of	$ 20,000,000
Bonds	10,000,000
Preferred stock	5,000,000
Commond stock (voting)	5,000,000

pany securities in the great crash of the early 1930s. Such abuses led to the Public Utility Holding Company Act of 1935, which ordered dissolution of all such public-utility holding-company systems.

Such familiar companies as American Tobacco, U.S. Rubber, American Can, and U.S. Steel were established as holding companies around the turn of the century. Since then, however, the holding-company approach to consolidating economic control has waned outside of finance. Now direct mergers account for most intercorporate combinations. During the 1960s, major corporate mergers averaged over 1,500 annually; in 1969 the total was about 4,000. Some of these were mergers among firms in the same line of business, but increasingly they were "conglomerates"—firms cutting across many different lines of business, some of giant size. In the years 1968 to 1969, conglomerates accounted for 88 percent of all corporate mergers.

Financial Control Groups in the Modern Economy

By means of large investments coupled with extensive use of financial holding companies and other minority-control devices, a few powerful financial groups have attained great power over the corporate structure of the nation. Grouping the 50 largest financial corporations with the 200 largest nonfinancial, the National Resources Committee found in the late 1930s that out of total assets of $115 billion for the whole lot, the J. P. Morgan–First National Bank of New York group controlled over $30 billion, and that the Kuhn–Loeb investment banking interest controlled over $10 billion, primarily railroads. Of the purely family groups, the Rockefellers controlled over $6 billion; the Mellons over $3 billion, and the Du Ponts over $2.5 billion.

Although their form has changed, such large financial control groups continue. Often they operate through interlocking directorates, which usually include directors of banks and nonfinancial businesses. Today the dollar amounts are much larger, though the total economy has grown so fast that the proportion controlled by such groups is probably smaller than a half century ago. Modern tightly knit control groups tend to center in major cities— New York, Chicago, Pittsburgh, and so on— where large corporations are headquartered.[2]

A big, and growing, share of all corporate stock is held by financial institutions—pension funds, bank trust departments, mutual funds, insurance companies, and the like. They probably now hold around a third of the total. To date, such financial institutions have seldom intervened directly in corporate management. But as savings pile up in such institutions, their potential power becomes enormous, far exceeding that of even the wealthiest families. Even corporations' and unions' own pension funds, amounting to billions of dollars, are now being invested in corporation stocks, posing intriguing problems of future corporate control. Who should watch over the managers of these vast accumulations of funds?

Conclusion

Concentration of business management in the hands of a small number of professional, salaried managers who have little direct contact with most of the owners of business is one of the major developments of twentieth-century industrial society. There is a parallel concentration of financial control over the modern financial and industrial worlds by a small fraction of the population, although stock ownership is widespread among small holders. But the American economy is so huge that no one, nor any subgroup, of these can effectively control prices, wages, and production in more than small parts of the economy.

It would be a mistake, moreover, to infer from these facts that the "insiders" are using their operating control to the disadvantage of either

[2]See P. C. Dooley, "The Interlocking Directorate," *American Economic Review*, June, 1969. Further details on concentration of economic power are provided by Chapters 29 and 31.

other stockholders or consumers. On the contrary, many big business concerns are now managed both more efficiently and with a greater view to social welfare than they were under the direct control of owner-operators. If you have $5,000 invested in General Motors, it is doubtful that your interests would be better protected were Messrs. James Roche and Edward Cole (the top executives of G.M.) larger stockholders than they in fact are, or if you could personally participate in the management of the business. In Messrs. Roche and Cole you are hiring a much-admired team of experts in managing a huge corporation. In general, it seems safe to assume that their goals are roughly what yours would be (making profits, for example), and that they are more expert at achieving the objectives than you would be.

Similarly, today's growing group of professional managers seems more concerned with serving the public well than was the typical captain of industry a half century ago. Certainly the drive to "feather his nest" on a large scale is less dominant with the professional salaried manager, because he personally has so much less to gain from such behavior than did the more picturesque industrial tycoon. The earlier attitude of "the public be damned" may still exist in some companies, but it has been largely replaced by a more responsible attitude among the professional managers. Nor is there much evidence that the dominant large stockholders use these positions to exploit other stockholders or the public. Indeed, many investors prefer such companies as Du Pont and Alcoa partly because they want the watchful guidance given these companies by the Du Pont and Mellon families. And, whatever the abuses of big business over the years—and we shall see that there have been some—the research and mass production underlying the present spectacular American standard of living generally trace back to these same industrial giants, whose monopoly powers consumers may have grounds to fear.

There is little likelihood that the modern corporation, with its vast accumulations of capital and its professional management divorced from most stockholders, will soon disappear from the American scene. This raises a big problem for every thoughtful observer. How shall we obtain the obvious advantages offered by such huge industrial concerns while at the same time avoiding the excesses which the American public has typically feared from large concentrations of economic power? This is the problem we will come to in Chapters 30 and 31.

Review

CONCEPTS TO REMEMBER

The concepts in this chapter deal largely with institutions and legal forms. Be particularly sure that you understand the following:

entrepreneur
plant
firm
industry
individual proprietorship
partnership
corporation

common stock
"plowed-back" earnings
preferred stock
bond
trust
holding company
merger

APPENDIX *THE ELEMENTS OF BUSINESS ACCOUNTING*

In order to understand the workings of modern business, you need to know something about the elements of business accounting. Although the details of modern accounting are complex, its fundamentals are simple. Only a knowledge of these fundamentals is essential for our purposes.

The Balance Sheet. A balance sheet is a cross-section picture of the financial position of a firm at some given point of time. It is an instantaneous snapshot. A second sort of picture, discussed below, is an "income" or "profit-and-loss" statement that summarizes the firm's operations over some period of time, say a month or a year.

The balance sheet of any business rests on a fundamental equation. One side of the balance sheet shows what the business owns—its assets. Exactly corresponding to the value of these assets must be their ownership, which goes on the other side of the balance sheet. Obviously the two are always equal—the balance sheet always balances.

It is not easy to say just *who* "owns" the assets of the business. At the one extreme, the common stockholders are commonly considered the "residual owners"—that is, the ones who would get all the cash left over if the business were liquidated and its debts paid off. But this statement makes it clear that the various creditors of the business (for example, the bank that has loaned it funds or the supplier from

whom it has bought on credit) also have a claim on the assets. Such "creditors," to whom the business owes money, are at the other extreme of the claimants on the business' assets—they generally get their funds first. Bondholders, whose interest is contingent on satisfactory earnings, have a less-preferred claim on the assets; preferred stockholders are still further down the list. Plainly the line between "creditors" and "owners" is indistinct. The two groups shade into one another as a continuum of claimants on the business' assets.

But fundamentally, the balance sheet reflects the basic accounting equation (or identity) that assets = liabilities + net worth; or put the other way round, that net worth = assets — liabilities. That is, the business is worth to the stockholders what assets they would have left over if all the liabilities were paid off.

Table A is the balance sheet of a hypothetical Gadget Manufacturing Company, as of December 31, 1970. The left-hand side lists all the assets of the company—everything of value that it owns. The right-hand side lists all claims against these assets, broken down into two groups: first, its liabilities (what it owes); and second, its capital and surplus accounts (sometimes called its "net worth" or "proprietorship") on this date.

Assets. Once you see the basic equation underlying the balance sheet, most of its items are self-

table a

GADGET MANUFACTURING COMPANY

Balance Sheet, December 31, 1970

Assets			Liabilities and Proprietorship		
Current assets:			Current liabilities:		
Cash	$2,000,000		Accounts payable	$ 500,000	
U.S. Government securities	1,000,000		Accrued taxes	900,000	
Accounts receivable	2,000,000		Total current liabilities		$ 1,400,000
Inventories on hand	2,000,000		Bonds outstanding		3,000,000
Total current assets		$ 7,000,000	Capital and surplus:		
			Preferred stock outstanding	$1,000,000	
Fixed assets:			Common stock outstanding	2,000,000	
Investment in affiliated company		300,000	Surplus	3,100,000	
Plant and equipment		3,000,000	Total capital and surplus		6,100,000
Patents and goodwill		200,000			
Total		$10,500,000	Total		$10,500,000

explanatory. For convenience, assets are often arranged beginning with the most liquid (the most readily convertible into cash) and ending with the least liquid. Those assets that are readily convertible (say within one year) are grouped together as "current assets." The others are called "fixed assets."

The last asset calls for special explanation. Two hundred thousand dollars is the value attached, for accounting purposes, to the patents and goodwill accumulated by the company. Obviously this is an estimated figure, a more or less arbitrary valuation determined by the company's officials and accountants. The item is so obviously intangible, albeit of tremendous importance for such well-established products as Coca-Cola and Lucky Strike, that it has become accepted conservative business practice to place a very low value on it.[3]

Actually, this is only the most conspicuously estimated item; others are estimated too. The current value placed on plant and equipment, as we shall see, is particularly susceptible to the vagaries of managerial and accounting judgment, because the "current value" shown is generally nothing but the original cost of the assets less an estimated amount of depreciation.[4] Current assets can be valued somewhat more precisely; but only cash is clearly and inevitably "worth" exactly the figure at which it is carried.

Liabilities and Net Worth. The liability side seems a little more tricky at first glance. "Accounts payable" is easy—these are debts owed to suppliers. "Accrued taxes" represent tax liabilities that have been incurred but have not yet been paid. The liabilities that will come due within a year or so are grouped together to facilitate comparison with current assets. Such a comparison gives a quick picture of the short-run financial position of the company— its "current ratio."

"Capital and surplus" (net worth) consists of three items in this particular balance sheet. Part of the company's funds were obtained by sale of preferred, part by sale of common stock. The amounts shown for each are the "par," or "face," value of the stock outstanding. This value is presumably the amount for which the stock was originally sold, though this is not always so.[5] Surplus reflects profits of the company

that have not been paid out as dividends to stockholders.

Surplus is a peculiarly misleading word. It seems to connote an extra fund of cash lying around somewhere, but such is far from the case. Surplus is nothing but a formal accounting subitem as part of the general capital and surplus (net worth) category. It could just as well be lumped in with common stock; its segregation is only a matter of accounting custom. Total "capital and surplus" is nothing but a derived figure that follows from the values placed on assets, less the company's "liabilities," which may also be partly estimated. The fact that capital plus surplus on December 31, 1970, was $3,100,000 more than the paid-in value of the stock reflects past earnings not paid out in dividends.

There is no reason to suppose that these past profits now repose in the cash account. More likely, as part of the firm's regular operations, they have been "reinvested" or "plowed back" into inventory, plant and equipment, or some other assets. Or they may be reflected in a reduced level of the firm's liabilities. It is essential to understand that there is no direct correspondence between individual items on the two sides of the balance sheet. Any attempt to link up individual items directly will lead to fallacious conclusions.[6]

One other crucial warning, suggested above: The values placed on most assets, and hence on the capital and surplus group as well, are estimated values. If every one of these values is accurate, then the capital and surplus figure is accurate. But it by no means follows even then that every asset could be liquidated (sold) at the value at which it is carried on the balance sheet. Many of the items have a "going value" only as part of the operating concern. If the concern were to close down, it would be very doubtful whether many of the assets could be sold for the stated values (for example, semifinished gadgets in the inventory item). Going concerns are seldom completely liquidated even when they "go broke." Instead, they are often reorganized with the injection of new capital, or transferred to some other going concern, in order to maintain as much as possible of their going value.

The Income (Profit-and-loss) Statement. The income, or profit-and-loss, statement is the accoun-

---

[3]United States Steel and American Tobacco (Lucky Strike), for example, carry "goodwill and patents" at $1. Coca-Cola, on the other hand, carried goodwill, trademarks, formulae, and so on, at their cost—$45 million in 1969.

[4]See the discussion of "depreciation" charges in the following section.

[5]In the 1800s, it was common practice to set a fictitiously high value on the capital stock. Part of this stock was issued to original founders who provided not money but goods and services that were overvalued. The term "stock watering" in reference to this practice came from the then common

practice of inducing cattle to drink as much water as possible just before being marketed in order to increase their weight temporarily. Although supervisory control now exercised by the U.S. government Securities and Exchange Commission has made such watering very difficult for stocks "listed" on the major exchanges, it still can be done with unlisted stocks.

[6]The common argument that higher wages should be paid out of surpluses is an example of such an inadequate understanding of the elements of accounting.

tant's summary view of a firm's operation over some time period, say a year.

Table B shows a hypothetical income statement for the Gadget Manufacturing Company during the year ending December 31, 1971, the year following the balance sheet shown in Table A. This is a straightforward account of the gross income received during the year and what was done with it. The first part of the statement summarizes the income from[7] and expenses of operations; then separate items are included for other income and expenses; then federal income tax liability is deducted, which gives net profit after taxes for 1971.

The last part of the statement shows how the corporation allocates this profit. Only $500,000 is paid out as dividends. The other $600,000 is reinvested in the company. Capital and surplus (net worth) will now be $600,000 higher than if all the profits had been distributed to the stockholders. Common stockholders—the corporation's "owners"—may thus be as well off one way as the other. In one case, they get cash dividends; in the other, the value of their investment accumulates. Such plowing back of earnings has long been commonplace in American industry, and many industrial giants such as Eastman Kodak and Ford have grown almost entirely through reinvestment of earnings.

[7]The "net sales" item corresponds to the revenue from sales shown by the "demand curves" in the following chapters.

One warning about the profit-and-loss statement: The income and costs shown are not necessarily cash receipts and outlays; the profits are not necessarily cash profits. This distinction between cash transactions and accounting records is illustrated by the "materials" item. The materials used may have been purchased long before and already have been in inventory at the year's beginning. Or materials purchased during the year might have been double the $2,000,000 shown, if the firm had chosen to build up its inventories during the year. The $2,000,000 materials cost is the accounting figure for materials used, not for materials bought during the year.

The same point is well illustrated by the cost item "depreciation." Every engineer and accountant knows that plant and equipment depreciate. If a truck bought in 1970 is expected to last five years, after each year it has one year less life. At the end of five years it has only scrap value if the original estimates were accurate. The concern will not have to buy another truck until 1975, but if it does not figure the using up of the truck as a current expense it is obviously understating its costs and overstating its profits in the intervening years. If no current depreciation is charged, in 1975 the entire cost of the new truck would have to be charged against 1975 income. Hence, accountants "charge" depreciation annually, even though no cash outlay is involved. Thus, one-fifth of the value of the truck might be charged off as a current cost each year, or some more

table b		
GADGET MANUFACTURING COMPANY		
Income Statement for Year Ended December 31, 1971		
Net sales		$10,000,000
Manufacturing and selling costs:		
Materials	$2,000,000	
Labor cost	3,000,000	
Depreciation	500,000	
Maintenance and repairs	400,000	
Administrative and selling costs	1,400,000	
Taxes (other than income taxes)	600,000	7,900,000
Net profit from operations		2,100,000
Other income — interest and dividends		150,000
Less interest charges — on own bonds outstanding		50,000
Net income before federal income taxes		2,200,000
Provision for federal income taxes		1,100,000
Net income (or profit)		$ 1,100,000
Allocation of net income:		
Dividends on preferred stock		$ 100,000
Dividends on common stock		400,000
Increase in surplus		600,000

complicated depreciation formula might be used. There need be no cash expenditure that matches the depreciation shown.

Since cost and income items are accounting entries rather than cash transactions, obviously there is no necessary cash accumulation at the year's end equal to net profit earned during the year. The firm's cash may be higher or lower, depending on what has seemed to the managers the best use of available funds. Managers need only be sure they have cash on hand to meet their obligations, one of which is dividends when dividends are to be paid. In fact, dividends may be paid in years when no profits have been made. A.T. & T., for example, paid its regular cash dividend of $9 per year straight through the depression of the 1930s, even though annual profits fell well below $9. Capital and surplus, of course, declined by the excess of dividend payments over net profits.

Relation between Income Statement and Balance Sheet.

These observations tell us a good deal about the relation between the income statement and the balance sheet. Suppose now we draw up a balance sheet for the Gadget Company at the end of 1971—another spot picture, linked to the earlier one by our income statement.

During the year, assets have been continually used up in the production of current output; sales or other sources of funds have continually rebuilt the firm's assets. Since a net profit of $1,100,000 after taxes was made during 1971, total capital and surplus (net worth) was up by this amount before payment of dividends. As emphasized above, the increase in assets over the year may have come in cash, inventories, accounts receivable, or any other item—or there may have been a decrease in liabilities. All we know from the income statement is that, on balance, assets less liabilities are up $1,100,000.

This $1,100,000 is reduced to $600,000 by the payment of dividends. On the asset side the reduction is in the cash item when cash is paid out; in the capital and surplus accounts it is in the surplus item, which would have shown a steady increase through the year if monthly balance sheets had been made. This leaves the surplus account up $600,000 over December 31, 1970. Together, the income statement and balance sheets provide an overall accounting of the firm's financial operations and status for the period.

There is one other tricky spot. On the income statement, $500,000 depreciation was charged as a cost. This means that "plant and equipment" will be carried at only $2,500,000 in the December 31, 1970 balance sheet, $500,000 less than before. Actually, many firms would show the entire calculation on the balance sheet, thus:

Plant and equipment
Original cost $8,000,000
Less reserve for depreciation . 5,500,000

Net plant and equipment . . $2,500,000

---

table c

GADGET MANUFACTURING COMPANY

Balance Sheet, December 31, 1971

Assets			Liabilities and Proprietorship		
Current assets:			**Current liabilities:**		
Cash	$2,100,000		Accounts payable	$ 400,000	
U.S. government			Accrued taxes	800,000	
securities	1,200,000		Total current liabilities		$ 1,200,000
Accounts receivable	2,600,000				
Inventories on hand	2,000,000		Bonds outstanding		3,000,000
Total current assets		$ 7,900,000	Capital and surplus:		
			Preferred stock	$1,000,000	
Fixed assets:			Common stock	2,000,000	
Investment in affiliated			Surplus	3,700,000	
company	300,000		Total proprietorship		6,700,000
Plant and equipment	2,500,000		Total		$10,900,000
Patents and goodwill	200,000				
Total		$10,900,000			

Here the $5,500,000 is the total amount of depreciation charged against the original cost of the company's existing plant and equipment to date; $500,000 of it was charged in 1971. The "reserve for depreciation" is carried as a deduction item on the asset side of the statement. It is crucial to remember, however, that the reserve is not a cash fund set aside and available for expenditure. It is merely the summation of depreciation costs charged against assets in making profit-and-loss calculations to date. Neither is it necessarily reinvested in plant and equipment. Whether and how it is ultimately reinvested will depend largely on the profit expectations of the concern's officials.

Throughout this appendix, we have been primarily concerned with the mechanics of business accounting. Stop now and look for a moment at what this all means economically. During 1970, the Gadget Manufacturing Company had a good year. It made $1.1 million of profits on its total net worth (capital and surplus) of $6.1 million at the beginning of the year. This is around a 17 percent return on net investment, even after paying taxes. Before taxes, the return was more than twice as high. If you compare this rate of return with that of many leading American corporations, you will find that it looks very good.

How did this good year show up for the common stockholders? They collected $400,000 of dividends on $5.7 million stated net worth to the common stockholders. This would be a return of 7 percent on money invested in the stock at that price, a very high rate. We can safely assume that the price of the stock has been bid up in the market by investors to reflect this high rate of return. Although market prices of common stock fluctuate widely, depending on many circumstances, an effective dividend yield of 4 or 5 percent on good small companies would have been reasonable in 1971; this would imply a market price for the company's shares totaling $8 million to $10 million, on which the $400,000 dividends would amount to 4 to 5 percent return. The price per share would depend on the number of shares into which the company's capital stock had been divided. Suppose there were 200,000 shares (giving an original-issue, or "par," value of $10 per share). At current market prices we might expect these shares to be selling for perhaps $40 to $50 apiece ($8 million or $10 million total value divided by the 200,000 shares).

The stockholders also gained from the $600,000 of profits plowed back into the business, which show up on the December 31, 1971, balance sheet as $600,000 additional surplus in the "Capital and Surplus" section. It means that the company now has either that many more dollars' worth of assets, or that much less debt, or some combination of both. This condition should make it a more profitable company in the future, with larger total profit figures in the years ahead. And generally this fact would be reflected in a correspondingly high value for the company's stock on the market.

Review

CONCEPTS TO REMEMBER

This appendix has introduced several important new concepts. You will meet many of the following terms not only throughout the course but in the newspaper as well:

balance sheet	profit-and-loss statement
assets	income statement
liabilities	dividends
proprietorship	depreciation
capital	reinvested earnings
surplus	net worth

FOR ANALYSIS AND DISCUSSION

1. Suppose you are planning to set up a small shoe repair shop. Will you be better off with a single proprietorship, a partnership, or a corporation as your legal form of business? What are the main considerations involved in choosing?
2. Single proprietorships and partnerships predominate in retailing

and agriculture, while corporations dominate the manufacturing industries. How do you account for these differences? How can you reconcile the above statement with the great success of such retail corporate giants as A&P. and Sears, Roebuck?

3. Public-opinion polls repeatedly indicate that the majority of the public view common stocks as a speculative and somewhat uncertain investment. How do you account for this fact, in view of the great growth in the aggregate value and earnings of American corporations over the past century?

4. If you are a stockholder in General Motors, would you prefer to have earnings paid out to you as dividends or directly reinvested by the management? Why?

5. Should individual stockholders in business concerns take a more active part in the management of the concerns involved? Why or why not?

6. *(Based on the appendix)* Construct the profit-and-loss statement of the Amalgamated Widget Company for 1970 from the following data.

(000's omitted)

Materials used	$ 400
Net sales	2,500
Selling costs	150
Dividends on common stock	50
Provision for income taxes	180
Wages and salaries paid	400
Interest paid on bonds	20
Real estate taxes	50
Administrative costs	300
Depreciation	150
Dividends on preferred stock	10
Maintenance and repairs	200

7. *(Based on the appendix)* ABC Corporation reports the following data on its position as of December 31, 1971. Construct its balance sheet. Note that the figure for surplus is missing and must be computed.

(000's omitted)

Buildings and equipment	$ 400
Inventories on hand	200
Bonds outstanding	250
Cash	200
Accounts payable	250
Common stock	400
Accounts receivable	450
Goodwill	10
Surplus	
Reserve for taxes	60
Loan from bank	180
U.S. Government bonds	50

twenty-one

Consumers and Market Demand[1]

Individual Demand
Equilibrium of the Consumer
Market Demand—Signals to
Producers
Elasticity of Demand

In our economic system the businessman is in business to make profits—not exclusively, but surely as one of his major objectives. By and large, he can make profits only by producing goods and services that people want to buy— autos, radios, dry cleaning services, movies, lamp shades, and thousands of others. If there is no consumer who is willing and able to "lay cash on the barrelhead," the businessman is pretty much out of luck. Maybe the government will temporarily come to his rescue with a subsidy, or maybe he can keep going by using up his own invested capital. **But over the long pull, it is the customer who is willing and able to buy** who directs production in a private-enterprise economy.

He directs it by the way he spends his money —the way he allocates his income among different goods and services. If consumers want yellow electric refrigerators, the chances are good that yellow electric refrigerators will be produced. If consumers want to rent cars at airports, the rent-a-car agencies will prosper. If consumers develop a taste for artichokes, enterprising farmers will soon be raising artichokes to gain a profit by meeting that demand.

Consumer demand is the mainspring of economic activity. But never forget—it is the consumer with money to spend who counts! Many of us would like to have a Cadillac, and T-bone steak for dinner. But unless we have the money

[1]Note to instructors: This chapter has a mathematical appendix at the end of the book, for those who want to assign it.

and are willing to spend it on these objects, our desires have little significance for General Motors or the corner meat market.

Thus, your "vote" on what gets produced in a private-enterprise economy is largely determined by your income, unless you have accumulated funds to supplement your income. The mill hand has a lot less influence than the rich man, even though the former may be a virtuous, hardworking father of five needy children and the latter a ne'er-do-well who has inherited his money through no effort of his own. This is not to imply that virtue resides in poor rather than rich souls, but merely to emphasize that the private-enterprise economy responds to what people have to spend, not to who they are.

Figure 21–1 shows who had the buying power in 1969. It emphasizes again the huge buying power of the "middle class" in America. Nearly two-thirds of all families fell in the $5,000-$15,000 income group in 1969, and the average income of this group is steadily moving up.

But Figure 21–1 points up the extremes too. Ten million families, one family out of five, had an income below $3,500. These families received only 5 percent of total personal income —far less than their proportionate say over what gets produced for the market. At the other extreme, about 1 million families (2 percent of the total) received incomes over $22,000 and about 10 percent of all income, giving them a large leverage over what the system produces.

The consumer is a powerful, and sometimes capricious, monarch. Table 21–1 shows what he

table 21-1		
Percentage Breakdown of Consumer's Dollar		
Spending Category	1929	1969
Food and drink	28	21
Housing	14	15
Clothing	12	9
Household furnishings	6	6
Medical services	4	9
Recreation	3	9
Autos and parts	3	7

spends on some major categories in the American economy. He still spends the biggest chunk of his income on food, housing, and clothing. But the proportion spent on food and clothing has dropped sharply since 1929 (to only 30 percent as against 42). Spending on services (medicine, transportation, recreation, and the like) has grown rapidly as we have become richer and able to devote more of our incomes to "nonessentials."

You may have heard of "the economic man" —a mythical individual who carefully calculates just what he should buy before he spends each dollar, comparing the satisfactions obtainable from every conceivable expenditure before he parts with his cash. Most of us don't operate this way, and everyone knows it. A lot of our spending is based on habit, some on impulse, and so on.

Still, most of us face a real problem of how to allocate our incomes among far more goods and services than we are able to pay for. Perhaps the

fig. 21–1

In 1969, three-fifths of all families fell in the $5,000–14,600 income range and they received 54 percent of the national income. But the one-fifth receiving over $14,600 had a big chunk of total consumer spending power. (Source: U.S. Bureau of the Census.)

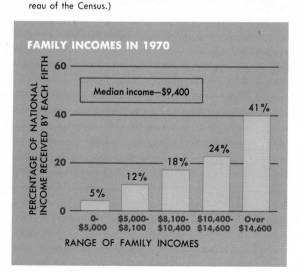

FAMILY INCOMES IN 1970

Median income—$9,400

PERCENTAGE OF NATIONAL INCOME RECEIVED BY EACH FIFTH

0-$5,000	$5,000-$8,100	$8,100-$10,400	$10,400-$14,600	Over $14,600
5%	12%	18%	24%	41%

RANGE OF FAMILY INCOMES

Aga Khan buys everything he wants without concern for what it costs. But most of us have to calculate how to divide up our incomes among the things we want to buy. You may devote most of your income to nourishing foods, college tuition, and durable clothes; I may spend most of mine on books, phonograph records, and airplane trips; our neighbor may prefer a dissolute life of wine, women, and song. Probably none of us is the human calculating machine envisaged in "the economic man," though the less money we have the greater is the pressure to act in a careful, calculating way.

The economist does not pass judgment on which pattern of expenditure is the proper one. Nor does he pretend to tell you how you should spend your income to lead a happier, healthier, more learned, or other kind of life. What he does do is assume that normally you spend your money on the things you want most. Thus, if you spent a dollar on the movies this afternoon, he takes that as evidence that you preferred going to the movies over buying a new necktie or paperback at the same price. If you stop and think about it, any other assumption leads to very strange results, as long as we assume freedom of individual action in spending incomes.[2]

These rather obvious observations become important later on when we try to evaluate how well the economic system works, since one of the main tests we will apply is: How well does the system respond to consumer wants? Unless we can assume that consumers' expenditures generally reflect what they want most, we will be at a loss for any measure of how well the system does in fact allocate its scarce productive resources to satisfying consumer wants. And later on, we shall need to look carefully at the importance of advertising in shaping consumer "wants," but disregard it for now.

[2]Some economists have worried about special difficulties in this connection. For example, suppose you buy a suit on the installment plan, and then decide you don't like the color. Is your payment of the ten-dollar installment due next month a fair measure of your preference then for the suit over other ten-dollar purchases? In this case, at the time of expenditure you don't have real freedom to allocate your income; the difficulty is avoided if you view the entire expenditure as being made at the time you buy the suit.

Individual Demand

Since consumer demand basically directs a private-enterprise system, it is important to define "demand" accurately at the outset. "Demand" is the schedule of amounts of any product that buyers will purchase at different prices during some stated time period. This definition takes some explaining, since it obviously isn't quite what the word means in everyday conversation.

What is your demand for sirloin steak? A little thought will tell you that this is a meaningless question until you ask, "At what price and over how long a time?" You'll surely buy more at fifty cents than at $1.00 a pound; and obviously you'll buy more in a year than in a week. Recognizing this need to specify prices and a time period, we might construct a hypothetical "schedule" of amounts you would buy at different prices during some particular time interval, say a week, as in Table 21–2. The table shows how much steak you will buy during the week at each price shown, assuming that other things (especially your income and the prices of other commodities) remain unchanged.

When we speak of your "demand" for steak, we mean this entire schedule of amounts that you would buy at various prices, other things equal. It is meaningless to say that your demand is one or three pounds a week. By "demand" we mean instead your entire state of mind as to how many pounds you would buy at

table 21-2	
Individual Demand for Sirloin Steak	
Price per Pound	Pounds Bought per Week
$1.20	0
1.00	1
.80	2
.60	2
.50	3
.40	4

different prices, other things remaining unchanged. In principle, we might list every possible price from zero to infinity. Table 21–2 pictures your demand only over the price range shown.

This state of mind (your demand) can be shown graphically, as in Figure 21–2. If we plot price on the vertical axis and pounds bought on the horizontal axis and connect the points, we can read off the resulting curve how many pounds you will buy during the week at any price shown, continuing the assumption of other things equal. Thus, at $1.20 you will buy no steak, at $1.00 you will buy one pound, and so on down the curve, just as the schedule above shows. If you haven't had much experience with graphs, it may be useful to practice plotting and reading off a number of such points.

Whether we use the schedule or plot the points graphically is a matter of convenience.

fig. 21–2

The demand curve shows how many pounds of steak this individual will buy in a week at different prices. He will buy more at lower than at higher prices.

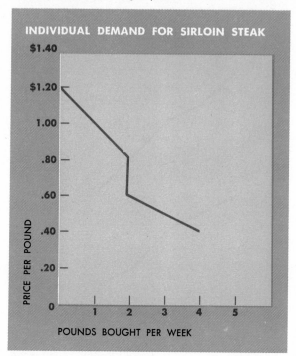

INDIVIDUAL DEMAND FOR SIRLOIN STEAK

They show the same thing. In making the graph, we merely join the plotted points. Since we knew only the points shown in the schedule, the readings from the curve between the points are only approximations. Only if the plotted points were very close together (say at one-cent intervals) would the curve properly be a continuous line, with the reading at every point meaningful and accurate. But most demand curves are shown as continuous lines because they are easier to work with that way and for our purposes are ordinarily good enough approximations between the points specifically plotted. And when we add together the demands of many people later, the bumps and corners in the individual-household curves are eliminated, so we tend to have smooth, continuous curves.

But watch out for one tricky point, whether you use schedules or graphs! Going back to your demand for steak, suppose the price is $1.00 and you are buying one pound per week. Now the local grocer lowers the price to eighty cents and you step up your weekly purchases to two pounds. **This is not a change in demand.** Your demand (your state of mind toward steak) has not changed. You have merely moved to a different point on your demand schedule, or curve, as a result of the lower price, as the original demand schedule or curve says you would do. This increased purchase at a lower price is merely a reflection of the downward slope of your demand curve.

Why Demand Curves Slope Downward

It seems obvious that you will buy more of anything at a low price than at a high one. Thus, on the kind of graph we have drawn, the demand curve will slope down, from northwest to southeast. Why? First, at a lower price for anything you can **afford** to buy more of it **out of any given income.** Second, at a lower price you are likely to **want** to buy more of it because it becomes relatively more attractive compared with other things you might spend your money on, **given unchanged prices of other things.** You will want to substitute sirloin for hamburger as their prices converge. And at low enough prices you may find new uses for sirloin—for example, feeding steak instead of dog biscuits to your dog. Thus, for both reasons, the quantity bought typically increases as the price falls.[3]

Looked at another way, the downward sloping demand curve says that you will be willing to pay a high price for a little steak each week, but the more steak you have the less you're willing to pay per additional pound to increase your weekly consumption still further. Many economists have associated this tendency with the decreasing satisfaction, or "utility," you get from each additional pound of steak you add to your weekly diet. We call it the law of diminishing marginal utility. The additional, or marginal, utility (or satisfaction) you obtain per unit falls as you get more units within the stated time period. Marginal utility is the want-satisfaction obtained from having one additional unit of some commodity per unit of time. Try applying the law to yourself—for oranges, movies, airplane trips home.

Changes in Demand

Remember that your "demand" for steak is your entire set of intentions about buying steak. These depend on how much income you have, your taste for steak compared with other things, and the relative prices of the alternatives you are considering. Now suppose that you get tired of steak and develop a taste for seafood. You will now buy less steak than before at each of the prices shown. This change in attitude is a change in demand. Your demand for steak has decreased.

[3]Three exceptions should be mentioned: (1) "Prestige goods," such as mink coats or exotic perfume, may be bought largely because their price is high. A decline in price might lead some persons to buy less as the goods come down into a price range open to the less-wealthy. (2) Some goods, called "inferior," are bought by poor people simply because they are cheap and useful. Potatoes in Ireland are the classic example. If the price of the food staple, potatoes, goes up, the Irish peasants may have to buy even more potatoes, which are still the cheapest food, because they have even less left than before to buy other more expensive foods. (3) When price drops, people may buy less because they expect the price to decline still further. But this is a dynamic effect that depends not on whether price is high or low but on the way it is changing.

A change in demand is illustrated easily by using demand curves. Begin with curve AA in Figure 21–3. Your lower demand for steak would be reflected in a new demand curve, to the left of, or below, the old curve. You will now buy only one pound of steak per week at sixty cents, and none at any higher price; only two pounds at fifty cents; and so on. This new, lower demand curve is shown in Figure 21–3 as curve BB, which is below AA. If something increases your demand for steak, say a fatter paycheck to finance such delicacies, the new, higher demand might be indicated by CC. A change in demand is shown by a move to another demand curve.

Why would your demand for beefsteak, or Buicks, or neckties change? There are three major reasons. First, your tastes may change. You simply decide you don't like beefsteak, or that now you prefer Buicks to other cars. Second, your income may change. As a beginning office

fig. 21–3

Curve CC shows an increase in demand from AA. Curve BB shows a decrease. How much steak would consumers buy at $1 per pound in each case?

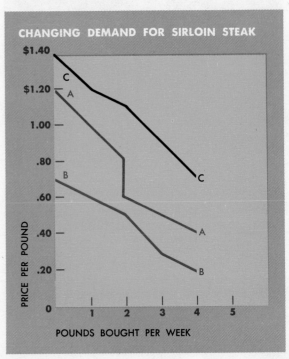

clerk, you may have to be satisfied with a secondhand Ford. With a doubled paycheck you may be in the Pontiac class. Third, changes in the availability and prices of other commodities may change your demand. If pork prices soar, your demand for steak may rise because you'll buy more steak than before now that pork costs more. Note that such changes in demand reflect changes in "other things" (your income and prices of other goods) which were previously being held unchanged.

It is important to distinguish between movements along the same demand curve and shifts in the curve itself. Many economic fallacies are perpetrated through slippery use of the concept of "demand." Try checking your own grasp with these questions: (1) Production of sheep rises, prices fall, and consumers buy more mutton. Is there an increase in the demand for mutton? (Hint: does the demand curve itself shift, or do customers merely buy more mutton on the same demand curve at lower prices?) (2) Chrysler comes out with a new, more powerful engine and Buick sales decline. Is there a drop in the demand for Buicks? (3) Philco raises the price of its TV sets and sales drop off. Is there a drop in demand? (4) Congress puts a new tax on movie admissions and movie attendance drops. Is there a drop in demand?[4]

Equilibrium of the Consumer

If we assume that consumers (households) generally try to maximize the utility (or satisfaction) they get by spending their incomes, two important propositions follow.

1. First, each consumer will change the pattern of goods and services he buys whenever he can get more utility by spending an extra dollar on item A rather than on item B. He will maximize his total utility when he allocates his income so that the marginal utility he receives from the last dollar spent on each item he buys is identical. When he so allocates his income, the consumer is "in equilibrium," in the sense that he is maximizing the satisfaction he can

obtain by spending his income. He has no incentive to change to another spending pattern.

This is only common sense. If the consumer can get a larger marginal utility by spending a dollar on A than on B, obviously he will spend it on A. Whenever the marginal utility of the last dollar spent on different commodities is unequal, he can increase his total utility by switching from the lower to the higher marginal utility commodities. If, to simplify, we assume that the price of every commodity is the same, he will so allocate his income as to obtain the same marginal utility from every commodity he buys. We could write this in equation form as follows: $MU_x = MU_y = MU_z$, and so on, where x, y, and z are the commodities bought.

If the prices of different commodities vary, as they do in actual life, the consumer in equilibrium would not expect to get the same marginal utility from each commodity, but only from the last dollar spent on each commodity. It would be nonsense to think of so allocating your income as to obtain the same marginal utility from a movie and an automobile. But if we divide the marginal utility from each by the price of each, then we have made them comparable. Then we can state our central proposition again: For the consumer to be in equilibrium, the marginal utility of the last dollar spent on each commodity must be equal. In equation form, the equilibrium condition is, therefore:

$$\frac{MU_x}{P_x} = \frac{MU_y}{P_y} = \frac{MU_z}{P_z}, \text{ etc.},$$

where P is the price of each commodity.[5]

We can extend this reasoning to other uses of households' incomes. Clearly each household has another alternative—you may save part of your disposable income rather than spending it. To be in equilibrium, you must so allocate your

---

[4]Answers: To (1), no; (2), yes; (3), no; (4), no.

[5]Wouldn't this lead the consumer to allocate all his income to x instead of y or z, if x has the highest marginal utility? No, because of the law of diminishing marginal utility. Remember that the marginal utility obtained from an additional unit of each commodity will tend to decline as the consumer gets more of it in any time period. Thus, spending more dollars on x will produce diminishing marginal utility for x, and will generally keep the consumer from switching all his expenditures to x (i.e., to any one commodity).

income between saving and spending that the marginal utility obtained from a dollar saved is equal to that obtained from a dollar spent on each item you buy. Equating marginal utilities works for all uses of the dollars we have to spend or save.

2. When consumers spend their incomes this way, their demand curves for different products accurately reflect the relative marginal utilities they think they will obtain from different products they might buy. If *A* spends a dollar for a necktie rather than for a movie ticket, we can safely assume he prefers the tie to the movie. His preferences are reflected in his demand curves for the two products, and his demands will reflect to producers the relative values he places on neckties and movies.

This is an extremely important point, since in our system we rely largely on consumer demand to give signals to producers on what should be produced and in what quantities. If the system is to perform efficiently, it should allocate resources in accordance with these consumer demands. This test will be applied to different types of markets and economies in later chapters.

Some Applications

Consider three simple applications of this reasoning that consumers will always tend to move toward an equilibrium condition. First, suppose that all consumers are in equilibrium, as described above. Now consumers' tastes change and they desire more beefsteak relative to pork chops. At existing prices, consumers are now out of equilibrium, and they will switch their purchases from pork chops to steak. This increase in consumer demand for steak will both push up the price of steak and signal farmers to produce more beef, while the reverse action occurs for pork. A new consumer equilibrium will be reached when, at the new prices for beef and pork, the marginal utilities obtainable from a dollar spent on each are again equal.

A second application: Begin again with consumers in equilibrium, and now assume that a disastrous drought in Latin America drastically reduces the world's coffee supply. This will raise the price of coffee relative to the price of tea and other drinks. At the new price ratios, consumers will be out of equilibrium and will switch from buying coffee to buying more tea, until at the new relative prices the marginal utilities obtained from spending a dollar on each are roughly the same. Changes in relative prices have signaled changes in the relative costs of supplying coffee and tea, and consumers have changed their purchases of the two to reestablish a situation in which they maximize the utility obtainable from the incomes they have to spend.

A third application: When a consumer is in equilibrium he is usually receiving a "consumer surplus" on the commodities he buys. Figure 21–4 shows a typical downward sloping consumer demand curve, say for bananas. The market price is ten cents per banana, and this consumer buys five per week. But this demand curve shows he would have been willing to pay twenty cents for the first banana, seventeen cents for the second, and so on. He gets a "consumer's surplus" of utility on each of the first four bananas, since he has to pay only ten cents

fig. 21–4

The consumer pays only 50 cents (gray rectangle) for his 5 bananas, but his demand curve shows he would have been willing to pay more than 10 cents for each of the first 4. Thus the red triangle measures how much more he would have been willing to pay to get the total utility provided by 5 bananas, and hence measures the "consumer's surplus" he obtains free.

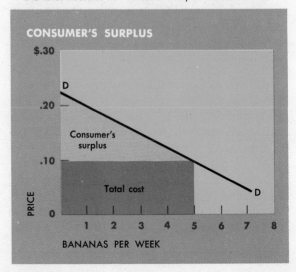

for each. The shaded area provides a measure of this consumer's surplus, if in fact the demand curve accurately reflects the marginal utility of each additional banana to this consumer. (Thought teaser: How much consumer's surplus do you get on each gallon of water you drink? On each cubic foot of air you breathe? Hint: the answer depends on the difference between total utility and marginal utility.)

Market Demand— Signals to Producers

Millions of consumers, each allocating his income so as to provide the greatest satisfaction to himself, provide the basic signals to producers telling what they want produced. The local department store isn't much concerned with your personal demand for shirts. But it is very much concerned with the aggregate market demand for shirts in its market territory. **Aggregate, or market, demand is the sum of all the individual demands in the market under consideration. Such market demand provides the main signal to producers as to what they should supply to meet consumers' wants, and thereby to maximize their own profits.**

Consider the market demand for sugar at the crossroads store of an isolated village with only three families. The demand schedules of the three families, and total demand, might look something like Table 21–3. The market demand schedule for sugar, as seen by the crossroads

grocer, is the sum of the individual demands of his customers. It could be plotted on a graph just like the individual demands' schedule. The total-expenditures column shows the grocer's total weekly sales of sugar at different prices. (For the moment, disregard the right-hand column.)

Note that if these individuals' demand schedules can be taken as indicators of the marginal utility consumers attach to an additional dollar's worth of sugar at different prices, then the market demand schedule provides an effective signal to producers of the relative importance attached by these consumers to getting more pounds of sugar at different prices (given their incomes and the prices of other products). And similar demand schedules exist for other products. All these demand schedules together represent the total set of signals from consumers to producers about how much consumers want of each product at each price.

Consider the entire national market demand for some commodity, say carrots. What determines the national demand for carrots? Five major factors determine the national demand (schedule, or curve,) for any commodity.

1. Demand will depend on the tastes (preferences) of all consumer units in the country— here, for carrots vis-à-vis other goods and services.

2. Demand will depend on the size of the population. Since the national demand for carrots is simply a summation of the individual

table 21-3

Crossroads Demand for Sugar

| Price per Pound | Purchases per Week by: | | | | | |
	A	B	C	All Three	Expenditures	Demand
20¢	3 lb	1 lb	2 lb	6 lb	$1.20	Elastic
15¢	4 lb	2 lb	4 lb	10 lb	1.50	Unitary
10¢	6 lb	3 lb	6 lb	15 lb	1.50	Inelastic
5¢	6 lb	4 lb	7 lb	17 lb	.85	

household demands, clearly the amount demanded at any given price will increase as the number of households increases.

3. Demand will depend on the level of income of households. This reemphasizes the central point above, that demand reflects the number of dollars that people have to spend on things they want, not just on their desires. The larger the total income of the American people is, the larger will be the national demand for carrots.

4. Demand will depend on the distribution of income among households. Rich and poor households demand different mixes of goods and services. For example, in a society with very unequal income distribution, we might expect there would be a large demand from the rich for Cadillacs, and a large demand from the poor for secondhand VWs. In a society with substantially equal income distribution, the automobile demand might be more concentrated in the middle-range cars.

5. Demand will depend on the prices of other commodities. The demand for butter will fall if the price of margarine (a close substitute) declines. The demand for gasoline will rise if the price of automobiles falls, inducing more people to buy automobiles, since gasoline is demanded as a complement to automobiles.

These five factors determine the demand (schedule or curve) for any commodity. Given this demand curve, a sixth proposition tells us how many carrots will be demanded at different prices:

6. The quantity demanded will depend on the price of the commodity in question (carrots). Other things being equal, the higher the price of carrots, the fewer will be bought. But note that this response of quantity bought to different prices of carrots is a movement along the demand curve for carrots, not a shift in the curve. The demand (curve or schedule) for carrots is determined by the five forces listed above.

The market system is an impressive device for channeling to producers the preferences of millions of different consumers. But remember that its effectiveness rests on the presumption that the demand curves do truly represent consumer preferences. Sometimes they don't, as we shall see later. If, for example, advertising should convince John Jones to buy (demand) something he hadn't previously wanted, does Jones's new demand curve truly reflect his wants? Critics of modern advertising say "no"; consumers are led to buy things they neither really want nor need. Defenders say that if a consumer spends his money without compulsion, that's the best measure we have of what he really wants, however the wants were originally established. More on this issue in Chapter 28; here the important thing is to see the critical role of market demands as signals to producers under our system, and the importance therefore that they be true signals.

Elasticity of Demand [6]

The preceding sections say the most important things about individual and market demands as signals from consumers to producers. But demands for individual products vary widely, and it is useful to be able to describe some of these differences precisely in analyzing how the economic system does respond to changing consumer demands.

Salt provides an interesting example. Suppose ordinary table salt sells for ten cents a pound and you use about a pound a month. If the price goes up to fifteen cents, how much less salt will you use? Probably no less at all. Unsalted beans and potatoes don't taste very good, and the fraction of a cent saved each day by not salting your food is trivial compared with the better taste of flavored cooking.

This is a case where quantity bought responds very little, or not at all, to price changes. Plotted on a graph, the demand curve for table salt at the local grocery store would be substantially vertical over the ten-to-fifteen cent price

[6]Mathematical Appendix III at the end of the book provides a precise mathematical statement of demand elasticity, which may be helpful to students who think readily in mathematical terms. Ordinarily, the appendix will be most useful *after* you have read the remainder of the chapter.

range. Try drawing it. We say that the demand for table salt is very "inelastic" over this price range. With a change in price, there is very little response, or stretch, in the quantity bought.

At the other extreme, take your demand for beefsteak at the local A&P if you are substantially indifferent about whether you eat beef or pork. Suppose beef has been $1.00 a pound but rises to $1.25 while other prices remain unchanged. The chances are you will cut back your steak purchases sharply and substitute pork. Here your demand for steak would be highly "elastic." In your purchases there would be a great response to the increase in the price of beef.

Loosely, "elasticity" is a measure that tells how much the amount bought will change in response to a change in price. Thus, elasticity of demand is a measure of the responsiveness of quantity bought to changes in price. (A more precise definition will be given on page 319.) Elasticity is one characteristic of any given demand curve or schedule. To say a given demand is elastic or inelastic is merely to describe it, just as you might describe your next-door neighbor as tall or short.[7]

For an illustration, look back at the last column of Table 21–3. A 25 percent price cut from twenty to fifteen cents a pound for sugar led to a 67 percent increase in sales—from six to ten pounds a week. Obviously the demand over this price range is quite elastic, since a relatively small price cut led to a relatively big increase in quantity bought. But a 50 percent price cut from ten to five cents a pound induced only a relatively small (13 percent) increase in quantity sold. Over this ten to five cent price range the crossroads demand for sugar is inelastic.

This example illustrates what we mean by elasticity. It also illustrates that the same de-

[7]Strictly, we should call this concept "price elasticity of demand." There is a related concept, "income elasticity of demand," that measures the response of quantity bought to a change in income received. However, throughout this book we shall use "elasticity" to mean "price elasticity." At a more advanced level, we can also speak of "cross-elasticity" of demand. This is the percentage change in the amount of product *A* that will be bought in response to a given percentage change in the price of product *B*.

mand curve may be elastic in some price ranges and inelastic in others. In most cases, it is not correct to speak of a demand curve as elastic or inelastic as a whole. You need to specify at what price or prices.

Total Revenue and Elasticity of Demand

The concept of demand elasticity helps us to predict what effect price changes will have on total expenditure for a commodity. Look again at the last column of Table 21–3. It's obvious that the crossroads storekeeper would be foolish to cut the price of sugar from ten cents to five cents. Although he would sell more sugar, his total revenue on sugar would decrease by almost 50 percent, because the quantity bought would rise very little in comparison with the big percentage cut in price where demand is highly inelastic. On the other hand, a price cut from twenty to fifteen cents might make more sense, since this change in the elastic demand range would bring an increase in total revenue.

By now, if you're reasonably good at figures, you will have seen that one measure of elasticity is what happens to total revenue when price changes. Specifically, if demand is inelastic, total expenditures on a commodity will change in the same direction as a change in price. If demand is elastic, total expenditures will change in the opposite direction from a change in price. Examine the reasoning.

1. **Inelastic Demand—Total Revenue Moves in the Same Direction as Price.** When the crossroads grocer cuts his sugar price from ten to five cents, he takes 50 percent less for each pound of sugar. Yet he sells only 13 percent more pounds. Obviously the volume increase, with such inelastic demand, is not great enough to offset the lower price per pound sold. Total revenue drops with a cut in price. Now reverse the process over the same price range. Suppose he raises the price from five to ten cents. Here he will get 100 percent more per pound and sales will drop by only two pounds, about 12 percent. Clearly, total revenue will increase. It will move in the same direction as the price

change, since demand is unresponsive—inelastic. The change in amount bought is not enough to offset the effect of the change in price in either direction.[8]

2. *Elastic Demand—Total Revenue Moves in the Opposite Direction from Price.* Now look at what happens when he cuts the price from twenty to fifteen cents. Although he gets 25 percent less per pound, he sells 50 percent more pounds. Total revenue increases, since the increased sales volume more than offsets the decrease in price. Demand is elastic. Reverse the process over the same price range and you will see again that total revenue moves in the opposite direction. Demand is elastic.

3. *Unit Elasticity—Total Revenue Is Unaffected by Price Changes.* The borderline case between elastic and inelastic demand is called "unit" elasticity. This occurs where an upward or downward shift of price is just offset by a proportional change in quantity bought, so that total revenue remains unchanged. The crossroads demand for sugar between ten and fifteen cents is a case in point. Total expenditure on sugar is identical at either price, since the shift in amount bought just offsets the change in price.

The Real-World Importance of Elasticity

The elasticity of demand for his product is a prime concern of every businessman, whether or not he uses that technical term. Consider two important real-world examples.

First, the farmer. Modern econometric studies show that the demand for most basic farm products is inelastic over the relevant price ranges. What does this mean if farmers all work hard, the weather cooperates, and a bumper crop rolls out? It means that the total revenue farmers get from selling their crops will be lower as a result of this bonanza, because the bigger crop can be sold only by cutting prices more than proportionately. This simple fact goes far to explain the continuing stream of government-sponsored crop-reduction plans, beginning with the New Deal AAA program, all aimed at raising total farm income. With inelastic demand, even a small crop restriction may induce a substantially higher price and more total revenue from crop sales.

Contrast this with the depression-period attempts of the railroads to increase their total revenues by raising passenger fares in the 1930s. Unfortunately for the railroads, the customers stayed away in droves. Either they stayed at home, or they traveled by bus or car. Demand turned out to be elastic and total revenue moved down, not up. Only when fares were **cut** did total revenue actually rise. Although this experience was also influenced by changing levels of national income, the impossibility of filling the coffers by raising price in an elastic-demand market is plain to see.

What Makes Demand Elastic or Inelastic?

Why people want what they want is beyond the realm of the economist. By and large, we take people's wants as given, leaving it up to the psychologist and others to explain this particular why. But we can say some things about circumstances where demand is likely to be elastic or inelastic. Briefly, demand is likely to be inelastic where (1) your outlay on the object is small, (2) your want for it is urgent, (3) good substitutes are unavailable, and (4) it is wanted jointly with some complementary item. For example, matches don't cost very much, and if you smoke a pipe or cigarettes you want them badly in case you don't have a functioning lighter. In general, wants are most urgent for goods and services for which no close substitutes are available. Nobody's want for Esso gasoline is likely

---

[8]Notice that the percentage change in price from ten to five cents is different from that from five to ten cents—50 percent compared with 100 percent. This is because the base with which we compared the five-cent change varies with the direction in which we are calculating. The difference really doesn't matter for our purposes, since the effect on total revenue will always give the right answer. (If you always take the percentage change on the bigger price or quantity figure you'll get around this directional problem.) Obviously, the discrepancy between the two ways of figuring percentage change will gradually vanish as we take smaller and smaller price intervals—for example, a price change between ninety-nine cents and $1.00. There is a more precise formula in the mathematical appendix.

to be terribly urgent as long as a similar grade of Gulf can be had for the same price across the street.

Conversely, demand is likely to be elastic where (1) the outlay involved bulks large in your total expenditures, (2) your want is not urgent, (3) close substitutes are available, (4) the commodity is durable or repairable, and (5) the commodity has multiple uses. The first three statements are reasonably obvious. You think a long time before you pay a 10 percent higher price for a hi-fi set, but not so long for a candy bar. You stop buying if the price of something you don't care much about goes up—say a certain brand of cornflakes. Other brands offer very similar products.

The points on durability and multiple uses take a little more thought. Autos are durable and repairable. At any given time, you can usually drive your old car a few thousand miles more; a new set of tires plus a motor tune-up costs a lot less than a new car. This alternative is likely to increase the elasticity of your demand for new cars. Lastly, any commodity that has multiple uses (like butter) is likely to have an elastic demand, because as price falls new uses and buyers may come into the market. At $1.00 a pound, butter is out of sight for any use at all by lots of families. Others can afford it on bread, but not on vegetables or for cooking. At fifty cents, the first group may start using butter on the dinner table, and the second may move butter on beans from the luxury to the everyday-use class. And so on for other uses, as the price falls further.

A Quantitative Measure of Elasticity

For some purposes it is useful to be able to say just how elastic or inelastic demand is. A ready measure can be worked out from the previous reasoning. Elasticity depends on the relative changes in quantity and price. If the percentage change in quantity bought (Q) is more than the percentage change in price (P), total revenue moves in the opposite direction from price; demand is elastic. Thus, we can easily get a numerical value for elasticity by the formula:

$$\text{Elasticity} = \frac{\%\ \text{change in } O}{\%\ \text{change in } P}$$

For example, if a cut in the price of steel ingots from $80 to $76 per ton (5 percent) leads to an increase in sales from 100 million to 101 million tons (1 percent), by inserting the 5 percent and 1 percent in the formula we get an elasticity of demand of .2. Any value less than 1 (unity) is called inelastic demand. Any value of more than 1 is called elastic demand. Unitary elasticity of demand means exactly offsetting changes in quantity and price. Go back and try out this approach on Table 21–3 to get the precise demand elasticities at different prices.[9]

Econometric estimates have been made of the elasticity of demand for many products, although many of these are very rough. Table 21–4 gives estimates for several common products (for price variations near their then prices). The section on what makes demand elastic or inelastic should help you explain the elasticities of the different products. Another study recently found the present demand elasticity for butter to be about 1.3, compared to a pre–

[9]Since price and quantity move in opposite directions, elasticity will always be a negative figure. The minus sign is customarily dropped in using elasticity measures. Strictly, our formula needs to be applied only to very small changes in price and quantity. For a more precise statement, see the mathematical appendix.

table 21-4

Estimated Elasticities of Demand*

Furs	2.6
Automobiles	1.5
Refrigerators	1.1
Local phone calls	1.0
Luggage	.8
Movie tickets	.4
Electric light bulbs	.3
Matches	0

*Treasury estimates presented before House Ways and Means Committee, 1960.

World War II estimate of about .6. Can you explain the difference? (Hint: consider possible substitutes then and now.)

Elasticity in Graphical Presentations

A perfectly inelastic demand curve would obviously be vertical. The same quantity would be bought at every price. An example might be your demand for insulin over a wide price range if you needed the insulin to keep alive. Highly elastic demand would be a nearly horizontal demand curve. Very small changes in price would lead to very large changes in the quantity bought. But in between these extremes, trying to read elasticity by the slope of a plotted demand curve is dangerous business. Look, for example, at the two charts in Figure 21–5. Both show the demand schedule seen by our old friend the crossroads grocer, but they use different horizontal and vertical scales. Exactly the same demand is shown on both.

Because the left-hand graph uses an extended horizontal scale, the demand curve is relatively flat throughout. Yet it is exactly the same demand as in the right-hand graph, and the elasticity at every point along it is identical with the corresponding points on the right-hand graph. Both curves are marked to show the elastic and inelastic areas. This example emphasizes the danger in trying to generalize that flat demand curves are elastic, whereas steep ones are inelastic. You have to remember that elasticity is a matter of relative (percentage) changes in price and quantity. Elasticity

changes continuously along a straight, diagonal demand curve. Check it for yourself if, as is likely, this statement seems to you intuitively wrong.[10]

Interacting Demands

If you buy a car, your demand for gasoline is pretty sure to increase. But, assuming that your total income stays unchanged, your demand for some other things (say bus rides) will drop.

The example illustrates the two main kinds of interrelationship among demands for different things: (1) complementary, or joint, and (2) substitutive, or competitive. When you buy the car, you take on a "complementary" demand for gasoline to run it. But now you don't need to ride the bus. Bus rides are "competitive" with cars in your demand pattern.

In the broadest sense, taking your income as given, the car must be a substitute for other expenditures lumped together. In this sense, all goods and services are competitive, or substitutive; since incomes are limited, any expenditure you make reduces your power to buy other things. But in many instances this effect is quite remote; for example, your car purchase may have little effect on your demand for potatoes. By contrast, the substitution of car rides for bus rides is very direct.

[10]For mathematicians: the curve which shows unitary elasticity at all points is a rectangular hyperbola. The equation is $xy = $ constant.

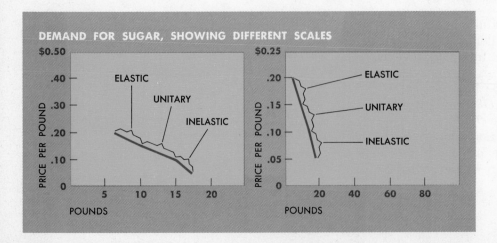

fig. 21–5

Trying to judge elasticity of demand by looking at the slope of a demand curve is tricky. These two curves show identical demands, plotted on different scales.

Review

CONCEPTS TO REMEMBER

This chapter has presented a string of important new analytical concepts that will be used repeatedly. Check to be sure you have them clearly in mind:

demand	elasticity of demand
individual and aggregate demand	elastic demand
the economic man	inelastic demand
marginal utility	competitive demands
total utility	complementary demands
equilibrium of consumer	unit elasticity

FOR ANALYSIS AND DISCUSSION

1. Calculate roughly how big a voice people in your own family's income group have in the allocation of the economy's resources. Does it seem to you to be a fair share? (Check the income data in Table 21-1.)
2. Do you act like the mythical "economic man" in allocating your income among alternative uses so as to maximize your satisfaction from it? If your answer is "no," are you saying that you are irrational?
3. Explain the concept of "equilibrium of the consumer." How useful does this concept seem to you in understanding consumer behavior? If you don't think it is useful, can you suggest a better one?
4. Since consumers' demand signals what is to be produced in America, it follows that consumers are responsible if our economy produces "wasteful" products like elaborate chrome trim on automobiles. Do you agree or disagree?
5. How elastic is *your* demand for the following, near the present price for each?

Required textbooks	Silk shantung suits
Gasoline	Lipstick
Airplane tickets home	Ford convertibles

   In each case, see if you can isolate the factors that make the elasticity what it is.
6. If the demand for wheat is inelastic, would a bumper crop raise or lower wheat farmers' total income?
7. What effect would a successful advertising campaign by the Campbell Company have on the elasticity of consumer demand for Campbell's tomato soup? Explain your answer.
8. Suppose unsold stocks of gasoline are piling up in the storage tanks of the major refineries. If you were regional sales director of one of the major companies, would you recommend a marked reduction in the filling-station price? How would you go about deciding?

321

Supply, Demand, and Market Prices

Chapter 4 provided a bird's-eye view of how producers respond to consumer demands in a private-enterprise, free-market economy. Now we need to examine in more detail the role of the marketplace and market prices in connecting consumers and producers. If you thought economics was going to be about "supply and demand," this is it.

The Role of the Market and Market Prices

In a loose way, it is easy to see how consumer demands get the goods and services produced that consumers want. If consumers buy more red barn paint, the immediate result is increased sales for paint stores, and these stores order more paint from wholesalers to replenish their stocks. The wholesalers in turn order more paint from the manufacturers. And the manufacturers, with joyous hearts, turn out more red barn paint, since their profits depend on producing and selling paint. The linkage may be jerky and imperfect, but each participant has an incentive to do his part—the profit incentive.

Sometimes the linkage between consumer and producer is direct. An example is the local laundry that washes your shirts. More often, consumer demand has to pass through several links before it hits the ultimate producer. An example is consumer demand for steel nails, which goes through at least the local hardware store and a wholesaler before it gets to, say, the

American Steel and Wire Company, which makes nails. But this is only part of the picture. American Steel and Wire in turn has to obtain iron ore, coal, and the other ingredients of steel, to say nothing of steel-making machinery, buildings for its operations, adding machines for its cost clerks, and stationery for its typists. Yet nails are a relatively simple commodity.

Try automobiles, or new houses, or air travel. If you chart the branching-out relationship that starts with consumer demand, you will soon find yourself rapidly running out of sheets of paper. The complex interdependence of the modern economic system surpasses the comprehension of even the most systematic human mind. Yet consumer demands must be relayed to producers through the intricate web if the system is really to turn out what consumers want to buy.

What ties all these myriad links together is a structure of markets and market prices. The grocer knows you want sugar when you walk into his store and buy five or ten pounds at the prevailing price. Similarly, there is a market that links grocers to wholesalers; one that links wholesalers and sugar refiners; one that links sugar refiners and sugar growers.

In each market, price acts as the adjuster between demand and supply. When you demand more, price tends to move up. When price rises, there is an increased incentive to produce more.[1] It is this interaction between demand, supply, and price that is the core of the self-adjusting mechanism of the private-enterprise system.

The world is far too complex to understand if we try looking at all the details at once. Thus, it is useful to concentrate first on some very simple cases, or models, of markets. The problem of understanding the real world is, then, one of using these models to help understand the more complex markets of the real world. In many respects, markets differ widely. But they all boil down to pretty much the same central problem of interaction between demand, supply, and price. A good understanding of the much-cited "law of supply and demand" is a powerful tool indeed for understanding how the modern economy works. Having looked at the consumer demand side, consider now the supply side of the picture.

Supply

Supply is analogous to demand. Supply is a schedule of amounts that will be offered for sale at different prices during some time period, other factors remaining unchanged. Supply can also be plotted on a curve with amounts on the horizontal axis and prices on the vertical one. But it differs from demand when it is plotted, since the supply curve ordinarily slopes uphill whereas the demand curve ordinarily slopes downhill. The upward slope of the supply curve reflects that fact that usually more units will be offered for sale at high than at low prices, in contrast to the reverse demand relationship.

Upward sloping supply curves may seem obvious to you. The higher the price, the greater will be the profit inducement to produce and sell more. Or they may seem anything but obvious. You may think of the economies of mass production and suspect that more units will be produced when demand increases, without any rise in price. This may, of course, be true under some circumstances, and sometimes—for example, in the automobile industry—to a significant extent.

The relation between firms' costs and the supply curves for their products is a major subject in economics. It is analyzed in detail in the following chapters. For the moment, take it on faith that most supply curves are flat or upward sloping, with the reasons to be examined later. And even if supply curves should turn out to be downward sloping in some cases, the type of interaction between supply, demand, and price described in the following pages would still be generally applicable and useful.

A simple example can show how supply

[1] This second statement is a more tricky proposition. Sometimes the entire response to increased consumer demand comes merely through more production at the same price. But usually, increased demand bids up the price, and this higher price helps in calling forth added supply to satisfy the increased demand. Chapters 23 to 25 provide a more thorough analysis of the relation between business costs and the goods they supply.

table 22-1

Supply Schedule for Milk

Price per Quart	Number of Quarts Supplied per Week by:			
	A	B	C	All
20 cents	50	50	20	120
15 cents	40	50	20	110
10 cents	40	40	0	80
5 cents	30	35	0	65

curves work. Suppose there are three dairy farms nearby. At various milk prices each will produce and offer different amounts for sale, as in Table 22–1. For the moment, we merely assume that each farmer will produce and offer more milk as the price rises.[2]

This supply schedule can be plotted on a graph just as the demand schedule was. Again putting price on the vertical axis and quantity on the horizontal one, we get the market supply curve shown in Figure 22–1.

[2]Farmer C is what some economists call a "marginal producer." He comes into the market only if the price rises to a relatively high level.

fig. 22–1

The supply curve shows how many quarts will be supplied each week at different prices.

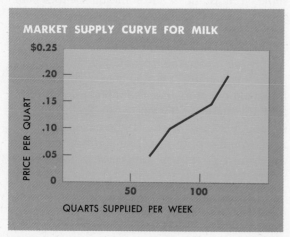

MARKET SUPPLY CURVE FOR MILK

PRICE PER QUART — QUARTS SUPPLIED PER WEEK

It is important to remember some of the same warnings on supply that apply to demand: (1) Supply is a schedule, not a single amount. Thus, more output at a higher price may be merely a movement to a new point on the supply schedule, not an increase in supply. A change in supply is a change in the schedule (a shift of the curve). (2) Supply has meaning only with reference to some time period. The period should always be specified. (3) A supply schedule or curve is always drawn on the assumption of "other things equal." Just what "other things" we hold constant will vary from case to case, depending partly on the time period involved. For a one-day period, the number of cows and the amount of mechanical equipment the farmer has must be taken as constants. If we're talking about supply per year, obviously such matters become variables. This would lead you to suspect that the supply curve per year might look quite different from the supply curve per day—and it does, as we shall see presently.

The Nationwide Supply of Carrots

Chapter 21 listed the major factors determining the national demand for carrots. We can list a similar set of factors controlling the nationwide supply of carrots. Remember that supply (like demand) is a schedule or curve, not simply an amount offered.

1. Supply depends on the costs of factors of production needed to produce that commodity (labor, raw materials, land, and so on). Other things equal, the lower the costs of the factors of production needed to produce any commodity are, the more of it firms will want to produce, because this would increase their profit or reduce their loss.

2. Supply depends on the state of technology. Other things equal, the greater the advances in technology related to producing any product are, the larger will be the supply of that commodity. For example, if a new invention decreases the costs of producing steel, other factors being the same more steel will be produced than before at any given price.

3. **Supply depends on the goals of business-men.** By and large, we assume that businessmen try to maximize their profits. In doing so, they try to maximize the difference between their costs and their sales revenues, and this action determines the supply of each of their products. But if a businessman decides that other goals are more important, for example promoting urban reconstruction or lessening injustices to minority groups, the supply curve of the firm's product will be different from what it would be if it were merely attempting to maximize profits.

4. **Supply depends on the prices of other (competing and complementary) commodities.** Suppose the demand for brussels sprouts rises while that for carrots remains unchanged, with a resulting increase in brussels sprouts prices relative to those of carrots. This will decrease the supply of carrots and increase that of brussels spouts as farmers shift their production to the more profitable commodity.

These four factors determine the supply of carrots, or any other commodity. Given this supply (schedule or curve), a fifth proposition tells us how many carrots will be produced and supplied at different prices:

5. **The quantity of carrots supplied will depend on the price of carrots.** Other things being equal, the higher the price of carrots, the larger the amount that will be supplied.

Elasticity of Supply

Supply can be elastic or inelastic, just like demand. This is true of both individual producers and market or nationwide supplies. If the amount put on the market is highly responsive to price changes, the supply is elastic. If the amount offered is little affected by price variations, the supply is inelastic. Except that the amount supplied and the price ordinarily move in the same direction, whereas for demand the amount demanded and the price move in opposite directions, the two concepts are parallel.

Elasticity of supply varies with the time period involved. Take an extreme case of inelastic supply first. Suppose you have a strawberry patch and a roadside stand, but no overnight

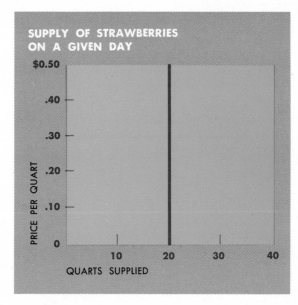

fig. 22–2

This chart shows completely inelastic supply. The same number of quarts is offered at any price shown.

refrigeration. If you picked twenty quarts this morning, you must sell them at whatever price you can get or let them spoil (neglecting the possibilities that you may eat them fresh yourself or preserve them). Thus your supply curve for the day may be completely inelastic—a vertical line at twenty quarts of strawberries. By the end of the day, if you have them left you're willing to sell your twenty quarts at any price from zero up—the higher the better, of course. Figure 22–2 pictures this simple assumption, where cost of production appears to play no role.

Now take a case at the other extreme. Suppose some simple commodity like lead pencils can be reproduced almost without limit at a certain cost, say three cents per pencil, merely by duplicating existing manufacturing facilities, materials, and workers. Given enough time to build new facilities, almost any given number of pencils will be produced for sale at a price of three cents or above. Thus, the supply curve might be completely elastic—a horizontal line, at three cents per pencil, as in Figure 22–3.

This case, like that of strawberries, is oversimplified; cost per pencil may not be quite con-

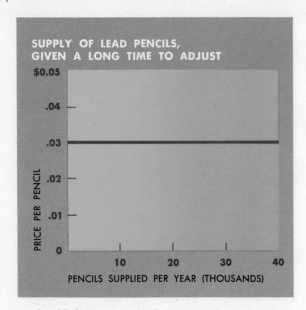

SUPPLY OF LEAD PENCILS, GIVEN A LONG TIME TO ADJUST

y-axis: PRICE PER PENCIL — $0.05, .04, .03, .02, .01, 0

x-axis: PENCILS SUPPLIED PER YEAR (THOUSANDS) — 10, 20, 30, 40

fig. 22-3

This chart shows infinitely elastic supply. Given a long time to adjust, any number of pencils can be produced for sale at three cents per pencil.

stant in the real world, and the resulting supply curve may not be perfectly flat. But both cases serve to indicate the variations that may prevail in the supply of different kinds of commodities, depending on the time period considered. Most cases and most time periods, of course, fall somewhere between these two extremes.

Supply, Demand, and Market Price

You may have visited the "wheat pit" at the Board of Trade in Chicago, which is one of the world's major wheat-trading markets. Here millions of bushels of wheat are bought and sold daily by a relatively small number of men, acting largely as dealers and agents for others. Suppose the supply and demand for wheat in the pit on some particular day are as shown in Table 22-2, and that these schedules are constant for the entire day.

Suppose that the first bid on this day is $1.50 a bushel for 1,000 bushels. It is readily filled, but it's clear that at this price there's going to be trouble, because buyers will demand 17 million

bushels, whereas sellers are willing to offer only 12 million bushels. Table 22-2 shows that lots of buyers are willing to pay more than $1.50 if they have to. And most of them soon discover they have to, because offerings are 5 million bushels short of demand at $1.50. We say there is an "excess demand" of 5 million bushels at $1.50. As buyers bid higher prices to get the wheat they want, the price will move up toward $2.00. As the price rises, those unwilling to pay the higher price will drop out and new sellers will come in, until at $2.00 the amount offered for sale just matches the amount demanded. There is no reason to suppose that the price will be bid higher this day, because everyone who is willing to pay $2.00 is getting his wheat and everyone who has wheat for sale at $2.00 sells it.

Try starting with a price of $3.00 to see whether that price could last long in this market. Where does the price stabilize?

This same analysis can be done graphically just as well. Figure 22-4 graphs these same demand and supply schedules. The curves intersect at a price of $2.00 with 14 million bushels traded. This is the only price at which the amount demanded just matches the amount supplied, and it is the price that will be reached through bargaining in the market. The reasoning is the same as with the schedules. Try any higher price, say $3.00, and you can see from Figure 22-4 that it can't last. At $3.00, 18 million bushels will be offered but only 8 million

table 22-2

Supply and Demand for Wheat, Chicago, on a Given Day

Bushels Offered (In Millions)	Price	Bushels Demanded (In Millions)
18	$3.00	8
16	2.50	11
14	2.00	14
12	1.50	17
10	1.00	20

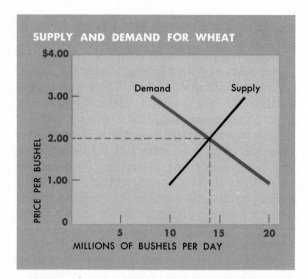

SUPPLY AND DEMAND FOR WHEAT

fig. 22–4

With these supply and demand curves, the equilibrium price will be $2, with 14 million bushels exchanged.

bushels demanded; there is an "excess supply" of 10 million bushels. Competition among sellers will push the price down. At any price higher than $2.00, there is excess supply. There will be too many sellers for the buyers, and sellers will shade their prices in order to find buyers. At any lower price, buyers won't be able to get the wheat they demand and will shade up the prices they offer.

Equilibrium Price and Market Equilibrium

When a price is established that just clears the market, economists call it an "equilibrium price." The amount offered just equals the amount demanded at that price. Price is in equilibrium when, with given demand and supply curves, it stays put at that level. At any other level, price will not be in equilibrium, since there will be excess supply or excess demand, and price will move up or down toward a level that will eliminate the excess supply or excess demand.

When an equilibrium price has been reached, with given demand and supply curves, we say the market is in equilibrium. At the prevailing price, all those who want to sell are selling and all those who want to buy are buying. There is neither excess supply nor excess demand. Unless either demand or supply changes, price will remain unchanged, as will the amount bought and sold each time period.

Consumer demands and producers' responses to those demands are meshed together through market adjustments toward equilibrium. Once a market has reached equilibrium, it has impersonally and automatically:

1. Reflected the wants of all consumers willing to spend their dollars in that market, weighting each want by the number of dollars that particular consumer will spend at different prices. If each consumer's demand schedule truly reflects the marginal utilities of different amounts of the product to him, the market has given him the largest utility obtainable for his dollars.

2. Led firms to produce as much of the product as consumers will buy, taking into account the costs of producing the commodity. These costs are reflected in the supply curve; the higher costs of production are, the less will be produced at each price offered by consumers.

Only when the market is in equilibrium are the combined wants of consumers and the costs of production meshed together so as to give consumers the most that can be obtained of the commodity, given the costs of producing it. And we can be reasonably sure this equilibrium accurately reflects the preferences of all the parties concerned, buyers and sellers, because the exchanges are voluntary. If any individual saw the purchase or sale as against his best interests, he would not have bought or sold at that price.

This evaluation of the results of market equilibrium is preliminary and oversimplified. But it's a useful first approximation to keep in mind as we look in more detail at the operation of different markets through the chapters to come.

Changes in Demand and Supply

Actually, of course, demand and supply seldom stay constant for long in an active market like the wheat pit, and one price may be hardly established before demand or supply changes and price slides up or down toward a new equilibrium level. Changes like this are easy to illustrate, as in Figure 22–5. Keeping the same supply curve as before, suppose that news of war sharply increases the demand for wheat on successive days. Common sense tells you that with constant supply and increased demand, the price will be bid up—and it is. On the second day, with increased demand D^1D^1, the price is bid up to $2.50 with 16 million bushels bought. Although the supply curve is constant, more wheat is supplied at the higher price. The result of the increased demand is both a higher price and more wheat traded. On the third day (demand D^2D^2) the price is still higher—up to $3.00 with 18 million bushels bought. The demand curve slides up the fixed-supply curve.

This example is useful as an exercise in analyzing the consequences of changing demand or supply curves. It is important also to point up the effective way in which market responses automatically link up demanders with suppliers and do so in a way that generates production and sales of just the "right" amount, given the demand and supply conditions specified.

Supply and Demand: Some Special Cases

Completely Inelastic Supply. Some extreme cases may help to clarify what is involved in market adjustments to different demand-and-supply relationships. Take first a case where the amount supplied is absolutely fixed. A favorite economists' example is that there are only four corners at State and Madison Streets in Chicago, sometimes called the busiest corner in the world. The supply curve for building space on this corner is thus completely inelastic —there's no more land available on the corner no matter how high land prices or rents may go. Suppose we graph the supply of land on this corner in square feet, and the demand *(DD)* for it on either a purchase or rental basis. The picture might look roughly like Figure 22–6, with annual rents in equilibrium at $1,000 per square foot.

Now suppose the demand for space on the corner increases. The demand curve moves up to D^1D^1. Property owners can now charge $1,100 per square foot. The amount of land rented is identical before and after the increase in demand. This outcome is very nice for the landowner, not so good for the consumer. But if demand falls, the full burden falls on the land-

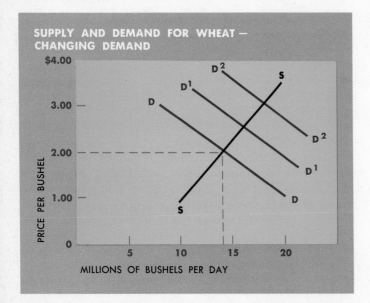

SUPPLY AND DEMAND FOR WHEAT — CHANGING DEMAND

MILLIONS OF BUSHELS PER DAY

PRICE PER BUSHEL

fig. 22–5

Increases in demand to D^1D^1 and D^2D^2 cause increases in both price and quantity traded. The new equilibrium with D^2D^2 involves a price of $3 and 18 million bushels exchanged daily.

owner. The price (rent) going to the supplier (landowner) is determined solely by the demand. Supply in this extreme case, and only in

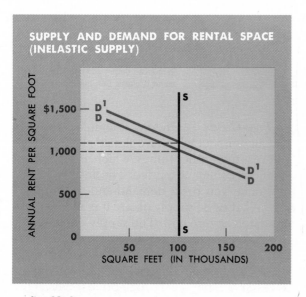

fig. 22–6

With completely inelastic supply, increased demand means merely a higher price.

fig. 22–7

With infinitely elastic supply, increased demand leads to more output with no increase in price.

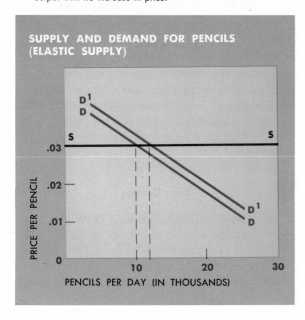

this case, has no active role in determining the price.

Completely Elastic Supply. Now take the other extreme—the pencil industry described before where the amount supplied could be increased at a constant cost merely by duplicating productive facilities. Given a long enough time period, the supply curve here would look perfectly flat, as in Figure 22–7. If *DD* is the demand, the price of pencils will be three cents and 10,000 per day will be made and sold. Suppose now that demand increases to D^1D^1. Here the price remains unchanged while production and sales rise to 12,000 daily. And this is clearly sensible. This is a case of "constant costs." Since more pencils can be produced at the same cost per pencil, increased demand will simply call forth more pencils without bidding up the price. This is the other extreme from the land-rent case above. Here consumers can be happy because rising demand brings more output without any rise in price. With the land, changing demand had no effect on the quantity sold, only on the price.

Most real-world cases lie between these two extremes—though many commodities approximate the pencil case, given a long time period for adjustment. If increased output can be obtained only by constructing more expensive factories, or by paying higher prices for raw materials and labor, the supply curve will slope upward. This is the case that economists call "increasing costs." If the increased output can be produced at the same cost per pencil, the long-run supply curve will be flat, as in the "constant-costs" case just above.

Try working out the results of increased demand in these cases. You will see that it makes a good deal of difference to you, the consumer, which kind of product you want more of. In one case, you get more at the same price; in the other, you get more only at a higher price. (With decreasing costs and a downward sloping supply curve, which we have temporarily ruled out, the consumer could be happier still, since then increased demand could mean more goods at a lower price.)

TAX EFFECTS WITH ELASTIC AND INELASTIC DEMAND

fig. 22–8

A new tax on whiskey is largely passed on to consumers if demand is inelastic (right-hand portion), but results mainly in reduced output and purchases if demand is elastic (left-hand portion).

An Example—The Effects of Taxes. Suppose we want to analyze the probable effects of imposing an additional $1.00 tax on each fifth of whiskey distilled for sale. Assume that the long-run supply curve before the new tax is the solid curve SS in Figure 22–8 (same in both halves). The left-hand diagram shows a highly elastic demand curve for whiskey, the right-hand diagram a highly inelastic one. Before the new tax the price is $5.00 per fifth, and 100,000 fifths are being sold weekly.

Now the government imposes the new tax. Consider its effects with the two different demand conditions. The tax raises the effective cost of producing whiskey by $1.00 per fifth; hence the supply curve moves up (to the left) by $1.00 at each level of output. Less will be produced at each selling price. S^1S^1 represents the new supply curve (after tax) in both halves of the diagram. But as supply is restricted, the results are very different with the two demand curves. With highly inelastic demand (right diagram), as price moves up consumers continue to buy nearly as much whiskey; the new equilibrium shows nearly as much whiskey produced and sold as before the tax, with the price to the consumer higher by nearly the full amount of the tax. With highly elastic demand (left diagram) the amount bought drops rapidly as price rises. The new after-tax equilibrium shows mainly a reduction in production and purchases, with the new price (including tax) only a little above the old $5.00 level. The main result is that consumers get less whiskey, while producers share $1 of the $5+ price with the government. Simple supply-and-demand analysis can produce highly illuminating results if we use it to examine particular markets.

"Free Goods." One last example: How is it that air, without which we should all die, is free, whereas most other things, which are much less essential, command a price? The answer is obvious, once you try a demand-and-supply analysis. What is the supply of air? It is substantially unlimited at zero cost. The supply curve would rise above the zero-cost line only at some very high-quantity figure for most real-world situations. Thus, even though we might be willing, if necessary, to pay a very high price for air, it just isn't necessary. Since the air available at zero cost is practically unlimited, any demand curve would cut the supply curve at a zero cost and price.

The Economics of Price Fixing

The law of supply and demand states that market price and quantity sold are determined by supply and demand under competitive conditions, such as in the wheat-market case above. But lots of times, people—labor unions, farmers, businessmen, congressmen—don't like the prices and quantities set by market demand and supply. And they want to do something about it. What then?

Price Ceilings

Most people don't like to pay high prices. When prices rise, the pressures mount on Congress and the president to hold them down. "How can I pay $1.00 a pound for butter and $125 a month rent for a poor apartment when my income is only $4,000 a year?" asks the mill hand. And he's not going to be very happy about getting an answer from the politicians in Washington that the law of supply and demand says it has to be that way. He wants something done, or he's easy picking for the other party next election.

So sometimes Congress enacts price ceilings. Suppose it slaps a price ceiling on butter below the equilibrium level. Suppose that the demand for and supply of butter are as shown in Figure 22–9. The equilibrium price would be about $1.00 a pound. But Congress has passed a law setting a maximum price of eighty cents.

At the legal price ceiling, clearly the amounts demanded and supplied don't match. There is excess demand; people want a lot more butter than they can buy. The amount demanded daily in this local market is about 2,200 pounds; that offered is only 1,600. At the ceiling price, excess demand is 600 pounds daily.

Who gets the butter? The price system is tied down—it can't allocate the butter by equilibrating supply and demand through higher prices.

"First come, first served" may be the answer. Housewives get the children off to school early and head for the grocer's. They stand in lines in the grocery store. This solution is not calculated to make anyone very happy, least of all the grocer who fast loses his friends when there isn't

fig. 22–9

When the government sets a legal maximum price below the market equilibrium price, there's trouble. More butter is demanded than is supplied at the artificially low price.

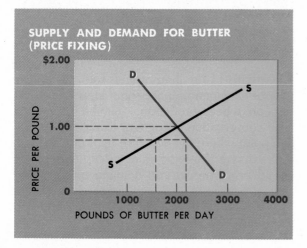

SUPPLY AND DEMAND FOR BUTTER
(PRICE FIXING)

PRICE PER POUND

POUNDS OF BUTTER PER DAY

enough to go around, and the working wives who can't do their shopping till evening.

In frustration, grocers may set up informal rationing systems of their own—say, only a half pound to a customer. Or they may decide to protect their regular customers, so they put away a few cases of butter for them. This is hard on wives who shop around, and disastrous for families that move to new neighborhoods.

If enough people get unhappy enough, the government may have to step in with a formal rationing plan, whereby the customer has to have a ration ticket as well as money to buy a pound of butter. Nobody is very happy about being rationed, and everybody complains about the red tape. Unless the government officials are both skillful and lucky, the number of ration tickets issued won't exactly match the supplies available, and a good many mix-ups can be counted on.

Lastly, the price system may sneak in the back door again and take over part of the equilibrating job outside the law. "Black markets" may develop. It's pretty hard for well-to-do consumers not to offer the corner grocer a little extra for an extra pound of butter. And it's pretty hard for the grocer, pinched between rising costs and fixed price ceilings, to refuse. Short of a regimented system like Hitler's Germany, it's hard to see how rigid price ceilings can be tightly enforced when excess demand is large. In World War II, such ceilings worked reasonably well in the United States, partly because of intense patriotic pressures and partly because the government gradually raised ceilings as pressures built up on various commodities. The surprising thing to most economists was not that black markets developed, but that the public's basic sense of fair play was so strong that black markets didn't blow the price-control system apart.

Whether the job is done by informal seller rationing, official government rationing, or black-market price increases, someone or something has to decide who is to get the butter when a price ceiling is imposed below the equilibrium market price. A price ceiling works no magic. It just transfers the equilibrating job to some other channel. You can't get rid of the basic supply-and-demand forces at work by passing a law.

Price Floors and Income Supports

Some people—usually sellers—worry because prices aren't high enough. Labor unions often try to set wages above free-market levels. Some business associations do the same thing with their prices. The government is a large-scale participant in the game of putting floors under prices above the free-market level; parity farm-support prices and minimum-wage legislation are two big examples.[3]

Supply and Demand for Wheat (Price Supports). Since the 1920s, the government has been supporting farm product prices to help the farmers. Suppose the government decrees that wheat shall not sell for less than $3.00 a bushel. But suppose the free-market price would be only $2.00, as pictured in Figure 22–10. It's clear that there is going to be a lot of unsold wheat around—excess supply at the $3.00 price is about 30 million bushels. Many buyers will pay $3.00, but a lot won't.

Suppose the government price floor is enforced and nobody undercuts the stated $3.00 price. Are wheat farmers better or worse off as a result? First, only about 80 million bushels will be bought. Another 30 million bushels are offered, and either the government will have to buy them up or strong price-cutting pressures will develop among the farmers with the unsold wheat. Second, our old friend elasticity-of-demand reenters. If demand is inelastic, total expenditures on wheat are larger at the higher price and total farm income is up (even though consumers get less wheat to eat). But if demand is elastic, the higher price leaves everyone worse off; then farmers get less total income from their wheat, and consumers get less wheat.

But even if demand is inelastic over the price range involved, this simple form of government price edict won't prove very satisfactory. If you

[3]This is not to say that parity price supports or minimum wage rates are always above free-market levels. They are not. But if they weren't intended to be at least part of the time, there would be little reason for their existence.

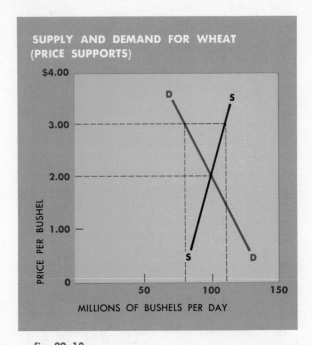

SUPPLY AND DEMAND FOR WHEAT (PRICE SUPPORTS)

fig. 22–10

When the government sets a minimum price higher than the market equilibrium price, there's also trouble. More is offered than customers will buy, so the government must step in to buy the surplus or to cut back production.

are one of the farmers with the millions of bushels of wheat that nobody bought, the higher total income of wheat farmers is small solace to you when you have no income at all. You want the government to help you, too.

So the governmental income-support program will probably take one of two basic courses. (1) The government may support the legal price through buying up the extra 30 million bushels of wheat. This would in effect move the total (private plus government) demand curve to the right, so the equilibrium price is $3.00 with 110 million bushels sold. Or (2) the government may impose some kind of restriction on wheat production (maybe through a "soil-conservation" program) to reduce supply to a point where the new free-market price will approximate the legal-edict price. This policy would bring supply and demand into equilibrium at a price of $3.00 with sales of 80 million bushels, by shifting the supply curve to the left. Combinations are of course possible.

In approach (1), the government ends up buying the 30 million bushels of wheat at $3.00 a bushel—at a cost of $90 million to the taxpayers. This result is nice for the farmers but not so nice for the taxpayers. Remember, too, where the consumer stands in this plan—with less wheat and a higher price for what he buys. Moreover, unless something changes, the government will keep on piling up wheat indefinitely.

In approach (2), this situation is avoided by requiring that 30 million fewer bushels of wheat are produced. Farmers will get more or less income, depending on the elasticity of demand. If the government merely required everybody to cut production by the required percentage, this would be the end of the matter. But actually, the government may well be expected (at least by some of the farmers) to pay those farmers who wanted to produce wheat but couldn't because of government restrictions. This was the case in the basic New Deal AAA farm programs through the 1930s, and it seems to be no less the case today. The government pays farmers for not producing. Here again the taxpayer picks up the bill for the subsidy paid to farmers for not producing the 30 million bushels of wheat. As under approach (1), consumers pay more and get fewer bushels of wheat. The government can keep the price up—if it's willing to eliminate excess supply by buying it up or by restricting output. But laws that fix prices above or below market-equilibrium levels without dealing with excess demand or supply soon face painful problems of which simple supply and demand analysis gives ample warning.

Summary: Supply, Demand, and Market Equilibrium

A surefire way to sound like an expert in economics is to observe sagely, "You can't repeal the law of supply and demand!" This remark is especially good if the argument is running against you, or you need a devastating blast against the political party in power.

The preceding pages should help to clarify both how meaningless such a statement is until it is carefully applied to the problem at hand, and how powerful an analytical tool supply-and-demand analysis can be. It doesn't provide ready-made answers to problems. Obviously the government and private groups can control market prices—they do it every day. But unless they recognize that they must do it ultimately through controlling either supply or demand, they're headed for some unhappy surprises.

Thus, supply-and-demand analysis provides a powerful tool in thinking through a wide range of economic problems. Market price plays a central role in compromising and meshing the multiple pressures exerted by demanders and suppliers in every market. And the concept of market equilibrium helps greatly to focus the way in which markets and market prices merge these conflicting interests toward a result that will be as nearly "optimal" for all as is feasible. This chapter provides the central tools for analyzing market forces at work. Over and over in the chapters ahead we shall be asking: What determines demand and supply in this market, how do they interact, and what is the equilibrium outcome toward which they move?

Review

CONCEPTS
TO
REMEMBER

Recheck your understanding of the important new concepts introduced in this chapter. They are:

market price	market equilibrium
supply	excess demand
supply curve	excess supply
elasticity of supply	constant costs
equilibrium price	increasing costs

**FOR ANALYSIS
AND DISCUSSION**

1. Is it demand or supply that primarily determines price? If your answer is, "different in different cases," give an example in which you would expect each to be the dominant force.
2. Explain carefully what is meant by saying that an equilibrium price "clears the market."
3. When demand is large, we can be sure the price of the commodity will be high. True or false? Why?
4. Why are diamonds so high-priced, when they serve for the most part only as decoration?
5. Are the factors determining the price of a Picasso painting the same as those determining the price of potatoes? Explain your answer.
6. Suppose that the demand for sugar is very inelastic and a new tax is imposed on sugar. Would the tax be passed on to consumers through higher prices? Compare this with a product for which the demand is highly elastic.
7. Suppose the demand for oleomargarine increases, without any corresponding increase in the supply. What effect, if any, would this have on the demand for butter?
8. How does elasticity of demand help to explain why historically governments often imposed a salt tax when they wanted to obtain more revenue?

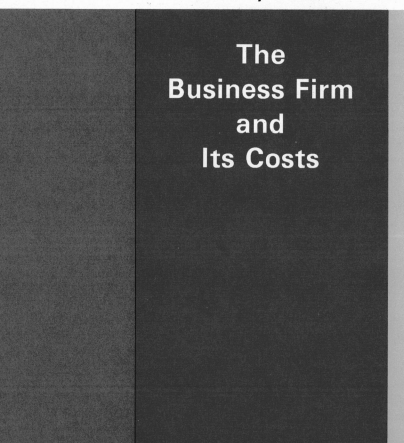

The
Business Firm
and
Its Costs

Why Worry about Costs?
What Are Costs?
Cost of Production and the Rate of Output
Unit-Cost Curves
"Short-Run" and "Long-Run" Views of Costs
How Big Is "Optimal"?
Social Costs and Private Costs
Appendix: Physical-Production Relationships Underlying Cost Curves

In a market economy, consumer demands direct what is produced. We turn now to look in detail at the way business firms respond to consumer demands—at the supply side of the demand and supply interaction.

General Motors supplies Chevrolets. You and I buy them. Westinghouse supplies light bulbs and we buy them. In most cases where a firm manufactures a physical product, wholesalers and retailers intervene between manufacturer and consumer. In others, consumers demand services rather than goods—for instance, shirt laundering and air travel.

Obviously, there are many different kinds of suppliers. To simplify, however, in the next few chapters we shall consider manufacturing firms as suppliers and consumers as demanders, with no intermediaries. This is unrealistic, but it

gives a simple first approximation to the working of the market system. And the goal here is to explain the main framework of how the economic system responds to changing consumer demands, changing cost conditions, and other such factors. You can see the main issues without getting enmeshed in the mass of detail that surrounds many markets in the real world.

Why Worry about Costs?

Why worry about costs? Because a businessman's costs will largely determine how much he will produce in response to different demands, and the lowest price at which he can sell and stay in business. If customers will only pay $1 for a widget and the minimum cost of producing a widget is $1.25, you don't need to be an expert economist to see that not many widgets will be produced. Thus, viewed fundamentally, costs are important because they exercise a restraint on production. If there were no costs in making a product, we could get unlimited supplies whenever we wanted them. But since it does cost something to produce almost everything, we can't expect everything we want free. And how far any business will go in producing what we want will depend on how much that article costs to produce relative to what we are willing to pay for it.

Business costs are important for another reason. Looked at as wages and salaries, rent, and interest payments, business costs are the incomes of workers and of resource owners. In explaining business costs, therefore, we are simultaneously explaining why most people receive the incomes they do.

This chapter considers the kinds of costs faced by business concerns. Chapter 24 then explains how these costs influence business production and pricing practices.

What Are Costs?

Since costs are so important, they deserve careful analysis. First, how do costs look to the businessman?

Back in the profit-and-loss statement on page 304, costs were broken down into materials, labor cost, depreciation on plant and equipment, maintenance and repairs, selling and administrative costs, taxes, and interest payments on borrowed funds. Every business has its own way of classifying costs, but these main categories show up in most such statements.

Most of these costs represent direct cash outlays—wages; payments for materials; tax payments; and so on. But it is important to remember that cash outlays are by no means identical with costs.

Depreciation is an example. Depreciation is merely a bookkeeping entry estimating how much of the value of plant and equipment has been used up in producing goods during a certain time period. It is not a cash outlay at all.

Cost of materials is another illustration. This item shows the cost of materials used to produce goods sold during the period. It may be more or less than the cost of materials bought during the period. For example, a business with big materials inventories might run a whole month without buying any materials. Yet it should obviously consider as costs the value of the materials used up from inventory during the month.

These examples emphasize another point. Many important business costs are necessarily estimated costs. What the accountant tries to do is to get the best possible approximation of the cost of producing one ton of steel or one quart of milk. But this is a more complex problem than it sounds, both because it is hard to allocate many types of cost accurately to individual units of output, and because cost per unit in most companies varies with the scale of output and the passage of time. The problem is especially acute when a company uses the same facilities, officials, and labor to produce a variety of products. For example, how much of the president's salary should be allocated to plows, harrows, and harvesters, respectively, in the International Harvester Company?

One other reminder about costs. The modern business has lots of costs not directly related to turning out its products. For example, as a practical matter, it must give to the community chest and keep its plant looking reasonably attractive if it wants to be a good citizen in the community—and most companies do. It probably has to contribute to health and retirement funds for its employees, in addition to direct wages. Partly these are just examples of managerial philanthropy, but competition also drives firms to make these expenditures, just as it drives them to pay the going wages and prices for their workers and materials.

Alternative Costs

The economist is interested in these calculations. But his concern with the overall allocation of resources in the economy leads him on to some further questions.

Thinking in "real" terms, the economist is

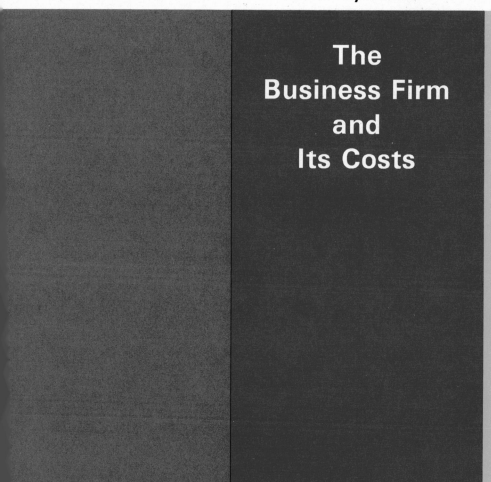

twenty-three

The Business Firm and Its Costs

Why Worry about Costs?
What Are Costs?
Cost of Production and the Rate of Output
Unit-Cost Curves
"Short-Run" and "Long-Run" Views of Costs
How Big Is "Optimal"?
Social Costs and Private Costs
Appendix: Physical-Production Relationships Underlying Cost Curves

In a market economy, consumer demands direct what is produced. We turn now to look in detail at the way business firms respond to consumer demands—at the supply side of the demand and supply interaction.

General Motors supplies Chevrolets. You and I buy them. Westinghouse supplies light bulbs and we buy them. In most cases where a firm manufactures a physical product, wholesalers and retailers intervene between manufacturer and consumer. In others, consumers demand services rather than goods—for instance, shirt laundering and air travel.

Obviously, there are many different kinds of suppliers. To simplify, however, in the next few chapters we shall consider manufacturing firms as suppliers and consumers as demanders, with no intermediaries. This is unrealistic, but it

gives a simple first approximation to the working of the market system. And the goal here is to explain the main framework of how the economic system responds to changing consumer demands, changing cost conditions, and other such factors. You can see the main issues without getting enmeshed in the mass of detail that surrounds many markets in the real world.

Why Worry about Costs?

Why worry about costs? Because a businessman's costs will largely determine how much he will produce in response to different demands, and the lowest price at which he can sell and stay in business. If customers will only pay $1 for a widget and the minimum cost of

335

producing a widget is $1.25, you don't need to be an expert economist to see that not many widgets will be produced. Thus, viewed fundamentally, costs are important because they exercise a restraint on production. If there were no costs in making a product, we could get unlimited supplies whenever we wanted them. But since it does cost something to produce almost everything, we can't expect everything we want free. And how far any business will go in producing what we want will depend on how much that article costs to produce relative to what we are willing to pay for it.

Business costs are important for another reason. Looked at as wages and salaries, rent, and interest payments, business costs are the incomes of workers and of resource owners. In explaining business costs, therefore, we are simultaneously explaining why most people receive the incomes they do.

This chapter considers the kinds of costs faced by business concerns. Chapter 24 then explains how these costs influence business production and pricing practices.

What Are Costs?

Since costs are so important, they deserve careful analysis. First, how do costs look to the businessman?

Back in the profit-and-loss statement on page 304, costs were broken down into materials, labor cost, depreciation on plant and equipment, maintenance and repairs, selling and administrative costs, taxes, and interest payments on borrowed funds. Every business has its own way of classifying costs, but these main categories show up in most such statements.

Most of these costs represent direct cash outlays—wages; payments for materials; tax payments; and so on. But it is important to remember that cash outlays are by no means identical with costs.

Depreciation is an example. Depreciation is merely a bookkeeping entry estimating how much of the value of plant and equipment has been used up in producing goods during a certain time period. It is not a cash outlay at all.

Cost of materials is another illustration. This item shows the cost of materials **used** to produce goods sold during the period. It may be more or less than the cost of materials **bought** during the period. For example, a business with big materials inventories might run a whole month without buying any materials. Yet it should obviously consider as costs the value of the materials used up from inventory during the month.

These examples emphasize another point. Many important business costs are necessarily **estimated** costs. What the accountant tries to do is to get the best possible approximation of the cost of producing one ton of steel or one quart of milk. But this is a more complex problem than it sounds, both because it is hard to allocate many types of cost accurately to individual units of output, and because cost per unit in most companies varies with the scale of output and the passage of time. The problem is especially acute when a company uses the same facilities, officials, and labor to produce a variety of products. For example, how much of the president's salary should be allocated to plows, harrows, and harvesters, respectively, in the International Harvester Company?

One other reminder about costs. The modern business has lots of costs not directly related to turning out its products. For example, as a practical matter, it must give to the community chest and keep its plant looking reasonably attractive if it wants to be a good citizen in the community—and most companies do. It probably has to contribute to health and retirement funds for its employees, in addition to direct wages. Partly these are just examples of managerial philanthropy, but competition also drives firms to make these expenditures, just as it drives them to pay the going wages and prices for their workers and materials.

Alternative Costs

The economist is interested in these calculations. But his concern with the overall allocation of resources in the economy leads him on to some further questions.

Thinking in "real" terms, the economist is

driven by the basic fact of scarcity to the conclusion that the "real" cost of producing anything is the alternatives that are foregone. For example, the real cost of producing an auto is the other commodities given up that might otherwise have been produced with the same steel, glass, rubber, and labor. The real cost is an "alternative cost"—the alternative uses of the resources that are given up when the resources are used in producing autos. Sometimes alternative cost is called "opportunity" cost.

This fact is most obvious in a war economy, when the guns-or-butter alternative stares us in the eye. We can make more tanks, but only at the cost of giving up trucks. The real cost of the tanks is the alternative use of steel and labor foregone—trucks, refrigerators, or other civilian hard goods. The same thing is true in a peacetime economy, unless unemployed resources are available. If we use our resources for one thing, we can't use them for another.

This concept of alternative, or opportunity, cost can be put into money terms. Thus, the cost of producing one TV set is the amount of money necessary to get the factors of production needed for the set away from alternative uses. For example, as a TV manufacturer, you have to pay enough for mechanics to get them away from auto and radar plants. You have to pay enough for copper wire to bid it away from telephone companies. And so it is for every resource you use. In economic terms, the total cost of the TV set is the amount necessary to bid all the required resources away from the strongest competing uses.

Accounting and Economic Costs

Use of an alternative-cost concept leads economists to different cost figures from the ones that businessmen and their accountants work with. These differences arise primarily because the economist includes several items that the accountant ordinarily doesn't consider as costs when he draws up his profit-and-loss statements.

A simple example is the independent corner grocer, who has bought a store with his own funds and runs it himself. In addition to the regular business costs in the profit-and-loss statement, the economist would say:

How about a return on your own investment and a salary for yourself? If you didn't have your money tied up in the store, you could be earning 5 percent on it in another investment. If you weren't working in the store, you could earn $5,000 a year working for Krogers. You ought to account as costs a 5 percent return on your investment and a $5,000 salary for yourself before you compute your profit for the year, because these reflect real alternatives that you're giving up when you stay in your business.

If the grocer does not include these costs and finds he's making a $4,000 annual "profit," he may think he's doing well—but actually he's kidding himself. The $4,000 doesn't even give him the salary he could earn working for someone else, much less the return he could get by doing that and investing his money somewhere else.

A similar, though less-obvious, situation is found in business corporations. Corporations pay salaries to their officers and employees, so there's no problem there. And they pay interest to their bondholders, which is considered a cost in computing profits. But what about the interest on the owners' (stockholders') investment, just as on the corner grocer's investment?

The usual accounting calculation of corporation profits omits the alternative cost of using the stockholders' capital in this firm rather than elsewhere. Profit is calculated before any dividends are paid to stockholders. The economist, however, includes in the firm's costs a reasonable rate of return on stockholders' investment (measuring the alternative return that is foregone elsewhere). He therefore considers as "economic profit" only the excess income over and above this basic alternative cost, because a reasonable rate of return is part of the cost required to keep funds invested in any business. Thus, part of dividends to stockholders should be counted as costs.[1]

The accountant's way of computing profits

---

[1] In economics, costs that show up in the usual accounting procedures are often called "explicit" costs, while alternative costs (like a return on stockholders' investment) which are not usually recorded in modern accounting are called "implicit" costs.

leads to some inconsistencies. Take two identical corporations, one financed by $1,000,000 of 4 percent bonds and $1,000,000 of stock, the other by $2,000,000 of stock. Suppose each earns $100,000 after all other costs are covered. Corporation A will now show an accounting profit of only $60,000, because the bondholders' interest takes $40,000 of the $100,000. Corporation B, identical except for financing arrangements, shows profits of $100,000. Not the least important consequence is the difference in income tax liabilities of the two substantially identical firms, since the law permits firms to deduct bond interest as a cost in calculating profits for income-tax liability, but not implicit return on stockholders' investment.

Through the rest of this book, we shall use the alternative-cost concept. Thus, costs of production will include the reasonable (or "normal") rate of return on investment necessary to keep the funds invested in any given concern rather than elsewhere. Costs will include the entrepreneur's salary if he is self-employed, and dividends equal to a normal return on capital invested by stockholders. Broadly, they will include all costs required to get and keep resources in the occupation under consideration. Most costs will be the same as those used by the accountant, but the differences noted above must be kept in mind. Especially, remember that the production-cost data and curves used here include a "normal" return on investment, if you want to avoid some dangerous pitfalls later on.

Cash vs. Economic Profits: A Managerial Application

A simple managerial example may help show the importance of these distinctions, as well as give you an impression of how basic economic analysis can help in day-to-day business. Suppose you're in business for yourself, doing miscellaneous repairs (carpentering, electrical wiring, and so on) at a minimum charge of $10 per call and $4 per hour additional after the first hour. Your only equipment is your family station wagon, the back end of which you have converted to carry your working tools. You are prepared to answer calls anywhere in your general area. You've spent $20 for an ad in the local paper and for a supply of mimeographed postcards mailed at random to names from the phone book.

After a month, you've collected a large amount of experience, considerable boredom waiting for the phone to ring, and $620. Have you made a profit? Should you stay in business?

The answer to the profit question hinges on what your costs have been. If you deduct the original $20 outlay, you have $600 left. Not bad for a summer month. But look again. There is clearly gas and oil for the station wagon. And wear and tear on the same, which may be appreciable from this use. Then, aside from any materials (for which you may have charged extra), there's the question of your own time.

Suppose gas and oil allocable to this work have cost $80. And you make a rough estimate of $50 a month extra depreciation on the car. That still leaves you $470. Is that more or less than a reasonable wage for your own full time and energy for the month? Here the concept of opportunity cost provides a guide to the answer. What could you hope to make elsewhere, doing work you consider about equally interesting, difficult, and convenient? If the answer is above $470, you've made a loss, even with $520 in the bank. If it's less than $470, you've made a profit, though maybe a very small one. Central concepts from economic analysis: the distinction between cash and income, and opportunity cost. Without them you're apt to pull a real business boner.

Cost of Production and the Rate of Output [2]

How do a business firm's costs vary with the amount it produces? Imagine a small company that produces a single product—say it assembles luxury-level hi-fi stereo sets. Suppose the company's only costs are raw materials, labor, depreciation on plant and equipment, mainte-

[2]The appendix to this chapter, "Physical Production Relationships Underlying Cost Curves," provides the logical foundation for this cost analysis. It should be assigned here by those instructors who wish a rigorous analytical foundation for this and the following chapter, but students can grasp the central issues in the text without it.

table 23-1

Fixed, Variable, and Total Costs

Output	Total Fixed Cost	Total Variable Cost	Total Cost
1	$1,000	$ 2,000	$ 3,000
2	1,000	2,500	3,500
3	1,000	3,000	4,000
4	1,000	4,000	5,000
5	1,000	5,000	6,000
6	1,000	6,600	7,600
7	1,000	10,000	11,000
8	1,000	16,000	17,000

nance, and return on stockholders' investment. Suppose further that, if we look at costs over the month ahead, we find that depreciation and a normal (implicit) return on stockholders' investment are "fixed" for the month—they go on whether the company operates at full capacity or part capacity, or shuts down. The other costs are "variable," depending on the company's rate of output.

Assume that the "fixed" costs amount to $1,000 per month, and that the "variable" costs vary with changes in output as in Table 23–1.

These same costs are plotted in Figure 23–1. Cost is shown on the vertical axis, output on the horizontal one. The fixed cost totals $1,000, the same no matter what output is produced. On top of this, we need to put total variable cost— zero at zero output, $2,000 for one set, $2,500 for two, and so on. The total-cost curve (top line) thus shows the sum of total fixed and total variable cost at each level of output.

It is easy to see that total cost does not rise at an even rate. It doesn't cost much more in total to produce two sets than one, or three than two. But as the firm gets up to six or seven sets per month, total cost begins to rise much more rapidly. It is obviously total variable cost that begins to shoot up. The reason may be that the company was set up with a capacity of only five or six sets a month, and to exceed this capacity involves expensive readjustments in equipment, hiring more workers or overtime labor, and other such special problems. Or there may be some other explanation. Nearly all plants see their variable costs shoot up if they try to produce beyond the plant's planned capacity.

Fixed, Variable, and Total Costs per Unit

The preceding data don't show costs per set produced, and you probably think of business output in terms of cost and selling price per unit. You may already have divided the total-cost figures by the number of stereo sets produced to see what the cost per set is at different levels of output. If you haven't, it's a sensible thing to do. The result is shown in Table 23–2. These are, of course, just hypothetical figures. But their general character is important, because in some ways they are typical of all such cost data.

Fixed cost per unit will always be a steadily decreasing series, because the constant total-fixed-cost figure (here $1,000) is divided by a steadily rising volume of output. This is what is commonly known as "spreading the overhead." The drop in fixed cost per unit is very rapid at

fig. 23–1

Total fixed cost is $1,000 at all outputs. Total variable cost rises as output increases. Total cost for any output is the sum of fixed and variable costs; it rises rapidly once the "capacity" of the plant is reached.

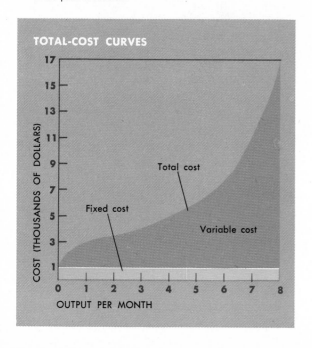

TOTAL-COST CURVES

COST (THOUSANDS OF DOLLARS)

Total cost

Fixed cost

Variable cost

OUTPUT PER MONTH

table 23-2

Fixed, Variable, and Total Costs per Unit

Output	Fixed Cost per Unit	Variable Cost per Unit	Total Cost per Unit
1	$1,000	$2,000	$3,000
2	500	1,250	1,750
3	333	1,000	1,333
4	250	1,000	1,250
5	200	1,000	1,200
6	167	1,100	1,267
7	143	1,430	1,573
8	125	2,000	2,125

first, but as volume grows the additional cost reduction per unit steadily decreases in importance.

Variable cost per unit will generally fall at the outset, then flatten out somewhat, and then rise again as plant "capacity" is approached. To produce one set, the company has to have labor and materials of all the types needed for the set. On the labor side, it will clearly be inefficient to try to call each type of skilled labor in just long enough to work on one set. If we try to use two or three jacks-of-all-trades, we get less-efficient work than by dividing the work up among experts on the various parts of the job. Similarly, it may be cheaper to buy materials in larger quantities than to buy just enough to produce one set per month. It's not efficient to produce only one or two sets a month.

At the other extreme, once the "capacity" for which the plant was planned has been reached, costs are likely to shoot up rapidly if we try to produce still more sets per month. "Capacity" is seldom an absolute limit in a plant. For example, steel plants may operate above 100 percent of capacity; rated capacity allows for an average amount of shut-down time for maintenance and repairs, which can be postponed temporarily. But expansion of output beyond plant "capacity" often means expensive overtime work, hiring of lower-skilled workers, more spoilage under pressure of speedup, and a variety of other such factors.

Thus, without going into details at the moment, it seems reasonable that with any given plant (which we have assumed) variable costs per unit will rise rapidly at some point beyond "capacity" output. Just when this point is reached depends, of course, on the individual firm. In many industries, variable costs per unit are apparently flat over wide ranges of output. In others, where small-scale operations are advantageous, increase in output beyond low levels may lead quickly to rising unit costs.

Total cost per unit is simply the sum of fixed cost per unit and variable cost per unit. Or it can be obtained by dividing total cost by the number of units produced. The decreasing fixed cost per unit will always pull down on total unit cost as output rises. At first, as long as both fixed and variable costs per unit are declining, clearly the total cost per unit is declining. But at some point total unit costs will begin to rise, often after a long flat area in which the fixed cost per unit declines slightly and the variable cost per unit is substantially constant or slightly rising. The rise in total unit cost will begin when variable cost per unit turns up more than enough to offset the downward pull of declining fixed costs per unit. This point is at the sixth unit in our hi-fi plant. Total unit cost is relatively stable over the output range of three to six units, with the minimum cost per unit at an output of five sets per month.

This simple example should warn you against one common fallacy—the idea that each firm has a cost of production for its product. In every firm, cost of production per unit varies with output. This is certain at the extremes of very low and above-capacity output. It often also occurs over the range of normal variation in operations.

A good many firms now use what they call "standard costs" in pricing their products and in keeping control over their production processes. A "standard cost" for our hi-fi set would be an estimate by our accountant and production man of how much it should cost to produce one set at a normal, or typical, rate of output. If we think of four sets monthly as about normal operation, our standard-cost figure would be $1,250 per set.

Such standard-cost estimates play a useful

role in modern industry. Many firms use them as a basis for setting prices, and we will meet them again in the chapters ahead. It is important, however, to remember that "standard cost" is only an estimate of unit cost at some selected level of output, not necessarily the minimum unit-cost level.

Unit-Cost Curves

All these per-unit-cost data can readily be plotted on graphs as cost curves. Figure 23–2 shows the per unit cost data for our hi-fi firm. The shape of the curves corresponds, of course, to the data. Fixed cost per unit falls steadily as the constant total cost is spread over more and more units. Variable cost per unit and total cost per unit are both U-shaped, for the reasons suggested above. In most firms, the *TUC* (total-unit-cost) curve is probably flatter than in this hypothetical case. That is, there is a wider range of output over which total cost per unit is substantially constant, between the low-output inefficiencies shown at the left of the graph and the above-capacity inefficiencies at the right. (For a large, real-world plant producing many units, the cost curves would be smooth and continuous, without the corners shown in the curves for our very small firm.)

Be sure you know just what the graph means. For example, at an output of five sets next month, the fixed cost per set will be $200 and the variable cost per unit $1,000, for a total of $1,200. This happens to be the lowest point on the total-unit-cost curve. It is called the "least-cost combination." It is the lowest cost at which these hi-fi sets can be made, given the existing plant and the firm's other commitments for the month ahead. This is the lowest price at which we can get resources away from alternative uses and still cover all costs.

"Short-Run" and "Long-Run" Views of Costs

Economists speak of the "short run" and the "long run." Time is an extremely important variable in the analysis of economic problems, and this distinction is an attempt to clarify the assumptions being made about the time period involved in any case. We mean by the "short run" any time period in which some costs (such as rent and interest on borrowed funds) are fixed and do not vary with changes in the firm's output. We mean by "long run" a time period long enough so that all costs become variable with changes in output. Thus, the distinction is an analytical one. In calendar time, the short run for one firm may be longer than a long run for another, depending on how long the cost commitments run in different cases.

Some examples will clarify this distinction.

fig. 23–2

Unit-cost curves are derived by dividing the corresponding total-cost curves by total output. Here fixed unit cost slopes downward continuously as the constant total fixed cost is spread over more units of output. Other curves are U-shaped.

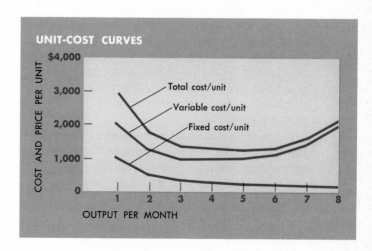

UNIT-COST CURVES

For our firm, next month is clearly a "short run." During that month certain costs are fixed no matter how many hi-fis we produce—depreciation on the factory building, for example. Given a longer time period, the existing plant will depreciate away or it may be sold, so the capital tied up in the plant becomes available for other uses. Similarly, the manager's salary may be a fixed cost for the next month or year, but over some longer time period his contract will expire and his salary will become a variable cost. If a firm has commitments for fixed costs extending for years ahead, the "short run" for that firm will be a long time. The other extreme would be a firm with no plant of its own, no leases or salary contracts, and no other forward commitments. The commonest way to think of the "short run" is the time period over which a firm has a fixed plant and equipment to which variable agents such as labor and materials are added to achieve different output levels. This is not a very precise way of drawing the distinction, but it conveys the general idea.

In the "long run," by contrast, all the firm's costs become variable. The entrepreneur can decide to build a new plant of different size if he likes. He can transfer his investment to another industry. He has complete freedom to move.

The Optimum Scale of Enterprise

The "long run" is thus a planning period, free from the short-run limitations imposed by fixed plant and other commitments. The big long-run planning problem is: What is the "optimum scale of enterprise" for the firm? How big a fixed plant, how big a labor force, how much equipment, what kind of management organization? The question involves everything related to planning the enterprise's scale of operations in the future.

Businesses seldom find themselves in a position to make all these decisions on future scale at one time. But they are continually reevaluating their positions and planning specific long-run changes. So they may replan their overall scale of enterprise much more frequently than would appear from a superficial glance.

Each possible scale of enterprise for any given firm can be shown as a U-shaped total-unit-cost curve associated with that scale. Clearly some scales of enterprise will be too small for reasonable efficiency. We may suspect that our hi-fi firm is such a producer. As the scale of enterprise becomes larger, more of the advantages of mass production and specialization of functions can be realized, bulk buying becomes possible, and skilled management can be afforded. The least-cost point on the cost curve for this larger plant will be lower than the least-cost point on the curve of a smaller enterprise. But after a certain size is reached, the firm may get too big. The least-cost point for the jumbo-sized firm may be higher than for a smaller-scale company. Why this is so, we shall consider in the next section.[3]

A set of five possible planning curves, showing expected costs for five different scales of enterprise, is given in Figure 23–3. Actually, there could be a much larger number of such curves, representing different scales of operation. Each *TUC* curve corresponds to a given scale of enterprise—a plant of certain size, equipment of certain sorts, and so on. The scale of enterprise giving the cost curve at the extreme left is obviously too small to be advantageous except for a very small market. In this figure, the scale corresponding to the fourth cost curve gives the lowest possible least-cost point. A firm of this size is the "optimum scale of enterprise," in the sense that it provides the possibility of the lowest cost per unit of output of any possible scale of enterprise. It is the lowest price at which this business can afford to bid the needed resources away from alternative uses. Note, however, that, if total market demand is small, it may still not be economical to build and operate a firm of this scale.

How Big Is "Optimal"?

Why are manufacturing companies typically bigger than dry-cleaning establishments?

[3]Throughout, we must assume some standard product being produced in order to keep the different scales of operation comparable.

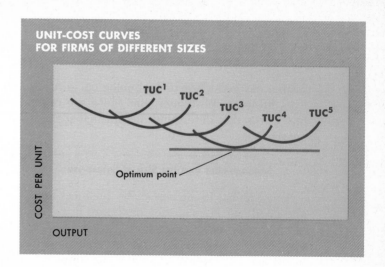

UNIT-COST CURVES
FOR FIRMS OF DIFFERENT SIZES

COST PER UNIT

TUC¹   TUC²   TUC³   TUC⁴   TUC⁵

Optimum point

OUTPUT

fig. 23–3

Larger firms have lower minimum total-unit-cost points until the optimal scale of firm is reached. Then still larger firms face higher minimum TUC's.

Why is retailing still carried on by many small-scale enterprises? Why do some firms remain small while others are huge?

These are hard questions, and the answers are complex. The primary reasons may be classed under four headings: technology, management, market opportunities, and financing channels.

Technology and the Size of Enterprise

America is the land of mass production. American industry is admired the world over for its fabulous equipment and its technical know-how. The mass-production revolution pioneered by Henry Ford with the famous Model T has never stopped spreading. The basic advantages of today's huge steel mills, oil refineries, and auto plants boil down to four factors:

1. **Specialization and Division of Labor.** Adam Smith pointed out in 1776, in his famous *Wealth of Nations*, that specialization and division of labor in making pins would reduce the cost of pins, compared with having one man do the whole job. This principle underlies mass production. Extensive specialization and division of labor are feasible only in reasonably large firms. Such specialization pays off most where the product being turned out is complex and where many different skills and operations are involved. The auto plants of Detroit are a spectacular example of how far specialization can profitably go.

2. **Use of Elaborate, Expensive Machinery and Equipment.** No small gasoline refinery can compete effectively with the massive, auto-matic, multi-million-dollar refineries now used by all the major oil companies. Only a large company can afford a "cat cracker." The machinery for a modern, efficient steel-rolling mill is very expensive; only a big firm that is able to spread the cost of the equipment over a large volume of output can afford it. No small establishment could afford to use such equipment, for without large-volume output the cost per ton produced would be prohibitively high.

3. **Balancing of Processes.** In a large firm, the various stages of a productive process can be fitted together to take advantage of the optimum scale for each stage of the operation. Suppose machine A feeds machine B, but A processes 100 units per hour while B handles 150 at optimal rates. The big company can install three A machines in line with two B machines, and thus be able to use all at maximum efficiency levels. The small company, unable to use more than one machine of each type, must either keep B idle part of the time or put A on an extra-shift basis of some sort.

4. **Utilization of By-products.** The big firm can make effective use of many by-products that may be wasted in small concerns. For example, a big meat-packing firm uses cattle hoofs to make glue and other products. In a small company the number of hoofs is too small to make this recovery worthwhile.

All these technological considerations point toward large concerns as being more efficient. But economies of size don't continue indefinitely. Once a company is big enough to take full benefit of all these factors, it can realize no further cost reduction on technological grounds from growing still bigger. But there are other factors too that determine the optimal scale of enterprise.

Management and the Size of Enterprise

Someone has to manage every business firm, and good managers are scarce. Large firms can afford highly skilled managers—in purchasing, sales, production, finance, personnel. This kind of managerial specialization is quite similar in principle to the technological specialization and division of labor mentioned above. And it's a big advantage.

But there is one crucial difference. Somebody in every business has to pull the whole business together. At some point any business may get so big that managerial efficiency drops—though this point may come only after the firm is very large indeed; witness the efficiency of General Motors. The larger and more complex the firm, the more essential and yet more difficult coordination becomes. It is harder to reconcile conflicting views on policy problems. There is too much red tape, too many levels between the managers in the executive office and the workers in the factory or on the road; the structure becomes top-heavy and inflexible. Modern management emphasizes decentralization of authority and responsibility to avoid this central managerial problem. And this approach has accomplished much. But the potential diseconomies of management are a major problem for giant firms.

These possible management diseconomies may be stated in a different way—as the positive advantages of managing a small business. In the small firm, decisions can be made more easily and more quickly. There are few specialists to consult, fewer difficulties in arriving at a mutual understanding of the problems faced. This fact gives a special advantage to small firms in fields where changes must be made frequently, as in the production of style goods like women's dresses. Channels of communication are more direct between worker and management, and supervision is easier. Blind spots where wastes persist are less likely. Not least important may be the special interest, energy and enthusiasm of men who manage their own businesses. Do these match the managerial advantages in bigness? Sometimes yes, sometimes no.

Market Opportunities and the Size of Enterprise

The size of the market may limit the size of firms. The potential market may not be big enough to permit even one firm to expand to its optimal scale. An example might be the light-and-power company in a small city. Often, where numerous firms compete, the share of the total market available to each places a direct limitation on the scale of enterprise. Such situations often lead to attempts by some firms to drive out competition in order to get the larger market needed to permit lower-cost production.

The big firm has obvious advantages in selling its products—large-scale advertising budgets, sales specialists, nationwide sales organization. Similarly, big firms can often buy more cheaply through ordering large quantity lots, as well as through having more expert buyers. Often, large firms integrate vertically so that they themselves can produce many of the materials used in their own processes, whereas smaller concerns must buy their materials in the market.

All these factors may lower costs for big concerns. But it's easy to overemphasize them. The small seller retains many advantages, especially in retailing—personal contact with the customer, special services, and so on. And expected advantages of vertical integration sometimes turn sour. Many big firms have found to their dismay that they were better off going back to the market for their raw and semifinished materials, after they had tried producing their own materials. There is no magic in producing steel for yourself if you are an auto manufacturer. The critical question is whether you can make the steel sheets cheaper than you can buy them from a steel company.

Financing Channels and the Size of Enterprise

It may be hard to get the funds necessary to start a big business. But once it is well established, it is likely to have an advantage over little businesses in getting more funds. This is partly because of its added prestige and attractiveness to investors, partly because the organized security markets are in effect accessible only to quite large firms, and partly because the costs of making large loans are less per dollar than those of making small loans.

How Big Is "Optimal"?

Thus, how big "optimal" is varies widely from industry to industry. It is clear that very large plants and firms are required in some industries to obtain peak efficiency—for example, in autos, cigarettes, petroleum, and steel. But the evidence is also clear that in many industries medium-sized or even small firms manage to achieve costs as low as the giants. Rates of return on invested capital do not appear to be consistently larger for huge than for medium-sized firms, though some of the giants are among the most profitable firms. An indirect test of the optimal scale of firm is provided by the size of firm that grows fastest. Here again the evidence is mixed. For the economy as a whole, the share of market obtained by the largest firms is growing, but only slowly—though nearly all firms are getting bigger as the economy grows. In only a few industries are the giants clearly increasing their dominance. In steel, for example, the share of the market held by U.S. Steel, the biggest firm, has fallen substantially over the last several decades. The empirical evidence shows clearly that there is no single, pat answer to the question: How big is optimal?

Do Businesses Operate at Optimal Scale?

If we look at all the firms in any particular industry, we will probably find a wide divergence in size. Why aren't all the firms the "optimal" size? There are many reasons. But a summary might look like this:

1. Optimal scale is only the lowest-cost scale of enterprise. It is not necessarily the most profitable scale. In many cases, the market simply isn't big enough to permit all firms to operate at optimal scale. In such cases, a firm may in fact operate at lower costs per unit with a small plant than it would with a large plant that was used at only partial capacity.

2. Firms may become overexpanded as part of a drive to attain dominance in their industry.

3. Some firms just want to be big. Men with dreams of industrial empire may expand beyond optimal scale in their drive for bigness and prestige. It is hard to measure this factor, but the last century of U.S. history has produced many cases where this motive appears to have been important.

4. Sometimes fear of government action holds firms back from profitable expansion. This is true when a firm fears that further growth may bring government action to break it up, under the Sherman Antitrust Act or other antimonopoly legislation. It is often alleged that this fear is what keeps General Motors from taking a still larger share of the automobile market.

5. Probably most important of all, errors in judgment and the inevitable slowness in adjusting to changed conditions mean that at any time most firms will not be at optimal scale. The most careful estimates in establishing a new plant are inevitably imprecise on a multitude of factors involved: new technology to be incorporated, future wage rates and prices, scale of market available, and so on. And even if the estimates could be precise, change is inescapable in economic life. Before long, new situations will arise, new technological changes will appear. Replanning optimal scale is a continuous process for the well-managed firm.

Social Costs and Private Costs

Profits in any industry are a signal that resources can profitably be moved into that industry from elsewhere. Losses are a signal that resources can earn more elsewhere and should be moved away. Profits and losses are thus crucial signals in the working of a free-market economy.

If the signals are to be correct, costs of producing goods should fully reflect the alternatives foregone in other economic uses.

Generally, the private costs incurred by the firm in hiring resources (wages, rents, interest, and so on) are a good measure of what it takes to get resources away from other industries. But in some cases "social costs" are involved in the production of a good or service in addition to the private costs paid by the firm. If, for example, a steel mill produces cold-rolled steel sheets for $100 per ton, but also spews out smoke and soot which cover the surrounding neighborhood, the $100 is not a complete measure of the real cost of producing the steel. The extra social cost involved in grimy windowsills and curtains, discolored paint, and smoke-filled lungs are all real costs for the people in that community. They are social costs, even though they are not included in the money costs that the steel company must pay to produce steel at $100 per ton.

In such a case, total real costs (social plus private costs) exceed the private costs seen by the producer. Thus, the total social cost of producing steel is not reflected to consumers in the price charged for steel. From the overall social viewpoint, the price of steel is too low, too much steel is produced, and too many resources are devoted to steel (and smoke) production. Only if the price fully reflects both social and private costs will profit or loss in the steel industry be an accurate guide to when resources should move into or out of the industry.

Often social costs are called "externalities." Thus, the smoke-and-dirt side effects of producing steel are "externalities," or "external diseconomies." They represent a real cost above and beyond the private costs that the steel producer pays.

Consider another example. Most paper mills are situated on streams because they use large quantities of water in the production of paper from wood pulp. The chemistry of papermaking is such that they pour back into the streams large amounts of polluted water, which destroys normal plant and fish life in the stream near the plant. It also spoils the appearance of the stream, and lessens the usefulness of the water to municipalities downstream, which have to build expensive water-purification plants to make the water safe for human use. Also, paper plants often create an odor that seems highly objectionable to many people, and that is extremely difficult to avoid for people living nearby. Such paper production has externalities; total social costs are in excess of private costs.

In such cases, it is clear that the competitive market solution does not provide an optimal allocation of resources from society's point of view. Government (or some other form of collective) action is called for to see that full social costs of producing steel or paper are covered in the price charged for the finished steel or paper. One possibility is for the government simply to pass a law imposing maximum tolerable limits on the air and water pollution. This will force the firms involved to incur the costs needed to eliminate the pollution. It will thus increase costs and the price of the product—and properly so, since without the government rule full social costs were not being reflected to buyers.

Alternatively, the government might impose a special tax on the steel or paper firm, approximately enough to cover the additional costs to the surrounding neighborhood. In principle, the special taxes should then be used to compensate the people who are injured by the externalities involved. Either way, the net result would be full payment of costs by the consumers of paper or steel; a higher price for the product involved; and protection of the people in the community against having to bear the costs of air and water pollution caused by the plant.

How important are such externalities in the world around us? This is an empirical question that must be answered separately in each particular case. Since water and air pollution seem to be widespread in a highly industrialized age like ours, calls for government action to bring social and private costs into line are understandably widespread. By and large, Americans appear to prefer the free-market system to government intervention unless there is a clear presumption that the latter is needed. But if the spread between social and private cost is, by popular consensus, large, widespread support for government regulation or taxation can be expected.

There may be external economies as well as

external diseconomies; that is, production may involve side benefits to the community instead of side costs. For example, if a lumbering company replants and improves the landscape after it has cut the trees, the real benefits from this act may exceed the expected monetary benefits to the company. The company may simply calculate that to stay in business over the long pull it must replenish its stock of trees. Whatever the motives, the total social benefits exceed the private benefits to consumers who buy the wood products. Society benefits from the replanted forest for the future, through better scenery, prevention of water runoff, and the like. In such cases, some special government payments to the lumber company that will encourage replanting beyond the test of the private marketplace are desirable to obtain a socially optimal allocation of resources. Other cases of positive externalities are easy to find—for example, with respect to education. We shall examine them in much greater detail in Part Five, "Public Goods and the Public Sector."

Review

CONCEPTS TO REMEMBER

This is another chapter of important concepts that will be used throughout the analysis of business-firm behavior. Be sure you understand the following:

cost	total costs
alternative cost	fixed cost per unit
opportunity cost	variable cost per unit
real costs	total cost per unit
accounting costs	least-cost combination
money costs	short run
fixed costs	long run
variable costs	optimal scale of enterprise

FOR ANALYSIS AND DISCUSSION

1. If you were operating a clothing store, would there be any significant difference between your cash outlays per month and your costs per month? If so, what items would account for the difference?
2. The XYZ Company has the following costs. From this information prepare a table showing the following: fixed cost per unit, variable cost per unit, and total cost per unit. Then plot your data on a graph.

Total fixed cost per month $2,000
Total variable costs:

Units Produced	Variable Cost
10	$ 500
11	1,000
12	1,400
13	1,750
14	2,000
15	2,400

3. You are considering the possibility of setting up a pizza parlor near the campus. Make a list of all the costs you ought to have in mind in estimating whether the expected demand will produce a profit.

4. Which of the costs in question 3 would be fixed regardless of how many pizzas you sold, and which would vary from week to week with sales volume? Using this dichotomy, draw rough approximations of your fixed- and variable-cost curves per pizza, indicating the general shape you would expect the curves to have. From these curves, draw a rough approximation of your total-cost (per pizza) curve.

5. Make a list of the reasons why manufacturing concerns are typically bigger than dry-cleaning establishments. Can you reconcile your list with the observed fact that some dry-cleaning establishments are bigger than some manufacturing companies?

6. "By and large, the competitive system sees to it that every firm is near the optimal size for producing its product." Do you agree with this statement? Explain carefully why or why not.

APPENDIX   *PHYSICAL-PRODUCTION RELATIONSHIPS UNDERLYING COST CURVES*[4]

This appendix provides a brief statement of part of the "theory of production," which underlies the cost of production in a firm and provides a foundation for understanding the distribution of income to different factors of production. The purpose here is to examine rigorously the physical and technological relationships involved as the businessman combines the various factors of production in turning out his product.

The simplest case arises when one variable factor of production (say, labor) is applied to a fixed amount of some other factor (say, land). Consider the results of applying an increasing number of units of labor to a fixed plot of land, abstracting from any other factors of production, such as fertilizer and tools. Table 23–3 shows what might happen in a hypothetical case. Such a table showing the physical output obtainable from various combinations of productive factors presents what economists call a "production function."

Column 1 shows the number of laborers used. Column 2 shows the total production—say, bushels of wheat—obtained as more workers are added. Total product rises until at some point (twelve workers with 3,300 bushels of output in this example) so many laborers are being used on this small plot of land that they get in each other's way and thereafter there is an actual decrease in the total output of wheat. Obviously, no intelligent farmer would ever carry production of wheat beyond this point, because by hiring

more laborers he would actually decrease the total crop he obtained.

Column 3 shows the average product (bushels of wheat) per worker on the land. This average product rises at first, because total product rises faster than in proportion to the number of workers used. But the average output per worker reaches a peak (at seven workers and 2,604 bushels in this example, which gives the maximum output per worker of 372 bushels). Thereafter, even though total product continues to rise for a while, the average output per worker falls.

Column 4 shows the "marginal product" as more workers are used. This column shows the additional, or "marginal," output obtained by adding each extra worker. Thus, adding the first worker increases total product by 100 bushels. For the second worker the marginal product is 250 bushels, as total product rises from 100 to 350. Marginal product reaches its peak at five workers. After this, adding workers (up to eleven) continues to increase total product, but not as rapidly as before; so the increment per additional worker falls.

These relationships can be seen readily in Figures 23–4 and 23–5. Figure 23–4 shows total product as additional workers are hired. It rises rapidly at first as production becomes more efficient, then gradually levels off, and finally (after twelve workers and 3,300 bushels) turns down, for there are just too many workers to avoid getting in each other's way.

Figure 23–5 plots average product and marginal product from Table 23–3. Marginal product reaches

[4]This appendix is intended for those who want a rigorous physical-output foundation for the previous and following sections on business costs.

table 23-3

Variable Output with Increasing Inputs

Units of Input (Labor)	Total Output (Bushels)	Average Output per Unit of Labor (Bushels)	Marginal Output of Labor (Bushels)
1	100	100	100
2	350	175	250
3	702	234	352
4	1152	288	450
5	1700	340	* 548
6	2190	365	490
7	2604	* 372	414
8	2908	364	304
9	3114	346	206
10	3240	324	126
11	*3300	300	60
12	3300	275	0
13	3250	250	—50
14	3080	220	—170

*Denotes highest point for each output series.

fig. 23–4

Total output rises fast at first as variable factors are added to a fixed factor, then levels off, and eventually turns down.

fig. 23–5

Marginal product shoots up rapidly as total output grows fast when the first variable factors are added. It turns down as the growth in total output slows, and becomes negative when total output turns down. Check it against Fig. 23–4.

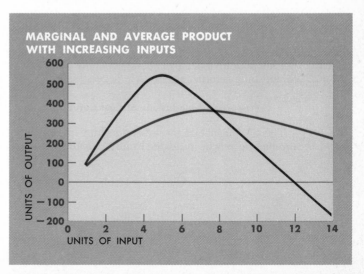

its peak first and then turns down as the rate of growth of total product begins to slow. Average output per worker shows a similar inverted U, but the peak is reached with more workers, as Table 23–3 shows.

Note that the marginal-product curve cuts the average-product curve at the latter's highest point. This is necessarily true because as long as marginal product is higher than average product, each additional worker is adding more to total product than the average of all workers up to that point. As soon as the marginal worker adds less to total product than the average up to that point, the marginal-product curve will be below the average-product curve. Thus, it will always cut the average-product curve at the latter's highest point.

The other significant point is when marginal product becomes zero. Comparing the two figures, we see that this is at twelve workers, which is just the point where total product turns down. This is clearly to be expected, because marginal product is merely the amount by which total product increases as additional workers are added. Thus, when adding another worker decreases total product, marginal product becomes negative.

The Law of Diminishing Returns, or Variable Proportions.

The preceding paragraphs provide a statement of Ricardo's famous "law of diminishing returns." They show just what happens when additional units of one factor of production are combined with a fixed stock of some other factor or factors.

Modern economists have come to a more general statement of these relationships, which they call the "law of variable proportions." As the proportion of one factor of production to other fixed factors increases, the average product of the increasing factor will first rise and then fall persistently; and the marginal product of the increasing factor will also first rise and then fall, cutting the average-product curve at its highest point.

Thus, if all factors increase in proportion, there is no reason to expect Ricardo's law of diminishing returns to set in. This is a critical fact, for it says that neither an individual firm nor an economy need face diminishing returns just because it gets bigger.

Production Foundations of Cost Curves.

The significance of these relationships for costs of production may be indicated briefly. Assume that the market prices of all factors of production are fixed—labor and land in our case. Then the total-fixed-cost curve (as in Figure 23–1) is obtained directly by multiplying the fixed amount of land used (fixed factor) by its rent per acre. The total-variable-cost curve is obtained by multiplying the number of workers (variable factors) by the wage per worker.

These total costs can readily be converted to the per-unit-cost curves of Figure 23–2 by dividing through by the number of units produced. Thus, the variable-unit-cost curve will be the inverse of the average-product-per-worker curve, since wage per worker is constant. When average product per worker is rising, variable cost per unit of output falls (we continue to assume that workers are the only variable cost involved). When average product per worker begins to fall, variable cost per unit of output begins to rise. Fixed cost per unit (rent on the land in the example above) steadily falls as more bushels are produced with the same total fixed cost for land.

The combination of the persistently declining fixed-cost-per-unit curve with the U-shaped variable-unit-cost curve gives the (flatter) U-shaped total-unit-cost curve. Thus, given the prices of the factors of production, the physical production relationships determine the shape of the fixed-cost-per-unit, the variable-cost-per-unit, and the total-cost-per-unit curves in any situation. The unit-cost curves are the inverses of the physical-production curves in Figure 23–5.

Chapter 23 has made no use of the marginal-product curve indicated above. This curve will become the physical basis for the "marginal-cost" curve introduced in Chapter 24.

The physical productivity of varying combinations of factors of production will become of major importance again in Part Four, which considers the distribution of income. This is because what entrepreneurs are willing and able to pay in wages, rent, and so on, depends directly on the contributions different factors make to total production. In determining unit costs of production in the present chapters, we take wages, rents, and the prices of the other factors of production as given; this means that the shapes of the various cost curves depend largely on the physical-production relationships involved. In Part Four, we reverse this process and take final product prices (demand curves) as given, and then analyze entrepreneurs' demands for the various factors of production. There again, these same underlying physical-production relationships will play a fundamental role in determining how many units of each factor of production it will pay entrepreneurs to hire, and how much they can afford to pay for each.

twenty-four

The Business Firm: Competitive Output and Price in the Short Run[1]

This chapter examines how business firms respond to consumer demands. We will focus on firms in highly ("perfectly") competitive industries, postponing until later a look at the partially monopolized sectors of the economy.

The Theory of The Firm

Traditionally, economists and other advocates of the private-enterprise system have pictured the business firm as, by and large, trying

to maximize its profits. If we accept this position, the "theory of the firm" is a relatively simple affair.

Our "model," or "theoretical," firm wishes to maximize profits. Profits are the difference between total cost and total revenue. Hence, the firm does what it can (within the legal rules and mores of society) to maximize this difference. It tries to sell more of its own product when the

---

[1]*Note to instructors:* Part Three of the mathematical appendix at the end of the text provides a concise mathematical statement (for students who know calculus) of the cost relationships of the preceding chapter and of the profit-maximizing behavior of the firm in the short run, as stated in this chapter.

Some instructors wish to concentrate on the long-run behavior of the firm and the economy, omitting the traditional marginal-cost–marginal-revenue apparatus in establishing short-run price and output. For them, the text is written so that Chapter 24 can be completely omitted. The preface indicates which other sections of the book rest directly on this chapter and should be omitted if it is not assigned.

price is high enough to exceed costs, and it tries to keep its costs as low as possible. That is, it tries to produce its output as efficiently as possible. Whenever the firm can increase its profits by increasing its revenues or by reducing its costs, it will do so. Only when it is maximizing its profits (at least to the best of its own ability) will the manager be satisfied. Then the firm will be in "equilibrium"—in the sense that it will not change its own actions unless conditions change. Actually, external conditions (for example, consumer demand and wage rates) do change frequently, so the business firm will seldom actually reach equilibrium and stay in it for long. But the firm will always be aiming at this maximum-profit position in conducting its day-to-day affairs and in its long-run planning.

We know, of course, that not all firms behave this way, and at the end of this chapter we will take a more detailed look at just how realistic this assumption is. But for the moment, assume that firms in our highly competitive industry have the single goal of profit maximizing. What, then, can we say about how they should make their decisions?

The Competitive Firm in the Short Run

In trying to maximize its profits, the firm tries to maximize the difference between its income from sales and its costs. Since we are assuming highly competitive conditions, in which our firm represents a very small part of the market and turns out a product just like its competitors', it must take the product price as given—fixed in the market by total demand-and-supply conditions over which no one firm has any significant control. Under this assumption, our firm can't charge a higher price than the one prevailing in the market. If it does, it won't sell any goods, since consumers can get all they want at the prevailing price from other sellers. In sum, the firm is a "price taker," not a "price maker."

This means that the firm sees the demand curve as a horizontal line at the prevailing market price. This assumption may seem to you rather extreme, and it is the limiting case of

table 24-1			
Total Cost, Total Revenue, and Profit: = $1,800			
Output	Total Cost	Total Revenue	Profit
1	$ 3,000	$ 1,800	−$1,200
2	3,500	3,600	100
3	4,000	5,400	1,400
4	5,000	7,200	2,200
5	6,000	9,000	3,000
6	7,600	10,800	3,200
7	11,000	12,600	1,600
8	17,000	14,400	−2,600

what economists call perfect competition. But it is an instructive case with which to begin. We will modify the assumption later.

Comparison of Total Costs and Total Revenue

If the stereo-hi-fi firm from Chapter 23 wants to maximize profits, it can compare its total cost with total revenue at each level of output, and thus determine the most profitable number of sets to produce. This is done in Table 24–1, assuming that the market price is $1,800. (Obviously the estimated total revenue will be different if the price is different, since total revenue is merely output multiplied by the price.) The table shows that the maximum-profit output is six sets per month. At only one set per month, total revenue doesn't cover costs. When the plant gets up to eight sets a month, costs shoot up so fast that they exceed even the big-sales income. In between, any output if profitable, but some more so than others. Profit is the largest if we produce and sell six sets.

This same comparison can be made graphically, as in Figure 24–1. *TC* is total cost, plotted from the second column of Table 24–1. *TR* is total revenue, plotted from the third column. Where *TR* is above *TC*, the firm makes a profit. The profit is largest where *TR* is farthest above *TC*—here at an output of six units monthly, just as in the table. The light yellow area between the two curves shows the range over which a

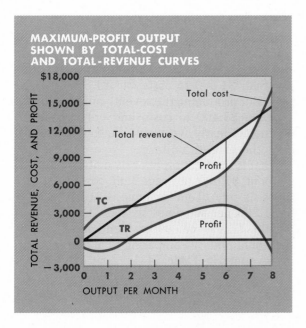

MAXIMUM-PROFIT OUTPUT
SHOWN BY TOTAL-COST
AND TOTAL-REVENUE CURVES

fig. 24–1

Maximum profit is where the total-revenue curve is farthest above (in vertical distance) the total-cost curve. Potential profit range is from 2 to 7 sets per month.

table 24-2		
Total and Marginal Costs		
Output	Total Cost	Marginal Cost
1	$ 3,000	
2	3,500	$ 500
3	4,000	500
4	5,000	1,000
5	6,000	1,000
6	7,600	1,600
7	11,000	3,400
8	17,000	6,000

profit is possible. The same area is shown separately at the bottom of the chart, where it is easy to see where the vertical distance (height of area) is greatest.

Marginal Analysis: Marginal Costs

The businessman may also approach his output decision another way. First, remember that he must take the market price of $1,800 as given by the market. He is a price taker. Now look again at his cost data. Some of the businessman's decisions are big ones—to operate or shut down, for example. Most of his decisions, however, are marginal ones—to take this new order at the going price or to refuse it; to cut back output 5 percent or 10 percent as price falls or unsold inventory piles up. In such decisions, how much additional cost is involved in expanding output moderately, or how much is saved by cutting output a little, becomes of special interest. The concept of "marginal cost," or "incremental cost," has been developed to help in this kind of analysis.

Marginal cost is the addition, or increment, to total cost involved in expanding output by one unit. For example, going back to the hi-fi-cost data in Table 24–1, if the total cost of producing three sets per month is $4,000 and that of producing four sets $5,000, the marginal cost of expanding production from three to four units is $1,000. That's how much extra it costs us to get the fourth set produced.[2] This calculation is shown in Table 24–2.

Most economic adjustments are marginal adjustments of some sort. Comparison of gains and losses "at the margin"—for example, comparison of the marginal income and marginal cost associated with increasing output from four to five sets monthly—is the core of intelligent decision making, in economics as elsewhere. The principle is the same as when you weigh the advantages of another hour's study before an exam against the disadvantages of giving up the hour's sleep. Applications abound in every field. In building a bridge, for example, the engineer must constantly weigh the advantages of getting increased strength against the related disadvantages of incurring additional weight and expense.

[2]Thus marginal cost is the logical counterpart of marginal product described in the appendix to Chapter 23. Other things equal, marginal cost will be lowest when marginal product is highest, and vice versa. As more variable productive agents are added to the fixed plant, the marginal product attributable to the variable agents first rises and then falls. By the same token, at given prices of the productive agents marginal cost will first fall and then rise correspondingly.

Maximizing Profits in the Short Run: Marginal Costs and Marginal Revenue

Table 24–3 reproduces the cost data for the hi-fi firm from Chapter 23, adding a column to show the marginal cost involved in increasing output by one set at each stage. This is simply the last column of Table 24–2 above. With the market price at $1,800, how many sets per month should we produce? Try to figure it out for yourself, by comparing how much we add to costs and to income as we increase output.

The answer again is six—neither more nor less. The figures for six sets are underscored in the table. The marginal-cost column tells how much extra is added to total costs by increasing output one more unit at each level of output. Now compare this with the extra income produced by each additional unit sold. Each unit we produce brings in $1,800.[3] This concept of incremental income is similar to the concept of marginal cost. Economists call the $1,800 added to total revenue by each additional set sold the "marginal revenue." Marginal revenue is the extra revenue added by the sale of one more unit.

So long as producing more units adds more to total revenue than to total costs, it pays to keep on increasing output. This is the same as saying that it will pay to keep on increasing output so long as marginal revenue is larger than marginal cost. At all levels of output up to and including six, producing another unit adds less than $1,800 to costs, but $1,800 to revenues. But producing the seventh unit would add an extra $3,400 to costs, and only $1,800 to revenue. Clearly we would be foolish to produce the seventh unit.

What is the total profit at six units? Total cost is about $7,600 (average unit cost of $1,267 times six sets). Total revenue is $10,800 (price of $1,800 per set times six sets). Profit is thus $3,200. This is, of course, identical to the answer obtained by comparing total costs and total revenues in Table 24–1.

The principle is: Profit will be maximized by carrying production up to the point where marginal cost equals marginal revenue (here, the price), and no further.

Ask yourself one more question, to be sure you understand. Wouldn't we be better off to produce seven units instead of six, getting the profit on the seventh, since the $1,800 price exceeds the total unit cost of $1,573 at seven units of output? The marginal-cost–marginal-revenue comparison gives the answer. The seventh set adds $3,400 to total cost and only $1,800 to total revenue. The fact that price is above total-unit cost tells us that we can make a profit at that output level, but not that we will make our maximum profit at that level. Trying

[3] Since this is a purely competitive market, we can sell all we produce at the market price, without worrying about forcing down the price by producing more.

	table 24-3			
	Hypothetical Hi-Fi Producer: Price = $1,800			
Output	Fixed Cost per Unit	Variable Cost per Unit	Total Cost per Unit	Marginal Cost
1	$1,000	$2,000	$3,000	$ 500
2	500	1,250	1,750	500
3	333	1,000	1,333	1,000
4	250	1,000	1,250	1,000
5	200	1,000	1,200	1,600
6	167	1,100	1,267	3,400
7	143	1,430	1,573	6,000
8	125	2,000	2,125	

to pick up the profit on a seventh set would be a mistake, since it would actually involve adding more to cost than to revenue; average total cost per unit would be higher on all seven units if we increase output to seven. Compute the total profit at seven units and you'll see that it's only about $1,600 ($12,600 revenue less cost of about $11,000), less than at six units.

Minimizing Losses in the Short Run

With the market price at $1,800 we're in clover. But suppose consumer demand for stereo-hi-fi sets nosedives, and the market price falls to $1,100. A quick look at Table 24–3 shows that we're going to lose money at this price, no matter what we do. The lowest total cost–unit at which we can produce is $1,200, at an output of five units.

What should we do to minimize our losses? One possibility would be to shut down. This way we'd lose $1,000 a month, the amount of our fixed costs, which continue whether we operate or not. But if we operate, producing three, four, or five units, we'll be getting $1,100 per set produced and only having to spend $1,000 per set in variable (out-of-pocket) costs. This income will provide $100 per set left over to apply on our $1,000 of fixed costs, which we have to pay in any case. So we'd better operate, even though we lose money. By operating, we lose less than by shutting down altogether.

If the marginal-cost–marginal-revenue principle is a sound one, it ought to tell us now how many units to produce again this time. And it does. The answer is five. Producing every unit up to and including the fifth adds more to revenue than it does to costs. Marginal revenue for the fifth unit is $1,100; marginal cost is only $1,000. But marginal cost for the sixth set is $1,600, above marginal revenue. Our total loss at a five-set production rate figures out at $500 ($6,000 total cost less $5,500 total revenue), or only half the loss involved in shutting down completely. The principle for minimizing loss is the same as for maximizing profit: **If you operate at all, carry production up the point where marginal costs equal marginal revenue, and no**

further. Compute the loss at any other level of output, and you'll see that the rule is right.

The Decision To Shut Down in the Short Run

Would it ever pay us to shut down in the short run? Obviously, yes. If price falls below $1,000, which is the lowest variable unit cost we can manage at any output level, we'd better close up shop. Suppose price is $900. No matter how many units we produce, our income is not even enough to cover our variable costs, much less provide anything to help cover the $1,000 of fixed costs. Suppose we produce three units. They will cost $4,000 but will bring in only $2,700, leaving a loss of $1,300 compared with only $1,000 if we just shut down. **At any price below the lowest variable-cost–unit point, we will minimize losses by shutting down altogether.** This rule does not contradict the marginal-cost–marginal-revenue principle for maximizing profits, since that principle tells us only what to do **if** we operate at all.

Graphical Analysis of Short-run Behavior

This analysis can readily be put in graphical form with, of course, the same answers. The cost curves in Figure 24–2 are plotted from Table 24–3, and are the same as in Figure 23–2 except for the addition of the marginal-cost curve. The marginal-cost curve, of course, shows the increment to total cost involved in increasing output by one unit at each stage. For example, the marginal cost involved in stepping up output from four to five units is $1,000; in going from five units to six it is $1,600.[4]

Three horizontal lines, *AA, BB,* and *CC,* have been added to show the market prices of

---

[4]For mathematically inclined readers: Marginal cost is the first derivative of total cost (not of total cost per unit). The marginal-cost curve will always cut the *TCU* curve at its minimum point. In nontechnical terms, this is so because the marginal cost is the increment to total cost. Whenever this increment to total cost is less than the existing cost per unit, the average cost per unit must be falling. Whenever the increment is larger than the existing cost per unit, the average cost per unit must be rising. The same reasoning holds for the relationship of the marginal-cost and variable-unit-cost curves. For more detail, see the mathematical appendix.

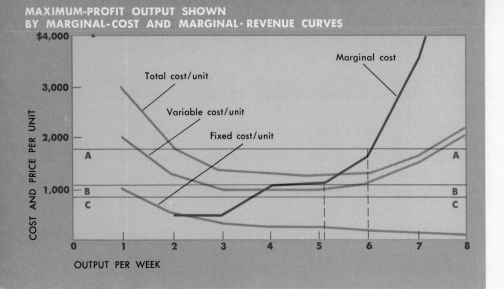

fig. 24–2

Profit is maximized by carrying production up to intersection of marginal-cost and marginal-revenue curves—if you operate at all. Horizontal price lines also show marginal revenue at each price.

$1,800, $1,100, and $900, respectively. These lines are the demand curves as seen by our firm when those are the prevailing market prices. The lines are also, of course, our marginal-revenue curves at the respective prices, since sale of one more hi-fi set adds just its price to our total revenue.

With this graph, we can readily determine the maximum-profit or minimum-loss output for any given market price. The principle is the same as before: It will pay to increase output whenever marginal revenue is above marginal cost, if we operate at all. We will minimize losses by shutting down completely if price falls below our lowest variable cost per unit.

Suppose the market price is $1,800 (line *AA*). At that price the marginal cost curve is still below marginal revenue (price) at six units, but above it at seven. We can tell by looking at the graph, therefore, that six units is the most profitable level of output. Since the $1,800 price line is above the total-unit-cost curve at this point, we can also tell that this is a profitable situation. The actual profit can be computed by multiplying the profit per unit ($533) by six units, giving the same $3,200 profit we got by tabular computation.

Similarly, with price at $1,100 (line *BB*), five units is the output that will minimize loss, given our fixed costs that must be paid whether or not we operate. Up to five units the marginal-cost curve is below the marginal-revenue (price) curve; at six units, it is above it. Clearly the firm

won't stay in this industry in the long run, but for the short run this is the best it can do.

And a quick glance at the $900 price situation will tell us to close down immediately. The $900 price line *(CC)* is everywhere below the variable-unit-cost curve. At $900 we can't even get enough revenue to cover variable costs, let alone accumulate anything to apply on fixed costs. If you can't cover variable costs, it is better to shut down and minimize your loss by just paying the fixed cost of $1,000.

For a quick answer to the most profitable levels of output, the graphical approach has real advantages. For computing exact profit-and-loss figures, tabular data are often more satisfactory. But the answers are the same either way.

Short-Run Equilibrium of the Firm

When will the business firm be in short-run equilibrium? When it is maximizing its profit or minimizing its loss, given consumer demand and given its fixed costs which it cannot alter in the short run. It will then be in short-run equilibrium when it is producing just up to the point where marginal cost is equal to marginal revenue (price). Only at that output is it maximizing its profit.

This concept of the equilibrium of the firm parallels the concept of the equilibrium of the household (or consumer) developed in Chapter 21. Both tell us the situation toward which an economic unit will move in trying to improve its economic position. In a real world of constant change, we would seldom expect to find firms actually in equilibrium for long. But whenever a household or firm is out of equilibrium, we can expect that economic unit to spend more or less, or produce more or less, so as to approach more closely its desired goal, be it maximum utility from spendable income for the household or maximum profit for the firm.

"Equilibrium" is thus an analytical concept. It is a position that would be achieved if the household or firm were free to adjust to the conditions specified, and if all other forces in the economy (the "givens") remained unchanged until the new equilibrium was reached.

Note that this chapter is only about the short-run equilibrium toward which the firm will move under the conditions assumed. The firm may be in short-run equilibrium when it is making a large profit, no profit at all, or even a loss, depending on its costs and the price given by the market. But, as we shall see in Chapter 25, the short-run equilibrium may not last in the long run. Long-run and short-run equilibrium may be different.

For example, if the firm's best short-run position unfortunately yields a loss (as with price B in Figure 24–2), it is clear that the firm will go out of business in the long run to avoid incurring a continuing loss. If the firm is making a large profit (as with price A in Figure 24–2), it is clear this will provide an incentive for new firms to move into the industry to make big profits too. If more firms do move in, we would expect the increased supply to push down the price and erode the short-run profit position of our firm. Remember: Short-run and long-run equilibrium positions may be different.

Short-Run Cost Curves and Supply Curves

If firms try to maximize profits in the short run, we can tell from a given firm's cost curves what output it will produce at any given price. The firm's marginal-cost curve will be its short-run supply curve anywhere above the minimum point on the variable-unit-cost curve. Thus, at any price below $1,000 our firm will supply zero units. At prices from $1,000 to $1,599, it will supply five units. At prices from $1,600 to $3,399, it will supply six units. And so on up the marginal-cost curve. The short-run marginal-cost curve is the firm's short-run supply curve.

If this is true for all firms, it is easy to get a short-run market supply curve for any industry, by adding together the short-term supply curves (or schedules) of all the individual firms. Suppose there were 1,000 identical firms in the hi-fi industry. Then the short-run industry supply schedule would look like Table 24-4. At each price the supply offered would be 1,000 times the supply offered by our own little firm.

Do Firms Try To Maximize Profits?

Do firms really try so logically and precisely to maximize their profits? Anyone who has spent much time around a business concern knows that this is only a rough approximation of the way businesses behave. A variety of deviations from the simple profit-maximizing model are easy to see, even in highly competitive industries.

1. The businessman who continuously adjusted his output and activities in response to every little change in affairs outside and inside the firm would have his business in a continual

table 24-4

Short-Run Industry Supply Schedule

Price	Output of Typical Firm	Industry Output
Under 1,000	0	0
1,000-1,599	5	5,000
1,600-3,399	6	6,000
3,400-5,999	7	7,000
Over $6,000	8	8,000

state of turmoil. He might also find himself overadjusting to small changes. Many businessmen follow a wait-and-see attitude; their responses are often far behind what an instantaneous-adjustment theory would presuppose.

2. Businessmen never know for sure what costs and demand in the future will be. They can only estimate, or sometimes guess—and sometimes they're wrong.

3. Cases of inefficiency in business, where better management would produce lower costs, are easy to find—at least until competition squeezes them out.

Where competition is less pressing, other deviations are likely to be added to the list, as we shall see later.

Use of a Profit-Maximizing Model of the Firm

Where does this leave the model of a firm busily maximizing profits? Certainly any reasoning based on the assumption that every firm is striving exclusively to maximize profits at every moment should be suspect, and anyone who uses such reasoning as a description of reality deserves the scorn often heaped by the man in the street on "armchair economists." Yet, through all these aberrations there is impressive evidence that the desire for profits is a dominant motive in most business concerns. Perhaps some businessmen don't carefully try to maximize profits in the way we have outlined. But few consistently and knowingly adopt policies calculated to cut profits substantially below levels they could otherwise achieve.

Indeed, one of the major arguments for the competitive system is that businessmen are forced to act as if they were trying to maximize profits, whether they want to or not. Any firm that continues to operate inefficiently will be undersold in the market and will be driven to either bankruptcy or greater efficiency. Any firm that does not respond efficiently to consumer demand will vanish from the business scene before long. Thus, even though some businessmen may not be very efficient or conscious profit maximizers, a competitive market

will force them by and large to behave the way the profit-maximizing model pictures them.

Bearing all these warnings in mind, we shall use an analytical model of business firms that act to maximize profits as a first approximation in our analysis of a competitive, private-enterprise economy. Remember, however, that the theory says only, if conditions are as they are postulated in the model, then the real-world results will be as described in the model. It is up to the user to see for himself in any given case how closely the real-world problem corresponds to the model he is using. Economic theory is an aid to thinking—not a substitute for it.[5]

The Firm As a Buyer of Productive Services

Before ending this chapter, it is important to look at the short-run output policies of the firm from a different angle. Whenever businessmen decide to produce 1, 10, or 1,000 units of output, they simultaneously decide to buy or hire the "inputs" of productive services needed to produce those units—labor services, raw materials, machinery, and so on.

If we liked, therefore, we could analyze the most profitable level of output in terms of units of productive inputs used, rather than in terms of units of output. For example, to simplify, assume that our plant needs only labor and raw materials, and that these are conveniently hired in units costing $100 per unit—perhaps one worker per week plus the material he uses. For each number of units of input, there will be some corresponding output of stereo sets. Thus, our cost schedules above could have been stated in terms of costs to hire varying amounts of labor-plus-materials input rather than in terms of producing one, two, three, or more sets per week as output.

How many units of labor–materials input should we hire each month at $100 per unit? The marginal-cost–marginal-revenue principle holds here as before. Whenever adding one

[5]For some examples of how useful the theory can be in practical business situations, see the appendix to Chapter 28, "Some Managerial Applications."

more unit of input adds more to revenue than to cost (i.e., when it adds more than $100), it pays to increase inputs and hence output. As soon as another unit of input adds more to cost than to revenue, you'd better stop expanding, because you have come to your best profit level. The marginal-revenue–marginal-cost principle here again tells you what the maximum-profit or minimum-loss production level is.[6]

---

[6]The marginal revenue from hiring an additional unit of variable input is based directly on its "marginal product," as described in the appendix to Chapter 23, although of course the marginal product needs to be converted to dollar terms to become marginal revenue.

Looking at the firm's decision making in terms of hiring labor and other productive services is particularly useful in analyzing how many workers will be hired and how wages are determined. Thus, as we shall see in Part Four, these two equivalent ways of looking at the firm's price–output decisions provide a means of integrating the theory of product prices with that of wages (prices of productive services).

The number of workers hired times the average wage determines the incomes received by workers. Similarly, the amount of land used times the average rent determines the incomes of landowners.

Review

CONCEPTS TO REMEMBER

The essence of this chapter is the way a profit-seeking firm would try to maximize profits in the short run by carrying production up to the point where marginal cost equals marginal revenue, and no further, if it operates at all. Check your understanding of the following concepts:

profit maximization
marginal cost
marginal revenue

incremental cost
equilibrium of the firm
unit of input of productive services

FOR ANALYSIS AND DISCUSSION

1. A competitive firm will always maximize profits by producing at the lowest possible total-unit cost. True or false? Explain.
2. Explain carefully why a firm will maximize its profits by carrying production up to the point where marginal cost just equals marginal revenue. If there are any exceptions to this rule, specify them.
3. You operate a roadside fruit stand. You have been selling strawberries at fifty cents a quart; they cost you forty-five cents to produce. It is now midafternoon and raining. With customers scarce, you now estimate your demand schedule for the rest of the afternoon as follows:

Price	Quarts
50¢	20
45	30
40	50
35	60
30	75
25	80

You have eighty quarts on hand and no storage facilities to avoid spoilage before tomorrow. What price should you charge to maximize profits? Explain. What is the importance of your costs in this case?

4. Convert the total-cost data in question 2 of Chapter 23 into unit costs. Calculate and add the marginal-cost curve.

5. You are managing the hi-fi plant shown in Figure 24–2 and are currently producing four sets a month. You have an order for one additional set a month, but the customer will only pay $1,050 a set, less than your minimum total cost per set. Should you accept the order? Show both graphically and through arithmetical calculations why your answer is sound.

6. "A rational businessman will always disregard his fixed costs in setting his prices and current rate of output. Sunk costs are water over the dam." Do you agree with this quotation from an economics textbook? Explain fully why or why not.

7. How should a manager decide how much to spend on civic causes like the Community Chest?

Long-Run Competitive Equilibrium and Economic Efficiency

This is a very important chapter. After our detailed look at individual households, firms, and markets, we now need to see how all the pieces fit together in a big picture of how a highly competitive economy would work in the long run. How efficient would a highly competitive economy be in allocating the economy's scarce productive resources in accordance with consumers' demands?

What economics has to say about long-run competitive adjustments is more reliable than what it has to say about the short run. In the short run, individual entrepreneurs may behave unpredictably. They may mistakenly adopt inefficient production methods. They may sell below costs. They may produce unwanted products. In most cases, entrepreneurs proba-

bly do the best they can to earn the large profits —but they may make all kinds of mistakes.

In the long run, on the other hand, in a highly competitive market we can be pretty sure about how businessmen will behave. They will act *as if* they were maximizing profits—by meeting consumer demands and by producing goods at the lowest possible costs. We know this is so because if they don't, competition will drive them out of business. And the "long run" is a period long enough for this to happen.

It was this long-run competitive pressure that led Adam Smith, in his famous *Wealth of Nations,* to speak of the "invisible hand" that leads businessmen who seek their own profits to produce the goods consumers want and to sell them at the lowest possible prices. It is the intellec-

361

tual core of the support for the private-enterprise economic system today. Although a purely competitive system has never actually existed, the model has long provided a loose approximation of how a largely competitive system might work; and many observers believe that the model is a good first, rough approximation to our own system. For some, it is a "norm" of ideal behavior against which to measure actual conditions.

The main purpose of this chapter is to examine how a purely competitive system would work in terms of long-term tendencies, and to consider some of the major virtues and failings of such a system. On the basis of this examination, you can judge for yourself whether you think Adam Smith set economists off on the right track with his talk about the "invisible hand"—or whether he gave us a bad steer.

But first we need to be clear on two important points that have been glossed over so far. Precisely what do we mean by "pure competition" and by "long-run equilibrium"?

Competition and Monopoly

No business firm is free from competition. A.T.&T., for example, is often cited as a complete monopoly in the field of telephone communication in most communities. This is true in one sense, but if people get unhappy enough with telephoning they can write or telegraph. There are only six major firms that produce aluminum today. But quite aside from the competition among the six, for many uses steel, copper, and other metals are potential substitutes for aluminum. Alcoa and the other aluminum companies are acutely aware of this fact. Competition is inescapable in business.

Nevertheless, it is obvious that competition is a lot more active in some industries than it is in others. The only grocery in an isolated rural village is a good deal less exposed to competition than is the corner grocer who has Kroger and Safeway supermarkets in the next block. At the competitive extreme, far from A.T.&T., we find the individual farmer producing such standardized products as wheat, corn, and hogs.

He has thousands of competitors, and his product is so standardized that the buyer has no interest in who the producer is—he is interested merely in the price he has to pay. If Farmer Jones prices his No. 2 hard northern wheat one cent a bushel more than other farmers, he just won't sell any.

There is a whole spectrum of market positions between the protected monopoly position of the public utility and the extreme competition of farmers. Most of the real world lies somewhere between these two extremes, and we will look at the less-competitive sectors later. Here we want to examine how the economy would function under "pure competition"— roughly the situation of the wheat farmer above, without government intervention.

Pure Competition

The essence of pure competition is that no single seller is important enough to have any appreciable influence over market price. Specifically, pure competition is characterized by:

1. Many sellers, each acting independently and each so small relative to the market as to have no appreciable effect on market price.
2. An identical product, so that the consumer is·indifferent about the seller from whom he buys.[1]
3. Freedom of entry for new sellers who wish to enter the market. (This assumption is not logically necessary where 1 and 2 hold, but most economists include it in analyzing pure competition.)

The same conditions define pure competition on the buyers' side of any market.

When there are many sellers of identical products, and when no one of them acting alone can exert a significant influence on the market price, each producer must adjust his activities to the market price. The individual firm is a "price taker," not a price setter or price maker.

---

[1]The added assumption is also usually made that all buyers and sellers have full knowledge of prices being quoted over the entire market.

It takes the market price as given, and considering its costs of production decides how much to produce in order to maximize its profit.

But although no one firm alone can significantly influence market price, the summation of all the individual producers' actions has a great influence on that price. If prevailing costs and market price lead each individual firm to restrict output, the summation of all the thousands of individual cutbacks will significantly reduce market supply and, other things equal, raise the price. Thus, quantity produced and sold along with market price are "automatically" determined by the impersonal mechanism of the competitive market as it responds to consumer demand. No one has to plan how much cabbage should be produced in the economy. The profit motive and the competitive market together decide how much, as farmers respond to what consumers buy in the market.

Why Study Pure Competition?

It's clear that there aren't many purely competitive industries in the modern American economy. Even agriculture, which has long been the standard example, doesn't quite represent pure competition any more, since the government has increasingly intervened to set prices and output levels. Why study pure competition, then? There are three reasons:

1. Economics is concerned with the overall performance of the economic system, and with the allocation of society's resources among alternative uses. To get at these problems, we must have some overall picture of the way the various parts of the economy fit together. The purely competitive model, in which all markets are competitive, has the great virtue of providing a reasonably simple and predictable picture of the way markets signal consumer demands to producers, and the way producers respond to those demands. Many economists believe that this picture also provides a rough approximation of the "ideal" way in which a private-enterprise system ought to work. They thus use the model as a standard of comparison to ferret out those areas of the actual economy that aren't operating as well as they ought to.

2. Pure competition, though almost nonexistent, does provide a rough approximation to the behavior of major sectors of the modern economy. Most of agriculture, broad areas of retailing, whosesaling, and service establishments, and important sectors of manufacturing where a moderate scale of plant is big enough for efficient production—all come reasonably close to the pure-competition model. To be sure, their products are not quite identical, and each producer has some control over the price at which he sells his product. But the pressures of competition are strong, and if he gets far out of competitive line the individual producer finds himself steadily losing out in the market.

3. We have to begin somewhere, and the basic analytical tools are pretty much the same in the competitive and partial-monopoly cases. Even where the pure-competition model is not directly applicable, the insights gained with this case will come in handy, when we look at the partial-monopoly cases.

Long-Run Equilibrium and Equilibrium Tendencies

Long-run equilibrium is an abstract analytical concept. Equilibrium is a situation that would be reached and maintained unless some external force came along to disturb it. Suppose we want to know how a purely competitive system, beginning from some equilibrium position, would respond to a change in consumer demand. Assume we can hold everything else constant—the supply of productive resources, society's technological know-how, all legal and social factors—as consumer demand for strawberries increases. The new position to which the system would move in response solely to the changed demand would be its new long-run equilibrium position.

To be complete, we should consider all the millions of interrelated effects throughout the economic system. But once we get far from the strawberry industry, these effects are likely to be negligible. Thus, economists generally concentrate their analysis on the effects on the industry directly concerned, here the strawberry industry. This emphasis leads us to a concept of the "equilibrium of the firm" within the industry, and to the "equilibrium of the industry."

For some purposes we are not safe in stopping with the industry and should instead go on to study the effects on other industries, looking toward "general equilibrium" for the economy as a whole. When, for example, the price of strawberries rises, people buy more raspberries, which are a competitive product. But let us begin with the conditions of equilibrium for the industry, and for firms within the industry.

Time is important in the economy's adjustment to changing demand. The immediate (very short-run) adjustment to a higher strawberry demand would be a higher price for strawberries. The short-run adjustment would give time for existing strawberry farmers to increase their outputs if they wished, but not to vary their fixed costs. In the long run there would be time for new firms to move into strawberry producing, for existing firms to vary their whole scale of operations, and for all productive factors in the economy to adjust fully to this shift in demand. Even in the long run we assume that no changes other than the new strawberry demand interfere with the full working-out of the adjustment process. We hold "other things equal" analytically—even if they don't stay that way in the real world. Long-run equilibrium is the new stable position finally reached by industry, other things being held unchanged except as they may change in response to the increase in strawberry demand.

Of course, in the real world there is no way to hold "other things constant," and the real world never reaches a state of economic equilibrium. Before farmers can get thoroughly adjusted to this increase in demand for strawberries, consumers switch to blueberries. Or scientists invent a new, cheaper way of producing strawberries. Or any one of a million other things may happen. Yet this analytical device of isolating the effects of a particular event is the best way we have for getting at those effects in a real world so complex, interrelated, and ever changing as ours is.

When we talk about long-run equilibrium, therefore, we are talking about the new situation toward which industry is moving and which would ultimately be reached if no other forces interfered. Long-run analysis gives us guides to the ultimate effects of particular changes—for example, the ultimate effects of a new tax on cigarettes, or of improved technology in quick-freezing vegetables. Will the lower costs of improved quick-freezing be passed on to the consumer or used to swell profits? Will more or fewer workers be employed in the frozen-food industry? In agriculture? Analysis of the way a competitive system moves toward new equilibrium positions can give us strong clues to the answers to such questions in a competitive world.

Long-Run Equilibrium: The Continuous Search for Profits

The mainspring of the private-enterprise economy is the businessman's continuous search for profits. This does not imply that the proprietor of the local grocery spends every waking hour worrying about how to squeeze the last nickel out of his business; or that the farmer doesn't decide to go visit his friends some afternoons when he could be working. But it does imply that, by and large, the desire to earn profits is a dominant one, and business concerns adopt those policies that they think will produce the largest profits for the company.

In the short run, some costs are fixed. The businessman's search for profits is limited by this fact. He can only make the best possible adjustment to market demand by varying output from his existing plant. If he has hired a group of employees on an annual basis, he must make the best of the arrangement until the end of the year.

In the long run, however, all costs become variable. Existing plant and equipment wear out. Wage and salary contracts come up for renewal. Long-term contracts for supplies and materials expire. Long-term bonds come due for payment or refinancing. With all costs variable, the entrepreneur is completely free in making his output decisions. He can expand, contract, change the nature of his productive processes, or go out of business altogether.

Thus, in the long run, firms will move into or drop out of any purely competitive industry until expectations of profits or losses have been substantially eliminated—until it is no longer possible for anyone to better his position by moving into or out of the industry.[2] Thus, as long as the expected market price is above the expected minimum cost of producing a commodity, firms will move into the industry and present firms may expand. Output will increase, and the price will gradually be forced down to about the minimum-cost point. But if the expected market price is below the minimum expected cost of production, firms will drop out of the industry, output will decline, and price will gradually rise toward the minimum-cost level. Under pure competition, with firms free to leave and enter the industry, market price cannot in the long run stay higher or lower than the minimum total cost per unit of producing the commodity. This is the long-run equilibrium price and output level toward which the industry will move.

Three points need special emphasis here.

1. It is expected market prices and production costs that matter. Change is the essence of economic life. Past and present prices and costs matter only as they provide evidence to the businessman of what the future will be like.

2. Any alert businessman will tell you that it is the long pull that matters. The businesses that last and pay good dividends to their shareholders year after year are seldom out to "turn a fast buck." They are the ones that hold back new products until they have worked out all the bugs, even though short-run profits are foregone. They are the ones who say that the customer is right, even when they're burned up at his unreasonable demand on return privileges. To assert that most businesses try to maximize profits each day, or month, or even each year would be naïve indeed. But this is not to say that the continuous search for profits is not pervasive in the competitive areas of the business world.

3. In assuming pure competition, we assume that there are no artificial barriers to the free movement of resources into and out of the industry on a par with those already there. This assumption, like the others of pure competition, is seldom found true in its pure form. But, like the others, it can serve as part of the analytical model of pure competition, subject to the same warnings that apply to all other theoretical models.

Long-Run Competitive Equilibrium— The Firm and the Industry

Consumer demand provides the signals to which businessmen respond. Given some pattern of consumer demand, when will firms be in equilibrium in adjusting to those demands?

The firm is in long-run equilibrium when there is no advantage in increasing or decreasing its output, either by varying utilization of existing plant or by changing the scale of plant. This equilibrium will be reached when (1) the firm is producing in the most efficient way available (otherwise there would be an advantage in shifting to more efficient operations), and (2) market price is equal to the least-cost point on the cost curve for that scale of enterprise. In this equilibrium position, profits have been eliminated by competition (remember that costs include a "normal" return on investment), and the firm will continue using just the same amount of all productive resources as it now uses.

It is important to notice further that in this equilibrium marginal cost just equals price for each firm. Remember that the marginal-cost curve necessarily cuts the average-unit-cost curve at the latter's minimum point,[3] which is also equal to price in long-run equilibrium. Thus, mc = price is a critical result of the competitive adjustment.

The entire industry is in long-run equilibrium when each firm is in equilibrium and there is no incentive for firms either to enter or leave the industry. We can thus define long-run equilibrium either in terms of movement of

---

[2]Remember that a "normal," or "going," rate of return (or profit) on investment is included in the costs of each firm.

[3]For proof, see Mathematical Appendix III.

firms or of movement of productive resources. In long-run equilibrium, there is no incentive for firms or for productive resources to enter or leave the industry. There is no incentive for entrepreneurs to hire more or fewer resources in the industry. Owners of productive resources (including people who sell their own labor) have no incentive to enter or leave the industry, since the returns they can earn there are about what they can earn in comparable circumstances in other industries—comparable working conditions and security for labor, comparable risk for capital investment, and so on.

Survival of the Fittest and Pressures toward Cost Minimization

The competitive market is an impersonal arbiter of who survives and who vanishes from the business scene. With a standard product, such as oats, the buyer is indifferent to who the producer is. He will pay the market price, and no more. Any farmer whose production cost is above the market price simply takes a loss, and in due course will vanish from the scene unless he improves his efficiency or receives a subsidy from someone. The fact that he may be a hardworking farmer with a good wife and six small children is irrelevant in the market. If his neighbor is a thoroughly unpleasant individual who throws stones at small children and refuses to contribute to the Community Chest but nonetheless produces oats at ten cents less per bushel, his neighbor will still prosper in the market. In long-run equilibrium, only those who can produce at a cost as low as market price will survive, and this price will be no higher than the least-cost point on the cost curve of firms using the most efficient methods.

At any time, any industry includes firms of varying efficiency, with different levels of profits and losses. This is partly because of the dynamic nature of the economic world; some firms are on the way up, some on the way down. Partly it is because many industries are far from being purely competitive; some firms do not have free access to markets and technological know-how. But if a purely competitive long-

run equilibrium position were actually attained, the lowest total-unit-cost points of all firms would be the same.

It is easy to see that in the long run inefficient firms will be eliminated by competition. But it would be unreasonable to assume that all firms become identical. Some entrepreneurs are more efficient than others. Some firms are located near good markets and pay high rents, whereas others are more distant but pay lower rents. Some firms are small and obtain efficiency through close personal supervision; others are large and count on mass-production methods to provide low costs. Such differences may exist in long-run equilibrium. It is not necessary that all firms be identical or have identical cost curves. It is only necessary that the method of production used by each permit it to produce at a total unit cost as low as its competitors. Persistent differences between firms are consistent with equal minimum total-unit costs because there may be compensating advantages and disadvantages.

For example, suppose that one manager of a textile firm is more effective in organizing production than anyone else in the industry. Won't his firm continue to make a profit even in the long run, and won't its costs remain below the costs of other firms, since none of the others can duplicate its efficiency? The answer is "no." When the manager is hired, his firm will have to pay him a higher salary than other managers receive in order to keep him away from other firms. Assuming active competition among firms, his salary will be bid up until it is higher than that of a less-efficient manager by roughly the differential advantage of his services. If the entrepreneur himself is the efficient manager, he must charge as a cost a salary for himself equal to what he would be able to get in alternative opportunities; this "implicit" or opportunity cost would be the compensating factor. This is true for all productive resources.

Illustration of Response to an Increase in Demand

Suppose that the purely competitive desk-blotter industry is in long-run equilibrium and that consumer demand for blotters increases. How will the industry respond?

The immediate effect will be (1) a higher price for blotters, with improved profit opportunities. (2) Then each firm will increase its output, since with a higher price it is now profitable to produce more blotters. (This is a move upward along the industry short-run supply curve, before there is time for new firms to move in.) (3) In the new short-run equilibrium, price will be higher, output larger, and profits in the industry greater than before the increase in demand.

This short-run adjustment is pictured in Figure 25–1. The left-hand portion shows the short-run industry supply of desk blotters (S^1S^1). Remember from Chapter 24 that the industry-supply curve is simply the sum of all the individual-firm-supply curves, and that the supply curve for each firm is its marginal-cost curve above minimum variable cost. Thus S^1S^1 is merely the horizontal summation of all the SS curves of individual firms on the right.

In the left-hand portion of the chart, D^1D^1 is the original demand for blotters, while D^2D^2 shows the new increased demand. The result of the increased demand is to raise the price from $.06 to $.08. At this higher price, each firm can increase its profits by increasing its output from 400 to 500 units, as indicated on the right-hand portion of the graph. That is, each firm increases output to the point where marginal cost

(the SS curve) again equals price, now $.08 per blotter. The summation of all these increases is shown in S^1S^1 on the left, which indicates the total increase in blotters supplied at the higher price of $.08.

The right-hand portion shows the happy result for each firm; it is now making a profit indicated by the shaded area. Consumers are now getting 62,500 blotters instead of the original 50,000, but they have to pay $.08 instead of $.06 per blotter. This increase results automatically from the independent actions of hundreds of purely competitive firms producing blotters.

But this situation is obviously unstable. New resources will be attracted to the industry by the generous profits available. As new firms enter and productive capacity is expanded, the industry supply curve (S^1S^1) will gradually move to the right; more will be produced as more resources move into the blotter industry in the long run.

With more blotters produced, the price will gradually fall back toward its original level. If unlimited productive resources can be attracted without having to pay more for them (that is, if new firms can enter without bidding up costs in the blotter industry), the new long-run equilibrium will be back at the original price but with more blotters being produced. This would be a case of long-run "constant costs" for the industry. If, however, the entrance of new firms raises costs for all firms,

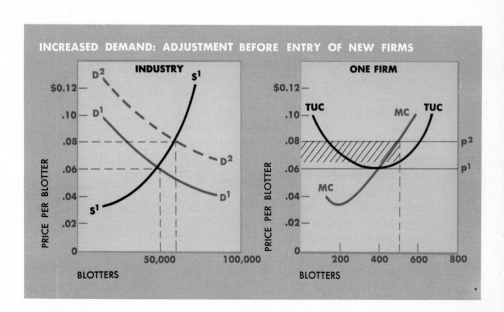

fig. 25–1

New increased demand (D^2D^2) raises the market price and makes increased output profitable for the individual firms.

fig. 25–2

Increased demand draws new firms into the industry and produces new equilibrium for the firms and the industry at a price of 7 cents. S^3S^3 is the long-run industry supply curve.

because higher payments are necessary to attract labor, materials, and other resources from other industries, we have the case of "increasing costs." Either way, as the price of the product falls back and costs rise, profits are gradually squeezed out. When the price is again equal to the lowest total unit cost, there will be no further inducement for new firms to enter. The new long-run equilibrium will probably be at somewhat higher costs and price than originally, with a larger industry output. That is, the industry may face long-run increasing costs.

These long-run adjustments are shown in Figure 25–2. S^2S^2 is the new short-run aggregate-supply curve after new firms have had time to come into the industry; it has shifted to the right. Under these new conditions, supply and demand are equal at a price of $.07 per blotter, with an output of 70,000 blotters in the industry as a whole. This is the new long-run industry equilibrium. It is long-run equilibrium because price is now just equal to the new higher TUC curve at its minimum point, shown in the right-hand portion of Figure 25–2. Thus, there is no longer any incentive for resources to move into or out of the industry. Note that the position of the typical firm is now changed, as shown in the right-hand part of the figure. Its cost curves have risen, because the increased production of blotters has bid up the price of labor and raw materials. On the demand side, price first rose from $.06 to $.08, and then fell back to $.07, the lowest point on the TUC curve. In the new long-run equilibrium, the typical firm is again producing about the same amount as before, again

at just its lowest-total-unit-cost point.[4] But since there are more firms than before, the aggregate output of the industry is greater than it was initially. In response to their increased demand, consumers are getting 20,000 more blotters, and are getting them at the lowest price that will cover costs. But they have to pay $.01 more per blotter because that much more was necessary to attract more productive resources from other uses into blotter making.

The adjustments following a decrease in demand would be the reverse. In the short run, price would fall and firms in the industry would suffer losses. After some firms had been eliminated and production reduced, price would rise back toward its original level, to a new equilibrium at the lowest point on the new total-unit-cost curve. Consumers would be getting fewer blotters, possibly at a lower price than before the decrease in demand if the smaller supply of productive resources could be obtained at lower prices.

Long-Run Industry Supply Curves

S^3S^3 in Figure 25–2 is the long-run supply curve for the blotter industry. It joins the points at which the demand and supply curves

[4]Figure 25–2 shows the new equilibrium output of the firm identical with the old—that is, the new average-cost curve is merely raised by $.01 for each level of output. This will be the result if the costs of all factors of production rise in the same proportion. This need not, of course, be the case, and the particular type of cost increase shown is not important for the basic analysis of the industry's response to an increase in demand.

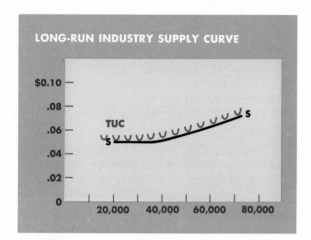

LONG-RUN INDUSTRY SUPPLY CURVE

fig. 25–3

Figure shows relationship between typical individual firm average cost curves and long-run industry supply curve over a wide range of outputs.

intersect before and after the increase in demand. More fundamentally, it joins the lowest points on the typical firm's average total-unit-cost curves as more firms enter the industry.

This is shown in Figure 25–3, which is patterned after Figure 23–3, which considered the optimal scale of enterprise for firms. These *TUC* curves show the average total-unit-cost curves for the typical firm as more firms enter the industry. Excluding the decreasing cost sector (which we will consider in the monopoly chapters ahead), clearly the supply of the industry at each point will be the sum of the outputs of all the firms, each producing at its minimum cost point, which is, of course, also the point where marginal cost equals price. The *SS* curve in this figure corresponds to the S^3S^3 curve in Figure 25-2. The industry is one of constant costs between 20,000 and 40,000 blotters, and one of increasing costs above 40,000 blotters.

"Constant-Cost" and "Increasing-Cost" Industries

When will unit costs rise if demand for a product increases? If an industry is very small, its chances of expanding output without bidding up productive service prices (wages, raw-material prices, and so on) may be good. Even if the industry is a large one, in the long run expanding output **may** not encounter substan-

tially rising costs. If we assume that the total income of society is constant, then more spending on blotters will mean less spending on something else—say, books. Thus, the expanding blotter industry can get needed workers and materials from the contracting book industry. Insofar as productive resources are relatively unspecialized (for example, common labor usable in one industry as well as the other), this shift can be made easily and without bidding up wages in the blotter industry. But if the blotter industry needs specialized resources (perhaps, skilled machinists who are not available from the contracting book industry), it will probably have to pay higher wages to lure more workers away from other industries.

Thus, the degree of specialization of resources needed, more than the size of the industry, is the critical factor determining the shape of the long-run industry-supply curve, though the two factors are often closely related. Since the long run is long enough to permit retraining workers and shifting production methods, the vast majority of industries can expand output over a wide range with only negligible increases in long-run costs.

When we talk about constant- and increasing-cost industries, we are talking about the shape of their long-run industry-supply curves. As Figure 25–3 indicates, the long–run industry-supply curve is the locus of the lowest points on the individual-firm unit-cost curves as more and more firms enter the industry. Since in the constant-cost case the new firms can enter without bidding up the lowest point on the unit-cost curve, the long-run industry-supply curve is a horizontal line joining the lowest points of the unit-cost curves of the new firms as they enter the industry. In the increasing-cost case, as industry output is increased the lowest unit-cost point gradually rises; thus the long-run industry-supply curve will slope gradually upward.

General Equilibrium of a Competitive Economy

Now an overview of the entire economy, still assuming that perfect competition prevails in all industries. Suppose the entire pattern of consumer demands for the economy is frozen, and a full "general equilibrium" adjustment to these demands has worked itself out in a purely competitive economy. What would be the main characteristics of the resulting general equilibrium?

1. **Each consumer (household) is in equilibrium.** Each household spends its income on the different goods and services it wants most, given the prices it must pay. Thus, if we assume that it allocates its income so as to maximize the total utility obtained, each household buys different products until their prices are proportional to the marginal utilities they yield. Hence, consumer demand in the marketplace provides an accurate measure of how much satisfaction each commodity yields, and an accurate signal to producers as to how much of each commodity consumers want produced at different prices. The price paid is a measure of the marginal utility of the product to consumers who pay for it.

2. **Each business firm is in equilibrium.** Each business firm is doing everything it can to maximize its profits. To achieve this position, it carries its output up to the point where marginal cost equals price. The price is set by overall market conditions—by consumer demand and by the prices it must pay for the resources it uses. But given these prices, each firm does the best it can to maximize profits.

3. **Each industry is in equilibrium.** The price of every commodity has been forced down by competition to the lowest point on the average unit-cost curve—that is, to the lowest total cost of production that is consistent with known technology, with the prices of productive resources used in the industry, and with the size of consumer demands. There is no longer any incentive for firms and resources to move into or out of the industry, since economic profit has been eliminated in every industry. (Remember that a normal return on investment is included in economic costs, so that accounting profits would remain in each industry in equilibrium.) Put in other words, each businessman is producing his output in the most efficient way possible, so the minimum amount possible of society's scarce resources is being used in producing each commodity demanded by consumers.

In equilibrium, thus, price equals marginal cost. This is so because marginal cost equals the minimum total cost per unit for each firm, and each firm must be producing at its minimum-cost level.

4. **Each market is in equilibrium.** In each market the amount being supplied is equal to the amount being demanded at the existing price. There is no unsatisfied demand or excess supply in any market.

5. How can we be sure that in general competitive equilibrium, the economy is (a) producing that combination of products which consumers want most, as measured by the prices they are willing to pay; and (b) using society's resources most efficiently in producing those products?

First, how much consumers buy at any price mirrors their preferences for different products. These purchases provide signals to producers. Price paid is the measure of the product's marginal utility to buyers.

Second, on the cost side, marginal cost in each firm provides an accurate measure of the additional cost it would take to produce one more unit of that output in responding to consumer signals. If marginal cost is below price, we know that too few resources are being used in that industry to satisfy consumer demand effectively. But if marginal cost is higher than price, too many resources are being used in the industry in response to consumer demand. In equilibrium, marginal cost is just equal to price, and price just covers the full cost of producing each product. Thus, marginal cost is just what it takes to produce the last unit here as compared to other industries, and price measures the marginal utility of the last unit bought (produced). When $mc = p$, no change in resource allocation could increase the total satisfaction gained by all consumers. (See the Appendix for a more rigorous statement.)

Put broadly, therefore, the combination of each consumer spending so as to maximize his own utility plus each businessman trying to maximize his own profits plus the force of competition in all markets has automatically:

(a) Forced each businessman to behave in the most "efficient" way if he is to remain in business;

(b) Led businessmen as a group to produce just as much of each product as consumers want to buy, at a price that just covers the cost necessary to attract the resources needed to produce that amount; and

(c) Obtained the maximum total output of wanted products from society's scarce productive resources.

6. We can now add another important proposition. **The income received by each factor of production (laborers, capitalists, and the like) is the largest possible, given the productive powers of each.** Assume that all workers and other resource owners (landowners and capitalists) work where the total monetary and "psychic" rewards are the highest. In other words, assume that each person does what he thinks is best for him.

Competition among businessmen for factors of production will bid up the return (wage, rent, and so on) on each to roughly the contribution it makes to the total revenue for the firm, and no higher. This is the "marginal product" of the worker or other productive resource.[5] Whenever the price of any productive service (say, the wage of a particular grade of labor) is lower than its marginal product, businessmen can increase their profits by hiring more of that factor, and this competition will bid the wage up. Whenever the price of a productive service is higher than its marginal product, businessmen will cut back on hiring that factor, and its price will fall until it just equals its marginal product. Moreover, each productive factor will have its highest marginal product (that is, it will add the most to the total output of wanted goods) when it is in the industry where its contribution is greatest—where its efficiency is highest in producing wanted products. Thus, **each productive factor will earn the most when it is in that industry where it can contribute most to satisfying consumer demands as reflected in the market.**

[5]Remember that marginal product is the addition to total output made by using one more unit of labor or capital.

7. Last, in general equilibrium the rate of capital accumulation (investment) will reflect the public's preference for the future relative to the present, as shown by the proportion of income saved rather than spent on current consumption. When the public saves, it indicates that it prefers to forego current consumption in order to obtain future benefits, given prevailing interest rates on savings and other motives for saving. Conversion of these savings into investment reflects a judgment by profit-seeking investors (businessmen) that future consumer demands will yield returns that more than cover the interest rates required to obtain savers' funds. Interest rates (the "price" of savings) will move up or down toward equilibrium in this market, as in others (though the adjustment process may be a complex one, as noted in Part Two). In equilibrium, the economy's rate of capital accumulation would thus reflect the combined preferences of the public (supplying savings) and business (estimating future returns from investing). Again, the result depends on compromise through the market of the millions of self-seeking decisions of individual units that make up our economy.

In such a general equilibrium situation, could we say that consumers first demand certain goods and services, then businessmen respond to those demands, then competition forces their prices down to minimum costs, then wages and rents are set, then incomes are paid out to workers, landowners, and capitalists? Obviously the answer is "no." **All these steps—millions of them each day—are being carried out simultaneously in the economy. The prices of all final goods and all factors of production are being set and adjusted continuously and simultaneously. Each depends on all the others.**[6]

[6]A more rigorous statement of these general equilibrium conditions is presented in the appendix to this chapter. Some economists describe general equilibrium conditions in mathematical terms. Since general equilibrium involves considering a vast number of demands, costs, markets, prices, and productive factors simultaneously, we can view the system as a large set of simultaneous equations and investigate the effects of different changes mathematically. Leon Walras, a French economist, was one of the first, a century ago, to use mathematics in analyzing economic problems and apparently the first to state the essential general equilibrium conditions for such a competitive economy.

"The Invisible Hand"

Such is the case for pure competition. Everyone looks out for his own interests. The result is an organization of society's scarce resources that looks amazingly as if it has been guided by some invisible hand for the welfare of society as a whole. Each individual, as consumer, laborer, or businessman, maximizes his own advantage. No individual consumer or resource owner has any appreciable influence over what gets produced and how much of it, but in the mass they determine the allocation of society's resources among all possible alternative uses. Individual incomes, outputs, and prices are simultaneously determined. And at the center of the process, trying to buy cheap and sell dear, is the entrepreneur, continually searching for profits and thereby (perhaps unwittingly) providing the organizing service that merges and compromises all these millions of different interests.

Purely Competitive Economy— Evaluation

The case for a purely competitive economy is an impressive one. If we want to avoid authoritarian control over what gets produced, where we work, and how we invest our savings, the purely competitive private-enterprise system offers a nonpolitical, individualistic way of making the millions of interrelated compromises required among the different interests involved.

Can we do better than Adam Smith's "invisible hand," the profit motive with competitive markets? Still assuming that pure competition might actually be attained for the entire economy and still putting aside the problem of business fluctuations, how, if at all, might such a purely competitive result be improved upon? Economists suggest several ways, which we can group under three main headings.

Problems in Making Competitive Markets Work Effectively

1. Resource allocation when social costs differ from private costs. To get the optimal al-location of resources among different products, the price of each product to the consumer should cover the total cost of producing it. In some cases, there are hidden costs (externalities) that are not paid by the producer and hence do not enter into the commodity's price but nevertheless are borne involuntarily by the rest of society. In such cases, price is lower than it should be and output is larger than is socially justifiable.

Air and water pollution is a leading example. Smoke and dirt produced by many industrial plants represent real costs to residents of the vicinity—through higher cleaning and painting bills, through impaired health, and through lessened contact with sunshine and fresh air. Yet these real social costs don't enter into the firm's accounting costs of producing its product. The added cost to society of the plant's dirt is not included in the manufacturer's "private" costs, and a market price that covers only the latter won't be high enough to cover the former.

The converse may also occur, where society gets special benefits from a producer for which it does not pay in the price of his products. An example is soil-conservation practices in agriculture. Suppose you own farm land along a stream, and you carefully plant and terrace your property to prevent erosion. This costs money, and you will spend only as much as is justified by the benefits you expect. But people downstream from you benefit from your outlays through the decreased likelihood of floods, in addition to your private benefits. Yet you have no way of collecting from them in the revenues you receive from the sale of your product, and the market provides no incentive for you to spend as much as would be socially desirable.

Where "private" and "social" costs and returns diverge (where there are externalities), a market system fails to produce an "ideal" pattern of resource allocation. Most economists believe that in such cases we should take collective (government) action to bring results nearer to the competitive ideal.

2. Imperfect information, immobility, and consumer control. For a purely competitive system to work well, consumers must be well informed about the goods and services available

at different prices, and resource owners must be well informed about employment opportunities that are open to them. Farm workers in Montana may know nothing of a shortage of laborers in Detroit's auto assembly plants. Secretaries in Chicago may not know about better jobs in St. Louis.

If the Montana farm worker knows about the auto jobs in Detroit and decides to stay in Montana, even at lower pay, his decision is perfectly consistent with "ideal" resource allocation under pure competition. The competitive system acts to reflect people's preferences among types of work as well as among consumption goods. But if the farmer stays in Montana because he just doesn't know about a better job in Detroit that he would have preferred, the situation is different. Then imperfect knowledge has blocked complete competitive adjustment of resources to consumer demands. The farmer is worse off as an individual. And too many of society's resources are being allocated to producing wheat in Montana, too few to producing cars in Detroit.

The same malallocation results if resources are immobile, even though information is freely available. If our farmer has a big family and no savings, he may be quite unable to take the better Detroit job, no matter how badly he wants it. The cost of getting from Montana to Michigan, of supporting his family between jobs, and of going through a retraining period may make the change utterly impractical. Yet both the farmer and society would be better off if he could somehow get over the hump into the new industrial job.

Both imperfect information and imperfect mobility are widespread in the modern economy, especially among the lower-income groups. Both block the economy from carrying out the wishes of consumers and resource owners.

Another problem is perhaps even more serious, if we temporarily drop the assumption of a perfectly competitive economy. In the modern world, sellers influence, and sometimes even determine, what consumers want. Modern advertising and selling methods not only provide information on products but also mold con-

sumer wants. Some people say, therefore, that the basic assumption of free consumer choice is increasingly violated. They say that producers tell us what we should want, rather than that they respond to our own wants. This is an important and complex issue, which will come to center stage in Chapter 27.

3. **The problem of minimum size for efficient production.** Pure competition requires that no one seller be large enough to have appreciable influence over market price. If he gets very big, there is a danger that he may react to increased consumer demand by putting up price and trying to shut out new competitors, rather than by expanding output.

This requirement means that there have to be lots of firms in every industry. We cannot, then, reasonably hope to have pure competition in many of the big mass-production industries. Take the flat-glass industry, for example. Eight or ten huge furnaces and glass-making tanks, together with appropriate modern rolling equipment, can apparently furnish all the flat glass the economy can use at peak production levels for the foreseeable future. Transportation costs are high for glass, so actually not more than half of these plants are in active competition in any one part of the country. Older methods of making flat glass are still usable, but only at substantially higher costs than the modern methods. Insisting on many firms would mean high production costs, and hence high prices, in such cases.

Even in small concerns, there is sometimes a conflict between competition and productive efficiency. For example, in a small town one large A&P supermarket may be able to sell at a lower price than would be forthcoming if the market were divided among four local competing grocers.

Where there are important economies of large-scale production that are unobtainable with a large number of firms, the public faces a difficult choice. We can insist on competition, but this will mean higher production costs than a smaller number of large firms would involve. Or we can tolerate some degree of monopoly, but lose some of the pressures of competition obtainable with large numbers of producers.

This dilemma poses a major issue of public policy, which is considered in detail in Chapter 29.

Public Goods and the "Public Sector"

There is a wide range of public, or collective, wants which most people feel cannot be satisfactorily provided through the marketplace. National defense is the clearest example. We agree that this is essential, and through the political process legislate taxes (compulsory payments) to see that resources are used to build missiles and to train soldiers. There is no practical way to leave it up to each individual to buy in the marketplace the amount and kind of national defense he wants. So it is with police protection, highways, and a variety of other public services that we agree are essential and that cannot, as a practical matter, be adequately provided through relying on individual purchases in the market. What we do directly through government action, we often call the "public sector" of the economy. This now totals over $300 billion annually.

Just how far we should go in using compulsory taxes to "buy" such public goods and services is a highly debatable issue. Even with schools, we leave part of the job to private choice and the marketplace, with private schools and tuition at state universities. When we come to other areas, like slum clearance, the issue gets even hotter. Is slum clearance a "public good," not salable through the market? For true public goods, there is no practical alternative to turning to the political process for making decisions.

We will take a detailed look at how big the public sector should be—at what the government should do—in Part Five, on "The Public Sector."

Equity and the Distribution of Income

Many observers believe that the distribution of income (wages, interest, profits, and the like) produced by a purely competitive economy would be inequitable, however "efficiently" the market might allocate resources in response to consumer demands. In a purely competitive economy, every man's income would rest on the economic contribution made by his own services or those of his property. Every man's power to direct the allocation of resources would thus depend on his marginal contribution to the economy's total output of wanted goods.

This is so because in a purely competitive economy there would be "consumers' sovereignty" over what gets produced. It would be a "one dollar, one vote" system—not a "one person, one vote" system such as we have in our political affairs. In the dollar-vote system the high-income man has lots of votes. When incomes are unequal, luxury hotels may be produced while millions are underfed and ill-clothed, all quite consistently with consumers' sovereignty.

In a purely competitive economy, moreover, there are many reasons why the incomes earned by some people would be much larger than by others. Some individuals inherit large fortunes, from which they obtain large incomes in the form of interest and profits from the funds invested. Some people have higher intellectual abilities than others, which tend to produce larger incomes for them. Some people are born into higher-income families, which means they tend to get better education and broader opportunities to develop earning power. Some people work harder and longer than others.

Some people argue that such an income distribution, based on "economic contribution," would be an eminently just and efficient arrangement. It would provide both incentives and equity for all. Whether you agree, you can decide for yourself. Lots of people don't, and support government intervention to distribute incomes and buying power more equally. We will consider the problem in detail in Part Four.

Review

CONCEPTS TO REMEMBER

Be sure you have a firm grasp of the new analytical concepts introduced in this chapter:

pure competition	**increasing-cost industry**
long-run equilibrium	**long-run supply curves**
equilibrium of the firm	**price takers**
equilibrium of the industry	**social costs**
general equilibrium	**private costs**
equilibrium tendencies	**externalities**
constant-cost industry	**public goods**
economic efficiency	

FOR ANALYSIS AND DISCUSSION

1. Explain briefly but concisely how the self-interests of individuals and businesses interact to produce a widely beneficial outcome under competitive market conditions.

2. "Under pure competition, the consumer is king. Prices of what he wants to buy can never stay for long above the minimum cost of producing any article." Is this quotation sound?

3. Under a purely competitive system, what incentive, if any, would remain for businessmen to do an efficient job, since competition would eliminate profits?

4. Pure competition, strictly speaking, does not prevail in any part of the economy. Then why study it?

5. "A purely competitive economic system would be ideal." Do you agree? Why or why not?

6. Suppose a tax of one cent per blotter has been included in the costs of all blotter producers. Now the tax is removed. Beginning from the situation in Figure 25–1, with price P^1P^1 and demand D^1D^1, trace through the adjustment to a new equilibrium.

7. Show how under long-run competitive equilibrium each household and business firm would be in its optimal (preferred) position, so that it could not gain by a different pattern of behavior.

8. "Most people would agree that a dollar means more to a poor man than to a rich man. Since this is so, an economic system that merely reacts to the number of dollars spent is a grossly unfair system in the way it allocates resources." Do you agree or disagree? Why? If you agree, how should we modify the system to get around the problem?

9. Suppose you are part owner of a steel company. The city asks you to install expensive smoke-control equipment to eliminate an alleged smoke nuisance caused by the mill. The cost will be $5 million, and most of your competitors in other cities have no such smoke eliminators. Would you agree? If you were a citizen in the community, would you favor a city ordinance requiring the mill to install the smoke eliminator?

10. How effectively would Adam Smith's "invisible hand" work for the general good under perfect competition? Explain your answer. What steps would be required to make the system work optimally?

APPENDIX *GENERAL EQUILIBRIUM AND ECONOMIC EFFICIENCY*

A purely competitive system of the sort described above would provide the most efficient possible allocation of resources in the sense described in the text of the chapter. More precisely, we can show that such a purely competitive system would allocate resources most efficiently, in the sense that no possible reallocation would increase the welfare of anyone in the system without harming someone else. This condition, which economists call "Pareto optimality" (after the famous French economist who first stated it precisely) seems to some observers a weak claim for an optimal system. But it is a major claim indeed, if you stop to think about it. For if Pareto optimality does not prevail, we could make someone better off without harming anyone else, thus unambiguously increasing the public's total utility. Any system which does not provide Pareto optimality is producing a socially inefficient allocation of resources that holds total utility for the economy below what it could otherwise be.

It is possible to demonstrate precisely that Pareto optimality will prevail under competitive general equilibrium (that is, no one can be made better off without injuring someone else); while under other market arrangements (e.g., with some degree of monopoly) it is generally possible to increase the welfare of someone without injuring anyone else. For simplicity, consider only two goods, x and y, although the argument can be generalized to many goods.

Assume that competitive general equilibrium prevails. We know then (from Chapter 21) that when a consumer is in equilibrium, maximizing his utility, he spends his income so that the marginal utility obtained from the last dollar spent on x is the same as that obtained from the last dollar spent on y. Alternatively, we can say that the marginal utilities of the two products must be proportional to their prices. In equation form:

$$(1) \quad \frac{MU_x}{MU_y} = \frac{P_x}{P_y}$$

We also know (from Chapters 24 and 25) that in long-run competitive equilibrium, each producer in each industry maximizes profits by producing up to the point where marginal cost equals price. Thus:

(2a) $P_x = MC_x$ (for industry x)
(2b) $P_y = MC_y$ (for industry y)

Combining equations (1) and (2), we can then write:

$$(3) \quad \frac{MU_x}{MU_y} = \frac{P_x}{P_y} = \frac{MC_x}{MC_y}$$

Equations (1), (2), and (3) state the conditions under which, with the competitive prices P_x and P_y, every consumer and business firm is in the best position it can achieve. No one can increase his utility or profits by changing his behavior. Equation (3) also emphasizes that prices provide the basic equilibrat-

ing link between consumers (expressing their preferences through expenditures) and businesses (maximizing their profits by hiring resources up to the point where marginal cost equals price).

Now, consider any situation where perfect competition does not prevail—for example, where a monopolist is restricting output and raising price to enlarge profits so that he holds his selling price above marginal cost. (We will demonstrate rigorously in the next chapter why he will do so in order to maximize his profits, once he is free from competitive pressure.) Suppose, for example, that monopoly prevails in industry y, so marginal cost in y is less than price. Then equation 2b will not hold, and hence neither will equation (3).

Suppose, for example, that

$$\frac{MU_x}{MU_y} = 2$$

but that

$$\frac{MC_x}{MC_y} = 3$$

because marginal cost is below price in industry y while MC equals price in industry x. Thus the marginal utility of one unit of x is twice that of one unit of y, but the marginal cost of producing one more y is only one-third that for x. This means that in terms of costs, producers could make three additional units of y by giving up one of x. By so shifting resources to produce one less x and three more y we can make consumers better off, by giving them more than the two units of y they view as equivalent to one unit of x in their utility functions. Similarly, for any other condition than the (competitive) one specified in equation (3), it will be possible to make someone better off without injuring anyone else. When equation (3) is satisfied, Pareto optimality will prevail.

Competitive equilibrium provides Pareto optimality, and monopolistic equilibrium does not except in some unlikely hypothetical cases which need not concern us here. Thus, economists presume that a monopolistic situation which holds price above marginal cost will generally lead to a less-efficient allocation of resources than would a competitive system.

But remember that a Pareto optimal competitive system would not necessarily be the best system, even though it provided the most "efficient" allocation of resources in response to consumer demands. You might still object to its failure to take into account externalities, to provide enough public goods, or to produce an "equitable" distribution of income. The substantial benefits from purely competitive markets do not necessarily imply that economically no government is the best government.

Agriculture: a Case Study in Competition

Changing Fortunes in Agriculture

The Farm Problem

Agriculture's Claims to Special Aid

The Farm-Aid Program

U.S. Agriculture and the World Food Problem

Agriculture in the Political Economy

Agriculture is the area of the American economy that comes closest to the model of pure competition. For most major farm products —wheat, corn, cotton, hogs, and many others— substantially the conditions of pure competition prevail except insofar as the government has stepped in to alter them. How well has substantially pure competition worked in agriculture? What accounts for the far-reaching government intervention to help solve "the farm problem"? In fact, is there any "farm problem" that the forces of competition would not resolve adequately if left alone to work themselves out?

Changing Fortunes in Agriculture

Some historical background helps in understanding the present situation. Five big facts stand out.

First, agriculture is a relatively declining industry. With our huge increases in population and income, the nation consumes more farm products than it did a century ago. But the percentage of our national income that we spend on farm products has persistently declined. A century ago, over half of the labor force was employed in agriculture. In 1970, only 5 percent of it was.

Second, technological change has been spectacular in agriculture, much faster than in industry where we tend to place the modern technological revolution. Annual output per farm worker has quadrupled since the 1930s, an increase of nearly 6 percent per annum compared to about half that figure for the nonagricultural sector of the economy. A century ago, one farmer could feed four people; today he feeds nearly thirty. New fertilizers, hybrid seeds, plant-disease control, modern farm machinery, and generally improved farming methods have accounted for a production revolution. The upshot is that 5 million farmers today can produce more than twice as much as 12 million could in 1930.

Third, this technological revolution means that big farms are required for peak efficiency in most crop and animal production. Farm experts estimate that in basic crops it is a rare farmer selling $10,000 of output per year who can cover all his costs; yet three-fourths of all farms are below this level, and over 40 percent of all farms have total sales (not profits) of less than $2,500 annually. Only about 30,000 of all the nation's 3 million farms sell more than $25,000 of product annually, a level at which modern farming apparently begins to yield a return on investment more comparable with other industries.

Fourth, farm incomes are low. Figure 26–1 presents the evidence. At the depth of the depression, per capita income of farm people was less than one-third that of the nonfarm population. Today it is about 70 percent of that of the rest of the population, but the narrowing of this income gap is due entirely to increasing government benefit payments to farmers and to gains by farmers' incomes from nonfarm sources (dividends, urban property, and the like); in addition, the number of farmers has fallen rapidly over the period. As Figure 26–1 shows, in 1969

farmers' incomes from farm sources excluding government payments was only a little over $1,000 per capita, compared to nearly $4,000 for the nonfarm population. Many farmers have made a lot of money since the 1930s, and most remaining farm families are in total better off than they've ever been before. But the millionaire livestock ranchers in Texas and the farm Cadillacs in the Iowa corn-hog belt are the exceptions, not the rule. In 1969, over 80 percent of all farm production came from the less than 1 million large farms; conversely, the 2 million small farmers together accounted for less than 20 percent of total farm production, and their living standards were comparably low.

Fifth, agriculture is highly susceptible to economic instability. In booms things are good, but in depressions the bottom falls out. The two world wars provided the biggest agricultural booms of modern times. Prices for wheat, corn, cotton, and hogs soared, far higher than those of industrial products. Farmland values skyrocketed.

But the depression of the 1930s was desperate. Farm prices fell to 44 percent of 1929 levels, but mortgage costs and taxes stayed up. Demand for many crops was insufficient to pay even for harvesting them. Mortgage foreclosures swept the country, until in desperation farmers in the Midwest began a wave of forcible resistance to foreclosures. Farm money incomes

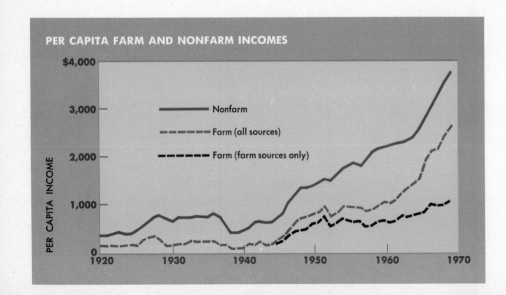

PER CAPITA FARM AND NONFARM INCOMES

Nonfarm
Farm (all sources)
Farm (farm sources only)

PER CAPITA INCOME

fig. 26–1

Per capita farm incomes have long been under nonfarm incomes. Recently a substantial part of total farm income has come from nonfarm sources. (Source: U.S. Department of Agriculture.)

plummeted below subsistence levels, and many farm families survived only by living off their land.

What would you do if you were a farmer and prices dropped? You'd be more likely to increase output than to decrease it. By planting more acreage next year you'd hope to increase your income enough to offset the lower price. But there, alas, enters the villain, inelastic demand for farm products. With inelastic demand, more total output sends prices and total farm income nosediving further. Falling prices don't increase the amount of food people buy very much.

So, relatively declining demand, rapid technological change, low incomes, and high sensitivity to instability have dominated the history of American agriculture over the past century. Prosperities have eased the gradual relative decline of agriculture; in depressions the adjustment has been dragging and painful.

The Farm Problem

Is there a "farm problem"? Or are the relatively low farm prices and incomes just evidence that the competitive system is working the way it is supposed to, pushing resources out of an area where consumer demand has fallen steadily relative to the rest of the economy? Whether you call agriculture sick or not, are its difficulties to be blamed on the fact that competition doesn't really work, or on the fact that it works very well indeed?

In a competitive economy, we would expect market forces to pull resources into areas where demand grew fastest, away from relatively declining areas. And this has happened in agriculture. In prosperity, people have migrated heavily from rural to industrial jobs. And the pattern of crops and animals produced by farmers has responded to shifting consumer demand. But in recessions, with the traditionally high farm birthrates, people pile up on the farms; they have no place to go. And even with heavy out-migration, mainly young people from the small-farm areas, the population left in agriculture has continually been too large to earn average incomes equal to more than about half those in the rest of the economy.

Insofar as there is a special "farm problem," it appears to arise primarily from a combination of the following circumstances:

1. Demand for farm products declining relative to the rest of the economy.
2. High birthrates in farm families, and limited mobility out of farming.
3. Rapid technological advance in agriculture.
4. Inelastic demand for most farm products.
5. Inelastic supply of farmland.
6. Active competition among farmers, with no one farmer big enough to do more than adjust to the market price.
7. Instability in farm prices, magnified by cyclical fluctuations in business and industry.
8. The uncertain weather.

If agriculture is sick, it boils down pretty much to this—too many resources, especially too many farms and farmers, in agriculture relative to the rest of the economy. Market pressures are steadily shifting resources (especially young people) and inefficient producers out of farming. But agriculture faces a tough, continuing adjustment problem, especially with such rapid increases in output per farm worker.

As everyone knows, the federal government has provided continuing large subsidies to farmers, partly through buying up farm surpluses to maintain prices at federal-support levels above free-market prices, and partly through paying farmers not to produce potential surpluses. But before we go on to examine agriculture's claims for special aid, ask yourself what you would expect to happen to agriculture if it were left free to shift for itself in the marketplace.

Private Enterprise or Intervention?

The core of the farm problem is presented in Figure 26–2. Let *SS* be the supply curve, and *DD* the demand curve for beans. Given these curves, the equilibrium price will clearly be twenty cents per pound with 20,000 bushels of beans produced each year. All farmers produc-

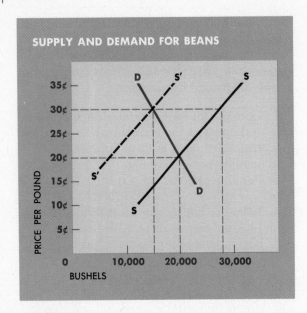

SUPPLY AND DEMAND FOR BEANS

fig. 26–2

Market-clearing price for beans is twenty cents. If price is fixed at thirty cents, there are 13,000 pounds of unsold beans.

ing beans will be doing so at a cost of no more than twenty cents per pound, because at any lower price their incomes would not cover their costs. Everyone who is willing to pay twenty cents per pound for beans is getting all he wants to buy at that price.

Suppose, however, that bean farmers protest that the price is too low and they are not really making a decent living at that price. They lobby for a price-support program for beans, and they get it—at a price of thirty cents per pound, which they allege will give them a decent living standard. What is the result?

The first result is that there is a large excess supply in the market. At thirty cents per pound, roughly 28,000 bushels of beans will be produced, but buyers will only take about 15,000 bushels. Those farmers who sell at thirty cents per pound may be very happy, but there are a lot of farmers holding the unsold 13,000 bushels of beans. Clearly they will have a large incentive to undercut the legal price, and offer their beans at twenty-eight or twenty-five cents a pound to get rid of them, albeit in violation of the law.

The government, considerate of the bean farmers' plight, has two main alternatives. First, it can simply buy up the overhang of 13,000 bushels of beans on the market, thereby supporting the price of thirty cents for all farmers who want to produce and sell their 28,000 bushels at that price. This is fine for the bean producers, but bad for the taxpayers who have to pick up the bill for the 13,000 bushels of beans. The government cannot sell the beans on the open market, because to do so would undercut the price it is trying to support. Thus, in all probability it will store them—or perhaps find a way to give them away to hungry people, here or in other parts of the world.

Alternatively, the government can simply pay bean farmers not to produce as much as they would like to at that price. Thus, the government might provide a "soil-conservation" payment of ten cents per bushel for beans on the condition that no more than 15,000 bushels are produced by the industry as a whole. This, in effect, moves the supply curve back to the left so that the total amount supplied at thirty cents per pound is the 15,000 bushels that the private market will take. This movement of the supply curve is shown by S^1S^1.

How do the various parties fare now? The bean farmers are happy. They are getting the equivalent of thirty cents per pound for their beans and they are permitted to either produce, or be paid for not producing, a total of 28,000 bushels. Alas, the taxpayers and the consumers are in a different position. Taxpayers end up spending ten cents per pound in subsidy for 13,000 bushels of beans not produced under the soil-conservation plan. And consumers must pay thirty cents per pound for beans, getting only 15,000 bushels at that price. Clearly, there are too many bean farmers and too many bean farms in the industry, but they are paid to stay there by the "soil-conservation" subsidy paid by the government to reduce supply and thereby maintain the thirty cents per pound price. A lot of farmers who would be submarginal at the competitive price of twenty cents are subsidized to stay in bean farming by taxpayers and consumers combined.

The government may recoup part of its loss by selling the surplus beans on the world market at a competitive world-market price, well below the thirty cents supported domestic price. But if it does so, it will encounter cries of "dumping" by foreign bean producers who will find themselves being undercut by what they consider a government-subsidized price from the United States. If the government can't sell the beans abroad, perhaps it can at least give them away to hungry countries. This will make the cost of the gifts quite clear, and the full amount of the subsidy is seen as a loss to the government. But don't forget that even then domestic consumers are only getting 15,000 bushels and have to pay thirty cents per pound for them.

Agriculture's Claims to Special Aid

Do farmers have any claim to such special subsidies from the taxpayers and consumers? Consider a few of the arguments.

1. **Low-income status.** Low farm incomes are a main argument. Farmers want a reasonable living and a fair return for a hard day's work, just as much as anyone else. If you believe that everyone should have at least some minimum income, this plea is understandable. But while many farmers are in the lowest income groups, many others are not. Thus, helping all farmers may be a shotgun approach that confuses personal needs with farming as an industry. As a practical matter, under both Democratic and Republican farm programs the rich farmers, not the poor ones, have received the big government checks. Moreover, aid programs based on staying in agriculture (that is, aid to the "industry" rather than to needy persons as persons) perpetuate the basic cause of low farm incomes by making farmers stay in farming to get government aid.

2. **Special susceptibility to business fluctuations.** Farmers are hard hit by depressions. Does agriculture have a special claim for help on this score? Surely the main approach must be through greater stability for the economy as a whole. This argument, you should note, is easy to confuse with the general low-income argument above. Don't count the same thing twice.

3. **The weather.** The vagaries of nature may upset the best-laid plans. Droughts and floods come. There's nothing new about this problem, of course. Centuries ago the emperors of China sought to establish something surprisingly like the modern "ever-normal granary" storage plan, to save up surpluses in bumper years for the shortage years to come. There's no doubt that the weather can make things tough for the farmer. ("Well, he can always move out and take a job somewhere else if he doesn't like it," say the objectors.)

4. **Special aid to offset advantages of other groups.** Farmers claim that they are injured by special privileges for other groups, and hence that they deserve offsetting special assistance. The American tariff on industrial products has long forced the farmer to pay higher domestic prices while his own foreign markets are weakened by the same tariffs. Monopolistic conditions have been tolerated by government officials in many industries, for businesses and labor unions. All these raise the prices paid by farmers and restrict movement from farms to urban occupations.

Many economists object to this argument for special aid to agriculture. They maintain that the answer lies in removing special privileges for other groups rather than in building up still more special privileges and restrictions. Fighting evil with evil leads to a self-feeding spiral of special privileges and restrictions, according to this counterargument. Besides, U.S. tariffs have been dramatically reduced since the 1940s (see Figure 42–1).

5. **The need for soil conservation.** Most Americans believe it is desirable to conserve our natural resources. Often the advantage of conservation to society as a whole exceeds the dollars-and-cents return to the farmer in undertaking soil-conservation measures; this is a case where the social benefits exceed those to the individual producer. Thus, much of the farm-aid program has been justified as soil conservation (for example, conserving soil by not planting part of the land each year). In fact, however, much of the conservation talk has served to disguise programs whose main goal is to raise farm income. And at the moment, the problem is too much farmland rather than too

little. But the conservation argument is an important one in many persons' minds.

6. **Agriculture as a way of life.** Many people look on agriculture as a stable, sound way of life, harking back to the ways of our fathers—an anchor to windward in a hectic world of assembly-lines, tenements, skyscrapers, and neuroses. The farmer is still an individual, not just a cog in a huge economic machine. This, they feel, is a way of life worth preserving.

However strong this case may seem to you, it raises some economic dilemmas. The very traits of the farmer and his life that are admired most in this view are the ones associated with small-scale, often inefficient, family farming. Large-scale commercial farming that promises a higher farm standard of living compromises these very virtues. Experts agree that only the bigger farms can provide reasonable family incomes with today's mechanized farming methods.

A closely related argument hinges on large farm families. There is no provision in the price system, say some, for paying farmers for the outlays of money and effort they make in bearing, rearing, and educating a large number of children who later move into other economic areas. Economically, the argument runs, human beings are capital resources of the nation just as much as are buildings and machines.

But on closer examination, this, like the low-income argument, is logically a personal, not an industry, argument. If we want to encourage and pay for large families, all right. But if we do, the aid should be based on size of family, not on the number of bushels of wheat not produced. Perhaps we think farm children are especially healthy and well brought up; if so, focus the aid on large farm families. Keeping our goals clearly in mind is essential if we expect public policies to do what we want them to do.

The Farm-Aid Program

"Parity"

The core of the New Deal farm-aid was the concept of "parity"—parity between farm incomes and prices and those in the rest of the economy. Parity is still the foundation of the farm-aid program today.

As it was developed in the New Deal legislation, farm parity meant that prices paid and received by farmers should be in the same ratio as in the "normal" years 1909 to 1914. If farm prices drop relative to other prices (or don't rise as fast as other prices), government action should push the farm prices back up to parity.

If you're a skeptic, you will recall that the period from 1909 to 1914 was the golden age of agriculture. You may ask, why not a parity program for buggies and women's high-buttoned shoes, based on the years 1905 to 1906, which saw the peak for the buggy and high-button shoe industries?

In the 1950s Congress finally shifted the parity base for each year to the ten preceding years. But at that same time it inserted wage rates and taxes in the index of prices paid by farmers, which effectively increased the rise in that index and with it the height of the parity price for farm products.

To the man from Mars, the parity farm program would be a strange phenomenon. It would be hard to explain to him why we should pay people not to produce things and buy up available food to hold prices at levels where people won't consume it. But the New Deal farm program was comprehensive. According to a joking description then current in Washington circles, the Agricultural Adjustment Agency paid the farmers not to raise the crops, then the Commodity Credit Corporation paid them (through loans) to store any surplus that AAA didn't prevent, and the Federal Surplus Commodities Corporation bought up and gave away what surplus was left over. Though only a half-truth, the description had an uncomfortably penetrating ring. And the basic nature of the government's farm-aid program has been much the same for every administration since—Democratic and Republican.

Production Control and Marketing Quotas

The core of the New Deal farm program was the effort to prevent crop "surpluses" and to hold up prices by restricting production. The designers knew about the effects of inelastic demand. Limitation of acreage planted was the primary method used in the original AAA, supplemented by a system of marketing quotas for cotton, tobacco, wheat, rice, and vegetables. The arrangement thus was strikingly similar to private industrial cartels where total output is limited, the market is "divided up," and price is maintained by agreement.

How effective have these production-control and marketing-control schemes proved? The answer is, not very effective. Not because smaller supplies would not have raised prices and farm incomes; with inelastic demand they would. But because the programs weren't very successful in restricting output. Acreage restrictions cut back the number of acres planted to wheat or corn, but profit-seeking farmers figured out ways to increase yields per acre. Development of hybrid seed corn alone offset the acreage-restriction program on corn; better fertilization and land-use practices helped; and farmers used the freed land to raise substitute crops. Yield per acre rose nearly 50 percent over the past decade alone.

Thus, production has stayed up or increased, while prices have been held above where private demand would clear the market. The result has been continued government accumulation of surpluses, leading to immense storage costs in addition to the basic costs of buying up the surpluses. Since the government cannot sell its stocks on the open market without depressing the supported parity price, it holds the surpluses, while consumers pay the high supported prices. Thus, the public pays two ways— through taxes to buy up the surpluses at supported prices, and through the higher prices on farm products at the supermarket. Look back at Figure 26–2 for the simple supply and demand economics of such price-fixing.

To get around part of this conspicuous waste, recent administrations have proposed plans whereby the government would, in effect, guarantee the farmer a supported price but still sell its surplus stocks at less than parity price. Thus, the surpluses would not go to waste and consumers would get farm products at lower prices,

even though taxpayers would subsidize farmers. What if this action produced a market price below the support level, as it almost certainly would? Then the government would give the farmers a subsidy for the difference. But these plans have received only lukewarm support, especially from farmers. Visible subsidies are not as popular as hidden ones, even if they're a cheaper way of getting the same results.

Crop-Storage and Loan Plans. One major device for supporting farm prices has been crop-storage "loans" for farmers, through the Commodity Credit Corporation. It works like this: The farmer can get a government loan on his major drop at, say, 85 percent of the parity price. He then seals the crop in storage. Anytime he likes, he can take the crop out of storage, sell it off, and pay back the government.

The exceptional thing about these storage loans is that they give the farmer a "Heads I win, tails you lose" setup. For example, if a farmer has a $2-a-bushel loan on his wheat and the market price falls to $1.75, he can turn the wheat over to the government, let it bear the loss, and keep the $2 as, in effect, a price for his wheat. On the other hand, if the price goes up to $2.50, he can sell the wheat, pay back the $2 to the government, and pocket the difference. Thus, the crop-"loan" program is in effect a guaranteed minimum price for the farmer, plus an option on any higher price that may appear.

The effects of over a quarter century of price support and production-control plans are hard to assess precisely. Presumably farm prices have been higher than they otherwise would have been. Billions after billions of dollars have gone into supporting farm prices and into paying farmers not to produce, mainly through withholding land from the production of particular crops. In 1971, nearly $5 billion was budgeted for price and income supports. Since nearly all these plans have been based on maintaining prices or on percentage reductions of previous acreage, they have consistently provided large benefits to the large farmers (with large crops to sell and large acreage to cut back) and small help for the little farmers who need help most. There is no clear evidence that total

COMMODITY CREDIT CORPORATION INVESTMENT IN FARM CROPS

BILLIONS OF DOLLARS

Other

Wheat

Cotton

Corn

1952　1960　1969

fig. 26-3

This chart shows the amount of government funds tied up in farm crop loans and surplus stocks each year. Tobacco and soybeans account for most "Other" in recent years. (Source: Commodity Credit Corporation.)

farm production has been held below the levels that would have prevailed without the programs. Many competent observers believe that the various government programs adopted have done more to stimulate farm production than to reduce it.

But two results are crystal clear. First, over the past ten years federal agricultural expenditures, mainly through price- and income-support programs, amounted to more than the entire increase in farm income over the period; even this support was insufficient to raise average farm incomes relative to nonfarm ones.

Second, the huge farm surpluses piled up by the government have been mute, if expensive, evidence of the difficulties of trying to maintain prices above market levels through government action. Figure 26–3 summarizes the evidence since World War II. By 1969 the Commodity Credit Corporation, the main agency supporting farm prices, had investments of about $3 billion in surplus crops.

Figure 26–4 looks at the problem another way —what percentage of the annual crop is loaned on or bought up by the government each year? The federal price-support program isn't just nibbling at the edge of farm production. The C.C.C. bought up (directly or through loans)

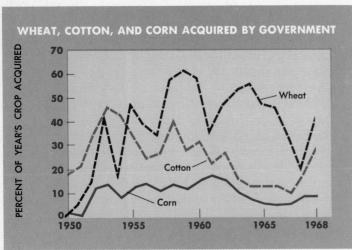

WHEAT, COTTON, AND CORN ACQUIRED BY GOVERNMENT

PERCENT OF YEAR'S CROP ACQUIRED

Wheat

Cotton

Corn

1950　1955　1960　1965　1968

fig. 26-4

A big proportion of the cotton, wheat, and corn crops has been bought up or loaned on by the government in most recent years. (Source: U.S. Department of Agriculture.)

384

table 26-1

Federal Government Aid to Agriculture*

Year	Federal Aid (In Billions)	Percent of Total Federal Budget	Farm Population (In Millions)
1961	$3.3	3.4%	14.8
1963	5.1	4.6	13.3
1965	4.8	4.1	12.4
1967	4.4	2.8	10.9
1969	6.2	3.4	10.3
1971	5.4	2.7	9.5

*Data from U.S. Budget for Fiscal 1971 and from *Economic Report of the President*. Figures are for fiscal years.

about 40 percent of the entire cotton crop and about 15 percent of the wheat crop over the last half of the 1960s. Wheat, cotton, and corn are the big three of the price-support program, but the legislation covers a total of 20 crops.[1] Even with a major program to dispose of the surpluses here and abroad through sale and gift, this has consistently piled up the surplus stocks.[2]

Table 26–1 summarizes the cost of price-support programs to the government over the past decade, and the beneficiaries; note that this does not include the costs to consumers in the form of higher prices.

What the table does not convey is the concentration of federal aid payments to a relatively small number of large farmers. For example, in 1968 one farm in Kern County, California received a federal farm-subsidy payment of $4.1 million for not growing cotton; this reflected crop-reduction payments on a farm covering 83,000 acres. In four San Joaquin Valley counties in California, 2,300 cotton farms received a total of $65.4 million in federal farm subsidies. While these are extreme cases, most poor small farmers, who need help most, get tiny, if any, subsidy payments at all, because "conservation" subsidies are based on the acreage or crop cutback, usually some proportion of previous output levels. In 1970, Congress limited payments per crop to each individual to $55,000. Whether this limit will be retained remains to be seen.

Programs To Promote Agricultural Efficiency

Long before the government set out to raise farm incomes by restricting production, the Department of Agriculture was busy telling farmers how to **increase** production. A broad program of scientific research, on-the-ground help for farmers through nationwide agricultural experiment stations, advice on soil-conservation practices, and a variety of other measures have played a big role in raising the efficiency of American agriculture to a level unparalleled in most other nations.

But by carrying out this eminently sensible program, the Department of Agriculture has been sabotaging its own crop-restriction programs. The American farmer is nobody's fool, and he has taken full advantage of modern methods to increase yields even while he is cutting back acreage under the income-support programs. From an individual point of view, that's the way to have the best of both worlds. Would you do differently if you were a farmer?

U.S. Agriculture and the World Food Problem

U.S. farm policy seems particularly anomalous in view of the total world food situation. As was indicated in the appendix to Chapter 19, over 2 billion of the world's population live in countries where malnutrition and undernourishment are widespread. While actual starvation is relatively uncommon except in periods of drought or other special disaster, inadequate food supplies lower health and energy levels for hundreds of millions of people. And actual starvation is never far away. In these countries, Malthus's predictions look about right.

---

[1] The others are barley, beans, butter, cheese, dried milk, honey, peanuts, flaxseed, sorghum, oats, rice, rye, soybeans, tung oil, tobacco, wool, and mohair.

[2] Surpluses are sold mainly abroad (where the world price is under the U.S. support price) and at low prices domestically when deterioration threatens. The average loss has been about 25 percent of the C.C.C. investment.

The world food situation reflects unbalance at least as much as total shortage. In fact, world food production has grown somewhat more rapidly than population over the past twenty-five years, and the doomsday criers who predict mass starvation over the entire face of the earth in the next decade or two appear to be wrong. But the U.S. problem of farm surpluses is special to only a few of the richer countries and those that depend heavily on agricultural production, such as Canada and Australia. The total food deficit is large for the less-developed nations of the world. Table 26–2 presents rough estimates of the share of the world food deficit that is centered in different areas.

Why should the United States not produce all the food it can and sell the "surplus" above our needs to the hungry less-developed nations? The answer is simple: the less-developed nations can't afford to pay for it at anything like world prices, so we have, in essence, the alternative of giving the food to them or of having it go into storage here. In fact, the United States has given away every year during the past two decades a large amount of "surplus" food, accumulated under the U.S. farm-price-support program. During the 1960s, for example, food aid to the less-developed nations averaged between $1.0 billion and $1.5 billion annually. More recently, the total has declined gradually, partly reflecting reduced congressional willingness to provide foreign aid, and partly reflecting the smaller surpluses being accumulated by the U.S. farm program.[3]

Critics point to what seems to them the nonsense and immorality of paying U.S. farmers not to raise crops while hundreds of millions are hungry. How much aid we want to provide to the less-developed countries, and how to provide it, is an issue that needs to be faced directly on its merits; the concluding pages of Chapter 19 summarized the issues. The principle of opportunity cost is the key here again. If in fact we can produce more food only at the cost of giving up other uses of the resources involved, there is a real cost to the American people in producing good and giving it to the less-developed countries. How much we want our government to spend this way is a question properly determined through normal democratic political channels. On the other hand, if there is no opportunity cost involved in using resources (men, capital, and land) to produce more crops (for example in a depression period), there is virtually zero opportunity cost to the United States in producing the extra food and sending it to less-developed nations. Since World War II, the United States has had no major depressions, so the alternative cost of producing more food to be sent abroad would surely have been positive—though exactly how large is difficult to estimate, given the persistent surplus of some types of labor and land in American agriculture. President Nixon's budget for fiscal 1971 included about $900 million of "Food for Peace."[4]

table 26-2

World Food Deficit — 1970*

Country	Share of Deficit (Percent)
Central and South America	2.3
Africa	5.1
India	13.2
Other South Asia	5
East Asia (excluding Japan)	12
Communist Asia	62.4

* Data from W. W. Cochrane, The World Food Problem, p. 47.

[3] Much of this food aid was provided under "Public Law 480," which, in essence, permits the United States to sell the surplus food abroad to less-developed countries and accept payment in local currency, which the U.S. government promises not to take out of the country by converting it into dollars. Thus, for example, huge stocks of wheat have been provided to India for many years in exchange for "payment" in rupees. But since the United States has accumulated vastly more rupees than there is any likelihood it will be able to spend in India for the foreseeable future, the food is close to a gift. Part of U.S. government expenses overseas have been met by P.L. 480 funds; "Fulbright aid" to American students and teachers to spend time in the countries involved is a well-known example in university circles.

[4] In addition to food transfers, the United States and other developed nations provide large financial grants and loans to the less-developed nations. Total direct U.S. government nonmilitary aid ran between $3 and $4 billion annually during the 1960s; it was contracted sharply after 1969, and is now budgeted at less than $2 billion per year, a small fraction of 1 percent of the gross national product.

Agriculture in the Political Economy

In the fiscal year 1971, the federal government spent over $5 billion on special aid for agriculture. In the same year, total farm income from farming (excluding income from investments and other nonfarm sources) was about $16 billion. Thus, approximately one-third of total income from farming was accounted for by federal-government aid. Yet in 1971 there were fewer than 3 million farm families in the United States, out of a total of over 60 million family units. As Table 26–1 indicated, total federal expenditures on farm aid have been relatively stable over the past decade, though the farm population has declined steadily relative to total population, to less than 5 percent now.

Is this expenditure for a small special-interest group justified? Agriculture may have some valid claims to special aid. But, at least by the standards of a free-market competitive economy, this is far from a blanket justification for helping the farmer every time he finds himself in trouble. If he raises lemons when the customers want oranges, does he have any more claim to special government help than any other businessman who guesses wrong? Even more fundamentally, if consumer demand for nonfarm products grows faster than for farm products, and if, simultaneously, farmers have lots of children, does the farm population have any better claim to being supported comfortably in agriculture all their lives by a government subsidy than had the buggy and bloomer manufacturers when consumer demand passed them by? In a competitive economy, resources must follow consumer demand if they are to be efficiently allocated. The basic farm problem is adjustment to shifting consumer demands and getting productive resources out of agriculture, not subsidies to maintain an uneconomically large number of people and farms in farming.

In perspective, three big facts stand out about the farm legislation of the past half century: One is the farmers' success in getting what they want. As one Washington correspondent put it, "As long as they act together the farmers can get anything out of the government short of good growing weather—and Washington is working on that through cloud seeding."

Anomalously, to give the individualistic farmers the things they wanted, the government had to make them the core of the first big central-planning movement in its peacetime history. But their own organizations had a big hand in the process. Never forget that the political process is a major part of political economy. Stuart Chase summed it up this way: "If any American believes that the New Deal farm legislation was the product of dreamers, long-haired professors, and agents from Moscow, he is a pretty good dreamer himself. It was the product primarily of local farmers crying to be delivered from free competition."[5] Some observers believe the political force of agriculture is weakening, and small reductions in annual farm-aid budgets give some support to this analysis. But this doesn't change the general picture painted above.

Second, it's clear that forty years of massive federal aid haven't solved "the farm problem." The data above speak for themselves. The farm problem today doesn't look much different from what it did a decade ago, and the arguments about farm aid sound about the same—unless we are more concerned than before about the world food situation.

The third striking fact is the widespread failure to distinguish between the economic problem of efficiency in resource allocation and the ethical problem of minimum income levels. On the economic side, there can be little doubt that agriculture has been overexpanded in the American economy over the last half century, except during war periods; the direction pointed by the price system has been clear and unequivocal. Economically, our efforts should have been devoted to increasing the mobility of resources out of agriculture. On the ethical side, you have to make up your own mind on whether poor farmers' incomes ought to be subsidized by the rest of the population.

Most farm aid has been consciously or subconsciously aimed at the farm-income problem, though it has focused on holding up farm prices. Failure to think through the separate economic and ethical aspects of the problem has produced poor results on both scores. On the eco-

[5]*Democracy Under Pressure* (New York: The Twentieth Century Fund, 1945), p. 99.

nomic side, farm-aid legislation has by and large required farmers to stay in farming as a condition of receiving aid. They have been paid for not raising crops and have been guaranteed prices that include government subsidies. If they leave agriculture, they lose the subsidies.

So tying benefit payments to products, not to people, has produced a grossly ineffective system for dealing with the ethical (income) problem. By raising farm prices, the program has given the biggest benefits to the biggest farmers, since they have the most to sell. By paying farmers for cutting back production in proportion to acres farmed, the program has handed the biggest benefit checks to the highest-income farmers, now including many huge corporate farms. This adds up to the anomalous result of passing out benefits in inverse relation to need. Only by recognizing the low-income subsidy objective as such, if that is a major objective, can we hope to make efficient use of government funds for that purpose.

There is no necessary contradiction between the economic objective of efficient resource allocation and the ethical objective of leveling up low incomes. We could pay direct subsidies to low-income farm families, finance greater mo-

bility out of farming, and encourage efficient, low-cost production by the remaining farmers prepared to meet the test of a free-price market. Economists and others have repeatedly advocated such programs, with elimination of farm subsidies spread, say, over five years to avoid excessive hardships on present inefficient farmers. But these proposals have drawn violent reactions from farmers and their supporters.[6] It is intriguing indeed that our farm-aid programs have helped most the well-off few among the farmers, yet they have apparently been popular vote getters among the millions of farm voters. It is easy to see why the political parties, in power and out, court the farm votes in the key agricultural states that have swung many an election. Why farm voters have not been more perceptive about who is helped how much by what farm aid is harder to understand. But simple supply-and-demand analysis points to glaring economic weaknesses in the expensive American farm program.

[6]See, e.g., the similar proposal advanced in 1962 by the Committee for Economic Development (a group of leading businessmen) and the sharp reply by Secretary of Agriculture Freeman, reprinted in Joseph, Seeber, and Bach, *Economic Analysis and Public Policy*.

Review

FOR ANALYSIS AND DISCUSSION

1. Is there a "farm problem" that public policy needs to be concerned about? If so, what is it?
2. In a competitive economy, resources are supposed to move where consumer demand is strongest, as individuals seek higher incomes. In the light of the comparative incomes shown by Figure 26–1, how do you explain the fact that so many families stay in agriculture?
3. In agriculture, output per man has recently grown at the rate of 6 percent per annum, twice that for the rest of the economy. Since we face a situation of continuing farm surpluses, would a slowdown of the growth rate in agriculture be a desirable solution to the farm problem?
4. If the demand for basic farm products is substantially inelastic, is there any way the government can help farmers except through output-restriction programs?
5. The Committee for Economic Development, an organization of leading businessmen, has proposed a gradual reduction of government support for farm prices, pointing out that this would both save

money and help induce the excess supply of farmers to move to other occupations. This proposal was followed by large-scale farmers' boycotts of some businesses represented in the C.E.D. The farmers' biggest complaint was that C.E.D. had suggested that there were too many farmers. Were these boycotts justified? Are there indeed too many farmers?

6. There are fewer than 4 million farm families in the United States. Yet Congress has repeatedly voted to grant huge subsidies to agriculture. How do you explain this fact?

7. If you were a congressman, what suggestions would you make with regard to the "farm problem"?

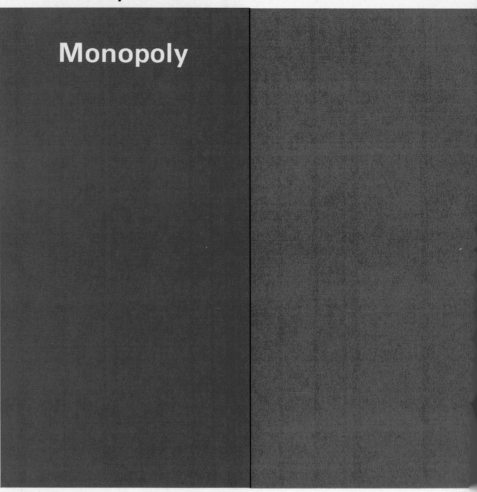

twenty-seven

Monopoly

The Bases of Monopoly
Pure Monopoly
Pure Monopoly—Evaluation

Monopoly is something like sin. Everybody says he's against it, but a lot of people aren't very clear just what it is they're against. Like sin, monopoly has to be defined before one can talk much sense about it, or decide what, if anything, ought to be done about it.

The Spectrum from Competition to Monopoly

Monopoly is generally defined as a market in which there is only one seller—as the Greek derivation of the word suggests. But this is deceptively simple. There is no commodity that doesn't have some substitutes, more or less close, and we have no sharp criterion of how close the substitute can be before we no longer have a monopoly. The Aluminum Company of America, up to World War II, was often called a monopoly in this sense: There was no other American producer of basic aluminum. But steel, wood, copper, and other materials are possible substitutes for aluminum, if the price of aluminum gets too high. Thus, Alcoa had a monopoly in producing aluminum, but certainly not in producing metals. Or consider General Motors. It has a monopoly in producing Chevrolets, but there is Ford next door producing close substitutes. In one sense, every producer who isn't in a purely competitive market has a monopoly in selling his own product. But the closer the substitutes produced by others, the less his "monopoly" matters as a practical matter.

Pure Monopoly

In spite of these problems, economists have defined a situation they call "pure" monopoly. Consider the local power company in a small town, as an example. It is the only producer of electricity in the town, and the substitution of candles, oil lamps, or gas lighting by consumers who rebel at high prices is not a very serious likelihood. (The big-city public utility is likely to be more exposed to potential competition, since industrial users of electricity do have less remote substitutes.) Clearly, Alcoa wasn't in as strong a position as is a public-utility company, but both approach the pure-monopoly classification, which is characterized by:

1. Only one seller of the good or service.
2. Rivalry from producers of substitutes so remote as to be insignificant.

Under these circumstances, the pure monopolist can set the market price himself, and customers don't have close substitutes to turn to. He is a "price maker," unlike the wheat farmer who is a price taker. But even the monopolist has to face up to the realities of elasticity of demand. He can put his price where he wishes. But unless demand is perfectly inelastic, the higher he puts his price the less he can sell. Partly, the elasticity of demand for any product reflects the presence of potential substitutes, and there is no monopoly so pure that it can escape completely the possibility of partial substitutes. Thus, completely pure monopoly is never quite found in the real world, and "pure monopoly" shades, albeit imperceptibly into "monopolistic competition," just as "pure competition" shades into lesser degrees of competition.[1]

Monopolistic Competition and Oligopoly

There is a spectrum from competition to pure monopoly. Where there are a good many sellers of only slightly differentiated products, but not enough to make the market perfectly competitive, we call the situation "monopolistic competition." There may be a dozen or a hundred sellers of substantially identical products. But the products vary somewhat. For example, breakfast-food manufacturers don't make just breakfast food. They make Wheaties, Cheerios, and all the rest. Even corn flakes aren't just corn flakes; Post and Kellogg put them in differently colored boxes under different names, and to the buyer they are at least somewhat differentiated. Or stores may provide 1i-erent services with the same product—say, free delivery. The degree of "product differentiation" gets to be more substantial for, say, television sets. Philco, RCA, and Sylvania may all show the same picture on the same-sized tube when turned on to Channel 4, but neither the makers nor the customers believe the sets are the same.

Where there are only a few competing producers, so each producer must take into account what each other producer does, we call the situation "oligopoly," which means few sellers. In the auto industry, with only a few big producers, obviously General Motors, Chrysler, and Ford have to pay a lot of attention to each other's policies in setting prices, even though their products are all somewhat differentiated. Firms in oligopolistic industries may compete actively, or they may get together ("collude") formally or informally to agree on prices and on sharing the market.

Most of the American economic system lies in between pure competition and pure monopoly. Each industry seems to be a little different. Yet we need to classify this huge "in-between" area into some major groups if we are to make any headway in analyzing how it operates. In looking at the world of monopolistic competition and oligopoly, economists often emphasize the following four questions:

1. How many producers are there of any

---

[1]The analogy to pure monopoly on the buyer's side is sometimes called "pure monopsony," which means one buyer. This case might prevail where there is only one buyer for labor services—say the mill in an isolated mill town. But like pure monopoly, pure monopsony is hard to find. For instance, workers are free to move to another town if the monopsonist exploits his position too much.

given commodity? The larger the number, the more likely competition is to be active.

2. **How close are the substitutes for the commodity?** The closer the substitutes are, the less real monopoly power any firm can exercise without losing customers.

3. **Do the producers involved compete on prices, or through nonprice channels such as quality and advertising?** In some cases producers may not compete at all—they may agree to maintain fixed shares of a market at some agreed price. But in the vast majority of cases firms do compete in some way—on price, on quality of product and services, through advertising, or in some other way.

4. **How easy is it for new firms to get into the industry, or into producing close substitutes for the industry's product?** A monopoly that can be invaded by anyone on short notice isn't much of a monopoly.

If we use these questions, we can immediately see some important subclasses under monopolistic competition and oligopoly. For example, the monopolistic-competition group is usually subdivided into cases where competition is primarily on prices, and those where it primarily takes the form of nonprice and advertising competition. Oligopolies seem to fall into three groups depending on whether they collude on prices and output (in which case they are often called "cartels"), follow a "leader" on price setting, or compete actively.

We come out with a division like this:

I. **Pure competition**—many sellers of an identical product (wheat).
II. **Monopolistic competition**—a substantial number of sellers of closely substitutable products.
   a. Price competition (vegetables in local grocery stores).
   b. Nonprice competition and "demand creation" (beer, men's suits).
III. **Oligopoly**—a few sellers of closely substitutable products.[2]

   a. Competition—on prices and through nonprice competition and demand creation (television, automobiles).
   b. Collaboration.
     1. Formal collusion on prices and on output—"cartels" (nickel, internationally).[3]
     2. Price leadership or informal price stabilization (steel, gasoline).
IV. **Pure monopoly**—one seller of a product without close substitutes (local water company).

The examples are intended merely to provide some concrete impressions to go with the analytical categories. Few real-world cases fit neatly and exclusively into any one of the intermediate categories. For example, there is some demand creation, and quality competition as well as price competition, in groceries (case IIa); and there is surely some price as well as nonprice competition in both beer and men's suits (case IIb). The main purpose of the classification is to give us a rough framework to organize analysis of the various types of market behavior. Where industries are hybrids, we may need to use two or more of the analytical models in thinking about them.

Broadly, most of the "service" industries (retail trade, legal services, banking, and so on) fall in the monopolistic competition category, as do a good many manufacturing firms. Much of the manufacturing (probably over half) falls under the oligopoly head. Only public utilities provide major examples of "pure monopoly."

The Bases of Monopoly

The basic test of an effective monopoly is its power to exclude competitors from the market. If a firm can keep out potential competitors, it can raise prices with relative impunity. The nearer the substitutes that competitors can put on the market, the weaker is the firm's monopoly position. The ideal monopoly (from

---

[2]Where there are only two sellers, another Greek word, "duopoly," is used. This is a special case of oligopoly.

[3]Formal collusion in setting prices or dividing up markets is illegal under the Sherman Act, as we shall see in Chapter 30.

the monopolist's viewpoint) would cover an absolutely essential product with no effective substitutes.

Government Action as a Basis for Monopoly

The strongest monopolies are the public utilities. An exclusive government franchise is about as airtight protection as any monopoly can hope for. This arrangement is found in most localities for water, electricity, gas, and telephone companies. Even where multiple companies are permitted by law, the market territory is usually divided up by law or regulatory commission. Having granted this enviable monopoly position, however, governments invariably regulate the prices the monopoly can charge. Often they maintain supervision over the company's whole operations, to protect the public's interest. Otherwise, the stockholders of the local water or gas company would be in a happy position indeed.

Governments intervene in other ways to provide partial bases for monopolies. The farm-aid programs of the past three decades have supported prices and induced farmers to behave like a cartel in restricting output. Local building codes, which specify particular types of construction and particular materials, are manifestly intended to protect the public against unsafe construction and poor work, but in fact provide a widespread basis for monopolistic practices by building suppliers and building-trade unions. The entire federal patent system, discussed below, protects the monopoly position of the inventor. Federal legislation establishes the right of workers to combine in unions that in essence act as monopolies in selling their labor to employers.

Patents and Research

The patent law gives the inventor exclusive control over his invention for seventeen years. If a patent gives effective control over production of some commodity, direct competition is almost impossible. Despite some recent limitations on their use as a basis for extending monopoly positions, patents can still provide a powerful basis for monopoly powers. For example, the United Shoe Machinery Corporation for years held exclusive control over the shoe-making machinery field through its patents.

Key patents underlie the industrial position of many major American concerns. Research has become part of the American industrial scene, and the "blue chips" of American industry come automatically to mind when we think of technological advance—General Electric, Du Pont, Standard Oil. These firms maintain their leading positions in oligopolistic industries in no small part by being first with the best in research. Over the past twenty years almost two-thirds of all patents have gone to corporations. General Electric alone, for example, received about 13,000; AT&T about 10,000.

Research is an expensive and cumulative process. It's hard for the little firm to compete, quite aside from the patent laws. For example, Du Pont's research laboratories alone would swallow up most of the business firms in the United States, and their stable of top-notch industrial scientists is the hopeless envy of all except a few leading rivals.

Control of Raw Materials

If you can get exclusive control over the raw materials needed to make your product, you're sitting pretty—at least until someone figures out a substitute material. A few major firms have managed to get such exclusive control. Two examples described in the late 1930s by the Temporary National Economic Committee provide examples.[4]

The International Nickel Company of Canada, Ltd., owns more than nine-tenths of the world's known reserve of nickel. The company produces more than 92 percent of the world's output of nickel.

Molybdenum is an element that finds its principle employment either in competition or in combination with other alloying metals, in the production of steels of exceptional toughness and strength. In Bartlett Mountain in Colorado, the Climax Molybdenum Company owns 95

[4]*Competition and Monopoly in American Industry,* TNEC Monograph No. 21, p. 79.

percent of the world's known store of commercially workable deposits of this metal.

Financial Resources and the Capital Market

The money needed to set up an efficient firm in many industries today is tens and even hundreds of millions of dollars. Not very many people have this much money, and it's hard to borrow ten million dollars unless you're already a very well-established person or firm, no matter how engaging a picture you paint of your prospects.

In a "perfect" capital market, funds would be available whenever the prospective borrower was willing and able to pay the going rate of interest on loans of comparable risk. In fact, however, it is hard for newcomers to raise funds in the market. Lenders are skeptical of unknown faces. Capital is rationed out to "desirable" borrowers rather than "sold" on the basis of borrowers' willingness to pay the quoted interest rates. Moreover, borrowing is especially expensive for small, new borrowers, even when they can get the funds.

The fact that large sums are often needed to set up new firms gives an important protection to established monopolists. The imperfection of the capital market, which often makes it especially hard for the newcomer and small producer to get funds, increases this protection.

Advertising

Advertising by itself would have a hard time establishing or even maintaining a monopoly on any product. But the entrenched positions of names like Cadillac and RCA-Victor in the mind of the American consumer are a cause of dismay to prospective competitors. Modern advertising has become increasingly "institutionalized." That is, ads aim primarily at building up the company's name and prestige, rather than at selling a particular product. Large-scale prestige advertising (for example, national TV advertising) costs big money, and only big and successful companies can afford it. The large company, which is often at least a partial mo-

nopolist, may find advertising a potent weapon for maintaining and extending its dominant position. Business outlays on advertising are large. They totaled $17 billion in 1970.

Unfair Competition

Running the little fellow out of business by unfair price cutting is one of the charges commonly brought against big business. If A&P prices groceries very low, it is accused of a devious intent to run the independents out and then to boost its own prices when competition is gone. And you don't have to look very far back into history to find plenty of cases where big business behaved this way. Such discriminatory price cutting, aimed to eliminate competition, often put price below cost. Often prices were cut only in areas where competition existed; high prices in other areas were used to keep profits up while competitors were being forced to the wall. The old Standard Oil Company provided some spectacular cases of such behavior —and with great success. But the practice was widespread during the late nineteenth and early twentieth centuries.

Such unfair price competition is now illegal. But the line between legitimate price cutting and unfair price cutting merely to eliminate competition is hard to draw in many cases. The more efficient producer always tend to eliminate the inefficient—unless, as is said to be the case in some modern industries, the dominant firm is already so big that it voluntarily chooses to encourage other firms in order to lessen the chance of antitrust prosecution by the government.

Large-Scale Production and Decreasing Costs

Low-cost mass production is the price of American industry. In many industries (steel, electrical equipment, automobiles, chemicals, and so on), maximum efficiency can be obtained only by large firms, each producing a substantial share of the total amount that can be sold on the market. In local areas, taking advantage of the economies of large-scale production may mean one or a few monopolistic firms—for example, the one grocery store a small town can reasonably support.

In extreme cases, the total market is not big enough to permit even one firm to operate at the optimal scale of output. Until a firm reaches this optimal scale, it is operating in its range of "decreasing costs." That is, by increasing output it can cut its cost per unit produced. This is described in common terminology as the "economies of large-scale production." In such cases, the pressures toward monopoly are great.

Figure 27–1 represents such an industry. The *TUC* curves are simply total-unit-cost curves for different scales of enterprise for a firm in the industry, say a local gas company. Scale TUC^3 is the most efficient scale in this case; its least-cost point is the lowest of any possible scale of enterprise. Each cost curve is drawn in a heavy line through the range in which it is lower than any other. The heavy scalloped line is therefore a curve that indicates the total unit cost at which each output can be produced as the size of the firm increases. This will be a decreasing-cost industry if demand is small relative to the scale of enterprise TUC^3—for example, if de-

mand is D^1D^1 or D^2D^2. It is a "decreasing-cost" industry because the economics of scale of enterprise within the single firm have not yet been fully exploited at any output less than *OM*, the least-cost point on TUC^3.

Under what conditions will our gas company remain a one-firm monopoly? Suppose demand is D^1D^1, and it sets a price well above average cost to produce a juicy profit. If it has no government-guaranteed monopoly, these large profits are likely to attract a competitor into the market. But in this market, with demand D^1D^1 it is obviously impossible for two or more firms to cover costs if they compete actively. Demand for gas in the area isn't big enough to support even one of them at optimal scale. If they get into a price war as each tries to get a bigger share of the market to permit lower unit costs of production, the likely result is bankruptcy for the weaker, with the stronger taking over the whole market again.

In such circumstances, instead of competing aggressively, the two firms may enter into a formal agreement or unspoken understanding to maintain price high and to restrict output. This arrangement is obviously wasteful of resources. Each firm is producing gas at a higher cost per cubic foot than if one firm alone were to produce the same total output. But under this market-sharing arrangement both companies may be able to make profits, and profits are likely to be the first concern of the managers. The social advantage of limiting the industry to one firm is obvious; this is the basis for most exclusive public-utility franchises.

How widespread decreasing-cost industries really are in the economy is a moot issue. Some claim that many firms could be more efficient if they were to expand further and take over more of the market. It is common gossip, for example, that General Motors could undersell the entire auto industry and eliminate all the other firms if it were not held back by possible antitrust action. But even if this rumor was true, in most industries the market appears to be adequate to support more than one firm of optimum size. Whether each market is big enough to support enough firms to guarantee effective competi-

fig. 27–1

This industry has decreasing unit costs up to output *M*. For any demand short of that amount, competition is unlikely to work effectively.

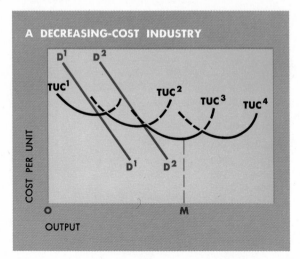

A DECREASING-COST INDUSTRY

tion is another question—a more difficult one that we will consider in detail a little later.

Pure Monopoly[5]

Where we draw the line between pure monopoly and monopolistic competition is arbitrary, since it depends on how close the available substitutes are. In the American economy, except in the public utilities, we seldom find only one firm, no available substitutes for the commodity produced, and no possibility that other firms may invade the market. Yet looking at such an extreme case is useful, because it shows up clearly some of the attributes of monopoly. It gives some insight into what the world might be like if pure monopolies were tolerated without regulation. It suggests rules for controlling public utilities. And it may be a quite realistic description of the short-run position in which firms temporarily find themselves because of special advantages of location, development of new products ahead of competitors, or other such circumstances.

Imagine a single electric-power company in an isolated community, free to charge whatever rates it pleases. Suppose you are the owner-manager of this hypothetical concern. You are a "price maker"; you can set your price where you wish. Waiving the fear that the local government will begin to regulate your rates, how would you go about maximizing your profits?

Costs

First, you'd want to know your costs. Your engineers and accountants will probably have estimates at hand or can produce some for you. Recognizing that these estimates are probably pretty rough, suppose the cost schedule looks like the one in Table 27–1. To simplify matters, the table shows only the estimates for producing at rates from 1,000,000 to 1,600,000 kilowatt-hours, in intervals of 100,000 kilowatt-hours. (To simplify the language, we will use merely the word kilowatts hereafter, for kilowatt-hours.)[6]

The table is self-explanatory. Columns 1 and 2 are the basic total-cost estimates. Column 3, which is simply 2 divided by 1, converts total cost to cost per unit. Column 4, marginal cost per 100,000 kilowatts, shows the additional cost

[5]The remainder of this chapter rests directly on the marginal-cost–marginal-revenue analysis of Chapter 24.

[6]Electricity producers often face demands that fluctuate widely through the day and seasonally. For simplicity, we neglect this problem here.

table 27-1

Hometown Electric Company — Cost Schedule*

Kilowatts (1)	Total Cost (2)	Average Cost per Kilowatt (3)	Marginal Cost Per 100,000 Kilowatts (4)	Per Kilowatt (5)
1,000,000	$50,000	5.0¢		
			$2,800	2.8¢
1,100,000	52,800	4.8		
			2,400	2.4
1,200,000	55,200	4.6		
			2,000	2.0
1,300,000	57,200	4.4		
			3,000	3.0
1,400,000	60,200	4.3		
			4,300	4.3
1,500,000	64,500	4.3		
			5,900	5.9
1,600,000	70,400	4.4		

*Unit-cost data are rounded to the nearest tenth of a cent.

involved in producing an extra 100,000 kilowatts. For example, it costs an extra $2,800 to raise production from 1,000,000 to 1,100,000 kilowatts weekly. Column 5 converts this marginal cost per 100,000 kilowatts to marginal cost per kilowatt.

Sales Revenue and Marginal Revenue

All this cost information doesn't do you any good unless you know something about the demand for electricity. So you have your market-research people get you the best estimates they can on the prices at which you can sell these various amounts. To simplify matters again, assume that you sell at the same price to everyone (not discriminating between residential and commercial users). Table 27–2 shows estimated demand over the same output range as Table 27–1.

This table is the counterpart of the cost table. Column 2 shows the prices at which different amounts of electricity can be sold. Column 3 shows the total revenue obtained by selling at those prices. Column 4 shows the extra revenue obtained by selling an additional 100,000 kilowatts—for example, $3,600 extra obtained by boosting sales from 1,000,000 to 1,100,000 kilowatts. And Column 5 converts this marginal revenue to a per kilowatt basis, by dividing the marginal revenue per 100,000 kilowatts by 100,000.

There is one special point in this table that merits attention. Under pure competition, price and marginal revenue to the seller are identical. If the farmer sells an extra bushel of wheat at $2 a bushel, he adds $2 to his total revenue. **But for the monopolist, marginal revenue is always less than price, assuming he sells his product at the same price to everybody. This is because he must lower his price to sell more units, and he must lower it not just on the marginal unit but on all units sold.**

For example, you can sell 1,500,000 kilowatts at 6.1 cents per kilowatt. To increase sales to 1,600,000 you must reduce the price to 5.7 cents on all 1,600,000 kilowatts. Thus, your marginal revenue is your income from selling the extra 100,000 kilowatts (100,000 times 5.7 cents = $5,700) minus the .4 of a cent loss on each of the other 1,500,000 kilowatts (1,500,000 times .4 cents = $6,000). In this case, then, marginal revenue on the 100,000 kilowatts is actually negative. Your total revenue will be $300 less if you cut price to 5.7 cents in order to increase sales to 1,600,000 units, even though you sell an extra 100,000 kilowatts at 5.7 cents each. All along the demand schedule, marginal revenue is less than price, for the same reason, though only when price is

table 27-2

Hometown Electric Company — Customer Demand Schedule

Kilowatts (1)	Price (2)	Total Revenue (3)	Marginal Revenue Per 100,000 Kilowatts (4)	Marginal Revenue Per Kilowatt (5)
1,000,000	8.0¢	$80,000	$3,600	3.6¢
1,100,000	7.6	83,600	3,400	3.4
1,200,000	7.25	87,000	2,700	2.7
1,300,000	6.9	89,700	1,300	1.3
1,400,000	6.5	91,000	500	.5
1,500,000	6.1	91,500	−300	−.3
1,600,000	5.7	91,200		

cut below 6.1 cents marginal revenue is actually negative.[7]

This relationship between price and marginal revenue is fundamental for every seller who is not in a perfectly competitive market. Whenever he faces a downward sloping demand curve, to sell more he must cut price both for the extra units he hopes to sell and for the units he could otherwise sell at a higher price. His gain from cutting price is never as big as it appears at first glance.

Maximizing Monopoly Profits

The monopolist can set his price where he pleases, and sell what the market will take at that price. Or he can decide how many units to produce, and sell them at the price that consumers will pay. But, given the market demand schedule, he cannot set both the price and the number of units he will sell. The market will determine one or the other for him.

How could you maximize your profits, if you were the manager?

[7]Marginal revenue is always zero when elasticity of demand is unity, positive when demand is elastic, and negative when demand is inelastic. Why? From this proposition it obviously follows that no perceptive monopolist will ever increase his output into the range where demand is inelastic, since in this range cutting price to increase output would *reduce* his total revenue from sales.

One answer is simple. You compare estimated total cost and estimated total revenue at each different level of output. When you find the level that gives the biggest total profit (revenue minus cost), that's it. You plan to produce that many units and sell them at the price indicated.

This calculation is shown in Table 27–3, whose first four columns reproduce the cost and revenue figures from the preceding tables. It's plain that profit is largest if you produce 1,300,000 kilowatts weekly and sell them at a price of 6.9 cents per kilowatt, which gives a profit of $32,500. Expected profit is lower for any other level shown—though there is the possibility that some level within the 100,000-kilowatt intervals on either side of 1,300,000 might be better.

Another way of calculating your maximum-profit position is by comparing marginal costs and marginal revenues. This comparison is made in the right-hand two columns. As long as the marginal revenue from selling an additional unit of output is greater than the marginal cost of producing the unit, obviously profit is increased by producing the extra unit. This gain is clear when you increase output from 1,000,000 to 1,100,000 units, on up to 1,200,-000 units, and then to 1,300,000 units. But if you try 1,400,000 units, the marginal cost is 3 cents per unit and the marginal revenue only

table 27-3

Hometown Electric Company — Profit Calculations

Kilowatts	Price	Total Cost	Total Revenue	Total Profit	Marginal Unit Cost	Marginal Unit Revenue
1,000,000	8.0¢	$50,000	$80,000	$30,000	2.8¢	3.6¢
1,100,000	7.6	52,800	83,600	30,800	2.4	3.4
1,200,000	7.25	55,200	87,000	31,800	2.0	2.7
1,300,000	6.9	57,200	89,700	*32,800	3.0	1.3
1,400,000	6.5	60,200	91,000	30,800	4.3	.5
1,500,000	6.1	64,500	91,500	27,000	5.9	—.3
1,600,000	5.7	70,400	91,200	20,800		

* Maximum total profit.

1.3 cents. This is a profit-reducing move, since it adds more to cost than to revenue—even though total profit would still be substantial at 1,400,000. The marginal approach gives us the same answer as the total-cost–total-revenue comparison. The two are simply alternative ways of getting the same profit-maximizing answer. Still a third way of getting the same answer would be by comparing marginal cost and marginal revenue per 100,000 units, instead of on a per unit basis.

Which was is better? Take you pick. They give the same result.

Graphical Analysis of Profit Maximization

If you think best in terms of graphs, you may ask your staff to present the cost and revenue data to you graphically. This is easy. Figure 27–2 plots the relevant per unit data for calculating your maximum-profit position graphically. *DD* is the estimated market-demand curve. *MR* is the associated marginal-revenue curve per unit, which shows the increase in your total revenue associated with each addi-

tional unit sold.[8] *TUC* is the estimated total-unit-cost curve for your lowest-cost scale of enterprise. And *MC* is the associated marginal-unit-cost curve, showing at each point the addition to your total costs involved in increasing output one unit. The solid part of each curve represents the data from Table 27–3; the dotted lines extend the curves hypothetically beyond the range of data we have.

Be sure you know how to read the various curves. Reading from the graph, for example, at 1,200,000 units output the total cost per unit is about 4.6 cents. According to the demand curve, this output can be sold at a price of about 7.25 cents per kilowatt. Obviously this is a profitable level of output—the demand curve is above the total-unit-cost curve. Now look at the margianl curves. The marginal-cost curve shows that to increase output by 1 kilowatt—to 1,200,001 kilowatts—would add about 2.4 cents to total cost. This additional unit would add about 3.4 cents to total revenue, according to the marginal-revenue curve. Thus, we can readily see from the graph: (1) that an output of 1,200,000 kilowatts is profitable, and (2) that a larger output would be still more profitable, since at the 1,200,000-kilowatt level marginal cost is still below marginal revenue.

Going on, you can easily determine the maximum-profit position. It will be the output where marginal cost just equals marginal revenue. This is a little above 1,300,000 kilowatts, which you could sell at a price of about 6.8 cents, reading off the demand curve at that output. If you want to compute your total profit from this graph, you can. You find your profit per unit by first taking the distance between the selling price and your total unit cost, and then multiplying this profit per unit by the total number of units sold. This would give a profit of about $33,000 at the best level—roughly 2.5 cents per kilowatt on 1,320,000 kilowatts.

Note that this is a slightly higher profit than the maximum shown by Table Table 27–3. The graph, which gives you data for all levels of output rather than just one estimate each

fig. 27–2

The monopolist maximizes profit by equating marginal cost and marginal revenue—here at an output of about 1.32 million kilowatts to be sold at a price just under seven cents.

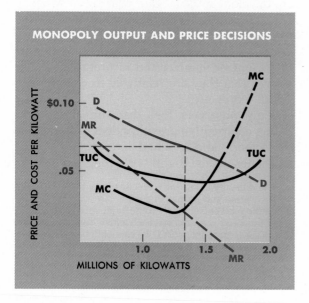

MONOPOLY OUTPUT AND PRICE DECISIONS

[8]As was explained above, the marginal-revenue curve is always below its demand curve, and slopes downward more steeply.

100,000 kilowatts, tells you to produce an extra 20,000 kilowatts beyond the prescription of the table. The price for the larger output will only be 6.8 cents, but the cost per kilowatt stays at about 4.3 cents, and your total profit is about $500 larger than at 1,300,000 kilowatts. The continuous curves on the graph give you a quick guide to the maximum-profit level of output and prices. Whether you use the graph or not, you clearly need to make calculations covering outputs within the 100,000-kilowatt intervals used in the tables. The graph is only a shortcut to these finer calculations.

Pure Monopoly—Evaluation

This look at the consequences of unregulated pure monopoly, protected against entry of competitive enterprises, illustrates the extreme case of monopoly's impact on the economy.

Resource Allocation

Monopoly leads to an inefficient allocation of resources from the consumers' point of view. If the monopolist restricts output and raises price to maximize his profits, he will be holding price above marginal cost. But Chapter 25 told us that mc = price is the condition for achieving the most efficient allocation of productive resources to satisfy consumers' demands. Thus, monopoly price is too high and too few resources are hired into the monopolized industry. Consumers get fewer resources devoted to producing the monopolized product than would be optimal to meet their demand for it, relative to other products. This is the basic economic criticism of monopoly.

Conversely, too many resources are used in other sectors of the economy. Resources shut out from the monopolized industry seek employment elsewhere. In restricting his output, the monopolist is failing to bid resources away from competitive industries, even though the marginal contribution of the resources to satisfying consumer wants would be greater in the

monopoly than in the competitive sector of the economy.[9]

Income Distribution

Monopoly tends toward inequality of income. Monopoly profits may swell the incomes of businesmen and stockholders in monopoly concerns at the expense of the rest of society. Monopoly restriction on output cuts the demand for labor in that industry and reduces average wages and prices of other productive services. But the basic evil of monopoly is the malallocation of resources explained above, not the special profits made by the monopolist.

To see this point, suppose the government taxed away, through a lump-sum tax, all special monopoly profits and returned the sum to the public through public services. The monopolist would have extracted no monopoly profit from the public. But the misallocation of resources would remain as a burden on the public; too few resources would be used in producing the monopolized product, too many in producing other products, as measured by what consumers want.

Efficiency and Progress

Pure competition forces each firm to be efficient or perish. If new production techniques are developed, the laggard who fails to keep up with the leaders soon loses out in the market. Under monopoly, these pressures are weak. It does not necessarily follow that monopolies are inefficient or uninterested in progress. It only follows that they are relatively free from competitive pressures.

Many observers feel that the absence of strong competitive pressures does often lead to inefficiency and lessened interest in meeting consumer needs. Rightly or wrongly, they cite

[9]The difficulty in making a precise comparison with competitive price and output in such a case should be clear. Since the market is unlikely to be large enough to support a large number of producers, each with a least-cost point as low as the large monopolist's, we cannot demonstrate rigorously that monopoly price is higher than competitive price would be.

the public utilities—railways, electric power, gas companies, and so forth—as slow to adopt new ideas and techniques, slow to respond to new consumer needs. Some argue that monopolists have intentionally retarded the development and introduction of new products that might increase the obsolescence rate of their existing equipment. And even though monopoly profits don't appear excessive, this fact may reflect inefficiently high costs, protected from the pressures of competition. On the other side, AT&T has large monopoly power in the telephone industry, yet it has provided a high rate of technological advance. The evidence is mixed. But the prod of competition is a powerful incentive to innovation and efficiency.

Either way, remember one earlier qualification: If the market is so small that only a few firms can be supported at efficient scales of operation, insistence on many firms would lead to higher-cost production and probably to oslcilating instability through periodic price wars. Limited markets seldom justify pure monopoly. But they often mean that the full conditions of pure competition cannot be met. Most of the world lies somewhere between the two extremes.

Review

CONCEPTS TO REMEMBER

Most of the major concepts used in this chapter were introduced in earlier chapters. But there are a few important new ones:

pure (simple) monopoly oligopoly
monopolistic competition decreasing-cost industry
price makers

FOR ANALYSIS AND DISCUSSION

1. Why have the American people traditionally distrusted both monopolies and big business? Is there any significant economic distinction between the two? How about IBM and A&P?
2. The post office and your local water company are examples of substantially pure monopolies. How would you go about deciding whether they are doing an efficient job of serving the consumer at reasonable prices? Do you have a better way of evaluating the performance of such big partial monopolies as General Motors and Alcoa?
3. A noted economist has argued that without government support, there would be little serious monopoly in America today. He cites public utilities, government support of unions, government-sponsored cartelization in agriculture, and "fair-trade" laws to hold up prices in retailing. How sound is this argument? Can you cite counterexamples?
4. Why do economists say that the basic *economic* criticism of monopolies is that they hold price above marginal cost?
5. If a monopoly is not making excessive (i.e., above-normal) profits, it is doing no serious harm to the public. True or false? Explain.

twenty-eight

Monopolistic Competition and Demand Creation

Do Partial Monopolists Maximize Profits?

Prices and Output under Monopolistic Competition

Quality Competition and Competitive Demand Creation

Measures of Market Performance

Almost nobody has a pure monopoly. But lots of firms have partial monopolies. The corner druggist has a partial monopoly in his neighborhood. He can charge several cents more a quart for ice cream than the big dairy stores downtown. And he can get it—because he is so conveniently located for people in neighborhood.

Coca-Cola has a partial monopoly. No one else can make a drink exactly like Coca-Cola without infringing the law, and for years "a Coke" has been the habitual mid-morning and mid-afternoon drink of millions. But Pepsi-Cola, Royal Cola, and a good many others look and taste enough like Cocal-Cola to have made Coca-Cola's share of the soft-drink market decline appreciably in the last two decades. The Coca-Cola people will tell you they're in a highly competitive field.

Bayer Aspirin has a partial monopoly. For years Bayer's held a substantial monopoly in the retail sale of aspirin, based largely on effective advertising that identified Bayer Aspirin with aspirin, even though all commercial aspirin is chemically identical. But here too other companies are after the customer's dollar and have steadily whittled away at the impression that only Bayer's is really aspirin.

A large part of the American economy is in the range between competition and monopoly —partly protected from competitors by trade names, location, tradition, quality of product, but far from perfectly protected; exposed to new competitors, but much less exposed than the wheat farmer. This is the area of "monopolistic competition." In it, each firm's product is "differentiated" from its competitors', but not enough to forestall active competition—on prices, selling costs, quality, or all three. As was indicated above, monopolistic competition does not include those cases where there are only a few firms in an industry; this few-firms case is called "oligopoly."[1]

How much of the economy is in the "monopolistic-competition" category? The lines are hazy, but a fair, though very crude, answer would be, perhaps one-half the private sector. This would include nearly all of wholesale and retail trade, finance, real estate, and personal services (legal, medical, and the like); a substantial sector of manufacturing (e.g., textiles, apparel, lumber, and printing); and most of construction and of trucking. By contrast, a large part of manufacturing (autos, steel, heavy electrical equipment, glass, and tobacco products) is oligopolistic; railroads, airlines, and all public utilities are regulated by government; and agriculture is a special case of nondifferentiated products with prices substantially influenced by government policies. It's a complex world, but "monopolistically competitive" describes a big part of it.

Before going on to examine monopolistic competition in this chapter and oligopoly in the next, we need to ask an important question that applies to both.

Do Partial Monopolists Maximize Profits?

Do these partial monopolists, operating with various degrees of protection from market competition under monopolistic competition and oligopoly, produce efficiently and maximize their profits? Maybe businessmen in highly competitive industries don't try to maximize profits. But if they don't make a fairly good stab at it, competition will remove them from the scene in due time. With the monopolist and partial monopolist, we can't count so fully on competition to exert this pressure. We need to know more about the firm's motives and patterns of behavior if we are to understand hot the partially monopolized sectors of the economy work.

If you asked most businessmen whether they try to maximize profits, they would probably tell you, "Yes, but...." The "but" might refer to lots of things, but especially to the fact that few businessmen like to say that they exploit their position by charging the last penny the traffic will bear. Playing for the long pull makes sense to many managers. It may be good business to forego higher profits today in the interest of long-run earnings.

But do partial monopolists generally maximize even long-run profits? Back in Chapter 25, four reasons were listed why even under pure competition many firms may not be maximizing profits at any given time. These apply equally here:

1. It takes time to adjust to change.
2. Businessmen never know what costs and demand in the future will be. They can only estimate, and often they're wrong.
3. Sometimes managers just aren't very efficient. They don't do a very good job of either minimizing costs or increasing revenues.
4. Firms sometimes can't get funds to undertake potentially profitable investments that require substantial cash outlays. The capital market is more open to large than to small firms.

Beyond these four reasons, there are some others that apply especially to firms holding partial monopolies, where the pressures of competition may be weaker:

5. Unusually large profits may be an invitation to new competitors, lured by the hope of winning some away. This danger may lead the monopolistic competitor to think twice before reaching for more profits that may invite more competition.
6. Unusually large profits may bring special

---

[1]Remember that "industry" is usually defined loosely to include all firms producing reasonably close substitutes, such as the aspirin industry, the ice-cream industry, and the steel industry.

scrutiny from the government's antitrust officials, who may suspect illegal behavior as the basis for the profits, especially if the firm has only a few major competitors.

7. Historians point to many firms that have grown big as the result of the promoters' and managers' desire for bigness as such. They focus on total sales and share of market, rather than on profits per se. Many observers rate growth as the dominant single objective of large corporate management today (though it is important to recognize that growth may also be highly profitable).

8. Some managements engage in "business statesmanship." They concentrate on improving the community where they exist, or on promoting better international understanding, or on advancing industrial relations. "Business statesmanship" and concern for the "social responsibilities" of management have become very stylish in recent years. These things cost money and don't necessarily increase sales. Management generally answers that these policies help long-run profits, and that such costs have become an essential part of doing business on the modern sense.

9. Lastly, some observers stress that the modern hired manager (as distinct from the owner-operator) often has important objectives in addition to profits—the desire to get along well with others in the company; the desire to avoid ulcer-producing arguments with the union; perhaps most important, the desire to avoid looking foolish by being wrong when he takes risks. Management has more freedom to follow these other motives if it is sheltered from vigorous competition.

There is some evidence that owner-controlled firms do achieve a higher rate of return on investment than do similar management-controlled firms. Between 1952 and 1963, owner-controlled firms earned a 12.3 percent rate of return on investment as against 7.3 percent for management-controlled firms.[2]

[2]R. J. Monsen, J. Chin, and D. Cooley, "The Effect of Separation of Ownership and Control on the Performance of Large Firms," *Quarterly Journal of Economics*, August, 1968, p. 441.

Clearly, there are wide differences from firm to firm and industry to industry. In the following pages, we will assume that by and large the drive of quasi monopolies for profits is a major factor in their behavior—as it appears to be. Actual or potential competition is seldom far away. But in using profit-maximizing models, don't forget that management may have other motives and all the slips that may occur between wish and achievement in maximizing profits.

In many ways, reason 2 above poses the toughest problems for the businessman. Maximum-profit estimates are no better than the demand and cost estimates on which they rest. Estimating the future is never easy, and it's the future that matters. Businesses spend millions of dollars keeping track of their costs in great detail and trying to get accurate forecasts of what costs and demand will be at different levels of output. Big corporations have thousands of employees in their cost- and sales-estimating departments. Yet many businesses lose more potential profit through inability to forecast their cost and demand situations accurately than through failure to act effectively on the basis of the costs and demands they estimate.

Business decisions have to be made on the basis of inadquate information and hunches more often than most people realize. When he has to guess at both future costs and revenues, no executive can calculate exactly what his optimum price and output positions are going to be. Yet he has to make these decisions, day in and day out. What does he do? Many managers look for some reasonable guiding rule to avoid the necessity of starting from scratch in solving each price problem. The practices of "standard costing" and "cost-plus pricing" have come into widespread use to meet this need.

"Standard Costing"

Cost per unit of output varies at different output levels, and you're never sure just what your output is going to be very far in the future. Yet you can't be jiggling your price up and down all the time, and usually you have to quote advance prices to customers. So a lot of businessmen ask their accountants and engineers to estimate as closely as possible the total cost of one unit of output at near-capacity operations. This estimate they call the "standard cost." It is the cost figure often used for price setting, even though output may vary markedly from day to day or from month to month.

"Standard costing" may not be very precise, and many economists explain that it may lead the firm to make less profit than it could, in principle, make by calculating all costs anew for each individual transaction. But standard costing is a way of getting the day's business done. It's a rule-of-thumb shortcut, albeit an imperfect one. Without such rules of thumb, the complexity of modern big-business operations might lead to utter confusion and organizational breakdown rather than to a more perfect approach to profit maximization.

"Cost-Plus Pricing"

Using standard costs as a basis, many firms engage in "cost-plus," or "full-cost," or "markup," pricing. They price their product by taking their standard-cost estimate and adding on some allowance or markup—5, 10, 50, or 100 percent—to provide a reasonable profit.[3] They are likely to use this same "full cost" to quote prices on all orders, regardless of substantial variations in the actual cost of filling the orders. This approach leads to reasonable simplicity in business operations, but it is easy to see how it may also lead to less-than-maximum profits on individual orders.

Actually, businessmen are often better economists than this would suggest. When standard-cost pricing gets them too far out of line with the results they would get through using an analysis based on a more direct cost calculation, they often modify, or give up entirely, their standard-cost pricing. In booming markets where standard-cost pricing clearly undershoots what the market will bear, larger markups or upward revision of quoted standard costs

[3]Often the standard-cost estimate covers only manufacturing costs. In such cases, the mark-up percentage must cover all nonmanufacturing costs, as well as an allowance for profits.

often result. In a serious depression when competition is sharp, pricing well below "full cost" becomes common.

"Break-Even Charts"

Some firms use another simplifying approach, "break-even charts" or "break-even analysis." In its simplest form, this technique compares total revenue at some constant market price with total cost for different levels of output. Total revenue will rise by a constant amount, say $5 for each unit sold if the price is $5. But total cost will rise at a different rate. The total cost (remember, **not** total cost **per unit**) is composed of two parts. Fixed cost is the same at any level of output—say $100 per week for rent and managerial salary. Variable cost in many firms seems to be about constant per unit of output over a considerable range—say $3 per unit for wages and materials. In such a case, total cost at any output is $100 plus $3 times the number of units produced.

Figure 28–1 is a simple break-even chart. Line *TR* shows total revenue, growing at $5 per unit sold. Line *TC* shows total cost, beginning at

fig. 28–1

With price at $5, *TR* is the total-revenue curve. Comparing this with the total-cost curve *(TC)*, the break-even point is fifty units per week. The firm makes a profit at any higher output.

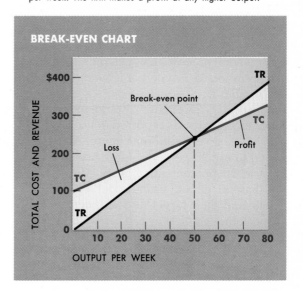

$100 for zero output and rising $3 per unit thereafter. The "break-even point" is at an output of fifty units. The yellow-colored areas show that a loss will occur at any output less than fifty, and a profit at any higher output. The profit or loss is the vertical distance between the total-cost and total-revenue curves at any given output.

Using this chart, the businessman can see quickly about what he would make or lose at any output, given his costs and the market price of $5. Using different prices with resulting different *TR* lines on the chart, he can compare how well-off he would be at different prices he might charge. The chart is one tool to help decide the best price to set.

Return on Investment

Increasingly in recent years, big corporations appear to have used some "target" return on capital investment as a rough guide to pricing policy (and to capital investment in new ventures as well). Du Pont and General Motors have for years followed this policy. G.M., for example, shoots for 20 percent on invested capital after taxes. This, of course, doesn't give any automatic guide to setting prices, but it does throw out some guidelines to the men who do the price setting. The company doesn't expect to get that return each year, through good times and bad. It takes the long view, and expects to do better than the target some years, and worse in others. Thus, current pricing and plans for expansion are all wrapped up in the same general process, in which the test of effective performance is whether it meets this profit-rate standard.

Why does G.M. choose 20 percent as the target rate? U.S. Steel is reported to use 8 percent after taxes, a very different figure. Alcoa is reported to use 20 percent before taxes; General Electric 20 percent after taxes. Maybe you'll say that, in effect, each is out to maximize profits, and their target rates are merely about the peak they think they can earn. Certainly we need to know more about how the targets are set to evaluate their impact on pricing. But for

better or worse, lots of big businesses use this approach as one major guide in pricing and investment planning generally.[4]

Prices and Output under Monopolistic Competition

The Bases for Product Differentiation

The essence of monopolistic competition is that each firm's product is a little different from those of its competitors, but not very different. Each producer tries to differentiate his product and increase the demand for it. To the extent he succeeds, he can get away with charging a little more for his product. He has set himself apart in a partially protected position.

Sometimes product differentiation involves actual physical differentiation. For example, Schlitz beer tastes different from Pabst; a Frigidaire is different from a G.E. refrigerator. But often the differentiation hinges on the things that go along with the product—convenience of the corner grocery's location, thick carpets on the floors of the best dress shops, well-groomed waitresses in some restaurants, easy-credit terms at some stores. Sometimes the differentiation is largely illusory—it exists in the mind of the customer but not in fact. Most smokers can't tell one standard cigarette brand from another when they are blindfolded. If you can really tell the difference between the various high-test gasolines in your car on the road, you're better than most of the experts. Often when you think you're getting special easy-credit terms you're paying just what is normal in the trade.

Some bases for product differentiation are more fundamental and longer-lasting than others. But whatever the reason, whenever one seller is differentiated from others in the customer's mind, that seller is able to charge a price higher than his competitors without losing all

[4]There is a large literature on business pricing practices. For a more detailed, easy-to-read account of some current big-business pricing policies, see A. D. H. Kaplan, Joel Dirlam, and R. F. Lanzillotti, *Pricing in Big Business* (Washington, D.C.: The Brookings Institution, 1958).

his market. His demand curve slopes downward; it is not horizontal as under perfect competition.

Short-Run Output and Prices

Given his costs, the monopolistic competitor's problem is to set his price so as to maximize his profits. He has some freedom to raise price above what his competitors charge for similar products, but if he goes too far his share of the market will drop sharply. The more successful he is in differentiating his product, the less elastic his demand curve will be. With an inelastic demand curve, he can boost his price without a corresponding drop in sales. But it's hard to convince customers that no substitute will do.

The firm's optimal price—output decision in the short run is hard to specify under these conditions. It will generally try to maximize the difference between total revenue and total costs by producing efficiently and by stimulating demand for its own product. But just what the demand curve for any one firm's product looks like is hard to estimate. For it depends **both** on what this firm does through advertising to change consumer demand **and** on what competitors do that also affects the demand for our firm's product. The demand curve we face will depend on consumers' total demand for the whole group of slightly differentiated products, and on our firm's share of the total. Palmolive can increase and steepen the consumer demand curve for its soap either by getting customers away from Lux, Sweetheart, and the rest, or by somehow increasing total consumer demand for toilet soap. If Palmolive succeeds in convincing people they should wash their faces oftener, this may increase the demand for other soaps as well as for Palmolive. The trick is to be sure you get the big share of the benefit if you go in for this kind of advertising. Conversely, increased advertising by Lux may leave Palmolive with a lower, flatter demand curve, even though Palmolive soap is just as good as before. And if Palmolive's advertising steals Lux's customers, retaliation is almost certain. **Thus, it should be**

clear that under monopolistic competition and oligopoly, the level and elasticity of any firm's demand curve depend both on what it does and on what the other firms in the industry do as well. It is not possible to draw a stable, unambiguous demand curve for the individual firm's product.[5]

Just how much any monopolistic competitor will spend on demand creation, trying to raise his demand curve and make it more inelastic to increase his profits, is hard to tell. Presumably he will increase his expenditures on advertising and other demand-creating activities as long as he estimates that the results will add more to his income than to his costs. But under monopolistic competition, uncertainty about what competitors will do makes short-run output and price behavior very hard to predict. Thus, as with pure competition, we are on much safer ground when we look at long-run adjustments than when we try to predict short-run behavior.

Long-Run Adjustments under Monopolistic Competition

In the long run, new firms enter industries and old firms leave. The search for profits goes on, with productive resources freely transfer-

---

[5]*Given* the firm's cost and demand curves, the technical conditions for maximizing profit in the short run are identical with those for the monopolist described in detail in the last half of Chapter 27. Thus, in the adjoining figure, to maximize profits the firm will set price and output where marginal cost equals marginal revenue. This gives output O to be sold at price P as the optimal position. But when we say *given* the demand curve, we are assuming away a big piece of the problem, as is explained in the text.

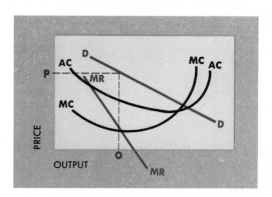

able throughout the economy. Monopolistic competition is like pure competition in that new firms can enter the industry. It is different in that new firms cannot exactly duplicate the product of existing fiirms. A new drugstore across the street from an established one might provide very close substitutes. But a new women's-wear store that sets up in competition with Saks Fifth Avenue will have a tougher time. For one thing, drugs, candy, and ice cream are relatively standardized as compared with women's clothes. For another, few drugstores have the prestige and location of Saks.

But even though newcomers face problems, high profits in any monopolistically competitive field will draw new competitors. As more firms enter, the total market is divided up more ways. The demand curve for each established firm is moved downward (to the left). Profits per firm are reduced by this sharing of the market. Gradually, as more firms enter, profits tend to be eliminated, just as under pure competition. A new (unstable) equilibrium with economic profits eliminated may be achieved.

This sounds just like pure competition. But it is different in two important respects. First, in this temporary equilibrium, under monopolistic competition each firm is restricting output a little to take advantage of its product differentiation. In each firm, marginal cost is less than price, since the demand curve is tangent to the cost curve to the left of the minimum point. Each firm is producing inefficiently; it is operating below its optimal capacity and producing at a cost above the least-cost point on its optimal-cost curve. As a result, the equilibrium market price is higher than it would be under pure

competition where price would be forced down to the least-cost point on the cost curve for the firm; and the resources are wasted through the excess capacity in each firm. From a social point of view, too little of the product is being produced and sold, since price is being held above marginal cost.

This result is illustrated in Figure 28–2. Suppose that case A pictures a typical firm in a monopolistically competitive area. The firm is making a good profit. Since its demand curve is well above its total-unit-cost curve over a substantial range, the manager can make some profit even if he isn't very alert in choosing the best short-run price and output. The demand curve is downward sloping, because this product is differentiated from its competitors.[6]

What will happen? Competition will pick up. As new firms enter the market, the demand curve for each old firm moves downward as its share of the market falls. Eventually, the demand curve for a typical firm will be pushed down far enough to be just tangent to the cost curve. All profit has been eliminated, and there is no further apparent incentive for new firms and new resources to enter the industry. Neither is there any incentive for existing firms to leave, unless some especially attractice opportunity opens up elsewhere in the economy. This is case C in Figure 28–2.

But, as was indicated above, here each firm is operating to the left of the minimum point on its cost curve. Price is higher than marginal cost. As long as the demand curve for each

[6]The graph in the preceding footnote shows precisely how much the firm should produce to maximize its short-run profits.

INDIVIDUAL FIRM UNDER MONOPOLISTIC COMPETITION

fig. 28–2

Figure shows firm making money on left, losing money in middle, and in no-profit temporary equilibrium on right.

firm is downward sloping (as it must be when each firm is big enough and different enough to have an independent influence on price), it must become tangent to the cost curve to the left of the minimum point. In economic terms, each firm will end up restricting its output below the competitive level to try to take advantage of its differentiated position—but market competition from new firms will tend to wipe out any special profits it might have hoped for.

Look now at *B* in Figure 28–2. Here existing firms are making losses. As firms gradually drop out of the industry, the demand for the products of each remaining firm gradually rises. It continues to rise until a no-loss situation has been reached, when there is no further incentive for resources to move out of the industry. This again is case *C.*

The similarity of these results to those under pure competition stems primarily form the free entry of firms into the industry. Incentives to maximize efficiency and to develop products to meet consumer needs are strong. The only important difference evident so far is the somewhat higher price to the consumer under monopolistic competition. But this difference is unlikely to be very important if the competing products are close substitutes.

Equilibrium Unstable under Competitive Demand Creation

But this is not the end of the story; the equilibrium is almost surely unstable. If you were running a grocery store and were in position *C* in Figure 28–2, what would you do? Maybe you'd just sit, but probably you'd try to figure a way to get more business. You might try improving your service to customers. Or putting in air conditioning. Or advertising more. All these attempts would cost you money. They might bring you more customers—that is, they might raise your demand curve—probably by drawing customers away from competitors. And they would upset the equilibrium situation shown in *C.* Such attempts to increase demand for products are apparent everywhere, keeping equilibrium (with the demand curve tangent to the cost curve) from being achieved or maintained.

Imagine a monopolistically competitive milk industry in a good-sized city, with fifteen milk companies of about equal size and no advertising. Company *A* begins an advertising campaign. It gets more customers by luring a few away from each competitor. *A*'s costs are now higher, but its profits are up because of increased volume.

It doesn't take a business genius to predict the reaction of the other companies. After spending a few well-chosen words on the manager of Company *A,* they will get busy on their own advertising campaigns, designed to get their customers back and (hopefully) to lure new customers into the fold. If every company just matched *A*'s advertising, we might think of a new equilibrium situation, with each producer having back just his original customers, but with every company's cost higher by the amount of the advertising and with price correspondingly higher to the consumer or company profits correspondingly lower.

But having tasted success, *A* is unlikely to sit quietly at the restored higher-price equilibrium. Nor are *B, C, D,* and all the others. Each will be busy contriving a new and better advertising campaign—at least to protect his sales against the selling campaigns he strongly expects from his rivals. If another round of advertising expenditures starts, or trading stamps with each gallon of milk are introduced, the result is likely to be similar. Everybody's costs go up. Nobody ends up with many more customers, or with any more profits. And consumers end up with higher prices. Now they're buying advertising and trading stamps along with their milk—without having anything to say about whether they really want to buy them or not. And nobody can tell where the whole process will stop.

Even in the happy event that the advertising campaign increases **total** spending on milk, a similar problem remains. Where do these additional funds for milk come from? Maybe the milk advertising stimulates total spending and raises the level of total spending and g.n.p., but this seems unlikely on the basis of our look at the determinants of national income and employment in Part Two. If total spending is unchanged, more spending on milk must mean less spending on something else. Producers in these other industries will fight back to regain sales.

This will cause another reshuffling of demand, with still other industries (possibly including milk) losing customers to the newest advertisers.

Overall, it is difficult for anyone to gain more than temporarily from large advertising outlays in an economy in which counteradvertising is general. The overall effect of advertising, on which we spent $18 billion in 1970, is to devote these productive resources (men, ink, billboards, and so forth) to producing advertising rather than to producing other goods and services.

Selling Costs and Production Costs

It is important to distinguish between "selling costs" and "production costs." The costs discussed in previous chapters were production costs, incurred to make products that meet expected consumer demands. By contrast, the selling costs discussed above are costs incurred in trying to increase the demand for a product. Production costs include costs of manufacture, transportation, financing, storage, and all other activities that are required to produce the commodity and to get it to the consumer. Selling costs include all forms of advertising and demand-creating activities—newspaper, television, magazine, and direct-mail advertising, window displays, salesmen, prize contests, and so on.

When all costs are production costs, the demand seen by any firm is not changed by the firm's own activities. But with selling costs, the seller can increase the demand for his product by spending more money—he can shift the demand curve for his own product. Whenever he tries, he is almost certain to cut the demand for his competitors' products, and you can guess what his competitors do then. They retaliate.

Quality Competition and Competitive Demand Creation

Every housewife knows about quality competition. She knows which stores have the freshest vegetables, and where there are enough clerks to provide quick service. When you buy a suit, you go to a store you know will stand behind it if something goes wrong. These are examples of quality competition, just as much as the more obvious cases of using better materials and better workmanship in the physical construction of products.

Alert businessmen are very much interested in knowing what quality consumers want. They spend thousands of dollars on market research to find out whether consumers want softer seats in autos, cellophane around fresh vegetables, more carbonation in ginger ale. A shrewd businessman will improve the quality of his product whenever he believes customers will want the improvement enough to pay for the extra cost—and a little bit more. He will put chromium trim on automobiles, foam rubber cushions on sofas, or fancier packages around candy if he thinks these steps will get him additional customers enough or let him charge enough higher prices to increase his profits. He will reduce product quality—for example, by putting his store on a cash-and-carry basis—whenever he believes that most customers would prefer to pay less and go without delivery service. But he will do more. He will spend money to induce present and potential customers to want the particular qualities he provides in his product.

Some observers believe that quality competition is the pervasive form of competition in modern America, and that price competition is of secondary importance. There is much evidence to support this point of view. Filling stations long ago learned that a clean rest room is more important to a touring family than a half cent off the price of gas. The first air-conditioned movie had an enormous quality advantage. Now they're all air-conditioned.

Such is often the case in quality competition. Once one firm pioneers, others feel they must follow—or risk losing their customers as a consequence of holding out. The result is higher "quality" all around, and higher prices to cover the higher costs involved in providing it. Then every manager starts scratching his head to figure out a new improvement that will give him at least a temporary jump on the field again.

Quality competition is a perfectly valid type of competition, just as much as price competition. Sometimes people don't want the extra "quality" built into new products. But they have the option of not buying. And with active competition, there's always a competitor ready to provide a cheaper, low "quality" product—witness the success of discount stores and of compact cars.

Annual Model Changes—Another Example

Each year the major auto manufacturers come out with new models, announced with great fanfare. In perhaps two years out of three there are no changes of significance for the performance or comfort given by the automobile. The roof line is lowered, the dashboard modified, the horsepower upped a little. The upshot is that last year's models are now out of date, and those of two years ago are quite passé—or at least so the auto companies hope. "Planned obsolescence" is the phrase many observers use. Your old car may be good for 50,000 miles more, but the auto manufacturers are spending hundreds of millions of dollars on new models each year to convince you that you really have an old car, inferior to the shiny new models.

There is no doubt that today's autos will do many things their predecessors would not—go faster, ride smoother, eat more gas. Most people believe that each year's model is really better than last year's. But the cost of annual model changes is large—hundreds of millions of dollars for new tools and dies each year that must be charged off in the price of cars that year, since new ones will be required next year. One study, which should be recognized as very rough, put the total cost of annual autos model changes to American consumers at $35 billion between 1949 and 1961.

Annual model changes are another example of competitive selling costs. Every auto company admits it could sell cars a lot cheaper if it didn't face the enormous cost of annual model changes. And it's not clear that total car sales are much larger because of the changes, though they probably are stimulated to some extent. But no major company (except Volkswagen and a few other foreign makers) feels safe in coming out each year without new models. The situation is much like that in competitive advertising, but with real quality changes mixed in.

Advertising Outlays

Advertising in 1970 totaled just over $18 billion. Figure 28–3 shows total outlays over the past decade, and the major types of advertising that make up the total.

Eighteen billion dollars is a very large amount; it would purchase a lot of alternative goods and services if consumers instead had the cash to spend. But looked at another way, we spend less than 2 percent of g.n.p. on advertising of all products and services.

Does Advertising Increase Total Demand?

Many people argue that advertising increases total demand, thereby helping to provide more jobs and making possible the advantages of large-scale production. Certainly advertising and other selling costs may increase the demand for individual products. But the illustrations above should warn against easy transfer of this reasoning to aggregate demand for the economy as a whole. When everyone advertises, a main effect is likely to be the neutralization described above. If advertising increases aggregate demand, it must increase consumers' collective propensity to consume out of disposable income. It **may** do so—for example, when the auto industry comes out with major style changes and massive sales campaigns to push them. But most economists are skeptical that advertising raises the aggregate propensity to consume much. They believe the evidence points mainly to the factors listed back in Chapter 8, with the major impact of advertising on sales of particular products and brands. Note that even if advertising induces people to buy more cars this year, we need to be sure this is a net addition to total spending and not merely a transfer from other goods or services.

Should we Give Up Competitive Advertising?

If advertising and many other selling costs are so largely neutralized by counteradvertising and counterselling costs, why don't competitors simply call the whole thing off? One big reason is that each hopes to stay ahead in the race and none dares to drop out. There is usually an advantage in leading, and always a danger in cur-

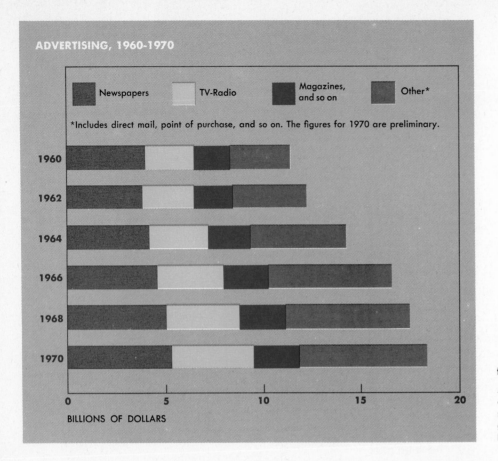

Newspapers   TV-Radio   Magazines, and so on   Other*

*Includes direct mail, point of purchase, and so on. The figures for 1970 are preliminary.

1960
1962
1964
1966
1968
1970

0   5   10   15   20

BILLIONS OF DOLLARS

fig. 28–3

Advertising has grown persistently over the past decade, though more slowly in recession years. Newspapers get the largest part of advertising dollars.

tailing. And it is very difficult to measure the results of selling costs, particularly those aimed at "goodwill" and "repeat customers." Once a firm has customers firmly tied to its product, it can afford to cut back on its advertising outlays for this purpose. But a good customer is far easier to keep than to get back once he's been lost. All this uncertainty leads to reluctance to experiment with reduced selling costs.

Measures of Market Performance

Monopolistic competition characterizes a large section of the economy. In summary, what can we say about the market performance of this sector?

Allocation of Resources

Under monopolistic competition every seller has a little bit of monopoly, little though it may be if his product is only slightly differentiated. Thus, given the downward sloping demand curve he faces, it pays him to set price higher than marginal cost. Price will tend to be forced by competition toward the level where the demand curve is tangent to the cost curve, to the left of the minimum-cost point. Too little of the product will be produced to satisfy consumer demand most efficiently. But if competition is active and products are only slightly differentiated, each firm's demand curve will be almost horizontal and this malallocation of resources may be negligible.

The Use of Resources in "Demand Creation"

More important is the large allocation of productive resources to demand creation. In 1970, advertising expenditures alone totaled $18 billion. In a full-employment economy, we must choose between alternative uses of resources. For our advertising dollar (paid in the price of the product) we get information on products, TV movies, sport events, billboards, the Metropolitan Opera, and a wide variety of other services, the worth of which might be disputed vigorously. Advertising expenditures make possible ten-cent daily papers, and a fifty-cent *Life* magazine; $18 billion spent on advertising provides many useful services and some not so useful. The amount spent on demand creation has soared. In 1940, total expenditures on advertising were less than $2 billion.

Is this "demand creation" wasteful? From the standpoint of resource allocation, the real question is: Are the services provided by advertising the services we want? No firm answer is possible. Eighteen billion dollars would buy a lot of other things—schools, houses, food, medical services. We can say firmly only that by financing these services through advertising, little effective choice is left to the consumer as to how much of each he buys. The cigarette smoker buys TV westerns even though he never looks at a TV screen. Still, almost everybody buys many advertised products and enjoys some of the fruits of advertising and demand creation. Perhaps, aside from cases of misleading advertising, everything pretty much evens out and consumers get just about the information and "entertainment" they would have bought anyway with their advertising dollars. But you may properly have your doubts.

Advertising and Consumer Information

One important benefit from advertising is the information it makes available. To spend their money efficiently in satisfying their wants, consumers must be well informed about the products available. The better informed consumers are, the better they are able to force producers to cater to their wants by spending on those products that best meet their needs. Advertising that informs consumers about new products is also useful. In a rapidly changing economy, this is an especially valuable service. Just how many resources should be devoted to making consumers better informed is a difficult question. The price mechanism doesn't provide a measuring stick by which consumers can automatically make the decision on this use of resources, since consumers don't have a chance to buy the information separately.

Much modern advertising makes little contribution to consumer information. Many advertisers are more concerned with attracting consumers away from competitors and with building a "corporate image" than with providing information on which consumers can make more intelligent choices. Watch TV a whole evening and record all the information you get that is of value in helping you decide among the products advertised. Read a copy of one of the big-selling magazines. Try the morning newspaper.

Figure 28-3 shows the relative importance of different kinds of advertising. Newspaper advertising, which generally contains useful information (grocery and clothing ads, want ads, and so on), makes up about one-third of the total. TV and magazine advertising, which is more commonly aimed at brand emphasis and prestige building, accounts for another 20–25 percent. The big remainder is a wide variety of types, some of which (direct trade magazines, and in-store advertising) include significant customer information, and others (e.g., direct mail) tend to have limited informational value.

Advertising and the "Management of Demand"

Recently social critics have leveled larger guns against modern advertising. The problem is not advertising's ineffectiveness; on the contrary, big corporations and marketing experts can control through advertising what we think we want, and what we don't. Businessmen "manage" consumer demand and thus dominate the whole economic process. Sellers determine what consumers want, in sharp contrast to the presumption of consumer sovereignty. Perhaps the best-known critic is J. K. Galbraith, in his best-selling *The New Industrial State.*

This attack challenges the very foundation of private-enterprise economics. If consumers really don't know what they want, and merely respond to producer demand-management, the whole intellectual case for a consumer-directed economy falls.

To deny that modern advertising influences our wants would be ridiculous. To claim that it completely dominates our desires is equally preposterous. Although 1 to 2 percent of the g.n.p. is a lot, it is hardly enough to dominate our entire spending pattern. If success were that easy, sellers would spend far more than the present $18 billion on advertising. Producers have repeatedly learned the hard way that consumer demand is often hard, even impossible to manage. A classic example is the debacle of the Ford-produced, massively advertised Edsel. Consumers just didn't buy them. American auto manufacturers in the 1950s saw their tail-finned behemoths increasingly challenged by small European imports in spite of hundreds of millions spent in advertising U.S. cars. Indeed, auto-makers' advertising budgets are only about 1 percent of sales. Soap and similar "small-ticket" brand items are the major examples of advertising costs reaching 5 or even 10 percent of sales. Look back at Table 21–1 that summarizes what consumers buy, and make your own judgment on what portion of total spending appears to be controlled by advertising.[7]

Selling Costs as a Basis for Monopoly

Product differentiation, whether based on real differences or illusions, help provide increased opportunities for profit by setting apart the seller's product. It lets each firm boost its price somewhat. Sometimes the result may approach pure monopoly; the classic case of Bayer Aspirin, which kept dominant control of the market even when competitors sharply undercut its price on pharmaceutically identical aspirin, was mentioned above. Although advertising is seldom so successful, cases of very strong consumer attachment to trade names are commonplace. Aggressive advertising serves both to keep alive these consumer attachments and to discourage new firms from competition. It can play some role in developing and protecting seller monopolies.

[7]These issues are considered in more detail in Chapter 31.

Quality Competition and Price Competition

For some products, quality competition has largely replaced price competition. Improvements in quality are of real benefit to consumers, and quality competition can be just as beneficial as price competition.

Some, however, view the shift toward quality competition with alarm because they feel that such competition often produces "improvements" more illusory than real. Are the annual model changes in autos worth the huge sums they cost? Why should the consumer be forced to pay for two or three fancy "crisper trays" in a new refrigerator when he could buy a less-elegant storage dish himself at one-third the cost? Indeed, many producers have pushed for "Fair Trade Laws" that forbid retailers to use price competition.

These criticisms suggest a real danger—that lively price competition may be atrophy, and that higher "qualities" may become so standardized that the buyer who prefers a lower-quality product at a lower price will be unable to buy it. But competition continually pushes sellers to give consumers what they want. Witness the success of compact cars as a reaction to the behemoths of the late 1950s. If you don't want delivery service, there are plenty of cash-and-carry supermarkets anxious to serve you. Ideally, for freedom of consumer choice, quality differentials should be available separately and charged for only when taken. To carry this principle to the extreme could lead to a chaos of products and prices, but to disregard it entirely would equally lead to serious restriction on consumer direction of resource allocation.[8]

[8]Note to instructors: Some of the examples in "Some Managerial Applications" at the end of Chapter 30 are equally useful here.

Be sure you have the following new analytical concepts firmly in hand:

standard costs	quality competition
cost-plus pricing	demand creation
break-even point	selling costs
product differentiation	unstable equilibrium

1. Is the absence of unreasonable profits in an industry satisfactory evidence that monopolistic competition is not injuring consumers of the product concerned? Explain your answer to a noneconomist.
2. "As long as there is relatively free entry to an industry, I can't get worried about the dangers of monopoly in that industry." Do you agree or disagree? Explain.
3. Some critics argue that we now have "producers' sovereignty" rather than "consumer sovereignty," because advertising now determines what we think we want. Marshal the evidence for and against this argument.
4. It is alleged that quality competition is increasingly replacing price competition in the American economy. From your own observation, is this a valid conclusion? Insofar as it is valid, is this development advantageous or disadvantageous for the consumer?
5. As a consumer, would you like to see aggressive price competition among sellers of all the products you buy? Under such competition, would you get the same breadth of display, rerutn privileges, and charge-account arrangements now provided by major department stores?
6. Do you get your money's worth out of the advertising expenditures for which you indirectly pay?

twenty-nine

Oligopoly,
Collusion,
and the
Mixed Economy

Three companies—General Motors, Ford, and Chrysler—make nearly all the automobiles produced in the United States. The top four companies account for over 90 percent of all flat glass and electric light bulbs produced. Over 75 percent of the total business in the industry is done by the top four producers in cigarettes, linoleum, and typewriters. In dozens of major industries, from half to three-fourths of the total business is done by fewer than ten firms. These are the oligopolies—industries where a few firms dominate the industry, though there may be many small firms that generally follow the leaders, or take what is left over. Figure 29–1 summarizes the degree of market domination by the leading four firms in a number of major industries.

These examples are all on a national scale. The number of oligopolists in local markets is far larger. Building materials (such as cement and bricks), for example, are produced by hundreds of different firms scattered all over the country. But in any one local market, production is usually concentrated in one or a few firms. The two or three druggists in a small town are oligopolists so far as drugs are concerned—though possibly not on ice cream and soft drinks (where groceries and others compete). Other examples are commonplace. The more important transportation costs are and the harder it is for cus-

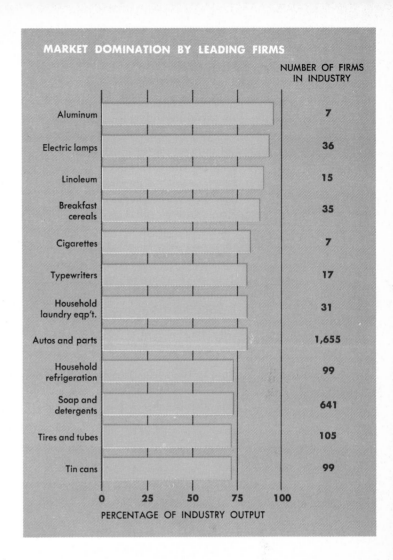

MARKET DOMINATION BY LEADING FIRMS

fig. 29–1

The largest few firms dominate the industry's output in leading U.S. industries. The total number of firms varies greatly from industry to industry. (Source: U.S. Department of Commerce; data are for value of shipments in 1966; number of firms data are for 1963.)

tomers to shop around, the more likely local oligopolies are to be found.

Economists consider "concentration ratios" (the percentage of total sales in a market or industry concentrated in the largest four, or sometimes eight, firms) an important indication of likely market performance. But it is important to recognize that this is only one rough measure of the degree of monopoly power held by the leading firms. Probable price–output behavior may be quite different, for example, in two industries with the same concentration ratio of 80 percent, if in one case the biggest firm has 60 percent of the market while in the other it has only 25. Similarly, the total number of firms in the industry outside the leaders may make a difference. The soap and match industries have similar concentration ratios, with the additional industry characteristics shown below. Which would you say is more concentrated?

	Soap	Matches
Total number of firms	267	14
Percentage of total industry sales by:		
Largest 4 firms	85	74
Largest 8 firms	89	93
Largest 20 firms	95	100

In general, economists suspect that monopoly-like results are more likely in highly concentrated than in less-concentrated industries. But this measure provides only a rough first presumption.

The degree of concentration in different industries has varied substantially over the years. But some industries, with the characteristics noted below, have been dominated persistently by a few large firms, and overall data on concentration show a surprisingly stable pattern for a dynamically changing economy. A more detailed analysis of these historical patterns is presented in Chapter 30.

International data on concentration are also illuminating. Table 29–1 compares concentration ratios for leading industries in five industrialized nations. Overall, concentration patterns are strikingly similar, which suggests common underlying factors in the industries concerned. But here again, there are numerous cases that don't fit the general pattern.

The Foundations of Oligopoly

At bottom, most oligopolies rest on one or both of two factors: (1) the necessity of large-scale production (relative to the size of the market) for low-cost output, and (2) barriers against the entry of new firms into the industry.

If total market demand will support only a few firms of optimum size, clearly the competitive struggle will tend to make a few big firms the winners. This situation rests fundamentally on the economies of large-scale production. In each of the industries in Figure 29–1, large-scale production is essential to obtain low unit costs.

How do these big firms maintain their positions, once attained? As we shall see presently, aggressive price competition is unlikely. Instead, the oligopolist tries to increase his market share and his profits by improving his product, by demand-creating activities, and by setting up barriers against the intrusion of new competitors. In many oligopolies, patents, established marketing organization, or control over raw materials may be of key importance in keeping out newcomers. The bases for oligopoly power are similar to those for other monopolies indicated in Chapter 27.

Dominant firms in an oligopoly are seldom completely safe from potential competition. It

table 29-1

Concentration Ratios in Five Nations*

	U.S.	U.K.	Canada	France	Japan
Primary aluminum	100	43	100	100	100
Automobiles	98	74	100	79	76
Cigarettes	82	74	85	100	
Trucks	77	86	100	78	
Matches	74	86	98	100	74
Steel ingots	64	32	81	40	52
Flour	40	46	35	12	53
Petroleum refining	32	93	79	72	41
Beer	27	11	49	25	98
Cement	31	89	100	52	48
Cotton textiles	18	4	60		7

*Ratios are for four firms in the United States, three firms in other nations. Figures show percent of total sales accounted for by leading firms. Data vary between 1950 and 1960 for different nations. Source: J. Bain, *International Differences in Industrial Structure* (New Haven: Yale University Press, 1966), pp. 67-106.

is the rare oligopoly that escapes for long the pressures of competition from new firms and new products. Even patents, large size, and technological dominance provide only partial insulation. For example, General Electric long held most of the basic patents in the electric light-bulb industry. It licensed these patents to small firms on condition that total production be controlled, and to Westinghouse under fewer restrictions. G.E. and Westinghouse dominated production and prices, and the market was, for all practical purposes, shared between them in stable proportions and without aggressive price competition. Finally, G.E.'s control was weakened by expiration of the seventeen-year period on some patents and by threatened antitrust action. Sylvania Electric, a small but alert firm, decided to brave the uncertainties of competition. It started with certain free patents, stressed efficient technology and aggressive selling, and by the end of World War II had become a third major firm in the industry, though still far smaller than G.E. and Westinghouse.

Oligopoly Prices, Output, and Profits

Analytically, the crucial thing about an oligopoly is the small number of sellers, which makes it imperative for each to weigh carefully the reactions of the others to his own price, production, and sales policy. Given the wide range of possible reactions of different sellers in most oligopolistic markets, it is difficult to predict precisely what these reactions will be, and therefore difficult for the oligopolist to determine what price-production levels will give him the largest profits. We have, therefore, no simple oligopoly theory to tell us reliably what the price-output equilibrium condition will be. The outcome will be different depending on the assessments each businessman makes of the likely reactions of his competitors to his own policies.

While many reaction patterns are possible, history suggests some central tendencies in oligopoly price–production decisions. In olig-

opoly, one attractive alternative for the rivals is collectively to establish the profit-maximizing price for the industry as a whole, and then divide up the market and profits among themselves. The law prohibits open collusion of this sort, so oligopolists must make secret agreements or rely on the willingness of all to "go along" with avoiding competition that would force price below the optimal (profit-maximizing) level. But in such a situation, it will also generally be to the self-interest of each individual producer to get a bigger share of the market for himself, which he might hope to do by cutting prices and luring away some of his competitors' customers. On the other hand, if he cuts price, there is always the danger that competitors will meet the price cut, and the only result will be a lower price and lower profit for all of the oligopolists. Against this background, the following hypotheses appear to have substantial support:

1. Under oligopoly, the greater the mutual recognition of interdependence among the firms is, the nearer price and output will be to the combined profit-maximizing price and output profits for the industry. Such mutual recognition of interdependence will usually be greater, the smaller the number of important sellers and the more nearly identical the product of the sellers.

2. The easier it is for oligopoly firms to reach a tacit (or collusive) agreement, the closer the price-output level will be to the combined profit-maximizing level for the industry. Generally, the smaller the number of firms is, the easier it will be to work out and maintain such agreements.

3. The greater the barriers to entry of new firms are, the closer oligopolistic industries will come to the combined profit-maximizing price. This is because the threat of entry of new firms may force existing firms to keep prices and profits lower than they would otherwise do. Competition among the oligopolists will be more likely to break out if new firms find entry relatively easy.

4. The weaker other barriers to entry of new

firms are, the greater nonprice competition among oligopolists will be. If no other barriers to entry exist, oligopolists will try to protect their positions by advertising and other forms of quality competition that deter new competitors.

5. Nonprice competition will be greater, the greater is the limitation on price competition. If firms see the disadvantage of involvement in "price wars," they will tend to compete instead through nonprice channels, such as advertising and quality changes.

Oligopoly Theory: Avoidance of Aggressive Price Competition

Suppose that you are the manager of a local brick factory, and that you have two competitors in the area. You are making a reasonable profit, and so are your competitors. Each of you sets the price at which he sells—an "administered" price. You are "pricemakers." Each of you knows he could make a larger profit if he could manage to increase his share of the market, because each of you is operating below capacity. Will you cut your price to get customers away from your competition?

Maybe you will. But you'd better think twice before you try it. Your competitors will almost surely retaliate by meeting your price cut. Maybe they'll undercut you if you stir them up by disturbing the stability of the market. Your price advantage can't last more than a day or two before they know about it, and you can't get very rich in that length of time. Heaven only knows just what will happen if you start a local price war, but three things looks reasonably sure: All three of you will end up with lower prices; none of you will have lured many customers away from the others; and everybody's profits will have taken a beating. In the end, you might just glower at each other in the local Rotary Club meetings, but probably you'd get together and agree to put prices back to some reasonable level near where you started.

This is only a small-scale, hypothetical example. But the questions are the same ones that the

presidents of huge corporations ask when they consider cutting prices in oligopolistic markets, in steel, automobiles, plate glass. With only a few firms in the industry, the forces toward letting well enough alone are strong. Most oligopolists hesitate to cut prices except to meet a price cut by another firm. Price reductions are likely to come only under severe pressures—seriously weakened overall market demand, for example. When firms do cut, they usually do so in the expectation that their cut will be met by rivals. Thus, the cut is made with the intention of moving the whole industry price scale to a lower level, in the hope of stimulating overall demand for the industry's product. In many cases, one major firm in an oligopolistic industry ordinarily acts as a "price leader," both upward and downward, in this way, although there may be no formal agreement.

It is not theoretically certain that oligopolistic price will be higher than competitive price would be in the same industry. But when facing a downward sloping demand curve, there is a strong incentive for oligopolists to keep price above the minimum average unit cost and above marginal cost. Oligopolists may price on a standard-cost mark-up system; they may shoot for a "satisfactory" return on capital investment; they may just follow customary price leaders. But active competition is what forces price down toward the minimum point on the unit-cost curve. In the absence of active price competition, the likelihood is strong that oligopoly price will be at least somewhat higher. If the industry has recently gone through a couple of price wars in which everyone has temporarily lost his shirt, there will be an especially strong tendency for everyone to let price alone at a level high enough to provide a "reasonable" profit. Price policy may also be affected by public opinion, and by the federal antitrust authorities lurking in the background.

Such a "live and let live" policy makes sense to most producers. It leaves room for each firm to try quality and advertising competition to increase its share of the market. It leaves room for some price shading and juggling when times are hard or when one firm is losing out badly in the market. But aggressive price competition will probably blow the situation wide open.

Oligopoly Theory: The Kinked Demand Curve

Economic theory helps present the price problem that faces the oligopolist. Go back to the brickworks case above. The current price is twenty cents a brick, and you are selling 10,000 bricks per week. As you sit in your office, you try to imagine what your demand curve looks like, as a basis for deciding whether to change your price. Chances are you will come out with something like Figure 29–2, a "kinked" demand curve—assuming that all bricks are substantially alike.

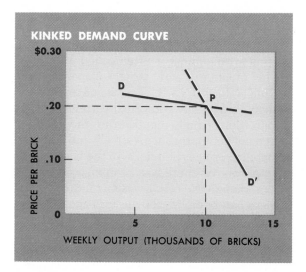

fig. 29–2

Kinked demand curve suggests that you will lose total revenue if you either raise or lower price. Demand is elastic above twenty cents, inelastic below it.

It says that if you raise your price and the others don't follow, your sales will fall off sharply because your customers will desert you; your demand curve looks highly elastic if you raise price above twenty cents. On the other hand, if you cut the price, you can be almost

sure your rivals will follow to avoid losing customers to you. Thus, a lower price may increase sales a little, since the market will take some more bricks at a lower price; but there's little reason to suppose you'll get a bigger share of the market away from your competitors. Your demand curve looks very inelastic if you cut price below twenty cents. This situation obviously puts a high premium on keeping the price where it is, just as the common sense reasoning above suggested.

Note now the critical assumptions. The first is that if you **raise** price, your rivals **will not** follow. It is this assumption that underlies the highly elastic curve to the left of the "corner" *P*. If, by contrast, you are a price "leader" and your rivals will follow your increase, the *DP* section of the curve will be much less elastic and will probably just extend directly on up from *D'P*, as in the dashed line. This is because you won't lose a share of the market to the others; the only loss in sales volume comes from the market as a whole, because fewer bricks will be bought at the higher price.

The second crucial assumption is that if you **cut** price, the others **will** also cut. If they do not, then *D'P* of your demand curve will probably be highly elastic, as your rivals' customers switch to you. Then the "corner" in the demand curve would again vanish and your demand curve will just be an extension of *DP*. This would be a wonderful situation for you, but it is not very likely unless you can hide your price cuts from your rivals. And that's hard in an oligopoly.

In summary, then, the kinked demand curve exists because you assume a **different** reaction from your competitors when you raise than when you lower your price. If you are the recognized price leader, there will be no kink, and you are merely moving price up or down along the demand curve for the whole industry. If you are so little that nobody reacts to your price changes, there is also no kink—but this case is really a violation of the oligopoly situation, since the essence of oligopoly is the existence of so few competitors that each must be concerned with the others' reactions. Lastly, your freedom to move price without immediately risking rivals' reactions is larger the more differentiated your product is.[1]

Oligopoly and "Game Theory"

Economic theory has no clear-cut answer as to where price will be set under oligopoly, although the kinked demand-curve analysis above gives some insight into likely behavior. Another approach is through "game theory." This likens competing oligopolists to participants in a game—a contest for market share and profits. In an oligopoly of, say five leading firms, there are many possibilities of partial collusion and different forms of competition. If you change your price, will all the others react together? May they "gang up" on you? If you have been the "price leader," will they follow your lead again this time? What devices are there for implicit collusion to avoid price competition when open collusion is illegal and each of you wants a bigger share of the market? How shall you play the game to avoid having newcomers break into your profitable circle of five?

"Game theory" explores systematically the

[1]Where the demand curve is kinked, the corresponding marginal-revenue curve has a break, or discontinuity. The attached graph shows the demand and marginal-revenue curves from Figure 29–2. Note that given this marginal-revenue curve, a marginal-cost curve *(MC)* could move up or down considerably without logically leading the firm to change its price. This fact may further explain the observed oligopoly tendency toward price stability, even when costs change substantially. (The lower half of the *MR* curve need not be negative, though of course it will be if *D'P* shows inelastic demand.)

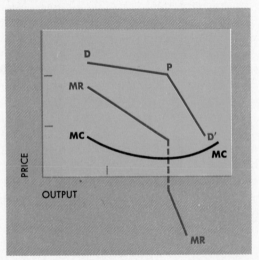

outcomes of different strategies and coalitions, depending on different assumptions about there actions of competitors. This approach suggests the outcome of different policies, but the combinations and permutations of different assumptions mount rapidly, and the theory becomes very complex—too complex for inclusion here. Thus, unfortunately, game theory gives no clear predictions of what profit-seeking oligopolists will do, although it helps to suggest some likely limiting cases. The best we can do at the elementary level consists of the broad predictions outlined in the two preceding sections.

Oligopoly Theory: Price-Fixing and Market-Sharing Agreements (Cartels)

Presumably, oligopolists would like to maximize profits for the industry as a whole, thereby obtaining the largest profit pie to divide by sharing the market. Such a price-fixing market-sharing arrangement is often called a "cartel."

This practice is now strictly illegal. But analyzing a formal cartel can suggest the consequences of today's informal cartellike price-stabilization arrangements. And the line between not competing aggressively and agreeing to stabilize price is nebulous. In the brick-works example above, there was no open collusion on prices, though the result was much the same as if there had been. Moreover, formal cartels are a dominant form of market organization in many European countries.

Cartels with Free Entry — a Simple Model. Assume a hypothetical furnace industry, in which there are only ten firms. What are the long-run results of a cartel in the industry, if the ten firms agree to "stabilize" prices and to share the market equally?

In effect, the firms will act like one pure monopoly in setting price and then divide up the business and profits.[2] Assume that the competitive price for furnaces of a particular type would be $400, the lowest point on the total-

[2]Logically, the cartel as a whole would maximize its profits by estimating its costs and revenues, and then setting price and output where marginal cost equals marginal revenue for the industry as a whole. See Figure 27–2 and Table 27–3 in Chapter 27 on "Monopoly."

unit-cost curve of each producer. At $400, consumers would buy 30,000 furnaces monthly. But by restricting output, the ten firms can make substantial profits. So they agree to raise the price to $500, at which level 20,000 furnaces can be sold monthly, this price being estimated to maximize profits for the group as a whole. Then each firm sells only 2,000 furnaces monthly, but at the higher price it reaps a profit of about $75 per furnace (the difference between the $500 price and the $425 total unit cost at the 2,000 output level). The situation is pictured in Figure 29–3.

Price is now higher than the competitive level; output is lower; employment of labor and raw materials is lower; and production is less "efficient." Each firm is operating to the left of its minimum total-unit-cost output, and for the industry as a whole price is too high and too few resources are used. By agreeing to eliminate price competition, the furnace makers gain; if they can keep new competitors out, they're sitting pretty. Consumers take a beating. Price is well above marginal cost. This can be an equilibrium situation as long as potential rivals can be kept from entering the furnace industry.

But suppose new firms can't be kept out. Oligopoly profits lure them in. The entry of new firms will divide up the same total sales among more and more firms. With ten firms, each pro-

ducer could sell 2,000 furnaces monthly; with twelve firms, individual monthly sales can be only 1,667 (assuming each firm gets the same share of the market). Thus, profits are eliminated as new firms enter, not by price reduction but by reducing output in each firm to a less and less efficient level. New firms will continue to enter, cutting down the market available to each, until finally the cost per unit has risen to equal the cartel price of $500 at an output of 1,333 for each of, say, fifteen firms.

This situation is illustrated in Figure 29–3, which shows the total-unit-cost curve of a typical producer. The original cartel members agreedto stabilize the price at $500. This permitted each producer to sell 2,000 furnaces monthly, and to make about $75 per furnace. But as more firms enter, building similar plants, the sales allotted to each producer fall lower and lower, until with fifteen producers each can sell only 1,333 furnaces monthly. At this output the average cost per furnace has risen to $500, the cartel price, because each producer's plant is used so far below the optimum level of output. Profits have been eliminated.

Now look at the results. Consumers are just as badly off as under the original ten-firm cartel, since price is still up at $500 and total output is still restricted to 20,000 furnaces. And with the entry of more firms, the profits of the oligopolists have been eliminated. Thus the producers are no better off than under competition, consumers suffer all the results of monopoly, and society bears the loss of extensive "overinvestment" in the industry, since far more productive facilities have been built than are required. Such a cartel arrangement with free entry, it might thus be argued, is not a halfway point between competition and monopoly, but rather an arrangement that combines the worst characteristics of each and the benefits of neither.

Obviously, this "equilibrium" would be highly unstable. Each producer sees a big potential gain from cutting his price, and he has little inducement to remain in the agreement, since profits have been eliminated. Thus, formal cartels without effective restrictions on entry seldom last long. Those with strong restrictions are more durable.

This example overstates the evils of cartels

fig. 29–3

At the cartel price of $500, firm first makes $75 profit per furnace. As more firms enter, each firm's market share and profit diminish.

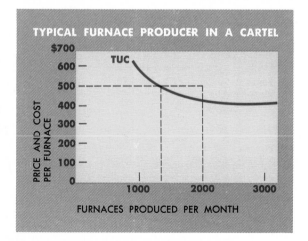

TYPICAL FURNACE PRODUCER IN A CARTEL

TUC

PRICE AND COST PER FURNACE

$700
600
500
400
300
200
100
0

1000   2000   3000

FURNACES PRODUCED PER MONTH

by failing to recognize the likelihood of quality competition. Cartels seldom fix market shares rigidly. Thus, producers, seeing their profits vanishing, would probably try hard to attract customers through quality improvements and other nonprice competition. These efforts would benefit at least some consumers, and might be a substantial offset to the cartel's price rigidity—through they would also raise costs.

Oligopoly Theory: Restrictions on Entry

The preceding section points up the importance of restrictions on entry of new firms in determining the price–output performance of an oligopolistic industry. If the furnace producers above had had some effective way of keeping new firms out of the industry, their original cartel would have worked out very nicely for them in terms of continuing profits—though there would always be the danger that one firm would become dissatisfied and cut prices to increase its share of market and profits. But once outsiders are free to enter, the end of the collusive price-fixing plan is sure to come. As more and more firms enter, profits are eroded for everyone, and the incentive to fight back becomes almost irresistible.

Thus, oligopolists, like other partial monopolists, try hard to insulate themselves against new competitors, by product differentiation, by patents, by developing secret productive know-how, by bringing out new products that are hard to reproduce. And in many cases they are helped by the basic technology of the industry. As was indicated above, oligopolies tend to develop where large-scale investment and production are required for efficient output, and it's hard for newcomers to break into such industries. Look ahead to Table 30–1 to get an impression of the big investments required to complete effectively in a variety of modern American industries, and to the text there for a classification of industries by relative ease of entry.[3]

Recent research suggests that barriers to en-

[3]For a more detailed account, see Joe Bain, *Barriers to New Competition* (Cambridge: Harvard University Press, 1956).

try are effective ways of protecting above-average profits, at least temporarily. Table 29–2 classifies major oligopolistic industries by the apparent barriers they have against new entrants, and shows the average rate of return on

table 29-2

Rate of Return on Owners' Investment in Oligopolies, 1950-1960*

Very High Barriers to Entry:	Average Profit Rate (Percentage)	
Automobiles	15.5	
Cigarettes	11.6	
Ethical drugs	17.9	
Flat glass	18.8	
Liquor	9.0	
Nickel	18.9	
Sulfur	21.6	
Class average		16.4
Substantial Barriers to Entry:		
Aluminum reduction	10.2	
Petroleum refining	12.2	
Steel	10.8	
Soap	13.3	
Copper	11.5	
Shoe machinery	7.4	
Class average		11.3
Moderate-to-Low Barriers to Entry:		
Glass containers	13.3	
Shoes	9.6	
Rayon	8.5	
Meat-packing	5.3	
Flour	8.6	
Beer	10.9	
Bituminous coal	8.8	
Class average		9.9

*Data from H. M. Mann, "Seller Concentration, Barriers to Entry, and Rates of Return in Thirty Industries," *Review of Economics and Statistics*, August, 1966. Table 29-2 shows only part of Professor Mann's entire list of industries. He also found that profit rates vary directly with the share of market held by the largest eight producers in thirty major oligopolistic industries.

owners'investment in each for the years 1950 to 1960. Those with the highest entry barriers generally showed the highest profit rates, though the experts disagree over the effectiveness of barriers in some industries.

Try one last check on oligopoly theory. Suppose the ten barbers in Hometown are pricing haircuts at $1.50 and making what seems to them a very bad living. So they get together and agree to raise the price of haircuts to $2.50. Predict the results of this cartel-type agreement — for barbers and for customers. Hints: What is the elasticity of demand for haircuts? What will happen to the number of barbers in Hometown?

Oligopoly in the American Economy

Collusion among firms to keep profits at profitable levels has been common since the earliest records we have of market-type economies. In the American economy, the "pools" of the nineteenth century were formal cartel arrangements in which all the output of the industry was pooled together, then priced and sold as if the industry were essentially one monopoly. The profits were divided among the members. Economic historians have compiled a long list of pools and "trusts" — in steel rails, lumber, whiskey, brass, iron pipe, envelopes, window glass, petroleum products, wallpaper, and many others. Most of these pools prospered temporarily, then disintegrated with price wars as more and more competitors tried to invade the industry.

In 1890, the Sherman Antitrust Act made price-fixing agreements illegal. Price "stabilization," with more informal sorts of market sharing, gradually supplanted the formal pools and "trusts." The prosperous decade of the 1920s saw informal price stabilization entrenched as sound business policy. The New Deal policies of the 1930s encouraged cartel-type arrangements in agriculture, coal, and in industry generally through the National Industrial Recovery Act. The search for ways to avoid disruptive price competition has been persistent.

Price Wars and Price Stabilization in High-Fixed-Cost Industries

High-fixed-cost industries have played a major role in the history of American oligopoly. Consider the case of the railroads between New York and Chicago before railway rates were regulated by the federal government. There were four main routes. Each had an enormous fixed investment in right-of-way, stations, rolling stock, and so forth. Variable costs associated with adding a few more cars to any given train, or even adding whole trains, were inconsequential compared with the fixed costs. The *TUC* curve for each (for ton-miles of freight or for passengers) was downward sloping far beyond the traffic level anyone of them could realize. Thus, marginal costs were low and the incentive was great to cut prices in order to get more of the available traffic.

Under these circumstances, the New York Central could boost its profits spectacularly if it could get traffic away from the Pennsylvania. Since shippers of heavy products are sensitive to freight costs, the conclusion was easy—by cutting its prices, the Central could lure business away from its three competitors. But exactly the same thing was true for each of the others. It was not surprising, therefore, that cutthroat competition was the rule rather than the exception.[4]

You might suppose that after about the third price war the railroads would get together and agree on a market-sharing price-stabilization policy. And they did periodically. But the lure of profits was great, and those were the days of the swaggering industrial tycoon. It was not until the government stepped in with the Interstate Commerce Commission to regulate rates that the price wars were ended and price discrimination against short-haul shippers was eliminated.

The steel industry today is a similar high-fixed-cost industry. The cost of a modern steel

[4]Throughout, the railroads kept up their short-haul rates to shippers who were served by only one of the four roads and who therefore had no alternatives. In many cases, it cost more to ship freight a few hundred miles between intermediate points than to ship the same freight all the way from Chicago to New York.

mill has to be spread over an enormous tonnage to keep cost per ton down to a reasonable figure. Steel demand is highly sensitive to business fluctuations, and only in good times do the steel companies run near capacity. Thus, much of the time each company can increase its profits markedly by increasing volume, since its *TUC* curve is downward sloping and marginal cost is low until reasonably high-level operation is reached. The pressure to shade prices is great.

Long ago, the leaders of the major steel firms recognized the problems involved. Price stabilization, with U.S. Steel acting as a "leader" in setting prices on basic products, has been the rule since the early part of the century. Over half a century, basic steel has avoided aggressive price competition much of the time—first by formal agreements, then by the famous "Gary dinners" (at which steel leaders apparently came to price agreements at sumptuous stag dinners given by Judge Gary, president of the leading steel company), and recently by more informal, tacit, "go-along" attitudes, facilitated by the American Iron and Steel Institute, the industry's trade association.

But the difficulties of avoiding aggressive price competition in a high-fixed-cost industry like steel have repeatedly led to undercover price cutting and periodically to open price wars. In the depression of the 1930s, for example, the quoted base prices on steel became little more than a beginning point for bargaining with major consumers as to how much the price would be shaded or what other special concessions would be made. The published prices confronting the little fellow might be firm and unyielding, but in effect steel had two price systems—the published prices and the actual bargains arrived at with big buyers. Even in good times, list prices are actual prices only for small, irregular buyers in many industries. Price stabilization as a business policy by no means eliminates all price competition, though it keeps it within restricted bounds as long as the "orderly market" holds.

Electrical Equipment and Cigarettes: Two Contrasting Examples

Heavy electrical equipment and cigarettes are both oligopolies, with concentration ratios exceeding 80 percent for the top four firms. In 1961, leading executives of General Electric, Westinghouse, and other major manufacturers of large generators, turbines, and circuit breakers were found guilty of price-fixing and market-sharing agreements over the preceding decade, carried out in secret meetings in hotels and motels around the country. Such equipment is sold on sealed bids, and the firms agreed in advance which was to get each bid and at what price. Periodically the cartel broke down under pressure of falling demand and profits in recessions, and resultant large excess capacity in the industry; the most spectacular case was the famous industry "white sale" of the middle 1950s when violent price competition broke out. But each time, the market-sharing arrangements were reestablished, until the court's findings in 1961 shocked the nation and, apparently, the top management of some of the companies involved.[5]

By contrast, apparently the leading firms in the cigarette industry, with a similar concentration ratio, have scrupulously avoided direct collusion on prices for many years. Yet severe price competition has seldom developed. Observers agree that price leadership generally prevails, with competition concentrated mainly on advertising and other forms of demand creation.[6]

Why have market practices developed so differently in these two industries with similar concentration ratios? The answer is complex, but the preceding sections on oligopoly theory can throw some light on the answer.

1. Cost structure. Both industries require a large investment in fixed plant and equipment for efficient production, but this investment is larger relative to the market for electrical equipment than for cigarettes. Thus, excess capacity posed an especially serious problem for electrical producers when demand slackened; marginal costs were far below market prices

---

[5]For a vivid account, see "The Incredible Electrical Conspiracy," *Fortune*, April and May, 1961.

[6]For a fuller description of the industry, see R. B. Tennant, *The American Cigarette Industry* (New Haven: Yale University Press, 1950).

when demand was slack, and the pressures to cut price to increase share of market were great.

2. **Nature of product and difficulties of effective collusion.** Big turbines and generators are built to order. Cigarettes are highly standardized, with the price per pack visible to everyone. Thus, in the cigarette industry, each firm can quickly check up on every competitor's prices; communication on prices is easy and substantially instantaneous. Cuts are readily observable if anyone breaks the stabilization pattern. Informal avoidance of price competition is thus easy, and no one risks getting undercut without his knowing about it promptly. But in electrical equipment, without a formal agreement among the producers there is no way to check up on how competitors are pricing until the contract is finally let. There is no effective way to manage market sharing and price stabilization without formal collusion. The practical problems of making informal (tacit) price and market collusion work are enormous for a nonstandard, special-order product like heavy electrical machinery, easier for standardized products.

3. **Number and size of firms.** The top four concentration ratios are similar in both industries. But for practical purposes, during the 1950s only the top three producers could compete for the big orders in heavy generators, circuit breakers, and turbines, while there were numerous smaller cigarette producers beyond the big four. Thus, formal collusion was easier to arrange in heavy electrical equipment than in cigarettes; but in lighter electrical equipment there were more producers and effective formal collusion was correspondingly more difficult to arrange and maintain. Secret, illegal meetings and communications are difficult at best. As the number of parties goes up, the difficulties and dangers mount geometrically.

4. **Ease of entry.** Where entry cannot be restricted, collusive oligopoly agreements seldom last. Thus, in spite of the large market concentration in the top three producers, entry of new competitors on lighter types of equipment continued to plague the electrical conspirators. Demands of smaller newcomers for market shares continually posed crises over the questions of which requests should be granted, and of how

to keep the newcomers from breaking the prices needed to maintain profits. As a practical matter, even without formal collusion the cigarette industry appears to have been more successful in discouraging new entrants, though new brands have been repeatedly introduced by existing firms. (Interestingly, with the establishment of completely noncollusive pricing in the heavy electrical industry following the court decision of 1961, all firms except the big two appear to have withdrawn from major sectors of the market rather than risk open competition on such large special-order items.)

5. **Nature of demand.** In heavy electrical equipment, demand varied markedly with the business cycle. Thus, firms are under severe profit pressure in recessions, with heavy investments in idle fixed plant and equipment. Growth in cigarette demand, by contrast, has been more stable, avoiding the severe price and excess-capacity problems which periodically plagued the electrical industry. Moreover, many consider the demand for cigarettes to be inelastic, so price cutting for the industry as a whole would provide no gain, and individual firms are loath to risk leading the whole industry price structure down by cutting their own prices. The demand for heavy electrical equipment looks more elastic; thus, the individual producer may be more ready to risk inducing an industry-wide price cut if this should be the result of his individual price cut, unless he is bound tightly by collusive agreements. In both cases the demand as seen by one producer is surely elastic if he could cut price without retaliation, but retaliation is almost certain as a practical matter.

This has been only a sketchy analysis of the electrical and cigarette oligopolies. If you want to really understand them, read the more thorough references noted. The purpose here has been merely to provide some "feel" for how the theoretical framework above can be used to study in more detail the enormously varied real-world cases of oligopoly which surround us. Oligopoly is the most unstable of all market structures and the hardest for which to predict output and price.

Research, Development, and Innovation

Oligopoly gets dubious marks on the criterion of efficiency in the allocation of resources. But there is another important kind of efficiency—efficiency in using resources to promote economic progress. How does oligopoly score on that test?

The general presumption of static economic theory is against monopoly in all its forms on this score as well. The pressure of competition is the greatest prod to progress. Adam Smith and his successors tell us. The more protected from competition any businessman is, the less-likely he is to work hard at producing new and better products.

But there is another side to the issue. Progress in the modern economy depends heavily on re-search and development spending. And only big firms have the resources to afford large R and D expenditures. Thus, as a practical matter, only with oligopolistic market structures are we likely to get the heavy R and D spending on which modern industrial progress depends.

What do the facts show? Figure 17–5 showed the rapid growth of R and D spending since the 1930s. Table 29–3 details the 1969 total by industry and federal financing.

Out of industrial R and D expenditures, less than 5 percent was in industries dominated by small firms—e.g., textiles and construction. Conversely, the great bulk of R and D is done by big firms, and by the same token in oligopolistic industries—e.g., aerospace, chemicals, and electrical equipment. (As was indicated in Part Two, much of this research is ultimately financed by government funds.) Only in agriculture among the industries approaching pure competition is there large R and D spending, and this is financed almost entirely by government and conducted largely in the universities.

But the picture is more complex. Among the large firms that do have research and development organizations, the middle-sized ones spend as large a fraction of their sales dollars on

table 29-3

Research and Development Spending, 1969*

Industry	R & D Spending (Billion $)	Percentage of All R & D	Federal Funds as Percentage of Total
Aircraft and missiles	$ 6.4	33.2%	83.4%
Electrical machinery	4.6	24.0	56.1
Other machinery	1.8	9.2	17.3
Chemicals	1.7	9.0	11.4
Autos, transport equipment	1.7	9.0	23.7
Instruments	.5	2.8	29.6
Petroleum products	.5	2.8	13.4
Food products	.2	1.0	8.9
Steel	.2	.9	.6
All other**	1.6	8.1	48.0
Total	$19.2	100.0%	50.7%

*Data estimated by National Science Foundation; federal share based on 1968 budget allocations. This series excludes certain commercial product-development activities sometimes included in R & D estimates.

**Includes mining, contruction, transportation, public utilities, agriculture, and others.

research as do the huge ones. Although modern industrial research is heavily concentrated in oligopolistic industries, increasing firm size above a certain level doesn't seem to increase the relative stress on research.

Whose research contributes the most to innovation and economic progress? Do the big firms make the advances that really count, or do the important innovations come from little and medium-sized firms? We have few clear measures of success. Researchers have looked especially at three measures—patents received, important innovations achieved, and the rate of increase in productivity.

Jacob Schmookler of the University of Minnesota has found that a few giants dominate the total number of patents awarded (Bell Labs, G.E., and Du Pont), but that in general big firms receive patents only in proportion to their larger expenditures on research. If anything, the middle-sized firms appear to have done a shade better in relation to their research spending, except for the few research giants.

A more important, but more difficult, measure is the number of important innovations actually produced by different-sized companies. Here Penn's Edwin Mansfield has studied three major industries intensively. He finds that in petroleum refining and coal mining, the larger firms have produced a larger proportion of the important innovations than their share in industry sales. But in steel, the reverse was true. He speculates on the basis of his evidence that large, but not giant-sized, companies are the most promising sources of major innovations—though this statement must be recognized as only a very tentative judgment.

Which industries show the highest rates of growth in productivity? Broadly speaking, those with the highest growth rates tend to be the oligopolies—chemicals, aerospace, and communications. Productivity has grown more slowly in industries dominated by small firms—the services, construction, and textiles. Agriculture is a strong counterexample, with a very high growth rate in productivity. But there the research is almost entirely financed by the government, done in the state universities, and dis-

seminated through state agricultural extension services.

How about the influence of entry barriers on the rate of innovation? As was indicated above, profits on invested capital tend to be higher where barriers to entry are high, which might suggest that oligopolists have been progressive in reducing costs. However, numerous cases can be cited where well-protected oligopolists have failed to introduce major innovations until the way has been charted by outsiders, often big firms in other industries. Examples are the early introduction of radio outside G.E. and Bell Telephone, the dominant communication firms; and the development of jet engines outside the established aircraft engine manufacturers. But there are numerous counterexamples, some involving the same firms. Pending more conclusive research, we are left with only a general theoretical presumption that pressures to innovate will be strongest where firms are not protected against the threat of new entrants.

What is the conclusion on oligopoly and economic progress? Clearly firms of substantial size are needed in most industries to undertake substantial R and D activities, if we expect the research to be done by private firms.[7] The evidence suggests that on this score some degree of oligopoly is probably preferable to either monopoly or many small firms. But just how big firms should be for optimal progress remains an unsettled issue.

The Dynamics of Oligopoly

Many rapidly growing industries are dominated (led) by one or a few firms. Rapid growth tends to come with the introduction of new products or new methods, and understandably the firms that innovate get a leadership position. Figure 29–4 shows a typical life-cycle curve for a new product. After introduction, sales grow slowly as it becomes better known on the market. Then, as it catches on, it grows rap-

[7]Some observers suggest introduction of government-financed research and dissemination for the business section, to parallel the arrangements that have worked so well in the small-firm agricultural sector.

TYPICAL PRODUCT, LIFE-CYCLE PATTERN

1-2% G.R. 7-20% G.R. 3-7% G.R. 2-(4) G.R.

Sales

Profit margins

30
22.5
15.0
7.5

Introduction Growth   Maturity   Decline

G.R. = Annual growth rate of sales
ROI = Percent return on investment, after taxes (right-hand scale)

fig. 29–4

Typically, sales of successful products grow rapidly at first, then gradually level off, and ultimately turn down. Profits peak earlier. (Source: *Economic Concentration,* Hearings before the Senate Subcommittee on Antitrust and Monopoly, 1964, p. 138.)

idly, often reaching rates of 10–30 percent per year; in extreme cases, growth rates are even higher. Profits soar, both because new products are often priced to "skim the cream" off the market and because of rising sales volume.

As the product matures and other producers come into the market, the growth rate tends to slow. Profit margins for the innovating firm tend to level off and fall. As the product reaches "maturity," the sales growth rate slows and

finally turns down, as new products and new methods tend to replace this one.

Table 29–4 is, of course, only illustrative. Some products never catch on in the market at all; others have short lives and are soon outpaced by competitive products. But the success stories usually look something like Table 29–4, and in such cases one or a few firms very often dominate the market.

Table 29–4 shows some of the great success

table 29-4

Growth Rates of Innovative Industries 1945-65*

Company	Product Line	Average Annual Growth Rate	
		Sales	Jobs
Texas Instruments	Transistors, integrated circuits	29%	10%
Xerox	Photocopiers	23	18
I.B.M.	Computers, office systems	18	12
3M	Tapes	15	8
Polaroid	Instant photography	13	8
Total economy		2.5 (g.n.p.)	1.4

*Source: U.S. Department of Commerce, *Technological Innovation: Its Environment and Management* (1967), p. 5.

stories of modern times. These concern companies that pioneered new product lines, and then stayed ahead of competitors during the rapid growth of their industries. Their net sales, and the jobs they provided, grew far faster than comparable figures for the economy as a whole, and their profits reflected their happy state. Each firm was dominant in its industry during this growth period.

The fact that each industry grew around one pioneering firm is not a coincidence. Competition has developed only as the successes became apparent. Oligopoly thus often comes with rapid growth, but oligopolies, of course, do not necessarily produce rapid growth.

One last observation on the dynamics of oligopoly. Alert firms know that spectacular growth rates for individual products must end. Thus, most large firms try to diversify with several or many products. They try always to have a new growth product in the wings as established lines reach maturity. Otherwise, they may fade as new competitive products make them obsolete, or at least they may grow slowly, if at all. The most successful oligopolists are those that keep a step ahead of their competition with new products and new production methods.[8]

---

[8]This suggests that oligopolists often make their biggest profits on new products, and they do. Prices are set to "skim the cream" of market demand when new products are introduced and there are no competitors. During the rapid growth period, price may be set far above marginal cost, and the wide profit spread continues as costs fall with production experience and rising volume. As the industry reaches maturity and competition intensifies, profit spreads narrow. Then the innovative firm may be willing to accept small profits or even losses, continuing production from its fixed plant as long as price exceeds variable cost. Multi-product firms, which include most big oligopolists, thus often follow significantly different pricing policies at different stages of product life cycles. The overall profits of such a firm may thus reflect a combination of large and small profits, and even losses, on different product lines. Unfortunately, most publicly available statistics do not make it possible to sort out these dynamic developments.

Review

CONCEPTS TO REMEMBER

This chapter reuses most of the analytical concepts introduced throughout Part Three. Beyond these, be sure you understand the following new ones:

administered prices   price leadership
cartel   price stabilization
concentration ratio   kinked demand curve

FOR ANALYSIS AND DISCUSSION

1. Suppose you were manager of one of the furnace firms originally forming the cartel described in Chapter 29. What policies would you follow to promote your own best interests as additional new firms entered the industry?
2. What are the main forces that determine whether there will be few or many firms in any given industry?
3. "The big oligopolies like General Motors, General Electric, Swift, and Alcoa have been primarily responsible for making better goods available to consumers. Breaking them up into smaller units to obtain more active price competition would be disastrous." Do you agree or disagree? Support your position against a critic.
4. Is the rate of profit earned on invested capital a good indication of whether an oligopoly is abusing its position?
5. In many of the major oligopolistic industries, entry is difficult for

new firms because of both the technical know-how and the large financial investment required for effective competition. Can you suggest desirable ways to overcome these difficulties?

6. Suppose that you are president of the largest firm in an industry where the great bulk of the business is done by the largest five firms. As the industry leader, your firm ordinarily initiates any price changes in the industry.

   a. How would you go about deciding what price to charge for your product?
   b. Is there a conflict or community between your interests and those of the other four firms in the industry?
   c. Would consumers be better off, by and large, if active price competition were enforced rather than price leadership in the industry?

APPENDIX   *SOME MANAGERIAL APPLICATIONS*

This is primarily a book of economics for the citizen. Its main goal is to examine how the economic system works and how we might make it work better. But these same economic concepts and principles can help the businessman make better decisions for himself and the stockholders.[9]

Elasticity of Demand and Product Pricing. Demand is often elastic. And when it is, a price policy that doesn't recognize this fact can mean disaster. But a price policy founded on full knowledge of demand elasticity can make life pleasant for the stockholders, and unpleasant for competitors.

The phonograph-record industry is a classic case. For decades classical records were high-priced luxury items, aimed at a small market. In 1938, Columbia reduced the price per record (on the old shellac 78-rpm records) from $2 to $1. The response was overwhelming. Total expenditure on classical records, to the amazement of almost everybody else, rose drastically. Demand turned out to be highly elastic, and the competition was left behind.

About the same time, the railroads, desperate for revenue, raised their fares. The result was equally impressive. The customers switched to cars and buses, or just stayed home in droves; total revenue dropped as the railroads learned about elastic demand the hard way.

Of course, individual product demand is sometimes inelastic. But over and over again, businessmen have underestimated the gain to be had from reducing prices and expanding markets where elastic demand prevails. Economists sometimes describe this as "elasticity pessimism." Mass markets based on low costs and low prices have been the foundation of the growing American economy.

New-Product Decisions—Marginal Cost vs. Average Cost. Suppose you manage a filling station. You have handled only gasoline, oil, and a few miscellaneous supplies like auto polish, windshield-wiper blades, and so on. The local wholesaler approaches you to put in a small line of batteries and tires. He argues there will be very little extra expense since you're not pressed for space, and that you have a small but ready-made market in your regular customers who don't want to go to the inconvenience of shopping around for these items.

You've had a course in economics and you know about costs. So you calculate carefully what the marginal (extra) cost of putting in these lines would be compared to the likely increase in revenue. The answer looks good. The only marginal cost you can see is the money tied up in keeping an inventory on hand, and it looks as if you might sell $200 to $300 a month worth of tires and batteries. At a markup over wholesale that will keep the final price roughly competitive with other retailers, this should yield an extra $50 to $75 a month even after allowing for interest cost on the money tied up in inventory. On the other hand, if you allocate against the tires and batteries their proportionate share of other costs (space, your time and that of the help, taxes, electricity, and so on), the line would probably show a small loss. Should you put in the tires and batteries?

The answer clearly hinges on whether you use marginal or average costs, assuming your estimates

[9]For more detailed analyses of the use of economic analysis in managerial decision making, see M. Spencer and L. Siegelman, *Managerial Economics* (Homewood, Ill.: Irwin, 1963); and M. Colberg, W. Bradford, and R. Alt, *Business Economics* (Homewood, Ill.: Irwin, 1965).

are reasonable. Adding the line will pretty clearly increase revenue more than cost for the enterprise as a whole, unless you've overlooked some new costs associated with the tires and batteries. Following the principles of Chapter 24, you'll increase your total profit by expanding, even though when you compare the "total" cost of the batteries and tires against their selling prices they wouldn't appear to provide a profit. If it's total profit that matters to you, the comparison based on marginal cost will point to the best answer.

But this is a rule to be used with care. It depends on careful analysis of costs, to be sure of what is truly marginal and what is not. Suppose you add the tires and they seem a great success, selling more than you'd expected and taking up more and more space and time. You have to add a new man and expand your building. Where do you allocate the cost—to the gasoline, the tires, where? You can look at any one part of your output first, and then the rest looks marginal.

Many businessmen use the above kind of marginal (or incremental) analysis in adding products, but only when the addition is small relative to their total activity, and understandably so. But when any product line becomes relatively large, they expect it over the long pull to carry its regular share of the "overhead," or the "burden," as indirect costs of running the business are sometimes called. In principle, comparing marginal cost with marginal revenue always gives the right answer in deciding whether or not to take on a new product or to expand output. The trick lies in applying the principle carefully, and being sure which costs are really marginal in the short run and in the long run.

Sunk Costs and Operating Decisions. Try another case—similar but different. You manufacture men's suits. Your costs fall roughly into two groups—those variable with the level of output (mainly labor and materials), and those fixed for a considerable period without reference to the level of output (rent, management salaries, and so on). You know that for the range of output in which you usually operate, you must add about 30 percent to your variable costs to get a price that permits you to break even; you normally price by adding 40 percent to variable costs, with the prices of individual suits varying largely with differences in cloth and the amount of hand labor.

This season, demand has been slow and you are operating well under your normal rate. It has been a bad year, and you probably will not even break even. You have a chance to make 1,000 suits on a special order from a wholesaler who is not a regular customer. However, he will only pay a price that would cover variable costs plus 20 percent. Should you take the order?

Your fixed costs are "sunk." That is, they go on and must be paid, at least for the short run, whether you operate or not. Since they are sunk, economic analysis says they should have no effect on your decision to accept or reject the order, if your goal is to maximize profits or minimize loss in the short run. By taking the order you will cover all your variable costs and will have the 20 percent addition to apply on your fixed costs. You may not make a profit on your total operations, but your loss will be smaller than without the order, as was explained in Chapter 24.

The logic is right. But many businessmen would think a long time before taking the order. They worry about the long run, and properly so. Suppose you cut the price on this order and your regular customers hear about it. Might this break your whole price line, with dire results for profits over the longer run? Or might it lead your competitors to cut their prices? If the answer is "yes," looking only at the particular gain from taking this order would be wearing blinders to the long-run result. In the short run you may minimize losses by taking orders at less than total cost, but both economic analysis and managerial common sense say that in the long run your price has to cover all costs or you'll end up in bankruptcy.

The Nature of Costs: Depreciation. You operate a fleet of taxicabs. With the hard use the cabs receive you estimate that after three years they will have depreciated to the point where it is no longer economical to operate them. At that time you anticipate you will be able to sell or trade them for about 10 percent of the original cost of $3,000 each. Thus, you account as a cost an annual depreciation charge of 30 percent ($900) each per cab, in addition to regular operating and maintenance costs.

At the end of three years you have fully depreciated the cabs, except for the small turn-in value. Yet they seem to be still in reasonably good condition. Should you turn them in on new cabs, using the accumulated depreciation reserve to finance the new cabs, or continue to use the old ones?

The forward looking nature of economics, and the principle above that "sunk costs are sunk," suggest the answer. The fact that you estimated a three-year life and have now accumulated a 90 percent depreciation reserve does not give you an answer to when you should replace these particular cabs. Don't be overimpressed by the bookkeeping. The optimal choice depends on analyzing the cost and performance of new cabs against the cost and performance of continued use of the old cabs. If the total profit by continuing to use the old cabs exceeds the profit with new cabs,[10] then keep the old ones. If not, buy new

---

[10] Remembering possible consumer preferences for new models and all such relevant considerations, and recognizing that the money can temporarily be used another way if it is not used to buy new cabs.

ones. The crucial point is the importance of the forward looking decision, not the fact that three years is the end of your estimated depreciation period. If you made a mistake in estimating the cabs' useful life, it may pay you to replace long before the the cabs are fully depreciated or to wait until long after. Depreciation charges represent only an estimate of the proper cost to be currently charged for the use of durable assets, not a determinant of when assets should be replaced.[11]

[11]For a precise analysis of how to decide the best time to replace durable plant and equipment, a more advanced text is needed. See, for example, E. L. Grant and W. Ireson, *Principles of Engineering Economy* (New York: Ronald Press, 1960), Chaps. 10 and 16.

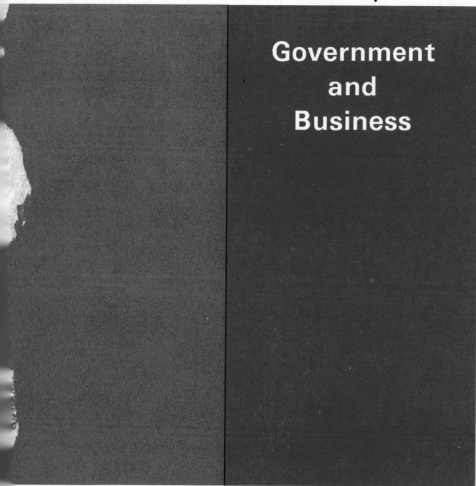

Government and Business

Is Monopoly Growing?

Bigness, Monopoly, and Public Opinion

The Law and Competition

Where to from Here?

Business and Government in the New Capitalism

Why should government intervene at all in business affairs? Adam Smith had one answer: Because self-seeking can be channeled to the common good only if competition prevails. Seldom do merchants gather together, he wrote, that their talk does not turn to means of getting higher prices for their produce. Without competition among sellers, more consumer spending may mean higher profits and not more products. It is the job of the government, representing all the people, to see to it that competition prevails.

Everyone agrees, moreover, that in an individualistic society there have to be some rules of fair play in economic life, just as in personal behavior. Without common consent to eliminate fraud, to respect property ownership, and

to honor contractual promises, business dealings would be carried on under a great handicap. By general agreement, it is the job of government to establish and enforce these basic rules to enable men to deal effectively together; just as it is the government's job to establish and enforce laws against murder, theft, and arson to enable men to live securely together. Among Adam Smith's nineteenth-century followers, "laissez faire" never meant that the government should do nothing, but rather that it should leave economic affairs alone within a framework of basic moral and governmental rules of the game.

There is wide agreement on these two basic governmental functions in relation to business affairs—to insist on competitive behavior and to establish the basic rules of the game. But what do they mean in practice? Does enforcing competition mean enforcing **pure** competition as we have defined it? Obviously not, for this would leave almost the whole economy outside the pale. Does it mean breaking up General Motors, General Electric, and United States Steel? Maybe, but if it does we'd better think such a radical step through carefully before we take it. Does it mean refusing to let present firms get any bigger through mergers?

The economic analysis of the preceding chapters provides a presumptive indictment against monopoly. Monopoly generally malallocates resources; it raises prices and restricts output in the monopolized industry. But most of the real world falls in between the areas of pure competition and pure monopoly, and the results suggested by the theoretical models in these in-between cases are less clear than at the two extremes. Don't forget the basic requirements for active price competition, including a market big enough to support many firms each operating near its "least-cost" point.

Economic theory gives no clear answer to just how much competition is enough, just how big is too big. Expert economists who have spent years studying the problem of "workable competition" come up with a reasonable consensus on some broad outlines of public policy against excessive monopoly, but they admit frankly they are perplexed about how to handle some of the in-between situations.

Is Monopoly Growing?

Is monopoly growing? Are big firms dominating more markets? The answer is mixed. In manufacturing, the share of total assets and total output produced by the biggest firms has increased substantially since World War II. Table 30–1 tells the story.

As measured by "value added," the big firms don't bulk quite as large, but the picture is similar. Between 1947 and 1968, the share of the largest 100 firms rose from 23 to 33 percent in manufacturing. On the other hand, the top is a slippery pinnacle. Table 30–2 shows the largest

10 industrial firms in 1909, and what had happened to them by 1969. Only 2 were still in the top 10, and 5 had vanished completely from the list of the largest 100 firms. General Motors, Ford, and IBM weren't even in existence in 1909.

In the rest of the economy, any trend toward concentration is less clear. In the rapidly growing services area, markets are generally divided among many relatively small sellers. Construction continues to be dominated by relatively small firms. There are still millions of farmers,

table 30-1		
Concentration in Manufacturing*		
	Share of Total Assets in:	
	1948	1968
largest 5 firms	10%	13%
largest 20 firms	21	26
largest 100 firms	39	48
largest 200 firms	48	61

*Data from Federal Trade Commission.

table 30-2		
Largest Ten Industrial Firms, 1909-1969*		
Rank		
1909	1969	
1	8	U.S. Steel Corporation
2	1	Standard Oil Co. (New Jersey)
3	52	American Tobacco Co.
4	**	International Mercantile Marine Company
5	44	Anaconda Co.
6	35	International Harvester Co.
7	**	Central Leather Company
8	**	Pullman Inc.
9	**	Armour & Co.
10	**	American Sugar Refining Co.

*Data from A.D.H. Kaplan, *Big Enterprise in a Competitive System* (Washington, D.C.: The Brookings Institution, 1964) and *Fortune*. Rankings based on total assets.
**No longer in top 100 firms.

though the market share of big commercial farms has been rising steadily. One striking development has been the explosive growth of the nongovernment but nonprofit sector, especially in the service areas—hospitals and Blue Cross, private education, research institutes, and the like. The share of the national income produced by private, profit-seeking corporations apparently reached a peak of 55 percent in the mid-1950s. By 1968 it was back down to 53 percent, its level of twenty years earlier. The problem of economic concentration, once we eliminate the public utilities, appears to be centered in the manufacturing sector.[1]

Mergers to form huge conglomerates, sometimes called mega-corps, have been the big news of the last decade. Table 30–3 tells the story for the manufacturing sector since 1950.

Many of the mergers involved large firms, especially in recent years. In 1968, firms with over $250 million assets accounted for 45 percent of all assets acquired by merger; firms with over $100 million for 62 percent. In earlier years, most mergers were "horizontal" (mergers between firms selling the same product) or "vertical" (mergers between suppliers and their business customers). In the last decade, "conglomerate" mergers (between firms producing

[1]Concentration statistics are tricky, and it is possible to convey signficantly different pictures by changing the groupings of products and measures used (assets, sales, value-added, and so on). When reading such statistics, it is generally wise to probe for possible biases of the writer.

table 30-3

Mergers in Manufacturing, 1950-1969*

Year	Number	Acquired Assets ($ billion)
1950	219	$ 0.2
1955	782	1.6
1960	966	1.8
1965	1,125	4.4
1969	3,000	16.0

*Source: Federal Trade Commission. Figures for 1969 are preliminary estimates. Acquired assets figures are the average for the 5 years surrounding the date, except for 1969.

different products) have accounted for over 80 percent of merged assets. This reflects in part, as we shall see presently, prohibition by the 1950 Antimerger Act of horizontal and vertical mergers when they might have any substantial tendency to lessen competition. The result has been huge conglomerates, like Litton Industries and Ling-Temco-Vought, which engage in a wide range of businesses, with only a central-management link among them. These mergers generally do not change the concentration ratios (degree of market power) for the products involved, since by definition conglomerates involve noncompeting products. But they raise other issues of economic and political power, to which we shall turn presently.

Bigness, Monopoly, and Public Opinion

In 1969, the General Electric Company had assets of $6 billion, and reported profits before taxes of $700 million on sales of $8 billion. It had over 300,000 employees. Although no exact figures are available, G.E. apparently accounted for nearly half the total sales in the country of heavy electrical machinery, light bulbs, and other major categories of electrical equipment. It was rivaled only by Westinghouse, another giant, with assets of over $2 billion and sales and profits about a third the size of G.E.'s. Big companies like Allis Chalmers in heavy equipment and Sylvania in bulbs and lighter equipment absorbed another sizable chunk of the market, but they were far short of the two leaders in overall size and market power.

Is G.E. a monopoly? Should it be broken up into several smaller concerns in the public interest?

Now consider Jones's Grocery Store, at the crossroads corner of an isolated village in northern Minnesota—population 150. Jones's total sales in 1969 were about $12,000, on which he realized a return after paying all costs (except his own salary) of about $3,000, as near as he could figure it. Jones had one employee—himself. His service was so-so. There is no other grocery store within thirty-five miles.

Is Jones's Grocery Store a monopoly? Should it be broken up into several smaller concerns in the public interest?

No reasonable person would answer that Jones's store ought to be broken up by antimonopoly policy in order to provide more competition in the village. This would be nonsense. The market can't support one respectable grocery, let alone two or three. Yet Jones's monopoly power over the customers in that village may far exceed G.E.'s power over its customers. If Jones takes advantage of Widow Smith down the street and slips in a bad potato with every peck, she's pretty much out of luck. She can say what she will about Jones—and it may be plenty—but that's about all she can do about it. Let G.E. treat one of its customers that way, and Westinghouse will get a phone call the next day from the outraged purchasing agent.

How about G.E.? If you think the Antitrust Division ought to look into G.E., why? Because G.E. clearly has a dominant position in its different products, with around half the market for many of them? Or because G.E. just seems to you too big—because you feel that no one business ought to control so much wealth, with the far-reaching economic and political power that goes with it?

It may be that you can't get very excited about G.E. one way or the other, if you're like a lot of other Americans today. G.E. is indeed a huge business, and you may sympathize with the workers when they strike for higher pay. But you know that G.E. has long been a pioneer in research and development of new and better products for consumers. It makes lots of money, but it turns out high-quality, reliable products, and you have at least a sneaking suspicion that it got that big by being better than its competitors. You know, too, that for every G.E. product you buy, you can find competing ones from Westinghouse and a bevy of other companies, depending on the item. And you're really not much interested in 10,000-horsepower turbines. G.E. is certainly an oligopolist, but it seems to be doing a pretty good job of serving the American consumer—and of providing a lot

of well-paid, stable jobs to American workers in the process.

If you stop to think about these two cases, you'll see that two different issues are involved. One is the question of how strong a monopoly does the seller hold? This is largely an issue of the size of the seller **relative** to the market in which he sells. The second is the question of **absolute size** which bears no necessary relationship to the degree of monopoly the firm possesses. Jones's Grocery has a pretty effective monopoly in its market, according to the economist's definition, but it's a tiny concern in absolute size. G.E. clearly holds some monopoly powers too—it's an oligopolist—but its monopoly power in its markets is less than that of Jones's Grocery. The striking difference is G.E.'s absolute size and economic power. The company affects immediately millions of consumers and hundreds of thousands of employees and stockholders by its economic actions. Its managers exert economic power—the power of $6 billion—over the lives of 300,000 workers, over the communities in which they live, and over the consumers who buy electrical products. Never forget that our analytical monopoly and quasi-monopoly models refer to the firm's positions **relative to its market**. The issue of absolute size and power in the society is related, but different and broader.

These chapters are devoted primarily to helping you do your own straight thinking on the **economic** aspects of monopoly and quasi monopoly. But it's important to recognize that public opinion—that potent force in controlling government action—often isn't very precise and logical. It often doesn't separate out the issues very sharply. If we could tap the thinking (partly subconscious) of the mythical man on the street about "monopoly," we might get something like this:

1. Is more competition practical? Would breaking up the big companies really give the consumer better products at lower prices? The cheapest products seem to come out of the mass-production industries with big firms.

2. How many firms does it really take to insure reasonable competition? Certainly not the

infinitely large number required by the economist's "pure competition." Maybe only three or four big producers with several little ones nipping at their heels.

3. Some of those corporation presidents certainly do get big salaries.

4. Can you really trust anybody with the power that goes with a billion dollars? Big business has taken it out on the worker and the public lots of times in the past. They'd probably do it again if they could get away with it.

5. The little fellow deserves a break. We ought to help him a little against the giants.

6. The "blue chips" of American industry are the ones that have produced most of the good products that underlie our high standard of living—automobiles, nylon, refrigerators, and so on. Still . . . there are those stories about how they hold products off the market—razor blades that would last two years, storage batteries that would never wear out.

7. They say that the big corporations dictate a lot of what goes into the laws made by Congress and the state legislatures. All that money surely gives them a way to buy votes that the little man can't afford.

8. Oh well, maybe with unions as strong as they are now, big business and the unions are about in balance.

This picture may not be accurate, but it does suggest the complex mixture of objectives, reasoning, and hearsay that makes up current American public opinion on "big business" and "monopoly." For the economist, big business and monopoly are far from synonymous. But the man in the street may not distinguish between them very sharply.

Elmo Roper and Lou Harris, the public-opinion pollsters, have repeatedly sampled the man-in-the-street's feelings about big business. Briefly, their conclusions are: (1) Americans on the whole believe that big business is good for the economy, and that on balance it does a good job of turning out good-quality products. (2) The American public doesn't quite trust big business, and feels that we need a government that keeps an eagle eye on the big businessman to see that he doesn't abuse his enormous potential power over workers, the public, and smaller competitors.

Let us turn now to a brief look at how the law has developed over the last century in the United States, both to support competition and to restrict it. Then we'll take a concluding evaluative look at the broad problem of public policy vis-à-vis competition, market structure, and market performance. Can we make the market system serve us better? Lastly, in Chapter 31, we will take a still broader look at big business in an analysis of the so-called "military-industrial complex."

The Law and Competition

The law is what is written down in the statute books, and more. It is what the courts say it is, what the long rows of past court decisions suggest, altered as the judge thinks proper in any particular case. It is what the Justice Department thinks it is; most law is enforced without ever coming near a court room. It is what the president and his advisers think it is, through the way they instruct the government's law-enforcement branches. Above all, it is what the people will obey and support. In our democratic system, no law that does not command widespread public support can long be enforced. Sometimes the law is changed when it loses support, but equally often its enforcement varies to mirror the times.

This description is especially accurate in the field of government-business relations. Here much of the law is in the mass of court decisions, and in the policies of the government's administrative agencies. Both reflect (with lags) what the public wants—often more accurately than we realize. Our antitrust laws seldom change by formal congressional action. But in fact they alter constantly—with changing congressional appropriations for enforcement, changing antitrust personnel, changing judicial attitudes—often to the frustration of businessmen, who protest that no one can tell when he is violating the law until he sees whether the government takes him to court and the judge finds him guilty.

The Common Law

Until 1890, there was no federal legislation that declared monopoly illegal. Nor did the states have any antimonopoly laws of consequence. Under the common (unwritten) law inherited from England, contracts to restrain trade unreasonably or to raise prices were unenforceable. But the common law did not hold monopoly practices to be criminal, nor did it even provide for damages to those harmed by the restraint of trade. The contracts were merely unenforceable. Thus, the common law provided little protection to the consumer or to the little competitor who got squeezed out by combinations in restraint of trade. Some judges held extreme and vicious forms of competition to be illegal, as an extension of the law against fraud and misrepresentation, but these decisions were of little general import.

Legislation

The last half of the nineteenth century saw the development of the great trusts. Standard Oil, American Sugar, American Tobacco, and dozens of others amassed huge empires that held almost complete monopolies over the products concerned. Standard Oil at its peak controlled over 90 percent of the country's oil-refining capacity, and the bulk of the pipelines. American Sugar controlled 98 percent of the country's sugar-refining capacity. American Tobacco had virtually complete control of tobacco manufacturing.

Moreover, the means used to build up these monopolies aroused widespread ire and fear. Standard Oil, for example, relentlessly drove small competitors to the wall by cutthroat competition, bought them up cheap, and then raised prices. Competitors who resisted found themselves up against ruthless force. Standard, with its vast resources, cut local prices to one-half of cost and made up the losses in noncompetitive areas. It bought up pipelines and refused transportation to competitors. Through its vast power, it forced railroads to give it rebates of 25 to 50 percent, not only on its own shipments but **on the shipments of its competitors.** When competing pipelines tried to gain a foothold, Standard bought up the refineries they served and refused to take oil from the pipelines.

The Sherman and Interstate Commerce Acts. With half a hundred trust giants on the American scene, popular resentment was reflected in two major acts—the Interstate Commerce Commission Act (1887) and the Sherman Antitrust Act (1890). The Interstate Commerce Act established federal control over railroad rates and services for the first time, eliminating the cutthroat competition and rate discrimination that had long characterized this industry. The Sherman Antitrust Act was aimed at industrial monopoly. It declared illegal every contract or combination in restraint of interstate trade—to protect both small competitors and consumers. It is the foundation for our treatment of public utilities.

The Interstate Commerce Act takes the alternative of strict, comprehensive government regulation of an industry that cannot operate satisfactorily on a competitive basis. By the late 1800s, it was abundantly clear that regulation of interstate railway rates and service through market competition was impracticable. At most, only two or three roads serviced most communities, and in many areas one railway had a complete monopoly. Even where two or more roads competed, as between Chicago and New York, competition was unsatisfactory because railroads are almost invariably decreasing-cost concerns and competition leads to price wars that drive rates far below total average cost. Most markets were simply not big enough to support two or more railway systems, each operating near its minimum-cost levels.

Under such circumstances, there was little point in trying to enforce competition. Instead, the I.C.C. Act made the railroads public utilities, under the regulation of a new government body, the Interstate Commerce Commission. General operating responsibility is left with the management elected by the private stockholders, but prices and output (that is, rates, and amount and quality of service) must be approved by the I.C.C. as in keeping with the public interest. Under this approach, the railroads are guaranteed monopoly positions, but how they use their monopoly powers is carefully regulated.[2]

The Sherman Act was aimed at the other part of the economy, where competition could reasonably be expected to do a good job of regulating prices, output, and quality for the public good. Here the approach was exactly the opposite of that in the I.C.C. legislation. In order to enforce active competition, the Sherman Act outlawed restraints of trade and attempts to monopolize, as follows:

Section 1. Every contract, combination in the form of a trust or otherwise, or conspiracy, in restraint of trade or commerce among the several states, or with foreign nations, is hereby declared to be illegal. . . .

Section 2. Every person who shall monopolize, or attempt to monopolize, or combine or conspire with any other person or persons to monopolize any part of the trade or commerce among the several states, or with foreign nations, shall be deemed guilty of a misdemeanor. . . .

This was broad and sweeping language. Inevitably, a wide range of questions arose over the years as to just what was actually outlawed. What is covered by "restraint of trade," by "monopolize, or attempt to monopolize"? Another complex set of questions arose over just what activities were included under "interstate" commerce, since the federal government's power to regulate covers only commerce between states.

As with all such legislation, such questions have been answered primarily through a long series of court rulings interpreting the law. We will look at some of these rulings in the following section. But first it is important to recognize the basic problem of regulatory policy that the Sherman Act illustrates. No legislation regulating the complex modern economy can hope to specify in detail every case and situation that is to be covered. Instead, Congress must do its best to state its intentions clearly, leaving to government administrative officials, to regulatory commissions, and ultimately to the courts the job of applying the law to individual cases.

[2]With modern truck, bus, pipeline, and airline competition, many economists now suggest that the day has come to try freer competition again, on the argument that competition provides more stimulus to efficiency and good service than does government regulation.

The substance of regulatory law is often developed more in its interpretive application over the years than through the original legislation.

The Clayton and Federal Trade Commission Acts. In 1914 two new acts were passed—the Clayton Act and the Federal Trade Commission Act—to clarify the Sherman Act by specifically prohibiting certain practices, regardless of the group or individual engaging in them, and by setting up new enforcement procedures.

The Clayton Act listed specifically as illegal (1) discriminatory price cutting; (2) tying contracts, which require buyers to purchase other items as a condition of getting one item; (3) acquisition of stock in competing companies to obtain monopoly powers; and (4) interlocking directorates in competing corporations. But each of these was prohibited only "where the effect may be to substantially lessen competition or tend to create a monopoly. . . ." Thus, the Clayton Act cleared the picture by defining some illegal acts. But it still left open the basic problem of interpretation for the courts in many individual cases.

The Federal Trade Commission Act created a commission to act as a watchdog against unfair competitive practices aimed at creating monopoly or injuring competitors. The commission was given power to hold hearings and to issue "cease and desist" orders that require offending firms to discontinue illegal practices. When the first major appeal from a commission ruling reached the Supreme Court in 1919, however, the Court held that it is for the courts, not for the F.T.C., to make the ultimate decisions in interpreting the law.

The effect of this ruling was to reduce sharply the F.T.C.'s powers. Major actions have reverted back to the courts, since everyone recognizes that an unfavorable F.T.C. decision can be appealed to the courts. The F.T.C. does, however, play an important role in policing cases of seller misrepresentation (for instance, artificial silk as silk, domestic lace as Irish lace), and in arranging voluntary agreements among business competitors on fair-trade practices.

New Deal Legislation of the 1930s. Not all legislation has been designed to encourage competition. In the Great Depression of the 1930s, the New Deal was mainly concerned with recovery, greater economic security, and helping the little fellow. Ending the depression seemed to call for measures to halt falling prices and cutthroat competition for shrinking markets. The National Recovery Act (N.R.A.) led businessmen to band together in formal cartels, aimed at raising prices. In agriculture, the Agricultural Adjustment Administration (A.A.A.) had a similar purpose—to raise farm prices and incomes by government-sponsored cartellike agreements to restrict production. The Bituminous Coal Act did the same thing for soft coal. In labor markets, the Wagner Act threw the full force of the government behind workers' right to unionize and bargain collectively, thus lessening the cutthroat price competition among workers for scarce jobs. Both N.R.A. and A.A.A. were later declared unconstitutional, but the powerful competition-restricting effects of the agricultural and labor programs have become central parts of our governmental policy on market structure and performance.

This desire to help the small competitor and avoid "destructive" competition was reflected in two new pieces of legislation. The Robinson-Patman Act of 1936 strengthened the prohibition against price discrimination that might act to the benefit of such large buyers as chain stores and permit them to undersell small retailers. In 1937, the Miller-Tydings Act guaranteed protection from Sherman Act prosecution to manufacturers and retailers who participated in "fair-trading" arrangements, whereby the manufacturer specifies that no retailer may sell his product below a specified price. Too much competition was feared more than too little, reflecting the widespread fear of unemployment and depression. Legislation sought to protect competitors—especially small firms—from competition, rather than to encourage competition.

The Celler Antimerger Act of 1950. After World War II, many corporations found that acquiring other companies outright was a profitable path of expansion as the economy grew. Such mergers were sometimes prompted by market-expansion goals, sometimes by special tax considerations, sometimes by the desire for diversification, sometimes by opportunities to make the acquiring company grow faster, with resultant rises in the price of its stock among investors. As indicated above, the annual rate of corporate mergers in manufacturing and mining alone rose from about 200 in 1950 to over 4,000 in 1969. The merger movement reflected again the adaptability of American businessmen in finding ways to achieve their aims.

Such extension of market power through merger was not limited by earlier antitrust legislation. But in 1950 the Celler Antimerger Act was passed forbidding the acquisition of, or merger with, other companies where the effect "may be substantially to lessen competition, or tend to create a monopoly."

The Antimerger Act showed again the response of the law to hold business within the broad antitrust goals of our time. And the first major court test under the new law showed its potency. Bethlehem Steel and Youngstown Sheet and Tube, the second- and sixth-largest steel producers, announced plans to merge and were brought to court in 1958 by the Justice Department. The court held that the proposed merger was prohibited. Subsequent cases have held that large companies may not merge with even very small ones in the same business; that mergers are illegal if they reduce competition between broadly competing products (e.g., glass and metal containers); and that mergers may be illegal if they threaten to reduce even **potential** competition. Moreover, the court has applied the potential-elimination-of-competition test to market areas as small as a single state or community, not merely to large areas or the whole country. Under these cases, any merger of competing firms above small size appears to be of doubtful legality, though each case is judged on its own circumstances. The application of the law to conglomerate mergers, where no direct competition is eliminated, is now being tested in the courts.

The Law in Operation

The law is what its administrators and the courts make it. And its administrators and the courts by and large make it what the public wants, often very roughly and with a considerable lag.

Nowhere has this been truer than in antitrust legislation. The first big enforcement campaign under the Sherman Act was President Teddy Roosevelt's, conducted with a total staff of seven lawyers and four stenographers. With this tiny staff, but with the big stick of aroused public opinion, the government tackled the biggest trusts. In 1911, the Supreme Court required both Standard Oil and American Tobacco to divest themselves of a large share of their holdings and to desist from numerous specific unfair competitive practices. But there, too, for the first time, the Court enunciated the now-famous "rule of reason." Only trusts that "unreasonably" restrained trade were illegal. In a series of earlier cases, the Court had given a broad interpretation to the interstate-commerce clause, permitting federal regulation to apply to all firms that had any direct dealing across state lines or (later) in products or materials crossing state lines; this interpretation brought most big businesses within the purview of federal antitrust legislation.

By 1920, the attitude toward big business had altered, with the checking of the flagrant abuses of the 1800s. In the *U.S. Steel* case of 1920, the Supreme Court refused to dissolve the company. It held specifically that neither mere bigness nor unexerted monopoly power was illegal as such; that actual unreasonable restraint of trade must be proved under the Sherman Act. The tenor of the 1920s was one of prosperity and "leave well enough alone." The total budget allocated the Antitrust Division averaged only $250,000 annually for the decade. Big business was popular during the twenties.

With the strong antibusiness sweep of the New Deal, the last major change in the application and interpretation of the antitrust laws began in the late 1930s. Under Thurman Arnold, Antitrust began an aggressive drive in the late 1930s against several of the industrial giants. Antitrust's budget was upped to $1 million (to police the entire economy). Its investigations in the construction field disclosed eye-openers that aroused the public, and actions were begun against labor, agricultural, and professional groups as well as against business. The government dissolved a glass-container monopoly based on patents in the Hartford Empire case in 1944 with a decision that greatly weakened the use of patents to support monopoly practices. In the Alcoa case of 1945, it obtained a strongly worded ruling that market dominance itself, even though not actively used to restrain competition, is illegal. It outlawed "basing-point pricing" (under which a few leaders set industry-wide prices f.o.b. at selected factory "basing points") in the Cement case of 1948. Application of federal legislation through the interstate-commerce clause was steadily broadened.

The Eisenhower, Kennedy, Johnson, and Nixon administrations have continued active prosecution under the antitrust legislation. Appropriations to both the Federal Trade Commission and the Antitrust Division of the Department of Justice have been further increased. Du Pont's ownership of approximately one-fourth of General Motors common stock was condemned. The Antimerger Act has become a powerful barrier to business growth through acquisition of competitors.

But the government does not win all the cases it brings. For example, in 1956 it argued that Du Pont had monopolized the manufacture of cellophane. But the Supreme Court held that competition should be construed to include reasonably close substitutes as well as the product itself. Du Pont produced about 75 percent of all cellophane, but cellophane constituted less than 20 percent of all "flexible packaging material" sales. Thus, the majority declared Du Pont's position legal, even though it was a monopolist in cellophane, because it held only a relatively small part of the total "flexible packaging material" market.

Nor should you assume that all economists, understanding the theoretical presumption against monopoly, agree that the antitrust always serves the public interest. Some economists, for example, argue that the court's strong interpretation of the Antimerger Act can give topsy-turvy results. To prevent mergers among relatively small firms may hinder useful, cost-saving combinations more than it protects consumers. In the 1966 Von's Groceries case the court forbade a merger between two Los Angeles grocery chains, which together held less than 8 percent of the Los Angeles market. Many economists fear that the result of such rulings will be to protect inefficient competitors, not competition.

Where does antitrust law stand now, as a practical matter? First, all price-fixing agreements are per se illegal. Second, oligopolies where a few firms dominate the market are probably legal so long as no leading firm tries to expand its market share by merger or by aggressive competition that endangers small firms.[3] Third, growth through merger in the same industry is virtually forbidden, except among very small firms—although growth through reinvestment of a firm's own funds is permissible. How far the law prohibits conglomerate mergers remains to be determined by the courts, or possibly through new legislation. Fourth, many specific practices (price discrimination, tying clauses in contracts, and the like) are illegal when they may tend to create a monopoly or significantly reduce competition. Fifth, retail price-fixing under "fair-trade" agreements is legal in many states, but fair-trading is of limited importance because retail competition has generally broken out in spite of the price floors set by manufacturers. A total picture of antitrust today would need a much longer list, with many more details and qualifications. This is intended merely to provide a broad overview.

Why has Antitrust again become a potent force since the 1930s? First, the budget given the Antitrust Division by Congress is now about $10 million, larger than ever before; Antitrust now has some 300 lawyers to police the entire economy. Looked at another way, however, this is still a tiny sum compared with the vast resources of the billion-dollar corporations it has to police. The budget reflects America's ambivalent attitude toward Antitrust. The public admires and wants big business, but it also wants the government watching closely to be sure that big business doesn't abuse its powers. Antitrust is one of the main tools the government has.

And the Supreme Court has generally supported the government's accusations in recent years.

One last point on the law in action. The main impact of the antitrust law is preventive, not punitive. Since 1890, only about 1,000 suits have been brought under the Sherman Act. Of these, the government has won about 600 and lost about 200, with the rest still in the courts. Total fines paid by defendants over the half century were only a few million dollars—very little compared to the billions of dollars of assets in the companies concerned. But in 1961 the business world was rocked by the federal court decision which sent top executives of G.E., Westinghouse, and smaller competitors to jail for conspiring to fix prices on electrical equipment. If this marks the beginning of a new trend in antitrust enforcement, the bite of the law may be strong indeed. Moreover, a company convicted of antitrust violation is liable for triple damages if customers or competitors can show they were injured by the illegal acts. G.E. and Westinghouse were sued for hundreds of millions of dollars by customers after their 1961 case.

Most observers agree that Antitrust has been a surprisingly powerful force in the American business scene since 1890. No business likes to be called criminal. It does not like to have its affairs dragged into open court, even though it thinks it may win out in the end. Besides, most businessmen are law-abiding citizens who are reluctant to break the law—though the G.E.-Westinghouse case raised widespread doubts on this point. Many American businessmen talk the strongest case for competition you can find anywhere.

But although Antitrust has been an ever present danger to monopolists, Congress and the state legislatures have eaten away at the Sherman Act's prohibition against price-fixing agreements in some areas, especially agriculture, labor, and retailing. The Robinson-Patman and Miller-Tydings acts specifically limit price competition and make price floors set by manufacturers legal for their own products. Some observers feel that the loss to consumers through such legalized price-fixing may outweigh all the

---

[3] J. K. Galbraith has argued vigorously that the effect of present antitrust is to let the big, established oligopolies go untouched while applying the Antimerger Act to smaller firms trying to grow through mergers.

gains provided by the Antitrust Division. But one strong ally for the consumer has stubbornly reappeared—the profit motive. Many retailers object to price-maintenance policies and cut prices surreptitiously or openly in defiance of manufacturers' rules. "Discount houses" are a major manifestation of this revolt. By the 1960s, most leading manufacturers had given up fair-trading because it was so hard to keep retailers from cutting prices in order to sell more goods.

Where to from Here?

Where to from here? Nobody thinks the modern American economy can look like the economist's perfectly competitive model. It never has, even back in the pre–Civil War days, and it certainly doesn't now. We're in for a mixed economy of some sort. How shall we assure that business performance is efficient and in the public interest?

Antitrust and Economic Efficiency

Would stronger antitrust action really produce a more "efficient" economy, in the sense of giving consumers the largest possible amount of what they want at the lowest feasible prices? More firms create a general presumption of more active competition. But no magic number of firms is needed to assure effective competition. Sometimes (for example, in the auto industry) there is aggressive competition with only two or three big firms. But most observers agree that more firms generally increase the likelihood of strong price and quality competition.

If more firms are generally good for competition, we need to face the issue of whether this condition is consistent with having firms big enough to be efficient, low-cost producers. Clearly, business has to be big for efficiency in many industries. But it's also true that business can get too big from the cost standpoint. Various studies have indicated that in many industries middle-sized to large companies have lower costs than gigantic ones. But not always. Table 30–4 summarizes a widely quoted research study on the problem of optimum (least-cost) size of plant and firm in a sample of manufacturing industries. It reflects the wide diversity just mentioned. Column 1 shows the percentage of national industry capacity contained in one plant of optimum size; the range indicates the variation in the best available estimates. Column 2 provides the same information for a firm of optimum size. Where the firm figure is larger than the plant figure, there are additional economies from combining a number of optimal-size plants in one firm. Column 3 shows the wide variation in the amount of capital needed to set up a new plant of about the optimum size in each industry, presumably some measure of what it would take a newcomer to enter the industry. Lastly, column 4 shows the percentage share of the national market actually held by the average of the largest four firms in each industry. This figure is obtained by dividing the total share of the largest four firms by four. The percentage so obtained is thus smaller than the actual share of the largest firm in the industry. For example, General Motors' share of the auto market approached 50 percent in comparison with the 23 percent average for the largest four firms. Similarly U.S. Steel had about 30 percent of the market compared to the average of only 11 percent for the top four firms.

The estimates of Table 30–4 suggest that the actual share of market held by many of the biggest firms is far above that needed to obtain lowest-cost production. This general finding is confirmed by George Stigler and T. R. Saving, using a different research technique. They postulate that by and large the most efficient sizes of plant and firm will win out in the competitive race. During the postwar period, medium-sized plants (relative to their total markets) have survived most effectively in most industries. This test therefore suggests that in most industries plants small enough to permit effective competition can produce efficiently.[4]

But the other side of the picture is impressive too. In several industries the cost of an efficient plant is so high that there is no point pretending that competition can be readily open to new

[4]See, for example, T. R. Saving, "Estimation of Optimum Size of Plant by the Survivor Technique," *Quarterly Journal of Economics,* November, 1961.

table 30-4

Estimated Size of Optimal Plants and Firms in Manufacturing Industries*

Industry	Percentage of National Industry Capacity in One Plant of Optimal Size	Percentage of National Industry Capacity in One Firm of Optimal Size	Capital Required For One Efficient Plant (in Millions)	Percentage Share of National Market Held by Average of First 4 Firms
Shoes	.14 to .5	.5 to 2.5	$.5 to 2	7
Canned fruits and vegetables	.25 to .5	.25 to .5	2.5 to 3	7
Metal containers	.5 to 3	No estimate	5 to 20	20
Cement	.8 to 1	2 to 10	20 to 25	7
Steel	1 to 2.5	2 to 5	265 to 665	11
Distilled liquor	1.25 to 1.75	No estimate	30 to 42	19
Petroleum refining	1.75	1.75	193 (without transport)	9
Gypsum products	2.5 to 3	27 to 33	5 to 6	21
Tires and tubes	3	No estimate	25 to 30	19
Cigarettes	5 to 6	15 to 20	125 to 150	23
Autos	5 to 10	5 to 10	250 to 500	23
Tractors	10 to 15	10 to 15	125	17
Typewriters	10 to 30	10 to 30	No estimate	20

*From J.S. Bain, "Economies of Scale, Concentration, and Entry," *American Economic Review*, March 1954, pp. 30, 36. Data as of about 1950; adjustment for the 1950-1970 inflation would at least double the figures in column 3, but should not change the other columns significantly.

table 30-5

Ease of Entry into Different Industries*

Very Difficult	Moderately Difficult	Relatively easy
Automobiles	Primary aluminum	Baking
Cigarettes	Copper	Beer
Ethical drugs	Cement	Canned vegetables and fruits
Flat glass	Farm machinery	Coal mining
Liquor	Oil refining	Flour
Nickel	Shoe machinery	Gypsum products
Sulphur	Soap	Meat-packing
	Steel	Rayon
		Shoes
		Textiles

*Source: M.Mann, "Seller Concentration, Barriers to Entry, and Rates of Return," *Review of Economics and Statistics*, August, 1966.

producers; note the figures for cigarettes, petroleum refining, tractors, autos, and steel. But there are a number of industries where the minimum cost of entry is so small that entry for potential competitors should be fairly easy; note the cases of canned fruits and vegetables, and of gypsum products.

Table 30–5 repeats from Table 28–2 a ranking of some major industries by overall ease of entry for potential competitors. It takes into account minimum scale of plant, capital requirements, established product names, distribution facilities needed, and other potential barriers to entry.

Many economists are highly critical of the Robinson-Patman and Miller-Tydings acts. Both were designed primarily to protect small competitors against large ones, and they often do so even when the large competitors are more efficient in satisfying consumer needs. They tend to protect small **competitors**, not **competition**. But from the economist's and the consumer's point of view, it's not clear why price cutting isn't just what competition is supposed to produce, so long as it isn't used as a device for driving out competitors by temporarily selling below cost just to gain a monopoly position.

Antitrust and Economic Progress

The other big question about monopoly and partial monopoly is what they do to the rate of economic progress—whether they contribute to, or impede, a dynamically growing economy. The issues and some of the facts were presented in the concluding sections of Chapter 29. Broadly speaking, those industries with the highest growth rates tend to be oligopolies—big firms with large R and D expenditures. Most research and development spending is done by large and medium-sized firms. Productivity has grown more slowly in industries dominated by small firms (except agriculture, with its government financing and distribution of research). But the picture is far from uniform; there are numerous exceptions, and industries protected against entry by new competitors clearly have the power to suppress innovations that might otherwise have been forced by competition.

What is the implication for Antitrust? Not clear. It seems certain that we can generally not expect much R and D spending from tiny firms in industries that approach perfect competition, however aggressively they may compete for the consumer's favor. If we want R and D in such industries, the pattern of government financing and dissemination of results in agriculture may be the best way. But remember that firms far short of giant size can spend heavily on research and obtain results that compete with the giants' in many industries. Even on the score of economic progress, few industries require such large firms for efficient R and D that they cannot support numerous sellers and effective price competition.

Bigness and the Concentration of Economic Power

Can Antitrust do anything about the problem of the sheer power of bigness? This is the most basic question of all for some people. Political power, economic power, power over other people's lives, just the power that goes with a billion dollars—these are the things that worry many people most about big business.

The power of big business seems especially alarming to some observers because in many firms "inside management" has a substantially free hand in exercising its vast power. While the stockholders theoretically direct the management, as a practical matter few stockholders know much about the details of management or have any interest in interfering in it. To whom is big management really responsible in the exercise of its economic power?

A. A. Berle, a long-time observer of the business corporation, has pointed up this problem. Only 500 corporations control approaching two-thirds of the entire manufacturing sector of the American economy, he writes, and within each of those 500 a relatively small group holds the ultimate decision-making power. "Since the United States carries on not quite half of the manufacturing production of the entire world today, these 500 groupings—each with its own little dominating pyramid within it—represent a concentration of power over economies which makes the medieval feudal system look like a Sunday School party. In sheer economic power this has gone far beyond anything we have yet seen."[5]

J. K. Galbraith, in his best-selling *The New Industrial State*, has argued even more—that big-business planning and parallel government planning are replacing market competition in modern America. He updates Berle's data on the massive role of the largest few hundred corporations, and points to a growing tendency of self-perpetuating management in the big oligopolies toward long-range planning for efficiency, for avoidance of vigorous price competition, and for stabler relations with organized labor. Solid, prosperous growth is the keynote, without undue, disruptive, old-style competition. With these policies, the big quietly grow bigger and more powerful. In essence, government protects and approves this secure, stable world for the giants, unless they abuse the mores unduly or openly try to aggrandize their positions by acquiring or squeezing out smaller firms. Antitrust acts mainly to prevent open collusion and mergers among the smaller competitors which, as a practical matter, are probably their only way of challenging the concentrated power of the giants.

Galbraith's solution? Not to break up the giants, for that would waste the economic benefits of modern technology which underlie the success of big firms. Rather he says that the answer is increasing government participation to provide the good life—more and better public services in the modern affluent society. Parks, modern housing, better education, state-supported symphonies and drama—through a bigger public sector we can improve the quality of modern life, not merely the quantity of g.n.p.

Most economists believe that Berle and Galbraith have badly overdrawn their case. Competition in most markets is far too pervasive to permit the comfortable life for the giants that Galbraith paints, except in a few industries. Manufacturing now accounts for only about one-third of total g.n.p., and big firms are far less dominant in the nonmanufacturing sectors of the economy. The turnover in firms at the top is too fast to support Galbraith's picture of comfortable security.

Yet Galbraith has touched a sensitive nerve. Many Americans are uneasy about the concentration of economic power in the big corporations, even though their achievements and their well-paid top managers are widely admired. Still, there is little evidence of public support for a radical extension of Antitrust to break up the blue chips of American industry just because they are so big, when there is no open abuse of market power to reduce competition or fence out new competitors. More on this broad issue of economic and political power in the next chapter.

The Dilemma of Modern Antitrust Policy

The dilemma of antitrust policy in the mixed economy can be summarized in two brief statements. The first is that of Henry C. Simons, one of the outstanding advocates of free-enterprise economics in the United States.[6] "Reasonable" monopoly, said Simons, is a contradiction in terms. There can be no such thing. Wide dispersion of political and economic power is the only foundation on which a democratic, free-enterprise system can long exist. The role of government is clear: (1) to maintain active competition within a general framework of free-enterprise rules of the game, which disperse economic power; and (2) to own and operate directly those few industries where competition cannot be made to function effectively. Specifically, said Simons, this implies:

1. Forbidding any manufacturing or merchandising corporation to own stock in any other such corporation, and elimination of interlocking directorates except between unrelated industries.

2. An upper limit on the asset size of all corporations, far below the size of the present giants. Writing in the 1930s, he suggested $100 million in assets as a presumptive upper limit for all firms; with today's prices, the equivalent

---

[5]*Economic Power and the Free Society* (New York: Fund for the Republic, 1958), p. 14. For some counterviews, see Chapter 31.

[6]See especially "A Positive Program for Laissez Faire," and "A Political Credo," in his *Economic Policy for a Free Society* (Chicago: University of Chicago Press, 1948).

figure might be $250 million. We may need big plants for productive efficiency, but we certainly don't need gigantic corporations controlling many similar plants.

3. Provision that no firm may be big enough to dominate its industry—the F.T.C. to determine this size limit in each industry. Moreover, we must recognize that cartels among a few large firms, however informal and "respectable," are probably the most wasteful of all monopoly arrangements, and strictly forbid them.

This may strike you as a completely impractical program, which only an ivory-tower college professor could take seriously. But many thoughtful observers of the American scene consider Simons the outstanding intellectual spokesman of our time for a free, private-enterprise economy.

The other statement is that of the Pittsburgh Plate Glass Company in its answer to the government lawyers in the trial brought against it and other leading glass manufacturers for alleged violations of the antitrust laws during the late 1940s.

We certainly are a big company, said the corporation's lawyer to the judge, and we can understand why the government wanted to investigate us. It's their job to see that the competitive system stays competitive, and we believe in competition just as strongly as they do. All we want to do is to tell you something about the flat-glass industry. Then he went on to demonstrate that today six huge, efficient glass-melting tanks and rolling lines can produce all the flat glass used in the United States. Pittsburgh Plate had three of these big plants, one to serve each part of the country, since transportation is a big cost on finished glass. He didn't deny that Pittsburgh Plate Glass might be called an oligopoly. He just pointed to modern technology in relation to the market, huge as it is in the United States today, and led the judge to wonder what was to be gained by going back to smaller-scale, less-efficient productive processes.

How did the case come out? It never went to a decision. After the company's presentation, the judge instructed the lawyers for both sides

to work out a consent decree for him to sign, making it clear that he was in no mood to find for the government and order dissolution of Pittsburgh Plate.[7]

Which road is better? Pittsburgh Plate Glass, or the one taken by Simons? Many economists would say somewhere in between, and that the best market structure will be different in different industries, depending on technology, the size of the market, and other factors. Indeed, it seems clear that few major sectors of the public really want an economy of rampant competition —neither farmers, labor, businessmen, nor consumers. Most people appear to be interested, not in a perpetual competitive struggle, but in a steady job at good pay, good profits, good-quality products, and predictable, stable times economically.

In conclusion, test out your own views on the best role for Antitrust over the years ahead by judging this proposal. *Fortune* magazine urges a major revolution in our antitrust laws and philosophy, as follows:[8]

Congress should amend the antitrust statutes to make it clear that the national policy is to foster competition by punishing restraints of trade, including conspiracies to fix prices, limit production, allocate markets, and suppress innovation; but that it is not the national policy to prefer any particular size, shape, or number of firms to any other size, shape or number; and that mergers—horizontal, vertical, or conglomerate—are entirely legal unless they spring from a manifest attempt to restrain trade.

Would this be a good substitute for our present antitrust policy?

Business and Government in the New Capitalism

Antitrust action is the most conspicuous government regulation of business. But government has a much wider range of impact on business in the modern American scene. The Federal Trade Commission regulates the kind

[7]This is a much oversimplified version of the controversy, but it illustrates the essential issue on this major part of the case. The company agreed to alter several of its marketing practices, which were claimed to restrain competition.

[8]Max Ways, "Antitrust in an Era of Radical Change," *Fortune,* March, 1966.

of advertising business may do. The Securities and Exchange Commission regulates its practices in issuing securities. The Federal Reserve controls the terms on which it can borrow money from the banks. Federal law sets the minimum wage it must pay its workers, and prescribes that it must deal with them in unions when they choose. Through its income tax, government takes half of all business profits, and in effect prescribes what kinds of accounting procedures must be followed. On the vast amount of government contracts issued to business (over $90 billion in 1969), it sets elaborate standards of performance; specifies that business cannot discriminate amongst employees on the basis of race, creed, or color; and often reserves the right to renegotiate prices downward retroactively if business profits appear to be excessive by government standards.

When labor disputes produce long strikes that disrupt the economy, government often calls business and labor together and brings pressure for settlement on terms that businessmen consider unfair. In 1962, President Kennedy brought the full force of the government and public opinion to force U.S. Steel to rescind price increases which, he thought, endangered the nation's antiinflation program. If the business is an airline, it is regulated in detail by the Civil Aeronautics Authority and the Civil Aeronautics Board as to where it can fly, how much it can charge, the kinds of equipment it can use, and the safety standards it must meet. At the local level, government tells business for what purpose land can be used, and how much taxes business must pay to help support schools and roads. Beyond all this, government constantly hovers in the background, ready to impose new restrictions or bring new pressures to

bear if a considerable portion of the public becomes seriously dissatisfied with what business is doing.

Some businessmen bitterly resent this government interference with the freedom of managers to manage as they please. They argue that it has sapped the essential force of private-enterprise "capitalism." But others believe that it reflects a gradual change in the role of business toward greater responsibility to the general public—a change that has modified the nature of "capitalism" but has not fundamentally altered the basic forces of the profit motive, self-interest, and private ownership of property. The old automobile has had its face lifted; horsepower has been stepped up and gas consumption along with it; a governor and safety padding are compulsory; the carburetor has been adjusted; power steering has become standard equipment. Sometimes the machine works better as a result of this tinkering, sometimes worse. But on the whole it is now a better automobile. And above all, the gasoline that makes it go is still the same—self-interest and the profit motive. Writers sometimes speak of "the new capitalism." Government in business is a big element in the new capitalism, but private capital and management still take the major risks, make the major economic decisions, and reap the major gains or losses those decisions produce.

Some look toward growing cooperation between big business and the state to solve our pressing social and economic problems—urban renewal, pollution, integration of minority groups, aid to less-developed nations. Perhaps imaginative, new, mixed government-business ventures are the path to the future.

Review

FOR ANALYSIS AND DISCUSSION

1. Do you think the problem of bigness as such is more important than the problem of monopoly?
2. What are the main characteristics that determine whether it is in

the public interest that a certain industry consists of a large or small number of firms?

3. Does big business, through advertising, effectively control what consumers want? How about products like the Edsel, Corvair, Packard, Hudson, and so on in the auto industry, which have vanished through lack of consumer acceptance?

4. Many businessmen argue that vigorous government prosecution under the antitrust laws is a sign of government antagonism toward business and profits. Is this a proper criticism? If you think it isn't, how would you convince such a critic?

5. Critics of big business often argue that the majority of large modern corporations could be broken up into several competing units without loss of productive efficiency because as a rule they control many different plants and each of these could just as well operate as a separate, competitive business. Is this argument a sound one? If so, how should we go about implementing the proposal?

6. Should conglomerate mergers be challenged under the antitrust laws, even though the merging firms handle noncompeting products?

7. Would you favor direct government conduct or support of all basic research, with the results freely available to all? List the advantages and disadvantages?

8. Trucks, buses, pipelines, and airlines now are at least as important as railroads in freight and passenger transportation in most areas. Has the time come to abolish the Interstate Commerce Commission and turn the transportation field back to open competition, to provide more effective incentives to efficiency and progress?

9. Would you favor tripling the congressional appropriation to the Department of Justice for antitrust enforcement?

thirty-one

Government, Business, and the Military-Industrial Complex

The case for an individualistic, highly competitive economy is an impressive one. In such an economy, government would need to make and enforce the rules of the game, as we saw in Chapter 30. In addition, there is a large area of the economy where the lines between private and government responsibilities are fuzzy. Where private production has "external" effects, that is, where social costs differ from private costs of production, clearly government intervention is called for to achieve a socially optimal allocation of resources. In the modern, increasingly complex economy, externalities have grown so rapidly in importance that many economists argue now that purely private goods are the exception rather than the rule. We shall look further into this problem in Part Five.

This chapter deals with another private–pub-lic mix problem—the "military-industrial complex." Big business plays a useful role and also raises serious problems in our modern economy. While much modern technology requires big-ness, big businesses may gain economic and po-litical power far beyond that considered in monopolistic share-of-market and price–output statistics. Critics of the American system have argued strongly that big business dominates our lives far beyond acceptable levels—both by controlling our wants through advertising, and by the exercise of vast political and economic power.

"The Military-Industrial Complex"

In recent years, the strongest criticism of this sort has focused on the "military-industrial complex." Government defense contracts make up a big part of many corporations' business, and the interaction between these companies and the government is often close. Recognizing both economic and political issues, General Dynamics or General Electric may be just too big for an individual-oriented, pluralistic society.

What Is It?

"The military-industrial complex" means different things to different people. To radical critics of the American system, it means a pervasive conspiracy of big business, defense contractors, the Pentagon, and "bought" congressmen, to maintain military domination of society, to swell arms makers' profits at the expense of the working poor, and to promote American imperialism abroad.

Among moderates, President Eisenhower's valedictory statement is widely quoted:

This conjunction of an immense military establishment and a large arms industry is new in the American experience. . . . In the councils of government we must guard against the acquisition of unwarranted influence, whether sought or unsought, by the military-industrial complex.

Two other influential statements can help define the problem. Senator George McGovern, a leading critic of the military-industrial complex, writes:

It includes all groups and individuals that have an interest in more arms spending. Defense contractors press for more business. Communities in which they exist or where defense installations are located seek to preserve and expand the local economic stimulus of arms dollars. Workers want job security. The scientists and technicians who work in the research phases have a built-in interest in seeing their work bear fruit. Politicians list, among their accomplishments, their successes in bringing military business to their districts. The military establishment headquartered in the Pentagon—in economic terms a bigger enterpirse than all but seven other countries in the world —is at the center . . . Trade and professional military organizations keep their members informed about arguments for new weapons.[1]

Professor Galbraith, whose *The New Indus-*

trial State has been influential in challenging the role of the large corporation in modern society, has spelled out his picture of the "military-industrial complex" at some length:

It is an organization or a complex of organizations and not a conspiracy . . . In the conspiratorial view, the military power is a collation of generals and conniving industrialists. The goal is mutual enrichment; they arrange elaborately to feather each others' nests. The industrialists are the *deus ex machina*; their agents make their way around Washington arranging the payoff . . .

There is some enrichment and some graft. Insiders do well . . . Nonetheless, the notion of a conspiracy to enrich the corrupt is gravely damaging to an understanding of military power . . .

The reality is far less dramatic and far more difficult of solution. The reality is a complex of organizations pursuing their sometimes diverse but generally common goals. The participants in these organizations are mostly honest men . . . They live on their military pay or their salaries as engineers, scientists, or managers, or their pay and profits as executives, and would not dream of offering or accepting a bribe . . .

The men who comprise these organizations call each other on the phone, meet at committee hearings, serve together on teams of task forces, work in neighboring offices in Washington or San Diego . . . The problem is not conspiracy or corruption, but unchecked rule. And being unchecked, this rule reflects not the national need but the bureaucratic need—not what is best for the United States, but what the Air Force, Army, Navy, General Dynamics, North American Rockwell, Gruman Aircraft, State Department representatives, intelligence officers, and Mendel Rivers and Richard Russell believe to be best.[2]

But lastly, many other observers believe the military-industrial complex is a fantasy of the alarmists. No one denies that a great deal of money is spent on arms, but the leap from that fact to the proposition that the military-industrial complex dominates our lives, or even the military budget, seems to them a large leap indeed.

The Facts

What are some of the major facts on the link

[1] *Christian Science Monitor,* July 12, 1969.

[2] J. K. Galbraith, *How To Control the Military* (New York: Signet Books, 1969), pp. 23–31.

between the military budget and America's corporate structure?

During the late 1960s, peak years for the military spending, the total defense budget ran between $70 billion and $80 billion, perhaps 7 to 10 percent of the total g.n.p. In fiscal 1968, defense contracts let by the Department of Defense (D.O.D.) totaled $39 billion. Of this total, the largest 100 companies in the United States and their subsidiaries received about two-thirds, or $27 billion—roughly 10 percent of their total 1968 sales.

Table 31–1 provides a more detailed picture. Two big companies (General Dynamics and Lockheed) depended heavily (over 80 percent) on D.O.D. contracts. United Aircraft is the only other with D.O.D. contracts exceeding 50 percent of sales. Only General Electric, of the real corporate giants, appeared near the top of this list, with D.O.D. contracts totaling 18 percent

of sales. The other two giants on the top ten list are AT&T (with D.O.D. contracts equal to 5 percent of sales) and General Motors (with D.O.D. contracts equal to 3 percent of sales). Standard Oil (New Jersey) was twenty-fifth on the list with $300 million in contracts, but this represented less than 2 percent of sales. IBM was 30th, with $200 million in contracts which accounted for only 3 percent of sales.

The top ten companies on this list are certainly not industrial pygmies; however, they do not include most of the real giants (by size) of American industry. Medium-sized corporations receive the largest share of Defense Department orders, and they depend most heavily on D.O.D. business. Without military business, their sales would slip heavily. But the widespread notion that the biggest American corporations depend primarily on military contracts for their business and profits is clearly incorrect.

table 31-1

Defense Contracts*

Company	Billion $	Percent of Total Contracts	Percent of Company Sales
Total D.O.D. Contracts	$38.8	100.0	—
Top 100 Companies	26.1	67.4%	10.0%
1. General Dynamics	2.2	5.8	84.3
2. Lockheed Aircraft	1.9	4.8	86.2
3. General Electric	1.5	3.8	17.7
4. United Aircraft	1.3	3.4	54.1
5. McDonnell-Douglas	1.1	2.8	30.5
6. A.T. & T.	.8	2.0	5.4
7. Boeing	.8	2.0	20.3
8. Ling-Temco-Vought	.8	2.0	27.4
9. North American Rockwell	.7	1.7	24.9
10. General Motors	.6	1.6	2.7
15. Raytheon	.5	1.2	37.5
20. Honeywell	.4	.9	28.6
25. Standard Oil (New Jersey)	.3	.7	1.9
30. I.B.M.	.2	.6	3.1

*Contracts let by D.O.D. in fiscal year 1968. Company sales data are for calendar year 1968. Source: Congressional Quarterly, November, 1968, and Fortune, August, 1969.

The top ten corporations in the United States, by size, depend on military contracts for less than 5 percent of their sales.[3]

Where was the work actually done on military contracts? Prime contractors subcontract a large portion of the work on their projects. It has been estimated that between 20,000 and 40,000 different U.S. firms are involved to some extent in the production of military-contract items. Defense Department business is very important to the American industrial scene. But perspective is needed too. Military business does not dominate the business of large or small companies to the extent often claimed by critics of the military-industrial establishment.

Consequences

Clearly a lot of companies have enough military business to make it of real concern to them, though only a handful sell predominantly to the military. It is not surprising that these companies, their communities, the people who work for them, and their congressmen try to increase the economic benefits they gain from D.O.D. business. And their combined political-economic interactions with the military clearly give them leverage on the size and composition of the military budget. What are the main consequences?

1. The military-industrial complex probably increases the allocation of resources to the military budget, away from civilian use. The political process is an imperfect mechanism for allocating resources most efficiently to supplying public wants. Pressure groups play a significant role in congressional and administration budget decisions. Critics argue that members of the military-industrial complex exercise an inordinate control over the allocation of resources. Too many get allocated to the military budget.

It is far from clear how important this pressure is in explaining the total military budget.

Hardly anyone believes that the military-industrial complex has no influence in maintaining a large military establishment. But quite aside from any military-industrial complex, the American people have long been willing to allocate vast sums of money to national defense; the votes in Congress have seldom been close on huge defense budgets, in times of war or peace. National defense is one public good where we have no reasonable way of comparing what the private marketplace would do to meet the same social needs. We shall look in more detail at the problem of achieving the optimal level of resources to producing such "public goods" in Part Five.

2. Some argue that profits are excessive on military contracts. Measurement of profits and their relationship to capital investment is a complex issue. A variety of studies have been conducted; some find profits "excessive," others "inadequate." Professor Murray Weidenbaum of Washington University conducted a widely noted study of the mid-1960s that showed that profits as percent of sales were only about half as large on military contracts as on nonmilitary business, but that profits as a percent of the owners' investment were larger on defense than on nonmilitary contracts. This difference results from the fact that the government provides part of the working capital and plant for many military contractors, so that the actual private investment was smaller relative to final sales than in many nonmilitary businesses.[4]

A larger study, breaking down the profits of different companies between their defense and nondefense business, is reported in Figure 31–1, covering the ten years from 1958 to 1968. Profits as a percent of sales on military contracts are consistently only about half as high as those on nonmilitary business. Profits on military and civilian business as a percent of private equity capital invested varied substantially over the decade. On the average they were not far apart, but from 1961 to 1968 profits as a percent of owners' investment were appreciably lower on defense than on general manufacturing business.

[3]Addition of the space contracts (N.A.S.A.) would increase the total volume by 12 percent and would change somewhat the rank ordering of the big companies; but it would not significantly change the overall picture presented in Table 31–1.

[4]M. L. Weidenbaum, *The Modern Public Sector* (New York: Basic Books, Inc., 1969), p. 56.

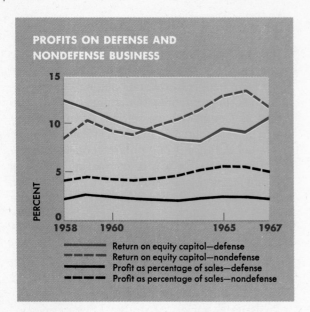

PROFITS ON DEFENSE AND NONDEFENSE BUSINESS

Return on equity capitol—defense
Return on equity capitol—nondefense
Profit as percentage of sales—defense
Profit as percentage of sales—nondefense

fig. 31–1

Defense profits as percentage of sales were consistently only about half those on nondefense business during the 1960s. As percentage of owners' equity capital invested, defense and nondefense profits have varied; recently those on defense business have been substantially lower. (Source: *Fortune,* August, 1969.)

As measured by the test of the stock market, military is less attractice than civilian business. The market places relatively low values on the shares of the primary military suppliers, despite their good earnings on major contracts; that is, price–earnings ratios on D.O.D.-oriented companies are substantially lower than for civilian-oriented companies. Defense is often a feast-or-famine business for individual companies. In the eyes of investors, the return on military contracts are not high enough to make the defense-oriented companies attractive investments compared to civilian companies.

3. Those who have worked most closely with military spending, both in the government and outside, agree that the huge volume of D.O.D. expenditures reflects primarily the huge military commitments the United States has undertaken, far more than inefficient use of federal dollars in buying national defense. Repeated congressional investigations have turned up waste in military spending, and this needs to be prevented. But when the "wasteful" items are totaled up, they still amount to only a small share of the total military budget. The painful fact is that if we want the huge military establishment we now have, it is going to cost a fantastically large amount. No doubt substantial further savings can be made; during the McNamara regime in the 1960s, the efficiency of military contracting increased substantially. But missile systems, modern aircraft, and the maintenance of a large U.S. armed force cost a huge amount of resources, no matter how efficiently defense procurement is carried out. It is important to remember, moreover, that well under 50 percent of the total military budget goes into "hardware," so that savings vis-à-vis the "industrial complex" can operate on only a fraction of the total military budget.[5]

Economics and Politics

Clearly national defense is a "public good." The optimal amount of national defense certainly must be set through the political process, not through the marketplace. The central economic issue is whether the political process allocates the right amount of productive resources to military activity (as judged by the real desires of the people) and uses those resources efficiently.

Nowhere is the inescapable interlinkage between economic and political processes more apparent.

Two separable issues are involved in the allocation of economic resources to defense. First, how much national defense do we "need"— that is, are we willing to pay for? Second, given that amount of national defense, are we producing it with the smallest possible use of productive resources, that is, most efficiently? Economic analysis can help to answer both questions. Comments by three distinguished economists throw light on these interlinked issues.

[5]Beyond these economic issues, it is a plausible inference that pressures by the military-industrial complex to maintain or increase military spending contribute to the long-run likelihood of war. On the other hand, some argue that a strong U.S. defense is the best deterrent to war in the future. This is clearly a question that the economist, as such, has no special ability to answer.

(1) Charles Schultze of Brookings, Director of the Budget for President Johnson, writes:

The uniformed armed services and large defense contracts clearly exist . . . Yet I do not believe that the "problem" of military budgets is primarily attributable to the complex. If defense contractors were always as disinterested in enlarging sales as are local transit magnates, if retired military officers all went to selling soap and TV sets instead of missiles, if the Washington offices of defense contractors were all moved to the West Coast, if all this happened and nothing else, then I do not believe that the military budget would be sharply lower than it now is. Primarily we have large military budgets because the American people, in the cold-war environment of the 1950s and 1960s, have pretty much been willing to buy anything carrying the label "National Security Necessity."[6]

(2) Weidenbaum suggests that the close and continuing relationship between the Department of Defense and its major suppliers is resulting in a convergence between them, which is blurring the distinction between public and private activities in that portion of the economy. Government participation in private-business decision making is great: D.O.D. virtually determines the choice of products a defense firm produces, strongly influences the source of capital funds that it uses, and closely supervises the firm's internal operations. Weidenbaum argues that this attempt to peer closely over the shoulders of defense contractors every step of the way is likely to cost the taxpayers more, not less, in the end. Elaborate procurement procedures and regulations govern the awarding of defense contracts. The D.O.D. reviews and may veto company decisions as to which activities to perform directly and which to subcontract, which firms to use as subcontractors, which products to buy domestically rather than to import, what internal financial reporting systems to establish, what minimum and average wage rates to pay, how much overtime work to authorize.

Weidenbaum concludes that contracting processes that give contractors strong economic incentives to reduce costs would lead to more efficient production on these contracts. Profit (personal or corporate) remains a powerful incentive. The great fear that the government may be fleeced on defense contracts has probably increased the average cost of the items procured. He concludes:

In some ways, the federal government is taking on the traditional role of the private entrepreneur, while the companies are behaving less like other corporations and more like government agencies or arsenals. Certainly, the detailed day-to-day government surveillance of internal company operations which is now so characteristic in the military market is a poor precedent to follow in establishing the future roles of industry and government in the public sector areas, both military and civilian.[7]

(3) Galbraith sees the military-industrial complex as a part of the general domination of economic-political life by the modern corporation and the technostructure of which it is a central part. His "solution" is essentially political.

The primary goal is to get the military power under firm political control. This means electing a president on this issue next time. . . . The Armed Services and Appropriations committees of the House and Senate must obviously be the object of special effort. . . . The goal of the campaign is not to make the military power more efficient or more righteously honest. It is to get it under control. These are very different objectives. The first seeks out excessive profits, poor technical performance, favoritism, delay, or the other abuses of power. The second is concerned with the power itself and the spending on which that power depends.[8]

Galbraith proposes a special body of highly qualified scientists and citizens called, perhaps, a "military audit commission," to oversee the military establishment. The military-industrial complex is a reflection of the increased bureaucratization of modern society, based as it is on vast economic and technological complexities in our system. We need to substitute new national priorities, he argues, and to override the natural biases of the military-industrial complex.

What does all this add up to? Economics tells

---

[6]C. L. Schultze, "Reexamining the Military Budget," *The Public Interest*, Winter, 1970, pp. 20–21.

[7]M. L. Weidenbaum, "The Military-Industrial Complex," *Vital Speeches*, June 15, 1969, pp. 523–28.

[8]Galbraith, *How To Control the Military*, pp. 72–75.

us to examine the allocation of economic resources, and the process that controls this allocation. It tells us that more resources should be allocated to any activity, public or private, of which the marginal return is higher than the marginal cost. American political processes are by no means a surefire way of achieving this allocation. The military-industrial complex no doubt exerts significant influence in increasing the flow of resources into the military establishment. But the biggest questions about defense spending have less to do with the much-discussed military-industrial complex than with the need for a hard reappraisal of U.S. strategic assumptions and potential enemy strength. If the military-industrial complex is indeed a costly threat to the U.S. economy, it is primarily because it exercises inordinate influence through the political process and thereby helps to overallocate resources to defense. More on this in Part Five.

Economic analysis suggests, too, that detailed government bureaucratic oversight of military spending may well be counterproductive. The record of competition in the private marketplace has been impressive over the years in driving down costs and providing efficient production. Substitution of economic incentive plans in government contracting, rather than increasingly detailed surveillance of operations, is likely to provide more defense output for the dollar. The convergence of D.O.D. and corporate roles that Weidenbaum stresses raises serious problems of both political power and economic efficiency. The basic goal for the nation is the provision of needed national defense with a minimum use of economic resources, not the minimization of defense contractors' profits.

Review

FOR ANALYSIS AND DISCUSSION

1. Is there a military-industrial complex? If your answer is "yes," define precisely what you understand by it.
2. Is there an education–Department of Health, Education, and Welfare complex? A medical care–government complex? How do these interest groups inside and outside government compare with the military-industrial complex?
3. How should we decide how much to spend each year on national defense and who should get the defense contracts? How about education? How about medical care and research?
4. Suppose a company like Lockheed or General Dynamics (which do over 80 percent of their business on military and government aerospace contracts) is faced with failure if government cuts its military-space spending next year. What, if any, responsibility does the government have to the workers and stockholders involved? What to keep the company in existence to meet future military-space needs?

As with the appendix to Part Two, the purpose here is to suggest a sample of recent research in economics that may be of interest to students who want to know more of what economists do, and especially of the excitement that goes with research—the probing for new knowledge and new understanding. Here again the items listed are merely a sample. They are not necessarily the best, nor even a cross section, of current research in the area. They are chosen because I hope some of them may be intriguing to you and make you want to look further. They vary widely in approach, substance, and difficulty.

Industry and Market Studies. You can find a research study on just about every major industry. Two interesting recent ones are MertonPeck's *Competition in the Aluminum Industry, 1945–1958* (Harvard University Press, 1961), and M. A. Adelman's *A&P: A Study inPrice–Cost Behavior and Public Policy* (Harvard University Press, 1959). For a very different industry (music, the theatre, and ballet), see W. Baumol and W. Bowen, *Performing Arts—The Economic Dilemma* (Twentieth Century Fund, 1966). Broader coverage is given by *Pricing in Big Business: A Case Approach*, by A. D. Kaplan, J. Dirlam, and R. Lanzilotti (The Brookings Institution, 1958); and Kaplan's *Big Enterprise in a Competitive System* (The Brookings Institution, 1964) provides a further readable overview.

The most controversial and lively study of modern business is J. K. Galbraith's *The New Industrial State* (Houghton-Mifflin Company, 1967), a best seller almost from its publication. For equally lively antidotes, see the review of Galbraith's book in *Fortune*, July, 1967 (pp. 90ff.) and the comments by businessman Eli Goldston and economist H. Demsetz in the *American Economic Review*, May, 1970, pp. 479–84.

Government Antitrust Policy. A sample of leading economists' analyses of some of the central problems of antitrust policy is provided by J. F. Weston and S. Peltzman, eds., *Public Policy toward Mergers* (Goodyear Publishing Co., Inc., 1969). Carl Kaysen's and D. Turner's *Antitrust Policy: An Economic and Legal Analysis* (Harvard University Press, 1959) illustrates the intricate interrelationships between economic and legal issues. A provocative proposal is advanced by Max Ways in "Antitrust in an Era of Radical Change" *(Fortune,* March, 1966). For a broader look at the issues involved, try Edward Mason's "Introduction" to his *The Corporation in Modern Society* (Harvard University Press, 1959); or Chapter 8 of Milton Friedman's *Capitalism and Freedom* (University of Chicago Press, 1962). On the military-industrial complex issue, sample *The Military-Industrial Complex*, O. Carey, ed. (Washington State University Press, 1969).

Economic Theory and Human Behavior. You can always start a lively dispute in economics by asking how well generally accepted economic theory corresponds to actual human behavior. One persistent question is how closely consumer spending actually mirrors consumers' free choices, and how well the market responds, therefore, to consumers' desires. See the symposium on "The Doctrine of Consumer Sovereignty," especially the paper by Tibor Scitovsky, in the *American Economic Review* for May, 1962. Then look at "The Costs of Automobile Model Changes Since 1949," by F. Fisher, Z. Griliches, and C. Kaysen, in the *Journal of Political Economy* for April, 1962. On the behavior of businessmen, see R. A. Gordon's classic *Business Leadership in the Large Corporation* (University of California Press, 1966). James Earley comes to the defense of marginalism in "Marginal Policies of 'Excellently Managed' Companies" *(American Economic Review,* March, 1956). J. Monsen and others argue in "The Effect of Separation of Ownership and Control," *Quarterly Journal of Economics,* August, 1968, that owner-managers make larger profits than comparable hired managers.

part four

The Distribution of Income

How Income Is Distributed: The Pricing of Productive Services

One of the hottest issues in economics has long been the distribution of the national income—between wages and profits, rich and poor, the farmer and the industrial worker, the "haves" and the "have-nots." Governments have risen and fallen on the struggle for income shares. The revolutionary doctrines of Karl Marx centered around the "exploitation of the worker" by the "rich and greedy capitalist." In a different setting, this same struggle over income shares is the issue when the United Steelworkers fight the steel companies for wage increases. It is the issue behind the race riots in the cities —and when Congress votes government support for "parity prices" on farm products. Over the centuries, history tells a recurrent story of the "have-nots" fighting for more and the

"haves" struggling to protect and increase their share.

Thoughtful observers of the private-enterprise economy point out that we're all in the same boat. If everybody pulls together—labor, capital, management—total output will grow and all can have more. No one who understands the basic interdependence inherent in the modern economy would deny this. There is an enormous community of interest in making the private-enterpise economy work effectively.

But part and parcel of that community of interest is a basic conflict that is rooted deep in our ethics and traditions of self-interest and competition. This is the struggle of each individual to get more for himself and his family. It is the struggle over who gets how much of the economic pie—at the level of the individual worker, his union, and his boss, and at the level of national policy. However rich or poor the nation is, we're all interested in our own shares —relative and absolute. Nothing is gained by refusing to face this fact.

Individual self-interest is at the core of the American economic tradition. We look with favor on the man who works hard, earns a good income, and provides well for himself and his family. Self-earned wealth brings widespread esteem. The man who can't earn a good living is viewed with a touch of contempt, or with sympathy if there is an obvious reason beyond his own control. The "Protestant ethic" of work and reward has been strong, though it has been challenged by many teen-agers and college students in recent years.

Yet Americans have agreed on limits to the financial success that should be permitted. Federal income tax rates in 1970 reached 50 percent on income above about $50,000, and a peak rate of 70 percent on income in excess of $200,000. Some government programs are expressly aimed at reducing income inequality— for example, aid to the poor. We want the incentives and productivity of an individualistic, income-motivated economy. But we apparently don't want the extremes of inequality in income and power that are the consequence of all-out adherence to individual self-interest. And we face some tough problems in compromising these desires for maximum incentive and limited inequality.

The first half of this chapter summarizes briefly some of the major facts about the distribution of income. The second half then outlines the theory that helps to explain why different people get the incomes they do; the theory turns out to be essentially an application of the same supply-and-demand analysis that was developed in Part Three. then the following chapters apply this theory to explaining wages and salaries, rents, interest, and, last but by no means least, the same profits that were the focus of much of Part Three.

Who Gets the National Income?

The Income Revolution

American incomes today are higher than ever before. Our standard of living is the highest in the world. Some economists have dubbed modern America "the affluent society."

Look at Figure 32–1 for some of the facts. Since World War II, the real national income

REAL INCOMES IN 1947 AND 1970

(Slices show percentage of families in each income range)

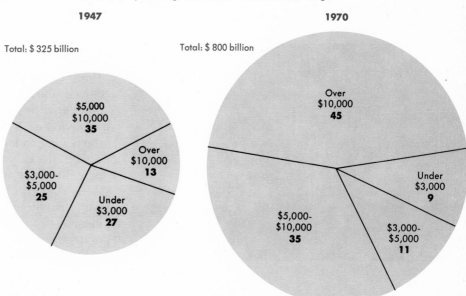

fig. 32–1

Total real income has more than doubled since World War II. Four-fifths of all families now receive over $5,000, compared to only about half in 1947. Forty-five percent now get over $10,-000, compared to 13 percent in 1947. (Source: U.S. Department of Commerce; all data in 1970 dollars.)

1947

Total: $ 325 billion

$5,000
$10,000
35

Over
$10,000
13

$3,000-
$5,000
25

Under
$3,000
27

1970

Total: $ 800 billion

Over
$10,000
45

Under
$3,000
9

$5,000-
$10,000
35

$3,000-
$5,000
11

has more than doubled—from $325 billion to $800 billion between 1947 and 1970, both in 1970 prices. In 1947, median family income was about $4,600 in 1970 dollars; in 1970 it was $9,400.[1] In 1947 over half of all families received less than $5,000, and only 13 percent over $10,000. By 1970, nearly 45 percent of all families received over $10,000, and only 20 percent less than $5,000. The most striking fact in the 1970 data is the rise of the huge middle-income class. Nearly two-thirds of all families received between $5,000 and $15,000. But the extremes are striking too. Five percent of all families received less than $2,000, and together received only about 1 percent of the national income. And at the other extreme, 19 percent of all families received over $15,000, and together received about 40 percent of the entire national income.

Figure 32–2 suggests an interesting question about this distribution of incomes in America. The regular, bell-shaped curve shows what statisticians call a "normal" distribution. Intelli-

[1]The median is the figure that divides the total number of families in half. Thus, in 1970 half of all families received over $9,400, half less. Remember that both these figures exclude nonmarket income (like housewives' services) not included in the national income accounts. Inclusion of all nonmarket income would increase both figures by as much as 50 percent, according to some estimates.

fig. 32–2

Ability and most other human characteristics seem to be "normally" distributed through the population, as shown by the regular bell-shaped curve. Incomes are much more unequally distributed. Why?

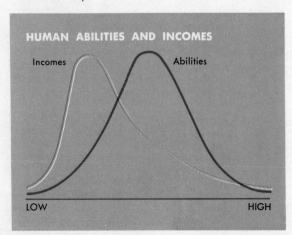

HUMAN ABILITIES AND INCOMES

Incomes   Abilities

LOW   HIGH

gence, physical traits, and many other phenomena seem to approximate closely this type of normal distribution, when large numbers are considered. More people are at the mid-point of the curve than at any other level, and those above and below the average shade off about equally either way.

We might assume that general ability is something like normally distributed in the total population. But incomes received, shown by the solid line, are "skewed." That is, there are many relatively poor individuals. These account for the big hump in the curve toward the lower-income end of the scale. There are a few very rich, who give the curve a long "tail" out to the right. Questions: Are incomes less "normally" distributed than human abilities? If so, why? Do differing economic opportunities for rich and poor explain the continuing skewedness of the income curve? Is it because some people work harder than others? Because some do more useful work than others? Why?

Is income becoming more or less equally distributed? Since the 1920s, more equally. (Before that the data are highly unreliable, although apparently the same comparison would apply.) The facts are shown by Figure 32–3, a "Lorenz curve" which shows the distribution of income. The income of all families is cumulated along the horizontal axis, beginning with the lowest-income family; the percentage of total income received by those families is cumulated along the vertical axis. For example, in 1929, the bottom 40 percent of all families received about 12 percent of the total national income; the lowest 90 percent of families received about 60 percent of total income. Of all income in 1969, the bottom 40 percent of families received about 15 percent, and the bottom 90 percent received about 75 percent.

Obviously, if all family incomes were equal, the points plotted would all fall on the diagonal. That is, the lowest 10 percent would receive 10 percent of the total income, and so on up the line. Thus, the more bowed out the Lorenz curve is, the more unequal the distribution of income is; the nearer it is to the diagonal, the more equally incomes are distributed.

Figure 32–3 thus shows that incomes are

DISTRIBUTION OF U.S. INCOMES, 1929-1969

Line of equality

1969

1935-36

1929

PERCENT OF INCOME CUMULATED FROM LOWEST TO HIGHEST

PERCENT OF FAMILIES CUMULATED FROM LOWEST TO HIGHEST

fig. 32–3

Incomes are somewhat more equally distributed now than in 1929 or 1935–36. The more bowed the curve is, the less equal the distribution of income was in that year. (Sources: For 1969, see Fig. 1–1; for earlier years E. C. Budd, *Inequality and Poverty* [Norton, 1967], p. xiii.)

somewhat more equally distributed now than either in 1929 (the peak of the boom) or in the years 1935–1936 (the Great Depression). It also shows that the distribution has changed only moderately over this tumultuous period. The three curves lie reasonably close together. Make your own judgment as to whether these are large or small changes. Many observers attribute most of the changes to New Deal measures (especially the progressive income tax introduced in the 1930s) and to increased union strength since the 1930s, but the factors responsible remain in dispute.

One last historical observation. Are the very rich—the millionaires—being squeezed out by high-income- and inheritance-tax rates? Apparently not. By 1968, there were apparently some 50,000 millionaires in the nation, compared to only a few hundred in the 1920s, and in 1968 about 900 people had annual incomes exceeding $1 million. But the share of total wealth held by the top ½ percent of all families was estimated at just under 30 percent in 1968, compared to 36 percent in 1929.

Occupational and Educational Differences

What jobs provide the best incomes? Table

32–1 provides part of the answer. It shows median incomes for a sample of occupations, as reported by the Census Bureau for 1969.

table 32-1

Median Incomes — Different Occupations, 1969*

Physicians and surgeons	$30,000
Dentists	18,000
Lawyers	17,000
Engineers	15,000
Managers and proprietors:	
Salaried	12,000
Self-employed	11,200
Foremen	10,500
Teachers — grade and high school	9,500
Skilled craftsmen	8,800
Operatives	7,600
Service workers — sales clerks, and so on	6,900
Secretaries	6,500
Unskilled workers — nonfarm	6,400
Unskilled workers — farm	3,300

*Preliminary estimates based on U.S. Census Bureau and Department of Labor data; median incomes for full-time workers. Some figures are averages of very diverse groups (e.g., "managers and proprietors") and should be viewed as only rough approximations. Figures do not include "fringe benefits." Incomes of part-time workers are typically much lower in the same occupations.

The table speaks for itself, but there are some surprises. Physicians, surgeons, lawyers, and other highly trained professionals undoubtedly top the list. The median figures for managers and proprietors don't look like the huge salaries you've heard about for corporation presidents. Answer: There are some huge salaries, but a lot of middle-level managers who earn lots less. Nor does the figure for self-employed proprietors look as if many people in business for themselves get rich quick; some succeed, others don't. At the bottom of the list, it's clear that farmers and unskilled laborers don't do very well, either absolutely or relatively.

Table 32–2 presents a more detailed breakdown for a sample of occupations. The figures are estimates of lifetime (age eighteen to sixty-four) earnings in 1970 dollars, based on Census Bureau Data. Note the high correlation between the amount of education and probable lifetime earnings, even when the long years of no-income schooling for professionals are figured in. The education figures show up directly, apart from the occupational break. In 1969, for example, the median income for all heads of families with eighth-grade education or less was about $6,000. That for family heads with college degrees was about $14,500, and the figure rises steadily with the number of years of schooling.

Regional income differences reflect these occupational and educational facts. The high incomes are concentrated in the urban areas, where high-income occupations are centered. Incomes are generally low in the south, especially in rural areas. Per capita incomes in the Deep South are still around the New York levels of a half century ago. But the South is pulling up. New England, the traditional high-income area, is slipping relatively. And the West Coast is rising rapidly.

The average income of working women is about two-thirds that for working men. Women generally get less pay than men do for similar jobs. But more than that, the difference reflects the heavy concentration of women in low-pay jobs—especially clerical and service work, and unskilled labor. More women are now showing up in higher-paid occupations—the professions, skilled labor, and middle management. But there are few in peak-income jobs.

Older workers are another special group whose incomes are generally below average. For the high skilled occupations—management, law, medicine—a man's earning power rises steadily until he reaches fifty or sixty. But for the commonplace jobs this is not true. Workers past forty find it hard to get new jobs, and often most move down the income ladder if they have to find another job. Unskilled laborers find the best-paying jobs in their twenties, or at the latest in their thirties.

Lastly, Negroes and other minority groups generally have incomes below whites. The median income for white families in 1970 was $9,800, that for nonwhites $6,200, only about two-thirds of the white median. But the relative position of Negroes has improved substantially over the past decade. In 1960, it was only about 50 percent of the white average. Available data for other minority groups are inadequate to justify national estimates, but evidence points clearly to the poverty of Mexican, Puerto Rican, Asiatic, and other unassimilated groups in the United States. Look at the slums of a big city. The issue of discrimination has rocked the nation in the last few years, and measures to de-

table 32-2

Estimated Lifetime Earnings in Different Occupations*

Doctors	$910,000
Lawyers	785,000
Managers and proprietors	750,000
Dentists	745,000
Economists	522,000
Aeronautical engineers	500,000
Accountants	396,000
High-school teachers	333,000
Electricians	318,000
Plumbers	299,000
TV mechanics	231,000
Clergymen	221,000

*From Herman Miller, *Rich Man, Poor Man* (New York: Thomas Crowell, 1964). Adjusted to 1970 prices. More recent data would raise the relative position of physicians.

crease discrimination against these groups have made headway, especially in periods of high employment and labor shortages. But the Negro or "foreigner" is still often the last to be taken on and the first to be laid off; and the best-paying jobs are only gradually opening up to these minority groups. Many of these income differentials go back to differences in educational opportunities. Chapter 37 analyzes these problems in detail.

Wages and Profits—Functional Shares

The American economy today doesn't look much like Karl Marx's picture of capitalism in its death throes, with the workers poised to seize ownership of the means of production. American labor and management exchange some violent words, and strikes are sometimes long and bitter. But the evidence is overwhelming that American workers want a basically capitalistic, free-enterprise system. In the showdown, management and labor get together; production goes on with the worker's rights pretty well looked out for and the capitalist's control over his investment substantially maintained. When the workers go to the polls, they vote Republi-

can or Democratic, not Communist. The radicals who want to destroy the capitalist system have usually been students and other young revolutionaries, who have found themselves lined up against management and workers defending the economic system.

But within this framework, labor and management wrestle constantly over the division of the consumer's dollar between wages and profits. In the big-union industries, this argument comes to a boil every two or three years, when the union's wage contract comes up for renewal. In nonunionized industries, the struggle is less sharply focused, and wages appear to follow the unionized leaders, such as in automobiles, steel, and coal.

Figure 32–4 gives an overall picture of the outcome of this wage–profit bargaining over the last four decades. The left-hand part of the figure plots the actual dollar shares of national income that go to wages and salaries, corporate profits, unincorporated business incomes (a mixture of salaries and profits), rents, and interest, all before payment of income taxes. The right-hand portion shows the percentage shares that go to these various groups.

fig. 32–4

Everyone's income has grown since 1929, but wages and salaries by far the biggest amount. They have also gradually increased their share of the total. Profits vanished in the Great Depression but have soared since then. (Source: U.S. Department of Commerce.)

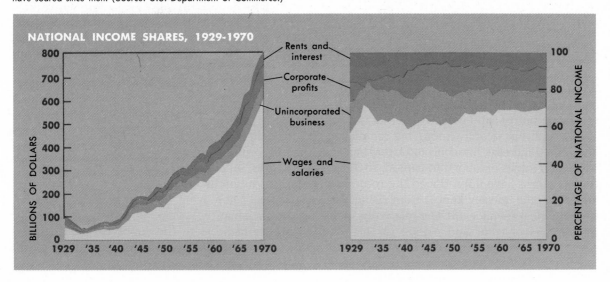

The first lesson comes from the left-hand chart. Everybody's income has grown rapidly, but in a serious depression everyone takes a beating. We're very much all in the same boat. The second lesson, from the right-hand chart, is the general stability in the major income shares except in big business fluctuations. The wage and salary share persistently hovered in the 60–70 percent range, although it has shown a long-term upward trend. In the late 1920s it was around 60 percent of the total. By 1969–1970, another prosperous period, it had approached 75 percent. The wage increases were concentrated in three quite different periods—during the depression of the 1930s when profits vanished, and during the later 1950s and 1960s when wages rose faster than profits despite generally good times. Partly, the rising wage share reflects the steady population shift from farms to urban jobs.

A rather different picture of the outcome of the labor–capital struggle for income shares is given by the bottom half of Figure 17–2, back on page 232. If we compare the return per unit of labor and capital used in the economy since 1900, real wages per hour are five times as high as in 1900, while the long-term interest rate (a crude measure of the return per dollar of capital invested in the economy) has averaged about the same as it was then. Looked at this way, it appears that virtually all the fruits of increased output have gone to labor and virtually none to capital.

How are these different ways of looking at the same world to be reconciled? The answer is back in Chapters 16 and 17 on economic growth. The total capital stock has grown much faster than the labor force. (1) Thus, the law of diminishing returns has acted to diminish the return per unit of capital relative to that per unit of labor. (2) But steadily improving technology has helped increase total output faster than the combined inputs of labor and capital, so diminishing returns have not reduced the return per unit of capital, merely kept it from rising with technological advance. (3) The relatively stable total shares of labor and capital in the total g.n.p. thus reflect the rapid growth in income per unit of labor, and a correspondingly faster growth in the capital stock than in the labor force, with the two factors just about offsetting each other to keep the labor and capital shares in g.n.p. roughly unchanged. The data are shown back in Figure 17–2.

The Theory of Income Distribution

Why do people receive the incomes they do—some large, some small; some stable, some insecure? The answer is complex, as with most other important issues in economics, and there is still much debate among economists on the finer points. But the core of the answer was laid out back in Chapter 25. In competitive markets, the prices of productive services (e.g., wages) are set through supply and demand so as to roughly equal the marginal productivity of the productive resource (e.g., labor). Whenever the price of, say, labor is below its marginal product (what one more worker would add to the firm's salable output), businessmen can increase their profits by hiring more labor. Competition among businesses for workers will bid up the wage rate toward the marginal productivity of that type of labor. Conversely, if the wage rate is more than labor's marginal product, it will pay businessmen to hire fewer workers, and the wage rate will fall. Only when the wage rate just equals labor's marginal product will business firms and the labor market be in equilibrium.

"Distribution theory," explaining why different productive resources earn the incomes they do, is thus merely price theory from Part Three, viewed from the reverse side. There we focused on the pricing of final products, like autos; here we focus on the pricing of productive services, like labor used to produce the autos. Obviously, when the businessman decides to produce 10,000 autos this week, he is *ipso facto* deciding to hire the labor and rent or buy the machines needed to do the job. Here, in distribution theory, we consider the decision in terms of how many workers and machines the businessman will demand. When we compare this demand with the supply of labor or machines offered, we can determine the price set for productive services through the same supply-and-demand mechanism as in Part Three. Obviously, the degree of competition or monopoly in the market will affect the outcome in markets for both productive services and final products.

The remainder of this chapter lays out a supply-and-demand framework for explaining the incomes received by owners of productive resources—labor, land, capital. The following chapters then apply this central theory to explain wages, rents, and profits in a variety of real-world circumstances.

This approach temporarily omits transfer payments—income payments that are not payments for goods or productive services. "Welfare," old-age, and unemployment benefit payments under social security are examples. Such transfer payments make up a substantial part of some people's incomes, but they reflect a transfer of claims to the nation's real income and wealth, not an increase in the size of that real output and wealth. Chapter 37, on "Poverty and Insecurity," at the end of this section puts together earned and transfer incomes, in an examination of how we try to deal with situations where society is not content with the distribution of earned incomes produced by the marketplace.

Incomes Are Payments for Productive Services

Most incomes (excluding transfer payments) are received as payments for productive services. Wages and salaries are payments for labor services. Rents are payments for services of land and buildings. Interest is payment for the use of money, but more fundamentally for the real productive services that the money will buy. Economic profits are the residual for businessmen and risk takers that's left over after all the other income payments are made out of business's receipts—and they're also the incentive to entrepreneurs that makes the private-enterprise system go.

Thus, most incomes are based directly on the prices received for productive services. Like others, these prices are determined by supply and demand. The following paragraphs map out a simple supply-and-demand model for analyzing productive service markets.

The Supply Side

First, we need a supply curve, or schedule. Look at the supply of some given type of labor in your community, say carpenters, as an example. The supply of such labor this month may be highly inelastic—fixed by the number of carpenters there and by their strong preference to work about forty hours a week. Or the supply may be elastic, if carpenters can readily be drawn in from neighboring areas. Or overtime work may be feasible. For some types of labor, unskilled workers can be easily upgraded. Another source of elasticity may be school children and retired old people, if the job is relatively unskilled. All these things together produce a labor-supply curve for the market for the time period under study, probably an upwardsloping supply curve indicating that more labor hours will be supplied at higher than at lower wage rates.

The Demand Side[2]

Next, we need a demand curve. The demand for productive services is primarily a derived demand. The local drugstore hires clerks because customers want clerks to wait on them— not because the druggist want clerks in the same way he wants shirts, bread, and the other consumer goods he buys. Businesses' demands for productive services thus reflect ultimate consumer demands. If consumers want lots of ice cream, the demand for drugstore clerks will be strong. But if the customers stay away, the druggist doesn't need many clerks.

How many workers will a firm demand at any given wage rate? If it is to maximize profits, it will hire additional workers as long as each additional worker adds more to the firm's income than he adds to its costs. If the wage the firm has to pay for another worker is more than what that worker adds to income, to hire him would lower the firm's profits. Workers' contri-

---

[2]The appendix to Chapter 23, "Physical Production Relationships Underlying Cost Curves," provides a rigorous logical foundation for this section. If you studied that appendix it may be useful to review it before proceeding. The "marginal product" of that appendix is identical with the "marginal *physical* product" of this chapter.

butions to the firm's profits will be maximized, therefore, when workers are hired just up to the point where the additional income equals the additional cost for the last worker taken on —no more workers and no fewer. It's the same old rule—maximize profits by equating marginal cost and marginal revenue.

The additional income obtained by hiring one additional worker and selling the output he adds is called marginal revenue or "marginal-revenue product" (or sometimes the "marginal-value product," and sometimes simply "marginal product"). Additional **physical** output ("marginal physical product") is what the worker adds to total output. But from management's point of view it is the increase in sales dollars that matters most; hence, it is the marginal **revenue** product in which we are most interested. It is the marginal-revenue product that the businessman compares with the marginal cost incurred by hiring another worker in deciding how many workers to hire to maximize his profits. To summarize, the marginal revenue product of any type of productive service sets the upper limit that a business will ordinarily pay for that service; and businesses will have an incentive to hire more productive services as long as the wage paid to each is less than its marginal productivity.[3]

Remember the process by which firms maximized profits through equating marginal cost and marginal revenue back in Chapter 24. It should be clear that the firm's decision on how much labor to hire at any wage so as to maximize profits is precisely the same process. The only difference is that here the marginal-cost–marginal-revenue comparison is made in terms of additional workers hired, whereas in Chapter 24 it was in terms of additional units of output produced. The logic of increasing output (hiring more resources) as long as the marginal cost is less than the marginal revenue obtained is identical in both cases; and the equilibrium level of output (of resources hired) will obviously be the same either way the firm analyzes the decision.[4]

It is important to note that, generally, the demand curve for any productive resource will be downward sloping. It will pay to hire fewer workers at a high than at a low wage.[5]

The Interaction of Supply and Demand

We now have the broad outlines of the market for productive services—a supply curve and a demand curve for each type of productive service in each market area, local or national. Deriving the supply curve of labor in our local area is, as we saw above, easy in principle though complex in practice. On the demand side, employers will hire more workers as long as their wage is below their marginal-revenue product. As long as the wage is lower than labor's marginal-revenue productivity, business will compete for labor. **This competition will bid wages up to about the level of labor's marginal productivity, and no higher. And so the wage will be set.**

Figure 32–5 pictures a simple supply-and-demand market equilibrium for one type of labor in a local market this week. The supply curve is inelastic; in one week not many more labor hours will be supplied at moderately higher wage rates. The demand curve slopes down for the reasons suggested above. A wage of $2 per hour just clears the market, at 400 hours of labor per week demanded and supplied. At a higher wage more would be supplied but less demanded; at a lower wage, the reverse.

---

[3]The existence of monopoly raises some special problems, which will be considered in the next chapter.

[4]Although the above statements indicate only how much of one single resource it will pay the business to hire, this approach can readily be generalized to cover all productive

resources the firm hires. It will pay to hire more of *each* resource as long as the additional cost involved is less than the revenue added (in technical terms, as long as its marginal cost is less than its marginal-revenue productivity). In equilibrium, therefore, each resource will be hired up to the point where its marginal cost just equals its marginal-revenue product, which is the same as saying that marginal cost equals marginal revenue for the firm as a whole, the profit-maximizing condition stated in Chapter 24. (For a more complete statement, see the appendix to this chapter.)

[5]This seems obvious. But to demonstrate it rigorously, we need to invoke the law of diminishing returns again. The firm's demand for workers rests directly on the workers' marginal-revenue productivity. If more workers are hired, their marginal-value product will fall as the ratio of workers to other factors of production rises. This is *both* because marginal physical product declines *and* because the price of the final output will drop as more units are put on the market with unchanged market demand. The same is true for land, machinery, or any other productive service.

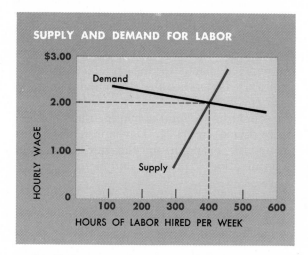

fig. 32–5

Wages, like other prices, are determined by the interaction of supply and demand forces. Here the equilibrium wage is $2 an hour, with employers hiring 400 hours per week.

The Integration of Price and Distribution Theory

The preceding section emphasized that price theory and distribution theory (Parts Three and Four of this book) are substantially the same. They both look at the pricing process and at the allocation of resources in response to consumer demands. But price theory focuses on consumer demand for final products, as businessmen strive to maximize profits by meeting those demands. Distribution theory looks at the same process, but focuses on its implications for the incomes received by owners of productive resources (labor, land, and capital). It is very important to see this close integration between price and distribution theory in understanding how a private-enterprise market economy works.

To see how the integrated system fits together, go back and reread the section "General Equilibrium of a Competitive Economy" on pages 369–372 in Chapter 25. They are the analytical core of this chapter as well. The pricing of productive services is part and parcel of the general equilibrium pricing process. The costs paid out by business firms are the incomes received by the factors of production. Thus, the profit-maximizing decisions of businessmen

simultaneously provide the goods most desired by consumers at the lowest feasible prices and provide to resource owners the largest incomes that are consistent with their abilities and willingness to contribute to producing what consumers want. The whole system relies on each individual (worker, capitalist, consumer, businessman) to look out for his own self-interest; it relies on competition in all markets to see that the end result is in the best interest of all. Adam Smith's invisible hand of self-interest and competition is a powerful mechanism for the compromise of millions of conflicting individual goals.

Wages, Rents, and Prices Simultaneously Determined

Wages, rents, and product prices are all simultaneously determined in the competitive market system. In Figure 32–6, let DD be the downward sloping marginal-revenue-product curve of labor. It shows how much labor will be hired by businesses at different wage rates, less at higher wage rates, more at lower. Suppose the wage rate is W, determined by the type of

fig. 32–6

Marginal productivity determines return to both labor and capital, though either can equally well be considered a residual after the other is determined.

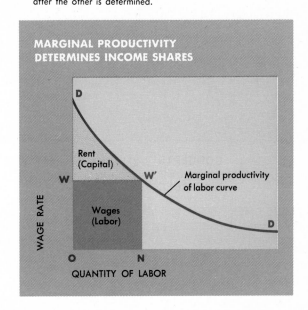

supply-and-demand interaction shown in Figure 32–5. At that wage, all workers willing to work at wage W are hired, a total of N workers. Total wages paid will thus be the rectangle DWW^1N.

But total output is the entire area under the marginal-productivity curve, ODW^1N. Who gets the rest of the product? The answer is capitalists—for simplicity assume they are all land- and machinery owners. They get the triangle DWW^1, labeled rent, as earnings on their capital. In competitive equilibrium all economic profits are eliminated. Rent is what is left over after wages have been paid.

Suppose now we had begun with the marginal-productivity curve of capital instead of labor. Although the shape of the curve might be different, the total area under it is the same as in Figure 32–6, since both show the possible total output of the economy using all its capital and labor. If we now compute the total rent paid to capitalists, what is left over will be wage for labor, just the inverse of the calculation in Figure 32–6.

Actually, we could take a case with several factors of production, say labor, land, and capital (other than land). The same marginal-productivity calculation will give us the income share of each. The marginal-productivity curve of each will depend on its own physical productivity working in collaboration with the others and on the final price consumers will pay for the product. Each will get a share of the total product (income) dependent on its own contribution interacting with other factors of production and consumer demands for final products. Product prices and factors are all determined simultaneously.[6]

Economists are fond of quoting the following little rhyme by H. J. Davenport, a famous economist, to point up the interdependent determination of product- and factor prices:

> The price of pig is something big;
> Because its corn, you'll understand,
> Is high-priced, too; because it grew
> Upon the high-priced farming land.
>
> If you'd know why that land is high,
> Consider this: Its price is big
> Because it pays thereon to raise
> The costly corn, the high-priced pig.

Consider the jingle. It tells an important truth.

We are ready now to use these principles to investigate more thoroughly some important real-world cases, beginning with wages and salaries.

[6]The appendix to this chapter provides a more rigorous statement of the marginal-productivity relationships involved. Mathematically inclined readers are referred to Mathematical Appendix IV at the end of the book, where the preceding theory of income distribution (factor pricing) is stated rigorously and some of its interconnections with the macro explanations of relative income shares are explored.

Review

CONCEPTS TO REMEMBER

Check your understanding of the following new concepts introduced in this chapter. You ought to be able to relate them directly back to Part Three, especially to the various cost-and-demand concepts there.

derived demand
marginal physical product
marginal-revenue product

marginal-value product
distribution theory
Lorenz curve

FOR ANALYSIS AND DISCUSSION

1. The biggest two shares of the national income are wages and profits. Are the basic interests of wage earners and of their employers competitive or complementary?
2. Explain carefully how incomes are distributed in a highly competitive, market-type economy.
3. Are most people's incomes a good measure of what they are worth?
4. Would a distribution of income based purely on marginal productivity give everyone about what he is worth? Explain.
5. Would the equalization of incomes in the United States, as is proposed by some Socialists, solve the problem of poverty? Use the figures on national income (in Chapter 5) and those on income distribution in this chapter, insofar as you think they are relevant, to support your answer.
6. According to Table 32–1, farmers and unskilled laborers have made substantially lower incomes than the other groups shown. If this is so, why do people continue to become farmers and unskilled laborers?
7. "The distribution of incomes to factors of production is no problem to one who has studied the behavior of business firms. In determining what prices to charge and what output to produce, the firm simultaneously determines how many workers to hire and what wages to pay out, what rents and interest charges to incur, and so on for the other income shares." Can you show how your analysis of Part Three (just preceding) has in effect explained the distribution of incomes?

APPENDIX *PRODUCTION THEORY, PRICE THEORY, AND DISTRIBUTION THEORY*

This appendix provides (for those who studied Chapter 24) a more rigorous statement of what economists call the theory of production and the way in which it underlies price theory and distribution theory.

The Theory of Production. The theory of production is concerned with the physical relationship between the factors of production used (input) and the product produced (output). The central principle is the law of diminishing returns, or of variable proportions. This law states (appendix to Chapter 23) that as the proportion of one input to other inputs rises, the additional units of output per unit of that input may rise at first, but will sooner or later begin to fall, and fall persistently thereafter (other things, such as technology, being unchanged).[7]

Since the law of diminishing returns applies to each productive factor as more of it is used relative to others, it constitutes a powerful analytical tool for deciding the optimal proportions among factors of production if we want to obtain the most efficient, or least-cost, production of any commodity. As more of each factor is added relative to the others, its marginal physical product will decline. To obtain the minimum cost of production for any given output, we should add more of each productive factor until the last (marginal) dollar spent on each provides the same addition to total output—that is, the same marginal physical product. This is so because under any other condition more physical product could be obtained for the same cost by switching a dollar from a lesser-contributing factor of production to a higher contributing factor. Thus, in equilibrium:

$$\frac{\text{Marginal physical product of } A}{\text{Price of } A} = \frac{\text{Marginal physical product of } B}{\text{Price of } B} \text{ etc.}$$

Another (equivalent) way of saying the same thing is that in the least-cost condition the marginal physical products of the factors of production must be proportional to their prices. That is:

$$\frac{\text{Marginal physical product of } A}{\text{Marginal physical product of } B} = \frac{\text{Price of } A}{\text{Price of } B} \text{ etc.}$$

---

[7] A more complete analysis of these relationships may be found in most economic theory textbooks. See, for example, M. J. Bowman and G. L. Bach, *Economic Analysis and Public Policy* (Englewood Cliffs, N.J.: Prentice-Hall, Inc., 1949), Chaps. 18 and 19.

This proposition implicitly underlies the discussion of the unit-cost curves back in Chapters 23 and 24. The U-shape of the firm's cost curve derives in part from the physical relationships described by the law of variable proportions. Most important, assuming the prices of factors of production to be given, the minimum-cost point on the firm's unit-cost curve can be achieved only when the factors of production are used in the proportions indicated above.

This theory of production also provides the answer to how a change in the price of any factor will affect its use. If the price of one resource (say, labor) falls, its use will be increased until its marginal physical product falls to the same proportion with other marginal physical products as the new proportion among the factor prices concerned. In other words, more labor will be hired until the marginal dollar spent on labor again produces the same marginal product as when spent on any other factor of production. Hiring more labor becomes desirable even though this reduces labor's marginal physical product under the law of diminishing returns.

Maximum-Profit Positions in Price Theory and Distribution Theory. The statement of the least-cost conditions above does not necessarily specify the maximum-profit position of the firm. It only specifies the conditions for obtaining the least-cost production for any given production level. The condition for maximum-profit (or minimum-loss) production is to increase production as long as marginal cost is less than marginal revenue (up to $mc = mr$). This is identical with the proposition that maximum profit (or minimum loss) will be obtained by adding units of each factor of production as long as its marginal cost (price, under competitive conditions) is less than its marginal revenue product. Each proposition follows because as long as spending another dollar on costs adds more to total revenue than it does to total cost, total profit must be increased. The statement in terms of individual factors of production merely specifies in more detail the mix of productive factors that must be used in arriving at the maximum-profit position. The $mc = mr$ proposition of earlier chapters is silent on the optimal factor combination; it implicitly takes the optimal combination for granted. We can now add the proposition that for maximum profit the marginal cost of each factor used must be equal to its marginal-revenue product and that the marginal costs of all the factors used must be proportional to their marginal-revenue products:

$$\frac{\text{Marginal cost of factor } A}{\text{Marginal cost of factor } B} = \frac{\text{Marginal revenue productivity of } A}{\text{Marginal revenue productivity of } B}.$$

Or, to put it another way, that

$$\frac{\text{Marginal cost of } A}{\text{Marginal revenue productivity of } A} = \frac{\text{Marginal cost of } B}{\text{Marginal revenue productivity of } B}.$$

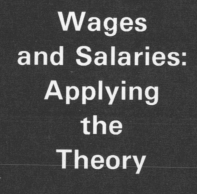

Wages and Salaries: Applying the Theory

Wages and salaries account for over two-thirds of the total national income, and for all of most people's incomes. By the same token, wages and salaries constitute around two-thirds of total business costs. So it is not surprising that people, ever since they began to write about economics, have been spinning out theories to explain why wages are what they are.

Economists' theories mirror the times in which they live, and over the last two centuries we have passed through at least three different widely accepted theories of wage determination. Today, we do not yet have a fully satisfactory theory of wages. Yet most economists agree that the simple marginal-productivity, supply-and-demand theory stated in the last half of Chapter 32 is a fruitful way to understand why

individual wages are what they are. This chapter is primarily an application of that theory to explain why different people get the wages and salaries they do.

Some Dubious Theories

But first let us turn briefly to three theories of wages that attained widespread acceptance during the last century, and that still have considerable influence in day-to-day thinking, even though economists consider them largely fallacious, or at least of dubious value.

The Subsistence Theory. Chapter 16 outlined Malthus's subsistence theory of wages, sometimes also called the "Iron Law of Wages" because of the inescapable hard fate it predicted. In essence, Malthus said that population will always tend to outrun the means of subsistence. Thus, the growing supply of labor will tend always to force wages down toward the subsistence level. Wages cannot permanently stay below the subsistence level, for obvious reasons. But they will not for long stay above it in the absence of artificial means to limit the rate of population growth. Karl Marx accepted much of the theory and predicted the downfall of capitalism, as workers become increasingly unwilling to accept their menial existence while capitalists appropriate the "surplus value" created by the workers whose wages fall increasingly short of the total value they create.

But history has shown an escape from this bitter prospect. In most Western industrialized nations, technological advance and capital accumulation have saved us from Malthus and Marx. In fact, real wages have risen rapidly and (except for cyclical fluctuations) steadily over the past century. Moreover, in the nations with the highest living standards, birthrates have fallen below the rates in less-advanced countries.

But we must not write off Malthus too fast. Even with modern technology and capital accumulation in the West, for well over half the world's population in the less-developed nations, Malthus's predictions on wages look perilously close to being right. Total output has grown in most nations, but for over half the world's population little faster than the number of mouths to feed, and starvation looms on the horizon each bad crop year.

The Lump-of-Labor Theory. Another widely held, but almost completely fallacious, theory is that there is some fixed amount of work to be done in the short run, so more people seeking work will merely bid wages down and steal jobs from those already at work. This theory, often unarticulated, lies behind widespread opposition to letting new workers into the labor market—foreigners, women, new apprentices, and so on. It lies behind union restrictions on entry to many occupations. Most importantly, it lies behind widespread resistance to "automation"

—to the introduction of machines which appear to replace human beings.

What is the fallacy in this lump-of-labor theory? The answer should be clear from Parts Two and Three. With proper monetary and fiscal policies, aggregate demand can always be expanded to match growing potential output. There can always be enough demand to provide jobs for as many workers as enter the labor market. At the level of the individual industry, the demand for labor is a function of the marginal productivity of that labor. Workers willing to work at a wage at or below their marginal productivity can always be employed profitably. The total amount of labor which will be hired is thus a function of both ultimate demand and the price (wage) of the labor. There is no fixed amount of work to be divided up; the number of jobs depends on aggregate demand and the real wage which workers demand.

The Bargaining Theory. A third theory, with an important element of truth, is that wages depend on the relative bargaining power of employers and employees. Clearly relative bargaining strength does matter sometimes, for example when the United Auto Workers sit down to bargain with General Motors. But the bargaining theory leaves one big question unanswered: What are the limits within which the bargaining can vary the wage, and what sets those limits? If the union is very strong, does that mean there is no upper limit as to how high it can push its members' wages? Obviously not. At some level, the employer would have an economic incentive to substitute nonunion labor or machinery for the high-cost union members, or eventually go broke. If there is no union, does that mean the employer can drive down the wage virtually to zero? Obviously not. If his wages go far below prevailing levels, his employees will look for jobs elsewhere. Thus, to say that wages depend on relative bargaining strength is an obvious half-truth. The following pages should go a long way toward defining the limits within which bargaining power may dominate under different conditions.

But to point out the inadequacies of these theories does not provide a satisfactory explanation of what does set wages. We need a theory that will encompass the cases where Malthus appears to be right, where "automation" occurs, where bargaining power varies, and where new workers enter the labor market. In short, we need a more general theory of wages.

Wages in Competitive Markets

What will your income be the year after you graduate? Five years later? Will you be a salesman, an accountant, an engineer, a secretary? Would the factors governing the answer be different for a factory worker?

Basically, your salary will be set by the forces of supply and demand in the market you enter —for beginning engineers, accountants, or secretaries, wherever you go to work. And the forces of competition on the demand side of the market will bid that salary up to roughly your marginal productivity—to roughly what you are "worth" economically to the firms hiring beginners like you. They won't pay you more, and if there is active competition in hiring, you need not take less. This is what the modern theory of wage determination says, and you can see that it will serve equally well to explain the wages received under a wide variety of conditions in any market economy.

Figure 33–1 shows the close correspondence between average output per man-hour and real wages in the American economy since 1900. Although this doesn't show the path of marginal productivity, it does suggest a basic fact: it is rising productivity that has made possible

the steadily rising wages of American workers. Even though there are many more workers seeking jobs now than in 1900, their average productivity is so much higher that businesses demand the larger number, and at higher wages as well.

But before we look at the application of our theory in more detail, two preliminary warnings. First, there are over 80 million people in the American labor force, and in some respects, every one of them is unique. No two people are exactly alike. Thus, it is meaningless to talk of "labor" and "wages" as if they were homogeneous. We need to look separately at many different types of labor, at people with different capacities, different education and training, different attitudes, living in different places. On the other hand, unless we lump individuals into different types of labor in different market areas, we're left with the job of looking separately at 80 million individuals. So we do group workers together where they are similar and in the same area.

Second, in this chapter, we shall be looking at the determinants of individual wages, or wages of particular groups of workers, in contrast to the macro issues of wage-profit shares in the national income and the relationship of wage levels to total g.n.p. Thus, this is a chapter mainly at the micro level. It takes the levels of aggregate spending and aggregate demand for labor as given, determined by the forces described back in Part Two. Later on, we shall drop this simplifying assumption.

Begin with a relatively simple case. What determines the wage received by William Welder,

fig. 33–1

Rising productivity has made possible the steadily rising real wages of American workers. (Source: Council of Economic Advisers.)

a hypothetical laborer who works for the Acme Plumbing Company, a small plumbing-fixtures manufacturer. There is no welders' union in the area. Will's abilities are substantially undifferentiated from those of many other welders. There are many businesses and construction contractors in the area who hire welders. And there are many plumbing-supplies manufacturers in the United States who compete actively with each other in the product market. So there is active competition at three levels—among welders for jobs, among businesses for the services of welders, and among businesses for the consumer's sales dollar.

What determines Will's wage? His boss sets the wage he pays, so we might ask him. He'd probably have a simple answer. Will gets the going hourly rate for welders—say, $3 an hour. Acme Plumbing doesn't haggle over wage rates with each man it hires. It pays the going rate.

Something beyond Acme determines the "going rate" for welders in the area. By now, the answer "supply and demand" ought to come easily to you as the framework for looking at this price.

The Supply Side

What determines the supply of welders in the area? In any real-world case we could write a book on the subject, but the essential points would probably boil down to these.

Number of Welders in the Area. Welding is a skilled trade. There are only so many people in the area who qualify as skilled welders at any given time.

Availability of Additional Welders. The existing group of welders might be expanded either by training new welders or by bringing in men from other areas. If a small increase in the wage rate draws welders into the area and draws new recruits into the three-month training programs required to pick up the minimal skills, the supply of welders will be elastic. But if welders are immobile and the field doesn't look attractive, the supply will be inelastic. The elasticity of supply will thus depend on the desirability of the job and labor's mobility into it.

Hours of Work per Welder. For the most part, welders either put in the workweek stated by their employer or they don't get the job. But there is some flexibility in the number of hours worked per week. Overtime pay can pull out more.

Elasticity of Supply Dependent on Time Period. On any given day, the supply of welders in our area is pretty much fixed. But given six months, training new welders becomes a practical possibility. In most cases, supply becomes increasingly elastic as a longer time period is considered. But in the professions and management, many years rather than a few months are required for big increases in supply. A doctor goes through about ten years of college, medical school, and internship before he is ready to go out on his own.

Figure 33–2 pictures the general relationship between short-run and long-run labor supply curves. In any particular market, the short-run supply is usually inelastic. Except for overtime and the possibility of getting workers away from other areas, higher wages won't greatly increase the amount of labor offered. See curve *SS*. But in the long run, there are many new

fig. 33–2

The short-run supply curve for labor is typically much less elastic than the long-run curve. If *OQ* labor is offered now at wage *OW*, a higher wage will increase labor offered only slightly in the short run, much more in the long run.

SHORT- AND LONG-TERM LABOR SUPPLY CURVES

sources of supply. The curve is likely to look more like S^1S^1.

The Demand Side

The demand for welders' services is a derived demand, derived from the ultimate consumer demand for the plumbing fixtures Acme produces. Acme (and other businesses) will demand more welders whenever they have unfulfilled demand for their product at profitable prices. More precisely, Acme will demand more welders as long as the wage is below welders' marginal revenue productivity to it. Other firms will do likewise. By aggregating the demands of all firms, we could draw a demand curve for welders' services at any time. Since welders' productivity may be different in different firms, some firms' demand will drop off rapidly as the wage rate rises; others' will drop off only slowly.

If the marginal revenue productivity of welders underlies employers' demand for welders, we need to look at the underlying determinants of marginal revenue productivity. Remember, m.r.p. is compounded of marginal physical productivity and a product price factor, though they may be hard to separate in some cases—for example, in engineering and selling.

Marginal Physical Productivity. Will Welder's marginal physical product is the additional physical product Acme Plumbing turns out by having Will on the job, compared with the output without him, all other productive factors being identical in both cases. This marginal physical product depends on Will's own mental and physical abilities, training, morale, and so on. It also depends, probably even more, on the other productive agents with which he works. With an old-style welding torch and poor working conditions, Will will have a low marginal physical product. If he is well equipped and works on a well-designed, balanced production line, his marginal physical product will be higher.[1]

Marginal Revenue Productivity. The production manager is interested mainly in how many sinks get turned out in a day. But the president and the stockholders are more interested in the profit figures—in dollars and cents rather than in numbers of sinks and faucets. For top-management purposes, physical productivity figures have to be converted into sales-dollar terms.

Will's marginal revenue productivity is the additional sales dollars brought in by employing him. If his marginal physical product is one sink per day, and the wholesale price of sinks is $30, then Will's marginal revenue productivity at Acme Plumbing, with the existing number of welders, is $30. Marginal revenue productivity is found by multiplying the marginal physical product by marginal revenue (price under pure competition). Consumer demand for the ultimate product is just as important as the worker's physical output in determining his value to the business.

The marginal revenue productivity of welders will eventually decrease as more welders are put to work producing sinks, for two reasons. First, the law of diminishing returns will bring decreasing marginal physical productivity as the ratio of welders to other factors of production increases (see footnote 1). Second, as more sinks are produced by this and competing firms, their price will fall, consumer demand remaining unchanged—although Acme alone is too

---

[1] A worker's marginal physical product depends on the *proportion* of workers to other productive agents, as well as on the quality of the machinery and tools he works with. For example, if welding is one operation on a metal-sink pro- duction line, the addition of the first welder to that line means a big increase in the firm's output. Addition of a second and third welder may skyrocket output further, until the line is roughly balanced between welders and other workmen. Beyond this point, adding more welders may increase output somewhat by speeding up the line or by having a spare welder around to spell anyone who takes a coffee break, but the additional (marginal) product is much lower than it was when the first few welders were added. This is the law of diminishing returns again. It means that adding more workers in any plant will sooner or later mean a declining marginal physical product for those workers, assuming the size of the plant and the combination of other productive agents remain unchanged. See the appendix to Chapter 23 for a more detailed statement.

Generations of economists have worried about all the angles. Suppose, e.g., we have five ditchdiggers and five shovels. What is the marginal product of a sixth shovel? Answer: Small, but positive. It has some value as a spare. How about a sixth ditchdigger with only five shovels? Same answer. He can fill in during rest periods, or he can go for beer.

FIRM'S DOWNWARD-SLOPING DEMAND CURVE FOR LABOR

D(MRP)

WAGE RATE

D(MRP)

LABOR HOURS DEMANDED PER WEEK

fig. 33–3

The competitive firm's demand curve for labor is downward sloping. The demand curve is labor's marginal-revenue product in the firm, since it will pay to hire more workers as long as marginal-revenue product is more than the wage.

small to influence market price. Thus, the demand curve for workers will generally be downward sloping, as in Figure. 33–3. Starting from any equilibrium position, firms will hire more labor only as wage rates fall, given an unchanged demand for sinks. In effect, the marginal-revenue-product curve for welders in the firm is that firm's demand curve for welders.[2]

Does Demand Really Depend on Marginal Revenue Productivity?

In a purely competitive labor market, the individual employer is a wage taker, not a wage maker. He has to pay the going wage; his problem is how many men to hire at that wage. This depends on the marginal product an additional worker will provide. But how can businessmen ever estimate anything so complex as a worker's marginal revenue productivity?

In a little firm like Acme Plumbing, with only a few employees, the boss may have a good idea

[2]Note that if firms are prepared to increase the amount of other resources with which welders work (for example, the scale of plant), the effect of diminishing physical productivity can be avoided. But the declining-price effect will nevertheless pull down marginal value productivity.

of how much his daily output will go up if he puts on an extra man. And he knows the price of sinks. This was the kind of situation economists had in mind when they developed the marginal-productivity approach to explaining the demand for labor.

But what about the marginal revenue productivity of a welder like Will in U.S. Steel? U.S. Steel has nearly 300,000 employees scattered over the United States, with hundreds of welders among them. Welders work on jobs many steps removed from the ultimate steel products sold to the company's customers. For example, one welder may do repair work on the company's railway cars that shuttle materials around the mills. What is his marginal productivity?

Obviously, no one knows. It would be impossible to isolate the effect on the ultimate production of cold-rolled steel sheets of laying off that one welder. And there are millions of workers in American industry who present similar problems in estimating marginal productivity.

Still, somehow U.S. Steel has to decide how many welders it will hire. Company officials might tell you it's simple. They hire enough welders to get the steel produced for which they have orders. But this answer, which is probably quite correct, drives us back to the question of the price at which U.S. Steel will book orders. Clearly, this decision depends in large part on the costs estimated by the steel people for producing steel sheets. Somehow all these interrelated variables have to be put together, and somehow the hiring officials down at the plant level have to decide when it will pay to hire another welder.

Where does all this leave us? First, it's clear that no very precise estimate of marginal physical productivity is possible in many cases. Second, hard as the estimating job is, businessmen have to make some such calculation (consciously or subconsciously) in their hiring and pricing decisions if they are intelligently trying to maximize profits. Third, in many cases several types of labor must be hired as a group to operate as a production unit. You either have the people it takes to run a modern assembly line, or you just shut the line down. In this common type of situation, it is very difficult to separate out the marginal physical product of each kind of laborer.

Out of all this emerges a rough notion that businessmen are willing to pay workers only what they are "worth," sometimes viewing workers as individuals but often as groups required for an integrated operation. What workers are worth logically boils down to a notion of marginal revenue productivity. Although this figure can't be estimated precisely in most cases, many businesses use their cost-accounting systems to get working ideas of when it pays to take new orders and hire more workers. Big concerns typically break down the cost of producing different commodities into a good deal of detail. Behind these money-cost data are time-and-motion studies of how much labor time should turn out how much product. Using these studies the the businessman can get a rough estimate of the "productivity" of workers of different types.

Supply, Demand, and Purely Competitive Wages

In a competitive market, price (here, the wage rate) is determined by the interaction of supply and demand. Will will get a wage about equal to the marginal revenue productivity of welders like himself. The market will see to it.

To demonstrate rigorously that this will result, assume (1) that welders are all identical, (2) that employment conditions are similar at different plants in the area, and (3) that information on wages at different plants is circulated freely. Then all plants will have to pay about the same wage to get welders, just as there tends to be a single price for any identical commodity within any given market area.

Suppose that the going wage for welders is $24 a day. However, Acme Plumbing and some other plants figure that welders are worth to them up to around $30 per eight-hour day. In technical language, they estimate that the marginal revenue productivity of such labor is more than $24 in their plants. What will happen? Those firms will try to hire more welders. When they do, (1) the wage rate will be bid up, and (2) the value (marginal revenue productivity) of welders in these plants will fall as more welders are added because of the law of diminishing returns and possibly a lower price for sinks. Each firm will bid for additional welders as long as the rising wage is lower than what it can afford to pay additional men. At some rate between $24 and $30 a new equilibrium wage will be established, with market supply and demand in balance at that new wage.

The left-hand portion of Figure 33–4 shows this equilibrium for the whole labor market; this is a summation of all the firms demanding welders. The right-hand portion shows that Acme hires ten welders when the daily wage is set by the market at $27; remember that Acme simply pays the going wage rate to get the welders it needs.

In this equilibrium situation, we would expect to find the following:

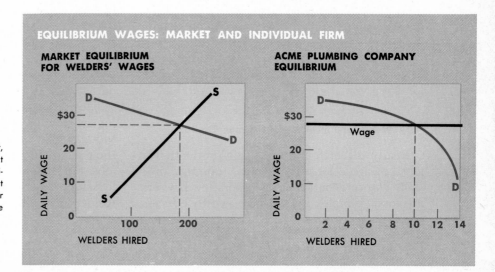

fig. 33–4

Welders' wages are set in the market, much like other prices (left portion). At a market wage of $27, Acme maximizes profits by hiring ten welders, at which point their wage equals their marginal-revenue productivity to Acme (right portion).

EQUILIBRIUM WAGES: MARKET AND INDIVIDUAL FIRM

MARKET EQUILIBRIUM FOR WELDERS' WAGES

ACME PLUMBING COMPANY EQUILIBRIUM

1. The wage rate is equal to welders' marginal revenue productivity in the plants where they are hired.

2. Welders' wages are identical at all plants in the area.

3. Each firm is hiring as many welders as it "can afford" at that wage, because each firm continues to hire welders as long as the wage is lower than welders' marginal revenue productivity to it.

4. All welders in the area who are seeking work at that wage are employed. If any were still looking for work at that wage or less, the market wage rate would be bid down, since employers could hire unemployed workers at less than they were paying employed welders.

Thus, the competitive market tends to establish a wage or salary for each class of labor equal to its marginal productivity, when all workers looking for jobs at that wage or less are employed. Each worker is earning what his type of labor is "worth," as measured by its marginal contribution to producing the goods and services consumers want to buy. But remember: Each individual's marginal revenue productivity, and hence his wage, depends on a lot of forces completely outside his own control. Any change in consumer demand (because a depression comes along or because competing companies turn out a better sink) will change Will Welder's dollar contribution to Acme's sales revenue. And any change in technology or in Acme's production setup can have the same result. The market pays each person about what he is "worth," but what he is worth to employers depends on a lot of forces over which he has no control.

Now try applying the same analysis to the original question. What will **your** starting salary be when you graduate? Five years later?

Wages and Investment in Human Capital

Nearly all high-pay and high-productivity jobs require a lot of education, training, and skill. The surgeon and the corporation lawyer are good examples. Both require a costly educa-tion, plus experience, before they can hope to hit the top in productivity and income. Such education and training are investment in human capital, just like purchase of machinery and buildings is investment in nonhuman capital.

Perhaps all humans are born equal, but by the time we reach working age we differ widely in terms of economic productivity. By middle age the differences are even wider; some people keep on growing, others level off early. Perhaps the biggest cause of these differences is the widely varying amount of investment in human capital represented by different individuals as the years go by. Modern economics analyzes investment in human capital much as it does investment in nonhuman capital. Note that investment may be made by the individual himself, his parents, or society. We shall return to this issue as a major explanation of differences in incomes in the modern market economy, and a major social problem as to how much investment should be made in what forms of human capital.

Wage Determination in Monopolized Industries

What difference does it make if the plumbing-supplies industry is monopolized by one or a few major producers? Continue the assumptions that each firm does the best it can to maximize profits, and that firms in this and other industries compete actively for welders.

As under competition, each firm will continue to hire more welders as long as the wage is lower than welders' estimated marginal worth to the concern. But the total number of welders hired in this industry will be lower than under competition, because the monopolist restricts output to get higher prices and higher profits.

Thus, fewer welders will have jobs in plumbing manufacture. If welders could work only there, clearly wages would be forced down by their competition for the reduced number of jobs. But welders forced out of plumbing can look for jobs elsewhere. Since we assume that welders are mobile, those forced out of plumbing will compete for jobs elsewhere, forcing down welders' wages there. Welders' wages will again be identical everywhere in the new equilibrium, but at a lower level than without the monopoly. **By restricting output below the competitive "ideal," the monopolist forces an inefficient allocation of labor, and this produces a lower wage for welders than under competition, both in the plumbing-supplies industry and elsewhere. Too few workers are employed in making plumbing supplies, too many in the rest of the economy. They are not efficiently allocated.**[3]

To test your understanding of this reasoning, suppose now a union comes in and forces welders' wages back up to the competitive level everywhere in the economy. What will be the effect on the number of workers hired?[4]

Wage Determination under Employer Monopsony

Now assume a different situation, where there is no competition among employers for labor. An example might be an isolated company mining town, where there is no significant alternative to working in the mine. The mine operator has a substantially complete "monopsony"—that is, a monopoly in hiring workers. Such a business is a wage maker, not a wage taker. There is no reason to suppose that he will pay a wage as high as the workers' marginal revenue productivity to him. If the workers are immobile, he may "exploit" them—that is, he may pay them a wage below their marginal revenue productivity to him. He may be able to offer a very low wage and still get all the labor he needs.

Even here the employer doesn't have a completely free hand. If his wages get too far below rates elsewhere, workers may move away to other areas where they can earn more. Thus, the monopsonist pays what wages he has to in order to keep his workers from leaving, or to lure others if he needs more help. But when he is forced to go outside his monopsony area, competition with other employers is likely to eliminate his ability to exploit the workers.

Economists define "exploitation" as a wage below a worker's marginal revenue productivity. Although such cases may seem unethical or improper to you, "exploitation" in economics is an analytical, not a moral, term. Willie Mays or a corporate executive may be exploited in this sense, just as may a secretary or steelworker.

To hear workers tell it, monopsony and exploitation is a common case; the worker needs a union to protect himself against such exploitation. According to employers this is a rare case. The evidence suggests a mixed world. But everywhere the strength of monopsony positions tends to diminish as job-information channels improve, and as workers have more time and money to move to new jobs. The more mobile workers are, the more likely it is that employers will have to pay competitive wages. Even though waitresses' wages are low in most cities, it is very difficult for employers to exploit such workers. There are hundreds of restaurants, so that collusion is difficult and any waitress will soon move elsewhere if her boss cuts wages below the going competitive rate.

A look ahead to implications for union behavior: Where monopsony exists, a union can clearly do a job for the workers. By banding together, the employees may be able to bargain their wages up to their full marginal revenue productivity without reducing employment. As long as the wage is less than the value of additional workers to the operator, even at the higher union wage, it will pay him to keep on hiring all the workers he was previously getting at a lower rate. The union may recoup for the workers the "exploitation" that had previously swollen the operator's profits.

[3]The argument can be stated rigorously, as follows. Since the monopolist always faces a downward-sloping demand curve, marginal revenue is always less than price. The marginal revenue product obtained by hiring more labor is therefore always less than marginal physical product times the product price; instead, it is marginal physical product times marginal revenue. Since the marginal-revenue-product curve is the firm's demand-for-labor curve, the firm's demand for labor under monopoly will always be less than in a comparable competitive case.

[4]Answer: Some welders will be unemployed. More details in Chapter 34.

Wage Determination under Bilateral Monopoly

The next model is one that comes close to real-world conditions in some of the big-union–big-business areas of today. "Bilateral monopoly" is the case where employers with substantial monopsony power bargain with unions with substantial monopoly power in selling labor. A simple case would be the mining-town example above after the workers formed a union to represent them as exclusive bargaining agent. A more realistic example, though not a "pure" case of bilateral monopoly, is wage bargaining in the steel industry, where the United Steelworkers represent most of the workers and the major firms in the industry in effect act together in bargaining for new contracts.

There are many other cases that might be called bilateral oligopoly, or bilateral oligopsony-monopoly. The auto industry, for example, has only three major firms, and they undoubtedly consider one another's positions as they bargain; but they do not bargain jointly as do the major steel firms.

Under bilateral monopoly or bilateral oligopoly the wage outcome is logically uncertain. The employer will be unwilling to pay more than the labor's marginal revenue productivity without cutting back the number employed; he will pay less if he can get the labor he needs at a lower wage, and without a union he can exploit the workers to some extent in this way. The union, with a monopoly in the sale of its members' services, pushes up wages as far as it can. If the wage is pushed above labor's marginal value product at the present employment level, fewer men will be hired. But the exact wage level is indeterminate between this marginal-value-product ceiling and a wage floor above which the employer could (without a union) get all the labor he needs. The outcome will depend on the relative bargaining strength of union and employer, on how badly the employer wants to avoid a strike, on the size of the union's strike fund.

A new union where the employer has "exploited" his workers can thus force up the wage rate without causing less employment. Just how far an employer may be able to hold the wage below the marginal productivity level—conversely, how high the union can force the wage toward that level—is a question to which economic theory has no answer. To a considerable extent labor is immobile. Workers do not move readily from one job or location to another. Thus, a major employer or group of employers can probably keep most of its labor supply at whatever wage rate is bargained, unless the wage is substantially below wages in alternative industries. But the union provides a strong force countering employer monopsony. Bargaining power holds the key to the outcome, within a fairly wide band.[5]

Wage and Salary Differentials

Now turn to another application of the marginal productivity theory—the explanation of wage and salary differentials. The huge salaries of T.V. stars, corporation presidents, and home-run hitters are always fascinating. Why should anyone get $100,000 a year when most of us have to be content with a small fraction of that? And especially, why should they get it when their work by and large looks so pleasant compared with ditchdigging or pounding a typewriter, which pay only a couple of dollars an hour? We shall see that marginal productivity again provides the biggest part of the answer.

Even within the range of occupations which seem reasonably likely for most of us, the differentials are big. Look again at Table 32–2. In lifetime earnings, the expectations of a doctor in 1970 were $907,000, of a lawyer $785,000, of an engineer $500,000, of a high-school teacher $330,000, of a plumber $299,000.

Supply and Demand Again

The most fundamental things about wage and salary differentials can be seen by using the

[5] A new analytical approach from mathematics—"game theory"—presents some interesting insights into alternative outcomes under different types of bargaining strategies.

same supply-and-demand, marginal-productivity model again. Give your theory a workout.

Salaries are extremely high where the supply is tiny and the demand is large. Wages are low where there are lots of workers relative to the demand. How "hard," how unpleasant, how tedious the job is—such considerations aren't very important except as they influence either the supply or the demand side of the picture.

Why does Willie Mays collect an astronomical salary just for playing baseball on warm summer afternoons? Mainly because he is better at hitting, catching, and throwing baseballs than almost anybody else; and we Americans lay our dollars on the line with enthusiasm to see good baseball players.[6] How can a surgeon get away with charging hundreds of dollars an hour? He gets away with it because his skills are very scarce, and the demand for them is very strong. His marginal productivity is very high. In contrast, it's easy to be a delivery boy or a retail clerk, and lots of people try these jobs. Their marginal productivity is low.

The biggest factor accounting for wage differentials thus lies in the ability of the individual to do something that few others can do —something that is demanded by consumers with money to pay for it. There are big differences in the capabilities of different people. Some of these differences we can't do much about. Joe Louis's split-second timing was largely born, not made, in spite of all the years of training that went into it. Psychologists tell us that our basic intelligence apparently changes little over the years, no matter how hard we study. But our capabilities also depend on education, hard work, and other things that are controllable. One obvious reason that top-notch

corporation lawyers are so scarce and their marginal productivity so high is that not many people have both the combination of brains and personality and the drive to put in the twenty-five years of hard work in college, law school and practice that it takes to make a fine corporation lawyer. The competition is tough for the top jobs, and most of them aren't won by fellows who work eight-hour days with Saturdays and Sundays off.

But ability and hard work aren't the whole story. Some occupations are hard to get into. You cannot become a lawyer or a surgeon unless you've got the money to get through law or medical school, however smart and ambitious you may be. The only way to become a senior airline pilot is to move up through a long period of training and experience. Becoming a plumber is almost impossible unless you meet the union's requirements in many areas, and the union may not want an increase in the number of plumbers. Many occupations are still substantially closed to Negroes, though the doors are gradually opening. Women are in effect excluded from many high-pay occupations.

Consider another example. When a new area develops and needs new workers, we would expect wages to be unusually high for a while. People are unlikely to give up other jobs and move across the country to take a fling in a new area unless the monetary incentive is clear. And this checks out. Wages in the Southwest are generally higher than in slower-growing sections. Most rapidly growing areas tend to bid up wages because labor is relatively scarce.[7]

Chapter 32 stressed the growing importance of education as a door to high-income occupations; investment in human capital again. Nine of the ten best-paid occupations on the 1960 Census list were professional or managerial, averaging over sixteen years of schooling. Salary studies consistently show the dollars-and-cents value of education. Roughly speaking,

[6]Anomalously, Mickey Mantle may have been more susceptible to wage exploitation than most common laborers. This is because there could have been little active competition for his services to force the New York Yankees to pay him more; almost no one else had a big enough ball park in a city large enough to push Mantle's salary up to what he was probably "worth" to the Yankees in marginal revenue productivity (marginal cash-drawing power). Moreover, under organized baseball's "reserve clause," other clubs couldn't hire Mantle away anyhow; they would have had to "buy" him from the Yankees. But Mantle obviously had a monopoly in selling his own services. Thus, the situation was one of bilateral monopoly.

[7]Per capita income in California in 1969 was about $4,300, in Missouri about $3,500, in Michigan about $3,900, in Vermont about $3,300, in South Carolina about $2,600, and in Mississippi about $2,200, the lowest in the nation. Can you explain these differences on the new-area hypothesis? If not, how can they be explained?

every year of additional school above eighth grade seems to be worth an extra $500 or so a year earning power over one's entire life-span. Over a working life-span, this means that college may be worth over $100,000, a nice return on investment by any standards. (There is some trickery in these figures, of course, since we know that those who go on to college are generally more able and would presumably earn above average even without the extra schooling. But even making a rough allowance to eliminate that factor, higher education pays well on the average.) But all the evidence points the same way. Investment in human capital pays off.

Unions have some influence on wage differentials. Especially where the situation approximates employer monopsony, it is clear that unions may improve the position of workers compared to nonunion shops. But just how much difference unions really make is a subject of much dispute, to be postponed till the next chapter.

A supply-and-demand model would predict that some particularly dirty, disagreeable, dangerous jobs will command high pay because these factors restrict the supply of labor for the jobs—not because the dirt, danger, or unpleasantness themselves justify higher wages. Extra-hazard pay often goes with dangerous jobs; sandhogs, for example, make good money, but not many people line up for the job of drilling tunnels underwater. Conversely, people like white-collar jobs. The wages paid to clerks in banks and other pleasant working places attest to the appeal of such jobs in increasing the supply even though wages are lower than elsewhere for comparable workers.

But the striking fact is that the cleanest, most attractive, most pleasant jobs are generally the ones with the **highest** pay—unless you classify responsibility as a disadvantage. Just about everybody would agree that the corporation president has a nicer job than the ditchdigger, that the lawyer leads a nicer life than the coal miner. Then why don't more people become corporation presidents and lawyers, so that the salaries there and in ditchdigging will move toward equality? Answering the question should give you some insight into the complex set of factors limiting the supply of certain kinds of abilities in our society, relative to the demand for those abilities. At the end, ask yourself one more question: Do existing income differentials (for movie stars, surgeons, corporation presidents, schoolteachers, dope peddlers, factory workers, farm laborers) reward most highly those who make the greatest contribution to human welfare?

Wages and Technological Advance

Technological advance is a dominant characteristic of the American economy, perhaps the single most important foundation of our rising standard of living. New methods, new machines, new products are the lifeblood of a dynamic, growing economy. Without the linotype we'd still be setting type by hand, and books and newspapers would still be for the elite few. Without the electric light bulb, we'd still be lighting our houses with candles, oil, and gas.

But "automation" (as technological advance is sometimes called when new automatic machines replace men) is often blamed for widespread unemployment. Big, electronically run, computers replace hundreds of clerks in processing checks and keeping records in banks and businesses. Modern chemical plants are almost fully automated. On a humbler level, spray guns and rollers get work done a lot faster than the old-fashioned paintbrush. Everywhere new factories produce more goods with fewer workers.

It is not surprising that many workers worry that automation may throw them out of a job. Actually, for the economy as a whole this worry is largely unfounded. But let us put the automation-unemployment issue aside for Chapter 45, and concentrate here on the relation between technological advance and wages.

Technological progress increases output per unit of input—output per worker or output per unit of capital, whichever way you wish to divide up total output. It would appear to raise the marginal revenue productivity of both labor and capital. Thus, we might expect it to raise both wages and the rate of return on capital—and so it generally will, other things equal. But how much of the gain goes to each under what circumstances is a more complex question, and there may be cases where either labor or capital income is actually reduced by a particular technological innovation.

But the overall upward push on wages is clear. Look back at Figure 33–1, which shows the steady growth of output per man-hour and of wages in the American economy. Moreover, the growth in total output has been much greater than the total input of labor and capital combined, as was shown by Figure 17–2. While the total incomes of both capital and labor have risen greatly over the past century, the return per unit of labor (the real wage rate) has gone up much more than the return per unit of capital (the interest rate), as the bottom half of Figure 17–2 shows dramatically. In the aggregate, labor has apparently been the great gainer from technological advance as measured this way. Measured as in Figure 32–3, the percentage shares of the total national income going to labor and capital have been relatively stable, because the quantity of capital has grown much faster than the quantity of labor.

Against this factual backdrop, let us examine the impact of automation on wages in a particular industry and occupation. Look back at Will, the welder. Suppose a new machine is invented that stamps out metal sinks, largely eliminating the need for welding. Let us trace through the results, assuming that all markets are perfectly competitive and all prices flexible both upward and downward.

1. Sink producers will adopt the new method if it's cheaper per sink produced than the old one was, and competition will force sink prices down to the lower cost level.

2. Many welders will lose their jobs in plumbing-supply companies. Will will be out of a job, at least temporarily. Welders' wages will fall as they compete for jobs elsewhere.

3. Employment will increase in plants that manufacture the new machine, in industries producing raw materials and parts, and in plumbing-supply companies that need men to install, service, and operate the new machines. This increased demand will tend to offset the downward pressure on welders' wages.

4. At the lower price of sinks, more sinks will be produced and sold, and consumers will be better off. More goods in total can be produced, since some welders are freed from plumbing supplies to help produce other products.

In all of this, what has happened to the wages of different labor groups and to the wage share in the national income? Note that this question now involves a return to macroeconomic issues, as well as the microanalysis we have just been using.

First, welders' wages drop. Some welders are thrown out of work, as the marginal value product of welders is reduced. They look for other jobs. If they stay unemployed, average wages of all welders are clearly down. Even if they get jobs as welders elsewhere, welders' wage rates and total wage incomes will tend to be pulled down as more welders seek jobs there.

Second, the demand for other types of labor rises—for workers to make the new machines and to service and operate them. Wages will rise in those other industries and occupations.

Third, if we assume constant total expenditures in the economy, welders thrown out of jobs will get work elsewhere or at different jobs in the sink industry, as consumers switch their expenditure patterns. Consumers will spend more on other products if they spend less on sinks, and more jobs will be available in other industries. This pleasant conclusion, however, depends on two critical assumptions: that workers are mobile in moving to new jobs, and that individual wages are flexible, so that the workers can be absorbed elsewhere. Thus, it skips lightly over the big interim problems of retraining and readjustment facing individual workers. Still, as a practical matter, probably the biggest help in assuring jobs and incomes elsewhere in the face of "automation" is government assurance that aggregate demand will remain strong.

Fourth, what happens to the total wage share in the national income will depend largely on the elasticity of demand for the product con-

cerned and on the ratio of labor to capital used in the innovating industry, relative to the rest of the economy. This gets pretty complicated. But since labor clearly benefits along with all of us in its role as consumer, in the real world it's reasonably clear that labor's real aggregate income is raised by technological advance, whatever happens to its relative share of the national income—though this is not necessarily so, according to our theory. The gradually rising share of wages and salaries in the national income over many years of rapid technological advance suggests that labor and nonlabor incomes both share the benefits of technological progress, and that if anything, the labor protion has grown a little. There's no doubt that, thus far at least, wage earners have benefited greatly from technological advance—or from automation, if you prefer that name. The data in chapter 17 and the theory here and there agree.

Marx and the Reserve Army of the Unemployed

One last application of the theory. Marx put great emphasis on the "reserve army of the unemployed" as a force inevitably driving wages down to a minimum subsistence level— his "iron law of wages." Unemployed workers would constantly force wages down toward that level, and the final result would be revolt and the overthrow of capitalism. How about it?

Suppose the demand for and supply of labor are as shown in Figure 33–5. Suppose the wage rate is W^1; then there is indeed unemployment, as shown on the chart. This unemployment, presuming competitive markets, will indeed push wages down, incidentally providing jobs for some of the unemployed workers at the lower wage rate. But will wages fall to W^3, assumed to be the minimum level of subsistence? Clearly not. They will fall to W^2, the level at which the amounts of labor demanded and supplied are just equal, but there is nothing to make them fall further. Quite possibly employers would like to pay still lower wages, but competition among them will prevent this outcome. Workers, on the other hand, might like to have wages higher than W^2, but at a higher wage fewer men will be hired and competition

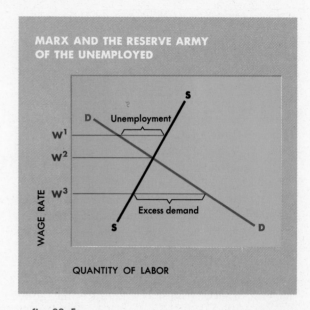

MARX AND THE RESERVE ARMY OF THE UNEMPLOYED

fig. 33–5

Marx argued that unemployment would always force wages down to the minimum subsistence level (W^3). But if we assume unemployment shown at some wage rate (W^1), competition for workers will keep wages from falling below W^2.

among the unemployed will push the wage rate back down to W^2.

Suppose, to examine a last possibility, wages were somehow depressed to W^3, the bare subsistence level. Would they stay there? They would not. At wage W^3 there would be a large employer excess demand for labor, and competition among employers would bid wages up. Only if competition among either employers or laborers is eliminated can the wage rate stay far below or above W^2 in the economy shown in Figure 33–5. Is this conclusion contradicted by the minimum-subsistence wage levels found in some of the less-developed economies, like India? No. The minimum-subsistence wage level is the equilibrium level there because productivity, given their populations, lack of education, and lack of capital, is so low. Marginal productivity is the fundamental determinant of the real wage level in both economies. The higher average wage in our Western economies reflects higher productivity; and given the productivity, the average real wage cannot be forced down to a minimum subsistence level by greedy capitalist employers as long as there is substantial competition for labor among them.

Review

FOR ANALYSIS AND DISCUSSION

1. Suppose you want to maximize your lifetime income. What factors should you take into account in selecting your occupation and in timing your entry into it?

2. "Labor is just another commodity, and wages are its price. All we need to explain wages is a basic understanding of supply and demand." Do you agree with this quotation from an economics textbook? Explain.

3. One theory holds that wages are merely the result of bargaining between workers and employers, and that the only important determinant of the outcome is the relative bargaining power of the two parties. Is this theory correct? If not, why?

4. Malthus argued that population would tend to outrun the world's food supply, and that wages would tend to be forced back down toward a bare subsistence level.
   a. Is this an acceptable theory of wages?
   b. How would you differentiate between its usefulness in explaining wages in America and in India?

5. To what extent are the "bargaining" and "subsistence" wage theories indicated above consistent with a supply-and-demand approach to the problem?

6. Is inequality of economic opportunity a major factor in the present unequal distribution of personal incomes in the United States? If it is important, what, if anything, should be done to reduce such inequality of opportunity?

7. Average wages are higher in the North than in the South. Would you expect this differential to persist or vanish? Why?

8. Define "exploitation" as it is used by economists. What are the factors that determine whether or not any worker is likely to be exploited?

9. Can you explain to a confirmed Marxist why the wages of workers need not be forced down to the subsistence level by the "reserve army or the unemployed"?

APPENDIX   *ECONOMICS OF THE DRAFT*

The military draft is a matter of considerable concern to most college students these days. This is especially so during the period of an unpopular war in Vietnam, but the draft has been with us in periods of less emotional turmoil as well. Clearly, the draft raises both ethical and economic issues. This appendix examines briefly how economic analysis can help throw light on the issues involved.

Supply and demand curves are useful tools in most matters of economic analysis, and they are here. Figure 33–1A shows the economics of the draft (using rough illustrative data). On the left-hand side, army pay is plotted on the vertical axis; the number of servicemen in the army on the horizontal axis. Since both are set by law, the equilibrium point (*E*) shows 2.5 million men in the army at an average rate of $2,500 per year. The supply curve is vertical, indicating that the required number of men will be forthcoming at whatever wage the army offers to pay, in this case $2,500 per year. The supply is perfectly inelastic. If Congress becomes more generous and raises the average salary to $3,500 per year, or conversely lowers the average wage to $1,500, the number of men in the army remains unchanged, while the tax bill for financing the army is increased or lowered correspondingly.

The right-hand portion of Figure 33–1A shows the supply and demand situation if we had a "voluntary" army—that is, one in which men volunteered to serve in response to the wage offered, just as they do for other jobs. Thus, the supply curve *(S')* slopes upward to the right, indicating that more men would volunteer for army service at a higher wage than at a lower one. In the same way, the demand for servicemen *(D')* slopes downward to the right, indicating that with high servicemen's pay it would pay the army to use civilians for many posts that servicemen might undertake under a draft; conversely that it would pay the army to use more servicemen relative to civilians and mechanical equipment at a lower service wage.

Assuming, again, that the army wants just 2.5 million men, given the supply and demand situation shown it would have to offer an average wage of $3,500 per year to obtain the servicemen needed. If it wanted more, it could get them by raising the wage offered; if it wished to get along with less, it could get the men needed at a lower average wage. The equilibrium E' is at $1,000 higher annual wage than E in the left-hand portion, indicating that in the draft many men are required to enter the armed services who would not do so voluntarily at that wage.

(a) The simple supply-and-demand apparatus helps to throw light on a number of issues about the draft. First, assume that the economy undergoes a recession, so that jobs become less plentiful in the private sector. In this situation, given a volunteer army, the number of men willing to volunteer for the draft at any given wage will increase, other things being equal, say to S'' The supply curve will shift out to the right, indicating that, at the same wage as before, more workers will volunteer. Since the military only need 2.5 million servicemen (by our original assumption), they can now get them by paying only $2,200 per year average wage. Conversely, if the private economy booms and wages there rise rapidly, the supply curve to the military would shift backward, to the left, and the military would have to offer a higher average wage than $3,500 to get the number of men needed.

(b) What can this analysis (going back to Figure 33–1A) tell us about the total welfare of society under the two plans?

Clearly, the cost of the army to the federal government is lower in the draft case. Two and a half million servicemen are drafted at an average salary of $2,500 per year, making total army pay $6.25 billion per year. With a volunteer army of the same size, the average wage is $3,500 per year, or a total annual wage cost for the army of $8.75 billion. The draft looks cheaper.

But think again. Suppose a star athlete, like basketball center Lew Alcindor, is drafted. He would have earned, say, $100,000 in professional basketball, but the army pays him $2,500. Clearly, Alcindor has been subjected to a concealed tax of $97,500—a tax rate of 97.5 percent on his potential earnings for the year. Or suppose a graduate of a good university is drafted; he could have earned $10,000 a year by taking a business job. In his case, the hidden tax is $7,500, or 75 percent. And so it is for everyone drafted who could earn more outside the army than the government pays him in it.

Many observers object strongly to this kind of unequal tax, which results from the draft. They say the cost of the army should be borne by the entire citizenry, presumably through the regular tax system, which is far less unequal than the result here. Funds should be collected through taxes and used to hire soldiers at whatever wage ratio is required to obtain volunteers. (This is, of course, in addition to any allowance one should make for the extra hazard of being in the army as against civilian life.)

(c) Can economic analysis tell us anything about the total cost to society of the two plans? The answer is yes. Although the draft looks cheaper and is cheaper in terms of government money spent on servicemen, overall it is a more costly arrangement for society than a voluntary army would be. The amount each individual can earn in the private marketplace is a rough measure of the contribution he makes to the welfare of society. That is, his wage tends to be equal to his marginal productivity, which in turn reflects how much society is willing to pay for his services—$100,000 for Alcindor, $10,000 for the university graduate. We can safely guess that neither Alcindor nor the university student would have volunteered for army service at $2,500 or even $3,500 per year. The "real" cost to society of putting Alcindor and the university graduate in the army is the civilian production foregone—$110,000 for the

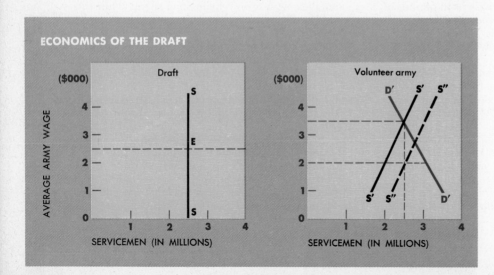

ECONOMICS OF THE DRAFT

Draft

Volunteer army

fig. 33–1a

With a drafted army of 2.5 million, Congress sets the wage and total government pay. For the same size volunteer army, annual army wage and total cost to the government would be determined by labor supply conditions (curve S'S' or S''S''), but total social cost would presumably be lower than with draft. Note that $2,200 with 2.5 million servicemen is not an equilibrium situation.

pair, not the $2,500 each paid draftees by the army.

But if Alcindor and the university man aren't drafted into the army, we still need 2.5 million men in uniform. Who puts on the uniform? The answer is that 2.5 million people are willing to volunteer for the army (in the assumed case) at the $3,500-per-year going rate. We can safely presume that these are people who would have made less, or certainly not very much more, in civilian life. Thus, the total civilian output foregone by having the men in the army is about $3,500 per man per year, possibly even less. In terms of overall economic efficiency, resources are best allocated by the voluntary service plan, leaving the choice up to each individual as to whether he prefers a $3,500 job in the army to what he can earn in civilian life. If the $S'S'$ curve supplying 2.5 million men at the $3,500 figure doesn't strike you as plausible, insert what seems to you a more realistic curve. The net real cost of the draft will change, but the basic argument will still hold.

There is a further efficiency argument in favor of the volunteer army. When men are drafted, they seldom stay in the army more than the required two years. If the army were on a volunteer basis, we can safely presume that more men would decide to undertake military careers, so the turnover in the armed services would be lower than it is with the draft. This would cut down the training costs involved.

Still a further reduction of real cost, which would not necessarily be reflected in the g.n.p. figures, would be the lower degree of uncertainty for everyone now potentially subject to the draft. He would go into the army if he wished, and the government would have to pay a high enough wage to be sure to induce the number of men in the army they need at that wage. If we accept the test of the market as measuring what all of us as consumers most want, it is clearly advantageous for Alcindor and the university graduate to sell their services in the private market, while young men who would otherwise be unemployed or work at menial jobs make up the army.[8]

(d) The draft is a study in economics, ethics, and politics. The economics are fairly straightforward, as outlined above. The ethical issues are complex. Many would object to a "voluntary" army on the grounds that it would end up being mainly low-income men, with a heavy representation of blacks. This is true, and in a period like that of the unpopular Vietnam War to many this would seem grossly inequitable. On the other hand, there are great inequities in the present draft situation. Note the marginal tax rates in

essence applied to Alcindor and the university graduate, and to anyone else who would have earned more in private life than he does in the army. It is far from obvious which way produces greater inequity.

For example, should we use a draft to preempt men for police, postal, and all other public-service duties, at a wage equal to that paid in the armed forces? Or, at a more extreme level, should we preempt workers through a draftlike plan to make steel and mine coal, rather than leaving it up to the private economy, where clearly firms have to pay more than army wage rates? A volunteer army would determine who serves by the same method as that by which labor is normally allocated to different industries in the United States.

(e) Strikingly, many Congressmen and administration officials in Washington have been reluctant to consider a volunteer paid army. The reason is more apparent if one looks at estimates of the real-world costs involved in switching the military services to a volunteer basis. Going back to 1964, before the Vietnam War raised so many special emotional issues, two economists made some very rough estimates of the costs involved. They are shown in Table 33–1A.

The table recognizes that one would have to raise military pay to get many of the enlisted men now in the army. We cannot assume that all present "volunteers" are really that; some are reluctant volunteers who enlist only because they fear the draft.

The table shows estimates separately for an economy of 5.5 percent and one of 4 percent unemployment. Of course it would take a higher level of military pay to obtain an all-volunteer army in a booming high-employment economy than in a 5.5 percent unemployment economy. Table 33–1A also provides rough estimates of the savings to the military services due to reduced turnover from going to an all-voluntary basis.

All things considered, the estimates suggest that the extra dollar costs to the government would be somewhere between $4 billion and $16 billion annually. In a reasonably prosperous economy, the "best" estimate made by the authors is an extra wage cost of about $8 billion for the all-volunteer army. Since both civilian and army pay have risen substantially since 1964, the year for which these estimates were made, the total cost figures probably ought to be increased by perhaps 50 percent for an army of the same size —2.65 million men.

These estimates are extremely rough, and their tentative nature is indicated by the wide variance between the low and high estimates. Still, they help explain why Congress, and politicians more generally, have been reluctant to plump for a volunteer army. In a period when taxes are already high and the federal budget is hovering near the deficit level, an added expenditure of $8 billion per year is not pleasant for Congress or the president to contemplate. This highly visible cost increase, plus the su-

---

[8]This of course presumes that all would give equally good service in the army. At the level of enlisted men, this may well be a good approximation; for officers, it's clear that high potential men do a better job than those with less ability and education, and in fact officer ranks are filled entirely on a volunteer basis.

table 33-1A*

**Estimated Increase in Payroll Costs Necessary to Obtain an
All-Volunteer Force of 2.65 Million****
(in Billions of Dollars)**

	5.5% Unemployment			4.0% Unemployment		
	Low	Best	High	Low	Best	High
Enlisted:						
Increase in active duty pay	$3.7	$5.4	$10.0	$5.6	$8.4	$16.5
Savings due to reduced turnover	−.3	−.4	−.5	−.4	−.5	−.7
Total enlisted	$3.4	$5.0	$ 9.5	$5.2	$7.9	$15.8
Officers increase in active duty pay***	$ .3	$ .4	$ .8	$ .3	$ .4	$ .8
Total officers and enlisted	$3.7	$5.4	$10.3	$5.5	$8.3	$16.6

*From S. Altman and A. Fechter, "The Supply of Military Personnel in the Absence of the Draft," *American Economic Review*, May, 1967, p. 30.
**Active duty pay estimates include increased retirement benefits. Estimates are for 1964.
***Savings due to reduced turnover assumed to be negligible for officers.

perficial impression of inequitable treatment to the poor and the minority groups in particular, make a volunteer draft a political hot potato. Moreover, the volunteer army would require a large income redistribution to young (draft-age) men from older taxpayers. Although the real economic cost of the present draft to society is certainly far in excess of the money cost to the federal government, the potential benefits of a volunteer army are largely invisible to the politician and the man in the street, though they are, hopefully, visible to you as a budding economist.

It is no accident that many economists support a volunteer army, while fewer politicians appear to do so.

(f) Few economists argue that we could manage with a voluntary army for a major war. At that point, the armed services become so large relative to the rest of the economy, and the risks of battlefield duty so high, that some form of draft seems the only practical alternative. This parallels the argument that in a war period, when the whole economy is on a war basis, it may be useful to ration some commodities (for example, bread and other necessities) and hold down their prices by law. Some economists would argue in favor of free market allocation of resources even in a war period, as economically most efficient. But in war the main job is to win the war, and adequate armed services plus war materiel understandably get top priority, even at the cost of, in principle, economic inefficiency.

thirty-four

Unions, Collective Bargaining, and Public Policy

Labor unions loom large on the current American scene. On the economic front, they exercise great pressures on wages, hours, and working conditions. They are behind the worker in his differences with the foreman, the day-to-day arguments that seldom reach the public's eye. Politically, their voice is heard in the selection of candidates, and their votes are felt in elections—usually on the Democratic side. Their lobbyists are among the most effective in Washington and the state capitals, and it is a secure congressman indeed who can afford to disregard what organized labor thinks.

Important as unions are, it is also easy to overrate their importance. Unions do indeed influence wages and hours. But supply and demand still set a confining framework for labor–management negotiations. Although the combined A.F.L.-C.I.O. loosely joins many unions, the member groups are still separate unions, often disputing among themselves. Less than one-third of all workers are unionized, and union membership has grown very little in recent years although the labor force has expanded steadily. Throughout the services, agriculture, and clerical and professional areas, unions have little hold. Whether they will become powerful in the public sector remains to be seen. Politically, the divisions within organized labor weaken the power it can exercise, and since World War II, labor has gone down to defeat on some of its most bitterly fought issues—notably the passage of the Taft–Hartley Act.

To understand organized labor's position, we

493

must remember history. With the present powers of big unions, it may be hard for you to realize that only forty years ago unions were hanging on by the skin of their teeth, with an active membership of only 3 million workers and little or no recognition in the great mass-production industries of the country; union leaders were tarred and feathered, heads were broken. But older union members and their leaders know it well. And that memory, though fading, colors union behavior today.

History of American Unionism[1]

The foundations of labor unionism in America lay in the skilled crafts during the early 1800s. In scattered localities, craftsmen banded together, in spite of public antagonism, bitter employer resistance, and susceptibility to prosecution as criminal conspirators. Their goals were direct—to cut the working day from twelve to ten hours, to obtain more tolerable working conditions, and to seek higher wages. But it was not until the 1870s that the first loose nationwide labor association appeared. This was the Knights of Labor, founded as a secret society (to avoid employer's reprisals against members). When the Knights foundered on dissension a decade later, the American Federation of Labor collected the stronger, skilled-craft elements and became the first effective national union organization. Under the leadership (from 1886 to 1924) of Samuel Gompers, a remarkable figure in American labor history, the federation became a significant force, with an outspoken philosophy of "practical" unionism. Gompers reflected the spirit of the times in organized labor—"Get more, now." Only this pragmatic, typically American attitude began to win a little grudging acceptance for unionism from employers and the public at large.

But it was Franklin Roosevelt and the New Deal that gave unions their place in modern industrial society. Depression was everywhere —massive unemployment, low wages, low pur-

chasing power. Higher wages and higher prices to promote recovery were cornerstones of the New Deal. The National Industrial Recovery Act for the first time gave workers the right to organize and bargain collectively with employers. Union organizers went to work and membership picked up fast, although N.I.R.A. was soon declared unconstitutional. The Wagner Act of 1935, passed soon thereafter, became the foundation of modern union powers. It spelled out workers' rights vis-à-vis employers, put teeth in the unions' powers to bargain collectively, and forbade prevalent employer anti-union practices. Unions were guaranteed recognition if they won a majority vote among the workers.

The labor history of the middle 1930s was stormy. The newly formed C.I.O., with the fiery John L. Lewis as its first president, opened big organization drives—violent, spectacular, and successful. Open defiance of management rather than workers' traditional subservience was the tone. The famous sit-down strikes, when the unions seized possession of the major auto plants, rocked the companies and the public. But in the bloodshed and bitterness that ensued, the unions won recognition time after time—with the open support of the Roosevelt administration and local Democratic government officials. The Who's Who of American industry fell to C.I.O. organizing drives one by one—U.S. and Bethlehem Steel, General Motors, General Electric, Goodyear, and so on down the list. By 1940, union membership had more than doubled, to about 10 million. By 1945 it was nearly 15 million, about one-third of the nonagricultural labor force.

Public sympathy during the 1930s was by and large prolabor, though many friends were lost by the violent sit-down strikes. But strong union wage demands during World War II, interunion jurisdictional quarrels and strikes, and open defiance of the federal government by a few leaders convinced the bulk of the public that organized labor's power had gone too far. In 1947 Congress passed the Taft–Hartley Act, restricting the powers of unions and restoring some rights that employers had lost during the preceding decade. And the years since World

[1]For a good account, see U.S. Labor Department, *Brief History of the American Labor Department* (Washington, D.C.: U.S. Government Printing Office, 1964).

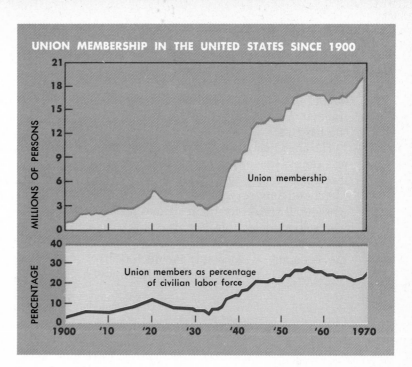

UNION MEMBERSHIP IN THE UNITED STATES SINCE 1900

fig. 34–1

The big growth period for unions was during the 1930s and 1940s. Since then, union membership has declined somewhat as a percentage of the civilian labor force. (Sources: National Bureau of Economic Research and U.S. Department of Labor.)

War II have seen a definite leveling of union power, with widespread public disapproval of gangsterism, jurisdictional disputes, and intraunion squabbles which made the headlines intermittently.

Figure 34–1 shows the picture. Union membership (excluding Canada) rose above 17 million in the mid-1950s, but then declined. Unions have made slow headway with white-collar workers and employees of the rapidly growing service industries. The bottom half of the chart shows the union problem more strongly. Union membership as a percentage of total nonagricultural labor force hit a peak of 33 percent in 1963, and has declined since to a level well below 30 percent. Union membership as a percentage of the total civilian labor force (shown in Figure 34–1) is of course still lower.

In 1955, the "merger" of the A.F.L. and the C.I.O. into one loose organization (the A.F.L.-C.I.O.) marked a major step toward a united labor movement. But interunion rivalries have kept the new organization from acting as an effective unit, economically or politically. Neither the United Auto Workers, nor the Teamsters, nor the United Mine Workers now participate. Jurisdictional disputes have been a persistent source of quarrels, and the member unions have been unwilling to give enough power to the combined organization to make it effective. The house of union labor, though over

16 million workers strong, shows bad cracks in its walls, and many observers believe they are getting wider.

Moreover, the unions face a new problem. The average union member has a good job, and often a house in the suburbs. He is one of the big middle-income class, well above the insecurity and poverty which threatened during the 1930s. He wants more pay, longer vacations, better fringe benefits. But the old class solidarity which once united workers against the capitalist employers is gone. There is an increasing gap between the goals of young union members and the militancy which motivated the now-aging leaders. Some describe the modern scene as "mailorder unionism." The members turn over their dues and want higher wages and other benefits delivered by union officials in exchange. Otherwise, many younger members feel little sense of belonging to the union as an organization. Different paths for the American union movement lie ahead. But militant union pressures for more **economic** benefits may be great, in both private and public sectors.

Union Wage Policy

From one point of view, a union is merely a monopoly that sells the labor services of its members. Neglecting for the moment all the other things that unions do, how effective is a union in raising wages under different circumstances? And how does the public come out in the bargain?

The analytical models of the last chapter give us a simple framework for examining the problem. Let us first assume that the union is a completely effective organization in controlling its workers. It speaks for them all, and it need not worry about defections from the ranks. Assume also for the moment that aggregate spending in the economy is constant, unaffected by the behavior of individual unions and employers.

Competition

First, consider the case where employers are highly competitive with one another both in selling products and in hiring workers. For example, suppose we look at unorganized retail clerks or restaurant waiters in an area where there are lots of stores and restaurants, so substantially perfect competition prevails in both labor and product markets. Here, in the long run, all economic profits will tend to be eliminated. Price will be forced down to about the minimum average cost at which each product can be produced. From the labor side, wages will be roughly equal to the marginal revenue productivity of each class of labor hired.

Suppose now that a union comes in and organizes all clerks and waiters in the area. It demands a wage increase and gets it. This raises costs, and forces up prices. At the higher prices, consumers will buy fewer restaurant meals and other retail products (assuming that aggregate income and spending are constant). With less output, there are fewer jobs for clerks and waiters as a result of the higher wages, though how many less will depend on the elasticity of demand for the products. This is the classic case in which union wage demands lead to fewer jobs for union members. In a highly competitive industry, there isn't much unions can do to push up wages without reducing employment in the long run (unless aggregate spending is somehow increased). The workers who keep their jobs have higher incomes, but those laid off bear the brunt. And it becomes harder for new job-seekers to find work in the industry.

Monopoly and Partial Monopoly

Second, consider the case where there is monopoly or monopolistic competition in selling products, but still active competition among firms for workers. Suppose, for example, there are only a dozen or so restaurants or stores in the area, or at the extreme only one. Can the new union now force the stores to pay higher wages without reducing the number of jobs? Our theory tells us, probably not. If the firms are maximizing profits before the union, they will be hiring workers up to the point where the wage equals the workers' marginal revenue product. If the union raises wages, it will, logically, pay employers to cut back on the number of workers hired and to raise price; the new maximum-profit output will be smaller than before. Again, logically, the union can obtain higher wages only at the cost of less employment.

But partial monopolists—especially oligopolists—often aren't maximizing profits in the precise sense above. Oligopoly is the world of live-and-let-live, of price leadership, of partially protected markets. Under these conditions, the effect of a wage increase on prices and employment is far harder to predict. Theory gives no clear-cut answer. Since prices are set by the leader on the basis of many tenuous variables, it is hard to tell when a wage increase will lead to a change in product price—and if it does, how much. If firms have a protected profit position, this special profit provides a melon over which the union and management can bargain, and higher wages need have no effect on either product price or output and employment. In oligopolies where firms behave as if they faced kinked demand curves, the union may have a considerable range over which it can force up wages without inducing higher prices and reduced employment. But wherever the union makes substantially the same bargain for all major firms in the industry, the facts will be obvious to all and all firms are likely to expect an increase by the price leader. Where this is true, the union thus faces much the same likely result on employment and prices as with a single monopoly firm; higher wages for union members will generally mean at least some reduction in the number of jobs available.

Monopsony and Bilateral Oligopoly

Consider now a different case, where workers are being "exploited" through a wage less than their marginal revenue productivity. For example, imagine an isolated mining town where there are few jobs outside the mines. The one mining company doesn't have to pay workers their full marginal product to get all the labor it wants. Now a union organizes the workers and demands a higher wage. What is the result?

Here in principle the union can push the wage up without decreasing employment.[2] Here the bargaining theory of wages applies. The employer is making a special profit by exploiting the workers and theoretically the union can grab this sum back for the workers. But the employer isn't going to be enthusiastic about turning his profits over to the workers. He'll fight to keep wages down. Where this struggle comes out is indeterminate so far as economic theory is concerned. To guess who will win, look at the relative bargaining power of employer and union. How big is the union strike fund? How adept are both parties around the bargaining table? How badly does the employer want to get his customers' orders out on time? Certainly the workers are better off with than without the union, though it is impossible to say by just how much. In cases like this, a monopoly union faces a monopsony employer, or perhaps a few big unions face a few big employers. The latter case might be called bilateral oligopoly.

Union Wages and Capital Substitution

The short-run effect of union wage pressures on the number of jobs in an industry is often hard to predict accurately. But a longer-range effect is highly predictable. Higher labor costs will lead businessmen to invest in labor-saving machinery more rapidly than they would with lower wages. It will pay to shift to coal-mining machinery to replace miners as hourly wages rise, to install mechanical dishwashers in restaurants, to replace farm laborers by automatic vegetable pickers. Higher union wages speeding "automation" clearly change the capital–labor ratio in the industries affected. But as was noted at the end of Chapter 33, remember that this need not mean unemployment for the economy as a whole. Don't fall into the trap of the fallacy of composition.

Do Unions Really Raise Wages?

This may sound like a silly question. Everyone has read of many cases where union demands for higher wages have finally been granted by employers. But such instances don't really answer the question. Maybe supply and demand would have produced the same raises in the market without any union. Don't forget the fallacy of *post hoc, propter hoc.*

Although any union man and most employers will tell you that of course unions raise wages, the dispassionate objective evidence is less clear. One careful study estimates that unions raised wages of their members by about 25 percent relative to nonunion workers in 1933 at the bottom of the depression (reflecting temporary union resistance to wage cuts), by about 5 percent in the inflationary boom of the late 1940s when all wages were bid up rapidly, and by 10–15 percent during the 1950s.[3] Another concludes that in perhaps one-third of all cases unions have raised wages by 15–20 percent; in another third by perhaps 5–10 percent; in the other third not at all.[4] The unions' effects are greatest when market demand is weak. In prosperous periods of strong demand, market forces pull up nonunion wages about as fast as, or even faster than, those of union members, whose wages are often governed by three-year contracts.

Note a commonly cited but unconvincing bit of evidence, that union wages are by and large higher than nonunion ones. But many union-

[2]In fact, the union theoretically might *increase* employment by eliminating exploitation. Without the union, the employer bargains wages down and gets as many workers as possible at his low wage. With a union, he must pay the going wage and he can get as many workers as he wants at that wage. Thus he hires workers up to the point where the wage equals their marginal revenue productivity; there is no longer any incentive to restrict output and employment to get the advantage of low wages.

[3]H. G. Lewis, *Unionism and Relative Wages in the United States* (Chicago: University of Chicago Press, 1963), p. 193.
[4]A. Rees, *Wage Inflation* (New York: National Industrial Conference Board, 1957), p. 27.

ized industries have been high-wage industries anyhow, even before they were unionized—big companies with lots of skilled workmen. One other interesting piece of evidence is that labor's share in the national income has increased somewhat since the 1920s, before the big modern union increase. But the shift is not enough to provide clear evidence that unions have raised the aggregate wage share.

Fringe Benefits

Increasingly, unions have coupled their wage demands with pressures for "fringe benefits"—paid vacations, pensions, health insurance, and a dozen other such benefits. All these cost the companies money. They all have to come out of somebody's pocketbook. In this sense, they all are, in effect, wage increases, though the worker takes his pay in special forms rather than directly.

Two issues are at stake here. First, should the workers get more pay, and what will be the impact of the higher costs in any given situation? Second, should the higher pay be in the form of fringe benefits? For example, should workers be allowed (or forced) to take part of their pay in health and old-age benefits? A lot of people think so, and both union contracts and the federal social security system require employers to pay part of total wages in this form. But make up your own mind. The benefits may look very different to young and old workers. One rough estimate is that fringe benefits now account for over 15 percent of the national wage bill; this would be around $75 billion annually. In manufacturing industries, fringe benefits in 1970 exceeded 70 cents per hour on an average hourly wage of about $3.40.

Collective Bargaining and Labor–Management Relations

The big wage negotiations and strikes always make the headlines and news broadcasts. But the great bulk of union–management collective bargaining and negotiation goes on unheralded behind the scenes. After a union contract is signed, the day-to-day relations of the foreman and his workers take over. Wage rates have to be set for individual jobs; broad contract wage provisions must be translated into elaborate wage structures in large firms. Decisions must be made as to which jobs are on a flat hourly pay basis and which "on incentive" where the pay depends on the number of units turned out. In the latter case, standard base rates must be established for "normal" output, above which bonuses are paid. Times and rates need to be established for new work. Arrangements have to be agreed on for handling the introduction of new machinery and new methods. Wrangles between foremen and individual workers have to be adjudicated. A thousand and one problems arise in a big plant that involve disputes between labor and management.

In these disputes, the union steward is the worker's first line of protection and negotiation, just as the foreman is management's. Good feeling and cooperation between foremen and stewards can do more for effective union–management relations than almost any amount of fine top-level policymaking. Bad relations between stewards and foremen can block any good intentions at top levels. Down in the plant is where the work gets done and where most of the disputes arise, except for the major wage and hour negotiations at contract-expiration dates.

Some union–management agreements provide elaborate machinery for handling worker–management disputes that can't be settled by the foreman and the worker. These often culminate in calling on an impartial arbitrator, paid jointly by union and management, whose decision is final on disputed issues under the contract. Other contracts set up other procedures. There is no point in trying to describe the vast variety of them. The main point is that they try to set up a body of rules under which workers and management can minimize friction and disagreement. The contract is something like the rules of law under which we operate our democratic system. This procedure has gone far toward creating stability and order in employee–management relations in thousands of industrial plants. But in industrial as in political democracy, the rules alone can't make the system work. They only provide a framework within which men of reasonable goodwill, with a reasonable agreement on common objectives, can live and work peaceably together.[5]

Union and Management Motivation in Bargaining

You don't need a course in economics to tell you the main reason why unions fight for higher wages. The members want more pay! But some other things aren't so easy to explain.

The thing that seems to amaze people most is that unions will strike for an extra few cents an hour pay, when third-grade arithmetic will show that it would take months or even years at the extra rate to make up for the pay lost in a long strike. Why are the union leaders willing to keep the men out over a few dollars? The same question can be asked the other way around, too. Why doesn't the company give in and end the divisive strike?

Try putting yourself in the worker's shoes. What would you think? You'd think: "That so-and-so who runs the company! He gets a big salary and has everything. His plushy stockholders are getting big dividends. Yet we have to scrape along on pay that just keeps the wolf away from the door. He won't even give us a couple of cents extra when he could save himself profits by doing it instead of trying to break this strike. We'll fight it out and lick him yet!"

Now turn around and see how you'd feel as the employer. You see the generous wages your

company is already paying. You see the workers stubbornly holding out for unreasonable demands. You may see the union leaders as self-seeking hypocrites, out to protect their own jobs. The whole business is just one more step in the union's attempt to dictate to management and to encroach on management prerogatives. Would you give in if you were the employer?

Now put yourself in the union president's shoes. You're probably sincerely out to do the best you can for your membership. You know that your best bet in the long run lies in getting along with management. But you also know that there's never enough money to go around, and that you're going to have to push hard to get the wages your members are (in your eyes) honestly entitled to. You know a strike is costly to everybody, but you know too that a threat often repeated but never carried out loses its force. And you don't quite trust the employer and his personnel men, even though by and large they're pretty decent people. You suspect that down underneath that surface friendliness they'd be delighted to see the unions go, and to return to the old preunion days when the employer told the workers to do what he said—or else!

You know some more things too. You know that unless you produce for your members, you're likely to be just an ex-president. If other unions have been getting 20 cents an hour plus fringe benefits, you've got to get about that much too, or you're going to have some disgruntled members. You know that your chance of rising in the union ranks, say to a position in the international, depends in part on your success in getting more than other unions do. You know that too much peace with the employer, even though it pays off handsomely in dollars and cents for your members, is going to be interpreted by some members as "selling out." As you sit across the bargaining table from management, with tempers frayed by a long strike, would you give in?

The issues at stake in a labor negotiation are seldom simple. Human motives are strong and complex. The quarrel that the public sees in the newspapers is often only part of the real issue. The fine speeches made by both sides—about the need for wage increases to prevent depres-

[5]One source of controversy between unions and management is the "union shop" and "right-to-work" laws. Under a union-shop agreement, everyone who works in the firm covered must join the union. The union's big argument for this arrangement is that if workers get all the benefits of union activities (higher wages, better working conditions, and so on), they should have to pay dues and bear their share of the union costs. Otherwise they get a "free ride," which makes no more sense than permitting a citizen to benefit from government but decide for himself that he won't pay taxes.

The counterargument says that union shops take away the individual worker's right to work without joining a union, and that this abrogates an important individual freedom. Make up your own mind. The union shop is legal under federal law but prohibited in a number of southern and western states which have enacted state "right-to-work" laws. Such right-to-work laws are fought bitterly by the unions.

sion, or the need to maintain a progressive free-enterprise system through large capital expenditures out of earnings—sound good on the news broadcasts but often have little to do with settling the dispute at the bargaining table. To look at the issue in terms of a simple dollars-and-cents comparison is naïve. There are few more complex jobs of compromise and good human relations than labor–management negotiations. The issues are real, and no purpose is served by pretending that nothing but common interest is involved. Unfortunately, there is seldom a clear, objective right-or-wrong answer.

The Changing Role of Strikes

Collective bargaining is a process of challenge and response. It includes innumerable variations as individual companies and unions shape it to fit their needs. For the most part it settles the disputes between employers and unions. But sometimes they can't, or won't, reach agreement. Tempers fray. Bitterness grows. Finally the union goes out on strike.

Strikes are rare events. With over 150,000 collective bargaining contracts in force, strikes over the last five years have caused a loss of less than ¼ of 1 percent of the total working time involved. Table 34–1 shows the record since

1935. Time lost exceeded ¾ of 1 percent in only one year—1947.[6]

Moreover, most of today's strikes are orderly and nonviolent, in sharp contrast to the bitter, bloody battles of thirty years ago. Strikes now arise largely over renewal of contracts and most often involve wage and work rule arguments, far less-explosive issues than the life-or-death organizing conflicts of the 1930s. Arbitration is now largely used to settle disputes that arise during the life of the contract. International officers generally try to help avoid or settle "wildcat" strikes, in which local unions strike in contravention of contract arrangements.

Thus, conflict resolution between labor and management has been moved increasingly to an orderly, peaceful procedural basis. But conflicts do persist, and the strike remains organized labor's weapon of last resort to enforce its views. Sometimes big strikes are enormously disruptive—for example, a long steel or public utility strike. But many labor observers feel that an occasional strike in most industries does no great harm and indeed may be a useful incident

[6]A Department of Labor study shows that higher wages were the main issue behind 44 percent of all strikes between 1964 and 1968; work rules or conditions, 15 percent; union recognition or union shop, 13 percent; and union jurisdictional differences, 11 percent.

---

table 34-1

Time Lost in Strikes, 1935-1969*

Period	Number of Strikes (Annual Average)	Workers Involved (Annual Average) (In Thousands)	Percentage of Working Time Lost
1935-39	2,862	1,130	0.27
1940-44	3,754	1,386	.16
1945-50	4,210	2,940	.61
1951-55	4,540	2,510	.31
1956-60	3,602	1,620	.29
1961-65	3,560	1,365	.14
1966	4,405	1,960	.15
1967	4,597	2,870	.25
1968	4,701	2,294	.22

* Data from U.S. Department of Labor.

in the continuing bargaining relationship between labor and management. A strike is a device for letting off steam, for reasserting bargaining powers. It is not necessarily a symbol of the failure of collective bargaining. Thus, few labor experts favor laws to outlaw strikes, except possibly strikes that clearly threaten the public interest. For to outlaw strikes would not resolve conflicts but merely force them into other channels. The main operational goal now is to further moderate conflict and contain it in orderly channels, looking toward a heightened sense of management and labor responsibility upon which ultimate peaceful working relationships must rest.

Union Power and Union Policies

Until a few years ago the above assessment seemed reasonably secure, and it is probably still accurate. But increasing violence over the past decade—in ghettos, on campuses, in business areas—has raised serious questions about the strength of democratic procedures of reason and negotiation in settling major social issues. Resort to sheer power and physical force in lieu of persuasion has spread from activist blacks and student radicals to other groups. Teachers, garbage collectors, and postal employees in New York openly defy the antistrike laws in order to force their demands on city and national officials, Congress, and the public. Hijackers use guns to divert planes to Cuba. Bombs explode in corporation offices to protest against "the establishment."

For the most part, unions as institutions and their members as individuals have avoided such tactics and have supported established labor–management conflict-resolution procedures. But many a union places self-interest above the national goal of stable prices when the government pleads for noninflationary wage settlements. And as resort to power tactics spreads in society, understandably union members turn to tough bargaining attitudes and strikes to get their wage demands when they see pressure tactics working for other groups. The public and quasi-public sectors, where strikes have long been illegal, pose special problems. Teachers, municipal employees, postmen, firemen,

bus drivers, airport controllers, and the like have begun to openly defy the antistrike laws. Clearly the status of public-employee unions remains to be defined, by law and practice, much as private-sector unions needed to develop an accepted set of practices during the 1930s, forties, and fifties. The comfortable middle-class status of most private-sector union members make them an unlikely bet for resort to radical, violent tactics. And their thrust must be toward generally conservative white-collar and service workers if they are to expand their membership significantly. But low-income service groups often present demands that seem reasonable to the public as well as to themselves in an affluent society. Public-sector laws will be enforceable only as long as they command general public support.

The paths to solution of social disputes over the decade ahead are uncertain. We cannot be sure that return to use of sheer power per se will not mark union tactics if rejection of reasoned discussion and negotiation continues to spread. In any event, reconsideration of the employer–employee power balance in the public sector seems certain to be a major issue over the next decade.

Government and Labor

Many labor–management disputes are now a test of strength between equals—sometimes equals of prodigious strength. When Leonard Woodcock sits down to bargain for the United Auto Workers, he speaks for a million men. Not millions, but billions of dollars are at stake in these bargains; not only wages, but also the pensions of tomorrow's retired families, workers' sickness insurance, their working hours, the vacations they take. In every election, the support of organized labor is eagerly sought. Labor lobbies in Washington and the state capitols are powerful and well organized. A nationwide Teamsters strike could bring the economy to a grinding halt in a matter of days. In local areas, small groups of union workers can achieve comparable results, especially in public-utility services. Many others can gravely disrupt economic activity and bring massive inconvenience through long strikes.

Great power is wielded by labor unions and their leaders. Is this power excessive? Many businessmen say "yes"; they stress that there are no antitrust laws to limit union power. When union rank and file, for example, in trucking, openly defied regularly negotiated wage agreements in the early 1970s to demand, and obtain, highly inflationary wage increases, this viewpoint gained support. Most laborers say "no." Do we need more stringent laws to limit union powers? Should government intervene when disruptive strikes occur, or when wage–price settlements threaten the government's own stable economic growth policies? If so, how? Labor–management relations have lots of unanswered questions.

Major Legislation

The Norris–La Guardia Act of 1932 was the first major national prolabor legislation. Employers had long been able to get court injunctions against labor groups to prohibit just about anything—for example, striking or picketing. Once the injunction was obtained, labor was the wrongdoer in the eyes of the law. Norris–La Guardia outlawed the injunction in federal courts as an employer weapon against a wide variety of union activities—strikes, joining a union, peaceful picketing, or giving financial aid to unions. The intent of the law was clear. It was to give unions support in achieving a more equal bargaining status with employers, and to eliminate one of the most powerful and misused employer weapons.

The New Deal, a year later, was frankly and aggressively prolabor. The National Industrial Recovery Act stated the legal right of the workers to organize and bargain collectively. But the N.I.R.A. was short-lived; it was declared unconstitutional in 1935. Congress wasted no time in replacing its labor provisions.

The Wagner Act. The National Labor Relations Act (the "Wagner Act"), passed in 1935, is the cornerstone of modern prolabor legislation. The Act:

1. Affirmed the legal right of employees to organize and bargain collectively, free from employer interference or coercion.

2. Required employers to bargain with unions of the workers' own free choosing.

3. Specifically prohibited a list of "unfair" employer practices.

4. Set up the National Labor Relations Board to provide a mechanism through which workers could gain recognition for unions of their own choosing, and to act as a quasi court to protect workers against unfair labor practices. (The N.L.R.B. does not act directly to mediate or settle labor–management disputes.) Employer intimidation, antiunion discrimination in hiring and firing, company attempts to influence union elections, and a variety of other practices were soon outlawed as unfair practices as N.L.R.B. and court decisions interpreted the new law.

By the early 1940s, the bitterest union organizing struggles were over, and industrial unionism in the mass-production industries was firmly entrenched. In the courts, labor also fared better. The Supreme Court, reflecting the changing temper of the times and the presence of several Roosevelt-appointed judges, in the *Apex* and *Hutcheson* cases (1940 and 1941) reversed a long line of judicial precedent and granted unions virtual immunity from the Sherman Act, though in the *Allen Bradley* case of 1945 an exception was made where they conspired with employers to fix prices or divide markets.

Public policy toward labor under the Wagner Act thus represents a 180 degree turn from public policy toward business combinations under the Sherman Act. The Wagner Act encourages workers to combine in unions in order to raise the prices at which they sell their labor, precisely the practice forbidden to business sellers by the Sherman Act. Should public policy face one way in labor markets and the other in commodity markets? Now is a good time to stop and ask yourself.

Fair Labor Standards Act of 1938. The Wagner Act was aimed at strengthening organized labor's power to deal with employers. The federal Fair Labor Standards Act of 1938 established minimum wages, maximum basic hours, and other fair labor standards for all labor in interstate commerce.

The core of F.L.S.A. was its mandatory-minimum-wage and maximum-basic-hours provisions. No covered employer could pay less than twenty-five cents an hour. A basic work-week of forty hours was established; employees could be worked longer, but overtime work required a higher pay rate. Other fair labor standards were spelled out, notably the first federal prohibition of child labor. F.L.S.A. has been periodically amended since 1938, both to widen the coverage and to raise the minimum wage ($1.85 in 1970).

The Taft–Hartley Act. Many called the Wagner Act labor's Magna Charta. All through the 1930s and in World War II, labor rode high. But the pendulum had swung too far. More and more middle-of-the-roaders began to feel that labor had overstepped its bounds; first in the sit-down strikes of the 1930s; then in the spreading jurisdictional disputes and strikes that the public and employers seemed powerless to halt; in its persistent wage demands during the World War II fight against inflation; and lastly, in its outright defiance of the federal government itself in disputes of critical importance to the national economy. The Taft–Hartley Act was passed, over President Truman's veto, in 1947, as an attempt to redress the balance of power between management and labor. Taft–Hartley defined unfair labor practices of unions to parallel those of employers. It clarified the powers of employers to speak against unions, so long as their pronouncement contained no threats or intimidations; and it prohibited the closed shop. It contained provisions to protect the individual worker against the union; unions may not coerce workers to join, disclosure of union financial affairs is required, and nonpayment of dues is the only ground on which a union can force discharge of a worker under union-shop contract. It permitted states to prohibit union-shop contracts. Last, it empowered the president under conditions of national emergency to petition a federal court for an injunction against any strike or lockout for an eighty-day cooling-off period, and required a secret union ballot on the latest company offer before the end of that period.

The Landrum–Griffin Act. By 1959, labor racketeering had become a national scandal, and Congress passed the Landrum–Griffin Act, again over the violent objections of union leaders. Nearly everyone agreed that the law was unnecessary to regulate many American unions, which are open and law-abiding organizations. But nonetheless, there was no resisting the public pressure generated by congressional committee disclosures of labor malpractices. Landrum–Griffin included a new "bill of rights" for individual union members, requirements for more detailed financial reporting by unions of all transactions with officials and members, a provision tightening restrictions on secondary boycotts and organizational picketing, a requirement for secret-ballot elections and limitations for the term of office of labor officials between elections, and a prohibition against any person who has been convicted of a felony or who has been a member of the Communist party serving as a union official for at least five years after conviction.[7]

Broadly speaking, strikes by government employees are illegal. The status of workers in quasi-public enterprises, like local transit systems and public utilities, is less clear, but generally similar. With few exceptions, no real procedures are established by law to resolve disputes between such employees and their employers. Public workers just aren't supposed to strike, even when they feel they aren't getting paid enough or treated right.

Recent events have highlighted this unsatisfactory state of affairs. Revised legislation seems certain, its details most unclear.

Labor and the Antitrust Laws

Unions are substantially exempt from the antitrust laws, except as they may collude with

[7]For a fuller account of the changing legal foundations of unions and collective bargaining, see L. G. Reynolds, *Labor Economics and Labor Relations* (Englewood Cliffs, N.J.: Prentice-Hall, Inc., 1969), Chap. 5.

employers to restrict output or fix prices. The Wagner Act put the National Labor Relations Board in the position of granting official patents of monopoly to the unions it certified as exclusive bargaining agents. Most businessmen, and many economists who believe in the efficacy of competitive markets, believe that the antitrust laws should, at least in part, be applied to unions as well as businesses.

But the difficulties are formidable. The essence of a union is to be a monopoly; unless it has exclusive power to borrow for its members it has little market power. One proposal is to forbid industry-wide bargaining, just as firms may not collude to fix prices and output. Union supporters retort that this would *de facto* emasculate unions, moving back to the old relationships where all the power was on the employer's side. Another approach would forbid union pressures on employers to restrict output and union "featherbedding" (for example, by work rules that prohibit use of paint sprays in place of brushes). But such distinctions have proven very hard to draw and enforce. Only legal reforms that command widespread public support have much chance of enactment and enforcement on such emotionally charged issues. And such widespread public support is hard to mobilize when the issue seems to be the working man against business, even where indirectly the ultimate consumer pays the bill.[8]

At bottom, the issue is one of union power versus employer power, and not infrequently versus the government. The massive construction workers' and teamsters' wage increases of 1970, supported by threats and local strikes to shut down the flow of goods, and widespread illegal public-employees strikes raised head-on the issue of whether collective bargaining can work acceptably in a high-employment, democratic society. Increased public demands for direct governmental wage and price controls, and

for reconsideration of union powers granted by the Wagner Act, seem probable in the decade ahead.

Mediation, Conciliation, and Arbitration

Often a skillful third party can soothe hot tempers and help get labor and management together when they are negotiating a contract or settling a grievance. The federal government and most state governments provide "mediators" and "conciliators" who serve as impartial go-betweens in trying to get disputes settled without resort to strikes. Sometimes these men enter at the request of labor and management; sometimes they are sent by public officials who want to be sure that work stoppages are avoided. Their work is generally unheralded and unspectacular, but it is successful in a great number of cases. To watch a skilled mediator at work is an intriguing experience. He has no power to force his views on either party. He must bring them together by winning their confidence, isolating the issues at stake, and somehow making each see the reasonableness of the other's position—as well as reminding both frequently of the public's interest in avoiding work stoppages.

Although governments frequently send in a mediator or conciliator, they have no general authority to act as "arbitrator" with power to prescribe settlement terms in labor disputes (except in the case of the railways). Nevertheless, as chief executive, the president has frequently stepped into disputes that vitally affect the national welfare, has appointed "fact-finding boards," and in effect has brought into play the full pressure of public opinion behind the settlement recommended. At the local level, governors and mayors often follow similar procedures.

The Government as Watchdog and Wage-setter

Congress has long been quick to investigate labor–management affairs. Labor racketeering and the wage-price spiral have been favorite subjects. Some investigations have been sober and careful. Others have focused mainly on the

---

[8]For economic surveys of the antitrust laws in relation to unions, see G. Hildebrand, "Collective Bargaining and the Antitrust Laws," in J. Shister, B. Aaron, and C. Summers, eds., *Public Policy and Collective Bargaining* (New York: Harper & Row, Publishers, 1962); and F. Machlup, *The Political Economy of Monopoly: Business, Labor, and Government* (Baltimore: The Johns Hopkins Press, 1952), pp. 339–417.

headlines. But either variety exerts a strong pressure on both labor and management to be prepared to defend in public the actions they take. The McClellan Committee of the late 1950s, for example, played a major role in exposing gangsterism, bribery, and hoodlumism in the affairs and practices of some unions.

But the bigger issues arise around disruptions of the national economy. Suppose a nationwide steel strike is in progress. The union, pointing to rising living costs, high profits, increasing productivity, and a sweeping variety of other considerations, argues that fifty cents an hour more in pay and fringe benefits is the lowest raise it will even consider. Management in the steel industry's Big Six say they won't offer a penny more than twenty cents. They say that profits are down, that capacity is up enormously and foreign competition is murderous, that steel wages have risen faster than prices, and that steelworkers are already among the best-paid workers in the nation. After long months of bickering back and forth with no progress, the union calls a strike. The strike has gone on now for two long months, and the steel shortage is shutting down not only civilian production but also arms production and construction of missile and other military facilities. If you were president, what would you do?

You might say, let the strike go on. It's none of the government's business. But with the economy grinding to a halt and critical defense needs, you probably wouldn't.

You might invoke the national-emergency provision of the Taft–Hartley Act. This probably would get the union back to work and would give you eighty days to bring all the pressure you could on both sides to settle their differences. You'd get your top assistants on the job, and focus as much public pressure as you could on the negotiators. If you felt strongly that right was mainly on one side or the other, you might tell the American people so and build up pressure on the other side to capitulate. But your position is especially tough if you're also worried about inflation, so you don't want to see a settlement that leads the companies to raise steel prices.

The power of the federal government is great, and chances are that this kind of pressure would bring some kind of settlement, hopefully noninflationary. No private business or union wants to fight the government. The odds are stacked in favor of the president. But . . . suppose this time neither the companies nor the union will give in. So the workers go out on strike again at the end of eighty days, more bitter than ever. What then?

Then is the tough time. By now tempers are really frayed. Labor and management have been over the issues *ad nauseam*. Each has been provoked into saying a lot of things better left unsaid. Everybody's dirty linen has been thoroughly aired before 200 million Americans.

You might decide to seize the steel industry and ask the workers to stay on the job. But this means seizing a vast, privately owned industry, against all the traditions of American freedom and probably against the Constitution. Or you might order the workers to stay on the job, in the interests of the public welfare. But you know perfectly well you can't make men make steel, either under the law or any other way, if they just won't go back to work and do it.

Well, what would you do?

This is an extreme example. But it dramatizes a problem that has arisen repeatedly in the last quarter century. Consider the government's continuing attempt to check wage–price inflation since the Korean War. The Eisenhower, Kennedy, Johnson, and Nixon administrations all repeatedly exhorted management and labor to reach noninflationary settlements and hold down prices. To keep the pressure on for such settlements, monetary and fiscal policy were run as tight as was consistent with trying to avoid unemployment and stimulate more rapid growth. President Kennedy's vigorous use of presidential pressure and public opinion to roll back announced steel price increases in 1962 raised violent objections among businesses, as have presidential pressures against inflationary wage increases from union members. Presidents Kennedy and Johnson increasingly used the "wage–price guideposts" to mobilize public opinion against inflationary wage settlements and price policies.

Lots of people worry over the governmental

power that can be brought to bear against unions and companies. But others say that the government has no alternative. No president, they say, could responsibly let the national interest—inflation control at home and a sound dollar abroad—be overridden by the wage and profit claims of one union or one industry. Often unions do what they please in spite of presidential pressure, for example in the longshoremen's crippling strikes for pay increases far above the guideposts. Should the president be given more power to deal with such cases? How should he exercise the power? Compulsory arbitration for major cases is the answer advanced by many. But this is not an area with any easy answer.

Improving Labor Markets

Fiscal and monetary policies have the primary governmental responsibility for helping to assure employment opportunities for those able, willing, and seeking to work. History shows that strong aggregate demand for labor works well in bringing unemployed workers and empty jobs together; that businessmen with unfilled orders show admirable efficiency in finding and training the workers they need. But increasingly the nation has felt that government should act to improve further the efficiency of labor markets in matching workers and jobs over time, space, and occupations.

The main federal step in this direction is the U.S. Employment Service, which operates cooperatively with the states through some 1,900 local employment offices to channel information on job openings from employers to potential workers. The Manpower Development and Training Acts (since 1962) and related antipoverty acts have provided funds to train unskilled workers for job vacancies, to retrain workers thrown out of jobs, and to otherwise improve the linkage between job vacancies and workers who need aid to find and fit the jobs.

Compared to the Wagner Act and the big shift of government labor policies outlined above, the impact of specific government measures to improve the efficiency of labor markets has thus far been small. It has been especially inadequate for the unemployed masses in the big-city slums. We have done little compared to most Western European nations, which manage much lower unemployment rates than ours. Improved job information, counseling, technical training, and labor mobility could help significantly to improve the efficiency of the economy, to facilitate adjustment to change, and to lower the margin of unemployment that is consistent with noninflationary growth in aggregate demand. Clearly, we must rely increasingly on steps to improve job markets as aggregate demand policies succeed in holding general unemployment to low levels.

Should the Government Get Out?

Ours is an economy of power groups. The unions and their leaders have great power. So do employers. Wage setting has moved from the competitive marketplace to the industry-wide bargaining table in many leading industries. The wage bargains set in steel, autos, electrical equipment, and coal go far to set the pattern for the rest of the economy. How can the government stand aside and see its antiinflation program split open, the operation of the whole economy periled by disputes in these industries? Less than 1 percent of the nation's labor force is employed in trucking. Yet that 1 percent could probably bring the economy almost to a dead stop in a few weeks.

But if it is drawn in, what can government really do? Many observers think that government intervention, especially when it becomes habitual, does more harm than good. They argue that when both sides know the government will eventually step in, there is little chance of settling the dispute beforehand. This is particularly true, they say, in inflationary periods when both labor and management know they will ultimately get much of what they want by putting on enough pressure, and the main question is how much prices will be pushed up for the consumer. One side or the other will nearly always feel it can get a better bargain by waiting to get government involved in the settlement. Thus excessive government intervention in bargaining may hide the need for management and labor themselves to accept basic responsibility in a free society.

The American economy has come a long way from the highly competitive, individualistic, free-market system described by the classical economists. Perhaps the present concentration of business and labor power is incompatible with a smoothly functioning, free-enterprise economic system and a truly democratic political system. But concentrated economic power is here, like it or not. The problem is somehow to develop a framework within which economic power is responsibly channeled to the public good. The hard fact is that we cannot order huge groups of workers around in a democratic society. Wage setting must be by consensus when two powerful groups face each other across the bargaining table. And it must be by political as well as economic consensus, once the government steps into the scene as a major participant in the process of wage setting.

Review

FOR ANALYSIS AND DISCUSSION

1. Over the past decade, union membership has declined slightly as the demand for labor has grown mainly outside the traditionally unionized areas. What is the outlook for union power over the decade ahead?
2. "Unions are justified where employers would otherwise be able to exploit employees, but nowhere else." Do you agree? Explain.
3. Should production employees be put on regular annual salary like those used for white-collar workers and middle management? If not, why not?
4. If you were a factory worker and union members in the plant put pressure on you to join the union, would you join? Would you consider such pressures an infringement of your personal freedom of choice?
5. Would it be better to give employees the extra money rather than all the fringe benefits commonly included in union contracts, so that each person could decide for himself how to spend the money?
6. Should compulsory arbitration be required by law to avoid strikes that involve government employees or otherwise affect the public interest? How would you define the public interest for this purpose?
7. Should labor unions be subject to the antitrust laws?
8. When the government intervenes in wage negotiations—for example, in steel—what criteria should it use in deciding what wage settlement to urge?
9. The Taft–Hartley Act requires unions and management to bargain "in good faith." Suppose an employer decides to make his best offer at the outset and thereafter refuses to improve the offer. Is he bargaining in good faith?

APPENDIX *THE ECONOMICS OF MINIMUM-WAGE LAWS*

What are the economic effects of a minimum-wage law covering all workers, in interstate commerce? This question provides an interesting chance to apply your economic analysis to an important issue of labor policy. Suppose, for example, that the minimum hourly wage under the Fair Labor Standards Act is raised to $2.00, in an attempt to raise the incomes of low-paid workers. Less than that will clearly not provide a decent standard of living. For the moment, assume a constant level of aggregate demand in the economy.

1. Assuming that the $2.00 is higher than the previous wage rate for some workers, economic theory says that the cost of hiring such workers will be raised, prices boosted, sales reduced, and employment cut. Those whose marginal productivity is less than $2.00 will lose their jobs, although workers who keep their jobs will get at least the $2.00 minimum rate. The new jobless may stay unemployed or they may go to work elsewhere in jobs not covered by the minimum-wage law (which applies only to firms in interstate commerce). If they do the latter, the uncovered substandard wages are forced even lower as the labor supply there rises without any increase in demand. The net result is to injure precisely the lowest-wage, lowest-income workers whom it was designed to help, since they are the ones with the lowest marginal productivities.[9]

2. However, if employers were "exploiting" labor before the law by paying wages below labor's marginal productivity, the minimum-wage law may simply boost wages without reducing employment. Wages get more of the consumer's dollar, profits get less. This is the situation implicitly assumed in most of the ardent arguments for minimum-wage legislation.

3. Even if there is no exploitation of labor, the law's upward pressure on wage rates may drive employers to more efficient methods, thereby absorbing the higher wages without reducing employment. This, too, is a favorite argument of minimum-wage-law advocates. How often it works this way is not clear from the evidence. A lot depends on how effec-

[9]Note that the effect here and in the following points is substantially the same as if an economywide union was enforcing the minimum wage.

tive businessmen have been at running their businesses without the pressures of the minimum-wage laws.

4. Minimum-wage laws tend to redistribute incomes—from employers to labor and mainly from workers who get pushed out to those who keep their jobs at higher pay. What happens to the total labor share in the national income depends basically on the elasticity of demand for labor. If employers' aggregate demand is inelastic, the law will mean higher total wage payments. Unfortunately, we don't know what the general elasticity of demand for labor is, though we do know that higher wages induce the substitution of capital for labor over extended periods. It's much easier to estimate what the elasticity may be in particular industries at particular times. The impact of a minimum-wage law is uneven, operating mainly against low-productivity workers wherever they are.

Repeal by Inflation. But don't stop with the theoretical analysis. Look at the real-world problem. As a practical matter, the minimum-wage law probably hasn't had much effect on the American economy. It has been repealed by inflation. By the time the act originally went into effect, minimum wages in most covered industries had already risen above the specified level. Wages in a few industries lagged behind the minimum figures, but these were mainly industries not covered by the law—agriculture, services, local shops, and so on, not in interstate commerce. Further inflation and rising wages robbed first a new $.75, then a $1.00, a $1.25, a $1.40, and a $1.60 legal minimum of much of their intended impact. Thus, there is little evidence that the law has thus far had a major effect on the wage structure for major industries. But it has clearly affected certain low-wage areas (especially in the South), scattered low-wage pockets throughout the economy, and such special low-productivity groups as uneducated workers and teen-agers.

thirty-five

Property Incomes: Rent, Interest, and Capital

Ours is a "capitalist" economy. One of its central tenets is the right of each individual to accumulate property (capital) of his own —a house, a factory, land, stocks, bonds.

Most such capital produces income for its owner—rent on land, interest on bonds, dividends on stocks. Some of the income may be consumed directly by the owner—housing services received by living in one's own house instead of renting. Indeed, every homeowner is a capitalist, just as is a bondholder or stockholder or an owner of his own farm or store. Nearly all the very rich receive much of their incomes from capital, and millions of families receive at least some income from such property.

In total, property incomes (including rent, interest, and profits) are about one-fifth of the national income, around $180 billion in 1970. What determines how big these incomes are? This chapter deals with rent and interest. It applies the same theory to the return on land and capital goods as we used to explain wages. Chapter 36 deals with profits alone.

Rent

In everyday usage, "rent" is the price paid for the use of land, buildings, machinery, or other durable goods. This is the way we shall use the term, except in one later section where a special meaning is given to the term "economic rent."

Rent paid for the service of property is

closely analogous to wages paid for the services of workers. The same kind of demand-and-supply, marginal-productivity analysis applies. There are important institutional differences—we don't have a slave economy, so we don't buy and sell workers the way we buy and sell land. But you should be able to transfer the general analytical framework for yourself from the wages-and-salaries area. This section raises only a few special points about rent.

The supply of nonhuman productive resources, like that of labor, varies widely from case to case. At one extreme, the supply of land at the corner of Madison Avenue and 42nd Street in New York City is completely inelastic—there's just so much and no more can be manufactured. At the other extreme, garden hoes, a simple productive resource, can be reproduced readily, and their supply is highly elastic. Most cases lie somewhere in between. By and large, the supply of any productive resource is likely to be reasonably elastic, given a long enough period for adjustment. Even farm land, for example, can readily be improved through the use of fertilizer, drainage, and so forth, if it pays to do so. For practical purposes, this is similar to making more land—you still have the same number of acres, but the acres have increased productivity.

The demand for the services of property depends basically on how much the service rendered is worth to the user. The same notion of marginal revenue productivity underlies the business demand for property services as for human labor. As in the case of labor services, marginal revenue productivity is often only a rough guide to thinking about the demand side of the picture—but a useful one nevertheless.

Competitive bidding by businesses tends to draw each resource into its most productive use. Each piece of land is rented to the highest bidder, and the high bidder must use the land where its marginal productivity is greatest to justify his paying the high rent. Under competition, the rent will approximate the marginal productivity of the land. Monopoly or monopsony may lead to inefficient allocation of resources, "exploitation" of resource owners, or to unemployment of some of the resources.

An Example

Take a simple example. What will be the rent on a ten-acre site on a highway near the outskirts of a good-sized town? Look at the demand side first. One demand may be for use in truck farming. How much renters will pay for this use will depend on the fertility of the soil, the water supply, and other such factors. Another demand may be for use as small individual business properties, such as restaurants, garden-supply stores, and so on. Here the amount of traffic passing by, the convenience of the location for potential customers, and other such factors will be especially important. Still another demand might be for use by a single supermarket, with surrounding parking area. Here again, traffic flows, convenience of location for shoppers, availability of adequate parking space, and desirability of nearby neighbors might be especially important. Each potential renter would make some estimate of how much he could afford to pay in rent for the site—logically, up to its estimated marginal revenue productivity for him.

Who will get the site, and at what rent? If there is active competition among the potential renters, the rent will be bid up until only the highest bidder is left. This will be the renter who estimates the marginal revenue productivity of the site to him as being the highest. Thus, the site will be drawn into that use which promises the highest return to the renter, and through this mechanism into the use where consumers value it most highly (since the estimated high marginal-revenue productivity reflects high consumer demand).

Will the rent be bid up all the way to the estimated marginal-revenue productivity of the highest bidder? Not necessarily, if the value to one user is substantially higher than to others. Suppose the site is ideal for a supermarket. Then the local Kroger manager needs only bid higher than the truck farmers and small shop operators, to whom the land is potentially worth less. Kroger's may get the site at a rent below its estimated marginal-value productivity as a supermarket site. On the other hand, Kroger's may not. Not if there's a local A & P or Safeway also in the market for sites. If there's active competition among potential renters, the rent is pretty sure to be bid up close to the land's highest estimated marginal-revenue productivity. Adam Smith's invisible hand again working through self-interest and competition in the marketplace!

"Economic Rent"—A Price-Determined Cost

Economists have one special definition of "rent" that differs from ordinary lay usage. "Economic rent" is the payment for the use of a scarce, nonreproducible resource. For example, the rent paid for one corner of Madison Avenue and 42nd Street in New York covers a mixture of "site value" and use of the building on the space, with all the improvements. If we could isolate the site value of a corner of Madison Avenue and 42nd Street —that is, the land itself exclusive of any of the improvements on it—we would have a resource that is scarce and completely fixed in supply; the supply is perfectly inelastic.

The rent on such nonreproducible productive agents is determined exclusively by the de-

mand for them. The supply curve is a vertical line. If there is no demand, there is no rent; the rent rises directly as demand rises, without relation to the original costs of producing the resource. Figure 35–1 illustrates the point. Since the supply is a fixed amount, SS is a vertical line. If the demand is D^1D^1, the rent will be $20 an acre. If demand is D^2D^2, rent is only $10 an acre. If demand is only D^3D^3, the land commands no rent as all. [1]

Is the "economic rent" on such a resource a cost of production? It is for the individual producer, since he has to pay the rent to the resource owner once a month. But from the viewpoint of the economy as a whole, such rents are purely price-determined (or demand-determined) costs. The economy can get exactly the same productive service from the nonreproducible scarce agent for any rent. In this sense, for the whole economy economic rent is not a cost that helps to determine the price of ultimate products.[2]

Outside the site value of land, few cases of pure economic rent exist. But there are many with some element of economic rent. If a firm patents a new productive process, for the life of the patent the process is much like the site value of land; it cannot be reproduced (except by consent of the patent holder). Indeed, if the firm has a temporarily protected monopoly position, part of the monopoly profits may better be considered a temporary rent on the monopoly position.

Interest

Most of us put our savings into financial assets, instead of buying real property directly.

fig. 35–1

When the supply is a fixed amount, price (rent) is determined solely by demand.

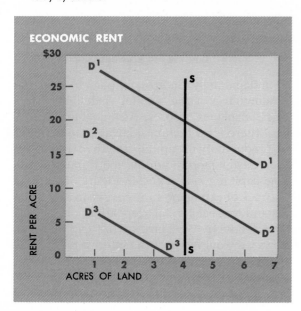

ECONOMIC RENT

[1]Economists often use the term "quasi rent" to describe the return on *temporarily* nonreproducible resources—for example, a patented production process. The return here is an economic rent, but one that will continue only so long as substitutes are not produced.

[2]Years ago, Henry George argued that all rents should be confiscated through a "single tax," since they reflect purely a bonanza to landowners that arises as society's demand for land grows. Some cities, for example Pittsburgh, still tax land more heavily than buildings on the remnants of single-tax reasoning. A few disciples still advocate this as the basis for our entire tax system.

We buy bonds, or put the money in a bank or a savings and loan association. Our property is then a financial asset—a bank account or a bond, on which we collect interest. Interest is the price paid for the use of money or credit, and indirectly for the capital or consumer goods that can be obtained with that money or credit.

Why are interest rates what they are? Fundamentally, they depend on the marginal productivity of the real capital goods obtainable with the funds involved. But temporarily they may be heavily influenced by monetary policy and other special factors. The same supply-and-demand framework is again the right one to use in answering our question.

Interest differs from rent and wages in two important respects:

1. Interest is paid for the use of money, or credit, rather than directly for the use of productive resources. Money itself has no productivity. It doesn't build buildings or dig ditches. We can't explain interest directly as a payment for money's productivity. But money does give its owner purchasing power to obtain men and machines that will build buildings and dig ditches, and demand for loan funds traces back in considerable part to their power to buy or rent real productive resources.

2. Interest is stated as a rate of return (4 percent) rather than as an absolute sum. To say that the interest rate is 4 percent is merely to say that the borrower pays $4 interest per year for each $100 borrowed. The statement in percentage terms as a rate permits ready comparison between the payments of different amounts for widely differing resources. You can easily compare the return on money invested in an office building and in a turret lathe by converting both returns into a percentage on the funds invested. For example, if the office building cost $1 million and provides an annual net return of $50,000 after depreciation and other expenses, the rate is 5 percent. If the lathe cost $1,000 and provides an annual net return of $40, the rate is 4 percent. According to these figures, funds invested in the office building provide a better return than funds invested in turret lathes.

The Structure of Interest Rates

There are hundreds of different interest rates. In 1970, for example, the government paid about 6½ percent on bonds. Bank loans ranged from about 8 percent for well-established business concerns to 10 percent on mortgage loans to buy houses, and as much as 18 percent on small loans to individual borrowers. Some consumer loan agencies charged up to 40 percent per annum. You got no interest on demand deposits, but most banks paid from 4 to 6 percent on savings deposits. The average short-term commercial loan rate at big banks in New York was about 8 percent, in southern and western cities about 8½ percent. Small business borrowers typically paid about 1 percent more than large ones.

These different rates reflect differences in risk, locality, length of loan, cost of handling the loan, and a variety of other factors, as well as the "pure" interest rate that is included in each. To simplify matters, economists often talk about "the" interest rate. They mean the interest rate on a long-term, essentially riskless loan. The rate on long-term U.S. government bonds is often considered a close approximation. At mid-1970, therefore, we might have said "the interest rate" was about 6½ percent. But don't make the mistake of assuming you could borrow money at this rate, or that most other borrowers could.

Interest and the Stock of Real Capital

Fundamentally, interest is paid for the use (productivity) of real capital—machinery, factories, airplanes, houses. Assume for the moment there is no technical advance to increase the productivity of capital; growth in the capital stock means merely adding more units of the same capital goods. Thus, in Figure 35–2, S^1 is the stock of capital now, S^2 next year. DD is the demand for real capital, dependent on its marginal productivity. Thus, as the capital stock grows we would expect the interest rate to fall, from i^1 to i^2, other things being equal.

Figure 35–2 can also show the effect of technical advance. Suppose that inventions occur that increase the productivity of capital—say, a

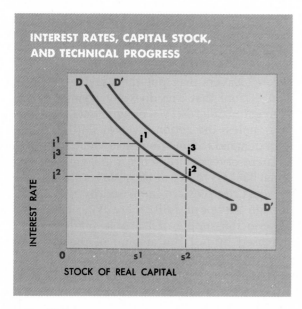

INTEREST RATES, CAPITAL STOCK, AND TECHNICAL PROGRESS

fig. 35–2

Given some level of technology and demand for capital *DD*, growth in the capital stock will reduce the interest rate from *i¹* to *i²*. Advancing technology partially offsets the growth in capital stock by increasing the demand for capital, and resulting interest rate in second year is *i³*.

new computer or improved programs ("software") for computer use. With higher marginal productivity, more capital will be demanded than before at the same price (interest rate). The *DD* curve will move to the right, say to *D¹D¹*. Thus, with **both** more capital and technical progress, the interest rate falls slightly, to *i³*, but much less than without technical progress. Of course, if the technical progress is very large, it may completely dominate the growth in capital stock, so that the interest rate would rise in spite of the increased stock of capital. In fact (look back at Figure 17–2) over the past century the two effects have been roughly offsetting; the interest rate has fluctuated cyclically but without any clear long-term trend.

Interest as the Price of Credit

Interest is the price of money, or of credit. Like any other price, it is determined by supply-and-demand factors in the market. But the factors determining the interest rate are complex on both the demand and supply sides. Be-

hind the scenes, the "real" forces determining the interest rate are the stock of real capital and the demand for capital based on the marginal productivity of capital goods. On the surface, however, monetary factors can exert a big influence. For example, an easy money policy by the Fed can increase bank reserves and the supply of credit available at the banks, thus temporarily driving interest rates below the level set by the underlying real forces.

The Demand for Credit

The biggest private demand for credit comes from business firms. Businesses borrow when they think they'll make money by doing so— when they expect to make a large enough return on the funds to pay back principal and interest, and something left over for profit. Basically, they are willing to pay interest because the borrowed funds give them control over real productive resources—machinery, buildings, labor, and so on. Their demand for funds is thus based directly on the marginal value productivity of the physical productive resources themselves. It is a derived demand.

Chapter 8 looked in detail at the factors determining the "marginal efficiency of investment," analogous to the marginal-revenue productivity of real productive agents. When a businessman sees an investment possibility with a marginal efficiency of investment much above the interest rate he has to pay, he will want to borrow additional funds if he doesn't have them already. Since it is the expected return that controls business planning, anything that affects business profit expectations will thereby affect the demand for credit.

The second big private demand for credit comes from individual households. In 1970, total consumer credit outstanding was $125 billion, and over half of all department-store sales were made on charge accounts or installment plans. Most house purchases involve borrowing part of the price; in 1970, total mortgage debt on houses was about $275 billion, rising about $15 billion annually.

The third major demand for credit is from governments—federal, state, and local. State and local governments borrow mainly to finance long-term capital improvements—highways, schools, water works. The federal government borrows for more purposes, partly to finance capital improvements but also for other purposes like national defense. Sometimes it borrows to finance deficits intentionally generated to combat depression.

The Supply of Credit

What determines the supply of credit? Your first inclination is probably to say, how much people and businesses save, and how the banking system behaves. This answer would be right, but not complete. We need also to consider other financial intermediaries as crucial links between saving and the offering of savings on the loan market. In addition, people and businesses often want to change the composition of their financial assets between money and other assets, and this shift swells or cuts the supply of borrowable credit.

Personal Saving. People save for all kinds of reasons—for old age, to put children through college, to buy a house, for a "rainy day," just because they feel they ought to save. A lot of personal saving is more or less automatic. In 1969, the 10 percent of families with the highest incomes apparently did around two-thirds of the total net personal saving in the country. At very high income levels, people save because they have money left over after buying all the things they want. Chapter 8 looked in detail at personal consumption and saving behavior; that analysis is equally applicable here.

Business Saving. Like individuals, businesses save for a variety of reasons. Mainly, they save because it is considered sound business practice to reinvest depreciation funds and to plow back a good part of earnings each year into expansion and long-term growth, rather than pay them all out as dividends. Firms could pay out all their profits in dividends and then go into the market to borrow money for expansion purposes—but they don't. Most of their savings flow directly on into real investment within the business; only a small part comes onto the open market for loanable funds.

Saving, Cash Balances, and the Supply of Credit. Savers may put their savings "in the bank." Note that this does not change either aggregate bank reserves or aggregate deposits. Thus, unless the action involves shifting funds from demand to time deposits (which have different reserve requirements), the saving will not signal bankers to expand their loans at all. Even if excess reserves are increased by the saving through a deposit shift, there is no reason to suppose the supply of loanable funds will be increased by just the amount of the new individual or business saving.

Savings may also be put into savings and loan associations, insurance, or other noncommercial banking financial intermediaries. Although, unlike commercial banks, such firms can't create and destroy money directly, they can pile up or spend down their money balances. There is no guarantee that savings flowing into these intermediaries will just match the funds being offered to borrowers by the intermediaries in any given period. They can increase the stock of loanable credit, much as banks can (See Chap. 12).

Similarly, individual and business decisions on the composition of the asset portfolios they hold may influence the supply of credit. When people decide to reduce the share of their assets held in the form of money, this puts the excess money into the loan market (or directly into the demand for real assets). Or they may shift their funds between commercial banks and other financial institutions. Such decisions can affect the supply of credit.

The Banks and the Supply of Credit. Chapter 12 described the power of the commercial banking system to create and destroy money. Here is a major force on the supply side of the loan-funds market. As long as the banks have excess reserves, they can make loans without regard to what individual and business savers do. They can contract their loans with comparable independence. If they don't have excess reserves, increased private saving won't permit

table 35-1

Credit Borrowed by and Advanced to Domestic Nonfinancial Sectors*

	1966	1968
Funds Borrowed	62.6	91.4
Private domestic nonfinance	62.0	79.7
Short-term debt		
Households	8.3	15.5
Businesses	13.6	13.0
State and local government	0.4	0.3
Long-term obligations		
State and local government	6.4	10.9
Households	11.0	15.4
Businesses	22.5	24.6
Federal government (net)	0.6	11.8
Funds Advanced	62.6	91.4
Private domestic nonfinance	20.1	17.0
Households	10.7	1.7
Businesses	3.2	7.7
State and local government	6.2	7.7
Financial institutions (net)	40.7	69.2
Banks	17.3	38.6
Nonbank saving institutions	8.7	15.1
Other	14.6	15.5
Rest of the world (net)	−1.6	1.6
Federal Reserve	3.5	3.7
Memorandum:		
Federal Reserve funds supplied as % of total	5.6	4.0
Bank funds supplied as % of total	28.8	42.1

*Source: Federal Reserve Flow-of-Funds data.

them to extend more loans (unless funds are shifted from demand deposits to savings deposits). The supply of credit in any time period is a complex matter. Fundamentally it depends on the economy's saving behavior, but as a practical matter a lot of different decisions are involved.

Credit Demanders and Suppliers. Table 35-1 summarizes the complex set of credit flows in the modern American economy. The top section shows who supplied credit in two typical years; the next section who borrowed it. Note the radically different role of federal-government borrowing in the two years. The memorandum at the bottom indicates the relative importance of the Federal Reserve and the commercial banks in the two years.

Determination of Interest Rates

Like other prices, interest rates are determined by the interaction of supply and demand in the markets concerned. Different markets may have different interest rates, though they are closely linked together, since it is relatively easy to transfer funds from one credit market to another.

If we look at all interlinked credit markets together, they have one quality that deserves special attention because of the important role given the interest rate by many theories of aggregate spending. In most markets price movements are a major factor in bringing about equality between the amount demanded and the amount supplied. But the interest rate may have only a very slight effect on the supply of credit (on personal and business saving), and much of the equilibrating mechanism may operate through other channels. For example, if the amount of loanable funds being supplied from current savings is in excess of the amount demanded, this excess intended saving may exert a strong downward push on aggregate spending and employment (see Chapter 7). Thus, equilibrium between the amount supplied and the amount demanded may be brought about more by changes in the level of national product that by mere fluctuations in the interest rate. [3]

Government Policy and Interest Rates

Since the 1930s, the federal government has exerted substantial influence on interest rates. Before the New Deal, interest rates were largely set in the market by the interplay of private supply and demand, though the Federal Reserve did intervene from time to time. But after 1933, federal fiscal and monetary policy became more important on both the demand and supply sides of the money market. The government became a heavy borrower in the 1930s, and the dominant borrower in the 1940s. At the same time, the Federal Reserve pumped new reserves into the banking system to supply the funds needed by the government to finance the spending voted by Congress. The result was substantial government influence over the level of interest rates. Since World War II, private forces have returned to dominance of the money markets. But, as was emphasized in Chapters 13 and 14, government monetary and fiscal policies remain powerful forces in the money market today.

[3] Advanced texts in economic theory explain that in equilibrium the interest rate must be equal to the marginal productivity of real capital (in the aggregate), must equilibrate the loanable funds market, and must equilibrate the market for money (currency and deposits), so that everyone is just willing to continue holding the existing amount of money, rather than spending it on goods and services or securities; and that it will simultaneously do all three.

Inflation, Money, and Real Rates of Interest. In inflation the market ("money") rate of interest exceeds the "real" rate. If you borrow $100 for one year at 6 percent and prices rise by 4 percent, in real purchasing power you pay only 2 percent interest. Thus, economists say the nominal or money rate is 6 percent but the real rate is only 2 percent. Conversely, if prices should fall the real rate will be higher than the money rate.

Presumably, if borrowers and lenders correctly anticipate inflation (say 10 percent per annum), they will both take this into account in making their contracts. If the real productivity of capital is 4 percent, they will add on the 10 percent inflation allowance, making a 14 percent market rate. If their anticipation of inflation is imperfect, the inflation allowance between money and real rates may be correspondingly imperfect. In fact, it is never possible to predict inflation perfectly. Econometric studies suggest that borrowers and lenders tend to extrapolate past experience, placing primary emphasis on the recent past but reaching back several years into the past for evidence—some economists say as many as twenty years or more. But the evidence is inconclusive, and particular events (say, a major change in monetary policy) may sharply alter expectations that merely extrapolate past inflation.

Thus, as Part Two emphasized, the monetary authorities can directly affect money (nominal) interest rates much more readily than real rates. Moreover, the channels of their impact are complex. The first effect of easier money (say a $10 billion open-market purchase by the Fed) will be immediately to raise security prices and lower interest rates. But more reserves will also lead to more spending and higher national income over, say, the next six months to a year; this will raise the (transactions) demand for money, thereby partly offsetting the original drop in interest rates. If, further, the increased spending comes with full employment and generates inflation, a resulting inflation allowance will also gradually be built into interest rates— so the ultimate effect of easier money in a period of high employment may well be to raise market interest rates, not to lower them. It is important to note, of course, that this does not necessarily raise real interest rates. In the years 1968 to 1970, for example, years of unprecedented high market interest rates (reaching 9 percent on top-quality corporate bonds), many corporate officials kept on borrowing, pointing out that with 5 percent or so inflation the real cost of borrowed money was very modest.

The Interest Rate, Resource Allocation, and Capital Accumulation

The interest rate helps potential business and individual investors allocate their funds among the millions of potential investment opportunities in the economy. When funds are allocated where the expected rate of return is highest, risk and other factors taken into account, the funds are optimally allocated from the consumer's viewpoint as well as from the investor's, since the highest returns will be found where consumer demand is relatively strongest. Unless an investment promises a return high enough to pay the going rate of interest under a private-enterprise economy, it does not justify exploitation, by the test of the market. Money capital is the fluid embodiment of real productive resources. Thus, the money market, by channeling funds into those investments throughout the economy where the potential return exceeds the interest rate, provides a most valuable service, to private investors and to the society as a whole.

The interest rate plays another, more subtle, role. The going interest rate provides a rough measure of the relative advantages of current consumption and saving—of the present against the future. By saving, the individual or business can get a continuing return of, say, 4 percent annually. If that return is enough to justify foregoing consumption now, it is advantageous to save. Without the interest rate to indicate the going return on saved funds in the economy, savers would have no standard by which to measure the relative advantages of current consumption and saving. How important this point is hinges on how important the interest rate is in consumer and business decisions to save.

Similarly, the interest rate helps businessmen and government planners decide among projects of different capital intensity. Suppose we can produce product A either with lots of labor and a simple plant, or with little labor working with long-lived, expensive machinery. Which is better? Only by calculating the "capital cost" (the interest rate times the dollar investment discounted back to the present—see the following section) of each and comparing the expected total labor-plus-capital cost of the two alternatives can we accurately choose between the two methods.

Lastly, perhaps most important of all, the interest rate exerts a powerful influence on the rate of economic growth in a capitalist economy like ours. A low interest rate encourages investment and faster growth. A high interest rate has the opposite effect.

Valuation of Income-Producing Property

Income distribution is concerned primarily with the pricing of productive services, not with the prices of the productive agents themselves—land, machinery, buildings, and the stocks and bonds representing their ownership. But income-producing assets are bought and sold daily in our economy, and the interest rate plays an important part in setting the prices at which they sell.

To estimate the price of an income-producing asset, we need to know (1) its net annual return, and (2) the going rate of interest.

Valuation of Perpetual Fixed Income ("Capitalization")

Take a simple hypothetical case first. Suppose we have a mine that will produce forever ore worth $100 annually, net after all expenses are met. Suppose further that the going rate of interest on substantially riskless investments is 4 percent. What will the mine be worth?

To get the answer, we simply "capitalize" $100 at 4 percent. That is, we find that sum on which 4 percent interest would amount to $100 annually. The arithmetic is simple. Four percent of x (the unknown value) is $100. In equation form, this is: $.04 \cdot x = 100$. Dividing the .04

into 100, we get $2,500 as the value of the mine. Put another way the formula is:

$$V = \frac{\$ \text{ Return}}{\text{Interest rate}}$$

Can we be sure the mine will really sell for $2,500? No, but we can be sure it will sell for something near that. No one will be willing to pay a much higher price, since by investing $2,500 anywhere else at equal risk he can get $100 annually. On the other hand, if the mine's price is much less than $2,500, people will find it a very attractive investment and the price will be bid up toward $2,500.

Valuation of Machinery

The principle involved in valuing nonperpetual assets is the same. Consider a machine that will last twenty years and whose marginal-revenue productivity (rent) per year is $60. The going rate of interest on comparable investments is 6 percent. Using the same approach as before, we might capitalize $60 at 6 percent, and find that $60 is 6 percent on $1,000.

But there's a catch. The $60 annual income here only lasts for twenty years, because the machine wears out. Our problem here is: What is the present, or capitalized, value of an income stream of $60 at 6 percent over twenty years, rather than in perpetuity? Mathematicians and industrial engineers have worked out a series of tables giving the answers for all combinations of interest rates and time periods for such problems. The answer here is $688.

The basic reasoning runs like this: At the end of the first year, we get $60. At the end of the second year we get another $60. And so on for the twenty years. Sixty dollars today is obviously worth $60, but $60 to be received, say, one year from today is clearly worth less than $60 today, since we do not have the use of it until a year hence. How much today is equivalent to $60 a year from today? If the interest rate is 6 percent, $56.60 invested today at 6 percent will amount to just $60 a year from now. And we can make a similar calculation to get the amount equal to $60 two years hence, and so on up to twenty years. If now we add together all these "present values" of $60 to be received at the end of each of the next twenty years, we will get how much we ought to be willing to pay now for the series of twenty annual $60 net returns anticipated from the machine. This calculation gives the $688 above, the "present worth" of the income stream promised if we buy the machine.

So you'd better not pay more than about $688 for the machine if you don't want to get stung. If you stop and think, you'll see why this amount has to be a good deal less than the $1,000 the machine would be worth if it provided the $60 annually in perpetuity. If you have to pay more than about $688, you could earn more on your money by investing it elsewhere at 6 percent for the twenty years.

One other point is needed to complete this example. Unless this is a patented machine, others like it can be produced. If the current cost of producing such machines, for example, is only $500, you can be pretty sure that even the $688 price won't last. At a price of $688, it will pay to produce more machines like this one. As more are produced, the price will gradually fall. Not until the price falls to $500 will a new equilibrium be established. With lots more machines, the marginal revenue productivity of each will be lower, both because of the law of diminishing returns and because the product of the machine will have fallen in price, so that the net annual yield per machine will no longer be $60.

To summarize: (1) At any time, the capitalized value of an income-producing asset will be based on its net yield and on the going rate of interest on investments of comparable quality. (2) In the long run, the value of any asset will tend to be equal to its cost of reproduction, although it may vary widely from this figure at any given time.

Valuation of Corporate Stocks: The Stock Market

The same general principle holds in valuing corporate stocks and bonds, which represent claims on income earned by the issuing companies. But don't take your nest egg and rush for the stock market with this new knowledge. Corporate securities are interesting illustrations of the capitalization principle especially because they point up so many of the pitfalls. So far, we've assumed that we knew the yield of each asset, its life, and the appropriate going rate of interest. But in the real world all three of these are usually uncertain, certainly on corporate stocks. The yield on most stocks fluctuates from year to year. There is no sure way of telling what it will be for any extended period ahead. Moreover, what rate of interest should we use in capitalizing? The appropriate one is the rate that prevails on other investments of comparable risk and other characteristics. But you pick it out.

Last, and most important, the market price of stocks is determined by thousands of other people who are all guessing at the same imponderables as you are. Many of them are in the market as speculators, looking for a quick dollar on the price rise rather than for a long-pull investment. There is no reproduction cost to set a fairly stable base level that anyone can count on. The actual market price will reflect what all those people think is going to happen. So you're betting on what other people will bet on, and they in turn are betting on what you and others will

bet on. The stock market is no place for neophytes. The capitalization principle can give you a rough steer and it can help you in comparing different securities. But the much-quoted statement of Bernard Baruch is relevant here:

> If you are ready to give up everything else—to study the whole history and background of the market and all the principal companies whose stocks are on the board as carefully as a medical student studies anatomy. If you can do all that, and, in addition, you have the cool nerves of a great gambler, the sixth sense of a kind of clairvoyant, and the courage of a lion, you have a ghost of a chance.

The point of this section is not to warn you against investing in common stocks. On the contrary, overall stocks have been a very good investment over the long pull. Rather, the point is to stress the wide range of special factors at work in determining the actual market price of some types of particular income-producing assets. The analytical framework outlined in the simple cases above can help in most cases, but like all analytical models it gives only a framework for analyzing any particular situation in detail.

Review

CONCEPTS TO REMEMBER

This is a difficult chapter. Recheck your understanding of the following concepts:

rent	"real" interest rates
economic rent	"money" interest rates
quasi rent	rate of return
interest	capitalization
"the interest rate"	"present worth" of an income stream

FOR ANALYSIS AND DISCUSSION

1. "Rent and wages are determined by substantially the same set of supply-and-demand forces, even though people are human and land is not." Do you agree? If not, what are the main differences?
2. "Rent is an unearned increment for any landowner, since he does not have to do any work for the rent he receives. Therefore the government should confiscate rents through special taxes." Do you agree? Why or why not?

3. "The profits made by a company on the basis of an exclusive patent are essentially rents, not profits." Do you agree or disagree?
4. Some economists predict persistent inflation over the years ahead. If they are correct, how would you expect this inflation to affect money and real rates of interest? Explain.
5. Other things equal, would you expect rapid technological advance to raise or lower the long-term rate of interest? Why?
6. Assume that you have $10,000 to invest. How would you go about deciding what is a reasonable rate of interest for you to receive in investing your money? What investments would you consider?
7. Suppose the Federal Reserve tightens bank reserves and raises interest rates. Would this increase or decrease real investment, other things equal?
8. Find out the "carrying charge" on some article you are considering buying. Then calculate the interest rate you would be paying on the funds you in effect borrow from the seller. Would you be better off to borrow the money at a bank? (See the appendix.)
9. Suppose you inherit an eighty-acre tract of farmland. You are uncertain whether to sell it, or to retain it and rent it out. How would you go about comparing the advantages of the best two courses of action?

APPENDIX *ACTUAL AND NOMINAL INTEREST RATES*

Interest rates aren't always what they seem to be. This appendix is intended to help you protect yourself against some common mistakes, by looking at two examples that arise frequently in everyday life.

1. Installment Charges. Most goods you buy on installment bear a "carrying charge" to pay the seller for extending credit to you. In essence, this is an interest rate, plus something extra for the nuisance of keeping the books and maybe having to dun you for the money. If you're smart, you'll compare carefully the interest rate hidden in the carrying charge with what the money would cost you if you borrowed it directly elsewhere.

Suppose you buy a $120 rug on the installment plan, with twelve months to pay and a carrying charge of $1 a month, or $12 for the year. This looks like 10 percent, a reasonable rate for such a loan. But look again. The actual rate is far higher. You pay a dollar each month, but the total amount you have on loan from the store goes down $10 each month. The last month you owe them only $10; yet you are still paying interest at the rate of $1 a month, or $12 per year. The actual rate on your unpaid balance during the last month is 120 percent per annum. The average for the year is 20 percent, twice the apparent rate, since the average loan to you is about half the purchase price of the rug.

The actual rate each month is calculated in the accompanying table.

	Unpaid Balance	Interest ($1 Monthly; $12 per Year)	Interest Rate on Unpaid Balance
1st month	$120	$12	10.0%
2nd month	110	12	10.9
3rd month	100	12	12.0
4th month	90	12	13.3
5th month	80	12	15.0
6th month	70	12	17.1
7th month	60	12	20.0
8th month	50	12	24.0
9th month	40	12	30.0
10th month	30	12	40.0
11th month	20	12	60.0
12th month	10	12	120.0

2. Bond Yields. Suppose you're thinking of buying a corporation bond that pays 4 percent. It is a $1,000 face value bond, so the annual interest is $40. Its current market price is $1,100, and it is due in ten years. Suppose your alternative is putting the money into U. S. government bonds, which pay 3¾ percent. Assume that the two investments are equally safe and attractive on all other grounds. Which one should you choose?

At first glance, the corporate bond seems to win hands down. But look again. You pay $1,100 for the bond, but you'll only get back $1,000 at the end of

ten years. To get the true net yield, you need to "write off" $10 of the value of the bond each of the ten years, so your actual net annual yield would be only $30 rather that $40. Now you can calculate the exact yield on the corporate bond. It's $30 per year on $1,100 invested. This figures out to 2.7 percent, appreciably under 3¾ percent. Better buy the government bond if yield over the next ten years is your main goal.

3. Inflation. Inflation, as the preceding chapter stressed, raises another situation where you may be tricked by the difference between actual and nominal interest rates. Suppose you have a bond which yields 5 percent annually over the next ten years. But prices rise 3 percent per year over the period. Thus, although the nominal rate of interest is 5 percent, the real rate is only 2 percent, since 3 percent of the return has been eroded by the price inflation.

Profits

Ours is a private-enterprise, profit-motivated economy—not entirely, but by and large. In 1970, total profits were about $100 billion, including net incomes of farmers, lawyers, doctors and the like, as well as business corporations. That's a lot of money. But was it enough to make the system function most efficiently? Or far too much, as most Marxists and many other radicals claim, since profits are nothing but an expropriation of value created by the workers?

Our look at the market system thus far has stressed two big roles for profits. They're the incentive to produce what consumers demand —the carrot that entices businessmen to perform their social function. And they're a major source of funds for the investment that makes the economy grow. Now it's time for a summary look at profits in their own right—and for at least a brief look at the anticapitalist, antiprofit views of radical critics.

Profits on the Modern Scene

Begin by remembering how economic profits are defined. Economic profit is the excess of income over all "economic" costs (including a normal return on investment). Profit is thus a residual, plus or minus—what's left over after the business has met all its costs.

Potential profit indicates where society wants more resources used. Thus, the individual businessman who predicts most successfully what the consumer will want, who meets consumer demand most effectively, who handles his production most efficiently, and who buys his labor and materials most adroitly will end up with the biggest profit. The inefficient producer who fails to respond to consumers' demands is likely to end up with red ink on his books. If a seller has a partial or complete monopoly position, he may be able to maintain positive economic profits over a substantial period without innovation, real productive efficiency, or close adaptation to consumer demands. But wherever other firms are free to enter the market, competition will tend to bid prices down and costs up, eliminating economic profits. The pursuit of profits plays a central organizing role for the entire economy.

If you ask the man in the street, he probably won't be very sure just what profit does mean, but there's a good chance he'll have a mildly antagonistic attitude. Public-opinion polls suggest this attitude toward profits. And it's highly likely he will have only a vague idea about how big profits are, in total, in return per dollar of investment, or in return per dollar of business sales. So a look at the facts may be in order.

The Facts

Figure 36–1 summarizes the course of corpo-

rate profits since 1929.[1] In 1970 they were almost $90 billion, a whopping amount. But many businessmen would protest vigorously. They'd say it's profits **after** taxes that we should look at. After taxes, profits are a lot less, only about half as much as the before-tax total. Corporate income taxes now take a much bigger share of profits than they did three decades ago. And of course inflation accounts for some of the big increases shown; prices have more than doubled over the period.

The aggregate dollar figures alone don't have much meaning. Everything in the economy has grown immensely since 1929. Have profits risen or fallen compared to other national-income shares? Are businesses making more or less profit these days per dollar of sales, or per dollar of investment? Figure 36–2 gives some of the answers.

It's clear that the profit share in the national income (based on reported corporate profits) has jumped all over the place in big business cycles. The average percentage for recent years has been a little above the 11 percent figure for 1929. Corporate profits were actually negative in the years 1931 to 1932 and hit a peak of

[1]Remember that these are much larger than *economic* profits, since total reported corporate profits include a large "normal" return on stockholders' investment as well as pure profits.

fig. 36–1

Corporate profits, in current dollars, have risen sharply but irregularly since 1929. Corporate income taxes now take somewhat less than half the total. (Source: U.S. Department of Commerce; 1970 is preliminary estimate.)

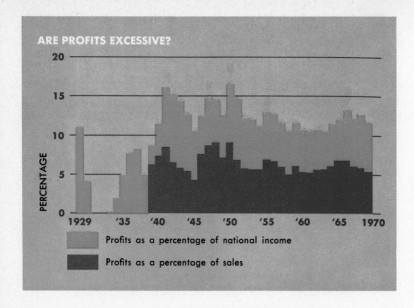

fig. 36–2

Corporate profits reached peaks during and after World War II. Since then they have fluctuated at somewhat lower levels relative to national income and sales, dropping in recession years. (Source: U.S. Department of Commerce. Profits as percentage of national income are before taxes, as percentage of sales after taxes.)

nearly 17 percent of the national income in the boom year of 1950. Lesson in statistics: Note how you can make the profit share look sharply rising or sharply falling, depending on which year you take as your starting point.[2]

The Two Roles of Profits

Profits as an Incentive

The number-one social function of profits is to give businessmen an incentive to produce what consumers want, when and where they want it, at the lowest feasible cost and price. This includes innovation of new products and new methods. The profit motive is at the center of a private-enterprise economy, and nearly everyone in the United States agrees that it ought to stay there.

But a lot of questions are raised about just how the profit motive does, and should, work as a practical matter. For example, with professional managers (rather than owner-operators) now running most big businesses, some people ask whether profit is still the most effective incentive to innovation and efficiency. The modern corporation president gets a salary plus a bonus

dependent on profits, but as president he gets only a fraction of 1 percent of the company's total profits. What motivates him? Moreover, the job big businessmen themselves do is mainly to organize and direct production. The wage earners and salaried employees, who do the great bulk of the company's work, have to have their carrots too if the overall job is to be done, and company profits may not rate very high on their motivation lists.

Second, remember that it's the expectation of profits that must be there to make the system tick, not the achievement of profits. Over the long pull, profits are smaller than you might guess. This is a profit-and-loss, not just a profit, system. Many a firm has gone broke. In prosperous times like recent decades it is easy to forget the big losses incurred across the board during past depressions.

Statistics on the rate of business failures even in prosperity are revealing. During 1969, for example, failures of incorporated businesses averaged about 1,000 per month. Total liabilities of these failures were $1.3 billion. Fewer than 25 percent of the businesses established during the immediate postwar years were still operating a decade later. Yet each year new thousands rush in, confident that they have the knack to succeed where others have failed. Big-business failures are less common than failures among small firms. People who have $50 million or $100 million to venture are rare, and profitability calculations on such investments are made with a great deal more care. But even for

[2]No official long-period series is available showing profits as a rate of return on invested capital. A private series (First National City Bank of New York) shows profits for a large sample of manufacturing corporations as 10 percent on net worth in 1929, about zero in 1932, a peak of 14 percent in 1948, between 9 and 13 percent for the years 1960 to 1965, and 14 percent in 1966.

big business the story is far from one of un-
broken success. Think of the automobile industry, with its spectacular growth over the present
century. The Oakland, Stanley Steamer, Max-
well, Hupmobile, and dozens of others were
once as much household words as Ford and
Pontiac are today. Yet only a few decades later
they are as extinct as the dodo. More recently,
Douglas Aircraft, a multibillion giant, was saved
only by merger with McDonnell Aircraft.

But hope springs eternal in the American entrepreneur's breast. Perhaps entrepreneurs are
by nature overoptimistic people. Their optimism leads to a good deal of waste in resources
devoted to ventures that don't succeed. But it
also helps give the American economy the dynamic vigor that has pushed the American standard of living far above its nearest competitor.
It is doubtful that dynamic progress in a private-
enterprise system is possible without widespread losses from bad business guesses as well
as widespread profits from good ones.

Profits as a Source of Investment and Growth

Profits have a second major social function.
Undistributed corporate profits (profits not paid
out as dividends) are one important source of
funds for business investment. In 1969, for example, they totaled $26 billion, and almost all
were plowed back into new plant, equipment,
and other such business uses. Corporation depreciation allowances are also considered by
most businessmen as sources of funds for business investments (though remember that a depreciation allowance is merely a bookkeeping
charge, not actual money set aside). Since businesses seldom replace worn-out assets with
identical assets, it is often hard to identify what
is replacement and what net new investment.
Thus, business investment is often viewed gross
(including replacement), as in the gross national
product accounts. In 1969, depreciation
charges totaled $49 billion, so net "internal"
sources for investment spending totaled $75
billion. Remember that each firm has considerable discretion as to just how much depreciation to charge in any given year, so the
distinction between profits and depreciation in
any given year is somewhat arbitrary.

In 1969, corporations also went "to the market" for another $30 billion of capital. That is,
they issued new stocks and bonds and went to
the banks for that amount. Thus, corporations
financed most of their gross investment from
"internal" sources (profits and depreciation),
but they were by no means free from reliance
on the capital markets.

The Theory of Profits

Profits in a Static Economy

In a static economy, without technological
advance, population change, capital accumulation, and changing consumer wants, only
monopoly profits would continue. Competition
would gradually eliminate all other economic
profits as resources were shifted into high-profit
industries. Capitalization would bid up the
prices and rents of especially productive resources until the rate of return on them was
equal to that on other resources. Throughout
the entire economy, economic profits would be
eliminated when equilibrium was achieved except for those industries where new businesses
were prevented from entering.[3] There, and
there only, monopoly and oligopoly profits
would continue indefinitely. In effect,
monopoly and oligopoly profits then would be a
kind of rent on exclusive monopoly position.

Even in such a static economy, it's hard to say
to whom, and for what, temporary profits are a
return. Increasingly, the job of making profits in
the modern economy falls on professional
managers. The return to these men is more
"wages of management" than profit, though
most of them have some sort of bonus plan under which they share in profits and lose take-
home pay when profits drop. Stockholders, who
put up most of the capital and get the profits
when there are any, are a very passive type of
entrepreneur in most modern corporations.
Thus, where to draw the line between profits
and wages of management is a difficult question. The functions of management, entre-

---

[3]Though accounting profits would, of course, continue,
since they do not include a normal return on stockholders'
investment as a cost.

preneurship, and providing capital are thoroughly entangled in modern business firms.

Profits in a Dynamic Economy

But continuous, unpredictable change is the dominant characteristic of the real world. Uncertainty is everywhere. Changing demands, new products, technological advance—all these and many more confront the entrepreneur or manager every day. He must somehow "guesstimate" the future demand for his product, his future costs, future changes in technology, future behavior of his competitors. Then he must keep an eagle eye out for how the government is going to behave—on taxes, government spending, antitrust policy, labor relations, and international affairs. In the midst of all this, he needs to worry about keeping his costs below those of competitors, keeping the union at least tolerably happy, being sure that his sales organization is on its toes, and so on.

If he does all these things better than his competitors, and especially if he has a partial monopoly position to help him, he'll end up with a good profit. If he misses on many of the important decisions, the red ink will appear. The biggest job of the modern entrepreneur is to live with and make the best of uncertainty. If he doesn't thrive on this kind of life, he'd better save himself a big doctor bill for ulcers and go to work for somebody else.

Insurable Risk and Uncertainty. Many kinds of risk can be insured against. In this way, the uncertainty can be eliminated by incurring a known dollar cost. The best-known example is the risk of loss from fire or theft. Without insurance, this uncertainty would be a major problem for any business concern. But the likelihood of fire loss is reasonably predictable for a large number of buildings of any given type, even though it is unpredictable for any given building. By pooling together the moderate insurance premiums on a large number of buildings, the insurance company has enough funds to pay off the fire losses on those few buildings that do burn each year. Long experience has reduced the likelihood of such occurrences to a scientific, statistical basis. Businesses can now con-

vert this type of uncertainty into a known cost through insurance.[4]

Professor Frank H. Knight has pointed out that insurable risks are really only another business cost to be included with other business costs, and that economic profits arise only from bona-fide cases of uninsurable uncertainty. Alas, the businessman can't go to his insurance agent and say: "I'm bringing out a new-style dishwasher; insure me against its being a flop." Economic profits beyond profits on monopoly positions, Knight argues, are thus analytically linked solely to a world of dynamic change and uninsurable uncertainty.

Profits and Dynamic Change. Since profits arise largely out of dynamic change and uncertainty, much of what happens to profits is outside the control of any individual manager or entrepreneur. The biggest profits arise in booms, the biggest losses in depressions. "Windfall profits" are widespread in a lusty boom; it's pretty hard for any reasonably well-situated business to avoid making good profits. In a bad depression, the best management in the world has a tough time making ends meet. The business cycle, with inflation and deflation, may well be the biggest single cause of profits and losses. The manager who can foresee business fluctuations and adjust successfully to them is worth his weight in gold.

Shifting consumer demand for individual products is a second big area of change largely outside the control of the individual businessman. Even General Motors is going to have a tough time making profits on automobiles if consumers decide to ride in helicopters instead. But the alert entrepreneur is far from helpless. He can change his product to keep in step with the times, and through his advertising he can influence what consumers want to buy.

Changes in costs are a third big area of uncontrollable uncertainty. What happens to the price of steel is pretty much outside the control of the Philco organization; yet steel repre-

---

[4]Very large firms may "self-insure." If a firm has hundreds of buildings itself, it may figure that the predictable likelihood of fire loss in any given year is less than the cost of buying commercial insurance on them.

sents one of the major costs in making Philco refrigerators. The same thing is true of most other costs. The businessman can bargain with his local union, but he isn't going to get far with a wage rate much below the rates that prevail elsewhere for similar work, any more than he can buy steel below prevailing market prices. Technological changes continually change costs.

Basically, it's the manager who does a good job of prediction under conditions of dynamic uncertainty, and who adjusts effectively to unforeseen conditions, who is likely to turn in good profits.

The Profits of Innovation. One noted economist, Joseph Schumpeter, has argued that profits boil down largely to payment for keeping a jump ahead of your competitors through innovation. The big profits come from big, successful innovations—the motor car, color TV, the diesel engine, and so on. The innovator needs both an idea and the ability to get it into operation. An invention or an idea alone makes no profits. But the utilization of that invention, if it leads to lower costs or to a successful new product, brings dollars into the coffers.

Unfortunately, no one has yet figured out a sure way of telling in advance whether a new mousetrap or a new railway car will succeed. First,there is the technological problem of developing the idea into a usable process or product. When this is licked, there is still that capricious monarch of all the surveys—the consumer. Business history tells a fascinating story of the sure things that flopped, and also of the thousand-to-one shots that have become the industrial giants of today.

Successful innovation in effect gives a temporary monopoly to the innovator, and often big profits. Like other monopoly profits, the economic profits of innovation persist only until competitors catch up and bring profits in the industry down to competitive levels. But innovations are often protected by seventeen-year patents. And a running start on your competitor is often more important than the legal protection of patents. The firm with the know-how and experience that go with a new product or

a new method is likely to have a new innovation at hand by the time competitors catch up on the last one. The continuing success of the industrial giants of today—General Motors, General Electric, Standard Oil, Du Pont—rests at least as much on this kind of continuing innovation as on any other single factor.

Conclusion

Profits go largely to those who manage most efficiently to give consumers what they want in a world of continuous change. How big do profits have to be to give the incentives to management and entrepreneurs that we need for a dynamic, progressive, private-enterprise economy? Nobody knows. Profits are big enough when businessmen and investors act as if they are big enough. What matters are two things: that businessmen desire to innovate and to run efficient enterprises aimed at meeting consumer demands—and that profits plus other savings be big enough to support the economic growth we want.

Some people nowadays say that individual and corporation income tax rates are so high that there's no use working too hard, no use taking big risks when the government takes half of the profit and shoulders you with any loss. Others complain that labor grabs all the gains from good management and new capital investment.

But the rough stability of aggregate wage and profit shares shows that profits have grown with the economy. And there is little evidence that the dynamic impetus is gone from the American economy. There are many incentives to fine management and pioneering entrepreneurship. Pride in achievement, the social acclaim for success, traditions of sound management, the development of professional standards, the pure joy of risk taking—all these incentives and others like them may be powerful supplements to the monetary incentive of profits. And one of the attributes of a shrewd businessman is the ability to manage affairs so as to take advantage of every possibility the law provides for minimizing taxes.

Human motivation is a very complex affair, and it varies widely from person to person. The long hours of unpaid toil that millions put in each year for causes they consider worthwhile are impressive evidence that money is far from everything. And the billions we spend each year on gambling devices we know are loaded against us provide impressive evidence of our love for risk taking. The Irish sweepstakes, slot machines, pari-mutuel betting on races—all are publicly announced to pay out less than the

contestants put in. Yet there is always the chance that you will be a big winner. If so many of us are willing to gamble when we know that as a group we must lose, we may hope that entrepreneurs continue their business risk taking undaunted. For with business innovation there is no reason to suppose that the dice are loaded against entrepreneurs in the aggregate. Indeed, the long record of rapid growth in the economy points strongly the other way.

Review

FOR ANALYSIS AND DISCUSSION

1. What are the main functions of profits in the modern American economy?
2. "By and large, continuing profits for any firm demonstrate it is doing a good job in satisfying consumer demand." Do you agree or disagree? Explain.
3. Are current profits excessive? (See Figure 36–2.) What are the best criteria as to whether profits are too large or too small?
4. "So long as we let businessmen think they have a chance to make profits, it doesn't matter whether they actually make any profits or not." Is this a sound analysis of the incentive role of business profits?
5. Who actually gets the profits made by the American corporations? (Refer back to Chapter 20 for some of the relevant information.) If it is not primarily the managers, how do profits serve their presumed incentive function?
6. Many economists say that Marxist criticism of capitalist profits as creating big incomes for stockholders is misplaced—that the main function of profits is as an incentive to get businesses to do what we (the consumers) want done, and we should expect successful businesses to earn substantial profits for serving this social function. Who is right?

APPENDIX: *MARX, "RADICAL ECONOMICS," AND PROFITS*

Marx, writing a century ago, argued that labor is the source of all value; that while capital goods may be "productive" in the sense of increasing the productivity of labor, they reflect merely the results of past labor; and that all interest and profits (all returns to owners of capital) thus represent expropriation of "surplus value" created by labor. Moreover, surplus value is seized from workers who would spend it on consumption by capitalists who will save (not spend on consumption) most of it. This will lead to a shortage of purchasing power ("underconsumption"), a

long-run decline in profits, ever greater depressions and unemployment as capital accumulates, with falling profits and the ultimate downfall of capitalism. The workers, long ground down under the oppression of the capitalists, will revolt and seize control of the system. Modern Marxists and "radicals" make many modifications on the argument, but this is the core.

Marxists have for a century persistently proclaimed the death throes of capitalism. Capitalism has been uncooperative. Indeed, all income and growth statis-

tics (e.g., Table 1–1) show the Western, capitalist economies dominating the list, with only the USSR of the Communist nations even in the upper income ranks. In the capitalist nations the poor have not become poorer and more numerous; on the contrary, the bottom-quarter income recipients in the Western capitalist nations are notably better off economically than even the middle classes in the Communist nations. Capitalist economies' income distributions have remained remarkably stable. "Property income,"depending precisely on how it is defined, has hovered around 25 percent of g.n.p. in the United States (see Figure 32–3), and not far from that in other major Western capitalist nations. Profits have not eroded from lack of mass purchasing power and overaccumulation of capital. Neither have they ballooned to sweep control over spendable income into capitalist hands. Aided by persistent technical progress, they have remained roughly constant as a rate of return on investment. The great middle classes look more and more stable and conservative, not increasingly ground down into an ever hungrier proletariat. Governments have not turned out to be merely agents of the rich; the income tax and the "welfare state" have proved more attractive to the masses than has the sword in dealing with the rich.

What went wrong with the Marxist predictions? Today, many Marxists and other radicals say, "Just wait!" They say that the capitalist statistics mask a growing sickness and economic instability, that modern capitalism with its profit motive is only temporarily shored up by wars and imperialism through which we live off the poor in other nations and at home.[5]

No one can know the future, but the Marxist arguments find limited support thus far in the data of history. Marx flatly denied any useful role for profits or interest in the operations of an economic system. Most modern economists, including many in the USSR and Communist Eastern Europe, agree that he was clearly wrong. Without the interest rate to help guide the choice between more-and-less-roundabout means of production (e.g., how much expensive machinery to use compared to labor-intensive production), Communist planners have made major errors in production processes. Similarly, without profits as an

incentive to efficient production, the Communist nations have faced increasingly serious difficulties in getting central plans carried out. Recently both interest and profits have been openly introduced into Soviet economic planning. The record of profits as an incentive to capital accumulation and the production of goods and services that the people want in the capitalist economies is far from flawless. But better-performing alternatives are not obvious, especially for those who value individual freedom and democratic political systems.[6]

Strikingly, most modern "radicals" indicate little interest in the problem of economic incentives. To many of them, the problem is easily manageable. If everyone, especially the rich, would only be less greedy and share what they produced, economists' persistent concern with "scarcity" and more efficient use of resources would be seen to be fatuous. In any event, others say, government planning can do whatever needs to be done. Besides, they argue that a lot of the apparent "scarcity" problem is that people think they want a lot of the things they have only because of capitalist corporation brainwashing.

Not surprisingly, economists and many others in the Western economies disagree with the analysis that only good will, plus maybe some all-powerful government planning, is needed. The optimal mix of planning and private economic incentives remains very much unsettled. But in a world with wants far in excess of the resources available to meet them, economic incentives lie inescapably at the heart of the problems faced by every society.[7]

[5]For some data on the "imperialism" issue, see appendixes to Chapters 19 and 37.

[6]Although Marx was quite explicit about the death throes of capitalism, his writings are devoid of any picture of how he would see a true "Marxist" economy functioning after the revolution. Thus, it is hard to compare actual capitalist and Communist developments with what Marx might have considered optimal. He predicted the gradual withering away of government after the workers' revolt, but failed to specify who would then run what parts of the economy how. Clearly, the USSR and Communist China today are far from the governmentless economy Marx forecast. Thus, some radicals would deny that the experience of such economies is relevant in comparing the effectiveness of "capitalist" and "Marxist" economies. But if they are not relevant, what is? For more detailed information on the USSR and the "mixed" economies, see Chapter 46.

[7]For a lively authoritative modern Marxist statement, see P. Baran and P. Sweezy, *Monopoly Capital* (Modern Reader Paperbacks, 1966).

Case Studies: Poverty and Insecurity

Poverty

Insecurity

Economic Perspective on Poverty
and Insecurity

Appendix: Black Economic
Development and Black
Capitalism

Poverty is as old as man. America is rich, and by the standards of most of the world poverty has been virtually eliminated here. Our "poor" in New York live as well as does the average worker in Leningrad or Mexico City. The visitor from India or the Congo would see nothing that even approaches the poverty that the mass of his people take for granted. Even by our own standards, today only about 10 percent of our people live in poverty. But even in the "affluent society" of modern America there is an economic underworld of poverty, and a widespread fear of economic insecurity.

These two problems—poverty and insecurity —provide two excellent opportunities to apply the economic theory you have learned thus far, in understanding why they exist and in evaluat-

ing what, if anything, we can do about them. For both are case studies that illustrate the intricate intermix of macro- and microeconomics in the real world, as well as the close interactions among economic, social, and political processes in our society. Both reemphasize the central point of economics that even in as wealthy a society as ours there are never enough resources to go around—to give everyone all he wants.

Poverty

Chapter 2 laid out one orderly approach to analyzing policy-type problems. First define the problem: Where are we now, and where do we want to go? Second, map out the main elements of the situation analytically, pointing up the main alternative policies for moving from where we are to where we want to be. Third, weigh the alternatives and decide which, all things considered, seems best.

Where are we now? What are the facts about poverty? In 1969 the median family income in the United States was about $9,100.[1] In that same year about 7 million families had money incomes of less than $3,800; their median income was $2,200, and over 1 million of the families were raising four or more children on that income. About 5 million people living alone had incomes below $1,800. Together, these two groups included about 23 million Americans, 11 percent of the population. These are the poor.

But there is much debate about how poverty should be defined, about where the borderline belongs between the poor and the reasonably well-off. The use of $3,800 for an urban family of four and $1,800 for an individual living alone as income cut-off points is an obviously arbitrary choice, but one that has been widely adopted in recent years. It was established by the Social Security Administration, and has risen each year to reflect rising prices. Thus the figure should be increased if inflation continues, in order to define a constant "real" poverty level.[2]

What is considered poverty changes with the times, and some people say we just define poverty so there will always be some. They argue that there's only a poverty problem in the eyes of the do-gooders. Twenty years ago, the median money income of all families was only about $4,000 (in 1969 prices), and $2,000 was often considered the poverty level. Then over a third of all families would have fallen below the $3,800 poverty level that we use now. Economic growth has steadily pushed most families above the minimum levels that seemed reasonable a generation or two ago. But our aspirations have risen with our rising incomes.

Who Are the Poor?

In 1962, Michael Harrington wrote a book, *The Other America*, which touched the conscience of many Americans. The other America, Harrington wrote, is the world of the poor in the midst of plenty—a world of desolation, of hopelessness, of bitterness and resentment, of slums, of discrimination. It is the world of Negroes and Puerto Ricans living in the great city slums; of old men and women living alone in rented tenement rooms; of poor southern farmers living in ramshackle huts without plumbing; of fatherless families whose mothers struggle to support their children; of failures and rejects for a dozen other reasons.

To understand poverty, Harrington argued, we must add sociology to economics. The poor, he wrote, live in a subculture of their own. Most of them feel—with apathy or resentment—that no one cares. It is a world whose inhabitants are isolated from the mainstream of American life and alienated from its values. It is a world whose occupants are literally concerned with day-to-day survival, where minor illness is a major tragedy, where fatback and cheap greens are a standard diet. Lastly, it is a world turned in on itself in its values and its habits, a world in which the poverty of the parents is visited upon the children.

Each year, many families move up from the ranks of the poor, and some families slide down below the imaginary line. But the great bulk of the poor stay poor.

To understand the problem of poverty, you must recognize that the poor differ widely. Five groups loom large.

Negroes. Although only 1.3 million of the 5 million poor families are nonwhite, over 30 percent of all Negro families are poor. Some 7 million of the 23 million poor persons in 1969 were Negroes. Many poor Negro families live in the rural South; over 60 percent of Negro farmers are in the poverty group. But increasingly, they

---

[1]The 1969 data are preliminary estimates, and may be changed somewhat when final figures become available.

[2]These poverty estimates are made by taking minimal food requirements and multiplying them by three. They vary for larger or smaller families, and are set at 70 percent of urban levels for farm families. Clearly, the standards are highly arbitrary, and many observers prefer to set other standards, correspondingly changing the number of families classified as poor. For a fuller description of S.S.A. procedures, with historical data, see U.S. Department of Commerce, *Poverty in the United States* (*Current Population Reports,* Series P-60), December 31, 1969.

have moved to the northern city slums. Those who live in the cities have incomes 35 percent below whites with comparable education. In the city slums, over half of Negro youths are high school dropouts. The breakdown of the Negro family in the city slums is a critical part of the problem of Negro poverty. Over half of all poor Negroes live in family units headed by females.

Farmers. Over 20 percent of all farm families are poor, about twice the urban rate. Rural poverty is concentrated in the South. A substantial portion of poor southern farmers are the Negroes mentioned above. Government aids to agriculture provide virtually no help to the poor farmers; the money goes largely to the big, well-capitalized farmers.

Old People. Old age brings poverty about as often as it brings adequate retirement. About 1.2 million families where the husband is over sixty-five are poor; this is about 16 percent of all such families, and it accounts for about 25 percent of all poor families. In addition, nearly half of all old people living alone have incomes below $1,800. Social security doesn't help much. The average benefit is only a little over $1,000 a year, and only half of the nation's poor receive such government benefit payments.

Fatherless Families. Nearly 40 percent of all women left alone to provide for their children are poor; for nonwhites the figure is nearly 60 percent. Fatherless families are common in the low-income groups, and the woman who has to earn her family's living must either leave her children alone (which she often does in the poverty groups) or find someone to look after them. She faces many lost workdays and consequently job instability. The breakdown of the family is near the core of the massive Negro problem in the city slums. Probably not one out of three Negro children in poor families who now reaches age eighteen has lived all his life with both his parents. Nationwide, the number of children on public "welfare" has risen from less than 1 million to over 6 million since 1950, with most of the increase during the 1960s, a decade of growing prosperity and falling unemployment. In New York City alone, over 1 million mothers and children were on welfare in 1970, out of a total population of under 8 million.

Others. About one-third of all poor families don't fit into any of the groups above. They live in depressed areas; they have poor motivation; they have low intelligence; most have had little education; they have chosen occupations which demand has passed. By the test of the market they are failures, the rejects of our modern economy.

One generalization applies to all these groups. Most come from poor families and have been poor all their lives.

The above picture is substantially accurate, but statistics can be misleading. Some observers argue that using money incomes as a test overstates the magnitude of the problem. The poor southern farmer with an annual income of $1,000 and six children eats better off the land than the arithmetic would suggest. Some poor families, especially the elderly, have accumulated assets, and draw on them to supplement their current incomes. Thus, their actual consumption is well above the incomes they report. As a college student, you are probably another example. In many ways, consumption would be a better measure of poverty than is current money income, and such a measure might show an appreciable number of the poor families better off than they seem. Clearly, families whose incomes drop temporarily may appear very poor by the income test, but they may maintain their consumption standards while waiting for a return to normal incomes. But with all these reservations, most of those who are poor by the income test above **are** poor by modern American standards.

Why Are They Poor?

There are many reasons why the poor are poor. In a brief analysis, we must simplify drastically. But, recognizing this warning, the theory of the preceding chapters should help you greatly in straightening out the causes of poverty.

Inadequate Aggregate Demand. When there is recession, unemployment raises the proportion of the population below the poverty line. Conversely, prosperity brings more jobs, especially for marginal members of the labor force who are last to be taken on. A major depression is a catastrophe for the poor.

But only a small fraction of the poor in the prosperous years 1968–1969 were "unemployed," as measured by the unemployment statistics. Over half the poor were simply out of the labor market. Children were the largest group. Many of the poor were elderly people, past their working years. Many in the slums, especially Negroes, had given up looking for work. Others were not in the labor force for a variety of other reasons. Rising aggregate demand and falling unemployment help to lessen poverty, but they give jobs and higher incomes only to those who have a service to sell. The best estimates suggest that reduction of the overall unemployment rate from 4 percent to 3 percent would reduce the population below the poverty line by only about 1 percentage point.

But the indirect effects of a prosperous economy are more important than this figure suggests in lessening barriers against minority groups as labor markets tighten, in providing more on-the-job training for marginal workers, in providing partial employment for the elderly, and in other indirect ways.

Low Productivity. The message of Chapters 32 and 33 was that individual incomes generally depend, to a rough first approximation, on the marginal productivity of the individuals concerned. If this is correct, given a reasonable level of aggregate demand, poor people in the labor market are by and large poor because their marginal productivity is low. They are poor because they are not worth more to employers in a profit-motivated economy. Or, if they are elderly, they are poor now because they did not adequately plan ahead, if they had an adequate life income to provide a reasonable retirement income through savings.

This is a harsh conclusion, and, as we shall see in a moment, one that is only partially correct. But it has a strong core of truth. Over 60 per- cent of all poor families are headed by an individual with less than an eighth-grade education; only 20 percent by individuals who completed high school. Many old people, even though seeking work, can offer only limited services in the market. Women attempting to support their children inescapably lose more time than others. Many of the adult poor have no skills, or obsolete ones.

Discrimination and Other Market Imperfections. A basic cause of nonwhite poverty is discrimination—in education, jobs, access to medical care, on nearly every score. Over 95 percent of nonwhites are Negroes. Negro incomes are 35–40 percent lower than those for whites at the same years of education, area of residence, and sex, and this overall spread has decreased only slightly. Just how much of nonwhite poverty is accounted for by discrimination is sharply debated by the experts. Some estimates suggest about $15 billion, but this is only a very rough approximation.[3]

But progress was made in the 1960s. Over a third of all black families received over $8,000 in 1969, compared to 15 percent in 1960 (in constant 1969 dollars). For black families headed by a male aged 25 to 34, incomes in 1969 were 87 percent those of comparable whites. The Negro unemployment rate declined sharply over the decade, though it remained roughly twice that for whites. The number of black "professional and technical" employees more than doubled during the 1960s, compared to a 40 percent increase for whites. Progress in reducing economic discrimination against nonwhites has been substantial. But the problem is still a massive one.

Apart from the special problems of market discrimination against nonwhites, immobility, apathy, and ignorance of job openings are generally characteristic of the poor. Poor southern farmers, both Negro and white, appear to be

---

[3]See, for example, J. Kain, *Race and Poverty* (Englewood Cliffs, N.J.: Prentice-Hall, Inc., Spectrum Books, 1969); L. Thurow, *Poverty and Discrimination* (Washington, D.C.: The Brookings Institution, 1969), especially Chaps. 7 and 9; and, at a much more technical level, G. Becker, *The Economics of Discrimination* (Chicago: University of Chicago Press, 1957).

highly immobile, except for the young. In Appalachia, there has been a massive exodus of population, but again almost entirely of young people. Thus, the poor of middle age and beyond tend neither to know about alternative job opportunities nor to be willing or able to move to them if the information is available. To move is expensive and uncertain. The subculture of the poor has little contact with the formal processes of employment exchanges and the information and mobility devices available to the middle classes. Even in the cities, the poor have little contact with the job markets of the middle classes.

Absence from the Labor Force. Nearly 60 percent of all poor families are headed by individuals who are not in the labor force. Many of these are elderly people, but many others are discouraged youths and mothers of fatherless families who have given up looking for work. Thus, the problems of poverty, family instability, and insecurity in old age are inseparably intertwined. Others are out of the labor force for a variety of reasons—because of ill health, lack of motivation, family circumstances, or simply because they have given up hope of finding a job. Until recently, "welfare" has helped both to break up poor families (since no aid could be given to a family headed by a male of working age) and to keep people out of jobs (since any earnings would lead to a dollar-for-dollar reduction in welfare benefits). Unless rising aggregate demand, lessened discrimination, improved aid practices, or improved information and mobility were to pull some of these individuals back into the labor force, no improvement in economic conditions or in the workings of the market can help alleviate their poverty.

Beyond these four economic causes, most observers add a socioeconomic analysis. Poverty breeds poverty, in a vicious circle. A poor individual or family has a high probability of staying poor. The poor live largely in slums or in backward rural areas. Their children do not learn to read, to write, even to speak well. They grow up to apathy or resentment, and they go to poor schools with other poor children. They lag far behind children in middle-class schools,

and their drop-out rate is high—not surprisingly, for there is little in their culture to make them care about education. When the poor are sick they stay sick longer because they have inadequate medical care. Thus they find it harder to keep jobs. Broken homes are common. Often there is little motivation or hope to rise from the vicious circle of poverty, either for the young or for adults.

Policies against Poverty

In 1964, President Johnson declared "unconditional war on poverty" as a major goal of his administration, and this goal has been widely reaffirmed since then. But to lessen poverty is a complex, difficult problem. We cannot explore all the many approaches that have been suggested. But the above analysis, together with the theory of earlier chapters, should suggest some broad lines of attack.

Maintaining High Employment. Macroeconomics tells us that maintaining high employment, a labor market in which demand for workers is strong, should be a powerful force for the reduction of poverty. Against poverty, as against many of our other problems, a combined attack on the macro and micro levels makes sense. To try to eradicate poverty without strong aggregate demand and general prosperity offers little hope of success. The case for high employment is further strengthened by the special problems of alleviating poverty.

Accelerating Economic Growth. Over the long run, faster growth in output per capita provides a fundamental approach to the erosion of poverty. This is shown dramatically by Figure 37–1. Over the past two decades, economic growth has reduced poverty by somewhat over 1 percent a year. If the rate of the 1960s could be maintained (remember that the decade included an upswing from a slack economy in the early 1960s), poverty would be entirely eliminated in less than ten years. But important as rapid growth is, the nearer poverty approaches zero the harder it will be to make further gains. The remaining poor will be increasingly those insulated from labor markets—the aged, the

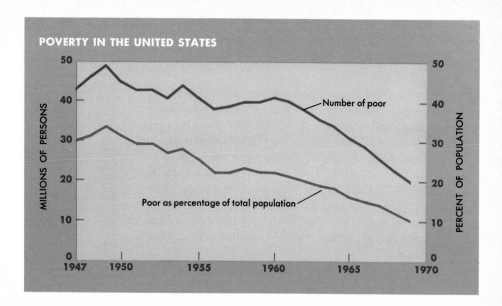

POVERTY IN THE UNITED STATES

Number of poor

Poor as percentage of total population

MILLIONS OF PERSONS

PERCENT OF POPULATION

1947 1950 1955 1960 1965 1970

fig. 37–1

Rapid economic growth has sharply reduced the number of poor people in the United States during the post-World War II years. (Source: Council of Economic Advisers and Social Security Administration.)

disabled, what some have called the "hard-core poor."

Improving the Productivity of the Poor. Probably the most basic reason for low incomes is the low productivity of the poor, certainly if we set aside the problem of children and the aged. By and large, investment in human beings increases their productivity, just as does investment in nonhuman wealth. For many reasons, society's investment in the poor falls far short of its investment in most individuals who rise above poverty. The poor live in slums, in squalor. They receive short and poor educations. They get little job training in schools or on the job, since they so often find no employment. They receive inadequate medical care. If we wish to raise the productivity of many of the poor, larger investment to develop their productive capacity is the first prescription that arises from standard economic analysis.

Lessening Discrimination. For nonwhites, lessening of discrimination is essential to long-run economic progress. Barriers to current jobs must be reduced. Still more fundamentally, better educational opportunities can improve minority groups' chances to break out of the vicious circle of poverty.

Debate over steps to eliminate racial discrimination far transcends issues of how best to reduce poverty. The answers are at least as much political and social as they are economic. The economic magnitude of the problem is

mapped out above, and some of its elements are examined in detail in the appendix to this chapter. Both government and private steps have made some headway in recent years, but it is only a beginning. The public sector has a better record than the private one; the ratio of blacks to total government employees far exceeds the comparable ratio in private business. Discrimination in education and housing poses even deeper problems, which are probably basic to the meaningful establishment of economic equality of opportunity. Reduction of discrimination makes economic sense; it would raise the real income of both whites and blacks. But economic measures alone will fall far short of solving the problem.

Improving Labor Markets. Many of the poor are effectively isolated from jobs by lack of information, immobility, and inertia, in addition to discrimination. This is especially true of the rural poor in the South. But it is also true in the slums of the great cities, where for thousands of unskilled and poorly educated teen-agers and adults there is no practical channel into the jobs that are opening up elsewhere in the economy, even in the same city. To say that individuals with proper motivation would seek out the jobs that may be open elsewhere is a very partial answer for the Puerto Rican or Negro teen-ager in Harlem or in the backwoods of Alabama.

Better job-training programs, employment exchanges, guidance and counseling services, and the like could help those who suffer merely from inadequate information or are immobile because of financial difficulties. Better information, better education, and better training programs for both youth and adults make sense both to fight poverty and on their own merits to improve the efficiency of our economic system. More subsidized day-care nurseries for poor working mothers could both improve their *de facto* economic productivity and get underprivileged youngsters off to a better educational start.

Many economists blame unions and the government itself for important job barriers. Many craft unions still have *de facto* barriers against nonwhites for apprenticeships and union membership and limit memberships for whites as well, thus in effect blocking them from higher-paying jobs. And the federal minimum wage law of $1.85 per hour as of 1970, however admirable its purpose, surely shuts many low-productivity workers out of jobs which might be there at lower wage rates for such workers, especially poorly educated, poverty-group teen-agers.

Money-Income Redistribution. Giving direct money grants of about $10 billion, or only about 1 percent of g.n.p., would be sufficient to raise every poor person above the $3,800-per-family or $1,800-per-individual poverty level indicated above. Assuming 3 percent per capita average growth in real income, if the nonpoor 90 percent of the population would forego one-half of 1 percent of that growth for four years, all poverty could be eliminated. And indeed some redistribution of income toward the lower groups has been occurring. Figure 38–5 in the next chapter shows the annual redistribution through government taxing and spending. Table 37–1 shows the general shift toward less income inequality over the past half century.

Some economists argue that direct income transfer (gifts) is the simplest attack on the poverty problem, and that it would have the great virtue of letting us see the full cost of the program. In addition, it would give recipients of aid freedom to spend their incomes as they wish, in contrast to programs that force them to take aid through housing subsidies, medical assistance, education, and the like.

table 37-1

Family Income Shares, 1929-1969*

	Percent of Total Income Received			
	1929	1950	1960	1969
Lowest fifth	13.0	4.5	4.8	5.7
Second fifth		12.0	11.7	12.4
Third fifth	14.0	17.4	17.4	17.7
Fourth fifth	19.0	23.5	23.6	23.7
Top fifth	54.0	42.6	42.6	40.6
All families	100.0	100.0	100.0	100.0

* Source: U.S. Department of Commerce.

But this approach would not raise society's total real income; it would merely redistribute what we now produce without using the productive potential of many poor. Moreover, such direct cash grants to all the poor might face serious problems on the incentive front, since individuals now earning more than the poverty level might prefer to take direct subsidies and avoid work. Thus, the actual cost of such a direct subsidy approach to the poverty problem would probably be larger than the $10 billion indicated. At the extreme, if everyone in the poverty range now earning stopped work, the total cost would go up to about $25 billion. But it would still be a small percentage of g.n.p.

The "Negative Income Tax." Recently a somewhat startling proposal to reform the welfare system has been advanced simultaneously by two such different economists as Chicago's Milton Friedman, an adviser to Barry Goldwater and President Nixon, and Yale's James Tobin, economic adviser to President Kennedy. It is to substitute a "negative income tax" for part or all of the present "welfare" system—to combine compassion with incentives by guaranteeing everyone a basic minimum income and permitting him to keep, say, half of all he earns in addition—up to some moderate income level, when he would slide over to regular taxpayer status.

The recent welfare system has had three big deficiencies: (1) It excludes a lot of poor people, mainly because they have an adult male in the family, even though he earns nothing or less than the poverty level. Thus, only about half the poor receive any welfare payments. (2) The system has in effect imposed a 100 percent marginal tax rate on any welfare-family earnings, since welfare payments have been reduced by the amount of any earnings. The result has been pressure to break up families, since welfare payments can be received only by fatherless families, and disincentive to work, since welfare payments are cut to match any earnings. (3) Moreover, benefits are largely set by the individual states, and they varied from $39 to $263 per person per month in 1969, with the very low benefit payments in the deep South.

The negative income tax proposal has many variations but two essential elements to correct these welfare-system weaknesses. First, it would guarantee some minimum income to everyone. Everyone would file a simple tax form, and the government would pay low-income people rather than collecting taxes from them. Second, this negative tax (subsidy) would decline if poor people earned in addition, but it would decline by only some fraction (say, half)

of those earnings, so the poor family would always have more after-tax income by working than by merely staying idle on government aid. Table 37–2 shows how it might work, assuming a guaranteed minimum income of $3,200 for a family of four and a marginal negative income tax rate of 50 percent, combined with the regular 1969 federal income tax.

If a family has no private income, it would receive from the government a $3,200 annual income (negative income tax), possibly in weekly or monthly checks like Social Security—see columns 4 and 5. If the family earns $1,000, it keeps the $1,000, but its payment from the government drops by half that amount. Net result: its after-tax income is $3,700, up $500. Since each family can keep 50 percent of all earned income, its dollar aid from the government will not fall to zero until its earned income is $6,400. Moreover, since its marginal tax rate is not to exceed 50 percent, exact after-tax equality with the present tax system would not be reached until an income of $7,920, when it is back on the regular tax system, with a tax of $711.

table 37-2

Negative Income Tax Example* (Family of Four)

| | Under 1969 Tax Law | | With NIT Added: | |
Private Income	Tax (−)	After-tax Income	Net Benefit (+) or Tax (−)	Income after NIT and Tax
$ 0	0	0	+3200	3,200
1,000	0	1,000	+2700	3,700
2,000	0	2,000	+2200	4,200
3,000	0	3,000	+1700	4,700
4,000	−140	3,860	+1200	5,200
5,000	−290	4,710	+ 700	5,700
6,000	−450	5,550	+ 200	6,200
** 6,400	−511	5,889	0	6,400
7,000	−603	6,397	− 300	6,700
*** 7,920	−760	7,160	− 760	7,160
8,000	−772	7,228	− 772	7,228

*On the assumption that the government would provide a minimum family income of $3,200, with a marginal negative income tax rate of 50 percent to supplement regular tax system; 1969 tax rates are without the special Vietnam "surtax" added for that year.
**End of government direct subsidy.
***Point of after-tax equality with 1969 system.

How much would the plan cost? The answer is unclear. A simple income transfer to eliminate the present "poverty income gap" would be less than $10 billion. But if every family were guaranteed at least $3,200 or $3,800, probably some who now work would work less, so the actual income transfer needed would substantially exceed $10 billion. If we want the maximum work-incentive effect from the N.I.T., the government out-of-pocket cost will be still higher, since the marginal tax rate on earned income should be kept low and the government would forego part of the taxes it would have otherwise collected from those in the income groups just above the poverty line. For the plan in Table 37–2, the probable cost has been estimated at around $25 billion annually, though advocates point out that present welfare programs could be eliminated. Obviously, the cost would vary greatly for different minimum income levels and marginal tax rates.

How about the other big question—wouldn't N.I.T. just lead a lot of ne'er-do-wells to loaf on the public purse? Why not require those able to do so to seek work as a condition of receiving government aid? N.I.T. advocates have two answers. First, a decent income is a right, not a privilege; free men and women should not be subjected to the indignity of being "investigated" by government agents as a condition to receiving this right. Second, even if you don't accept the preceding argument, trying to check up on the relatively small number of slackers just isn't worth it. The administrative morass of the present welfare system is evidence of what happens when the government tries to administer such a "spy system," as its critics call it.[4]

The Government as Residual Employer. Following the destructive riots of the 1960s, another dramatic proposal was advanced by some observers, namely, that the government step in as residual employer for the poor—that it guarantee jobs for all who want them. The government might employ the jobless directly, in city clean-up work, in providing more mail deliveries, or in other jobs useful to the public. Or it might subsidize private businesses to employ the unemployed. Jobs, incomes, and a feeling of personal usefulness, these observers argued, are essential if we are to break the syndrome of poverty, especially in the city "ghettos." Another million jobs for the currently unemployed, especially young people, could make the difference between constructive forward movement and increasing social disintegration, riots, and blight in our central cities. The expense, they argue, while immediately large, would be small compared to the enormous social and economic costs of inaction.

Direct Aid in Kind. One objection to all money-aid programs is that the poor may not spend the money wisely. Welfare mothers may buy TV sets and new clothes for themselves instead of nourishing food and medicine for their children. Under N.I.T., beneficiaries might buy booze, drugs, and expensive automobiles.

Some observers say that each man is the best judge of what he wants and needs, and that he should be free to spend as he wishes. Most societies agree only in part. We provide direct free education for all children to be sure they get it. We provide minimal health services for the elderly poor. We provide food stamps for the poor so they can use their aid only in buying certain classes of nourishing foods.[5] It's easy to see that the aid-in-kind principle could be extended to the entire welfare program, though with substantial administrative costs and problems as the "in-kind" list lengthened.

The War on Poverty

In 1964, Congress passed the Economic Opportunity Act, responding to President Johnson's call for an all-out "war on poverty." Since

---

[4]A large-scale experimental N.I.T. project now under way suggests that N.I.T. recipients work at least as much to obtain private incomes as do a comparable "control" group of families without N.I.T. The three-year experiment is indirectly financed by the federal government but largely conducted by a special University of Wisconsin research group, and covers some 1,000 families in New Jersey. But only preliminary returns are in so far.

[5]Contrast this with a common practice in many West European countries of giving a specific "children's allowance" for each child, to poor and rich families alike.

table 37-3

Selected Major Income-Maintenance Programs, Fiscal Year 1969 [a]

Program	Total Outlays (Millions of Dollars)	Beneficiaries	
		Number (Thousands)	Percent in Poverty Households [b]
All programs	58,679	(d)	(d)
Aid to families with dependent children	3,206	6,146	100
Unemployment insurance:			
Federal — state unemployment compensation	2,300	5,196	20
Federal employees and ex-servicemen	111	489	10
Railroad	52	92	(d)
Disability programs:			
Workmen's compensation	1,686	(d)	(d)
Federal employees	57	40	15
Veterans' compensation	2,611	2,390	24
Railroad	77	41	(d)
Social security	2,691	2,278	39
Aid to the blind	92	84	100
Aid to the permanently and totally disabled	726	721	100
Assistance to those sixty-five and over:			
Social security retirement and survivors' benefits	24,681	21,931	31
Old-age assistance	1,833	2,123	100
Military retirement	2,265	681	(d)
Civil service retirement	2,364	918	(d)
Railroad retirement	1,542	969	34
Veterans pensions	2,127	2,252	80
General assistance	32	700	100
Federal assistance-in-kind	10,226	(e)	(e)

[a] Source: *Economic Report of the President*, 1969, p. 164.

[b] Income including cash benefits.

[c] Data exclude state and local government retirement systems and all private retirement and charitable programs.

[d] Not available.

[e] Includes $8.5 billion for medical benefits, to 24 million individuals of whom perhaps half are poor. Other major items are food and housing programs, affecting about 14 million beneficiaries. Nearly all food aid goes to poverty families, perhaps two-thirds of public housing and rent supplement expenditures. Excludes all spending on education.

then, public attention has centered on the poverty problem, and Congress has enacted a variety of measures aimed at lessening poverty for various groups through various programs. Many of these programs (for example, increased social security benefits) help both "poor" and those above the arbitrary poverty line, so it is impossible to say just how much has been spent annually in fighting poverty. Moreover, the figures involved change substantially year by year.

Table 37–3 presents an analysis of many of the relevant expenditures for fiscal 1969. Note that it includes most, but not all, of the major government "income-maintenance" programs. For example, spending on education is not included in the last category of "assistance-in-kind" because it goes so broadly beyond income maintenance per se. The first column shows total government expenditures, the second the number of beneficiaries involved, and the third rough estimates of all beneficiaries who were in the poverty group. Many of the programs were aimed 100 percent at the poor, but several others (including some of the biggest, like Social Security and Medicare) went to numerous non-poor persons as well.

President Nixon's fiscal budget for 1971 proposed $50 billion for "income security," about 25 percent of the total budget (compared to $18 billion a decade earlier). This figure included about $42 billion for social security and unemployment insurance benefits, $7 billion for direct public aid to the poor, and $1.5 billion for vocational rehabilitation and the like. These "income-security" figures cover only part of the programs in Table 37–3, whose total for 1971 would exceed $70 billion. Rough estimates suggest that about $33 billion represented direct aid to the poor in fiscal 1971, as is indicated in Table 37–4.

table 37-4

Federal Aid to the Poor, 1971*

Education	$ 2.7 billion
Employment assistance	2.3 "
Health assistance	6.4 "
Direct income assistance	17.8 "
Other	3.7 "
	$32.9 billion

* Source: U.S. Budget Bureau

Focusing specifically on poverty and the "welfare" problem, President Nixon in 1969 proposed a revolution of the welfare system which, he said, has failed us. Citing the deficiencies indicated above, he proposed a modified, experimental negative-income-tax plan (carefully avoiding use of those possibly inflammatory words), with a $1,600 guaranteed family minimum, no tax on the next $720 of private income, and a 50 percent marginal tax rate above that. Under this plan, a four-person family would be back on the regular income-tax schedule just below the $4,000 income level. He proposed that all able-bodied males must register for jobs as a condition of receiving aid. The administration estimated the annual cost of the program at $4–$5 billion, far below that of the Table 37–2 example with much higher benefit levels.

As this is written, the fate of this proposal remains uncertain. One big issue is the requirement that all states meet at least the minimum levels specified, though the federal government would pay the costs above existing state levels. The great bulk of the federal outlays would go to the southern states, a provision noted with unhappiness by many northern states whose citizens would provide most of the funds and receive few of the benefits. The newspapers will record the outcome. The economics and politics of poverty are intertwined.

Insecurity

The second big problem—insecurity—is similar to, yet different from, poverty. Here again, economic theory can help to explain why the problem exists and what we might do about it. But here, too, using economic theory is only one part of the task. We must understand the present situation and how it came to be; we must clarify our objectives; and we must weigh carefully economic and noneconomic considerations in assessing the merits of alternative policies.

The Causes of Insecurity

Severe depressions, rapid technological change, and especially modern industrialization have over the past century brought nearly all groups face-to-face with the problem of economic insecurity at one time or another. The family farm, reasonably secure against hunger and physical privation, has nearly vanished. With increased mobility, the tradition of family care for aged parents and relatives has been drastically weakened.

Until only a half century ago, private charity, plus some state-local government help, was depended on to shoulder the burden of caring for persons unable to support themselves. Inability to provide for self-support was considered a social stigma. The general attitude was, "If he can't make his own way, why should we look out for him?" Workers were expected to take jobs at their own risk; compensation for injuries on the job was almost impossible to collect. The specter of poverty in old age was an uncomfortable subject to be avoided in polite conversation. Though every county had its "poor house" and local "poor" laws existed in most communities, they were usually so ineffectual as to be only a sop to the consciences of the more fortunate.

In the Great Depression of the 1930s, a quarter of the labor force was completely unemployed; probably not more than half had regular full-time jobs. There were hunger and privation across the land. Whatever people's previous attitudes about every man looking out for himself, it was clear someone had to do something; and the only someone with significant power to attack such a massive problem seemed to be the federal government.

President Roosevelt's desire to help the "underfed and underprivileged third" culminated in the Social Security Act of 1935, which provided a long-run program of aid for the aged and other needy groups. This act, which is still the cornerstone of the nation's governmental social-security program, had two main facets: a nationwide program of unemployment insurance, and compulsory old-age insurance for workers and self-employed persons. In 1965, thirty years later, "Medicare" was added for the aged, and then "Medicaid."

One big cause of insecurity is the risk of unemployment. Modern fiscal and monetary policy have apparently gone far to keep the economy nearer a stable growth path; the role of unemployment insurance as an "automatic" fiscal stabilizer and aid to the unemployed was examined in Chapter 14. The special problems of insecurity arising from rapid technological change ("automation") will be analyzed in Chapter 45, on "The Economics of Change." Let us focus here on the biggest dollar sector of the "Social Security" problem, public and private aid for the aged, including Medicare. In 1970, federal payments under these programs exceeded $50 billion to over 35 million elder citizens. Moreover, totals of both dollars and persons affected are scheduled to skyrocket in the years ahead. Social Security is very big business for the American economy.

The Economic Issues in Old-Age Insecurity

The essence of an individualistic, private enterprise system is its willingness to let people make their own economic decisions, take their own risks, reap the benefits of good choices, and make their own mistakes. Some personal economic insecurity—the chance that individuals will make mistakes and face painful consequences—thus is of the essence of such a system. It is a central issue of public policy whether we are prepared to let people suffer the consequences of their own actions—conversely, to what extent we should prevent them from taking dangerous chances or guarantee them against painful consequences (like hunger in old age). It is clear that the issues in old-age insecurity are only partly economic; how we define the problem and assess alternative policies depends heavily on personal value judgments.

Economic analysis suggests three main reasons why the market system may produce socially unacceptable low asset and income levels for people past sixty-five. First, some people have such low lifetime total incomes that there is no way they could allocate their incomes to provide above-poverty levels before and after retirement. Second, some people have high enough lifetime total incomes to be able to provide for above-poverty-level postretirement incomes, but intentionally or haphazardly allocate too much of the total to preretirement consumption, too little to saving. Third, some markets discriminate against older workers, so that above-sixty-five individuals find it difficult to supplement their retirement savings, even though they have productive abilities that could be sold on the market in the absence of such discrimination.

Consider the three causes separately.

Lifetime Poverty. If, for any of the reasons suggested above, an individual's or family's total lifetime income is below the poverty level, society cannot expect him to provide an adequate postretirement income for himself. In such cases, the fundamental remedies lie in raising the lifetime productivity of such individuals, in assuring growing and open markets for their services, and in providing income transfers to raise their living standards to socially acceptable minimum levels.

Adequate Lifetime Incomes but Inadequate Private Provision for Old Age. It is the second case that raises tough additional issues. Suppose John Doe has an above-poverty-level lifetime income, but chooses to live too well (save too little) before retirement, or perhaps risks his savings on bad investment choices. Shall society provide a guaranteed minimum postretirement income, or force him (through compulsory government social security) to save for his own retirement? Can we think of ways to induce him to choose voluntarily to save the required amount? Or shall we let him suffer poverty in old age, since he's responsible for his own plight?

The answer in the United States, and in most of the other Western industrialized nations, is mainly a combination of the first and second alternatives—a compulsory social security program for old age, supplemented by direct income grants in special cases not covered adequately by social security. You should be clear that this answer rests largely not on economic grounds per se, but on the social "value judgment" that society should insist that people save for their own retirement and guarantee at least a minimum income to the aged. We are unwilling to let most people risk making a mistake that might entail abject poverty after retirement—or, more likely, might require a direct income transfer from others in society to avoid postretirement poverty and destitution. In economywide terms, this amounts to large annual real-income transfer from current workers to those who are idle.

Market Discrimination against Older Workers. Markets that are closed to potentially productive workers both waste potential output and make it difficult for the excluded workers to earn reasonable incomes. Many persons over sixty-five are unable or unwilling to work. But others are able and anxious, even at jobs below the level they held before retirement. In America, we take retirement at about sixty-five as the normal path, and many workers want it so. Moreover, our government social-security program withholds benefits from those between sixty-five and seventy-two who continue to earn above $1,800 of income for themselves. But the cost of enforced retirement in terms of total g.n.p. lost may be appreciable, and barriers against those who want to work after sixty-five mark a discrimination similar to that against the other groups noted in the poverty section above. Maximum output in a market system calls for freedom of all productive resources to compete openly for employment.

The Federal Social Security Program

What have we done about the problem of old-age insecurity? Figure 37–2 summarizes governmental social-security programs as of 1970. Old-age and Survivors' Insurance (O.A.S.I.)[6] is the biggest element of the program. In 1970 there were nearly 30 million beneficiaries who received nearly $40 billion; and nearly 100 million people are now covered by O.A.S.I. and related programs. About 95 percent of all employees in the United States are in "covered" occupations. Medicare covers roughly the same group. Moreover, 60 million workers are covered by unemployment insurance. In addition, other benefits, especially public assistance to the needy not receiving benefits under the other programs, reach another 7 million people.

Thus, government social security now provides minimum protection against unemployment, poverty in old age, and destitution from lack of support for most (though not all) of the

[6]Including such special retirement programs as the Railway Retirement Fund.

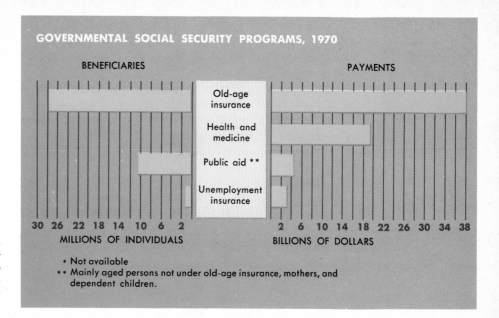

GOVERNMENTAL SOCIAL SECURITY PROGRAMS, 1970

BENEFICIARIES   PAYMENTS

Old-age insurance
Health and medicine
Public aid **
Unemployment insurance

30 26 22 18 14 10 6 2   2 6 10 14 18 22 26 30 34 38
MILLIONS OF INDIVIDUALS   BILLIONS OF DOLLARS

* Not available
** Mainly aged persons not under old-age insurance, mothers, and dependent children.

fig. 37–2

Old-age benefits dominate the governmental social-security picture, but health and other welfare benefits also run into the billions. (Source: Department of Health, Education, and Welfare.)

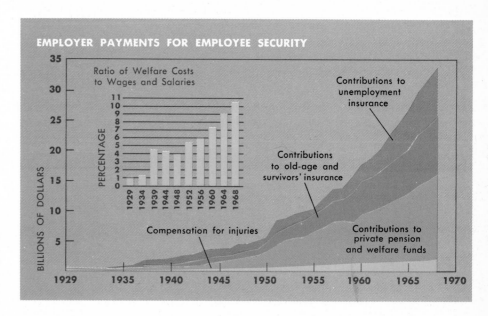

EMPLOYER PAYMENTS FOR EMPLOYEE SECURITY

Ratio of Welfare Costs to Wages and Salaries

Contributions to unemployment insurance

Contributions to old-age and survivors' insurance

Compensation for injuries

Contributions to private pension and welfare funds

1929 1935 1940 1945 1950 1955 1960 1965 1970

fig. 37–3

Employer payments for employee pensions and other benefits have soared. Private pension and welfare funds now make up the biggest category. (Source: National Industrial Conference Board.)

nation's population. But the benefits under all these programs are small, and workers have increasingly pressed for supplementary private retirement plans. In 1929, employer contributions to employee security programs took less than 1 percent of the total wage bill, almost entirely for executive pensions and workmen's compensation for injuries. Figure 37–3 shows what has happened to such contributions since then. In 1969 they totaled about $40 billion, over 10 percent of the entire wage bill. Of this, about one-third went into O.A.S.I. About half represented employer contributions to private

employee pension and welfare funds, and this total is growing faster than O.A.S.I.

O.A.S.I. and Medicare. In 1970, about 20 million people in the United States were sixty-five or over and presumably out of the active labor force; another 95 million were under twenty, most of them also not in the labor force. Thus, in a population of 205 million, fewer than half were between twenty and sixty-five, the years of main contribution to the nation's economic output. If we allow for housewives and others of the twenty to sixty-five group who

543

were not looking for jobs, only about 80 million were in the labor force. Viewed fundamentally, the problem of providing economic security for the aged is the question of how much of the nation's current real g.n.p. we will transfer to help support those past sixty-five.

The average monthly old-age benefit payment is only about $125, since many employees still have only modest benefits built up from their past tax premiums.[7] Inflation and steadily rising income levels have repeatedly led Congress to raise benefits under the program, and to raise payroll tax rates to provide the needed revenue. In 1970 a single retired man got a minimum of $64 to a maximum of approximately $185 monthly, depending on how long he had been contributing tax payments. For husband and wife, the comparable figures were $96 and $277. For a widow with two dependent children the maximum, but by no means average, amount was $434.40, and other benefits varied according to number of beneficiaries and period of tax contribution.

[7]O.A.S.I. was originally thought to parallel an ordinary private insurance plan. A payroll tax on the employer, matched by an equal tax on the worker (currently 4.8 percent on each on the first $7,800 of income, and scheduled to rise gradually in future years) provides the funds. The premiums must be invested in special U.S. government securities.

Under a private insurance plan, the insurance company would build up a "reserve" out of which to pay beneficiaries on retirement. But O.A.S.I. was so big that accumulation of the reserve fund appropriate by private insurance standards would have created an enormous drag on aggregate demand as the population paid in tax "premiums" for years before it gradually reached retirement age. In spite of persistently increasing benefit levels, the O.A.S.I. reserve was over $40 billion by 1970, and set to rise rapidly—to over $75 billion by 1975. To avoid this large drag on the economy (and, happily, to make friends with both beneficiaries and taxpayers), Congress will predictably increase benefit levels. In essence, Social Security has lost most of the characteristics of private insurance (where reserves are accumulated and individual policyholders' benefits depend on their premiums) and become primarily a massive annual income redistribution between taxpayers (workers) and retirees.

Medicare and Medicaid. In recent years, soaring medical costs have become a major threat to the financial and physical security of the aged—and increasingly to others as well. Figure 37–4 pictures the problem dramatically. A week in the hospital with drugs and medical

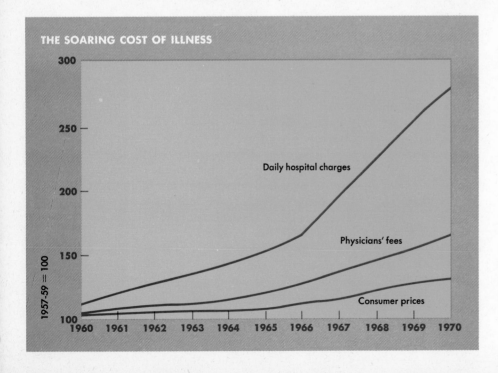

THE SOARING COST OF ILLNESS

fig. 37–4

The cost of being sick has soared astronomically in the last half dozen years. (Source: U.S. Department of Labor.)

services can easily cost from $500 to $1,000, half—or more—the full annual income of many O.A.S.I. beneficiaries.

Old people are sick more than young people, and they stay sick longer. Many, especially those who live alone, must spend their declining years in nursing homes. Link up these observations with the very low income of many old people and it is clear that even moderate illness may mean financial disaster, given today's soaring costs of medical care.

In 1965, Congress added "Medicare" to the basic O.A.S.I. program, providing guaranteed minimum medical care to those over sixty-five. The act has three major parts. The first provides compulsory hospital and nursing insurance, up to sixty days per year, with the individual paying only the first $50. These benefits are financed by matching employer–employee payroll-tax contributions, added to earlier O.A.S.I. taxes. Funds go into a separate trust fund, parallel to the O.A.S.I. fund. The second section of "Medicare" provides a voluntary "insurance" plan to cover doctor bills, under which the government will pay most but not all of the cost of such medical insurance. The third section provides additional federal aid to states through "Medicaid" to assist them in providing medical aid for welfare cases of all ages.

The Medicare–Medicaid programs are still so new that accurate predictions of their costs are difficult. In 1970, combined federal costs were $11 billion, with aid to over 20 million people, including widows, disabled, and others under age sixty-five. Costs have skyrocketed at 10-15 percent per annum with rising medical costs per se and increasing numbers of beneficiaries. With growing pressures to extend public health protection to the entire population, it seems likely that drastic changes in the entire medical-services area will occur over the next decade, possibly including a sweeping national health "insurance" plan supplementary to the present program.

Economic Evaluation of O.A.S.I. Economically, O.A.S.I. represents a massive, politically established, forced-saving plan for most of the population, or it can equally be seen as a massive government-enforced annual income redistribution from working taxpayers to retirees and health beneficiaries. Although a $40-billion reserve fund has been accumulated, O.A.S.I. is substantially on a pay-as-you-go basis, with current tax collections about equal to current benefit payments.

From the viewpoint of the worker, O.A.S.I. looks somewhat like a private annuity plan. But on five important points, it is significantly different.

First, participation in the federal old-age insurance program is compulsory. The worker has no voice in how he allocates his earnings as between this "insurance" and other uses; we force ourselves to save for retirement. Make up your own mind whether this compulsion is desirable; most people think it is.

Second, half the cost is financed by a payroll tax on employers. This would appear to represent a redistribution of income from businesses to workers. But more likely the tax is shifted onto the workers involved or onto consumers (see Chapter 40). Merely putting the tax on employers does not guarantee they will ultimately pay it.

Third, individual benefits are not determined solely by that individual's contributions, as they would be under a private old-age retirement annuity. Once a person has made contributions for a certain number of years, he is entitled to at least the minimum benefit whether he contributes all his life or only the required minimum period. Benefits are more generous in relation to contributions for low-income than for high-income earners. Indeed, O.A.S.I. pays less benefits, or sometimes no benefits at all, to age sixty-five to seventy-two participants who continue working—this in contrast to private annuity plans where benefits are fixed, regardless of earnings, after a person's retirement age is reached.

Fourth, Medicare and Medicaid pose a special problem. By sharply reducing the marginal cost of medical services to the aged, they may induce wasteful recourse to such services and thereby intensify an already serious "shortage" of doctors and medical facilities.

Fifth, looking back to the macroeconomic

analysis of Part Two, whether the government accumulates a surplus or runs a deficit in the O.A.S.I. program clearly may have a substantial impact on the government's total cash surplus or deficit. The financing of government Social Security is inescapably intermingled with issues of stabilizing fiscal policy.[8]

Private Pension and Welfare Plans

Twenty-five years ago private pension and welfare plans were almost nonexistent. Today, as Figure 37–3 showed, their burden on employers has substantially outdistanced even the burgeoning O.A.S.I., and their lead is growing. Since World War II, unions have stressed pension plans as part of the "package" to be bargained for at each contract negotiation. By 1970, private employer contributions to employee pension and welfare funds were $18 billion annually, and were growing at a rate of over $1 billion per year. Most of these plans, unlike O.A.S.I., are fully financed by company contributions. Plans typically cover retirement pensions, death benefits, and accident, hospital, and health insurance. Figure 37–5 shows what has happened to the assets of both the public

[8] J. Pechman, H. Aaron, and M. Taussig, *Social Security* (Washington, D.C.: The Brookings Institution, 1968) and J. G. Turnbull and C. A. Williams, *Economic and Social Security* (New York: Ronald Press, 1967), provide thorough descriptions and analyses of the American social security system. For a more thorough analysis of the impact of the present unemployment insurance program, see G. L. Bach, *Economics*, 4th edition (Englewood Cliffs, N.J.: Prentice-Hall, Inc., 1963), pp. 700–705.

and private pension funds. Private pension fund reserves now far exceed $100 billion.

What, beyond the obvious pension benefits for the workers, is the economic significance of these burgeoning private pension plans?

First, although they have as yet paid out only relatively small benefits, the private pension plans will gradually lead to a further allocation of currently produced real income to the retired portion of the population, just as governmental old-age insurance does. They involve the same kind of burden on wage costs as does O.A.S.I. Many observers are beginning to ask: How big a cost burden can the employed sector stand without cutting incentives to increase total output?

Second, private pension plans are rapidly piling up vast reserves. These represent net withdrawals from the income stream which must be offset by new investment unless they are to be a net drag on aggregate spending. Some firms invest their pension reserves in government bonds, some in mortgages, many in common stocks. All these raise the vital macro problem (from Part Two) of assuring a continuous, stable flow of savings into real investment.

Third, the mere existence of such huge funds poses big new problems. Where should they be invested? In stocks, to protect pensions against erosion from possible inflation? In bonds, to give security of dollar income? Elsewhere? What are the implications for control of companies as more and more pension billions are poured into common stocks? Will the managers of pension funds come to wield vast power over

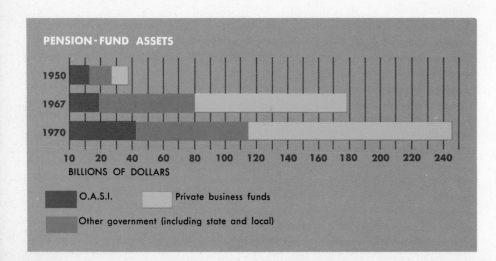

fig. 37–5

Total assets of private and public pension funds have reached astronomical figures already, and are growing by more every year. (Source: Securities and Exchange Commission.)

the management of American business? With over $100 billion of assets already under their control, some fear that pension and private trust-fund managers may become the new financial power center in our economy.[9]

Fourth, the plans may significantly reduce the flexibility and efficiency of the market economy. Few of the programs "vest" the pension benefits in individual workers as funds are set aside to provide future benefits. That is, if the worker leaves the company, he loses his accumulated pension rights. As potential pension benefits mount over the years, the incentive to stay in the same job mounts accordingly. Yet, rapid technological change and shifting demands require more mobility for a smoothly functioning economy. At the executive level, where pension plans are oldest, nonvesting pension plans are clearly a major barrier to job changes, as many companies intend them to be. For the mass of workers, the effect is not yet clear. Vesting benefits in individual workers (so they could take the benefits with them to other jobs) would eliminate the mobility restraint, but companies understandably fight this more expensive provision. Under present plans, less than half the workers currently covered by private corporate pension plans will actually draw benefits from the plan they are now under, because they will change jobs.

Economic Perspective on Poverty and Insecurity

Five concluding observations may help provide perspective on the problems of poverty and economic insecurity in modern America, and on our sweeping efforts to deal with these problems in recent years. As with most other big economic problems, these reflect the dynamic mix of macro- and microeconomic forces at work in today's complex world.

1. Our widespread social security and antipoverty programs represent a major modification of our traditional individualistic philosophy of letting individuals fend for themselves, risk where they will, reap the gains, and suffer the consequences of failure. They control the use of a substantial part of the public's income, producing a large redistribution of real income from workers to persons unable or unwilling to provide an adequate income for themselves. Unless these programs increase total g.n.p., they necessarily involve such a transfer of real income. Remember the first principle of economics: With limited resources, more for one use means less for others.

This redistribution of real income is not necessarily an argument against social security or antipoverty programs. The programs themselves rest largely upon ethical and moral foundations. Their major premise is that it is the responsibility of society to care for those who for some reason are temporarily or permanently unable to care for themselves, or at least to force the improvident to save as to be better able to care for themselves.[10]

2. A high-employment, prosperous, rapidly growing economy is the strongest single weapon against both poverty and insecurity in our economy. Over the past century, economic growth has steadily eroded poverty in America. Prosperous times wipe out the insecurity of unemployment for most workers, and permit them to build reserves against future insecurity. Only those effectively out of the labor market are not aided significantly by general prosperity. But it is also important to remember that general prosperity will not eliminate poverty; nor will it completely eliminate insecurity rising from rapid technological change, from shifting demand, and from failure to provide adequately for old age, unforeseen disability, or other such contingencies.

3. It is important to keep the goals of reduc-

---

[9]For a lively discussion of the whole pension problem, see Robert Tilove's *Pension Funds and Economic Freedom* (New York: Fund for the Republic, 1959), which sees no crisis ahead. However, A. A. Berle, in *Economic Power and the Free Society*, cited in Chapter 20, finds cause for alarm.

[10]A few years ago the American public joshed about the British "cradle-to-the-grave," or "womb-to-tomb," social security, introduced by the newly elected Labor government. With over $60 billion annually already being set aside in America through public and private channels by the working portion of the population to take care of the voluntarily or involuntarily "idle" and "poor," now the critics say that we're there too.

ing insecurity and reducing poverty separate in your mind. Many people jump to the conclusion that our sweeping social security program in effect will take care of the poverty problem as time goes on. But this is far from true. Remember that less than half of the poor, as defined above, in 1969 received any kind of social security benefits, and only about 4 million people currently draw old-age pension benefits under organized, private-business pension programs. The federal social security program, as a practical matter, benefits the middle and lower-middle classes more than the poor. Many of the very poor do not work in covered occupations, and hence have accumulated no social-security benefit rights, although the 1969 Nixon proposals would extend benefits to substantially all.

4. It is unclear whether the social security and antipoverty programs on balance increase or decrease current g.n.p. Unemployment insurance, which helps temporarily unemployed workers, helps to reverse recessions and clearly contributes to maintaining a stabler, high-employment economy. Other social security and antipoverty expenditures help directly to increase future productive power—retraining and rehabilitation, public health, child care, and educational expenditures are examples. On the other hand, as the government provides medical care, low-cost housing, better education, and minimal money incomes, the incentive to work and earn is surely diminished for some recipients. It is a basic premise of the social security and antipoverty programs that, by and large, the American people want to work and will take productive jobs when they can find them at anything like reasonable wages. But what will happen if government-guaranteed real-income levels continue to move upward remains to be seen.

5. Last, the social security and antipoverty programs carry strong social and political, as well as economic, overtones. By and large, they appear likely to produce greater social stability, by lessening the likelihood of interincome-level strife and the resentment of those who would otherwise bear the insecurity and poverty of a rapidly changing industrial society. But in recent years, the poverty issue has been strongly intertwined with the issue of civil rights. Some feel that "welfare state" advocates have promised too much too fast, and have raised hopes and aspirations that will be disappointed. Failures have already been painfully numerous, and costs are soaring toward astronomical levels. If so, these promises to lessen poverty and insecurity may produce a backlash of bitter resentment and social unrest on the part of those intended as beneficiaries.

On the other side, as benefits under such programs rise, and as the middle- and upper-income groups become increasingly aware of the costs of financing such benefits for others, some predict a backlash effect here too. If society turns against the poor and the insecure after their aspirations have been raised, bitter strife may result.

Review

FOR ANALYSIS AND DISCUSSION

1. Should the government do something about the poverty problem? If so, what criteria should we use to decide who deserves help?
2. "The simplest and cheapest approach to eliminating poverty would be simply to give a tax-financed direct subsidy to each poor individual to the prescribed minimum level, perhaps through the negative income tax proposal. This would avoid the waste and misdirection of elaborate programs and would give each individual

freedom to spend his income as he pleases." Do you agree? Why or why not?

3. List the advantages and disadvantages of a massive "Marshall Plan" to rebuild the slum areas of our major cities through federal government aid, as a fundamental step toward alleviating the poverty problem.

4. Would you favor government action to raise the legal minimum wage to $3 per hour as a step toward raising low incomes and eliminating poverty, since lower wages generally produce poverty-level incomes? Explain.

5. What is your program to lessen or eliminate poverty in the United States?

6. Should basic medical care be guaranteed to all persons under an extended Medicare program? If so, who should pay for it? Who should set the prices charged by doctors, hospitals, and other providers of medical services?

7. Why is it the responsibility of government to do anything about economic insecurity? Can't we count on individual self-interest to lead people to look out for themselves? Explain your position on these questions.

8. "A strong aggregate demand policy to assure high employment would solve the poverty and insecurity problems, and eliminate the need for the hodgepodge of government measures adopted over recent years." Do you agree?

9. How good a living can the current workers in our society afford to provide for nonworkers, like children, the aged, and unemployed? What criteria should you use in answering?

APPENDIX   *BLACK ECONOMIC DEVELOPMENT AND BLACK CAPITALISM*

The median income of black families in the years 1969 to 1970 was about $6,000, about 60 percent of that of the median white family. Of about 5 million nonfarm businesses in the United States, 2.9 percent were nonwhite-owned, mainly by blacks. The share of nonwhite ownership was largest in personal services (barbershops, dry cleaning establishments, and the like) where nonwhites owned 7.2 percent of all businesses. But they owned only 0.8 percent of manufacturing businesses, 1.5 percent of construction businesses, 1.5 percent of wholesale trade firms, and 3.2 percent of retail trade establishments. Reflecting the mass migration of Negroes from the rural South to the urban North, Negroes comprised only about 6 percent of all farm operators in the late 1960s, as compared to over 15 percent in 1940. Negro participation in professional and technical occupations rose from 3.7 to about 6 percent, in clerical work from 1.2 to over 6 percent, in crafts from 2.7 to 6.3 percent, in semiskilled labor from 5.8 to about 13 percent, and in farm labor from 17.5 to just over 20 percent.

Black unemployment rates in the cities averaged about twice that of whites. But in Cleveland the unemployment rate in the Hough slum area in 1968 was about 16 percent, compared to 3.5 percent in all

of Cleveland; in Detroit the ghetto unemployment rate was 10 percent, compared to 4 percent in the city at large; in Los Angeles it was 12 percent in the ghetto compared to 6 percent in the city at large. In some blocks of the ghetto slums, unemployment rates as high as 40 percent was reported for blacks. But there are brighter statistics too, noted in Chapter 37.

It is in the predominantly black cores of the central cities that the vicious circle of poverty and discrimination seems most apparent. One sympathetic observer has described the black ghetto as an "underdeveloped, decadent economy":

"Economic anarchy is most visible in the important matter of jobs and employment. . . . The ghetto core do not respond to the simple opportunity of a job. . . . The militant and status-conscious young man in East Harlem calls his neighbor an 'Uncle Tom' if he takes a job, especially a menial one. He doesn't line up at the employment gate, because he believes it is a waste of time and he won't be hired. He is certain that, for blacks, all jobs are dead-end jobs. . . .

"In the slum economy, many commonplace events interfere with a man's ability to get or hold a job. Ghetto residents are constantly fighting off finance companies and arguing with the car dealers who have cheated them. Their cars break down and are towed off the street. These conditions not only interfere with an employee's on-the-job reliability, but they also build more theft, crime, inability to meet rent payments, evictions, and bad credit—the very obstacles that prevent people from getting and holding jobs. Plainly, the system of anarchy is self-perpetuating....

"Businessmen framing programs for new industry in ghetto areas are frequently bewildered by another unpredictable aspect of the slum economy—the implacable and illogical Negro opposition to programs for enrichment of the slums. When a major Wall Street firm announced in July, 1968 that it had signed a ten-year, half-million dollar lease for space in a Harlem furniture store to operate a branch brokerage office.... and had committed 7.5 percent of the slum's branch's gross commissions to a foundation organized to provide capital for ghetto businesses and new job opportunities, the company was denounced by blacks as 'A conspiracy by state, municipal, and Wall Street interests to take over Harlem. White power sees Harlem as the potentially most valuable piece of real estate in New York City.... Harlem is too valuable to leave in black hands....'

"The Negro economy is not simply underdeveloped; it is determinedly so and hostile to efforts to change it.... Meetings of black militants teach the advantages and techniques of bankruptcy."[11]

Credit is available to ghetto enterprises only at high rates. The risks of establishing a business in the slums are so great that stockholders or bank examiners cannot ignore the probable erosion of capital. But if the banker or merchant sets a price on his production or his capital high enough to cover the extra risks, ghetto residents understandably complain of white discrimination. Bankers are reluctant to make high-risk loans since foreclosure will predictably bring a charge of white discrimination against blacks.

Black Economic Development. The preceding chapter suggests three main paths to breaking this vicious cycle of ghetto poverty and decay, toward black economic development—steps to raise productivity of ghetto residents, including more capital investment; transfer payments to raise ghetto incomes; and improvements in labor markets to lessen discrimination, increase information on job opportunities, and improve the mobility of ghetto workers. But more and more in recent years, blacks and their supporters have argued that the only real answer is black economic development—development of the ghet-

tos as separate black economic units. At the extreme, this would mean complete black separatism.

The argument for black economic development in the ghettos has been put strongly by Roy Innes, national director of the Congress of Racial Equality:[12]

"Black people must seek liberation from the dominance and control of white society.... We black nationalists must speak of separating ourselves. We live in a setting where one group—not our own—controls the institutions, and a flow of goods and services. We can change our position by liberating ourselves and placing the vital instruments of social and economic change in our own hands. This is what we mean by separation....

"Black people are not talking about black capitalism, black people are talking about economic development. We are talking about the creation and acquisition of capital instruments by means of which we can maximize our own economic interests.... The question of autonomy is critical.... Extensive areas like Harlem in New York, Roxbury in Boston, Watts in Los Angeles... exist as colonial appendages of the urban center.... The urban centers are managed by political and institutional barons who include our piece of 'turf' in their domain.... Whenever we make any attempt to change that relationship—political, social, or economic—we meet the massive resistance of these barons....

"There is a very striking similarity between the so-called underdeveloped countries and our underdeveloped black communities. Both have always been oppressed; almost always there is an unfavorable balance of trade with the oppressors or exploiters; both suffer from high unemployment, low income, scarce capital, and we can point to a number of other similarities."

Surely healthy economic development of the black ghettos is preferable to the creeping decay which permeates many of our central cities. What can economic analysis tell us about the promise of "black economic development" as a device for raising incomes and improving the economic and social status of Negroes in the central cities? Is the parallel drawn with the so-called "developing" economies an accurate and helpful one? Is movement toward substantially separate black economic communities, controlled by blacks, a promising path toward the elimination of black poverty and the vicious circle of decay in the great city slums?

First, clearly a program of continuing mass income

[11]T. L. Cross, *Black Capitalism* (New York: Atheneum Publishers, 1969), pp. 22–25.

[12]Roy Innes, "Separatist Economics: A New Social Contract," in *Black Economic Development*, eds. W. H. Haddad and G. D. Pugh (Englewood Cliffs, N.J.: Prentice-Hall, Inc., 1969), pp. 51–53.

transfers (gifts) from the rest of the economy to the poor residents of the ghetto could raise ghetto incomes, both relatively and absolutely. It might also stimulate healthier ghetto economies. Many observers urge such large income transfers, on both ethical and economic grounds. The case for them stands or falls quite apart from separate "black economic development."

Second, elimination of discrimination could help reduce black poverty. Perhaps one-third to two-thirds of the difference between white and black and income distributions may be due to discrimination; only very rough estimates are feasible. But even if all discrimination were eliminated, substantial black poverty would remain, as would the arguments of many blacks in favor of economic separatism.

Third, consider the economic arguments for black economic separatism per se. (Note that this analysis is an economic one; it temporarily sets aside social and political issues that may be very important.) The economic analysis of Chapters 32–37 tells us that higher real incomes depend fundamentally on higher production. Low black ghetto incomes reflect a multitude of causes, but most of these causes are summed up in low productivity of workers and scarcity of capital in the ghetto, plus discrimination. The fundamental road to more income for ghetto families lies in higher productivity of their breadwinners. It lies in more capital, either white or black-owned, since most rising worker incomes reflect cooperation with increasing amounts of capital per worker. It lies in facilitating the movement of both capital and labor to those markets where their marginal productivity is highest.

Both economic analysis and history warn against black economic separatism as the approach to raising ghetto incomes. The ghetto is poor mainly because its workers' productivities are low and because its inhabitants own little capital of their own. To shut off economic flows between the ghetto and the rest of the economy will not raise ghetto productivities; indeed it will lower them insofar as it limits movement of ghetto residents to jobs outside the ghetto and flow of capital into the ghetto. To build an economic wall around the ghetto is to guarantee its continued poverty.

The economic fallacy that regions or nations can improve their economic lot by "keeping the money at home" is an old one. Many observers, but few economists, argue that the ghetto is poor merely because it is bled by white capitalists, withdrawing their ill-gotten gains. Undoubtedly many slum landlords behave this way. But in fact the rate of return on business investment in the ghetto is generally below that on nonghetto investment in spite of what seem to be discriminatory high prices. And profits comprise only a small part of most sales' dollars. To insist that all profits made in the ghetto be reinvested there would only reduce further the attractiveness of the ghetto as an area for outside investment funds, which are so desperately needed. If ghetto residents spent their money only within the ghetto, shutting off the flow of funds between the ghetto and the rest of the economy, it would merely further impoverish the ghetto. For example, Harlem would soon be very hungry indeed if it were to shut off all outpayments from local grocery stores for food products. To raise its own wheat, grind its own flour, and bake its own bread would mainly raise the price of bread to very high levels, even if it were feasible to raise the wheat in Harlem. So it is with other production. The cheapest food is that produced where it can be raised most efficiently. Ghetto residents will generally obtain the highest real incomes by specializing on the work they do best, in or out of the ghetto, and using their earnings to buy goods and services most efficiently produced by others. This principle of specialization in accordance with relative productivities to maximize wanted output is called the "principle of comparative advantage." It has been a central principle in Parts Three and Four, and will again be the center of attention in Part Six.

It is important to reemphasize that this is purely an economic analysis. Psychologically and politically, black economic independence may be so important as to overcome the economic advantages of interdependence with the white economy. If so, it should be so recognized on its own merits, with recognition of the economic costs involved. Economic progress for most blacks in the ghettos will depend heavily on their effective interaction with the total economy and their active participation in the total economic process.

Some Constructive Steps. What policies, then, does economic analysis suggest to speed black economic development? The answers are much the same as the general ones for the attack on poverty outlined in the preceding chapter.

1. Black ghetto incomes will rise if workers are combined with more capital resources than now exist in the ghettos. This points strongly toward steps to improve the mobility of ghetto inhabitants into jobs outside the ghetto, where their productivity will be higher, and to entice more capital to the ghetto to raise productivity there. Whether the capital belongs to whites or blacks is far less important than that it come. As a practical matter, it will belong largely to whites, since the capital owned by blacks is so pitifully small in today's economy. The unfortunate fact is that the ghetto economy, with undeniable assistance from white racism, has now substantially eliminated most profit and investment attractions. White investors, intent on providing help, will often need to do so with limited profit prospects, and frequently without thanks, indeed against often-unfair black criticism.

2. Since higher incomes depend fundamentally on higher productivity, improved education and training for ghetto inhabitants form a second high-priority path to development. In the short run, this highlights the need for subsidized education and training for low-skilled ghetto workers to start on the road up, and for better information and mobility between the ghettos and job opportunities outside. Over the longer run, it points to increased emphasis on early, improved schooling for ghetto children, to replace the present patterns that in essence train ghetto youngsters out of productive paths before they are old enough to enter the labor market.

3. There is no doubt that low ghetto incomes are partly caused by past and present white discrimination against blacks in economic life. On economic, as well as on social and political grounds, such discrimination is indefensible, and massive collective action should be taken to correct it as rapidly as possible. Perhaps black activist pressures are needed. Unfortunately, this is not a task that can largely be undertaken by the ghetto inhabitants on their own; it calls primarily for the good will and economic cooperation of the larger white community.

4. Since low productivity in the ghetto for both labor and capital to an important degree reflects the stagnant ghetto environment, which traps its inhabitants and repels outside investment, overall improvement of the ghetto environment is a necessary step for substantial economic development. Changing attitudes toward work, reduced crime rates, superior self-respect for inhabitants—such steps will be essential parts of substantial ghetto economic development. The ghetto problem is an incredibly complex and multifaceted one. It is unlikely that any one or two measures will make a significant difference. But combined, coordinated action on many fronts can make a difference, economically and sociopolitically.

5. Overall, thus, economic analysis suggests stress on rapid economic integration of black ghetto inhabitants into the white economy as the most promising path to higher incomes and economic development. This does not necessarily imply a movement of all blacks out of the ghetto to jobs elsewhere, nor does it imply exclusive reliance on white capital to finance ghetto businesses and housing. Nor does it necessarily imply more social integration. But black economic separatism, whatever its attractions may be socially and politically, makes little sense economically in the present, basically market-oriented, American economy.[13]

Black Capitalism. "Black economic develop-

ment" and "black capitalism" are often used interchangeably. "Black capitalism," however, also has a more narrow definition—the ownership and operation of business by black owner-managers, whether or not employees and customers are black.

Many enthusiasts for private enterprise and for black advancement support the establishment of more black businesses and encouragement of black entrepreneurs. President Nixon's campaign in 1968 called for active steps to aid black capitalism, and the Johnson regime also officially supported the move. In particular, the Small Business Administration and other arms of the federal government have been directed to aid in the establishment of black capitalism, through advice and investment of government funds. Moreover, since the riots of the mid-1960s, numerous white firms have aided the establishment of black-owned and operated firms, through loans, equity capital, management assistance, and guaranteed markets for black firms' output. The Watts Manufacturing Company, established by Aerojet-General in Watts, is an example of such a black firm, and one of the more successful ones. Most firms so established have been small retail establishments or simple manufacturing operations, which have made use of readily available low-wage black labor.

In spite of these efforts to aid black entrepreneurs, progress has been slow. Some ventures are succeeding, but loan loss rates have run between 10 and 15 percent, compared with an expected loss rate of about 3 percent for other Small Business Administration loans and of less than one-half of 1 percent on normal bank loans. Virtually all black businesses have been established in black neighborhoods. Only a few have sold much of their output outside the black community, except in cases where white firms have made such purchases specifically to help new black firms. Their impact on the total black economic development problem has been tiny.

Three major problems have confronted most new black businesses. First, most new firms have great difficulty obtaining "front-end money"—loans to get started and to continue operations during the years before the firm is well established. The loss rates indicated above explain why. Shortage of working capital has been one of the two biggest reasons for the failure of black firms.

Second, running even a simple business establishment calls for managerial skills, and few blacks have the background or experience that provides such skills. This is not surprising in light of the long discrimination against blacks in both educational and economic affairs.

Third, black firms have often been limited in their markets by discrimination. Whites do not normally go into black ghettos to buy consumer or producer goods. Indeed, at the retail level, they are often not welcome. At the business level, black firms often cannot offer the reliability of production and delivery

---

[13]Lively analyses, pointing toward ghetto dispersal, are provided by J. Kain and J. Persky, "Alternatives to the Gilded Ghetto," and A. and R. Wohlstetter, "'Third Worlds' at Home and Abroad," both in *The Public Interest*, Winter, 1969.

that is critical for white purchasers; to provide orders for new black firms, white buyers often must frankly undertake higher-cost procurement. Some whites simply do not want to buy from blacks, just as blacks may be discriminated against as workers.

Yet interest in black capitalism as a form of self-help is widespread, and some steps have been taken to meet all three problems. First, numerous government programs have been established to provide front-end money for new black businesses. Many banks, including some of the nation's largest, have set aside substantial sums specifically for high-risk loans to new black businesses. The insurance industry of America in 1969 allocated $1 billion for investment in black communities, in both housing and black businesses.

Second, in the last few years widespread efforts have been made to help blacks develop management and entrepreneurial skills. Hundreds of American junior and senior business executives have volunteered to help black businessmen. White business and law-school students have helped thousands of small black businesses. Often, well-meaning white helpers have been ineffective; the new black businessman frequently needs the most elementary tools —how to keep the books, how to apply for a bank loan, how to order and keep inventory records—not modern managerial techniques used by the large corporations and taught by the nation's leading business schools. White firms providing financial help have sometimes found themselves bitterly resented; collection of loans may be seen as gouging by the black community.

Third, both the federal government and some white firms give special preference to black suppliers where black firms can produce the goods required. Thus far, this has been limited to a few simple products, and many critics charge American white businesses with tokenism—talk big but place few orders.

Without white assistance in providing funds, managerial assistance, and markets, the probability that large numbers of black businesses will succeed is painfully small. There is little likelihood that black capitalism will provide jobs and higher incomes for more than a tiny part of the black community for the years just ahead. Nonetheless, black capitalism may be an important link in black economic development. Business success may give a feeling of achievement and self-pride that is hard to obtain in any other way. Blacks understandably want to be their own masters, to stand on their own feet, and not be beholden to whites. Just as other minority groups in American life have used success in the marketplace as a means of climbing out of poverty and discrimination, so black capitalism can play a useful role in the economic development of the black community and in keeping open the door to economic success for blacks with initiative and developing skills.[14]

[14]There are many useful books on black economic development and black capitalism. For example, W. Haddad and D. Pugh, eds., *Black Economic Development* (Englewood Cliffs, N.J.: Prentice-Hall, Inc., 1969); T. L. Cross, *Black Capitalism* (New York: Atheneum Publishers, 1969); and K. R. Clark, *Dark Ghetto: Dilemmas of Social Power* (New York: Harper & Row, Publishers, 1965). Cross provides a helpful bibliography.

appendix to part four | Current Research

Wages, Unions, and Collective Bargaining. Chicago's H. G. Lewis summarizes the quantitative impact of unions on wages in "The Relative Employment Effects of Unions" (*American Economic Review*, May, 1964). A controversial analysis, *Collective Bargaining in the Steel Industry*, by Harvard's R. Livernash, looks closely at one leading industry. A lively collection of analyses is assembled in *Unions, Management, and the Public*, E. Bakke, C. Kerr, and C. Anrod, eds. (Harcourt, Brace & World, Inc. 1967). There is a vast literature describing unions and the attitudes and behavior of organized labor groups. M. Perlman's *The Machinists* (Harvard University Press, 1962) is a good recent example. A collection of leading studies focused on union attitudes and behavior is assembled in *Labor and Trade Unionism*, eds. California's W. Galenson and S. Lipset. Interesting studies of grass-roots union politics and policies are presented by I. Sayles and G. Strauss, *The Local Union* (Harper & Row, 1961); see also J. Barbash's *Structure, Government, and Politics of American Unions* (Random House, Inc. 1967).

Poverty. Chapter 5 of the *Economic Report of the President*, January, 1969 provides a good introduction to research on the poverty problem. For important historical perspective, see the studies by Friedman, Solow, Goldsmith, and Lampman in E. C. Budd, ed., *Inequality and Poverty* (W. W. Norton & Company, Inc., 1967). Another useful collection is H. P. Miller, ed., *Poverty: American Style* (Wadsworth Publishing Co. Inc., 1968). Part III of this volume also offers a good introduction to antipoverty policy measures. James Tobin, who, with Milton Friedman, has been a chief protagonist of the "negative income tax," analyzes the entire issue in "Raising the Incomes of the Poor," *Agenda for the Nation*, Kermit Gordon, ed. (The Brookings Institution, 1968). Other lively volumes are P. Moynihan, ed., *On Understanding Poverty* (Basic Books, Inc., Publishers, 1969), and J. Sundquist, ed., *On Fighting Poverty* (Basic Books, Inc., Publishers, 1969). A series of case studies is presented in P. Doeringer, *Programs to Employ the Disadvantaged* (Prentice-Hall, Inc., 1969).

At the other end of the income structure, R. Barlow, H. Brazer, and J. Morgan of the University of Michigan have studied the richest families in *Economic Behavior of the Affluent* (The Brookings Institution, 1966).

Racial Discrimination and Black Economic Development. A factual introduction to problems of blacks in getting jobs is provided by H. Northrup and others in *The Negro in the Automobile Industry* (University of Pennsylvania Press, 1968), and a parallel series of studies of other major industries. Estimates of the economic effects of racial discrimination abound. One of the most thorough analyses is Lester Thurow's, *Poverty and Discrimination* (The Brookings Institution, 1969). Broader analyses of the problems of "black capitalism" and "black economic development" are presented by A. and R. Wohlstetter, "Third Worlds Abroad and At Home," and J. Kain and J. Persky, "Alternatives to Gilding the Ghetto," both in *The Public Interest*, Winter, 1969. See also *Black Economic Development* (Prentice-Hall, Inc., Spectrum Books, 1969), especially Chapters 3, 4, and 7; and T. Cross, *Black Capitalism* (Atheneum Publishers, 1969).

Public Goods and the Public Sector

thirty-eight

Public Goods, Externalities, and the Public Sector

The Four Big Functions of Government

Government Expenditures and Revenue

What Should the Public Sector Do?

What should the government do in economic affairs? How much should it tax and spend? The influential nineteenth-century English liberals argued that the primary function of the state was merely to set up and enforce certain "rules of the game" under which private enterprise could then be counted on to get goods efficiently produced and distributed. At the other extreme, the Communists argue that all productive resources should be owned by the state, and that production and distribution should be directed in detail by the government.

The present attitude in America is in between, but much closer to the private-enterprise position. Most Americans believe strongly in capitalism and the virtues of a free, private-enterprise economy. Yet government action has grown far beyond the minimal regulatory duties prescribed by the laissez-faire advocates.

The Four Big Functions of Government

Modern government has four big economic functions. People disagree violently on how far government should go on each front, but just about everyone agrees that government needs to play all four roles.

Government as Stabilizer: Stably Growing Aggregate Demand

Two centuries ago Adam Smith didn't worry about booms and depressions, because they didn't exist. But with modern industrial society, economic instability became a major problem. There is no reason why aggregate spending (consumers plus businesses plus governments) will automatically just match the output potential of the system at stable prices. Clearly, no private agency can assure the needed stable growth in aggregate demand. Government has to help, through monetary and fiscal policy, if we are to avoid the massive depressions and inflations that have marred the past. This was the topic of Part Two.

Government as Policeman: The Rules of the Game

Even Adam Smith said that government has to act as policeman—to spell out some rules of the economic game and see that people obey them. To live effectively together in a complex economic world, we have to agree that contracts will be respected. Equally important, competition must prevail in the marketplace to assure the benefits of private enterprise, and only government can undertake this kind of regulation.

Where externalities bulk large, moreover, the marketplace will fail to produce the optimal output. If a paper mill produces dirty water and an objectionable odor as well as paper, government action is needed to see that paper buyers, in addition to paying the private costs of producing the paper, pay for keeping the water and air clean. One standard way of doing this is governmental regulation that forbids the discharge of dirty water, or air pollution. Thus, the manufacturer's total cost will include pollution-control measures as well as labor, raw materials and the like. Another approach is to impose a special tax on polluters and use the funds to clean up the air or water.

Some would have government go further, for a variety of economic and ethical reasons, and regulate hours of work and child labor, the prices airlines can charge, and the wage bargains unions and management can strike. The role of government in setting and enforcing the rules of the competitive game was a main theme of Parts Three and Four. It's a vital role if a system like ours is to work effectively.

Government as Provider of Services: The Public Sector

There are some things a private-enterprise, profit-motivated system clearly won't provide adequately—national defense, education, highways, moon shots, police protection. Partly, these are instances of large externalities—social costs or benefits larger than private costs or benefits. At the extreme are pure "public goods" and "public services"—cases, like national defense, where we clearly want the "product" but where there is no practical way of producing and selling it through the market. The critical point is the inability to withhold the benefits from anyone who wouldn't pay voluntarily. Provision of a court system and general government are other examples of pure public services.

In essence, the government needs to act as both policeman and a public store. Instead of relying on the private store to produce everything we want, we set up a public store alongside to handle things that the private store can't or won't stock under the profit incentive. The public store is the "public sector." It allocates resources to producing desired public goods that are voted through the political process, alongside the private sector where the profit motive allocates resources to meeting consumer demands expressed through the market. The public sector allocates about 20 percent of all resources in the United States today through taxes and government purchase of goods and services, although most of the actual production (say, of highways) is contracted out to the private sector.

Government as Income Distributor: Transfer Payments

The fourth major economic function of government is to redistribute money income directly—by taxing some persons and making transfer payments to others. The aged, the poor, the helpless, the farmers, the unemployed—all receive government transfer payments financed mainly by taxes on others, and these money transfers provide a corresponding shift in control over resources. Since the payments go mainly to lower- and middle-income groups, and our tax system is "progressive" (that is, the rich pay a higher percentage of their incomes than the poor), these transfer payments broadly shift income from the upper- to lower-income groups. Government redistribution of money income is the second big activity of the public sector. It currently involves between 5 and 10 percent of the total national income.

Part Five is about public goods, externalities, and the public sector. This public store plus direct money-income transfers accounts for somewhere around 30 percent of total economic activity. The public sector is a big and growing part of the modern American economy.

Government Expenditures and Revenues

First, a look at the facts of our involvement. In 1970, federal, state, and local governments spent about $330 billion, and their expenditures are rising year after year. These expenditures have been roughly matched by growing tax collections. Thus taxes, including social-security taxes, are now over $1,500 annually for every man, woman, and child in the United States. Governments bought 23 percent of all goods and services produced in 1970. In addition, government transfer payments accounted for about 8 percent of personal income re-

ceived. Including military personnel, some 12 million workers—one out of every seven—are on government payrolls. You may not like government involvement on such a large scale, or you may consider it insufficient. But there it is.

The Growing Role of Government

It's useful to begin with a historical perspective. Figure 38–1 shows the growth in expenditures of all governments—federal, state, and local—since 1914. The increases are phenomenal, even allowing for the price increase of about 250 percent, which would pull the final figure down to about $140 billion in 1914 prices. What accounts for the growth?

1. One major answer is war—past, present, and future. War is fabulously expensive. Today, about half of the annual federal budget (over $100 billion) is directly or indirectly attributable to fighting present wars, preparing for future ones, and fulfilling the obligations of past ones. This compares with total federal expenditures for all purposes of about $15 billion for the entire period from 1789 to 1900.

2. Government expenditures for civilian goods account for over two-thirds of the combined federal-state-local total—for education, highways, public welfare, and many other things. Population has grown fast. Even if per capita government expenditures had remained

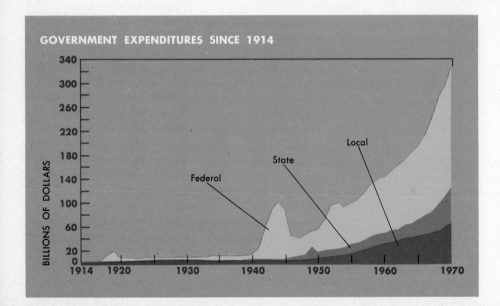

GOVERNMENT EXPENDITURES SINCE 1914

BILLIONS OF DOLLARS

Federal

State

Local

1914 1920 1930 1940 1950 1960 1970

fig. 38–1

Federal spending has shot up during wars and grown more slowly in peacetime. State and local spending has grown fast since World War II. (Source: U.S. Treasury Department. Figures are for fiscal years and include social security.)

constant, the doubling in population since 1914 would have meant an enormous increase in government spending.

3. We want more public goods and services today. And externalities have become pervasive in our big, high-technology economy. We want more government spending on sewers, streets, police, and so on. The nation's shift from a rural to an urban economy accounts for a big share of the state-local increase. The desperate plight of the big cities, with snowballing needs for funds—for welfare, education, police protection, and slum renewal—may soon become the nation's number one problem of public finance. But there's a lot more than just the cities involved. Now we want six-lane highways instead of dirt paths. Universal education and modern medical care are enormously expensive everywhere. Social security has become a government responsibility with higher minimum standards than would have been dreamed of a century ago.

4. Partly, the increase shown simply reflects higher prices. Today's price level is the highest in our history and more than double that of 1914. Look back at Figure 5–3 to find out how important this factor is over the long pull. Adjustment to eliminate inflation would cut the growth shown by more than half.

The Public Sector Today

Now look in more detail at the public sector today. Figure 38–2 summarizes what governments spent in 1970 and the taxes they collected to pay the bills. The length of each bar shows the size of the tax or expenditure involved. Although Figure 38–2 speaks for itself, $330 billion deserves a closer look.

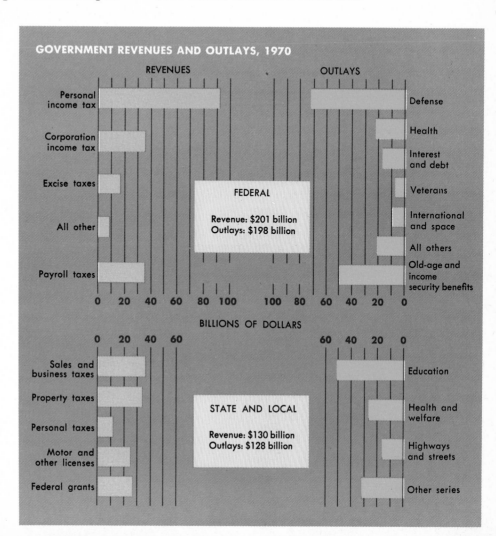

fig. 38–2

Federal, state, and local governments collected and spent about $350 billion in calendar year 1970 including social-security programs. Each bar shows a major tax or expenditure program. Chart does not include government-operated businesses (such as public utilities), but does overstate net government outlays by including state-local spending of federal grants totaling $26 billion. (Sources: U.S. Treasury and Commerce Departments; preliminary estimates.)

1. About 60 percent of all government spending is federal, about 40 percent state and local. But state and local governments now spend substantially more on nondefense goods and services than the federal government does. And contrary to many misconceptions about the federal bureaucracy, of the 9 million people who hold civilian government jobs, over 6 million work for state and local governments, less than 3 million for the federal government. This distribution reflects the fact that the great bulk of federal spending is on goods and services (for example, missiles and aircraft) produced in private industry, and on the payment of military personnel. Large federal transfer expenditures, like interest on the national debt and farm subsidies, require relatively few employees.

2. What are the major government expenditures? Foremost is spending on defense. Figure 38–3 presents the evidence. Defense, space,

fig. 38–3

Defense, education, and social security-welfare payments together account for nearly three-fourths of all federal, state, and local government spending. (Sources: U.S. Treasury and Commerce Departments; preliminary estimates.)

TOTAL GOVERNMENT SPENDING, 1970
Total: $326 billion (slices show percentages of total)

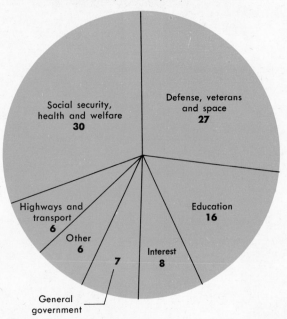

and spending on veterans comprise 27 percent of all government outlays. They comprise nearly half of federal spending. Elimination of war-related spending could annually make $1,500 of extra income available to every family in America, or could permit us to clear vast slums, build new systems of superhighways, nearly double our expenditures on education.

The next biggest budget item—old-age and other income security—mainly consists of transfer payments under the national social-security system. Health and education, together $63 billion, are a mixture of federal and state-local outlays; education is nearly $50 billion of the total. State-local spending has grown much faster than federal nondefense spending during the last two decades.

Old-age and unemployment benefits are financed mainly by special taxes on the persons who receive the benefits; and receipts are placed in special trust funds, separate from regular government tax collections. But by 1970 total annual payments had reached the huge sum of $40 billion, with the payroll taxes to finance these benefits at roughly the same level. Moreover, other health and welfare programs totaled another $40 billion at federal, state, and local levels. Social security and health and welfare programs have been the fastest-growing nondefense part of the public sector. They have surpassed education and are second in size only to national defense.

3. It is important to recognize that there are two different types of government expenditures, "real" (or "exhaustive") expenditures on currently produced goods and services, and money "transfer payments" (or "nonexhaustive" expenditures). "Real" expenditures use up ("exhaust") goods and services—for example, purchases of raw materials or trucks, hiring workers or soldiers, and the like. Transfer payments are merely monetary shifts—for example, old-age pension payments and interest on the national debt. Obviously, the immediate effect on the economy is different in the two cases; although the money transfers redistribute purchasing purchasing power, they do not **directly** reallocate, or use up, productive resources. In

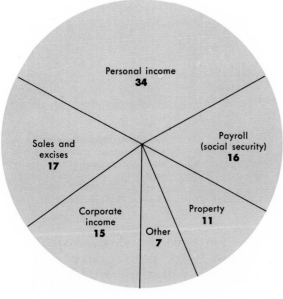

THE TAX BILL, 1970

Total: $331 billion (slices show percentages of total)

Personal income
34

Payroll
(social security)
16

Property
11

Other
7

Corporate
income
15

Sales and
excises
17

fig. 38–4

Personal-income and payroll taxes produce half the nation's tax revenue; corporation-income and sales taxes most of the rest. (Sources: U.S. Treasury and Commerce Departments.)

1970 government real expenditures totaled about $225 billion. The other $105 billion consisted of transfer payments.[1]

4. Figure 38–4 shows what taxes provided the revenue in 1970, combining federal, state, and local governments. Ours is increasingly a personal tax system. Half of all taxes are raised that way—34 percent through personal-income taxes and another 16 percent through payroll taxes. At the federal level, these personal taxes brought in two-thirds of all revenue. Another 12 percent came from corporate-income taxes. Sales, excise, and property taxes accounted for most of the rest, mainly at state and local levels. If you feel you're taxed wherever you turn,

you're right. We can't collect nearly a third of a trillion dollars to finance the services we want our governments to provide without making nearly everybody pay.

Redistribution of Incomes through the Public Sector

The public sector allocates resources away from private to public use—to producing defense and school buildings rather than factories and private houses. It does this partly by transferring money income (which shifts purchasing power) and partly by directly reallocating resources.

We are all taxpayers and all beneficiaries of government services. But we are not all affected equally. On balance, who pays what and who receives what benefits in this massive transfer? Figure 38–5 answers the question, with a very rough set of estimates. The very poor get a large part of their real income indirectly through government money grants and directly from government services, but they pay taxes equal to only about 30 percent of their income. At the other extreme, over-$15,000-income families pay about 40 percent of their incomes in taxes, but receive benefits comprising only about 20 percent of their real incomes. Putting taxes paid and benefits received together, it's clear that the net impact of the public sector is "progressive." That is, it tends to transfer income from the rich to the poor, to equalize incomes. Most of this effect obviously comes from the expenditure side. Percentage tax burdens are surprisingly similar at the different income levels shown; this reflects a clearly progressive federal tax structure but a somewhat regressive one at state and local levels.

Figure 38–5 gives a roughly accurate picture, but don't take the precise figures too seriously. Both tax burdens and expenditure benefits are very hard to estimate accurately. On the tax side, the man who turns the money over to the government often doesn't ultimately pay the tax; he may simply pass it on to someone else. Well-known examples are the taxes on movie admissions and on cigarettes, which are noted separately in the price. To obtain the estimates

[1]The distinction between "real" and "transfer" payments corresponds to that used in the g.n.p. accounts; "real" government expenditures are those on currently produced goods and services. The distinction is not, of course, the same as that between "real" and "money" g.n.p. when we compare g.n.p. in current prices with that in constant prices.

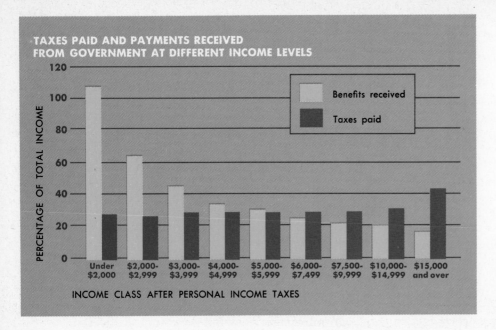

TAXES PAID AND PAYMENTS RECEIVED FROM GOVERNMENT AT DIFFERENT INCOME LEVELS

Legend:
- Benefits received
- Taxes paid

Y-axis: PERCENTAGE OF TOTAL INCOME (0, 20, 40, 60, 80, 100, 120)

X-axis: INCOME CLASS AFTER PERSONAL INCOME TAXES
Under $2,000 | $2,000-$2,999 | $3,000-$3,999 | $4,000-$4,999 | $5,000-$5,999 | $6,000-$7,499 | $7,500-$9,999 | $10,000-$14,999 | $15,000 and over

fig. 38–5

Low-income groups receive much more from government in services and payments than they pay in taxes. The reverse is true for high-income groups. Estimates, for 1965, are rough. (Source: Tax Foundation.)

in Fig. 38–5, we need to know who ultimately pays the tax, and on this score we have only rough estimates. On the expenditure side, it is even harder to estimate who gets the ultimate benefits from government spending. Old-age pensions to retired people are relatively easy. But for services like national defense, foreign aid, education, and general government, about all you can do is make an arbitrary allocation that seems not unreasonable. Thus, others have come up with estimates that disagree on the details. For example, another study shows the percentage tax burden at over 40 percent for the lowest-income groups (reflecting heavy sales, payroll, and property taxes), then sliding down in the $4,000–$15,000 range, and then rising sharply for higher incomes. But the general picture remains the same. Net real-income transfers through the public sector are substantially progressive as between very low and very high incomes but apparently not through the large middle-income range of $4,000 to $15,000.[2]

What Should the Public Sector Do?

What should the public sector do? Who should pay the taxes, and who receive the bene-

[2]Council of Economic Advisers, *Economic Report of the President,* January, 1969, p. 161. Note that the "benefits" shown here only include money transfer payments received from the government.

fits? How can governments best serve the "public interest"? To answer these questions meaningfully, we must ask first: What are we trying to achieve through government action? Until we're clear where we want to go, it's hard to say how we can get there the best way.

Goals for the Public Sector

Chapter 3 suggested five fundamental social goals are guideposts to help in evaluating how the economic system works. If these are useful in judging the entire economic system, they should be useful too in evaluating what the public sector can contribute. The goals were suggested because they seem to have widespread acceptance. But if you don't agree with them, substitute your own.

1. Progress: A rising national standard of living.
2. Freedom.
3. Security.
4. Production in accordance with consumer demands.
5. Equity in the distribution of income.

In a basically private-enterprise economy, the main job of achieving these goals has to fall on the private sector. But when should government help by stepping in with taxes and expenditures? Here we leave aside government stabilization and regulatory goals, focusing on the public sector, per se.

What Should Governments Do?

In the United States we have a strong tradition of trying private enterprise first and calling on government only where private enterprise clearly would fall short. This philosophy has provided a continuous, powerful restraint on expansion of the public sector in this country. But economists often stress three broad circumstances where collective (public) action is needed if the public is to achieve its desired allocation of resources and incomes.

1. "Public Goods." Some goods and services are viewed as essential and, as a practical matter, can only be provided collectively. National defense is a good example. Almost everyone agrees we need it, and there's no practical way for it to be provided through the marketplace.

Such "public goods" have two special qualities. First, they are widely viewed as essential. Second, there is no practical way in which the benefits of the collective service can be withheld from someone who does not pay. Even though Joe Doaks pays no taxes, he still benefits from national defense; there is no feasibility to charge him for it through the market. Other examples of "public services" are foreign aid, exploration of space, and police protection.

2. Externalities. In some cases, the costs or benefits to society are greater than those to any one individual who may undertake a particular activity. Air and water pollution in producing private goods are classic cases where social costs exceed private costs. Education is another major example of external economies. It is really advantageous to each individual to make an expenditure on his own education. But the advantages to society as a whole are greater than the private benefits to each individual because with a well-educated populace we will have a more productive, stabler political economy and social system. As Chapter 25 emphasized, where externalities are large, private markets cannot be expected to allocate resources properly.

Very large and risky undertakings provide a special case. Although the probable benefits exceed costs, as a practical matter nobody except the government can be expected to take them on. The famous Tennessee Valley Authority (TVA) is a controversial example. In retrospect, the TVA has turned out to be a largely self-financing regional development project, providing valuable electricity and industrial development for a large area, whether or not one accepts the much-debated government-accounting system on actual TVA costs. Yet the venture was an extremely large and risky one that no private capitalist would undertake. A recent comparable example may be the mixed public-private financing of the international communications space-satellite concern, "Comsat."

It should be clear that at one margin externalities shade into pure public goods. On the other, a vast range of private goods and services involve at least some small externalities. Thus, increasingly the line is blurred between "private" and "public" goods, and with it the clear presumption in favor either of the market or of government-produced output.

3. Altered Patterns of Production and Consumption. Virtually everything the public sector does alters the pattern of production and consumption. This alteration may be against consumer wishes. But in many cases the government wants to discourage or encourage some particular resource use, over and above the considerations just enumerated. For example, most people agree on compulsory free public education for all youngsters through some minimum age, regardless of ability or willingness to pay. Thus, we require that all children attend school to gain both private and social benefits, and we levy general taxes to pay the bills, whether or not the taxpayers have children.

Today most people agree that they want a wide range of public services, and that government should directly redistribute money incomes. But the three guidelines above provide only a broad framework for analyzing particular cases, and there is violent disagreement on many areas (for example, medicare, urban renewal, and foreign aid), and on how far income redistribution should go. Moreover, there is a proper concern that "the test of the market," i.e., the ability of the producer to make a profit by meeting consumer demand, is absent in the public sector. Thus, when we give up the market for the public sector, we lose a major and automatic test of whether resources are being used efficiently. Nor do the three guidelines tell us how much the government should provide of even the agreed-on public services like police protection, education, and national defense. These issues need further exploration.

Balancing Costs and Benefits in the Public Economy

With total output fixed (we assume full employment) and leaving aside temporarily the problem of externalities, all the government can do through the public sector is to reallocate resources and incomes, away from where they would go through the market economy. This means a transfer of resources from private to public use—from taxpayers to recipients of government services. This fact reemphasizes the ever-present need to economize—to allocate our resources most effectively, here as between private and public use, to satisfy our wants.

Can "Social Welfare" Be Maximized? In this situation, the principle of maximizing utility by equating returns at the margin suggests a rough guide to how big the public sector should be. Government expenditures should be increased up to the point where the marginal loss in giving up resources in the private sector is just equal to the marginal benefit from public expenditures. As long as the marginal gain is greater than the marginal loss, there is a net gain in overall welfare. Unless the marginal unit of each resource yields the same economic value in all possible uses (public and private), welfare could be increased by switching the resource to a higher-yielding use.

If society were a single unity, and if government were the all-comprehending brain of that unity, application of this principle would be feasible. The government could then weigh satisfactions lost against those gained. But in fact there is no such all-comprehending brain.

Practical application of this principle would involve comparison of the marginal satisfactions of millions of different people who might gain or lose from any proposed policy. Obviously no precise interpersonal comparison of satisfactions is possible. At best, we can make only the roughest sort of approximation. Even (especially) a very wise man would quail before the task of evaluating precisely the marginal effect of taxing and spending another $100 million on the interstate highway system. Yet, somehow we must agree on the amount we spend on this purpose. However rough its application, the marginal principle of economizing the use of scarce resources poses one of the important questions to ask in thinking about the right size for the public sector.

Cost–Benefit Analysis: Planning-Programming-Budgeting

In recent years, economists have begun to tackle this problem empirically through "cost–benefit analysis," an approach pioneered especially under Defense Secretary Robert McNamara. Shall we spend $10 billion on a nationwide missile-shelter system? Economically, the answer involves a comparison of marginal costs and marginal benefits, just as a private-market calculation does. First, a careful statement of goals is required: How much protection for whom and for what is desired? What would be the savings, in terms of life, property, and ability to recover rapidly, in the event of atomic attacks of various sorts? Then a comparable set of costs for different sorts of shelter systems to provide the desired results would be calculated. If the costs exceed the benefits, economically the civilian-shelter project is a dubious one. But if the cost–benefit balance is the other way, economically the project gets a green light.

Another example is cost–benefit analysis of the big dam system to provide water from the high Sierras for the cities and fields of California. Costs of alternative dams and water distribution systems could be calculated. Benefits could be estimated—for irrigation, for industrial use, for household use in cities, for electricity generated at the dam. For a multi-billion dollar water system, the job of fully estimating the complex intermesh of costs and benefits is a complex, difficult one. But cost–benefit analysis is one of the most intriguing, fastest-growing branches of modern economics.

Another interesting example is the new U.S. supersonic transport plane given the go-ahead, mainly on government money, in 1967. The case is interesting partly because most cost–benefit analyses raised serious questions about the economic case for the SST, even weighing the long-range future benefits generously. But Congress and the administration chose to go ahead anyhow, arguing that the international political advantages swung the balance; we just couldn't afford to let the French, British, and Russians develop an effective SST far ahead of us. And they suspected that the net economic benefits will be greater than the economists calculated, in spite of sonic booms, airport problems, competition from subsonic planes, and the like.

To implement careful cost–benefit analysis of proposed governmental programs, President Johnson instructed the Budget Bureau in the mid-1960s to push the spread of "Planning-Programming-Budgeting" (P-P-B), through the civilian agencies of the federal government. Should the post office automate its handling of mail? Should the Antipoverty Program spend more on retraining programs for the poor? Should the subsidy to U.S. shipbuilders be dropped, or expanded? P-P-B can provide an economic foundation for wiser governmental decisions on such issues. But P-P-B is still merely a lusty infant. How big a role government administrators and legislators will give it remains to be seen.

At least, this kind of marginal "cost–benefit" analysis assures that we ask the right economic questions. It warns against taking on government projects where expected marginal costs exceed expected marginal benefits. And it helps to avoid the nonsense often heard in public discussion of such issues. Consider these two examples: (1) The assertion is often made that we "need" more police protection, or more classrooms, or wider streets. But this gives no basis for intelligent economic judgment about whether the government should meet these "needs." To make this decision, the additional costs must be compared with the anticipated benefits. (2) Equally foolish is the common assertion that "we can afford" better schools and urban renewal; therefore we should have them. There are many things we "can afford." Their limit is set by our total productive resources. What resources should be used in the public sector, and for what, can be decided rationally only by asking how expected costs on each venture compare with expected benefits.

Consumers' Sovereignty and Citizens' Sovereignty: Two Approaches

For the answer to what the public sector should do, we need to look beyond economics. At the most fundamental level, the issue is whether the political process or the market process does a better job of expressing people's desires on how our productive resources should be used in each case, and whose desires should have the most weight.

The allocation of resources through the private economy occurs primarily in response to consumers' money demands for goods and services. This is "consumers' sovereignty."[3] But government services are generally made available without any market price at all. Instead, we as citizens express our preferences for roads, rockets, zoos, and so on, through voting for representatives who subscribe to our views. They in turn should vote funds to procure resources to produce the goods and services that we have indicated we want. Thus—through the public sector—there is, ideally, a "citizens' sovereignty," somewhat analogous to "consumers' sovereignty" in the private economy. But there are some very significant differences. Four, especially, deserve attention.

1. In the marketplace, voting for resource allocation is on a **one-dollar-one-vote** basis. In the public sector, in a democratic country, it is on

---

[3]Note that the government, although it seldom does so, might follow the same policy in the public sector, selling the services it provides so as to maximize profits in response to consumer demand. Or a government enterprise, such as a public utility, may be operated to satisfy consumer demand at cost, rather than attempting to maximize profits. In these cases, allocation through the public and private sectors might not differ much.

a **one-person-one-vote** basis. Thus, in the private sector the rich man has many more votes than the poor man. In the public sector a democratic system attempts, though not always with complete success, to give each citizen equal voting power, regardless of whether he is rich or poor. Which way provides the better machinery for determining what to produce with our productive resources is a very fundamental question.

2. In the public sector, it is difficult for individuals to weigh specific benefits and costs, as we do daily in the private economy. In private life, Mr. X can consider carefully whether he prefers to spend $10 on football tickets, an electric razor, a new pair of shoes, or nothing at all. But when Mr. X votes to elect his representative, he votes on a whole group of economic and noneconomic issues. He has little opportunity to distinguish in detail between the things of which he approves and those of which he disapproves—he votes for one complex, ill-defined combination against another when he chooses among candidates. And once he has voted, he has to take the package of virtues and failings rolled up in his representative—and pay the taxes levied whether he thinks he gets his money's worth or not. Only when a specific decision is put up to the voters there is an exception—for example, when a special bond issue to finance a new school must be approved by the voters. And even then the individual has to accept the majority verdict. Consumers' sovereignty clearly gives him a greater power to discriminate on what he wants for his dollars.

3. The public sector thus involves a big element of compulsion. Even with democratic processes, once the elected representatives decide we're going to put a man on Mars, you and I must pay the taxes to support the project, however foolish we may think it is. Not so in the private sector. There I'm not forced to pay for something I don't want.

Admirers of the market process stress the ability of the market to give effective representation to majority votes while adequately protecting minority interests. The market has a built-in protection for every interest. The rich man gets the most votes, but the little fellow has his say too **in proportion to the dollars he has to spend.** One dollar counts one vote, no matter how large or small the number of votes registered for any commodity. No man needs to spend a dollar on any product unless he personally decides it's worth a dollar to him. A simple, political majority-vote procedure is weaker in reflecting minority wishes, for the reasons indicated in the preceding paragraph.

In some ways, we have pragmatically adjusted our political processes so that minority interests aren't lost. For example, at both state and national levels representatives are elected from fairly small areas, which gives local minorities a chance to be heard. In legislatures, business is largely done by committees and in informal discussions, which work out compromises on important issues that can command majorities among legislators representing widely diverse interests. But this doesn't eliminate the advantage of the market on the score of reflecting "minority" voting interests.

4. The legislative and administrative processes of government favor some groups over others. Our governments are more responsive to the folks back home than we often give them credit for. But in the legislative process, pressure groups and logrolling play an important role, sometimes a dominant one. Contary to widespread impressions, this situation is often more true at state and local levels than in the federal government, which operates more nearly in a goldfish bowl. The groups that are well organized receive more benefits than the rest. The "little man," the consumer, the great unorganized masses, often get the short end of the stick.

And without the test of the market there is no assurance that any public service will actually render benefits greater than its cost. Many public services, once enacted, are continued indefinitely, even though their main rationale may have vanished and their costs exceed the benefits expected by the public that voted them in years before. But here again the case can be overstated. At least in the federal government, a new budget is enacted each year, with widespread publicity about major items. The arguments aren't all on the side of either the private sector or the public sector.[4]

What Is the "Public Interest"?

What is the "public interest"? How is it best achieved? (1) Traditional economics (modernized Adam Smith) implies that the public interest is a summation, or compromise, of millions of individual interests, weighted by dollars spent in the marketplace, possibly after incomes have been more equitably redistributed. The public interest (social welfare) is thus a consensus, or summation, of individual utility functions. Public goods and externalities are seen as special cases, where governmental action is required in order to remedy failures of the private market to reflect accurately individual preferences. Most of the economy can rely on market expenditures to guide resource allocation efficiently.

(2) If we turn to the political process to determine the public interest, citizens' votes through the ballot box are seen as a better guide. Emphasis is placed on private market failures, because externalities and public goods bulk large. But here, too, there are serious questions about how well the voting process guides resources to the "best" uses.

Suppose that each individual knows how he ranks items A, B, and C. Take the following three individuals, each of whom prefers A, B, and C in the order shown. Suppose they collectively must choose to consume A, B, or C. What would be proper social choice so as to maximize their social welfare or "the public interest"?

Individual	Individual's Preference Ordering		
I	A	C	B
II	C	B	A
III	B	A	C

In this case there is no clear collective preference. Two-thirds prefer A to C, and two-thirds prefer C to B. If they first choose between B and C and then between A and C, A will com-

mand a majority. But two-thirds prefer B to A, and if they first choose between A and B, then C will command a majority. But two-thirds prefer A to C. A different order of choosing can produce any one of the three as the final choice. Clearly, even if every voter knows just what he wants, a democratic voting process may not produce satisfactory decisions.[5] And to make the problem worse, often voters aren't sure how their preferences rank on proposed government actions. Moreover, voters have strong preferences in some cases, weak ones in others, but the preference table assumes that all preferences are weighted equally.

Some political scientists argue that "the government" is actually itself an entity, which makes its own choices rather than merely serving as a quasi market for reflecting voter preferences. Any viable democratic government is *de facto* a coalition of representatives of different socioeconomic interests, this analysis runs. Government officials never know, and sometimes don't even care, just how their constituents feel on every issue. They make and carry out decisions, subject only to the constraint that no important group be treated so badly that it withdraws its support from the coalition. Thus the common practice of viewing "the government" as an operating organization, separate from the voters it formally represents, may be in large part correct. Whether the outcomes of such a process can meaningfully be said to reflect the "public interest" is open to argument. Government is a process both of implementing constituents' wishes and of searching to find a viable combination of choices acceptable to the coalition.

What "the public interest" is, is thus a more complex issue than simple majority voting in either elections or the marketplace. Neither the private market nor a democratic political process will always provide a suitable response to the public's wishes, and to make matters worse

---

[4]See, e.g., *Economic Analysis and the Efficiency of Government*, Report of the Joint Economic Committee, U.S. Congress, 1970.

[5]The theorem demonstrated is that transitivity in all individual ordering is not sufficient to assure a collectively transitive set of choices. This is sometimes called the Arrow impossibility theorem, after Professor Kenneth Arrow who first stated it sharply.

often the public isn't very clear as to just what it wants. The problem of social choice among alternative uses of limited productive resources will need different answers for different circumstances, often a combination of public and private measures.[6]

Social Choice: The Problem of Social Balance

One last look at the central issue of consumers' versus citizens' sovereignty and the public interest from another angle may be helpful. Those who say the public sector is too big have a basic assumption that individual freedom to spend incomes in the marketplace should guide the allocation of resources; any other allocation of resources is presumptively inferior.

Professor Galbraith has made a forceful counterargument in a best-selling book, *The Affluent Society*. He argues that such general distrust of the governmental process has led to a serious underallocation of resources to the public sector (leaving national defense aside). In the world's richest economy, we allocate only about 20 percent of our gross national product to satisfying all nondefense collective wants through public goods and services.

Galbraith argues that our economy is so rich we can readily afford more and better public services, that we need them badly, and that indeed the alternative is generally wasteful civilian consumption just to keep our economic machinery going. Yearly model changes on automobiles, plush night clubs, and mink coats are symbols of conspicuous consumption, meeting demands developed by pervasive advertising. Yet our public services are barely adequate. Our cities are marred by slums. Our streets are jammed. Our police forces and local governments are often peopled by incompetent individuals, so poorly paid as to be constant targets for graft. Few of our symphonies and art museums receive adequate public support. The scientist who invents a new gadget is greeted with public acclaim, but the politician who suggest a new public service is deemed a wastrel. All this, Galbraith argues, reflects a basic social unbalance in the affluent American economy. Somehow, we have no effective machinery to translate the obvious need for greater public services into reality.

Why do we so often assume that a dollar spent on taxes is wasted, while a dollar spent in the market provides a valuable return? Galbraith suggests that people have become so accustomed to assuming that any government spending is prima facie bad that they do not really examine the alternatives carefully. As taxpayers each of us sees the cost of public services to himself, but the benefits are often so widespread and generalized that it is hard for the individual to value them. This is true, for example, even of highways, which we tend to take for granted without realizing the benefits we receive from them. It is equally true of police protection, education, and the like. Foreign aid to underdeveloped nations is an even more extreme case.

Galbraith challenges, too, the widespread belief that all government activities are conducted wastefully. To be sure, there is inefficiency in government, as in private business. But there are many counterexamples. The Veterans Administration now handles its millions of insurance policies with computers and only 3,000 employees instead of the 17,000 it took in 1950. Annual operating costs per policy have been cut from $9.03 to $3.88. The Department of Defense achieved massive cost reductions under the McNamara regime and P-P-B.

America can clearly "afford" more public services and the end to such negative externalities as pollution if we want them. The test of Galbraith's position lies in whether we collectively do want them badly enough to pay for them.

Public Services in the United States and in Other Countries

In conclusion it may be useful to look at a few special facts about public services in the American economy now, and how we compare with

---

[6]For an excellent summary of these issues, see Peter Steiner, "The Public Sector and the Public Interest," in *The Analysis and Evaluation of Public Expenditures* (Joint Economic Committee of Congress, 1969), Vol. 1.

other nations. Figure 38–6 shows government nondefense purchases of goods and services as a percentage of total nondefense g.n.p. since 1929. Though total government spending has

than in most West European nations—around 6 percent of g.n.p. compared to nearly twice that ratio in West Germany and Sweden. In all the industrialized Western democracies, clearly the

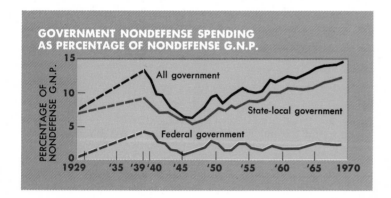

fig. 38–6

Government spending on nondefense goods and services has risen gradually since World War II as a percentage of total nondefense g.n.p. Most of this increase has been at the state-local level. (Sources: F. Bator, *The Question of Government Spending* [New York: Harper & Row, Publishers, 1960] and U.S. Department of Commerce.)

grown immensely, nondefense spending has grown only gradually as a share of nondefense g.n.p. Federal spending on nondefense collective services except social security has remained a very small percentage of total g.n.p. (less than 2 percent in most years if we leave out the social security system); this percentage has declined since 1939. State-local spending (mainly on education, streets, and highways) is larger and has grown steadily in recent years.

How big is the public sector (including defense expenditures) in the United States compared to other leading Western nations? Table 38–1 provides a rough summary, and includes a few less-developed nations for comparative purposes. These figures show tax collections as a percentage of gross national product in 1965, including taxes used to finance both real and transfer expenditures.

If we look at "real" government expenditures alone, the U.S. figure was about 20 percent of g.n.p. This compared with about 22 percent in West Germany and the United Kingdom, and around 20 percent in Belgium, Sweden, and Canada. But U.S. government transfer payments (largely welfare payments) were smaller

public sector plays a big role. In the United States, this role is smaller than in most of the leading West European nations, but much larger than in the less-developed countries.

table 38-1	
The Public Sector in Different Nations*	
Country	Tax Collections as a Percentage of G.n.p.
Sweden	39
France	38
West Germany	34
United Kingdom	30
Italy	30
United States	27
Canada	27
Japan	20
Mexico	10
India	8

*Data for 1966 from Organization for Economic Cooperation and Development, except for Mexico and India.

CONCEPTS
TO
REMEMBER

Some new analytical concepts are introduced in this chapter, and important old ones are reused. Be sure you understand the following:

"the public sector"
real (or exhaustive) expenditures
transfer (or nonexhaustive)
    expenditures
external economies and
    diseconomies (externalities)

consumers' sovereignty
citizens' sovereignty
balancing alternatives at the
    margin
cost-benefit analysis

FOR ANALYSIS
AND DISCUSSION

1. What are the main economic functions of government?
2. Does government spend too much? What are your criteria for deciding?
3. Does consumers' sovereignty or citizens' sovereignty provide a better process for allocating society's productive resources?
4. If a copy is available (e.g., in the *New York Times* of about the third week of each January, or in the *Federal Budget in Brief*), read over the president's most recent budget message to Congress. What are the major increases and decreases proposed from the preceding year? Do these changes seem desirable to you? What criteria have you used, implicitly or explicitly, in making these judgments?
5. Many argue that our national priorities should place a higher value on better public services—education, slum clearance, public health, and so on—than on more consumer goods. Analyze this argument.
6. Locate your family income level roughly on Fig. 38–4. Assuming that these data are roughly accurate, do you feel that your income level is being treated equitably in the government's overall redistribution of income?
7. What are externalities? Give three examples of cases where probable externalities provide a basis for government provision of goods or services.
8. What is cost–benefit analysis? How can it help in deciding what projects government should undertake?
9. Recently, much concern has been expressed that our educational facilities are inadequate in many areas, especially in some rural areas in the South. Should the federal government spend more money to improve these educational facilities, say by building new schoolhouses or making grants to raise teachers' salaries? If your answer is yes, how much would you be willing to see your taxes raised to help pay for such new expenditures?
10. a. Many people believe that there is always a presumption in favor of reducing government expenditures. Do you agree?
    b. Why, if at all, is the above presumption more defensible than a presumption that government spending to provide public services should be increased?

APPENDIX   *THE URBAN CRISIS*

The problems of the modern public sector are nowhere more vividly apparent than in the urban crisis—the plight of the great cities that already, with their sprawling appendages, include well over half our total population and may encompass 80 percent or more by the year 2000. Consider New York, the largest metropolis of all, with the biggest problems of all. It has nearly 1 million dilapidated housing units, with private construction of housing in the central city at a virtual standstill—it simply isn't profitable to build new housing, given city building restrictions, land prices, taxes, and the flight to the suburbs of the middle and upper-middle classes. Worse, it doesn't pay to keep much of the existing slum-area housing stock in repair. Landlords, with existing conditions and rent controls, are generally better off to let their apartments deteriorate, collecting rents as long as they can, and then just abandon the property.

City taxes are already so high they drive investment and households away. Yet city services are clearly inadequate. Crime and dirt seem to be everywhere. Teacher pay rates are among the highest in the nation; yet teaching vacancies go unfilled and the city's slum-area schools sometimes resemble minor battlefields rather than educational establishments. Racial groups quarrel incessantly over control of their schools.

Transportation threatens a gigantic breakdown as the ratio of autos to space soars, and millions of auto exhausts pollute the atmosphere. Public transportation, while plentiful compared to many cities, is noisy, dirty, and increasingly expensive for the poor who must use it since they have no cars.

Welfare rolls have soared during the last decade, in spite of a booming economy and low overall unemployment. Over a million residents are on welfare, more than one of eight in the city's population. Puerto Ricans and Negroes from the southern states have poured in during recent years, partly in search of the nation's highest welfare payments. Harlem and Bedford-Stuyvesant bubble with racial tensions.

The city's problems are complicated by the exodus of the upper and middle classes to the suburbs, where they live in more pleasant surroundings, send their children to school, and pay their property taxes, and from whence they commute daily, complaining loudly about the bad facilities. The metropolitan area is a mass of overlapping local authorities, towns, counties, school districts, sewer districts, water districts, and dozens more. Each is concerned to maintain its own tax base, and to maximize the services it obtains while minimizing the costs to its own members. Understandably, coordinated metropolitan area planning is extremely difficult.

The list could go on. New York is the nation's urban crisis on display. To deal adequately with this one aspect of the public sector problem would take another book at least as large as this one; the problems are economic, political, social, physical. But before going on to the next chapter, consider briefly how you would advocate solving the city's slum housing problem—a major, complex problem but only one of many. Are less-greedy landlords the answer? Public housing? Stricter rent controls—or abolition of rent controls? Rent supplements to the poor, or subsidies for private construction of low-cost apartments? A federal negative income tax to guarantee minimum incomes? State aid? New mass-production housing construction? Renovation of existing housing? Better schools to stop the exodus to the suburbs? Abolition of discrimination against minority groups?

Obviously, this is too hard a problem for easy answers. But it provides an illuminating case study of the problems of applying the principles of Chapter 38 to a tough real-world situation. What are the central principles? For an interesting analysis of this particular problem, see G. Sternlieb, "New York's Housing: A Study in Immobilism," in *The Public Interest* (Summer, 1969), pp. 123–42; the entire issue is devoted to "Focus on New York." J. Kain and J. Persky, "Alternatives to the Gilded Ghetto," *The Public Interest* (Winter, 1969), focus on problems of the central city and dispersal possibilities. Broader summary looks at the nation's housing problem are provided by A. Downs, "Moving Toward Realistic Housing Goals," in *Agenda for the Nation* (Washington, D.C.: The Brookings Institution, 1969); and M. Schussheim, *Toward a New Housing Policy* (Committee for Economic Development, 1969).

thirty-nine

Case Study: Pollution and the Environment

National concern for the deteriorating quality of the environment has snowballed in recent years. Concern for economic growth has been supplanted by the question, growth for what? Air and water pollution are pervasive by-products (externalities) of modern industrial society. On every side there are cries for the government to "do something" to halt pollution. Insofar as 200 million people can be said to have a national commitment, to clean up the environment and halt its dangerous deterioration has emerged as a major national commitment in the last few years. And little wonder! Examples:

1. **Water.** In 1969, the oily, chocolate-brown Cuyahoga River, which runs through Cleveland into Lake Erie, burst into flames. The Cuyahoga is so laden with industrial and municipal waste that not even the leeches and sludge worms that thrive in many badly polluted rivers are found in it. Lake Erie is described as "dead." Along the entire southern shore, there are virtually no fish left and most other forms of marine life have vanished. Once called "the beautiful river," the Ohio is now perhaps the most contaminated of all our rivers, the receptacle for thousands of tons of pollutants from plants and cities along its valley. Swimming, even boating, in many of our inland waterways has become too dangerous to risk.

The Public Health Service warns that the United States is "rapidly approaching a crisis stage with regard to drinking water." Although the nation has invested about $15 billion since 1952 in the construction of thousands of municipal sewage-treatment plants, sewers, and industrial-pollution control and related facilities, over 40 percent of the nation's sewage is dumped, raw and untreated, into the streams and water resources of the nation. Only about 25 percent of the total receives what sanitary engineers call "two-stage treatment"—which may, under ideal conditions, satisfy 90 percent of the biochemical oxygen demand before the sewage is released into the streams of natural water. The remaining 30 to 35 percent of communities have "one-stage" treatment, which merely takes out the solids from the raw sewage. In the great majority of sewage systems, the same facilities are used for rain runoff and industrial and household sewage, so when heavy rainstorms exceed the capacity of sewage-treatment plants, the city's raw sewage bypasses the sewage plant with the street-water runoff and is washed directly into the waterways without treatment.

2. **Air.** Each year, America's industries, homes, and cars spew over 200 million tons of smoke and fumes into the air. Autos account for about half of this total, and in some areas, particularly Los Angeles, for nearly all of it. As long ago as 1952, 4,000 deaths were recorded in London in one period of massive smog, when air conditions held down close to the earth all the pollutants being poured out by furnaces, fireplaces, industrial plants, and autos. The famous New York Thanksgiving Day smog of 1966 reached almost the same danger level, as air inversion held the smog motionless over the metropolitan area. Scientists warn that Los Angeles hovers on the brink of a similar danger. Because of the particular location of that sprawling city, it is peculiarly susceptible to air inversion, which holds down the enormous mass of pollutants poured into the atmosphere daily by millions of autos and trucks. Air pollution is not new, nor peculiar to the United States. Ancient Romans complained of the smoke that enveloped their city. But the magnitude of the problem has increased vastly in recent decades.

3. **Solid waste.** As a result of America's mas-

sive production of goods and services that make up our incredible g.n.p., every year we junk 7 million cars, 50 million tires, 20 million tons of paper, 28 billion bottles and 48 billion cans. Just to collect the nation's garbage costs nearly $3 billion a year. Every year, U.S. plants disgorge 165 million tons of solid waste along with the tons of smoke and fumes they gush into the air. Graveyards of junked cars are the most visible symptom of our massive waste-disposal problem. But the problem is even worse than it seems, for increasingly packaging materials (cans and the like) have been shifted to a "no-return" basis and to materials that are virtually indestructible (for example, plastics and aluminum instead of steel). Every major city faces a crisis on the disposal of its massive wastes already, or in the years near ahead.

4. **Noise.** Especially in the cities, noise is approaching the level of persistent intensity that threatens both the mental and physical well-being of the inhabitants. According to a widely cited standard, 85 decibels represents the level above which continuous noise can cause deafness. A typical subway train produces 95 decibels, a power mower 110 decibels, and a jet aircraft at takeoff 150 decibels. Electronically magnified rock and roll reaches well above 100 decibles. When sonic booms come with the supersonic transport, the noise problem will dramatically worsen. Noise at a level of 165 decibels can kill animals such as rats and cats. Experts warn that it can damage human ears, nerves, and general bodily functioning.

5. **The ecological system.** Ecologists, who study the interactions of entire systems of living things, note all the above problems and go far beyond them. They suggest that population growth and modern technology have gone so far so fast that they threaten man's very existence on this globe. Partly they point to the rapid using-up of natural resources. More fundamentally, they argue that our throw-offs of all forms of waste are interacting so as to make the planet uninhabitable. For example, chemical fertilizers and pesticides used in farming are only partly absorbed by growing plants; many of them wash into the streams and oceans where they may seriously affect both marine life

and those who consume the water. Thus, attempts to increase the output of agricultural land through the use of such modern methods may boomerang. The destruction of Lake Erie is due more to washoff of agricultural chemicals than to industrial pollution. The natural balance of living things is said to be a delicate one, and man's incredibly rapid development of the past century threatens to disturb these fundamental balances. At the extreme, some argue that our massive burning-up in a few years of fossil fuels that took millenia to compose may change the basic heat balance of the earth and its atmosphere and result in fundamental changes in climate, including the melting of the polar glaciers and massive flooding as ocean levels rise. Most ecologists consider these predictions extreme. But the fundamental problem is real, and the doomsday predictions help to focus attention on it.

Deterioration in the quality of the environment is not confined to the United States, although our massive increases in real g.n.p., modern technology, and rising living standards make the problem most vivid for us. Nor is the problem confined to capitalist systems. Soviet newspapers complain of the same conditions in the USSR, and Soviet cartoonists are equally caustic in their drawings of pollution as it envelopes the Russian man in the street. Their rivers vie with ours for the title of dirtiest.[1] And the Rhine, fabled in song and verse, is possibly the dirtiest of the world's major rivers. Moreover, pollution is far from new. Early Roman writers complained of filthy drinking water. Early Spanish explorers noted that campfire smoke hung thick and low in what is now the Los Angeles basin. Open sewers and cesspools are common in the world's underdeveloped nations, many of which are neither rich nor capitalist.

[1]For example, see K. Iosifob, "The Vokhna River Flows," and O. Volkov, "A Writer's Notes: A Trip to Baikal," reprinted in M. Goldman, ed., *Controlling Pollution* (Englewood-Cliffs, N.J.: Prentice-Hall, Inc., Spectrum Books, 1967).

The Problem

If the American public is so seriously concerned about the deteriorating quality of the environment, why does the system continue to produce environmental deterioration rather than improvement? This is a complex question, but much of the answer goes back to "externalities"—the fact that private production costs do not include the full costs to society, such as the pollution of rivers by industrial wastes. Thus, in responding to market demands, businessmen do not charge the full social cost of their operations in their prices to consumers. The result is that the price of industry's products is too low, consumers buy too much paper and steel produced by the riverside plants. In effect, we make the losers from pollution subsidize users of steel and paper. In the same way, the price of automobiles does not reflect their full cost to society; car users do not have to pay for the air pollution they create. Pollution and deteriorating environment reflect in large part market failure because of the existence of externalities —social costs substantially in excess of private costs.

Put another way, manufacturers and auto drivers treat clean water, clean air, and quiet as if they were free goods, when in fact they are increasingly scarce and are overconsumed at a price of zero. We should be able to charge users of clean air and clean water for the privilege of making them dirty, but we don't. We should be able to charge users of quiet for the privilege of polluting it with noise, but we don't. So far we have developed no feasible way of recognizing these public goods as property and directly charging a price for their use.

In principle, to provide an optimal allocation of society's resources in response to the public's wishes, costs should include both private costs and by-product social costs. The price of cars, for example, should include a charge for clean-exhaust engines—in effect a price for the clean air we wish to keep clean. Similar analysis can be applied to most other cases of pollution, for example, the social cost of smoke and dirty water in many industrial areas.

Fundamentally, the deteriorating environment reflects our rapidly growing population, rapid movement toward high-technology production, and, above all, the enormous demand of American citizens for a bigger and better life —bigger and better cars, bigger and better airplanes, bigger and better household appliances, more electricity and man-made energy, redder apples, greener beans. The villain of the piece is not some profit hungry industrialist who can be fined into submission, nor some lax public official who can be replaced. The villain is the failure of free markets to take into account full social costs. And the villains are consumers themselves who demand (or let themselves be persuaded to demand) new, bigger, cheaper things without counting the cost in the dirtier environment that results as a by-product. The quips of critics are often telling. Smog, they say, is the Air Apparent. Paraphrasing Perry's famous battle report from Lake Erie, they quip "We have met the enemy, and he is us." As population grows and living standards rise, more people and more modern technology mean a nonlinear increase in environmental problems. Ours is an effluent, as well as an affluent, society.

Much of the pollution problem traces to a simple proposition: You can't get rid of matter. We can change the form of matter, in the earth, on it, and in its atmosphere, but we can't do more than transform it. Thus, we can change coal into heat and pollutants such as fly ash, gases, and soot, but the same amount of matter remains in a different form. This is most obvious in the form of solid wastes, but it is equally important in pollution of the air and the water, which are the recipients of some of the by-products in transforming materials.

This fundamental fact is emphasized by Figure 39–1. This is a schematic diagram of the inflow of organic and inorganic materials produced by mines, farms, forests, and wildlife areas, which, with oxygen, are transformed into fuel, food, and raw materials. These in turn are partly transformed into final goods (solids, liquids, and gases) and partly into by-products in the form of gaseous residuals and solid and liquid wastes.

Figure 39–1 points up several important propositions. 1) Externalities in the form of gaseous, solid, and liquid residuals are a fundamental part of the entire production process, and must be recognized as ubiquitous, not special cases. 2) Such external diseconomies become progressively more important as population and the level of output increase. 3) They can be properly dealt with only by considering the entire system of transformations in toto not by looking independently at the air, water, and solid waste problems. 4) Since by-product residuals from transformation of materials are inescapable, these must either be minimized through regulations or, more fundamentally, be recycled back into the production process in some useful form. For example, the fly ash from burning coal might be rechanneled into compressed building blocks, rather than spewed out to pollute the atmosphere. It is important to note that the final products of the

THE POLLUTION PROBLEM

fig. 39–1

Technological external diseconomies in the form of residuals are inherent in our production and consumption processes.

process (consumer and investment goods) also ultimately become residuals deposited into the environment, which are either maintained in the form of waste (aluminum cans and plastic containers) or recycled into the productive process (reclamation of sulfur from gaseous residuals in the production of steel).

Pollution Policy

Pollution, Population, and Economic Growth

It is important to remember from Chapter 18 that pollution, population growth, and economic growth are intimately related—but also that they are analytically separable and need not come together. Economic growth means growth in total economic output per capita—it is growth in generalized productive capacity. We may use the increased capacity to produce useful things that nonetheless involve pollution (e.g., leaded gasoline), things that involve no pollution (e.g. art museums), or things that reduce pollution (e.g., smoke filters on chimneys). Though growth in output of some goods inescapably involves pollution (e.g., solid waste from many products), in general we can use our productive capacity to produce the combination of goods, services, and cleanliness we want and are willing to pay for. Choice of more clean air will mean less steel and auto transportation from the resources available, but more steel and autos need not mean dirtier air. G.n.p. in total and per capita will not be as large as with pollution, since cleaner air (less pollution) doesn't get included as we compute g.n.p.; but this does not change the fact that we can allocate our productive resources as we wish to maximize our satisfaction from them. Indeed, the more we grow (increase productive capacity), the greater will be our ability to have both cleaner air and water and more of the other goods and services we want. To oppose economic growth because that seems the only way to lessen pollution is shortsighted indeed.

Population growth is different. More population, other things equal, means less output per capita—a lower standard of living. It also inescapably means more crowding of the environment, since the total amount of space to be shared is substantially fixed.

As a practical matter, combined population and economic growth have brought a devastating amount of environmental pollution over the last half century. But this does not mean that zero economic growth, or even zero population growth, is the best way to clean up the environment. On the contrary, we need to be careful not to throw the baby out with the bathwater. If these basic analytical distinctions are not clear, go back and review the first half of Chapter 18.

The rest of this chapter deals mainly with the problem of how best to obtain the combination of environmental cleanliness (or pollution) and g.n.p. that we want from our given amount of productive capacity at any given time.

Pollution Policy and Externalities

Private-market failure is to be expected when externalities are large. Clean air, clean water, and quiet are no longer free goods and should not be treated as such. When private costs and prices do not fully reflect social costs, too much of the product involved will be produced and used. If autos, for example, were (a) produced with no air or water pollution side effects, and (b) were redesigned to eliminate all undesirable exhaust emissions, the cost of producing cars and their prices would be substantially higher, and consumers would presumably buy fewer cars. In substance, auto makers and users would have to pay the price of maintaining clean air. To expect one auto company individually to be social-minded and offer only pollution-free but more expensive cars misses the core of the problem. Any one producer who added on these extra costs without his competitors' doing so would soon find that he was pricing himself out of the market.[2] Nor is it reasonable to expect the individual consumer to invest voluntarily in an expensive smog-control device for his car when other auto users are not required to do so.

---

[2]A small example of this occurred in the late 1950s, when Ford put expensive safety features in its production-line cars and lost sales heavily to G.M. and Chrysler, which offered cheaper cars without the safety features.

Alone, he can do no measurable good in reducing the overall level of smog. Only if all, or most, consumers are required to add smog-control devices is the general problem of smog alleviated and can each individual feel he is paying his part of the price of clean air, with assurance than other car users are doing the same.

Effective action to alleviate pollution therefore must be collective action—action through the political process. Only collective action can assure compliance and uniformity for antipollution policies. Fundamentally, four channels appear to be open to us.

1. **Persuasion.** Well-intentioned social reformers urge that if only businessmen and consumers would behave properly, the pollution problem could be eliminated. But to count primarily on persuasion would be a misguided hope indeed, for the reasons suggested just above. And to condemn businessmen because they produce what consumers are most willing to pay for misconstrues the incentive role of profits in our system.

2. **Regulation-prohibition.** If society wants to assure minimum pollution standards, the simplest approach is to set legal standards that producers or users must meet. Auto manufacturers could be required to build only smog-free engines, even though they cost more; basically auto users would have to pay the higher price to get new cars. Equally, minimum exhaust-emission standards could be established for all used cars, perhaps by requiring installation of smog-control devices with annual inspection to assure compliance; the major part of the auto-smog problem comes from old, not new, cars. Both steps would raise the effective cost of driving and would presumably lessen the total use of autos. Similar regulations can be readily imagined for maximum permissible pollutants discharged into streams by industrial producers, and for other externalities.

Three problems: (a) Such regulations are hard to write and enforce equitably. (b) Many of the worst offenders are local governments themselves, which contribute to pollution through inadequate sewage- and waste-disposal systems. (c) Direct regulation doesn't necessarily

impose the correct social cost on users; regulation that eliminates all undesirable externalities (side effects) may cost more than the public would choose to pay if they were given the choice of different levels of pollution at different prices. Pollution is a matter of degree, not of all-or-none, as a practical matter.

3. **User-taxes.** In principle, the optimal allocation of resources would be obtained when the price of each product just covered the full social cost (i.e., both private and externality costs) of producing and using it. This could be achieved by imposing a special tax on each producer or user that just covers the external costs that he imposes on society. For industrial water pollution, for example, a tax of so much per ton of pollutants discharged could be imposed, with the tax rate set to cover the estimated social cost of cleaning up that pollution if it occurs. Consumers would have to pay more for the firm's products, but just enough more to cover the full social cost of producing or using it. Thus, the externalities would be internalized into the production-and-price system.[3]

Problems: (1) Such tax charges are difficult to set accurately and equitably for all concerned. Though in principle better than specific regulations, user taxes raise such difficult administrative problems that many experts are inclined to accept the simpler, albeit second-best, approach of uniform minimum standards. (2) Again, municipalities themselves are among the worst offenders, so such charges would need to be imposed by national or state governments.

---

[3]Public or private appropriation of property rights to clean water and air so these can be "sold" to users (polluters) is, though in principle desirable, very difficult. A possible exception is property rights to quiet near modern airports. The cost of noise created by aircraft on approach and takeoff patterns could be roughly measured by the drop in value of affected property sites before and after construction of the airport. Thus, a "price" equal to the difference between "before and after" property values might be charged airlines using up the quiet over these properties, with the proceeds paid to the injured property owners.

The actual case is, as always, more complex. The airlines might argue in return that their presence at the airport actually increases property values nearby (provides positive externalities) through drawing travelers and tourists to the area, creating demand for motels, restaurants, service stations, and the like. It should be clear that both negative and positive effects could exist simultaneously, with differential effects on different property owners near the airport.

But such user-charge systems can work, in spite of these problems. For example, pollution in the Ruhr River valley in Germany, one of the world's most concentrated industrial complexes, has for over forty years been controlled by just such a set of charges—and highly effectively, in the eyes of most observers.[4]

4. **Payments-subsidies.** Where social benefits exceed private benefits, precisely the opposite policy is appropriate. Subsidies should be paid to producers to encourage larger production than the private market would call forth. For example, education has large positive externalities, and these are recognized in large governmental subsidies through provision of free, or below-cost, education. Another example: More effective soil-conservation practices by farmers upstream would lessen the danger of floods downstream and thereby provide benefits to individuals and municipalities downstream that could not be charged for in the private marketplace. Thus, a special subsidy to upstream farmers to finance the improved conservation practices, with the funds obtained by special charges on the beneficiaries downstream, would increase the incentive for upstream farmers to carry out the socially desirable conservation practices. As in the case of special taxes and charges, the practical application of the principle might be very complex. But its theoretical justification is sound, and simple approximations may be quite feasible.

An Example

Urban sewage disposal, an unglamourous but central part of the water pollution problem, illustrates cleanup potentialities and problems. As was indicated at the beginning of this chapter, in many American communities, raw sewage is dumped directly into flowing streams. In about 35 percent, sewage is passed through a one-stage treatment, in another 25 percent through a two-stage treatment, which removes perhaps 90 percent of the pollutant qualities of the sewage before it is dumped into streams. In

[4]For a brief description, see L. E. Ruff, "The Economic Common Sense of Pollution," *The Public Interest*, Spring, 1970, pp. 84–85.

virtually all cases, common sewers are used for rainwater runoff and sewage waste. Thus, heavy rainstorms may produce such flooding that the combined sewage plus rain runoff must be bypassed around the treatment plants, pouring directly into flowing streams or lakes without any sewage treatment at all.

Use of sewers for both waste and rain runoff is sensible; at most times, the same sewer system is quite adequate to carry both and both are funneled through the sewage-treatment plants. But increasingly, sanitary engineers point out that a completely separate runoff system for rainwater would be a major safeguard against massive water pollution in storms. An alternative would be to build sewage-treatment plants so large that they would handle even the massive runoffs in large storms, but this would be extremely expensive. Cost estimates vary, but a total of $35 to $50 billion would possibly suffice to build completely separate rain-runoff sewage systems for the nation and provide two-stage sewage treatment for all major municipalities. This would, of course, fall substantially short of 100 percent water purification for the nation. Providing separate runoff systems alone might cost from $20 to $30 billion, with a wide range of uncertainty about these figures.

How clean is clean? To clean up sewage completely before it is dumped into flowing streams would be fantastically expensive, far beyond the $35-50 billion figure indicated above. Costs mount astronomically as we move toward 100 percent clean. Clean water is not an all-or-nothing proposition. As almost everywhere in economics, the question is one of degree, and of the costs of achieving varying degrees of the desired goal.

A simple example may emphasize this point. Johnny's mother tells him to wash his hands before he comes to dinner. When she sees the result she says he has not *really* washed his hands. Johnny protests that he has; he has passed his hands through a stream of cold water before coming to the table. His mother sends him back, to use hot water, soap, and a towel, and then his hands pass inspection. Yet Johnny's hands, even after a two-stage treatment, are far from clean enough to meet the standards insisted on by a surgeon in a hospital operating room. He would demand a third-stage process to meet his standards of cleanliness. Johnny measures cleanliness by the fact of washing his hands. His mother's measure is a visual one—how much dirt she can see. The surgeon is interested in bacterial count. To insist on a third level of cleanliness in day-to-day life for most of us would be incredibly expensive in terms of time, energy, and money, and pointless. Just so, completely cleaning up all sewage to 100 percent purity before its discharge would mean buying more cleanliness than we really want to pay for.

How can the thousands of municipalities involved afford to lay out the vast sums of money required to improve their sewer systems or their sewage-treatment facilities? Should they? Will they do so?

The capital costs involved are very large compared to the likely willingness of many communities to pay. Taxpayers are reluctant in any event to see tax rates go up; and such outlays would require enormous tax increases or bond issues that might be difficult to sell at reasonable interest rates. Part of the problem is that water pollution is a case of massive externalities. If city A on river B cleans up its sewage, it somewhat helps the residents of city A but mainly the communities downstream that benefit from A's cleanup program. If A cleans up but city C upstream does not, the water flowing through city A is just about as dirty as before it put in its own sewage-disposal program. And so it is with other cities up and down the river.

Thus, without some concerted effort that coordinates the activities of all the communities involved, effective action is unlikely. And given the fact that most metropolitan areas are masses of overlapping municipalities and other political jurisdictions (water districts, school districts, and the like), the outlook is practically hopeless without either a massive alteration of our local governmental systems or federal intervention to finance and oversee area water-cleanup programs. The private market obviously provides no mechanism for allocating costs and benefits so as to get the overall desired result of cleaner water. Unfortunately, neither do the local polit-

ical processes of the many communities involved.

How shall the federal government decide how much it should spend combating water pollution in the thousands of different areas throughout the nation? Cost-benefit studies (studies comparing the estimated cost of installing water-cleanup facilities in comparison with the estimated benefits in the form of cleaner water, higher property values, and the like) provide an answer in principle. But it is easy to see that the practical problem of making such studies for the entire United States is enormous, and even then it is not sure that the voting process will provide a clear answer that will guide the federal government in allocating just the right amount of tax money to clean up streams and avoid industrial and household-sewage pollution in the thousands of communities involved. Another approach would be to rely on laws setting minimum standards of cleanliness, with legal sanctions to enforce compliance by all. But there would be very tough political problems in setting and enforcing federal standards on states and localities.

Some Estimates of Total Cost

It should be obvious by now that estimated costs to clean up air, water, and other forms of pollution are extremely nebulous, and that the amounts involved are vast, whether they are paid by taxpayers, by business firms, or by final consumers of the products involved. Table 39–1 provides one set of estimates of the annual cost of pollution control, covering air pollution, water pollution, and solid-waste disposal, at a minimal level of acceptability. (Note the vagueness of the words "minimal level.")

Other estimates are vastly higher. Starr and Carlson,[5] for example, report that $100 billion may be a modest estimate of the total cost of providing thorough cleanup of water pollution and sewage waste disposal throughout the nation; some pessimists place the figure nearly twice that high. Substantial elimination of air

[5]R. Starr and J. Carlson, "Pollution and Poverty: The Strategy of Cross-Commitment," *The Public Interest*, Winter, 1968.

table 39-1

Estimated Annual Cost of Pollution Control*
(Billions of Dollars)

	Capital	Operating	Total
Air pollution:			
Automobile afterburners	$1.5	$1.0	$2.5
Sulfur dioxide removal from stack gases	0.3	1.0	1.3
Industrial control equipment	0.3	—	0.3
Total	$2.1	$2.0	$ 4.1
Water pollution:			
Reservoirs for seasonal equalization of river flows for waste oxidation	0.4	—	0.4
Municipal sewage collection and treatment	0.9	0.6	1.5
Industrial effluent treatment	1.1	0.5	1.6
Separation of combined sewers and storage of storm waters	0.5	—	0.5
Electric utility cooling towers	0.1	0.6	0.7
Total	$3.0	$1.7	$ 4.7
Solid-waste disposal:			
Collection of municipal wastes	—	2.6	2.6
Incineration of municipal wastes	—	0.7	0.7
Landfill of municipal wastes	—	0.3	0.3
Junk-auto disposal	—	0.2	0.2
Demolition-waste disposal	—	0.9	0.9
Total	$ —	$4.7	$ 4.7
TOTAL	$5.1	$8.4	$13.5

*Source: Harvard Center for Population Studies.

pollution (again, absolute cleanliness is neither obtainable nor needed) is cheaper but still vastly expensive. Elimination of solid waste (discarded automobiles, beer cans, and the like) involves costs that are extremely difficult to quantify; alternatives include massive transfers of wastes to desert areas with landfills, dumping waste far out in the oceans, and, most hopefully, recycling many residuals into productive uses, though such recycling would be very expensive.

Economics and Politics

Pollution control points up the inescapable mix of economic and political factors in many major social problems. It is clear that the private market provides no adequate mechanism for eliminating pollution in America; externalities are vast and private-market failures are to be expected in such a case. On the other hand, it is not clear that the regular political process provides an effective alternative. Eighty million voters cannot indicate directly their preferences for each pollution cleanup area in the nation, and announce how much they would like to see spent on it. Each locality understandably hopes to get large federal assistance with a minimum layout of its own resources. In assessing the benefits and costs of pollution-control projects, the federal government usually finds itself in the middle. Those who will have to pay for environmental improvements, such as businesses, municipalities, and general taxpayers, tend to inflate potential costs and deflate benefits. Those who particularly want the improvements—for example recreationists—can be counted on to do just the opposite, arguing on moral grounds man's right to a truly clean environment.

A wealthy nation like the United States finds itself increasingly searching for decision processes that will provide an acceptable allocation of resources to meet new national priorities. There is a vast area between cases clearly appropriate for the private marketplace alone and those for government action alone. The problem is one for economics and politics.

Awareness of air and water pollution has snowballed in the past few years. On President Johnson's recommendation, Congress passed the Water Quality Act of 1965 and the Clean Water Act of 1966, stating high standards for water cleanup and allocating millions (not billions) of dollars of federal money to help. Between the mid-1950s and 1970, federal spending to reduce water pollution rose from about $1 million to $300 million annually, while the outlays for air-pollution control rose from about $3 million to about $90 million annually. In 1969, Congress established a Council on Environmental Quality, parallel in many respects to the Council of Economic Advisers established in 1946. Reflecting the growing sense of national urgency, President Nixon submitted in 1970 a broad program of environmental restoration to Congress, proposing thirty-seven different action steps covering four major categories: water-pollution control, air-pollution control, solid-waste management, and parklands and public recreation. He wrote:

The fight against pollution is not a search for villains. For the most part, the damage done to our environment has not been the work of evil men, nor has it been the inevitable by-product with advancing technology or of growing population. It results . . .

from failure to take into account the full consequences of our actions.

. . . By ignoring environmental costs, we have given an economic advantage to the careless polluter over his more conscientious rival. While adopting laws prohibiting entry to a person's property, we have freely allowed entry to our shared surroundings.

The tasks that need doing . . . call for a fundamentally new philosophy toward land, air, and water use, for stricter regulation, for expanding government action, for greater system involvement, and for new programs to ensure that the government, industry, and individuals are all called upon to do their share of the job and pay their share of the costs.

To achieve these goals, President Nixon proposed radically stiffer minimum air-pollution requirements for automobiles and industrial plants; and a water-pollution cleanup program whereby municipalities would spend some $10 billion over the next five years, with the federal government prepared to support bonds issued by municipalities to finance these expenditures. He proposed major fines ($10,000 per day) for polluters who disobey the new antipollution standards. He urged rapid development of research on the problem of recycling wastes into productive uses.

Supporters hailed the message as a national mission for a cleaner America, and a blueprint to achieve that goal. Critics accused the president of rhetoric without back-up federal money to carry out the vast improvements he mentioned. Eliminating pollution in America will be a long, hard struggle, both economically and politically. You will need to decide for yourself how much money and inconvenience you are willing to pay for how much cleanliness, and how involved you want to be in the political processes of achieving the goals you set.[6]

---

[6]*Fortune*, February, 1970, provides a lively, more complete survey of the pollution problem. See also especially L. E. Ruff, "The Economic Common Sense of Pollution," *The Public Interest*, Spring, 1970, for a vivid application of the economic analysis outlined here.

1. Explain why you would expect "market failure" in case of large externalities.
2. Devise a workable program to eliminate unwanted air pollution in your own community, including an acceptable means of financing your program.
3. Should Lake Erie be cleaned up so that its south shore is again attractive for swimming, boating, and fishing? If so, how, and who should pay for the reclamation?
4. Many critics argue that the auto manufacturers are responsible for smog and air pollution in the cities. They argue that the auto companies should be required to bear the cost of eliminating the auto-exhaust contribution to smog.
   a) Is this a correct analysis of responsibility?
   b) If you believe the cost of eliminating auto air pollution should be placed on the auto manufacturers, how would you accomplish this? (Remember your price theory from Part Three.)
5. How shall we get a "national priority" like a cleaner and more pleasant physical environment implemented?

The Public Sector: Taxes

Nearly everyone complains about high taxes. But if we want public goods and services, we must get resources transferred from private to public use. If we assume full employment, taxes are the most straightforward way to get the funds needed, since they reduce private incomes that would otherwise bid for the resources. With full employment, more government spending without more taxes means increased total spending and inflation, as more government spending bids resources away from private use. Resources are taken away from those whose incomes fall behind in the inflation.

Government spending sets the general level of taxes we need to collect. By the same token, the amounts our governments can spend are roughly limited by the taxes we are willing to pay. With government spending at present levels, and probably headed higher, construction of a sound and equitable tax system is of foremost importance. The multibillion dollar federal budget may not mean much to you—the figures are too big. But the fact that you, when you leave college with an average middle-class income of perhaps $10,000, will start turning over to Uncle Sam and to local governmental units over $2,500 each year puts the dollars and cents in more meaningful terms.

Distribution of the Tax Burden

Who pays the taxes? Figures 40–1 and 40–2 summarize the answer on one basis—what taxes provide the revenue for federal, state, and local governments?

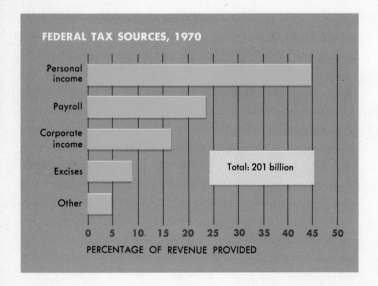

FEDERAL TAX SOURCES, 1970

Personal income

Payroll

Corporate income

Excises

Total: 201 billion

Other

0 5 10 15 20 25 30 35 40 45 50

PERCENTAGE OF REVENUE PROVIDED

fig. 40–1

This figure reemphasizes the dominant position of personal and corporation income taxes in financing federal government activities. (Source: U.S. Budget Bureau.)

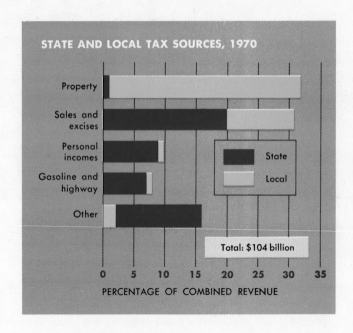

STATE AND LOCAL TAX SOURCES, 1970

Property

Sales and excises

Personal incomes

State

Gasoline and highway

Local

Other

Total: $104 billion

0 5 10 15 20 25 30 35

PERCENTAGE OF COMBINED REVENUE

fig. 40–2

Property taxes provide almost all local tax revenues, while sales taxes and excises provide most state funds. (Source: Preliminary estimates based on U.S. Department of Commerce data.)

At the federal level, direct personal taxes (on incomes and payrolls) dominate the picture, together providing about 60 percent of all tax revenue. The other main source is the corporation income tax. But for local governments the property tax (mainly on land and buildings) dominates; it provides nearly 80 percent of all local taxes, and about a third of state and local taxes combined. At the state level, sales taxes are the big revenue source, accounting for half of all state taxes.

But we're at least as interested in who pays the taxes, as in what taxes provide the revenue. To get this information, we must estimate who finally pays each tax, as distinct from who turns the money over to the government. Once we make the adjustment as best we can, the combined federal-state-local tax burdens on some typical families are roughly as follows. As a background, look back at the overall picture in Figure 38–5.

Typical family A, with a poverty-level income of around $2,000, paid about $600 in taxes, nearly a third of its total income. Most of this

$600 was "hidden" in the form of higher prices paid for taxed products, higher rents, and the like, in payroll taxes, or in the form of lower wages received. About half the total went to local governments, largely through the property tax (whether paid directly or through higher rents).

Typical family B, with $8,000 income, paid over $2,000 in taxes. This family paid only $900 or so in federal income tax, but it was hit hard by payroll taxes and the hidden excise and property taxes that caught family A as well. In total, family B paid a lot more taxes than A, but it is striking that in percentage of income paid the two are close.

Typical family C, with an income of $20,000, paid $7,000 or so in taxes, perhaps 35 percent of its income. Family C had a nice income; only one family in ten was as well off. Here the federal income tax began to bite in, though it was still only $3,500 or so. Family C also bore a small chunk of the corporation income tax, plus its share of all the same payroll, sales, and property taxes that hit A and B.

Family D, with an income of $100,000, can't be called typical, since there are only few such families. Moreover, its tax burden depended so heavily on the way in which it received its income and how adeptly it utilized tax loopholes that no typical tax figure is possible. Probably it paid between $35,000 and $50,000 in taxes, somewhat less than half its income. Its federal income tax would normally be nearly $40,000 if all its income came from salary, but if part of the income was received on tax-exempt securities or as "capital gains" (see below) the tax would be much smaller. D, being a substantial corporate stockholder, also may have paid heavily through the corporation income tax. In addition, it was subject to most of the same hidden taxes as the lower-income families.

Remember that these figures tell only what "typical" families paid, not where the government's total tax revenue came from. The wealthy family pays a substantial share of its income in taxes. But for every rich family there are millions of poor and middle-income families. Thus, in 1969, about one-third of all taxes were ultimately paid by the half of all families

below the $9,000-income level, even though the tax per family wasn't large; nearly another quarter by the $9,000 to $15,000 group; and the rest by the 6 million families with incomes over $15,000. Put another way, about 60 percent of all taxes came from the under-$15,000 group. The reason was simple—that's where about two-thirds of the income was.

Good and Bad Taxes

Few subjects generate as much heat in popular discussion as taxes. All too often the heat is unaccompanied by light. You can't judge intelligently what are good and what are bad taxes until you've clarified the criteria by which you're judging. Since many people don't bother, it is little wonder that they often disagree violently on what taxes should be.

The same broad social objectives we've used before can be pointed up conveniently in three questions in analyzing the tax system:

1. Progress. Does the tax encourage or hinder investment, employment, and stable economic growth?

2. Freedom and Individual Choice. Does the tax hinder or aid the allocation of resources in accordance with consumer preferences? How much does it interfere with the free choices of individuals and businesses in earning and spending? Note that taxation may aid in achieving the public's wishes if the taxes deter production of goods with large externalities (by-product social costs).

3. Equity. How equitably is the tax burden distributed? Government taxing and spending significantly affect the distribution of income. Unless government tax collections exactly equal the benefits provided to each family, the issue is not whether the government shall redistribute income, but how.

Progress: Stable Economic Growth

Economic growth depends on an intricate complex of factors, but especially on technological advance, on saving and investment, on education, and on hard work by the labor force (see

Chapters 16–18). Any tax is a drain on someone's income from work or investment, and in general taxes will deter economic growth (although of course the related government expenditure may have an offsetting effect). But the government must generally levy taxes to pay for its expenditures, and one tax **structure** may be less restrictive on (more conducive to) rapid growth than another.

Theory tells us that taxes that bear on profits and other returns from investment will discourage **growth** compared to taxes that fall on personal income and consumption. Similarly, taxes that give special advantages to expenditures on investment, research and development, and education, are an incentive to faster growth. We have learned over the past decade how to provide such incentives—the special "investment tax credit" of 1962, and the more generous depreciation guidelines for plant and equipment are examples.

Tax contribution to **stability** is equally important. We want taxes which tend to keep after-tax incomes growing at a reasonably stable rate, not fluctuating sharply. Individual and corporate income taxes, for example, provide such "built-in tax flexibility." When national income rises, these tax liabilities rise even more rapidly, since individual income-tax rates are progressive and since corporate profits subject to tax rise sharply in business expansion. The opposite is true when national income falls. This built-in flexibility tends to damp the swings in private incomes and spending. By contrast, a tax that is insensitive to income changes (for example, the property tax or a fixed "headtax") makes no contribution to stabilizing private spending.

Noninterference with Free Choices

If we want free private choices to determine the allocation of resources and the distribution of income, a "good" tax system should be neutral in the sense that it does not affect these results. But a tax system as pervasive as ours cannot be truly neutral. People do take tax considerations into account in their business and personal decisions. In a few cases—for example, taxes on tobacco and liquor—we consciously discourage the use of particular products through heavy taxation. Similarly, we may impose taxes to discourage production that has associated external diseconomies—for example, a tax on pollutants discharged into a stream. In these cases the tax is used to bring resource allocation into line with our social preferences.

But in most cases, the distortions produced by taxes on individual commodities (excise taxes) are considered unfortunate. These distortions occur because higher taxes on particular commodities lead people to buy less of that commodity than they would otherwise buy, relative to other commodities. Or they lead people to work less in particular occupations than they would otherwise choose to do. By distorting resource use this way, a tax may thus produce a "deadweight" loss to the economy—a cost against which there is no offsetting gain. Such a cost is in excess of the resources given up by the private sector through taxation to finance public expenditures. The economy is misled into producing the wrong combination of goods, that is, into producing too few of those that are heavily taxed and into allocating resources in a nonoptimal way.

To minimize this deadweight loss while raising any given amount of revenue, we should use taxes that produce the smallest changes in private production and consumption behavior (excluding cases with externalities). A "head" tax (simply a lump-sum tax on each person regardless of income or expenditure) would rate high on this criterion. Since no one could avoid it, it would not affect his economic behavior much, if at all. Taxes on commodities with highly inelastic demand (for example, a salt tax) are similar, since people buy about as much of the product at the higher (taxed) price as before. Conversely, excise taxes on commodities with elastic demand are apt to be highly distorting in their effects.[1]

---

[1] By this same criterion, to avoid distorting effects, marginal tax rates should be low relative to average rates; on this score, our progressive personal income tax rates low.

"Equity" in Taxation

A tax system should be equitable as well as nondistorting and conducive to stable growth. Three tests of equity are often advanced. One is to levy taxes on the people who get the benefits. Another is to levy taxes according to ability to pay. The third stresses equal treatment of taxpayers equally situated. Equity means different things to different people, and economics cannot say which is right. It can only clarify the effects of different taxes so each person can judge for himself which result is most "equitable."

The "Benefit" Principle. It seems fair to a lot of people that those who benefit from government services should pay for them. No one argues that this benefit principle should be rigidly applied, but would it be a good general rule?

One obvious problem is how the principle could be applied practically. If a city is putting in a new sewer, it's easy to see who the primary beneficiaries will be and to assess the cost against these property owners through a "special assessment." But how can the benefits derived from national defense, or the judicial system, be divided up among the citizens?

An even more fundamental question: Would we really want the benefit principle applied? Look at education, for example. Now we have free public schools for everyone. But suppose we put all education on a benefit-tax basis. Then each parent would have to pay a special school tax depending on how many children he had in school—for example, $500 per child. This policy might work out fine for the local banker and doctor. But how about the poor family on the other side of the tracks, with eight school-age children? The well-to-do could continue sending their youngsters to school (and more cheaply than now), but millions of poor children would be priced out of the market. Government activities like poor relief would be completely ruled out by the benefit principle, since there would be little point in imposing special taxes on the poor just to return the funds to them.

Broad use of the benefit principle would thus be far more revolutionary than it sounds at first blush. It would mean in effect direct sale of government services to the user. It would preclude any redistribution of income through the public economy. As soon as government deviates from strict benefit-principle taxation (that is, direct sale of all government services at cost), it is in effect redistributing income, whether we like to admit it or not. This is the meaning of the statement above that, for practical purposes, the issue is not **whether** the government will redistribute incomes, but rather **how** it will redistribute them.

The "Ability To Pay" Principle. Taxation according to ability to pay is widely favored. But how should we measure ability to pay? Net money income received in the current year is a widely accepted criterion.

Even if we agree on net income as the best measure of ability to pay, there is still the problem of the rate at which different incomes should be taxed. Some argue that the rate should be **proportional**—that is, the same percentage of each person's income. For example, the tax rate might be 1 percent, giving a $10 tax on $1,000; $100 on $10,000; $1,000 on $100,000. Though the rate is proportional, this procedure of course takes more dollars from high- than from low-income groups. More argue that rates should be **progressive**—that is, a higher percentage tax on high incomes than on low (for example, $5 on $1,000; $100 on $10,000; $2,000 on $100,000). This places a still heavier burden on the well-to-do. All ability-to-pay advocates argue against **regressive** taxation, in which a larger percentage of income is taken from the lower-income groups (for example, $20 on $1,000; $100 on $10,000; $500 on $100,000).

It is important to see that ability to pay as a base for taxation has no exactness or "absolute" validity. There is no objective way of deciding whether rates should be proportional or progressive, or, if progressive, how steeply progressive. The "ability" phrase is, however, convenient for working purposes, since in

America we generally agree that progressive taxation of income and inheritances represents the primary application of the ability-to-pay principle. When the term is used in this book, therefore, it will mean progressively higher tax rates as net income rises, without specifying any particular rate of progression. Many writers have attempted to reach some more basic justification underlying the ability-to-pay principle, but without success. In the last analysis, the issue of how much progression is "equitable" is an ethical and moral one. It boils down largely to the question of who should get how much of the limited national-income pie—a fundamental and explosive question. This issue of relative tax burden at different income levels is often called the issue of "vertical" equity.

"Equal Treatment of Those Equally Situated." A third principle of equity states that persons equally situated should be taxed equally. This is a powerful guide to tax policy, and one that is accepted by most observers. But what is "equally situated"? Are two people with the same income always equally situated? For example, is a disabled, retired man with an annual pension income of $5,000 equally situated with a healthy single man in his twenties with the same income? Are both equally situated with the $5,000-a-year laborer who has a wife and ten children to support? Does it matter where the income comes from? For example, is a factory superintendent who earns $15,000 a year equally situated with a rich young man who gets $15,000 by clipping bond coupons on a fortune left him by his father? How about a gain of $15,000 on General Motors stock that has gone up in price between your buying and selling it? Our tax laws treat the first two identically, but apply a much lower tax rate to the "capital gain" on the General Motors stock. Should they? This is the issue of "horizontal" equity.

Loopholes and "Tax Expenditures"

Taxes affect the economic behavior of taxpayers. Indirectly, so do taxes they don't pay. The Internal Revenue Code is full of special deductions, exemptions, and provisions that permit citizens and businesses to pay less than they otherwise would. For example, state and municipal bondholders are exempt from federal taxation on their interest. Capital gains are taxed at lower rates than regular income. The aged and the blind are given special exemptions. Interest on mortgages and other borrowed funds is exempt.

These legal loopholes can be looked at as much the same thing as federal government subsidies to the affected taxpayers and functions. They are sometimes called "tax expenditures." Table 40–1 shows the magnitude of these federal tax expenditures on different groups and functions for fiscal 1970. They totaled about $50 billion, compared to about $200 billion of actual expenditures.

These "tax credit" loopholes not only cost the government foregone taxes. They also distort economic behavior and the allocation of resources toward tax-exempt activities, such as owning rather than renting homes. We shall return to the problem of tax loopholes presently.

How Much Taxation Can We Stand?

Hardly a day goes by but someone complains that we've reached the limit of our ability to pay taxes—that for the government to raise taxes further would be the last straw. Is there some definite limit to how much taxation the country can stand? Are we approaching it?

The general answer to both questions is "no." But to answer more fully, we have to ask, What is the meaning of "what we can stand?" The usual connotation is that with more taxes the system would slow its growth, people would stop working, there'd be no incentive for businessmen to invest. Faced with predictions of such a debacle, the economist asks, how will it come about, and why?

Economic analysis suggests that if more taxes are going to bring disaster, it will probably be through one or more of the following effects:

1. **Heavier taxes may reduce the incentive to work.** If the government takes too big a share of the income you earn, you may just quit working

table 40-1

Federal "Tax Expenditures," 1970*

Budget Function	Regular Budget (In Billions)	Tax Expenditures (In Billions)
Health and welfare (personal deductions for children, age, blindness, and so on; for charitable contributions; for medical expenses, and so on)	$ 55.0	$ 19.5
Commerce and transportation (investment credit; interest, excess bad debt, and excess depreciation deductions; small corporation exemptions, and so on)	9.0	9.7
Housing and community development (deduction of mortgage interest and property taxes, excess depreciation on owner-occupied homes)	2.8	5.2
Natural resources and agriculture (oil depletion allowances, deduction of exploration costs, and so on)	7.1	2.7
Other functions	101.0	2.7
Aid to state and local governments (federal income tax exemptions for interest on securities and for direct taxes paid to these governments)		4.6
Lower capital gains rates for individuals, not distributed above		5.5-8.5
Total tax revenue foregone		$50.0-53.0

*Source: U.S. Treasury Department, Estimates are for fiscal year 1970.

—or at least work less. Maybe there is some level of taxation at which there'd be no more incentive at all to work—but then there's always the pressing problem of how to eat. As long as something remains after taxes and most people still have much less than they want, the incentive to earn is a powerful one, even when earnings must be shared with the government. But for well-to-do people who feel less income pressure, the amount of work may fall off as tax rates rise. And this holds even for middle-income people, when it's a question of overtime work or a second job. The evidence we have doesn't settle the question. Most formal studies find little evidence that higher income taxes seriously reduce the work at any income level. But this runs contrary to many people's intuitive notions. More on this subject later.

2. Heavier taxes may reduce the incentive to invest, especially if the taxes fall heavily on profits. Again, this prediction seems intuitively reasonable, but the evidence is unclear. If taxes fall differentially on one type of investment, investors will flee from it in droves. But taxation on all corporate income leaves few alternatives to which investors can escape. They may turn to partnerships or individual enterprises, or to tax-exempt state and municipal bonds. But corpora-

tions are the only practical form of organization for most big businesses, and government bonds have limited appeal to profit-seeking investors.

There's little evidence that corporations and wealthy individuals just consume more instead of investing. More likely, they complain bitterly about the low return on investment, and go on investing—if sales are good (which is the more fundamental stimulus to investment). But here too there is surely some deterrent marginal tax effect, and the impact of differential taxes is substantial in shifting investment among alternatives.

3. **Heavier taxes may lead to legal tax "avoidance."** The law provides many loopholes for people who feel taxes heavily enough to hire a good tax lawyer. The preceding section described the alternatives. Congressional tax committees have repeatedly been told that almost no one, no matter how rich, needs to pay more than half his income in taxes, although the personal income tax reaches a 70 percent peak rate. The capital-gains provision is the big loophole, but there are many others. A large amount of resources goes into legal tax avoidance. At last count, the Treasury listed about 100,000 tax counselors and tax lawyers whose business was to help on income tax returns. And the effort pays off. In spite of the 70 percent peak rate on incomes over $200,000, Treasury statistics show that less than 35 percent of all income above that level is collected in personal income taxes. What is worse, desire to avoid high tax rates often leads to distortions in investment and diversion of earning activities into special channels (like oil drilling) that permit wealthy people to avoid peak tax rates under the law.

4. **Heavier taxes may lead to illegal tax "evasion."** The case of France is often cited, where for years the government has been able to collect only a modest fraction of the taxes due because of the expense and energy required to run down the individuals who just don't pay. By and large, we Americans report and pay our taxes without being pursued. But a recent National Bureau of Economic Research estimate suggested that 5 percent of all wages, 30 percent of unincorporated business incomes (farmers, doctors, lawyers, and so on), 13 percent of divi-

dends, and no less than 63 percent of interest on bank deposits went unreported. This would mean a total of perhaps $75 billion in an $800 billion national income. How much harder it would become to collect taxes at higher rates nobody knows. Introduction of widespread employer reporting and computerized checking of all tax returns has made tax evasion increasingly difficult for most people, and most dividend and interest income is probably now caught.

5. **Higher taxes may lead to inflation.** This seems a perverted argument, since modern fiscal policy rests on the premise that higher taxes check inflation. This argument is that if taxes get too high everyone will raise his asking price to offset them—unions, businessmen, lawyers, farmers, everybody. Careful thought will show that this behavior can result in continuing inflation only if the government helpfully puts in more money to support total purchasing power at the higher prices. Still, don't forget the pressures on government to do just that, if the price of inaction or restraint is unemployment and recession.

What do all these points add up to? Not a conclusion that we can't stand any more taxation. Clearly we can, and a lot more if we want more public goods urgently enough. Our standard of living is so high we could divert far more resources to the public sector and still have the highest private-consumption standard in the world. But they do point to some real dangers as the level of taxation climbs relative to the national income.

Our governments—federal, state, and local—face a tough practical political job finding new tax revenues with taxes as high as they are now. This is a major barrier to voting new government expenditures. But remember from the last chapter that our total tax take as a percentage of g.n.p. is still one of the lowest among the Western industrialized nations—around 27 percent compared to over 30 for many European nations—out of a per capita income level far higher than theirs. One interesting difference may help explain why Americans complain so much about taxes. Most of our federal taxes are direct and highly visible—on personal and busi-

ness incomes—while in Europe more taxes are indirect and "hidden." On the whole, our federal tax system is probably the most "progressive" in its impact on higher incomes of any in the major industrialized nations. This combination worries those who are concerned about work and investment incentives, and pleases those who are most interested in ability-to-pay approaches to equity.

Who Must Pay?

This analysis leads to one last point, which creates some of the sharpest controversy among people who don't look at the facts. If we want a lot more tax revenue it has to come from the middle- and lower-income groups, because that's where the income is. Thomas Jefferson's ideal of "a country made a paradise by the contribution of the rich alone" won't work any more—the country's too big and there aren't enough rich. Complete confiscation of all personal incomes over $1 million would add less than $5 billion to the total federal tax take. So if someone is going to "stand" more taxes, it has to be the general public, not just a super-rich few.

Sharing and the "Fiscal Dividend"

Except for national defense and social welfare payments, the big increases in government spending have come at state and local levels since World War II. Educational costs have soared with the population surge and the move to the suburbs. Highway and street costs have risen nearly as fast. Rising public assistance and welfare benefits, hospitals, and general government costs have reflected widespread demands for more and better public services. Total state-local spending has risen over 600 percent since World War II and is currently increasing at nearly $15 billion a year.

State and local tax revenues have risen too. Local governments rely almost entirely on property taxes; rates on land and buildings have soared and property owners have protested increasingly. Worse for the cities, as city tax rates have soared, families and businesses have fled to the suburbs. State sales taxes have been somewhat more flexible revenue sources, since taxable sales have grown with the economy. But here too rate increases have pushed total burdens to 5 percent in many states. More and more state and local governments have faced fiscal crises.

Federal spending has soared too. But the federal individual and corporate income taxes have proved enormously productive revenue producers. Individual rates are progressive, so rising national income automatically and promptly produces more than proportional increases in tax revenues. In total, the federal tax system automatically produces a "fiscal dividend" of over $10 billion annually in increased tax revenues without any increase in tax rates, when the economy grows at its average rate.

Increasingly, the state and local governments have complained that the best revenue sources have been preempted by the federal government. And increasingly, Congress has responded with bigger direct subsidies to state and local governments—up from about $7 billion to $25 billion annually during the 1960s. Some have close federal controls over spending, many do not.

Figure 40–3 shows the picture. Highway and public assistance grants have been massive federal transfer programs. Education and the antipoverty program are lusty newcomers to the federal grants arena.

As the state-local tax pinch became more stringent in the early 1960s, Walter Heller of the University of Minnesota and others proposed that the federal government use a big part of its annual "fiscal dividend" from economic growth for direct, no-strings-tied grants to the states. This tax sharing would, he argued, face fiscal and political realities; somehow the powerful federal revenue system must be tapped to help the foundering states and cities without a further extension of federal power over state government activities. Nontied tax sharing to distribute the federal fiscal dividend was his answer.

In 1969, President Nixon proposed such a revenue-sharing program, rising by 1976 to about $5 billion annually, in addition to existing

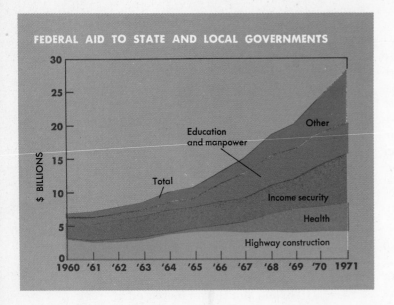

FEDERAL AID TO STATE AND LOCAL GOVERNMENTS

$ BILLIONS

Education and manpower

Other

Total

Income security

Health

Highway construction

1960 '61 '62 '63 '64 '65 '66 '67 '68 '69 '70 1971

fig. 40–3

Federal aid to state and local governments has soared during the last decade. (Source: U.S. Budget Bureau. Data are for fiscal years.)

federal aid programs. Some critics termed this merely a token proposal; others attacked the no-ties aspect of the bill. The degree of control over spending the federal government should retain remains a disputed issue—for example, insistence on racial integration as a condition for education grants to the states. Some see federal aid as a weapon to force states and localities to meet specific federal standards. But as the plight of the states and municipalities steadily worsens, increased federal aid of some sort seems more and more inevitable.[2]

Shifting and Incidence of Taxation

Often the person who pays the funds over to the government does not actually bear the burden of the tax. The federal tax on liquor, for example, is paid to the government by distillers. But it may be "shifted" forward to consumers through higher prices, or backward to workers through lower wages, and to owners of other resources used in the industry through lower rents or prices. The final "incidence" (or resting

[2]Note that this "fiscal dividend" is identical with the "fiscal drag" of Chapter 14. From the point of view of fiscal policy, this growing federal tax take will exert a deflationary drag if the funds are not spent. The funds, transferred to state governments that badly need them for their expenses, become a fiscal dividend to those governments. Obviously, they could equally well be considered a fiscal dividend available for spending by the federal government.

place) of a tax may be far from the man who turns the money over to the government. Obviously it is this final incidence that is most important.

It is safe to assume that in most cases a taxpayer will shift a tax whenever he can. The question generally is, therefore, when can a tax be shifted? A tax can be shifted only when, as a result of the tax, the taxpayer is able to obtain a higher price for something he sells or to pay a lower price for something he buys. Hence a price transaction of some sort is essential if shifting is to occur.

Generally, taxes do nothing to increase demand for taxed commodities (remember that we are examining the impact of the tax alone, apart from what is done with the money collected). But particular taxes do often raise costs and prices. If, as a result of a tax (for example, on cigarettes), the price a taxpayer receives or pays is higher or lower than it otherwise would have been, the tax has been shifted to that extent.

Since tax shifting depends on the prices charged and paid, it is largely an application of the general supply-and-demand analysis of Part Three. If an excise tax is considered a part of business costs, will these higher costs be passed on in higher prices? In a competitive market? In a monopolistic market? How about a tax on business net profits, which doesn't change busi-

592

ness costs as usually defined? It's supply-and-demand analysis and the theory of the firm that you need to answer the questions.

Two warnings are necessary. First, a rise in price following the imposition of a tax in the real world is not necessarily proof that the tax has been shifted. The price rise may have come from some other cause. (Remember the fallacy of *post hoc, propter hoc.*) Empirical verification of tax shifting is very difficult, since it is hard to isolate one cause and its effects in the multitude of forces simultaneously at work in economic life. Analytically, however, we can trace through the effects of any tax assuming "other things equal"—that is, assuming the tax to be the only new element in the situation. Such theoretical analysis is of necessity oversimplified, and the conclusions drawn are only tentative. But unless we know at least roughly the final incidence of any tax, there is little sense in talking about its place in a good tax system.

Second, special care is needed when we analyze the incidence of a major, economywide tax like the corporation income tax or a national sales tax. In such cases, it is not safe to use partial-equilibrium analysis, which holds "other things" equal while we analyze the impact on a typical firm or household. If a city sales tax is added, it is generally reasonable to argue that the new higher costs will be shifted forward to consumers through a higher price that includes the tax. But if the sales tax is nationwide and all sellers raise prices to pass on the tax, clearly this will lead to an economywide decrease in the number of units that can be sold given any level of aggregate demand, and to resulting unemployment, unless government monetary-fiscal policy increases aggregate demand enough to permit the same number of units to be sold at the new higher prices.

Thus, when we assume in analyzing such economywide tax changes that aggregate demand stays constant, it makes a big difference how aggregate demand is kept constant. For example, suppose we raise personal income taxes by $10 billion. Other things equal, this will cut private spending and aggregate demand will fall. To keep aggregate demand unchanged the government could either increase its own spending or cut some other tax by $10 billion, say the corporation income tax. Obviously, the overall incidence of the personal income tax increase will be significantly different depending on which way the government compensates to keep aggregate spending unchanged.

Some economists argue that it therefore makes no sense to talk about the incidence of such economywide taxes without specifying what happens to other government taxes and spending—in short, without specifying a complete general-equilibrium solution for the economy. But here we will nonetheless analyze the incidence of individual major taxes, presuming that you will remember the importance of compensating changes in taxes or spending.

A Look at the Main Taxes [3]

The best way to get a good feel for how the tax system really works is to look in detail at some of the main taxes that bring in most of the revenue. The following sections do this. However, this material on individual taxes is set in smaller type to indicate that it involves a considerable level of detail. The big ideas of the chapter are contained in the preceding and concluding pages of the chapter. The look at each individual tax is essentially an application of the preceding criteria on incidence, effects, and equity. It also provides a practical exercise in applying price theory to predict who will really pay each tax when we look through to its final incidence.

Personal Income Taxes [4]

Ours is increasingly an income-tax system. Personal income taxes alone account for one-third of all tax revenues. They are levied by the federal government, by about two-thirds of the states, and even by a few cities, but about 90 percent of the revenue is accounted for by the

[3]Note to instructors: This section on individual taxes is written to be optional, depending on instructor preferences.
[4]Details of different taxes and their rates change from year to year. Information in this chapter is as of 1971.

federal tax. Payroll taxes directly on wages and salaries account for about the same share. Altogether, the three taxes produce two-thirds of total tax revenues.

The federal income tax applies to all money income in excess of certain deductions. (1) A personal exemption is allowed for the taxpayer and for each dependent member of his family ($650 per person in 1971); thus, low-income families escape the tax altogether. (2) Additional deductions are permitted for expenses necessary to earning one's income (such as traveling expenses for traveling salesmen and operating expenses for farmers). (3) Deductions are also allowed for gifts to charitable and nonprofit institutions, for most other taxes paid, for interest paid, for exceptionally large medical expenses, and for certain other expenses; an automatic deduction of 13 percent of income (up to $1,500) is given whether or not the taxpayer actually makes such payments.

The tax is progressive—large incomes are subject to higher tax rates than small ones. In 1971, an average family of four would have paid no income tax unless its income exceeded about $3,500—$2,600 personal exemptions for four persons plus an automatic deduction of about $900 for gifts, interest, medical expenses, and the like. On the first $2,000 of income over these exemptions, the family was taxed 14 percent; on the next $1,000, 15 percent. Rapidly increasing marginal rates applied on higher incomes. The marginal rate was 50 percent at $44,000, and it reached a maximum of 70 percent on all income over $200,000.

It is important to note that the **effective average rate** actually paid is always less than the top applicable **marginal rate.** For example, a family receiving $22,000 in salary income would appear to face a marginal rate of 32 percent, but its income tax bill would actually be only about 18 percent of its income. The first $4,000 or so of income would be free of tax because of exemptions. The next $2,000 would be taxed at only 14 percent, and so on up the rate structure. Only that portion of taxable income over $20,000 (presumably none after exemptions) would be taxable at 32 percent.

The law has several provisions that permit taxpayers to cut their actual rates further below those listed. The three most important are:

1. **Capital-Gains Provision.** Capital gains (profits on assets bought and sold) on assets held over six months are taxed at only half the rate on other income, and at a maximum rate of 25 or 35 percent, depending on the size of the capital gain. This provision encourages investment in growing industries, and it seems to many people more equitable than taxing such special gains as regular income. But by the same token it provides a major escape from peak rates for wealthy persons who invest their funds in growing firms, the stock market, or other assets where they can obtain capital gains rather than current income. Wealthy investors often thus prefer companies that plow back their earnings and thereby grow faster. The growing value of the company's stock represents merely a capital gain, subject to tax at the reduced rate when sold to realize the gain, while dividends are currently taxed as regular income. To take advantage of this law, part of executive salaries are often paid in the form of a privilege for the executive to buy the company's stock at the present market price at a later date. If the stock goes up (as it probably will for a growing company), he can buy in later and take the profit on the stock's value as a capital gain rather than as regular income taxable at full income tax rates.

2. **Tax-Exempt State and Local Bonds.** Traditionally, interest on state and local government securities has been exempt from the federal income tax. For the rich man, this makes a whopping difference. If you are in the 66 percent marginal tax bracket, a tax-exempt yield of 6 percent on a local bond is equal to a yield of 18 percent on a taxable security. This provision makes state and local bonds easier to sell, but it provides a large loophole for the well-to-do to avoid high federal income tax rates on income from their investments.

3. **Expense Accounts.** Today's corporate executive travels in luxury, holds membership in the best clubs, and has frequent health check-ups, all at company expense. A star goes to London, ostensibly to advertise a new movie. Are these really necessary business expenses,

or merely concealed employee income that doesn't get taxed? No one doubts the legitimacy of business expenses, and the mores of the times are that business executives entertain well and do a lot of business out of the office. But sometimes those with access to expense accounts stretch them pretty far. What worries the Treasury as much as the income that goes tax-free through plush expense accounts is the resentful feeling of millions of other taxpayers who don't have expense accounts, but who may feel it's all right to fudge a little when they think of those big fellows who seem to get away with so much.[5]

At high income levels it pays to take advantage of these legal loopholes. A good tax lawyer is worth his weight in gold if you're rich enough.

Figure 40–4 indicates how important these special provisions can be for wealthy taxpayers. The top line shows the steady rise of stated marginal tax rates under the law. The shaded areas show the effective tax reductions provided by exemptions, deductions, and capital gains at different income levels. Thus, a typical millionaire might end up paying less than 30

[5] A variety of other tax-reducing alternatives is available to the very rich, including establishment of family foundations and investment in oil drilling where a special "depletion allowance" exists.

percent through judicious use of tax-exempt gifts and capital gains. But not all high-income receivers escape this way. If your $200,000 income is entirely from your salary, you have no way to escape the 55 percent effective rate shown by Figure 40–4, even after taking full advantage of deductions and exemptions.

Incidence. The incidence of the personal income tax is generally on the taxpayer; the tax is hard to shift. Neither the demand for nor the supply of any good or service is likely to be so much affected by the tax that it would permit shifting. If individuals are receiving the maximum income they can before the tax, no change will enable them to make more merely because of the tax.

The only important exceptions arise where the tax does lead people to work less, where the taxpayer's ability to get more income was not being fully exploited before imposition of the tax, or where for some reason employers are willing to pay higher wages after imposition of the tax on employees.

Effects on Growth and Stability. Present high marginal income-tax rates are often said to reduce the incentive to work at upper income levels. These may be crucial levels for rapid growth; they include managers, entrepreneurs,

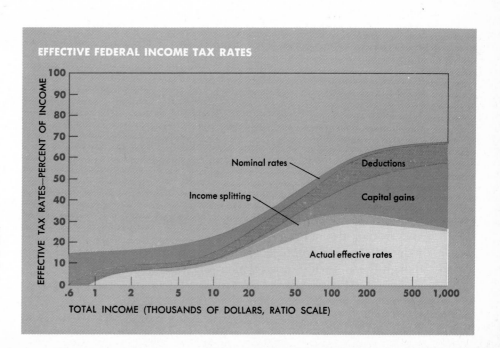

fig. 40–4

Nominal income-tax rates specified by the law are much higher than actual rates paid by most taxpayers. (Source: J. Pechman, *Federal Tax Policy* [Washington, D.C.: The Brookings Institution, 1968], p. 66.)

596 Public Goods and the Public Sector

and top scientists. Empirical studies have failed to show this deterrent effect. But people in high tax brackets generally claim that high tax rates do affect their behavior, and the evidence is not yet sufficient to brush their arguments aside. Many economists and sociologists believe that the desire to improve one's relative position will keep most people working hard, even when Uncle Sam gets a big chunk of the increase. Moreover, most high-income jobs are closely associated with social prestige, power, and status. At the top of the income scale, these incentives to work and advancement may rival the importance of more take-home pay.

At lower income levels, higher tax rates may cut down on overtime work and second jobs and reduce the number of working wives. But here the pressures for more income are strong, and it is not clear that taxes are a major deterrent to work in most cases, as long as the earner keeps the bulk of the marginal income for himself.

A parallel argument is that peak marginal tax rates seriously deter risky investment. If you win, the government takes most of the killing; if you lose, you bear the loss. So why take the chance? This argument may deter investors from risky ventures—but remember that most such gains would be subject only to the maximum capital-gains rate of 25 to 35 percent, and substantial offsets of losses against gains are permitted in computing taxable income.

The income tax rates high as a built-in stabilizer to damp down instability. When national income soars in a boom, income-tax receipts rise even faster, because a bigger proportion of people's incomes falls in the higher tax brackets. This puts a damper on the boom. Conversely, when national income slides in a recession, personal income-tax receipts slide even faster, thus cushioning the recession's impact on personal disposable income.

Equity and Nondistortion. The personal income tax is generally thought to be an equitable tax, though the special loopholes drastically reduce its progression for many taxpayers, and though there is wide disagreement on the optimum rate structure. It is a progressive tax on the basis of net income received, probably the best-available single indicator of ability to pay. Moreover, we can be surer than with other major taxes that the incidence will be where it is intended. Further, it probably involves less interference with free consumer, investor, and worker choices than any other major tax. Although the income tax takes a certain percentage of net income, this percentage is the same whatever the source of income, with the very important qualifications noted above as to loopholes. The taxpayer is left free to spend or invest his remaining income wherever he pleases without government interference. The personal income tax may stimulate leisure as against work, since it can be avoided by not working, but, as was indicated above, there is limited evidence to substantiate this effect.[6]

Corporation Income Taxes

The federal government and many states levy corporation income taxes; these yielded over $45 billion in 1970. The federal tax applies to all corporate net income, with a 48 percent rate in 1970—except that the first $25,000 of income was taxed at only 22 percent and over 80 percent of the nation's million corporations make less than $25,000 annually. But the big companies, which do the great bulk of corporate business, paid the 48 percent rate. Companies may offset losses in bad years against profits in good years to a considerable extent.

Two big issues arise in calculating a firm's "taxable income." One is "depreciation allowances."[7] How fast should companies be permitted to depreciate new plant and equipment for

---

[6]Death and gift taxes supplement the personal income tax. The federal government levies a progressive "estate tax" on the estate of everyone who dies with property totaling more than $60,000. Above that level, rates climb rapidly to 77 percent on that portion of estates over $10 million, but the large exemption, plus a further special exemption of half the estate if it's given to one's husband or wife, keeps most families free from the tax. Most states have comparable taxes on the inheritance received by beneficiaries in estates, but at much lower rates, and there is a partial exemption under the federal tax for state taxes paid. The federal tax is accompanied by a gift tax to limit evasion of death taxes by giving away property before death, though there are generous exemptions for gifts spread out over several years.

[7]For a review of depreciation, look back at the appendix to Chapter 19.

tax purposes? If they can accelerate depreciation, depreciation charges (allowance as business costs) will be larger and taxable profits correspondingly smaller during the years immediately ahead. This practice permits the corporation to postpone taxes, giving it funds for current reinvestment instead. If the government wants to speed up investment, accelerated depreciation privileges on new investment appear to be an effective device.

Second, how large should "depletion" allowances (that is, a special type of depreciation allowance) be for drilling and mining companies that use up such natural resources as oil and coal. Under present law, oil companies can charge as a business cost a special depletion allowance of 22 percent of the gross income received from their oil wells. This special income exclusion is supported as necessary to encourage expensive exploration and drilling activities. Depletion allowances totaled about $2 billion in 1970 and succeeded in holding the average tax rate on oil company incomes down to about 20 percent, compared to just under 48 percent for most major companies. Critics of the provision attack it as a blatant subsidy to the oil interests. Similar, though smaller, percentage depletion allowances are provides for most other minerals.

Incidence. The incidence of the corporation income tax is uncertain. First, assume a highly competitive economy. If a company was maximizing profits at some price–output level before the tax, this would still be the best level after the tax. The government would take some of the profits, unfortunately for the stockholders, but their profits after taxes would still be maximized at the same output and price. The new income tax might drive investment completely out of the corporate form into other kinds of investment opportunities. But for big business, incorporation is essential, and comparable investment possibilities at lower tax rates are hard to find. Or it might lead stockholders to give up investment and to consume their funds. But this too seems unlikely on any large scale. This reasoning says the tax cannot be shifted.

But the real world is one of oligopolies and partial monopolies, of imperfect information on costs and markets, of multiple motives for corporate management among which profit maximization is only one. Here the incidence of the corporate income tax is much less certain. Prices are set administratively, markets are shared, big buyers bargain with big sellers. It's not clear that firms are acting very precisely to maximize profits. If a firm does not want to disturb its position in the industry, it may be willing to absorb a modest increase in income taxes. Or the tax increase may prod the firm into breaking the inertia of established prices and venturing a big price increase.

Here the government's aggregate demand policy, and macro adjustments more generally, may play a crucial role in determining tax incidence. A rise in corporate tax rates will push corporations toward higher prices. With an expansionary monetary-fiscal policy, higher prices may stick and the tax is shifted forward. With constant aggregate demand, on the other hand, business volume will drop off at higher prices and both employment and profits will fall; the likely result is a triply shared burden through lower profits, retarded wages, and possibly somewhat higher prices.

What has in fact happened to posttax corporation profits when corporation tax rates have been increased in the past? In general, profits have been squeezed, compared to lighter tax periods. This is far from convincing evidence on incidence, since many other factors influenced corporation profits in each period. But it is evidence that taxes have eaten away at profits available for stockholders and for reinvestment.

High marginal tax rates encourage current corporation expenditures, whatever the incidence of the tax itself. With a 50 percent marginal tax rate, each dollar spent on advertising, research, or other such business purposes costs the company only 50 cents. The government in substance pays the other 50 cents (and, of course, takes 50 percent of any increase in profits). There is no way of estimating precisely the importance of this effect, but tax experts and businessmen agree that business takes a more lenient attitude on spending when the marginal tax rate is high. This was vividly demonstrated during World War II, when peak tax rates were 82 percent and corporations could spend "18-cent dollars." But as long as the corporation keeps part of each dollar of profits, it has an incentive to hold down costs. Spending "cheap" dollars costs less than spending tax-free dollars, but it still costs potential profits.

All in all, economic analysis suggests that corporation income taxes are borne partly by stockholders, partly by consumers of corporate products, and possibly to some extent by workers whose wages rise more slowly. In addition, the expenditure-inducing effects of high marginal tax rates may place the cost of some business expenditures on taxpayers rather than on the consumers or stockholders.

Effects on Growth and Output. A tax on corporate net income imposes no direct burden on costs and hence does not have the same direct deterrent effect on output and employment as do sales, excise, and payroll taxes. On the other hand, the level of business investment depends largely on profits and the expectation of profits. A tax on profits surely has some effect in slowing investment and growth. Just how much is not clear.

Most of the Western European nations and Japan have lower corporation income tax rates and more lenient depreciation policies than we do. Businessmen urge that we permit businesses (as some European nations do) to depreciate assets as fast as they wish for tax purposes, and rely more on indirect, nonbusiness taxes. Tax experts generally agree that our corporate tax rules and rates are relatively restrictive, and that easing them should speed investment and growth. But that doesn't answer the hard question of who does pay the taxes if businesses don't.

On the score of built-in countercyclical flexibility, the corporation tax rates as excellent. With good times, corporation profits rise rapidly, pushing up tax liabilities and draining off funds to the government. When business declines, corporate profits drop fast, and there is a correspondingly fast reduction in corporation tax liabilities.

Effects on the Distribution of Income. Taxes on corporate income conform well to the criterion of ability to pay. The tax falls partly on corporate stockholders, and most such securities are held by the upper- and middle-income groups. But dividend income is an imperfect measure of tax-paying ability. For example, Mr. A may have an income of $5,000 annually, and own a few shares of General Motors. He loses about 50 percent (at 1970 rates) of his potential income from dividends because of corporate income taxes. The millionaire owner of General Motors stock loses the same percentage. Clearly, high-income stockholders are taxed less progressively than if all corporate income had been paid out to them for taxation as personal income, and low-income ones more so.

Under the present corporate income tax some argue that there is "double taxation" of dividends; they are taxed first as corporate profits and then as personal income to the stockholder. They assert that this arrangement is highly inequitable. Such double taxation seizes a major share of the profits from the stockholder, and discourages precisely the type of enterprise and risk taking that we need for economic growth and innovation. Supporters of the present arrangement retort that these are merely arguments for reducing the tax burden on the rich (the stockholders), and shoving a bigger share of total taxes back onto the poor.[8]

Payroll Taxes

Payroll taxes are used largely to finance the federal old-age insurance program and the combined federal-state unemployment insurance plans. At $47 billion in 1970 they were second only to the personal income tax as a revenue producer.

Most payroll taxes fall in two equal parts, half levied on the employee and half on the employer. Note that payroll taxes differ significantly from personal income taxes, in that payroll taxes fall on only one type of income—

[8]A new type business tax—the "value added" tax—has been widely discussed in recent years. This tax would require each firm to pay a flat-percentage rate on the value it adds to its products. These taxes would, in essence, be added to the final price of each final product.

wages and salaries. Dividends, rents, interest, and all other nonpayroll income are exempted. This focus on payrolls is justified by the use of funds collected for the special benefit of the workers. Indeed, the payroll taxes to finance the federal old-age retirement program are not officially termed taxes. Instead, Old-Age and Survivors' Insurance is considered an insurance plan in which payroll taxes are compulsory premiums. Second, payroll taxes are almost always at a flat rate and the federal tax of 4.8 percent each for employers and employees applied only to the first $7,800 of income, as of 1970.

The incidence of both parts of the payroll tax (that deducted from wages and that paid by employers) is primarily on the workers covered. But the widespread imperfections in the labor market make the process of shifting uncertain and jerky. Where wages are inflexible downward, moreover, the incidence may take the form of unemployment for some workers involved. Again, monetary-fiscal policy sets the aggregate demand framework. Look separately at the tax collected out of wages and that imposed on the employer.

1. The incidence of the tax deducted directly from the employee's wage is almost sure to be on the employee. There is no one to whom he can shift it backward, and there is nothing in the tax to increase the demand for labor. Powerful unions may be able to use the tax as an excuse to demand wage increases—but if they can get higher wages after the tax we have to explain why they couldn't do it before. There is little likelihood that the tax will be shifted to the employer by a withdrawal of labor to "noncovered" occupations, partly because there are few such areas and partly because workers don't want to give up the benefits of the social security program.

2. The likely incidence of the tax on the employer is also on employees, unless expansionary monetary-fiscal policy makes it easy for employers to shift the tax forward through higher prices. The tax increases the effective wage cost. If the firm was previously in a maximum-profit adjustment, after the tax it will be advantageous to raise selling prices or to curtail employment directly, both restricting output and substituting machinery for labor. If wages are flexible, they may move down to permit the same number of workers to be employed after the tax as before. If wage rates are inflexible, one likely effect of the tax is unemployment. Notice that this analysis holds for either competitive or monopolistic conditions where economic profits have been eliminated. When firms have a protected profit position, unions may be able to bargain wages up to offset part or all of the higher payroll taxes.

A simple diagram makes clear that the incidence of the payroll tax is the same in both cases under competition—on the workers. In Figure 40–5, let D^L be the demand for labor

fig. 40–5

Payroll taxes are generally borne by workers, whether they are imposed on workers or employers.

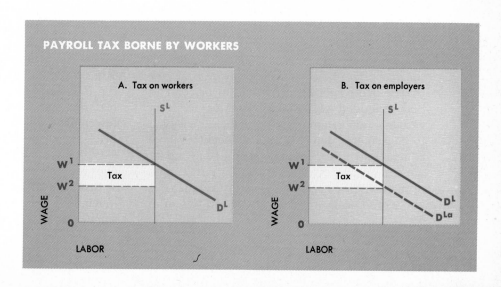

and S^L its supply, fixed in amount. Part A shows that the wage will be W^1 without any tax. Now suppose a payroll tax is imposed on all workers, which they must pay to the government. Neither demand nor supply is changed, so the wage paid by employers is unchanged. Unhappily, workers' wages after taxes are only W^2, lower by the amount of the tax they must pay.

Part B starts with the same S^L and D^L curves, and the same wage, W^1. Now the government imposes the same wage tax on employers. Workers are worth no more than before to employers, so the employers' demand curve shifts down at all outputs by the amount of the tax, to D^{La}. If employers must pay the tax on all employees, their wage without tax will again fall to W^2, just as in Part A. In both cases, employment stays constant and the wage after tax is reduced just by the amount of the tax. It should be easy to see that the critical factor underlying the full incidence on workers is the fixed stock of labor, the perfectly inelastic labor-supply curve. The same result would follow for a tax imposed on the wage (or rent) of any other fixed resource.

If we want workers to bear the major costs of unemployment and old-age insurance, payroll taxes may be a good means of financing social security. They are widely supported. But don't forget that putting the tax on the employer in the present fashion, even though we **want** him to pay, doesn't necessarily mean that he **will** pay it.

Excise and Sales Taxes

Excises are taxes on particular commodities—liquor, tires, cigarettes, movie admissions. They are often collected from the manufacturer or wholesaler, so that many of them are hidden in the final price of the product, although some are by law quoted separately from the price. The bulk of federal excise tax revenue comes from gasoline, liquor, and tobacco taxes, all "visible" to consumers. Many states and localities have comparable taxes, ranging all the way up to general sales taxes which levy a flat percentage of the sales price on all items sold at retail. Sales and excise taxes produced about $45 billion in 1970.

Incidence. Most people assume that excise taxes will be passed on to the consumer, and much of the time they're right. But not always. The answer comes directly from an application of the supply-and-demand analysis of Part Three. It depends on how competitive the industry is, on the demand for its product, and on the supply of labor and raw materials to the industry, given the assumption that aggregate demand is constant, so that partial equilibrium analysis is usable. Use the price theory from Chapters 21–29.

Competition. Suppose an excise tax is applied to playing cards. If competition is active in the industry, so that economic profits tend to be eliminated, the tax will be shifted. It raises costs and does nothing to increase demand, so net losses will result until the tax is shifted. Firms may put prices up by the amount of the tax, or may reduce their costs by paying less for labor and raw materials, or a combination of both.

Simple supply-and-demand analysis helps to explain what happens. The solid lines in Figure 40–5 show the playing-card market before the tax, with 100,000 decks being produced and sold daily at $1 per deck. Now a tax of twenty-five cents per deck is imposed on producers. This increases their costs accordingly, and reduces the amount it will pay them to produce (supply) at any given price. The new industry supply curve is the dashed line S^1S^1, which is twenty-five cents lower (to the left) at each point. Thus, the tax leads to a reduced supply and a higher price (including tax). The after-tax equilibrium is about 75,000 decks daily at a price of about $1.15. Note that the new price is higher than the old by only fifteen cents. The other ten cents are shifted backward through the industry's reduced demand for labor, raw materials, and other productive resources, since fewer playing cards can be sold at the higher price after tax.

Which way will the tax be shifted? Whichever way is "easier." If demand is highly elastic, so that sales fall off rapidly as price is put up, not much of the tax will be shifted forward to consumers. If there is a strong union in the industry, so that wages are hard to push down (that is, so that the supply of productive resources is highly elastic), backward shifting is difficult. How much of the tax goes each way depends on the relative elasticities of demand and supply in the two directions. The common presumption of forward shifting implicitly assumes that the supply of productive resources to the taxed industry is more elastic than consumers' demand for the taxed product. Change the slopes of the demand and supply curves in Figure 40–6 and you can readily see the importance of different elasticities.

In industries using highly specialized resources, backward shifting is more likely than elsewhere. Suppose the playing-card industry takes the whole output of some grade of paper pulp that is not useful in any other industry. Then the supply of pulp to the card industry would be very inelastic, at least in the short run; even if the card industry offered a lower price it would still get about as much pulp, since there are few other places for the pulp to be sold. The tax would be largely shifted backward in lower pulp prices. But the more unspecialized and mobile resources are, the less they are forced to take lower payments as a result of decreased demand. And in the long run, most resources are unspecialized. Thus, in the long run a big portion of the tax is probably shifted forward to consumers.

Monopoly and Oligopoly. In monopolistic or oligopolistic markets where competition has not eliminated economic profits, the final outcome is less certain. Part of the tax may fall on profits and stay there without driving resources out of the industry. Here we are up against the uncertainty of price making in imperfectly competitive areas. The partial monopolist may immediately add the tax to his price. Or he may absorb it rather than chance driving away his customers. Or he may use the tax as an excuse for an even larger price boost.

But through all this uncertainty, two fundamental facts stand out: (1) A large tax cannot be absorbed by monopoly profits and will be largely shifted, as under competition. (2) A nonshifted tax eats into profits, and few businessmen like to see profits sink; they will shift the tax whenever they feel they reasonably can. Most substantial excise taxes are shifted.

Effects on Growth and Employment. The direct impact of sales and excise sales is highly deflationary. They impose a direct burden on costs or effective purchasing power. But if we are mainly interested in rapid growth and still most obtain some given amount of tax revenue, sales and excise taxes may nevertheless be the best bet. For they bear directly on consumption, while leaving investment untaxed.

By the same token, a general sales tax is a strong antiinflation weapon. It hits directly at the massive consumption expenditures of the lower- and middle-income groups

But in both cases, as with incidence analysis, we can make reasonable forecasts only when we know what the stance of monetary-fiscal policy will be.

Effects on Income Distribution and Resource Allocation. A general sales tax is regressive. A $2,000-income family will spend almost the en-

fig. 40–6

Under competition with these supply and demand curves, new tax is partly shifted forward through a higher price and partly reduces output and consumption of cards. What would this do to the industry's demand for labor and raw materials?

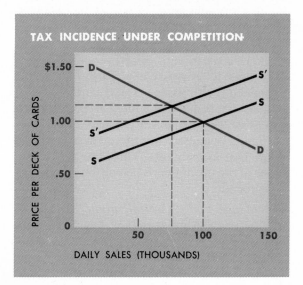

TAX INCIDENCE UNDER COMPETITION

PRICE PER DECK OF CARDS
$1.50
1.00
.50
0

DAILY SALES (THOUSANDS)
50   100   150

tire amount, except for rent payments, on taxed consumption. Assuming a forward-shifted tax of 5 percent, it will pay a tax of $100, disregarding rent—5 percent of total income. But a $100,000-income family will spend only part on consumption goods (say $40,000). The wealthy family is thus taxed 5 percent on only $40,000, making a total sales tax burden of $2,000, or only 2 percent of total income. Even though the wealthy family pays many more dollars, it pays a smaller percentage of its income.

But increasingly, major "necessities" like food and clothing have been exempted to soften this inequity. With these exemptions, plus rent, sales taxes lose most of their regression, and don't differ greatly, except at high income levels, from raising the same funds with a broad-based income tax. As a result, popular acceptance of sales taxes has risen considerably, even among "liberals" who generally favor the most progressive taxes that will raise the revenue needed.

Excise taxes discourage consumption of the taxed products. In some cases, like liquor and tobacco, the tax is specifically intended to discourage consumption. We call these "sumptuary" taxes. But it is easy to mix up economics and morals here. For example, many people think we ought to avoid taxing "necessities," but that it is all right to tax "luxuries." Taxes on "necessities" are thought to be regressive; taxes on "luxuries" progressive. These loose generalizations depend, however, on how "necessities" and "luxuries" are defined. If "necessities" are goods that everyone consumes heavily (for instance, bread), taxes on necessities are clearly regressive, since a larger proportion of income will be spent on them by low- than by high-income groups. But consider taxes on two major "luxuries"—liquor and tobacco. In fact, the demand for these products by rich and poor is relative inelastic. The cigarette tax of about eight cents per pack in many states often leads to lower expenditures on clothing and food, not to less smoking; many people give up what are usually called "necessities" rather than cigarettes. The same is true of liquor. Thus, liquor and tobacco taxes (on "luxuries") may be among the most-regressive taxes. Elasticity of demand,

rather than morals, is critical in determining who actually pays excise taxes.

Any excise changes (often distorts) the allocation of resources. Excises tend to produce a relatively big "deadweight loss." Or, where production has large by-product social costs (externalities), excises can be an effective way of adding on the extra costs needed to induce the optimal level of output.

Property Taxes

Property taxes on land and buildings were, until World War II, the most important single tax source in the United States. They are also the oldest major source of tax revenue. The federal government levies no property taxes, and state governments now receive only a small sum annually from them. But local governments depend on property taxes for almost their entire income.

Administration. How does the property tax work in practice? Most local units—cities, school districts, and the like—annually or biennially estimate the expenditures required for the coming year or two. Meanwhile, the property to be taxed has been assessed. The amount to be raised is compared with the assessed property values, and the tax rate necessary to raise the funds is determined. For example, if $1 million is to be raised and the local assessed valuation is $100 million, a tax rate of 1 percent on assessed valuation is necessary.

Low-priced real property is widely overassessed relative to high-priced property (that is, assessment is "regressive")—partly because of "influence" with assessors and partly because most assessors have no idea of the value of expensive properties and hence depend on the figures suggested by the owners or simply follow past assessments. Thus, the actual incidence of the tax depends heavily on administrative procedures.

Incidence and "Capitalization." There is nothing peculiarly hard about figuring out the incidence of many property taxes. Taxes on buildings will be gradually shifted if the tax drives investment out into other areas where taxes are lower, thereby reducing the supply and raising the prices of these taxed buildings. This is the same analysis as in the case of other taxes that hit other special areas or products. This effect is plainly visible in big-city slums, where effective property tax rates rise as buildings age, but dollar assessments are not reduced while tax rates rise. Property owners just let their buildings run down and transfer their investment elsewhere.

An interesting point concerns the tax on land itself, as distinct from improvements on it. The first effect of the tax on land is the same as on any other investment opportunity—the net return on the property is correspondingly reduced. Thus buyers will be willing to pay less for the land after the tax has been levied. The capital value of the land is thus decreased by the imposition of the tax.

The tax is then said to have been "capitalized." Any future buyer of the land will not invest in the land unless the price is low enough to provide a net return after real-estate taxes equal to that obtainble on investment elsewhere. Capitalization thus puts the burden of the capitalized tax exclusively on the owner of the land at the time the tax is levied, by forcing him to pay the unshiftable tax and by forcing down the capital value of his property. Any future buyer will not bear the burden of the tax, because he anticipates the tax in the price paid for the land. Future owners buy "tax-free."

Although capitalization often does not work out so precisely, it is an important factor in connection with the real-property tax. Consider a proposal to decrease the tax on real property. Present owners have bought at lower figures because of the tax, capitalizing the burden on earlier owners. To lower the property tax now would be to give a subsidy to present owners through increasing the capital value of the land. The fact of capitalization is a strong argument against drastic reductions in long-established property-tax rates.

The real-property tax is often supported on the "benefit" principle. Owners of real property receive many important special benefits, such as police and fire protection; and the larger the property holdings, the greater are the benefits received. The property tax has some virtues on the benefit criterion, and a few on ability-to-pay. But the main case for it is that it's there, and everything is pretty well adjusted to it. There is no other local tax source that looks better, which would realistically replace it for local governments.

A "Model" Tax System

What would a model tax system look like? What changes would you make in our tax system? As a citizen, this is one issue on which you will repeatedly get a chance to say your piece. At federal, state, and local levels, tax changes are continually being made.

It's clear that different taxes look good on different criteria. Recognizing that what is considered a "good" tax system must depend heavily on each individual's weighting of different objectives, some economists have proposed a "model" tax system along the following lines. It would make some drastic changes in the present system, and it is presented only to stimulate you to think through your own views on what an ideal tax system would be.

This "model" tax system would have four major taxes:

1. A progressive personal income tax would account for at least two-thirds of all tax revenue. This would mean more than doubling present income-tax revenues. Much higher rates would reach down through the middle-income groups, and the bulk of the income-tax yield would necessarily come from these groups, where the income is. This tax places the burden directly on individuals where it ultimately must rest, and it makes clear who is paying how much. The exact rate structure would depend on our collective judgments on equity, together with recognition of the importance of adequate income incentives. The tax would be supplemented by progressive death and gift taxes. To encourage incentive and economic growth and to improve equitable treatment of similarly situated people, the present punitively high peak rates of the federal tax would be lowered to

about 50 percent, but at the same time the sieve of avoidance loopholes for high-income taxpayers would be closed.

State income taxes would be added to the federal income tax, with the funds returned to the states concerned, in order to simplify tax reporting and collection procedures. Thus, the personal income tax base would be shared by federal and state governments.

2. Both to stimulate economic growth and to improve equity by switching to the personal income tax, present corporation income tax rates would be lowered substantially. The new tax would fall on all businesses, not merely corporations. At the same time, again to encourage growth, depreciation restrictions would be eased to permit faster charge-offs. But major loopholes like the present "depletion allowance" would be closed. Undistributed profits above generous reinvestment levels would be prorated out to stockholders for taxation, to avoid use of corporations as tax-avoidance devices.[9]

3. Taxes on real property would be continued at roughly present levels, not so much because the property tax is a good tax as because it is a major revenue source for local governments to which economic life has become well adjusted, and because its removal would mean a large subsidy to present real-property owners.

4. There would be special "user charge" taxes that are clearly justifiable either to cor-

[9]Some would substitute a value-added tax for the business-income tax.

rect externalities or on the benefit principle. In this group would be: (a) special assessments; (b) highway taxes (on fuel and on vehicles), with the revenue to be spent on highways and streets; and (c) payroll taxes on the worker (not the employer) to finance social security benefits. All three have strong claim to use as benefit levies.

Could such a tax system yield adequate revenue to pay the governments' bills? The answer is clearly "yes," since personal income tax rates could be set to produce any desired yield. Could it yield the revenue without impairing the incentive to work and earn? This is a big question raised by critics of the income tax, which in this system would supplant hidden excise and sales taxes, plus part of present corporation taxes. One way of putting the question is: Do we really want as many government services when we recognize individually what we have to pay for them?

Taxes are going to take over a quarter of the income you earn during the rest of your life, if something like present conditions continue. Every time we tell our governments to do something more for us, we're in effect saying there'll have to be more taxes collected. Thus, getting a good tax system is one of the most important problems we face, as a nation and as individuals. So stop and ask yourself: What does **your** model tax system look like? Even more fundamentally, how big should the public sector be, and what should it do? For that is what will determine how many taxes we as a nation must ultimately pay.

Review

CONCEPTS
TO
REMEMBER

Public finance involves mainly the application of analytical concepts already learned in the preceding chapters. But it has some concepts and terms of its own that you need to have firmly installed in your economic tool kit:

incidence
shifting
benefit principle
ability-to-pay principle
progressive taxation
regressive taxation
"deadweight loss"
"fiscal dividend"

vertical equity
horizontal equity
Incentive effects
"tax expenditures"
capital gain
tax capitalization
tax sharing

FOR ANALYSIS AND DISCUSSION

1. Are taxes too high? What is your criterion?
2. Can you suggest ways of minimizing the negative incentive effects of rising taxes as government expenditures grow?
3. Some tax experts argue that taxes should be highly visible (like the personal income tax) in order to make citizens keenly aware of the taxes they are paying. Others argue that indirect and hidden taxes (e.g., excise and sales taxes) are better because taxpayers don't feel the burden so strongly and are less unhappy about the costs of government services. Analyze these arguments. What are the main issues, and where do you stand on them?
4. "The government's taxing and spending policies should leave the distribution of income roughly as it would be through the private economy."

   "Every child should receive a good education at least through the grade-school level."

   Can you consistently accept both these propositions? Analyze carefully why or why not, examining specifically any apparent inconsistencies.
5. What are tax loopholes? Should all tax loopholes be closed by Congress? (See Figure 40–4 in answering.)
6. Suppose a new excise tax were imposed on the following products, at the producer's level:
   a. Steel (where there is mixed price leadership and competition, plus strong labor unions).
   b. Potatoes (where the market is highly competitive and little unionized labor is involved).
   c. Ladies' garments (where the market is highly competitive and there is a strong labor union).
   d. Refined oil and gasoline (where the market is oligopolistic and little strongly unionized labor is involved).

   Explain in each case whether you would expect the incidence of the tax to be on the consumer, labor in the industry, the producing firm, or some combination.
7. Assume a period of strong inflationary pressures as a result of government arms spending. Which of these alternatives would you consider the more equitable, and why?
   a. A general sales tax to balance the budget.
   b. Inflation.
8. Given a full-employment situation and the need for more taxes to finance more defense spending, what tax program would you propose to raise an additional $10 billion? Defend your program against likely criticism from those who would bear the major burden.
9. What is your model tax system?

Research in the area of public finance has since the decade of the 1930s focused heavily on fiscal policies to avoid depression and inflation (see Part Two). But in recent years, research aimed at the allocative and distributional effects of government taxes and expenditures has come back into fashion, as it becomes increasingly clear that big government spending and taxes are here to stay.

Government Expenditures. Murray Weidenbaum's *The Modern Public Sector* (Basic Books Inc., Publishers, 1969) is a good introduction to the whole area of public goods and expenditures. Charles Schultze, economist and former U.S. Budget Director, provides a sobering analysis in *Setting National Priorities: The 1971 Budget* (The Brookings Institution, 1970). *Fortune* devotes half an issue (August, 1969) to the military budget and the "military-industrial complex," here and in the USSR. R. McKean's *Public Spending* is a penetrating analysis of the problem. On cost–benefit analysis, Stephen Enke's "Government-Industry Development of a Commercial Supersonic Transport" in the *American Economic Review* (May, 1967) provides an accessible introduction; and the following articles on water resources and the federal antipoverty program are examples of other applications. More advanced analyses are presented in the Joint Economic Committee's *The Analysis and Evaluation of Public Expenditures: The PPB System*, Vol. 1, especially the articles by Steiner, Davis and Kamien, and Bonnen.

Pollution and Externalities. A. Kneese's and R. d'Arge's "Pervasive External Costs and the Response of Society," in the volume just cited, is a penetrating analysis of externalities. L. E. Ruff's "The Economic Common Sense of Pollution," *The Public Interest*, Spring, 1970, applies the principles understandably. Two useful additional collections on the pollution problem are M. Goldman, ed., *Controlling Pollution* (Prentice-Hall, Inc., Spectrum Books, 1967), and H. Wolozin, ed., *The Economics of Air Pollution* (W. W. Norton & Company, Inc., 1966). The February, 1969 issue of *Fortune* provides a detailed layman's overview of the issue.

Urban Problems. The cities' problems reach far beyond economics, but economic issues are near the center of the problems. *The Metropolitan Enigma*, J. Q. Wilson, ed., offers a readable introduction; see especially the pieces by Meyer and Netzer. The National Commission on Urban Problems' *Building the American City* (U.S. Government Printing Office, 1968) provides a good overview of the issues, with the commission's recommendations. A number of leading economists join in *The Quality of the Urban Environment*, H. Perloff, ed. (Resources for the Future, 1969). The analysis by J. Kain and J. Persky, "Alternatives to Gilding the Ghetto," *The Public Interest*, Winter, 1969, is relevant here as well as on the race problem. Last, the entire Summer, 1969, issue of *The Public Interest*, "Focus on New York," illuminates the awesome problems facing our biggest city.

Taxes. *Federal Tax Policy for Economic Growth and Stability*, a volume of papers prepared by seventy-five leading tax experts for the Joint Economic Committee of Congress in 1955, but still timely, provides a detailed cross section of research in the field of taxation. For a beginning, try R. A. Musgrave's "Incidence of the Tax Structure and Its Effects on Consumption," or Keith Butters's "Effects of Taxation on the Investment Capacities and Policies of Individuals." J. Pechman's "The Rich, the Poor, and the Taxes They Pay," *The Public Interest*, Fall, 1969, updates incidence analysis and argues for greater progression. California's George Break looks further at the alleged deterrent effect of high personal income taxes on work, without finding much evidence of it, in "Income Taxes and Incentives to Work" *(American Economic Review*, September, 1967). H. Grubel and D. Edwards report a study of Stanford students' behavior in "Personal Income Taxes and Choice of Professions" *(Quarterly Journal of Economics*, February, 1964).

part six

The International Economy

forty-one

International Trade and Lending

In the "one world" of today, the close interdependence among nations is painfully obvious. The dominating problem is war—how to assure international peace? But big economic issues fill the newspapers too. What happens if we lose more gold? Should we raise or lower our tariffs? Do low foreign wages threaten our standard of living? Is our foreign-aid program too big or too small?

Since prewar days, our sales of goods and services abroad have soared—from $4 billion in 1939 to $56 billion in 1969. Our imports from abroad have grown nearly as fast, to $54 billion in 1969. The best estimates indicate that perhaps 4–5 million American workers owe their jobs directly to export sales, and exports come from every state in the union. Our exports of goods and services total only about 5 percent of the g.n.p., but to many industries foreign trade is the blood of life—we export half of our cotton crop and import over 90 percent of the tin and nickel we use. More important, our foreign economic policies in a world of international tension are inseparable from our political and military policies. For to most of the world, foreign trade is far more urgent that it is to us. England must import most of her food or starve, and she can pay for her imports only by selling her exports abroad. And so it is with other nations; their living standards depend heavily on foreign trade.

In spite of the pressing importance of foreign trade, governments have long followed policies that restrict rather than encourage such trade—tariffs, quotas, exchange controls. Prima facie, the case for international division of labor and exchange is clear, as it is in domestic affairs. On the surface, there would appear to be no reason to suppose that human welfare could be improved by obstructing the processes of specialization and exchange. Why, then, have the laymen and the lawmaker so often distrusted foreign trade and favored the tariff? Why have nations so often flown in the face of apparent economic reason? Nowhere in economics is there a better opportunity to apply relatively simple economic analysis to popular fallacies.

It is well to begin by looking at what foreign trade means to the United States today—at what we export and import. Then we can analyze the basic case for international trade and lending, going on to the entire "balance of international payments" and the policy issues it raises.

The Balance of Trade

Look first at our exports and imports of commodities. Figures 41–1 and 41–2 summarize the goods we exported and imported in 1969. The figures speak for themselves. They show the huge sales abroad by many of our basic industries, mainly manufactured goods, but farm products as well. It's easy to see why a lot of American businessmen, workers, and farmers are all for foreign trade. Figure 41–2 shows the other side of the picture—the goods we import. Look at the list. It's easy to see why some businessmen and workers are opposed to foreign trade that competes directly with them. But never forget one basic fact. Our exports (and the jobs they support) are bigger than our imports, $2 billion bigger in 1969.

Figure 41–3 throws more light on this comparison. It shows exports and imports of goods and services as a percentage of g.n.p. During the prosperous 1920s, about 7 percent of all goods and services produced in the United States were exported. During the depression, this figure fell off to around 4 percent, partly because of bad business conditions and partly because of growing trade barriers here and in other countries. After World War II, the ratio rose sharply, then fell back to around 5 percent, and has climbed slowly since.

fig. 41–1

Machinery, autos, chemicals, and other manufactured products dominate our exports, but farm products also continue to be important. (Source: U.S. Department of Commerce. Excludes government military aid, but includes farm products financed through U.S. foreign aid.)

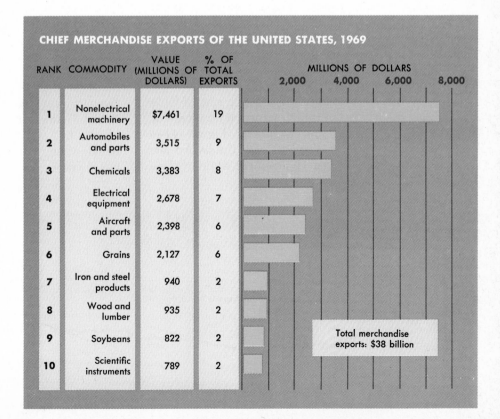

CHIEF MERCHANDISE EXPORTS OF THE UNITED STATES, 1969

RANK	COMMODITY	VALUE (MILLIONS OF DOLLARS)	% OF TOTAL EXPORTS
1	Nonelectrical machinery	$7,461	19
2	Automobiles and parts	3,515	9
3	Chemicals	3,383	8
4	Electrical equipment	2,678	7
5	Aircraft and parts	2,398	6
6	Grains	2,127	6
7	Iron and steel products	940	2
8	Wood and lumber	935	2
9	Soybeans	822	2
10	Scientific instruments	789	2

Total merchandise exports: $38 billion

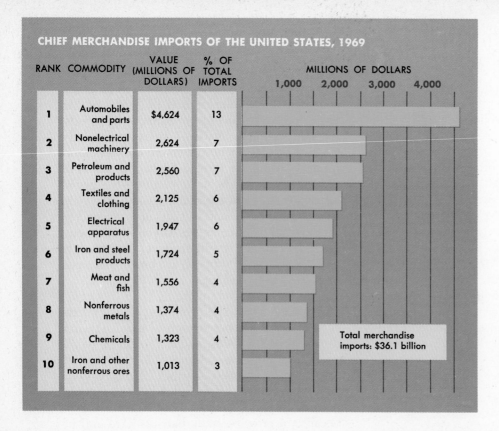

CHIEF MERCHANDISE IMPORTS OF THE UNITED STATES, 1969

RANK	COMMODITY	VALUE (MILLIONS OF DOLLARS)	% OF TOTAL IMPORTS
1	Automobiles and parts	$4,624	13
2	Nonelectrical machinery	2,624	7
3	Petroleum and products	2,560	7
4	Textiles and clothing	2,125	6
5	Electrical apparatus	1,947	6
6	Iron and steel products	1,724	5
7	Meat and fish	1,556	4
8	Nonferrous metals	1,374	4
9	Chemicals	1,323	4
10	Iron and other nonferrous ores	1,013	3

Total merchandise imports: $36.1 billion

fig. 41–2

Manufactured products also dominate our imports, though raw materials and food are also important. Note that the same manufactures rank high in both our exports and imports. (Source: U.S. Department of Commerce.)

Don't jump to the conclusion that international trade isn't very important. Remember those huge export figures in Figure 41–1. And it is virtually impossible to get some goods except from abroad (for example, coffee and tin). To most nations abroad in a tense, uncertain world, U.S. demand in world markets and U.S. policies on foreign aid and investment are matters of vital concern.

There is still another interesting way of looking at our foreign trade picture: Who were our main customers and suppliers? Figure 41–4 gives the answer. Canada leads the list by far, and other Western Hemisphere nations com-

bined add up to a third of all our customers. But Western Europe is equally important and Japan has been coming up fast. "Developed" countries account for about three-fourths of our exports and imports, "developing" countries for about one-fourth. The fact is that our foreign trade blankets the world.

The commodities we buy and sell abroad are the most visible part of our foreign trade, and the part most directly related to American jobs. But in Figures 41–3 and 41–4, over $15 billion of sales of American services abroad (shipping, banking, and similar services, plus returns on U.S. investments abroad) were added to the $38

U.S. EXPORTS AND IMPORTS AS A PERCENTAGE OF G.N.P.

fig. 41–3

U.S. exports of goods and services have consistently exceeded imports. During the last decade, both have stayed generally in the range of 4 to 6 percent of g.n.p. (Source: U.S. Department of Commerce.)

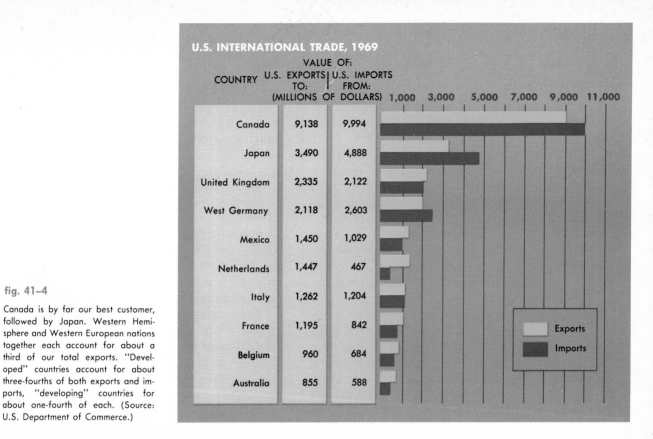

U.S. INTERNATIONAL TRADE, 1969		
COUNTRY	VALUE OF: U.S. EXPORTS TO: (MILLIONS OF DOLLARS)	U.S. IMPORTS FROM:
Canada	9,138	9,994
Japan	3,490	4,888
United Kingdom	2,335	2,122
West Germany	2,118	2,603
Mexico	1,450	1,029
Netherlands	1,447	467
Italy	1,262	1,204
France	1,195	842
Belgium	960	684
Australia	855	588

fig. 41–4

Canada is by far our best customer, followed by Japan. Western Hemisphere and Western European nations together each account for about a third of our total exports. "Developed" countries account for about three-fourths of both exports and imports, "developing" countries for about one-fourth of each. (Source: U.S. Department of Commerce.)

billion of merchandise exports. To get a complete picture of the international "balance of payments," we will need also to add "capital movements" (the transfer of short- and long-term monetary investments) and, lastly, gold. But first, let us consider the basic analytical case for free international trade and lending.

The Case for International Trade

Florida produces oranges, Iowa produces corn and hogs, Pittsburgh produces steel. Each sells its products to the others. When each specializes on what it does best, we produce more in total and all have more to consume than if each tried to be self-sufficient. In the same way, Chile sells us copper, we sell machinery to England, England sells cotton cloth to Chile. When each nation specializes on what it does best and then exchanges with others, we produce more in total and each of us ends up consuming more than if each tried to be self-sufficient.

The advantages to all in the first case—to Florida, Iowa, and Pittsburgh—are obvious. No one would question them. For each area to try to live alone, barring trade with the others, would be foolish. The advantages to nations from specialization and exchange are identical; more is produced for all to consume. The case for free international trade is that simple, and that powerful. By using our total resources most efficiently through specialization and exchange, the world can move all the way out to its combined production-possibilities frontier. But it seems very hard for voters and legislators to see and remember this simple truth.

Interregional and International Trade

Nations (like regions within a nation) vary greatly in efficiency in producing different goods, differences that persist largely because of international immobility of resources. These differences arise largely out of five considerations:

1. Over the face of the earth climatic and geographical conditions vary widely. Brazil is admirably suited for raising coffee, the lower Nile valley for cotton production. Texas and

Oklahoma are great oil-producing centers. Chile has rich nitrate deposits. Such geographical and climatic differences alone would justify worldwide specialization.

2. Human capacities vary over the globe. Some groups are large and strong, adept at physical labor. Others excel at dexterity and manual skills. Still others stand out in enterprise and organizational ability. These differences may be due to long-standing racial characteristics, or to the varying political, social, and economic environment. Whatever the reasons, they constitute a reason why international specialization and trade will be beneficial.

3. The accumulated supply of capital goods varies greatly from nation to nation. In some countries, centuries of accumulation have produced large supplies of fixed and mobile capital —railroads, buildings, machinery, and so forth. Examples are the United States and England; they specialize in industrial products. In other countries—for example, Greece and Nigeria— capital is scarce; they specialize in farming and simple production that requires little elaborate equipment. Moreover, vast differences exist between the kinds of capital accumulated in different nations.

4. The proportions among different resources vary widely from country to country. Australia has vast plains but relatively few people and capital goods. Therefore, she specializes in farm products that require a high proportion of natural resources to labor and capital goods. In England, land is scarce relative to human beings and capital. Therefore, she is best fitted for manufacture and industry, even though her soil may be as good as Australia's for wheat growing.

5. In addition to these "economic" considerations, great differences exist in the political and social climate in different countries. In countries of stable government, vast industrial organizations requiring large long-period capital commitments are likely to grow up. In backward, illiterate, badly governed areas, conditions virtually prohibit mass-production industry. A hustling, mechanical-minded nation like the United States could hardly be expected to be satisfied again with a small-unit, predominantly rural economy, any more than we would expect the South Sea islanders to be happy or efficient auto makers.

The Principle of Comparative Advantage

Given these differences among nations, it is clear that some international trade will be advantageous. But how far each nation should specialize and how much international trade is to its advantage is not so obvious. Neglect costs of transport between nations for the moment in answering that question.

The greatest possible advantage for all from trade will be obtained if each nation devotes itself to what it can do relatively most cheaply. In the simple case of Iowa and Florida, where the cost advantage of each in its representative products is clear and large, and with only two products, Iowa should raise all the corn, Florida all the oranges. The greatest total of corn plus oranges will be obtained in that way. But such money-cost comparisons don't provide much guidance when it comes to comparing costs between different nations that have different monetary units, different proportions of the factors of production, different qualities of labor, and different productive techniques. Perhaps as between coffee and factory machinery, Brazil has an "absolute" advantage in the former, the United States in the latter. But even in such an extreme case, it is hard to be precise on just why we are sure that these absolute advantages exist and what they mean. When less-striking differences are considered, such as textiles in the United States and England, the difficulty of such comparisons becomes insurmountable. Monetary comparisons mean little, since different monetary units prevail in the two countries.

But fortunately, as David Ricardo demonstrated a century-and-a-half ago, the advantages of international trade don't depend on such absolute cost calculations at all. Even though one nation were more efficient than another in the production of everything, it would still be to the advantage of both to specialize and engage in international trade. Each, and both combined, will gain most when each specializes in production of those commodities of which **comparative,** or **relative,** costs of production are lowest.

Let us first illustrate this "principle of comparative advantage" with a simple case involving only two countries and two commodities, the United States and France producing wheat and cloth. To simplify, let us assume that labor is the only factor of production (or that a day of labor is a shorthand measure of a bundle of land, labor, and capital used in producing things). Assume further that in the United States one man-day can produce one bushel of wheat or one yard of cloth. Thus, in the United States we can obtain one bushel of wheat by giving up the production of one yard of cloth, and vice versa.[1]

Assume that in France one day of labor also produces one bushel of wheat, but only a half yard of cloth. In this sense, American labor is more productive than French labor, but, as we shall see, this is not the critical factor. The critical factor is that in France two bushels of wheat must be given up to produce one more yard of cloth. This situation in the two countries is shown in Table 41–1.

them to begin specializing and trading? The answer is "yes." In the United States, we can obtain **one** more bushel of wheat by giving up one yard of cloth. But in France they can obtain **two** more bushels of wheat by giving up one yard of cloth. Therefore, there will be an increase in total world output if the United States uses more of her labor to produce cloth while resources in France are shifted to raising wheat. By transferring labor from cloth to wheat in France, Frenchmen produce two additional bushels of wheat for each yard of cloth they forgo; by transferring labor from wheat to cloth, the United States produces an extra yard of cloth for each bushel of wheat she foregoes. Obviously, we should shift more of our resources to producing cloth, France should shift more of hers to wheat. Then by exchanging we can both live better.

A simple example may help demonstrate the point. Assume that there are 100 workers each in the United States and France. At the beginning, in each country half are producing wheat and half cloth. Total world output is 100 bushels of wheat and seventy-five yards of cloth, as in Table 41–2.

Now suppose that we specialize completely on cloth and France specializes completely on wheat, as the principle suggests. As Table 41–3 shows, the result is 100 bushels of wheat and 100 yards of cloth, an increase of 25 yards of cloth to divide between us.

It might appear from these tables that the

Suppose first that there is no trade between France and the United States; each country produces all its own wheat and cloth. Will it pay

[1]Temporarily, assume that wheat and cloth are industries of constant costs both here and abroad. That is, unit costs of production do not increase or decrease as output in the country changes. This is sometimes called the assumption of constant returns to scale.

table 41-1

Comparative Costs of Production, in Man-Days

	In the U.S.	In France
Wheat (1 bushel)	1	1
Cloth (1 yard)	1	2

table 41-2

World Output Before Specialization

U.S.
50 workers on wheat = 50 bushels
50 workers on cloth = 50 yards

France
50 workers on wheat = 50 bushels
50 workers on cloth = 25 yards

table 41-3

World Output After Specialization

U.S.

100 workers on cloth = 100 yards

France

100 workers on wheat = 100 bushels

United States has an absolute advantage in efficiency over France, since in France it takes two man-days to produce a yard of cloth, whereas here it takes only one. But it is easy to show that these absolute differences are not the critical point at all. Suppose, instead, that we had begun with the assumption that French labor was the more efficient—that one man-day in France would produce two bushels of wheat or one of cloth. Total world output can be larger because of the higher productivity of French labor. But work out the new example, and you will see that it pays each country to specialize just as before, where its comparative advantage is higher, and then to exchange parts of its production.

The principle is that gain in total world output is possible from specialization and trade if the cost ratios of producing two commodities are different in different countries. This same principle would have applied in the above example had the cost ratios for producing wheat and cloth been 3:2 in the United States and 5:1 in France, or any other set of differing ratios. To repeat, absolute costs in the two countries are not relevant. It would make no difference, for example, if U.S. labor were vastly more efficient than French. Total output could be increased by further U.S. specialization on cloth, because the cost ratios differ and our comparative advantage is greater in producing cloth. This is the principle of comparative advantage: total output will be maximized when each nation specializes in the lines where it has the greatest comparative advantage or the least comparative disadvantage. [2]

From this statement we can tell also how far it is advantageous to carry specialization and trade. Gain from trade is possible until the cost ratios of producing the two commodities are the same in the United States and France. With constant costs complete specialization would occur; the cost ratios never become equal, since they are fixed by the constant-cost assumption. But now, realistically, drop the assumption of constant costs. As production of cloth increases in the United States, and that of wheat increases in France, the cost ratios will move together. Here the cost of producing cloth will rise relative to that of producing wheat as more cloth is produced. In France, the cost of producing wheat will rise relative to that of producing cloth. Finally, at some levels of output the cost ratios will become identical here and in France. Thereafter, there is no advantage in further specialization and exchange, since no further increases in total output can be obtained thereby. (Realistically, we should introduce transport costs between nations, which would correspondingly reduce the potential gains from international exchange.)

When the law of comparative advantage is generalized to many countries and thousands of products, no new principles are introduced, but the picture becomes more complex. Gain will still be maximized if each country specializes in those goods and services where its comparative advantage is greatest or its comparative disadvantage least, and if this specialization is carried to the point where the cost ratios involved are equal to those of other countries producing the same products. In any given country, produc-

---

[2] Note that we use this principle all the time in our domestic economic life. Suppose that in a business firm the president is also a whiz at typing, better than any of the secretaries. Should he do his own typing? Obviously not. He should specialize where his comparative advantage is greatest, in managing the firm, leaving the typing to his secretary even though she types slower than he does. Or suppose a fine surgeon is also the best driver in the community. Should he drive the hospital ambulance instead of spending all his available time in the hospital operating room?

tion of many products will never take place, because the country's comparative disadvantage in their production is so great and because of international transportation costs. Most nations will find it advantageous to produce a variety of products.[3]

You may have noted that thus far we have said nothing about the division of the gains from international trade. For example, in the case of Table 41–3, will France or the United States get the extra twenty-five yards of cloth obtained by specialization, or will they be divided between the two nations? In most cases, the gain will be divided, with the division depending on a complex set of considerations, mainly the relative cost structures of the countries involved. In extreme cases, it is possible to demonstrate logically that all the gain would accrue to one country, but this requires some highly unlikely assumptions.

The Law of Comparative Advantage, Free Trade, and the Price System

In world markets, the search for profits and the price system tend to bring about this international specialization and optimal allocation of resources in each country automatically. If we are relatively inefficient in producing coffee but very efficient in producing machine tools, American producers are going to have a tough time competing with Brazil in the world's coffee markets, but we'll beat out other machine-tool makers in the marketplace. Under an international free-trade system, in each country the greatest profits can be obtained by producing those commodities most desired by consumers at home and abroad. If our comparative advan-

tage is great in producing automobiles, this fact will be reflected in high returns to resources in the automobile industry. If our comparative advantage is low in producing spices, American spice producers will be unable to pay wages high enough to bid resources away from the more efficient automobile industry, since the world prices for spices are set by relatively efficient East Indian production. Thus, under a free-price system and free trade, the resources of each nation would tend to be drawn into its most efficient industries. No one would manage or direct international trade. Each producer would simply try to maximize profits and each buyer would simply buy where the price was lowest for the commodity he wanted. The central mechanism is the same as domestically with Adam Smith's invisible hand.

Worldwide Multilateral Trade

To provide the full advantages of international specialization and exchange, trade must be multinational, or "multilateral." That is, goods and services must move freely among all nations. This eliminates the necessity that the exports and imports between any two nations must be in balance, which would severely restrict the degree of international specialization. Vis-à-vis all other countries combined, a nation's exports and imports must roughly balance (omitting "capital movements"), but with multinational trade this balance may result from a combination of export and import imbalances with different individual nations, depending on the individual-country comparative advantages involved.

This fact is illustrated by Figure 41–5, which shows the pattern of multinational trade among major areas of the world. The United States, for example, exports more to Europe, Canada, and nontropical Latin America than it imports from them. But our imports from the tropical nations exceed our exports to them. The data may change from year to year, but Figure 41–5 illustrates the importance of multinational trade.

---

[3]If this were an advanced treatise, we would introduce the fact that different industries in different countries may use differing ratios of labor to capital, and note that this raises interesting, intricate problems of exactly how far each country should go toward specialization in different industries. But these complications do not change the general principle of comparative advantage, and we need not become involved in them here.

fig. 41–5

The yellow arrows show the directions of flow of exports where they exceed imports, while the red arrows represent the smaller amounts moving in the opposite directions. (Source: United Nations.)

The Case for International Lending

Society benefits when individuals and institutions save and invest, because useful capital goods and durable consumer goods are thereby accumulated. The saver gains individually from the return on his investment, and society gains from the increased efficiency of roundabout, mechanized production. Both the saver and society gain most when savings are invested where their productivity is highest.

In the domestic economy, we mainly trust the price system to allocate savings to the most desirable investments. Those who save invest their funds (either directly or through such institutions as banks) where the combination of safety, liquidity, and rate of return seems most attractive. Since the rate of return tends to be highest where investments fulfill the strongest consumer demands, savings are drawn into those industries where consumers most want output increased. Consumer choices direct the allocation of savings among investments.

Internationally, as domestically, society is generally best off if savings are allocated where their marginal productivity is greatest. International loans are "better" than domestic loans when the anticipated rate of return on them (including liquidity and risk allowance) is greater. For decades, both England and the New World gained from heavy loans by Britishers to the rapidly developing Western Hemisphere. British lenders gained by receiving good returns on their investments; U.S. borrowers gained by getting capital to combine with the plentiful natural resources of the New World. The overall result was a faster growth in world output, divided between the United States and Britain. Today the United States is the big international lender, but the general result is similar. Internationally, as domestically, lending may be unwise if the loan is unsafe, or undesirably illiquid, and the risk is often greater on international investments. But here again national political boundaries do not invalidate basic economic principles: we gain as individuals and as nations from having savings invested where their marginal productivity is highest.

The Foreign-Trade Multiplier and Domestic Employment

Thus far we have been implicitly assuming that full employment prevails, and that the problem is to allocate our fully employed resources most efficiently. But in the real world of intermittent underemployment and inflation, international trade can affect the level of domestic employment and output as well.

Export sales provide jobs, just as do domestic sales. Conversely, imports replace domestic jobs. Thus, the net excess of exports over imports("net exports" in the g.n.p. accounts) is one component of aggregate demand that calls forth production and employment. And like any other autonomous expenditure, such as private investment, it tends to have a multiplier effect on g.n.p. Thus the net export balance produces jobs in its own right and also has a further multiplier effect tending to create more jobs.

But this "foreign-trade multiplier" is smaller

than the regular domestic-investment multiplier, because our increased exports, by increasing domestic income, will indirectly induce increased imports into the United States. We import more when our incomes rise and these induced imports partially offset the original multiplier effect. The final foreign-trade multiplier is reduced by the extent to which induced imports offset the original export balance.

This reasoning makes it easy to see why nations with unemployment especially want to increase their net export balances, by increasing exports and/or reducing imports. Either way the result will be more jobs at home. Creation of a net export surplus is a way of exporting unemployment to the nation that buys more U.S. goods or has its exports to the United States cut. For this reason, it is often called a "beggar-my-neighbor" policy for increasing domestic employment.

But if any nation tries to export its unemployment in a world of widespread unemployment (as in the 1930s), say by raising its tariffs to shut out imports, it's easy to predict the result. Rather than importing unemployment, other nations will retaliate by raising their tariffs too. Obviously it is not possible for all nations to increase their exports and none to increase their imports, for each export is somebody else's import. Thus the main result of import restrictions aimed at exporting unemployment is likely to be retaliation abroad, higher tariffs everywhere, and a shrinkage in the total volume of international trade with no more than transient gains to any nation. This was exactly the result in the disastrous 1930s, when snowballing trade restrictions cut world trade to a small fraction of its level during the 1920s.

The Balance of Payments

Table 41–4 summarizes the complete U.S. "balance of payments" in 1969, including foreign investments, government foreign aid, and

table 41-4

U.S. Balance of International Payments, 1969 (Liquidity Basis)*

		In Billions
I. U.S. exports (payments due United States):**		
Merchandise	$38.0	
Services	8.7	
Income from investments abroad	8.8	
Total		$55.5
II. U.S. imports (payments due to foreigners):		
Merchandise	$36.1	
Services and U.S. travel abroad	8.1	
Military purchases abroad	4.9	
Income on foreign investments here	4.5	
Total		$53.6
III. Net balance due United States on goods and services		$ 1.9
IV. Foreign investment in United States (long term)		$ 4.1
V. U.S. government grants**	$ 3.8	
VI. U.S. net capital exports and private remittances	6.6	
VII. Errors and omissions	2.9	
VIII. Net capital outflow, plus omissions		$ 9.2
IX. Balance due others (payments "deficit" — liquidity basis)		$ 7.2
X. Accumulation of short-term foreign capital in United States***		$ 8.4
XI. Increase in U.S. gold and other official assets		1.2

*Data from U.S. Department of Commerce. Data are rounded to nearest $100 million, so figures may not add or subtract exactly.
**Excludes direct military aid; see footnote 4.
***Sometimes considered a short-term capital inflow to United States. See text.

gold movements, as well as exports and imports of private goods and services. Basically, the table shows what we paid to foreigners and what they paid to us. The dark shading (I and IV) shows what they paid us, for goods, services, and interest on our investments abroad and on new investments in the United States. The light shading (II, V, VI, and VII) shows what we paid them—for goods and services, in government and private aid, and in net new U.S. investments abroad, plus "errors and omissions" which were probably largely short-term capital exports. Item III is merely a memorandum item included to show where we stood on exports versus imports of goods and services alone; and VIII is another memorandum item to show where we stood on all reported payments. Since VIII shows that our payments out exceeded payments to us, we had a basic balance of payments "deficit" of $7.2 billion in 1969, calculated on this basis.

The bottom two items (X and XI) show how the deficit was financed. Foreigners could have taken either dollars (in bank deposits or short-term investments like U.S. government bills) or gold. In 1969 they chose to take the entire $7.2 billion in dollar balances, and in addition sold us about $1.2 billion of their gold in exchange for additional dollar balances. Clearly they preferred to build up their dollar holdings (on which they earn interest) to accumulating more gold (on which they earn nothing).

Look at some of the individual items. We exported $1.9 billion more goods and services than we imported. But we gave foreigners $3.8 billion through government grants, and invested abroad the huge sum of $9.5 billion (assuming that most of the "errors and omissions" are unreported short-term capital outflows). While foreign investments here of $4.1 billion partly offset this outflow, clearly the big U.S. payments deficit reflected largely U.S. capital flows abroad.[4]

[4]U.S. direct *military* aid is excluded completely from the tables. Such exports of military equipment (planes, missiles, and so on) might have been included in the exports figure (I) and in the balancing government grants figure (V). But such goods are not considered regular exports, and if they're not included in exports they can't be included either under government grants, since to do so would throw the balance-of-payments figures out of balance.

"Liquidity" and "Official Settlements" Payments Concepts

Table 41–5 illustrates how balance-of-payments statistics can be presented in more traditional balance-sheet form. The dark-shaded items on the left show payments to the United States; the light-shaded items on the right payments from us to other nations; and the unshaded items show the "deficit" and how it was financed. It also calculates the U.S. deficit for 1969 somewhat differently—on an "official settlements" basis whereas Table 41–4 was on a "liquidity" basis.

The official-settlements basis calculates the deficit as only what we owe to foreign governments and central banks, since officially we are only committed to pay gold or other official reserves to them—not to private foreign holders of dollars. On the official-settlements basis, our 1969 deficit was only $2.7 billion. The big difference in the two payments deficits lies in the treatment of short-term dollar balances (bank deposits and short-term U.S. securities) owned by foreign individuals and businesses. The liquidity balance considers them a claim against our basic liquidity, not a private investment in the United States; thus, when private foreigners accumulate U.S. dollars, it shows as part of the U.S. payments deficit. The official-settlements basis (used by most foreign governments) considers such short-term currency accumulation a short-term investment in the country concerned, to be treated parallel to long-term investments. As we shall see in Chapter 44, the issue becomes one of major importance in deciding how to deal with balance-of-payments deficits in U.S. international monetary policy. Neither concept is entirely satisfactory.

The "Balance of Payments" and the "Balance of Trade"

These tables point up the importance of being clear about the difference between the "balance of payments" and the "balance of trade." The balance of payments includes all payments between the countries concerned (all of Tables 41–4 and 41–5). The balance of trade includes only trade in goods and services (I and II of the tables).[5] Popular discussion, which generally runs in terms of the balance of trade, is often confused because of failure to consider the entire balance of payments. For example, the massive $15 billion gold inflow into this country during the 1930s, which accounts for most of our current gold stock, was due primarily to a huge flow of funds to this country for long- and short-term investment and simply for safekeeping—not to a "favorable balance of trade," as a surplus of exports over imports is popularly called. Similarly, the outflow of gold during the 1960s obviously wasn't on account of the balance of trade, since we exported some $40 billion more than we imported. Rather, it reflected governmental aid and U.S. private investment

abroad. You must keep the distinction between the balance of payments and the balance of trade clear to think straight about international economic problems.

Since World War I, the United States has generally had a net export surplus—that is, exports of goods and services have consistently exceeded imports. But the total balance-of-payments picture has varied widely. During the 1920s and 1930s, we generally accumulated gold and short-term balances abroad, because payments were due us on balance. Since about 1950, by contrast, we have run a persistent balance-of-payments deficit. Thus, foreigners have steadily accumulated gold, U.S. bank deposits, and short-term investments here ("dollar balances"), as we have made large investments abroad and have annually given foreign nations a large amount of economic and military aid. Since 1950, foreigners have taken about $13

[5]It is the difference between these two (that is, III in Table 41–4) which is the "net exports" figure shown separately in the g.n.p. accounts. When not shown separately, it is usually included as part of gross private investment.

table 41-5

U.S. Balance of Payments, 1969 (Official-Settlements Basis)*

Payments to United States (In Billions)	
U.S. exports:	
Merchandise	$38.0
Services	8.7
Income on investments	8.8
	$55.5
Foreign private investments in United States (long- and short-term)	8.8
Foreign official long- and short-term claims on United States	1.5
Decrease in U.S. gold and other resources	1.2
	$66.9

Payments from United States (In Billions)	
U.S. imports:	
Merchandise	$36.1
Services and travel	8.1
Military purchases abroad	4.9
Income on foreign investments here	4.5
	$53.6
U.S. government grants	3.8
U.S. capital outflow and remittances	6.6
Errors and omissions	2.9
	$66.9

*See footnotes for Table 41-4

billion in gold and increased their "dollar balances" by about $40 billion. We still have about 25 percent of the world's known monetary gold stock. As we shall see in Chapter 44, our persistent balance-of-payments deficit has become a serious problem in the past few years. But it should be clear that international payments imbalances are settled in large part by foreign currencies, only in small part by gold transfers.

International Community and Conflict of Interests

Free international trade and lending are in the interest of the world as a whole. This is the big lesson to be learned. Since World War II the Western non-Communist world has moved persistently toward freer trade, with the United States a leader. And the results have been satisfying. Since 1950, world trade has more than tripled, from less than $60 billion to about $200 billion in 1970. This is a substantially faster growth rate than in the domestic production of most of the individual countries.

For the most part, freer trade and lending also benefit each of the individual countries concerned while world output increases, but not always. It is possible, though unlikely, that an individual nation may temporarily increase its domestic employment by shutting out competing foreign goods and increasing its export surplus. But, assuming that relatively full employment exists, some other possible conflicts of interest deserve attention here, as qualifications to the general argument.

1. *Personal Migration.* If the "economic welfare" of the world as a whole is our aim, then international migration probably should occur whenever real wages obtainable in one country are higher than in another. But for workers in high-wage countries, immigration of workers from low-wage countries might prove a major blow. Assume such an influx into the United States, and assume that the immigrants are substitutable for American workers. Work out the supply-and-demand analysis yourself. Average real wages for workers throughout the world would rise, but the influx of foreign workers would surely lower the incomes of present American workers. **Given the international distribution of resources,** the law of comparative advantage applies. But the law does not say that each nation must gain from an international shift of resources, even when the shift raises the world's average standard of living.

2. *Monopoly-Type Action by One Country.* Just as a domestic monopolist can benefit himself by restricting output, so a country may be able to benefit itself by restricting trade. But the attempt may not work. For one thing, the international monopolist must always face the potential competition of other countries. More important, any country's restrictions on imports are likely to provoke retaliatory restrictions by other countries, and then both are worse off.

The extreme cases of nations acting as monopolists are those where foreign trade is centralized under government control—Soviet Russia, for example. But to a smaller extent, other countries have also centralized their foreign-trade activities. Brazilian coffee is an example.

3. *Growth of Less-Developed Areas.* When a rich country lends to less-developed areas, the lender **may** find itself worse off because of the loans. This result may occur if the new areas develop industries which compete with the lender's. More often, however, the new industries are not directly competitive. In any case, as the developing country sells abroad it can begin to buy abroad, and the law of comparative advantage ultimately applies as stated above. Three-fourths of U.S. trade is with other highly industrialized nations. But the problem of the less-developed countries vis-à-vis the industrialized nations is a major one for the decades ahead.

4. *War.* The most important potential conflict goes beyond economics. It centers around war and preparation for war. No nation wants to be dependent on potential enemies for vital raw materials and finished goods, or to help build up the strength of potential enemies. With this major exception, however, economic and political considerations point in the same direction. Wide-ranging international trade and finance

are probably the soundest bases for lasting peace.

The Great American Responsibility

In the century before World War I, England was the world's great creditor nation and the financial center of the world. This was an era of free international trade. Trade was multilateral—based on an intricate web of exchanges in which no two countries balanced out directly with each other. The gold standard assured stable exchange rates among the world's currencies, to facilitate foreign trade. The British pound provided a standard currency and, along with gold, comprised the basic monetary reserves of most leading nations. London was the financial center of world trade and lending, the banker to the world. The system was complex, but it operated, like the free-price system, in a mainly automatic fashion—through the multitude of buying and selling activities of individuals in the many countries of the world.

The day of British leadership has passed. On the United States falls the enormous responsibility of providing leadership in the twentieth-century world economy. The dollar has become the international reserve currency of the free world, along with gold. Our task is incomparably more difficult than was Britain's in the nineteenth and early twentieth centuries. Nations no longer accept unquestioningly the "discipline" of international gold flows in regulating their domestic money supplies. "Planned" domestic economies have replaced free private enterprise in many countries. Maintenance of domestic high employment has become the first objective of most nations' economic policies. Many nations have come to look upon the United States as a continuing source of military and economic aid.

In the face of these conditions, it has been widely suggested that the United States must do four things:

1. Maintain a stable, prosperous U.S. economy as a foundation for international economic prosperity.

2. Maintain a strong, stable dollar internationally, as the world's major "key," or "reserve," currency.

3. Continue to lead the way toward reducing trade barriers.

4. Help to strengthen international institutions for supporting international monetary stability and for facilitating investment in less-developed countries.

What is America's responsibility in these matters? In today's world, few questions are more important to the American citizen. The next three chapters analyze some of the issues.

Review

CONCEPTS TO REMEMBER

International economics is essentially fundamental economics applied to international economic activity. But it has some new terms and concepts that you need if you want to be able to operate effectively on international problems:

law of comparative advantage
comparative costs
balance of payments
balance of trade
"trade surplus or deficit"
"liquidity deficit"

"official-settlements deficit"
foreign-trade multiplier
multilateral trade
capital movements
beggar-my-neighbor policies

**FOR ANALYSIS
AND DISCUSSION**

1. State the basic case for specialization, division of labor, and free exchange. Are there reasons why this case applies differently within a nation and across national boundaries?
2. Explain the difference between the balance of payments and the balance of trade. On which do the data in Figures 44–1 through 41–4 throw most light?
3. What industries in your area are most affected by international trade? (See Tables 41–1 and 41–2.) How important is such trade to your immediate area?
4. Suppose U.S. imports were reduced by half through new tariffs or import quotas. What effect would this probably have on jobs in export industries in your area? (See Table 41–1.)
5. "Anyone who believes in free trade ought to believe in free international migration of labor, unrestricted by immigration barriers." Do you agree? Why or why not?
6. What is the principle of comparative advantage?
7. Why is multilateral trade more advantageous than bilateral?
8. If you were wealthy, would you invest any of your money abroad? Why or why not?
9. Why is the "foreign-trade multiplier" ordinarily smaller than the domestic-investment multiplier?

forty-two

Tariffs, Quotas, and Free Trade

The Tariff
Quotas and Export Subsidies
Intergovernmental Agreements To Expand Trade
Current U.S. Trade Policy

Adam Smith's *Wealth of Nations* in 1776 was a major attack on barriers to free international trade. The case for free trade internationally is the same as the case for free trade domestically, Smith argued. It is that specialization and division of labor with free exchange of the resulting products makes possible a higher standard of living for everyone. Tariffs or other barriers to free international trade impede such mutually advantageous specialization and exchange and reduce living standards throughout the world, just as would barrier to free trade within a nation. Only with unfettered specialization and exchange can each nation and the world move out to be on their maximum production-possibilities curves.

Yet from Smith's day to this, many have re-mained unconvinced. Support for tariffs to "protect the American standard of living and the high wages of American workers" is still widespread. Why, if the case for free trade is so clear, have nations retained tariffs that restrict trade?

The Tariff

A tariff is a tax on imports. The major goal of modern tariffs is to restrict imports—to protect domestic industry and workers from foreign competition. A secondary effect is to produce revenues for the government. But the two effects conflict—the more the tariff keeps out imports, the less revenue it raises. If the

623

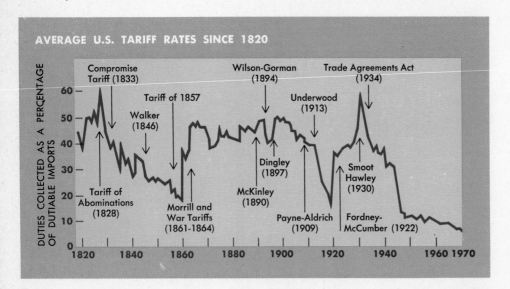

AVERAGE U.S. TARIFF RATES SINCE 1820

y-axis: DUTIES COLLECTED AS A PERCENTAGE OF DUTIABLE IMPORTS

Compromise Tariff (1833)
Tariff of 1857
Walker (1846)
Wilson-Gorman (1894)
Trade Agreements Act (1934)
Underwood (1913)
Tariff of Abominations (1828)
Morrill and War Tariffs (1861-1864)
Dingley (1897)
McKinley (1890)
Smoot Hawley (1930)
Payne-Aldrich (1909)
Fordney-McCumber (1922)

x-axis: 1820 1840 1860 1880 1900 1920 1940 1960 1970

fig. 42-1

U.S. tariff rates have fluctuated with changing times and attitudes. Since 1934 they have been reduced sharply to the lowest levels in our history. (Source: U.S. Department of Commerce.)

tariff is mainly for protection, it won't be much of a revenue producer.

Figure 42–1 shows average U.S. tariff rates on dutiable imports since 1820. This shows clearly the peaks of restrictionism and the major attempts to whittle away barriers to free international trade. From peak rates of about 60 percent under the Tariff Act of 1833 and the Smoot-Hawley Tariff of 1930, average tariff rates on products that are covered by the tariff have been cut to below 10 percent in the last two decades, including a last downward push by the "Kennedy round" in the 1960s. These figures understate the real restrictive effect of the tariff, because some products are shut out completely by the tariff, and they don't show up in Figure 42–1. But any way you look at it, major progress has been made in reducing U.S. tariff barriers since the early 1930s. The United States, after a spotty history of restrictionism, has been the leader in a worldwide push toward freer trade.

The history books are full of accounts of the tariff acts battled through Congress over nearly two centuries, and of the regional and political issues underlying them. Our job is to look objectively at the economics of tariffs—to apply the economic analysis of the preceding chapters to the major arguments advanced in support of tariffs. And the central principle to use is the law of comparative advantage.

Some Partially Valid Arguments

The Infant-Industry Argument. A protective tariff may help "infant industries" until they are able to stand on their own feet. This was the most stylish argument for tariffs in the early 1800s. For example, the newly formed iron industry found it difficult to get established in the face of strong competition from British iron makers. If foreign competition were shut out for a few years, it was argued, the American iron industry could soon not only meet, but outstrip, foreign competitors.

There is some validity to the "infant industry" argument. It is hard for a new industry to establish itself in the face of vigorous competition from older competitors, even though the new industry once established may compete effectively with the old. The protective tariff on iron probably speeded the growth of an industry that would in any case have prospered.

But a tariff once on the books is hard to get off. The steel industry today, still protected a century and a half later, is a very mature infant.

The National-Self-Sufficiency Argument. In a world of international tension, every nation wants to be as nearly self-sufficient as possible in the event of war. The desire for economic self-sufficiency may overbalance all other considerations, regardless of what the costs may be.

The economist cannot say whether a nation should try to become self-sufficient in the face of such considerations. But he can point out what self-sufficiency costs in terms of poor allocation of resources and a lowered standard of living so that this factor will be weighed with others in deciding whether or not we will seek more self-sufficiency. And the cost for most nations would be great.

The Diversified-Economy Argument. When a nation is highly specialized in producing one or a few major products, its economy is highly vulnerable to variations in foreign demand. Brazil's coffee economy is an example; usually such one-product nations export a foodstuff or raw material. If foreign markets weaken, the result is domestic disaster. For such nations, greater economic diversification may be desirable, even though the new industries are comparatively inefficient. Tariffs may be used to shelter them in a diversification program. But for widely diversified countries like the United States, this argument has little relevance.

Over the last century in the United States these partially valid arguments have carried little weight in tariff controversies. Let us now turn to the arguments that have been the important ones in support of the tariff. As we shall see, they turn out to be largely fallacious.

The Favorable-Balance-of-Trade Argument

Most naïve of all the tariff arguments is the desire for a "favorable balance of trade" for its own sake. It goes back to the old mercantilist desire to gain more gold and silver as national wealth. Two major fallacies are involved.

First, there is nothing generally favorable about a "favorable" balance of trade. A continued "favorable" balance means that we continually give foreigners more goods and services than they give us; we receive in exchange gold (often to be held idle at considerable storage expense) or investments abroad. Thus, it means a reduced standard of living for the country sending away goods and services, certainly in the short run, and indefinitely if the "favorable" balance of trade continues without willingness to accept goods from abroad. We don't eat gold.

Our standard of living is made up of the goods and services we have.

Second, a favorable balance of trade is impossible as a continuing policy, if we consider only the goods-and-services portion of the balance of payments. Foreigners can't buy from us unless they get dollars to pay for our products. The way they get dollars is by selling us their goods and services. It is only by buying from foreigners that we can expect to sell to them.

There is no point more fundamental than this —that we can sell abroad only if we buy abroad. It is basic to understanding the fallacy in nearly every argument for protective tariffs and other trade-restriction policies. Figure 42–2 shows where other countries obtained the dollars to buy our exports from 1929 to 1970 (U.S. exports are indicated by the heavy black line). Private investments abroad and government aid helped foreigners finance their purchases from us. But our purchases of foreign goods and services have always been the big source of dollars with which foreigners bought our exports. To sell abroad we must buy abroad. We cannot shut out foreign imports and continue to export.

The Protect-Home-Industry Argument

Perhaps the most popular argument for the tariff is that we need it to protect American industry against low-cost foreign competition.

A domestic industry asking for tariff protection argues that without protection its market will be lost to foreign competitors. This will force the domestic industry out of business, throwing workers out of jobs, and decreasing our national welfare. Suppose that the industry is right; if it does not receive protection it will lose its market to foreign competitors. What are the effects of giving the tariff protection the industry wants?[1]

The first effect is that domestic consumers must pay more for the protected product than if it had come in free. If sugar comes in over the

---

[1] Often industries seeking protective tariffs would be able to retain their markets without tariffs; tariffs enable them to raise domestic prices with lessened fear of foreign competition. Indeed, the tariff has been called "the mother of monopolies," since it helps domestic monopolies to exist without fear of foreign competition.

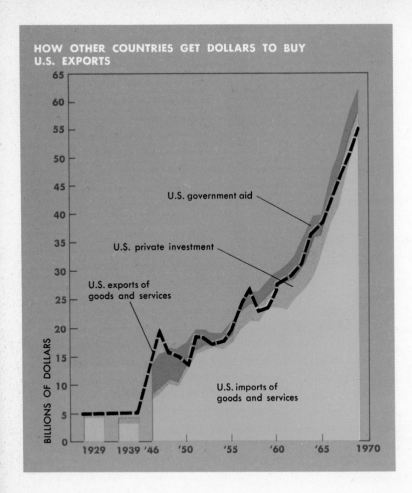

HOW OTHER COUNTRIES GET DOLLARS TO BUY U.S. EXPORTS

U.S. government aid

U.S. private investment

U.S. exports of goods and services

U.S. imports of goods and services

BILLIONS OF DOLLARS

1929 1939 '46   '50   '55   '60   '65   1970

fig. 42-2

Other countries get dollars to buy U.S. exports mainly through our payments for imports. But U.S. investments abroad and government foreign aid also provide a good many dollars. (Source: U.S. Department of Commerce. Military aid and exports excluded.)

tariff, consumers must pay the regular price of the foreign sugar plus the tariff duty. If the tariff shuts out foreign sugar, domestic consumers must pay a higher price for domestic sugar. We know it's higher because domestic producers cannot, without a tariff, produce and sell at a price low enough to meet foreign competition. If they could, they wouldn't need the tariff.

Second, domestic sugar producers are subsidized by the tariff; they are enabled to charge higher prices than would have been possible if foreign competition had not been shut out. It's clear that domestic producers are the great gainers from a tariff on their product.

In effect, therefore, a tariff is a subsidy to domestic producers, financed by consumers through higher prices for the protected product. Moreover, the more inefficient domestic producers are, the higher tariff they need to protect them against foreign competition and the larger subsidy they receive.

Indeed, industry's argument for a tariff is often for a "scientific" tariff that would just "equalize domestic and foreign costs of production." A suggestion in Congress that special taxes be levied on consumers to finance subsidies to producers, each subsidy to be based on the producer's inefficiency, would horrify everyone. Yet this is substantially the result of a "scientific" protective tariff designed to equalize foreign and domestic costs of production.

A noted economist, Frederick Bastiat, put the free-trade case against "protection" tellingly over a century ago in his satirical "Petition of the Candlemakers." We need protection, said the candlemakers of Paris in their petition. Foreign competitors are bad enough, but it is the sun that is the most unfair competitor of all. Each day it shines and throws light over all, at no cost at all. If you only shut out the sun, pleaded the candlemakers, we can have a magnificent candle industry, giving jobs to untold numbers of workers.

Should we protect American domestic industry against cheap foreign competition today, using the same arguments as Bastiat's candle-makers a century ago?

The Protect-Our-High-Wages Argument

American wages are the highest in the world. Therefore, it is argued, unless we have a protective tariff, competition from low-wage nations will push down high American wages to the level of wages abroad.

The "Petition of the Candlemakers" should suggest a fallacy here. Would the real wages of French workers have been raised by shutting out the sun? Would the French people have been better off? As the principle of comparative advantage says, the maximum real output will come when we allocate our resources to their most efficient, not their least efficient, uses. Look at the argument in more detail.

First, why are wages now higher in the United States than in other countries? Fundamentally, because of the high productivity of American workers. Anything that raises their productivity makes it possible for them to receive higher real wages. And each worker can receive his highest possible wage when he works where his marginal productivity is highest.

What happens when a tariff is passed to "protect" high American wages? The tariff shuts out foreign products and permits relatively inefficient American industries to grow up where otherwise they could not have existed, giving new jobs to American workers. But, as a result, American exports will fall off because foreign countries cannot buy from us unless we buy from them. (Remember Figure 42–2.) Therefore, fewer workers are employed in the export industries. The net result is a shift of workers from relatively efficient export industries (where they would be situated under free trade) into less-efficient protected industries. As workers move to lower-marginal-productivity positions in protected industries, the wages they can receive in the new jobs are necessarily lower than they could have been before the shift. The long-run result of a protective tariff is to lower real wages, not to raise

them. People earn the most when they work where they are most efficient.[2]

To be sure you understand this point, consider an extreme example cited by proponents of a tariff to protect American wages. Suppose that Japanese labor is paid only one-tenth as much as U.S. workers and we remove all tariffs on Japanese imports. Won't American workers be forced to take much lower wages to compete?

In analyzing this case, first we need to recognize that even though Japanese daily wages are much lower, it is not necessarily true that the labor costs of Japanese producers are correspondingly lower. The Japanese worker gets lower wages, but he also produces less in a day. Therefore, the labor cost per unit of output may be as much, or more, for the Japanese producer as for the American. For example, suppose the average hourly wage of Japanese industrial workers is about 35 cents, that in America about $3.50. But suppose, for example, in the china-ware industry, that the hourly output per worker in Japan is 10 plates; then the labor cost per plate is 3.5 cents. If the hourly output per American worker is 100 plates, the labor cost per plate would be only 3.5 cents too. Wage cost per plate (per unit of output) is the one that counts.

The evidence is clear that although wages are lower everywhere else than in the United States, our unit costs are highly competitive in many industries. Our $40 billion of annual merchandise exports and our persistent export surplus are unmistakable evidence of that. Table 42–1 presents data on comparative wage costs and output per man-hour in manufacturing for a sample of countries, data which illustrate why U.S. manufacturers do very well in world markets in spite of paying the highest wages in the world.

American wages are by far the highest, but so is American output per man-hour. If you compare the wage cost per dollar of output in the

[2]This is not to deny that a protective tariff on a particular product may raise the real wages of workers *in that industry* by increasing the demand for labor there, so long as there are immobilities in the domestic labor market that keep other workers from moving in to take advantage of the higher labor demand provided there by protection.

table 42-1

International Wage Costs
Per Unit of Manufacturing Output*

Country	Net Output per Man-hour	Hourly Earnings	Wage Cost per Dollar of Output
United States	$3.89	$2.68	$0.69
Canada	2.56	1.89	.74
Belgium	1.33	.74	.58
Norway	1.29	.90	.70
United Kingdom	.97	.77	.79
West Germany	.96	.70	.73
Italy	.96	.61	.64
Japan	.40	.29	.72

* Data from J. Dunlop, ed., *Automation and Technological Change* (Englewood Cliffs, N.J.: Prentice-Hall, Inc., 1962), p. 137. Figures are for 1960 and 1961, with national currencies converted to U.S. dollars. Hourly earnings in all cases include "fringe benefits." Conversion of currencies is based on official exchange rates, and should be recognized as only a rough approximation. See text for later data.

third column, you'll see that the higher American productivity roughly offsets the higher American wage costs, as compared to other nations with lower wages but also lower productivity. The estimates are very rough (see the footnote to the table), but they illustrate the basic point. It's wage cost per unit of output that counts, and on this vital score we're highly competitive on a wide range of products.[3]

What happened to comparative unit labor costs during the 1960s? During the first half of the decade, the United States made substantial gains. Wages here rose only moderately while productivity soared. Inflation pushed up wages rapidly in most other major Western economies. During the last half of the decade, the picture was reversed. For the whole decade, official figures show some relative gain for the United States on unit labor costs.

These figures show that the problem of competing with low-wage foreign labor is less dramatic than it may seem. But they don't answer the whole tariff argument, for per unit labor costs on many articles may be lower in Japan in spite of the higher output per worker here. But even then, the principle of comparative advantage shows that we would be better off as a nation without tariffs on Japanese goods.

Suppose, to continue the hypothetical example, that Japan can far undersell us on china plates, and that we remove the tariff on such plates. This move, of course, would throw workers in the American chinaware industry out of jobs. But since Japan would then be selling more to us, she could now buy more from us. She would buy from us those goods that we are able to produce most efficiently—say, machine tools. Workers thrown out of jobs in making china would gradually be drawn into the machine-tool industry. But since the United States is, by assumption, comparatively more efficient in producing machine tools than china, workers can receive higher wages making machinery. Workers in the china industry would surely be temporarily unemployed and, if personally unadaptable, might never be reemployed. But the general public would gain by obtaining cheaper china, and more workers would be drawn into the high-productivity industries where wages are highest. Removal of an existing tariff may ruin protected producer groups; yet in the long run average wages and the standard of living for the economy as a whole will be raised.[4]

This reasoning, however, rides easily over some tough "short-run" adjustment problems. Higher average wages for the economy don't help the fifty-year-old china maker thrown out of work by the new imports. Where will he get another equally good job, or even one at all? The offsetting new jobs producing for export may not come immediately. The Japanese may temporarily accumulate dollars, or spend them elsewhere instead of here. Sooner or later, our expanded imports will mean new export mar-

[3] Note that this statement does not say that all the higher output per man-hour in America is attributable to workers, but merely that, all things considered (including more and better capital goods in America, American management, and the like), our labor costs per dollar of output are competitive with those of other nations. Much of our high productivity clearly depends on our high technology and large capital investment.

[4] This argument applies strictly only if labor costs are the same proportion of total costs in the two industries concerned. In most real-world cases in the United States, this approximation is close enough to permit the above example to apply in substance.

kets. But with these uncertainties and delays, and the pain felt in the displaced industries, it's easy to understand why some labor opposition to tariff cuts is bitter. Nor does the higher national standard of living help those china-company stockholders whose investment is destroyed by the cheap imports. The opposition comes from investors and businessmen as well as from workers.

The Increased-Employment Argument

In the long run, it should by now be clear, a protective tariff neither increases nor decreases employment, but merely shifts resources from more efficient to less efficient industries. However, the short-run adjustments in moving toward the new long-run equilibrium may be slow and painful (as with any shift in demand). Removing an existing tariff may result in temporary unemployment, unemployment that may persist stubbornly if aggregate demand is weak.

But the protectionist argument claims more. It says that, at least in the short run, raising tariffs will create more jobs as domestic firms begin selling to the customers who previously bought imported goods. And the foreign-trade multiplier will amplify the creation of domestic jobs. Even though in the long run this may not increase total employment, temporarily the new tariff will raise exports relative to imports and create jobs.

But this is a short-sighted argument. Suppose America puts on a tariff to shut out foreign goods and to export our unemployment. What would you do if you were Belgium, or England, or France? You'd come right back with higher tariffs or quotas against American exports. And that's just what they did during the 1930s. If we can increase our exports relative to imports in a period of unemployment, this may temporarily raise employment and real g.n.p. But it's unlikely that higher tariffs will do the job, and likely that the main result will just be less trade for everybody.

Summary

From this analysis, we can draw a broad summary of the economic effects of tariffs. In the long run, a protective tariff lowers real wages and the standard of living. It diverts resources from self-sustaining export industries to less efficient, protected domestic-consumption industries; and it forces consumers to pay higher prices. In the short run, advantages may be gained from imposing new tariffs to aid infant industries or to reduce unemployment. However, new tariffs will increase domestic employment only if almost inevitable retaliatory steps are not taken by other nations.[5]

Tariff Making in the United States

If the protective tariff is open to such serious criticism, and if it benefits only particular groups at the cost of the rest of society, why did we have high protective tariffs so long? There are two chief answers.

First, public opinion on the tariff has been greatly influenced by self-seeking propaganda, and many citizens are uninformed on the nature of international trade. Groups seeking protection have presented their case effectively in Congress and to the general public, and the appeal to nationalism against foreigners is a potent rallying cry.

Second, the benefits of freer trade are widespread—lower prices, and more jobs in export industries tomorrow. But the costs are concentrated and direct—on the businessmen and workers who lose out to cheaper foreign imports. The threatened interests are alarmed, organized, and vocal. Consumers as a whole are not organized to speak effectively. Congress passes acts covering thousands of products, and most of the actual decisions are made by small subcommittees in the House and Senate. No congressman can know about more than a comparatively small number of these thousands. But each congressman is pressed by his constituents to vote for protection for the goods that they produce. Thus, the congressman from one state will agree to vote for a tariff on shoes if his colleague from another state will vote for one on sugar. The tariff is the classic example of congressional lobbying and logrolling.

[5]Though as a practical matter U.S. tariff reductions are usually advocated on the presumption of reciprocal reductions by other nations, the logic of comparative advantage shows that under most circumstances even unilateral tariff reductions can benefit the country making them.

Thus, the big tariff reductions since 1930 have come through congressional delegation of tariff-cutting authority to the president. Under the Reciprocal Trade Agreements Act of 1934 and the Kennedy Trade Expansion Act of 1962, the president was authorized to bargain down U.S. tariffs in return for similar reductions by other nations. The results are shown in Figure 42–1. Similar reductions have been made since the 1930s by most other major Western nations with whom we trade heavily.

Quotas and Export Subsidies

Tariff barriers have been dramatically reduced since World War II. But many nations retain other restrictions on foreign trade, especially import quotas that limit absolutely the quantities of particular commodities that can be imported per year. Japan makes extensive use of import quotas, and during the late 1960s and early 1970s retaliatory use of quotas showed signs of a resurgence of protectionism. Many European countries have quotas on at least some commodities, as does the United States.

Quotas, rather than tariffs, limit petroleum imports into the United States, our next-to-largest import, to protect American firms. Textiles are the other major U.S. industry protected by quotas, but U.S. legislation permits retaliatory imposition of quotas, and in 1970 Congress was debating adoption of new legislation to impose import quotas for all cases in which imports increase their U.S. market share by more than 5 percent in two years and thus reach a total of more than 15 percent. Steel, bicycles, flat glass, and consumer electronic products are among the major products that might obtain import quota protection under such legislation.

Free traders find import quotas more objectionable than tariffs. With a quota, additional foreign goods cannot enter, no matter how inefficient (high-cost) domestic producers may be. With a tariff, at least foreign competitors may enter if their cost advantage becomes large enough.

Export subsidies are another device widely used to provide domestic producers a special advantage over foreign competitors in world markets. U.S. legislation permits the use of "countervailing duties" against such subsidies given by foreign nations that sell in this country. Such countervailing duties have been levied on a variety of food imports from Europe, and quota negotiations with Japan have grown rapidly in recent years, including such major commodities as textiles, steel, and numerous farm products. U.S. farm price support programs are considered by many foreigners to provide, in effect, a large export subsidy to U.S. farm exporters. Moreover, the United States calculates its tariff duties on major chemical imports by pricing them at U.S. market levels, in effect thereby imposing a higher tariff barrier; this is the controversial so-called "American selling price" provision. Conversely, some nations (especially Japan and many developing economies) use foreign-exchange controls to limit the purchase of particular products from foreigners.

Nontariff barriers to trade constitute the major current threat to continued progress toward free world trade. Unfortunately, countries often find it easier to retaliate against such barriers by imposing similar restrictions than to negotiate them down. And rising nontariff barriers dot the international scene.

Intergovernmental Agreements to Expand Trade

The International Trade Organization and GATT

After World War II the spirit of internationalism was strong. All the victorious nations except the USSR moved to extend their wartime collaboration into economic cooperation that would reverse the restrictionist wave of the 1930s. Within the framework of the United Nations, member nations pushed for an International Trade Organization, which would attempt to expand and stabilize the volume of world trade.

Prolonged debate failed to bring agreement on a charter for ITO that could command support of most of the nations concerned. Out of these discussions, however, came the General Agreement on Tariffs and Trade (GATT), now with some forty signatory countries. GATT provides for regular discussion of means to reduce international trade restrictions among the members, and each member nation agrees to work toward freer trade practices, insofar as these practices are not in conflict with the country's national legislation.

The European Common Market

The biggest postwar move toward international economic cooperation is the European Common Market, and a major move it is. After earlier cooperation on coal, iron, and atomic energy, in 1958 six European nations—Belgium, France, Italy, Luxembourg, the Netherlands, and West Germany—banded together in the European Economic Community, generally called the Common Market. This precedent-shattering agreement has eliminated all tariff and similar trade barriers against one another and has gradually equalized all their restrictions on trade with nations outside the six, so they present a common tariff to the outside world. Barriers against internal movement of capital and labor are being abolished. Other economic policies will be "harmonized." A common anti-trust policy is provided to eliminate long-time restrictions on competition, though here considerable freedom is left for national differences. In essence, the Common Market is a new massive free-trade area, nearly as large as the United States.

Together, "The Six" have a total population of 190 million, just under that of the United States and only about 25 percent below the USSR's. In 1970 they accounted for about one-fourth of the world's exports, substantially more than the United States, and together they are by far the world's largest importer. Their combined gross national product is about half ours, and about the same as that of the USSR.

In its first years the Common Market has been a major success. Its g.n.p. has grown at over 5 percent per year, well above our growth rate and higher than that in most surrounding European countries. Between 1958 and 1968 internal trade rose from $6 billion to nearly $30 billion, though tariffs were only gradually reduced over the decade. Investment in industrial facilities was high as a percentage of g.n.p., and heavy foreign investments (especially from the United States) were augmenting domestic

expansion of facilities. Gold reserves by 1970 exceeded $14 billion, more than those of the United States, plus another $7 billion of dollar balances. The German mark is increasingly viewed in world financial circles as being nearly as sound as the dollar. The darkest cloud has been France's growing reluctance to push forward except on terms especially favorable to her economy, and substantial nontariff barriers remain within the six.

Seven other European nations—Britain, Norway, Sweden, Denmark, Switzerland, Austria, and Portugal—in 1960 formed a parallel organization, the European Free Trade Association (EFTA). These nations for one reason or another had not joined in formation of the Common Market, mainly because they were unwilling to move as far toward economic integration as the Common Market envisioned. Britain faced an especially serious problem because of her long-standing tradition of special preferences on foreign trade to British Commonwealth nations, preferences which would have to be renounced as a condition of membership in the Common Market. EFTA, therefore, stressed elimination of internal tariff barriers among member nations almost as fast as within the Common Market. But there was no provision for a common external tariff or for the increasingly close general economic integration envisaged for the Common Market nations.

Britain has twice applied for admission to the Common Market pact. France both times in essence vetoed the British bid, but negotiations are still in progress. If, in fact, Britain and the other EFTA nations join the Common Market, the result will be a large economic free-trade area indeed, with a population of over 250 million, and a g.n.p. of perhaps two-thirds ours and considerably larger than the USSR's. It will be by far the world's largest importer and exporter. And it could be largely self-sufficient in agriculture, raw materials, and industrial products if it should choose the path of high protection against outside products.

Current U.S. Trade Policy

The success of the Common Market, with the possibility of an even larger European free-trade area and perhaps even a United States of Europe, has confronted American business firms and American trade policy with a new challenge. American export markets inside the Common Market are in serious danger, since our products must pay the common external tariff while competitive products made within the Common Market pay no tariff. Intra–Common Market trade is booming and entire new patterns of trade are developing. Parisian department-store counters are loaded with Italian fashions and shoes, German leather goods and housewares, Dutch clothing and pottery. The same is true in other cities throughout the Common Market. Thanks to reduced tariffs, prices on many basic items are dramatically lower throughout the Common Market area. A revolution of consumer buying habits is under way. The comparison is widely drawn with the mass consumer market that is the foundation of the American economy.

America's first response was the "Kennedy round" negotiations with some forty nations, including the Common Market, for sweeping mutual tariff reductions. In 1967, after arduous, often acrimonious, negotiations, the results were announced. The United States agreed to reduce tariffs an average of 35 percent on over 6,000 items accounting for $8 billion of imports in 1966, and widespread reciprocal reductions were obtained. This represented a sweeping further step toward complete free trade, especially on a wide variety of manufactured products. But on numerous important items, especially farm products, substantial tariff barriers remain between us and the Common Market nations. And frictions over quotas and export subsidies continue, with retaliatory actions by both the United States and Common Market countries.

Over the past decade, U.S. foreign trade has grown from $16 to $40 billion annually. Total world trade has grown even faster, however, and U.S. exports have declined slightly to about 16 percent of the world total. Although U.S. wages are by far the highest in the world, each year we have had an export surplus. Freer trade has served us well.

Review

FOR ANALYSIS
AND DISCUSSION

1. What is the fallacy in the "Petition of the Candlemakers" for protection against the sun? Is the same fallacy present in other arguments for protective tariffs?

2. List the factors that explain the high wages received by American workers in the steel and chemical industries. Which, if any, would be affected, and in which direction, if American tariffs were raised on steel and chemicals?

3. Under the "Kennedy round," U.S. tariffs have been reduced sharply. Using the figures in Chapter 41, which major industries and areas are most likely to be helped and which injured? Should workers and firms presently protected by tariffs receive government subsidies for retaining and compensation for loss of markets when tariffs are reduced?

4. Are there any industries in the United States today that seem to you clearly to deserve tariff protection as "infant industries"?

5. One leading economist has argued: "Removal of tariffs is clearly desirable, but the associated transition effects would be tolerable only in times of prosperity and in the absence of monopolistic restrictions in the more efficient American industries." Can you explain this apparently paradoxical statement?

6. Can you suggest any ways whereby, in a period of depression, the United States could raise its tariffs against foreign goods so as to avoid probable retaliation?

forty-three

International Adjustments and the Balance of Payments

Financing Foreign Transactions
Exchange Rates
International Economic Adjustments
The United States—World Creditor

Domestic and international trade are essentially similar, but in foreign trade two different currencies are involved. This chapter explains first how international transactions are financed, and then how international economic adjustments occur under different international monetary systems.

Financing Foreign Transactions

If you buy woolens from England, the English seller wants British pounds, not American dollars. You need to convert your dollars into pounds if you're going to buy his cloth. What do you do?

There is a continuous demand for this sort of currency conversion, and the big New York banks stand ready to sell you pounds, or almost any other foreign currency, for dollars. If you go to your local bank to buy pounds, it will simply pass the transaction along to a big bank in the foreign-exchange business.

Suppose that you want to pay a Britisher £1,000 in British money for the woolen goods. You go to a bank, say the Chase Manhattan in New York, to buy 1,000 British pounds. The Chase Manhattan is a regular dealer in foreign currencies. It sells you the pounds at the going rate—say £1 for $3. You pay the Chase Manhattan Bank $3,000 and get a special check, made out to the bearer, for £1,000. This special type of check is called "foreign exchange."

Then you send the check over to the British

manufacturer. He takes it to his bank in London and gets his £1,000. His bank presents the check to the Chase Manhattan's London branch for payment, and the transaction is completed (except that we have omitted the small commission charged you by the Chase Manhattan on the deal). You have paid $3,000. The seller has received £1,000.[1]

The rate at which you can buy British pounds with American dollars is called the "exchange rate." When you buy pounds with dollars, you are purchasing foreign exchange. Foreign exchange is merely a claim on some foreign currency, and the rate of exchange is the number of units of one currency it takes to purchase one unit of another currency. If the franc–dollar exchange rate is 5 to 1, for example, then it takes five francs to buy one dollar; the price of one franc is twenty cents.

Like other prices, exchange rates are determined by supply and demand. Suppose American importers need large numbers of pounds to pay British manufacturers. When they try to buy these pounds with dollars, the increased demand will force up the price of pounds, say to $4 for £1. Conversely, when Britishers want to make heavy payments here, they buy dollars. This bids up the price of dollars, and the exchange rate moves toward $2 to £1.

This situation can readily be represented by a simple supply-and-demand diagram, as in Figure 43–1. With the solid supply and demand curves, the price of pounds is $3. If demand increases to D′D′ (when American importers need more pounds to pay for their British woolens), the price of pounds goes up to $4, given the supply of pounds shown. Try for yourself to show the effect of an increased British demand for dollars to pay for movies imported from America.

There are always Americans buying British pounds with dollars, and Britishers buying dollars with pounds. This is what keeps things reasonably well in balance on both sides of the

[1]This example is not an exactly accurate statement of how such a transaction would be executed. However, the actual procedure, though sometimes more complicated, follows the same general principle.

THE FOREIGN EXCHANGE MARKET

PRICE IN DOLLARS

BRITISH POUNDS

fig. 43–1

The supply and demand for British pounds looks just like the supply and demand for a commodity.

Atlantic. The demand for pounds in America comes from American importers, people planning to travel or invest in Great Britain, and people owing other debts in Great Britain. The British demand for dollars comes from comparable British sources. Thus, there might be an exact offset to your payment of £1,000 to the British manufacturer—say, by a $3,000 payment to General Motors in Detroit by a British auto dealer, who bought the dollars at the Chase Manhattan's London branch. In effect, the two payments would be canceled off against each other. Fundamentally, goods would be exchanged for goods (woolens for autos), with the help of the foreign-exchange markets.

Of course, the British auto-parts dealer might not have gone to the Chase Manhattan branch in London, but instead to some other foreign-exchange dealer. This would have caused no difficulty. In both London and New York there are regular foreign-exchange markets, in which foreign-exchange dealers buy and sell foreign currencies. As long as the total demand for pounds in New York equals the total demand for dollars in London, all transactions can be settled without any change in the exchange rate or any shipment of gold. Here again the market place does the complex job more or less automatically.

Exchange Rates

Freely Fluctuating Exchange Rates

Exchange rates are set by the demand for, and supply of, the currencies in question, except where rates are somehow fixed by government decree. In a completely "free" exchange market, exchange rates would fluctuate freely ("float") in response to varying demands for the different currencies. With fluctuating demands for currencies, swings in foreign-exchange rates could be expected, especially since capital movements (for instance, shifts of funds for investment abroad) affect exchange rates as directly as do merchandise exports and imports. As long as supply and demand for the various currencies remained in balance, stable exchange rates would prevail.

Exchange Rates under the Gold Standard

For many years before World War I and again during the 1920s, most important countries were "on the gold standard." During these periods, no direct control was exercised over exchange rates by governments, but through the gold standard exchange fluctuations were held within narrow bounds.

Under the gold standard, each monetary unit "contained" (was convertible into) a fixed number of grains of gold. For example, the prewar dollar was 23.22 grains and the prewar British pound 113 grains of fine gold. Thus, the pound had 4.86 times as much gold as the dollar, a relationship that established a par of exchange between the currencies. And remember, from Chapter 13, that domestically the money supply varied roughly in proportion to changes in each nation's gold stock.

Under these circumstances, suppose there was an increased demand for dollars which sent the price of dollars up so that one pound would buy less than $4.86 (say the exchange rate

moved to 1 to 4.80). Then, instead of buying dollars and getting only $4.80 for £1, Britishers could simply convert their pounds into gold, send the gold to America, and there get $4.86 for the 113 grains of fine gold in each pound. Obviously, therefore, the exchange rate could not vary far from 4.86 to 1 or gold would be shipped instead of foreign exchange being used at all. Actually, shipping costs and interest losses in transit made it unprofitable to ship gold unless the exchange rate varied more than three cents either way from the 4.86 to 1 ratio. Hence, exchange rates could fluctuate within these "gold points" of 4.89 and 4.83, but no farther.

This stability of exchange rates was a great boon to international traders. They always knew just what foreign currencies would cost to make payments abroad and just what price they could get for foreign currencies received. Such stable exchanges may prevail without the gold standard, but as soon as one country is off the gold standard the guarantee of stable rates vanishes.

The International Gold-Reserve Standard

In the Great Depression of the 1930s, every major nation went off the gold standard. Facing massive unemployment, each chose to go its own way, refusing to be bound by international gold flows. Exchange rates fluctuated widely. Country after country imposed controls on capital outflows to conserve its scarce gold. Together with widespread tariff increases designed to stimulate domestic employment, these capital controls increasingly stifled international trade and lending, without, in retrospect, significantly helping any of the nations participating in the economic warfare.

Following World War II, everyone agreed that the folly of the 1930s must not be repeated. International cooperation, beginning with the Bretton Woods Conference of 1944, reintroduced stable exchange rates among the major currencies and gradually reduced restrictions on capital outflows. Finally in 1958, substantially free convertibility of currencies at fixed exchange rates was restored among the major nations of the "free world." Some controls over capital movements still exist, and no major nation has restored the prewar gold standard with its rigid linkage of the domestic money supply and economic conditions to international gold flows. But most major currencies were made freely convertible into gold at fixed prices, and rates of exchange among major free-world countries were fixed by international agreements, based on the dollar as the key currency. Gold was exchanged freely among central banks in settlement of international balances.

In 1968, the leading central banks modified this arrangement by agreeing they would neither buy nor sell gold to private holders or producers. This substantially fixed the amount of monetary gold in the Western world and shut off private speculation in gold vis-à-vis the central banks, but retained free exchange of gold among central banks and fixed exchange rates among those currencies. The move was coupled with important parallel agreements to supplement gold as an international monetary reserve with a new international reserve ("Special Drawing Rights") created cooperatively by international agreement, much as new domestic reserves are created by the Federal Reserve in the United States. These moves are examined more thoroughly in Chapter 44.

This arrangement is commonly called an "international gold-reserve standard." Gold serves as an international reserve for each country, which it can use to meet its international payments. Exchange rates are fixed by international agreement and the various currencies are convertible into gold at fixed prices for official settlements, as under the old gold standard. But nations do not necessarily tie their domestic monetary policies to gold flows, nor do central banks guarantee to buy gold from or sell it to private individuals and businesses.

International Economic Adjustments

International trade and capital flows link together the economies of the world. It is important to understand these linkages in the modern world. For they have a major impact on most economies, and play an important role in the United States, even though foreign trade totals only about 5 percent of our gross national product. Consider first the international adjustment process in a simple case involving only commodity trade, at the start under the gold standard and then under fluctuating exchanges; and finally introduce international capital movements and the entire balance of payments.

Under the Gold Standard

The full gold standard provided a more or less automatic procedure for keeping different countries "in balance" with one another. Suppose the United States begins to buy more goods and services from France without a corresponding increase in exports to France, both countries being on the gold standard. The United States will need an increasing number of francs to pay for its imports, and francs will become increasingly expensive in terms of dollars. But as soon as the dollar–franc rate moves to the gold point, U.S. importers will begin to ship gold rather than francs to pay for their additional imports from France.

What happens when gold moves from America to France? In America there is less gold backing for the money supply; currency and credit are contracted. In the absence of offsetting action, this movement will mean depressed prices, costs, and incomes here. In France, the reverse effect occurs. The new gold provides more bank deposits and more excess reserves. Currency and credit expand, with rising incomes, costs, and prices.

As these effects proceed, it will become harder for U.S. importers to buy from France, and easier for the French to buy here. Frenchmen have larger incomes to spend on U.S. goods, and prices of U.S. goods are falling. Conversely, we have lower incomes to spend on French goods and French prices are rising. This combination gradually shuts off the excess of U.S. imports from France, pulling the exports and imports of the two countries back into balance. When exports and imports are restored to balance, the gold flow ceases and equilibrium has been restored in both American and French balances of payments.

But remember that gold flows tend to bring equilibrium only if they are permitted to affect prices, costs, and incomes in the countries involved. If central banks offset these gold flows their equilibrating effects are negated.

Under Fluctuating ("Floating") Exchanges

How do international adjustments take place when exchange rates are free to fluctuate? Assume the same United States–France situation as before, with American imports overbalancing exports to France. As before, Americans will buy francs to pay for their imports, and will thereby drive up the exchange rate—that is, the cost of francs in terms of dollars. French goods become more expensive to us, and our goods become cheaper to France. French incomes rise because of their increased exports, without any such corresponding increase in America. These circumstances will gradually cut down on U.S. purchases from France, and will increase French purchases from us, until finally exports and imports between the two countries are restored to balance. As under the gold standard, there is an automatic tendency for the payments between the two countries to be brought back into equilibrium.

But the adjustment process is restricted to a smaller segment of each economy in the flexible-exchange case. The rising price of francs effectively raises the price of French exports to us, but it does so without raising French domestic prices generally in terms of dollars, as a gold inflow would have done by expanding the French money supply under the gold standard. Similarly, the falling dollar-exchange rate effectively lowers the price of U.S. exports to French buyers, but it does so without imposing deflationary pressure on the whole U.S. economy, as a gold outflow from the United States would have done.

All this makes a floating exchange standard sound very attractive. But it has one very important drawback. International traders and investors would have to live in a world of uncertainty about the rates at which they convert their foreign receipts into domestic currency. Would you invest abroad with no assurance of what your foreign dividends would buy in terms of U.S. dollars? More on this dilemma in Chapter 44.

Under the International Gold-Reserve Standard

How do adjustments to eliminate disequilibrium occur under the international gold-reserve standard, which now prevails? The answer is not simple, and we shall mainly postpone it until Chapter 44 that deals with modern balance-of-payments problems. But the central points can be outlined here.

Suppose the same U.S.–French case, with U.S. imports exceeding exports. The deficit in the U.S. balance of payments will again lead to gold being transferred to France. But now the United States need not accept a deflationary contraction of her money supply, nor France an inflationary expansion of hers unless each country feels this would fit in with its domestic stabilization goals. Each nation attempts to balance its international and domestic goals.

A big country like the United States, where gold reserves are large and international trade is a small part of g.n.p., can afford to give dominant weight to domestic goals for a long time in the face of a balance-of-payments deficit and gold outflows. Smaller countries that depend heavily on foreign trade have little option; their prices and costs must be closely in line with balance-of-payments needs or they will exhaust their limited international gold reserves and be unable to pay their bills. But either way the international adjustment process is less direct and predictable than under either the gold standard or fluctuating exchange rates. The pressures for international adjustment build up on any country that continually runs a balance-of-payments deficit, and the nation may eventually run out of reserves to pay its international bills. But it is vital to recognize that any nation may postpone adjustment to international pressures as long as its reserves hold out, in order to pursue its own domestic policies.

Capital Movements and International Adjustments

Now introduce capital movements into the picture. U.S. investment abroad involves foreign payments, just as when we buy goods abroad. If Westinghouse decides to build a plant in Holland, for example, it must have the Dutch guilders to pay its bills there. It uses dollars to buy guilders. If an individual American buys Royal Dutch Shell stock on the Dutch stock exchange, the same is true. And the effect is similar if the American government provides foreign aid to our allies or to less-developed countries (unless we give them goods outright). Our foreign aid provides them dollars, just as they would get dollars if they sold goods to us.

A look back at Tables 41–4 and 41–5 will show the importance of capital movements and foreign aid in the total balance of payments. Although in 1969 we had a $1.9 billion surplus of exports over imports (which means net payments due us), our net private investments abroad totaled $6.6 billion and U.S. government foreign aid totaled $3.8 billion. Thus, these capital transfers more than offset our export surplus, and, with 'errors and omissions" which were probably unrecorded capital exports, we were left with a huge $7.2 billion "deficit" in our basic "liquidity" balance of payments. Other years have been different in detail, but the general picture has been the same. Exports and imports are by far the biggest parts of our total balance of payments, but capital movements also reach into the billions annually and have recently more than offset our surplus on goods and services.

Do the same adjustment mechanisms outlined above still work? The answer is "yes," but with complications. Take the 1960s. We have exported over $40 billion more goods and services than we imported. But our capital exports and government grants were so large, that we nevertheless have had a big payments deficit. Under gold-standard rules, we should have lost gold and put deflationary pressure on our economy, restricting imports and encouraging exports so as to bring the balance of payments back toward equilibrium. And gold did flow out. But note that the U.S. problem was not to bring imports and exports back into balance. Rather, it was to get exports up even farther ahead of imports, to provide a payments surplus there big enough to cover the large payments deficit

on capital account. The pressure of the gold outflow pushed us in the right direction—to get exports up relative to imports.

But we had over 5 percent unemployment until mid-1965, and we were unwilling to accept a decline in U.S. incomes, prices, and costs in order to cut our imports. Letting an international-payments deficit generate a recession to close the deficit, when the economy already had unemployed men and factories, seemed like killing the patient to cure him. Moreover, it wasn't even clear that the medicine would work if used, since capital movements were such a big cause of the difficulty. After 1965 with substantially full employment and growing inflation, both domestic and international pressures called for tighter money.

The 1960s illustrate two basic points. First, we must always look at the entire balance of payments, not merely at the balance of trade, to understand what is going on. Second, few nations are now willing to let balance-of-payments adjustments automatically dictate the level of their domestic economies, especially when capital movements are the main disequilibrating force.

Reserves, Exchange Rates, and the Adjustment Process

Under all fixed-exchange-rate systems, including the one now in use, the participating central banks or governments agree to keep the values of their own currencies fixed in relationship to gold or to some key currency. Under the present system, established at Bretton Woods in 1945, the U.S. agrees to keep the dollar pegged to gold at $35 per ounce, and the other countries agree to keep their currencies pegged to the dollar at stable rates.

Day-to-day transactions in exchange markets (reflecting payments for goods and services, capital transfers, and the like) push the prices of different currencies up and down vis-à-vis one another. It is the job of each central bank to intervene if the price of its currency deviates very far from parity. This it does by buying or selling its own currency or other currencies it holds as part of its international reserves.

For example, suppose there is a heavy demand for dollars by pound-holders in London, and the price of pounds vis-à-vis dollars falls below its parity of $2.40, say to $2.38. Then the Bank of England would "protect" the pound by buying pounds with dollars it holds as part of its international reserves. Conversely, if the pound were to rise above parity in the open market the Bank of England would sell pounds, accumulating dollars or some other foreign currency.

In order to protect its currency, each central bank must have a big enough international reserve in gold or other currencies to be able to buy its own currency and maintain its price at parity if need be. (As a practical matter, most central banks hold the bulk of their reserves in gold, S.D.R.'s, and dollars, since these are all readily convertible into any other other currency that might be needed.) If a nation's balance of payments is near equilibrium, normally market forces will keep its currency near parity; private purchases and sales will roughly balance off. But if its balance of payments is in persistent deficit, a nation's currency will normally "weaken"—that is, its price will tend to fall. Thus, its central bank will need substantial reserves to keep the currency at parity. If a nation runs out of reserves, it can no longer keep its currency at par, and must either borrow reserves temporarily or "devalue" (that is, let the price of its currency fall).

Clearly, nations with large international reserves can tolerate substantial balance of payments deficits merely by drawing on their reserves. Nations with low reserves, like individuals and businesses with small bank accounts, feel themselves in precarious, exposed positions. Understandably, every nation tries to maintain a reasonable supply of international reserves.

The United States—World Creditor

Growing nations tend to pass through four stages of economic development. Each produces a different payments position for temporary balance-of-payments equilibrium.

1. *Early Borrower.* A less-developed country often borrows heavily abroad to obtain the capital goods it needs to develop its natural resources. For example, until about 1873 the United States apparently was a substantial capital importer from Europe. Imports of supplies, machinery, and consumption goods exceeded exports. In this stage, the trade balance must be "unfavorable" (imports must exceed exports) if the needed goods and supplies are to be obtained, and this "unfavorable" balance is covered by borrowing.

2. *Mature Debtor.* After about 1873, debt repayment by the United States began to exceed new borrowing, though we were still a heavy debtor. In this stage, exports tend to exceed imports—the trade balance is "favorable." Our net export balance transferred the real goods to other nations as we paid off our debts. As in stage 1, money transfers are only the first step. It is the real transfer of goods and services that counts.

3. *Early Creditor.* Stage 3 is entered when the nation shifts over to a net creditor basis—when total investments abroad exceed foreign investments here. World War I and the 1920s thrust the United States abruptly into this stage, as we made heavy loans to our European allies. Government and private lending during and after World War II repeated the World War I experience with billions upon billions of dollars. Today, the United States is the one great creditor nation of the world. In this stage, a continued export surplus is to be expected. This surplus transfers abroad in real form the loans we make as we increase our creditor position.

4. *Mature Creditor.* In stage 4, the creditor nation's outstanding loans are so great that current income on foreign investments more than offsets the net new loans being made abroad. In this stage, the trade balance must shift to an import surplus in order to transfer to the mature creditor nation the excess of its current return on investment over new loans being made abroad. England was a mature creditor early in this century; we are moving toward that condition.

As a nation passes through these four stages, a changing trade balance is normal and essential. Whether a "favorable" balance of trade is in fact favorable depends basically on how well it fits in with the country's overall balance-of-payments position. Severe disequilibrium will result if the trade balance is maintained (by tariffs or other controls) in a position unsympathetic to general balance-of-payments equilibrium requirements.

We, like other nations, must keep our balance of payments roughly in equilibrium over extended periods, though, as during the decades following World War II, it may show a substantial deficit for years if we have accumulated large reserves of gold and other currencies. Today, already the world's great creditor nation,

we continue to invest huge sums abroad under the private profit incentive, and to provide billions annually in governmental foreign aid. Under these circumstances, we are still in stage 3, and one basic fact is sure: Unless we continue our heavy capital transfers abroad, we cannot hope to maintain our present huge export surplus of goods and services. Or the matter can be put the other way round: Unless we have a huge export surplus, we cannot continue to send so much capital abroad without facing a continuing payments deficit and likely depletion of our gold reserves.

What shall we do about it? That is the subject of Chapter 44.

Review

CONCEPTS TO REMEMBER

This chapter adds a few more important concepts to the list at the end of Chapter 41

exchange rate
flexible ("floating") exchange rates
international gold reserve standard

foreign exchange
gold points
controlled exchange rates
balance-of-payments equilibrium

FOR ANALYSIS AND DISCUSSION

1. Explain how balance-of-payments disequilibrium tended to be eliminated under the gold standard, with fixed exchange rates. How would disequilibrium be eliminated in a system of flexible exchange rates?
2. Using Figure 42-1, trace through the effects of the following, beginning from the equilibrium shown by DD and SS:
   a. General Motors decides to buy a British automobile plant to get production facilities there.
   b. British students come to study in America.
   c. British citizens decide to buy General Electric stock in America at the same time as American imports from England decline.
3. Suppose that you and many others decide to travel to France next summer. Trace through carefully the effect your trip might have on dollar–franc rates, gold flows, and prices in each country under:
   a. An international gold standard.
   b. A flexible exchange-rate system.

4. Domestically, free-price movements serve to equilibrate supply and demand in the markets concerned. Since foreign exchange rates are substantially frozen under the gold standard, how can the gold standard be said to be an international equilibrating system?

5. "Short-term capital movements (hot money) seeking protection from monetary and political uncertainty first in one country and then in another were the real cause of the downfall of the gold standard. No country could afford to let its monetary system be subjected to such unpredictable, violent shocks." Does this argument, based on the 1930s, apply to the United States today? Explain.

forty-four

Gold and Current Balance-of-Payments Problems

In recent years, gold losses and the deficit in our balance of payments have been front-page news. Are the predictions of impending disaster overdone? How worried, if at all, should we be? Above all, what should we do about it?

One of the first things to recognize is that economic problems change rapidly. Two decades ago, the big international problem was the "dollar shortage" and too much of the world's gold accumulated in the United States. As this is written, it is the U.S. payments deficit and our gold losses. By the time you read this, the problem may have changed again. A brief look at history, therefore, is a useful background for understanding the problems we face today.

The Downfall of the Gold Standard

Before 1914, the international gold standard ruled the international monetary scene. It was, in theory and to a substantial degree in practice, an "automatic" system. A balance-of-payments deficit would lead to a gold outflow, which in turn would usually reduce the nation's money stock and lower its costs, prices, and incomes, thereby cutting imports and stimulating exports so as to restore equilibrium in its balance of payments. Central banks "managed" the money supply to a limited extent, but gold was the center of a "religion" of money. It was accepted by most economists and the public alike as an ultimate repository of value. In the rapidly expanding, reasonably flexible pre-1914 world, this gold standard supplied an important element of international-exchange stability, and the requisite domestic price and income adjustments were generally accomplished without excessively painful consequences.

The monetary disruptions of World War I were extreme. Wild inflations occurred in several European nations, serious inflation in all. Reestablishment of the international gold standard in the 1920s was thus fraught with difficulties. What should the reestablished gold values, or "contents," of the various national currencies be, in light of the preceding inflations? In other words, what should exchange rates be? In Britain, the financial center of the prewar world, the pound was finally put back "on gold" in 1925 at the prewar gold content, and the prewar dollar–pound exchange rate of $4.86 = 1 was restored. In other countries, new gold contents were prescribed for currencies in an endeavor to place these currencies in "equilibrium" balance-of-payments positions vis-à-vis the rest of the world. The Western world went back "on gold."

But the depression of the 1930s dealt the deathblow to the prewar gold standard. Losing gold in a period of growing unemployment meant even further deflationary contraction of national money supplies. First England in 1931, then most other major nations, decided this price was too high to pay. They "went off gold," devaluing their currencies relative to gold and to other currencies in order to avoid the domestic deflation implicit in adherence to the gold standard, and to encourage foreign purchases of their domestic products. The American dollar was devalued in 1934 to 59 percent of its earlier gold content. Eventually every major currency was devalued, exchange and capital movement controls were established, and domestic currencies were cut loose from gold flows.

In retrospect, three major factors led to the downfall of the gold standard:

1. The Great Depression of the 1930s, with massive unemployment, made the domestic price of gold-standard orthodoxy too high to pay.

2. Downward cost–price rigidities served to aggravate the impact of price and income deflation, and to thwart the equilibrating forces previously at work under the gold-standard system. Unions, industrial monopolies, agricultural groups—all contributed to holding up prices when incomes fell in the depression.

3. With waning faith in the gold-standard religion, and with growing political instability, capital flights to "safer" countries became common. Huge "hot-money" drains were more than any nation could stand. The religion of gold worked admirably so long as no infidels entered the temple to whisper misgivings. Once doubt spread, however, capital flights never envisaged in a stable, well-behaved international system spelled doom to the gold standard in a rigid, depression-conscious world.

Exchange Depreciation and Exchange Controls

Widespread desertion of the gold standard and currency devaluations failed to bring the results expected. One country acting alone could expand its exports by depreciation. But when everyone's currency was depreciated, the actions offset one another and this resulted in fewer, not more, exports.

In retrospect, thus, the main result of the competitive depreciation race of the 1930s was disruption of international trade and investment, widespread friction and ill will, and no very important gains to any of the competitors. As with tariff increases, exchange depreciation was a "beggar-my-neighbor" attempt to shift unemployment to other nations. And it was doomed to defeat by the virtual certainty of retaliation.

As exchange depreciation failed to eliminate the unemployment that plagued the Western world, crosscurrents of conflict and cooperation were everywhere apparent in international economic relations. New types of exchange controls proliferated. Nations set their exchange rates at varying levels, searching for the one to maximize their gain from foreign trade. Many countries, especially Nazi Germany, "blocked" the use of foreign exchange received from their foreign sales, and rationed the foreign exchange received to control its expenditure. Every major nation introduced controls over capital exports.

The International Monetary Fund

To the nations mapping peacetime reconstruction at the end of World War II, the international monetary disruption and conflict of the 1930s were bitter memories. There was little sentiment for restoring the old gold standard. But there was widespread agreement on the need for reasonable exchange stability and for reduced restrictions on international trade and capital movements.

In 1945, some forty nations established the International Monetary Fund to help attain these goals; the total membership is now over 100.[1] The fund consists of about $30 billion of gold and member-country currencies made available for stabilization activities in accordance with the fund's charter. Each country's contribution was based on its national income; the United States put up about one-third of the total. As world trade has grown, the size of the fund has been increased three times. Voting control over the fund is roughly in proportion to contributions to its capital.

The officially stated purposes of the fund are:

1. To promote international monetary cooperation through a permanent institution that provides the machinery for consultation and collaboration on international monetary problems.

2. To facilitate the expansion of international trade and thereby to promote and maintain high levels of employment and real income.

3. To promote exchange stability, to maintain orderly exchange arrangements among members, and to avoid competitive exchange depreciation.

[1]After participating in the planning, the Soviet-bloc countries did not join.

4. To assist in the establishment of a multilateral system of payments on current transactions and in the elimination of exchange restrictions.

5. To provide temporary loans to members so they will have more opportunity to correct payments maladjustments gradually, without resorting to measures destructive of national and international prosperity.

6. In accordance with the above, to shorten the duration and lessen the degree of disequilibrium in the international balances of payments of members.

Organization and Operations

The primary operating purpose of the fund is to help member nations maintain exchange-rate stability, coupled with reasonable flexibility to make any long-run adjustments required. In this respect, the philosophy of the fund differs substantially from that of the old gold standard, whose keynote was exchange stability at all costs.

The fund is intended to help member countries meet temporary exchange deficits only— to give them time to correct balance-of-payments maladjustments without being forced to adopt depressive measures under exceptional strains. The fund can thus lend foreign currencies to a country that is caught temporarily short of exchange. Whereas previously the only likely alternative would have been devaluation or imposition of exchange controls, with the fund's assistance such controls may be avoided. The fund stands ready to lend to any member country up to one-fourth of its quota in any year, if the proposed use of the exchange is in keeping with the fund's stated objectives.

If any country faces a lasting disequilibrium in its balance of payments, more fundamental steps are called for. Here the fund tries to play a different role. First, member countries agree that they will consult through the fund on all major international monetary problems, and that each will continuously submit to the fund's expert staff full information on its own international monetary position. Second, any country may, if it finds its balance of payments in fundamental disequilibrium, devalue its currency by as much as 10 percent on notification, but without official permission, of the fund. But any greater devaluation must be approved by the fund, which will judge on the basis of the need for such a step to restore equilibrium. This is the second aspect of the basic philosophy underlying the fund—exchange stability, but with flexibility where required to correct fundamental disequilibrium.

The fund does not prohibit member-country controls over capital movements. Most participants agreed that hot-money movements may be too disruptive to tolerate, and retained their freedom to control them individually.

The Fund in the Postwar World

On the experience thus far, the fund appears to be a significant step toward international monetary collaboration and stabilization after the disastrous decade of the 1930s. But it can work satisfactorily only in a relatively stable world, where cases of "fundamental disequilibrium" are rare. Indeed, member countries (for example, France in the 1950's) have already defied the fund's regulations, devaluing their own currencies when they thought it essential, without the fund's approval. But the fund has repeatedly helped to tide member countries over temporary balance-of-payments pressures that otherwise might have generated major international financial crises or disruptive domestic deflations.[2]

Special Drawing Rights

During the 1960s, the need for some collective means to increase international monetary reserves became increasingly clear. Newly mined gold became available erratically, and reliance on the U.S. balance-of-payments deficit was an obviously unsatisfactory way of obtaining reserves for other countries, as will be explained presently. Thus, in 1968, the leading free-world nations agreed to give the I.M.F. power to create "Special Drawing Rights"—in essence, new international reserves (official-settlements money) created outright, much as new money might be printed. Member countries can then draw their shares of these new reserves as needed. New "S.D.R.'s" can be created only by an 85 percent vote of the fund's shareholders, which gives both the United States and the Common Market countries (if they vote together) a veto over new issues. Countries' quotas correspond roughly to the general fund borrowing quotas (the United States' is about 25 percent of the total). But S.D.R.'s, unlike regular loans, need not be repaid to the fund. About $3 billion of S.D.R.'s were issued in 1970, with the expectation that more would be approved as needed, probably annually.

U.S. Foreign Lending

A major development of the postwar financial world has been the massive growth of U.S. lending abroad. Our large recent payments deficits have been attributable mainly to our heavy private foreign investments and to government loans and foreign-aid programs, since we have continually had an export surplus on trade and services. At the same time, U.S. investors have acquired ownership of a huge volume of assets abroad—factories, oil refineries, assem-

---

[2]Parallel to the International Monetary Fund, the same forty countries also established the $8 billion International Bank for Reconstruction and Development. It was set up to facilitate foreign lending for postwar reconstruction and for development of less-developed areas. The organization and management of the bank closely parallel those of the fund. The bank's operating head is from this country, in recognition of the United States' large contribution to the bank's capital and the dominant demand for dollar loans. There are now seventy member nations, and total capital is about $20 billion. In 1969, new loans to the less-developed economies totaled $1.3 billion.

Although the IBRD may lend out its own capital, it oper-

ates primarily through two other channels—attaching its guarantee to private loans, and borrowing funds in the various member countries to finance its loans. For example, if Peru wants a loan to develop its industries and plans to spend most of the loan in the United States, the bank will either try to arrange a direct loan for Peru from American lenders, attaching its own guarantee to the loan, or it will float a bond issue in the American market to obtain funds for the Peruvian loan. In either case, the U.S. representative on the bank's board would have to approve, since every loan must be approved by the major country in which the loan is to be raised and spent, as well as by the bank's officers.

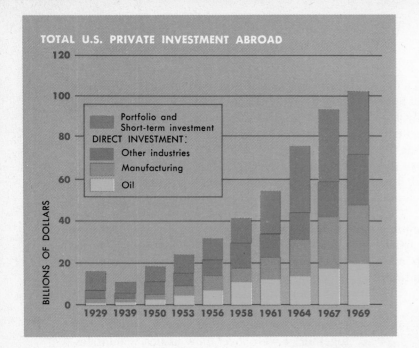

TOTAL U.S. PRIVATE INVESTMENT ABROAD

BILLIONS OF DOLLARS

Portfolio and
Short-term investment
DIRECT INVESTMENT:
Other industries
Manufacturing
Oil

1929 1939 1950 1953 1956 1958 1961 1964 1967 1969

fig. 44–1

Since the 1930s, U.S. private investment abroad has soared. Oil is the biggest single industry, but investments
have been widely diversified. (Source:
U.S. Department of Commerce.)

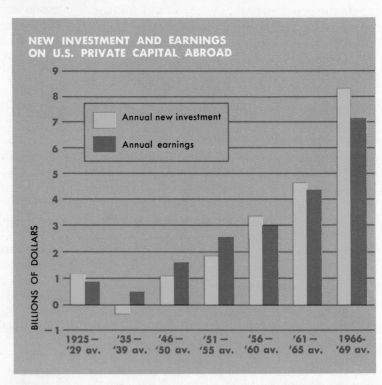

**NEW INVESTMENT AND EARNINGS
ON U.S. PRIVATE CAPITAL ABROAD**

Annual new investment
Annual earnings

BILLIONS OF DOLLARS

1925 – '35 – '46 – '51 – '56 – '61 – 1966-
'29 av. '39 av. '50 av. '55 av. '60 av. '65 av. '69 av.

fig. 44–2

Annual new U.S. private investment
abroad has grown rapidly, but returns
on such investments abroad have
grown about as fast. (Source: U.S. Department of Commerce.)

bly plants. Thus, it is important to look carefully
at international capital movements if we are to
understand recent international economic
events.

U.S. private investment abroad has bur-
geoned since World War II. Figure 44–1 shows
the data for selected years since 1929. The
three lower areas in each bar are direct Ameri-

can investments. The blue area at the top is
investment in securities, including short-term
investments. Even allowing for inflation, the
rise since World War II has been phenomenal.

Figure 44–2 shows the picture in terms of
annual new U.S. investment abroad and annual
earnings on total American foreign investments.
The earnings bars show that our earnings each

year on investments abroad equal our new investments abroad. Foreign investments are profitable business. As with domestic firms, a big part of new U.S. investment abroad each year consists of plowing back earnings on the investments already there. In recent years, this reinvestment has been about three-fourths of total new investment, and new funds from the United States only about one-fourth. About three-fourths of U.S. private investment since World War II has been in the developed nations (mainly Canada and Western Europe), about one-fourth in the less-developed economies.

Figure 44–2 also suggests a central fact about foreign lending. To collect earnings and amortization on loans and investments abroad, we must either accept payment through importing goods and services or be prepared continually to reinvest the principal and earnings abroad. (Remember the early and mature creditor positions from Chapter 41.) Government and private lending abroad has been a major factor in permitting us to continue our traditional export surplus of goods and services. If we ever stop our annual net lending abroad, we will be able to collect our earnings and repayments on principal only by running a net import surplus of goods and services.

The International Gold-and-Dollar Reserve Standard

What kind of international monetary system has evolved out of these circumstances, and what is the role of the dollar in it? To answer, we need to review one more piece of history, the period since World War II, with particular focus on the dollar and the U.S. balance of payments.

The Post–World War II "Dollar Shortage"

Western Europe, Russia, and Japan emerged from World War II tired, devastated, with their foreign assets depleted, and heavily in debt. The United States emerged powerful, prosperous, unbombed, and a massive international creditor. Our real g.n.p. more than doubled under the pressures of war from the depression of the late 1930s, so that we not only provided a large portion of the war materiel for our allies but simultaneously substantially raised the American standard of living in terms of consumer goods between 1940 and 1946. Until our allies used up their ability to pay, we sold war materiel and civilian supplies to them, and later provided many of them on loans and "lend-lease," rather than as gifts or our contributions to the common war.

Thus, in 1946 the reconstruction needs of Europe, Russia, and Japan were enormous. The unscathed American economy offered vast productive power to meet these needs. But foreign nations, faced with the job of rebuilding their war-torn factories and feeding their people, had little to offer in exchange for our goods. Their gold and dollar reserves had been exhausted by the war, and they were already heavily in debt to us.

The resulting "dollar shortage" dominated the international scene. No nation seemed to have enough dollars to pay for the goods and services it needed from America. The Marshall Plan, under which we extended billions in reconstruction aid to allied nations, was our major answer to helping foreign nations rebuild and to alleviating this dollar shortage. Our exports of goods and services soared, financed partly by growing imports, partly by U.S. government aid, and partly by growing U.S. private investments in the rebuilding nations.

With our aid and their own effective work, Europe, Japan, and the USSR recovered at an almost miraculous rate. Factories were rebuilt, employment was restored, prosperity was everywhere, and their economic growth rate soared to more than twice our own. With growing prosperity and profits, Europe and Japan increasingly drew American private capital for investment, and large-scale government aid continued. After about 1950, the U.S. balance of payments showed a persistent deficit. Exports of goods and services continually exceeded imports, but our private capital investment abroad plus our government aid exceeded even the growing export surpluses.

Thus, each year foreign nations received more payments from the United States than they made to us. With the option of taking gold or accumulating dollar balances, they mainly chose dollars through the 1950s. The dollar was better than gold. It could be freely exchanged for gold at $35 an ounce; one could earn interest on dollar balances held in New York banks or invested in short-term U.S. securities; much of what nations wanted to buy was available in the United States and dollars were needed to pay; and throughout the world dollars were as acceptable as gold.

Figure 44–3 shows the steady accumulation of short-term dollar balances by foreign nations after 1950 and the decline in the U.S. gold stock as foreign nations took some payments in gold.

The U.S. Payments Deficit and the Dollar Glut

By the middle 1950s, the rehabilitation of Europe and Japan was substantially complete, and their economies were booming. The U.S. balance-of-payments deficit rose rapidly in the late 1950s to over $3 billion per year. Foreign nations, with their own international-reserve

fig. 44–3

Since 1950, foreign nations have steadily built up their holdings of U.S. dollars and short-term claims on dollars, but since the late 1950s have taken part of their dollar claims in gold. Do we have enough gold? (Source: Federal Reserve Board.)

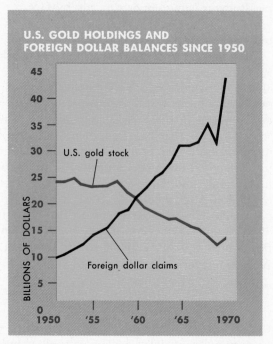

U.S. GOLD HOLDINGS AND FOREIGN DOLLAR BALANCES SINCE 1950

BILLIONS OF DOLLARS

U.S. gold stock

Foreign dollar claims

1950 '55 '60 '65 1970

balances substantially rebuilt, continued to hold growing amounts of short-term balances in New York, but they also began to take increasing amounts of gold. Although the United States was still carrying the major burden of defense spending for the free world and of providing economic aid to the less-developed nations, increasing concern was voiced abroad over our continuing large payments deficit. International bankers and conservatives at home warned direly of dangers to the dollar and that we must "put our house in order" if we were to maintain confidence in the dollar and avoid a crisis in our international situation. Specifically, they urged tighter money and fiscal restraint in spite of the slack U.S. economy.

In 1960, widespread speculation that the dollar might be devalued caused a sharp run on our gold stock through withdrawal of short-term dollar balances. Since 1957, our gold holdings have declined from $23 to $11 billion, and short-term foreign dollar balances held in the United States have risen to $43 billion. Central banks abroad (with $14 billion in 1970) considered these dollars part of their international reserves, substantially as good as gold and convertible into gold on demand. But increasingly during the 1960s, foreign central banks and private holders had all the dollars they wanted, and more! There was, the critics said, a dollar glut. The United States found itself precariously exposed to a run on gold from unwilling dollar holders.

The International Gold-and-Dollar-Reserve Standard

The international monetary system that evolved is sometimes called the "international gold-and-dollar-reserve standard." Most nations of the Western world held both gold and dollars as their basic international reserves, with the two freely convertible into one another. The total international reserves for the world were thus supplied by gold and by short-term dollars balances, the latter produced, in effect, by U.S. international payments deficits. The very U.S. international deficits which were so often criticized were thus the source of about one-third of the Western world's entire basic

international monetary reserves since World War II. By 1968, total free-world monetary gold-holdings were about $43 billion, and total U.S. short-term dollar liabilities to foreign central banks and international monetary organizations were about $16 billion.

The United States thus, without conscious planning, became the banker to the free world. The dollar became the "key," or "reserve," currency of that world. It was critical to this arrangement that dollars be freely convertible into gold by official holders, even though in some nations (for example, the United States) gold was not available domestically in exchange for currency. In many nations—for example, France and Switzerland—any large holder who had dollars could convert them into gold—by first converting the dollars into (say) francs at the fixed exchange rate and then buying gold with his francs. This would in turn, reduce the Bank of France's gold stock and build up its supply of dollars, so that the Bank of France was likely to exchange some of its increased dollars for gold from the United States. Thus, in essence, under the gold-dollar reserve system of the 1960s, foreign dollar holders could demand gold in exchange on short notice. Figure 44–3 shows how far our short-term dollar liabilities exceeded our gold holdings.

The Two-Tier Gold System and S.D.R.'s

In 1968, two major modifications to the international gold-and-dollar reserve standard were agreed on by the major Western nations. First, S.D.R.'s were adopted to provide for rational, managed growth in international reserves, supplanting newly mined gold and dollar deficits as the main sources of expansion in international liquidity, as was noted above. Second, repeated speculative runs on the dollar (conversions of dollar balances into gold) emphasized the basic instability of the prevailing system, and the leading nations agreed to stop buying and selling gold vis-à-vis private holders and miners. This meant that private speculators could no longer count on getting gold for their dollars or other major currencies, but gold was continued as an official international reserve, freely ex-

changed by the major central banks to settle international balances at the established price of $35 per ounce. The amount of official monetary gold was thus substantially fixed at the amount held by the central banks, with additions to reserves to be provided by S.D.R.'s.

This was called a "two-tier" gold system, because gold held by the central banks was fixed at $35 per ounce, while all other gold became, in effect, just another commodity, to bring whatever price market supply and demand might set. Gold speculators, who had accumulated large gold holdings, complained bitterly. So did South Africa, which mines most of the world's gold and had long happily counted on a guaranteed price support of $35 per ounce, without a ceiling if private holders would pay more. But thus far the leading central banks have stood firm, and increasingly it appears that gold has moved a long step toward reduced status as a monetary metal, much as silver did several decades ago. Central banks and the fund, however, hold $43 billion of gold and there is little likelihood that it will vanish from the monetary scene in the near future. Indeed, some observers predict a breakdown of the two-tier plan and a return to pre-1960 arrangements, arguing that different prices for the same commodity cannot coexist for long.

Gold and the U.S. Payments Problem

Where does this leave the United States? We still have about $12 billion of gold (1970), and foreigners hold over $40 billion of dollar balances. While our gold is no longer exposed to the raids of private speculators, we are still committed to provide gold at $35 an ounce for all dollars presented by other leading central banks. It is unlikely that any of these will want to create a crisis by drawing U.S. gold reserves to critically low levels. But if, say, the German central bank accumulates a huge volume of dollars because German nationals convert large dollar balances into German marks, will the German authorities be willing to hold ever larger dollar balances? Clearly, the whole plan puts pressure on the United States to eliminate our balance-of-payments deficit so as to avoid the piling-up of still more dollars in foreign hands.

But don't jump to the conclusion that we're internationally bankrupt and the dollar of dubious value. Far from it! The dollar is backed fundamentally by the powerful U.S. economy, by far the most efficient and productive in the world. And our total foreign assets, once we add in our vast long-term investments overseas, far exceed our total liabilities, as is shown by Table 44–1.

The United States is in much the position of any other banker. Though our basic position is excellent, our short-term liabilities substantially exceed our reserves and other short-term assets. Widespread confidence makes such systems work well. But we are a banker without deposit insurance. Internationally there is no FDIC to insure deposits or Federal Reserve to assure liquidity to temporarily frozen assets in case a confidence crisis develops. More on this dilemma in the following sections.

The Persistent U.S. Payments Deficit

Why has the United States had a persistent, large balance-of-payments deficit for two decades? There is no one simple answer; on the contrary, there have been many important forces at work. A brief summary might look like this.

1. *U.S. Foreign Aid and Government Loans.* Since World War II, we have provided government direct aid and loans totaling $100 billion to the rest of the world. This aid has had military, economic, and humanitarian goals, widely approved by the American people. But the net result has been a vast outflow of dollars.

2. *U.S. Inflation.* Since World War II, U.S. inflation has pushed up prices and costs here but other countries have had inflations as well. U.S. inflation was rather rapid during the early 1950s and slowed down from 1955 to 1965. Since then, it has once again picked up steam. In total, inflation in the United States since 1950 has been somewhat less severe than in

table 44-1

Total Foreign Assets and Liabilities of the United States, January 1, 1967*

	In Billions	
Assets:		
Gold	$ 12	
U.S. short-term private investments abroad	14	
U.S. long-term private investments abroad	100	
U.S. government claims abroad	32	
Total assets abroad plus gold		$158
Liabilities:		
Short-term balances of central banks and international organizations	14	
Short-term private balances	28	
Long-term foreign investments here	44	
Total liabilities to foreigners		86
Excess of assets over liabilities		$72

* Preliminary data, from Department of Commerce and Federal Reserve Board.

most European countries and far less severe than in Japan. However, over the same period the rise in labor productivity in the United States has been slower than in most competing nations, and noticeably slower than in Japan. Thus, our overall international competitive position, price- and costwise, has deteriorated to some degree over the past two decades. But remember that we have had a substantial trade surplus nearly every year.

3. *U.S. Private Investment Abroad.* In recent years, the largest single element contributing to our payments deficit has been an enormous outflow of private capital seeking profitable investment in Western Europe, the Americas, and Japan. These private investments obviously seemed economically sound to the investors, else they would not have been made. And in the long run they produce a large countervailing flow of interest and dividends. But in the short run, their net effect is to increase the size of the U.S. payments deficit.

4. *Slower Productivity Growth Here Than Abroad.* Since World War II, productivity has grown at a spectacular rate in Japan, and rap-

idly in Western Europe and (apparently) the USSR. Our production technology is still ahead of theirs. But starting from a postwar low their heavy new investment and rapid technological advance has lessened this gap, even though U.S. productivity has continued to grow at somewhat above its long-run rate. During the 1950s the higher rate of productivity growth abroad was a fundamental cause of our persistent payments deficit. But recently our productivity growth rate has speeded up while those in Western Europe and the USSR have slowed down somewhat. If this continues, our export surplus should widen again as American productivity resumes its long-run leadership position—though note that it is the combination of wage increases and productivity that determines our competitive position in world markets.

5. *Lack of Confidence in the U.S. Economy and the Dollar.* Foreign capital will not be invested in the United States, either at long or short term, if foreigners do not have confidence in the American economy and the stability of the dollar. Over the postwar period as a whole, both the dollar and the American economy have been widely agreed to be the soundest in the world. But as our efforts to reduce our payments deficit fell short in the 1960s, criticism was widespread. After 1968, the criticism receded, but it could easily rise again. Whatever the talk, foreigners continue to hold large volumes of dollars, and to invest large sums here. And they are anxious to borrow American dollars.

6. *An Overvalued Dollar.* Looking at all these factors and at the continuing U.S. payments deficit, some economists argue that the U.S. dollar is "overvalued." That is, the present exchange rates between the dollar and other major currencies make it too hard for foreigners to buy American products and too easy for us to buy foreign products and to obtain foreign currencies for investment abroad. This reasoning suggests that we could eliminate the balance-of-payments deficit by devaluing the dollar relative to other currencies and to gold. But other economists point to our continuing export surplus and agrue that the present exchange rates

are not the basic problem; rather the basic difficulty consists of the underlying "real" factors above, especially capital flows, which bulk large in U.S. payments difficulties.

There is another difficulty—it's far from clear that the United States could devalue the dollar relative to other currencies even if we wanted to. We could devalue relative to gold—that is, raise the price we will pay for gold (though, as is explained below, there would be major disadvantages to doing so). But this would change our competitive position internationally only if other nations did not correspondingly change their currencies' gold prices. Or we could announce a devaluation of the dollar vis-à-vis (say) the mark and the pound. But it takes two to devalue. Unless the Germans and the British were willing to see their currencies rise in value relative to the dollar (an unlikely event, since that would worsen their international competitive positions), they could simply announce offsetting devaluations of the mark and the pound against the dollar. Little countries can often get away with devaluing against major currencies. But major countries upset the whole international competitive scene if they devalue, and they can avoid retaliation only if other nations agree that the devaluation is in their mutual interests.

Conflict and Compromise between Foreign and Domestic Goals

Domestically, we want a high-employment, stably growing economy. Internationally, we want to preserve the stability of the dollar as a foundation of a stable international payments system. Often these domestic and international goals are consistent, and the policy prescription is clear. If we have an inflationary boom, which leads to a growing import surplus and international payments deficit, we should use tight money and fiscal policy to solve both problems simultaneously. This was the U.S. situation during the late 1960s. Similarly, the policy need is clear if we have unemployment and a payments surplus; then we need expansionary monetary and fiscal policy. But the United States in the first half of the 1960s provided a vivid example of the policy dilemma when domestic and international goals conflict.

At home, the problem was a slack economy. The standard domestic policy prescription was budgetary stimulus and easier money. Wholesale prices were stable, and the economy seemed extraordinarily well balanced except for the underutilization of labor and industrial capacity. But internationally our continuing large payments deficit and substantial gold outflow called, under traditional gold-standard rules, for restrictive monetary and fiscal policy. These would check the rise in American incomes and prices, and decrease our imports while expanding our exports. But the U.S. deficit position of the 1960s didn't fit the textbook pattern. Under the traditional theory, a nation's deficit should reflect falling exports and rising imports, usually resulting from an inflationary boom at home that raises costs and prices relative to other nations. However, the U.S. export surplus was enormous; our businesses were competing effectively in foreign markets. The U.S. payments deficit reflected huge private investments abroad and government aid, not a deteriorating export position.

In this situation, most American economists rejected tight money and restrictive fiscal policy to reduce the international payments deficit. Although higher U.S. interest rates might have reduced the capital outflow, they would also have checked private investment at home and worsened unemployment. Moreover, higher interest rates here might simply have induced other nations to raise their interest rates correspondingly. Indeed, tighter money might have increased the capital outflow if it had generated recession and falling profits in the United States, since then both American and foreign funds might have moved abroad to seek higher profits there. In fact, much of our overseas investment is in equities and direct purchase of plant and equipment, for which the profit rate, not the interest rate, is the major inducement.

Still, nearly everyone agreed that doing nothing was also unacceptable. What would you have done? Remember that unemployment in-volves vast economic waste at home and loss of prestige and position abroad. But remember, too, the position of the dollar as the foundation of the international-payments system, and our responsibility as leaders of the free world's struggle against totalitarianism. The life of a central banker is not easy, nor is that of his fellow economic policy makers in the Treasury and the White House. Nor, indeed, is that of the college economics student confronted with such dilemmas.

Are Fixed Exchange Rates and Independent National Policies Compatible?

The United States and the other Western nations are trying to learn how to live under a new international-payments system, one with fixed exchange rates (the core of the old gold-standard adjustment system), but with reservation of each nation's right to take independent monetary and fiscal action to fit its own domestic needs. It is not clear how basic international adjustments are to be assured under this system. In the world of today, when either surplus or deficit nations find the gold-standard prescriptions out of line with their domestic needs, they insist on freedom to decide for themselves between meeting domestic and international needs.

The difficulties are compounded by today's international mobility of capital. Since World War II, European capital markets have developed that compete actively with New York for funds, and small interest-rated differentials or rumors of instability in particular nations can trigger massive capital movements. A new "Eurodollar market" has developed in Western Europe where dollars can be invested and where both short- and long-term loans of dollars can be obtained. Dollars move freely between the United States and that market, which totaled over $25 billion in 1969. "Hot money" currency shifts are an ever present danger.

A nation with large international reserves can avoid steps to correct a deficit for years—the United States in the 1960s was an example. The new two-tier gold system hopefully removes the disruptive pressures of private speculators. But each nation must be prepared to meet its payments vis-à-vis other nations through official (central bank) channels, and even cooperating central banks and treasuries will tolerate the accumulation of deficit foreign currencies only so long.   Recent developments have substantially improved the resiliency of the international-payments system and have assured more time for deficit nations to adjust to disruptive pressures that earlier might have required devaluation, exchange controls, or drastic domestic measures. But the basic dilemma remains. Ultimately a deficit country must either eliminate its deficit, however painful this may be, convince other nations to hold more of its currency, or fail to meet its international-payments obligations.

The problem is especially important for the United States because of its key international status. The dollar is the key reserve and general-transactions currency for the Western world. Our capital markets dominate the world. Our exports and imports are of vital importance to many nations. Maintenance of stable prosperity in the United States is probably essential to stability in the other major Western nations. If we would fail to meet our liabilities under the present international monetary arragements, it would probably bring the entire structure tumbling down. Whether we like it or not, we are largely responsible for the successful operation of world monetary arrangements.[3]

U.S. Payments Policy

U.S. policy during the 1960s illustrates a very basic fact. Wise policy makers, when confronted by painful dilemmas, do not necessarily

[3]Nearly everone lectures the administration that it must nudge the U.S. balance of payments back toward "equilibrium." But, on top of all the problems noted above, the experts disagree on the best indicator of equilibrium. Some use the liquidity balance, some the official-settlements balance, and some still other measures of the size of the deficit. Everyone agrees that no one measure is ideal. Whichever measure is used, the further issue remains as to just what deficit or surplus is most consistent with equilibrium in any given year. While U.S. deficits have probably been appropriate in most years since World War II, as S.D.R.'s take over the role of providing needed increases in world liquidity the case for U.S. deficits will largely vanish.

choose one or the other of the unattractive alternatives, but search for other ways. So, U.S. policy has neither accepted the traditional fixed-exchange deflationary prescription for a payments deficit, nor has it ignored the deficit and concentrated on domestic policy. Instead, we have followed a multifaceted policy aimed at making the best of both situations while avoiding the worst aspects of each traditional policy alternative.

1. First, U.S. officials persistently and firmly stated our intention to maintain the free official convertibility of the dollar into gold at the present price. Maintenance of confidence in the integrity of the dollar among foreign holders is obviously essential to the success of the entire system. Even if we were to eliminate our basic deficits tomorrow, there would still be a large overhang of dollar balances.

2. The Federal Reserve and the Treasury worked cooperatively with other central banks to assure stability of their dollar balances and to get their aid in calming down fears and uncertainties abroad. A ten-nation agreement was worked out to supplement the lending facilities of the International Monetary Fund, to be sure the United States or other nations could borrow foreign currencies to meet any crisis situation. Other special arrangements among central banks were developed to insure against calamitous runs on the dollar or on other currencies. (The effectiveness of these international cooperative arrangements was demonstrated repeatedly—for example, in 1964 when, in the face of an impending confidence crisis, a $3 billion loan to support the British pound was arranged among the ten on two-days' notice. An even more important example was the quick development of the two-tier gold system in the face of a speculative gold crisis in 1968.)

3. Longer-run steps to eliminate the basic payments deficit were pushed. Government officials exhorted American businessmen and workers to hold down American costs and prices, and to push exports in every way possible. The Kennedy–Johnson wage–price guideposts were made a major part of this push to improve America's position in export markets.

In the Nixon administration, these were supplanted by restraint on aggregate demand.

4. Government spending abroad was substantially reduced, partly through cutting back military outlays in Europe and aid to less-developed nations. Moreover, most of our overseas aid was "tied," requiring recipients to spend the aid dollars in the United States.

5. To lessen long-term private-capital outflows, a special "interest-equalization tax" was placed on foreign borrowing in U.S. markets in 1963, and in 1965 an extensive program of "voluntary" restraints was established, under which U.S. businesses and financial institutions would restrict their foreign investments to a modest increase over the preceding year. In 1968, most of these controls were made mandatory.

6. A new monetary-fiscal policy mix was developed. Fiscal policy was given the main job of stimulating the domestic economy, mainly through the tax cuts of 1964 and 1965. Meanwhile, monetary policy nudged short-term interest rates up while holding long-term rates stable. This mix was intended to stimulate domestic employment and output through tax reduction, to avoid counteracting effects from rising long-term interest rates, and to hold volatile short-term foreign balances in this country through higher short-term interest rates.

7. Radical measures were generally rejected. Devaluation of the dollar (against gold or against other major currencies) was rejected out of hand, as being unjustified and disruptive to the entire international monetary system. Drastic reduction of government foreign aid was rejected, because the aid was considered desirable on its own merits, but by "tying" aid its negative pressure on our international payments was essentially eliminated. Drastic deflationary measures, in line with gold-standard prescriptions, were rejected because of their unacceptable impact on domestic employment and output until inflation became the main problem after 1965.

8. International agreement in 1968 on S.D.R.'s plus the two-tier gold system marked, in most observers' eyes, an imaginative and basic response to fundamental weaknesses in the preceding international-payments system. U.S. officials played a leading role in developing these changes.

Long-Range Reforms

Three big problems have plagued the international monetary system since World War II. Basic reform proposals have concentrated on these three. We may hope that the reforms of the 1960s have made substantial progress on the first two; most experts believe the third has yet to be solved.

The Liquidity Problem

World trade increased from $50 billion to over $200 billion between 1950 and 1970. International lending grew even faster. Yet the world's monetary gold stock grew only from $36 billion to $41 billion. Gold production was far more than $5 billion over the period, but the remainder went into the hands of speculators and hoarders, jewelry, industry, or other nonmonetary uses. Morever, speculators could, until 1968, add or detract from the monetary gold stock at will by exchanging currencies for gold or vice versa.

The other main source of new international reserves consisted of U.S. payments deficits, which added $32 billion to foreign dollar balances over the twenty years. But this was an erratic and obviously unsatisfactory way of providing needed increases in world liquidity.

Adoption of the S.D.R. plan in 1968 appears a major step toward a more rational, collective plan for gradually increasing international monetary reserves. The plan is new and remains to be tested. The experts do not agree on just how fast reserves should be increased. Some argue that a generous supply is the best protection against confidence crises for individual currencies and against undesirably drastic pressures on deficit countries to restore balance through precipitous action. Others argue that excess liquidity makes it too easy for deficit countries to avoid painful steps needed to put their houses in order. But nearly everyone agrees that the S.D.R.'s are a sensible step in the direction of rational, managed growth in international reserves.

The Confidence Problem

A confidence crisis occurs when foreign holders of some currency (say, francs) lose confidence that they can exchange their francs for gold or other safer currencies at existing exchange rates. They fear that the franc will be devalued. Such rumors spread rapidly, and the result is likely to be a massive run on the franc. Francs are presented for gold or other safer currencies; the result can be a massive drain on French gold and foreign currency reserves. If the speculative run continues, France may have to devalue or temporarily stop all gold payments for francs to protect her reserves. Moreover, such currency crises tend to spread. Uncertainty about francs can easily spread to, say, the pound and the lira, precipitating runs there.[4]

Such major confidence crises occurred for the pound in 1964 and 1967, for the franc in 1967, and for the dollar in 1968. Since other nations fear the spread of the collapse of confidence, the leading Western central banks have banded together to come to each other's aid with gold and currency loans to meet and stop currency crises. Massive credits, totaling billions of dollars, can be extended almost overnight to nations in trouble, and this aid has helped greatly in keeping currency crises from cumulating. Equally important, general awareness of the cooperative plans helps maintain confidence by currency holders that they can in fact count on converting their currencies at par when they wish to do so.

The greatest danger has come from private holders of weak currencies, who may be spurred on to speculative runs by rumors, even unfounded ones. Such speculators represented a threat to even strong currencies like the dollar. In 1968, a billion dollars in gold was paid out for dollars in a single day in the confidence crisis preceding adoption of the two-tier gold system. The new system eliminated the possibility that private currency holders could directly mount such speculative raids on the participating nations, since the central banks now refuse to buy or sell gold vis-à-vis private individuals or organizations. The threat, however, is not completely gone. British dollar holders, for example, however irrationally fearing a dollar devaluation, might still convert their dollars into pounds on a massive scale. The Bank of England would thus accumulate huge dollar holdings, which it might be reluctant to hold and seek to convert into gold from the United States.

A confidence crisis might also arise if foreign central banks or treasuries would lose confidence in some currency they hold—for example, the dollar. They could then demand gold from the United States for their dollars at $35 an ounce—and they can still do so under the two-tier agreement of 1968. While such an official run on the dollar might occur, it is unlikely. The leading central banks know that by and large they stand or fall together. The entire international monetary system rests on mutual confidence (as do domestic monetary systems). A speculative run that would lead the United States to devalue or to go off gold completely would almost certainly destroy the whole present international-payments system and plunge the financial world into disorder and uncertainty.

Recognizing this fact, the leading Western central banks have moved ever closer in their cooperation to avoid such a cumulative disaster. Their large mutual loan commitments were mentioned above. They share major responsibility for the effective operation of the I.M.F. Any major central bank or treasury will ponder a long time before it chances destroying the confidence system on which its own stability also depends.

Thus, major progress has been made toward managing the confidence problem—by the two-

[4]The fear of devaluation is not necessary an irrational one. During the century preceding 1914 major currency devaluations were rare, but not so since 1929. The U.S. dollar's gold value has been unchanged since 1934, the longest recent stretch of any major currency. Only the Swiss franc approaches this record. The French franc has been devalued six times since the mid-1930s. The British pound, Spanish peseta, Danish krone, Canadian dollar, Dutch guilder, USSR ruble, German mark, Mexican peso, Swedish krona, Italian lira, Japanese yen, and many others have all been devalued at least once since World War II.

tier gold agreement, by assuring adequate total liquidity through S.D.R.'s, and through elaborate central-bank cooperative arrangements. But long history, reaching far back from this generation, warns us that confidence in money and monetary systems is a precarious thing.

The Adjustment Problem

The present mixed international monetary system, combining fixed exchange rates and national independence, provides an uncertain mechanism for bringing about international adjustments. Sooner or later, deficit nations must face up to their loss of reserves, even under the new two-tier gold system. But payments deficits may persist for long periods where (as in the United States) nations have large reserves. The refusal of surplus nations to permit inflationary domestic expansions (as in Western Europe over the past decade) equally blocks the effectiveness of the adjustment mechanism. Above all, if we are to live with this system we must learn to expect adjustments to come more slowly and to avoid crises because adjustments do not occur rapidly.

Many economists argue that the basic system itself must be changed to facilitate international adjustments. Academic attacks on the present system generally point toward two basic reforms: substitution of flexible for fixed exchange rates, or adoption of a "sliding, or crawling peg" whereby exchange rates are adjusted gradually to fit shifting international cost–price relationships.

Flexible ("Floating") Exchange Rates. Freely fluctuating ("floating") exchange rates would automatically reflect excess demand or supply of any currency. As the price of that currency moved up or down, it would correspondingly discourage or stimulate imports into the country, and conversely for exports—thus directly pulling the country's balance of payments back into equilibrium. Moreover, the floating exchange rate would directly affect the prices of the nation's exports and imports. This is in contrast to the fixed exchange system, where the adjustment is brought about by an expansion or contraction of aggregate demand affecting the whole economy. With floating rates, no central bank or treasury needs to intervene to help achieve equilibrium; freely fluctuating exchange rates do the job automatically. Here again, the marketplace will do the job if we free it from restrictions.

But there is strong objection from men of affairs. Floating rates would impose major barriers to international trade and lending, because creditors would never know what their future receipts would be in terms of their own currency. Importers, lenders, and borrowers alike would face serious uncertainties on all except the shortest-term transactions. While floating rates might make overall international adjustments easier, as a practical matter they'd kill the goose that lays the golden eggs—trade and lending itself.

Economists have an answer. Just as in the markets for wheat and copper, organized "futures" markets in different currencies would develop in which importers and exporters could buy and sell currencies for delivery at the future date needed, thus eliminating the uncertainty produced by possibly fluctuating rates. They could "hedge" against the possibility of higher or lower prices for the foreign currency involved.

But there is a counteranswer. Businessmen and bankers doubt that effective forward markets would actually develop in all major currencies, especially for long-term commitments. And both they and some economists fear that speculation on such forward markets might be destabilizing instead of stabilizing to rates themselves. With commodities, the cost of production provides a central level around which prices tend to move. With foreign exchange rates, there is no cost of production to serve as a stabilizing force. Instead, if the dollar weakened, speculators might lose confidence in it and all decide to sell dollars at once, driving the dollar rate far down.

Today little serious consideration is given to completely floating exchange rates by government officials in any major nation, or by many academic economists as a practical matter. But clearly, the issue of fixed versus flexible exchange rates is a complex one. It is likely to be a source of lively controversy for many years to come.

The "Sliding Peg." Facing this dilemma, many economists, and recently government officials as well, favor a compromise—the "sliding, or crawling, peg." This policy would recognize the need to keep exchange rates substantially stable as a foundation for foreign trade and lending. But it would deviate from fixed exchanges in two ways. First, it would permit exchange rates to fluctuate moderately (say by 1 to 3 percent on each side of parity) under market pressures, so they could do part of the equilibrating job. Second, if a currency consistently moved above or below par vis-à-vis other currencies, the par (peg) itself would automatically be adjusted gradually, say by ½ or 1 percent a quarter or half year. This sliding peg would be responsive to the fact that costs and prices do move differently in different nations, for example reflecting different rates of technological progress. But the changes would be gradual enough to retain most of the benefits from fixed rates.

The sliding peg doesn't solve the basic dilemma if one nation gets badly out of international equilibrium—say, because its technical progress is very slow or because it tries to live beyond its international means by importing much more than it exports. But it does offer a more flexible system than the present one, without running the risks involved in a more drastic shift to a floating rate system.

The painful fact is that no one has discovered a surefire system for assuring basic balance-of-payments adjustments without unwanted pressure on domestic economies. Assurance of adequate international liquidity, to avoid crises while adjustments are taking place, can help. And we must recognize that under the present system international adjustments to eliminate payments disequilibriums may be very slow, compared to earlier expectations. If we want the system to work, we must learn to suppress alarm and disruptive speculation merely because deficits are not eliminated overnight. But the present system does not seem fully satisfactory to almost anybody, and there is little doubt

that the search for more effective arrangements will be active over the years ahead.

The Future Role of Gold

What is the future role of gold in the world's international monetary system? To answer, one needs a crystal ball, especially because so much of gold's present role depends on centuries-old tradition and "psychology." Given the mixture of myth and reality that surrounds gold, what can we say of its future role? The following predictions seem probable.

1. Gold has declined greatly in monetary importance since the 1920s, but it will not soon vanish from the near-center of world monetary arrangements. It remains the one universally acceptable means of international payments, and central banks now hold over $40 billion of gold reserves. On the other hand, nations are unlikely to return gold to a position of control over their domestic monetary policies.

2. Gold **plus** key currencies and S.D.R.'s will probably constitute the international monetary reserves of most "free world" nations, with a relatively declining role for gold. Different countries will prefer different mixes of gold and other reserves, depending on their individual trade and financial relationships.

3. What about the proposal that the United States simply "go off gold," eliminating our commitment to other central banks to exchange gold for dollars at a fixed rate? If fear of a gold drain prevents us from taking overwise desirable domestic policies, this may appear an attractive course. But it seems unlikely in the near future, for three main reasons.

First, such a step would be highly disruptive to free-world trade and investments. Dollars now serve as the basic trading currency for most of our major friends and trading partners, reflecting in considerable part our repeated commitment to provide gold for the dollars on demand. International trade and, still more, long-term investments rest on confidence in the predictable convertibility of the foreign currencies received. As the devaluation of the British pound in 1931 triggered worldwide uncertainty and runs on other major currencies, so, probably, would an announcement of our refusal to continue redeeming dollars in gold at the promised rate.

Second, going off gold would threaten, possibly destroy, the dollar's position as the free world's key reserve currency, and with it this nation's profitable position as the world's banker. If other nations were unsure about the redeemability of dollars in gold, they would be far less likely to hold excess dollars as reserves. With this uncertainty, less of the world's trade would probably be carried on in terms of dollars. How much this development might injure our international trading and banking position is hard to say. Certainly it would be a blow to our international prestige and that of the dollar as "good as gold." Unfortunately, such a step would especially penalize our friends and economic allies who have continued to hold dollars rather than asking for gold. It would help nations (like France) that have refused to cooperate in strengthening the dollar–gold international system; and, if the price of gold rose as a result, major gold producers like South Africa and the USSR would be major beneficiaries.

Third, there seems little need to incur these costs and risks, since our present gold policy leaves us wide flexibility for monetary policies designed to meet domestic needs. Domestic monetary policy is now tied only loosely to the state of our gold stock—although as the gold stock dwindles the tie will become even closer if we maintain our promise to redeem all officially presented dollars at the established price of $35 an ounce.

4. One last comment. It is important to recognize that the case for a fixed gold–dollar tie and that for fixed exchange rate are related, but different. We could fix our exchange rates vis-à-vis other currencies by international agreement and appropriate domestic monetary and fiscal policies, without any commitment to buy or sell gold at a set price. Adherence to a fixed price for gold imposes the added discipline upon us that we must ultimately adopt domestic policies consistent with maintaining stable exchange rates and avoiding depletion of our gold reserves.

Review

<table>
<tr><td>CONCEPTS
TO
REMEMBER</td><td colspan="2">This chapter reuses the central concepts of both domestic macroeconomics and Chapters 41–43 and adds the following important concepts and institutions:</td></tr>
<tr><td></td><td>devaluation
International Monetary Fund
special drawing rights (S.D.R.'s)
two-tier gold system
adjustment problem</td><td>floating exchange rates
sliding, or crawling, peg
liquidity problem
confidence problem</td></tr>
</table>

FOR ANALYSIS AND DISCUSSION

1. Should the United States be concerned about its continuing balance-of-payments deficit? If so, what should we do about it?
2. Do we now have enough gold for domestic and international reserve purposes? How much do we really need? Explain.
3. Describe the two-tier gold system of 1968. What are its presumed advantages? Is it fair to private holders of dollars abroad?
4. Given our persistent payments deficit, should we tighten credit and raise interest rates here to reduce the heavy outflow of American capital, both short- and long-term? In your answer consider both

possible effects on domestic economic activity and possible actions by foreign nations in response.

5. How can we have a continuing balance-of-payments deficit when our exports exceed our imports by a wide margin?

6. Should we reduce our military expenditures abroad in order to protect our gold stock?

7. "Our continued balance-of-payments deficits clearly say that we are not competitive enough abroad and that restrictive monetary and fiscal policy is needed to restrain American prices and wages so we can become more competitive." Do you agree? What would be the likely consequences of such a policy?

8. Why shouldn't we simply go off gold, discontinuing our purchase and sale of gold at $35 an ounce even vis-à-vis central banks, to eliminate any possible pressure on us from a future gold shortage?

9. What are SDR's? Are they "as good as gold" to the countries that get them through the IMF?

Research in the area of international economic affairs has snowballed since World War II. The U.S. balance-of-payments deficit and our gold position have been front-page news, and interest in the European "Common Market" and "Eurodollars" has not lagged far behind. Leaving aside our problems vis-à-vis the less-developed areas (covered in Part Two), the following sample may provide some impression of the lively probing into international economics in recent years.

Gold and the Balance of Payments. A useful, relatively simple beginning is provided by the *Economic Report of the President*, January, 1970, pp. 126–42. Then try Milton Friedman, "The Advantages of Flexible Exchange Rates," and Henry Wallich, "In Defense of Fixed Exchange Rates," before the Joint Economic Committee, *Hearings on the U.S. Balance of Payments* (1963), pp. 451–59 and 495–99. Richard Cooper's "The Dollar and the World Economy," in K. Gordon, ed., *Agenda for the Nation* (The Brookings Institution, 1968), though written just before adoption of the two-tier gold system, is a thorough analysis of the entire problem. Gold is the focus of M. A. Kriz's interesting *Gold: Barbarous Relic or Useful Instrument* (Princeton International Finance Section, 1967).

A complete description and analysis of "Eurodollars" is provided by the Federal Reserve Bank of Cleveland's *Economic Review*, for March, April, and May, 1970. "Measuring the U.S. Balance of Payments," in the Federal Reserve Bank of Chicago's *Business Conditions*, June, 1970, gives a brief analysis of the different major balance-of-payments concepts.

U.S. Trade Policies and the World. Pennsylvania's Irving Kravis presents a readable introduction to the European Common Market in "Common Market—Lesson in Trade Expansion," *Harvard Business Review,* March, 1962. An authoritative, thorough recent analysis is L. Krause's *European Economic Integration and the United States* (The Brookings Institution, 1968).

A broad and still up-to-date picture of research on U.S. tariff policy is provided by *Foreign Trade Policy*, a compendium for the Foreign Trade Policy Subcommittee of the House Committee on Ways and Means (1958). Many of the papers are partisan pleas by industry representatives, but the papers by Piquet, Salant, and Kravis are readable, analytical research pieces. On the effects of widely differing national growth rates in productivity, try Richard Cooper's "International Aspects," in *Automation and Technical Change* (Prentice-Hall, Inc., 1962). Lastly, *A New Trade Policy for the United States*, by the Committee for Economic Development (1962), though not original research, provides a good example of how economic analysis and related data can be used at a nontechnical level in reaching reasoned policy conclusions.

Both the United States and other nations, nonetheless, continue to impose barriers to free trade, in order to help their own economies. "How the Japanese Mount That Export Blitz," *Fortune*, September, 1970, explains some of the devices used by Japan in obtaining a bigger share of total markets. R. Baldwin's *Nontariff Distortions of International Trade* (The Brookings Institution, 1970) measures the impact of these measures. Edward Shaffer's, *The Oil Import Program of the United States* (Praeger Publishers, Inc., 1968) attempts to assess the effects of U.S. oil import quotas.

A quite different aspect of our foreign economic relationships is pictured by Charles Kindleberger in *American Business Abroad* (Yale University Press, 1969); and by T. Geiger in *The General Electric Company in Brazil* (National Planning Association, 1961), one of a series of studies of U.S. private firms operating in other lands.

part seven

Perspectives on Economic Change

The Economics of Change

*Midway and O'Hare Airports:
Chicago*
"Automation"
Disarmament
Conclusion

Change is evident everywhere in economic life. It is the blood of a dynamic economy. On the world front, we face a population explosion of staggering dimensions. By the year 2000 the world's population may soar to 6 billion people, most of them in the poverty-striken non-Western nations that today look askance at our wealth and power. At home, a century ago 60 percent of our jobs were in agriculture, now only 5 percent are. Massive population concentrations in urban areas are creating problems never dreamed of before. "Automation"—rapid technological advance—is revolutionizing manufacturing processes. Patterns of consumer demand have changed dramatically over our lifetime. Spending on services has skyrocketed, so that today more people earn their living by producing consumer services than physical commodities. One family in five moves each year. I.B.M., a tiny unknown twenty-five years ago, last year had a market value on the New York Stock Exchange exceeding those of General Motors and U.S. Steel. Fifty years ago, International Mercantile Marine was the nation's fourth largest business, U.S. Leather the seventh; who knows them today? General Motors, the largest manufacturing corporation in the world today, did not even exist.

The process of economic change presents an unrivaled opportunity to apply the economic concepts and theory developed earlier in this book. This chapter consists of three brief case studies; then a final section summarizes some of the central elements of the way our economy adjusts to rapid economic change. The first case is a simple, though dramatic, one—the precipitous shift of virtually all airline travel into and out of Chicago from the old Midway Airport on the south side to the new O'Hare Airport on the north. The second is the impact of rapid nationwide technological change—some call it "automation." The third is a case where the change is government-induced—the impact of rapid disarmament—say complete withdrawal from Vietnam.

Like the earlier studies of poverty and insecurity, these cases call for an orderly job of problem solving, using the tools of both macro and micro theory. We need to define the problem: where are we, how did we get there, and what are our objectives? We need to analyze the situation, using the theory at our command, and to lay out promising alternative policies to achieve our objectives. We need to evaluate these alternatives carefully and to decide which looks best. A crucial part of the job is to clarify your objectives and balance them against one another when you must accept less of one to have more of another. Particularly in looking at economic change, potential conflicts crop up everywhere among the goals of growth, economic security, and different notions of equity in the distribution of income.

Midway and O'Hare Airports: Chicago

Fifteen years ago, Midway Airport on the south side of Chicago was the world's busiest field. During rush hours planes landed and took off one a minute. Millions of passengers passed through in a year. Virtually every major airline flew into and out of the airport, and most maintained passenger service and other facilities in its sprawling buildings. Nearby were elegant motels, restaurants, hot-dog stands, filling stations, parking lots, and a multitude of other exterprises, all aimed at speeding the traveler on his way and earning a profit from him en route.

Then came the jets! Midway, barely large enough for big propeller-driven planes and squeezed on all sides by residential and business areas, was obsolete overnight. The huge new O'Hare International Airport, far out in the farmlands north of Chicago was rushed to completion. Miles of runways, acres of shining steel and glass, the most modern facilities for passengers and planes—all these made O'Hare by 1962 one of the model airports of the world, capable of handling huge planes and an enormous volume of traffic.

By 1962, a walk through Midway's sprawling terminals was a walk through a graveyard—long, dusty corridors, closed-down shops and restaurants, a few local airline counters. From being the world's busiest airport, suddenly Midway became a field used only by local feeder lines and private and freight planes. Nearby, motels permanently displayed vacancy signs. Parking lots were empty. Restaurants and hot-dog stands struggled to keep alive or closed their doors. Property values plummeted; bankruptcies soared.

The most complete displacement of Midway by O'Hare in four short years is a classic case of economic change on a local level. With the jets, consumer demands for modern air travel simply could not be met at Midway. The federal government, as with other major airports, financed much of the basic landing facilities and equipment at O'Hare. The major airlines and a wide variety of auxiliary services, speeded by the profit motive, lost little time in shifting to O'Hare where full advantage could be taken of technological advances and excellent service could be rendered to customers. Capital and jobs moved swiftly from Midway to O'Hare.

Since the airports are only thirty miles apart, it was relatively easy for workers to move if they chose to do so. Most of the airlines offered all Midway workers jobs at O'Hare, though for many older workers uprooting residences of many years' standing in south Chicago and making the long move out into the suburbs was difficult and uninviting. Much capital was more immobile. Owners of valuable land near the airport saw a big part of their wealth wiped out overnight. Land cannot move; when demand for it drops, its value drops accordingly. (Remember the analysis of capitalization in Chapter 35.) So it was for other relatively fixed investments at Midway—airline facilities, restaurants, shops, motels, and the like. If they could not be moved their value dropped as demand moved away. Investments in new expensive enterprises were especially hard hit. Such investors,failing to foresee the change, paid the price for their mistake in sharply reduced returns (and hence also plummeting capital values) on their buildings and facilities.

At O'Hare, just the opposite happened. New jobs opened up by the thousands. Land values around the airport soared. Motels and filling stations sprang up like mushrooms. Valuable concessions were let in the huge new terminal buildings. The airlines invested millions of dollars in facilities for passengers, freight, and equipment, all with an eye to more profits by handling more customers and cargo.

What was the end result of the move? A rapid response to shifting technology and changing consumer demand, implemented partly through government investment in the new airport itself but mainly through profit-seeking private enterprises. Improved service for airline customers. Windfalls for property owners near O'Hare, and big profits for those who foresaw the change. Headaches, heartaches, and financial disaster for property owners and others left behind in Midway. Greater profits for the airlines who moved to O'Hare and invested in the new facilities.

What is the lesson of Midway and O'Hare? Many would say it is a shining example of how well our system can adjust to dramatic technological change and rising consumer demands, under the impetus of private enterprise with a little government assistance. Few argued for government aid to those left behind, or government measures to seize windfall gains from those who benefited in and around O'Hare. Because the move was local and airlines offered new jobs at O'Hare, information on new jobs and mobility to them posed relatively small problems for airline workers. Related enterprises, like the motels and restaurants, had to do the best they could. If they looked far ahead and bet right on the jets, they were among those first on the scene at O'Hare and prepared to move out of Midway as the market fell. If they didn't see ahead, they were left behind.

Chicago is a big city, and Midway was a tiny part of the area job market. Airports produce a mass of externalities—both costs and benefits. Should government—federal, state, or local— have done less or more?

"Automation"

Next consider "automation," the name some observers give to rapid technological advance that appears directly to displace workers. You see the headlines everywhere. "Electronic Computer Displaces 200 Clerks." "Fully Automated Assembly Line Installed." Ninety per cent of the nation's light bulbs are turned out by glass-blowing machines tended by fourteen operators. A machine run by ten workers produces the same number of auto engine blocks as were turned out by 400 men ten years ago. Automation has been widely hailed as the foundation of modern industrial progress, and as widely decried as a monstrous threat to the jobs of millions of workers. Some claim that modern technology is destroying the human elements of our society.

Technological Advance, Progress, and Unemployment

Does "automation" raise the nation's standard of living? The answer is yes. Over the past century, output per man-hour in private employment has grown about 2½ percent per annum, reflecting technological advance, capital investment, improved education and skills of workers, and the variety of other factors outlined in the chapters on economic growth. Since World War II, this rate has stepped up to between 3 and 4 percent. If this recent rate continues (reflecting, remember, technological advance and other factors), over the decade ahead each year nearly 3 million workers will be freed by rising productivity to produce additional products—or society can have 3–4 percent more leisure and the same real output as the preceding year. That is, in 1970 the $980 billion g.n.p. was produced by 78 million civilian workers, but in 1971 the same output could be produced by only 75 million people, since on the average each worker could produce about 3–4 percent more. Technological advance is vital to economic progress and our rising standard of living. Freeing 3 million workers each year to produce other wanted goods, or to permit more leisure for all with the same output, looks impressive indeed.

But technological advance is a two-edged sword. If you're a worker thrown out of a job by a new machine, you don't care much about the gross national product. You have to find another job to keep the paychecks coming in. And especially if you're middle-aged with only one skill, finding another job at equal pay, or any job at all, may be difficult indeed. Technological progress is a boon to society, but it may be a disaster to some individuals in that society.

Does "Automation" Cause Unemployment?
Obviously automation may cause unemployment for the man thrown out of work by a new machine that does his job better or cheaper. But remember the oft repeated warning above about the fallacy of composition. Just because Joe Doaks is thrown out of work doesn't necessarily mean that there will be more unemployment in the whole economy. Indeed, both economic theory and experience give the same answer: The alarmist cries that machines will soon consign millions of men to involuntary unemployment rest far more on fancy than on fact.

The historical record is clear. Over more than a century of increasingly rapid technological progress, there is no evidence that the unemployment rate has increased. On the contrary, our economic system has shown impressive ability over the decades to provide useful jobs not only for displaced workers but for new additions to a growing labor force as well. There has consistently been some unemployment, reflecting in part lags in the adjustment to economic change. More vividly, there have been intermittent periods of mass unemployment, but these have come with recessions and weak aggregate demand, not with periods of especially rapid technological advance. On the contrary, rapid technological advance and *falling* unemployment have generally come together in business

upswings, while relatively slow technological advance and rising unemployment have come together in downswings.

The Two Faces of Automation. Clearly, society benefits if we have technical advance without unemployment, and if displaced resources move quickly and smoothly to new jobs producing what consumers want most. We want to maintain high employment and to have resources allocated efficiently to meet consumers' demands.

Part Two above taught the big lesson about large-scale unemployment: Mass unemployment generally reflects a shortage of aggregate demand, and we can avoid it through rational monetary and fiscal policy. Second, the final section of Chapter 33 showed how, if there is adequate aggregate demand, automation will lead to a redistribution of workers among industries and types of jobs, but to little if any change in the level of total employment. New machines will replace people in some jobs, but the same total stock of workers will continue to find employment through shifting to jobs where their comparative advantage is highest. But a necessary condition, remember, is that displaced workers do not insist on wages above their (possibly reduced) marginal-value products.

Given market imperfections, inadequate information on job opportunities, and worker immobility, the adjustment process may be slow, and some individual workers may never be reabsorbed. But in such cases, the finger of blame should be placed where it belongs—on market imperfections and immobilities (for example, on prejudices against hiring older workers or on poor information about job openings elsewhere), not on technological advance per se. Adequate total demand assures that the total labor force can be employed, making reasonable allowance for immobilities and delays,so long as workers do not insist on wages above their marginal-value products. And the micro market mechanism helps wages and prices to allocate new machines and workers into those productive channels where the comparative advantage (marginal product per dollar of cost) of each is highest. (Go back and review the underlying analysis on pp. 486–488 if the process isn't clear in your mind.)

Can We Trust the Market?

In 1962, a prestigious President's Advisory Committee on Labor–Management Policy, composed of top businessmen, labor leaders, and professional economists, reported unanimous agreement on these "fundamental points" about automation:

1. Automation and technological progress are essential to the general welfare, the economic strength, and the defense of the nation.
2. This progress can and must be achieved without the sacrifice of human values.
3. Achievements of technological progress without the sacrifice of human values requires a combination of private and governmental action, consonant with the principles of a free society.

If we accept this general position, what combination of private and governmental measures does economic analysis suggest? Can we have rapid progress, economic security, and an equitable distribution of the fruits of progress, all three?

Aggregate Demand Policies

Stably growing aggregate demand is the first requisite for progress through technological change without unemployment. In periods of prosperity, workers displaced by technological advance find it relatively easy to move to new jobs. Indeed, then few workers are actually displaced; with growing market demand and advance planning, employers can generally shift displaced workers to other jobs in the firm as such jobs open up through normal labor turnover and retirements. New entrants into the labor force move into new job openings elsewhere. The shift in labor induced by technical progress is accomplished smoothly, with little need for older workers to move to new companies and new locations.

But note that total demand must grow enough to provide new jobs for the workers displaced by technological advance if long-run unemployment is to be avoided. If displaced workers were willing to accept lower wages in new jobs, a correspondingly smaller increase in aggregate demand would be enough to avoid unemployment. But widespread wage reductions in our economy seem unlikely, and most economists recommend growing aggregate demand to match technological advance. Wise governmental monetary and fiscal policies are the first-line defense against technological unemployment, as against other general unemployment.

Government Policies To Improve Labor Markets

Even with adequate aggregate demand, technological progress may force difficult adjustments on displaced workers, especially older workers and those heavily committed to now obsolete skills. The market provides no guarantee that each individual worker will find a new job as good as the one he loses. But it is to everyone's advantage that he find a new job as promptly as possible where he can make his greatest contribution to total output. If the displaced worker stays unemployed because of poor information on other job openings, lack of opportunity to learn new skills, or geographical immobility, both he and society suffer. He is unemployed, and society wastes potential output.

Many economists urge greater government aid to displaced workers in finding new jobs. Most European governments do much more than we to provide information on job openings, to help retrain unemployed workers, and to provide funds for moving expenses. These governmental activities would be very difficult for the individual to undertake efficiently on his own, but they promise to benefit society as a whole as well as the individual—externalities again. There is a public good to be served, over and above the case for helping the worker as an individual.

On a longer-term basis, government can also help by providing better education and training for both youths and older workers. In a rapidly changing society, most workers will have to learn new job skills one or several times during their lives. In an individualistic society, we largely count on individuals to obtain skills for themselves after they leave school, and on employers to provide training in new skills where this will augment their profits. But this may be a haphazard process, which leaves many displaced workers without retraining. Thus, many observers ask, why should government's educational role end with young people? Wouldn't governmental responsibility for skill training over the individual's entire productive career make sense for the general welfare?

In Western Europe, nations also do more than we to bring investment to depressed areas and to unemployed workers, instead of moving displaced workers to jobs elsewhere. Italy, West Germany, France, Denmark, Belgium, and the United Kingdom all adopted legislation during the 1950s to assist local economic development. Government loans, grants, and tax concessions are used to channel new investment into areas of unemployment. In the United States, the Area Redevelopment Act of 1961 and the Appalachian Program of 1965 represent tentative moves in the same direction here. TVA in the depressed Tennessee Valley during the 1930s was a major example of this approach.

Private Employer-Employee Agreements on Automation

The President's Labor-Management Advisory Council of 1962 urged management and labor to work out their own plans jointly to permit rapid technological change while softening the impact on individual workers. Agreements covering the introduction of new methods and new machines are now common in union contracts. Many contracts provide that management must notify the union in advance when new processes and machinery are to be introduced; often, displaced workers are guaranteed any other jobs in the company before any new employees can be hired for them. Many companies provide extensive retraining for their own workers. Increasingly, technological change is managed so that it occasions few layoffs. The burden of adjustment is thrown on new entrants into the labor force, generally young people who are reasonably mobile and who may suffer less from temporary unemployment than do older workers with families.

Unions are often adamantly opposed to automation that threatens their members' jobs. For example, for years the newspaper unions have delayed, or blocked completely, the introduction of highly automated devices for setting type, and have enforced their demands through effective strikes, though the new methods are far cheaper. The railway workers' brotherhoods have permitted technological advance (for example, diesel locomotives) but have fought to maintain their jobs even where the work was no longer needed. Some employers, faced by strong unions adamantly opposed to rapid technological advance, have worked out novel agreements that in effect buy union acquiescence to rapid technological change by providing generous benefit payments to displaced workers. The West Coast longshoremen are one example. They have extremely generous layoff and other benefits in exchange for their cooperation in introducing cost-saving changes. The Kaiser Steel agreement of the early 1960s gives union members a direct share with stockholders in the gains from technical progress. In 1970, all major steel companies agreed to a plan that pays adjustment allowances to all workers who are shifted to lower-paying jobs, covering a full year before the new lower rate prevails. Over many years, the United Mine Workers have cooperated in introducing technological change in return for high wages and generous retirement and medical-aid plans. Question: If you were president of a steel company, would you agree to a plan like Kaiser's to share the benefits of automation with your workers?

How far employers find it advantageous to go in buying labor cooperation in introducing automation varies from industry to industry. Employer resentment at worker resistance to cost-saving improvements runs high. But it is clear that the mores of the times have changed. The employer's right to hire and fire is no longer absolute. The "rights" of employees to their jobs have become a moral and legal reality, increasingly built into union contracts.

But private union-management agreements

protect only the interests of workers in the firm or union concerned. Job security for these workers merely throws the burden of adjustment to technological progress on new job seekers who as yet have no jobs to protect.

The Shorter Workweek and Barriers to Automation

It is not surprising that workers worry about technological change that threatens their jobs. One major response, on both the national and individual-industry levels, has been a strong union push for a shorter workweek "to create more jobs." Union leaders argue that a shorter workweek, with the same weekly wage, would create jobs for displaced workers and new entrants into the labor force, and would simultaneously maintain aggregate demand for the products of those workers. Increasing union pressure has been brought on employers to cut the normal workweek from forty to thirty-five hours, and on the government to reduce the legal workweek above which employers must pay premium overtime rates.

What does economic analysis tell us about the likely consequences of such proposals?

First, suppose that the workweek in industry is cut from forty to thirty-five hours, with no change in the hourly wage rate. (Note that this is not the union proposal.) This plan obviously would just spread the existing amount of work among more people. Average weekly wages would fall, but the total wage bill and the output of the industry would be unchanged. The change would not significantly change either the unit labor cost of output or demand for the industry's product. It would "solve" the unemployment problem by taking some work and pay away from those who would otherwise work forty hours and spreading it to include those who might otherwise be unemployed.

It should be clear that the net effect is to reduce the total potential g.n.p. by the five hours of work given up by each worker. Real g.n.p. would be larger if everyone worked forty hours, not thirty-five. Perhaps, if it were impossible to provide jobs for the labor force on a forty-hour basis, it would be better to spread the work around. But if there is an unemploy-

ment problem, it would be better to raise aggregate demand to provide higher total employment at existing wage rates. Unless we really want more leisure instead of more jobs and more goods produced, this shorter-workweek approach would just accept wastage of potential productive capacity.

Second, suppose the industry workweek is cut from forty to thirty-five hours, but the weekly wage is kept unchanged. This is the proposal unions generally make. Here the picture is significantly different. Unless hourly output per worker increases one-eighth with reduced hours, labor costs per unit of output are raised by the change. Under competitive conditions, this will require higher prices; and the result will be reduced sales and production unless demand for the product increases. Unfortunately, there is nothing in the picture to lead to such an increase in demand for the industry's product. Even if the industry's workers receive higher total wages, they will spend most of their new incomes on the products of other industries. The predictable result, therefore, is fewer hours of work available.

Most union leaders disagree with this analysis. In many industries, they say, price need not rise. Most firms have generous profits, so they can afford to pay higher wages and keep prices stable. Then more workers would have to be taken on to continue producing the goods that are sold. Or employers can increase efficiency to offset higher wage costs. But this appears to most economists to be wishful thinking. Profits are seldom large enough to absorb big wage increases per unit of output, and there is often too little "slack" in efficiency to permit such cost absorption.

Third, suppose a thirty-five-hour workweek were somehow introduced for the entire economy, cutting the average workweek from forty hours. Again, unless hourly productivity was correspondingly increased by the shorter hours, wage costs per unit of output would rise and either other costs would have to be reduced, or profits would be reduced, or prices would have to be increased. Since profits in the economy at large are unlikely to be cut to absorb such a large wage increase and since it is unlikely that the pressure could induce such massive cuts in other costs (remember that wages account for around two-thirds of total costs for the economy), higher prices would be the likely response. If, then, monetary-fiscal policy stepped in to raise aggregate demand proportionately, the net result would be mainly inflation to match the higher wage cost per unit of output. Prices and money wages would be higher, but the total real g.n.p. would be only that producible by a thirty-five-hour week, significantly lower than the output of a forty-hour week. Inflation and lower production would be the main results.

Alternatively, suppose the government stands firm against inflation and refuses to validate the higher prices through expansionary monetary-fiscal policy. Then the net result of the higher labor costs and higher prices would be a reduced volume of sales, less work available, and unemployment. Again, the result would be less real g.n.p. and less work because of the thirty-five-hour workweek.

The economist's answer to these problems is reasonably clear. If we voluntarily choose to reduce the workweek to thirty-five hours because we prefer leisure over the products of the extra five hours of work, this can be a rational individual and social choice. But to accept a reduced standard of living (either with or without higher money wages) as an imagined solution to the threat of automation would be shortsighted policy indeed.

Progress, Security, and Equity

The nation benefits through greater output from technological advance. But what is an equitable and efficient distribution of burdens and benefits in this complex world of externalities? Should displaced workers and investors whose capital equipment has been made obsolete by automation bear the bulk of the cost, even if they did no wrong? Should management that introduces the innovation reap the lion's share of the benefits through higher profits? Should the gains be shared with labor in the same industry? Or should they be distributed generally to the population through lower prices as costs

fall? Broadly, how high a reward do we want the system to provide for those who correctly anticipate change under uncertainty, and how far should government go to aid those injured by technological change?

In broad perspective, the macro facts are clear. Both wages and profits gain from technological progress. More advanced theories tell us this will happen under a wide range of conditions, and the facts of history back up the theories. The issues on automation mainly involve its micro effects on the relative positions of different workers and industries, and how much of the total gain will go to profits and to wages at the macro level.[1]

A widespread policy of price reductions as costs fall with technical progress could spread the benefits widely to all users. But this would imply stable money wage rates and profits in the industry, a result neither unions nor management would like, and we have no practical means of enforcing such a policy. Far more likely, profits and wage rates will rise with technical advance, on the average enough to absorb the direct cost savings and to keep product prices from falling much. This stable-price approach will divide the main benefits of automation between wages and profits, with nothing going to fixed-income groups, since prices do not fall. If inflationist fears are right, then wages, profits, and prices will all creep upward in spite of cost-reducing technical advance.

In recent years, unions have successfully demanded job security for their members and costly benefits as their price for agreement to technological change. Even so, many union leaders argue that we have not gone far enough to protect the innocent individual worker against technological change over which he has no control. In addition to his case as a human being and a worker, they say he will cooperate better if his interests are protected in a reasonable way. But management counterargues that, as the costs of technological innovation are increased, the rate of innovation will be slowed, to the detriment of everyone.

[1] For an excellent elementary treatment of this issue, see H. A. Simon, *The Shape of Automation* (New York: Harper & Row, Publishers, 1965), Chaps. 1 and 2.

It is clear we need some combination of private and governmental policies that will allay the fears of workers, employers, and the general public that automation may generate large-scale unemployment. For unless these fears are allayed, resistance by individual workers and unions will slow technological advance, often with the support of the general public. The American people want faster growth and a better life. But they also have a long history of concern for the underdog. And without better understanding, this concern may well mistakenly and unintentionally check that very technological change on which our economic progress rests.[2]

Disarmament

The third case of economic change is disarmament—reconversion to peace. Would, say, complete withdrawal from Southeast Asia bring unemployment and economic disaster? This may seem a shocking question, but the Communists argue that a major reason for our large defense program is to avoid unemployment and depression. Marxist doctrine says that massive depression arising from shortage of consumer buying power will bring the downfall of the capitalist system, and today's Communists say we dare not end the arms race because the result would be massive unemployment at home.

In 1970, defense spending was about $75 billion, 7 to 8 percent of our g.n.p. Suppose a peaceful settlement in Vietnam permitted us to cut this defense spending by $20 billion. Twenty billion dollars is about 2 percent of g.n.p. which would give every family in the

United States about $400 more to spend as it pleases if taxes were cut correspondingly. Or with $20 billion we could substantially eliminate poverty (as it is officially defined), or clear and rebuild vast slum areas in every major city in the United States. We could dramatically improve the quality of education from kindergarten through college.

Would we dare cut Vietnam or other arms spending by $20 billion to get these benefits? Here again we need to use both macro and micro theory to understand the likely results. What will be the impact on aggregate demand, and on the allocation of resources and incomes? And like the other cases we have analyzed, disarmament raises difficult questions of trade-offs among social goals, especially among progress, security, and equity.[3]

Aggregate-Demand Policy

Macro theory tells us that a $20 billion cutback in government spending would reduce g.n.p. and employment, unless it were offset by some other force. Indeed, multiplier effects might lead to a drop of two or three times the $20 billion cutback. This analysis says we must have offsetting increases in other spending to avoid unemployment. It is clear that a cutback of $20 billion in defense spending would mean layoffs for the 2 to 3 million defense workers and others whose jobs directly depend on those expenditures, in addition to released military personnel—unless other spending holds up aggregate demand.

The government has three main macro alternatives if it cuts defense spending by $20 billion: (1) It can increase its spending on civilian goods and services by $20 billion, offsetting the arms reduction; (2) it can cut taxes by $20 billion; or (3) it can maintain taxes and use the hoped-for resulting budget surplus to retire the national debt. Our theory suggests that these three policies would have different results in-

---

[2]Why is the automation case different from Midway–O'Hare, where most people were content to let private initiative and the market work out the problems largely unaided? First, automation is nationwide, not merely local. Second, with automation there is no guarantee short of government action that aggregate demand will be maintained; whereas the Midway–O'Hare shift occurred in response to strong consumer demand in the economic sector involved, so there was no danger of a shortage of the relevant demand. Third, job information and worker mobility were high in the local Midway–O'Hare shift, whereas nationwide automation raises difficult and far-reaching problems on these scores.

[3]A $20 billion cut now would be about the same percentage of g.n.p. as was the cut made immediately after the Korean War. It would be far less than the huge ($75 billion) reduction in the years 1945 and 1946, after World War II.

deed. The monetarists suggest a fourth approach: (4) Keep the money stock growing stably, they say, and aggregate spending and employment will sag little as the transition occurs (whatever our budget policy) — though they too are concerned about the micro effects to be noted below.

Increase in Government Nondefense Spending. Suppose first that government spending on slum clearance, highways, and education is increased by $20 billion as defense spending is cut back, and that the government announces this policy when it announces the arms cutback. This looks like Midway-O'Hare writ large. It would maintain aggregate demand roughly unchanged. New jobs would be created in the expanding civilian-goods industries to offset those lost in the contracting arms industries, and businessmen and consumers would know this in advance.

But unlike the Midway-O'Hare case, the new jobs might be in quite different industries and localities, involving quite different skills. And investors in defense industries would be subject to disastrous losses. Possibly these "transfer" problems would result in a lot of temporary unemployment, and the next section analyzes them in detail. But if aggregate demand is kept roughly stable through the shift, there is little reason to expect continuing large-scale unemployment, tough though the transition might be (remember the automation analysis).

Keeping aggregate demand up is the biggest single safeguard against large-scale unemployment. But even continued high aggregate demand will not guarantee us against unemployment from the spending cut unless individual wage rates are reasonably flexible. Again, remember the automation analysis above. If men thrown out of work in defense industries insist on equal wages before they will accept another job, unchanged aggregate demand may leave some of them permanently unemployed. Their specialized skills have been made obsolete, so their marginal products are lower when they shift to different jobs. If they refuse to take wage cuts, they stay unemployed; and the new nondefense spending that might have given them jobs instead then goes to bidding up wages of other workers whose skills are in higher demand where spending increases.

Since even unemployed workers may resist accepting lower wages, many economists suggest that major demand shifts should be accompanied by gradually rising, not merely stable, aggregate demand, in order to ease the required job transfers. This would mean an increase of more than $20 billion in government nondefense spending.

Tax Reduction. A second alternative would be to cut taxes by $20 billion. Here the macro outcome is less obvious. If private households and businesses increase expenditures by $20 billion, the result is much as above, except that the expanding industries are those where private spending goes up, instead of highways, education, and slum clearance.

But will private spending rise by $20 billion? Probably not. Consumer spending normally rises by only a fraction of an increase in disposable income; part of the increased income is saved. Thus, spending would rise by less than the cut in individual tax liabilities. It is more difficult to predict the result of a major corporation income tax reduction. Look back at the complex determinants of investment-spending in Chapter 8 for the considerations. Perhaps business investment-spending would rise by more than the amount of a corporate tax cut, but this is unlikely. This is the balanced-budget multiplier case; with a balanced budget, the cut in government spending will generally reduce g.n.p. Most economists, therefore, would urge cutting tax liabilities by more than $20 billion. And the lag in private spending might create severe temporary problems.

Pay off the National Debt. Third, we might use the $20 billion saving on defense spending to reduce the national debt. Again, go back to macro theory to predict the consequences. Twenty billion dollars of taxes are a withdrawal from the income stream. They exercise a deflationary impact unless they are replaced by someone's spending. Using the $20 billion tax receipts to repay $20 billion of a national debt would partially offset the withdrawal, but only partially.

First, suppose the bonds paid off are held by individuals and businesses. Repayment of this debt would return the tax money to the public, but it would also buy up from them $20 billion of government bonds. Thus, the net result of the tax collection plus debt retirement would be to reduce the net wealth (liquid assets) of the public, just as the federal borrowing had originally increased the economy's net wealth in the form of government securities. Alternatively, suppose the bonds paid off are held by banks. Then the effect of the total tax-plus-debt-retirement policy is to wipe out $20 billion of demand deposits that were created when the banks bought the bonds—although the banking system's reserves are unchanged, so it has the power to reexpand its loans and deposits to the earlier level. The next effect is highly deflationary, unless bank loans are miraculously expanded without delay, leading to $20 billion more of private spending.

Stable Growth in M. Harking back to Part Two, we can predict what the monetarists would say—keep the money stock growing at about 4 percent annually (roughly the growth rate in productive capacity) and aggregate demand will continue to grow reasonably stably, whichever fiscal policy is followed. If growing bank reserves, loans, and investments are assured by monetary policy, a big cutback in arms spending might, of course, lead to payoffs and a temporary aggregate-demand slump. But the slump would be temporary, because money g.n.p. moves roughly in proportion to M.

How can the monetarists brush aside fiscal policy effects (only the extremists would go that far)? Clearly, they would say, fiscal effects would pose no particular problems in cases 1 and 2 above. What about case 3, where tax rates are kept up but government spending drops by $20 billion? (a) If publicly held bonds are redeemed, the public's money holdings are unaffected. In case the reduced wealth effect tends to reduce spending, introduce a little more M to offset the effect. (b) If bank-held bonds are redeemed, the volume of bank reserves is unaf-

fected, and banks will soon reexpand loans and investments. In case they delay, it is the central bank's job to assure that the money stock does not contract but is kept expanding. Lastly, note that the large repayment of public debt will flood the market with lendable funds in the hands of previous bondholders. Thus the interest rate will fall, stimulating private borrowing and investment.

These are the same issues debated by the monetarists and neo-Keynesians back in Part Two. The outcome remains unsettled. Here the main point is that both agree that proper monetary and fiscal policy can avoid serious recession and unemployment if reconversion to peace comes. Though they stress different policies, there is no incompatibility between their proposals. (Both, of course, recognize the serious micro adjustment problems involved, which we have postponed to the next section.)

The World War II Experience. This analysis suggests that positive government action to keep aggregate demand up would be needed to avoid unemployment if arms spending were to be cut $20 billion. But between late 1944 and late 1946, federal war spending fell from a peak annual rate of nearly $90 billion to about $15 billion, a drop of $75 billion, or about a third of the entire g.n.p., in two years. Eight million men were demobilized from the armed forces, in addition to the cuts in defense procurements. Over the same period, federal tax receipts fell by only $3 billion, from an annual rate of $46 to $43 billion. Still, reconversion unemployment was short, and soon the economy was booming again.

How shall we reconcile this history with our analysis? Would the private market do the job again if we cut defense spending drastically today? Very unlikely, most economists answer. The post–World War II transition was a very special case. First, there was a huge pent-up demand for consumers' goods and housing after five years of war shortages. Second, the public had a huge accumulation of money and securities from government borrowing during the war, ready to pour out onto the market; M had grown very rapidly during the war while spending opportunities were blocked off. Without these special circumstances, it is highly unlikely that the precipitous transition from war to peace would have occurred without at least temporary heavy unemployment.

Conclusion. A big cut in spending by any sector of the economy threatens deflation and unemployment. This is true for government, as it is for the private sector. Massive reductions like $20 billion throw the spotlight on the need for measures to offset the deflationary impact. There is no mechanism by which private spending will automatically generate the right aggregate demand to assure the gradually rising aggregate demand needed for a prosperous economy. We need wise, positive monetary and fiscal policy to assure a stably growing economy in such a case.

The Problem of Micro (Structural) Adjustments

Maintaining adequate aggregate demand can help smooth the adjustment to a big cut in defense spending, but it cannot do the whole job. In our economy the main job of transferring resources in response to changing demand falls on private initiative, the profit motive, and the marketplace. And with the assumed $20 billion cut in arms spending, the job would be a big one.

Table 45–1 shows the distribution of jobs depending on Vietnam War spending as of 1969. It shows separately all industries where more than 25,000 jobs were involved.

Table 45–1 answers the radical criticism that the American economy must depend on the Vietnam War to keep it from collapse—that we dare not make peace. Total Vietnam War spending at its peak was only between 2 and 3 percent of U.S. g.n.p. Only 2 percent of all workers' jobs depended on Vietnam War spending. The average annual growth in U.S. g.n.p. over the years 1965 to 1970 exceeded $60 billion. The argument that American capitalism would collapse without this $20 billion of Vietnam War spending is obvious nonsense.

But that is not to say there will be no problems of converting back to peace. To face the

table 45-1

Jobs Dependent on Vietnam War Spending, 1969*

Industry	Vietnam-related Jobs (In Thousands)	Percent of Industry's Employment
Aircraft	233	27 %
Transportation services	165	6
Ordnance	140	42
Wholesale-retail trade	76	0.5
Communications equipment	74	11
Business services	50	2
Electronics	41	11
Textiles	41	10
Medical, education, nonprofit	36	0.7
Primary iron-steel manufacture	33	4
Machine-shop products	33	14
Construction	29	1
All other	650	—
Total	1,600	2

*Rough estimates by U.S. Labor Department. Includes secondary effects of Vietnam spending. Total for last column shows percent of total civilian employment.

problem at its most difficult level, consider the impact of total defense spending of about $75 billion in the late 1960s. Approximately 95 percent of employment in aircraft and missiles, 60 percent in shipbuilding, and 40 percent in radio and communications equipment depended directly on total defense spending. Missile and aircraft production alone in 1968 provided over 80 percent of the manufacturing jobs in the San Diego area, 70 percent in Wichita, 50 percent in Seattle. About 30 percent of all manufacturing employment in Kansas, Washington, and California depended directly on defense spending. About three-quarters of a million workers in aircraft and missiles, nearly a half million in electrical equipment, and a quarter million each in shipbuilding and ordnance works would have been out of jobs without defense spending. All this says nothing of the jobs indirectly dependent on defense spending through what these defense workers buy.

Even if civilian demand did increase $20 billion to fill the entire gap left by reduced defense spending, it's easy to see that the impact on some industries, some regions, some individual firms, and some classes of workers could be disastrous. This is Midway-O'Hare writ large. Suppose the public decides it wants more new homes and more vacation trips with its $20 billion windfall. Maybe Seattle and San Diego can turn on the advertising and pick up some of the tourist trade, but that's not going to give jobs to many of the unemployed missile workers and electronics engineers. There are going to be lots of jobs in the construction industry across the land, but most places are a long way from San Diego, Seattle, and Wichita, to mention only those three examples; and bricklaying is very different from wiring electrical relays for missile guidance systems. A lot of workers and business firms could shift readily to meet a growth in civilian demand. But to pretend there wouldn't be a major problem of structural adjustment would be nonsense.

Moreover, at least temporarily there might be serious shortages and price increases in civilian goods industries. In home building, the demand for materials and skilled workers could soar. Swords do not convert easily to plowshares.[4]

A prestigious task force of government, industrial, labor, and academic economists in the 1960s came up with the following recommendations to mitigate painful and disruptive impacts on workers, communities, and investors in defense industries in the event of major disarmament.

1. Strengthen our system of employment offices to provide faster, more accurate information on job opportunities.

2. Strengthen our unemployment insurance

program to assure a higher minimum standard of payments and duration of coverage.

3. Establish better government-aided retraining facilities.

4. Consider measures to bring new industries into hard-hit areas, rather than trying to move displaced workers out.

5. Permit defense industries to provide more generous severance allowances for laid-off workers, and charge them as costs on government contracts.

6. Encourage defense contractors to plan ahead for peacetime reconversion possibilities for their plants and workers.

These proposals have a familiar sound. They're much like the proposals to improve the performance of the labor market mentioned in the earlier sections on automation and poverty.

The Special Problem of Research and Development

Since the Korean War, the federal government has financed over two-thirds of all research and development spending in the American economy, and nearly all the basic research. Nearly 90 percent of these federal R and D outlays have been under the national defense and space programs. Jet aircraft, atomic energy, electronics, computers, and a variety of other widely used civilian goods were originally developed under defense R and D contracts. Thus, an across-the-board cutback in defense spending could wipe out a big part of the nation's research and development activities, including most of our basic research.

In a big defense cutback, should we leave it up to the individual initiative, the profit motive, and the marketplace to reallocate the quarter million scientists and engineers now working on defense-financed research and development? Many experts argue that the national interest is at stake here in a unique way. Basic research has massive positive externalities, hence (on the analysis of Chapter 38) direct government financing may be socially desirable. In any event, the case of R and D in a big defense cutback illustrates the fact that the problems of adjustment to change are seldom simple, espe-

[4]For an intriguing set of estimates of the possible impact of disarmament made through the use of "input–output" tables, see W. Leontief and M. Hoffenberg, "The Economic Effects of Disarmament," in *The Scientific American* for April, 1961; or a simpler version with the same title in *Disarmament and the Economy*, E. Benoit and K. Boulding, eds. (New York: Harper & Row, Publishers, 1963).

cially when the changes are large and fast. Not many people would like to see our whole basic research effort go down the drain, however enthusiastic they are about cutting government defense spending.

A Final Question

With this background, a final question on disarmament. Suppose worldwide peace should come—a happy day for mankind. U.S. defense spending is now about $75 billion annually. How would you advise the government to go about the job of converting this $75 billion peace bonus to the public good?[5]

Conclusion

Change is everywhere in economic life. It is the essence of a dynamic economy. Without it, our economy would stagnate. Yet every change brings problems, often painful ones. When change is big and fast, the problems may envelop the whole economy.

Over the past century, rapid, flexible adaptation to change has been an outstanding mark of the American system. How to continue this dynamic performance, and to improve on it, is one of the largest challenges facing us today. For tomorrow's changes are sure to be different from the ones we have learned to cope with, though we cannot know today what they will

[5] If you want to explore the problem further, *Defense and Disarmament*, R. E. Bolton, ed. (Englewood Cliffs, N.J.: Prentice-Hall, Inc., 1966) provides a readable set of analyses of different facets of the economics of transition to peace. The *Economic Report of the President*, 1969, pp. 187–211, contains a detailed report on plans for conversion to peacetime activities after the end of the Vietnam War.

be. Abraham Lincoln wrote, a century ago: "The dogmas of the quiet past are inadequate to the stormy present. . . . We must disenthrall ourselves and then we shall save our country."

The three examples in this chapter are intended as illustrations, to stimulate you to think through analytically what an economy must do to adapt effectively to change—shifting consumer demands and social needs, technological advance, changing patterns of international economic competition, the world population explosion. If you think back, the whole book has been a steady stream of cases of economic change and how well or badly our economy adjusts to them.

Every case is different, but some central strands run through most of them. First, to understand them, we need to look at both macro and micro aspects. To focus on either alone is likely to miss a substantial part of the adjustment problem unless we are concerned with only a small segment of the total economy. Second, policies to deal with most important economic problems involve balancing off two or more social goals against one another—progress, freedom, security, and others you may rate high. Your personal values will go far in determining how big a role you believe government should take in aiding the market process to adjust to economic change. Third, don't be content with clichés and first-glance answers. Most important economic problems involve complex, interacting issues. Thus, the simple black-or-white answer is seldom the best one. The world is more often grey than pure black or white. For complex problems, complex policies often make the most sense.

Review

FOR ANALYSIS AND DISCUSSION

1. "Since society at large is the main beneficiary of rapid technological advance, we should provide reasonable government aid to workers and industries who, through no fault of their own, are displaced by such advance." Do you agree or disagree? What government aid, if any, should be provided? Who should pay?

2. Should we place primary emphasis on assuring strong aggregate demand or on retraining and relocation of displaced workers if we are concerned about unemployment resulting from rapid automation?

3. Organized labor argues that the thirty-five-hour workweek with no reduction in pay is the best way to eliminate unemployment resulting from rapid technological advance. Businessmen reply that this would be self-defeating and would in fact cause increased unemployment, since it would raise wage costs per unit of output. Which is right? Justify your answer.

4. Is it better to move displaced workers to jobs elsewhere, or to bring capital (jobs) to workers who have lost their jobs? Explain.

5. Is the likely disruption from a rapid cutback in arms spending so serious that we should avoid such a cutback, even though world tensions ease? How fast could we afford to reduce our arms spending? What criteria would you use in deciding?

6. Since they are heavily dependent on government spending and were largely developed to meet government needs, do we owe the aircraft, missile, and electronics industries (workers or stockholders) special aid in case government military spending is drastically cut back? If so, what kinds of aid? Who should pay?

7. Do external economies create a convincing case for continuing government support of research even if we cut back government arms and space spending? Explain.

8. What is your program for converting to peace on the end of the Vietnam War?

9. What general rule should we follow in deciding when market forces are inadequate to handle rapid economic change satisfactorily?

Comparative Economic Systems: USA, USSR, and the Mixed Economies

The Comparison of Economic Systems

How Does the Soviet Economy Work?

Comparative Economic Systems in Perspective

Planning With Private Enterprise: The New Look?

Conclusion

What type of economic system serves man best? On the evidence of Tables 1–1 and 19–1, it is private enterprise, market-directed capitalism. Of the top twelve nations in real income per capita, every one has basically this type of economy . Yet one-third of all the world's people live in Communist nations (mainly China and the USSR,) and over the last half century Soviet Russia has become the world's second great industrial and military power. Many of the smaller nations are hovering as to the type of economy they prefer.

What is the Russian Communist system, and how does it work? Will an even more extreme form of communism in mainland China dominate the Communist-Socialist world? Are the mixed economies the harbingers of the future?

Who will win the respect and emulation of the world's uncommitted billions in the less-developed nations? At the end of a long book devoted mainly to our largely private-enterprise system, it is well to look in detail at these questions—to compare how the two leading systems get their jobs done.

The Comparison of Economic Systems

To us, ours is the normal way of life; private enterprise is the usual type of economic system. A half century ago this feeling would have been substantially justified for the whole Western, industrialized world. World War I was over. The postwar revolutions were done. Capitalism seemed securely reestablished everywhere except in Russia, and the new Communist regime there tottered precariously. Millions of Russians died of starvation; total Russian production was scarcely higher than it had been far back in the 1800s under the czars.

Today, though the United States and the other market-directed, Western-style economies have clearly won the race for economic well-being, communism is the economic pattern for more of the world's population than the private-enterprise system we know is. The democratic planning of India typifies another large fraction of the world's population. We must learn to see other systems as the people who live in them do—to recognize that many millions do not share the ideals and values we Americans hold so dear. But this recognition is a first step toward understanding how other economic systems work.

Capitalism and Communism[1]

Communism today has heavy overtones of politics as well as economics. To look at the economic side of any "ism" alone is to miss its essence. Communism has become inseparably associated with political and economic dictatorship because we see them together in Soviet Russia and Communist China, the countries that dominate our thinking about communism today. Yet in its original form, Marxian socialism was highly democratic in spirit. Karl Marx's famous *Das Kapital,* the foundation of modern communism, provided a detailed critique of capitalism, but he was conveniently vague when it came to blueprinting the Communist economy to be. Still, one thing is sure. Marx wasn't looking for any political or economic dictatorship except the dictatorship of the proletariat—of the whole working class. Evolutionary socialism comes from the same roots, but it is today found in varying degrees in Australia, New Zealand, Sweden—all countries with the highest traditions of political democracy and protection for individual rights.

From an economic viewpoint, there are two big differences between capitalism and communism. Under private-enterprise capitalism as we know it, most productive resources are privately owned, and economic activity is largely directed by the interaction of supply and demand in the market. Under communism, conversely, most productive resources are publicly owned, and economic activity is directed largely by central planning; this type of economy is often called a "command economy." The two critical questions, then, are: (1) Are productive resources privately or publicly owned, and (2) is economic activity directed by individual choice and the price system or by governmental planning?

Obviously, both are matters of degree. Not all productive resources are privately owned under American capitalism—governments own land, highways, dams, buildings, and so on. Nor

[1]There are many volumes on comparative economic systems and on the "isms." Three readable ones are G. Grossman, *Economics Systems* (Englewood Cliffs, N.J.: Prentice-Hall, Inc. 1970); W. Ebenstein, *Today's Isms* (Englewood Cliffs, N.J.: Prentice-Hall, Inc. 1964), which stresses the politico-economic mix; and P. J. Wiles' *The Political Economy of Communism* (Cambridge: Harvard University Press, 1961). For comparative looks focused primarily on the American economy, try Calvin B. Hoover, *The Economy, Liberty, and the State* (New York: Twentieth Century Fund, 1959); F. A. Hayek, *The Road to Serfdom* (Chicago: University of Chicago Press, 1944); and J. A. Schumpeter, *Capitalism, Socialism, and Democracy* (New York: Harper & Row, Publishers, 1942).

are all resources publicly owned in Russia. Similarly, not all economic activity is directed by the price system in the United States, nor is all economic activity centrally planned in Russia. Also, an economy can have private ownership of resources and nevertheless be centrally planned. The American economy during World War II was a partial example. Hitler's fascism in Germany was a more complete example. India makes substantial use of central planning today, with primarily private ownership of resources.

Thus, economic systems fall along a spectrum on both these conditions, something like the arrangement shown in the diagram above. The location of the countries is only approximate, but it is intended to suggest the variation on the two scores. The American and Russian systems differ widely on both. They are thus especially worth careful comparison. But don't forget that most of the world's economies lie in between, on one or both of the spectrums shown. Nor is Russia at the extreme of communism.

The Tests of a Good Economic System

Every economic system has to do four main jobs. It must decide and then carry out the decisions on:

1. What is to be produced?
2. How is it to be produced?
3. Who is to get the goods and services produced?
4. When—how many of society's resources should be devoted to current consumption (the present) and how many to investment (the future)?

Every economic system gets these jobs done somehow, whether it's the United States, the USSR, or a primitive South Sea island economy. If we want to evaluate the different systems, the question is, how well does each system do these jobs? And to answer rationally we need to set up criteria for judging.

At the beginning of the course, five broad socioeconomic criteria were tentatively suggested:

1. Progress: Does the system provide a progressively higher standard of living—stable economic growth? (How big is the economic pie?)
2. Individual direction: Does it produce the goods and services consumers want? (Who decides what's in the pie?)
3. Equity: Does it provide an equitable distribution of income? (Who gets a big slice of the pie and who a little one?)
4. Freedom: Does it provide economic free-dom for the individual? Is power widely dispersed?
5. Security: Does it provide reasonable economic security for all?

Substitute your own criteria if you don't like the five listed. But keep some set in mind as you read on.

The following pages are mainly an analysis of how the Soviet economy operates, and an evaluation of how well it does its job. But throughout there's a running comparison with the way the American economy accomplishes the same tasks. And at the end there's a final, comparative look at some of the in-between economies and at our own economy. A major purpose is to help you to pull together your own understanding and evaluation of the American economy.

How Does the Soviet Economy Work?

Objectives

The modern Soviet economy rests on the doctrines of Karl Marx. "From each according to his abilities, to each according to his needs," was Marx's foundation for the Communist society. The rule of the masses, with productive resources used for the common benefit of all, remains, on paper, the foundation of the modern Communist economies—of China as well as the USSR.

The goals stressed by modern Communist leaders look very much like the five listed above for the American economy. While there is no one set of official USSR goals, the following have been repeated many times by Soviet leaders:

1. Expansion of the productive capacity of the nation, to raise the Russian standard of living and to permit an adequate national defense against aggression.
2. Improvement in literacy and higher cultural levels.
3. Improvement in national health standards.
4. Reduction in hours and unpleasantness of work.
5. Reduction of economic insecurity.

Soviet leaders eulogize democracy and personal participation in achieving the goals of the factory, the community, and the state. Freedom of speech and assembly and all the other basic freedoms of the American Constitution are guaranteed in the Soviet Constitution—plus some others we don't include. From the words, it is hard to distinguish Soviet Russian from the Western democratic societies.

In fact, the USSR appears to most outsiders a "command" economy, with the big commands issued by a small group of Communist officials over whom the great mass of people have little control. The centralization of political power in Russia is especially significant for our economic survey, because all basic economic plans and policies are made by the controlling political group. Even after recent steps away from central control, among the major nations the Soviet economy is still the most highly planned and controlled in the world, save that of Communist China. In America, we leave everyone pretty much free to use his private property and his income as he wishes within the law, and we accept the outcome as being by and large the best one for the public welfare. The Russian leaders decide what they want to happen economically, and they use a comprehensive system of plans and controls to make it happen.

So much for Russia's stated objectives and basic approach. How do the Soviets go about solving the four big economic problems?

(1) Deciding What To Produce and (2) Getting It Produced[2]

In the USSR, the central planners decide what is to be produced. They do this through an elaborate system of planning. After the Russian revolution of 1917 to 1918, the Communists made an almost fatal mistake. They assumed that central economic control was easy—that all they had to do was confiscate private productive resources, use a little common sense in shifting over to a Communist system, tell people

in general what to produce, and everything would go along nicely. It didn't! Russian total output in 1919 to 1920 dropped back to near the 1890 level. The Russian peasants didn't see why they should produce just to have their crops taken away and given to someone else. There was virtually no modern industrial capacity in Russia. The economy was thrown into chaos.

The central planners made many mistakes, but the vast complexities of a completely planned economy were gradually realized. After years of experimentation and a series of "five-year plans" for economic development since 1928, the Soviets developed this general pattern:

First, the basic policy decisions are made by the central Communist authorities—what industries to develop, which to let lag, how much to allocate for consumption, how much for industrial expansion, how much for the military. Then the lower-level planners map out detailed directions for units in the economy to follow in implementing these decisions. Lastly, these plans have to be carried out by millions of Soviet officials, managers, and workers throughout Russia.

In the last decade, this process has been substantially modified in order to reduce the amount of detailed planning at the top and to place more responsibility on individual managers. This shift has reflected the growing difficulties of detailed planning in an ever more complex Soviet economy, and the need to provide more individual incentives to the local managers who have to carry out the broad plans made at the top. During the 1960s, the Soviets admitted having serious problems with the top-heavy planning system. The "new look" was to retain central control over the big allocative decisions but to delegate more detailed planning to the factories and the local ministries, especially for industries not vital to Soviet defense or the national welfare.

It is still hard to tell how far this "new look" in Soviet planning will change the detailed planning process developed over the past quarter century. At first, Soviet leaders spoke of major changes, but by 1970 problems with the new

[2]Two good studies of the Russian economy are H. Schwartz, *An Introduction to the Soviet Economy* (Columbus, Ohio: Charles E. Merrill Publishing Co., 1968); and Alex Nove, *The Soviet Economy* (New York: Praeger Publishers, Inc., 1968).

system apparently strengthened the hand of those who favored retaining strong central control. At the moment the process is substantially this.

Making the Plan

The broad goals for the economy are set by the Praesidium and the Central Committee of the Communist Party. Since 1928, these goals have been contained in a series of comprehensive five-year plans, each concentrated on a few special objectives (mainly defense and industrialization) and focused on major product goals for the economy. Table 46–1 shows some major elements of the plan for the years 1966 to 1970. Overall, the goal was an annual increase of 8.5 percent in industrial production and of 5 percent in agriculture. In fact, performance fell substantially short of this goal, and as of late 1970 no plan for the years 1971 to 1975 had been announced.

Within these broad objectives, the plan for each year is developed by the "Gosplan" (State Planning Commission), working with a huge Central Statistical Administration which provides data on available resources and productive capacities. Imagine their job. Suppose you

had to plan only aircraft. How would you plan production of all the hundreds of thousands of components that go into a single modern airplane, scheduling each to be on hand just when it was needed? Now back up and decide how you would plan the production of all the subcomponents to produce the parts you need for the airplanes. By now you'll be up in the millions of individual decisions, just for one major product. And the complexities multiply geometrically when you add other products, because of all the interlinkages between materials, labor, and manufacturing facilities needed. It's this vast complex of decisions we leave to supply and demand in the marketplace in our private-enterprise economy. And these difficulties have pushed the Soviets to simplify their planning process. How do they do it now?

First, the Soviets don't start from scratch each year. They use last year as a bench mark, which greatly simplifies the task. Second, they apparently concentrate largely on some 1,500 major commodities (industries). For each of these, they construct a "materials balance," a "labor balance," and a "geographical balance." These show the materials, labor, and other resources needed to produce the desired output throughout the economy, and the net output required to add to present inventories in order to meet the plan goals. By combining these balances for all major products, they have a reasonably complete picture of the overall materials, labor, facilities, and regional balances for the entire economy. From this "input–output" model, they can see roughly where there are likely to be materials shortages, where labor surpluses, and so on, and they can then adjust accordingly.

But the Gosplan apparently focuses each year primarily on some fifty basic products and industries that are of critical importance in attaining the prime goals of the overall plan.[3] We can safely assume, for example, that the military missile program is currently on that list. With central planning, the Russians can, and do, put first things first. We, or even the Russian people,

table 46-1

Soviet Economic Plan, 1966-1970

Commodity	1970 Output	Average Annual Percentage Increase
Electrical power (billion KWH)	950.0	10.6
Oil (million tons)	390.0	7.6
Steel (million tons)	145.0	6.8
Cement (million tons)	122.0	7.2
Natural gas (million cubic meters)	318.0	12.5
Autos (millions)	0.6	29.6
Refrigerators (millions)	7.5	26.0
TV sets (millions)	8.5	17.6
Grain (million tons)	190.0	4.6
Meat (million tons)	13.0	4.8
Sugar (million tons)	84.0	2.0

[3]During World War II, when the U.S. industrial economy was extensively but by no means completely planned, the whole planning process hinged largely on allocation of three major materials—steel, copper, and aluminum.

may not agree that they're the right first things —but it's clear that planning does get resources devoted effectively to the prime planned objectives.

Once the broad outline of an annual plan is completed, it is sent to regional and industry councils throughout the economy. They check their quotas against the productive capacities in their region or industry to see whether the plan appears feasible. If they think the quotas are too high, or if they believe their tentative allocations of materials and equipment would be inadequate to meet them, they have the right to protest . . . and they do! Local plant managers often argue that the goals are too high and that inadequate raw materials and new machinery are being allocated to meet them. The local workers may protest that they are already speeded up to the limit of their capacity. Then it's a subject for negotiation with the regional and industry-level planners, and after that between them and the national planners at the Gosplan. We know that the Soviet planning process involves lots of talk. Some observers have called it the most gigantic collective-bargaining process in history.

Finally, all this information gets reflected back up to Moscow, where the Gosplan must settle on the final plan so that everything balances out for the whole economy. The planners do the best they can, using some modern mathematical and electronic-computer techniques, and making adjustments in minor industries to accommodate the major goals.

The final stage, after the plan has been approved by top Communist officials, is to send it back down to the regional and industry councils for implementation.

We know the planners make mistakes. Plans are continuously adjusted. If the small-machinery plan runs into labor shortages while that for electric light globes turns up a surplus, the planners don't wait until next year to make an adjustment. This doesn't make for a quiet life among Gosplan employees or for managers throughout the economy, and the number of adjustments has apparently snowballed in recent years as the Russian economy has grown in complexity. Complaints from below have become increasingly bitter. Industry plans are changed dozens of times a year. These crises have led the pragmatic rulers in the Kremlin to consider delegating more responsibility and freedom to local managers in carrying out the broad goals handed down from above.

Carrying Out the Plan

The annual plan is a physical blueprint for the use of productive resources and production of intermediate and final products for the year. (Note that nothing has been said so far about money, prices, or profits.) How do the Soviets get their plans carried out? In essence, by telling people what to do and by paying them for doing it.

Managerial Incentives. Under the prevailing system, the plant manager has received a quota, together with detailed information on the supply of materials he will receive, the equipment that will be allocated to him, the labor he is to use, and so on. But it's up to him to get the final product out. His job is to meet the quota, not to question why. If he exceeds his quota, he is praised by the party and gets substantial economic rewards, including money, better housing, a car, paid vacations, and other such benefits not available except through the official reward system. These are powerful incentives in a low-consumption society. On the other hand, if his plant ends the year below quota, or if he requires more labor and materials than have been allocated to him, he has done a bad job. His income goes down; his special perquisites are taken away; in extreme cases he may be demoted or even expelled from the party, of which he is probably a member if his is an important plant. Under the "new look" in planning, managers in some industries are also urged to make a "profit" by using their resources more efficiently, but apparently the physical goals still dominate the planning and rewards system.

The Soviets are thoroughly aware of the importance of good managers to the success of their plans. Managers get among the largest incomes in the economy. They receive medals and public commendation for exceeding quotas. But the Communists are also harsh critics when managerial performance falls short. In the widespread Soviet self-criticism during the shortfalls of the late 1960s, managers were publicly criticized and poor performances were penalized by demotions, loss of special prerogatives, and reductions in pay. Managers are very important under communism, the Soviets have found, just as they are under capitalism.

How has this differed from the American scene? In some respects, not much. In both cases, it's up to the manager to run the plant effectively, though the Soviet test has been real output in relation to resources allocated, while the American test is low costs and high profits. In terms of rewards, the Soviet manager can't accumulate property and live well off interest and dividends to supplement his salary and bonus. His absolute standard of living, and certainly his ability to save for his children and his future, are much lower. But relatively speaking, he does a good deal better.[4]

But the Soviets have had major problems on managerial incentives. Since rewards have depended mainly on meeting physical output quotas, managers try to conceal production possibilities so as to get lower quotas, to hoard materials, to avoid doing too well lest quotas be raised for next year. There is no penalty for wasteful use of materials or manpower so long as it doesn't violate the plan. Fulfilling the plan has to come first, to the detriment of quality of product if need be.

"Blat" (using influence with higher-ups in industry) and "tolkachi" (special purchasing agents from plants who go around buying up scarce materials and parts outside the plan) are well-known, if technically illegal, parts of the Russian industrial scene. Russian managers have learned to make their own performances look good by hoarding labor and materials, bootlegging scarce materials outside the plan, and even fudging the basic performance reports on which they are judged. This is not utterly different from the American case, where

[4]For a lively comparison of Soviet and American managers, see David Granick, *The Red Executive* (Garden City, N.Y.: Doubleday and Company, Inc., 1960).

local managers sometimes try to make their own units look good by devices that reduce rather than increase total corporate profits. Either way, it's tough to make middle managers stick to top-level plans. But in America the dollars and cents on the income statement at year-end, the percentage return on investment, and the per share earnings for the stockholders provide visible measures that facilitate evaluation of management performance.

Innovation has been another special managerial problem. New ideas involve risks, and the Soviet system has lacked effective rewards for risk taking. In the Soviet climate, doing reasonably well is more conducive to the manager's peace of mind than taking a chance on a new idea that may flop. There's nothing like the American private-enterprise entrepreneur out to make a million (or go broke) in a gamble on a new product or new method. Soviet criticism of managers for lack of imaginative innovation has been bitter. American corporations not infrequently face the same problem with their managers.

The problem of how much decentralization of decision making and operating authority is optimal remains unsettled in spite of the "new look" experiments. The parallel to the problem faced by a large American corporation, like General Motors, is striking. In America, decentralized decision making and authority, under only broad rules from headquarters, have been widely accepted as the best way of maintaining local managerial initiative and of coupling the advantages of central planning with local, first hand management. The Soviet "liberals" have urged dramatic changes in the same direction. But Gosplan still makes all the basic plans, and the blueprints for carrying them out for most of the economy.

Labor Incentives and Labor Unions. How do the Soviets get the workers to carry out their plans? Just as in the United States, money is the big incentive, but it is supplemented by continuous emphasis on national price and party loyalty for members.

The planners decide how much should be paid for each type of work, and they do it so as to get the plan carried out effectively. The biggest pay goes to scientists, artists, inventors, and managers who overproduce their quotas. About 75 percent of all industrial workers are on "piece rates," whereby each worker gets paid according to how much he turns out. This is a much higher percentage than in the United States. Money wages thus play much the same role in pulling labor into jobs and stimulating good performance as they do in America, except that in Russia they are set by the planners to channel workers where the planners want them, rather than freely by market supply and demand. It is stiking that money incentives—differential pay for workers turning out more output—are used more strongly than in such "capitalist" countries as the United States. And resulting pay differentials for workers are considerably wider in the USSR than here, where union pressures have tended to lessen them.

Table 46–2 shows incomes received by various Soviet groups. It is useful mainly to suggest relative incomes for different jobs. Since the figures shown are for the early 1960s, they should probably be increased by 50–75 percent for 1970 incomes in 1970 U.S. dollars. The Soviet authorities have stated that average Soviet monthly wages and salaries for 1967 were 105 rubles (about $120 at the official exchange rate).

How free are Soviet workers to work where they wish? Substantially free, given the immobility inevitably associated with low incomes and limited geographical fluidity—except for farm workers who are not free to move to industrial jobs because of the major Soviet problem in raising farm output, and workers who have been "recruited" for special projects or have received special training or education at state expense. The complaints of managers about labor turnover suggest that labor moves from job to job with considerable freedom. The main coercion used to hold workers in particular jobs is preference on desirable housing, which may be lost if the worker leaves. With a nationwide housing shortage, this is a powerful incentive.

Most Soviet workers belong to unions. But they are quite different from unions in America.

table 46-2

Soviet Incomes*

	Monthly Earnings in Rubles
Leading scientist	800-1500
Senior government official	700
Opera or ballet star	500**
Professor (science or medicine)	400-1000
Plant manager	300-1000
Engineer	100-300
Worker (skilled)	100-250
Physician	85-180
High school teacher	85-100
Worker (semiskilled)	60-90
Worker (unskilled)	27-50

*Data for early 1960s from U.S. Department of Labor; see text. One ruble equals $1.11 at the official exchange rate; this exchange rate understates the real buying power of Russian incomes in our money. Figures do not include extra perquisites such as special housing, cars, and the like, or social services such as free vacations, health services, and subsidized housing for all.
**Plus outside earnings to 2,000 rubles.

Soviet unions have nothing to do with setting wages; wages are established by the central planners. The unions are worker organizations that are expected to help in implementing government plans. As such, they apparently have a substantial role in urging workers to meet quotas and in channeling labor from surplus to shortage occupations. They administer most worker benefits. They handle worker grievances. But they are more like workmen's clubs than like the unions we know. Make your own comparison with the role of unions in America, where there is far more union power—and far more conflict.

Checking on Performance: The Gosbank and the State Control Commission. Basic planning is done in physical terms. But the Gosplan also makes up a complete set of "value" (or financial) plans to parallel the basic physical plans. Using these financial plans, the Gosbank (state banking system) provides the money to managers needed to pay for labor and materials to carry out the production plans. For example, if the annual plan calls for 10 million pairs of shoes, the Gosbank provides shoe-plant managers just enough rubles to pay for the labor, leather, and so on, allocated to the production of those shoes. It does the same for all other products. And managers must deposit their receipts in the Gosbank, except for cash payments made to workers. Except for wages and citizens' purchases of consumer goods, all transactions in Russia are made by check through the Gosbank.

The Gosbank plays two significant roles. First, it provides a financial control over managers. If they run out of money, this is a sign they are buying more than the inputs allocated to them under the physical plan. And since they can get materials and labor only by paying for them, the control is close and effective. When the manager deposits his receipts in the Gosbank, this provides an automatic check on whether he has produced the amount specified in the plan. Second, the Gosbank provides a regular banking function, transferring funds, advancing working capital, and creating a money supply for the economy.

In some respects, the Gosbank with its local branches is thus like banks in the United States. It advances working capital to carry out productive processes, transfers funds, and creates money for the economy. But it is strictly government-operated, and its main goal is to help implement the physical plan. It advances new checking accounts (creates money) when they are needed to facilitate production, and it reduces funds to industries that have been absorbing too much labor or material. (Its policies are also designed to help insure that total purchasing power is about equal to goods and services available at the desired state prices, as we shall see presently. Thus, it is a little like our Federal Reserve, but with more direct control over the supply of money.)

The other official watchdog over managers and regional officials is the State Control Commission, whose representatives function as inspectors through periodic visits and through reviewing Gosbank checking accounts. Lastly, there are the ever present Communist party officials, who may report lax or improper behavior to party headquarters. Often these are overlapping groups, for high officials of the planning and control agencies also often hold party office.

How does this checking on performance compare with the private-enterprise process? In America, too, the availability of funds to carry out any economic service exercises a basic control over what is done and who does it. In America, the firm gets funds continuously from selling its product; thus consumers (rather than the government) exercise a continuous check on whether any firm is doing its job effectively. If a firm wants to expand, it must either have stored up its own profits to risk or it must go to the competitive capital market for funds. There its project is evaluated by bankers, private investors, and other lenders against other alternative demanders of funds. If the firm's prospects look good, it will be able to borrow; if they look bad, it will have trouble raising funds. The capital market controls who can expand and who cannot.

Which process is more effective? It obviously depends on your point of view. Who should check on whom? The Soviet procedure gives a direct control to the planners through the Gosbank and the control commission. In America, we place most of our faith in the impersonal market, where lenders and business firms are counted on to look out for their own incomes and thereby to get resources allocated most effectively. Here the Socialists criticize the American economy vigorously. They say our capital markets are not competitive—that capital is rationed out by monopolistic lenders to big, favored borrowers in a way that makes it hard for new, smaller firms to compete effectively with the established giants. But even fewer officials decide who gets the capital to expand in the USSR. Think back to the chapters on monopoly and competition and on the American banking system to decide how much weight to give this criticism.

The Recalcitrant Problem of Agriculture. Agriculture has been the Communists' knottiest problem. Their early attempts to collectivize

Russian agriculture, carried through by bloody force during the 1920s and 1930s, met bitter and sullen resistance. Forced to work on collective farms, farmers produced less than before and kept crops and animals for themselves rather than turning them over to Soviet authorities for export to the cities. Frustrated Communist planners tried one tack, then another—but with little success in meeting expanded food goals for the rapidly growing industrial population or in freeing farm labor for industrial jobs.

In theory, a collective farm is a cooperative, democratic association of farmers who have pooled their land, tools, and labor to make a large farm, which they operate in common. Proceeds are shared in proportion to the quantity and quality of work they do. Large-scale operation produces the economies of large-scale mechanized farming, eliminating the waste and inefficiency that for centuries have characterized Russian agriculture.

It sounds fine, but not to the Russian peasants. Soviet planners found crops vanishing into farm consumption and total production declining. Bloody reprisals brought only temporary compliance and smoldering resentment. Over millions of acres and widely scattered farmers, effective control was impossible.

There are now some 100,000 collective and state farms, compared to perhaps 25 million small peasant farms four decades ago. About 5,000 of these are huge state farms of many thousand acres, operated outright as "business" firms by the Ministry of Agriculture in much the same pattern as prevails for industrial production. The rest are collective farms, ranging from a few "communes" (which involve complete sharing of property, labor, and results) to many cases where the collective farm is scarcely more than a sharing of major machinery and some exchange of labor. In most cases, part of the land is farmed collectively but each family retains a small plot for its own individual operation. These private plots make up only 5 to 10 percent of the total land under cultivation, but they apparently produce nearly one-third of total farm output of vegetables, eggs, meat, milk, and other such products that are suited to labor-intensive production and that can be sold in small lots in markets.

Payments to farmers are calculated on a complicated basis. For work on collective farms they receive partly payment in kind, partly money income that varies above a guaranteed minimum, depending on how much they produce. Apparently about a third of total output is delivered directly to the state, about a third is used on the farms for further output (seed, feed for animals, and so on), and about a third is given to the farmers themselves. A substantial portion of the latter finds its way onto the free market for food consumption in the cities. This supply is augmented by products from the millions of small family holdings, as indicated above. Private initiative is far from dead in Russian agriculture.

In any case, farm output has persistently lagged far behind the plan goals, in spite of one "reform" after another. The 1970 farm output goals in Table 46–1 are viewed by most outsiders as unrealistic. Most outsiders estimate that since 1950 Soviet farm output has grown not more than 2 or 3 percent a year, if that much. In the mid-1960s Russia, historically a large wheat exporter, had to import large quantities of wheat for food. Food output per capita has barely held stable over the last decade.

The importance of agriculture in Russia is great. Nearly 40 percent of the Russian labor force is in agriculture—39 million workers, compared to 5 million in the United States. Yet U.S. total farm output substantially exceeds Russia's. U.S. farming is highly mechanized and capital-intensive; Russia's is technically backward and labor-intensive, with limited use of modern fertilizers and mechanical equipment. The Soviets badly need more efficiency on the farm, to increase output and to free labor for work in industry.

"Profits" and the New Look in Soviet Planning

In recent years, evidence has piled up that the Soviet planners have been increasingly overwhelmed by their task. As the size and complexity of an economy increase, the number of interconnections among products, labor, and materials increases exponentially. The sheer volume of work requires that it be divided among more and more offices and locations, even when modern computers are used. Mistakes and inconsistencies inevitably increase, and the number of plan modifications snowballs, wreaking havoc on the day-to-day operations of plant managers and the production process. Soviet growth slowed significantly after the late 1950s.

About 1960, a few academic economists, notably Professor Y. Liberman, began to question tentatively whether more reliance on a kind of "profit motive" for individual managers couldn't help the top planners, avoid the local wastes of physical planning, and increase total output. To the amazement of many Western observers, this possibility was discussed openly during the early 1960s by intellectuals and planners alike. And in 1964 the Communists announced an experiment that freed managers in the shoe and food-processing industries from planned quotas, and directed them to maximize their profits, much as in America, with their own bonuses based on the profits they make. Each manager was substantially free to set the price of his product and the wages he will pay, and to choose his own production methods. The profits themselves, above the special awards to the successful manager, of course revert to the state.

At first, tales of spectacular increases in efficiency abounded. Increased managerial freedom, reliance on "profit" incentives, and freer prices were extended to other noncritical areas of the economy. By 1968 apparently about one-fourth of Soviet industry was operating on this basis, though Gosplan still set the major priorities for the system and controlled in detail the areas vital to national defense, industrial expansion, and other high-priority objectives.

But the "new look" raised basic issues for the Soviets. Whether they can manage a system half planned and half market-directed remains to be seen. Widening of the experiment inevitably involves direct conflicts with centrally planned uses of productive resources for specific national goals. It has been far from clear how these conflicts could be resolved without destroying the new managerial freedoms or compromising major goals in the fully planned sectors. And troubles arose. In the late 1960s, industrial output fell increasingly short of the goals set by the 1966 to 1970 plan. Soviet leaders and the official press embarked on a striking campaign of self-criticism and analysis, focused on waste, managerial and worker inefficiency, faulty planning, alcoholism among workers, and agricultural deficiencies. The trend seems clearly to be back toward more central control. Support for the new "liberalism" has faded, at least temporarily. But it will be surprising if the Soviets are not driven back to further experiments with managerial decentralization and "profit" incentives.

(3) Deciding How Income Is To Be Distributed

Marxist doctrine says: to each according to his need. The Soviet leaders today season this liberally with: to each according to how hard he works and how much he contributes. Incomes are more equally distributed than in the United States, because in Russia income from property is very limited, whereas many of the highest American incomes are from dividends, interest, and capital gains on private property. There are no millionaires in modern Russia. But money incomes derived from work are about as unequally distributed in Russia as in America. This inequality reflects the strong use made of incentive payments to achieve the goals established by the central planners.

Table 46–2 above tells the story. Artists, scientists, professors, managers, and government officials receive the highest incomes, including special supplements in premium housing, use of government automobiles, paid vacations, and so on. As in America, common labor is at the bottom of the totem pole—except for farmers, many of whom take much of their income in kind from their farms. Within the ranks of factory workers and comparable laborers, apparently the spread between the lowest and highest monthly incomes is nearly one to eight, far wider than in America.

Wage rates are adjusted up and down frequently for different occupations and industries, to help implement the overall plan. The Soviets may be good Marxists on paper, but their behavior on wages suggests they have learned a good deal too about the power of monetary incentives.

Government Services and Income Redistribution. Although it uses money incentives freely to stimulate production and allocate resources, the Soviet state provides widespread free social services to help the masses. Soviet authorities claim that one-third of the income of low-income groups is provided by free government services. Nearly all housing is government-owned, and rents are extremely low; on the average, Soviet citizens apparently pay only about 2 to 3 percent of their income for housing, far under the 15 to 25 percent common in America. A Moscow two-bedroom apartment rents for $20–$30 a month—if you can find one. Russian housing is generally bad, but it's very cheap. Paid vacations, government nurseries, special grants to large families, free education, and extensive health services all supplement money incomes.

But to evaluate these government services we have to ask, who pays for them? A general sales ("turnover") tax accounts for over half of all government income. Profits on state enterprises provide most of the rest. Direct personal taxes (mainly an income tax) take only 8 percent of personal income. All told, government collections and expenditures comparable to our combined federal-state-local government taxes and expenditures apparently amount to about 35–40 percent of the gross national product, though estimates vary substantially.

Since the turnover tax varies widely from product to product and from year to year, estimation of its incidence by income levels is extremely difficult. Increases and decreases in the tax are used to adjust the prices of individual products up and down so as to discourage or stimulate consumption. This way the planners make consumer demand match the goods produced under the plan, somewhat as free market prices provide this adjustment in the United States. This tax, therefore, substantially offsets the apparent big government supplement to low incomes.

On the other hand, the Soviets use especially low prices on some major commodities in addition to housing to subsidize low-income consumers. This means that such goods are sold below "cost." Prices are set very high on such luxuries as automobiles. Here again, pricing is used by Soviet planners to promote the goals they consider important—stimulation or restriction of consumption, redistribution of income, and equating aggregate spendable income to aggregate supply available for purchase.

(4) Deciding Between Current Consumption and Economic Growth

In America the choice between current consumption and economic growth depends on a complex set of factors, including consumer saving, business investment decisions, private educational and research decisions, and government tax and investment behavior. In Russia, the decision is made and implemented by the central planners. And their choice has been in favor of rapid industrialization and growth, at the expense of current consumption.

Since the early 1920s, Russia's g.n.p. has grown at about 4 percent annually, about the same as the U.S. rate. But Soviet growth during the 1950s was spectacular—about double that rate—with a substantial slowdown since 1960. To press its postwar growth, the USSR allocated an extraordinarily large portion of its output to capital formation. Until recently private consumption was held below 50 percent of g.n.p. and nonmilitary investment apparently was 20 to 25 percent. Soviet consumption was so repressed that per capita real consumption was no higher in 1958 than it had been in 1928; only during the 1960s the average Russian has benefited through higher consumption from the last half century of Soviet economic growth. But this Soviet policy produced an average annual increase of 11 percent in the Russian capital stock, probably the primary factor that accounts

for rapid Soviet growth. Russia was also able to borrow a large amount of technology from the West.

Since 1960, Russian growth has slowed considerably. This has apparently reflected in substantial part a decline in the capital accumulation rate, as more was allocated to satisfying consumer wants. Even with central planning and control rather than individual choice and the price system, Russia faces the same fundamental problem in growth as does any other economy—she must divert scarce resources from consumption to investment, improve her technology, and step up the ability and performance of her labor force. There is no other way, for either communism or capitalism. As post-Stalin liberalization has opened up the Soviet economy to Western standards and Western ideas, the pressure has intensified on Communist leaders for more consumption goods.[5]

How fast the Russian economy grows depends on the decisions of the central planners, but it also depends on fundamental political forces—on how long the population will be content to see most of the increased output go into capital expansion and military products. In the American economy, the public speaks on this division continuously, through its own savings–spending behavior and through its directions to congressmen on government spending and taxes. Under the Soviet system there is little evidence that the man in the street has much voice in the decisions. Yet the Soviet leaders constantly face the need to keep the masses reasonably content if they are to stay in power.

[5]Under Marxist doctrine, only labor is truly productive. Thus, interest on money or real capital plays no role in Communist doctrine. Western economists properly point out that this position, if followed, will lead Soviet planners to improper decisions in allocating resources. Some methods involve a heavy use of productive resources per unit of output, others a low investment. Only by taking these differences into account can optimal decisions be made as to what capital goods should be produced. And the interest rate, as was pointed out in Chapter 35, is the price system's tool in making such comparisons among such alternatives. Interestingly, the pragmatic Soviet planners (who are smart fellows too) are now slipping the interest rate into their calculations through the back door.

Recent increases in consumption-goods output per capita attest to this concern.

Soviet planning for growth extends to every phase of economic life. Soviet education, in the European pattern, is deadly serious from kindergarten on. Although all youths go through elementary- and high-school-level education, only those with special capacities are sent on to what corresponds to our college-level training. For these, education is more specialized and more sharply focused on specific job training than ours is, but it is intense and thorough in those specialties, especially science, engineering, medicine, and the like. The National Science Foundation reports that Russia is currently training twice as many scientists and engineers as we are (about 125,000 a year as against our 60,000), and that her margin is apparently growing. Again, the contrast with the privately determined, free-choice advanced education system of the United States is striking.

No reliable estimates of total Soviet expenditure on research are available, but apparently, with a national income about half ours, Russia spends at least as much as we do on basic research.

Government Monetary and Fiscal Policy and Economic Stabilization

The Soviet central planners do not program men or machines into unemployment. If there is unemployment, it is because planning has gone awry or because someone is not behaving according to plan. And there has been very little official unemployment in the USSR—though many observers say the forced retention of low-income labor in agriculture is close to hidden unemployment. But there is still the problem of keeping total spending power roughly equal to goods available for purchase. If buying power gets too large, inflationary pressures will mount. If buying power is too low, prices must be cut or unsold inventories will pile up.

The Soviets manage this balance largely through the turnover tax (fiscal policy) and the Gosbank (monetary policy), the same two tools we use. In Russia, most of the burden falls on the turnover tax. If total demand is excessive and inflationary pressure exists, the turnover tax is raised all along the line, or on those products where demand seems most excessive, raising prices and siphoning off income to the government. If total demand is inadequate, turnover taxes are lowered. In a real sense, the Russians have adopted "functional finance" as the core of their stabilization and allocation mechanism.

In spite of this plan, inflation has been a persistent problem for the Soviets. The Russians are human beings too, and when there isn't enough to go around they apparently tend to plan a little more resources for all the demands than there are to parcel out. The result is a demand pressure that tends to bid up prices all along the line as shortages occur; black markets spring up everywhere. Twice since World War II, the Soviets have virtually repudiated their national debt, thereby wiping out bondholders' accumulated savings. The basic pressures that make for inflation—shortage of goods relative to the purchasing power provided by incomes paid out—are the same in Communist and capitalist societies.

Russia faces no serious danger of depression because of a collapse of private investment and consumption spending; there isn't any private investment to collapse. There is little doubt that the American private-enterprise market economy is more vulnerable to the economic instability and the waste of recession unemployment. This is a price we pay for our individual freedom and our spectacular economic success to date. However, if the Soviets expand the "profit-motivated" sector of their economy and consumers are given a wider range of choice in retail stores, unsold inventories and unemployment will pose increasing problems for the planners.[6]

---

[6]A complete report on the recent performance of the Soviet economy is provided by *New Directions in the Soviet Economy*, a compendium prepared for the Joint Economic Committee of Congress (Government Printing Office, 1966), especially Part II-A and II-B, on "Economic Performance."

Comparative Economic Systems in Perspective

At the end of a long book, it may be useful briefly to compare our performance with that of the USSR, and to look briefly at three interesting "mixed" economies, which represent different mixes of capitalism and communism. The main goal is to provide a last chance for you to organize your own ideas on the performance of the American system and what, if anything, you think needs to be done to improve it.

Progress—Stable Economic Growth

Which economic system has provided the highest standard of living for its people? However you measure, the United States is far out in front. In 1970, the U.S. g.n.p. was $980 billion. The USSR's, with a vastly larger area and 40 million more people, was only $425 billion, measured in U.S. dollars. Per capita g.n.p., a more significant measure of individual economic well-being, was $4800 in the United States, $1700 in the USSR. Such comparisons may be substantially off because of measurement problems and currency conversion difficulties; if a black-market, rather than the official, currency conversion rate is used, Russian per capita income may be as high as 60 percent of ours. Some experts, facing this statistical uncertainty, rate USSR per capita income as about half ours.

The Soviets have made impressive economic headway since the 1920s. Yet housing, especially outside the major cities, is appallingly poor. Nearly 50 percent of city families still live in a single room, sharing a kitchen and bath with others. Food for the masses is no more than adequate, with little variety. Consumer "hard goods" are scarce. Only the very powerful have private automobiles. In the late 1960s, less than 10 percent of all Russian families owned private refrigerators and washing machines, compared to over 95 percent in the United States. Russia had 18 vacuum cleaners per thousand people, the United States 211. For television sets the comparable figures are 56 and 318; for sewing

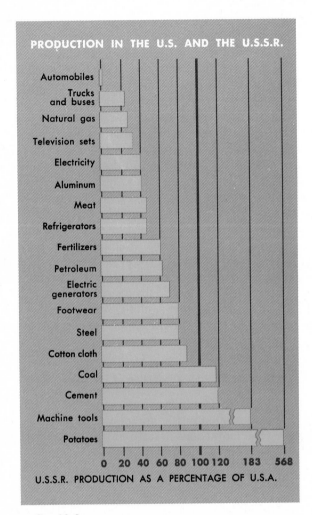

PRODUCTION IN THE U.S. AND THE U.S.S.R.

U.S.S.R. PRODUCTION AS A PERCENTAGE OF U.S.A.

fig. 46–1

U.S.S.R. production of most commodities is far below ours; but they surpass us in a few. What do you infer about Russian priorities from this partial list? (Source: Joint Economic Committee; *Soviet Economic Performance: 1966–67* [May, 1968].)

fourteen times as much for nylon stockings, eleven times as much for a refrigerator.

All in all, modern Russia is a study in contrasts. Space capsules go into orbit; accountants still use the abacus. Shiny new apartment buildings go up with antiquated elevators. Factories close down for lack of a few vital parts, but total industrial output soars impressively. Karl Marx's doctrine are everywhere, but if he gets in the way of what seems to be needed practically, he's quietly pushed aside.

Comparing U.S. and USSR growth rates was one of the favorite statistical games of the last decade. The Soviets didn't begin their five-year economic plans until 1928, but during the 1930s Russia grew far faster than the United States, which was bogged down in its worst depression. During World War II the picture was reversed, as the U.S. economy became prodigiously productive. The decade after World War II turned the tables again. Starting from low wartime levels, the USSR economy spurted, while the U.S. economy grew only gradually. By 1955, the postwar adjustments were largely completed, and Table 46–3 shows comparative data for the 1955 to 1970 period. For comparative purposes, the table also includes information on a sample of other economies, including the "mixed" economies

machines 100 and 135. Life in Russia is repeatedly described as drab.

Figure 46–1 provides a comparison of recent output in the United States and USSR of a range of producers' and consumers' goods in real terms, undistorted by price and currency quotations. Another way of comparing is to ask how many hours of common labor is required to obtain typical consumer goods. In the late 1960s, it took twelve times as much labor time to obtain a man's shirt in Russia as in the United States,

table 46-3

Comparative Growth Rates, 1955-70*
(Percentages per Year)

Country	Gnp per Capita	Investment	Consumption per Capita
Japan	10.5	21.0	5.4
Yugoslavia	5.6	**	**
West Germany	4.4	8.0	4.2
USSR	4.1	8.3	3.5
France	3.8	6.0	3.4
United States	3.1	4.8	3.0
United Kingdom	2.3	3.9	2.4

* Source: O.E.C.D. Data for 1970 are author's estimates.
** Not available.

examined briefly toward the end of the chapter. But don't forget the long-term comparative growth rates in Table 16–1, which give a quite different ranking.

Premier Khrushchev, back in the 1950s, boasted that Russia would overtake the United States in total output by 1970. He was wrong. Although Russia has grown faster than the United States over the last decade by perhaps 1–2 percent a year, the absolute lead of the United States in total and per capita output has substantially widened. At growth rates of the late 1960s, the USSR will still be far behind by the end of the century. Only Japan of the nations shown could threaten the U.S. lead if its recent growth rates should continue at a similar pace.

On the score of stability and avoidance of waste through unemployment, the American system doesn't come off as well. The Great Depression of the 1930s and even the smaller recessions of 1948, 1954, 1958, and 1961 have no direct parallels in the Soviet system. Although Soviet steel capacity was less than half of ours, in our recession year of 1961 Soviet production of steel was nearly as high as ours because our mills were running below 60 percent capacity. The "new economics" says we can have stable economic growth through intelligent use of fiscal and monetary policy, and the record of the 1960s is encouraging. But our past business cycles are a weakness the Communists are fond of emphasizing.

On inflation, neither communism nor capitalism can point to a clean slate. Inflation has plagued both systems through the postwar period. It is not clear that either has the problem effectively in hand. So, a nagging question: Does either capitalism or communism have a satisfactory answer to the problem of high employment without inflation?

But these problems in our economy don't change the basic picture. On the record to date, American capitalism has far outdistanced its competitors. Recessions slow us down, and we could be a lot better off without them. Another debacle like the 1930s could pull us back down near the Russians' level. But short of that, the record of the American economy is plain for all

to see. Other economies may be growing faster, but they have a long way to go to catch up.

One last comparison. Some critics argue that g.n.p. per capita is an inadequate measure of economic well-being. They are right, though it's the best we have. G.n.p. doesn't take into account leisure, such real costs as pollution, and a variety of other factors, noted at the end of Chapter 5. But as best we can tell, the USSR is no better off than we are on these unmeasured factors. Their press and their officials complain about water, air, and noise pollution, much as we do. Inclusion of leisure in g.n.p. would clearly worsen Russia's relative position. While the industrial workweek is about the same in both countries, a much larger proportion of the total population works in Russia. In particular, nearly all wives have jobs there, compared to less than half in the United States. No other non-g.n.p. factor would appear to change the relative standard of living comparison much.

Consumer Control—Dispersion of Economic Power

Clearly the American economy produces the biggest economic pie for consumers and for growth. How does it rate in giving the individual citizen control over what is produced, over the allocation of productive resources? On this issue the Soviet system rates low, ours much higher. In Russia, the Communist central planners, not the consumers, decide what is to be produced. Any "free choice" of consumers in spending their money is strictly limited—they can spend it only on goods available and at the prices set by the planners. The plan determines how much will be produced of all major products, and consumers have little to say about the division of resources between present and future. Only since the late 1950s have the Russian people had any increase in their real standard of living, out of the large increase in output since 1928. Perhaps in the Russians' eyes a centrally planned allocation of resources makes more sense than the unplanned allocation that we get through the market system, but it's hard to rationalize the argument that the typical Russian citizen has much control over what his system produces.

Does the American system produce the goods and services consumers want? By and large "yes" if we take "one dollar, one vote" as our criterion. About three-fourths of the gross national product is allocated through the private economy, pretty much in response to consumers' dollar demands. The American system produces fewer bicycles and potatoes than does the Russian, twice as much meat, twice as many washing machines and refrigerators, forty times as many autos. Look back at Figure 46–1 for the data on a list of individual products.

The way our market system responds to consumer demands is far from perfect. Varying degrees of monopoly and monopsony throughout the economy impede allocation of resources in accord with the purely competitive "ideal" of consumers' sovereignty. Some critics argue that businesses dictate what consumers "want" through advertising and other selling techniques; while the criticisms are often overdone in relation to the facts of the market, there is certainly some truth in them. Social costs and social benefits not mirrored in prices and costs distort resource allocation. But overall, consumer choice is the powerful director of economic production in our basically market-directed, unplanned economy.

Lastly, there is the quarter of the gross national product channeled through the public sector—presumably on a "one person, one vote" criterion rather than "one dollar, one vote." We say this one-fourth reflects what the people want as reflected through our democratic political processes. There are obvious problems in the public sector; they were spelled out in Part Five. Here the economist cannot answer alone. Answer for yourself how far we should go in substituting the public sector for the market, and how our public sector compares with the Russians' in permitting individual citizens to express their preferences.

Equity

Which system does a better job in slicing up the national economic pie among competing claimants? Does the Russian system provide a more equitable distribution of income than ours? By substantially eliminating incomes from property, the Communists have eliminated most of the very high incomes of capitalist systems. Worker money incomes, on the other hand, are more unequally distributed than in the United States, but then somewhat equalized by subsidized government services and pricing policies. This fact reflects the heavy emphasis placed on monetary work incentives by the Communists.

How about American capitalism? Our incomes are unequally distributed, before and after taxes. But the emergence of the huge, reasonably well-to-do middle class is the most striking development of recent American economic history. And the past half century has seen a tendency toward greater income equality.

How equal should incomes be? Partly, this is an ethical issue; make up your your own mind. Partly, it is an economic issue. If we want to live comfortably, we need to retain effective incentives to work and invest. Remember the Russian experience that individual money rewards seem to be a more powerful economic incentive than the Communists used to admit. Any income redistribution that reduces total output is very hard to defend. Table 19–1 shows how the spectacular growth of the Western, market-directed economies has dominated all distributional issues. Even the poor at the bottom of the income scale in the wealthy Western economies have higher incomes than the middle-income citizens in the less-developed, command-type economies. Individual initiative based on individual reward has been the foundation of most successful economic growth in the nineteenth and twentieth century world.

Individual Freedom

The American economy provides almost complete freedom on where to work, where to live, how to spend your money, and other economic choices. The freedom to go into business for yourself is completely unmatched in the Soviet system. American unions are a powerful device for equalizing the economic power of employers and employees. Government taxes are heavy and to this extent economic freedom may be said to be curtailed—though less so than in Russia.

How much "economic freedom" the Soviet economy provides for the individual depends on what you mean by the phrase. Today, the Soviet citizen has considerable freedom to move to another job and apparently freedom to spend his income on whatever he can find to buy. But the meaning of this freedom is subject to dispute, since the government determines what goods will be available for purchases and indirectly tells him where he should work. America has nothing like the Soviet insistence that workers stay on farms in spite of incomes there well below those available in the cities— because the plan calls for raising farm output. Further, Russian unions have no voice in determining the wages at which the citizens will work.

It seems obvious to us that our individual economic freedom far surpasses that available in Russia. But the question "through whose eyes?" is relevant again. The following quotation from a speech by then Premier Khrushchev illustrates how different things can look to someone else. He said:[7]

Indeed, there is freedom in the capitalist countries, but for whom? Of course, not for the working people, who are forced to hire themselves out to capitalists on any conditions to avoid finding themselves in the huge army of people who are unemployed. Neither is there freedom for the peasants, who are constantly threatened by "liberation" from their holdings as a result of bankruptcy. Nor is there freedom for the intelligentsia, whose creative activity is in the grip of material dependence on the moneybag.... Freedom in the capitalist countries exists only for those who possess money and who consequently hold power.

Related criticisms are advanced by American radicals who argue that in this country only the rich have economic freedom while the poor, and especially minorities, must simply do as they are told by members of "the establishment." Clearly, political and economic freedom are intimately intertwined. If in fact the Russian

people completely controlled the Soviet officials who make the nation's economic plans, the Communists could reasonably claim a high degree of individual economic freedom, exercised through voting for central economic planning rather through the marketplace. In America we freely choose to have our governments tax away part of our incomes and provide highways, schools, and the like through nonmarket channels; and there is no reason why for others to do likewise would imply lack of economic freedom. But without effective democratic control over the central planners, the Soviet system can hardly be rated high on economic freedom. Nor have the Soviets shown concern for their minorities and dissenters that compares favorably with the American record. Concern for human rights goes far beyond economics, but the economic component is an important one.

Security

What is economic security? Is it freedom from the fear of unemployment? Freedom from the fear of arbitrary discharge? Freedom from the fear of poverty and disaster in old age or ill health? Is economic security separable from political security?

How economic security is defined will partly determine the rating of the American and Soviet systems on this score. By one test, the Soviet citizen is secure economically. The state will not let him and his family starve. He is assured of a minimum of public services and of a job if he works reasonably hard and conforms to the rules of the leaders in power. In a planned economy, workers aren't planned into unemployment. Probably the Soviet leaders believe their system provides more economic security than does capitalism, where (to them) the worker lives in constant fear of discharge by the all-powerful capitalist and of unemployment in periodic depressions.

The United States has moved a long way toward similar security (see Chapter 37). But fundamentally, the greatest existing protection to economic security under the American system is the vast productive power it provides—the

[7]Speech before twenty-first Party Congress in Moscow, January 31, 1959.

high per capita incomes that make it possible for workers to look out for themselves. Beyond our basic reliance on individual initiative, our governmental social-security system now offers protection against most of the types of economic insecurity likely to strike the average individual. And private welfare and pension funds have developed rapidly in recent years. Still, the capitalist system has some unwanted insecurity that will persist until we learn to substitute stable economic growth for intermittent recessions and inflations (a problem the Soviets also still have to conquer).

How much security should an economic system provide? Many Americans believe the system ought to deal out big rewards to those who work hard and "produce," and that those who don't produce have no right to economic security. This is the incentive that has made the American economic system a spectacular success, they argue, and to substitute guaranteed economic security would undermine the very foundation of the system. But most voters disagree, arguing that elimination of unnecessary insecurity and uncertainty will make our system work better—and even if it didn't, we can now well afford the cost of reasonable economic security.

Planning With Private Enterprise: the New Look?

Most of the world's economies lie somewhere between America's private enterprise and Russia's communism. Some, like Yugoslavia, are near the Communist end of the spectrum, but with a new twist that allows widespread individual initiative and market guidance, with collective ownership of productive resources. Others, like France, are basically private-initiative, market-directed economies that are experimenting with combined government-private enterprise planning. Japan, the great economic success story of the postwar period, also makes heavy use of individual initiative, profits, and the market, but with a special kind of government-private enterprise cooperation that goes far beyond either Yugoslavia or France.

Yugoslavia

In 1948, Yugoslavia under Tito broke with the Stalin regime for both political and economic reasons. Economically, she was unconvinced of the value of strict central control over all economic activity, she could ill afford the inefficiencies apparent in Soviet industry and agriculture; nor did she have an educated and trained elite of central planners. Since then she has pragmatically evolved a different and successful mixed system, in which most productive resources are state-owned and there is some overall state planning (especially of investment and growth), but in which most production is worker-managed and market-directed and most incomes are heavily dependent on the individual's own performance.

Central Planning. The central authorities today retain control over about two-thirds of all investment—both as to overall level and allocation among old and new industries. Investment funds are obtained largely from taxes levied on business profits and individuals throughout the economy. This investment control is exercised mainly by spending investment funds in expanding old companies or establishing new ones, which then operate as independent enterprises. Public services are extensive, but less so than in the Soviet Union. The central planners use control over the banking system both to enforce investment allocations and to maintain overall balance between aggregate demand and supply.

Agriculture. At first, the Yugoslavs followed the Russian pattern of collectivizing farms. Like the Russians, they met widespread hostility and sullen resistance. Farm output fell. Rather than use force, the Yugoslavs in 1953 abruptly reversed their stand, returning most land to private ownership and operation, and shifting the remaining publicly owned land to cooperative (rather than state-directed) operations. The result has been moderately successful. Yugoslavia has avoided the persistent problems faced by the Soviets, and farm output has grown around

5 percent annually—more than in the USSR, but less than in the leading Western economies.

Industry—Workers' Management. At first, the Yugoslavs also tried central government control over production and distribution. But they rapidly moved toward decentralized management of individual enterprises and substantial reliance on the market system to mirror consumers' preferences and to allocate finished products. This reflected a pragmatic recognition of the independence of the people, widespread inefficiencies in trying to make central planning work, and inadequate expertise to carry out the elaborate central functions needed to run a command economy.

Today, most production and distribution is done by worker-managed individual enterprises that try to make as large profits as they can. The workers collectively own the enterprise and collectively select and oversee the manager. Broadly, the manager's job is to maximize profits by equating marginal cost with price, but also to keep the workers reasonably satisfied. The firm must pay substantial taxes to the government (see above), but thereafter it can either distribute its profits to the workers or reinvest them in the enterprise. Each worker receives (under state rule) a minimum income, but above that his income depends on the success of the enterprise. Officially there are no "wages," only profit-sharing, since the enterprise belongs to the workers. But in essence the guaranteed minimum is close to a minimum standard wage.

What has been the result? Most observers agree the system has worked well. From a backward, agrarian Balkan economy with a very low standard of living, Yugoslavia (according to official statistics) has grown at over 8 percent annually since World War II. Probably this is an overstatement; and some of the growth represents recovery from war disruption and from widespread unemployment. But the growth rate is well above that of her neighbors, and the mixed system appears to be an imaginative response to Yugoslavia's problems. The system provides effective incentives for most individuals, it appears to stimulate workers' morale, and

it avoids the enormous administrative burden involved in planning and controlling an economy on a centralized basis. Since the Yugoslav economy is a relatively simple one, conflicts between the investment priorities of the central planners and the operating activities of individual enterprises have been manageable without extending central controls.

Some problems have developed. Some of the worker-managed firms have become excellent profit maximizers and have seen advantages in growing larger to obtain monopoly powers and profits. There has been inadequate incentive to organize new firms, with the result that the central planners have had to assume primary responsibility for finding and developing new products. Lastly, with reliance on the market enterprise managers have made mistakes, and unemployment has intermittently appeared, much as it would in a capitalist society.

France

After World War II, France faced economic problems on every side—inadequate foreign-exchange reserves, intermittent unemployment, inflationary pressures, and inadequate government finances at home. Not least, she was humiliated and frustrated by her failure to play a significant role in the war against Germany. To revitalize the French economy, French government officials, in informal consultation with business and labor leaders, began to develop informal plans to encourage recovery and more stable growth for the economy. By 1960, a combined planning process had been widely accepted.

The French planning process is the outgrowth of a continuing search for means to "rationalize" economic investment and private capitalism through combined private-public planning while maintaining the right of private business to make its own decisions. Essentially, private business, labor unions, farmers, and government officials work out together a plan for stable economic growth that seems reasonable to all of them. These consultations now extend over two years for each five-year plan and normally involve some 4,000 businessmen, labor

leaders, farmers, governmental officials, and academicians. Then the resulting plan is accepted as a basis for both public and private policies. But individual firms are left free to make their own decisions within this broad plan, knowing that if others go along they can count on roughly the growth and markets outlined in the plan.

Look at the 1966–1970 plan. First, government economists mapped out three alternative patterns of French growth up to 1970, postulating 4, 5, and 6 percent annual growth rates. Each one covered not only total g.n.p., but also estimates of exports and imports, consumption and investment spending, materials and labor requirements, and the like, for twenty-eight major sectors of the economy. Second, these broad alternatives were discussed within the government and with the Economic and Social Council, an assembly of leaders of industry, labor, farmers, consumers, and other private economic groups. This Council, after much discussion, tentatively decided that a 5 percent growth rate looked feasible, and suggested that a more detailed plan be worked out on that basis. In the third stage, this more detailed 5 percent plan was sent out to some twenty-five joint public-private working committees, each of which examined the requirements and implications in detail for its sector of the economy. This involved widespread consultations with individual firms on expansion plans, labor requirements, import and export assumptions, and the like. (Remember American antitrust policy?) In the fourth stage, all these committees reported back to Paris, where the reports were combined and reworked into a final consistent plan for the whole economy for the years 1966 through 1970, with the 5 percent overall growth rate. Lastly, the plan was adopted by the French cabinet and by the National Assembly as the basis for French government and private planning.

Up to this point, the plan may sound more like Moscow than Paris, except for a broader French private participation in determining the goals. But despite its official adoption, the French plan does not bind the government, business, or anybody else. Yet early evidence suggests that

it is being taken most seriously as a basis for both public and private economic decisions. The Bank of France and the government ministries will hardly disregard it when their top officials were instrumental in putting it together. Private businessmen and labor leaders were similarly involved, agreeing that it was both good for France and reasonable for their sectors. Businessmen know that if the plan is adhered to, France will be prosperous and they will find markets for their own expansion called for by the plan. Moreover, most investment capital in France flows through government-controlled channels, so the government can exercise pressure if it chooses. Thus, while the plan is neither a forecast nor a binding program, it is intended to provide a widely accepted basis for combining more stable growth with private freedom. Sometimes it's called "indicative" planning. Others call the French approach "soft" planning to differentiate it from the Russian variety.

Since 1960, France has grown at the rate of about 5 percent annually, about the same as the other Common Market countries, faster than the United States. But indicative planning has not been able to contain French wage increases or to prevent inflation; and the French were forced to devalue the franc and to establish a variety of direct controls in 1967. How France will modify her planning remains to be seen.

Japan

Japan is the economic success story of the postwar world (see Table 46–3). Her growth rate in recent years has been spectacular, and she grew at a rapid, though much slower, rate over the century preceding World War II. To analyze this Japanese growth performance would take a chapter or a book itself. Here we are primarily interested in the role played by Japan's economic organization—a type of mixed economy that is uniquely Japanese.

Growth experts suggest that Japan's recent performance reflects an unusual set of forces, woven together in a carefully planned national growth policy—a mighty surge of capital investment; effective use of modern technology from other nations; extraordinarily efficient use of her national labor force (hard work, good management, and continuing shifts from low- to high-productivity industries); reliance on market incentives, with firm commitment to the principle of comparative advantage internationally; shrewd use of monetary and banking policy; and an unparalleled, peculiarly Japanese, collaboration between government and big business. Consider especially the latter factors.

Financial Growth. Adequate financing is a first requirement for capital investment. Japanese firms finance most (up to 85 percent) of their investment through bank loans, an extraordinarily high figure. This heavy debt ratio leaves them badly exposed in case the banks ever run short of funds and call their loans. The banks in turn operate with nearly 100 percent of their deposits offset by loans. How can the economy operate so precariously? The answer is that the Bank of Japan (fundamentally, the Japanese government) stands firmly committed to financing rapid growth and to providing the reserves needed to support it through bank loans. This financing system works especially well for the giant industrial groups (zaibatsu) that dominate the Japanese economy. Each group is tied closely to a major bank or financial group, which is directly responsible for assuring finance to the wide-ranging industrial activities of the group, and which also helps to see that financial resources within the zaibatsu are channeled to those activities that promise the highest yield. Since only a few zaibatsu dominate much of Japanese industry, it is easy for them and the big banks to work directly with the government and the Bank of Japan in making their plans for expansion and national economic growth.

Government–Business Relations. The relations between big businesses and the government are very close, peculiarly Japanese, and difficult to describe in Western terms. The zaibatsu at once compete vigorously and work together and with the government on plans for domestic and (especially) foreign markets. Japa-

nese profit rates have been high, and foreign investors have found Japanese corporate stocks attractive. Direct government intervention in day-to-day business activities is moderate, probably less than in the United States, though the Japanese government does operate the railroads, the major airline, telecommunications, and the cigarette and salt monopolies. But the government ministries and the Bank of Japan on the one hand and the major business groups on the other comprise an intricate planning net, which interacts closely and continuously on major economic decisions for the economy.

Broad economic plans are developed by the Economic Planning Agency, working with business organizations. Some 300 consultative committees of government and trade association officials work out detailed implementation of these plans. All Japanese industry is organized into trade associations, which in turn combine into a prestigious federation of economic organizations, which represents all industry. Neither government nor business is monolithic. Different government ministries and different industries have different needs and approaches. Yet, as compared to all Western economies, Japanese business and government plan and operate very closely together; some American businessmen call the result "Japan, Inc.," as if the nation were one big integrated economic firm.

Japan's spectacular success in world markets shows this cooperation most clearly. The Japanese export offensive has produced a 15 percent annual increase in exports over the past decade. The Japanese Supreme Trade Council is headed by the premier himself; top business executives and government officials personally set export goals. The government backs corporations with special tax incentives and credit facilities. Cartels of Japanese exporters are encouraged to fix prices and make collaborative plans for invading foreign markets. Giant trade companies market Japanese products throughout the world, often at prices that are substantially below Japanese domestic prices. At the same time, the government has imposed import quotas on a wide range of products and limits foreign investment in Japan in many industries to protect Japanese firms. Little wonder that businessmen in the United States and Europe complain that competing with Japanese exports seems almost impossible, and that they in turn need government help to let them compete on even terms.

Employment Practices. Japan is the only non-Western economy to industrialize successfully, but in the process she has become only partly westernized. When the typical Japanese factory worker, clerk, or minor manager is employed, it is for life. His salary depends almost entirely on age, education, and seniority, not on his job or productivity. In effect, he becomes a member of that business family for the rest of his life, with both benefits and responsibilities. Strikingly, the system produces high labor productivity. Workers identify themselves closely with their companies, and the Japanese tradition of hard, careful work is strong. Although union membership is about as widespread as in the United States and union leaders are often left wing, strikes are rare and generally mild. Since pay and status do not depend on job assignments, managers have great freedom in moving workers among jobs, and employment flexibility is high, in spite of the apparent rigidity of the traditional arrangement. Union work rules and "featherbedding" are almost unknown. Clearly, this employment system would work only with continuing high-level employment; firms would go bankrupt rapidly if they had to keep on paying workers when markets vanished. Again, the system depends on the government's commitment to maintain high employment and to sustain rapid growth, and the commitment is a firm one.

National Commitment to Growth. Japan, Inc. is committed to rapid growth as a keystone of national economic policy. During the late 1960s, investment totaled a spectacular 34 percent of g.n.p.; profits have boomed; output and incomes have risen rapidly. Has Japan found the key to success through its own brand of mixed economy? The record is impressive, but there are problems and many experts predict that Japanese growth will slow substantially over the decades ahead. Inflation has proved a persistent problem to the Japanese as they operate their high-pressure economy. Consumers appear increasingly anxious to get a bigger share of the growing national output for higher living standards. Stronger retaliation by other nations in foreign markets seems likely. A few Westerners predict a popular uprising against big business–strong government domination of economic life, but even Japanese left-wingers challenge only particular parts of the highly successful Japan, Inc.—not the system itself. Japanese nationalism is an important part of the mix that has produced Japan's postwar economic growth.[8]

Convergence of Economic Systems?

Other nations have tried their own approaches to economic "rationalization" over the postwar period. Britain has moved toward a pervasive government-sponsored "incomes policy" prescribing growth rates for wages and profits in a stably growing economy, though without detailed indicative planning. Even West Germany, commonly considered far over on the private-enterprise side, does a lot of behind-the-scenes planning. During two postwar decades 56 percent of Germany's net investment was financed by the government—directly, or indirectly through government loans and special tax privileges to industries that followed policies consistent with the plans for German growth. Many other countries have tried their own public-private mixes.

Some observers say that these experiments are the new look for the democratic societies—planning combined with private enterprise. But others take a dimmer view. They question whether such planning may not be an entering wedge for more governmental control over the private economy. At first the plan is voluntary.

[8]Lively popular accounts of the modern Japanese system are provided by J. C. Abegglen, "The Economic Growth of Japan," *Scientific American,* March, 1970; and "How the Japanese Mount that Export Blitz," *Fortune,* September, 1970. For a more scholarly and complete treatment, see L. Klein and K. Ohkawa, *Economic Growth; The Japanese Experience since the Meiji Era* (Homewood, Ill.: Richard D. Irwin, Inc., 1968). See, also, M. Bronfenbrenner, "Japan's Galbraithian Economy," *The Public Interest,* Fall 1970.

But after a while, when some private firms or unions decide not to play the roles assigned them under the plan, it is a short step for the government to exert pressure, or even to shift the plan to a compulsory basis through legislation.

American observers raise another question: What about antitrust laws? In Japan and France, cartelization rests on a long history of firms working together in the major industries. In the United States, not only is that tradition lacking but collusive price-and-output planning by competing firms is strictly illegal. Should we abrogate our antitrust laws for planning?

Lastly, informal planning sooner or later requires agreement on an "incomes policy," which specifies the shares of the growing g.n.p. that should go to labor and to profits. The unions in other nations may be a lot less agreeable than those in France, where workers are less unified than in many other nations, and even France is having serious wage problems. Dutch cooperative planning essentially blew up in the early 1960s when the unions refused to accept the wage holddowns provided in the official plans. The Kennedy-Johnson wage–price guideposts represented a tentative approach to such an incomes policy in the United States, but not one that retained widespread support.

Currently, a debate rages among economists over whether capitalist and communist economies are converging on a middle ground. No one argues that all nations will soon have identical mixed economies. It is unlikely that Russia, Yugoslavia, France, Japan, and the United States will soon look the same. But after a survey of European economies, Stanford's J. E. Howell and U.C.L.A.'s Neil Jacoby advance the following two hypotheses:[9]

(1) Optimum performance by advanced economies requires a judicious and probably changing blend of central economic management and decentralized competitive market direction.

(2) There is an increasing appearance of con-

[9]*European Economics: East and West* (New York: World Publishing Company, 1967).

vergence among the economic management systems of advanced countries.

Time will tell whether Howell and Jacoby are right. Do their hypotheses point the optimal path for the United States?

Conclusion

Since the beginning of recorded history, men have sought the perfect society. In the books that fill the libraries, many of these utopias promise peace and plenty for all. But it is a long step from dream to reality. In the real world, the utopias that look best in the writing sometimes turn sour for quite unforeseen reasons.

Over the years, some economists have worked out the details of an "ideal" democratic economy. In it, resources would be allocated in accordance with consumer market demands, individuals would be free to work and spend as they wish, state-owned capital resources would be devoted to producing what consumers want, and the proceeds from state enterprises would be distributed among the people to provide as much income equality as the public desired. This is much like the utopia of the early Socialists, with state ownership of resources and operation of enterprise, with political democracy, and with economic implementation through the price system. Its advocates claim it combines the best features of private enterprise and of socialism.

But in the real world, are centralized economic control and democratic freedom in fact compatible? The Russian official blueprint looks surprisingly like this model, but in operation it looks different. Wise observers have often noted that dispersion of economic and political power are usually handmaidens to each other—that centralized economic power and political democracy seldom live long together. If this is true, the attempt to "plan" and centrally control economic activity toward the goals we want may be a false dream, likely to lead to political and economic slavery rather than to organized plenty.

The economic system must be our servant, not our master, in an effective society. If the society has fundamentally democratic, individualistic ideals, most people must be at heart satisfied with the way the system works— not in detail and all the time, but by and large. Lewis Carroll, in *Alice in Wonderland*, puts his finger tellingly on the basic problem:

The Dodo suddenly called out, "The race is over!" and they all crowded round, panting, and asking, "But who has won?"

This question the Dodo could not answer without a great deal of thought, and it sat for a long time with one finger pressed upon its forehead, while the rest waited in silence. At last the Dodo said, "Everybody has won, and all must have prizes."

In a working, democratic society most must win, and most must have prizes. What shall the prizes be, and how can the economic system keep everyone satisfied with his reward? The American economy provides prizes in abundance, compared with all the other nations of the world. Any reasonable evaluation must count it highly successful. But to be pleased should not make us smug. The American economic system is not perfect. And it will change over the years ahead, as it adapts to changing needs and objectives.

You should now be able to do a good share of your own thinking on how the American economy should steer over the years ahead. Economic analysis alone cannot give you answers to the hard problems we face. But it can help greatly to illuminate the way in a changing world.

Review

<table>
<tr><td>FOR ANALYSIS
AND DISCUSSION</td><td>

1. In the light of your study of the American economic system and alternative systems, make a careful list of the major defects, if any, you see in the American system. What, if any, reforms do you think are needed, and how feasible do you think each of your reforms is?

2. During the past half century, the economic climate of the world has shifted toward central economic planning and collectivism. What factors do you think have been most important in bringing about this change?

3. Recently the USSR has apparently moved toward a limited profit motive for managers in some consumer-goods industries. If this experiment is broadened, do you think it will be compatible with basic planning for the rest of the economy? Explain your answer.

4. Since World War II, three of the nations showing the highest growth rates are Russia (a Communist state), West Germany (a basically private-enterprise economy), and Yugoslavia (a modified Socialist country). How do you account for this fact? Does it indicate that the two types of economic organization are equally fitted for producing continued, rapid growth? Or that other factors are the important ones in determining growth rates? Is there another explanation?

5. In Russia, wages are set by the central planners to keep total purchasing power about in line with the supply of goods to be bought. Would some variant of this plan be a good approach to our problem of avoiding creeping, wage push inflation? If you think so, defend your answer against the likely attack of a union member.

6. Make a list of those attributes of present-day Communist Russia that

</td></tr>
</table>

seem to you most objectionable. How many of these attributes are economic, how many social, how many political?

7. Do you believe the United States should adopt some of the informal planning approaches of France or Japan? What seem to you the main advantages and disadvantages?

8. What does your own utopia look like?

The two chapters in Part Seven raise a wide range of problems on which active research is in progress. Again, these are only samples that will, hopefully, stir interest for more.

Adjustment to Change: Automation and Disarmament. Chapters 1 and 2 of H. A. Simon's *The Shape of Automation* (New York: Harper & Row, Publishers, 1965) provide a good introductory overview of the impact of "automation," with special emphasis on the likely role of the computer; reversing the order of the chapters may make them easier reading. C. Silberman's *Myths of Automation* (New York: Harper & Row, Publishers, 1966) brings the arguments to bear on current issues. Paul Hartman, *Collective Bargaining and Productivity* (Berkeley and Los Angeles: University of California Press, 1969) analyzes experience with the West Coast longshoremen's pioneering plan to eliminate resistance to technical change in return for a share of the savings.

Several recent studies illustrate different analytical approaches to the impact of disarmament, when and if it comes. In *Defense and Disarmament*, R. Bolton, ed., see especially the analysis by Washington University's M. Weidenbaum and others in Part III. "Input–Output Analysis of Disarmament Impacts" by W. Leontief and M. Hoffenberg, in *Disarmament and the Economy*, E. Benoit and K. Boulding, eds. (New York: Harper & Row, Publishers, 1963), shows how a new mathematical technique (input–output analysis) can be used to predict the impact of changes in government spending on all sectors of the economy; for a more thorough description of the technique and its results, see the *Scientific American*, April, 1961. See also the footnote references in the text.

The USSR and the Mixed Economies. Several paperbacks provide good summaries of the Soviet economy; see the footnotes to the text above. *New Directions in the Soviet Economy*, a five-volume compendium by Congress' Joint Economic Committee in 1966, provides a mass of detail on recent Soviet developments; it is updated in the Committee's *Soviet Economic Performance, 1966–67*, May, 1968. On the "new look" in Soviet planning, see G. Burck, "The Toughest Management Job in the World" *(Fortune,* July, 1966); Marshall Goldman looks further ahead in "The Reluctant Consumer and Economic Fluctuations in the Soviet Union" *(Journal of Political Economy*, August, 1965), which predicts that the Soviets may soon face problems of unemployment and business fluctuations Western style. At a more advanced level, A. Bergson's *Economics of Soviet Planning* (New Haven: Yale University Press, 1964) provides an authoritative analysis of the entire planning process; and R. Powell's "Economic Growth in the USSR," *Scientific American*, December, 1968, illustrates how skilled researchers probe such a difficult area.

A readable introduction to mixed private-public planning in Europe is provided by N. Jacoby and J. E. Howell's *European Economics: East and West* (New York: World Publishing Company, 1967); and by N. Chamberlain, *Private and Public Planning* (New York: McGraw-Hill Book Company, 1966). Lively, popular analyses of the Japanese system are footnoted in the text above. For more thorough analyses, try A. Maddison's *Economic Growth in Japan and the USSR* (New York: W. W. Norton & Company, Inc., 1969), and J. McArthur and B. Scott's "Industrial Planning in France," *Harvard Business Review*, 1969.

Cutting across both the Soviet and Western "mixed" economies, two studies, *The Red Executive* and *The European Executive* (Garden City, N.Y: Doubleday & Company, Inc., 1959 and 1963) by Wisconsin's David Granick, draw an intriguing parallel between managerial problems and behavior in the two types of economies.

Lastly, though to us many of its articles smack more of propaganda than of research, sample the publication, *Problems of Economics*, if your library has it. This is a monthly translation into English of current papers by leading Soviet economists on all phases of Russian economics and the performance of the Soviet economy.

Mathematical Appendixes[1]

In economics, as in many other disciplines, mathematics has important uses. Mathematics provides a convenient, concise language for stating complicated ideas and relationships. It facilitates the analysis of complicated interrelationships and helps in reaching "correct" conclusions from sets of assumptions or premises. It provides a language for stating "models" or theories in a precise way that makes them testable by rigorous statistical analysis of empirical data ("econometrics").

Since an increasing number of college students know some mathematics, these brief appendixes use mathematics (through elementary calculus) to state precisely and rigorously some of the concepts and arguments developed verbally or graphically in the text. Each appendix relates directly to the chapter or section of the text indicated. If you know some mathematics and especially if you find the language of mathematics a helpful one, the following appendixes may prove a useful supplement to the verbal and graphical exposition of the same ideas in the chapters concerned.

The appendixes show, in very elementary forms, how mathematical language and mathematical reasoning can simplify and illuminate the (sometimes complex) interrelationships with which economic analysis must deal. Although a half century ago there were virtually no economists interested in applying math-

[1] Prepared in collaboration with Professor Michael Lovell of Wesleyan University.

704

ematical analysis to economic problems, today use of mathematics in economics has become commonplace; and, as the appendix to Chapter 10 indicates, "econometrics" (the use of mathematically stated models as the basis for quantitative measurement in analysis of economic variables) has become the fastest growing branch of modern economics. The following appendixes give a small indication of how mathematics can help in stating clearly and precisely some of the important concepts and relationships in economics.[2]

[2]If you find these appendixes interesting and want to investigate mathematical economics a bit further, R. G. D. Allen, *Mathematical Economics* (New York: The Macmillan Company, 1956) provides an excellent introduction for students who know calculus. Lawrence Klein's *Introduction to Econometrics* (Englewood Cliffs, N.J.: Prentice-Hall, Inc., 1962) is a comparable introduction to the field of econometrics, though it is designed primarily for readers who have also had a course in elementary statistics.

APPENDIX I *G.N.P. DETERMINATION AND THE MULTIPLIER*
(to Chapter 7)

Chapter 7 presents a simple algebraic model showing how, in an economy assuming no government or foreign trade, private investment and the marginal propensity to consume interact to determine the level of g.n.p. This appendix first states the model quite generally in mathematical terms, and then develops more rigorously "the multiplier" and the way in which it helps explain the impact of changes in investment on g.n.p.

A. The Income-Determination Model. In Chapter 7 two consumption functions were presented. In one, consumption *(C)* was simply a fixed proportion of g.n.p. *(Y)*. In the other, a somewhat more general form was used:[3]

$$C = a + bY \qquad (I.1)$$

(Of course, if $a = 0$, then this reduces to the simpler consumption function.) As in Chapter 7, since all of g.n.p. is either consumed or invested *(I)*

$$Y = C + I \qquad (I.2)$$

Now substitute the consumption function into this last equation in order to obtain

$$Y = a + bY + I \qquad (I.3)$$

Next, subtract bY from both sides:

$$Y - bY = (1 - b)Y = a + I \qquad (I.4)$$

Dividing both sides by the marginal propensity to save, $1 - b$, gives us

[3]You will remember from the text discussion that $0 < b < 1$.

$$Y = \left(\frac{1}{1-b}\right)(a + I) \qquad (I.5)$$

as the equilibrium level of g.n.p., in which consumption is at the level prescribed by the consumption function (equation I.1) for the given level of *I* and the resulting level of *Y*. In particular, if $a = 40$, $b = .6$, and $I = 100$ (as in Chapter 7), this last equation reveals that gross national product must be 350:

$$\left(\frac{1}{1-.6}\right)(40 + 100) = 350$$

B. The Multiplier. The "multiplier" tells us what happens as a result of a rise in investment to a new level *(I*)*. Clearly g.n.p. will rise, and as people receive more income, consumption will rise as well. Let *Y** denote the new equilibrium level of income and *C** the new equilibrium level of consumption, when the increase in *I* has exercised its full effect.

Since these new equilibrium values, *Y** and *C**, must satisfy both equations I.1 and I.5, the same line of reasoning as before implies that

$$Y^* = \left(\frac{1}{1-b}\right)(a + I^*) \qquad (I.5^*)$$

Subtracting equation I.5 from this last expression yields

$$Y^* - Y = \left(\frac{1}{1-b}\right)(I^* - I) \qquad (I.6)$$

The expression in large parentheses, the reciprocal of the marginal propensity to save, is the multiplier. It tells us by how much the change in investment $(I^* - I)$ must be multiplied in order to determine the change that it will induce in g.n.p.

C. Addition of Government Spending and Taxes.
Government spending and taxes can readily be introduced into this multiplier analysis. Government spending, G, then represents purchases of one part of the current g.n.p. Consequently, we must rewrite equation I.2 to read

$$Y = C + I + G \qquad (I.7)$$

In addition, we must now recognize a distinction between gross national product and disposable income. Specifically, let T denote tax revenue, and suppose that consumption depends on disposable (after-tax) income, so that $C = a + b(Y - T)$. Then

$$Y = a + b(Y - T) + G + I \qquad (I.8)$$

Proceeding as before, we obtain

$$Y = \left(\frac{1}{1 - b}\right)(a - bT + G + I)$$

as the equation explaining the equilibrium level of g.n.p. as determined by private investment, consumption behavior, government expenditure, and taxes. Note that for any given tax take, government spending and investment both have the same multiplier. On the other hand, the effect of an increase in taxes is to change g.n.p. by a negative "tax multiplier" of $-b/(1 - b)$. Thus, if government expenditure and taxes both increase by \$3 billion, we would have

$$Y^{\circ} = \left(\frac{1}{1 - b}\right)[a - b(T + 3) +$$
$$(G + 3) + I] = Y + 3$$

That is, income increases by the same amount as taxes and government spending, which in Chapters 7 and 14 is called the "balanced-budget multiplier."

D. Dynamics of the Multiplier. This exercise tells us nothing about the nature of the adjustment process. Let us now consider the dynamic process by which Y rises as a result of the increase in I. This corresponds to the discussion of successive rounds of consumption spending out of rising income in Chapter 7 on page 78. Let time be measured in discrete units, say months, and suppose that the level of consumption during the current month depends upon the income earned in the immediately preceding month. Thus

$$C_t = a + bY_{t-1} \qquad (I.9)$$

where the subscripts serve to indicate the time period.

Now let us suppose that the marginal propensity to consume, b, is $\frac{3}{4}$; that $a = 20$: and that initially, at time zero, investment is 67.5, $G = T = 0$, and income $Y_o = 350$. From equation I.9 we find that, in period one, consumption will be

$$C_1 = 20 + \frac{3}{4} \times 350 = 282.5$$

If investment were to remain constant at 67.5, there would be no tendency for g.n.p. to change from 350. (Check that $C_1 + I_1 = Y_1 = 350$). This is the sense in which the economy is said to be in equilibrium. But suppose that instead investment increases by 10, to 77.5. Our initial equilibrium is disturbed, and the economy will gradually adjust to the disturbance. The nature of the adjustment process is suggested by the following:

Period	$I_t - I_o$	$C_t - C_o$	$Y_t - Y_o$
1	10		10
2	10	7.5	17.5
3	10	13.1	23.1
4	10	17.3	27.3
.	.	.	.
.	.	.	.
.	.	.	.
.	.	.	.
∞	10	30	40

Each increase in income induces additional consumption in the next period, which constitutes additional income to the seller of goods or services, and so on ad infinitum. Will the process stop? The total increase in income is

$$10 + 7.5 + 5.6 + 4.2 + \ldots$$

But this is readily seen to be a sum of an infinite number of terms. More generally, of course, for any arbitrary marginal propensity to consume, the change in income resulting from a change in investment will be

$$\Delta I + b\Delta I + b^2\Delta I + b^3\Delta I + \ldots =$$
$$\Delta I(1 + b + b^2 + b^3 + \ldots) \qquad (I.10)$$

The conditions under which such a sum will be finite can be determined if we recall the procedure for deriving the sum of a geometric series. Let S_n be the first n terms in such a series; i.e.,

$$S_n = 1 + b + b^2 + \ldots + b^n \qquad (I.11)$$

Multiplying by b gives

$$bS_n = b + b^2 + \ldots + b^{n+1} \qquad \text{(I.12)}$$

Subtracting equation I.12 from I.11 yields

$$S_n - bS_n = (1 - b)S_n = 1 - b^{n+1}$$

Consequently,

$$S_n = \frac{1 - b^{n+1}}{1 - b} \qquad \text{(I.13)}$$

It is now obvious that

$$\underset{n \to \infty}{limit} \, S_n = \frac{1}{1 - b} \qquad \text{(I.14)}$$

if and only if the marginal propensity to consume is less than unity. This limiting expression is, of course, the multiplier of equation I.6. If the marginal propensity to consume were greater than unity, something which is conceivable but not likely except in temporary special cases, g.n.p. would increase without bounds in response to an increase in private invest-ment spending, at least under the simple assumptions used here.[4]

More advanced analysis would recognize that rising g.n.p. and business sales might well induce a further rise in investment spending, and thus increase the stimulative effect of any of the above assumed increases in I or G. Such further "induced" investment is often called the "accelerator" effect, and is considered more completely in Chapter 10. See especially the second appendix to that chapter for a simple mathematical model incorporating both multiplier and accelerator effects.

[4] Readers interested in the complexities of dynamic analysis will note that equation I.6 correctly tells us that equilibrium g.n.p. will decrease as a result of an increase in investment spending if the marginal propensity to consume is greater than unity; i.e., if, somehow, g.n.p. did decline to the level suggested by that equation it would remain there indefinitely. But if $b \geq 1$ this equilibrium is *unstable*, and with the passage of time g.n.p. will diverge further and further from its equilibrium as a result of the increased consumption induced by the augmented level of investment spending. This, however, while it is analytically interesting, is extremely unlikely, since empirical studies show that the marginal propensity to consume is less than unity except under very special circumstances.

APPENDIX II — DEMAND FUNCTIONS AND ELASTICITY OF DEMAND
(to Chapter 21)

The demand curve for any commodity shows how many units will be bought at each price. Looked at another way, it represents the function indicating how price responds to changes in the quantity of a commodity offered for sale, given buyer preferences and incomes, and may be denoted as $p(q)$. [This function might also be denoted by p, or by $f(q)$.] It will be assumed that this function is differentiable.

As is explained in Chapter 21, demand curves are ordinarily negatively sloped; i.e., $dp/dq < 0$. This information does not tell precisely how the total revenue obtained by the sellers will respond to changes in price and quantity sold, but simple analysis of the demand function can provide an answer to this important question.

Total revenue, denoted by $r(q)$, is simply price times quantity:

$$r(q) = p(q)q \qquad \text{(II.1)}$$

Differentiating with respect to quantity yields

$$\frac{dr}{dq} = p(q) + \frac{dp}{dq} q \qquad \text{(II.2)}$$

This derivative, which economists call **marginal revenue**, may be either positive or negative (remem-ber, $dp/dq < 0$). Selling more at a lower price will reduce total revenue if the fall in price is not offset by the increase in the quantity of the commodity purchased; i.e., if the demand is "inelastic." (Note that this is equivalent to saying that a reduction in price will increase the number of units sold less than proportionately.)

What level of output with its resulting price would maximize total revenue (but not necessarily profits)? We can tell by examining the demand function with the aid of a few rules of elementary calculus. Remember that a necessary condition for a maximum is that the first derivative of revenue with respect to quantity be zero.

$$\frac{dr}{dq} = p(q) + \frac{dp}{dq} q = 0 \qquad \text{(II.3)}$$

This maximum can be defined in terms of the elasticity of the demand function. Economists, following the reasoning on elasticity in Chapter 21, customarily denote elasticity more precisely as[5]

[5] If, as for the inidividual seller under perfect competition $\frac{dq}{dp} = \infty$, then we say elasticity is infinite.

$$\eta = - \frac{dq}{dp} \cdot \frac{p}{q} \qquad (\text{II.4})$$

Thus, when elasticity of demand is unity, revenue is maximized.

If demand is "inelastic" (i.e., $\eta < 1$), note that a reduction in the quantity of the commodity offered on the market would increase total revenue. Thus, a businessman with control over his selling price and output would be foolish to produce at a point where the demand for his commodity is inelastic, for then he could obtain more revenue by producing and selling less!

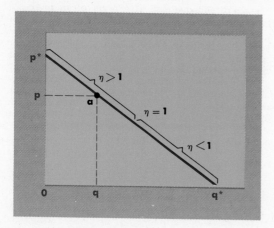

It is easy to determine graphically the elasticity of demand. Consider the demand curve q^*p^*, first graph above. To find the elasticity of demand at any point a (corresponding to price p and quantity q) we note that $- dq/dp = (q^* - q)/p$; hence

$$\eta = - \frac{dq}{dp} \cdot \frac{p}{q} = \left(\frac{q^* - q}{p} \right) \frac{p}{q} = \frac{q^* - q}{q} \qquad (\text{II.5})$$

From the last equality we see that for a linear demand curve, the elasticity of demand is simply the ratio of the excess of the quantity that could have been sold at a zero price over actual sales [i.e., $(q^* - q)$, divided by quantity sold (q)]. Note that, although this demand curve has a constant slope, it is not characterized by a constant elasticity. The elasticity changes along the curve. If q^* units were sold at zero price, the elas-

ticity of demand would be zero; for higher prices, less is sold and elasticity increases without bound as the price approaches p^*.

To determine the elasticity of demand at some point on a nonlinear demand curve, such a point a on curve DD on the second graph, draw a straight line tangent to the demand curve at that point, and from it determine the location of point q^*. Since at point a the demand curve and the tangent line have the same slope, as well as the same p and q values, they have the same elasticity at that point; hence formula II.5 again applies:

$$\eta = \frac{q^* - q}{q}$$

Is it possible for a demand curve to have constant elasticity throughout its entire length? Yes. Suppose that $q = \alpha p^\beta$, $\beta < 0$;

then $dq/dp = \left(\beta \alpha p^{\beta - 1} \right) = \beta \frac{q}{p}$

and $\eta = - \left(\beta \frac{q}{p} \right) \frac{p}{q} = - \beta.$

I.e., the parameter $-\beta$ of the demand curve is the elasticity of demand. For example, a rectangular hyperbola has a constant elasticity $= 1$.

APPENDIX III   COST CURVES AND PROFIT MAXIMIZATION
(to Chapters 23–24)

To determine what level of output will maximize profits, production costs in relation to demand con-

siderations must be analyzed. This appendix analyzes this interrelationship mathematically.

A, Key Cost Concepts. In Chapter 23 the dependence of production costs upon the level of output was examined in detail, and a number of basic concepts were explained. Table 23–1 reported hypothetical cost figures for a firm producing a single commodity. In such cases, the total cost function, $c(q)$, reveals how the total costs incurred by the firm depend on the level of output; we assume that the function is differentiable. Other cost concepts discussed in the text may be expressed in terms of $c(q)$, as shown in the following list.

Fixed costs: $c(0)$
Variable costs: $c(q) - c(0)$
Total unit cost: $c(q)/q$
Variable unit cost: $[c(q) - c(0)]/q$
Fixed unit cost: $c(0)/q$

Marginal cost: $\dfrac{dc(q)}{dq}$

B. Maximizing Profits. Profits, at any level of output, $\pi(q)$, is simply the excess of total revenue over total cost; i.e.,

$$\pi(q) = r(q) - c(q) \qquad \text{(III.1)}$$

where $r(q)$ is the total revenue function discussed in Mathematical Appendix II; the three curves are plotted in Figure 24–1 on page 353. From elementary calculus we know that if profits are maximized at some level of output $q > 0$, it is necessary that

$$\frac{\partial \pi(q)}{\partial q} = \frac{\partial r(q)}{\partial q} - \frac{\partial c(q)}{\partial q} = 0 \qquad \text{(III.2)}$$

Equation III.2 implies

$$\frac{\partial r(q)}{\partial q} = \frac{\partial c(q)}{\partial q} = 0 \qquad \text{(III.3)}$$

This states mathematically the fundamental proposition that a necessary condition for profit maximization at $q > 0$ is that marginal cost equals marginal revenue.

It is essential to note that condition III.2 does not necessarily yield a level of output, q, at which profits will be positive. In the short run, before the firm can liquidate its fixed investment, it may be worthwhile to operate at a loss rather than shut down. Remember that zero output involves fixed cost, $c(0)$, in the short run. Would a zero output minimize losses (negative profits) when there are fixed costs? Not if

$$\pi(q) = r(q) - c(q) > \pi(0) = -c(0) \qquad \text{(III.4)}$$

or equivalently:

$$r(q) - [c(q) - c(0)] > 0 \qquad \text{(III.5)}$$

In other words, the firm will produce a positive output at a loss if revenue exceeds total variable costs. Dividing both sides of III.5 by q yields, since $r(q)/q = p$, an equivalent condition:

$$p - [c(q) - c(0)]/q > 0 \qquad \text{(III.6)}$$

This is the condition (on page 355) that the firm will minimize losses by shutting down altogether only if there is no positive level of output where price would exceed average variable cost.

C. Some Observations on Competitive Equilibrium. Under competitive conditions, the output of the individual firm constitutes an insignificant contribution to the total market sales of the commodity. Consequently, the price the firm receives for its output is unaffected by variation in the quantity it offers for sale; its demand curve is horizontal (i.e., $dp/dq = 0$), and from equation II.2 we have marginal revenue equal to price $(dr/dq = p)$. Hence, equation III.3 implies that if firms maximize profits under competitive conditions, they produce at the point where marginal cost equals price.

This constitutes a basic proposition of economic theory which explains the general presumption of economists in favor of competition: When firms maximize profits under competitive conditions, the increment to total cost incurred in producing the last unit sold is exactly equal to the price, which is precisely as it should be. For the price reflects the consumer's evaluation of the benefits he will obtain from the purchase of that last unit; if the benefits were less he wouldn't buy the unit, and if they were greater he would buy more units.

Chapter 25 points out that, in long-run competitive equilibrium, price is equal to the minimum point on the total-unit-cost curve. This must be the case, for a higher price would encourage new firms to enter the industry in search of profits, while a lower price would yield continued losses and induce firms to leave the industry. But if price is to be equal to the minimum point on the total-unit-cost curve, can we be sure it also equal marginal cost, as required under competition (condition III.3, with $dr/dq = p$)? It is easy to show that the answer is, necessarily, yes. If output is at the minimum total-unit-cost level, then marginal cost will be equal to total unit cost. To establish this proposition, we note that the condition that output be at the minimum total-unit-cost level implies:

$$d\frac{\left[\dfrac{c(q)}{q}\right]}{dq} = \frac{\dfrac{dc(q)}{dq}}{q} - \frac{c(q)}{q^2} = 0$$

Multiplying through by q yields:

$$\frac{dc(q)}{dq} = \frac{c(q)}{q}$$

Thus, marginal cost is equal to average cost if output is at the firm's lowest average-unit-cost point. The marginal-cost curve cuts the average-cost curve at the latter's minimum point.

APPENDIX IV (to Chapters 32–33) — PRODUCTION FUNCTIONS AND THE DISTRIBUTION OF INCOME

Most firms have alternative ways to produce any given output. Thus, within limits, the services of machinery may be substituted for labor in the production of steel, or vice versa. A "production function," which states the relationship between various combinations of inputs and the resulting outputs (products), can be a helpful concept for exploring the way in which technological considerations influence the distribution of income among different factors of production (labor, capital, and so on).

A. Simple Production Functions. For simplicity, suppose that only two factors of production, labor *(L)* and machinery *(M)*, are used in producing a commodity. The output *(q)* produced each period depends on the quantity of labor and machinery services employed. We assume that this "production function" can be described by a differentiable function of the two inputs:

$$q = f(L,M) \qquad (IV.1)$$

Such functions can be estimated empirically from business and engineering production data or derived from engineering or physical principles.

We wish to determine the optimal (i.e., highest profit) mix of labor and machinery to produce any output. We will maximize profits (π) by maximizing the excess of revenue over cost. If we assume that labor and machinery services are purchased on competitive markets at prices w and p_m we have:

$$\pi = r(q) - wL - p_m M \qquad (IV.2)$$

or, substituting from IV.1,

$$\pi (L,M) = r[f(L,M)] - wL - p_m M \quad (IV.3)$$

If the optimal quantity of labor is indeed being employed, it must be impossible to increase profits by either increasing or decreasing the amount of labor used. Consequently, a necessary condition for profit maximization is that

$$\frac{\partial \pi(L,m)}{\partial L} = \frac{dr}{dq} \cdot \frac{\partial q}{\partial L} - w = 0 \qquad (IV.4)$$

Similarly, if the optimal quantity of machinery services is being employed,

$$\frac{\partial \pi(L,m)}{\partial M} = \frac{dr}{dq} \cdot \frac{\partial q}{\partial m} - p_m = 0 \qquad (IV.5)$$

As Chapters 32 and 33 indicate, economists call

$$\frac{\partial r}{\partial q} \cdot \frac{\partial q}{\partial L}$$

the **marginal-revenue product** of labor. Thus, equation IV.4 shows that to maximize profits, a firm hiring on a competitive market must hire additional workers just to the point where the marginal-revenue product of labor equals the wage rate (pages 470 and 481).

It follows from IV.4 and IV.5 that

$$\frac{\frac{\partial q}{\partial m}}{p_m} = \frac{\frac{\partial q}{\partial L}}{w} \qquad (IV.6)$$

The economist calls

$$\frac{\partial q}{\partial L}$$

the marginal productivity of labor; similarly,

$$\frac{\partial q}{\partial m}$$

is the marginal productivity of machinery services. Equation IV.6 thus shows that under profit-maximizing equilibrium conditions in competitive markets, each factor of production is rewarded in proportion to its marginal productivity (pages 468–474).

B. The Cobb-Douglas Production Function: An Example. As an illustration, let us consider a much discussed conjecture of Professors C. W. Cobb and Paul H. Douglas (later U.S. senator) that the total industrial output of the American economy may be described by a simple production function of the form:

$$q(L,M) = a\, L^\lambda\, M^{1-\lambda} \qquad \text{(IV.7)}$$

Statistical investigations have disclosed that a function of this form fits the historical data quite precisely with $\lambda = .75$. Note that this function is characterized by constant returns to scale; i.e., if the initial inputs are all multiplied by some scale factor $\rho > 0$, then output will also increase by ρ; more precisely:

$$q(\rho L, \rho M) = \rho\, q(L,M) \text{ for all } \rho \geqslant 0 \qquad \text{(IV.8)}$$

What are the implications of the Cobb-Douglas analysis for the shares of labor and machinery (capital) in the national income? Not only did Cobb-Douglas find that equation IV.7 provides a reasonable explanation of how capital and labor contribute to the generation of industrial output. They also found that this function, in conjunction with equation IV.4, embodying the assumption of competition, helps to explain an important observed fact—that labor income (wages and salaries) has been a roughly stable percentage of total income over many decades.

Their explanation of the rough constancy of labor's share can be appreciated if we first observe that the marginal productivity of labor is

$$\frac{\partial q}{\partial L} = \lambda a L^{\lambda-1} M^{1-\lambda} = \lambda \frac{Q}{L} \qquad \text{(IV.9)}$$

Similarly, the marginal productivity of capital services is

$$\frac{\partial q}{\partial M} = (1-\lambda)\, aL^\lambda M^{-\lambda} = (1-\lambda)\frac{Q}{M} \qquad \text{(IV.10)}$$

If output is sold on a competitive market at price p (so that $dr/dq = p$), then condition IV.4 implies

$$p\lambda\, \frac{Q}{L} = w \qquad \text{(IV.11)}$$

Hence

$$\frac{Lw}{Qp} = \lambda \qquad \text{(IV.12)}$$

Now remember that Lw is labor income while Qp is the value of total output; consequently equation IV.12 implies that the ratio of labor income to total income, labor's share, is equal to the parameter λ of the Cobb-Douglas production function.

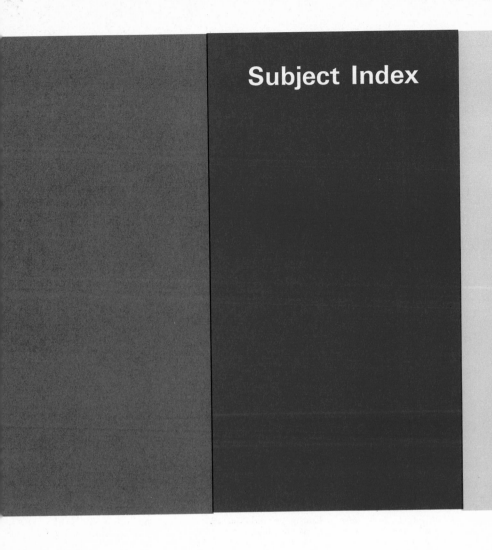

Subject Index

Labor (*cont.*)
Act, 494, 502 (*see also* Wagner Act)
productivity, 206, 224, 250, 468ff.
share of national income, 467ff.
technological change (automation), 476
union membership, 494f.
in USSR, 683
wage determination, 477ff.
wage differentials, 466ff.
women in labor force, 237, 466
working hours, 237
Labor–Management Relations Act, 493f. (*see also* Taft–Hartley Act)
Labor theory of value, 528f.
Labor unionism:
collective bargaining, 494, 498ff.
history, 494f.
job security, 667f.
Landrum–Griffin Act, 503
membership, 494f.
motives in wage bargaining, 499ff.
National Labor Relations Act, 493f., 502
New Deal, 494, 502
Norris–LaGuardia Act, 502
power, 497ff., 501
research, 554
responses to technological change, 497ff.
strikes, 494, 500ff.
Taft–Hartley Act, 493f.
union shop, 499n.
wage policy, 495ff.
Wagner Act, 494, 502
working hours, 140
Lags (*see* Monetary policy; Fiscal policy)
Laissez-faire, 41, 435
Land resources (*see* Resources)
Landrum–Griffin Act, 503
Leading indicators, 417
"Leakages," 80
Leisure, 237
Less-developed countries, 8, 258ff.
analytical framework, 261ff.
balanced vs unbalanced growth, 272f.
capital accumulation, 263f., 268ff.
development policy, 267f.
inflation, 266
infrastructure, 266
international comparisons, 259f.
international trade, 279
monetary–fiscal policy, 274f.
planning vs price system, 274ff.
population, 264ff., 283ff.
prospects, 278ff.
research, 289ff.
sociocultural factors, 266ff., 278

Less-developed countries (*cont.*)
U.S. policy, 279ff.
vicious circle of poverty, 267
Liabilities, 154, 303 (*see also* Accounting)
Liquid assets, 303
Liquidity trap, 178
LM curve, 111ff.
Logarithmic scale, *defined*, 57
Long run, *defined*, 342
Long-run equilibrium, 361ff.
Lorenz curve, 464f.

M
Macroeconomics, *defined*, 292
Management (*see also* Entrepreneur; Firm, business):
of corporations, 295ff.
labor–management relations, 498ff., 667f.
in less-developed countries, 267ff.
managerial economics, 432ff.
motives, 403f.
size of enterprise, 344
in U.S. growth, 239f.
in USSR, 682f.
wages, 465
Managerial economics, 432ff.
Manpower policies, 208
Marginal cost, 353ff., 432
Marginal efficiency of investment, 93
Marginal equivalency conditions, 348, 469, 469n.
Marginal physical product, 370, 376, 398, 473
Marginal productivity, 467ff., 473ff., 479 (*see also* Labor; Productivity)
Marginal propensity to consume, 77f., 119
Marginal propensity to save (*see* Marginal propensity to consume)
Marginal revenue, 354, 397
Marginal revenue product, 470, 479ff.
Marginal utility, 106, 313
Margin requirements, 166
Market performance, 412ff.
Markets (*see also* Demand; Prices; Supply):
disequilibrium, 331
equilibrium, 327
for productive services, 462ff.
research, 459
role, 36ff., 322ff.
in USSR, 486
Market sharing, 422
Market structure (*see* Competition; Monopolistic competition; Monopoly; Oligopoly)
Market system (*see* Price system; Private enterprise)
Marshall Plan, 647
"Marxist" economics, 528ff.
Mediation, 504
Medicare, 541, 544ff.

Mergers, 298ff., 437
Microeconomics, *defined*, 292
Military–industrial complex, 452ff.
Miller–Tydings Act, 444
Mineral resources (*see* Resources)
Minimum-wage laws, 507
Mixed economy, 42, 678, 695ff.
Models:
in economic analysis, 14ff.
simultaneous-equation, 83n.
single-equation, 83n.
stability properties, 228f.
Monetarists, 90, 98, 105, 173, 179, 191
Monetary policy (*see also* Federal Reserve System; Interest rates):
aggregate demand, 174ff.
central-bank policy, 160ff., 173ff.
debt management, 182ff., 214
differential effects, 176
employment, 172ff.
expansionary, 177ff.
fiscal-monetary policy mix, 191, 200ff.
gold standard, 172, 185ff.
guides, 174, 178f.
history, 179, 180ff.
interest rates, 173ff., 179
in less-developed countries, 274f.
money supply, 173ff., 179
open-market operations, 163ff., 182
outside lag, 209
portfolio balancing, 173
qualitative controls, 166
reserve requirements, 156ff.
restrictive, 174ff.
role of the Treasury, 181, 182ff.
for stable growth, 172ff.
theory of, 172ff.
timing and lags in, 176ff.
in USSR, 689f.
in World War II, 99, 158, 181f.
Money (*see also* Banks; Federal Reserve System; Gold standard; Interest rates; Monetary policy):
aggregate demand, 98ff., 147ff., 173ff.
banking system, 150ff.
business cycles, 100, 110, 122f.
cash-balances approach, 104ff.
changing value, 56ff.
credit creation, 153ff.
currency, 99, 152
defined, 99, 150
demand, 104ff., 173
equation of exchange, 102, 173
Federal Reserve policy, 172ff.

Money (*cont.*)
foreign exchange, 635ff.
gold standard, 172, 185ff.
history, 99f., 110, 180ff.
in the income-expenditures model, 96, 105, 173ff.
money-velocity approach, 102ff., 173ff.
motives for holding, 104
near-monies, 149f.
portfolio balancing, 105ff.
price level, 99ff.
quantity theory, 101
real balances, 104ff., 173
research, 108
reserve ("key") currency, 636
supply, 90, 99ff., 150ff., 173ff.
tight, 174ff.
value, 56ff.
velocity, 102ff.
Money-flow accounts (*see* Flow-of-funds accounts)
Monopolistic competition:
costs, 403ff.
defined, 391
evaluation, 412ff.
prices and output, 406
product differentiation, 402f., 406ff.
profit maximization, 403f.
quality competition, 410f., 414
Monopoly (*see also* Antitrust laws; Mixed economy; Monopolistic competition; Oligopoly):
advertising, 394
bases, 392ff.
bigness, 394f., 445f.
bilateral, 484, 485n.
capital markets, 344f., 394
cartels, 422f.
competition, 362, 436ff.
control of raw materials, 393
decreasing costs, 394f.
defined, 391f.
efficiency, 373, 394f., 400f., 436
evaluation, 400f., 445ff.
government regulation, 393, 435ff.
income-distribution effects, 400
patents, 393
profit maximization, 398f.
public utilities, 392, 394f.
"pure," 391
selling costs, 410, 414
in union wage policy, 496
wage determination, 482ff., 496f.
Monopsony, 483
"Moral suasion," 167
Multiplier, 77f., 108, 189ff., 705
balanced-budget multiplier, 190f.
foreign-trade multiplier, 616
Multiplier–accelerator model, 130ff., 706

Name Index

Expenditures

Govern ment
$302

$215
Purchases of goods
and services

$62
Transfer
payments

$29
Interest
payments

$87
Indirect
business taxes

**Gross
national
product**

$932

**Net
national
product**

$854

**Nationa
incom**

$771

$78
Capital
consumption
allowances

$141
Gross investment,
inc. foreign

$142

Investment   Gross   Savings

Consumer outla

$594